ESE 2024

UPSC ENGINEERING SERVICES EXAMINATION

Main Examination

Electrical Engineering

Topicwise *Conventional* Solved Papers

Paper-II

23 Years SOLVED PAPERS

- ✓ Thoroughly revised and updated
- ✓ Fully solved with explanations
- ✓ Also useful for State Engineering Services Exams

MADE EASY PUBLICATIONS

www.madeeasypublications.org

MADE EASY Publications Pvt. Ltd.

Corporate Office: 44-A/4, Kalu Sarai (Near Hauz Khas Metro Station), New Delhi-110016
E-mail: infomep@madeeasy.in
Contact: 9021300500
Visit us at: www.madeeasypublications.org

ESE-2024 : Main Examination
Electrical Engineering : Paper-II | Conventional Solved Questions : (2001-2023)

1st Edition : 2008
2nd Edition : 2009
3rd Edition : 2010
4th Edition : 2011
5th Edition : 2012
6th Edition : 2013
7th Edition : 2014
8th Edition : 2015
9th Edition : 2016
10th Edition : 2017
11th Edition : 2018
12th Edition: 2019
13th Edition: 2020
14th Edition (Feb) : 2022
15th Edition (July) : 2022

16th Edition: 2023

B. Singh (Ex. IES)

Director's Message

In past few years ESE Main exam has evolved as an examination designed to evaluate a candidate's subject knowledge. Studying engineering is one aspect but studying to crack prestigious ESE exam requires altogether different strategy, crystal clear concepts and rigorous practice of previous years' questions. ESE mains being conventional exam has subjective nature of questions, where an aspirant has to write elaborately - step by step with proper and well labeled diagrams and figures. This characteristic of the main exam gave me the aim and purpose to write this book. This book is an effort to cater all the difficulties being faced by students during their preparation right from conceptual clarity to answer writing approach.

MADE EASY Team has put sincere efforts in solving and preparing accurate and detailed explanation for all the previous years' questions in a coherent manner. Due emphasis is made to illustrate the ideal method and procedure of writing subjective answers. All the previous years' questions are segregated subject wise and further they have been categorised topic-wise for easy learning and helping aspirants to solve all previous years' questions of particular area at one place. This feature of the book will also help aspirants to develop understanding of important and frequently asked areas in the exam.

I would like to acknowledge the efforts of entire MADE EASY team who worked hard to solve previous years' questions with accuracy. I hope this book will stand upto the expectations of aspirants and my desire to serve the student community by providing best study material will get accomplished.

B. Singh (Ex. IES)
CMD, MADE EASY Group

ESE 2024 Main Examination

Electrical Engineering
Conventional Solved Questions
Paper-II

Contents

■■■■

1 Analog Electronics

Revised Syllabus of ESE: *Operational amplifiers – characteristics and applications.*

1. Operational Amplifier-Characteristics and Application

1.1 In an ideal operational amplifier, the voltage gain for the common mode signal is

(a) 0 (b) 0.5

(c) 2.0 (d) infinite

[2 marks : 2002]

Solution: (a)

For an ideal operational amplifier, the voltage gain for the common mode signal is equal to zero.

1.2 The magnitude of the gain in the inverting operational amplifier circuit shown in figure is Y, with the switch open.

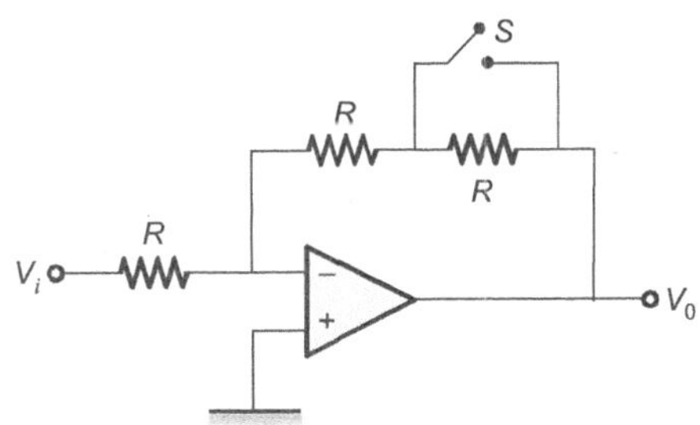

When the switch is closed the magnitude of the gain is

(a) $-Y$ (b) $Y/2$

(c) $2Y$ (d) $-2Y$

[2 marks : 2003]

Solution: (b)

For inverting operational amplifier

$$V_0 = -\left(\frac{R_f}{R_1}\right)V_i$$

For switch is open, $$Y = \frac{V_0}{V_i} = -\left(\frac{2R}{R}\right) = -2$$

For switch is closed, $$Y' = \frac{V_0}{V_i} = -\left(\frac{R}{R}\right) = -1 = \left(\frac{Y}{2}\right)$$

1.3 The operational amplifier circuitry is given below. Determine its gain and indicate its applicability.

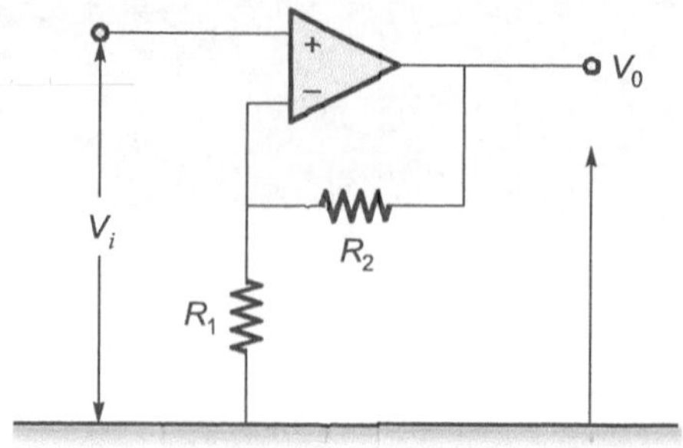

[7 marks : 2003]

Solution:

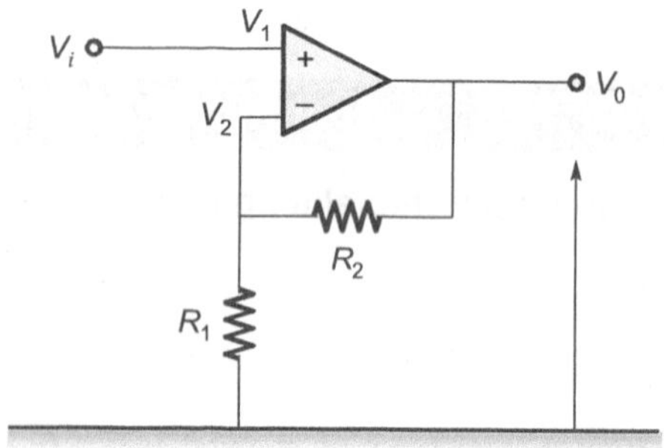

$$V_1 = V_i$$

and $$V_2 = \frac{V_0 \times R_1}{R_1 + R_2}$$

By virtual ground concept,

$$V_1 = V_2$$

$\therefore$ $$V_i = \frac{V_0 \times R_1}{R_1 + R_2}$$

$\therefore$ $$V_0 = \left(\frac{R_1 + R_2}{R_1}\right) V_i$$

Applications:
1. Used as comparator
2. As a zero crossing detector
3. Used as voltage follower circuit
4. Used in active peak detector
5. Used in rectifier circuit
6. Used in S-H circuit

1.4 Explain the operation of a Schmitt trigger circuit using an operational amplifier. Discuss the effect of hysteresis in such a circuit.

[8 marks : 2003]

Solution:

Schmitt trigger or wave shaping circuit:

It is a switching circuit which converts non-rectangular wave form into rectangular waveform.

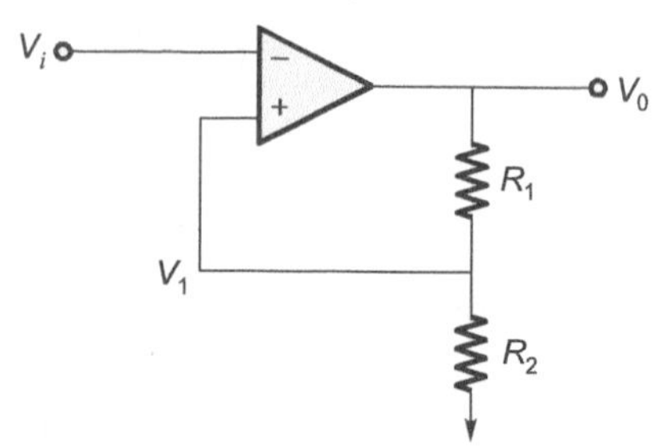

$$V_{UT} = \beta V_{sat} = \frac{R_2}{R_1 + R_2} V_0$$

$$V_{LT} = -\beta V_{sat} = \frac{-R_2}{R_1 + R_2} V_0$$

Schmitt trigger circuit:

$$V_1 = \beta V_0$$

where, $$\beta = \frac{R_2}{R_1 + R_2}$$

Transfer characteristics of schmitt trigger exhibit hysteresis characteristics.

Let us consider voltage V_i is less than (V_1) we get the output of $(+)$ $(V_{saturation})$ and if 'V_i' is increasing, then V_0 remains $(+V_{sat})$ until $(V_i = V_1)$, at this critical value, output voltage switches to $V_0 = (-V_{saturation})$ and remain at this value, as long as $(V_i > V_0)$.

The difference between V_{UT} and V_{LT} is defined as

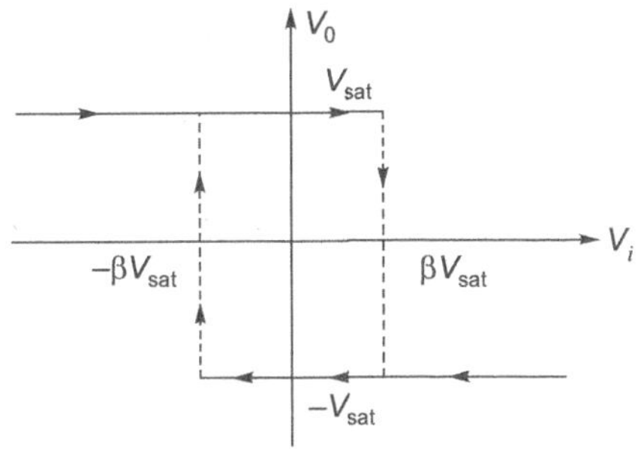

hysteresis V_H and given as

$$V_H = V_{UT} - V_{LT} = \frac{2R_2 V_0}{R_1 + R_2}$$

In such a circuit due to hysteresis loop, no transaction can takes place when $-\beta V_{sat} < V_i < \beta V_{sat}$

1.5 The most appropriate value of 'R' in the circuit shown is

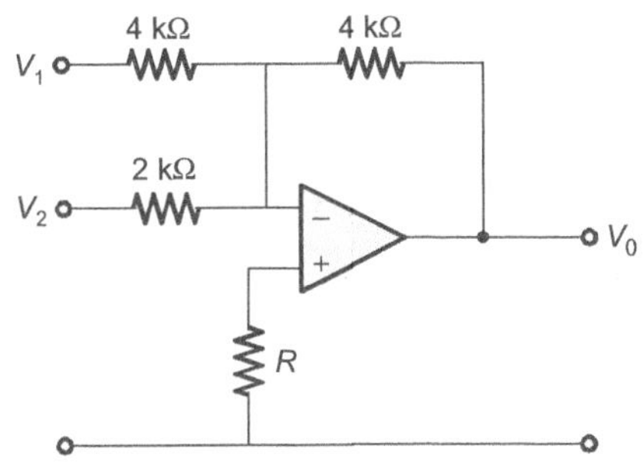

(a) 0 (b) 1 kΩ
(c) 2 kΩ (d) 4 kΩ [2 marks : 2004]

Solution: (a)

R is the dc resistance seen from the –ve terminal by removing all the sources by its internal resistance.

$$\therefore \quad R = 2\text{ k}\Omega \parallel 4\text{ k}\Omega \parallel 4\text{ k}\Omega = 1\text{ k}\Omega$$

1.6 The correct match between the pin numbers of an Op-Amp μA 741 in the left column and their functions in the right columns are

	Pin number		Functions
(A)	2	(P)	output
(B)	3	(Q)	non-inverting (+1 N)
(C)	4	(R)	inverting (–1 N)
(D)	6	(S)	$-V_{CC}$
		(T)	$+V_{CC}$

[5 marks : 2004]

Solution:

2 – (R) – inverting (–1 N)
3 – (Q) – non-inverting (+1 N)
4 – (S) – V_{CC}
6 – (P) – output

1.7 A non inverting operational amplifier summer is shown in the below figure. The output voltage V_0 is

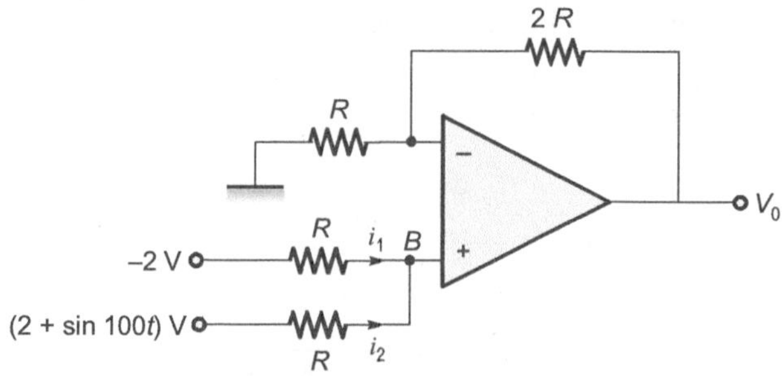

(a) $\frac{3}{2}\sin 100t$ (b) $3\sin 100t$

(c) $\sin 100t$ (d) $2\sin 100t$

[2 marks : 2005]

Solution: (a)

$$R_2 = 2R$$
$$R_1 = R$$

According to concept of non-inverting amplifier

$$V_0 = V_B\left[1+\frac{R_2}{R_1}\right] = V\left(1+\frac{2R}{R}\right) = 3V_B$$

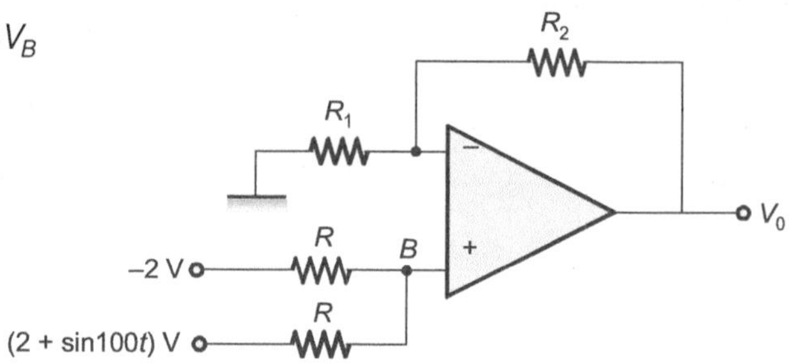

Now,
$$V_B = -2\times\frac{R}{2R}+(2+\sin 100t)\times\frac{R}{2R}$$
$$= -1+1+\frac{\sin 100t}{2}$$
$$V_B = \frac{\sin 100t}{2}$$

$\therefore$
$$V_0 = 3V_B = \frac{3}{2}\sin 100t$$

1.8 Describe with necessary diagrams:

(i) an Integrator, and

(ii) a differentiator using operational amplifier circuits. How the offset voltage can be minimized in an integrator at the output, and what is to be done to reset the integrator?

Discuss how in a practical differentiator high frequency oscillation can be prevented? How the outputs of a differentiator varies when (a) Ramp input is used, (b) Rectangular input is used?

[20 marks : 2005]

Solution:

$$V_0 = \frac{-1}{RCs}V_{in}$$

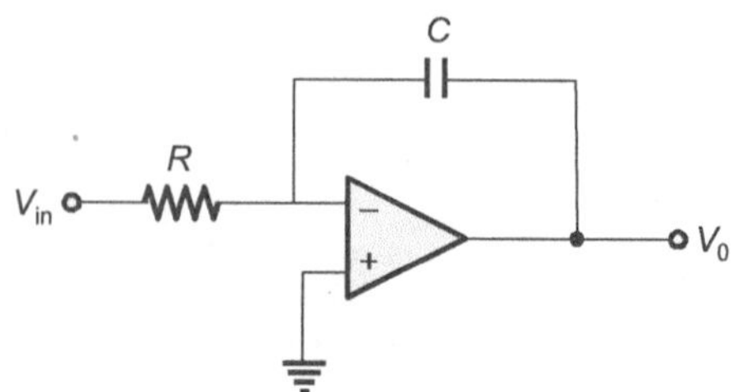

Integrator circuit

$\therefore$
$$V_0(t) = \frac{-1}{RC}\int V_{in}\,dt$$

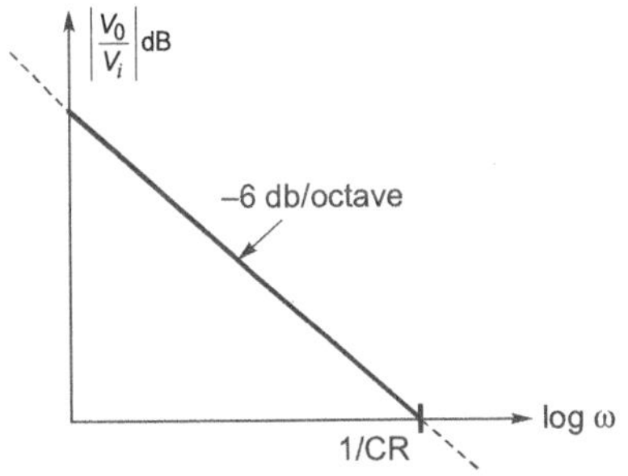

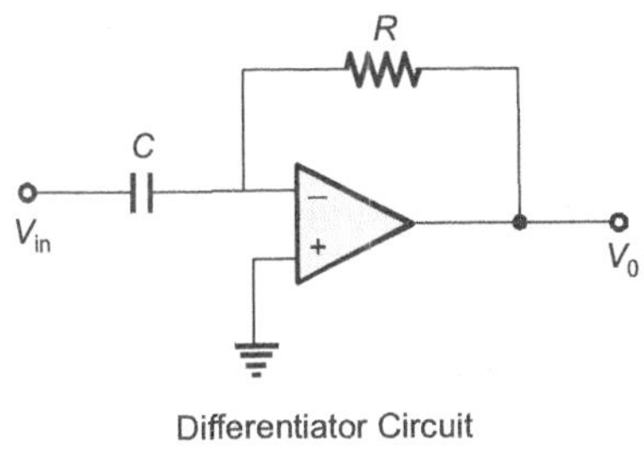

Differentiator Circuit

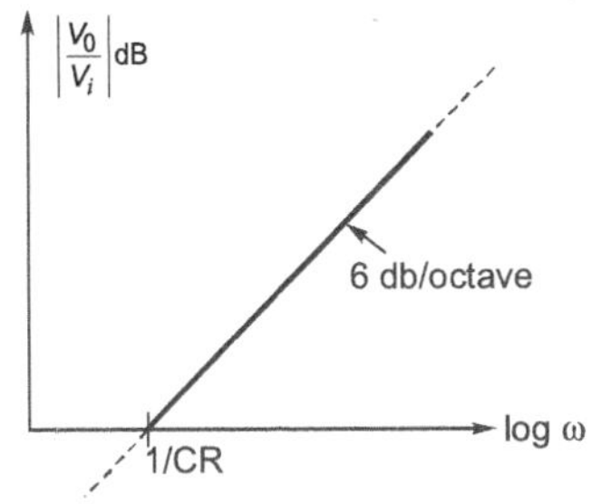

$$\therefore \quad V_0 = -RCs \times V_{in}$$

$$\therefore \quad V_0 = -RC\frac{d}{dt}V_{in}$$

In integrator, feed back element is capacitor and thus at dc, where the capacitor behaves as an open circuit, there is no negative feedback. The offset voltage can be minimised using a resistance connected across the integrator capacitance C.

Practically we consider differentiator circuit as a 'noise magnifier. This is due to the spike introduced at the output every time there is a sharp change in $V_i(t)$.

For this reason it suffers stability problems. Otherwise for high frequency (ω_0), input applied to differentiator will get multiple of factor $-(RC\omega_0)$. Hence for a differentiator, level at the output increase immensely. We use an external circuit to reset the integrator as:

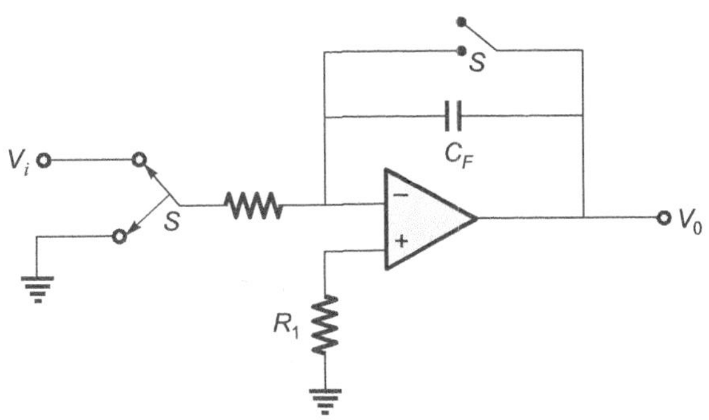

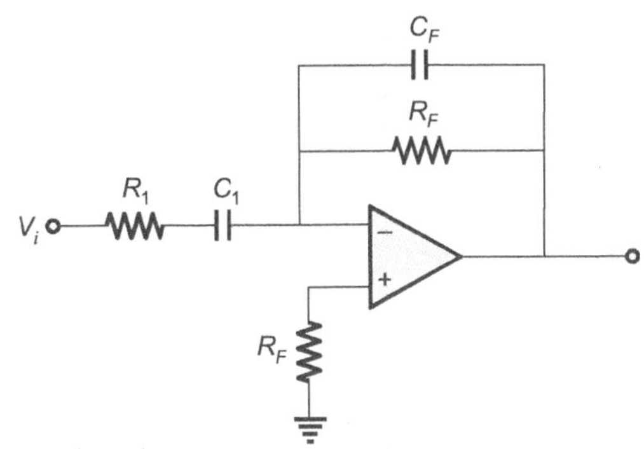

To eliminate the problem of high frequency oscillation in a differentiator circuit, circuit of differentiator is modified as:

and we take $\quad R_1C_1 = R_FC_F$

For this we get, $\quad f_b = \dfrac{1}{2\pi R_1C_1}$

So, till frequency f_b gain of differentiator increases but as frequency further increases above f_b, gain decreases at rate of –20 dB/decade so problem of instability at high frequency is solved.

(i) The output of the differentiator due to ramp input will be step signal.

$$r(t) = t$$

Output, $\quad c(t) = \dfrac{d}{dt}r(t) = u(t)$

(ii) For a rectangular input,

$$r(t) = u(t) - u(t-T)$$

$$\therefore \quad \text{output} = \delta(t) - \delta(t-T)$$

1.9 An operational Amplifier is basically a
(a) Low gain A.C. Amplifier
(b) High gain D.C. Amplifier
(c) High gain R.C. coupled Amplifier
(d) Low gain Transformer-coupled Amplifier

[2 marks : 2007]

Solution: (b)

An operational amplifier is basically a high gain DC amplifier.

1.10 Derive an expression for the closed loop gain V_0/V_i of the circuit shown below. Assume ideal Op-amp.

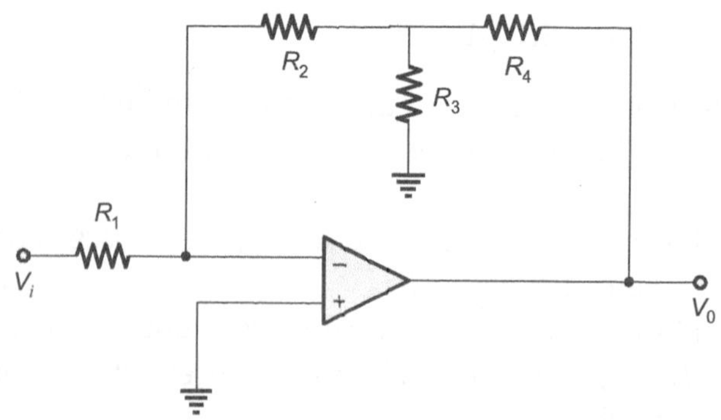

[10 marks : 2007]

Solution:

By applying KCL at node (1)

By Virtual ground concept, voltage at node 1 = 0 V

$$\frac{0-V_i}{R_1}+\frac{0-V}{R_2} = 0$$

$$\therefore \quad V = -\left(\frac{R_2}{R_1}\right)V_i$$

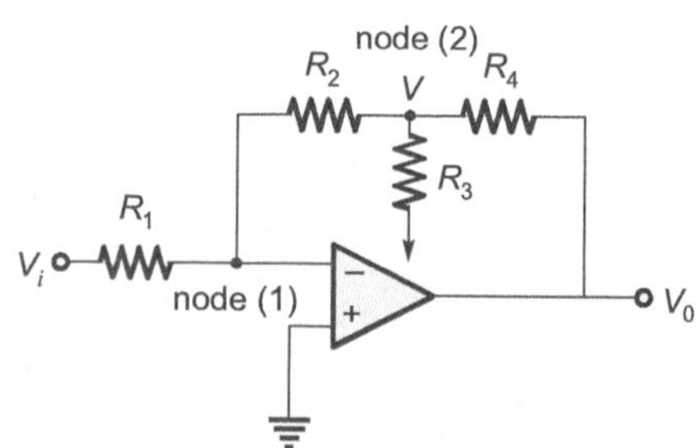

Applying KCL on node 2,

$$\frac{V-0}{R_2}+\frac{V-V_0}{R_4}+\frac{V}{R_3} = 0$$

$$V\left(\frac{1}{R_2}+\frac{1}{R_4}+\frac{1}{R_3}\right) = \frac{V_0}{R_4}$$

$$V\left(\frac{R_3R_4+R_2R_3+R_2R_4}{R_2R_3R_4}\right) = \frac{V_0}{R_4}$$

Putting value of V_i in above expression,

$$\frac{-R_2}{R_1}\left(\frac{R_3R_4+R_2R_3+R_2R_4}{R_2R_3R_4}\right)\times R_4 = \frac{V_0}{V_i}$$

$$\therefore \quad \left(\frac{V_0}{V_i}\right) = \frac{-(R_3R_4+R_2R_3+R_2R_4)}{R_1R_3}$$

1.11 (i) Draw a single-stage, double-ended, transistorized differential amplifier and define offset and drift. What are the measures taken to minimize offset and drift?

(ii) Sketch a single-stage, R.C. coupled, transistorized, common-emitter amplifier using npn transistor. Draw its frequency response. Why the gain is low at very low and very high frequencies? How the bandwidth of the amplifier is determined from this response?

[8 + 7 = 15 marks : 2007]

Solution:

(i) Basic building block of op-amp [differential amplifier]

Common mode gain of the amplifier depends upon the value of (R_E), where R_E increases, common mode gain will decrease.

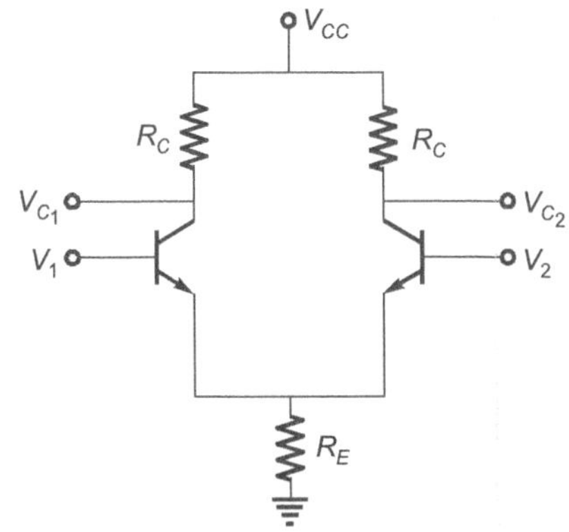

Terminology:

1. **Input offset voltage:** It is that voltage, which must be applied between the input to balance the amplifiers to get output voltage zero.
2. **Input offset current:** It is defined as the two biasing current entering the input terminal of the balanced amplifier.
3. **Input bias current:** It is the average of two bias current flowing into the two input terminal of the balanced amplifier.
4. **Output offset voltage:** It is the voltage at the output terminal, when the two input terminals are grounded.

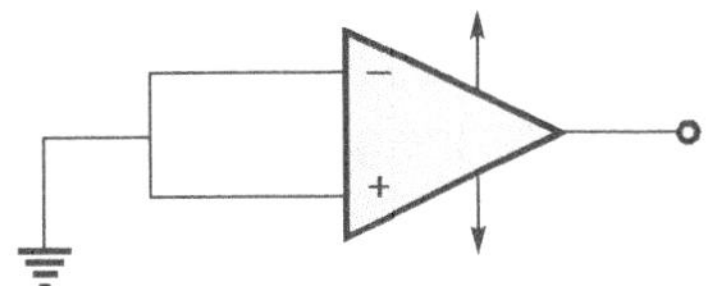

V_{00} - output offset voltage because transistor are not identical

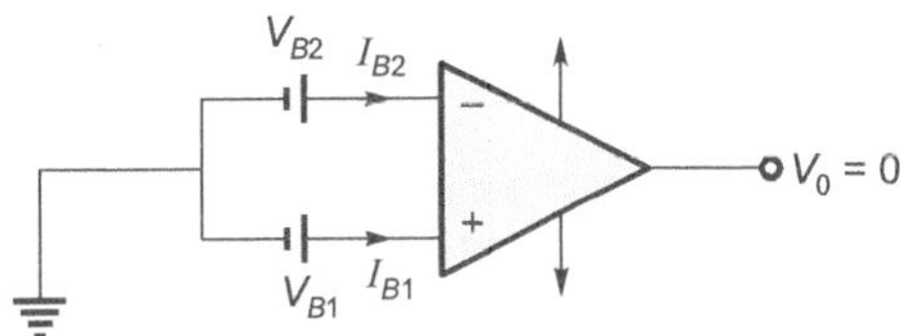

V_{i0} = (Input offset voltage) = $V_{B1} - V_{B2}$

Input offset current = $I_{i0} = I_{B1} - I_{B2}$, input bias current = $\frac{I_{B1} + I_{B2}}{2}$.

Offset: Shift in values of voltages and current in practical circuit with respect to ideal case is called offset voltage or current. To minimize the effect of offset voltages we add some additional voltage sources in circuit.

Similarly to minimize the effect of input offset current on output we introduce a resistance at +ve terminal whose value is equal to dc resistance seen from the –ve terminal by replacing all the sources by their internal impedances.

Drift: Change in bias current, offset current, and offset voltages due to change in temperature is called drift.

Offset current drift is expressed as μA/°C.

Offset voltage drift is expressed as μV/°C.

Careful printed circular boards are used to keep op-amps away from heat sources to minimize the problem of drift.

Sometimes forced cooling is also used to minimize the effect.

(ii)

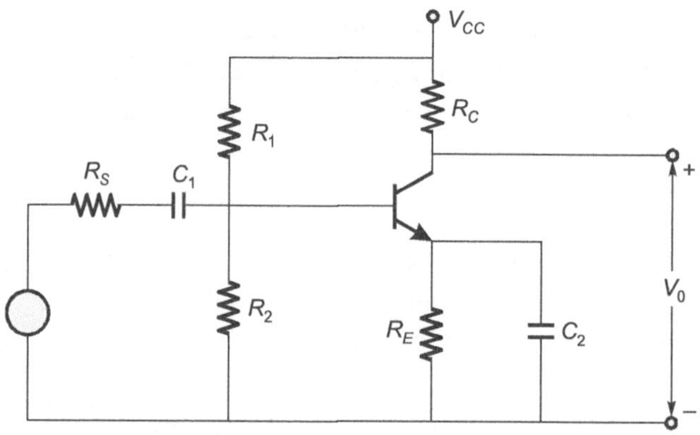

Single-staged *RC* coupled common-emitter amplifier

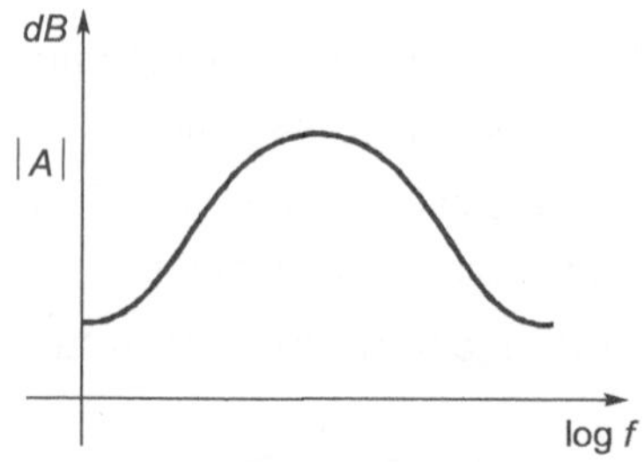

Because of degeneration caused by 'R_E', the gain is low at very low and at very high frequency.

$$\text{Bandwidth} = f_H = \frac{0.35}{t_r}$$

Where 't_r' is rise time of the circuit. Gain is low at low frequencies due to voltage drop across coupling and bypass capacitors. Gain is low at high frequencies because of internal junction capacitances which has finite impedance at high frequencies.

1.12 **Draw the circuit diagram of a transistorzed collector-coupled astable multivibrator and explain the generation of square wave. In a symmetrical collector-coupled astable multivibrator $R_1 = R_2 = 1$ MΩ and $C_1 = C_2 = 0.01$ μF find the frequency of operation.**

[10 marks : 2007]

Solution:

Circuit diagram:

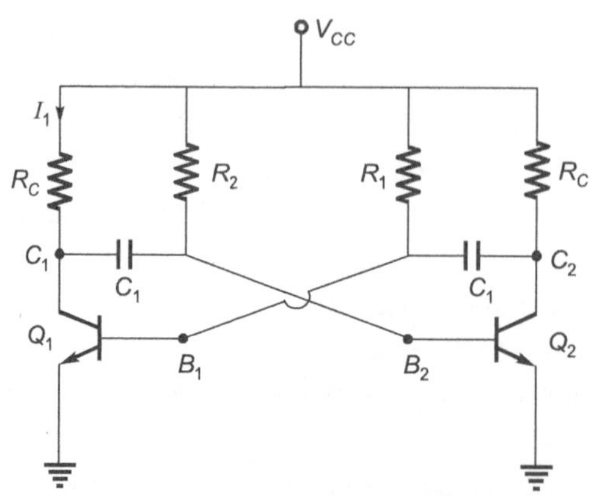

Waveform will be as

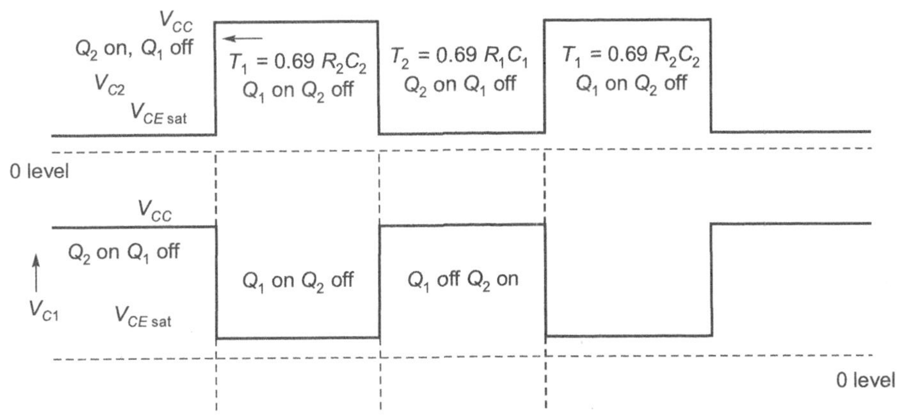

We consider immediately before $t = 0$, transistor Q_2 is in saturation and Q_1 is below cutoff. Hence for $t < 0$, $V_{c2} = V_{CE\,sat}$ (low output) and $V_{c1} = V_{cc}$ (high output).

Now capacitor C_1 will charge through R_1 and transistor Q_2 and voltage V_B, start increasing, when V_{B1} reaches cut-in voltage V_γ, Q_1 starts conducting and draws a large current I_1 so that V_{c1} immediately falls to $V_{CE\,sat}$ so that V_{B2} also falls by amount I_1R_C and $V_{B2} < V_\gamma$ so Q_2 goes in cutoff and voltage V_{c2} suddenly rises to V_{CC}. This charging and discharging of capacitor continuous and conduction transfers from one transistor to another transistor after a certain time as to produce square wave (duty cycle may or may not be 50%).

We know that, $T_1 = 0.69R_2C_2$

$T_2 = 0.69R_1C_1$

Now given that, $R_1 = R_2 = 1\ \text{M}\Omega = 10^6\ \Omega = R$

$C_1 = C_2 = 0.01\ \mu F = 10^{-8}\ F = C$

∴ Time period, $T = T_1 + T_2 = 0.69\ (R_1C_1 + R_2C_1) = 0.69 \times 2\ RC = 1.38\ RC$

$$\therefore \quad f = \frac{1}{T} = \frac{1}{1.38\,\text{RC}} = \frac{1}{1.38 \times 10^6 \times 10^{-8}} = \frac{100}{1.38}\ \text{Hz}$$

1.13 **A monostable multivibrator is to be constructed using an OP-AMP. Draw the diagram generating a positive pulse and explain its working with the help of waveforms. Derive an expression for the period of the pulse in terms of the circuit parameters.**

[16 marks : 2009]

Solution:

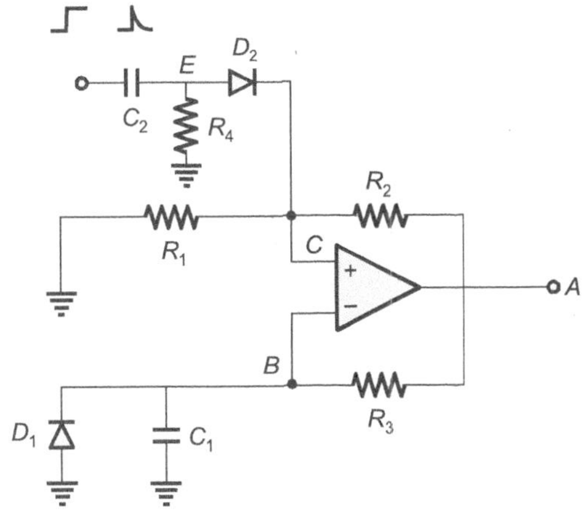

An OP-AMP monostable circuit:

Monostable multivibrator has one stable state and the other is quasi stable state. The circuit is useful for generating signal output pulse of adjustable time duration in response to triggering signal. The width of the pulse depends only on external components connected to the OP-AMP.

To analyse the circuit, let us assume that in the stable state, the output voltage is at $-V_{sat}$ [For getting positive pulse]. The diode 'D_1' conducts and 'V_B' the voltage across the capacitor 'C' gets clamped to (–0.7 V). The voltage at the positive input terminal through R_1 R_2 potentiometric divider is $-\beta V_{sat}$ or $[\beta L^{(-)}]$. Now if a trigger of magnitude 'V_i' is applied to the positive input terminal is greater than (–0.7 V).

∴ The output of the OP-AMP will switch from $-V_{sat}$ or $L^{(-)}$ to V_{sat} or $L^{(+)}$. The diode gets reverse biased and the capacitor starts charging exponentially to $(+V_{sat})$ through the resistance (R_3). When capacitor voltage (V_B) becomes just slightly more positive than $(+\beta V_{sat})$ or (βL^{+}), the output of the OP-AMP switches back to $-V_{sat}$. The capacitor 'C', now starts charging to $-V_{sat}$ or $-L^{(-)}$ through R_3 until V_B is (–0.7 V) as capacitor (C_1) gets clamped to the voltage. We observe that a five pulse is generated at the output during the quasi-stable state. The duration T of the output pulse is determined from the exponential waveform of V_B.

$$V_B(t) = L_+ - (L_+ - V_{D1})e^{-t/C_1R_3}$$

By substituting,

$$V_B(t) = \beta L_+$$

$$\beta L_+ = L_+ - (L_+ - V_{D1})e^{-T/C_1R_3}$$

which yields,

$$T = C_1R_3 ln\left(\frac{V_{D1} - L_+}{\beta L_+ - L_+}\right)$$

for $|V_{D1}| << |L_+|$ this equation is approximately

$$T \cong C_1R_3 ln\left[\frac{1}{1-\beta}\right]$$

1.14 Design a circuit using minimum number of OA to realize the equation:

$$V_0 = 2V_1 + 5V_2$$

[10 marks : 2012]

Solution:

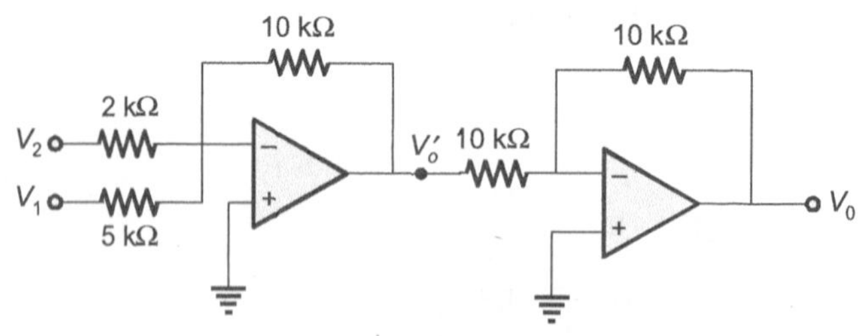

The output of first (OA) will be

$$V_0' = -\left(\frac{10}{2}V_2 + \frac{10}{5}V_1\right) = -(5V_2 + 2V_1)$$

The second OA will acts as inverter,

$$V_0 = -\frac{10}{10}V_0'$$

∴

$$V_0 = 2V_1 + 5V_2$$

1.15 A circuit has the following voltage transfer characteristic. Design a circuit to realize this characteristic.

Plot the waveforms for V_0 when

(i) $V_i = 5 \sin\omega t$

(ii) V_i = Half-wave rectified of 5 sinωt

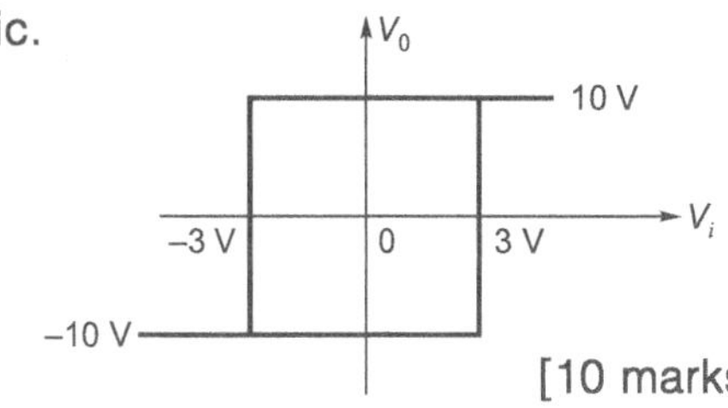

[10 marks : 2012]

Solution:

Circuit for the given voltage transfer characteristic.

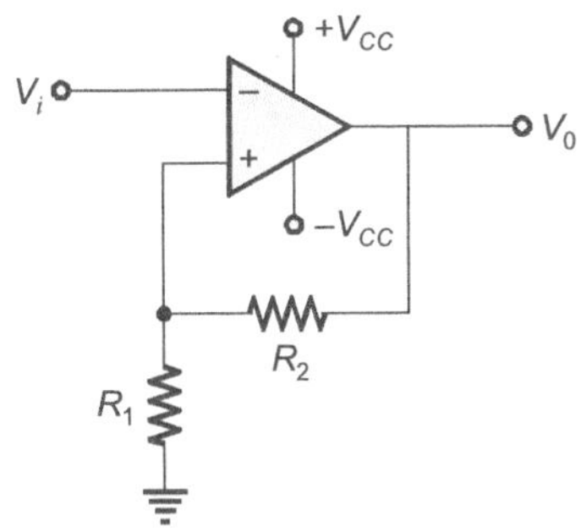

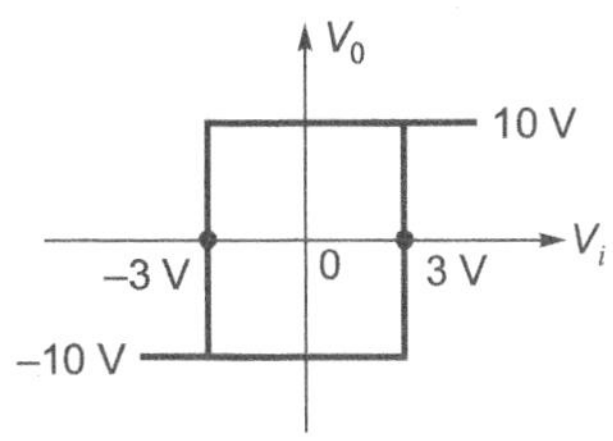

From given transfer characteristic,

$$\text{Upper trip point (UTP)} = 3\text{ V}$$

$$\frac{R_1}{R_1 + R_2} V_{sat} = 3\text{ V}$$

and $$V_{sat} = 10\text{ V}$$

$\therefore$ $$\frac{R_1}{R_1 + R_2} = \frac{3}{10}$$

$\Rightarrow$ $$1 + \frac{R_2}{R_1} = \frac{10}{3}$$

$$\frac{R_1}{R_2} = \frac{3}{7}$$

We can choose $R_1 = 3\text{ k}\Omega$ and $R_2 = 7\text{ k}\Omega$

(i) When, $V_i = 5 \sin\omega t$

When the input voltage exceeds the UTP on the upward swing of the positive half cycle, the output voltage switches to $-V_{sat}$. Half a cycle latter, the input voltage become more negative than the LTP, and the output switches back to $+V_{sat}$.

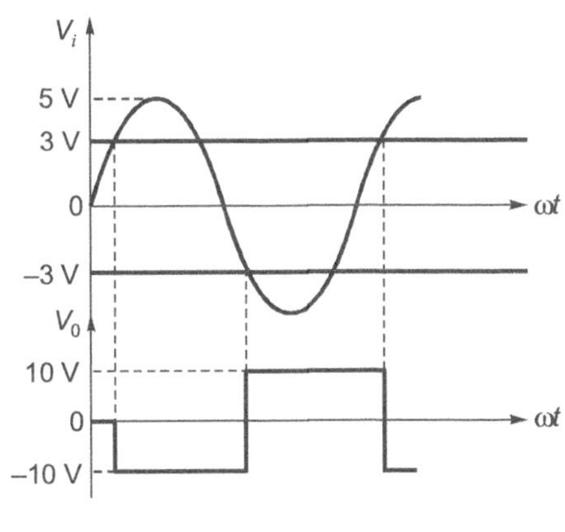

(ii) When V_i = half-wave rectified of 5 sinωt

As the input voltage will never become more negative then LTP, the output will never switch back to $+V_{sat}$.

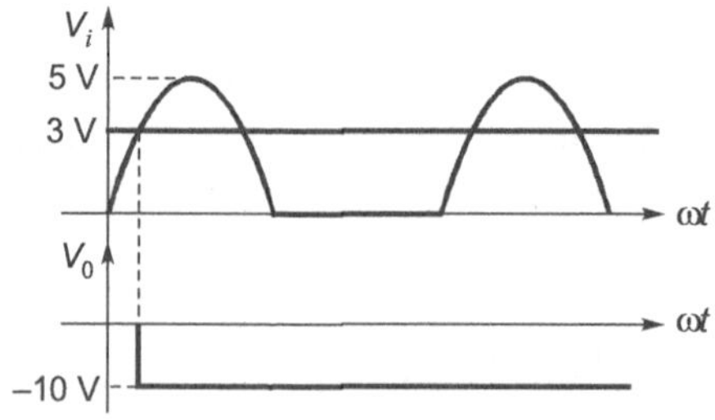

1.16 Determine the output voltage V_0 of the circuit shown in the figure.

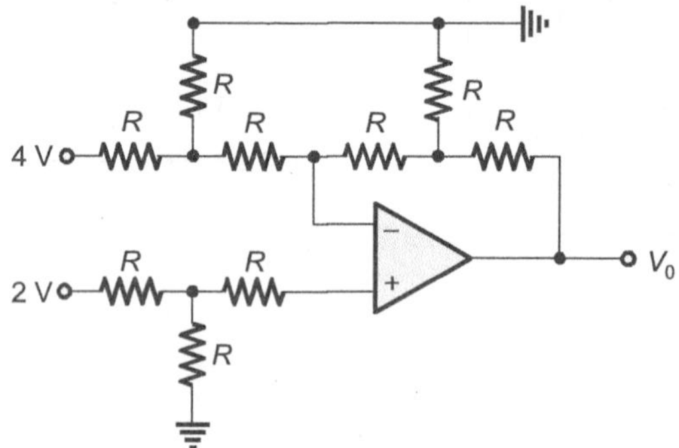

[10 marks : 2012]

Solution:

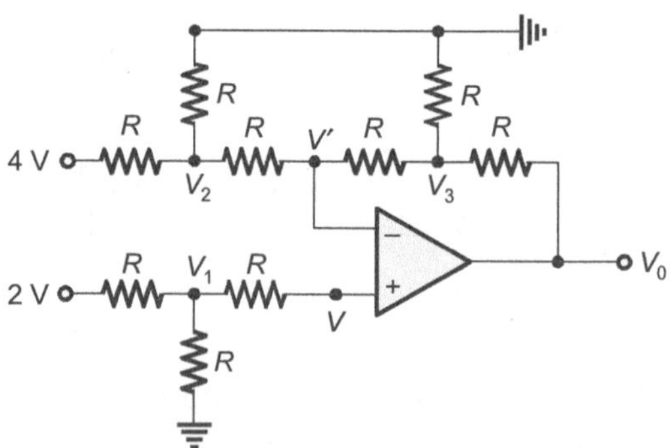

Applying KCL for V_1,

$$\frac{V_1-2}{R}+\frac{V_1}{R}+\frac{V_1-V}{R} = 0$$

$$\Rightarrow \quad 3V_1 = 2 + V$$

Since, no current flows into the op-amp,

$$V_1 = V$$

$$\therefore \quad 2V = 2$$

$$\Rightarrow \quad V = 1\text{ V} \quad ...(1)$$

Also, due to internal short, $V' = V = 1$ V

Applying KCL for V_2,

$$\frac{V_2-4}{R}+\frac{V_2}{R}+\frac{V_2-1}{R} = 0$$

$$3V_2 = 5$$

$$\Rightarrow \quad V_2 = \frac{5}{3}\text{ V} \quad ...(2)$$

Applying KCL at node voltage V',

$$\frac{V'-V_2}{R}+\frac{V'-V_s}{R} = 0$$

$$2V' = V_2 + V_3$$

$$\Rightarrow \quad V_3 = 2-\frac{5}{3}$$

$$V_3 = \frac{1}{3}\text{ V} \quad ...(3)$$

Now, applying KCL and node V_s,

$$\frac{V_3 - 1}{R} + \frac{V_s}{R} + \frac{V_3 - V_0}{R} = 0$$

$$V = 3V_3 - 1 = 0\text{ V}$$

1.17 **Define slew rate and PSRR of an operational amplifier. Explain clearly the difference between Bandwidth, transient response and slew-rate of an op-amp.**

[4 marks : 2013]

Solution:

Slew rate: It is defined as the maximum rate of change of output voltage per unit of time and is expressed as volt per micro second. An ideal op-amp has infinite slew rate.

PSRR: The PSRR is defined as the ratio of the change in supply voltage to the equivalent (differential) input voltage it produces in the op-amp, often expressed in decibles. An ideal op-amp has infinite PSRR.

$$\text{PSRR} = \frac{\Delta V_{\text{supply}}}{\Delta V_{IOS}}$$

Bandwidth: It is the range of frequency for which amplifier can faithfully amplify the signal.

Transient Response: When the system is subjected to an input, the output tries to reach to steady state value. This process of achieving steady state value is called transient response.

1.18 **Find an expression for the output V_0 of the amplifier circuit shown below. Assume an ideal op-amp. What mathematical operation does the circuit perform?**

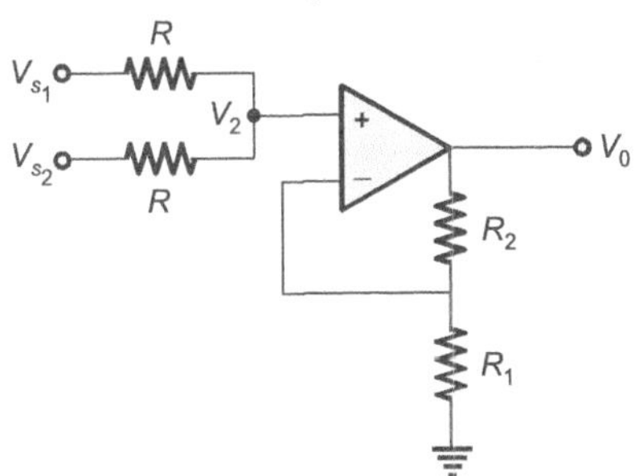

[4 marks : 2013]

Solution:

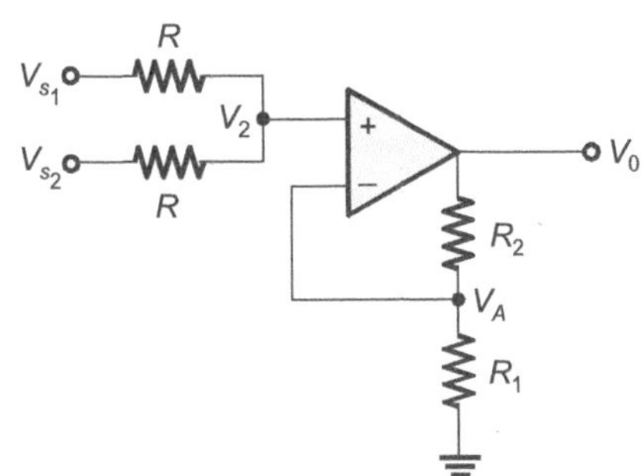

$$V_2 = \frac{V_{S_1} + V_{S_2}}{2}$$

By virtual ground theory, $V_2 = V_A$

$$V_2 = \frac{V_{S_1} + V_{S_2}}{2} = V_A$$

$$V_A = \left(\frac{R_1}{R_1 + R_2}\right) V_o$$

$$\Rightarrow \quad V_0 = \left(\frac{V_{S_1} + V_{S_2}}{2}\right)\left(\frac{R_2 + R_1}{R_1}\right)$$

$$\Rightarrow \quad V_0 = \left(\frac{V_{S_1} + V_{S_2}}{2}\right)\left(1 + \frac{R_2}{R_1}\right)$$

If $R_1 = R_2 = R$

$$\Rightarrow \quad V_0 = V_{S_1} + V_{S_2}$$

So mathematical operation performed is addition.

1.19 A voltage $v_i = 1 + 2\sin\omega t$ is applied to the circuit shown in figure. Draw the output voltage and capacitor voltage waveforms. Find the average output voltage. Assuming $\omega = 1$ rad/sec.

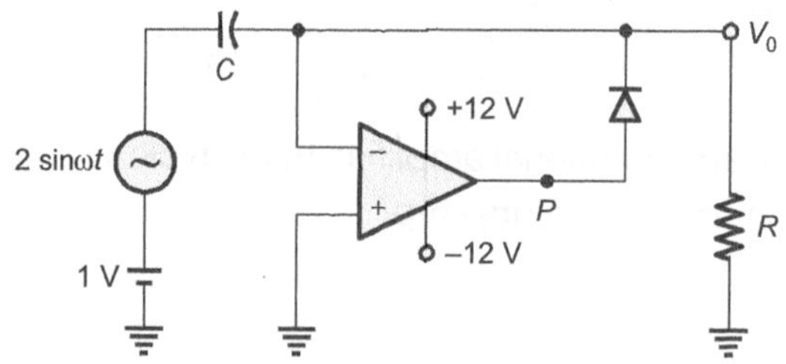

[4 marks : 2014]

Solution:

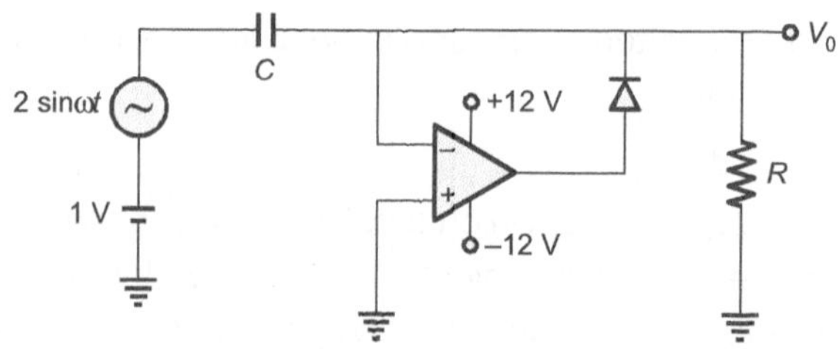

At $2\sin\omega t = -1$, the circuit becomes:

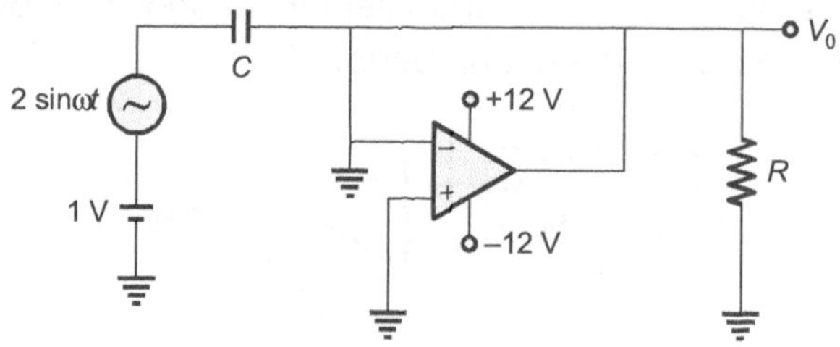

At $2\sin\omega t = -2$, the circuit becomes:

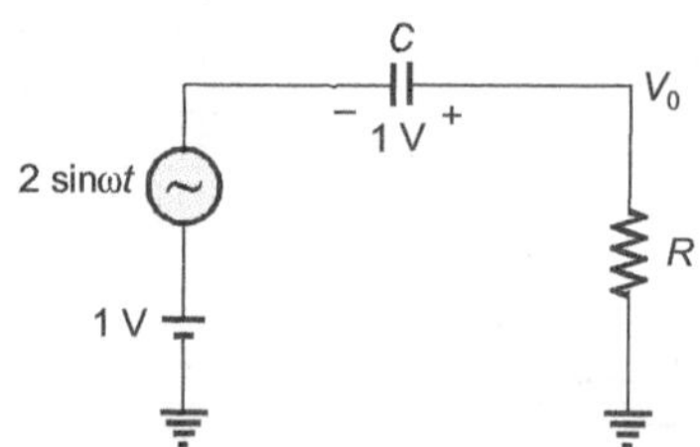

$V_0 = 2 + 2\sin\omega t$

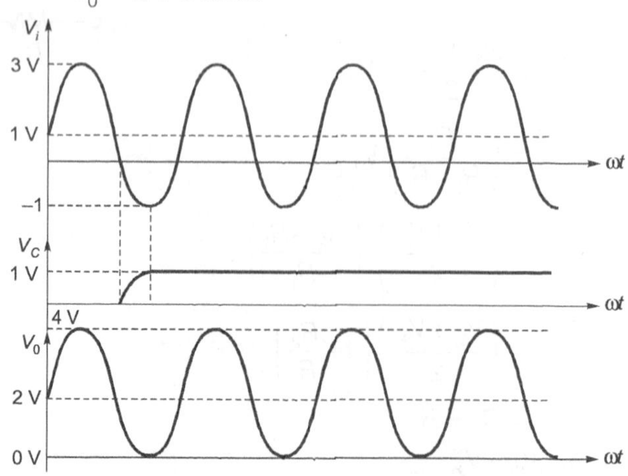

Average output voltage = 2 volts

1.20 Discuss the operation of the relaxation oscillator circuit shown in figure with relevant waveforms. Derive expressions for the

(*i*) *UTP* (V_H) and (*LTP*) (V_L)

(*ii*) Frequency and duty cycle in terms of *UTP* and *LTP*.

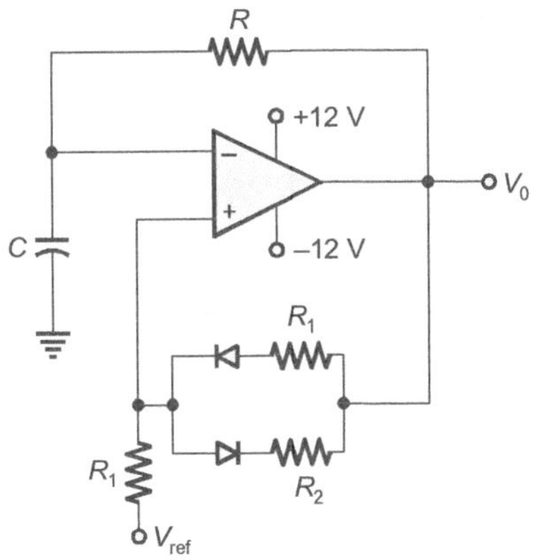

[15 marks : 2014]

Solution:

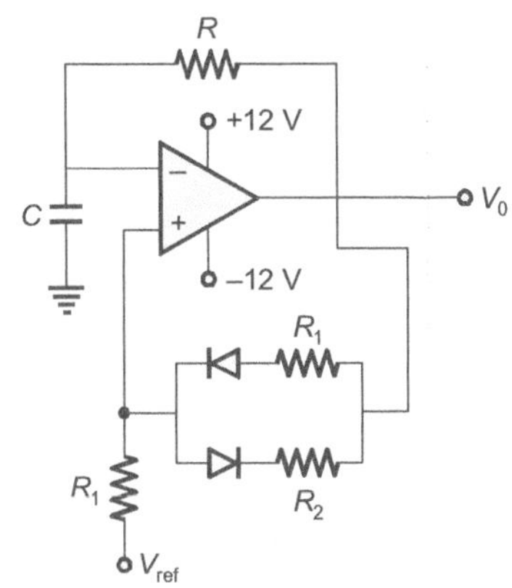

When, $V_0 = 12\text{ V}$

$$I_1 = \left(\frac{12 - V_{ref}}{2R_1}\right)$$

$$V^+ = 12 - I_1 R_1 = 12 - \left(\frac{12 - V_{ref}}{2}\right)$$

$$V^+ = \left(\frac{24 - 12 + V_{ref}}{2}\right) = \left(\frac{12 + V_{ref}}{2}\right)$$

When, $V_0 = -12\text{ V}$

$$I_2 = \left(\frac{V_{ref} + 12}{R_1 + R_2}\right)$$

$$V^+ = V_{ref} - I_2 R_1 = V_{ref} - \left(\frac{V_{ref} + 12}{R_1 + R_2}\right) R_1$$

$$V^+ = \left[\frac{V_{ref}(R_1 + R_2) - (V_{ref} + 12)R_1}{R_1 + R_2}\right]$$

$$= \left[\frac{V_{ref} R_2 - 12R_1}{R_1 + R_2}\right]$$

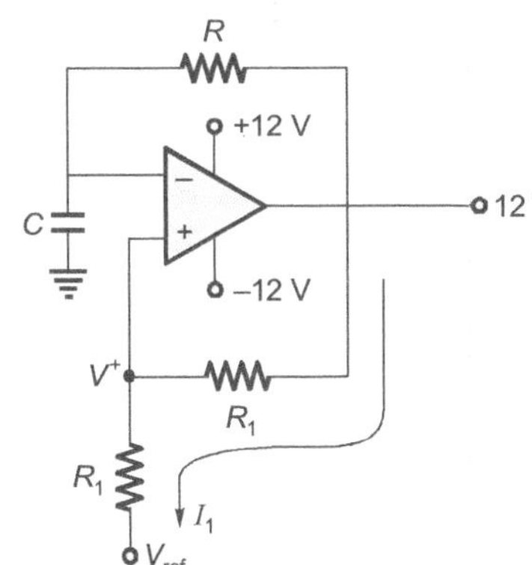

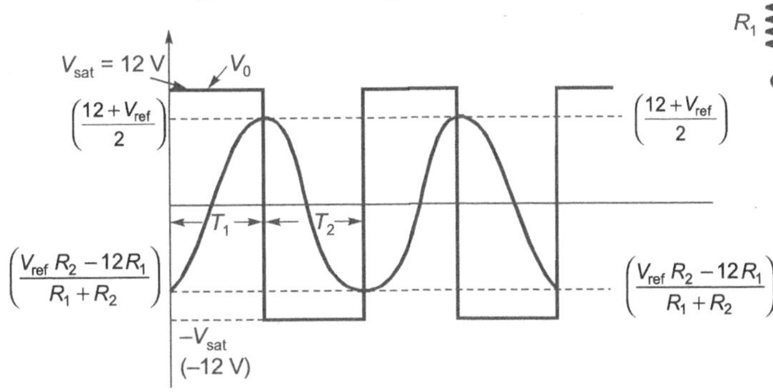

Calculation of T_1:

The voltage across capacitor is given by the expression

$$V_c(t) = V_c(\infty) + (V_c(0) - V_c(\infty))\, e^{-t/\tau}$$

where,
$$\tau = RC$$

$$V_c(t) = \left(\frac{12 + V_{\text{ref}}}{2}\right)$$

$$V_c(0) = \left(\frac{V_{\text{ref}} R_2 - 12 R_1}{R_1 + R_2}\right) V_c(\infty) = 12 \text{ V}$$

On solving,
$$T_1 = RC\, In\left[\frac{2(V_{\text{ref}} R_2 - 24 R_1 - 12 R_2)}{(R_1 + R_2)(V_{\text{ref}} - 12)}\right]$$

Calculation of T_2:

Here,
$$V_c(t) = \frac{V_{\text{ref}} R_2 - I_2 R_1}{R_1 + R_2}$$

$$V_c(\infty) = -12$$

$$V_c(0) = \left(\frac{12 + V_{\text{ref}}}{2}\right)$$

Solving,
$$T_2 = RC\, In\left[\frac{(24 + V_{\text{ref}})(R_1 + R_2)}{R_2(12 + V_{\text{ref}})}\right]$$

$$\text{Frequency} = \frac{1}{\text{Time period}} = \frac{1}{T_1 + T_2}$$

$$T = \frac{1}{RC\left\{In\left[\frac{2(V_{\text{ref}} R_2 - 24 R_1 - 12 R_2)}{(R_1 + R_2)(V_{\text{ref}} - 12)}\right] + In\left[\frac{(24 + V_{\text{ref}})(R_1 + R_2)}{R_2(12 + V_{\text{ref}})}\right]\right\}}$$

$$\text{Duty cycle of } T_1 = \left(\frac{T_1}{T}\right)$$

$$\text{Duty cycle of } T_2 = \left(\frac{T_2}{T}\right)$$

1.21 The following circuit is used for simulation of inductance by OP-AMP:

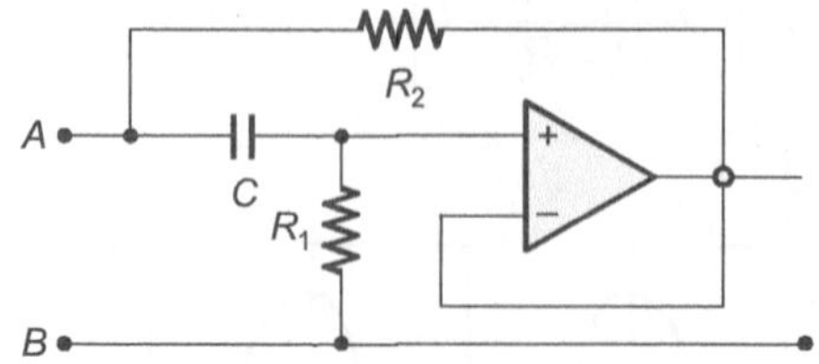

Show that we can have a tuned circuit, if we connect a capacitance between A and B and the maximum Q of the inductance is obtained when $\omega = \dfrac{1}{C\sqrt{R_1 R_2}}$.

[10 + 5 marks : 2015]

Solution:

First of all we will find the inductance seen between *A-B* terminals:

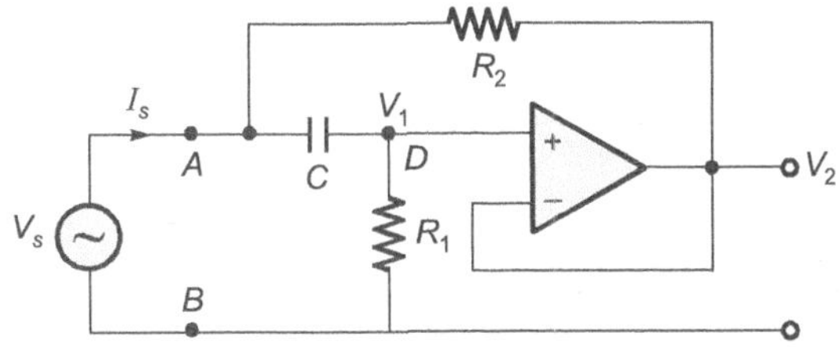

To find out impedance seen at terminals *A-B*, we apply a voltage source V_s and assume I_s current coming out of the voltage source. Since op-amp is in negative feed back, we can apply virtual short concept and $V_2 = V_1 = V$.

So, KCL at node A,

$$I_s = \frac{(V_s - V)}{R_2} + \frac{(V_s - V)}{1/sC}$$

$$I_s = \frac{(V_s - V)}{R_2} + sC(V_s - V) \quad ...(1)$$

and KCL at node *D*,

$$\frac{(V_s - V)}{1/sC} = \frac{V}{R_1}$$

$$V_s - V = \frac{V}{R_1 sC}$$

$$V_s = V\left(1 + \frac{1}{R_1 sC}\right)$$

$$V = \left(\frac{V_s}{1 + \frac{1}{R_1 sC}}\right) \quad ...(2)$$

Using equation (1) and (2),

$$I_s = V_s\left(\frac{1}{R_2} + sC\right) - V_s\left(\frac{1}{R_2} + sC\right) \cdot \frac{1}{\left(1 + \frac{1}{R_1 sC}\right)}$$

$$I_s = V_s\left(\frac{1 + R_2 sC}{R_2}\right) - V_s\left(\frac{1 + R_2 sC}{R_1 sC + 1}\right)\frac{R_1 sC}{R_2}$$

$$I_s = V_s\left[\frac{(1 + R_2 sC)(1 + R_1 sC) - R_1 sC(1 + R_2 sC)}{R_2(R_1 sC + 1)}\right]$$

$$= V_s\left[\frac{1 + R_1 sC + R_2 sC + R_1 R_2 s^2 C^2 - R_1 sC - R_1 R_2 s^2 C^2}{R_2(R_1 sC + 1)}\right] = V_s\left[\frac{1 + R_2 sC}{(1 + R_1 sC)R_2}\right]$$

So,

$$Z = \frac{V_s}{I_s} = \frac{(1 + R_1 sC)R_2}{(1 + R_2 sC)}$$

Now suppose $R_2 sC << 1 \Rightarrow Z = R_2 R_1 sC + R_2$

So above opamp circuit is equivalent to an inductance ($L = R_2R_1C$) is series with a resistor (R_2). Now, a capacitance is connected between A and B then the circuit will become a series RLC circuit with capacitance (C), inductance (R_2R_1C) and resistor (R_2).

The resonant frequency will be $\omega_0 = \dfrac{1}{\sqrt{LC}} = \dfrac{1}{C\sqrt{R_1R_2}}$ and the maximum Q (Quality factor) is obtained when

$\omega = \omega_0$ so it is obtained at $\dfrac{1}{C\sqrt{R_1R_2}}$.

1.22 **Draw the transfer characteristic V_0/V_{in} of the OP-AMP circuit shown in the following figure.**

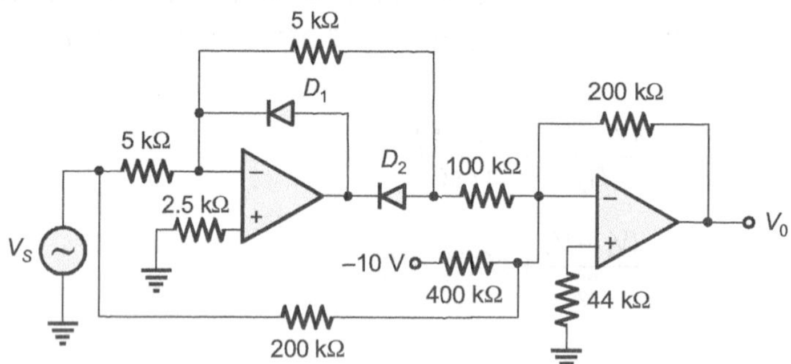

[10 marks : 2016]

Solution:

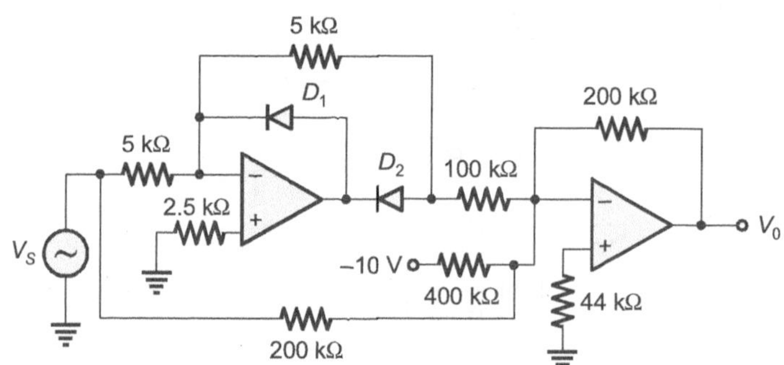

During positive half cycle, diode D_1 is off and D_2 is ON.

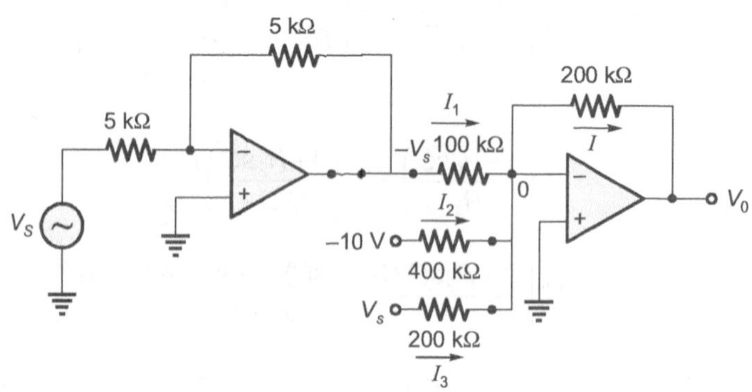

Output of the first op amp is

$$V_0' = \left(\frac{-5\text{k}\Omega}{5\text{k}\Omega}\right)V_s = -V_s$$

$$I_1 = \frac{(-V_s)}{100\text{k}\Omega}, \qquad I_2 = \left(\frac{-10}{400\text{k}\Omega}\right)$$

$$I_3 = \frac{V_s}{200\text{k}\Omega}$$

By KCL,
$$I = I_1 + I_2 + I_3$$

$$I = \frac{-V_s}{100\text{k}\Omega} + \left(\frac{-10}{400\text{k}\Omega}\right) + \frac{V_s}{200\text{k}\Omega}$$

$$I = 10^{-3}(-5 \times 10^{-3}\,V_s - 0.025)\text{ A}$$

$$V_0 = 2\,V_s + 5 - V_s$$

$$V_0 = V_s + 5 \qquad \text{(for positive half cycle)}$$

For negative half cycle diode D_1 is on, D_2 is off.

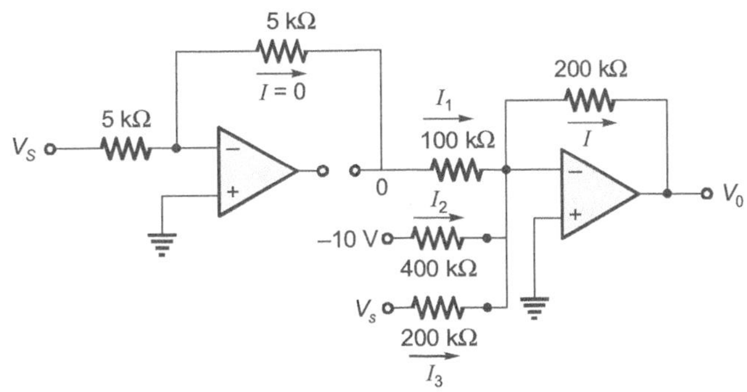

$$I = I_1 + I_2 + I_3$$

$$I = 0 + \left(\frac{-10}{400\text{k}\Omega}\right) + \left(\frac{V_s}{200\text{k}\Omega}\right)$$

$$I = (5 \times 10^{-3}\,V_s - 0.025)\,10^{-3}\text{ A}$$

$$V_0 = 5 + (-V_s) = -V_s + 5$$

$\therefore$ $V_0 = -V_s + 5$ from negative half cycle.

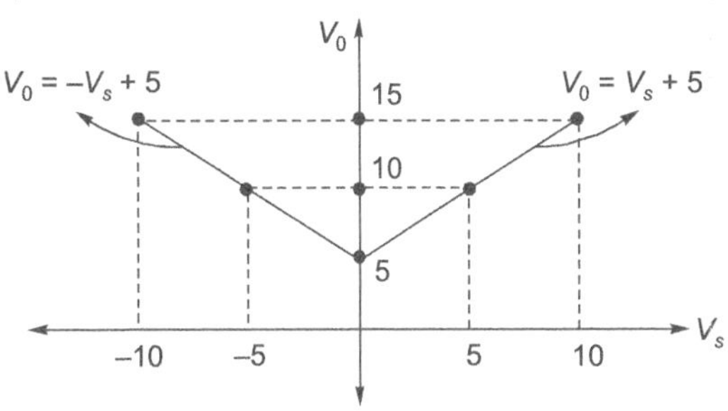

1.23 Find the gain v_0/v_i for the ideal Op-amp shown in the figure below.

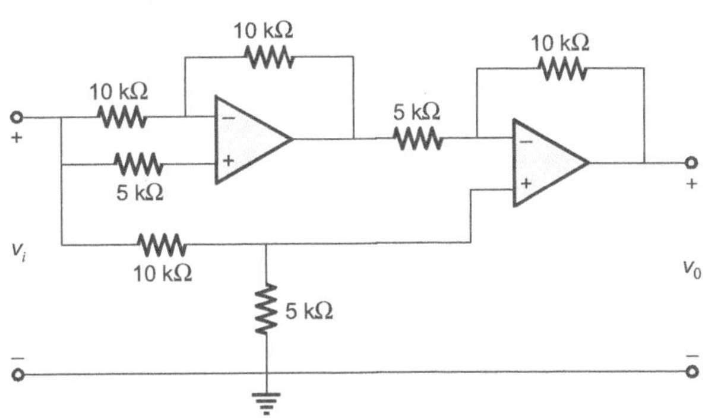

[12 marks : 2017]

Solution:

$$V_0 = -\frac{10\text{ k}}{5\text{ k}}V_i + \left[1 + \frac{10\text{ k}}{5\text{ k}}\right] \times V_i\left[\frac{5\text{ k}}{10\text{ k} + 5\text{ k}}\right]$$

$$= -2V_i + \left(3 \times \frac{V_i}{3}\right) = -2\,V_i + V_i = -V_i$$

$$\frac{V_0}{V_i} = -1$$

1.24 For the circuits shown below, calculate the output voltage:

$R_1 = 1$ kΩ, $R_2 = 2$ kΩ, $R_3 = 3$ kΩ

$R_4 = 10$ kΩ, $R_5 = 10$ kΩ, $R_6 = 1000$ kΩ

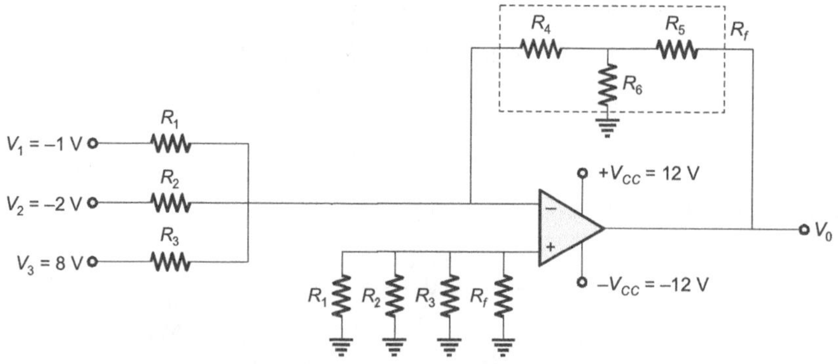

$V_1 = -1$ V $V_2 = -2$ V $V_3 = 8$ V

[20 marks : 2018]

Solution:

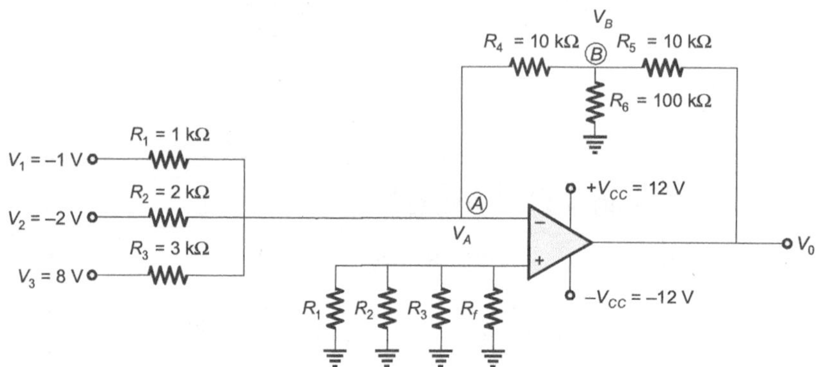

Assuming ideal opamp and respective node voltages V_A and V_B,

$$A_{OL} = \infty$$

Hence, $V_d = 0$

$\therefore$ $V^+ = V^-$

Applying KCL at (A),

$$\frac{-1-V_A}{R_1} + \frac{-2-V_A}{R_2} + \frac{8-V_A}{R_3} = -\frac{V_B}{R_4}$$

As, $V_A = V^- = 0$, putting given values we get

$$\therefore \quad V_B = -\frac{20}{3}\text{ V} \quad \text{...(i)}$$

Applying KCL at B, $$\frac{-V_B}{R_4} = \frac{V_B}{R_6} + \frac{V_B - V_0}{R_5}$$

From equation (i), $$V_B = -\frac{20}{3}$$

Putting given values $$\frac{20/3}{10k} = \frac{-20/3}{100k} + \frac{-20/3 - V_0}{10k}$$

$\therefore$ $V_0 = -14$ V

As V_0 exceeds the saturation voltage of opamp hence opamp works in saturation region.

Hence, $V_0 = -12$ V

1.25 Determine the values of slope K_1, K_2, K_3 and the voltages L_+ and L_- for the amplifier and its transfer characteristics shown in the figure given below:

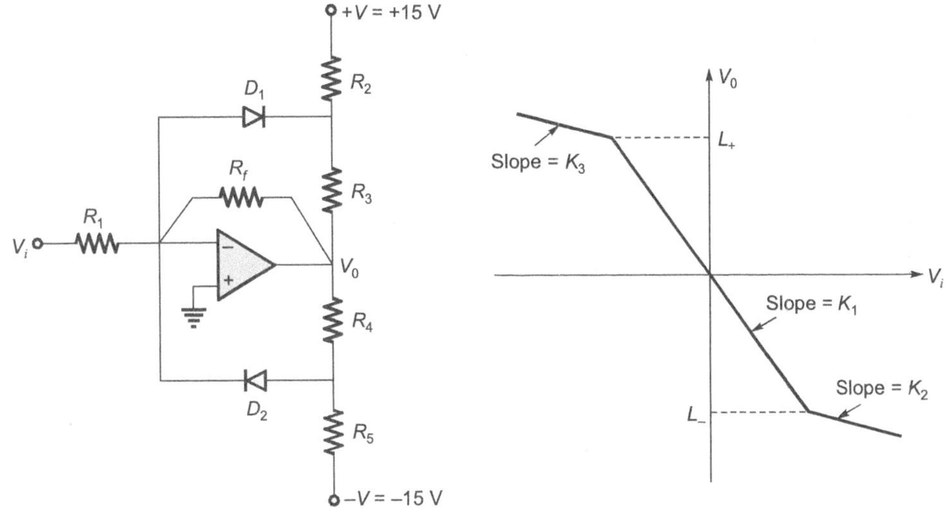

(R_1 = 30 kΩ, $R_2 = R_5$ = 9 kΩ, $R_3 = R_4$ = 3 kΩ, R_f = 60 kΩ).
The diodes may be assumed to be ideal.

[12 marks : 2019]

Solution:

Assume D_1 and D_2 off

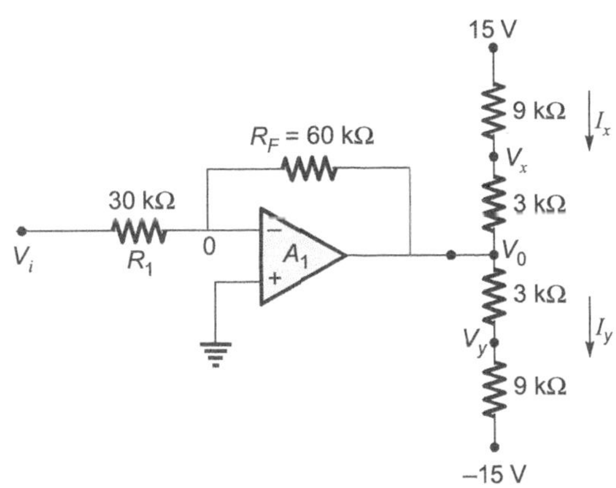

Op-amp A_1 is inverting amplifier,

$$V_0 = -\frac{R_F}{R_1}V_i = -\frac{60k}{30k}V_i = -2\ V_i$$

Case-1:

$$I_x = \frac{15 - V_0}{9k + 3k} = \frac{15-(-2V_i)}{12k} = \frac{15+2V_i}{12k}$$

$$V_x = 15 - 9k \times I_x$$

$$= 15 - 9k \times \left(\frac{15+2V_i}{12k}\right)$$

$$V_x = 15 - \frac{3}{4}(15 + 2V_i)$$

When, $V_x < 0$, D_1 ON

Keep, $V_x = 0$ (boundary) for slope change

$$0 = 15 - \frac{3}{4}(15 + 2V_i)$$

$$15 = \frac{3}{4}(15 + 2V_i)$$

$$\frac{60}{3} = (15 + 2V_i)$$

$$2V_i = 5$$

$$V_i = 2.5 \text{ then } L = -2V_i = -5\text{ V}$$

Similarly,

$$I_y = \frac{-2V_i - (-15)}{12k} = \frac{15 - 2V_i}{12k}$$

$$V_y = I_y \times 9k - 15$$

$$= \frac{(15 - 2V_i)}{12k} \times 9k - 15$$

When, $V_y > 0$, D_2 ON

Keep, $V_y = 0$ (Boundary) for slope change

$$0 = (15 - 2V_i)\frac{3}{4} - 15$$

$$15 = (15 - 2V_i)\frac{3}{4}$$

$$\frac{60}{3} = (15 - 2V_i)$$

$$-2V_i = 5$$

$$V_i = -2.5\text{ V then } L_t = -2V_i = +5\text{ V}$$

when D_1 on

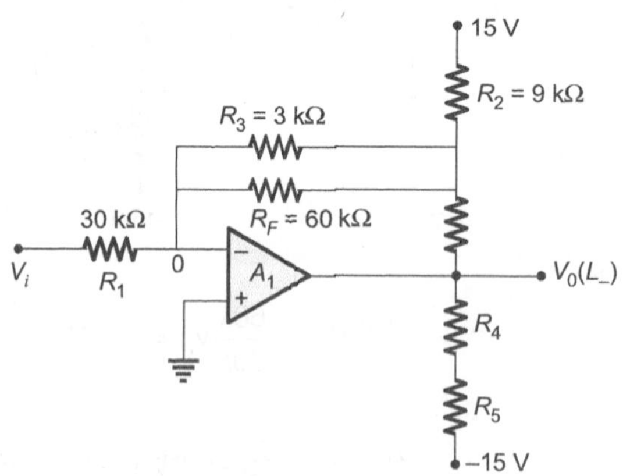

$$= -\frac{60k \,||\, 3k}{30k}V_i = -\frac{2}{21}V_i$$

Similarly, when D_2 on $V_0(L_+) = +\frac{60k \,||\, 3k}{30k}V_i = \frac{2}{21}V_i$

$$k_3(\text{slope}) = \frac{2}{21}$$

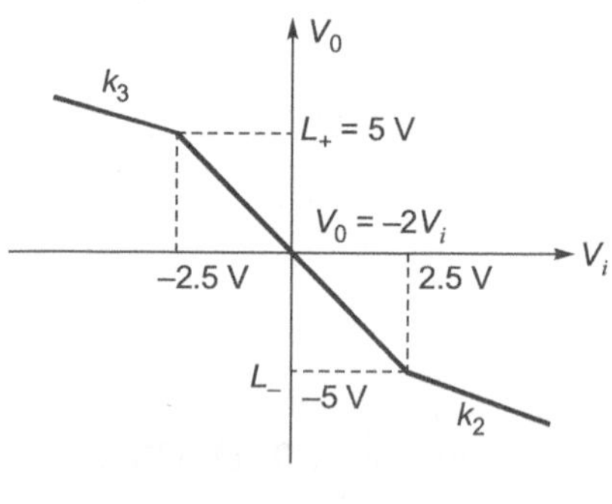

1.26 Determine the value of v_p, v_n and v_{out} in the circuit given below which uses an ideal operational amplifier. Find a resistance R that, when connected in parallel with the 1 mA source, will cause v_{out} to drop to half its value when R is not present.

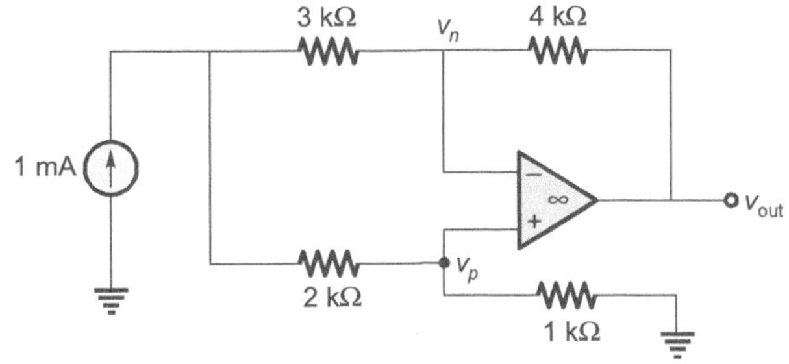

[20 marks : 2019]

Solution:

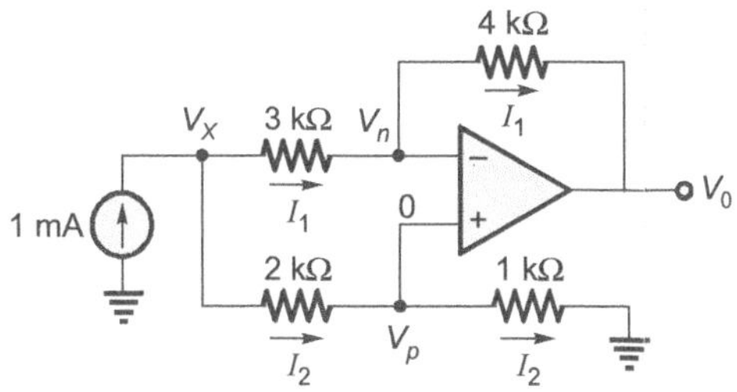

$$\frac{V_X - V_n}{3\text{ k}\Omega} = I_1 \qquad (\text{where } V_P = V_n)$$

$$\frac{V_X - V_p}{2\text{ k}\Omega} = I_2$$

$$I_1 \times 3\text{ k}\Omega = I_2 \times 2\text{ k}\Omega$$

$$\frac{I_1}{I_2} = \frac{2\text{ k}\Omega}{3\text{ k}\Omega} = \frac{2}{3}$$

$$I_1 + I_2 = 1\text{ mA}$$

$$I_1 = \frac{2}{5}\text{ mA}$$

and $$I_2 = \frac{3}{5}\text{mA}$$

$$V_P = I_1 \times 1\text{ k}\Omega$$

$$= \frac{3}{5} \times 1\text{ k}\Omega = \frac{3}{5}\text{V}$$

$$V_p = V_n = \frac{3}{5}\text{V}$$

$$V_0 = V_n - 4\text{ k} \times I_1$$

$$= \frac{3}{5} - 4\text{k} \times \frac{2}{5}\text{ mA} = \frac{3}{5} - \frac{8}{5} = \frac{-5}{5} = -1\text{ V}$$

$$V_0 = -1\text{ V}$$

$$V_p = \frac{3}{5}\text{ V}$$

$$V_n = \frac{3}{5}\text{ V}$$

Similarly, If R is connected in parallel to 1 mA current source where

$$V_0 = \frac{-1\text{ V}}{2} = -0.5\text{ V}$$

1.27 For the circuit shown in the figure below, derive the expression for output voltage and sketch the nature of the output when $V_2 = 10$ V and $V_1 = 5$ V.

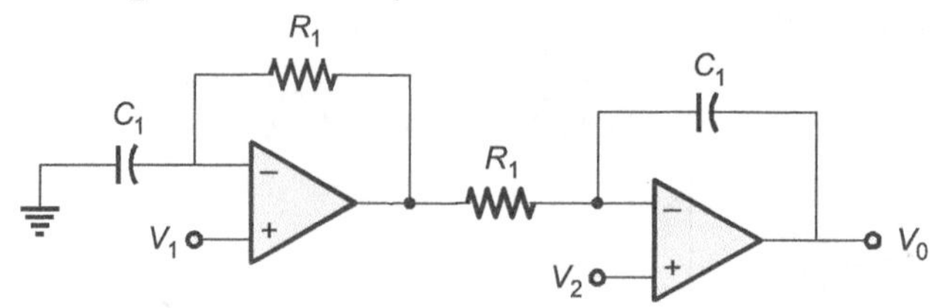

[12 marks : 2020]

Solution:

Assuming output terminal of first op-amp be at node voltage V_{01}.

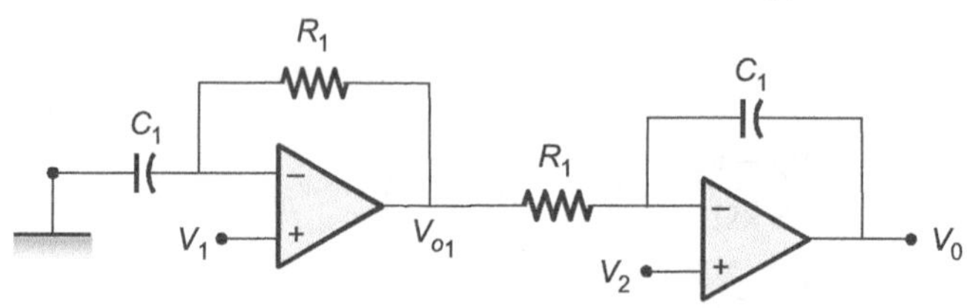

For op-Amp (1)

$$V_{o_1}(s) = \left[1+\frac{R_1}{\frac{1}{sC_1}}\right]\cdot\frac{V_1}{s}$$

$$= [1+sR_1C_1]\cdot\frac{V_1}{s}$$

For op-Amp (2)

$$V_o(s) = -\frac{\frac{1}{sC_1}}{R_1}V_{o_1}(s)+\left[1+\frac{\frac{1}{sC_1}}{R_1}\right]\cdot\frac{V_2}{s}$$

$$V_o(s) = -\frac{1}{sC_1R_1}V_{o_1}(s)+\left[1+\frac{1}{sC_1R_1}\right]\cdot\frac{V_2}{s}$$

$$V_o(s) = -\frac{1}{sC_1R_1}[1+sC_1R_1]\cdot\frac{V_1}{s}+\left[1+\frac{1}{sC_1R_1}\right]\cdot\frac{V_2}{s}$$

$$= -\frac{V_1}{s^2R_1C_1}-\frac{V_1}{s}+\frac{V_2}{s}+\frac{V_2}{s^2R_1C_1}$$

On taking inverse Laplace transform.

$$V_o(t) = -V_1\frac{t}{\tau}-V_1\ u(t)+V_2\ u(t)+V_2\cdot\frac{t}{\tau} \quad [\because\ \tau = R_1C_1]$$

$$= (V_2-V_1)\cdot\frac{t}{\tau}+(V_2-V_1)\cdot u(t)$$

$$V_o(t) = (10-5)\frac{t}{\tau}+(10-5)\cdot u(t) = \frac{5t}{\tau}+5u(t)$$

$\Rightarrow$ at $t = 0$

$V_o = 5V$

$\Rightarrow$ at $t = \tau,\ V_o = 10$

$\Rightarrow$ at $t = 2\tau,\ V_o = 15$

Output waveform:

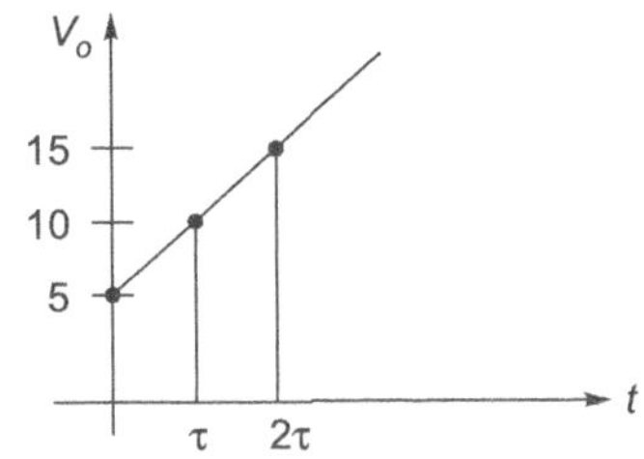

1.28 The current of an induction motor is sensed through a suitable arrangement and converted to equivalent voltage. The current contains fundamental and higher order 5th and 7th harmonics. In order to separate the fundamental, the equivalent voltage waveform is passed through the following circuit as given in figure. Find the (i) cut-off frequencies of each section, (ii) overall gain attenuation in dB for fundamental, 5th and 7th harmonics, and (iii) overall phase shift of the measured fundamental current.

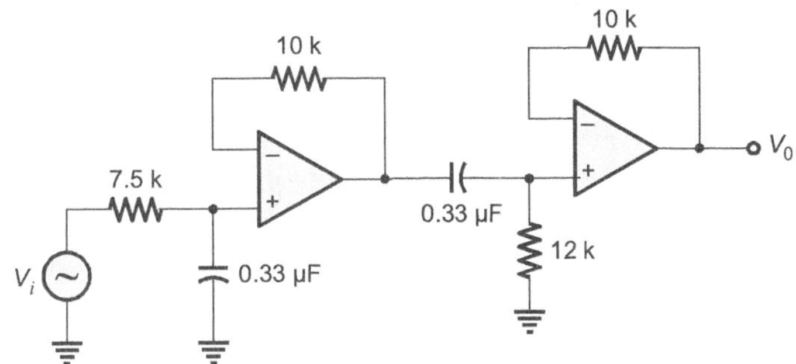

[20 marks : 2020]

Solution:

Current sensed by arrangement is $i_s(t)$

$$i_s(t) = I_1 \cdot \sin \omega t + I_5 \cdot \sin 5\omega t + I_7 \cdot \sin 7\omega t$$

This current is converted into equivalent voltages $V_s(t)$

$$V_s(t) = V_1 \sin \omega t + V_5 \sin 5\omega t + V_7 \cdot \sin 7\omega t$$

$$V_i = V_1 \cdot \sin \omega t + V_5 \cdot \sin 5\omega t + V_7 \cdot \sin 7\omega t$$

(i) For cut-off frequency of 1st section, f_{c1} [Low pass filter]

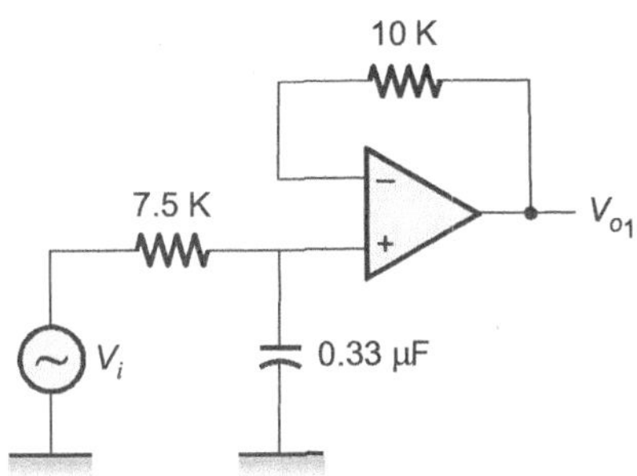

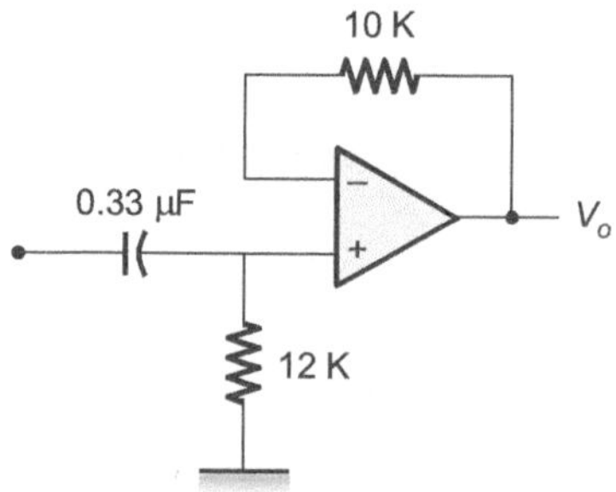

Cut-off frequency for given LPF is f_{c1}

$$f_{c1} = \frac{1}{2\pi\tau}$$

$$\tau = R_{eq} \cdot c$$

where R_{eq} is the resistance across c

So, $$f_{c1} = \frac{1}{2\pi\times 7.5\times 10^3 \times 0.33\times 10^{-6}} \quad (R_{eq} = 7.5 \text{ K})$$

$$f_{c1} = 64.30 \text{ Hz}$$

For cut-off frequency of 2nd section f_{c2} [High pass filter]

$$\tau = R_{eq} \cdot C \qquad R_{eq} = 12 \text{ K}$$

$$\tau = 12 \times 10^3 \times 0.33 \times 10^{-6} \qquad C = 0.33\ \mu\text{F}$$

$$\tau = 3.96 \times 10^{-3} \text{ sec}$$

Cut-off of 2nd stage is f_{c2}

$$f_{c2} = \frac{1}{2\pi\tau} = \frac{1}{2\pi\times 3.96\times 10^{-3}} = 40.19 \text{ Hz}$$

So cut-off frequencies are

$$f_{c1} = 64.30 \text{ Hz}, \ f_{c2} = 40.19 \text{ Hz}$$

(ii)

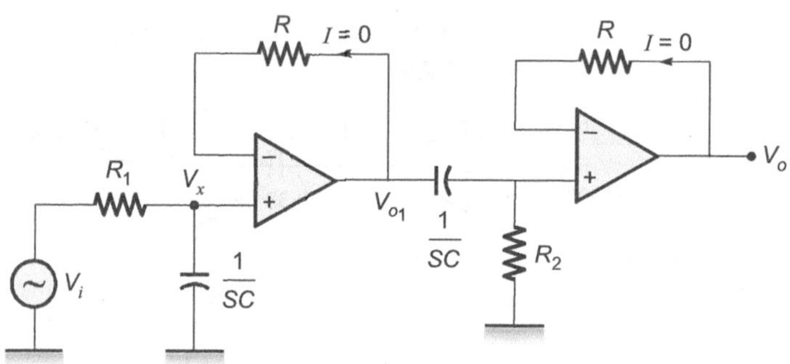

$$V_x = \frac{\frac{1}{sC}}{R_1 + \frac{1}{sC}} \times V_i$$

Due to virtual ground

$$V_x = V_o \qquad [\because I = 0 \text{ to } \infty \text{ input impedance of op-amp device}]$$

$$V_{o1} = \frac{V_i}{1+sR_1C} \qquad \text{[for LPF]}$$

Also, $$V_o = \frac{R_2}{R_2 + \frac{1}{sC}} V_{o1}$$

$$\frac{V_o}{V_{o1}} = \frac{sR_2C}{1+sR_2C} \qquad \text{[for HPF]}$$

Overall gain of given band pass filter is

$$\frac{V_o}{V_i} = \frac{V_{o1}}{V_i} \times \frac{V_o}{V_{o1}} = \frac{sR_2C}{(1+sR_1C)(1+sR_2C)}$$

$$\frac{V_o(s)}{V_i(s)} = \frac{sR_2C}{(1+sR_1C)(1+sR_2C)}$$

On putting values of C, R_2 and R_1

$$\frac{V_o(s)}{V_i(s)} = \frac{3.96\times10^{-3}s}{(1+2.475\times10^{-3}s)(1+3.96\times10^{-3}s)}$$

Put, $s = j\omega$

$$\frac{V_o(j\omega)}{V_i(j\omega)} = \frac{j3.96\times10^{-3}\omega}{(1+j2.475\times10^{-3}\omega)(1+j3.96\times10^{-3}\omega)} \quad \text{...(i)}$$

⇒ Overall gain (β_1) for fundamental frequency (f = 50Hz) is

$$\beta_1 = \left|\frac{V_o(j314)}{V_i(j314)}\right| = \left|\frac{j1.24344}{(1+j0.777)(1+j1.24344)}\right| = 0.6153$$

Attenuation for fundamental frequency,

$$\alpha_1 = \frac{1}{\beta_1} = 1.625$$

Attenuation (α_1) in (dB) = 20 $\log_{10}(\alpha_1)$ = 4.21 dB

⇒ Overall gain for 5th harmonic = β_5

$$\beta_5 = \left|\frac{V_o(j1570)}{V_i(j1570)}\right| = \left|\frac{j6.2172}{25.2662\angle156.43}\right| = 0.2460$$

$$\text{Attenuation } \alpha_5 = \frac{1}{\beta_5} = 4.06$$

α_5 in (dB) = 20 log 4.06 = 12.17 dB

⇒ Overall gain for 7th harmonic = β_7

$$\beta_7 = \left|\frac{V_o(j2198)}{V_i(j2198)}\right| = \left|\frac{j8.704}{48.46\angle163.39}\right| = 0.1269$$

$$\text{Attenuation in (dB)} = 20\log\left(\frac{1}{\beta_7}\right) = 37.92 \text{ dB}$$

So overall attenuation for fundamental frequency = 4.21 dB

5th harmonic = 12.17 dB

7th harmonic = 37.92 dB

(iii) Since filter is passing fundamental component of frequency only.

Output of filter = I_{o1} [only fundamental component of frequency]

$$I_{o1} = I_1\times\left|\frac{V_o(j314)}{V_i(j314)}\right|\times\sin\left(314t+\angle\left(\frac{V_o(j314)}{V_i(j314)}\right)^\circ\right)$$

$$I_{o1} = 0.6153\, I_1 \sin(314t + 0.9597^\circ) \text{ A}$$

So phase shift provided by band pass filter in fundamental component of current is 0.9597° only.

1.29 For a non-inverting amplifier with $A_0 = \infty$, calculate the closed loop gain. What happens to the result when $R_1 \to 0$ and $R_3 \to 0$?

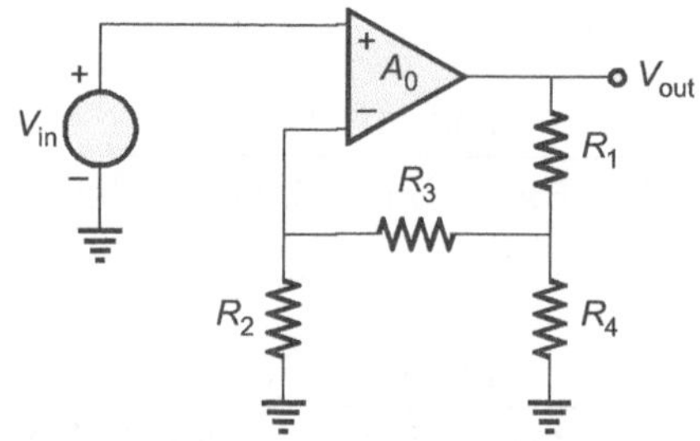

[12 marks : 2021]

Solution:

Given non-inverting amplifier is below :

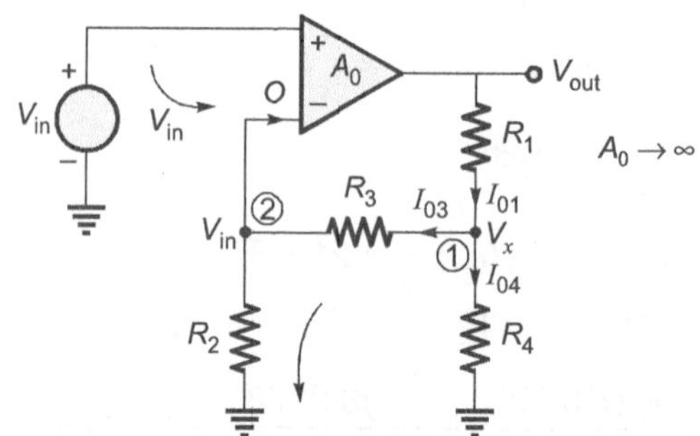

By applying virtual short concept because it is negative feedback amplifier.

Applying KCL at Node (1) :

$$\frac{V_0 - V_x}{R_1} = \frac{V_x}{R_4} + \frac{V_x - V_{in}}{R_3}$$

$$\Rightarrow \quad \frac{V_0}{R_1} = \left(\frac{V_x}{R_1} + \frac{V_x}{R_3} + \frac{V_x}{R_4}\right) - \frac{V_{in}}{R_3} \quad \text{...(i)}$$

Applying KCL at Node (2) :

$$\frac{V_x - V_{in}}{R_3} = \frac{V_{in}}{R_2}$$

$$\Rightarrow \quad \frac{V_x}{R_3} = \frac{V_{in}}{R_2} + \frac{V_{in}}{R_3}$$

$$\Rightarrow \quad V_x = V_{in} + \frac{R_3}{R_2}V_{in} = \left(1 + \frac{R_3}{R_2}\right)V_{in}$$

$$\Rightarrow \quad \frac{V_0}{R_1} = V_{in}\left(1 + \frac{R_3}{R_2}\right)\left[\frac{1}{R_1} + \frac{1}{R_3} + \frac{1}{R_4}\right] - \frac{V_{in}}{R_3}$$

$$\Rightarrow \quad V_0 = V_{in}\left(1 + \frac{R_3}{R_2}\right)\left(1 + \frac{R_1}{R_3} + \frac{R_1}{R_4}\right) - \frac{R_1}{R_3}V_{in}$$

The closed loop gain is

$$\frac{V_0}{V_{in}} = \left(1 + \frac{R_3}{R_2}\right)\left[1 + \frac{R_1}{R_3} + \frac{R_1}{R_4}\right] - \frac{R_1}{R_3}$$

When $R_1 \rightarrow 0$ and $R_3 \rightarrow 0$

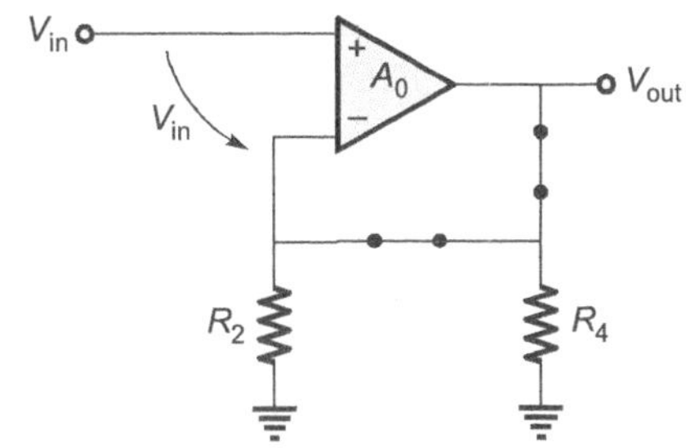

$\therefore$ The output voltage is given as for $R_1 \rightarrow 0$ and $R_2 \rightarrow 0$

$$V_{out} = V_{in}$$

1.30 (i) Analytically prove that following Op-Amp circuit does the function of differential integrator:

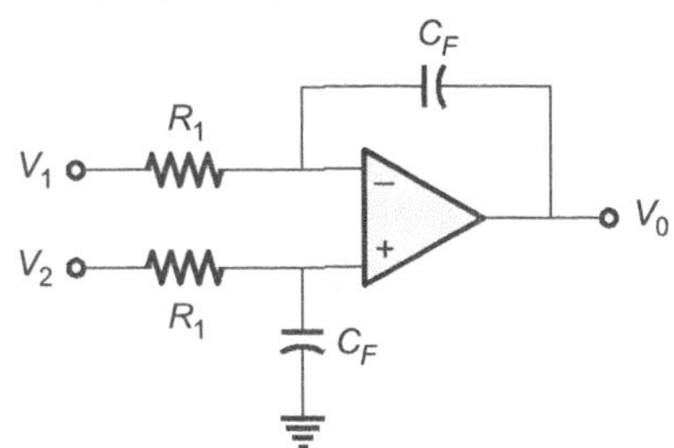

(ii) A. What is the full scale output of R - $2R$ ladder for 4-bit numbers with $R_F = 3R$ and state $0 \rightarrow 0$ V state $1 \rightarrow 5$ V?

B. What is output of above converter with input : 1001?

C. An analog signal sensed by a sensor needs to be digitized. The range of analog signal is 0 - 2 V, it is desired that variation of 0.01 V be detected. Assuming maximum frequency content in analog signal is not more than 2 kHz samples, calculate conversion time and resolution required.

[8+12 = 20 marks : 2021]

Solution:

(i) Given op-amp is :

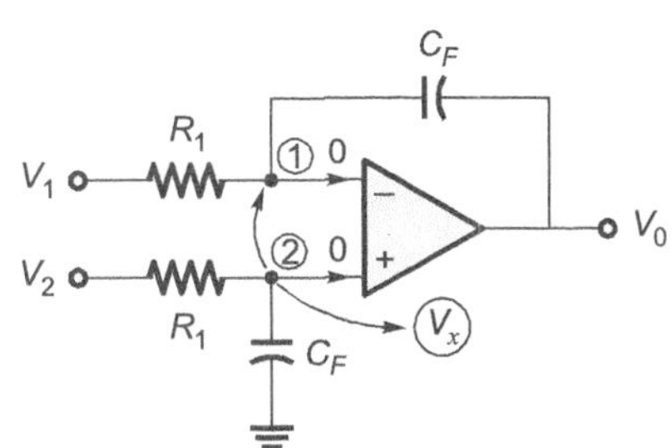

By applying voltage division rule at Node (2) :

$$V_x = \frac{V_2\left(\frac{1}{C_F s}\right)}{R_1 + \frac{1}{C_F s}} = \frac{V_2}{1 + R_1 C_F s}$$

Applying KCL at Node (1) :

$$\frac{V_1 - V_x}{R_1} = 0 + \frac{V_x - V_0}{\left(\frac{1}{C_F s}\right)}$$

$$(V_1 - V_x) = (R_1C_Fs)(V_x - V_0)$$
$$V_1 = (1 + R_1C_Fs)V_x - R_1C_Fs\,V_0$$
$$R_1C_Fs\,V_0 = (1 + R_1C_Fs)V_x - V_1$$
$$V_0 = \left(\frac{1+R_1C_Fs}{R_1C_Fs}\right)\left(\frac{V_2}{1+R_1C_Fs}\right) - \frac{V_1}{R_1C_Fs} = \frac{V_2}{R_1C_Fs} - \frac{V_1}{R_1C_Fs}$$
$$V_0 = \frac{1}{R_1C_Fs}(V_2 - V_1)$$
$$V_0(t) = \frac{1}{R_1C_F}\int(V_2 - V_1)dt$$

Output is integration of difference of input. Therefore, circuit functions as differential integrator.

(ii) A. For R-$2R$ ladder type

Full scale output $\Rightarrow$ V_{0f} = Resolution × Gain × Decimal equivalent of [1111_2]

$$V_{0f} = \frac{V_r}{2^n}\times\frac{R_f}{R}[1111_2 = 15] = \frac{15\times15}{16} = 14.0625\text{ V}$$

V_0 = Resolution × Gain × Decimal equivalent of binary data

B. $$\text{Output voltage} = \frac{V_r}{2^n}\times\frac{R_f}{R}\times[1001_2 = 9]$$

$$\text{Output voltage} = \left|\frac{5\text{V}}{2^4}\right|\left[\frac{3R}{R}\right][9] = \frac{5}{16}\times3\times9 = 8.4\text{ V}$$

C. Given :

Resolution = 0.01 V

$f_{m(\max)}$ = 2 kHz

$f_{s(\max)} = 2\times f_{m(\max)}$

$= 2 \times 2$ kHz = 4 kHz

$$\text{Conversion time, } t_c = \frac{1}{f_{s(\max)}} = \frac{1}{4\text{kHz}}$$

Conversion time will be, t_c = 0.25 ms

1.31 Draw the transfer characteristic of the circuit shown below. Assume the op-amp to be ideal.

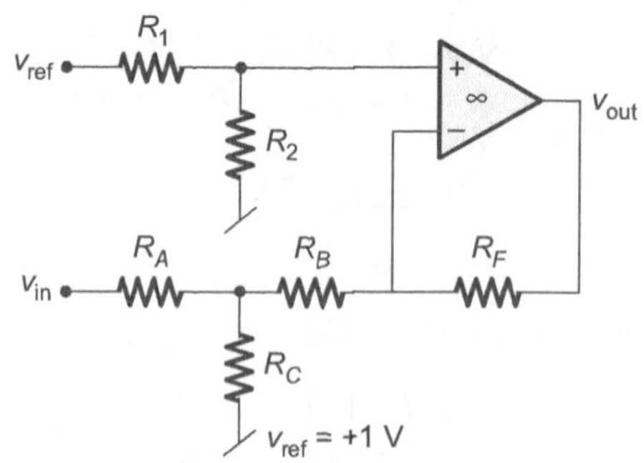

$$R_1 = R_2 = R_A = R_C = 100\text{ k}\Omega$$
$$R_B = 50\text{ k}\Omega,\ R_F = 1\text{ M}\Omega$$

[12 marks : 2022]

Solution:

Given :

V_{ref} = 1 V

$R_1 = R_2 = R_A = R_C = 100\text{ k}\Omega$

$R_B = 50\text{ k}\Omega,\ R_F = 1\text{ M}\Omega$

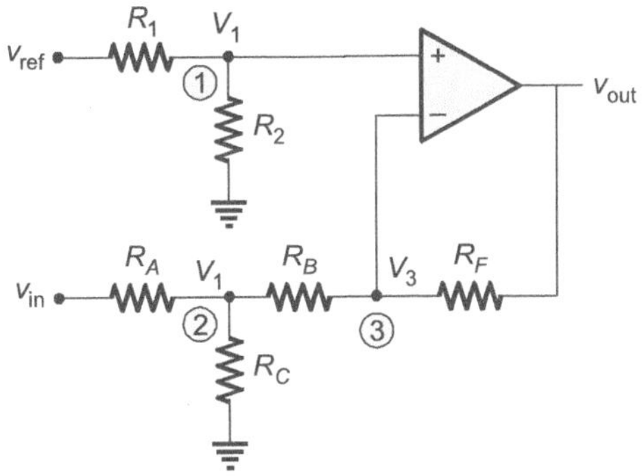

At node (1), apply voltage divider rule

$$V_1 = V_{ref} \times \frac{R_2}{R_2 + R_1}$$

$$= 1 \times \frac{100k}{100k + 100k} = \frac{1}{2}\text{V} \qquad ...(1)$$

At node (3), apply nodal analysis,

$$\frac{V_3 - V_2}{R_B} + \frac{V_3 - V_0}{R_F} = 0$$

$$V_3\left(\frac{1}{50k} + \frac{1}{1000k}\right) = \frac{V_2}{50k} + \frac{V_0}{1000k}$$

$$V_3 = \frac{20}{21}V_2 + \frac{V_0}{21} \qquad ...(2)$$

At node (2) apply nodal analysis,

$$\frac{V_2 - V_{in}}{R_A} + \frac{V_2}{R_C} + \frac{V_2 - V_3}{R_B} = 0$$

$$V_2\left(\frac{1}{100k} + \frac{1}{100k} + \frac{1}{50k}\right) = \frac{V_{in}}{100k} + \frac{V_3}{50k} \qquad ...(3)$$

$$V_2 = \frac{V_{in}}{4} + \frac{V_3}{2} \qquad ...(3)$$

Put eqn. (3) into eqn. (2)

$$V_3 = \frac{40}{21}\left(\frac{V_{in}}{4} + \frac{V_3}{2}\right) + 21V_0$$

$$\frac{11}{21}V_3 = \frac{5}{21}V_{in} + 21V_0$$

By using virtual ground theory, $V^+ = V^-$

$$V_3 = V_1$$

$\therefore$
$$V_3 = \frac{1}{2}V$$

$\therefore$
$$\frac{11}{21} \times \frac{1}{2} = \frac{5}{21}V_{in} + \frac{V_0}{21}$$

$$V_o = -5V_{in} + 5.5$$

Transfer characteristic of the circuit,

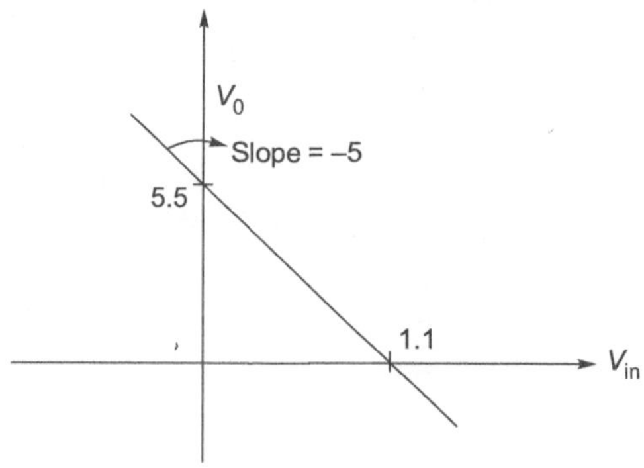

1.32 Determine the transfer function of the circuit shown below and determine therefrom, the function performed by the circuit. Also determine the input impedance $Z_{in}(s)$, as indicated in the figure.

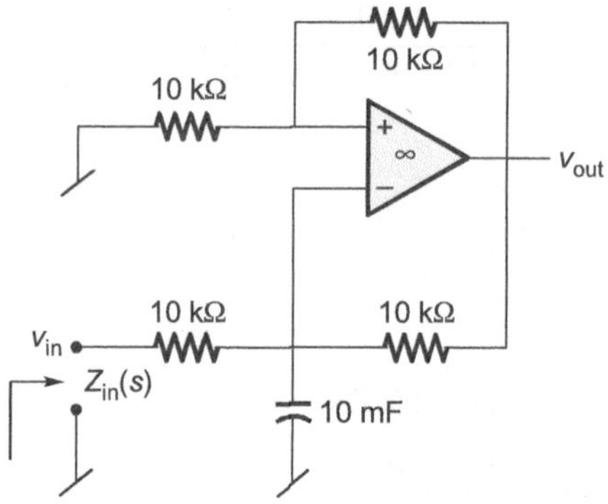

[12 marks : 2022]

Solution:

At node (1), apply KCL,

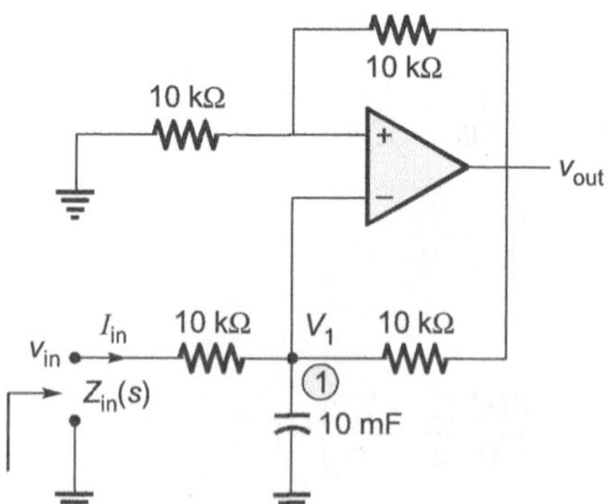

$$\frac{V_1 - V_{in}}{10k} + \frac{V_1}{\frac{1}{s} \times (0.01)} + \frac{V_1 - V_{out}}{10k} = 0$$

$$V_1\left(\frac{1}{10k} + 0.01s + \frac{1}{10k}\right) = \frac{V_{in}}{10k} + \frac{V_{out}}{10k}$$

$$V_1 = \frac{V_{in} + V_{out}}{2(1+50s)} \qquad \text{...(1)}$$

We know that, for non-inverting amplifier,

$$V_{out} = \left(1+\frac{R_2}{R_1}\right)V_1 = \left(1+\frac{10k}{10k}\right)V_1 = 2V_1$$

$$\therefore \quad V_{out} = 2\left(\frac{V_{in}}{2(1+50s)}+\frac{V_{out}}{2(1+50s)}\right)$$

$$V_{out}\left(1-\frac{1}{1+50s}\right) = \frac{V_{in}}{1+50s}$$

$$V_{out}\times\frac{50s}{1+50s} = \frac{V_{in}}{1+50}$$

$$\frac{V_{out}}{V_{in}} = \frac{1}{50s}$$

$$I_{in} = \frac{V_{in}-V_1}{10k} = \frac{V_{in}-\dfrac{(V_{in}+V_{out})}{2(1+50s)}}{10k}$$

$$= \frac{V_{in}(2(1+50s))-V_{in}-\dfrac{V_{in}}{50s}}{2\times 10k(1+50s)}$$

$$= V_{in}\left(\frac{2+100s-1-\dfrac{1}{50s}}{20k(1+50s)}\right)$$

$$= V_{in}\left(\frac{(1+100s)(50s)-1}{(50s)(20k)(1+50s)}\right)$$

Input impedance, $Z_i = \dfrac{V_{in}}{I_{in}}$

$$\therefore \quad Z_i = \frac{1000s(1+50s)}{5000s^2+50s-1}\ \text{k}\Omega$$

1.33 For the circuit given below, find the value of the components. Gain is 5 at a frequency of 32 kHz.

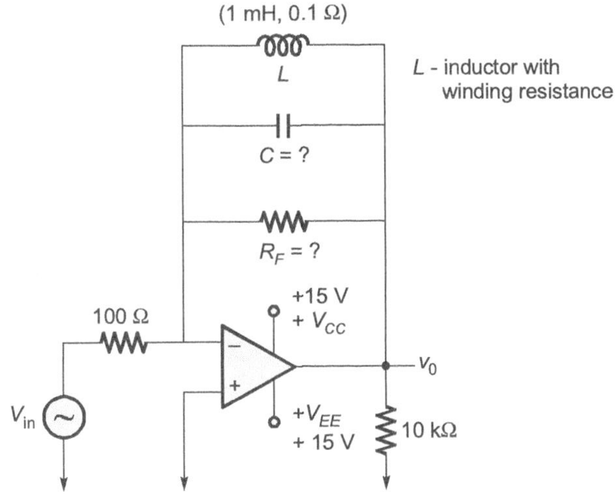

[20 marks : 2023]

Solution:

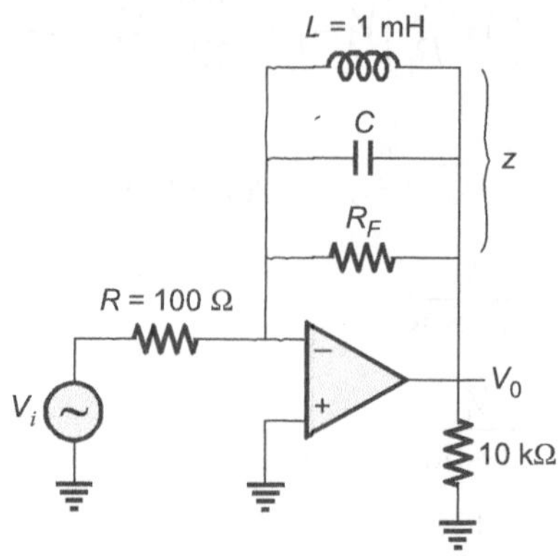

Assume resonant frequency of parallel RLC network as 32 kHz.

Since, frequency is very high so we can neglect internal resistance of inductor.

$$f_o \cong \frac{1}{2\pi\sqrt{LC}}$$

$$C = \frac{1}{4\pi^2 f_o^2 L} = 24.736 \text{ nF}$$

At $f = f_o$, L and C become open circuit.

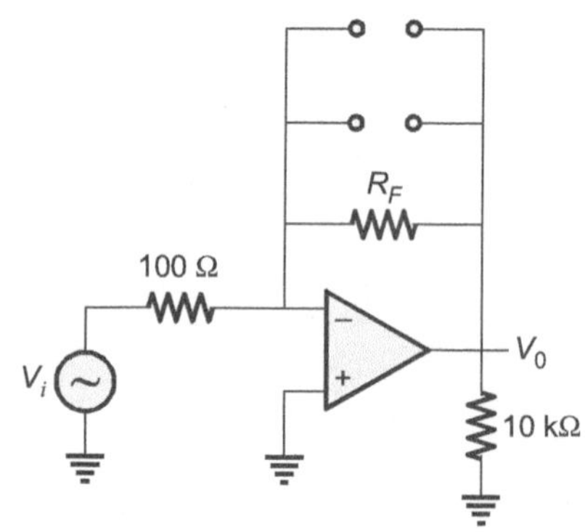

$$\frac{V_o}{V_i} = \frac{-R_F}{R}$$

$$\left|\frac{V_o}{V_i}\right| = \frac{R_F}{R} = 5$$

$$R_F = 5 \times R = 500\ \Omega \qquad (\because R = 100\ \Omega)$$

1.34 Design a second order low pass filter using Op-Amp with feedback gain 1.586. High cut-off frequency is 10 kHz. Assume capacitor 0.1 μF and R_1 = 10 kΩ (resistor connected between input source to input terminal of Op-Amp). Draw the circuit diagram and plot the frequency response.

[20 marks : 2023]

Solution:

Standard second order low pass filter

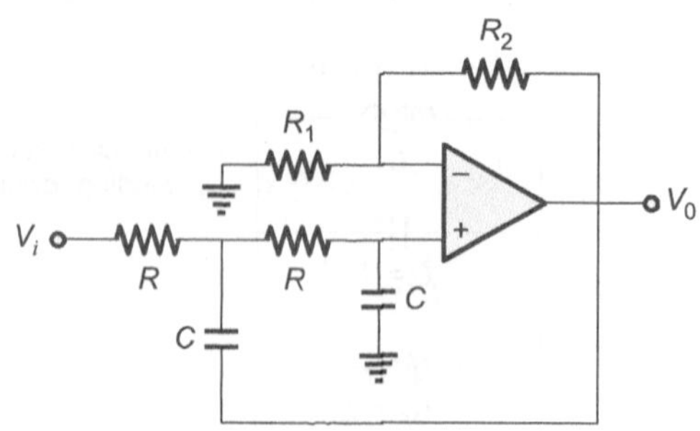

Given : $C = 0.1\ \mu\text{F}$, $R_1 = 10\ \text{k}\Omega$

$f_C = 10\ \text{kHz}$, $A_{max} = 1.586$

We know that cutoff frequency,

$$f_C = \frac{1}{2\pi RC}$$

$$\Rightarrow \quad R = \frac{1}{2\pi C f_C} = \frac{1}{2\pi \times 0.1 \times 10^{-6} \times 10 \times 10^3} = 159.15\ \Omega$$

Feedback gain, $A_{max} = 1 + \frac{R_2}{R_1} = 1.586$

$\Rightarrow$ $R_2 = 0.586 \times R_1 \Rightarrow R_2 = 5.86\ k\Omega$

Frequency Response :

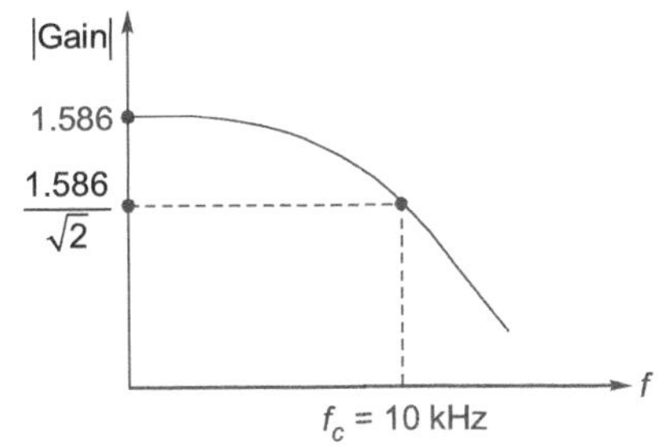

1.35 Draw a 4-bit digital to analog (D-A) converter circuit diagram using Op-Amp and binary weighted resistors. Derive the output voltage equation to get bidirectional signal output. Assume digital input 5 V and bias power supply are ±15 V.

[20 marks : 2023]

Solution:

By using Op-amp and binary weighted resistors we can draw a 4-bit analog (D-A) converter circuit is :

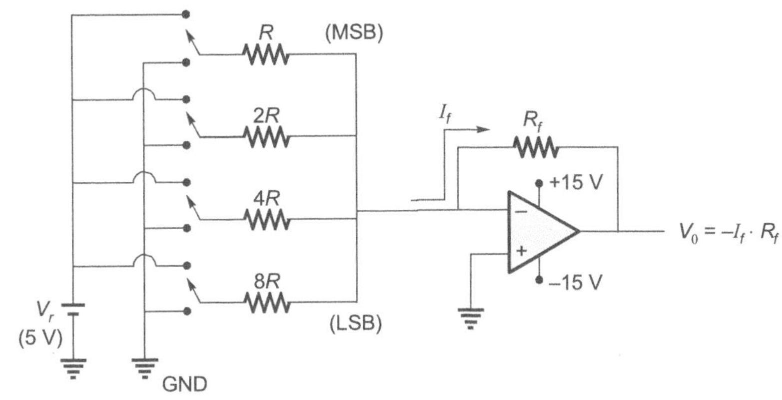

Output voltage, $V_o = -I_f R_f$

$$V_o = -R_f[I_3 + I_2 + I_1 + I_0]$$

$$= -R_f\left[\frac{V_r}{R} + \frac{V_r}{2R} + \frac{V_r}{4R} + \frac{V_r}{8R}\right]$$

$$= -R_f\left(\frac{V_r}{R}\right)\left[\frac{1}{2^0} + \frac{1}{2^1} + \frac{1}{2^2} + \frac{1}{2^3}\right]$$

$$= -\frac{V_r}{R}\cdot R_f\left[\frac{1}{2^0} + \frac{1}{2^1} + \frac{1}{2^2} + \frac{1}{2^3}\right]$$

$$= \left|\frac{V_r}{2^3}\right|\cdot\frac{R_f}{R}\underbrace{[2^3 b_3 + 2^2 b_2 + 2^1 b_1 + 2^0 b_0]}_{\text{Decimal equivalent of binary data}}$$

V_o = (Resolution).(Gain).(Decimal equivalent of binary data)

Required output voltage equation is,

$$V_o = \frac{5}{2^3}\cdot\frac{R_f}{R}[2^3 b_3 + 2^2 b_2 + 2^1 b_1 + 2^0 b_0] \quad [\because V_r = 5\text{ V}]$$

■■■■

2 Digital Electronics

Revised Syllabus of ESE: *Combinational and sequential logic circuits, multiplexers, multi-vibrators, sample and hold circuits, A/D and D/A converters, basics of filter circuits and applications, simple active filters; basics of linear integrated circuits.*

1. Logic Gates and Switching Circuits

1.1 Implement the following operations: $\vec{F} = \bar{x}\,\bar{y} + xy + \bar{y}\,z$

Using:

(i) NAND gates only (ii) NOR gates only

(iii) AND and NOT gates (iv) OR and NOR gates

[10 marks : 2001]

Solution:

(i)

$$F = \bar{x}\,\bar{y} + xy + \bar{y}z$$
$$F = x \odot y + \bar{y}\,z$$
$$\bar{F} = \overline{x \odot y + \bar{y}\,z}$$
$$\bar{F} = x \oplus y + \bar{y}\,z$$
$$F = \overline{\underbrace{x \oplus y}_{A} + \underbrace{\bar{y}\,z}_{B}} = \overline{A \cdot B}$$
$$A = x \oplus y$$
$$B = \overline{\bar{y}z}$$

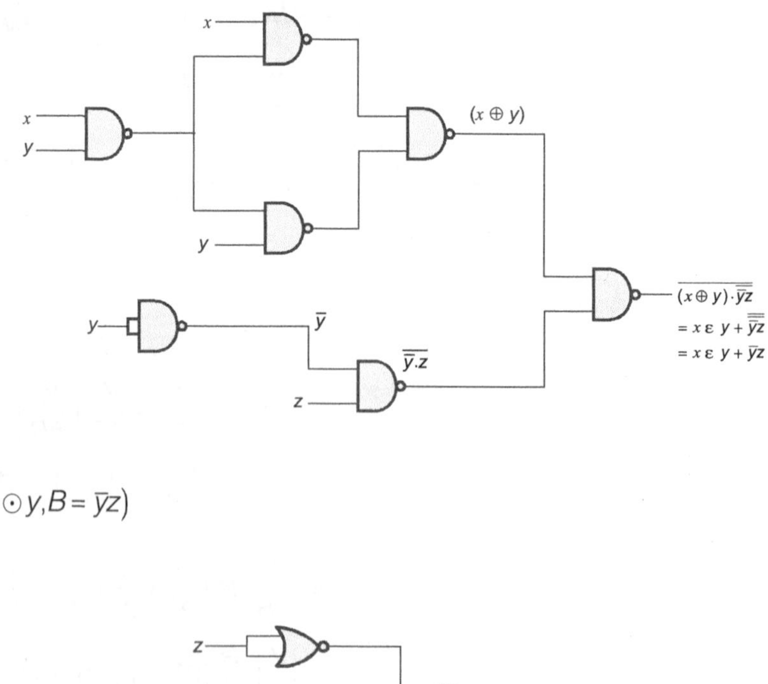

(ii) Using NOR gates:

$$F = \overline{xy} + xy + \bar{y}z$$
$$F = x \odot y + \bar{y}z$$
$$= A + bA + B(A = x \odot y, B = \bar{y}z)$$
$$\bar{F} = \overline{x \odot y . \bar{y}\,z}$$

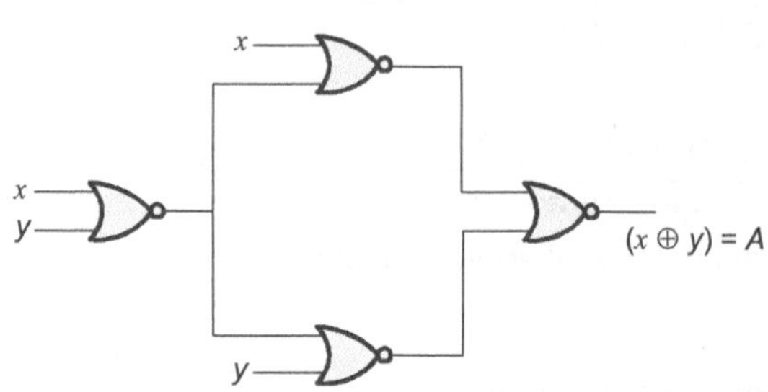

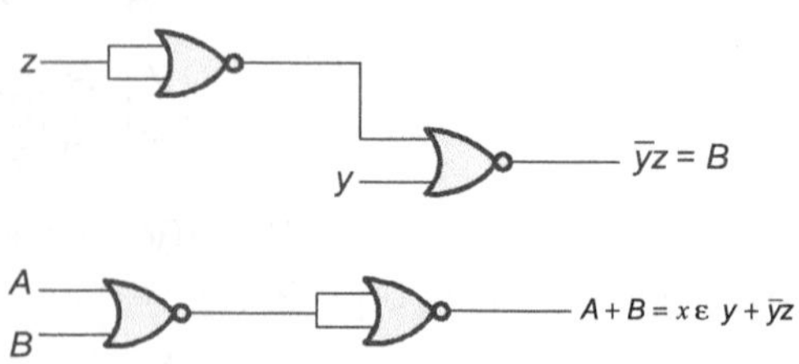

(iii) ∵ NAND = AND + NOT → So replace all NAND gates in (i) part by AND + NOT

(iv) ∵ NOR = OR + NOT → So replace all NOR gates by OR + NOT.

1.2 (i) An equality detector gives the output $Y = 1$, if both the inputs A and B are either 1 or 0

(a) Construct the truth table.

(b) Write the Boolean expression for Y

(c) Implement the circuit using NAND gates only

(ii) Prove: $A + \bar{A}B = A + B$

[10 marks : 2004]

Solution:

(i) (a) Truth table of Y

A	B	Y
0	0	1
0	1	0
1	0	0
1	1	1

(b) Constructing K-map

A \ B	0	1
0	1	0
1	0	1

$$\therefore \quad Y = \bar{A}\bar{B} + AB$$

(c) For constructing the required circuit, using NAND gates,

$$Y = \overline{\overline{\bar{A}\bar{B} + AB}} \quad \text{(By De-Morgan's law)}$$

$$= \overline{\overline{\bar{A}\bar{B}} \cdot \overline{AB}}$$

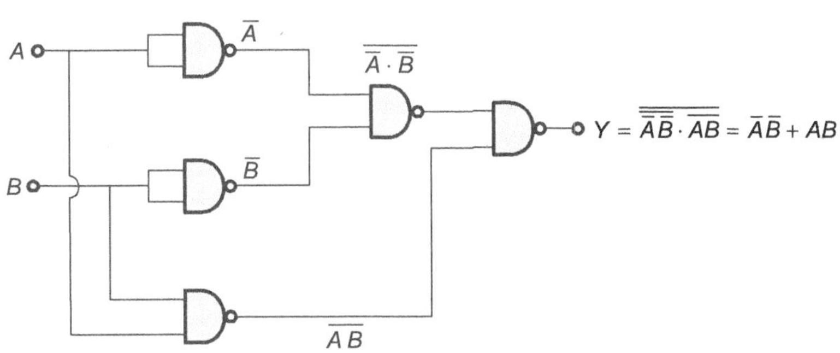

(ii) Prove, $\quad A + \bar{A}B = A + B$

where, $\quad A + \bar{A}B = A(B + \bar{B}) + \bar{A}B$

$$= AB + A\bar{B} + \bar{A}B + AB = A(B + \bar{B}) + (\bar{A} + A)B = A + B$$

1.3 Construct a logic circuit to give an output $X = (\overline{AB} + \bar{A}C)(\overline{AD + C})$ without any reduction in number of gates. Give the logic circuits in step by step.

[8 marks : 2011]

Solution:

$$X = (\overline{AB} + \bar{A}C)\,(\overline{AD + C})$$

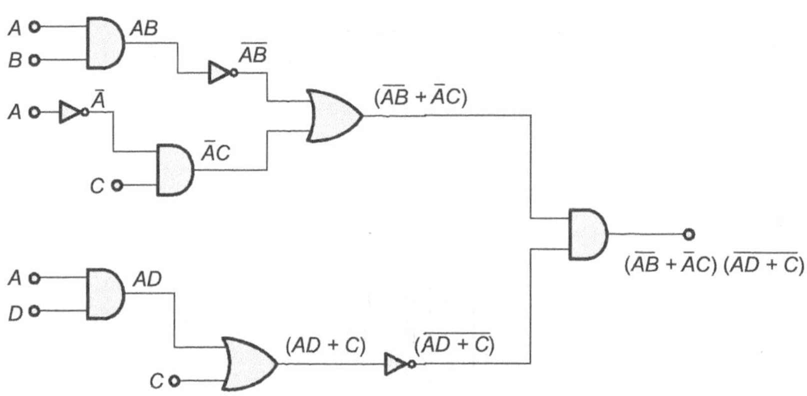

1.4 Determine the simplest (minimal) expression for *Y* for the logic circuit shown.

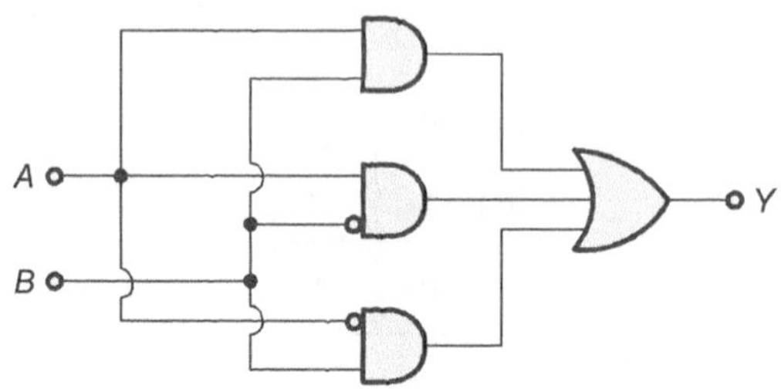

[4 marks : 2012]

Solution:

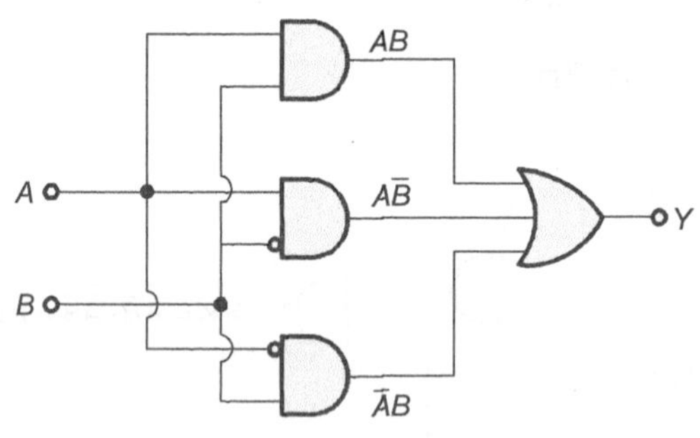

The expression for *Y* is, $Y = AB + A\bar{B} + \bar{A}B = A + B$

1.5 Define XNOR gate and write the truth table for exclusive-NOR (XNOR) gate.

[5 marks : 2013]

Solution:

The 'Ex-NOR' gate:

It is also called **"Equivalence gate"** or **"Coincidence logic circuit"**. It acts like an **"even number of 1's detector"** when number of input variables are **even** and also called **"odd number of 1's detector"** when number of input variables are **odd**.

Symbol:

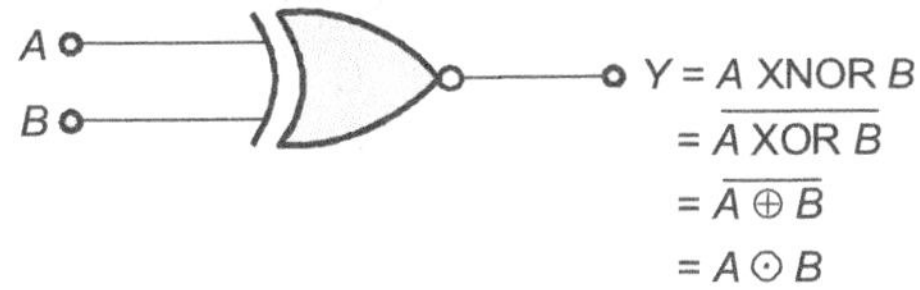

Boolean function of 2-input **Ex-NOR** operation is as,

$$Y = A \odot B$$

$$\therefore \quad \boxed{Y = AB + \bar{A}\bar{B}}$$

Truth table:

Inputs		Outputs
A	B	$Y = A \odot B$
0	0	1
0	1	0
1	0	0
1	1	1

1.6 (i) Draw the truth table of the three input logic gate shown below :

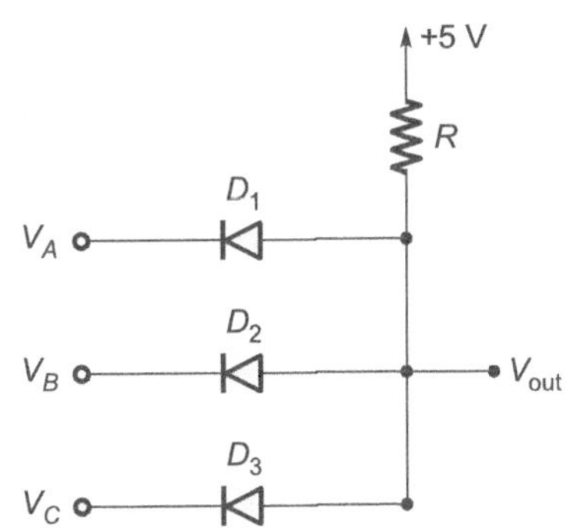

+5 V may be taken as logic '1' while 0 V may be taken as logic '0'. The diodes D_1, D_2 and D_3 are ideal diodes.

(ii) Given the logical function of three variables

$$f(A, B, C) = A + \bar{B}C$$

express f in the standard product-of-sum form.

[6 + 6 marks : 2022]

Solution:

(i) If $V_A = 0$, then diode D_1 will be on, then $V_{out} = 0$ V, irrespective of V_B and V_C.
Similarly, $V_B = 0$, then diode D_2 will be on, then $V_{out} = 0$ V. Same applies for V_C also.
But if $V_A = V_B = V_C = 1$, then D_1, D_2 and D_3 will be off, then $V_{out} = 1$.

Truth Table :

A	B	C	V_{out}
0	0	0	0
0	0	1	0
0	1	0	0
0	1	1	0
1	0	0	0
1	0	1	0
1	1	0	0
1	1	1	1

(ii) $f(A, B, C) = A + \bar{B}C$

A \ BC	$\bar{B}\bar{C}$	$\bar{B}C$	BC	$B\bar{C}$
$\bar{A}$	0	1	0	0
A	1	1	1	1

POS from $f = (A + C)(A + \bar{B})$

Standard POS form.

2. Combinational Logic Circuits

2.1 Draw the logic symbols and explain the operations of a *D*-type and a *T*-type flip-flop.

[8 marks : 2003]

Solution:

D-Flip Flop:

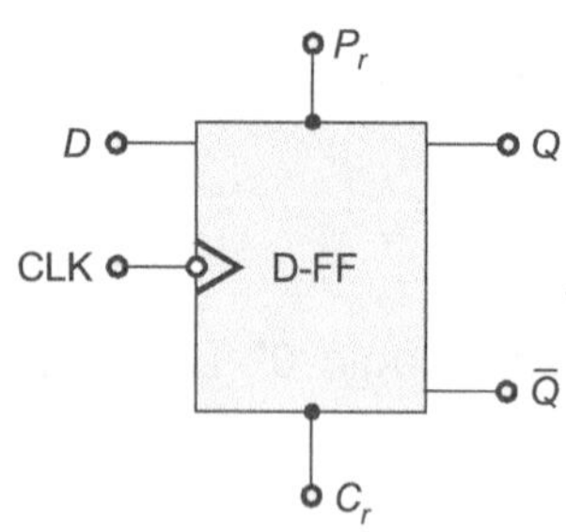

D(input)	Output (Q_{n+1})
0	0
1	1

$$Q_{n+1} = D$$

In a *D*-Flip Flop, the transfer of data from input to output is delayed by one clock pulse and hence its name is delay (*D*) Flip-Flop.

T-FF:

In a T-FF, if 'T' input is equal to 'zero' then the output (Q_{n+1}) is equal to (Q_n), (there is no change in output value) and if ($T = 1$) then, it acts as a toggle switch. For every clock pulse, the output Q changes.

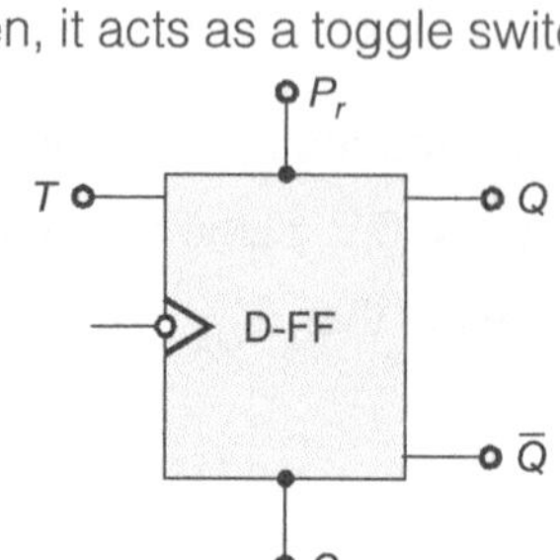

Truth table

T (input)	Output (Q_{n+1})
0	Q_n
1	$\bar{Q}_n$

$$Q_{n+1} = T \oplus Q_n$$

2.2 Explain briefly the functions of "De-multiplexer" and "Multiplexer". Explain with necessary diagram the operation of a 4 to 1 line Multiplexer.

[12 marks : 2003]

Solution:

A multiplexer is a circuit that accepts inputs from several different channel and feeds all of them into a single output channel in a sequential order. The input is selected by the value of select input or control inputs.

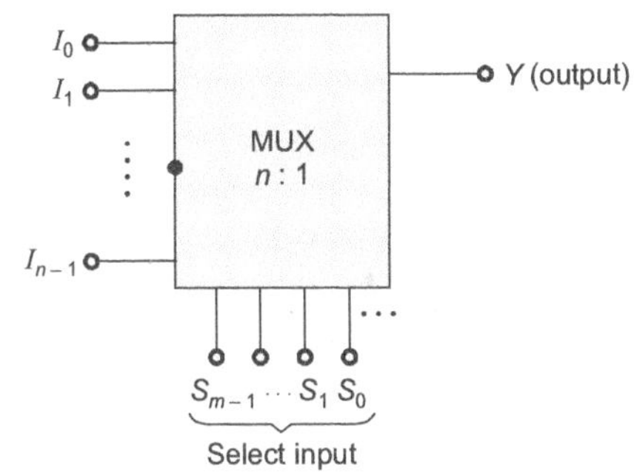

The demultiplexer performs the reverse of operation of a multiplexer. It accept a single input and distributes it over several outputs. The select input or control input code determines the output line in which data input will be transmitted.

Where ($2^m = n$)

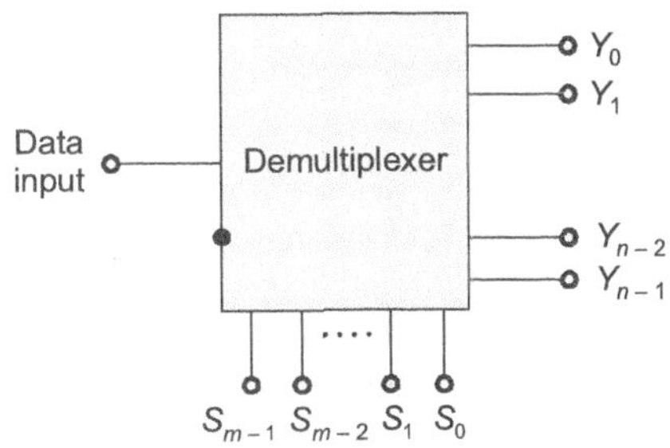

4 : 1 Multiplexer with low input at 'G' (enable)

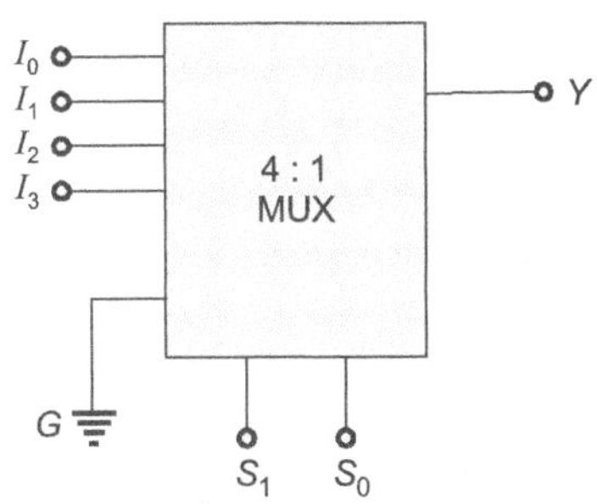

S_1	S_0	Y
0	0	I_0
0	1	I_1
1	0	I_2
1	1	I_3

$$Y = \bar{S}_1 \bar{S}_0 I_0 + \bar{S}_1 S_0 I_1 + S_1 \bar{S}_0 I_2 + S_1 S_0 I_3$$

2.3 Implement the function: $F(W, X, Y, Z) = \Sigma m(0, 1, 3, 4, 8, 9, 15)$ using an 8 : 1 multiplexer.

[4 marks : 2009]

Solution:

$$F(W, X, Y, Z) = \Sigma m(0, 1, 3, 4, 8, 9, 15)$$

For using 8 : 1 multiplexer for 4 variables.

	I_1	I_2	I_3	I_4	I_5	I_6	I_7	I_8
$\overline{W}$	(0)	(1)	2	(3)	(4)	5	6	7
W	(8)	(9)	10	11	12	13	14	(15)

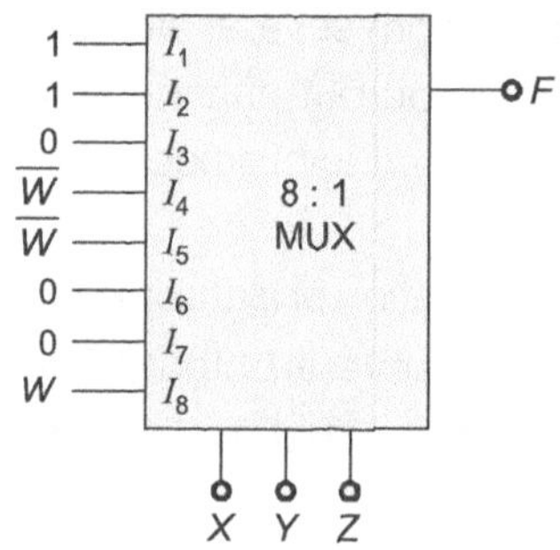

$I_1 = 1$ $\quad$ $I_2 = 1$

$I_3 = 0$ $\quad$ $I_4 = \overline{W}$

$I_5 = \overline{W}$ $\quad$ $I_6 = 0$

$I_7 = 0$ $\quad$ $I_8 = W$

2.4 A logic circuit implements the following Boolean function:

$$F(A, B, C, D) = \overline{A}C + A\overline{C}D$$

It is found that the circuit input combination $A = C$ can never occur. Find a simpler expression for F.

[10 marks : 2014]

Solution:

A	B	C	D	F
0	0	0	0	0
0	0	0	1	0
0	0	1	0	1
0	0	1	1	1
0	1	0	0	0
0	1	0	1	0
0	1	1	0	1
0	1	1	1	1
1	0	0	0	1
1	0	0	1	1
1	0	1	0	0
1	0	1	1	0
1	1	0	0	1
1	1	0	1	1
1	1	1	0	0
1	1	1	1	0

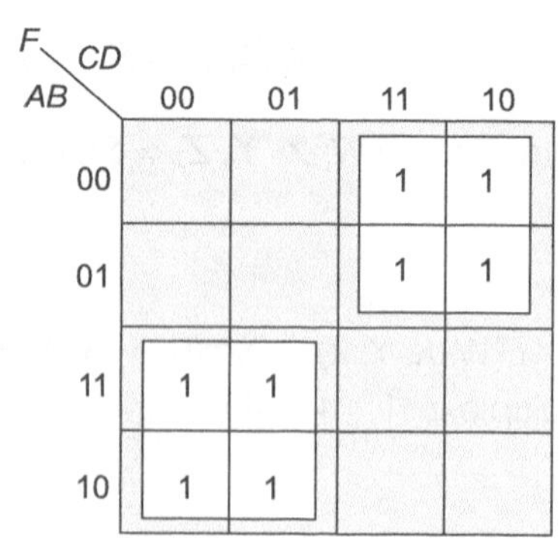

$$F = \overline{A}C + A\overline{C} = A \oplus C$$

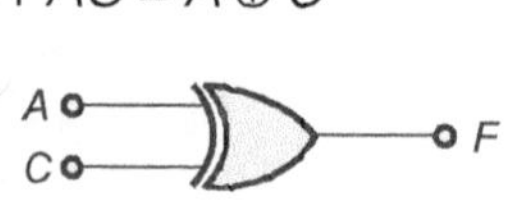

2.5 Draw a logic diagram showing how four exclusive-OR gates, four AND gates and two OR gates can be connected to construct a 2-bit parallel adder.

[10 marks : 2015]

Solution:

We need to design a two bit parallel adder.

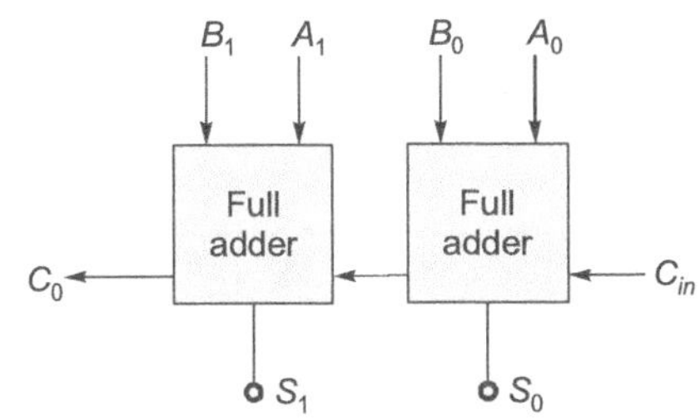

The figure show the block diagram of the two bit parallel adder.

Now we know that each full adder can be designed using two XOR gates, one OR gate and two AND gates so the whole system need 4 XOR gates, 2 OR gates and 4 AND gates.

The logic diagram is

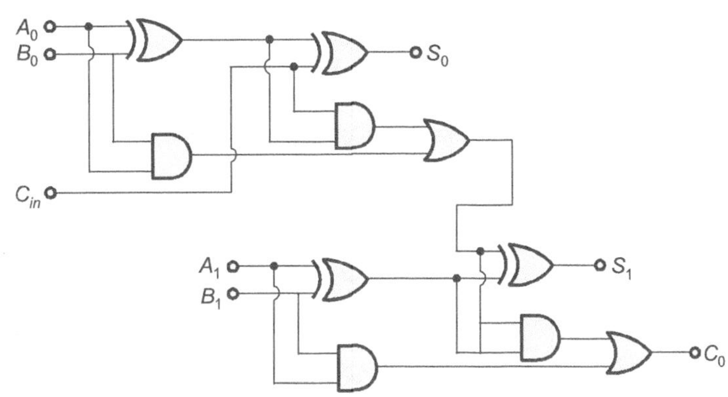

2.6 Design a circuit that takes as input two 2-bit numbers, N_1 and N_2 for comparison and generates three outputs:

$N_1 = N_2$, $N_1 < N_2$ and $N_1 > N_2$. These three binary outputs are represented by F_{eq}, F_{lt} and F_{gt} respectively. Realize the outputs in Sum of Products (SoP) form.

[20 marks : 2019]

Solution:

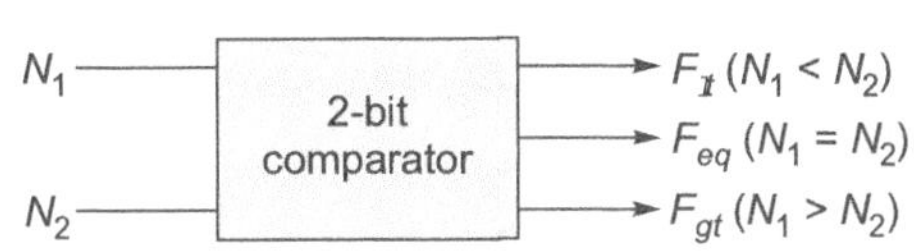

N_1 and N_2 are two inputs for which the output of the comparator is specified by three binary variables. That indicate whether,

$$N_1 > N_2,\ N_1 = N_2 \text{ or } N_1 < N_2$$

If, $$N_1 > N_2$$

$$F_{gt} = \sum(m_4, m_8, m_9, m_{12}, m_{13}, m_{14})$$

$$= A_1\bar{B}_1 + (A_1 \odot B_1)\, A_0\bar{B}_0$$

If, $$N_1 < N_2$$

$$F_{lt} = \sum(m_1, m_2, m_3, m_6, m_7, m_{11})$$

$$= \bar{A}_1 B_1 + (A_1 \odot B_1)\,\bar{A}_0 B_0$$

If, $$N_1 = N_2$$

$$F_{eq} = \sum(m_0, m_5, m_{10}, m_{15})$$

$$= (A_1 \odot B_1)\,(A_0 \odot B_0)$$

Minterm	A_1	A_0	B_1	B_0	F_{gt}	F_{eq}	F_{lt}
m_0	0	0	0	0	0	1	0
m_1	0	0	0	1	0	0	1
m_2	0	0	1	0	0	0	1
m_3	0	0	1	1	0	0	1
m_4	0	1	0	0	1	0	0
m_5	0	1	0	1	0	1	0
m_6	0	1	1	0	0	0	1
m_7	0	1	1	1	0	0	1
m_8	1	0	0	0	1	0	0
m_9	1	0	0	1	1	0	0
m_{10}	1	0	1	0	0	1	0
m_{11}	1	0	1	1	0	0	1
m_{12}	1	1	0	0	1	0	0
m_{13}	1	1	0	1	1	0	0
m_{14}	1	1	1	0	1	0	0
m_{15}	1	1	1	1	0	1	0

Logic circuit:

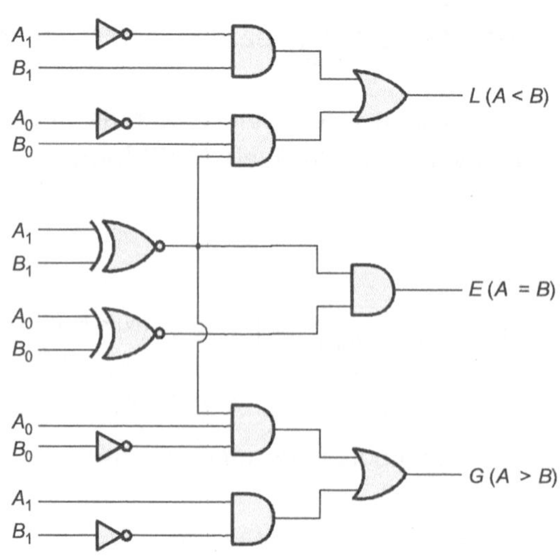

2.7 Consider the function $Y(A, B, C)$ given in the truth table:

A	B	C	$Y(A,B,C)$
0	0	0	1
0	0	1	0
0	1	0	0
0	1	1	0
1	0	0	1
1	0	1	1
1	1	0	0
1	1	1	1

(i) Write a logic expression for $Y(A, B, C)$.

(ii) Implement $Y(A, B, C)$ using only 2-input gates.

(iii) Implement $Y(A, B, C)$ using only 2-input NAND gates.

[20 marks : 2021]

Solution:

Truth table for given function $Y(A, B, C)$

	A	B	C	$Y(A,B,C)$
0	0	0	0	1
1	0	0	1	0
2	0	1	0	0
3	0	1	1	0
4	1	0	0	1
5	1	0	1	1
6	1	1	0	0
7	1	1	1	1

With the help of K-map

(i)

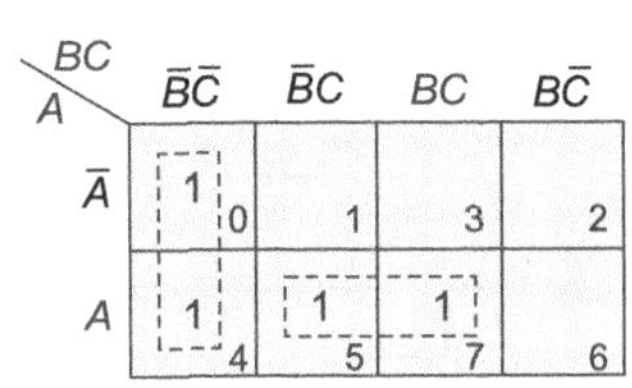

$$f = \bar{B}\bar{C} + AC$$

(ii) With the help of 2-input gate

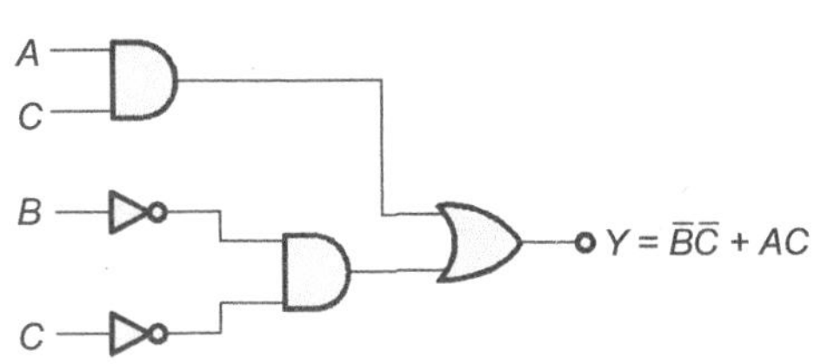

(iii) With the help of 2-input NAND GATE

$$f = \overline{B}\overline{C} + AC$$

$$f = \overline{\overline{\overline{B}\overline{C} + AC}} = \overline{\overline{\overline{B}\overline{C}} \cdot \overline{AC}}$$

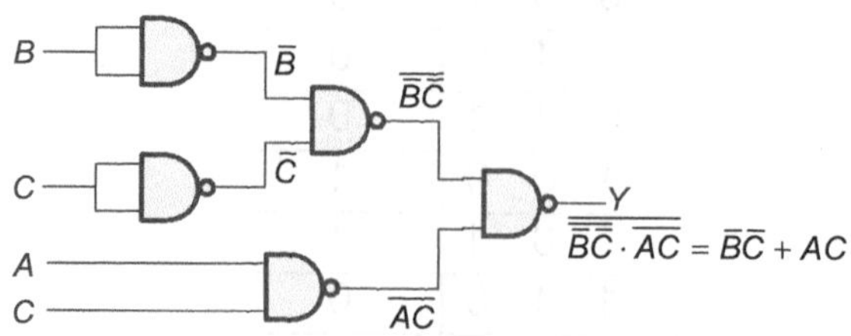

3. Sequential Logic Circuits

3.1 If the inputs P_1, P_2 to the circuit shown are 1, 1 determine the outputs Q_1 and Q_2.

[5 marks : 2004]

Solution:

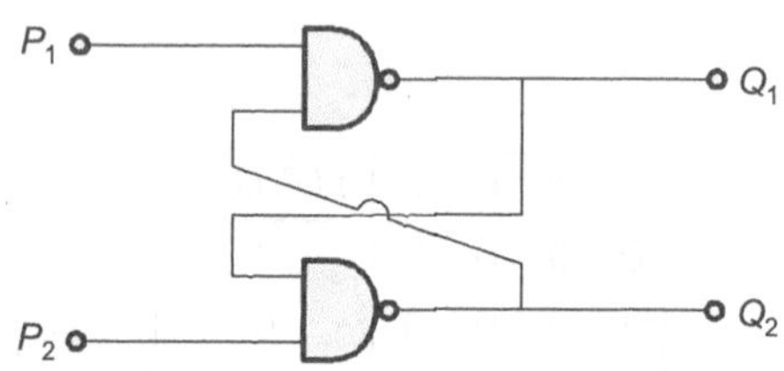

When inputs (P_1, P_2) are (1, 1) then

P_1	P_2	Q_1	Q_2
1	1	0	1
1	1	1	0

The output, $Q_1 = P_1 P_2 \overline{Q}_2$ or $Q_2 = P_1 P_2 \overline{Q}_1$

3.2 The waveforms

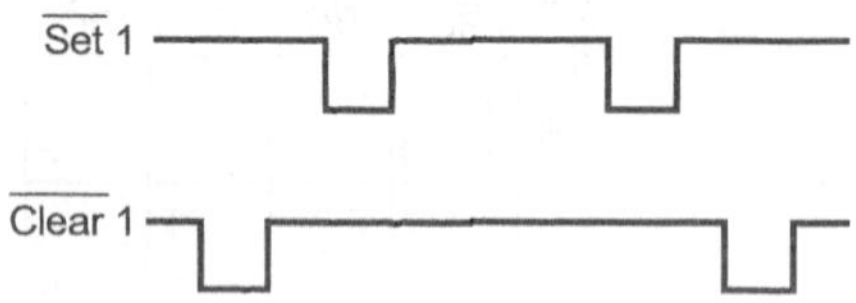

are applied to the inputs of the latch.

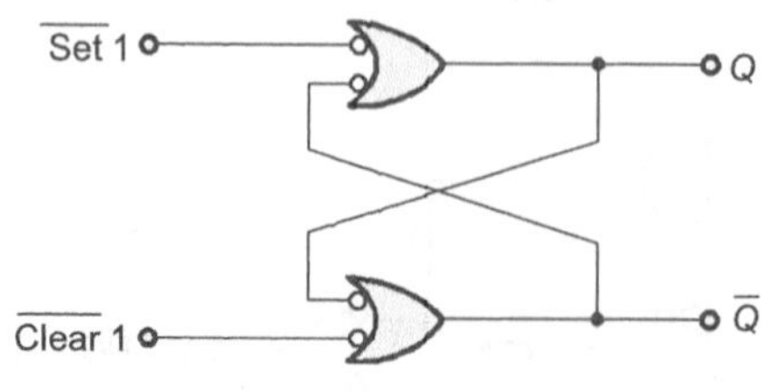

Draw the waveform at Q and explain.

[14 marks : 2006]

Solution:

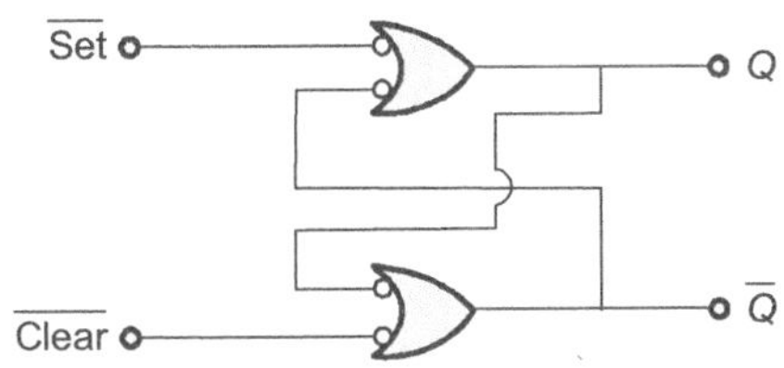

$\overline{Set}$	$\overline{Clear}$	$Q(n)$	$Q(n+1)$
1	1	0	0 } Q_n
1	1	1	1 }
1	0	0	0 } 0
1	0	1	0 }
0	1	0	1 } 1
0	1	1	1 }

Input waveform and output 'Q' waveform.

Let us take initial [Q = 1]

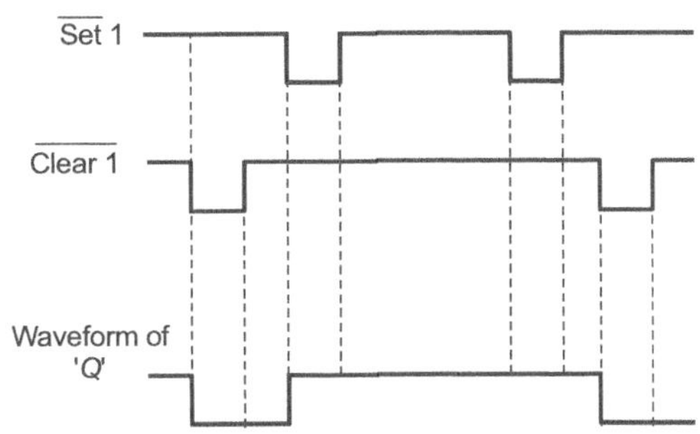

3.3 In a J-K flip-flop, race around condition occurs when

(a) both J and K inputs are 0
(b) both J and K inputs are 1
(c) J = 1 and K = 0
(d) J = 0 and K = 1

[2 marks : 2009]

Solution: (b)

Race around condition occurs when both input J and K are equal to one and clock period is greater than the delay of flip-flop.

3.4 Using T flip-flop and logic gates, design a L-M edge triggered flip-flop having a truth table as given below:

L	M	Q_+
0	0	0
0	1	$\overline{Q}$
1	0	1
1	1	$\overline{Q}$

[10 marks : 2014]

Solution:

Excitation table of T flip-flop:

Present state	**Next state**	
$Q(t)$	$Q(t-1)$	T
0	0	0
0	1	1
1	0	1
1	1	0

		Present state	Next state	
L	M	$Q(t)$	$Q(t-1)$	T (Based on $Q(t)$ & $Q(t-1)$)
0	0	0	0	0
0	0	1	0	1
0	1	0	1	1
0	1	1	0	1
1	0	0	1	1
1	0	1	1	0
1	1	0	1	1
1	1	1	0	1

Getting the value of T interms of L, M and $Q(t)$:

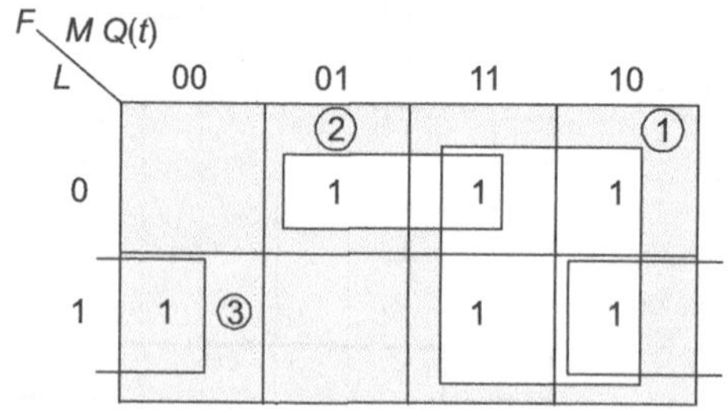

$$T = M + L\overline{Q} + \overline{L}Q = M + (L \oplus Q)$$

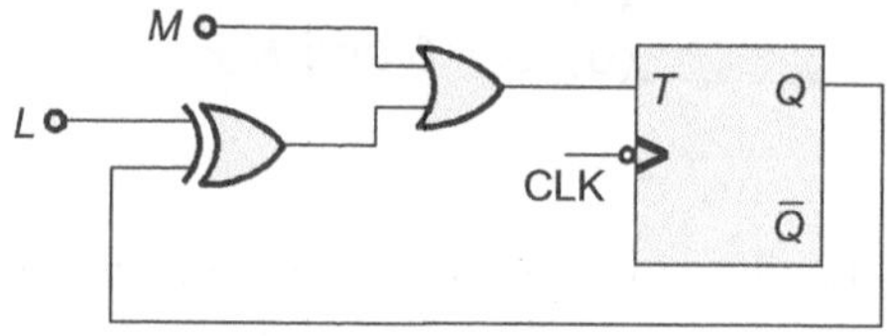

3.5 The following figure shows two master-slave RS flip-flops having a common clock input. Construct a timing diagram showing the responses of master and slave latches in each flip-flop to two clock pulses. Assume all latches are initially reset.

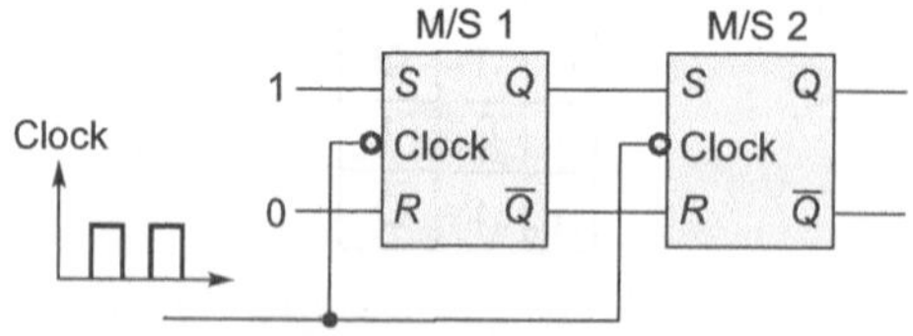

[4 marks : 2015]

Solution:

Single Master slave flip flop (working at negative edge of the clock) can be replaced by two latches, Master latch (working at positive level) and slave latch (working at negative level).

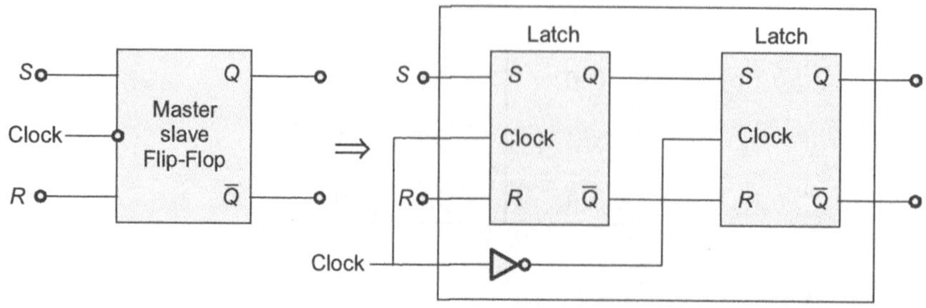

So the circuit shown in the question can be represented as

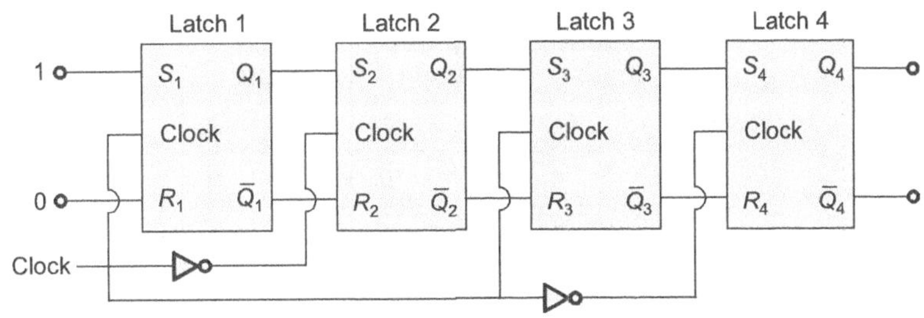

*Initially all the latch are reset.

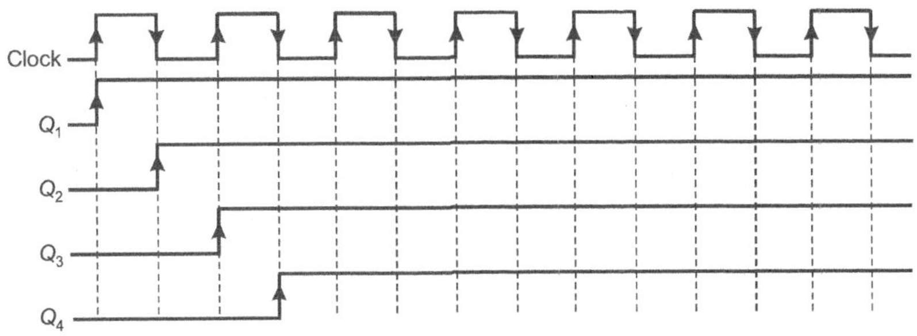

3.6 Show that a full adder can be constructed with two half adder circuits and a logic gate.

[10 marks : 2016]

Solution:

Full adder:

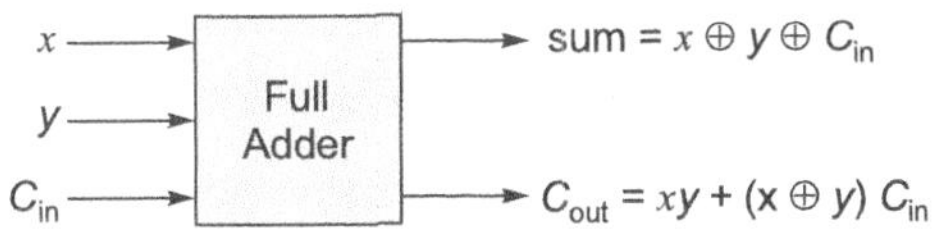

Using two half address, we can construct a full adder as below.

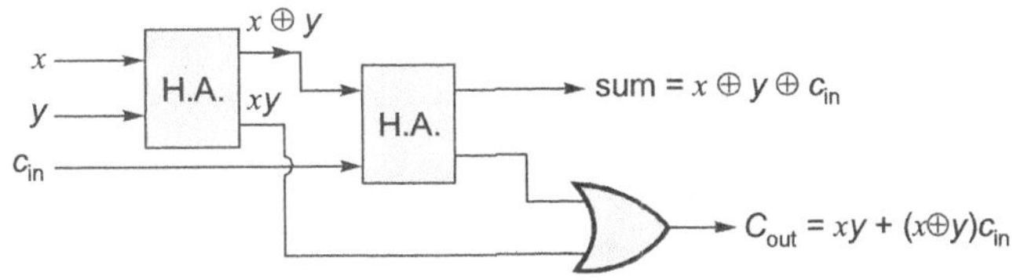

3.7 A *T*-flip-flop and a *D*-flip-flop are interconnected as shown in the following figure. Draw a timing diagram showing their operation through six complete clock cycles. Assuming $Q_AQ_B = 00$ initially.

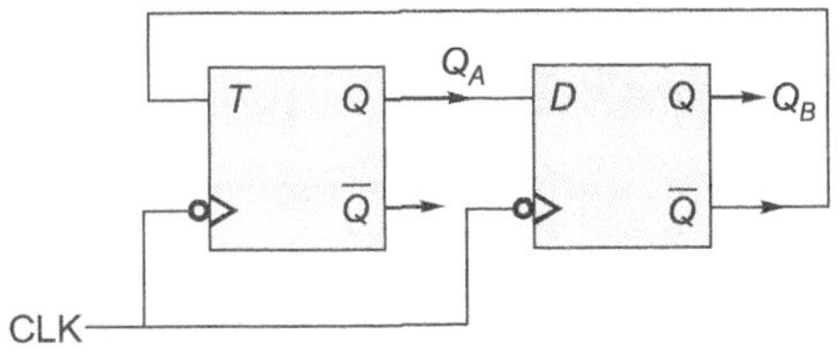

[10 marks : 2016]

Solution:

The state table of the counter circuit is shown below.

	Present State		Flip-flop Inputs		Next State	
Clock	Q_A	Q_B	T_A	D_B	Q_A	Q_B
0	0	0	1	0	1	0
1	1	0	1	1	0	1
2	0	1	0	0	0	0
3	0	0	1	0	1	0
4	1	0	1	1	0	1
5	0	1	0	0	0	0
6	0	0	1	0	1	0

The timing diagram is shown below.

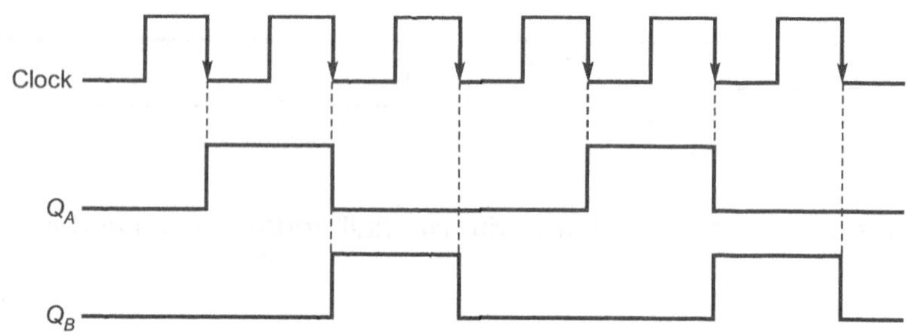

3.8 Convert a *D* flip-flop into a J-K flip-flop. Use additional logic gates. Draw the implementation.

[12 marks : 2017]

Solution:

D flip-flop into a J-K flip-flop:

J	K	Q_n	Q_{n+1}	D	Q_n	Q_{n+1}
0	0	0	0	0	0	0
0	0	1	1	0	1	0
0	1	0	0	1	0	1
0	1	1	0	1	1	1
1	0	0	1			
1	0	1	1			
1	1	0	1			
1	1	1	0			

J	K	Q_n	Q_{n+1}	D
0	0	0	0	0
0	0	1	1	1
0	1	0	0	0
0	1	1	0	0
1	0	0	1	1
1	0	1	1	1
1	1	0	1	1
1	1	1	0	0

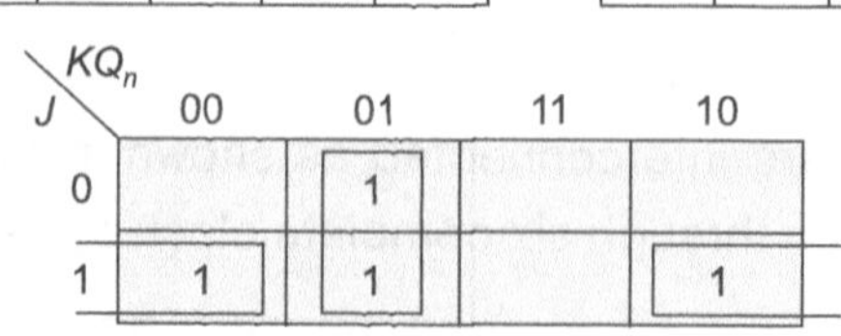

$$D = J\bar{Q}_n + \bar{K}Q_n$$

D	Q_n	Q_{n+1}
0	0	0
0	1	0
1	0	1
1	1	1

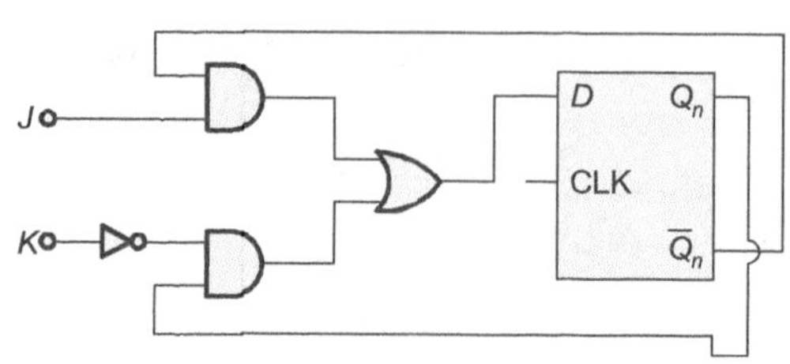

4. Counters

4.1 A ripple counter consists of 6 *FFs* and the first *FF*, F_0 receives the pulses from clock and gives an output Q_0. Other FFs are connected giving Q_1, Q_2, Q_3, Q_4 and Q_5.
(i) Determine the counter's mode
(ii) Frequency of Q_5 output , when the clock frequency 1 MHz
(iii) If the initial counter state is 101010, what would be the state after 256 pulses?
(iv) Draw the circuit of a 1-bit comparator

[10 marks : 2004]

Solution:

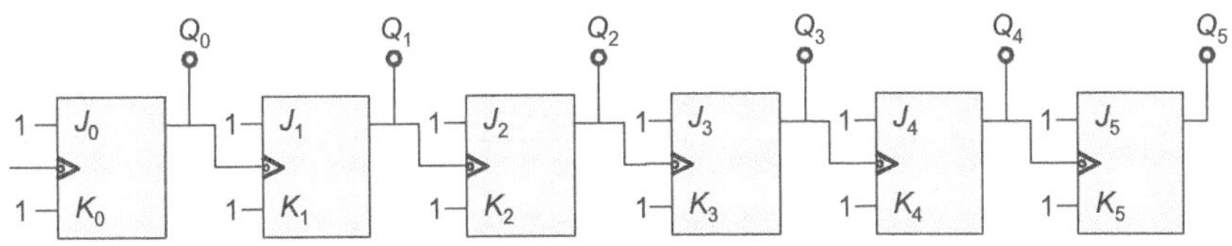

Ripple counter

(i) Counter mode = $2^N = 2^6 = 64$
(ii) Time period of Q_5 = 64 *T*in

$$f \text{ of } Q_5 \text{ output} = \frac{f_{in}}{64} = \frac{F_{CLK}}{64} = \frac{1}{64}\text{MHz}$$

(iii) Since the counter repeats its same state after 64 pulses, therefore after 256 pulses, the counter state will be same state. $\because \frac{256}{64} = 4$ integer.

(iv) One bit comparator

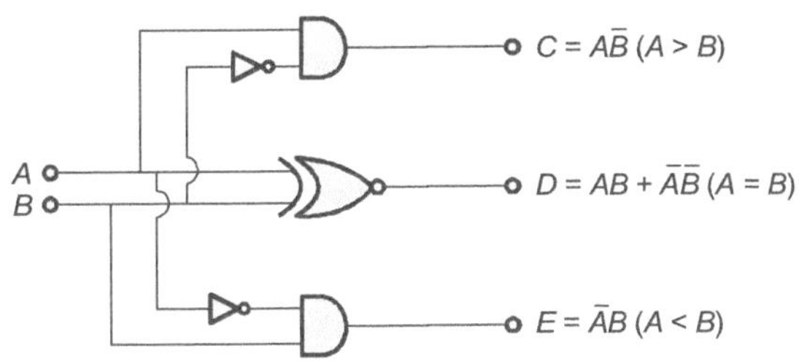

4.2 The output frequency of a decade counter that is clocked from a 50 kHz signal is
(a) 12.5 kHz
(b) 50 kHz
(c) 5 kHz
(d) 500 kHz

[2 marks : 2006]

Solution: (c)

$\therefore$ Output frequency a Mod *N* counters is f = fin/N

$\therefore$ The output frequency of a decade counter (i.e. Mod –10 counters)

$$= 50 \text{ kHz} \div 10 = 5 \text{ kHz}$$

4.3 Consider a two stage synchronous counter (both stages receive the pulses at the C_K input). In each counter $K = 1$. If $J_0 = \bar{Q}_1$ and $J_1 = Q_0$, draw the circuit. From a truth table of Q_0 and after each pulse, demonstrate that this is a 3 : 1 counter.

[12 marks : 2006]

Solution:

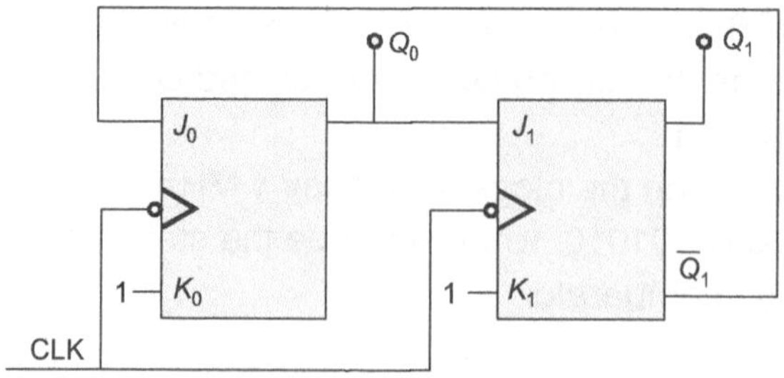

2-Stage synchronous counter

Present state Q_1	Q_0	J_1	K_1	J_0	K_0	next stage Q_1	Q_0
0	0	0	1	1	1	0	1
0	1	1	1	1	1	1	0
1	0	0	1	0	1	0	0

So, state diagram of the counter

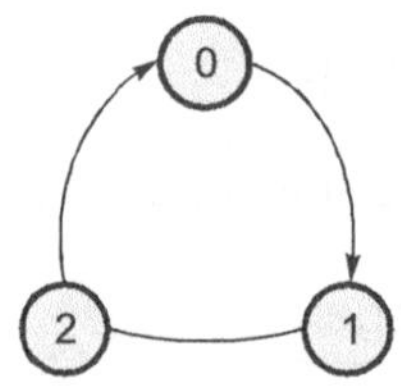

From this, our synchronous counter is 3 : 1 counter.

∴ it has 3-states.

4.4 **Using J-K flip-flop, design a counter which has the following count sequence:**

0	0	0
0	0	1
0	1	0
1	0	0
1	0	1
1	1	0

Draw the excitation table, logic diagram and state diagram. [15 marks : 2007]

Solution:

Excitation table of J-K Flip-Flop

Truth table

J	K	Q_{n+1}
0	0	Q_n
0	1	0
1	0	1
1	1	$\overline{Q_n}$

⇒

Excitation table

Q_n	Q_{n+1}	J	K
0	0	0	x
0	1	1	x
1	0	x	1
1	1	x	0

Design of synchronous counter using J-K flip-flop

State diagram

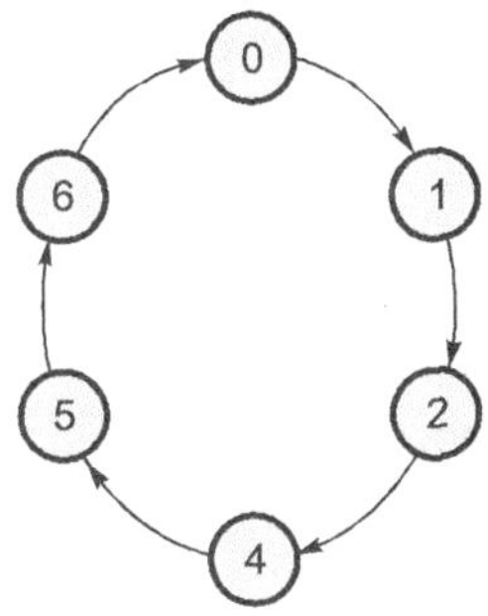

State assignment

0 — 000
1 — 001
2 — 010
4 — 100
5 — 101
6 — 110

	Present state			Next state								
	Q_2	Q_1	Q_0	Q_2	Q_1	Q_0	J_2	K_2	J_1	K_1	J_0	K_0
0	0	0	0	0	0	1	0	x	0	x	1	x
1	0	0	1	0	1	0	0	x	1	x	x	1
2	0	1	0	1	0	0	1	x	x	1	0	x
3	1	0	0	1	0	1	x	0	x	x	1	x
4	1	0	1	1	1	0	x	0	1	x	x	1
5	1	1	0	0	0	0	x	1	x	1	0	x

From close analysis, we get (K_0 = 1) and (K_1 = 1)

(J_0)

Q_2 \ $Q_1 Q_0$	00	01	11	10
0	1	x	x	0
1	1	x	x	0

$\therefore J_0 = \overline{Q}_1$

(K_0)

Q_2 \ $Q_1 Q_0$	00	01	11	10
0	x	1	x	x
1	x	1	x	x

$\therefore K_0 = 1$

(J_1)

Q_2 \ $Q_1 Q_0$	00	01	11	10
0	0	1	x	x
1	0	1	x	x

$\therefore J_1 = Q_0$

(K_1)

Q_2 \ $Q_1 Q_0$	00	01	11	10
0	x	x	x	1
1	x	x	x	1

$\therefore K_1 = 1$

(J_2)

Q_2 \ $Q_1 Q_0$	00	01	11	10
0	0	0	x	1
1	x	x	x	x

$\therefore J_2 = Q_1$

and

(K_2)

Q_2 \ $Q_1 Q_0$	00	01	11	10
0	x	x	x	x
1	0	0	x	1

$\therefore K_2 = Q_1$

$\therefore$

$$J_2 = Q_1,\ K_2 = Q_1$$
$$J_1 = Q_0,\ K_1 = 1$$
$$J_0 = \overline{Q}_1,\ K_0 = 1$$

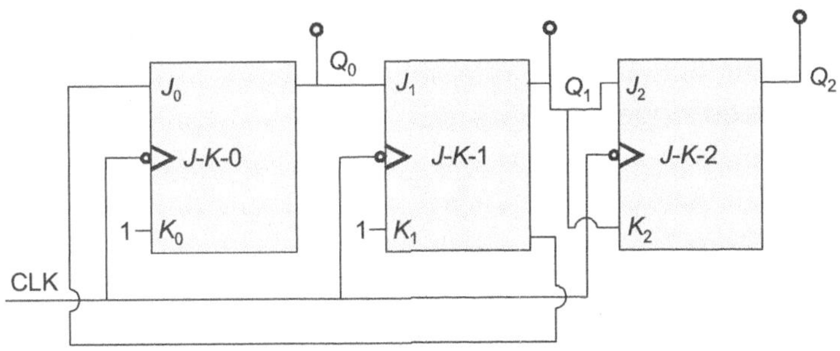

Logic diagram

4.5 Draw the state diagram, logic diagram and timing diagram for a decimal *BCD* ripple counter. Explain the operation mentioning the conditions for state transition of each flip-flop.

[15 marks : 2007]

Solution:

Asynchronous counter or ripple counter:

An asynchronous counter is one whose Flip-Flops do not depend upon a clock pulse transition for changing their states instead, they depend on the outputs from their previous state to change their present state. This counter is also known as ripple counter, since the input pulses ripple through the counter circuit to reach the output.

States of the output of the counter

Clock	States of Output			
	Q_A	Q_B	Q_C	Q_D
0	0	0	0	0
1	0	0	0	1
2	0	0	1	0
3	0	0	1	1
4	0	1	0	0
5	0	1	0	1
6	0	1	1	0
7	0	1	1	1
8	1	0	0	0
9	1	0	0	1

In a modulo-10 (or) decimal *BCD* ripple counter is one that counts number from (0 to 9). This can be constructed from a modulo-16 counter by resetting the counter at the tenth pulses.

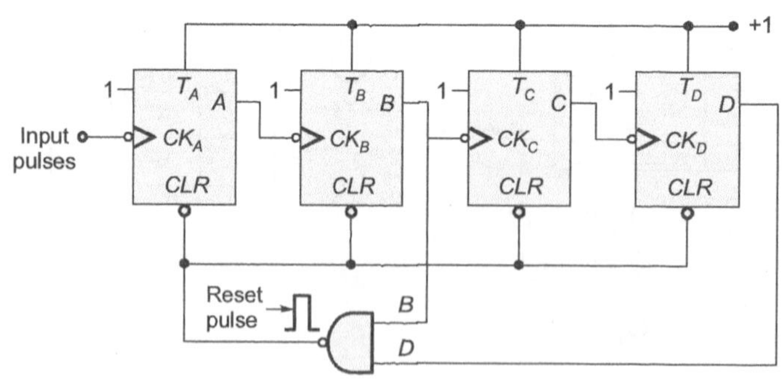

Fig. (1) : Decade ripple counter from modulo-16 counter

All the flip-flops are –ve edge triggered.

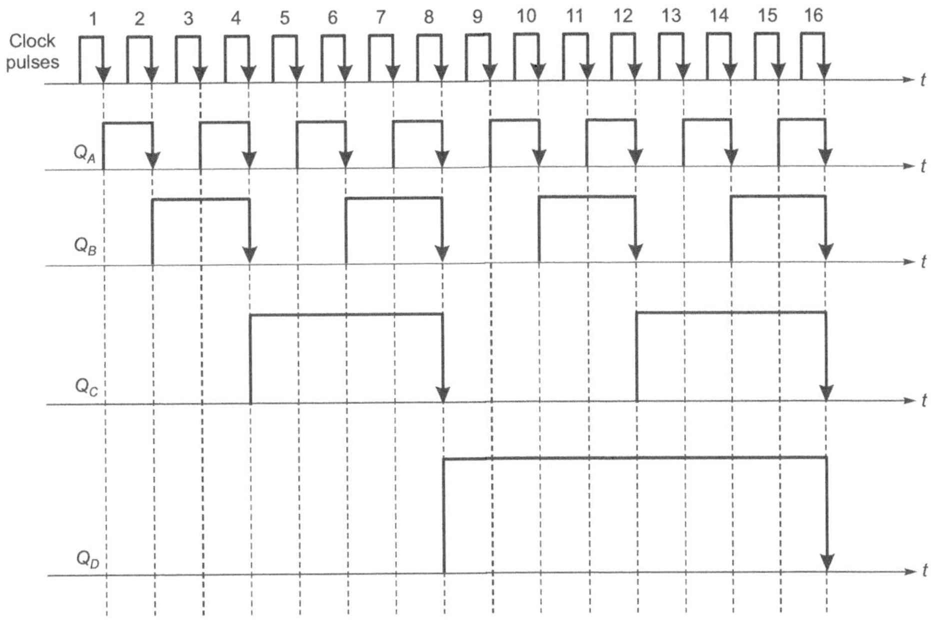

Fig. (2) : Waveforms of the asynchronous counter

From the figure, the input pulses to be counted being applied to the clock input (CK_A) of the first-*T-FFS*. The output of the (Q_A), drives (CK_B) and the output (Q_B) of Flip-Flop *B* drives (CK_C). As explained above ($T\text{-}FF)_A$ will deliver one output pulse for every 2 input pulses at Q_A. Two such pulses from Q_A will produce one output pulse at Q_B. Which means that four input clock pulses at (CK_A) will produce one pulse at Q_B. Following this argument, two output pulse of (Q_B) will produce one output pulse in Q_C and so, on. Here we use negative trailing edge triggering in Flip-Flops.

4.6 Design a MOD-10 synchronous counter using J-K flip-flops giving state diagram excitation table, K-maps and circuit diagram.

[20 marks : 2008]

Solution:

Truth table

J	K	$Q(n+1)$
0	0	$Q(n)$
0	1	0
1	0	1
1	1	$\overline{Q(n)}$

Excitation table

$Q(n)$	$Q(n+1)$	J	K
0	0	0	x
0	1	1	x
1	0	x	1
1	1	x	0

Design of synchronous counter using J-K flip-flop.

State diagram

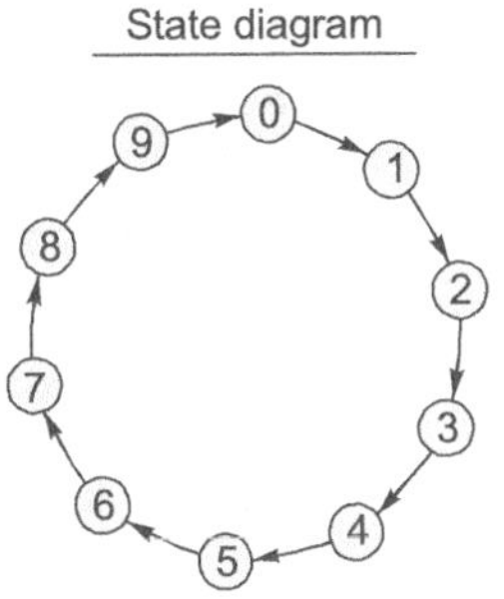

State assignment

0 — 0 0 0 0
1 — 0 0 0 1
2 — 0 0 1 0
3 — 0 0 1 1
4 — 0 1 0 0
5 — 0 1 0 1
6 — 0 1 1 0
7 — 0 1 1 1
8 — 1 0 0 0
9 — 1 0 0 1

	Present stage				Next stage											
	Q_3	Q_2	Q_1	Q_0	Q_3	Q_2	Q_1	Q_0	J_3	K_3	J_2	K_2	J_1	K_1	J_0	K_0
0	0	0	0	0	0	0	0	1	0	x	0	x	0	x	1	x
1	0	0	0	1	0	0	1	0	0	x	0	x	1	x	x	1
2	0	0	1	0	0	0	1	1	0	x	0	x	x	0	1	x
3	0	0	1	1	0	1	0	0	0	x	1	x	x	1	x	1
4	0	1	0	0	0	1	0	1	0	x	x	0	0	x	1	x
5	0	1	0	1	0	1	1	0	0	x	x	0	1	x	x	1
6	0	1	1	0	0	1	1	1	0	x	x	0	x	0	1	x
7	0	1	1	1	1	0	0	0	1	x	x	1	x	1	x	1
8	1	0	0	0	1	0	0	1	x	0	0	x	0	x	1	x
9	1	0	0	1	0	0	0	0	x	1	0	x	0	x	x	1

J_3

$Q_3 Q_2$ \ $Q_1 Q_0$	00	01	11	10
00	0	0	0	0
01	0	0	1	0
11	x	x	x	x
10	x	x	x	x

$J_3 = Q_2 Q_1 Q_0$

$K_3 = Q_0$

K_3

$Q_3 Q_2$ \ $Q_1 Q_0$	00	01	11	10
00	x	x	x	x
01	x	x	x	x
11	x	x	x	x
10	0	1	x	x

J_2

$Q_3 Q_2$ \ $Q_1 Q_0$	00	01	11	10
00	0	0	1	0
01	x	x	x	x
11	x	x	x	x
10	0	0	x	x

$J_2 = Q_1 Q_0$

K_2

$Q_3 Q_2$ \ $Q_1 Q_0$	00	01	11	10
00	x	x	x	x
01	0	0	1	0
11	x	x	x	x
10	x	1	x	x

$K_2 = Q_1 Q_0$

J_1

$Q_3 Q_2$ \ $Q_1 Q_0$	00	01	11	10
00	0	1	x	0
01	0	1	x	0
11	x	x	x	x
10	0	0	x	x

$J_1 = \overline{Q}_3 Q_0$

K_1

$Q_3 Q_2$ \ $Q_1 Q_0$	00	01	11	10
00	x	x	1	0
01	x	x	1	0
11	x	x	x	x
10	x	x	x	x

$K_1 = Q_0$

J_0

$Q_3 Q_2$ \ $Q_1 Q_0$	00	01	11	10
00	1	x	x	1
01	1	x	x	1
11	x	x	x	x
10	1	x	x	x

$J_0 = 1$

K_0

$Q_3 Q_2$ \ $Q_1 Q_0$	00	01	11	10
00	x	1	1	x
01	x	1	1	x
11	x	x	x	x
10	x	1	x	x

$K_0 = 1$

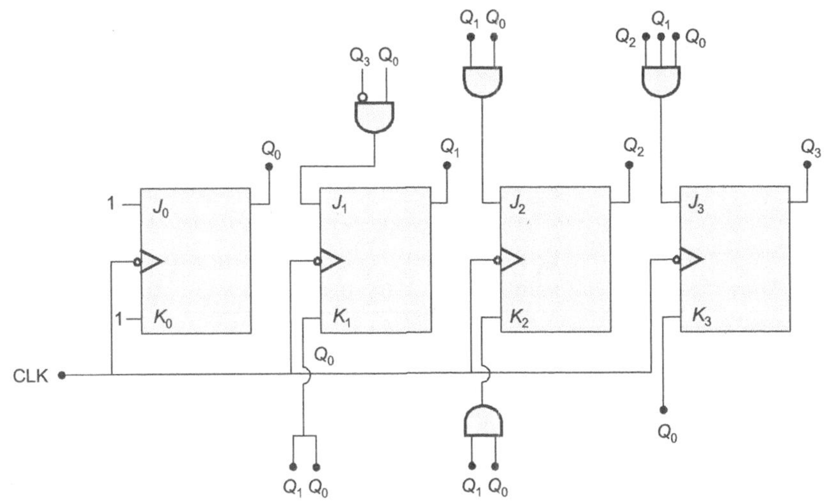

4.7 Design a mod-6 counter to go through the sequence of states as given in the table below using S-R flip-flop:

Sequence No.	Required state sequence		
0	0	0	0
1	0	1	0
2	0	1	1
3	1	1	0
4	1	0	1
5	0	0	1 → Repeat from 0 0 0

Show the state table indicating the present state, the next state for each present state along with the input requirements of each of the S and R inputs. Show clearly the minimization of logic requirements using *K*-maps. Write the logical expressions for each excitation input of all the flip-flops. Draw the logic diagram of the counter designed by you.

[16 marks : 2009]

Solution:

Excitation table of (*S-R*) Flip-Flop.

Truth table

S	R	Q_{n+1}
0	0	Q_n
0	1	0
1	0	1
1	1	x

$Q(n)$	$Q(n+1)$	S	R
0	0	0	x
0	1	1	0
1	0	0	1
1	1	x	0

Design of mod-6 counter state diagram.

State diagram

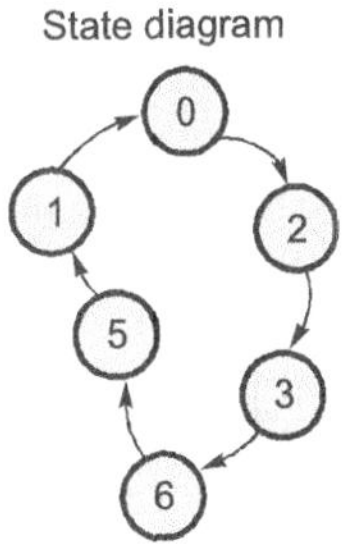

State transition table:

	Present stage			Next stage								
	Q_2	Q_1	Q_0	Q_2	Q_1	Q_0	S_2	R_2	S_1	R_1	S_0	R_0
0	0	0	0	0	1	0	0	x	1	0	0	x
2	0	1	0	0	1	1	0	x	x	0	1	0
3	0	1	1	1	1	0	1	0	x	0	0	1
6	1	1	0	1	0	1	x	0	0	1	1	0
5	1	0	1	0	0	1	0	1	0	x	x	0
1	0	0	1	0	0	0	0	x	0	x	0	1

S_2

Q_2 \ Q_1Q_0	00	01	11	10
0	0	0	1	0
1	x	0	x	x

$\therefore \; S_2 = Q_1 Q_0$

R_2

Q_2 \ Q_1Q_0	00	01	11	10
0	x	x	0	x
1	x	1	x	0

$R_2 = \overline{Q}_1$

S_1

Q_2 \ Q_1Q_0	00	01	11	10
0	1	0	x	x
1	x	0	x	0

$S_1 = \overline{Q}_1 \overline{Q}_0$

R_1

Q_2 \ Q_1Q_0	00	01	11	10
0	0	x	0	0
1	x	x	x	1

$R_1 = Q_2$

S_0

Q_2 \ Q_1Q_0	00	01	11	10
0	0	0	0	1
1	x	x	x	1

$S_0 = Q_1 \overline{Q}_0$

R_0

Q_2 \ Q_1Q_0	00	01	11	10
0	x	1	1	0
1	x	0	x	0

$R_0 = \overline{Q}_2 Q_0$

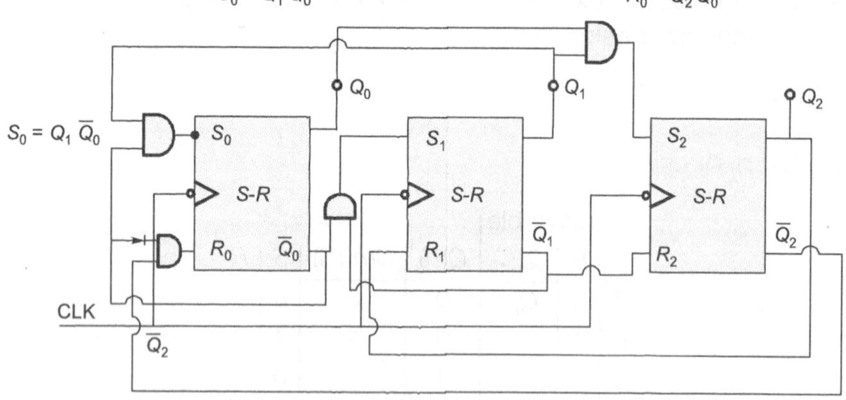

Logic diagram

4.8 Show how the counter shown in the following figure can be configured to operate as a mod-12 counter:

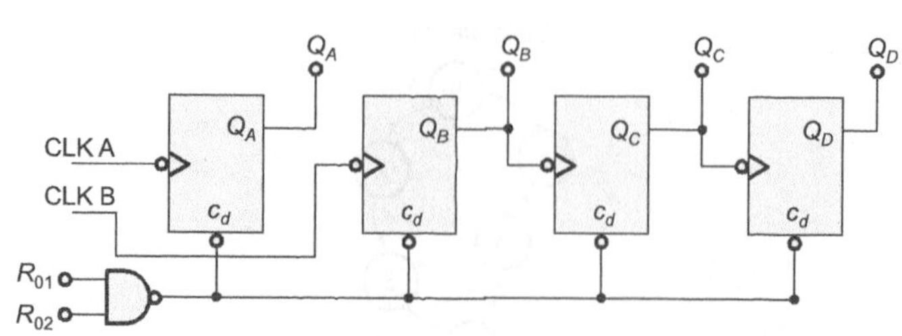

[10 marks : 2015]

Solution:

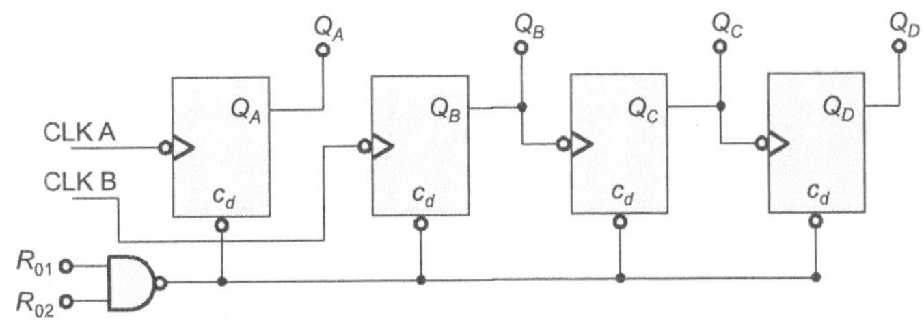

We need to design the above circuit to work as the MOD 12 counter, Each flip flop is a JK flip flop working in toggle mode. So, Q_A will toggle on each clock, so this will be *LSB* of the output.

$Q_BQ_CQ_D$ form an asynchronous counter which work on clock *B*, so Q_D is the MSB of output. Now the requirement of system to work as the mod 12 counter is that

(*i*) time period of clock *B* should be two times time period of clock *A*

(*ii*) when $Q_DQ_CQ_BQ_A$ = 1100 then all the flip-flop should be cleared, so $R_{O1} = Q_D$ and $R_{O2} = Q_C$.

5. Logic Families

5.1 **Give the comparison of different logic families in terms of propagation delay, power dissipation, fan-in fan-out and noise margin.**

[8 marks : 2008]

Solution:

TTL gates:

1. It is the fastest saturating logic family. TTL gates are available in the form of high-speed, high-speed Schottky, low-power, low-power Schottky, and a variety of other types.
2. It has good noise immunity.
3. Power dissipation is in the milliwatt range. With low-power Schottky, this is reduced to 2mW/gate.
4. Good fan out; can drive up to 10 gates.

Disadvantage:

1. Noise immunity is not very high; so it cannot be used in areas where large noise voltages prevail.
2. Power dissipation is much higher than MOS gates.

ECL gates

Advantage:

1. Since transistors operate in the active region, highest speed among all logic families

Disadvantage:

1. Very low noise-margin.
2. Highest power dissipation among all logic gates.
3. Capacitive loading limits fan-out.

NMOS gates

Advantage:

1. Very low power dissipation (nW).
2. Large fan-out capability (20 gates).
3. Very high noise-margin. Suitable for use in industrial atmosphere.

Disadvantage:

1. Large propagation delay per gate.
2. Higher power dissipation than CMOS gates.

CMOS gates

Advantage:

1. Extremely large fan-out capability (> 50).
2. Lowest power dissipation of all gates (a few nano watt).
3. Very high noise-immunity and noise-margin (typically, $V_{DD}/2$).
4. Lower propagation delay than NMOS.
5. Higher speed than NMOS. Currently computer chips operation at 1.5 GHz has been introduced into open market.

Disadvantage:

1. Delays are more compare to bipolar transistor logic families.

5.2 **Show how n-channel enhancement MOSFETs can be connected to obtain (i) NOR logic and (ii) NAND logic. Verify the logical operation in each case.**

[8 marks : 2009]

Solution:

NMOS NAND:

Figure shows a two-input NAND gate using NMOS field-effect transistors. Transistors T_1 and T_2 are of the enhancement type and T_3, which acts as the load resistance, is of the depletion type.

If $A = 0$ and $B = 0$ (i.e. A and B have 0-V inputs), transistors T_1 and T_2 will remain OFF. Then, output $Z = V_{DD}$ (logic 1). The same situation prevails, when $A = 0$, $B = 1$; and $B = 0$, $A = 1$ (here logic 1 = V_{DD}). Now, if $A = B = 1$, then both T_1 and T_2 conduct and the output $Z = 0$. This may be summarized as

$$\left.\begin{array}{lll} A=0, & B=0, & Z=1 \\ A=0, & B=1, & Z=1 \\ A=1, & B=0, & Z=1 \\ A=1, & B=1, & Z=0 \end{array}\right\} \quad \ldots(i)$$

The logic relations in equation (*i*) are seen to be that of the NAND operation. So, we conclude that the logic gate shown in figure performs positive logic NAND operation.

NMOS NOR:

In this case, we connect the transistors in parallel as shown in figure.

We notice that,

$$\left.\begin{array}{lll} A=0, & B=0, & Z=1 \\ A=0, & B=1, & Z=0 \\ A=1, & B=0, & Z=0 \\ A=1, & B=1, & Z=0 \end{array}\right\} \quad \ldots(ii)$$

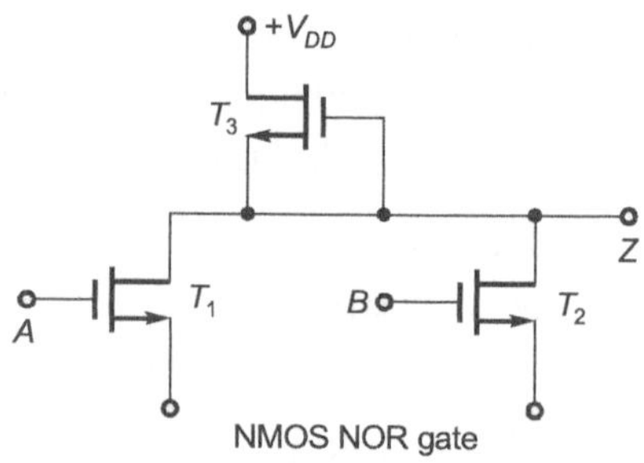

NMOS NOR gate

where logic 0 represents zero volt and logic 1 represents $+V_{DD}$. When 0 volt is applied at the inputs of the transistors they remain OFF, and when V_{DD} is applied at the inputs, the transistors conduct. We find that equation (*ii*) represents a NOR function.

5.3 **Among DTL, RTL, ECL and CMOS logic families, ECL has the propagation delay and power dissipation/ gate respectively as**

(i) low, high **(ii) low, low**

(iii) high, low **(iv) high, high**

[2 marks : 2011]

Solution:

ECL is fastest logic family so propagation delay will be low but due to use non-saturated region of transistor power dissipation is high. So (i) is correct option.

5.4 Prove the two open collector TTL inverters when connected together produce the NOR gate.

[4 marks : 2014]

Solution:

A and *B* are the outputs of the two open collector devices. Either open collector output "Pulls down" the voltage at *Y*.

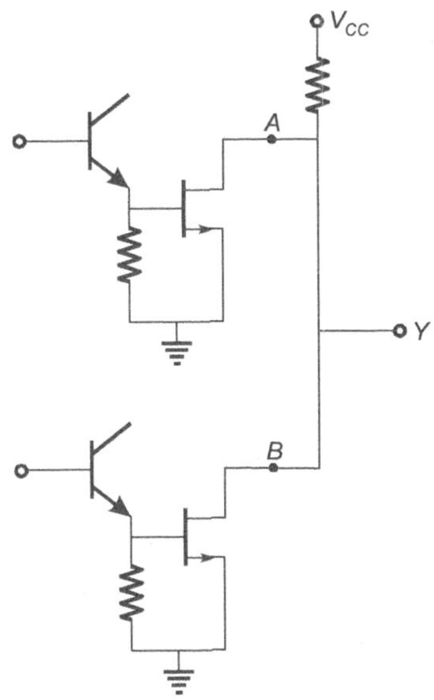

Truth table:

A	B	Y
0	0	0
0	1	0
1	0	0
1	1	1

$Y = AB$

From above, we see that the outputs of two open collector gates, when put in parallel, create an AND function. So, $Y = A'B'$. But by, DeMorgan's law, $A'B' = \overline{A+B}$. Thus, two open collector inverters in parallel create a NOR function.

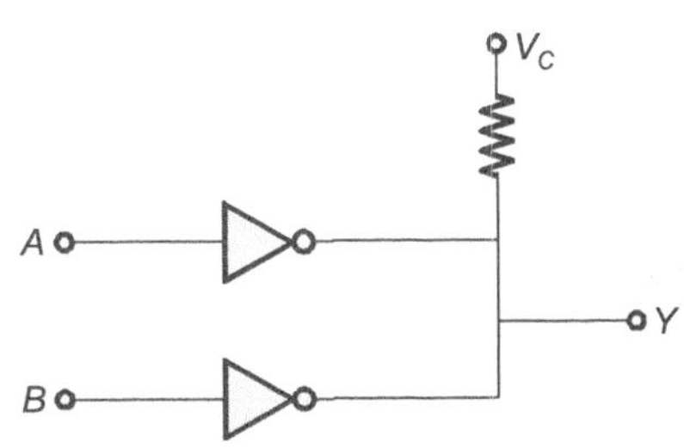

6. A/D and D/A Converters

6.1 Explain with diagram the principle of operation of an A/D converter based on successive approximation method". How it is better that A/D converter based on counter type?

[12 marks : 2003]

Solution:

The successive approximation converter is one of the most widely used types of ADC. It has more complex circuitery than the digital ramp ADC but a much shorter conversion time.

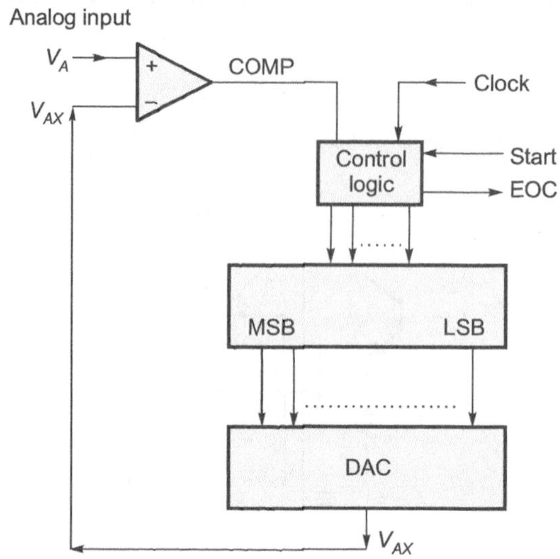

In addition SACs have a fixed value of conversion time that is not dependent on the value of the analog input. Simplified block diagram is shown above. The control logic modifies the content of register bit by bit until the register data are the digital equivalent of the analog input V_A within the resolution of converter.

Let us explain this by considering a four bit SACs.

Let analog input is 1.04 V.

DAC's step size is 1 V.

The operation begin with clearing all the register bits i.e

$$Q_3 = Q_2 = Q_1 = Q_0 = 0$$

or $$[Q] = 0000$$

This makes the DAC output

$V_{AX} = 0$ V with $V_{AX} < V_A$ the comparator output is high.

At the next step control logic sets the MSB of the register to 1 so that $[Q] = 1000$ this produces $V_{AX} = 8$ V because $V_{AX} < V_A$ the COMP output is still high. This high tells the control logic that the setting of MSB did not make V_{AX} to exceed V_A so that MSB is kept at 1.

The control logic now proceeds to next lower bit Q_2. It sets Q_2 to 1 to produce $[Q] = 1100 = 12$ V, because $V_{AX} > V_A$. The COMP output goes low. This low signal tell the control logic that value of V_{AX} is too large and control logic then clear Q_2. So register content back to 1000.

The control logic sets the next lower bit Q_1 so that $[Q] = 1010$ and $V_{AX} = 10$ V, with $V_{AX} < V_A$ COMP is high and tells the control logic to keep Q_1 at 1.

In final step where the control logic sets the next lower bit Q_0 so that $[Q] = 1011 = 11$ V because $V_{AX} > V_A$, COMP goes low to signal that V_{AX} is too large and the control logic clear Q_0 back to 0.

At this point, all the register bits have been processed, the conversion is complete and control logic activates its EOC output to signal that digital equivalent of V_A is now in the register i.e. 1010.

It is better than counter type ADC in the sense that average conversion time is much less than that of counter type ADC.

6.2 **A 12 bit dual-slope ADC utilizes a 1 MHz clock and has $V_{ref} = 10$ V. Its analog input voltage is in the range of 0 to –10 V. Find out the time required to convert an input signal equal to the full scale value. Also find the integrator time constant if the peak voltage reached at the output of the integrator is 10 V.**

[12 marks : 2019]

Solution:

$$T_1 = 2^{N+1}\,T_c$$

Here, $f_c = 1$ MHz

$$T_c = \frac{1}{10^6}\text{ sec} = 10^{-6}\text{ sec}$$

Here, $N = 12$

$\therefore$ $T_1 = 2^{13} \times 10^{-6} = 8192 \times 10^{-6}$

$= 0.008192$ sec

Also, $\dfrac{V_a T_1}{\tau} = 10$ V

$\Rightarrow$ $\dfrac{10 \times 2^n \times T_{clk}}{\tau} = 10$

$\tau = 2^{12} \times 10^{-6}$

$\tau = 4.096$ msec

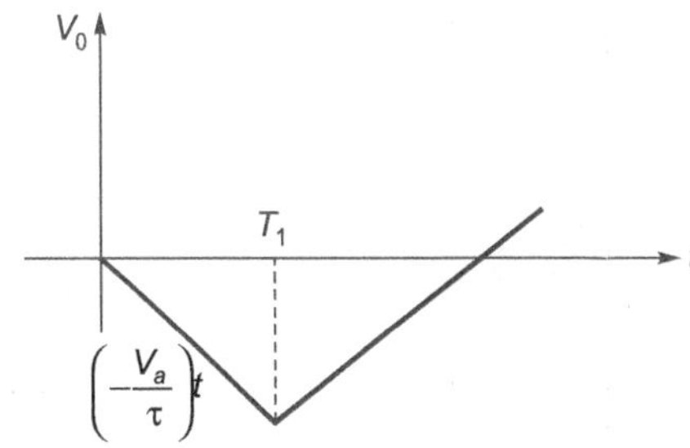

■■■■

3 Microprocessors

Revised Syllabus of ESE: *Microprocessor basics- interfaces and applications.*

1. Introduction to 8085 and Its Functional Organization

1.1 Draw the programming model of an Intel 8085 microprocessor and explain its different parts. Explain why address bus is time multiplexed? Explain also why 'ALE' signal is used? How the microprocessor communicates with a slow speed peripherals with the help of 'Ready ' signal?

[18 marks : 2003]

Solution:

The program model of 8085:

ALU (Arithmetic and Logic Unit): It is logical unit which can perform arithmetic and logical operations. It includes accumulator, temporary register, AL unit, stage register, flag register, stack pointer and programme counter.

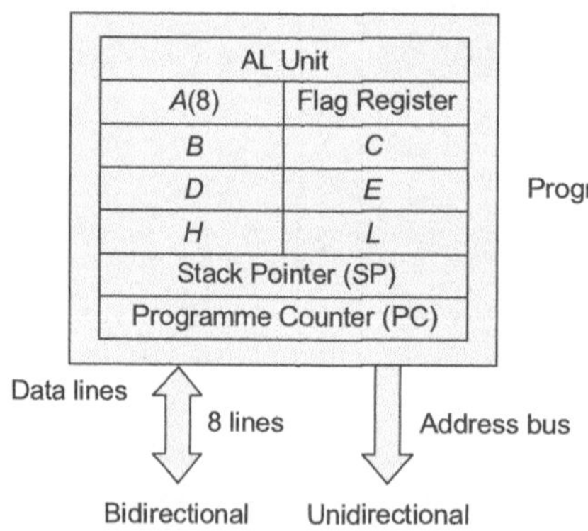

Programme Model

Flag register → It is also '8 bit register'.

5 bits used as flag

D_7	D_6	D_5	D_4	D_3	D_2	D_1	D_0
S	Z	X	A_c	X	P	X	C_y

Flag Register

Remaining general registers (B, C, D, E, H and L) are also 8 bit registers, can also used as register pair.

1. PSW – Programme status word – AF
2. B – BC
3. D – DE
4. H – HL

Programme Counter: (PC) It stores the address of the next instruction to be executed.

Stack Pointer (SP):

It stores address of the top of the stack.

For a 8085, ($AD_0 - AD_7$) lines are multiplexed and the lower half of address ($A_0 - A_7$) is available only during

(T_1) of the machine cycle. This lower half of address is also necessary during T_2 and T_3 of machine cycle to access specific location in memory or I/O port. This means that the lower half of an address bus must be latched in T_1 on the machine cycle. So that it is available throughout the machine cycle. The latching of lower half of an address is done using external latch and ALE signal from 8085.

In some application, speed of input/output system is not compatible with the microprocessor timing. This means that it takes longer time to read/write data. In such situation, the microprocessor has to confirm whether a peripheral is ready to transfer data or not. If the 'Ready' pin is high, the peripheral is ready otherwise 8085 enters WAIT STATE.

1.2 In 8085 microprocessor, how many interrupts are maskable?

(a) Two (b) Three

(c) Four (d) Five [2 marks : 2004]

Solution: (c)

In 8085 microprocessor, four interrupts are maskable (RST 7.5, RST 6.5, RST 5.5 and INTR)

1.3 What is function of signals at pin marked $IO/\overline{M}$ in 8085 microprocessor? [4 marks : 2004]

Solution:

Signal at pin $IO/\overline{M}$ is used to select, I/O devices or memory for data transfer.

If signal at this pin is low, data transfer takes place between mp and memory.

If signal at this pin is high, data transfer takes place between mp and I/O devices.

1.4 Which signal of 8085 microprocessor is used to insert wait states?

(a) Ready (b) ALE

(c) HOLD (d) INTR [2 marks : 2007]

Solution:

'READY' is used by the microprocessor to sense whether a pheripheral device is ready for data transfer or not. If not the processor waits, for synchronize with (slow) pheripherals.

1.5 Explain steps followed by microprocessor, when there is an interrupt signal applied at INTR pin. [10 marks : 2008]

Solution:

INTR is a maskable interrupt but not a vector interrupt. It has the lowest priority. The following sequence of events occur when INTR signal goes high.

1. 8085 checks the status of INTR signal during execution of each instruction.
2. If INTR signal is high, the 8085 completes its current instruction and sends an active low interrupts acknowledge signal $(\overline{INTA})$ if the interrupts is enabled, and disables the interrupt enable flip-flop.
3. In response to the $(\overline{INTA})$ signal, internal logic places an instruction OPCODE on the data bus. In the case multibyte instruction additional interrupt acknowledge machine cycles are generated by the 8085 to transfer the additional bytes into the microprocessor.
4. On receiving the instruction, the 8085 serves the address of next instruction on stack, executes received instruction. (This is done after serving the interrupt subroutine).

1.6 In microprocessor-based systems, DMA facility is required to

(a) increase the speed of data transfer between the microprocessor and the I/O devices.
(b) increase the speed of data transfer between the microprocessor and the memory.
(c) increase the speed of data transfer between the memory and the I/O devices.
(d) improve the reliability of the system.

[2 marks : 2009]

Solution: (c)

The DMA data transfer will be useful to transfer large amount of data between memory and I/O device in a short time.

1.7 In 8085 microprocessor, there are 3 sets of communication lines, called buses. Which are they? Explain each of them in brief.

[12 marks : 2009]

Solution:

8085 consists of 3 buses which are:

Address Bus: The address bus of 8085 consists of 16 parallel signal lines. On these lines the CPU sends out the address of the memory location that is to be written to or read from. If the CPU has N address lines, then it can directly address 2^N memory locations. When CPU reads data from or writes data to a port, it sends the port address out on the address bus.

Data Bus: In 8085 data bus consists of 8 parallel signal lines which are bidirectional. This means that the CPU can read data in from memory or from a port on these lines, or it can send data out to memory or to a port on these lines. Many devices in a system will have their outputs connected to the data bus, but only one device at a time will have its output enabled.

Control Bus: The CPU sends out signals on the control bus to enable the outputs of addressed memory devices or port devices. To read the byte of data from a memory location, the CPU sends out the memory address of the desired byte on the address bus and then sends out a memory read signal on the control bus. The memory read signal enables the address memory device to output a data word into the data bus. The data word from memory travels along the data bus to the CPU.

1.8 Draw memory read machine cycle of 8085 microprocessor and explain.

[12 marks : 2023]

Solution:

Microprocessor 8085 machine cycles are :

1. Opcode fetch; 2. Memory read; 3. Memory write; 4. I/O Read; 5. I/O Write

Required machine cycle timing diagram, i.e., Memory Read

Memory Read indicates to read/access data from memory into microprocessor.

e.g., MVI A, 90 H; 2B instruction to move 90H into accumualtor.

Machine cycles, i.e., Fetch and memory read.

Assuming the instruction at 4000H, 90H would be at 4001H.

Control signals : $\overline{RD}$, i.e., 0 (active) in T2 and T3 states.

Status signals : $S_1 = 1$; $S_0 = 0$

$IO/\overline{M}$ for 0; Memory operation

XX for Opcode of instruction

	Memory
4000H	XX
4001H	90H

Considering fetch as 4 T-states.

Memory Read starts from T5 and till T7.

If f_{CLK} = 3 MHz, $$T = \frac{1}{f_{CLK}} = \frac{1}{3 \times 10^6} = 0.33\ \mu s$$

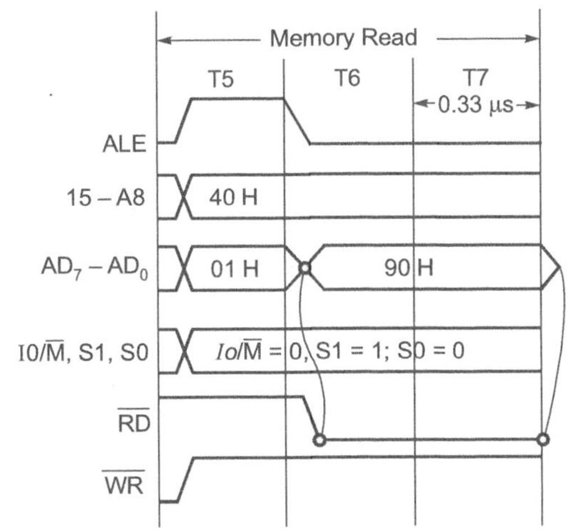

In T6 and T7, $\overline{RD}$ = 0, i.e., active.

Data is accessed into Reg-A in T7 as per example.

After opcode is decoded in T4 of opcode fetch machine cycle, the microprocessor interpretes the instruction as 2B and knows that fetch and memory read cycles are required.

Memory Read Cycle :

T5 : When ALE is 1, all 16 address lines carry the address 4001H as per consideration.

$\therefore A_{15} - A_8$ = 40H $\{AD_7 - AD_0$ = 01 H.$\}$

Status lines, $\frac{IO}{\overline{M}}$ = 0; S_1 = 1 and S_0 = 0 for memory read.

$\overline{RD}$ = 1; Inactive as there is not data bus available.

$\overline{WR}$ = 1; Inactive.

$T_6 \rightarrow$ ALE = 0, $A_{15} - A_8 \rightarrow$ Higher by of address, i.e., 40H but $AD_7 - AD_0 \rightarrow$ Data Bus.

As data bus is available, $\overline{RD}$ = 0, Active (or) $\overline{MEMR}$ = 0; Active, i.e., Memory Read Control Signal : active.

Data from memory location is accessed onto data bus of memory chip.

$T_7 \rightarrow$ Data from memory chip data bus is accessed into microprocessor register A.

2. Microprocessor Interfacing

2.1 In a 8085 microprocessor based system, the maximum number of memory and I/O devices that can be addressed to

(a) 2^8 (b) 2^{16}

(c) $2^8 + 2^{16}$ (d) infinite [2 marks : 2002]

Solution: (c)

In 8085 microprocessor, we are using 8 bit address for input/output (I/O) devices and 16 bit address for memory. So the maximum number of I/O devices and memory is ($2^8 + 2^{16}$).

2.2 Explain Memory mapped I/O. [15 marks : 2011]

Solution:

Memory Mapped I/O:

- In this type of input, the MPU uses 16 address lines to identify an input device.
- MPU used same control signal (memory read or memory write) and instructions as those of memory.
- In some microprocessors as the motorola 6800, all input have 16 bit address, inputs and memory share the same memory map (64 K).
- In memory mapped MPU follows the same steps as if it is accessing a memory register.
- To transfer data between MPU and input devices, memory related instructions (such as LDA, STA, MOV m, LDAX an STAX) and memory control signals ($\overline{MEMR}$ and $\overline{MEMW}$) are used.
- The μp communicate with an input devices as if it were one of the memory location.
- More hardware needed to decode 16 bit address.
- Arithmetic or logical operations can be directly performed with input data.

2.3 **An 8085A system is configured using 74LS373 data latch, two 2732 EPROM, two 6116 RAM and two 8255 PPI. The relevant control pins of these chips are given below:**

2732 A EPROM (4k × 8) : $\overline{OE}, \overline{CE}$

6116 RAM (2k × 8) : $\overline{OE}, \overline{WE}, \overline{CE}$

8255A PPI : $\overline{RD}, \overline{WR}, \overline{CE}, A_1, A_0$, RESET

The peripheral devices are interfaced with the processor using memory I/O. Draw a neat connection diagram for interfacing these chips to the system bus including Power-ON RESET circuit. Use 74LS138 for decoding. Give the addresses of all memory chips and peripheral devices.

[10 marks : 2016]

Solution:

Given:

74LS138 : 3 × 8 decoder

74LS373 : Data latch

2732 EPROM (4 k × 8)

∴ 2(4 k × 8) ⇒ 8 kB

For 4 kB ⇒ ($2^n = N$)

$$2^n = 4\text{ kB} = 2^{12}$$

$n = 12$ ⇒ 12 address lines are required for one chip

6116 RAM (2 kB)

∴ 2(2 k × 8) ⇒ 4 kB

For 2 kB ⇒ $2^n = N$

$$2^n = 2\text{ kB} = 2^{11}$$

$n = 11$ ⇒ 11 address lines are required for one chip.

Decoding logic of 74 LS 138

A_{14} C	A_{13} B	A_{12} A	Output
0	0	0	$y_0 \rightarrow \overline{CE}$ of EP ROM_1
0	0	1	$y_1 \rightarrow \overline{CE}$ of EP ROM_2
0	1	0	$y_2 \rightarrow \overline{CE}$ of RAM_1 and RAM_2
0	1	1	$y_3 \rightarrow \overline{CE}$ of 8255 A_1
1	0	0	$y_4 \rightarrow \overline{CE}$ of 8255 A_2

Memory map of 4 kB EPROM 1 $\rightarrow$ 0000 H – 0FFFH

A_{15}	A_{14}	A_{13}	A_{12}	A_{11}	A_{10}	A_9	A_8	A_7	A_6	A_5	A_4	A_3	A_2	A_1	A_0
0	0	0	0	0	0	0	0	0	0	0	0	0	0	0	0
0				0				0				0 H			
0	0	0	0	1	1	1	1	1	1	1	1	1	1	1	1
0				F				F				F			

Memory map of 4 kB EPROM 2 : 1000 H - 1 FFF H

A_{15}	A_{14}	A_{13}	A_{12}	A_{11}	A_{10}	A_9	A_8	A_7	A_6	A_5	A_4	A_3	A_2	A_1	A_0
0	0	0	1	0	0	0	0	0	0	0	0	0	0	0	0
1				0				0				0 H			
0	0	0	1	1	1	1	1	1	1	1	1	1	1	1	1
1				F				F				F			

Memory map of RAM1 (2 kB) $\rightarrow$ 2000 H – 27 FF H

A_{15}	A_{14}	A_{13}	A_{12}	A_{11}	A_{10}	A_9	A_8	A_7	A_6	A_5	A_4	A_3	A_2	A_1	A_0
0	0	1	0	0	0	0	0	0	0	0	0	0	0	0	0
2				0				0				0			
0	0	1	0	0	1	1	1	1	1	1	1	1	1	1	1
2				7				F				F			

Memory map of RAM_2 (2 kB): 2800 H – 2 FFF H

A_{15}	A_{14}	A_{13}	A_{12}	A_{11}	A_{10}	A_9	A_8	A_7	A_6	A_5	A_4	A_3	A_2	A_1	A_0
0	0	1	0	1	0	0	0	0	0	0	0	0	0	0	0
2				8				0				0			
0	0	1	0	1	1	1	1	1	1	1	1	1	1	1	1
2				F				F				F			

Address of 8205 A_1 : 3000 H

A_{15}	A_{14}	A_{13}	A_{12}	A_{11}	A_{10}	A_9	A_8	A_7	A_6	A_5	A_4	A_3	A_2	A_1	A_0
0	0	1	1	0	0	0	0	0	0	0	0	0	0	0	0
3				0				0				0			

A_1 and A_0 of 8255 are connected to A_2 and A_0 of 8085

$\therefore$ Port A $\rightarrow$ 3000 H

Port B $\rightarrow$ 3001 H

Port C $\rightarrow$ 3002 H

CWR $\rightarrow$ 3003 H (control word register)

Address of 8255 A_2 : 4000 H

A_{15}	A_{14}	A_{13}	A_{12}	A_{11}	A_{10}	A_9	A_8	A_7	A_6	A_5	A_4	A_3	A_2	A_1	A_0
0	1	0	0	0	0	0	0	0	0	0	0	0	0	0	0
4				0				0				0 H			

A_1 and A_0 of 8255 are connected to A_1 and A_0 lines of 8085.

$\therefore$ Port A $\rightarrow$ 4000 H

Port B $\rightarrow$ 4001 H

Port C → 4002 H
CWR → 4003 H

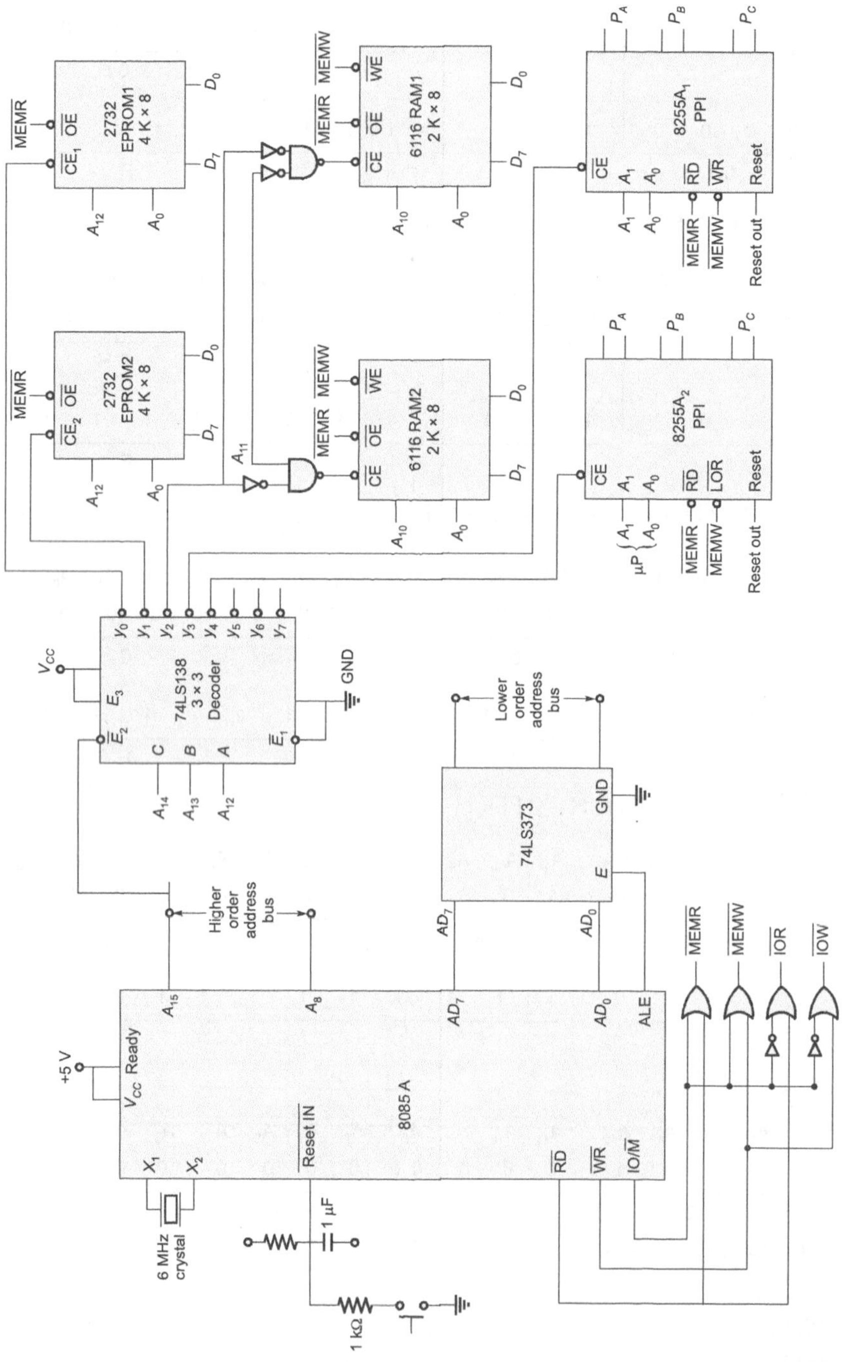

3. Instruction Sets and Data Formats

3.1 What do the following instructions do? What happens if RET is removed from location 2106?

2000	START :	MVI A, C0 H
2002		SIM
2003		CALL 2100 H
2006		MVI A, 40 H

```
2008                 SIM
2009                 CALL 2107 H
200C                 JMP START
2100                 MVI B, 2AH
2102        MOON  :  DCR B
2103                 JNZ MOON
2106                 RET
2107                 MVI C, 9FH
2109        SUNY:    DCR C
210A                 JNZ SUNY
210D                 RET
```

[15 marks : 2001]

Solution:

1. MVI A, C0H → Move immediate C0H to the accumulator.
2. SIM – Set interrupt mask

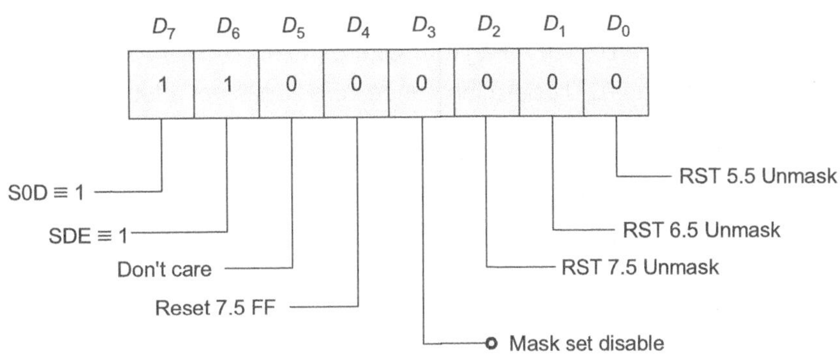

3. CALL 2100 H – The program will go to the location 2100 H.
4. MVI A, 40 H – Load accumulator with 40 H.
5. SIM – Same instruction as (2), except SOD = 0.
6. CALL 2107 H – Go to location 2107 H.
7. JMP START – Jump unconditionally to START.
8. MVI B, 2AH – Move immediate 2AH to register B.
9. DCR B – Decrement register B contents by 1.
10. JNZ MOON – Jump to MOON if result is non-zero.
11. RET – Return unconditionally.
12. MVI C, 9FH – Move immediate 9FH to register C.
13. DCR C – Decrement register 'C' contents by 1.
14. JNZ SUNY – Jump to 'SUNY' if result is non-zero.
15. RET – Return unconditionally.

'RET' is removed from the location '2106' Then, the program delay time will increase.

C0H = $(11000000)_2$, $D_7 = 1$

40H = $(01000000)_2$, $D_7 = 0$

SIM instruction is used to send D_7 bit at SOD.

∴ delays introduced by MOON & SUNY subroutines are unequal and 1 & 0 are alternatively send at SOD with unequal delay so we get a square wave of unequal duty cycle.

3.2 **Which bit of the eight-bit flag register is effected when during the execution of an arithmetic operation, there is a carry out of bit 3 to bit 4?**

(a) Carry flag (b) Zero flag
(c) Sign flag (d) Auxiliary carry flag

[2 marks : 2002]

Solution: (d)

When carry is generated from bit 3 (D_3) pass on through bit 4 (D_4) then Auxiliary carry flag will be set.

3.3 **Why is the z-flag of a 8085 microprocessor not affected after execution of the instruction MOV D, B?**

[4 marks : 2002]

Solution:

In 8085 microprocessor, zero flag is used to indicate the result of arithmetic or logic operation of ALU is zero or non-zero. If the result is non-zero, then Z-flag will be zero (reset) and if the result is zero, then Z-flag will be 1 (set). Here 'MOV D, B' is not an ALU operation hence zero flag is not affected.

3.4 **In eight-bit-unipolar D/A converter is connected to an output of 8085 microprocessor based system. The port address is 21H. Write a program to generate a continuous waveform at the output of the D/A converter as shown below. For a maximum input signal to the converter the output voltage is 5 V.**

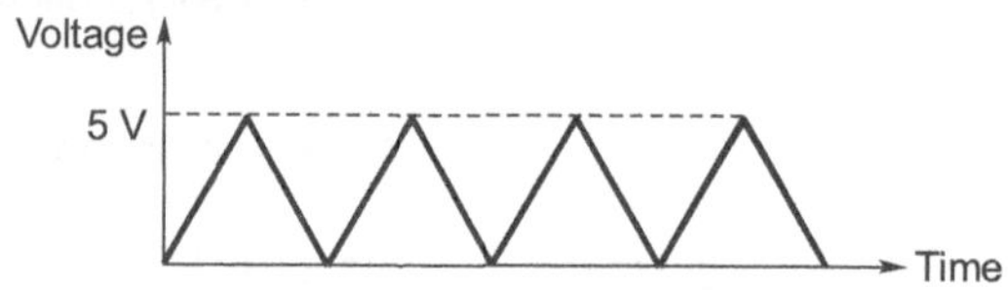

[4 marks : 2002]

Solution:

Start:	MVI A 00H	–	Move immediate 00H to accumulator
Ascent:	OUT 21H	–	Output the content of the accumulator.
	ADI 01H	–	Add immediate 01H to accumulator
	JNC Ascent	–	Jump on no carry to ascent
	MVI A FEH	–	Move immediate 'FEH' to accumulator.
Descent:	OUT 21H	–	Output the content of the accumulator.
	SUI 01H	–	Subtract immediate '01H' from accumulator.
	JNC Descent	–	Jump on no carry to descent
	JMP Start	–	Unconditional jump to start.

3.5 **An 8085 microprocessor polls an 8-bit input port having an address of 03 H. If the LSB of the data is high, the microprocessor operates a relay by sending a high MSB-signal to an output port with an address of 02 H, otherwise the polling continues. Write a program to implement it.**

[20 marks : 2002]

Solution:

Poll:	IN 03H	–	Input the content of the port '03' to accumulator.
	ANI 01H	–	Immediate AND operation with 01H and accumulator.
	JZ Poll	–	Jump on zero to poll.
	MVI A, 80H	–	Move immediate 80H to accumulator.
	OUT 02H	–	Output the content of accumulator port '02H'.
	JMP Poll	–	Unconditional jump to poll.

3.6 Write down the Addressing modes of the following instructions:

(i) ACI 20 H (ii) CMA

(iii) STA 2500 H (iv) LXI H, 2005 H

(v) XCHG (vi) MOV E, L

[1 × 6 = 6 marks : 2003]

Solution:

Instruction	—	Addressing mode
(i) ACI 20 H	—	Immediate
(ii) CMA	—	Implicit
(iii) STA 2500 H	—	direct
(iv) LXI H, 2005 H	—	Immediate
(v) XCHG	—	Implicit
(vi) MOV E, L	—	Register

3.7 Determine in each case the final values in Accumulator and Carry flags after the following instructions are executed:

	Accumulator	Carry
initial state	95 H	1

(i) RAL, (ii) RRC

(iii) XRI A5 H, (iv) CPI A 9 H,

(v) ORI C9 H, (vi) ANI 33 H.

In each case it may be assumed to start with the same initial values of Accumulator and Carry flags.

[1 × 6 = 6 marks : 2003]

Solution:

Initial state of accumulator (Acc) is equal to 95 H and carry (Cy) is equal to 1 then,

RAL – Rotate accumulator left to carry

(i)

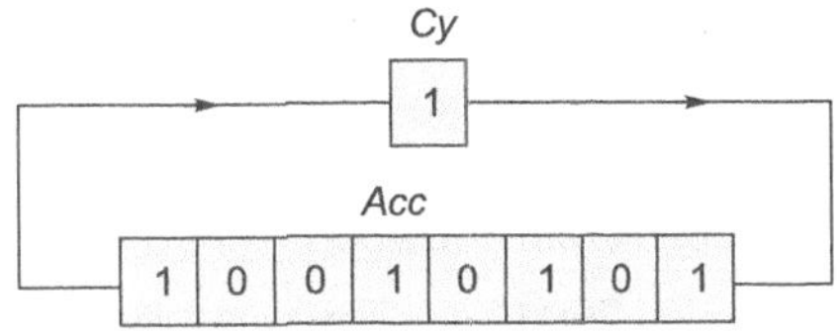

Acc: 0010 1011, $Cy = 1$

(ii) RRC – Rotate accumulator right

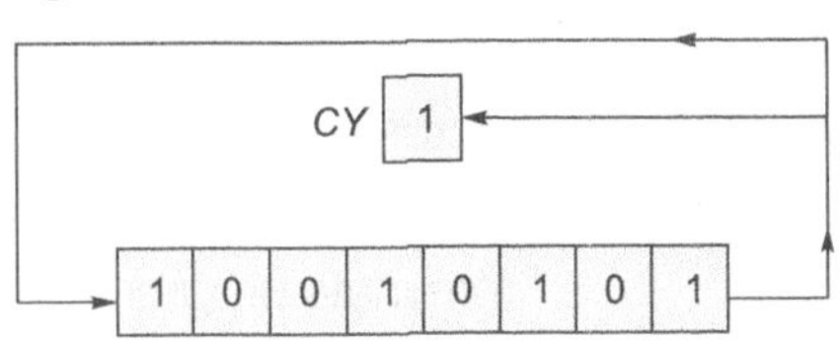

Acc: 1100 1010, $Cy = 1$

(iii) XRI – Ex-OR operation immediate with accumulator

```
            1 0 0 1 0 1 0 1 ⊕
            1 0 1 0 0 1 0 1
Acc ──►     0 0 1 1 0 0 0 0 ──► 30 H
```

For (Ex:OR) operation, carry flag will be in reset (0) state irrespective of any result.

(iv) CPI – Compare immediate with accumulator

After the execution of CPI instruction, content of accumulator is not changed. For the concern of flag affected ,'CPI' instruction we considered as 'SUI' instruction. Here accumulator content is small so, $Cy = 1$ (set).

(v) ORI C9H

For 'OR' operation, Cy (carry flag) is always zero (rest) and accumulator (Acc) becomes

```
            1001  0101
            1100  1001
Acc ──►     1101  1101 ──► DD H
```

(vi) ANI – 33H – AND immediate accumulator

For AND immediate accumulator instruction carry flag (Cy) always be in reset (0) state and content of the accumulator (Acc).

```
            1001  0101
            0011  0011
Acc ──►     0001  0001 ──► 11 H

Cy  ──► 0                  (irrespective of result in is reset)
```

3.8 **The sign-flag of 8085 microprocessor is set to 1, if**

(a) the result of an arithmetic operation is 1.

(b) the most significant bit of the result of an arithmetic or logic operation is 1.

(c) there is a carry from addition or borrow from subtraction.

(d) the result of an operation carriers Four 1s in accumulator.

[2 marks : 2004]

Solution: (b)

The sign flag of 8085 microprocessor is set to 1, if resultant of accumulator is negative, that means most significant bit of the result of an arithmetic or logic operation is 1.

3.9 **Write an assembly language program, starting at location 2100, to find Two's complement of an 8-bit number. The number 96 is stored at location 2501. The result is to be stored at location 2502.**

[15 marks : 2004]

Solution:

Memory	Op code	Operand	Comments
2100	LDA	2501	The number 96 H is loaded to accumulator from the memory location 2501H.
2103	CMA		Complementary accumulator
2104	INR	A	Increment the accumulator by 1
2105	STA	2502 H	Store the result at memory location 2502 H
2108	HLT		terminate program

3.10 Show diagrammatically the flow of signal of FETCH and execute cycle for ADI A, 05 indicated by arrow.

[10 marks : 2004]

Solution:

2000 : ADI, 05 H

Hex code of ADI is C6H

i.e.

2000	1	1	0	0	0	1	1	0	→ C6H
2001	0	0	0	0	0	1	0	1	→ 05H

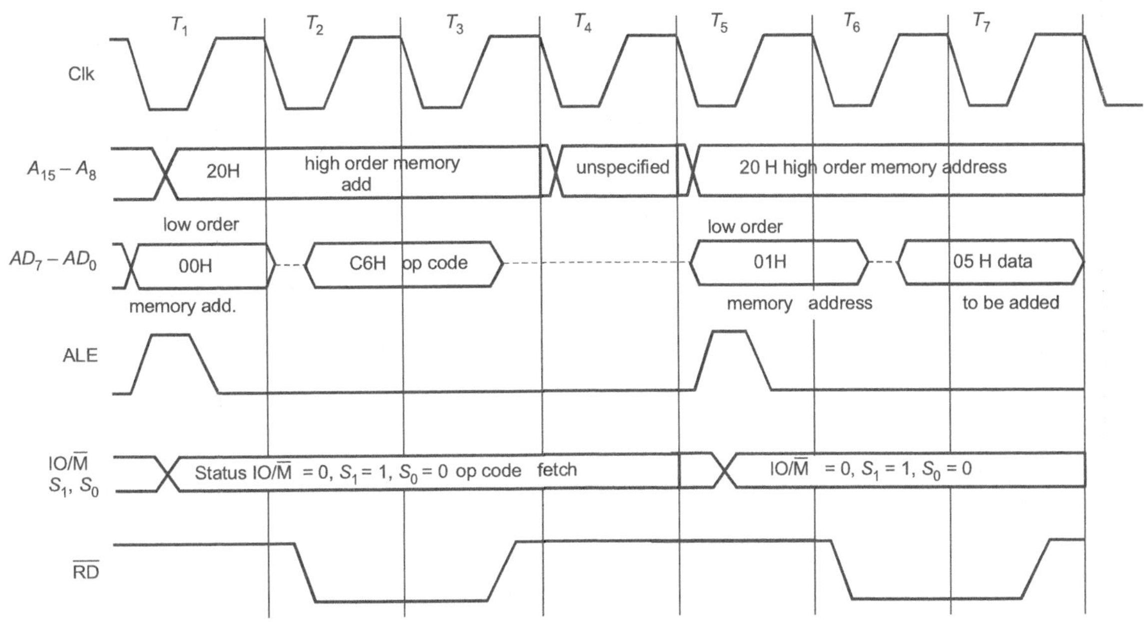

3.11 Two 8 bits Hex numbers are stored in Memory locations 2000 H and 2001 H respectively. Develop a suitable program with proper comments in assembly level language to multiply these two Hex numbers by shift and add technique. Store the 16 bit results in two memory locations 2002 H and 2003 H respectively with 'hi-byte' in 2002 H and 'lo-byte' in 2003 H. In which way "Shift and Add" technique used for multiplication is better suited for multiplication than "repeated addition" method?

[18 marks : 2005]

Solution:

Main Program:

```
LXI SP, STACK
LHLD 2000H      :  Place contents of 2000H in L register and contents of
                :  2001H in H register
XCHG            :  Place multiplier in D and multiplicand in E
CALL MLTPLY     :  Multiply the two numbers
MOV A, H        :  Store the product in locations 2002H and 2003H
STA 2002
MOV A, L
STA 2003
HLT
```

Subroutine:

MLTPLY : This subroutine multiplies two 8-bit unsigned numbers

Input : Multiplied, in register *E* and multiplier in register *D*
Output : Results in HL register

```
MLTPLY:   MOV A, D      :  Transfer multiplier to accumulator
          MVI D, 00H    :  Clear D to use in DAD instruction
          LXI H, 0000H  :  Clear HL
          MVI B, 08H    :  Set up register B to count eight rotation
NXTBIT:   RAR           :  Check if multiplier bit is 1
          JNC NOADD     :  If not, skip adding multiplicand.
          DAD D         :  If multiplier is 1, add multiplicand to HL and place
                        :  partial result in HL.
NOADD:    XCHG          :  Place multiplied in HL
          DAD H         :  And shift left
          XCHG          :  Retrieve shifted multiplied
          DCR B         :  One operation is complete, decrement counter
          JNZ NXTBIT    :  Go back to next bit
          RET
```

In case of add and shift no. cycles required are less, we have to execute the subroutine 8-times while in case of repeated addition we have to execute subroutine several times equal to decimal equivalent of multiplier.

3.12 **The purpose of different flag and their working in an intel 8085 microprocessor.**

[10 marks : 2005]

Solution:

There are five flags in 8085 μp. These are Sign Flag [*S*], Zero Flag [*Z*], Auxiliary Carry Flag [*AY*], Parity Flag [*P*] and Carry Flag [*CY*].

The microprocessor uses these flags to test data conditions.

These flags have critical importance in decision making process of the microprocessor.

The condition set or reset of the flags are tested through software instruction. For example, the instruction *JC* (Jump on Carry) is implemented to change the sequence of a program when *CY* flag is set.

These flags are affected by execution of an arithmetic or logical operation, data copy instructions do not affect any flags. Its working is as below.

Zero Flag: The zero flag is set to 1 when result is zero otherwise it is reset.

CY (Carry Flag): If an arithmetic operation results in a carry, the *CY* flag is set, otherwise it is reset.

Sign Flag (*S*): The sign flag is set if bit D_7 of the result = 1 otherwise it is reset.

Parity Flag (*P*): If the reset has even on. of 1s, the flat is set, for an odd no. of 1s the flag is reset.

AC (Auxiliary Carry): In an arithmetic operation, when a carry is generated by digit D_3 and passed to digit D_4 the AC flag is set otherwise reset. This flag is used for *BCD* operations, there is no jump instruction associated with this flag.

3.13 **A single pole 8 way rotary switch is connected to port *A* of 8255 chip, starting from bit 0 to 7 positions. When the switch is manually rotated to position 3 a fan connected bit position 3 of port *B* is to be switched on. Further when the manually rotated switch is changed to bit position 5 a television is to be made on whose switch is connected bit 5 of port *B* associated with 8255 chip. It is to be assumed that necessary 'control word' for making port *A* in input mode and port *B* in output mode have been done via the control port. Further latching circuits have been provided in port *B*, so that once the fan and television set is on, they will remain on, unless the switch position comes to bit 7 of port *A*. When both of them will be made automatically off by sending bit '0s' to bit position 3 and 5 respectively to port *B*. Develope the necessary program in assembly language.**

[15 marks : 2005]

Solution:

The addresses of ports and control register is

Port A	$(8000)_H$	$(A_1 = 0, A_0 = 0)$
Port B	$(8001)_H$	$(A_2 = 0, A_0 = 1)$
Port C	$(8002)_H$	$(A_1 = 1, A_0 = 0)$
Control register	$(8003)_H$	$(A_1 = 1, A_0 = 1)$

Port $A \rightarrow$ input mode and $1 \rightarrow$ means switch is on.

Port $B \rightarrow$ output mode and $0 \rightarrow$ means switch is off.

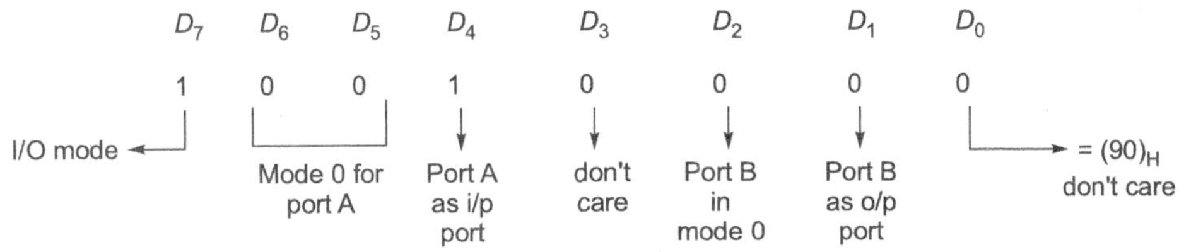

Program:

MVI A, 90 H: Load accumulator with control word

STA 8003 H: Write word in control register to initialize the ports.

LOC 1 : LDA 8000 H: Read the switch positions from port A.

ANI 08 H: Mask other bits except D_3 to check whether it is 1 or 0.

CPI 08 H: To check whether D_3 is 1 or not.

JNZ LOC1: It D_3 not 1, then wait until it be come?

MVIA, 08 H:

STA 8001 H: Set bit D_3 at port B to on the fan.

LOC2 : LDA 8000H: Read the switch position from port A gain.

ANI 20 H:

CPI 20 H : To check whether D_5 is 1 or not.

JNZ LOC2: It D_5 is not 1 wait till it become 1.

MVI A, 28 H:

STA 8001 H: Set bit D_5 to turn on fan but D_3 should also be 1 otherwise fan will be turn off.

LOC 3: LDA 8000 H: Read the switch position.

ANI 80 H:

CPI 80 H: Check whether D_7 is 1 or not i.e. switch is at portion 7 or not.

JNZ LOC 3: It switch is not at D_7 wait.

MVI A, 00 H:

STA 8001 H: Send 0 at bit position D_3 and D_5 to turn off the fan and TV.

HLT.

3.14 The ______ instruction allows control to transfer to a subroutine, which when complete, issue the ______ instruction to return control to the main program.

(a) CALL, JMP
(b) CALL, RET
(c) CALL, RSTI
(d) EI, DI

[2 marks : 2006]

Solution: (b)

The CALL instruction allows to transfer to a subroutine, which when complete, issue the RET instruction to return control to the main program.

3.15 **(i) Interpret the following instructions and mention their addressing mode and flag affected, if any: XRA A; DAA; DCR M; ADD B.**

(ii) What is the difference between Accumulator (ACC) and instruction Register (IR)?

[8 + 4 marks : 2006]

Solution:

(i) XRA R : Logical Ex : OR operation with accumulator.

Here

XRA $A \Rightarrow A \oplus A = 0$

The content of the accumulator becomes zero.

∴ Zero, parity flag, become set and remaining flags reset.

Here we have register addressing mode.

DAA : Decimal adjustment accumulator

It adjust an 8 bit number in accumulator to form two BCD numbers. Both carry and auxiliary carry flag is using to perform it. All flags are affected and it has implicit addressing mode.

DCR M: This instruction is used to decrement the content of a memory data whose address is in HL pair.

Address mode: Indirect

Carry flag does not affected. All other flags are affected.

ADD *B* : This instruction executes contains of '*B*' is added contents of *A* and result is stored in '*A*' and contents of '*B*' has no change. All flags are affected and it has register addressing mode.

(ii) Accumulator: It is an 8 bit register. In all arithmetic and logical operation, accumulator as one operand.

Instruction register: This functions on the instruction cycle of fetch/execute. An instruction is first fetched from the memory through the data bus and stored in the instruction register. It is then decoded by the internal decoder and fed to the control logic for execution.

3.16 **A BCD no. between 0 and 99 is stored in a R/W memory location called the input buffer. Write a main program & a conversion subroutine (BCDBIN) to convert the BCD no. into its equivalent binary no. in 8085. Store the result in a memory location defined as output buffer.**

[12 marks : 2006]

Solution:

Program:

Start:	LXI SP, STACK	—	Initialize the stack pointer
	LXI H, INBUF	—	Point HL index to the input buffer memory where binary no. will be stored.
	MOV *A*, *M*	—	Get BCD No.
	CALL BCDBIN	—	Call BCD to binary conversion routine.
	STAX *B*	—	Store binary no. in the O/P buffer.
	HLT		
	BCDBIN	—	**Function:** This subroutine converts a BCD number into its binary equivalent.

Input: A 2-digit packed BCD number in accumulator
O/P: A binary no. in accumulator.
NO other register contents are destroyed.

```
          PUSH B        —  SAVE BC registers
          PUSH D        —  SAVE DE registers
          MOV B, A      —  SAVE BCD No.
          ANI 0FH       —  Mask significant four bits
          MOV, C, A     —  Save unpacked BCD, in C
          MOV A, B      —  Get BCD again
          ANI F0H       —  Mask least significant four bits
          JZ BCD1       —  If BCD2 , the result is only BCD2
          RRC           —  Convert most significant bits into unpacked BCD2
          RRC
          RRC
          RRC
          MOV D, A      —  SAVE BCD2 in D
          XRA A         —  Clear accumulator
          MVI E, 0AH    —  Set E as multiplier of 10
SUM:      ADD E         —  Add 10 unit (D) = 0
          DCR D         —  Reduce BCD2 by one
          JNZ SUM       —  Is multiplication complete, if not go back and add again.
BCD 1:    ADD C         —  Add BCD1
          POP D         —  Retrieve previous contents
          POP B
          RET.
```

3.17 An 8085-8155 based micro-computer is required to drive on LED connected to bit 0 of port A based on two switches inputs connected to bits 6 and 7 of port A. If both switches are either high or low turn the LED ON and that a LOW will turn it off. Use port addresses of CSR and port *A* as 20 H and 21 H respectively. Program starts from 2000 H. Write an 8085 assembly language program.

[12 marks : 2006]

Solution:

Address of control register — 20 H

Address of port *A* — 21 H

Control words for port A as i/p and o/p port.

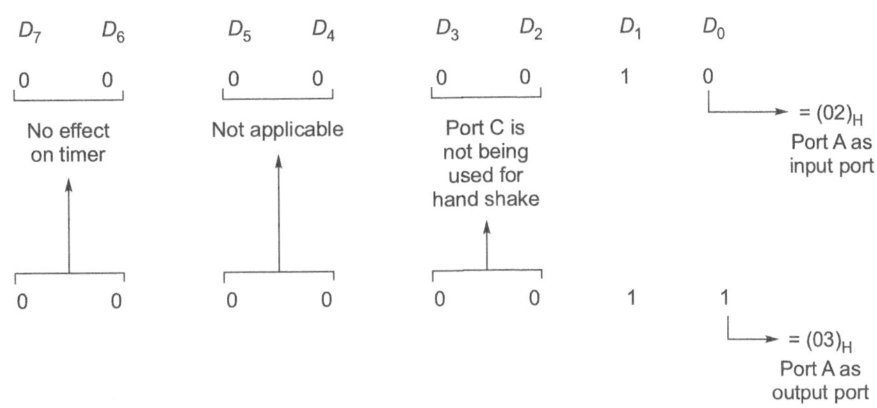

Switches are connected to D_7 and D_6 of port A.

Program:

	MVI A, 02 H		
	OUT 20 H	—	initialize port A as i/p port.
	IN 21 H	—	read the data of port A.
	ANI COH	—	mark all the bits except D_7 and D_6.
	RAL	—	rotate left so that carry bit becomes D_7.
	JC LOC1	—	If D_7 is at logic 1 i.e. CY = 1 go to LOC 1.
	XRI 00 H	—	If D_7 is at logic 0 then take XOR with 00H so that to check whether D_6 is same as D_7 or not.
	JP ON	—	It D_7 and D_6 are same ON the LED
	MVI A, 03 H		
	OUT 20 H	—	initialize A as O/P port.
	MVI A, 00H		
	OUT 21 H	—	$\because D_0 = 0$ — 80 LED will be off.
	HALT		
LOC1:	XRI 80 H		
	JP O N		
	MVI A, 03 H		
	OUT 20 H	—	initialize A as o/p port
	MVI A, 00 H		
	OUT 21 H	—	$\because D_0 = 0$ — So LED will be off.
	HALT		
ON:	MVI A, 03 H		
	OUT 20 H	—	initialize A as o/p port.
	MVI A, 01 H		
	OUT 21 H	—	$\because D_0 = 1$ — So LED will be turn on.
	HALT		

3.18 **Write the meaning of the following instruction used in 8085:**
MOV M< r
INR r
RLC
CMA

[4 marks : 2007]

Solution:

MOV m, r	—	Move data from register (r) to memory whose address is in HL register pair.
INR r	—	Increment the content of register (r) by 1
RLC	—	Rotate accumulator left
CMA	—	Complement accumulator.

3.19 **Draw the flow chart and write the assembly language program in 8085 to add two numbers of 8-bit data using direct addressing. The data is stored in memory locations $(4200)_H$ and $(4201)_H$ and the result is to be stored in memory locations $(4202)_H$ and $(4203)_H$.**

[10 marks : 2007]

Solution:

```
          LHLD 4200 H   – Load HL pair direct
          MVI, C,00H    – Move 00H to register 'C' immediately.
          LDA 4200H     – Move content of 'H' register to accumulator.
          MOV B, A
          LDA 4201
          ADDB
          JNC Ahead     – Jump if no carry
          INR C         – Increment content of 'C'
Ahead:    STA 4202H     – Store accumulator content in location in
                          location 4202 H directly.
          MOV A, C      – Move content of 'C' to accumulator.
          STA 4203      – Store accumulator content in location 4203 H
                          directly.
          HLT           – Terminate the programme execution.
```

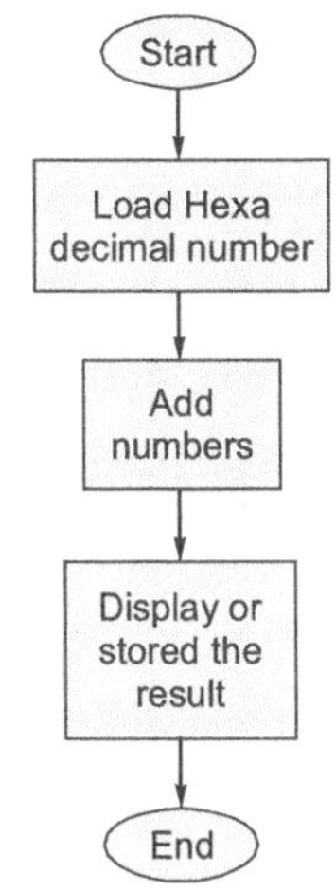

3.20 **The addressing mode used in the instruction STAX B is**

(a) direct
(b) immediate
(c) implicit
(d) indirect

[2 marks : 2008]

Solution: (d)

The addressing mode used in the instruction STAX *B* is register indirect. Because the content of accumulator is copied to a memory location whose address is given by content of register pair *BC*.

3.21 **Define addressing modes of a microprocessor system. State and explain addressing modes supported by 8085 microprocessor.**

[4 marks : 2008]

Solution:

Every instruction of program has to operate on a data. The method of specifying the data to be operated with an instruction is called addressing.

8085 has the following addressing modes:

(i) Immediate addressing mode: In an immediate addressing mode, 8 or 16 bit data can be specified as a part of the instruction.
Example : MVI *B*, 20 *H*

(ii) Register addressing mode: The register addressing mode specialties the source operand, destination operand or both to be contained in an 8085 register.
Example: MOVE *B*, *A*

(iii) Direct addressing mode: The direct addressing mode specify 16-bit address of the operand with in the instruction itself. Since, this address is a part of the instruction, the second and third byte of this instruction contain this 16-bit address. e.g. LDA 2050 H

(iv) Indirect addressing mode: In indirect addressing mode, the memory address where two operands are located is specified by the contents of a register pair.
Example : LDAX B

(v) Implicit addressing mode: In implicit addressing mode, op-code specifies the address of the operands.
Example : CMA, RAL

3.22 A serial device connected to 8085 at SID pin for serial data transmission. The device uses a synchronous communication with 11 bit format (1 start, 7 data, 1 parity, 2 stop). Write a program for 8085 to receive one character from the device and store it in the memory location 2500 H. Assume that delay routines are available

[15 marks : 2008]

Solution:

```
SI DATA:    RIM             — Read the SID line
            RAL             — Place D7 into CY
            JC SI DATA      — If D7 = 1 this is not a start bit go back and read again.
            CALL HAFBIT     — If D7 = 0, this is a start bit wait for half bit period.
            MVIC, 0BH       — Counter for 11 bits
NEXT BIT:   CALL BITT TIME  — Wait for one bit period
            RIM             — Read input bit
            RAL             — Save bit in CY
            DCR C           — One bit is read
            JZ RETURN       — If all bits are read return to main program
            MOV A, B        — Place the bits so far is A
            RAR             — Place the bit in CY into position D7 and shift all other bits by
                              one position.
            MOV B, A        — Save bit in B
            JMP NEXT BIT    — Get the next bit
```

After returning from this program into main program

```
We have           MOV A, B
RETURN:           STA 2500 H
                  HALT
```

3.23 A single instruction to clear the lower four bits of the accumulator in 8085 microprocessor is

(a) XRI 0FH (b) ANI F0H
(c) XRI F0H (d) ANI 0FH

[2 marks : 2009]

Solution: (b)

```
              xxxx  xxxx  [AND] operation
F0H ——→       1111  0000
              xxxx  0000
```

3.24 For the 8085-based micro-computer, define and stack pointer, and describe their uses.

[4 marks : 2009]

Solution:

For application programs, the internal memory of the microprocessor is not sufficient to store the intermediate results. These intermediate results can be stored temporarily on the stack and can be referred back when required. This stack is implemented with help of special memory pointer register (stack pointer). The stack pointer (SP) is a 16-bit register in the 8085 μp which is manipulated by the microprocessor control sections during stack related instructions example. During PUSH and POP operation, stack pointer gives the addresses of memory where the information is to be stored or to be read. The stack pointer contents are automatically manipulated to point to stack top. The memory location currently pointed by stack pointer is called as top of the stack.

Basically used to store the intermediate results like in case of call instruction address of next instruction is stored in stack and after returning, read from the stack using stack pointer, POP and PUSH operations.

3.25 **The memory location 2050 holds the data byte F7H. Write instructions to transfer the data byte to the accumulator using 3 different op-codes MOV, LDAX and LDA. Also show the register contents for all 3 op-codes. After examining all of them, find which method is more efficient by giving your comments.**

[12 marks : 2009]

Solution:

Since the memory location 2050 H holds the data byte F7H. So we can use these instruction to transfer the data byte to the accumulator.

1. LDA 2050 H – Load accumulator direct.
   Here we are given the address of data byte directly. By this single instruction we can use to transfer the data byte from memory location to accumulator.
2. LDAX R_p – Load accumulator indirect
   Before using this instruction, we should store the address of the data byte in register pair except (HL) pair.

   Example: $\begin{cases} \text{LXI B, 2050H} \\ \text{LDAX B} \end{cases}$

   Here content of the BC become – 2050H
   and content of the accumulator becomes – F7H
3. MOV A, M – Move the content of the memory location whose address is in HL pair. Here also before using this instruction, we should store the address of the data byte in (HL) pair.

   Example: $\begin{cases} \text{LXI H, 2050H} \\ \text{MOV A, M} \end{cases}$

   Here content of the HL become 2050H
   And content of the accumulator becomes F7H
   T-states required in case 1 is 13 *T*-states (4-machine cycle)
   T-states required in case 2 and 3 is 17-*T* states overall (5-machine cycles)

So LDA 2050 is more efficient because it take lesser time to transfer the data.

3.26 **A set of 12 voltage readings is stored in memory locations 2070H to 207BH. The readings are expected to be positive and less than 100_{10}. Write a program to:**

(i) check each readings to determine whether it is positive or negative;
(ii) reject all negative readings;
(iii) add all positive readings;
(iv) output FFH to port 1 at any time, when the sum exceeds FFH to represent overflow, otherwise, display the sum.
(v) If no output port is available in the system, then store FFH in memory location 2090H, when the sum exceeds FFH, otherwise store the sum in memory location 2090H. Write comments for each instruction.

[16 marks : 2009]

Solution:

$(12)_{10} = (0C)_{16}$

	LXI H 2070 H	–	Initialize memory pointer
	MVI C, $(0C)_H$	–	Initialize counter
	MVI D, 00 H	–	Initialize the value of sum
BACK:	MOV A , M	–	Get the number

```
         ANI 80 H     -  Check for positive
         JNZ SKIP     -  If negative, jump to (Skip)
         MOV A , M    -  Get the number
         ADD D        -  Add the positive value
         MOV D, A     -  Store in register D
SKIP:    MVIA, FFH    -  Move immediate FFH to accumulator
         CMP D        -  Compare D with accumulator
         JC OUT       -  Jump if non zero to (Back)
         INX H        -  Increment pointer
         DCR C        -  Decrement counter
         JNZ BACK     -  Jump on carry to (Out)
         MOV A, D     -  Move data 'D' to accumulator
OUT:     OUT port 1   -  Output the accumulator through port 1
         STA 2090 H   -  Store accumulator data in memory address 2090 H
         HLT          -  Terminate the program
```

3.27 Which one of the following has the highest priority?

(a) RST 7.5 (b) RST 5.5

(c) TRAP (d) HOLD

[2 marks : 2011]

Solution: (c)

Priority level is as TRAP > RST 7.5 > RST 7.5 > RST 5.5 > INTR and HOLD is also one of the INTR type interrupt.

So (c) is correct option.

3.28 List the machine cycles of 8085.

[10 marks : 2011]

Solution:

Machine Cycles:

- Machine cycle is defined as the time required to complete one operation of accessing memory, input or acknowledging an external request.
- This cycle may consists of three to 6-T states.

Op-code Fetch Machine Cycle:

The first operation in any instruction is op-code fetch.

- The microprocessor needs to get (fetch) this machine code from the memory register where it is stored before the microprocessor can begin to execute the instruction.
- This op-code fetch cycle is called the M_1 cycle and has four T-states. The first 3 states $T_1 - T_3$ of fetch the code and T_4 to decode and execute the op-code.
- In 8085 instruction set, some instruction have op-codes with 6-T states.

Memory Read Machine Cycle:

- The memory read cycle requires three T-states and is in many way similar to the op-code fetch cycle. Both use the same control signal to read contents from memory but it read 8-bit data or address.

Memory Write Machine Cycle

- In the memory write cycle the 8085 writes (stores) data in memory, using control signal $\overline{WR}$ and the states signal input/$\overline{M}$.
- It also requires 3-T states.

3.29 For 8085 microprocessor, if the stack pointer points to 0000 *H*, in which memory location will stack contents be stored, if the stack is to be used?

[4 marks : 2012]

Solution:

While storing stack contents, the stack pointer always first decrement and then the memory location pointed by the stack pointer is filled up. After decrementing 1 from 0000 H, FFFFH is obtained, hence stack contents will be stored from the memory location FFFFH onwards on progressively decreasing memory location addresses.

3.30 By drawing a suitable waveform, explain a typical instruction cycle (IC) of an 8085 microprocessor.

[8 marks : 2012]

Solution:

When a processor executes a program, the instructions (1 or 2 or 3 bytes in length) are executed sequentially by the system. The time taken by the processor to complete one instruction is called the ***Instruction Cycle*** (IC).

An IC consists of Fetch Cycle (FC) and an Execute Cycle (EC). Thus IC = FC + EC. It is shown in Figure Depending on the type of instruction, IC time varies.

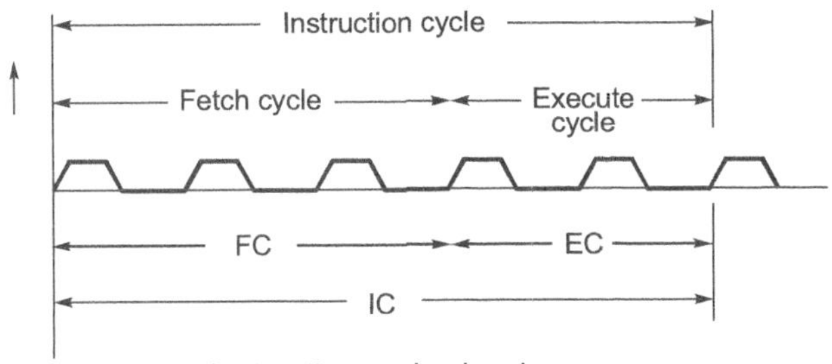

Instruction cycle showing FC, EC and IC

The time required to fetch an opcode from a memory location is called Fetch Cycle. A typical FC may consist of 3T states. In the first T-state, the memory address , residing in the PC, is sent to the memory. The content of the addressed memory (i.e., the opcode residing in that memory location) is read in the second T-state, while in the third T-state this opcode is sent via the data bus to the instruction register (IR). For slow memories, it may take more time in which case the processor goes into 'wait cycles'. Most microprocessors have provision of wait cycles to cope with slow memories. A typical FC may look like the following:

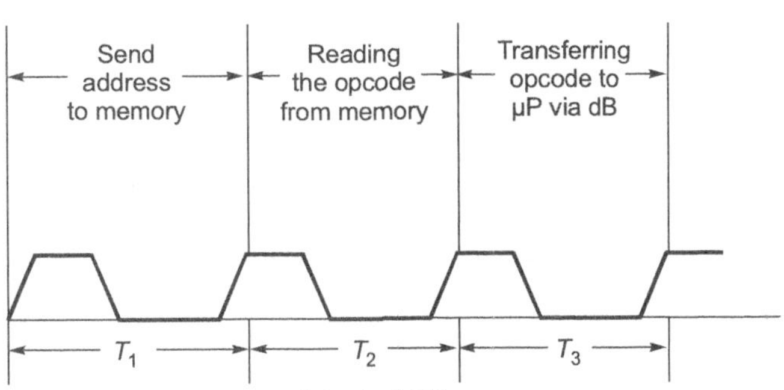

A typical FC

For execution of DAD, 10 T-states are needed. Instead of having a single machine cycle having 10 T-states, it consists of the Opcode Fetch machine cycle (4T states) and 6 extra T-states divided into two machine cycles. These two extra machine cycles are Bus Idle Machine cycles which do not involve either memory or I/O.

The timing diagram for DAD instruction is shown below:

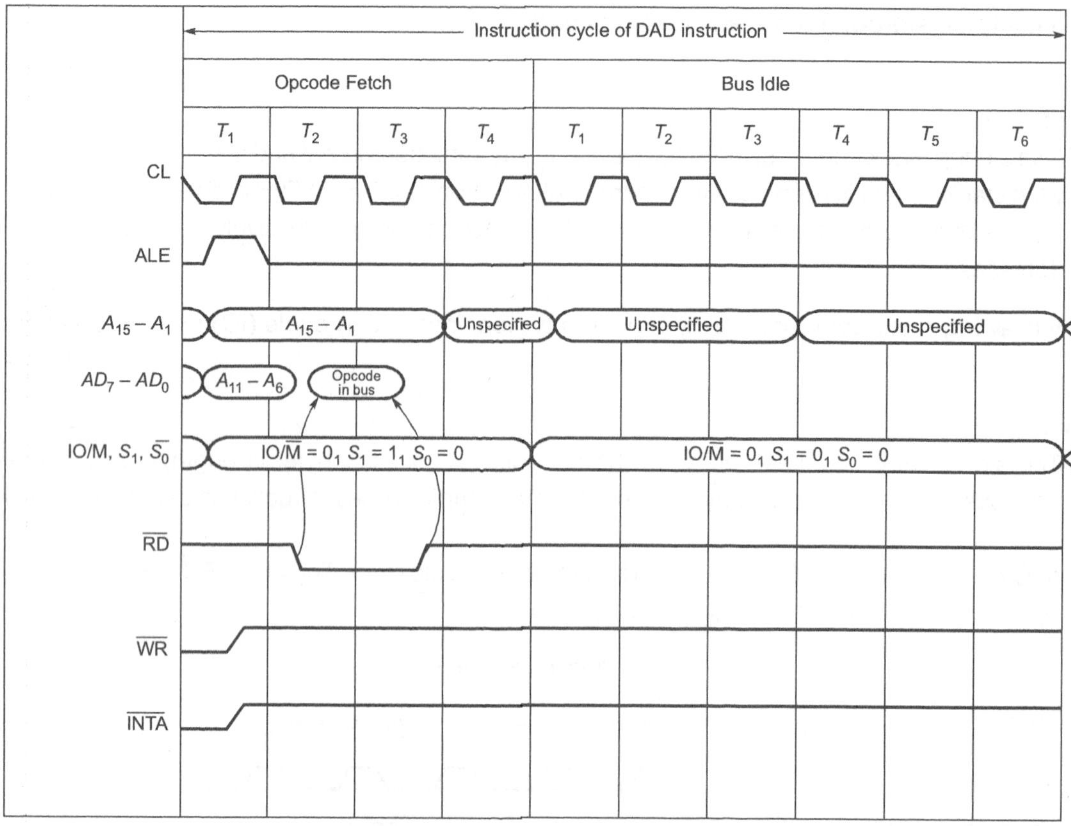

Timing diagram for DAD instruction

3.31 **Write an assembly language program for an 8085 microprocessor, which will store the contents of accumulator and flag register at 2000 H and 200 H memory locations respectively using PUSH and POP instructions. Write comments for selected instructions.**

[10 marks : 2012]

Solution:

The following is the program for the above, using PUSH-POP instructions:

LXISP, 4000 H	:	Stack pointer is initialized at 4000 H.
PUSH PSW	:	Accumulator and flag register contents pushed into stack
POP B	:	Accumulator content goes to *B* and flag register content goes to *C* register.
MOV A, B	:	Content of *B* taken to accumulator.
STA 2000 H	:	Accumulator content stored into memory location 2000 H.
MOV A, C	:	Content of *C* moved to accumulator.
STA 2001 H	:	Accumulator content stored into memory location 2001 H
HLT	:	Program halted.

3.32 **When returning back to the main program from Interrupt Service Routine (ISS), in 8085 microprocessor, the software instruction EI is inserted at the end of the ISS. Why?**

[6 marks : 2012]

Solution:

When an interrupt (either via RST 7.5, RST 6.5, RST 5.5, INTR) is acknowledged by the microprocessor, 'any interrupt acknowledge' signal resets the interrupt enable F/F. It thus disables RST 7.5, RST 6.5, RST 5.5 and INTR interrupts. Thus any future interrupt coming via RST 7.5, RST 6.5, RST 5.5 or INTR will not be acknowledged unless the software instruction EI is inserted which thereby sets the interrupt enable F/F.

3.33 For an 8085 microprocessor, write an assembly language program for the multiplication of two 8-bit numbers by shift-add routine method. Two 8-bit binary numbers are stored in two 8-bit registers and the result is stored in a register pair. Write comments in selected instructions.

[16 marks : 2012]

Solution:

Multiply the 8-bit unsigned number in memory location 2200H by the 8-bit unsigned number in memory location 2201H. Store the 8 least significant bits of the result in memory location 2300H and the 8 most significant bits in memory location 2301H.

- LXI H, 2200 : Initialize the memory pointer
- MOV E, M : Get multiplicand
- MVI D, 00H : Extend to 16-bits
- INX H : Increment memory pointer
- MOV A, M : Get multiplier
- LXI H, 0000 : Product = 0
- MVI B, 08H : Initialize counter with count 8
- MULT: DAD H : Product = product x 2
- RAL
- JNC SKIP : Is carry from multiplier 1 ?
- DAD D : Yes, Product =Product + Multiplicand
- SKIP: DCR B : Is counter = zero
- JNZ MULT : no, repeat
- SHLD 2300H : Store the result
- HLT : End of program

3.34 Write an 8085 assembly language program to perform a parity check on an 8-bit word in location 4000_{16}. If the parity is ODD, store DD_{16} in location 4000_{16}. However if the parity is EVEN, store EE_{16} in location 4000_{16}.

[10 marks : 2013]

Solution:

```
        LXI H, 4000H    (H, L load with 4000H)
        MOV A, M        (content of memory location 4000H copied to accumulator)
        ADI, 00H        (Add immediate 00H)
        JPE : Odd
        MVI M, DDH      (If parity is odd shore DDH, in 400H)
Odd :   MVI M, EEH      (Move EEH to 4000H is parity even)
HALT :  HLT             (End of program)
```

3.35 An array of 8-bit signed numbers (in 2's complement) is sorted in sequential memory locations starting from SGNDNOS. The length of the array is N(<255). Draw a flow chart and write an assembly language program to count positive non-zero numbers and store the result in sequential memory location 'POS'. Include the necessary remarks in the ALP.

[10 marks : 2016]

Solution:

Program to find the No's from 'N' bytes @ SGNDNOS.

- Consider 'HL' pair as memory pointer to profit SGNDNOS
- 'DE' register pair to point POS

- Register 'C' as counter to count 'N' bytes
- Register 'B' – To count positive values
- Required flow chart is

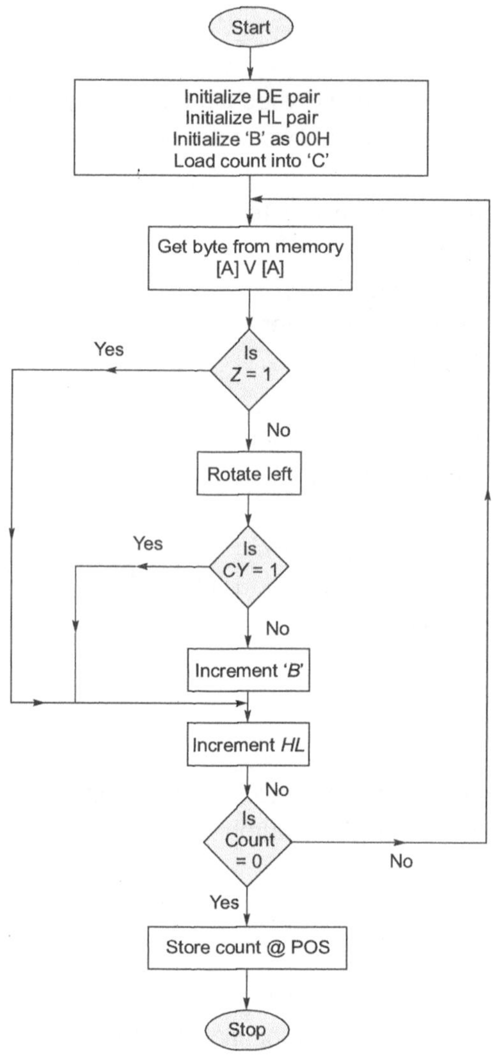

Program:

```
        LXI H SGNDNOS   ;  Initialize HL pair @ SGNDNOS
        LXI D, POS      ;  'DE' pair @ POS
        MVI C, N        ;  Load 'C' register with count
        MVI B, 00H      ;  To store result
Kept :  MOV A, M        ;  Get the data byte from array
        ORA A           ;  Check for a non-zero value
        JZ Next
        RLC             ;  Check if cy = 1 i.e. to neglect negative values
        JC Next
        INR B           ;  If cy = 0; positive value so increment 's'
Next:   INX H           ;  Increment pointer and check if count = 0
        JNZ Rept
        MOV A, B        ;  Store result in register 'B' @ POS pointed by 'DE' pair.
        STAX D
        HLT             ;  Stop
```

Notes:

In signed representations if

D_7 = 0 ; positive value
 = 1 ; negative value

3.36 A set of 10 readings whose individual values are less than $(127)_{10}$ is stored in memory location starting at XX80H. Write an assembly language program:

(i) to check each reading to determine whether it is +ve or –ve.
(ii) to reject all negative readings.
(iii) to add all +ve readings.
(iv) to output this sum to PORT 1, at any time when the sum exceeds eight bits to indicate overflow, otherwise display the sum to PORT 2.

[20 marks : 2017]

Solution:

```
MVIC, OA H
LXI D, XX80 H
NEXT : LDAX   D       ]
       INX    D       |
       MOV    B, A    |
       ANI    80 H    |
       CZ     POS     | Selecting positive number
       DEC    C       |
       JNZ    NEXT    |
       CALL   ADD     |
       HLT            ]
POS :  MOV    A, B    ]
       LXI H  2000 H  | Placing +Vc number in
       STAX H         | continuous memory
       INR M          |
       RET            ]
POS :  OUT    PORT 1  ]
       RET            |
ADD :  XCHG           |
       MOV    A, E    |
       ANI    0F H    |
       MOV    C, A    |
       MOV    B, 00 H |
AO :   LDAX   D       | Adding positive number
       ADD    B       | and result at OUTPUT 2
       CMP    B       |
       JC     OUT     |
       MOV    B, A    |
       DEC    C       |
       DCX    D       |
       JNZ    AO      |
       OUTPORT 2  RET ]
```

3.37 Explain the mathematical function that is performed by the following instructions of 8085 microprocessor :

MVI A, 07H
RLC
MOV B, A
RLC
RLC
ADD B

[10 marks : 2022]

Solution:

→ MVIA, 07H, move the data immediately to accumulator

[A] ← 07H

→ RLC

Rotate the elements of accumulator to left without carry,

A → 0000 0111 ⇒ 0000 1110

[A] 0EH (Data is multiplied by 2)

→ MOV B, A

[B] ← [A], More contents of A to B

[B] ← 0EH

→ RLC

Rotate contents of accumulator to left without carry

$$00001110 \Rightarrow \underbrace{0001}_{1}\ \underbrace{1100}_{C}$$

[A] ← 1CH (Multiplication by 2)

→ RLC

$$00011100 \Rightarrow \underbrace{0011}_{3}\ \underbrace{1000}_{8}$$

[A] ← 38H (Multiplication by 2)

→ ADD B

[A] ← [A] + [B],

$$\begin{array}{r} 38 \\ \underline{06} \\ 47 \end{array}$$

[A] ← 47H

At last we can see that the decimal value of [A] is almost 70 which is 10 times the initial value. Hence, we can say that multiplication by 10 is performed in above instructions.

4. Peripheral Devices and Semiconductor Memory

4.1 Explain why an interrupt controller is required with microprocessor systems. How many interrupts can be handled by one chip?

[12 marks : 2002]

Solution:

Interrupts can be used for a variety of applications. Each of these interrupt applications require a separate interrupt. For 8085 we have five interrupt pins where as 8086 has only one interrupt pin. For applications where processor interrupts are sufficiently large we have to use external device called programmable interrupt controller. 8259 A is a commonly used priority interrupt controller.

Earlier because of use of single interrupt pin and hardware requirement to decide priorities the 8085 interrupt I/O is limited to overcome this programmable interrupt controller such as 8259 is used to implement and retuned the capability of 8085 interrupt.

Features of 8259 A:

1. It can manage eight priority interrupts. This is equivalent to providing eight interrupts pins on the processor in place of INTR pin.
2. By cascading nine 8259s, it is possible to get 64 priority interrupts.
3. Interrupt mask register makes it possible to mask individual interrupt request.
4. Interrupts can mask or unmask individually.

4.2 **Write control word format for Intel-8253 programmable Counter/Interval Timer. Use 8253 for generation of square wave using BCD counting. Write control word and an assembly language program starting address 2000. Take N = 20 decimal and select Counter-2 for wave generation.**

[15 marks : 2004]

Solution:

Given that count, $N = 20_{10} = (14)_H = (0014)_H$

i.e. $$\frac{\text{clock frequency}}{\text{square wave frequency}} = \text{Count } N$$

$$\text{Square wave frequency} = \frac{\text{clock frequency}}{20} = \frac{3\text{MHz}}{20} = \frac{3\times10^6}{20}$$

$$\text{Square wave frequency} = 150 \text{ kHz}$$

We have to use counter 2 for

Wave generation

∴ Control word

D_7	D_6	D_5	D_4	D_3	D_2	D_1	D_0
1	0	1	1	0	1	1	1
Select counter 2		Load 16 bit count		Mode 3			BCD count

Program:

Port addresses for control register and counter 2 register.

For A_1A_0 = 11 control register is selected

For A_1 A_0 = 10 counter 2 register is selected

Assuming $A_6 - A_2$ address lines at logic 0 and chip is selected when A_7 = 1.

Then address for control register = $(83)_H$

Then address for counter 2 register =$(82)_H$

Program:

MVIA, $(10\ 11\ 0\ 111)_2$ control word mode 3 and counter 2

OUT 83 H → write in 8253 control register

MVIA, 14 H → lower byte of count

OUT 82 H → load counter 2 with low order byte

MVIA, 004 → higher order byte of count

OUT 82 H → load counter 2 with high order byte

HALT.

4.3 Draw a schematic block diagram of a programmable interval timer (8253). Explain operation of each block. State and explain control word format with emphasis on operation modes.

[10 marks : 2008]

Solution:

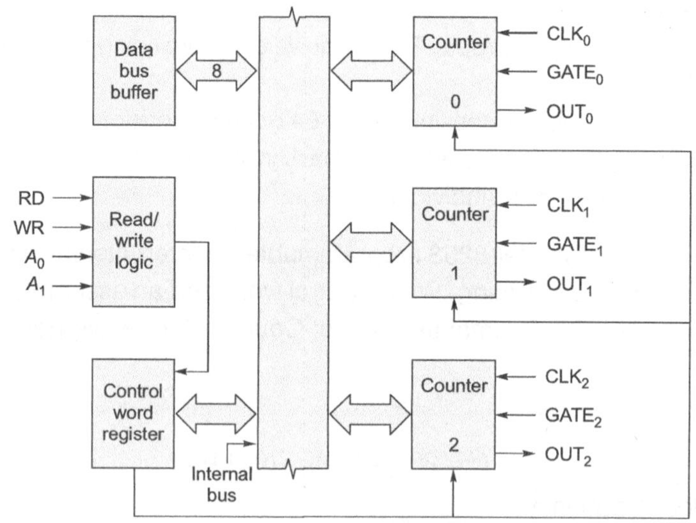

Block Diagram of 8254 (8253)

1. **Data Bus Buffer:** This tri-state, bidirectional, 8 bit buffer is used to interface the 8253/54 to the system data bus.

   Functions:

   (i) Programming the 8253/54 in various modes.

   (ii) Loading the counter register.

   (iii) Reading the count values.

2. **Read/write logic:** The read/write logic has five signals, $\overline{RD}, \overline{WR}, \overline{CS}$ and the address lines A_0 and A_1. In the peripheral I/O mode, a $\overline{RD}$ and $\overline{WR}$ signals are connected to $\overline{IOR}$ and $\overline{IOW}$ respectively. In memory mapped I/o, these are connected to $\overline{MEMR}$ and $\overline{MEMW}$.

   The control word register and counters are selected according to the signals on the lines A_0 and A_1.

A_0	A_1	Selection
0	0	Counter-0
0	1	Counter-1
1	0	Counter-2
1	1	Control word register

Control Word Register: This register is accessed when lines A_0 and A_1 are at logic 1. It is used to command word which specifies the counter to be used, its mode and either read or write operation.

Counters: These three functional blocks are identical in operation. Each counter has two input signals clock and GATE and one output signal OUT. Each counter consists of a single, 16 bit preset table down counter. The counter can operate in either binary or BCD and its input gate and output are configured by the selection of modes stored is the control word register. The counter is fully independent.

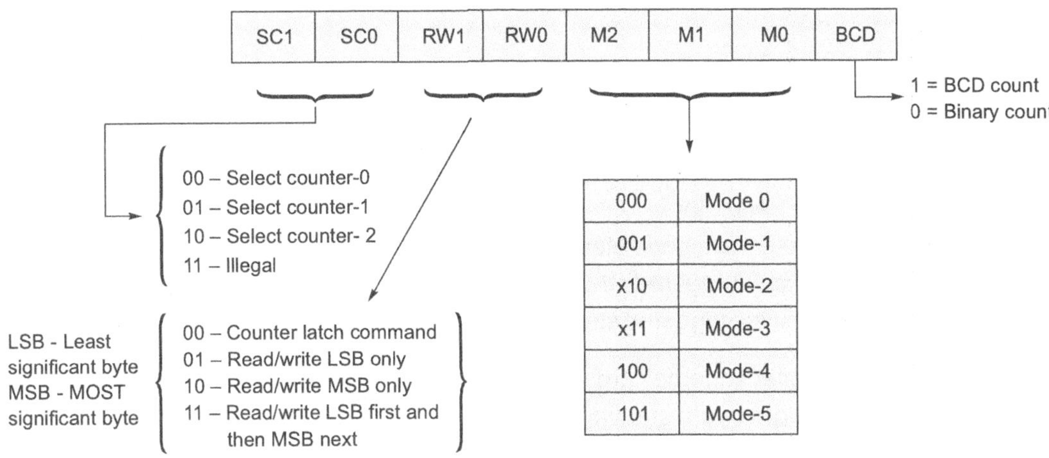

Format of control word for timer 8254

4.4 Explain Interrupts and Serial I/O of 8085. [15 marks : 2011]

Solution:

- The interrupt input is a process of data transfer whereby an external device or a peripheral can inform the processor that it is ready for communication and it requests attention.
- The process can be initiated by an external device and it is a asynchronous process.
- Interrupt requests are of two type maskable and nonmaskable interrupts.
- 8085 mp includes 4 maskable and 1 nonmaskable interrupt.
- Among 4 maskable interrupt one is nonvectored which requires external hardware to supply a call location to restart the execution. Other 3 are vectored to specific location.
  - ⇒ μp can ignore or delay a maskable interrupt request if it is performing some critical task, however it has to respond to a nonmaskable request immediately.
  - ⇒ The interrupt process allows the microprocessor to respond to these external request for attention or service on a demand basis and leaves the microprocessor free to perform other tasks.
  - ⇒ EI instruction is used to set the enable flip-flop.
  - ⇒ DI instruction is used to reset the enable flip-flop.
  - ⇒ SIM is used to set interrupt mask (i.e. used for maskable interrupts).
  - ⇒ RIM is used to read interrupt mask.

Serial I/O of 8085

- For long distance communication parallel data communication is expansive so we go for serial data communication. In these situations the serial input mode is used whereby one bit at a time is transferred over a single line.
- In serial transmission 8 bit parallel word should be converted into a stream of eight bit (serial bits) this is parallel to serial conversion.
- After conversion one bit at a time is transmitted over a single line at a given rate called baud (bit-per second).
- On other hand in serial reception, MPU receives a stream of 8 bits and they should be converted into an 8 bit parallel word this is known as p serial to parallel conversion.
- The illustrations include both software and hardware controlled serial input as well uses of the SOD (serial output data) and SID (serial input data) pins are specially designed signals for serial input in 8085.
- RIM & SIM instructions are also used in serial input communication in 8085.

4.5 Write the different modes of 8253 IC. [4 marks : 2015]

Solution:

The different mode of operation of 8253 IC are

(1) Mode 0 : Interrupt on terminal count
(2) Mode 1 : Programmable one shot
(3) Mode 2 : Rate generator
(4) Mode 3 : Square wave generator
(5) Mode 4 : Software triggered strobe
(6) Mode 5 : Hardware triggered strobe

4.6 What type of data transfer schemes are used when there is a speed mismatch between microprocessor and I/O devices? Explain cycle stealing technique.

[10 marks : 2015]

Solution:

Programmed Data Transfer-Asynchronous Mode:

When the I/O device speed and μp speed do not match, asynchronous mode may be used. The key feature of this mode is that, the MPU initiates data transfer by requesting the device to get ready and then goes on checking its status. The I/O instruction is executed only when the I/O device is ready to accept or supply data. So each data transfer is preceeded by a 'request ready' signal generated by the MPU and an acknowledgment signal issued by the I/O device. The method is known as handshaking mode of data transfer, as it resembles the back-and-forth movement of hands involved in handshaking, to coordinate the data transfer.

The asynchronous mode is ideal for reconciling the timing differences between the MPU and I/O devices. However, an important disadvantage is that a lot of precious MPU time is wasted during the looping to check the I/O device status. The wastage of the MPU time may be prohibitive or impractical in many situations.

Flowchart for the asynchronous mode of data transfer

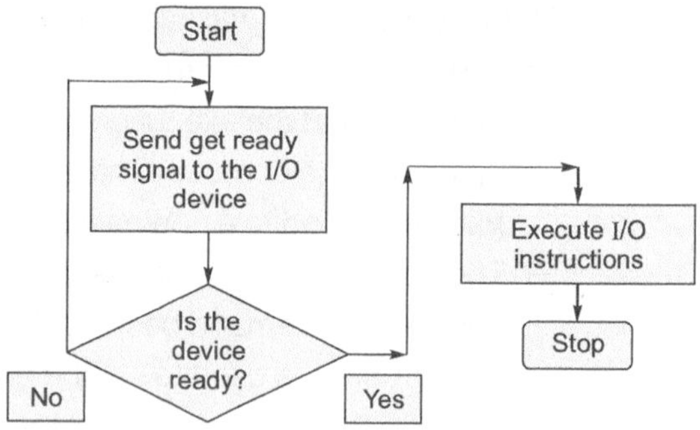

Direct Memory Access (DMA):

If a large block of data is to be transferred between memory and a fast I/O device, the overhead incurred may be prohibitive.

The direct memory access (DMA) mode has been designed to overcome this problem. The main idea underlying this method is that, the MPU is dissociated from the data transfer process by tristating its system bus. A direct link is established between the memory and I/O device, and an external circuit known as DMA controller controls data transfer. Here, the data transfer rate is only limited by the minimum speed of either of the two devices. However, to facilitate DMA mode of data transfer, the MPU must be equipped with the following features:

1. An input control line, through which the I/O device, via the DMA controller, requests the MPU for DMA data transfer.
2. An output control line, through which the MPU informs the DMA grant.
3. The MPU must be able to tristate the address, data and necessary control lines throughout the DMA data transfer duration.

   Flowchart of the data transfer in DMA mode:

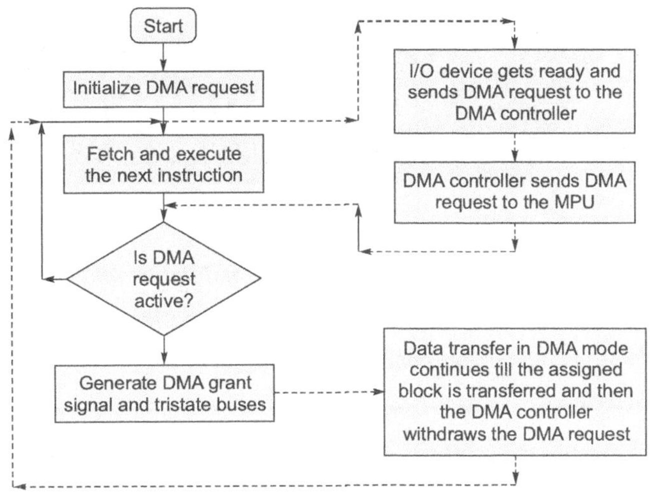

4.7 **What are the internal registers of 8259? Explain each one of them.**

[10 marks : 2016]

Solution:

The 8259 Microcontroller family is a set of Programmable Interrupt Controller (PIC), Integrated Circuits (ICs) The 8259A has several internal registers, similar to the processor.

Command Register:

This is a write only register, which is used to send commands to the microcontroller. There are lot of different commands that you can send. Some commands are used to read from other registers, while other commands are used to initialize and sending data, such as End of Interrupt (EOI).

Status register:

This is a read only register that can be accessed to determine the status of the PIC.

Interrupt Request Register (IRR):

This register specifies which interrupts are pending acknowledgment.

If a bit is set, the interrupt has been signaled by a device, and the PIC has signaled the CPU, but is awaiting acknowledgment from the CPU to go ahead with the interrupt.

In-Service Register (ISR):

This register specifies which interrupts have already been acknowledged, but are awaiting for the End of Interrupt (EOI) signal. The EOI signal is very important as it determines the end of an interrupt.

If a bit is set, the current IRQ has been acknowledged by the CPU to go ahead and begin executing. The PIC uses this register to determine what IRQ is currently being executed.

Interrupt Mask Register (IMR):

This specifies which interrupts have to be ignored, and not acknowledged. This allows us to focus on executing certain, more important interrupts before executing the interrupts specified in this register.

This is an 8 bit register, where each bit determines if an interrupt is disabled or not. If the bit is 0, it is enabled. If the bit is 1, the interrupt device is disabled.

This is an important register, as it allows us to enable and disable interrupts from certain devices.

■■■■

4 Communication Systems

Revised Syllabus of ESE: *Analog communication basics, Modulation and demodulation, noise and bandwidth, transmitters and receivers, signal to noise ratio, digital communication basics, sampling, quantizing, coding, frequency and time domain multiplexing, power line carrier communication systems.*

---

1. Introduction to Communication System

1.1 The signal to noise ratio of one communication link is 60 dB. If three such identical links are used in tandem the overall signal to noise ratio will be

(a) 180 dB
(b) 64.77 dB
(c) 55.23 dB
(d) 20 dB

[4 marks : 2009]

Solution: (c)

(S/N) for one communication link is = 60 dB

i.e.
$$10\log_{10}\frac{S}{N} = 60$$

$$\frac{S}{N} = 10^6$$

$$S = 10^6 N$$

Let noise power added in one communication channel is P.

$\therefore$
$$S = 10^6 P$$

$\therefore$ Signal power will be constant through out the link (i.e. through three common links) if there is no attenuation provided by link.

But noise gets added every time it passes through link.

$\therefore$ Total noise power, $P_t = P + P + P = 3P$

$$\left(\frac{S}{N}\right)_{dB} = 10\log_{10}\frac{S}{P_t}$$

$$= 10\log_{10}\frac{10^6 P}{3P} = 60 - 10\log_{10} 3$$

$$= 55.23 \text{ dB}$$

So option (c) is correct.

2. Amplitude Modulation

2.1 Show that the efficiency of single tone AM is 33.3% for the modulation index to be equal to unity.

[10 marks : 2001]

Solution:

We know that,

Transmission efficiency, $\eta = \dfrac{\text{useful power}}{\text{total transmitted power}}$

$$\%\eta = \frac{P_{SB}}{P_t} \times 100\%$$

For single tone AM, $P_{SB} = P_c \dfrac{m_a^2}{2}$

$$P_t = P_c\left(1 + \frac{m_a^2}{2}\right)$$

$$\eta = \frac{P_c \dfrac{m_a^2}{2}}{P_c\left(1+\dfrac{m_a^2}{2}\right)} \times 100\% \quad \text{or} \quad \eta = \frac{m_a^2}{2+m_a^2} \times 100\%$$

if $m_a = 1$ (given)

$$\eta = \frac{1}{3} \times 100\% = 33.3\%$$

2.2 What would be the value of gain k in figure below to yield the suppressed carried DSB signal?

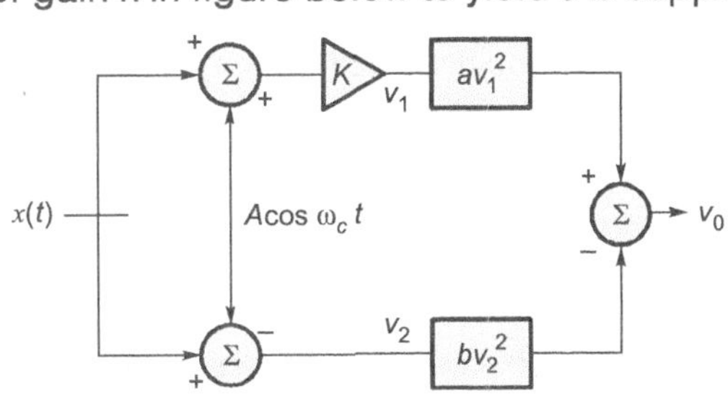

[10 marks : 2001]

Solution:

The signals v_1 and v_2 from the figure are,

$v_1 = k[x(t) + A\cos\omega_c t]$

and $v_2 = [x(t) - A\cos\omega_c t]$

and $v_0 = a\,v_1^2 - b\,v_2^2 = ak^2[x(t) + A\cos\omega_c t]^2 - b[x(t) - A\cos\omega_c t]^2$

$= ak^2[x^2(t) + A^2\cos^2\omega_c t + 2A\,x(t)\cos\omega_c t] - b[x^2(t) + A^2\cos^2\omega_c t - 2A\,x(t)\cos\omega_c t]$

Putting, $ak^2 = b$

we have $v_0 = b[x^2(t) + A^2\cos^2\omega_c t + 2A\,x(t)\cos\omega_c t] - b[x^2(t) + A^2\cos^2\omega_c t - 2A\,x(t)\cos\omega_c t]$

$v_0 = 4\,bA\,x(t)\cos\omega_c t$

which is a suppressed carrier DSB signal.

The condition for k is,

$$ak^2 = b \text{ or } k = \sqrt{\frac{b}{a}}$$

2.3 **What do you understand by vestigial sideband where it is used?**

[5 marks : 2001]

Solution:

Vestigial - sideband modulation is a compromise between SSB and DSB modulations. In this modulation one sideband is passed almost completely where as just a trace of the other sideband is retained.
The figure shown below is for VSB modulation.

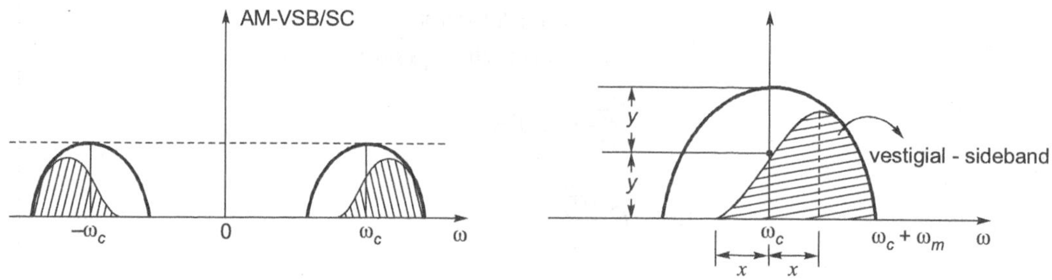

VSB is used for video signal transmission in commercial television broadcasting.

2.4 **Define "Amplitude modulation" and "Modulation index". Write down the equations for the**
(a) amplitude and
(b) the instantaneous voltage of the amplitude modulated wave.
Sketch the graph of an amplitude modulated wave.

[10 marks : 2003]

Solution:

Amplitude Modulation: "In amplitude modulation, the amplitude of the carrier is varied in accordance with the instantaneous value of amplitude of the modulating signal keeping the frequency and the phase constant"
Formally, AM is defined as the system of modulation in which the amplitude of the carrier is made proportional to the instantaneous amplitude of the modulating voltage.

Modulation Index: Modulation index is defined as the ratio of modulating voltage to the carrier voltage i.e., modulation index,

$$m = \frac{V_m}{V_c}$$

The modulation index is a number lying between 0 and 1, and is very often expressed as a percentage and called the percentage modulation.
Practically, the value of m lies between 0.4 to 0.6.

Equation for the amplitude of amplitude modulated voltage: Let the carrier voltage and the modulating voltage, V_c and V_m respectively, be represented by,

$$v_c = V_c \sin \omega_c t \quad \text{... (i)}$$
$$v_m = V_m \sin \omega_m t \quad \text{... (ii)}$$

and
$$m = \frac{V_m}{V_c}$$

The equation for the amplitude of the amplitude modulated voltage is given as,

$$A = V_c + v_m = V_c + V_m \sin \omega_m t = V_c + m V_c \sin \omega_m t$$

or
$$A = V_c(1 + m \sin \omega_m t)$$

Equation for the instantaneous voltage of the amplitude modulated wave

$$v = A \sin \theta = A \sin \omega_c t$$
$$v = V_c(1 + m \sin \omega_m t) \sin \omega_c t$$

Graph of the amplitude modulated wave:

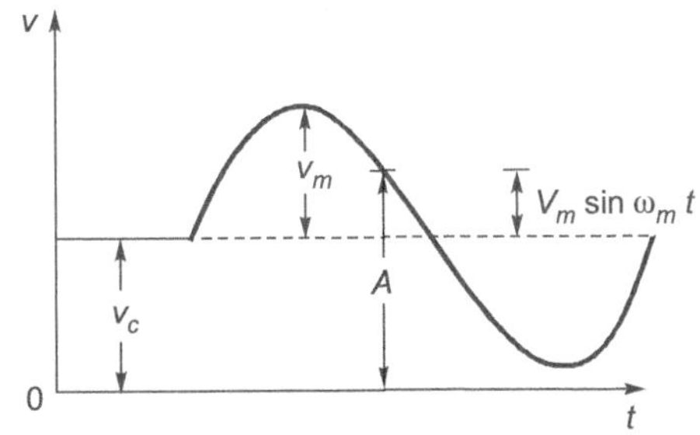

2.5 The antenna current of an AM transmitter is 7.5 A, when only the carrier is sent, but it increases to 8.65 A, when the carrier is sinusoidally modulated. Find the percentage modulation. Determine the antenna current when the depth of modulation is 0.75.

[15 marks : 2003]

Solution:

The antenna current, I_t = 8.65 A
and carrier current, I_c = 7.5 A
modulation index, m = 0.75

$$I_t^2 = I_c^2\left(1+\frac{m_a^2}{2}\right)$$

$$m_a = \sqrt{2}\sqrt{\left(\frac{I_t}{I_c}\right)^2 - 1} = \sqrt{2\left[\left(\frac{8.65}{7.5}\right)^2 - 1\right]} = 81.2\ \%\text{ or } 0.812.$$

For the second part we have,

$$I_t = I_c\sqrt{1+\frac{m_a^2}{2}} = 7.5\sqrt{1+\frac{(0.75)^2}{2}} = 8.489\text{ A}$$

2.6 (a) Write an expression for AM wave $V(t)$.
(b) Draw the waveform for $v(t)$.
(c) Show that modulation index.

$$m = \frac{V_{\max} - V_{\min}}{V_{\max} + V_{\min}}$$

(d) A 400 W (P_c) carrier is modulated to a depth of 75%. Calculate the total power P_t in the modulated wave.

[20 marks : 2004]

Solution:

(a) Expression for AM wave $v(t)$:

Let, $v_m(t) = V_m \cos \omega_m t$ .... modulating signal

$v_c(t) = V_c \cos \omega_c t$ .... carrier signal

modulated or AM signal is given by,

$$v(t) = [V_c + k_a v_m(t)] \cos \omega_c t$$

where, $v_c + k_a v_m(t)$ = new amplitude of carrier signal and is the function of modulating signal

$$v(t) = [V_c + k_a V_m \cos \omega_m t] \cos \omega_c t$$

$$v(t) = V_c[1 + m_a \cos \omega_m t] \cos \omega_c t$$

$$m_a = \frac{k_a V_m}{v_c}$$

(b) Waveform for v(t):

Case-I : AM-DSB/FC and AM-SSB/FC.

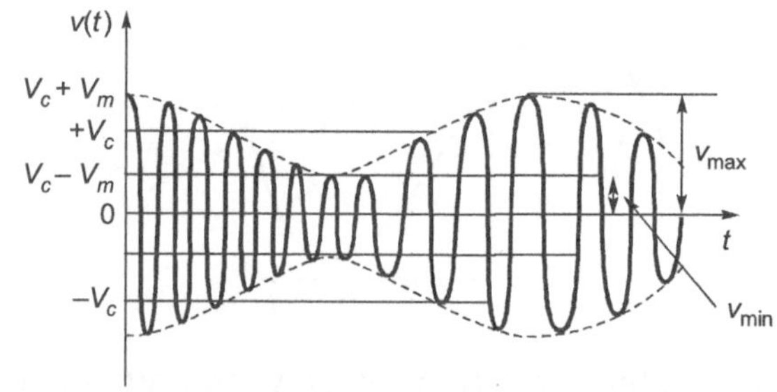

for $k_a = 1$

Case-II : AM-DSB/SC and AM-SSB/SC

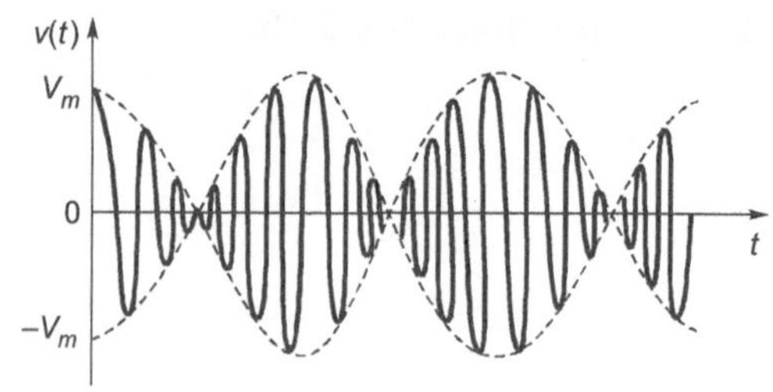

(c) Modulation Index:

$$m = \frac{V_{max} - V_{min}}{V_{max} + V_{min}}$$

It will be recalled that,

$$V_m = mV_c \qquad \text{For } k_a = 1 \qquad \therefore\ m = \frac{V_m}{V_c}$$

and $$V_m = \frac{V_{max} - V_{min}}{2} \qquad ...(i)$$

and waveform for the AM-DSB/FC shows that,

$$V_c = V_{max} - V_m = V_{max} - \frac{V_{max} - V_{min}}{2}$$

here $\because$
$$V_{max} = V_c + V_m$$
$$V_{min} = V_c - V_m$$
$$V_c = \frac{V_{max} + V_{min}}{2} \qquad ...(ii)$$

dividing equation (*i*) by equation (*ii*)

$$m = \frac{V_m}{V_c}$$

$$m = \frac{(V_{max} - V_{min})/2}{(V_{max} + V_{min})/2} = \frac{V_{max} - V_{min}}{V_{max} + V_{min}}$$

(d) Given that,

$$P_c = 400 \text{ W};\ m_a = 75\% \text{ i.e. } 0.75$$

$$P_t = P_c\left(1 + \frac{m_a^2}{2}\right)$$

$$P_t = 400\left[1 + \frac{(0.75)^2}{2}\right] = 512.5 \text{ Watt}$$

2.7 (a) Explain the working of diode detector. Show that RC time constant should be chosen as

$$RC \leq \frac{\sqrt{1 - m^2}}{\omega_m \cdot m}$$

where, ω_m = the frequency of modulating signal
m = modulation index

(b) Justify, sampling operation is equivalent to multiplication of two signals.

[20 marks : 2004]

Solution:

(a) **Working of Diode Detector:** When a carrier is modulated, the envelope of the modulated carrier is of the same form as the modulating signal. Conversely, a diode may be reversed - biased by the charge on a capacitor shunted by a resistance and the rectifying action of the diode follows the envelope.

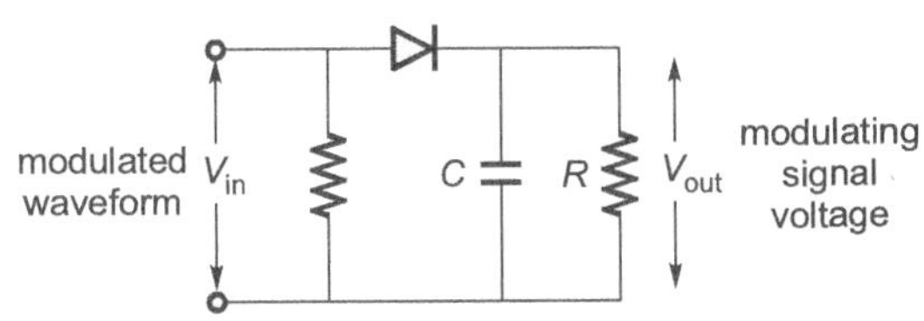

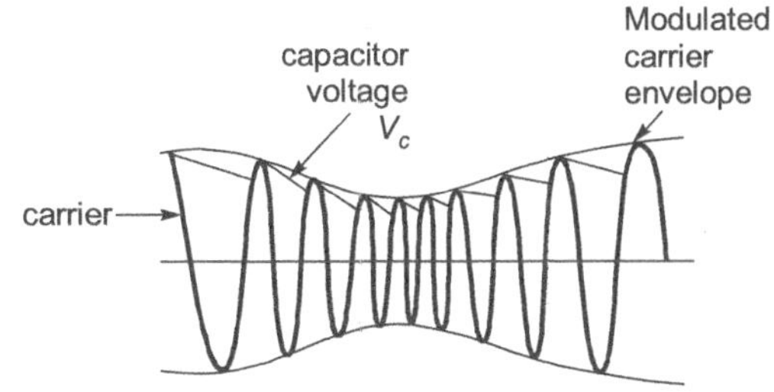

At first let the unmodulated carrier be applied to the diode. The positive rectified pulses will charge the capacitor to 0.636 V_m and the diode is reverse-biased to this value. This is similar to reintroduction of dc carrier voltage transmitted. But the resistance R across C will discharge this voltage. In order to kept discharge to minimum, the RC time constant is made large for carrier frequency $RC >> (1/\omega_k)$. If a modulated carrier is applied to the diode, the diode will conduct for positive swings of the modulating signal above the dc carrier level and a varying voltage corresponding to the signal envelope will be available at the capacitor. The diode will conduct during negative swings also as the average dc of the carrier gets reduced. This varying voltage should be quickly discharged for different levels of modulation upto a maximum of 1. For this the RC time constant should be small compared to the lowest modulating frequency say 50 Hz $RC << (1/\omega_m)$. As the varying voltage across R follows the envelope, it is called envelope detector $(1/\omega_k) << RC << (1/\omega_m)$.

The rectification efficiency, $\eta = \dfrac{V_\theta}{V_{in}} = \dfrac{I_{dc} \times R}{I_m(R_D + R)}$.

For efficiency to be high the load resistance R must be high as compared to diodes forward resistance. Let the input modulated voltage be,

$$e_0 = e_{km} = E_k(1 + m\cos\omega_m t_0)$$

Where ω_m is the highest modulating frequency at any time t_0.

The slope of the envelope is,

$$\left.\frac{de}{dt}\right|_{t_0} = -m\,E_k\,\omega_m \sin\omega_m t_0$$

After getting charged to e_0 at t_0 the capacitor discharges as

$$e_c = e_0 \exp - \frac{t - t_0}{RC}$$

and the rate of decay is,

$$\left.\frac{de_c}{d(t-t_0)}\right|_{t=t_0} = -\frac{e_0}{RC}$$

To satisfy the condition that the capacitor voltage should be less than the envelope voltage at time t_0.

$$-\frac{de_c}{d(t-t_0)} \leq -\frac{de_{km}}{dt}$$

$$-\frac{e_0}{RC} \leq -m\,E_k\,\omega_m \sin\omega_m t_0$$

or
$$\frac{e_0}{RC} \geq m\,E_k\,\omega_m \sin\omega_m t_0$$

substituting for
$$e_0 = E_k(1 + m\cos\omega_m t_0)$$

$$\frac{1}{RC} \geq \left[\frac{m\sin\omega_m t_0}{1+m\cos\omega_m t_0}\right]\omega_m \text{ or } RC \leq \frac{1}{\omega_m\left[\frac{m\sin\omega_m t_0}{1+m\cos\omega_m t_0}\right]} \leq \frac{1+m\cos\omega_m t_0}{\omega_m(m\sin\omega_m t_0)}$$

RC is minimum when $\cos\omega_m t_0 = -m$ and $\sin\omega_m t_0 = \sqrt{1-m^2}$

or
$$RC \leq \frac{1}{\omega_m}\frac{\sqrt{1-m^2}}{m}$$

(b) Let us take a signal $m(t)$ whose base-band is from 0 to f_M. It is to be sampled by a pulse train $s(t)$ of unit amplitude, width τ and period T_s. For sampling the signal, the pulses are modulated by the signal by passing through a multiplier. Product modulation yields the baseband signal $m(t)$ and DSBSC signals with a pair of sidebands around each harmonic of the pulse sampling frequency.
$s(t)$ is a periodic signal of period T_s and by Fourier expansion

$$s(t) = \frac{\tau}{T_s} + \frac{2\tau}{T_s}\left(\cos 2\pi\frac{1}{T_s} + \cos 2\times 2\pi\frac{1}{T_s} + ...\right)$$

$\frac{\tau}{T_s}$ is called the duty cycle k,

$$k = \frac{\text{Pulse width or duration}}{\text{Pulse period}}$$

We have taken the amplitude as 1. If the amplitude is V, all terms will be multiplied by V.

$$\therefore \quad s(t)\,m(t) = \frac{\tau}{T_s}m(t) + \frac{\tau}{T_s}[2m(t)\cos 2\pi(2f_M)t + 2m(t)\cos 2\pi(4f_M)t + ...]$$

The first term is the baseband signal $m(t)$ and the second, third terms, DSBSC signals with carrier frequency $2f_M$, $4f_M$ etc.

2.8 Define "Amplitude modulation" and "Modulation index". Write down the equations for the
(a) amplitude and
(b) the instantaneous voltage of the amplitude modulated wave.
Sketch the graph of an amplitude modulated wave.

[10 marks : 2005]

Solution:

Amplitude Modulation: "In amplitude modulation, the amplitude of the carrier is varied in accordance with the instantaneous value of amplitude of the modulating signal keeping the frequency and the phase constant". Formally, AM is defined as the system of modulation in which the amplitude of the carrier is made proportional to the instantaneous amplitude of the modulating voltage.

Modulation Index: Modulation index is defined as the ratio of modulating voltage to the carrier voltage i.e., modulation index, $m = V_m / V_c$

The modulation index is a number lying between 0 and 1, and is very often expressed as a percentage and called the percentage modulation.

Practically, the value of m lies between 0.4 to 0.6.

Equation for the amplitude of amplitude modulated voltage: Let the carrier voltage and the modulating voltage, v_c and v_m, respectively, be represented by,

$$v_c = V_c \sin \omega_c t \quad \text{... (i)}$$

$$v_m = V_m \sin \omega_m t \quad \text{... (ii)}$$

and $$m = V_m / V_c$$

The equation for the amplitude of the amplitude modulated voltage is given as,

$$A = V_c + v_m = V_c + V_m \sin \omega_m t = V_c + m \times V_c \sin \omega_m t$$

or $$A = V_c (1 + m \sin \omega_m t)$$

Equation for the instantaneous voltage of the amplitude modulated wave

$$v = A \sin \theta = A \sin \omega_c t$$

$$v = V_c (1 + m \sin \omega_m t) \sin \omega_c t$$

Graph of the amplitude modulated wave:

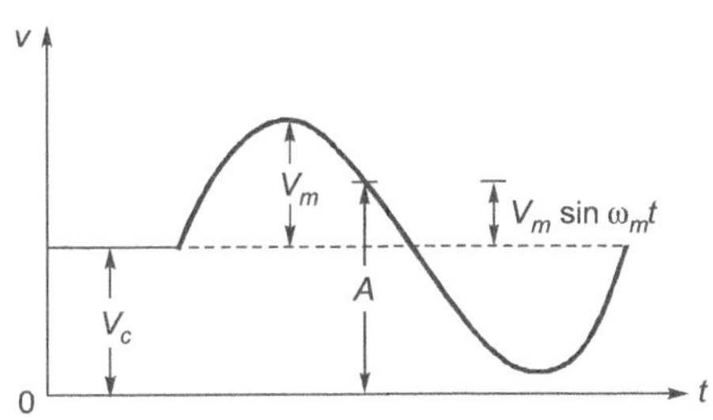

2.9 **The current in an antenna of an AM transmitter is 8.0 A when only the carrier is sent, but it increases to 9.0 A, when the carrier is sinusoidally modulated. Find the percentage modulation. Determine also the antenna current when the depth of modulation is 0.77.**

[15 marks : 2005]

Solution:

The antenna current, $I_t = 9.0$ A

and carrier current, $I_c = 8.0$ A

modulation index, $m = 0.77$

$$I_t = I_c \sqrt{1 + \frac{m_a^2}{2}}$$

or $$m_a = \sqrt{2\left[\left(\frac{I_t}{I_c}\right)^2 - 1\right]} = \sqrt{2\left[\left(\frac{9.0}{8.0}\right)^2 - 1\right]} = 0.728 \text{ or } 72.8\ \%.$$

For the second part, $$I_t = I_c \sqrt{1 + \frac{m_a^2}{2}} = 8\sqrt{1 + \frac{(0.77)^2}{2}} = 9.108 \text{ A.}$$

2.10 (a) List the major factors influencing the choice of the intermediate frequency (IF) in any particular system.

(b) Which are the frequency band for AM, SW and FM broadcast system? Mention the IF values for these systems.

[6 + 6 marks : 2006]

Solution:

(a) Major Factors influencing the choice of the IF:

1. If the intermediate frequency is too high, poor selectivity and poor adjacent-channel rejection results unless sharp-cutoff filters are used in the IF stages.
2. A high value of IF increases tracking difficulties.
3. As the IF is lowered, image-frequency rejection becomes poorer.
4. A very low IF can make the selectivity too sharp, cutting off the sidebands.
5. If the IF is low, the frequency stability of the local oscillator must be made correspondingly higher.
6. The IF must not fall within the tuning range of the receiver.

(b) Frequency band for AM, SW and FM broadcast system:

1. **For AM:** 540 kHz – 1650 kHz
   IF range: (438 – 465) kHz
2. **For SW:** Have Ist IF often in the range about 1.6 to 2.3 MHz or else above 30 MHz.
3. **For FM:** (88 – 108) MHz
   IF range: 10.7 MHz

2.11 An AM transmitter radiates 10 kW with carrier unmodulated and the antenna current is 10 A. The antenna current increase to 11 A when the carrier is modulated by a single sine wave. Find the percentage of modulation. The antenna current increases to 12 A as a result of simultaneous modulation by another sine wave. What is the modulation index if the carrier is modulated using only the second sine wave? Determine the total radiated power when the carrier is modulated using both the sine wave simultaneously.

[14 marks : 2008]

Solution:

Given that, Carrier power $\frac{A_c^2}{2} = 10 \text{ kW}$

$$P_c = 10^4 \text{ W}$$

In case of unmodulated carrier current,

$$I_c = 10 \text{ A}$$

In case of modulated signal current,

$$I_t = 11 \text{ A}$$

Equation of AM modulated signal is

$$s(t) = A_c[1 + k \sin 2\pi f_m t] \cos 2\pi f_c t$$

$\therefore$ Power of modulated signal,

$$P_t = \frac{A_c^2}{2}\left[1+\frac{k^2}{2}\right] \quad (k \text{ is modulation index})$$

Now,

$$P \propto I^2$$

$$P_c \propto I_c^2$$

$$P_t \propto I_t^2$$

$$\therefore \quad \frac{P_c}{P_t} = \frac{I_c^2}{I_t^2}$$

$$\frac{I_t^2}{I_c^2} = \frac{P_t}{P_c}$$

$$\frac{I_t^2}{I_c^2} = 1+\frac{k^2}{2}$$

$\therefore$
$$k = \sqrt{2\left[\frac{(I_t)^2}{(I_c)^2}-1\right]} = \sqrt{2\left[\frac{(11)^2}{(10)^2}-1\right]} = 0.648$$

$$\%\text{modulation} = 64.8\%$$

Now, $I_t' = 12$ A (due to simultaneous modulation by two sine waves)

$\therefore$ Now equivalent modulation index

$$k' = \sqrt{2\left[\frac{(I_t')^2}{(I_c)^2}-1\right]} = \sqrt{2\left[\left(\frac{12}{10}\right)^2-1\right]} = 0.938$$

$\therefore$ overall modulation index,

$$k' = \sqrt{k^2+k_1^2}$$

$k \rightarrow$ modulation index due to first sinusoidal wave
$k_1 \rightarrow$ modulation index due to second sinusoidal wave

$\therefore$
$$k_1 = \sqrt{k'^2-k^2} = \sqrt{(0.938)^2-(0.648)^2} = 0.678$$

total power when carrier is modulated by both the sine wave simultaneously

$$P_t = \frac{A_c^2}{2}\left[1+\frac{k'^2}{2}\right] = 10^4\left[1+\frac{(0.938)^2}{2}\right] = 14.40 \text{ kW}$$

2.12 In an amplitude modulation process, the carrier and modulating signals, respectively, are
$e_c = E_c \sin \omega_c t$

$e_m = E_m \sin \omega_m t + \frac{E_m}{2} \sin 2\,\omega_m t + \frac{E_m}{3} \sin 3\,\omega_m t + \frac{E_m}{4} \sin 4\,\omega_m t$

Derive an expression to show that for every modulating frequency component, the AM wave contains two sideband frequencies in addition to the carrier. Draw the frequency spectrum of this AM signal. Also find the value of composite modulation index.

[14 marks : 2009]

Solution:

Given that,

$e_c = E_c \sin \omega_c t$ .... carrier signal

$e_m = E_m \sin \omega_m t + \frac{E_m}{2} \sin 2\,\omega_m t + \frac{E_m}{3} \sin 3\,\omega_m t + \frac{E_m}{4} \sin 4\,\omega_m t$ .... modulating signal

modulated signal or AM signal,

$$e = [E_c + K_a e_m]\sin \omega_c t$$

where, $A = E_c + K_a e_m$ = new amplitude of carrier

or amplitude can be written as,

$$A = E_c + E_m \sin \omega_m t + \frac{E_m}{2} \sin 2\,\omega_m t + \frac{E_m}{3} \sin 3\,\omega_m t + \frac{E_m}{4} \sin 4\,\omega_m t$$

or $$A = E_c[1 + m\sin\omega_m t + \frac{m}{2}\sin 2\omega_m t + \frac{m}{3}\sin 3\omega_m t + \frac{m}{4}\sin 4\omega_m t]$$

where, $$m = \frac{E_m}{E_c}$$

Now, $$e = A\sin\omega_c t$$

or $$e = E_c[1 + m\sin\omega_m t + \frac{m}{2}\sin 2\omega_m t + \frac{m}{3}\sin 3\omega_m t + \frac{m}{4}\sin 4\omega_m t]\,.\sin\omega_c t$$

$$e = [E_c\,.\sin\omega_c t + mE_c\sin\omega_m t\,.\sin\omega_c t + \frac{mE_c}{2}\sin 2\omega_m t\,.\sin\omega_c t$$
$$+ \frac{mE_c}{3}\sin 3\omega_m t\,.\sin\omega_c t + \frac{mE_c}{4}\sin 4\omega_m t\,.\sin\omega_c t]$$

or $$e = E_c\sin\omega_c t + \frac{mE_c}{2}[\cos(\omega_m - \omega_c)t - \cos(\omega_m + \omega_c)t] + \frac{mE_c}{4}$$
$$[\cos(2\omega_m - \omega_c)t - \cos(2\omega_m + \omega_c)t] + \frac{mE_c}{6}[\cos(3\omega_m - \omega_c)t - \cos(3\omega_m + \omega_c)t]$$
$$+ \frac{mE_c}{8}[\cos(4\omega_m - \omega_c)t - \cos(4\omega_m + \omega_c)t]$$

Here it is clear that for every modulating frequency

$$\omega = \omega_m, 2\omega_m, 3\omega_m, 4\omega_m$$

There are two sidebands around carrier at $\omega_c + \omega_m$ and at $(\omega_c - \omega_m)$

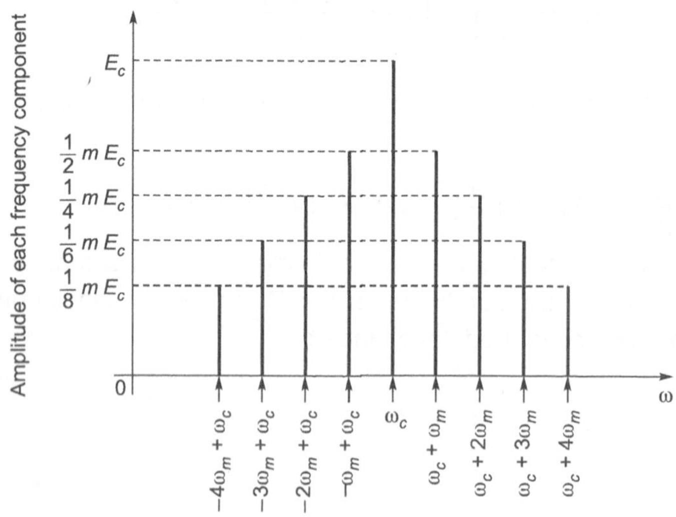

The value of composite modulation index is,

$$m_c = \sqrt{m_1^2 + m_2^2 + m_3^2 + m_4^2}$$

Where $$m_1 = m,\ m_2 = m/2,\ m_3 = m/3,\ m_4 = m/4$$

$$m_c = m\sqrt{1 + \frac{1}{4} + \frac{1}{9} + \frac{1}{16}} = 1.19\text{ m}$$

2.13 **With a neat circuit diagram and waveforms, explain how envelope detector detects AM signal.**
[16 marks : 2011]

Solution:

Circuit Diagram of Envelope Detector

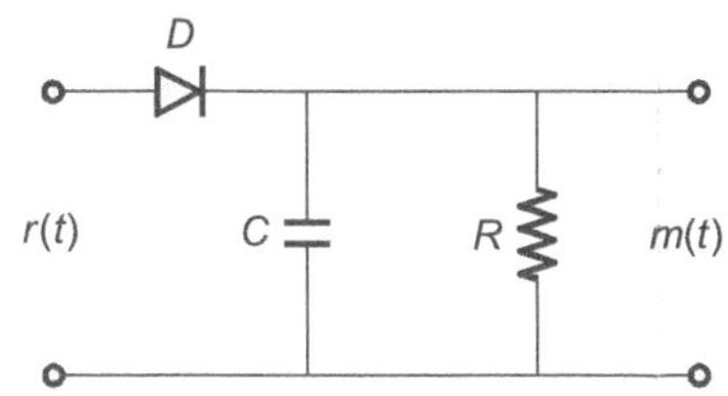

$r(t)$ — received signal at receiver end.

envelope detector is equivalent to rectifier + low pass filter.

- What we do in envelope detector is basically we rectify the received signal to eliminate the negative values without affecting the message signal.
- The rectified signal is $u(t)$ when $r(t) > 0$ and zero when $r(t) < 0$.
- The message signal is recovered by passing the rectified signal through a low pass filter whose bandwidth matches to that of message signal.

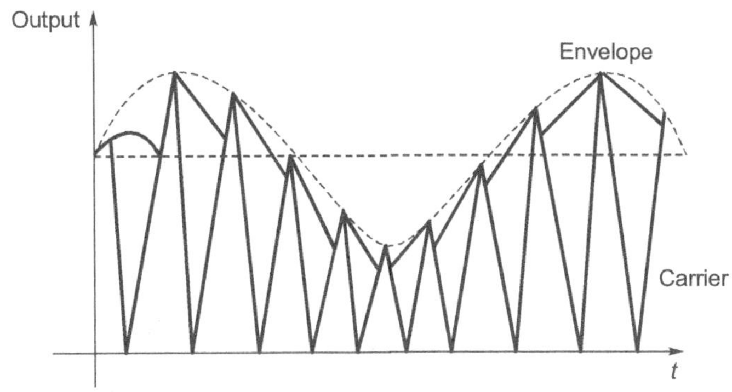

Envelope detection of conventional AM signal ideally result an output signal in the form

$$d(t) = g_1 + g_2 m(t)$$

where g_1 represents dc component and g_2 is gain factor due to the signal demodulator.

- The dc component can be eliminated by passing $d(t)$ through a transformer whose output is $g_2 m(t)$.
- The time constant RC must be selected so as to follow the variations in the envelope of the carrier modulated signal, in effect

$$\frac{1}{f_c} << RC << \frac{1}{W}$$

Where, f_c – carrier frequency
W – message signal's bandwidth.

- In such case capacitor discharge slowly through resistor and thus the output of the envelope detector closely follow the message signal.

2.14 **The antenna current of an AM transmitter is 8 A when only the carrier is sent, but it increases to 8.93 A when the carrier is modulated by a single sine wave. Find the percentage modulation. Determine the antenna current when the depth of modulation changes to 0.8. Derive the expressions used.**
[10 marks : 2016]

Solution:

$$I_{carrier} = 8\text{ A} \quad \text{and} \quad I_{AM} = 8.93\text{ A}$$

$$P_{total\,(AM)} = P_{carrier}\left(1 + \frac{m_a^2}{2}\right) \quad ...(i)$$

where, m_a = modulation index

Here we can write;

$$P_{\text{total}} = I^2_{AM} \times R_{\text{antenna}}$$

Similarly;

$$P_{\text{carrier}} = I^2_{\text{carrier}} \times R_{\text{antenna}}$$

Now from equation (i),

$$I^2_{AM} \times R_{\text{antenna}} = I^2_{\text{carrier}} \times R_{\text{antenna}}\left(1+\frac{m_a^2}{2}\right)$$

$$\left(\frac{I_{AM}}{I_{\text{carrier}}}\right)^2 = 1+\frac{m_a^2}{2}$$

and

$$m_a^2 = 2\left[\left(\frac{I_{AM}}{I_{\text{carrier}}}\right)^2 - 1\right]$$

From the given values:

$$m_a^2 = 2\left[\left(\frac{8.93}{8}\right)^2 - 1\right] = 0.492$$

$$\% \, m_a = \sqrt{0.492} \times 100 = 70.145\%$$

For $m_a = 0.8$;

$$I^2_{AM} = I^2_{\text{carrier}}\left(1+\frac{m_a^2}{2}\right) = 8^2\left(1+\frac{0.8^2}{2}\right) = 84.48$$

$$I_{AM} = 9.19 \text{ A}$$

2.15 (i) Obtain an expression for the total average power of a sinusoidal AM wave

$$V_c = V_c \sin\omega_c t$$
$$V_m = V_m \sin\omega_m t$$

(ii) An AM transmitter broadcasts a carrier power of 100 kW. Determine the radiated power at the amplitude modulation index of 0.8.

[12 marks : 2018]

Solution:

(i) Given,

$$V_c = V_c \sin\omega_c t$$
$$V_m = V_m \sin\omega_m t$$

We know that,

$$S_{AM}(t) = V_c[1 + K_a V_m] \sin\omega_c t$$

Power of message signal, $P_m = \dfrac{V_m^2}{2}$

Now,

$$P_{\text{total}} = \frac{V_c^2}{2} + \frac{V_c^2 k_a^2 V_m^2}{4} = \frac{V_c^2}{2}\left[1+\frac{(k_a V_m)^2}{2}\right]$$

Modulation index, $\mu = k_a V_m$

and let P_c be power of carrier signal,

$$P_c = \frac{V_c^2}{2}$$

$$\Rightarrow \quad P_{\text{total}} = P_c\left[1+\frac{\mu^2}{2}\right]$$

(ii) Given,

$$P_c = 100 \text{ kW}$$
$$\mu = 0.8$$
$$P_{Total} = P_c\left(1+\frac{\mu^2}{2}\right) = 100\times10^3\left[1+\frac{0.8^2}{2}\right]$$
$$= 132 \text{ kW}$$

2.16 **A signal $m(t) = 2\cos(20\pi t) - \cos(40\pi t)$, where the unit of time is millisecond, is amplitude modulated using the carrier frequency (f_c) of 600 kHz. The AM signal is given by**

$$s(t) = 5\cos 2\pi f_c t + m(t)\cos 2\pi f_c t$$

(i) Sketch the magnitude spectrum of $s(t)$. What is its bandwidth?

(ii) What is the modulation index?

(iii) The AM signal is passed through a high-pass filter with cut-off frequency 595 kHz (i.e., the filter passes all frequencies above 595 kHz, and cuts off all frequencies below 595 kHz). Find an explicit time-domain expression for the quadrature component of the filter output with respect to a 600 kHz frequency reference.

[20 marks : 2020]

Solution:

(i) Message signal, $m(t) = \cos(20\pi t) - \cos(40\pi t)$

Carrier frequency, $f_c = 600$ kHz

$$s(t) = 5\cos 2\pi f_c t + m(t)\cos 2\pi f_c t$$
$$= 5\left[1+\frac{m(t)}{5}\right]\cos 2\pi f_c t$$
$$= 5\left[1+\frac{2}{5}\cos(2\pi\times10t)-\frac{1}{5}\cos(2\pi\times20\times t)\right]\cos 2\pi f_c t$$
$$s(t) = A_c[1+\mu_1\cos 2\pi f_{m1}t+\mu_2\cos(2\pi f_{m2}t)]\cos 2\pi f_c t$$
$$A_c = 5,\ \mu_1 = \frac{2}{5},\ f_{m1} = 10 \text{ kHz},\ \mu_2 = \frac{1}{5},\ f_{m2} = 20 \text{ kHz}$$

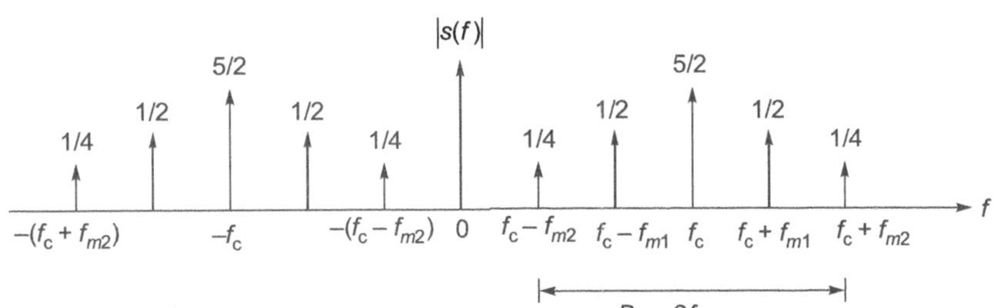

$$B_\omega = 2f_{m2}$$
$$B_\omega = 2\times20 \text{ kHz}$$
$$B_\omega = 40 \text{ kHz}$$

(ii) Modulation index of multitone AM signal is given as μ_T

The resultant modulation index/total modulation index is

$$\mu_T = \sqrt{\mu_1^2+\mu_2^2+\ldots\mu_n^2}, \qquad 0 < \mu_T < 1$$

Modulation index,

$$\mu_T = \sqrt{\mu_1^2+\mu_2^2} = \sqrt{\left(\frac{2}{5}\right)^2+\left(-\frac{1}{5}\right)^2} = \frac{1}{\sqrt{5}}$$

(iii) The output of high pass filter will contain the SSB-USB components only

$$s(t) = \frac{5}{2}[\delta(f - f_c) + \delta(f + f_c)] + \frac{1}{2}[\delta(f - 610\text{ K}) + \delta(f + 610\text{ K})]$$
$$-\frac{1}{4}[\delta(f - 620\text{ K}) + \delta(f + 620\text{ K})]$$

Apply IFT

$$s(t) = 5\cos(2\pi\ 600\text{ Kt}) + \cos(2\pi\ (610\text{ Kt}) - \frac{1}{2}\cos(2\pi\ (620\text{ Kt})$$
$$= 5\cos(2\pi\ 600t) + \cos(2\pi\ 610t) - \frac{1}{2}\cos(2\pi\ 620t)$$

The quadrature component of the filter output is 0.

$$s(t) = 0$$

3. Angle Modulation

3.1 **A modulating signal $E_m \sin \omega_m t$ passes through a square law device before entering the FM modulator. The FM modulator is characterized by its deviation in frequency as,**

$$f = f_c + k\, e_m(t)$$

where, k = **constant,**

$e_m(t)$ = **signal entering FM modulator**

Determine the FM signal.

[15 marks : 2001]

Solution:

The input modulating signal is,

$$x(t) = E_m \sin \omega_m t$$

The output of the square law device,

$$e(t) = x^2(t) = E_m^2 \sin^2 \omega_m t$$

The frequency deviation characteristic of the FM modulator is,

$$f = f_c + k\, e_m(t) = f_c + kE_m^2 \sin^2 \omega_m t = f_c + \frac{1}{2\pi}\frac{d\theta(t)}{dt}$$

comparing, we have

$$\frac{1}{2\pi}\frac{d\theta(t)}{dt} = kE_m^2 \sin^2 \omega_m t$$

or
$$\frac{d\theta(t)}{dt} = 2\pi\, kE_m^2 \sin^2 \omega_m t$$

or
$$\theta(t) = \int_0^t \frac{d\theta(t)}{dt}dt = 2\pi kE_m^2 \int_0^t \sin^2 \omega_m t\, dt$$
$$= \frac{2\pi kE_m^2}{2}\int_0^t (1 - \cos 2\omega_m t)dt = \pi kE_m^2\left[t - \frac{1}{2\omega_m}\sin(2\omega_m t)\right]$$

The envelope of the modulated FM signal is, FM signal will be

Now
$$s(t) = A_c \cos[2\pi f_c t + \theta(t)]$$
$$= A_c \cos\left[2\pi f_c t + \beta t - \frac{\beta}{2\omega_m}\sin 2\omega_m t\right]$$

$$= E_c e^{j\pi k E_m^2 t} e^{-j\frac{\pi k E_m^2}{2\omega_m}\sin(2\omega_m t)} = E_c e^{j\beta t} e^{-j\beta_1 \sin(2\omega_m t)}$$

where, $\beta = \pi k E_m^2$

and $\beta_1 = \dfrac{\pi k E_m^2}{2\omega_m} = \dfrac{\beta}{2\omega_m}$

3.2 In a commercial broadcasting system the FM signal has a centre of frequency 105 MHz and the highest frequency of 105.03 MHz, when modulated by a signal 5 kHz, determine

(a) frequency deviation
(b) carrier swing
(c) modulating index
(d) percent modulation

[12 marks : 2002]

Solution:

(a) Frequency Deviation:

$$\Delta f = f_H - f_C = [105.03 - 105] \text{ MHz} = 0.03 \text{ MHz or } 30 \text{ kHz}$$

(b) Carrier Swing:

$$= 2 \times \text{Max. frequency deviation} = 2 \times 30 \text{ kHz} = 60 \text{ kHz}$$

(c) Modulation Index:

$$\beta = \frac{\Delta f}{f_m} = \frac{30 \text{ kHz}}{5 \text{ kHz}} = 6$$

(d) Percent Modulation:

$$= 100\,\beta = 600\%$$

3.3 A 20 MHz carrier is modulated by a 450 Hz audio sine wave. If the carrier voltage is 4.5 V and the maximum deviation is 10 kHz, write down the equation of this modulated wave for (a) FM, and (b) PM. If the modulating frequency is only changed to 1.8 kHz, all else remaining constant, write down the new equation for (c) FM and (d) PM.

[15 marks : 2003]

Solution:

Given that, $f_c = 20 \text{ MHz} = 20 \times 10^6 \text{ Hz}$

$f_m = 450 \text{ Hz}$

Carrier voltage, $A_c = 4.5 \text{ V}$

Maximum frequency deviation,

$$\Delta f_{max} = 10 \text{ kHz} = 10^4 \text{ Hz}$$

Let message signal (modulating signal) is $m(t) = A_m \cos 2\pi f_m t$

$\therefore$ For FM $\rightarrow$ $f_i = f_c + k_f m(t)$

$f_i = f_c + k_f A_m \cos 2\pi f_m t$

Max. frequency deviation $\Delta f_{max} = k_f A_m = 10^4$ Hz

$$\therefore \quad \phi(t) = 2\pi f_c t + \frac{k_f A_m}{f_m}\sin 2\pi f_m t \qquad \left(\because f_i = \frac{1}{2\pi}\frac{d\phi(t)}{dt}\right)$$

$$\frac{k_f A_m}{f_m} = \frac{\Delta f_{max}}{f_m} = \beta_f \text{ (modulation index)}$$

$$\therefore \quad \beta_f = \frac{10^4}{450} = 22.22$$

$\therefore$ eq. of FM signal $s(t) = A_c \cos[\phi(t)]$

$$s(t) = 4.5\cos[2\pi\times f_c t + \beta_f \sin 2\pi f_m t]$$

$\therefore$ $$s(t) = 4.5\cos[2\pi\times 20\times 10^6 t + 22.22\sin 2\pi\times 450t]$$

$$s(t) = 4.5\cos[40\pi\times 10^6 t + 22.22\sin 900\pi t]$$

For PM signal $$\phi(t) = 2\pi f_c t + k_p m(t)$$

$$\phi(t) = 2\pi f_c t + k_p A_m \cos 2\pi f_m t$$

$k_p A_m \rightarrow$ max. phase deviation = modulation index for PM signal β_p.

$\therefore$ $$d(t) = 2\pi f_c t + \beta_p \cos 2\pi f_m t$$

Now $$f_i = \frac{1}{2\pi}\frac{d\phi(t)}{dt} = f_c + \beta_p(-f_m)\sin 2\pi f_m t$$

$\therefore$ max. frequency deviation = $\beta_p f_m$

$\therefore$ $$10^4 = \beta_p \times 450$$

$$\beta_p = 22.22$$

$\therefore$ equation of PM signal

$$s(t) = A_c\cos[2\pi f_c t + \beta_p\cos 2\pi f_m t] \qquad [\therefore s(t) = A_c\cos\pi(t)]$$

$$s(t) = 4.5[\cos\{40\pi\times 10^6 t + 22.22\cos 900\pi t\}]$$

Now, $$f'_m = 1.8 \text{ kHz}$$

$\because$ k_f, A_m and k_p are constant

So max. frequency deviation

$$\delta f_{max} = k_f A_m = 10^4 \text{ Hz}$$

$\therefore$ $$\beta'_f = \frac{10^4}{f'_m} = \frac{10^4}{1.8\times 10^3} = 5.55$$

$\therefore$ FM signal $$s(t) = 4.5[\cos(40\pi\times 10^6 t + 5.55\sin 2\pi f'_m t)]$$

$$s(t) = 4.5[\cos\{40\pi\times 10^6 t + 5.55\sin 3600\pi t\}]$$

$\because$ k_p and A_m are constant

So, $$\beta'_p = k_p A_m = \beta_p = 22.22$$

$\therefore$ PM signal $$s(t) = 4.5[\cos\{40\pi\times 10^6 t + \beta'_p\cos 2\pi f'_m t\}]$$

$$s(t) = 4.5[\cos\{40\pi\times 10^6 t + 22.2\cos 3600\pi t\}]$$

3.4 **An 18 MHz carrier is modulated by a 400 Hz audio sine wave if the carrier voltage is 5.0 V and the maximum deviation is 12 kHz. Write down the equations of this modulated wave for (a) F.M., (b) P.M. If the modulating frequency is only changed to 1.6 kHz all other data remaining constant, write down the new equations for (c) FM and (d) PM.**

[15 marks : 2005]

Solution:

Given that, $$f_m = 400 \text{ Hz}$$

$$A_c = 5 \text{ V}$$

Max. frequency deviation,

$$\Delta f_{max} = 12 \text{ kHz}$$

Let the message signal (modulating) signal is

$$m(t) = A_m\cos 2\pi f_m t$$

So for FM modulated signal frequency

$$f_i = f_c + k_f m(t)$$

$$f_i = f_c + k_f A_m\cos 2\pi f_m t$$

$\therefore$ $$\phi(t) = 2\pi f_c t + \frac{k_f A_m}{f_m}\sin 2\pi f_m t \qquad \left(\because f_i = \frac{1}{2\pi}\frac{d}{dt}\phi(t)\right)$$

Here, $k_f A_m \Rightarrow$ Max. frequency deviation

$\frac{k_f A_m}{f_m} \Rightarrow$ Modulation index for FM

$\therefore$ $$\beta_f = \frac{k_f A_m}{f_m} = \frac{12\times10^3}{400} = 30$$

$\therefore$ Equation of FM signal,

$$s(t) = A_c[\cos\phi(t)]$$
$$s(t) = A_c[\cos 2\pi f_c t + 30\sin 2\pi f_m t]$$
$$s(t) = 5\cos[2\pi\times18\times10^6 t + 30\sin 2\pi\times400t]$$
$$s(t) = 5\cos[36\times\pi\times10^6 t + 30\sin 800\pi t]$$

For PM signal, $$d(t) = 2\pi f_c t + k_p m(t)$$
$$d(t) = 2\pi f_c t + k_p A_m \cos 2f_m t$$

Max. phase deviation = Modulation index $\beta_p = k_p A_m$

Now, $$f_i = \frac{1}{2\pi}\frac{d\phi(t)}{dt}$$
$$f_i = f_c + (-k_p A_m f_m)\sin 2\pi f_m t$$

So max. frequency deviation,

$$\Delta f_{max} = k_p A_m f_m = \beta_p f_m$$

$\therefore$ $$\beta_p = \frac{\Delta f_{max}}{f_m} = \frac{12\times10^3}{400} = 30$$

$\therefore$ Equation of PM signal, $$s(t) = A_c\cos[\phi(t)] = A_c[\cos\{2\pi f_c t + \beta_p \cos 2\pi f_m t\}]$$
$$= 5[\cos\{2\pi\times18\times10^6 t + 30\cos 2\pi\times400t\}]$$
$$s(t) = 5\cos[36\pi\times10^6 t + 30\cos 800\pi t]$$

Now, $$f'_m = 1.6\text{ kHz}$$

$\therefore$ Now, $$\beta_f' = \frac{\Delta f_{max}}{f_m} = \frac{12\times10^3}{1.6\times10^3} = 7.5$$ ($\because k_f$ and A_m are const. so $Df_{max} = k_f A_m$ const.)

$\therefore$ Equation of FM is, $$s(t) = 5\cos[36\pi\times10^6 t + 7.5\sin 3200\pi t]$$

$\because k_p$ and A_m are constant so $\beta_p = k_p A_m = 30$

$\therefore$ PM signal will be, $$s(t) = 5\cos[36\pi\times10^6 t + 30\cos 3200\pi t]$$

3.5 **(a) Justify that frequency modulation is much more immune to noise than amplitude modulation.**

(b) Sketch the typical IF characters response for colour TV receiver. Indicate frequency and signal levels on curve.

[8 + 6 marks : 2006]

Solution:

(a) **To justify that the FM is much more immune to noise than AM:** A number of consideration must be taken into account. The first of these is that $m = 1$ is the maximum permissible modulation index for AM, where as in FM there is no such limit. It is the maximum frequency deviation that is limited in FM, to 75 kHz in the wideband VHF broad casting service. Thus, even at the highest audio frequency of 15 kHz, the modulation index in FM is permitted to be as high as 5. It may of course be much higher than that at lower audio frequencies. For example when the modulating frequency is 1 kHz. If a given ratio of signal voltage to noise voltage exists at the output of the FM amplitude limiter when $m = 1$, this ratio will be reduced in proportion to an increase in modulation index thus, when m is made equal to 2, the ratio of signal voltage to noise voltage at the limiter output in the receiver will be doubled it will be tripled when $m = 3$ and so on. This ratio is thus proportional to the modulation index, and so the signal to noise (power) ratio in the output of an FM receiver is proportional to the square of the modulation index. Hence, when $m = 5$ (highest permitted when $f_m = 15$ kHz), there will be a 25:1 (14 – dB) improvement for FM where as no such improvement for AM is possible. The second consideration is, that FM has properties which permit the trading of bandwidth for signal to noise ratio, which cannot be done in AM. Under ordinary circumstances (that is, $2V_n < V_c$ impulse noise is reduced in FM to the same extent as random noise. The amplitude limiter found in AM communications receivers does not limit random noise at all and it limits impulse noise by only about 10 dB, thus FM is better off in this regard also.

(b)

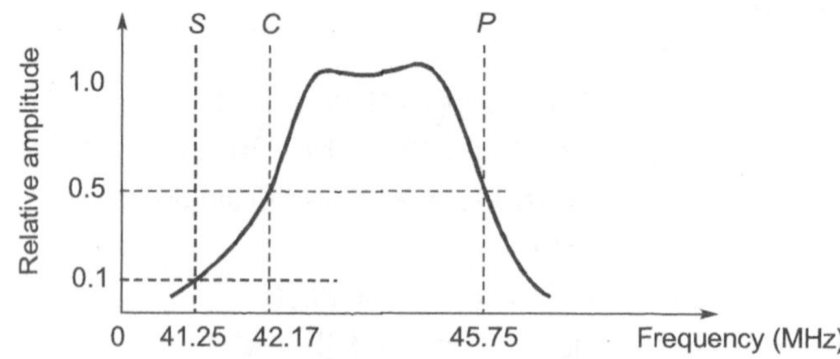

As in other receiver, the IF amplifiers provide the majority of the sensitivity and gain before demodulation. In figure, the IF bandwidth is some what lower than might be expected - three facts governs this. At the upper end relative response is down to 50 percent at the picture carrier frequency, to counteract the higher powers available at the lowest video frequencies because of the vestigial sideband modulation used. At the lower end, relative amplitude is also down to 50 percent at the chroma subcarrier frequency, to minimize interference from this signal. At the sound carrier frequency of 41.25 MHz, response is down to about 10 percent, also to reduce interference.

3.6 **(a) Explain foster-seeley discriminator with neat circuit diagram and waveforms.**

(b) When the modulating frequency in FM system is 400 Hz and the modulating voltage is 2.4 V, the modulation index is 60. Calculate the modulation index, when the modulating frequency is reduced to 250 Hz and the modulating voltage is simultaneous raised to 3.2 V?

[6 + 6 marks : 2006]

Solution:

(a) **Foster-Seeley Discriminator Circuit Diagram:** The FS discriminator circuit is drawn. The secondary coil is split into two by centre tapping. At resonance the voltages in the two halves are equal and there is no output voltage. The centre tap is fed with the primary voltage by C_1, L_4 combination and so the voltage at resonance becomes the reference voltage for the two diodes.

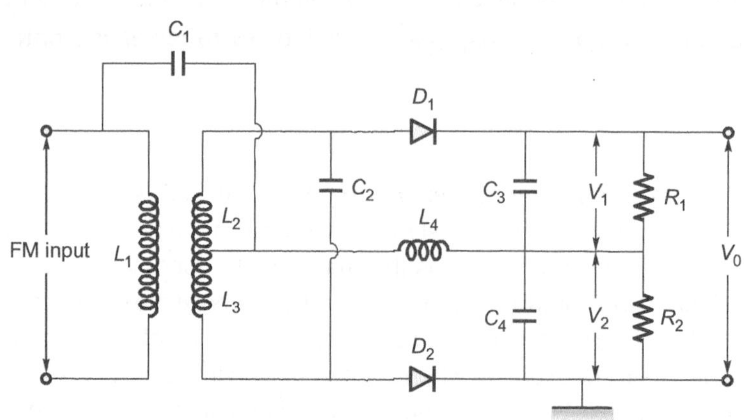

The vector diagram at resonance is

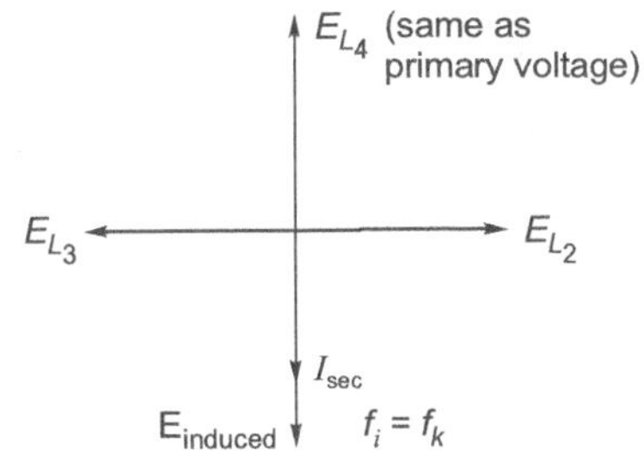

Above resonance, considering the series resonant circuit of L_2, L_3, C_2 for the induced voltage, it is inductive and so current in secondary I_s will lag E induced. But E_{L_2} and E_{L_3} will lead I_s by 90° as in any inductance voltage V_1 across L_2 is greater than V_2 across L_3.
The vector diagram is shown

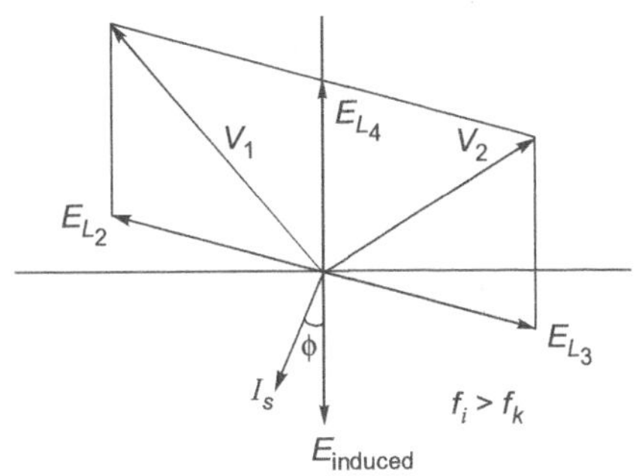

The greater the frequency deviation greater the inductive reactance and greater the angle ϕ from the induced voltage. V_1 becomes larger than V_2. The output voltage is positive. Below resonance, the impedance is capacitive and so secondary current I_s leads the induced voltage. Now V_2 is greater than V_1. The output voltage is negative.

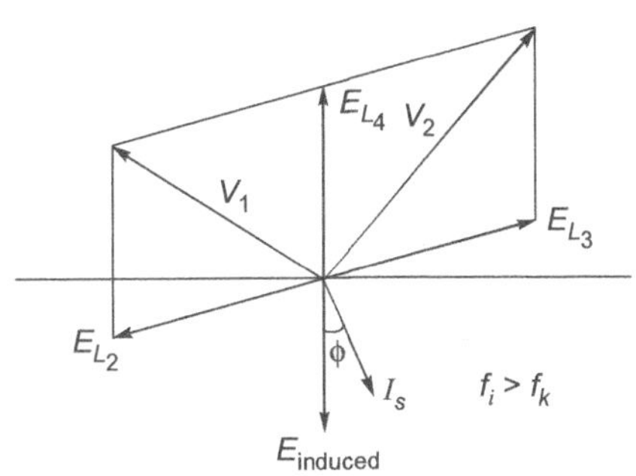

Condensers C_3, C_4 by pass the IF so that it does not reach the subsequent amplifier.

(b) $\delta \propto V_m$ we may write, ($\because$ max. frequency deviation $\delta = k_f A_m$), $\delta \propto A_m$ or $\delta \propto V_m$)

Given that,

$$f_m = 400 \text{ Hz}$$
$$\beta_f = 60$$
$$A_m = 2.4 \text{ V}$$

$\because$ Maximum frequency deviation,

$$\Delta f_{max} = k_f A_m$$

$$60 = \frac{k_f A_m}{400}$$

$$k_f = \frac{24\times10^3}{2.4} = 10^4 \text{ Hz/V}$$

Now, $f'_m = 250$ Hz

and $A'_m = 3.2$ Volt

$\therefore$ Maximum frequency deviation,

$$\Delta f'_{max} = k_f A'_m$$
$$= 10^4 \times 3.2 = 32 \text{ kHz}$$

$\therefore$ Modulation index, $\beta_f = \dfrac{\Delta f'_{max}}{f'_m}$

$$= \frac{32\times10^3}{250} = 128$$

3.7 In FM broad cast, maximum deviation is 75 kHz and maximum modulating frequency is 15 kHz. In view of Carson's rule, the maximum required bandwidth is

(a) 15 kHz (b) 30 kHz

(c) 150 kHz (d) 180 kHz

[2 marks : 2007]

Solution: (d)

$$\text{BW} \cong 2(\delta + f_m) \text{ Hz}$$
$$= 2(75 + 15) \text{ kHz}$$
$$= 180 \text{ kHz}$$

Option (d) is correct.

3.8 An FM signal is given as $s(t) = A_c \cos\omega_c (1 + m_f \cos\omega_m t)\, t$. Determine the instantaneous frequency of the given FM signal.

[6 marks : 2007]

Solution:

Given, $s(t) = A_c \cos \omega_c (1 + m_f \cos \omega_m t)\, t$

Comparing with,

$$s(t) = A_c \cos \theta_i (t)$$

we get $\theta_i(t) = \omega_c (1 + m_f \cos \omega_m t)\, t = (\omega_c + m_f\, \omega_c \,.\, \cos \omega_m t)\, t$

$\because$ $\omega_i = \dfrac{d\theta_i}{dt}$

$$\omega_i = (\omega_c + \text{m}_f\, \omega_c \cos \omega_m t)\, [m_f \omega_c (-\sin \omega_m t)\omega_m]$$

$$\omega_i = (\omega_c + \text{m}_f\, \omega_c \cos \omega_m t)\, [m_f \omega_c\, \omega_m (-\sin \omega_m t)]$$

$$\omega_i = -\text{m}_f\, \omega_c^2\, \omega_m \sin \omega_m t - m_f^2\, \omega_c^2\, \omega_m \cos \omega_m t \sin \omega_m t$$

$$\omega_i = -m_f \omega_c^2\, \omega_m \sin \omega_m t - m_f^2\, \omega_c^2\, \omega_m \left(\frac{\sin 2\omega_m t}{2}\right)$$

$$\omega_i = -m_f \omega_c^2 \omega_m \left(\sin\omega_m t + \frac{m_f}{2}\sin 2\omega_m t\right)$$

3.9 **Draw the circuit diagram of a Foster-Seeley discriminator and explain how this can be used for FM demodulation. What are Pre-emphasis and De emphasis?**

[12 marks : 2008]

Solution:

Circuit-Diagram:

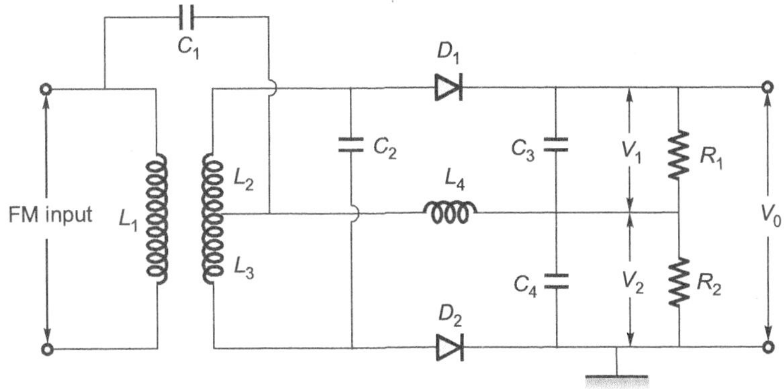

Foster-Seeley Discriminator: In FS discriminator, the difference in phase voltage between primary and secondary of a transformer is made use of, we know from the basic electrical theory that voltage leads current by 90° in a coil. Let this be the primary, In the secondary, a voltage is induced due to rate of change of flux (current) in the primary and this change is maximum when the current varies from positive peak to negative peak. Hence the primary applied voltage and secondary induced voltage are 180° (π rad) out of phase.

In this FS discriminator, the output v_0 is the difference of the two voltages v_1 and v_2. So whatever be the increase in v_1 and v_2, the ratio v_1/v_2 remains the same. So if there were no limiter, any increase in input voltage such as noise would give a corresponding increase in v_1 and v_2.

Although the individual component voltages will be the same at the diode input at all frequencies, the vector sum will differ with the phase difference between primary and secondary windings. The result will be that the individual output voltages will be equal only at f_c. At all other frequencies o/p of one diode will be greater than that of other. Which diode has larger o/p will depend entirely on whether f_{in} is above or below f_c. As for the output arrangements, it will be noted that they are the same as in balanced slope detector. Accordingly overall o/p will be +ve or –ve according to input frequency. As required the magnitude of o/p will depend on the deviation of the i/p frequency from f_c i.e. o/p is proportional to $m(t)$. So demodulation can be done using this discriminator.

Pre-emphasis and De-emphasis: Noise has a greater effect on the higher modulating frequencies than on the lower ones. Thus, if the higher frequencies were artificially boosted at the transmitter and correspondingly deamplified at the receiver, an improvement in noise immunity could be expected. This boosting of the higher modulating frequencies in accordance with a pre arranged curve, is termed preemphasis and the compensation at the receiver is called de-emphasis.

3.10 **Explain what is meant by *Y, I, Q* signals in colour TV. With the aid of a circuit diagram of a simple matrix show how the *I, Q* and *Y* signals are generated in a colour TV transmitter.**

[14 marks : 2008]

Solution:

Y(White): White may be synthesized by the addition of blue (*B*), Green (*G*) and Red (*R*).

It may equally will synthesized by the addition of voltage that corresponds to these colours in the receiver picture tube. However it is not just a simple matter of saying white (*Y*) equals 33(1/3) percent each *B*, *G* and

R. This is because, optically our eyes have a colour frequency response curve which is very similar to the response curve of a single - tuned circuit. Red and blue are at the two edges, and green is right in the middle of the response curve.

The 100% white is given by

$$Y = 0.30\,R + 0.59\,G + 0.11\,B \quad \ldots(i)$$

From equation (*i*), *Y* has an amplitude that correspond to 12.5 percent modulation of the carrier, the receiver will reproduce white since three primary colour must be capable of being indicated, two more signals must be sent. These clearly cannot be pure colour, since Y is already a mixture. In the NTSC system ,the remaining two signals are

$$I = 0.60\,R - 0.28\,G - 0.32\,B$$
$$Q = 0.21\,R - 0.52\,G + 0.31\,B$$

I stands for "in phase" and *Q* for "quadrature phase".

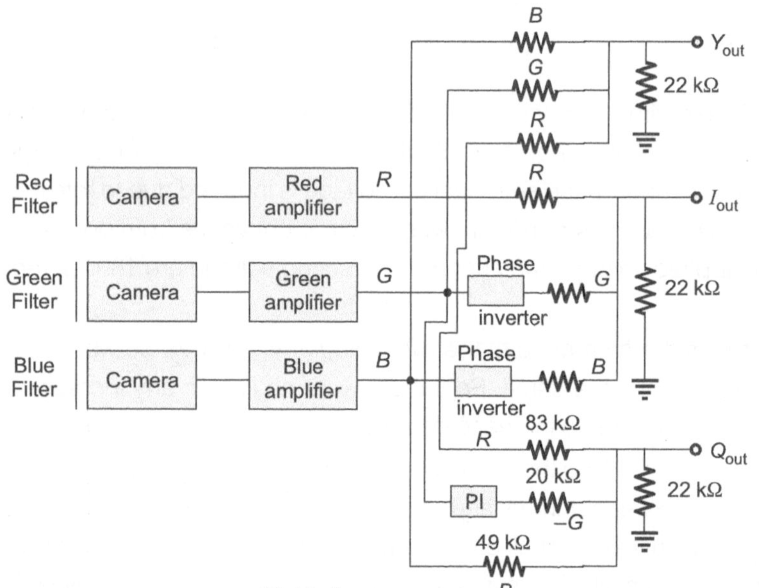

Matrix Arrangement

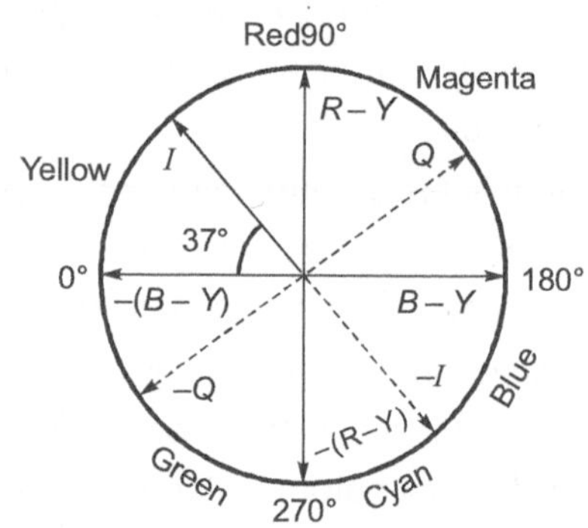

Colour phasor relationship

3.11 **A 25 MHz carrier is modulated by a 400 Hz audio sine wave. If the carrier voltage is 4 V and the maximum frequency deviation is 10 kHz, obtain the equation of frequency modulated wave. Now, if the modulating frequency is changed to 2 kHz, keeping all other parameters same, write the new equation of FM wave.**

[8 marks : 2009]

Solution:

Given that carrier frequency,

$$f_c = 25\text{ MHz} = 25 \times 10^6\text{ Hz}$$

Frequency of audio sinusoidal wave,

$$f_m = 400\text{ Hz}$$

Carrier voltage, $A_c = 4\text{ V}$

Max. frequency deviation,

$$\Delta f_{max} = 10\text{ kHz} = 10 \times 10^3\text{ Hz}$$

We know that modulation index,

$$\beta_f = \frac{\Delta f_{max}}{f_m} = \frac{k_f A_m}{f_m} = \frac{10 \times 10^3}{400} = 25$$

Let sinusoidal wave is

$$m(t) = A_m \cos 2\pi f_m t$$

From FM modulation instantaneous frequency,

$$f_i = f_c + k_f\, m(t)$$

$$f_i = f_c + k_f A_m \cos 2\pi f_m t \qquad \left(f_i = \frac{1}{2\pi}\frac{d\phi(t)}{dt}\right)$$

$$\phi(t) = 2\pi f_c t + \frac{2\pi k_f A_m}{2\pi f_m} \sin 2\pi f_m t$$

$$\phi(t) = 2\pi f_c t + \frac{k_f A_m}{f_m} \sin 2\pi f_m t = 2\pi f_c t + \beta_f \sin 2\pi f_m t$$

∴ Equation of FM signal,

$$s(t) = A_c \cos[2\pi f_c t + \beta_f \sin 2\pi f_m t] \qquad (\because s(t) = A_c \cos \phi(t))$$

$$s(t) = 4 \cos[2\pi \times 25 \times 10^6 t + 25 \sin 2\pi \times 400 t]$$

$$s(t) = 4\cos [50 \times \pi \times 10^6 t + 25 \sin 800\, \pi t]$$

Now modulating frequency is changed $f'_m = 2$ kHz

$$\beta_f' = \frac{\Delta f_{max}}{f'_m} \qquad (\because k_f, A_m \text{ are constant so } \Delta f_{max} \text{ constant} = 10 \text{ kHz})$$

$$\therefore \qquad \beta_f = \frac{10}{2} = 5$$

∴ Now equation of FM signal is

$$s(t) = A_c \cos[2\pi f_c t + \beta_f' \sin 2\pi f'_m t]$$

$$s(t) = 4 \cos[2 \times \pi \times 25 \times 10^6 t + 5 \sin 2 \times \pi \times 2 \times 10^3 t]$$

$$s(t) = 4 \cos[50 \times \pi \times 10^6 t + 5 \sin 4 \times \pi \times 10^3 t]$$

3.12 Explain the need of synchronizing pulses in TV. Also mention the basis for deciding the synchronizing frequencies.

[8 marks : 2009]

Solution:

The need of synchronizing pulses, to ensure that TV receivers scan correctly, it is very involved process. All systems have the same general principle in common. In each, blanking is applied before, and removed after, synchronizing pulses. A front porch precedes a horizontal sync pulse, and a back porch follows such a pulse, in all the systems.

The horizontal frequency is obtained by dividing 31,500 Hz by 2. Similarly, the 60 Hz field frequency is achieved by dividing 31500 Hz by 525 (i.e. 7 × 5 × 5 × 3). This point acquires added significance in colour television. The procedure for inserting synchronizing pulses is fundamentally the same as used in blanking pulse insertion. Horizontal and vertical pulses are added appropriately on top of the blanking pulses, and the resulting wave form is again clipped and clamped. The tips of horizontal and vertical synchronizing pulses reach a level that corresponds to 100 percent modulation of the picture carrier.

We have thus hypothetical video between 1.25 and 6.75 V, the blinking level at 7.5 V and the sync pulse tips at 10 V.

The horizontal sync information is extracted from the overall wave form by differentiation pulses corresponding to the differentiated leading edges of sync pulses are actually used to synchronize the horizontal scanning oscillator. The receivers after use monostable type circuits to generate horizontal scan, so that a pulse is required to initiate each and every cycle of horizontal oscillation in the receiver.

3.13 A sinusoidal modulating wave of amplitude 5 V and frequency 1 kHz is applied to a frequency modulator. The frequency carrier frequency is 100 kHz. Calculate

(i) frequency deviation

(ii) modulation deviation

(iii) instantaneous frequency of the FM wave

Also write the expression of the FM waveform. [16 marks : 2011]

Solution:

Given that, $A_m = 5\text{ V}, \quad f_m = 1\text{ kHz}$

Frequency sensitivity, $k_f = 40\text{ Hz/V}$

Carrier frequency, $f_c = 100\text{ kHz}$

(i) Frequency deviation $= k_f m(t) = 40\, A_m \cos 2\pi f_m t$

Maximum frequency deviation $= k_f A_m = 40 \times 5 = 200\text{ Hz}$

(ii) Modulation index, $\beta = \dfrac{\text{Max. frequency deviation}}{f_m} = \dfrac{200}{1\times 10^3} = 0.2$

(iii) Instantaneous frequency f_i of F_m wave

$$f_i = f_c + k_f m(t)$$

$$f_i = 100 \times 10^3 + 40 \times 5 \cos 2\pi \times 10^3 t$$

$$f_i = 10^5 + 200 \cos 2\pi \times 10^3 t$$

∴ Phase, $d(t) = 2\pi\int f_i\, dt$

$$d(t) = 2\pi\int 10^5 dt + 2\pi + 200\int \cos 2\pi \times 10^3 t\, dt$$

$$d(t) = 2\pi \times 10^5 t + \frac{2\pi \times 200}{2\pi \times 10^3}\sin 2\pi \times 10^3 t$$

$$d(t) = 2\pi \times 10^5 t + 0.2 \sin 2\pi \times 10^3 t$$

∴ Expression for FM wave

$$s(t) = A_c \cos\{\phi(t)\}$$

$$s(t) = A_c\left[\cos\left\{2\pi \times 10^5 t + 0.2 \sin 2\pi \times 10^3 t\right\}\right]$$

3.14 What are the limitations of the first order PLL for FM demodulation? Explain how this is overcome in second order PLL?

[4 marks : 2015]

Solution:

General phase locked loop structure is

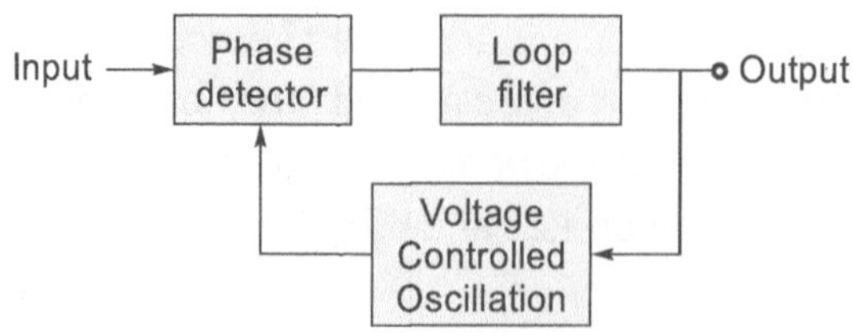

The loop filter decide the order of the PLL, when the loop filter is having transfer function $H(s) = k_o$ i.e., transfer function is a constant then the system is called first order PLL.
Limitation of first order PLL is that the loop gain parameter k_o control both the loop bandwidth and the hold in frequency range of the loop. The above problem can be solved by using loop filter $H(s) = \left(1+\frac{a}{s}\right)$, now the phase locked loop behave as a second order feedback system.

3.15 **What is the difference between PM and FM? Explain how FM can be generated using PM?**

[4 marks : 2016]

Solution:

PM signal is generated by modulating the phase of carrier signal with modulating signal or baseband signal.

$$s(t)_{PM} = A_c \cos(\omega_c t + k_p.x(t))$$

where, $x(t)$ = modulating or baseband signal

Whereas FM signal is generated by the modulation of the frequency of carrier signal by baseband signal.

$$s(t)_{FM} = A_c \cos(\omega_c t + k_f \int x(t))$$

Generation of FM using PM:

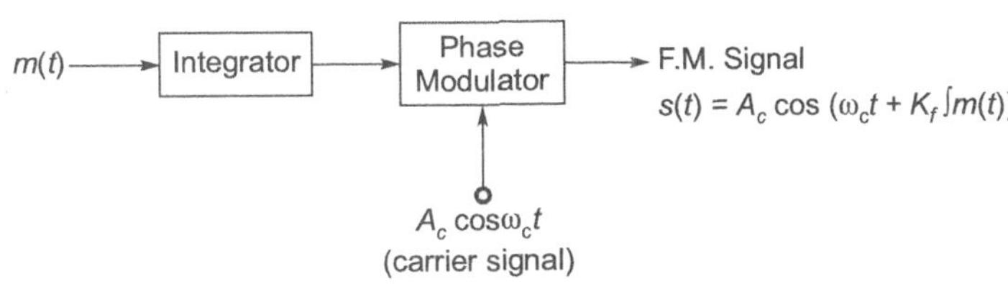

3.16 **An angle-modulated signal has a carrier,**

$$V_g = 6\cos(2\pi\ 110\ \text{MHz}\,t)$$

that produces a frequency deviation of 75 kHz due to information signal and a single interfering signal,

$$V_n = 0.3\cos(2\pi\,109.985\ \text{MHz}\ t)$$

Determine the:

(i) frequency of the demodulated interfering signal.

(ii) peak phase and frequency deviations due to interfering signal.

(iii) improvement in the voltage signal-to-noise ratio at the output of the demodulator compared to signal-to-noise ratio at the input.

[20 marks : 2017]

Solution:

$$V_g = 6\cos[2\pi\ 110\ \text{MHz}t]$$
$$V_n = 0.3\cos(2\pi\ 109.985\ \text{MHz}t)$$
$$E_g = 6\ \text{V},\ f_c = 110\ \text{MHz},\ \Delta f = 75\ \text{kHz}$$
$$E_n = 0.3\ \text{V},\ f_n = 109.985\ \text{MHz}$$

(i) Frequency of demodulated interference Signal,

$$f = f_c - f_n = (110 - 109.985)\ \text{MHz} = 0.015\ \text{MHz} = 15\ \text{kHz}$$

(ii)

$$\Delta f_{peak} = f \times \frac{E_n}{E_g} = 15 \times 10^3 \times \frac{0.3}{6} = 750\ \text{Hz}$$

$$\Delta\phi_{peak} = \frac{E_n}{E_g} = \frac{0.3}{6} = 0.05\ \text{rad}$$

(iii) S/N due to interfacing tone: $\frac{S}{N} = \frac{E_g}{E_n} = \frac{6}{0.3} = 20$

$\frac{S}{N}$ after demodulation: $\frac{S}{N} = \frac{\Delta f_{signal}}{\Delta f_{noise}} = \frac{75 \times 10^3}{750} = 100$

Voltage S/N improvement: $\frac{100}{20} = 5$

in dB = 20 log5 = 14 dB

3.17 A modulated signal is represented below as :

$$e(t) = 1500 \sin(2\pi \times 10^9 t + 2 \sin \pi \times 10^4 t)$$

Determine :

(1) type of modulation.
(2) carrier frequency.
(3) transmitted power, if the signal is applied to a 75 Ω antenna.
(4) modulation index.
(5) frequency deviation.

[10 marks : 2022]

Solution:

$$e(t) = 1500 \sin(2\pi \times 10^5 t + 2 \sin(\pi \times 10^4 t)) \quad ...(1)$$

For angle modulated signal, expression is given as :

$$s(t) = A_c \sin(2\pi f_c t + \beta \sin 2\pi f_m t) \quad ...(2)$$

$$A_c = 1500,\ f_m = \frac{10^4}{2}\text{Hz}$$

(1) Type of modulation is angle modulation because angle of the carrier signal is changing with respect to the signal $m(t)$.

(2) Comparing (1) and (2) equn.

$$f_c = 10^9 \text{ Hz}$$

(3) $$\text{Transmitted power} = \frac{\left(\frac{A_c}{\sqrt{2}}\right)^2}{R} = \frac{A_c^2}{2R}$$

$$= \frac{(1500)^2}{2 \times 75} = 15000 \text{ W}$$

(4) Modulation index = β, comparing eqn. (1) and (2), we get

$$\beta = 2$$

(5) $$\text{Frequency deviation} = \Delta f = \beta \times f_m$$

$$\therefore \quad \Delta f = 2 \times \frac{10^4}{2} = 10^4 \text{ Hz}$$

4. AM Transmitters and Receivers

4.1 What is meant by "heterodyning"? Draw the block diagram of a super heterodyne AM radio receiver and mention the role of I.F.

[10 marks : 2007]

Solution:

Heterodyning: Heterodyning is the technique by which the performance of the receiver is improved. The receiver based on this technique is known as superheterodyne receiver.

Block Diagram:

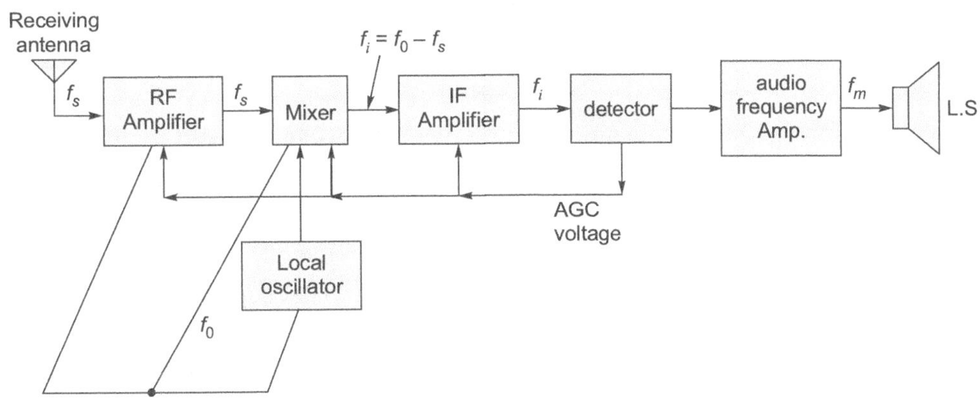

Role of IF: Radio signals at IF frequency itself can be heard at the output of radio receiver along with the dial-tuned signal, if such signals are able to reach the mixer tube with sufficient amplitude. This can be prevented by making RF stages highly selective so as to discriminate again radio signals in the region of the intermediate frequency itself.

If we will not use a IF frequency then for different tuning frequency for different stations, we need to change our filter circuit, amplifier circuit in accordance to different frequency range. When we convert all stations frequency to a single IF frequency so we require a filter, amplifier all according to IF frequency in receiver circuit so receiver circuit will be simpler.

IF Amplifier:

(a) This group constitutes the first detection by providing conversion from any input RF to a predetermined fixed signal frequency called intermediate frequency. IF = $f_0 - f_s$.

(b) This conversion is to enable adequate RF amplification of the signal within a bandwidth of an amplifier without distortion.

(c) This section provides selectivity, which is determined by the characteristics of the intermediate frequency amplifier.

5. Pulse Modulation

5.1 **(a) How sigma-delta modulation system is developed from delta modulation? Explain with block schematic.**

(b) A PCM system is to have SNR of 42.93 dB. The signals are speech and an rms to peak ratio of −10 dB is allowed for. Find the number of bits per code word required.

[8 + 6 marks : 2006]

Solution:

(a) **Sigma-Delta Modulation:** $\Delta\Sigma$ modulation (SDM) is inspired by Δ modulation (DM), as shown in figure. If quantization was homogeneous (e.g., if it was linear), the following would be a sufficient derivation of the equivalence of DM and SDM:

(i) Start with a block diagram of a Δ-modulator/demodulator.

(ii) The linearity property of integration $[\int a + \int b = \int (a + b)]$ makes it possible to move the integrator, which reconstructs the analog signal in the demodulator section, in front of the Δ-modulator.

(iii) Again, the linearity property of the integration allows the two integrators to be combined and a $\Delta\Sigma$-modulator/demodulator block diagram is obtained.

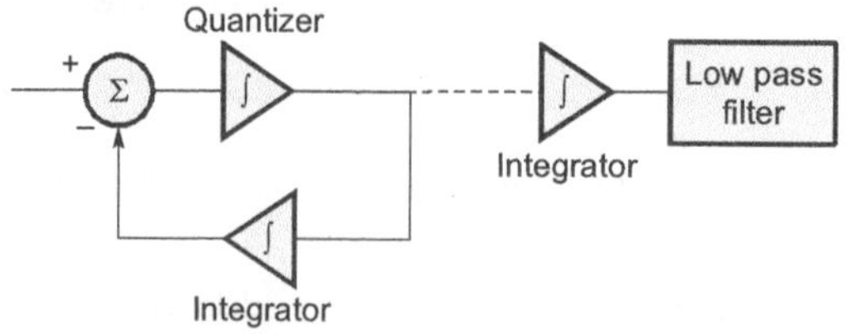

However the quantizer is not homogeneous, and so this explanation is flawed. Its true that $\Delta\Sigma$ is inspired by Δ-modulation, but the two are distinct in operation. From the block diagram, the integrator in the feedback path can be removed if the feedback is taken directly from the input of the low-pass filter. Hence for delta modulation of input signal u, the low-pass filter sees the signal

$$y_{DM} = \int \text{Quantize}(u - y_{DM})$$

However, sigma-delta modulation of the same input signal places at the low-pass filter.

$$y_{SDM} = \text{Quantize}[\int (u - y_{SDM})]$$

In other words, SDM and DM swap the position of the integrator and Quantizer. The net effect is a simpler implementation that has the added benefit of shaping the quantization noise away from the signals of interest (i.e., signals of interest are low – pass filtered while quantization noise is high-pass filtered). This effect becomes more dramatic with increased over sampling, which allows for quantization noise to be some what programmable. On the other hand, Δ-modulation shapes both noise and signal equally. Additionally, the quantizer (e.g. comparator) used in DM has a small output representing a small step up and down the quantized approximation of the input while the quantizer used in SDM must take values outside of the range of the input signal.

(b) $$(\text{SNR}) = 1.76 + 6n$$

Given that, $$\text{SNR} = 42.93 \text{ dB}$$

$\Rightarrow$ $$n = \frac{42.93 - 1.76}{6} = 6.86$$

$$n = 7 \text{ bits per code word.}$$

5.2 State and explain sampling theorem for base-band signals. Compare natural sampling with flat-topped sampling.

[10 marks : 2007]

Solution:

Sampling Theorem: According to the sampling theorem, if a modulating signal is bandlimited to B Hz (i.e. there are no frequency components beyond B Hz in the frequency spectrum of the modulating signal), the sampling frequency must be atleast - 2B Hz and, hence the frequency of the carrier pulse train must also be at least 2B Hz.

The spectral range occupied by the basic signal is called the baseband frequency range or, simply baseband. Hence, the basic signal is sometimes called as baseband signal.

Natural Sampling: When the modulated pulses follows the natural waveform of the modulating signal during the respective pulse interval the natural sampling takes place.

Flat-top Sampling: The electronic circuitry needed to perform natural sampling is some what complicated because the pulse-top shape is to be maintained. These complications are reduced by flat-top sampling. In this tops of the pulses are flat. Thus the pulses have a constant amplitude within the pulse interval. The constant amplitude of the pulse can be choose at any value of $f(t)$ within the pulse interval.

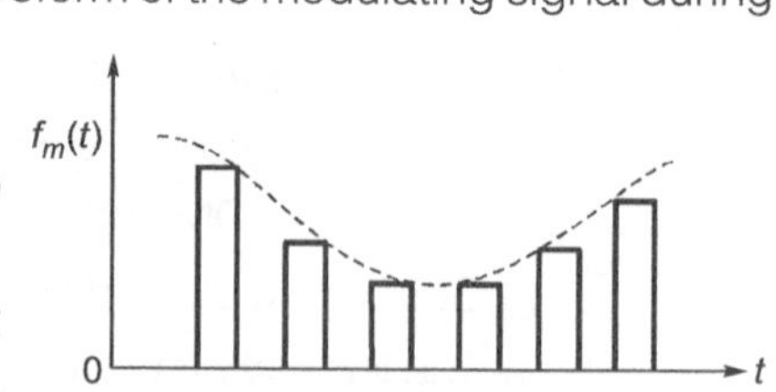

The value at the beginning of the pulse is chosen. By making the value of the pulse amplitude constant within the pulse interval, some distortion is introduced as there is a deviation from the actual value of $f(t)$ during the pulse interval.

5.3 **Explain the advantages and disadvantages of digital communication over analog communication.**
[10 marks : 2009]

Solution:

Advantage: Use the repeaters which minimized the effect of noise in channel.

1. The effect of noise can be minimized.
2. Microwave transmission systems are easily employed for digital communication because of its wide bandwidth requirement.
3. Ease of processing.
4. Ease of multiplexing.
5. Digital data is transmitted at relatively high rate.
6. SNR is very high.
7. The detection process is simple.
8. Probability of error in detecting a bit is very small..

Disadvantage:

1. The digital signal does not provide continuous representation of the original signal.
2. Such signals can not be transmitted through antenna these can be transmitted through coaxial cable or parallel wire transmission line. Therefore, range of transmission is limited.

5.4 **With a block diagram, explain the basics of transmitter and receiver of PCM system.**
[4 marks : 2011]

Solution:

LPF: Low Pass Filter at transmitter end is used to eliminate insignificant higher frequencies.

Sampler: Sampler samples the signal at a rate f_s, sampling frequency is selected sufficiently above Nyquist rate to avoid aliasing. The output of sampler is $m[nTs]$

L-Level Quantizer: A L-level quantizer compares the input $m[nTs]$ with fixed digital level. It assigns one of the digital level to $m[nTs]$ with its fixed levels. The difference between fixed level and input is called quantization error.

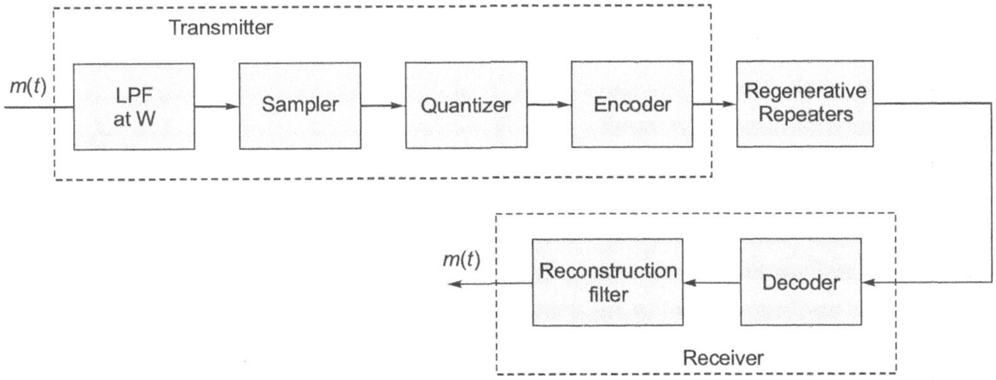

Encoder: The quantized signal level $m_q[nTs]$ is given to binary encoder which converts it into n bit binary code.

Decoder: It is on the receiver side. It converts code word into analog value, this analog value is passed through a reconstruction filter.

Reconstruction Filter: The input to low pass filter at the receiver is the sampled signal with quantization error. Due to this error signal distortion occur.

5.5 **In PAM, the carrier wave consists of a periodic train of rectangular pulses and the carrier frequency is equal to**

(i) the bandwidth of the modulating signal

(ii) the sampling rate of the modulating signal

(iii) atleast ten times greater than the bandwidth of the modulating signal

(iv) twice the bandwidth of the modulating signal

[2 marks : 2011]

Solution:

Carrier frequency must be much higher than the modulating signal bandwidth or (highest frequency component of message signal) in any modulation scheme.

So, f_c carrier frequency must be atleast ten time greater than the bandwidth of the modulating signal.

So, (iii) is correct option.

5.6 **Explain and differentiate Pulse Code Modulation (PCM) and Pulse Position Modulation (PPM).**

[5 marks : 2014]

Solution:

Difference between pulse position modulation and pulse code modulation.

PPM:

- PPM is a pulse modulation system which the position of the pulse changes according to the instantaneous value of the baseband message signal by keeping the amplitude and width of the pulse constant.
- PPM is an analog pulse modulation in which the indication of sample amplitude may be infinitely variable.
- Noise immunity is very less.
- They are used in telemetry and instrumentation.

PCM:

- PCM is a pulse modulation system in which message 1 signal is represented by a sequence of coded pulse, which is accomplished by representing the signal in discrete form in both time and amplitude.
- PCM is a digital pulse modulation in which a code that indicates the sample amplitude to the nearest predetermined level is used.
- They have much better noise immunity.
- They are used in broadband networks and in space communication.

5.7 **(i) Find the resolution and the bit rate in the sampling of a signal with dynamic range of 1 volt if the sampling rate is F_s = 20 samples/sec and 8-bit A/D converter is used. Determine the maximum frequency that can be present in resulting digital signal.**

(ii) In a signal processing system shown below, sampling periods of the Analog to Digital and Digital to Analog converters are T = 5 m sec and T' = 1 msec respectively. Find the output $y_a(t)$ of the system if the input is

$$x_a(t) = 3\cos(100\pi t) + 2\sin(250\pi t)$$

(Post-filter removes frequency components that are above $\frac{F_s}{2}$).

[6+14 = 20 marks : 2021]

Solution:

(i) Given, dynamic range = 1 V

Sampling rate, f_s = 20 sample/sec

Total bits, n = 8 bits/sample

$$\text{Resolution} = \frac{\text{Dynamic range}}{2^n - 1} = \frac{1\text{ V}}{2^8 - 1} = \frac{1}{255} = 0.0039 \text{ volts}$$

$$\text{Bit rate } (R_b) = nf_s$$

$$= 8 \times 20 = 160 \text{ bits/sec}$$

$$f_s \geq 2f_m \rightarrow 20 \geq 2f_m$$

$$f_m \leq 10$$

$$(f_m)_{max} = 10 \text{ Hz}$$

Maximum message frequency allow = 10 Hz

(ii)

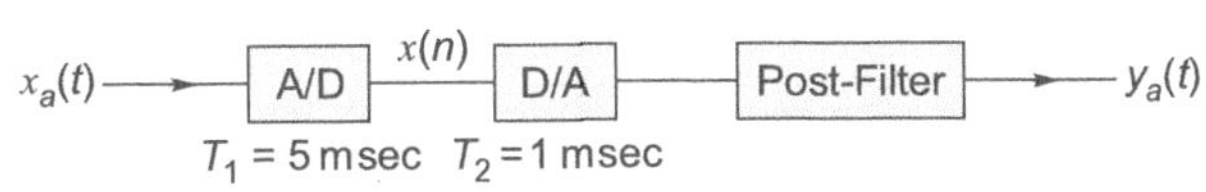

Given that, $x_a(t) = 3\cos 100\pi t + 2\sin 250\pi t$

Now, $x(n) = x_a(t)\big|_{t=nT_1} = 5 \times 10^{-3} n = \frac{5n}{1000}$

$$x(n) = 3\cos\left[100\pi\left(\frac{5n}{1000}\right)\right] + 2\sin\left[250\pi\left(\frac{5n}{1000}\right)\right]$$

$$x(n) = 3\cos\left(\frac{\pi}{2}n\right) + 2\sin\left(\frac{5\pi}{4}n\right)$$

$$x(n) = 3\cos\frac{\pi}{2}n + 2\sin\left[\left(2\pi - \frac{3\pi}{4}\right)n\right]$$

$$x(n) = 3\cos\frac{\pi}{2}n + 2\sin\left(2\pi n - \frac{3\pi}{4}n\right)$$

$$x(n) = 3\cos\frac{\pi}{2}n - 2\sin\left(\frac{3\pi}{4}n\right)$$

[$\because \sin(2\pi n - \theta) = -\sin\theta$ where, n = an-integer]

Output of post-filters:

$$y_a(t) = x(n)\big|_{n=\frac{t}{T_2}=\frac{t}{10^{-3}}=1000t}$$

$$= 3\cos\left[\frac{\pi}{2}(1000t)\right] - 2\sin\left[\frac{3\pi}{4}(1000t)\right]$$

$$y_a(t) = 3\cos(500\pi t) - 2\sin(750\pi t)$$

6. Data Transmission Schemes

6.1 What is multiplexing of signals and when it is employed? Discuss the principles of two multiplexing schemes.

[12 marks : 2002]

Solution:

Multiplexing: Multiplexing is a technique whereby several message signals are combined into a composite signal for transmission over a common channel. For the signals, not interfering with each other, they must be kept apart. This is employed when we have to sent several signal through a single channel.

There are two multiplexing techniques:

(a) **FDM (Frequency Division Multiplexing):** In FDM by taking a bandwidth adequate for the number of channels required and allocating each channel to a frequency "slot" adjacent to the previous channel. However, for reasons of flexibility, economy and simplicity, such frequency translations are not performed in one step. Instead, standardized grouping of channels are used, and several steps of frequency translation take place before all the channels have been placed in their locations in the frequency spectrum that is transmitted in a particular link.

Employed in telephone, telix and data transmission.

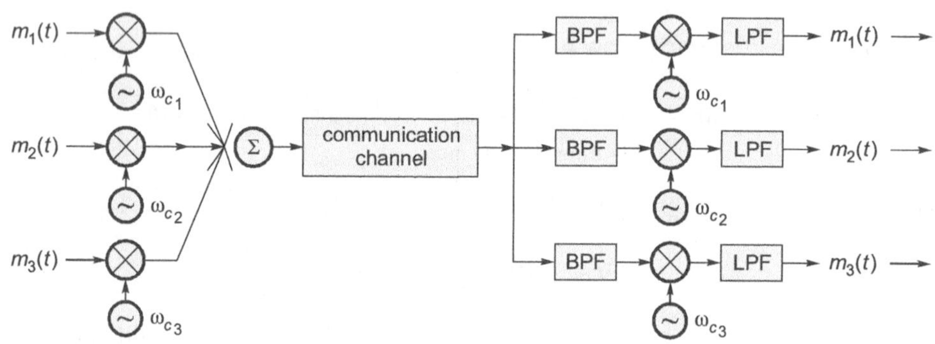

(b) **TDM (Time Division Multiplexing):** TDM is a method of interleaving, in the time domain, pulses belonging to different transmissions. That is to say, use is made of the fact that pulses are generally narrow, and separations between successive pulses is rather wide.

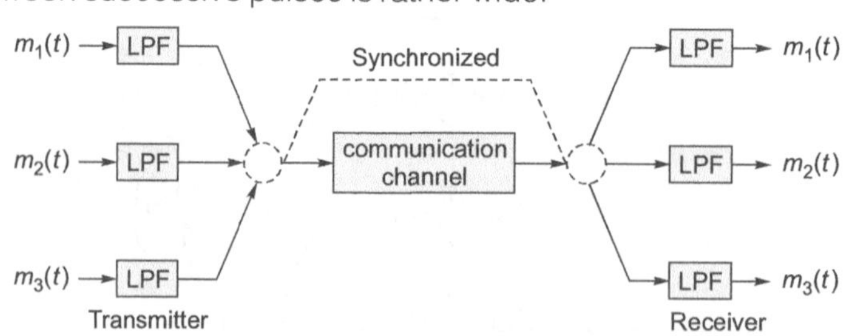

6.2 Consider an FDM system using AM-SSB modulation to transmit 24 independent voice inputs. Assume a bandwidth of 4 kHz for each voice input. Determine the transmission bandwidth. Compare the bandwidth with that of a standard 8-bit PCM with TDM. Assume bit duration is 0.647 μs.

[8 marks : 2011]

Solution:

Total number of voice inputs = 24

For each voice input B.W. = 4 kHz

Since AM-SSB is used BNW of AM-SSB modulated

Signal = BW of each voice input = 4 kHz

∵ there is no guard band is used so required bandwidth for

$$\text{FDM} = 24 \times 4 \text{ kHz} = 96 \text{ kHz}$$

$$\text{Number of bits in PCMn} = 8 \text{ bit}$$

bit duration $T_b = 0.647\ \mu\text{sec} = 0.647 \times 10^{-6}$ sec

$$\text{Number inputs } N = 24$$

$$W = 4 \text{ kHz}$$

B.W. of each message signal.

∴ Sampling frequency, $f_s = 2\text{W} = 2 \times 4 = 8$ kHz

(for each message signal) (sampled at Nyquist rate)

∴ Bit rate $R_b = N.nf_s = 24 \times 8 \times 8 \times 10^3 = 1536\ k_{\text{bits}}/\text{sec}$

required B.W. $= R_b/2 = 768$ kHz

So bandwidth required for 8 bit PCM-TDM for sending same 4 message B.W. requirement is high compare to AMSSB – FDM system.

6.3 **What is time-division multiplexing? With reference to pulse communication system, show the use of time-division multiplexing by drawing a block diagram.**

[4 marks : 2012]

Solution:

Time-division multiplexing is a type of digital (or rarely analog) multiplexing in which two or more signals are transferred apparently simultaneously as sub-channels in one communication channel, but are physically taking turns on the channel. The time domain is divided into several time slots of fixed length, one for each sub-channel.

The TDM system is highly sensitive to dispersion in the common channel that is, to variations of amplitude with frequency or lack of proportionality of phase with frequency.

Block diagram:

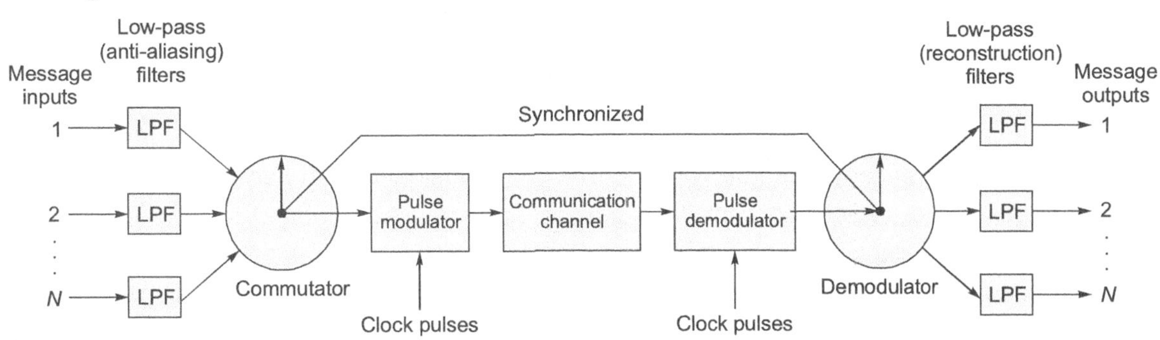

Block diagram of TDM system

6.4 **Why is TDM superior to FDM in PAM system? Draw the circuit diagram of a PWM modulator using 555 timer.**

[5 + 5 marks : 2015]

Solution:

Advantage of TDM over FDM are:

1. TDM offers bandwidth saving and there is low interference between the signals that are multiplexed. In FDM we need to provide guard band so bandwidth is wasted.
2. FDM is analog multiplexing technique and thus it has all disadvantages of analog modulation, TDM is a digital multiplexing technique and thus it has all advantages of digital modulation.

PWM modulator using 555 timer ⇒

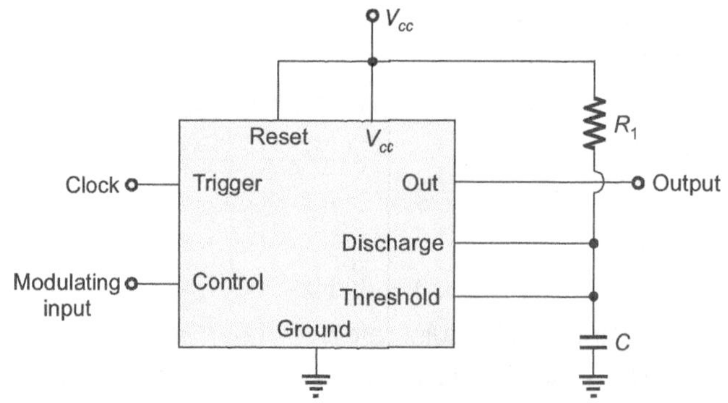

The diagram show the 555 timer wired up in monostable multivibrator mode. We know that in this mode the output is in a form of pulse in response to trigger at input. The duration of output depend on the control input, thus we get pulse width modulated wave at output.

7. Information Theory and Coding

7.1 **State the law that provides the limit for information capacity of a communication channel for given signal to noise ratio and name it.**

[4 marks : 2007]

Solution:

Shannon-Hartley theorem gives a formula for the capacity of a channel when its BW and noise level are known. This capacity is

$$c = \delta_f \log_2(1 + S/N)$$

where, c = channel capacity, bits/sec

δ_f = bandwidth, Hz

S/N = ratio of total signal power to total random noise power at the input to the receiver, within the frequency limit of this channel

This Shannon-Hartley theorem shows a limit that cannot be exceeded by the signaling speed in a channel in which the noise is purely random.

Capacity was increased, but certainly not doubled, when the bandwidth was doubled. This implies that the useful possibility of trading bandwidth for signal - to - noise ratio exits. Indeed, such trade off are often made in system design, especially in power limited situation. It also should be realized that, if channel capacity seems low in a given situation, this does not mean that a wanted amount of information cannot be sent over a given channel.

■■■■

5 Control Systems

Revised Syllabus of ESE: *Principles of feedback, transfer function, block diagrams and signal flow graphs, steady-state errors, transforms and their applications; Routh-hurwitz criterion, Nyquist techniques, Bode plots, root loci, lag, lead and lead-lag compensation, stability analysis, transient and frequency response analysis, state space model, state transition matrix, controllability and observability, linear state variable feedback, PID and industrial controllers.*

1. Modelling of a Control System and Transfer Function Approach

1.1 Describe a zero-order sample and hold circuit. Obtain the Laplace transform of the output of S/H circuit when discrete inputs are sampled at regular intervals of T seconds.

[8 marks : 2001]

Solution:

Sampling Process:

The sampling process is process in which a continuous signal into a sequence of pulses where in the magnitude of the pulse gives the value of the input signal at the instant of sampling.

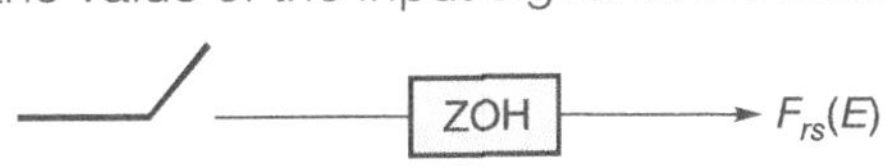

Pulse sampler with ZOH

Where (ZOH) zero order hold is a hold circuit in which the signal is reconstructed such that the value of reconstructed signal for a sampling period is same as the value of last received sample.

Consider a pulse sampler with zero-order hold (ZOH). Let the output of sampler be a pulse train width Δ. For each pulse, the ZOH produces a pulse direction T.

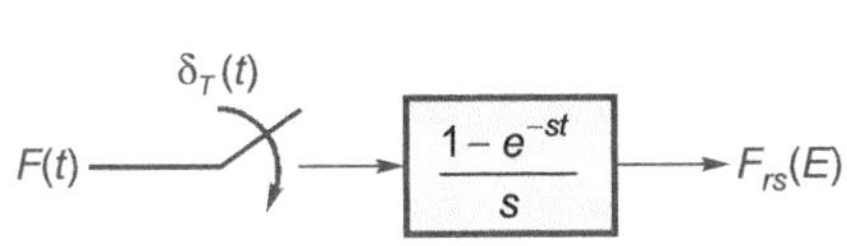

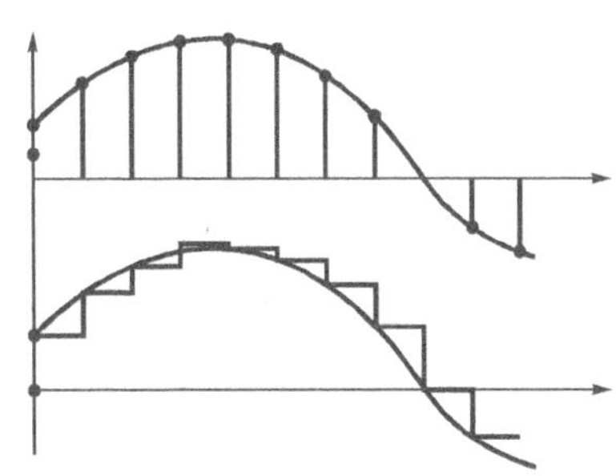

As the output of ZOH is a unit step function appearing into T.

$$h(t) = u(t) - u(t-T)$$

$$H(s) = \frac{1}{s}(1 - e^{-st})$$

$$\text{Transfer function of (ZOH)} = \frac{L\{\text{Output of ZOH}\}}{L\{\text{Input of ZOH}\}} = \frac{\frac{1}{s}-\frac{1}{s}e^{-st}}{1} = \frac{1-e^{-st}}{s}$$

Hence the pulse sampler with ZOH can be replaced by an equivalent system consisting of an impulse sampler and a block with transfer function $\left[\left(\frac{1-e^{-st}}{s}\right)\right]$.

1.2 **Briefly describe the working of a two-phase servomotor. Derive its transfer function and sketch its torque-speed characteristics.**

[12 marks : 2003]

Solution:

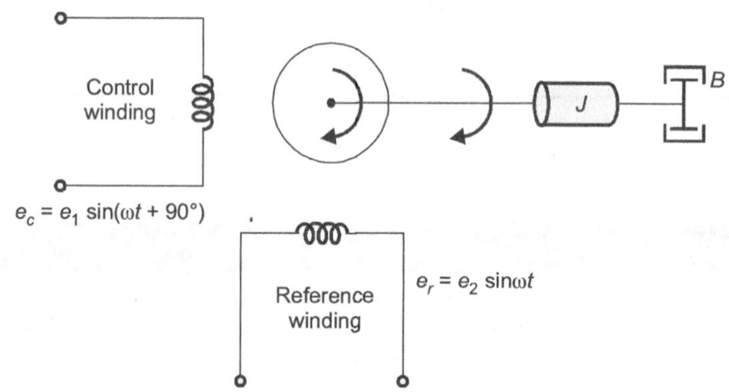

- An a.c. servomotor is basically a two-phase induction motor. The rotor is the servomotoris built with high resistance so that is X/R ratio is small and the torque-speed characteristic is nearly linear.
- The rotor construction is usually squirrel cage or drag-up type.

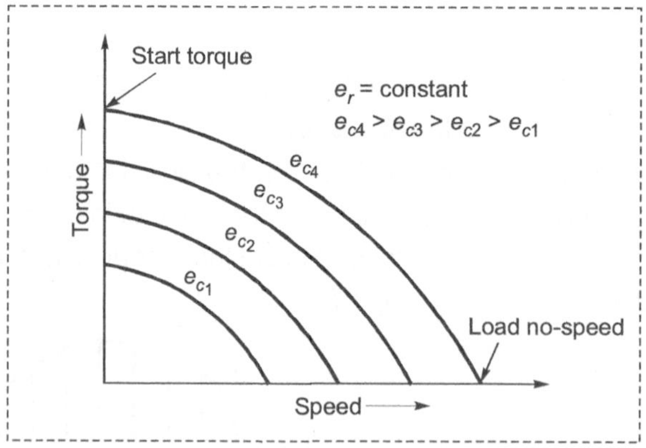

- The two-phase servomotor has 2 windage at right angles to each other and the two windings are supplied with voltages with 90° phase difference through a capacitor.
- One winding called reference winding is supplied with a fixed voltage and frequency from a constant voltage source. To the other winding is applied the voltage whose amplitude can be varied but of the same frequency. The axes of the coil are in space and phase quadrature and voltages in time quadrature. On account of this there will be a resultant flux. This resultant flux will be rotating at the frequency of supply at the synchronous speed, $\frac{120f}{p}$. This rotating flux cuts the conducting bars of rotor and causes a varying current. This varying current in turn produces a varying flux and reacts with the stator flux causing the rotor to rotate in a smooth manner.

Transfer Function of the Servomotor:

- Torque developed by motor

$$T_m = K_1 e_c - K_2 \frac{d\theta}{dt}$$

Load torque, $$T_l = J\frac{d^2\theta}{dt^2} + B\frac{d\theta}{dt}$$

- At equilibrium the motor torque is equal to the load torque.

$$T_l = T_m$$

$$\Rightarrow \quad J\frac{d^2\theta}{dt^2} + B\frac{d\theta}{dt} = K_1 e_c - K_2 \frac{d\theta}{dt}$$

- On taking Laplace transform of the above equation, assuming zero initial conditions,

$$Js^2\,\theta(s) + Bs\,\theta(s) = K_1\,E_c(s) - K_2 s\,\theta(s)$$

$$\Rightarrow \quad [Js^2 + Bs + K_2 s]\,\theta(s) = K_1\,E_c(s)$$

$$\text{Transfer function} = \frac{\theta(s)}{E_c(s)} = \frac{K_1}{s(Js + B + K_2)}$$

$$= \frac{K_1/(B+K_2)}{s\left(\dfrac{J}{K_2+B}s + 1\right)} = \frac{K_m}{s(\tau_m s + 1)}$$

where, $$K_m = \frac{K_1}{B+K_2} = \text{motor gain constant}$$

$$\tau_m = \frac{J}{K_2+B} = \text{motor time constant}$$

1.3 Why is it necessary to truncate a Taylor series expansion of a non-linear function after the first term, if the linear approximation is desired?

[10 marks : 2004]

Solution:

A Taylor series expansion is given by

$$f(x) = f(a) + (x-a)\,f'(a) + \frac{(x-a)^2}{2!}f''(a) + \frac{(x-a)^3}{3!}f'''(a) + \ldots\ldots\ldots$$

Its curve may be drawn as

Taylor's series expresses the height of a curve at a distance at $a + h$ form the origin in terms of its height at a distance a from the origin.

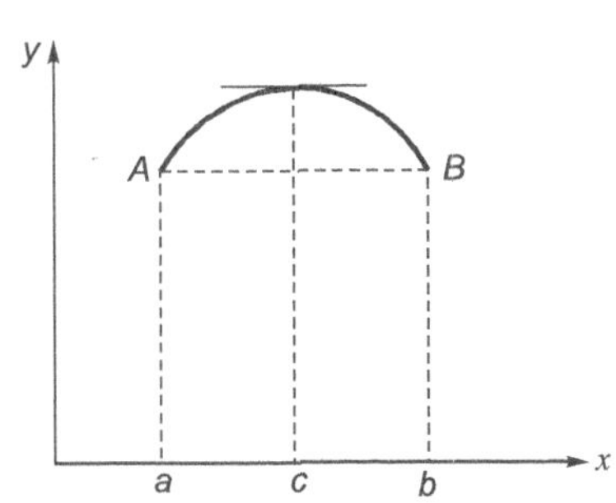

Another method of writing Taylor's series is by writing the series in terms of 'h' rather than 'x'.

$x = a + h$ or $h = x - a$. Substituting for x in equation (i) gives,

$$f(a+h) = f(a) + h f'(a) + \frac{h^2}{2!} f''(a) + \frac{h^3}{3!} f'''(a) + \ldots\ldots\ldots\ldots$$

If h is considered a small increase in the non-linearity, the higher orders may be neglected as being very small.

1.4 Draw a neat sketch of a hydraulic proportional controller and explain its working.

[10 marks : 2006]

Solution:

Hydraulic actuator:

Hydraulic actuator shown in Fig. (1) controls large displacement power at the shaft of main piston. The input power requirement is very small and provided by the displacement of the valve piston. The linear motion of the valve piston controls the flow of oil either side of the main piston.

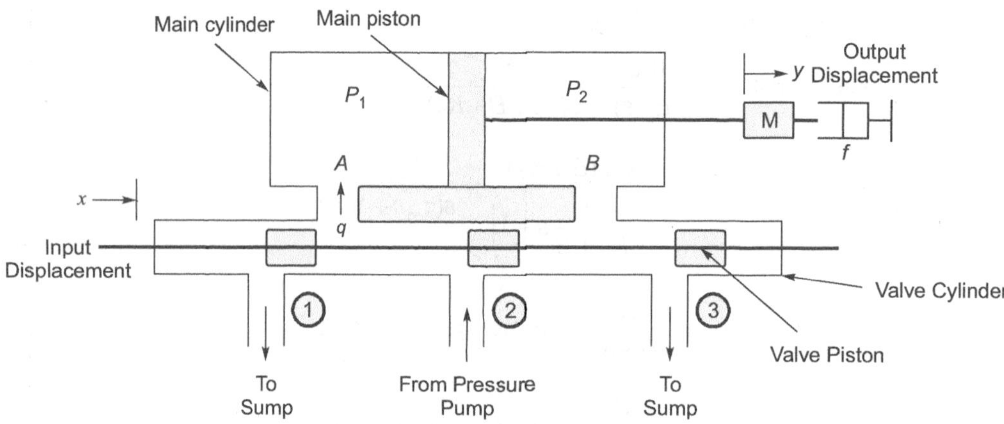

Fig. (1) : Hydraulic actuator

When the input force through the displacement x is applied to the valve piston, the valve piston moves to the right. Piston valve ports (2) and (3) are thus uncovered and oil higher pressure from port (2) enters to the left side of the main piston through main port A. At the same time the main port B is connected to the sump through port (3). The pressure P_1 on the left side of the main piston is higher than the pressure P_2 on the right side of the piston. The pressure difference $(P_1 - P_2)$ causes the main piston to move from left to right and the resulting displacement of the mass attached to main piston is y.

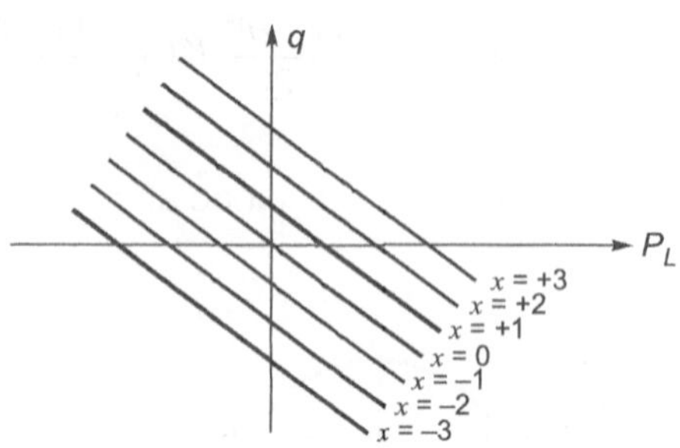

Fig. (2) : Linearized performance characteristics of hydraulic actuator

The mathematical relation between the input displacement x and the output displacement y gives the model of the system.

The linearized performance characteristics of hydraulic actuator relating the oil flow q (m^3/sec) and the pressure difference $(P_1 - P_2) = P_L$ (N/m^2) acting on the main piston as a function of valve displacement x is shown in Fig. (2).

1.5 Differentiate clearly between 'tracking control' and 'regulatory control' problems, with the help of an example and diagram.

[10 marks : 2010]

Solution:

Regulatory Control Problem:

With the system initially displaced from equilibrium will return the system to the equilibrium state in such a manner so as to minimize a given performance index.

Example: A radar antenna control system with the antenna subject to wind gusts.

Tracking Control Problem:

This is used to cause the state of a system to track as close as possible some desired state time history in such a manner so as to minimize a given performance index. This is the generalization of the regulatory control problem.

Example: When a radar antenna is to track an aircraft.

1.6 For a liquid level tank system shown in figure, write the dynamical equations and obtain a variable model. The liquid levels in the tanks may be assumed as output. Also draw the block diagram and obtain transfer function $H_2(s)/Q_1(s)$ for transient state.

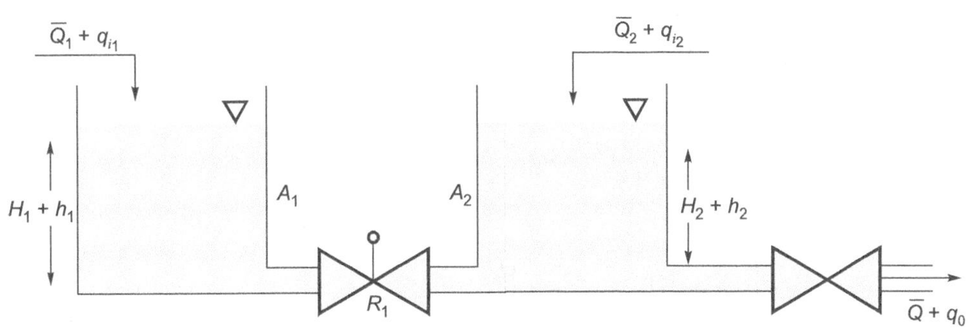

[10 marks : 2010]

Solution:

Assuming flow through the value of resistance R_1 is q_x.

Dynamical equations:

$$q_x = \frac{h_1 - h_2}{R_1} \quad \ldots(i)$$

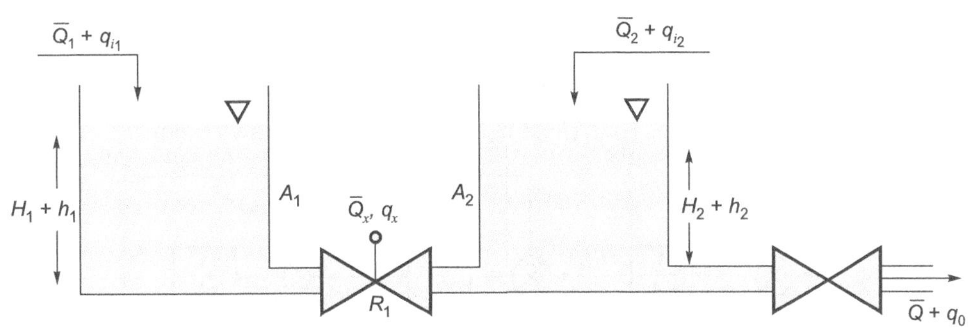

$$q_0 = \frac{h_2}{R_2} \quad \ldots(ii)$$

$$A_1\frac{dh_1}{dt} = q_{i_1} - q_x = q_{i_1} - \left(\frac{h_1 - h_2}{R_1}\right)$$

$$\Rightarrow \quad A_1\frac{dh_1}{dt} = -\frac{h_1}{R_1} + \frac{h_2}{R_1} + q_{i_1} \quad \text{...(iii)}$$

$$A_2\frac{dh_2}{dt} = q_x + q_{i_2} - q_0$$

$$= \left(\frac{h_1 - h_2}{R_1}\right) + q_{i_2} - \frac{h_2}{R_2}$$

$$= \frac{h_1}{R_1} - \left(\frac{1}{R_1} + \frac{1}{R_2}\right)h_2 + q_{i_2} \quad \text{...(iv)}$$

equation (*i*), (*ii*), (*iii*) and (*iv*) are the dynamical equations of the system.
Rewriting equations (*iii*) and (*iv*),

$$\frac{dh_1}{dt} = -\frac{h_1}{A_1R_1} + \frac{h_2}{A_1R_1} + \frac{q_{i_1}}{A_i} \quad \text{...(v)}$$

$$\frac{dh_2}{dt} = \frac{h_1}{A_2R_1} - \frac{1}{A_2}\left(\frac{1}{R_1} + \frac{1}{R_2}\right)h_2 + \frac{q_{i_2}}{A_2} \quad \text{...(vi)}$$

Choosing h_1 and h_2 as state variables.

$$x_1 = h_1 \text{ and } x_2 = h_2$$

Output, $y_1 = h_1$ and $y_2 = h_2$

Rewriting equations (*v*) and (*vi*),

$$\dot{x}_1 = -\frac{x_1}{A_1R_1} + \frac{x_2}{A_1R_1} + \frac{q_{i_1}}{A_1} \quad \text{...(vii)}$$

$$\dot{x}_2 = \frac{x_1}{A_2R_1} - \frac{1}{A_2}\left(\frac{1}{R_1} + \frac{1}{R_2}\right)x_2 + \frac{q_{i_2}}{A_2} \quad \text{...(viii)}$$

$$\begin{bmatrix}\dot{x}_1\\ \dot{x}_2\end{bmatrix} = \begin{bmatrix}-\frac{1}{A_1R_1} & \frac{1}{A_1R_1}\\ \frac{1}{A_2R_1} & -\frac{1}{A_2}\left(\frac{1}{R_1}+\frac{1}{R_2}\right)\end{bmatrix}\begin{bmatrix}x_1\\ x_2\end{bmatrix} + \begin{bmatrix}\frac{1}{A_1} & 0\\ 0 & \frac{1}{A_2}\end{bmatrix}\begin{bmatrix}q_{i_1}\\ q_{i_2}\end{bmatrix}$$

$$\begin{bmatrix}y_1\\ y_2\end{bmatrix} = \begin{bmatrix}1 & 0\\ 0 & 1\end{bmatrix}\begin{bmatrix}x_1\\ x_2\end{bmatrix}$$

On the basis of dynamical equations (*i*) to (*iv*), the block diagram is drawn below:

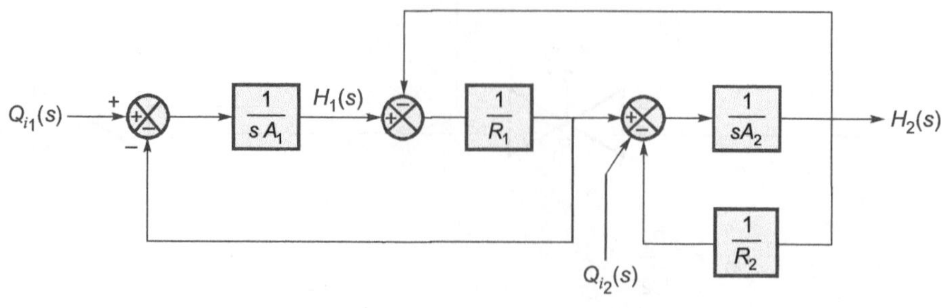

For obtaining transfer function $\frac{H_2(s)}{Q_{i_1}(s)}$, $Q_{i_2}(s)$ is assumed to be zero and signal flow graph is shown below:

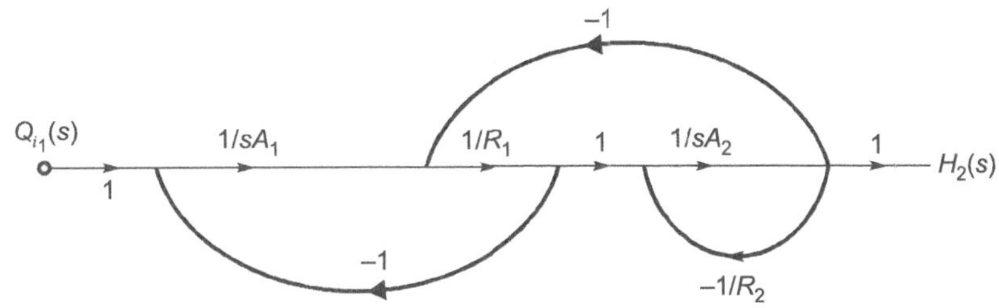

Forward path $= P_1 = \frac{1}{s^2 A_1 A_2 R_1}$ and $\Delta_1 = 1$

$$\Delta = 1-\left\{\left(-\frac{1}{sA_1 R_1}\right)+\left(-\frac{1}{sA_2 R_2}\right)\right\}+\frac{1}{s^2 A_1 A_2 R_1 R_2}$$

Applying Mason's Gain formula =

$$\frac{H_2(s)}{Q_{i_1}(s)} = \frac{\left(\frac{1}{s^2 A_1 A_2 R_1}\right)}{\left(1+\frac{1}{sA_1 R_1}+\frac{1}{sA_2 R_2}+\frac{1}{sR_2 R_1}+\frac{1}{s^2 A_1 A_2 R_1 R_2}\right)}$$

$$\frac{H_2(s)}{Q_{i_1}(s)} = \frac{1}{A_1 A_2 R_1 s^2+\left(A_2+\frac{A_1 R_1}{R_2}+\frac{A_1 A_2}{R_2}\right)s+\frac{1}{R_2}}$$

1.7 **Show the electrical connection diagram and model the armature voltage controlled d.c. motor in a block diagram form. Assume the necessary variables and obtain transfer function for change in position of armature to the change in armature voltage. Express the transfer function in standard form.**

[10 marks : 2011]

Solution:

Connection diagram of armature voltage controlled d.c motor.

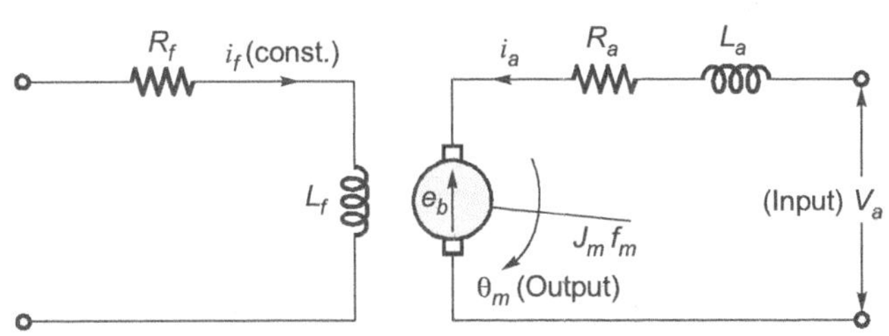

where,

V_a = Input voltage,
R_a = Resistance of armature,
J_m = Moment of inertia
θ_m = Angular shift in the motor shaft
I_a = Armature current
I_a = Inductance of armature
f_m = Coefficient of viscous friction

As the field current is kept constant the relationship between the developed motor torque T_m and the armature current is given by,

$$T_m \propto i_a \Rightarrow T_m k_T i_a$$

where, k_T = motor torque constant

The relationship between back e.m.f. e_b developed in the armature and the motor speed ω_m is given by

$$e_b \propto \omega_m$$

$$\omega_m = \frac{d\theta_m}{dt}$$

$$e_b = k_b \frac{d\theta_m}{dt}$$

where, k_b = back e.m.f. constant

The related dynamic equations are | **The corresponding Laplace transformed equations are**

$$V_a - e_b = R_a i_a + L_a \frac{di_a}{dt} \qquad V_a(s) - E_b(s) = R_a I_a(s) + s L_a I_a(s) \quad ...(i)$$

$$e_b = k_b \frac{d\theta_m}{dt} \qquad E_b(s) = s k_b \theta_m(s) \quad ...(ii)$$

or

$$e_b = k_b \omega_m \qquad E_b(s) = k_b \omega_m(s) \quad ...(iii)$$

$$T_m = k_T i_a \qquad T_m(s) = k_T I_a(s) \quad ...(iv)$$

$$T_m = J_m \frac{d^2\theta_m}{dt^2} + f_m \frac{d\theta_m}{dt} \qquad T_m(s) = s^2 J_m \theta_m(s) + s f_m \theta_m(s) \quad ...(v)$$

$$T_m = J_m \frac{d\omega_m}{dt} + f_m \omega_m \qquad T_m(s) = s J_m \omega_m(s) + f_m \omega_m(s) \quad ...(vi)$$

From equations (*i*) to (*vi*) the block diagram relating the output $\theta_m(s)$ and the input $V_a(s)$ is drawn below:

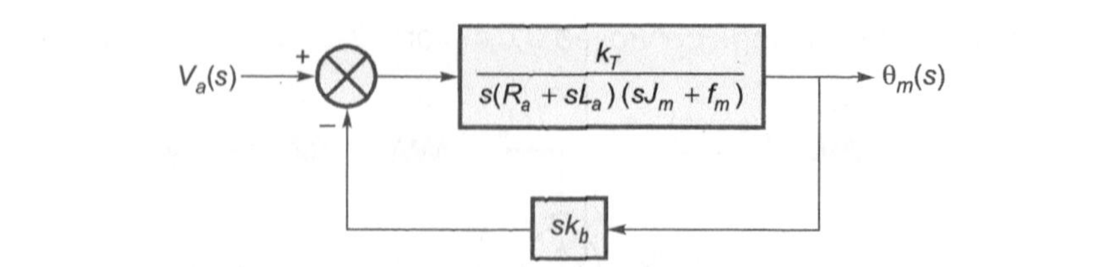

The block diagram is reduced and shown below:

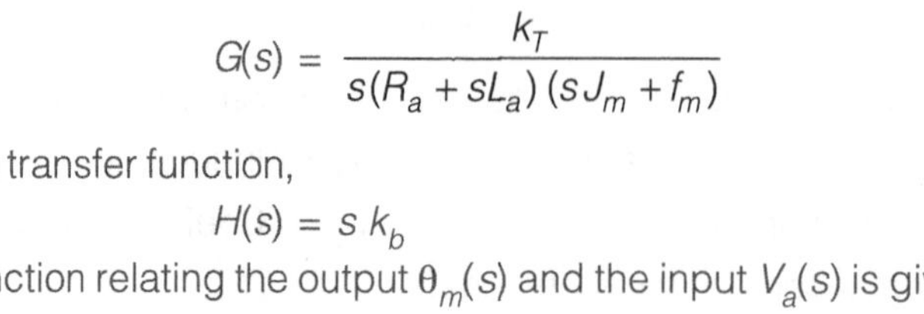

In the block diagram, the forward path transfer function,

$$G(s) = \frac{k_T}{s(R_a + sL_a)(sJ_m + f_m)}$$

and the feedback path transfer function,

$$H(s) = s\, k_b$$

The overall transfer function relating the output $\theta_m(s)$ and the input $V_a(s)$ is given by the relation,

$$\frac{\theta_m(s)}{V_a(s)} = \frac{G(s)}{1+G(s)H(s)}$$

$$= \frac{k_T / s(R_a + sL_a)(sJ_m + f_m)}{1 + \left\{\frac{k_T}{s(R_a + sL_a)(sJ_m + f_m)}\right\}\cdot(sk_b)}$$

Required transfer function,

$$\frac{\theta_m(s)}{V_a(s)} = \frac{k_T}{s(R_a + sL_a)(sJ_m + f_m) + s(k_T k_b)}$$

If the armature inductance La is neglected,

$$\frac{\theta_m(s)}{V_a(s)} = \frac{k_T}{s^2 R_a(sJ_m + f_m) + sk_T k_b}$$

$$\Rightarrow \quad \frac{\theta_m(s)}{V_a(s)} = \frac{k_T}{s(sR_a J_m + R_a f_m + k_T k_b)} = \frac{\left[\frac{k_T}{(R_a f_m + k_T k_b)}\right]}{s\left[\frac{sR_a J_m}{R_a f_m + k_T k_b} + 1\right]}$$

Transfer function is the standard form,

$$\frac{\theta_m(s)}{V_a(s)} = \frac{k_m}{s(1 + sT_m)}$$

where, $$k_m = \frac{k_m}{(R_a f_m + k_T k_b)} \qquad \text{(Motor gain constant)}$$

and $$T_m = \frac{R_a J_m}{(R_a f_m + k_T k_b)} \qquad \text{(Motor time constant)}$$

1.8 **Draw the schematic diagram of a 2-phase servomotor and draw the torque-speed characteristic. What care is taken to obtain linear characteristic? Derive the linearized transfer function under load condition.**

[10 marks : 2011]

Solution:

Schematic diagram of a 2-phase servomotor,

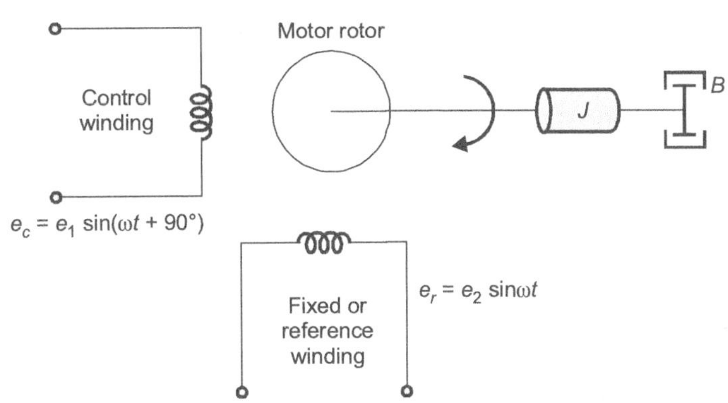

- The torque-speed characteristic of the servomotor are non-linear but may be considered linear for practical purposes.

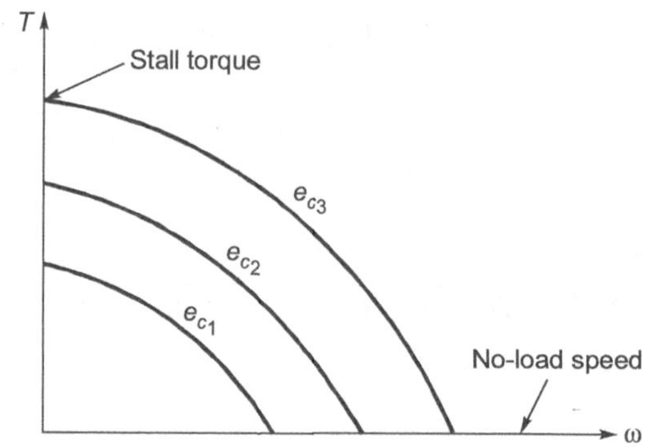

- The rotor of the servomotor is built with high resistance so that its X/R ratio is small and the torque-speed characteristic is nearly linear.
- **Transfer function of AC servomotor**

Torque developed by motor $T_m = k_1 e_c - k_2 \frac{d\theta}{dt}$

The rotating part of motor and the load can be modelled by the equation.

$$\text{Load torque} = T_l = J\frac{d^2\theta}{dt^2} + B\frac{d\theta}{dt}$$

At equilibrium the motor torque is equal to load torque

$$J\frac{d^2\theta}{dt^2} + B\frac{d\theta}{dt} = k_1 e_c - k_2\frac{d\theta}{dt}$$

On taking Laplace transform of equation with zero initial conditions we get,

$$Js^2\,\theta(s) + Bs\,\theta(s) = k_1\,E_c(s) - k_2 s\,\theta(s)$$

$$[Js^2 + Bs + k_2 s]\,\theta(s) = k_1\,E_c(s)$$

Transfer function of the servomotor =

$$\frac{\theta(s)}{E_c(s)} = \frac{k_1}{s(Js+B+k_2)} = \frac{k_1/(B+k_2)}{s\left(\frac{J}{B+k_2}s+1\right)} = \frac{k_m}{s(T_m s+1)}$$

where, $k_m = \frac{k_1}{B+k_2}$ = motor gain constant

and $T_m = \frac{J}{B+k_2}$ = motor time constant

1.9 **What are the properties of linear systems not valid for non-linear systems? Explain each briefly?**

[10 marks : 2011]

Solution:

- Linear systems satisfy properties of superposition and homogeneity. Any system that does not satisfy these properties is non-linear.

Property of superposition:

When the output corresponding to v_{in_1} is v_{out_1} and the output corresponding to v_{in_2} is v_{out_2} then the output corresponding to $av_{in_1} + bv_{in_2}$ is $av_{out_1} + b_{out_2}$.

Property of homogeneity:

It states that for a given input x in the domain of the function f and for any real number k

$$f(kx) = kf(x)$$

- Linear systems have one equilibrium point at the origin. Non-linear systems may have many equilibrium points.

1.10 Obtain the transfer function on the mechanical system shown in Fig. (a) and show how that it is analogous to the system shown in Fig. (b) below?

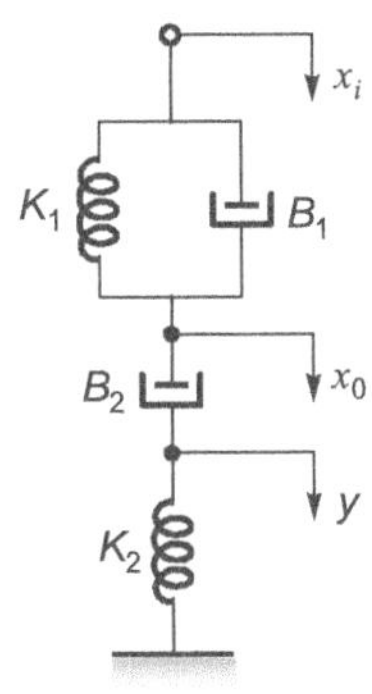

Fig. (a)

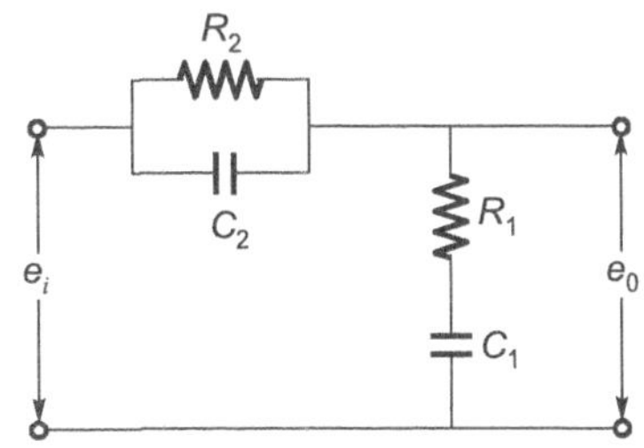

Fig. (b)

[10 marks : 2016]

Solution:

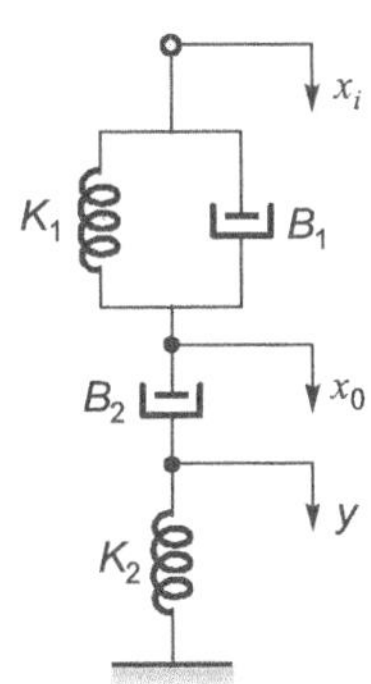

Fig. (a)

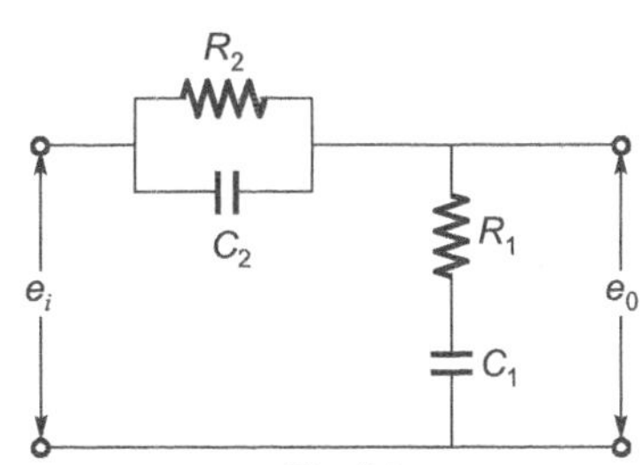

Fig. (b)

Transfer function to mechanical system nodal diagram,

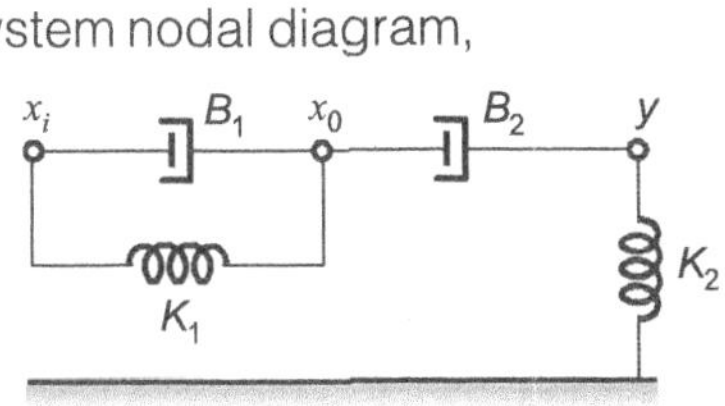

At node y:

$$0 = K_2 y + B_2 \frac{d}{dt}(y - x_0) \qquad ...(i)$$

At node X_0:

$$0 = B_1 \frac{d}{dt}(x_0 - x_i) + K_1(x_0 - x_i) + B_2 \frac{d}{dt}(x_0 - y) \qquad ...(ii)$$

Applying L.T. to equation (i) and (ii),

$$0 = (K_2 + B_2 s)\, Y(s) - X_0(s)\, B_2\, s.$$

$$Y(s) = \left[\frac{B_2 s}{K_2 + B_2 s}\right] X_0(s) \qquad ...(iii)$$

$$0 = [B_2 s + K_1 + B_1 s]\, X_0(s) - B_2 s\, y(s) - X_i(s)\,[K_1 + B_1 s]$$

Substitute $Y(s)$ in equation (*iii*),

$$0 = [B_2 s + K_1 + B_1 s] X_0(s) - \left[\frac{B_2^2 s^2}{K_2 + B_2 s}\right] X_0(s) - X_i(s)\,[K_1 + B_1 s]$$

$$X_i(s)\,[(K_1 + B_1 s)(K_2 + B_2 s)] = X_0(s)\,[B_1 B_2 s^2 + s(B_1 K_2 + K_1 B_2 + B_2 K_2) + K_1 K_2]$$

$$\frac{X_0(s)}{X_i(s)} = \frac{(K_1 + B_1 s)(K_2 + B_2 s)}{B_1 B_2 s^2 + s(B_1 K_2 + K_1 B_2 + B_2 K_2) + K_1 K_2}$$

$$= \frac{K_1 K_2\left[1 + \frac{B_1}{K_1}s\right]\left[1 + \frac{B_2}{K_2}s\right]}{K_1 K_2\left[\frac{B_1 B_2}{K_1 K_2}s^2 + s\left(\frac{B_1 K_2}{K_1 K_2} + \frac{K_1 B_2}{K_1 K_2} + \frac{B_2 K_2}{K_1 K_2}\right) + 1\right]}$$

In F-V. Analogy

$$B_1 \rightarrow R_1$$

$$\frac{1}{K_1} \rightarrow C_1$$

$$B_2 \rightarrow R_2$$

$$\frac{1}{K_2} \rightarrow C_1$$

$$\therefore \quad \frac{X_0(s)}{X_i(s)} = \frac{(1 + R_1 C_1 s)\,(1 + R_2 C_2 s)}{R_1 C_1 R_2 C_2 s^2 + s(R_1 C_1 + R_2 C_2 + R_2 C_1) + 1}$$

This is nothing but the transfer function of given network.

$$\frac{E_0(s)}{E_i(s)} = \frac{(1 + R_1 C_1 s)(1 + R_2 C_2 s)}{R_1 C_1 R_2 C_2 s^2 + s(R_1 C_1 + R_2 C_2 + R_2 C_1) + 1}$$

1.11 **Given the system shown below, find J and D to yield 20% overshoot and a settling time of 2 seconds for a step input of torque $T(t)$.**

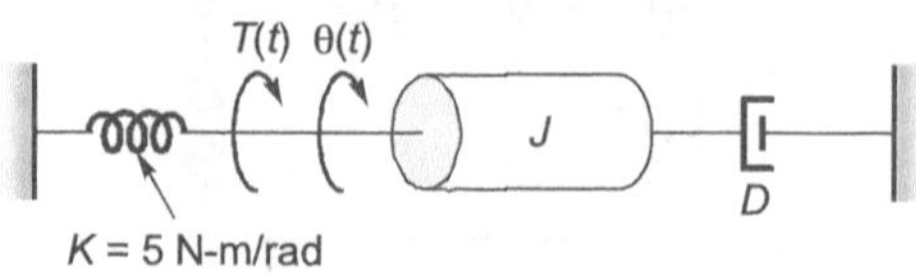

[10 marks : 2016]

Solution:

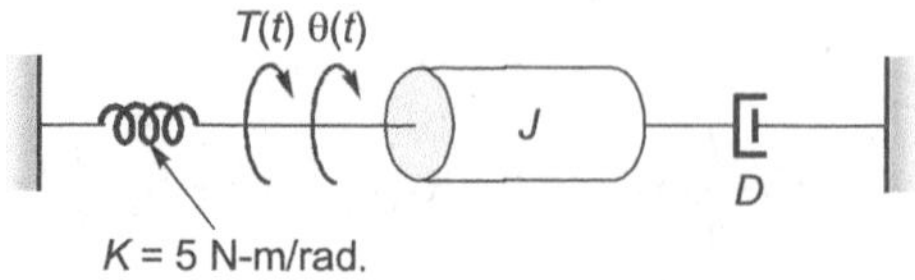

$$\%\text{ overshoot} = 20\% = M_P$$

Settling time, $$T_s = \frac{4}{\xi\omega_n} = 2 \text{ sec}$$

$\therefore$ $$M_p = e^{\frac{-\pi\xi}{\sqrt{1-\xi^2}}} = 0.2$$

$$\frac{\pi\xi}{\sqrt{1-\xi^2}} = 1.609;$$

$$\frac{\xi}{\sqrt{1-\xi^2}} = 0.5123$$

$$1-\xi^2 = 3.81\,\xi^2;$$

$$1 = 4.81\,\xi^2$$

$$\xi = \frac{1}{\sqrt{4.81}};$$

$$\xi = 0.456$$

and $$\frac{4}{\xi\omega_n} = 2;$$

$$\omega_n = \frac{4}{2 \times 0.456} = 4.3863 \text{ rad/sec}$$

From given system, torque balance equation is;

$$T(t) = \frac{Jd^2\theta(t)}{dt^2} + \frac{Dd\theta}{dt} + K.\theta$$

taking Laplace transform and simplifying it; we get,

$$\frac{\theta(s)}{T(s)} = \frac{1}{(Js^2 + Ds + K)}$$

Comparing characteristic equation with standard second order equation we get:

$$\omega_n^2 = \frac{K}{J};$$

$\Rightarrow$ $$\frac{K}{J} = (4.386)^2$$

$$J = \frac{K}{(4.386)^2} = \frac{5}{19.237} = 0.26$$

and $$\frac{D}{J} = 2\xi\omega_n$$

$\Rightarrow$ $$D = 2 \times \xi\omega_n \times J$$

$$D = 1.04$$

1.12 Determine the mechanical time constant of rotor of an electrical machine in terms of its moment of inertia J kg-m^2 and windage cum friction coefficient f N-m/rad/s. Also explain the method to determine mechanical time constant experimentally in laboratory.

[12 marks : 2018]

Solution:

Consider a field controlled separately excited DC motor,

Constant armature in field into the motor,

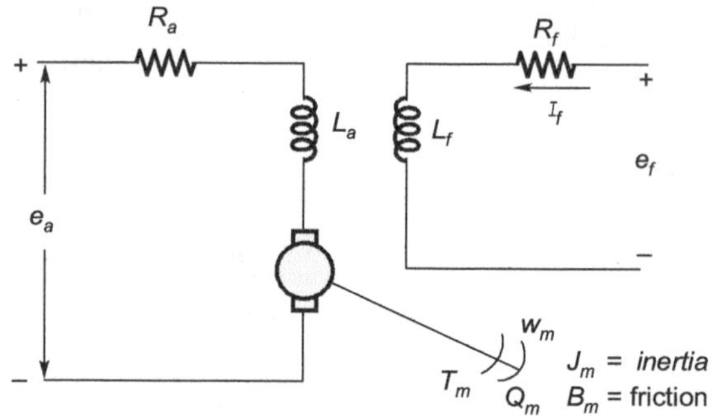

$$\phi_f \propto I_f$$
$$\phi_f = k_f I_f$$
$$T_m \propto \phi_f I_a$$
$$T_m = K\phi_f I_a$$
$$T_m = K k_f I_f I_a$$
$$T_m = k_m k_f I_f$$

where, $k_m = KI_a$ = constant

$$e_f = L_f \frac{di_f}{dt} + R_f I_f$$

$$T_m = J_m \frac{d^2\theta_m}{dt^2} + B_m \frac{d\theta_m}{dt}$$

$$T_m(s) = J_m s^2\theta_m(s) + B_m s\,\theta_m(s)$$
$$T_m(s) = (J_m s^2 + B_m s)\theta_m(s)$$
$$E_f(s) = (sL_f + R_f)\, I_f(s)$$
$$= (sL_f + R_f)\frac{T_m(s)}{k_f k_m}$$

$$E_f(s) = \frac{(sL_f + R_f)(J_m s^2 + B_m s)\,\theta_m(s)}{k_f k_m}$$

$$\frac{\theta_m(s)}{E_f(s)} = \frac{k_m k_f}{s(sL_f + R_f)(J_m s + B_m)} = \frac{k_m k_f}{B_m R_f s\left(1 + \frac{J_m}{B_m}s\right)\left(1 + \frac{sL_f}{R_f}\right)}$$

$$\frac{\theta_m(s)}{E_f(s)} = \frac{k_m k_f}{sB_m R_f(1+\tau_m s)(1+\tau_f s)}$$

τ_m = motor time constant = J_m/B_m

τ_f = field time constant = L_f/R_f

1.13 Consider a mechanical vibratory system as shown in Figure (a) below. Two kilograms of force is applied to the system in the form of step input resulting in the oscillation of mass. Determine the system parameters *m*, *b* and *k* of the mechanical vibratory system if the step response curve obtained is as shown in Figure (b). Displacement 'x' may be measured from the equilibrium position.

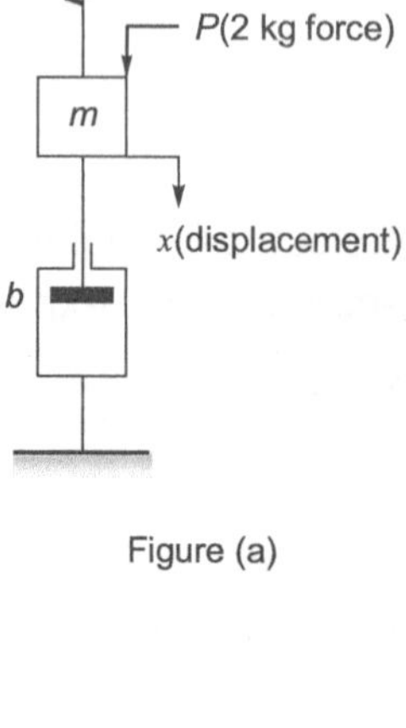

Figure (a)

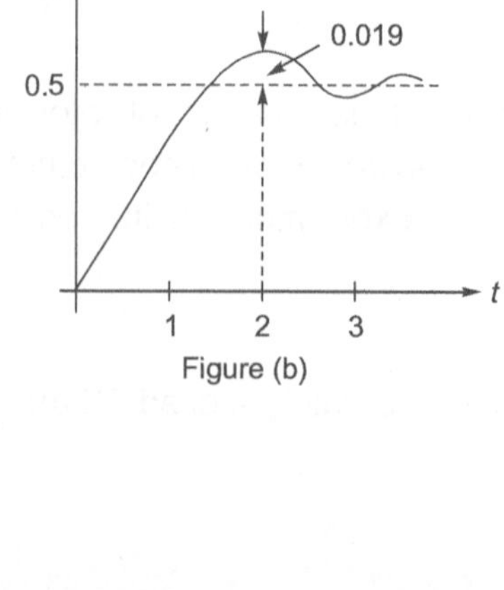

Figure (b)

[20 marks : 2022]

Solution:

We know,
$$F = m\frac{d^2x}{dt^2} + b\frac{dx}{dt} + Kx$$

Take Laplace transform of above

$$F(s) = ms^2X(s) + bsX(s) + KX(s)$$

$$\frac{X(s)}{F(s)} = \frac{1}{ms^2 + bs + K}$$

$$= \frac{1/m}{s^2 + \frac{b}{m}s + \frac{K}{m}} \quad \text{...(i)}$$

From the graph,

$$\% M_P = \frac{0.019}{0.05} \times 100$$

$$= 38\%$$

$$e^{-\frac{\pi\xi}{\sqrt{1-\xi^2}}} = 0.38$$

$$\pi\xi = \ln\left(\frac{1}{0.38}\right)\left(\sqrt{1-\xi^2}\right)$$

Squaring both sides,

$$(\pi\xi)^2 = \left(\ln\frac{1}{0.38}\right)^2 (1-\xi^2)$$

$$(\pi\xi)^2 = 0.9362(1-\xi^2)$$

$$\xi^2 = \frac{0.9362}{\pi^2 + 0.9362}$$

$$\xi = 0.2943$$

From graph peak time (t_p) = 2 sec

$$t_p = \frac{\pi}{\omega_d} = 2$$

$$\omega_d = \frac{\pi}{2} = 1.57 \text{ rad/sec}$$

$$\omega_d = \omega_n\sqrt{1-\xi^2}$$

$$\omega_n = \frac{1.57}{\sqrt{1-(0.2943)^2}} = 1.642 \text{ rad/sec}$$

From eqn. (i) characteristic equation is

$$s^2 + \frac{b}{m}s + \frac{K}{m} = 0 \quad \text{...(ii)}$$

Standard second-order characteistic equation is given by

$$s^2 + 2\xi\omega_n + \omega_n^2 = 0 \qquad ...(iii)$$

Steady state value = 0.05

From eqn. (i)

$$\frac{X(s)}{F(s)} = \frac{1/m}{s^2 + \frac{b}{m}s + \frac{K}{m}}$$

$$X(s) = \frac{1/m}{s^2 + \frac{b}{m}s + \frac{K}{m}}F(s)$$

Here, $F(t) = 2u(t)$

$$F(s) = \frac{2}{s}$$

$$X(s) = \frac{1/m}{s^2 + \frac{b}{m}s + \frac{K}{m}} \cdot \frac{2}{s}$$

Steady state value, $X(s) = \lim_{s \to 0} sX(s)$

$$= \lim_{s \to 0} s\frac{1/m}{s^2 + \frac{b}{m}s + \frac{K}{m}} \cdot \frac{2}{s}$$

$$= \frac{1/m}{K/m} = \frac{2}{K} = 0.05$$

$$K = \frac{1}{0.05} = 40$$

Now, compare eqn. (ii) and eqn. (iii)

$$\frac{b}{m} = 2\xi\omega_n$$

$$\frac{K}{m} = \omega_n^2$$

$\Rightarrow$ $$\frac{40}{m} = (1.642)^2$$

$\Rightarrow$ $$m = 14.83$$

$$\frac{b}{14.83} = 2 \times 0.2943 \times 1.642$$

$$b = 14.32$$

Hence,

$$m = 14.83 \text{ kg}$$

$$b = 14.32$$

$$K = 40$$

2. Block Diagram, Signal Flow Graph and Feedback Characteristics of Control Systems

2.1 The block diagram of a control system is shown in figure.

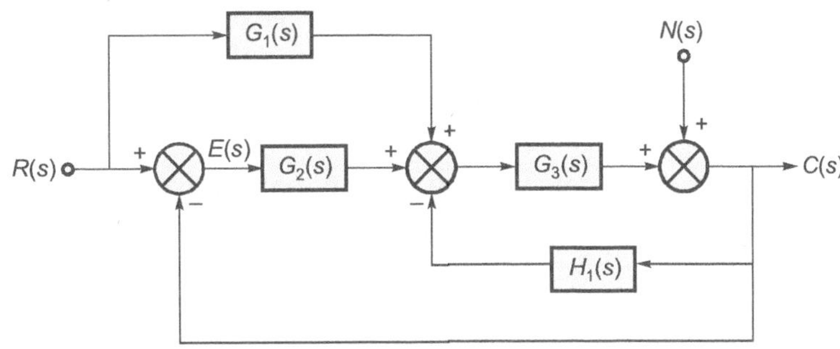

(i) Draw the Signal Flow Graph of the control system shown in figure.

(ii) Obtain the transfer functions $\left.\frac{C(s)}{R(s)}\right|_{N=0}$ and $\left.\frac{C(s)}{N(s)}\right|_{R=0}$

[14 marks : 2001]

Solution:

(i) Signal flow diagram,

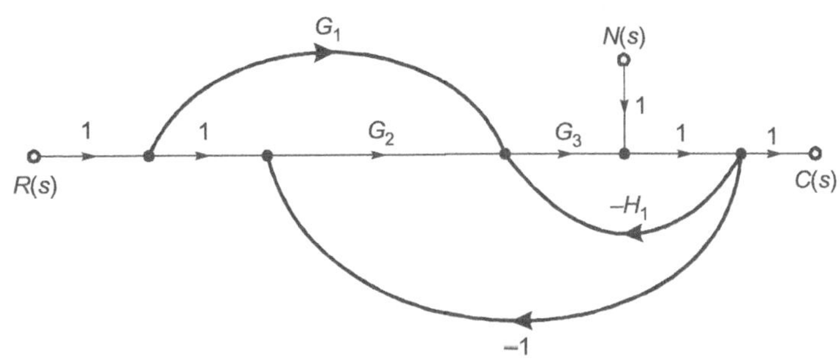

(ii) To find $\frac{C(s)}{R(s)}$ when $N(s) = 0$

The two forward paths are

$$P_1 = G_1G_3$$
$$P_2 = G_2G_3$$

The closed loop touches both the forward paths, therefore, path factors are

$$\Delta_1 = 1 \text{ and } \Delta_2 = 1$$

The individual loops are, $L_1 = -G_3H_1$ and $L_2 = -G_2G_3$

The graph determinant is, $\Delta = 1 - \{L_1 + L_2\} = 1 - \{-G_3H_1) + (-G_2\,G_3)\}$

$$= 1 + G_3H_1 + G_2G_3$$

Applying Mason's gain formula the closed loop transfer,

$$\left.\frac{C(s)}{R(s)}\right|_{N(s)=0} = \frac{\Sigma P_k\,\Delta_k}{\Delta} = \frac{P_1\Delta_1 + P_2\,\Delta_2}{\Delta} = \frac{G_1\,G_3 + G_2\,G_3}{1 + G_3\,H_1 + G_2\,G_3}$$

To find $\left.\frac{C(s)}{R(s)}\right|$ when $R(s) = 0$

There is single forward path having gain,

$$P_1 = 1$$

The path factor, $\Delta_1 = 1$

The individual loops are

$$L_1 = -G_3H_1 \text{ and } L_2 = -G_2\,G_3$$

The graph determinant,

$$\Delta = 1-\{L_1 + L_2\} = 1 + G_3H_1 + G_2G_3$$

$$\left.\frac{C(s)}{R(s)}\right|_{R(s)=0} = \frac{P_1\Delta_1}{\Delta} = \frac{1}{1+G_3\,H_1+G_2\,G_3}$$

2.2 In a feedback system shown in the below figure $G_P(s)$ denotes the controlled process and $G_C(s)$ and $H(s)$ are the controller transfer functions. There are two inputs namely $R(s)$ and $N(s)$.

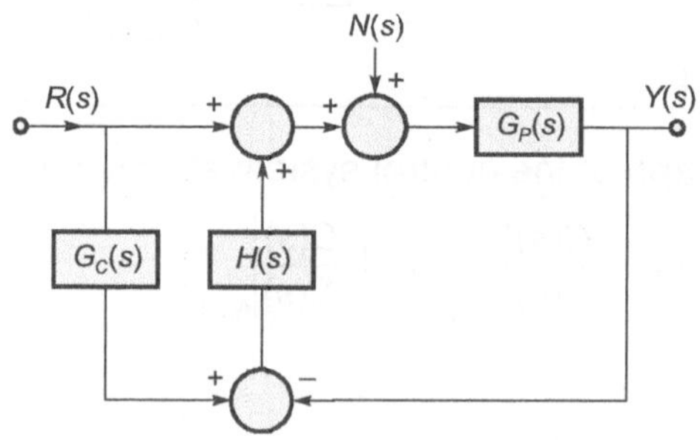

Derive the following transfer functions:

(i) $\left.\frac{Y(s)}{R(s)}\right|_{N(s)=0}$ (ii) $\left.\frac{Y(s)}{N(s)}\right|_{R(s)=0}$

and also find the output response $y(t)$ when $n(t) = 0$ and $r(t)$ = unit step. Assume $G_P(s) = G_C(s) = \frac{100}{(1+s)}$.

[10 marks : 2006]

Solution:

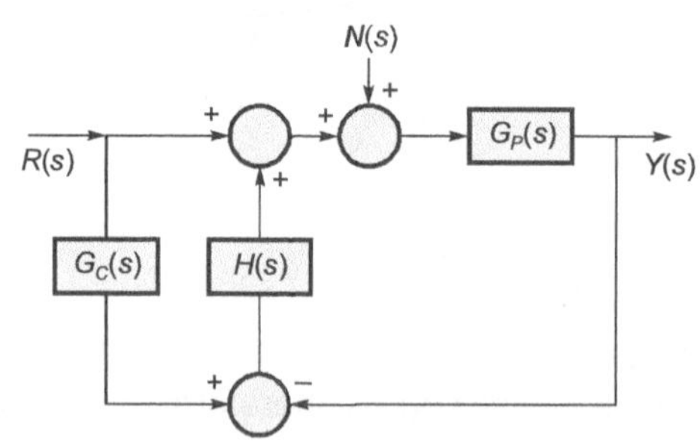

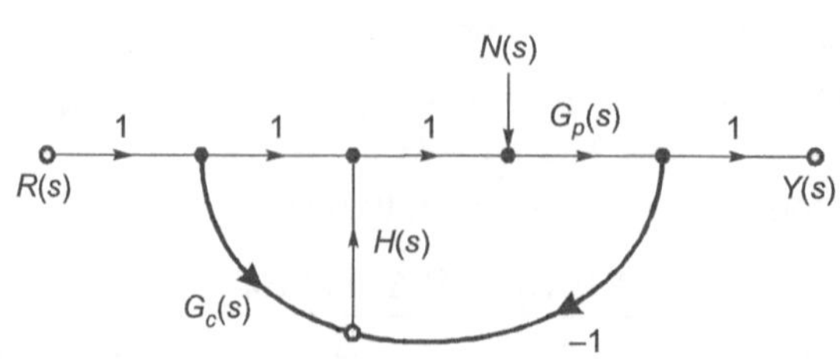

For finding $\frac{Y(s)}{R(s)}$ when $N(s) = 0$

Number of forward path and its gain = $G_p(s)\ G_c(s)\ H(s)$ and $G_p(s)$

Number of loop and its gain = $-G_p(s)\ H(s)$

$\therefore$ By mason's gain formula,

$$\left.\frac{Y(s)}{R(s)}\right|_{N(s)=0} = \frac{G_p(s)+G_p(s)\,G_c(s)\,H(s)}{1+G_p(s)\,H(s)} = \frac{G_p(s)(1+G_c(s)H(s))}{1+G_p(s)H(s)}$$

For finding $\frac{Y(s)}{N(s)}$ when $R(s) = 0$

Number of forward path and its gain = $P_1^1 = G_p(s)$

$$\text{loop gain} = -G_p(s)\,H(s)$$

$$\left.\frac{Y(s)}{N(s)}\right|_{R(s)=0} = \frac{G_p(s)}{1+G_p(s)\,H(s)}$$

For finding the output response $Y(t)$, for $r(t)$ = unit step and $n(t) = 0$, and $H(s) = 1$

$$\therefore \quad \frac{Y(s)}{R(s)} = \frac{G_p(s)(1+G_c(s)H(s))}{1+G_p(s)H(s)} = \frac{\left(\frac{100}{s+1}\right)\left(1+\frac{100}{s+1}\right)}{\left(1+\frac{100}{s+1}\right)}$$

$$\therefore \quad Y(s) = \frac{1}{s}.\frac{100}{s+1} = 100\left[\frac{1}{s}-\frac{1}{s+1}\right]$$

$$\therefore \quad y(t) = 100[1-e^{-t}]\,u(t)$$

2.3 **Draw the signal flow graph of the shown system and verify the results by using Mason's gain formula.**

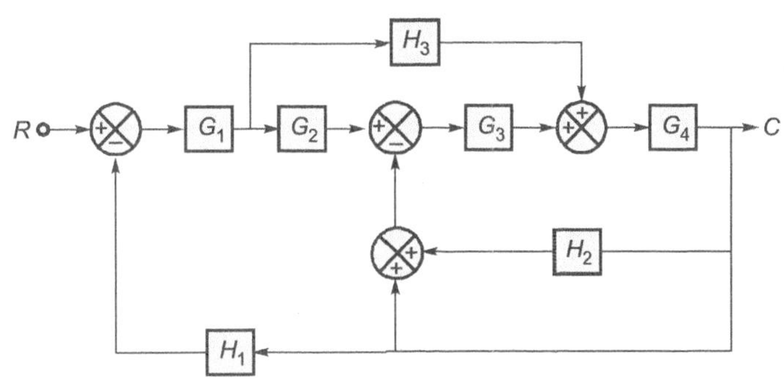

[10 marks : 2007]

Solution:

Signal flow graph of the block diagram.

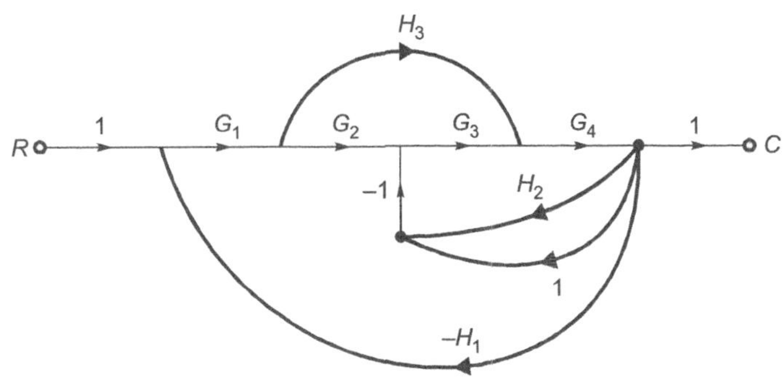

Number of forward path and its gain

$$P_1 = G_1 G_2 G_3 G_4 \qquad P_2 = G_1 H_3 G_4 \qquad \text{and} \quad \Delta_1 = \Delta_2 = 1$$

Both forward path touches all the loops.

Individual loop gain $\rightarrow -G_3 G_4, -G_3 G_4 H_2, -G_1 G_2 G_3 G_4 H_1 - G_1 G_4 H_3 H_1$

There is no non-touching loop

$$\Delta = 1 - \{-G_3 G_4 - G_3 G_4 H_2 - G_1 G_2 G_3 G_4 H_1 - G_1 G_4 H_3 H_1\}$$

By mason's gain formula,

$$\therefore \qquad \text{overall}\left(\frac{T}{F}\right) = \left(\frac{C}{R}\right) = \frac{G_1 G_2 G_3 G_4 + G_1 H_3 G_4}{1 + G_3 G_4 + G_3 G_4 H_2 + G_1 G_2 G_3 G_4 H_1 + G_1 H_3 G_4 H_1}$$

By signal flow graph, we verified the result.

2.4 Determine the overall transfer function C/R of the system shown below figure by block diagram reduction technique.

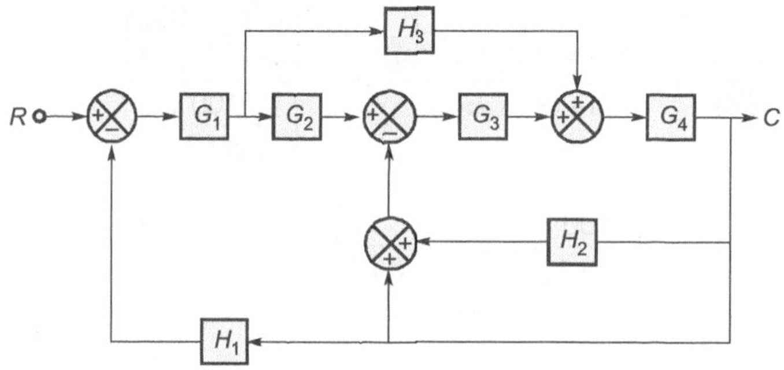

[12 marks : 2007]

Solution:

By taking a block before summing point,

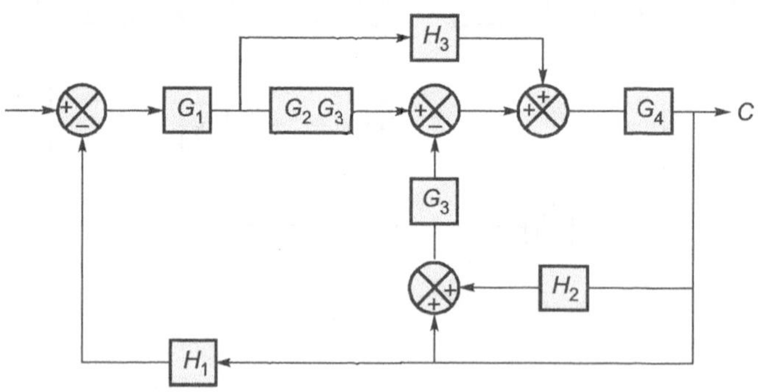

By combining parallel path, and alternating the summing point,

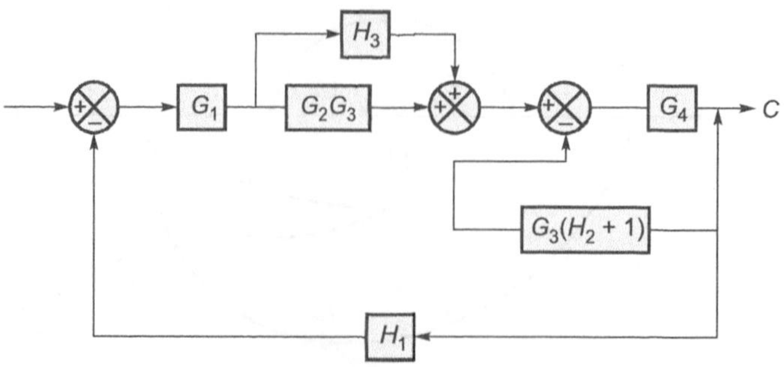

By reducing,

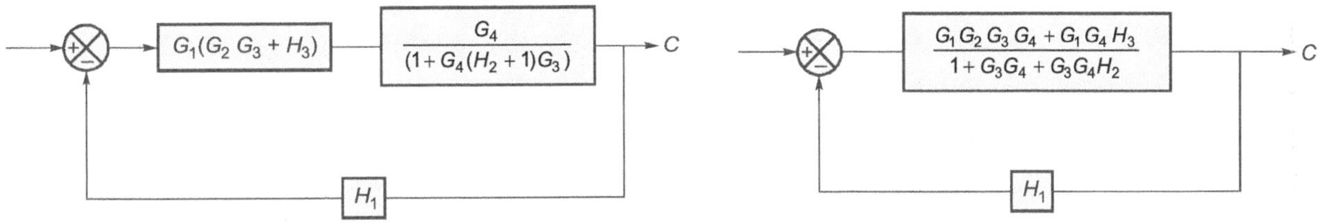

The overall $\left(\frac{T}{F}\right) = \left[\frac{C}{R}\right] = \frac{G_1 G_2 G_3 G_4 + G_1 G_4 H_3}{1+G_3 G_4 + G_3 G_4 H_2 + G_1 G_2 G_3 G_4 H_1 + G_1 G_4 H_1 H_3}$

2.5 **Using Mason's gain formula, calculate the transfer function *C/R* of the signal flow graph shown below in the figure.**

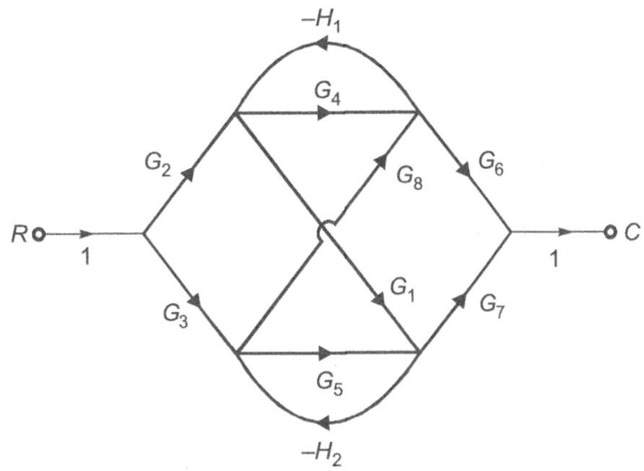

[10 marks : 2008]

Solution:

Number of forward path and its gain

$$P_1 = G_2 G_4 G_6,$$
$$P_2 = G_3 G_5 G_7$$
$$P_3 = G_2 G_1 G_7,$$
$$P_4 = G_3 G_8 G_6$$
$$P_5 = -G_2 G_1 H_2 G_8 G_6,$$
$$P_6 = -G_3 G_8 H_1 G_1 G_7$$

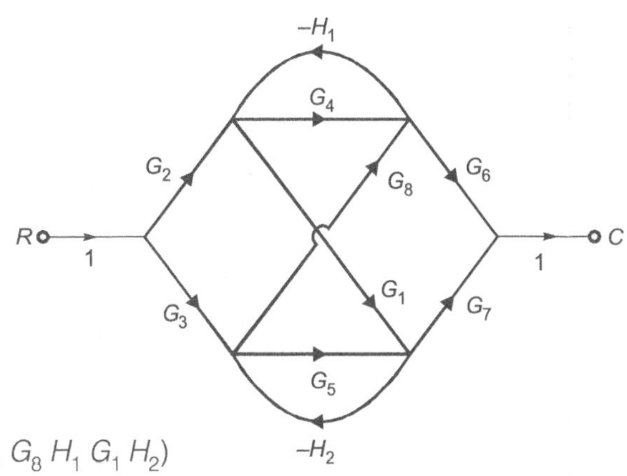

The forward path (P_1) is not touching loop ($-G_5 H_2$) and forward path (P_2) is not touching loop ($G_4 H_1$)

Number of individual loops = ($-G_4 H_1, -G_5 H_2, G_8 H_1 G_1 H_2$)

Gain of non-touching loops = $G_4 G_5 H_1 H_2$

Overall Transfer Function, $\left(\frac{T}{F}\right) = \left(\frac{C}{R}\right)$

$$= \frac{G_2 G_4 G_6 (1+G_5 H_2) + G_3 G_5 G_7(1+G_4 H_1) + G_1 G_2 G_7 + G_3 G_8 G_6 - G_2 G_1 H_2 G_8 G_6 - G_3 G_8 H_1 G_1 G_7}{1+G_4 H_1 + G_5 H_2 + G_4 G_5 H_1 H_2 - G_8 H_1 G_1 H_2}$$

2.6 Obtain C/R from the signal flow graph shown in the below figure using Mason's Gain formula.

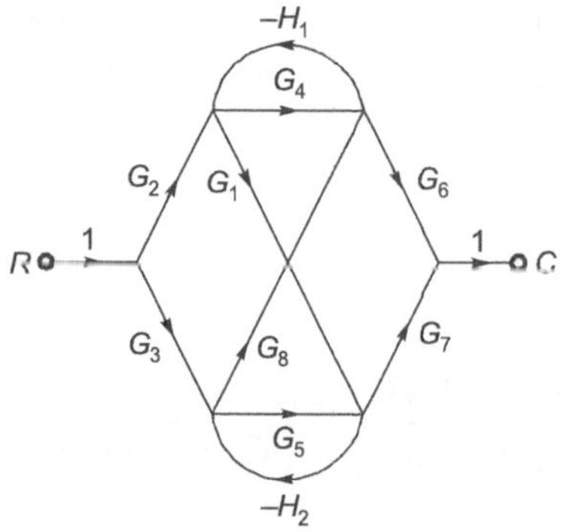

[5 marks : 2012]

Solution:

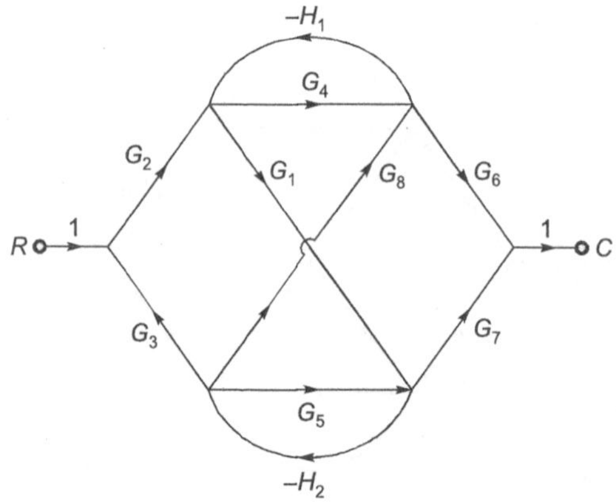

Number of forward path and its gain,

$P_1 = G_2\, G_4\, G_6,$ $\quad P_2 = G_3\, G_5\, G_7$

$P_3 = G_2\, G_1\, G_7,$ $\quad P_4 = G_3\, G_8\, G_6$

$P_5 = -G_2\, G_1\, H_2\, G_8\, G_6,$ $\quad P_6 = -G_3\, G_8\, H_1\, G_1\, G_7$

The forward path (P_1) is not touching loop ($-G_5H_2$) and forward path (P_2) is not touching loop (G_4H_1)

Number of individual loops = ($-G_4\, H_1$, $-G_5\, H_2$, $G_8\, H_1\, G_1\, H_2$)

Gain of non-touching loops = $G_4\, G_5\, H_1\, H_2$

overall Transfer function, $\left(\dfrac{C}{R}\right)$

$$= \frac{G_2\, G_4\, G_6\,(1+G_5\, H_2)+G_3\, G_5\, G_7(1+G_4\, H_1)+G_1\, G_2\, G_7+G_3\, G_8\, G_6-G_2\, G_1\, H_2\, G_8\, G_6-G_3\, G_8\, H_1\, G_1\, G_7}{1+G_4\, H_1+G_5\, H_2+G_4\, G_5\, H_1\, H_2-G_8\, H_1\, G_1\, H_2}$$

2.7 Draw the signal flow graph corresponding to the Block Diagram of the system given below. Evaluate the closed loop transfer function of the system using Mason's gain formula.

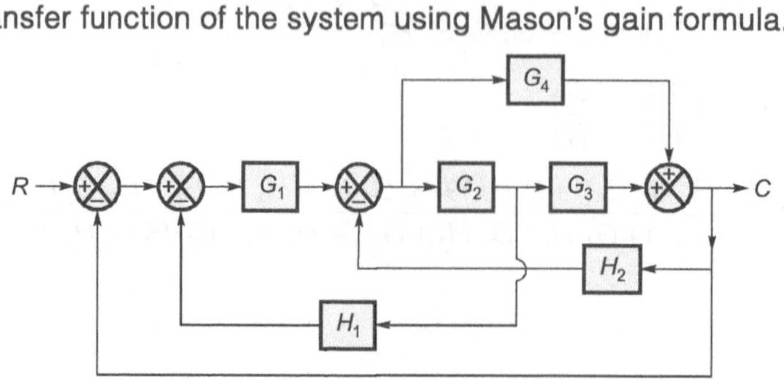

[10 marks : 2013]

Solution:

SFG of given graph:

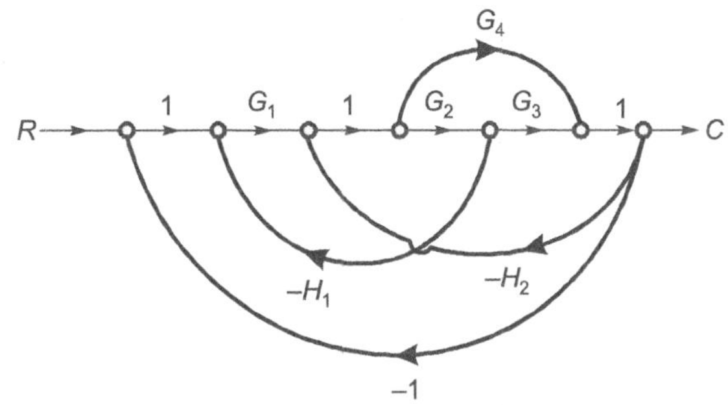

Forward pam, $P_1 = G_1 G_2 G_3$

$P_2 = G_1 G_4$

5 non-touching loops are $= -G_1 G_2 G_3$

$-G_1 G_4$

$-G_2 G_3 H_2$

$-G_1 G_2 H_1$

$-G_4 H_2$

Using Mason's gain formula,

$$\text{T.F.} = \frac{P_1 \Delta_1 + P_2 \Delta_2}{1-(L_1 + L_2 + L_3 + L_4 + L_5) + (2 \text{ non-touching loops}) \cdots}$$

So,

$$\text{T.F.} = \frac{G_1 G_2 G_3 + G_1 G_4}{1 + G_1 G_2 G_3 + G_1 G_4 + G_2 G_3 H_2 + G_1 G_2 H_1 + G_4 H_2}$$

2.8 A negative feedback control system has $G(s) = \dfrac{10}{s(s+1)}$ and $H(s) = 5$. Determine sensitivity of closed loop transfer function with respect to G and H, for $\omega = 1$ rad/sec.

[10 marks : 2013]

Solution:

$$G(s) = \frac{10}{(s)(s+1)}$$

$$\text{C.L.T.F.} = \frac{G(s)}{1 + G(s) H(s)}$$

$$S_{G(s)}^{CLTF} = \frac{G(s)}{F(s)} \frac{\partial F(s)}{\partial G(s)} = \frac{G(s)}{\dfrac{G(s)}{1+G(s)H(s)}} \left(\frac{1 + G(s) H(s) - G(s) H(s)}{(1 + G(s) H(s))^2} \right)$$

$$= \frac{1}{1 + G(s) H(s)} = \frac{1}{1 + \dfrac{50}{(s)(s+1)}}$$

$$\left| S_{G(s)}^{CLTF} \right|_{\omega = 1 \text{rad/sec}} = \frac{1}{\left| 1 + \dfrac{50}{(j)(1+j)} \right|} = 2.88\%$$

$$S_{H(s)}^{CLTF} = \frac{H(s)}{G(s)} \left(\frac{-(G(s))^2}{[1 + G(s) H(s)]} \right) = \frac{-G(s) H(s)}{1 + G(s) H(s)} = \frac{\dfrac{-50}{(s)(s+1)}}{1 + \dfrac{50}{(s)(s+1)}} = \frac{-50}{s(s+1) + 50}$$

$$\left| S_{H(s)}^{CLTF} \right|_{\omega = 1 \text{rad/sec}} = \frac{-50}{\sqrt{(50 - \omega^2)^2 + \omega^2}} = \frac{50}{\sqrt{(50-1)^2 + 1^2}} = 102.2\%$$

2.9 Using Mason's Gain formula, find C/R of the SFG shown in the below figure.

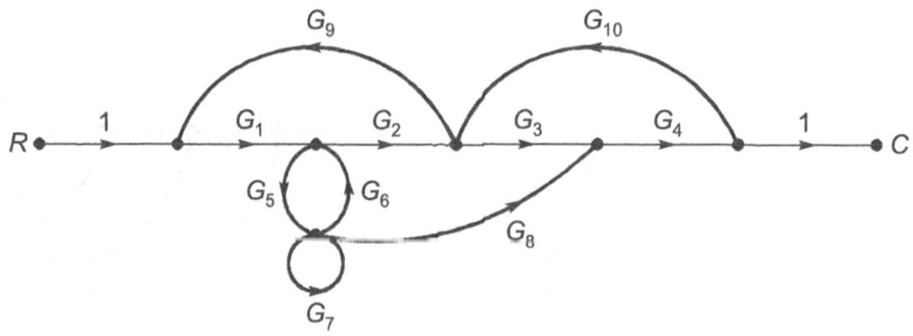

[10 marks : 2014]

Solution:

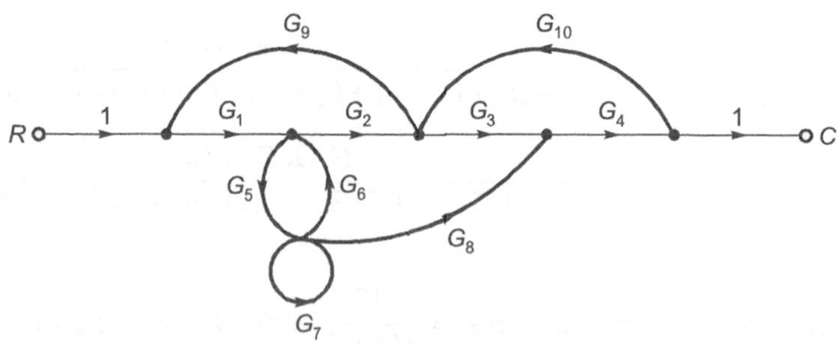

$$\frac{C}{R} = \frac{M_1\Delta_1 + M_2\Delta_2}{\Delta}$$

$$= \frac{G_1G_2G_3G_4(1-G_7) + G_1G_5G_8G_4(1-0)}{1-G_1G_2G_9 + G_2G_4G_{10} + G_5G_6 + G_5G_8G_4G_{10}G_9G_1 + G_7) + (G_1G_2G_9G_7 + G_3G_4G_{10}G_7)}$$

$$= \frac{G_1G_2G_3G_4 - G_1G_2G_3G_4G_7 + G_1G_5G_8G_4}{1-(G_1G_2G_3 + G_3G_4G_{10} + G_5G_6 + G_5G_8G_4G_{10}G_9G_1 + G_7) + (G_1G_2G_9G_7 + G_3G_4G_{10}G_7)}$$

2.10 Determine the output C for the below system using block reduction technique and signal flow graph technique.

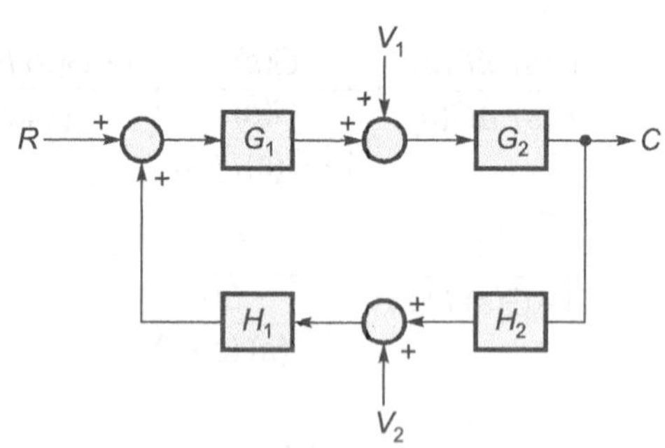

[8 marks : 2014]

Solution:

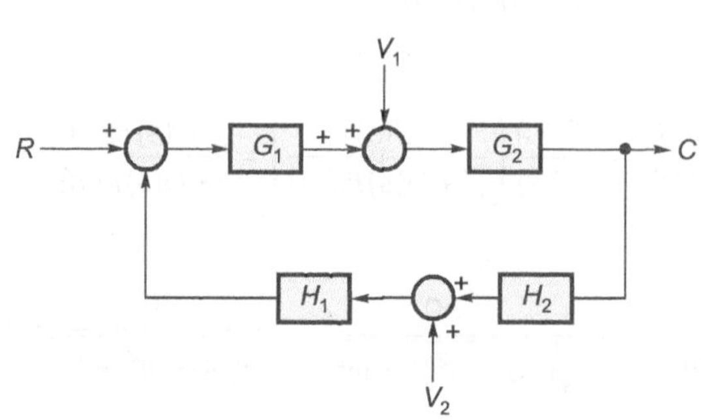

Block reduction technique:

Making V_1 and $V_2 = 0$

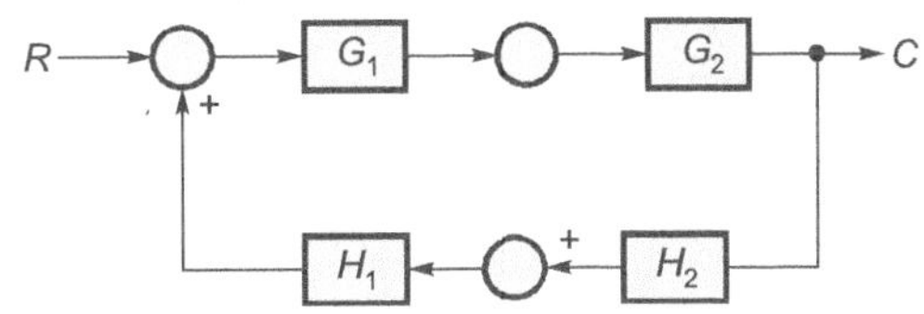

Here, G_1 and G_2 are the blocks in series and H_1 and H_2 are blocks in series. Replace them by one block.

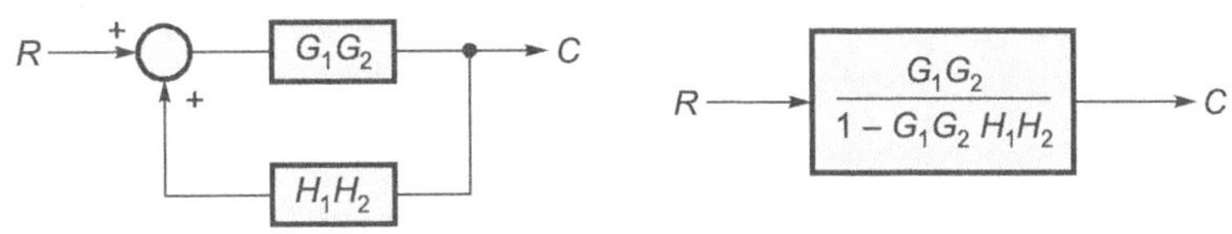

$$\frac{C}{R}\bigg|_{V_1=V_2=0} = \left(\frac{G_1G_2}{1-G_1G_2H_1H_2}\right)$$

Making V_2 and $R = 0$

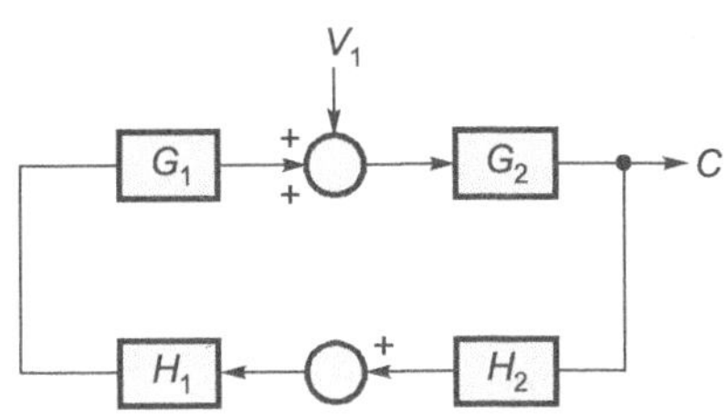

Here, G_1, H_1, H_2 are in series,

$$\left(\frac{C}{V_2}\right)\bigg|_{V_2=C=0} = \frac{G_2}{(1-G_1G_2H_1H_2)}$$

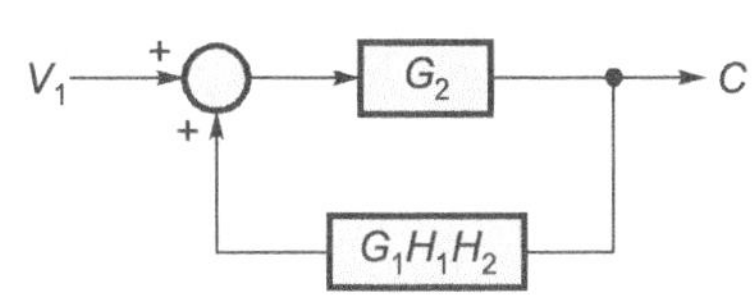

Making V_1 and $R = 0$

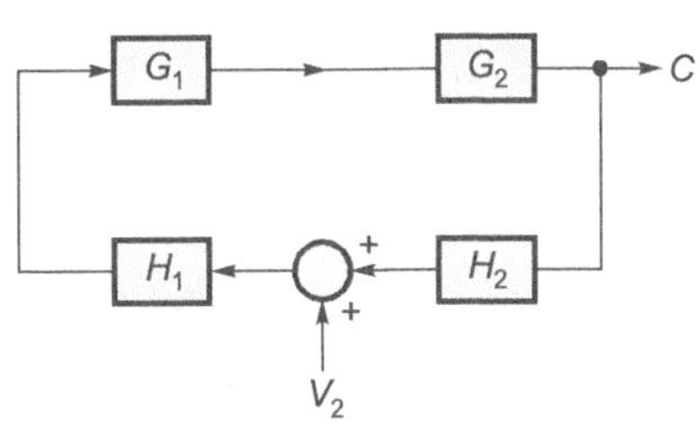

Here, G_1, G_2, H_1 are in series

$$\left(\frac{C}{V_2}\right)\bigg|_{V_1=0,R=0} = \left[\frac{G_1G_2H_1}{1-G_1G_2H_1H_2}\right]$$

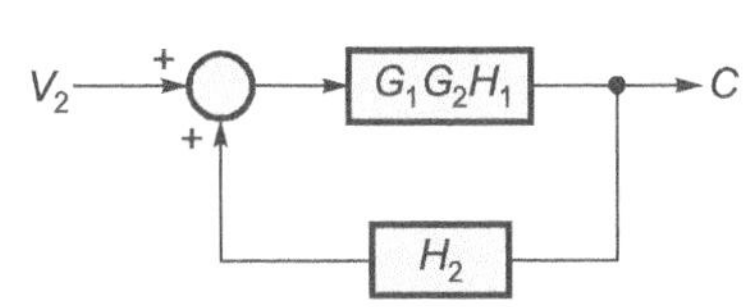

$$C = \left(\frac{C}{R}\right)\bigg|_{V_1=V_2=0} + \left(\frac{C}{V_1}\right)\bigg|_{V_2=R=0} + \left(\frac{C}{V_2}\right)\bigg|_{V_1=R=0}$$

$$\boxed{C = \left(\frac{G_1G_2}{1-G_1G_2H_1H_2}\right) + \left(\frac{G_2}{1-G_1G_2H_1H_2}\right) + \left(\frac{G_1G_2H_1}{1-G_1G_2H_1H_2}\right)}$$

Signal flow graph:

Mason's gain formula,

$$T/F = \frac{P_K \Delta_K}{\Delta}$$

$P_K = K^{th}$ forward path

$\Delta_K =$ Non-touching loops of Kth forward path

$\Delta = 1$ (individual loops) + (Two non-touching loops)

(Three non-touching loops)

Converting the given block diagram into signal flow graph

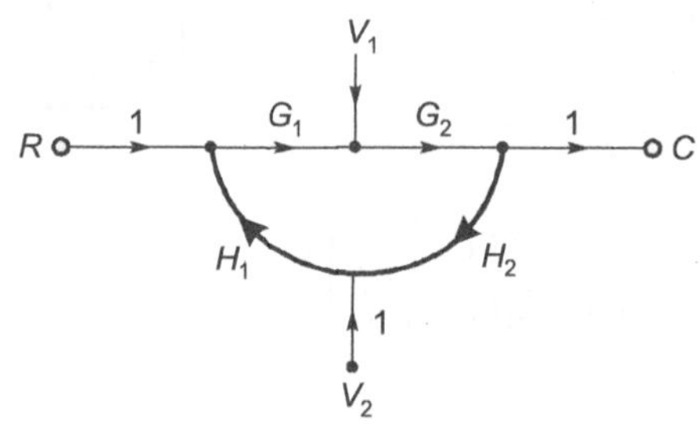

Making V_1 and $V_2 = 0$

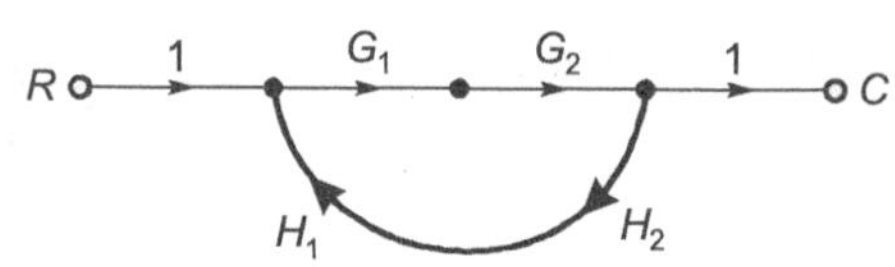

$$\text{Forward path} = G_1 G_2$$

$$\text{Loop} = G_1 G_2 H_1 H_2$$

By using Mason's gain formulae:

$$\left.\frac{C}{R}\right|_{V_1 = V_2 = 0} = \frac{G_1 G_2}{1 - G_1 G_2 H_1 H_2}$$

Making V_2 and $R = 0$

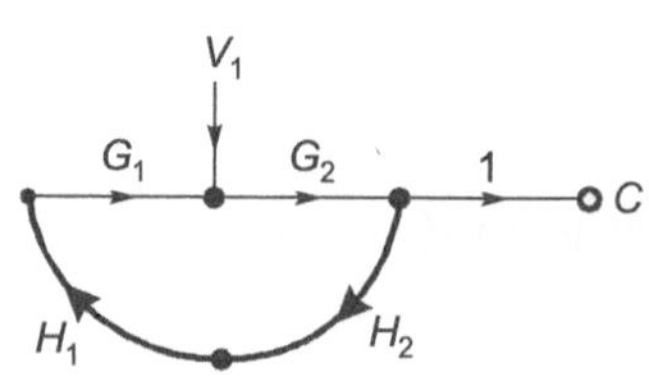

$$\text{Forward path} = G_2$$

$$\text{Loop} = G_1 G_2 H_1 H_2$$

$$\left.\frac{C}{V_1}\right|_{V_2 = R = 0} = \frac{G_2}{1 - G_1 G_2 H_1 H_2}$$

Making V_1 and $R = 0$

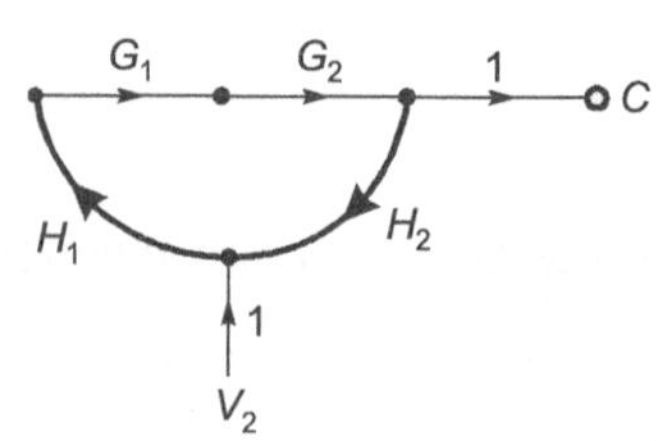

$$\left.\frac{C}{V_2}\right|_{V_1 = R = 0} = \left(\frac{G_1 G_2 H_1}{1 - G_1 G_2 H_1 H_2}\right)$$

$$C = \left(\frac{C}{R}\right)_{V_1 = V_2 = 0} + \left(\frac{C}{V_1}\right)_{V_2 = R = 0} + \left(\frac{C}{V_2}\right)_{V_1 = R = 0}$$

$$= \frac{G_1 G_2}{1 - G_1 G_2 H_1 H_2} + \frac{G_2}{1 - G_1 G_2 H_1 H_2} + \frac{G_1 G_2 H_1}{1 - G_1 G_2 H_1 H_2}$$

2.11 For the feedback control system shown below.

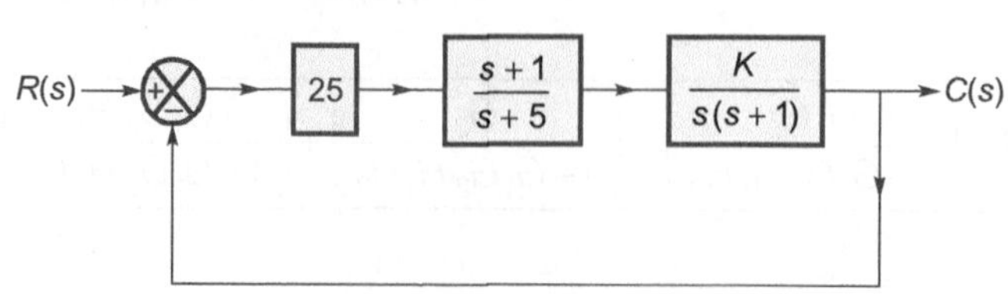

Determine the sensitivity of closed loop transfer function with variation in parameter 'K' at ω = 1.5 rad/sec. Assume, the normal process parameter value of K is 1.

[10 marks : 2015]

Solution:

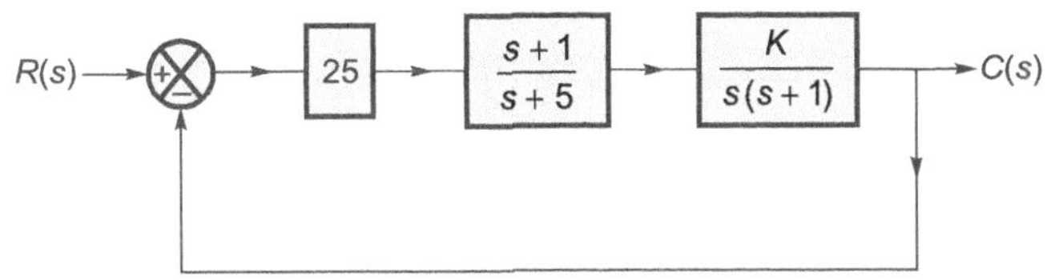

Closed loop transfer function,

$$\frac{C(s)}{R(s)} = \frac{25K}{s(s+5)+25K} = \frac{25K}{s^2+5s+25K}$$

Sensitivity of closed loop transfer function with respect to parameter 'K',

$$S_K^T = \frac{\partial T/T}{\partial K/K} = \left(\frac{\partial T}{\partial K}\right)\times\frac{K}{T}$$

$$T = \frac{25K}{s^2+5s+25K}$$

$$\frac{\partial T}{\partial K} = \frac{(s^2+5s+25K)(25)-25K(25)}{(s^2+5s+25K)^2}$$

$$\frac{\partial T}{\partial K} = \frac{25s(s+5)}{(s^2+5s+25K)^2}$$

$$S_K^T = \frac{25s(s+5)}{(s^2+5s+25K)^2}\times\frac{K}{\dfrac{25K}{(s^2+5s+25K)}} = \frac{s(s+5)}{(s^2+5s+25K)}$$

For K = 1, and ω = 1.5 rad/sec;

$$\left|S_K^T\right|_{S=j\omega \text{ and } K=1} = \frac{\omega\sqrt{\omega^2+25}}{\sqrt{(25-\omega^2)^2+(5\omega)^2}}$$

$$\left|S_K^T\right| = \frac{1.5\sqrt{(1.5)^2+25}}{\sqrt{(25-2.25)^2+(7.5)^2}} = \frac{7.83}{23.954} = 0.327$$

2.12 Determine the output C due to U_1, U_2 and R for block diagram shown below.

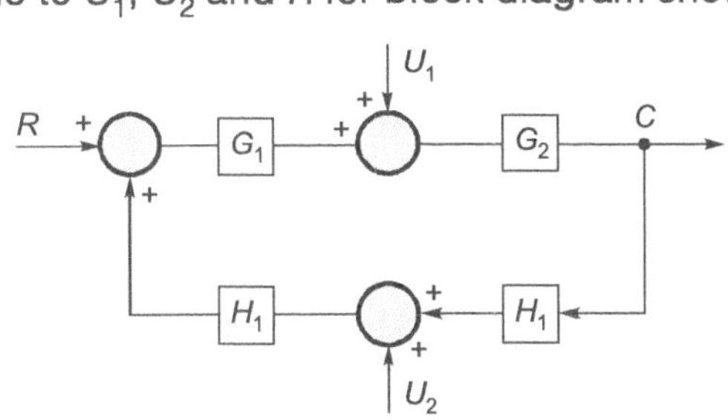

[10 marks : 2016]

Solution:

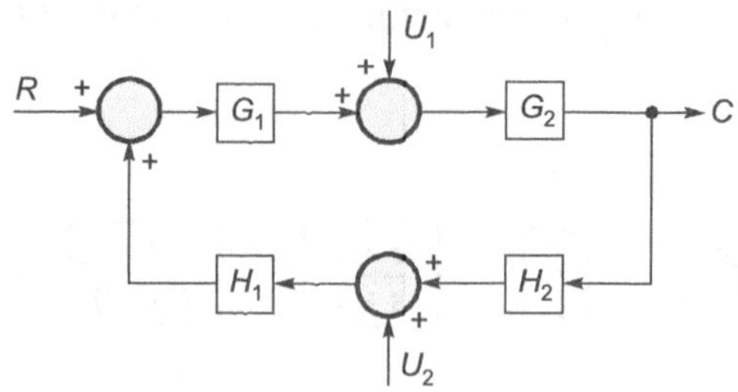

Output, $$C(s) = T_1(s) \,.\, R(s) + T_2(s) \,.\, U_1(s) + T_3(s).\, U_2(s)$$

$\therefore$ $$T_1(s) = \left.\frac{C(s)}{R(s)}\right|_{U_1 \text{ and } U_2 = 0}$$

and $$T_2(s) = \left.\frac{C(s)}{U_1(s)}\right|_{R \text{ and } U_2 = 0} \quad \text{and } T_3(s) = \left.\frac{C(s)}{U_2(s)}\right|_{R \text{ and } U_1 = 0}$$

(i) U_1 and U_2 are zero:

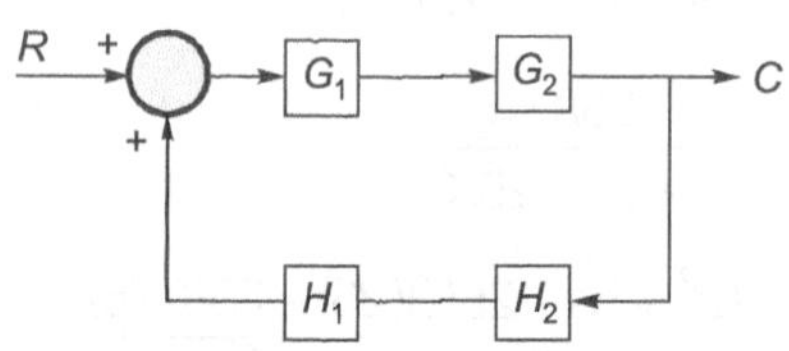

$$T_1(s) = \frac{C}{R}$$

$$T_1(s) = \frac{G_1 G_2}{1 - G_1 G_2 H_1 H_2}$$

(ii) R and U_2 are zero:

$$T_2(s) = \frac{C}{U_1}$$

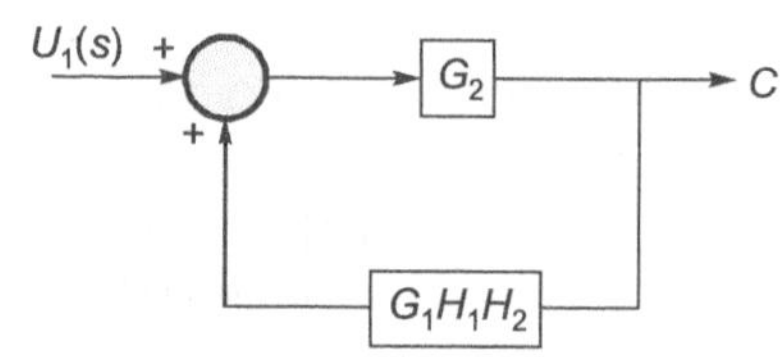

$$T_2(s) = \frac{G_2}{1 - G_1 G_2 H_1 H_2}$$

(iii) R and U_1 are zero:

$$T_3(s) = \frac{C}{U_2}$$

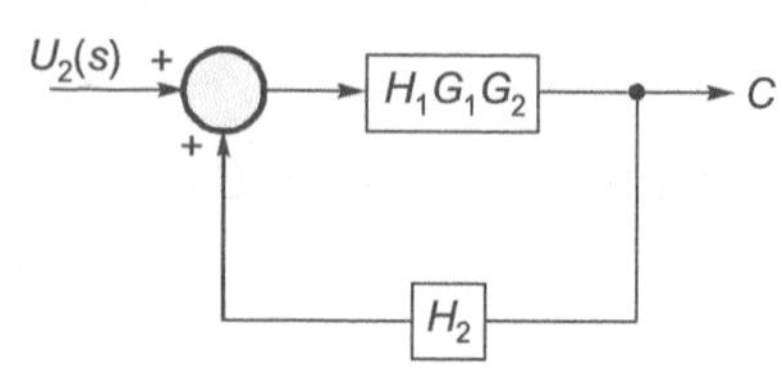

$$T_3(s) = \frac{H_1 G_1 G_2}{1 - H_1 H_2 G_1 G_2}$$

Total output, $$C(s) = \frac{1}{(1 - G_1 G_2 H_1 H_2)}[G_1 G_2 \cdot R(s) + G_2 \cdot U_1(s) + H_1 G_1 G_2 \cdot U_2(s)]$$

2.13 Evaluate the transfer function of the block diagram shown below using block diagram reduction techniques.

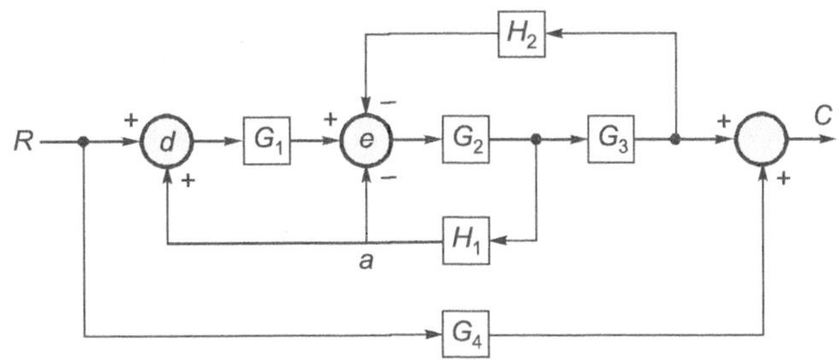

[10 marks : 2016]

Solution:

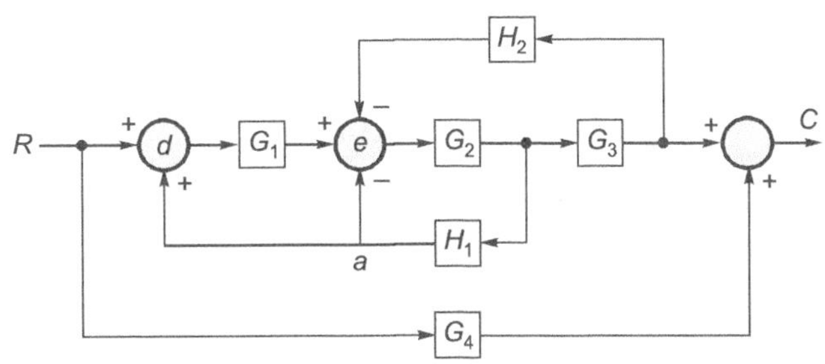

⇒ Shifting the take off point to the right of G_3.

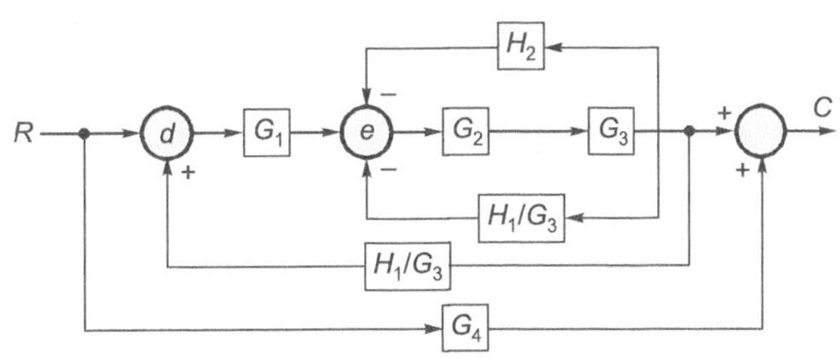

⇒ Solving inner closed loop;

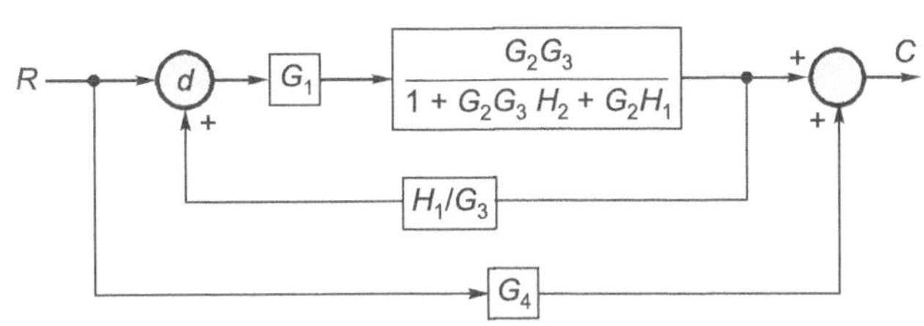

⇒ Solving inner closed loop, we get,

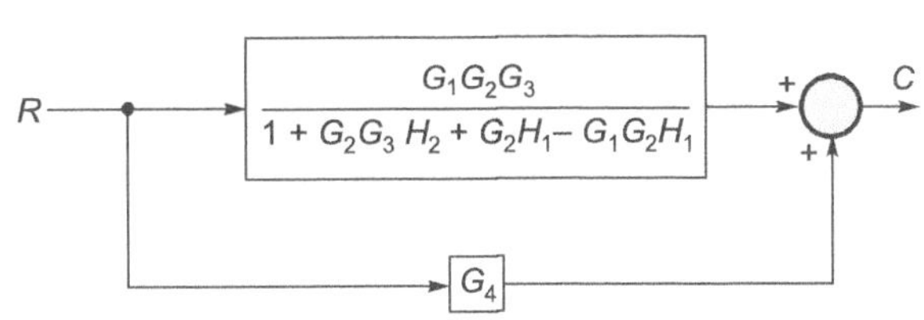

Transfer function,

$$T(s) = \frac{C}{R} = G_4 + \frac{G_1G_2G_3}{1 + G_2G_3H_2 + G_2H_1 - G_1G_2H_1}$$

2.14 Find the transfer function $Y(s)/U(s)$ using Mason's Gain formula. Also find $X_5(s)/U(s)$.

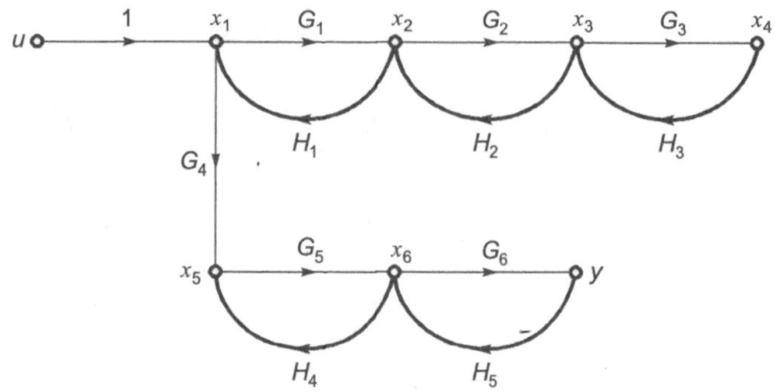

[20 marks : 2019]

Solution:

$$\frac{Y}{U} = \frac{G_4G_5G_6[1-(G_2H_2+G_3H_3)]}{1-[G_1H_1+G_2H_2+G_3H_3+G_5H_4+G_6H_5]}$$

$$+ [G_1H_1 \times G_3H_3 + G_1H_1 \times G_5H_4 + G_1H_1 \times G_6H_5 + G_2H_2 \times G_5H_4$$

$$+ G_2H_2 \times G_6H_5 + G_3H_3 \times G_5H_4 + G_3H_3 \times G_6H_5]$$

$$- [G_1H_1 \times G_3H_3 \times G_5H_4 + G_1H_1 \times G_3H_3 \times G_6H_5]$$

$$\frac{X_5}{U} = \frac{G_4[1-(G_2H_2+G_3H_3+G_6H_5)+(G_2H_2\times G_6H_5)+(G_3H_3\times G_6H_5)]}{1-[G_1H_1+G_2H_2+G_3H_3+G_5H_4+G_6H_5]}$$

$$+ [G_1H_1 \times G_3H_3 + G_1H_1 \times G_5H_4 + G_1H_1 \times G_6H_5 + G_2H_2 \times G_5H_4$$

$$+ G_2H_2 \times G_6H_5 + G_3H_3 \times G_5H_4 + G_3H_3 \times G_6H_5]$$

$$- [G_1H_1 \times G_3H_3 \times G_5H_4 + G_1H_1 \times G_3H_3 \times G_6H_5]$$

2.15 (i) For the signal flow graph shown in figure, determine overall transfer function $M(s) = \frac{C(s)}{R(s)}$.

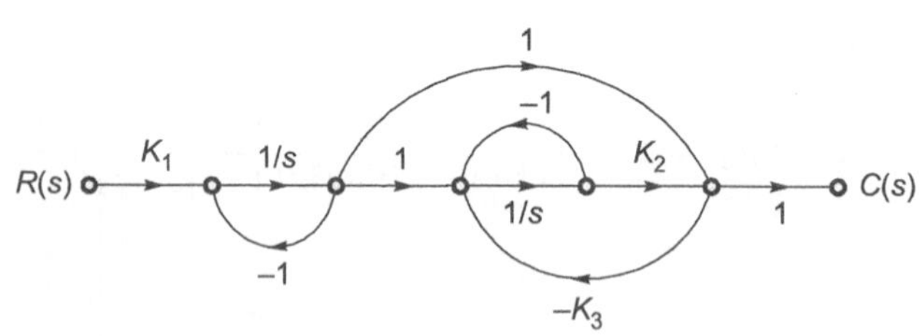

(ii) For a system represented in the figure, response to a unit step with $K = 1$ is given. For what value of K does the steady state error become zero?

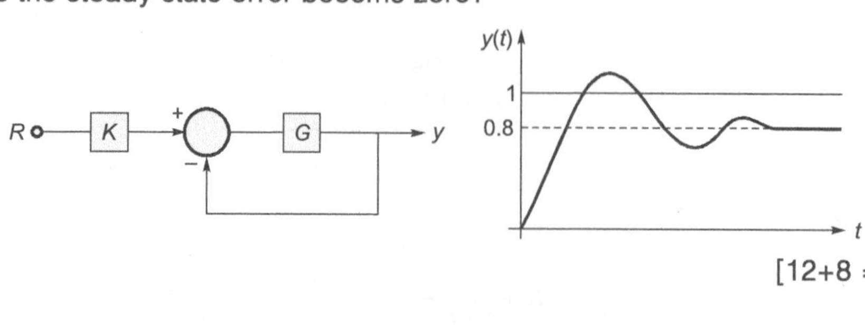

[12+8 = 20 marks : 2021]

Solution:

(i) Given signal flow graph is

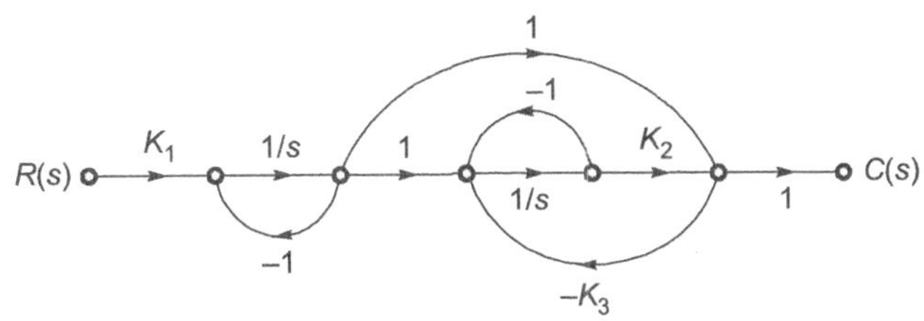

The transfer function, $\frac{C(s)}{R(s)}$ of a system represented by a signal flow graph is

$$\frac{C(s)}{R(s)} = \frac{\sum_K P_K \Delta_K}{\Delta}$$

where

K = Number of forward path

P_K = K^{th} forward path gain

Δ = 1 – (Σloop gain) + (Σnon touching loops gain taken two at a time) – (Σnon touching loop gains taken three at a time) + so on

Δ_K = 1 – (loop gain which does not touch the forward path)

There are two forward path gain.

So,

$$P_1 = \frac{K_1K_2}{s^2}; \qquad \Delta_1 = 1 - 0 = 1$$

$$P_2 = \frac{K_1}{s}; \qquad \Delta_2 = 1 - \left(-\frac{1}{s}\right) = \left(1 + \frac{1}{s}\right)$$

Now, there are 3 individual forwarth paths

$$L_1 = \frac{-1}{s}$$

$$L_2 = \frac{-1}{s}$$

$$L_3 = \frac{-K_2K_3}{s}$$

So, Value of $\Delta = 1 - [L_1 + L_2 + L_3] + [L_1L_2 + L_1L_3]$

$$\frac{C(s)}{R(s)} = \frac{P_1\Delta_1 + P_2\Delta_2}{\Delta}$$

$$\frac{C(s)}{R(s)} = \frac{\frac{K_1K_2}{s^2}(1) + \left(\frac{K_1}{s}\right)\left(1 + \frac{1}{s}\right)}{1 + \frac{1}{s} + \frac{1}{s} + \frac{K_2K_3}{s} + \frac{K_2K_3}{s^2} + \frac{1}{s^2}}$$

$$\frac{C(s)}{R(s)} = \frac{K_1(s + 1 + K_2)}{s^2 + s(K_2K_3 + 2) + (K_2K_3 + 1)}$$

(ii) The given step response is below :

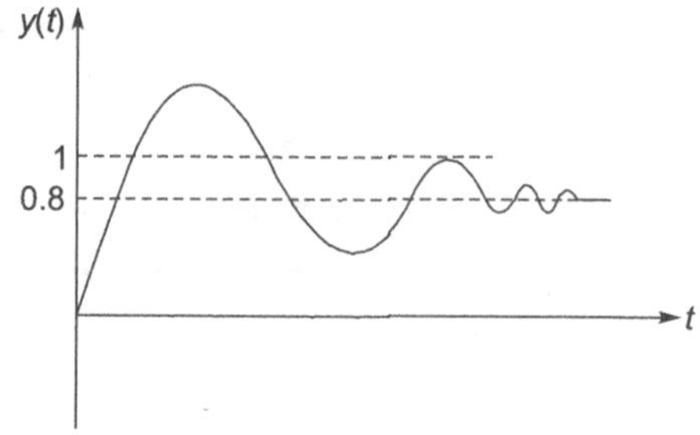

The steady state error, $e_{ss} = C - R = 1 - 0.8$

$e_{ss} = 0.2$ (for type = 0 and $K = 1$)

$\therefore$ For $e_{ss} = 0$, either type has to be 1 or $K = \infty$

Since $e_{ss} \propto \dfrac{1}{K}$

So, $K = \infty$

So, in order to make $e_{ss} = 0$, we have to increase gain (K) to infinite.

2.16 Reduce the block diagram shown below, using block diagram reduction technique and find the transfer function $\dfrac{C(s)}{R(s)}$.

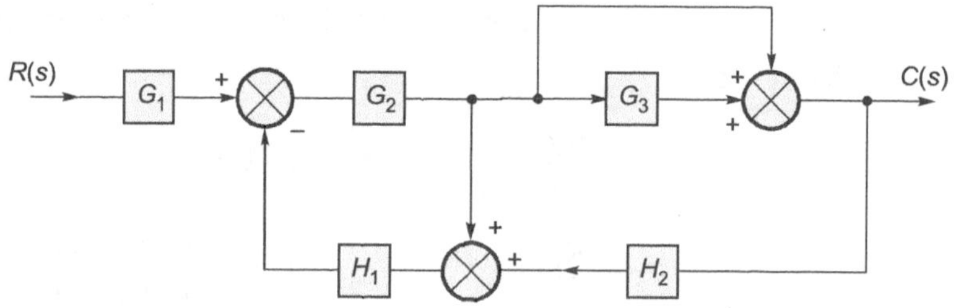

[12 marks : 2023]

Solution:

From the given block diagram, we can reduce :

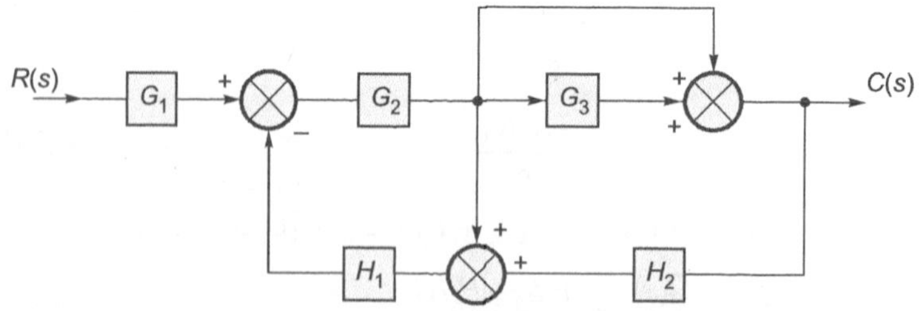

As G_3 and 1 are parallel, we can simplify feedback forming by H_1 and H_1H_2.

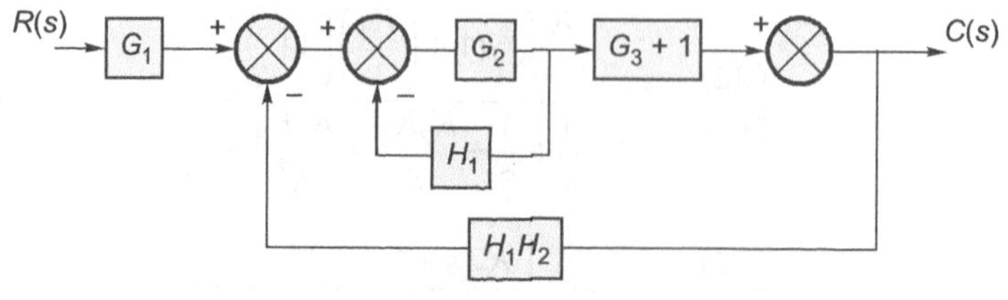

Solving the loop forming G_2 and H_1

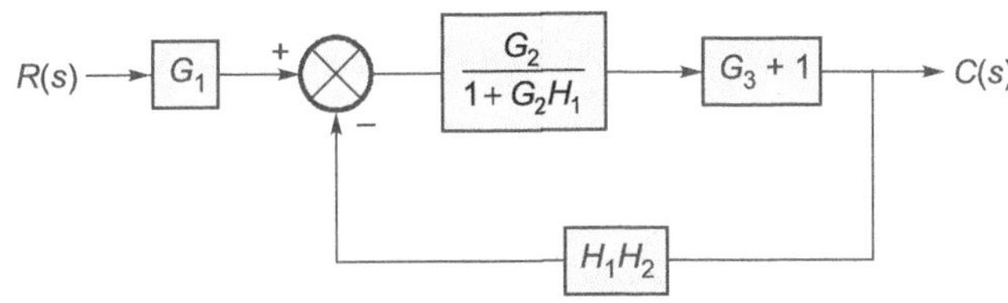

Cascading block $\dfrac{G_2}{1+G_2H_1}$ and $G_3 + 1$

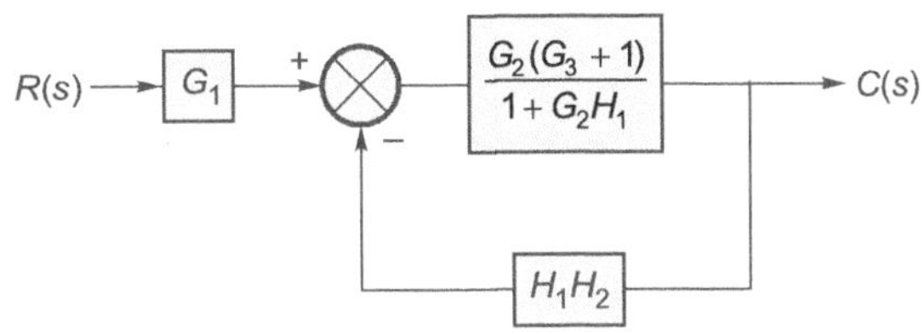

Required Transfer function is

$$\frac{C(s)}{R(s)} = \frac{G_1G_2(G_3+1)}{1+G_2H_1+G_2H_1H_2(G_3+1)}$$

3. Time Response Analysis

3.1 A circuit has the following transfer function $\dfrac{C(s)}{R(s)} = \dfrac{s^2+3s+4}{s^2+4s+4}$. Find $c(t)$ when $r(t)$ is a unit step. State if the circuit is undamped, underdamped, critically damped or over-damped.

[10 marks : 2002]

Solution:

$$\frac{C(s)}{R(s)} = \frac{s^2+3s+4}{s^2+4s+4} \qquad \text{[where } R(s) = (1/s)]$$

$$\therefore \quad C(s) = \frac{1}{s}\cdot\frac{s^2+3s+4}{s^2+4s+4} = \frac{1}{s}\left[1-\frac{s}{s^2+4s+4}\right] = \left[\frac{1}{s}-\frac{1}{s^2+4s+4}\right] = \left[\frac{1}{s}-\frac{1}{(s+2)^2}\right]$$

Taking inverse Laplace transform of $C(s) \Rightarrow L^{-1}[C(s)] = C(t) = 1 - te^{-2t}$

On comparing with,

$$s^2 + 2\xi\omega_n s + \omega_n^2 = s^2 + 4s + 4$$

From the given equation,

$$2\xi\omega_n = 4$$

and $\omega_n = 2$

then, $\xi = 1$

Hence, the circuit is critically damped.

3.2 Find the steady-state error in the output of any linear control system with unity feedback when the input is given by $r(t) = r_0 + r_1t + r_2t^2$

[10 marks : 2004]

Solution:

$$\text{Steady state error} = e_{ss} = \lim_{s\to 0}\left[\frac{sR(s)}{1+G(s)}\right]$$

Input, $r_1(t) = r_0$

$$R_1(s) = \frac{r_0}{s}$$

$$e_{ss1} = \underset{s\to 0}{Lt}\frac{r_0}{1+G(0)} = \frac{r_0}{1+k_p}$$

where, $k_p = G(0)$ = position error constant

Input, $r_2(t) = r_1\,t$

$$R_2(s) = \frac{r_1}{s^2}$$

$$e_{ss2} = \underset{s\to 0}{Lt}\frac{r_1}{s+sG(s)} = \underset{s\to 0}{Lt}\frac{r_1}{sG(s)}$$

$$= \frac{r_1}{k_v} \qquad \text{[where } K_v = \underset{s-0}{Lt}\, sG(s) = \text{velocity error constant]}$$

Input, $r_3(t) = r_2 t^2$

$$R_3(s) = \frac{2r_2}{s^3}$$

then,

$$e_{ss3} = \underset{s\to 0}{Lt}\cdot\frac{2r_2}{s^2+s^2G(s)} = \underset{s\to 0}{Lt}\frac{2r_2}{s^2G(s)} = \frac{2r_2}{k_a}$$

where, $k_a = \underset{s\to 0}{Lt}\, s^2 G(s)$ – acceleration error constant

Hence, the overall-steady state error

$$e_{ss} = e_{ss1} + e_{ss2} + e_{ss3}$$

$$= \frac{r_0}{1+k_p} + \frac{r_1}{k_v} + \frac{2r_2}{k_a}$$

3.3 Consider unity feedback control system whose open-loop transfer function is $G(s) = \dfrac{0.4s+1}{s(s+0.6)}$.

Obtain the response to a unit step input. Also determine damping ratio (ξ), and undamped natural frequency (ω_n).

[12 marks : 2008]

Solution:

$$H(s) = 1 \text{ and } G(s) = \frac{0.4s+1}{s(s+0.6)}$$

$$\frac{C(s)}{R(s)} = \frac{G(s)}{1+G(s)\,H(s)} = \frac{\dfrac{0.4s+1}{s(s+0.6)}}{1+\dfrac{(0.4s+1)}{s(s+0.6)}\times 1} = \frac{0.4s+1}{s^2+s+1}$$

$$C(s) = R(s)\times\frac{0.4s+1}{s^2+s+1} = \frac{0.4s+1}{s(s^2+s+1)}$$

The R.H.S. of the above equation can be expanded into partial fraction.

$$\frac{(0.4s+1)}{s\cdot(s^2+s+1)} = \frac{A}{s} + \frac{Bs+1}{s^2+s+1}$$

$$A(s^2+s+1)+s(Bs+C) = 0.4s+1$$

$A+B=0$, $A+C=0.4$ and $A=1$

Hence, $A = V$, $B=-1$, $C=-0.6$

$$C(s) = \frac{A}{s}+\frac{Bs+1}{s^2+s+1} = \frac{1}{s}-\frac{s+0.6}{s^2+s+1} = \frac{1}{s}-\frac{(s+0.5)+0.1}{(s+0.5)^2+0.75}$$

$$= \frac{1}{s}-\frac{(s+0.5)}{\left(s+\frac{1}{2}\right)^2+\left(\frac{\sqrt{3}}{2}\right)^2}-\frac{2}{\sqrt{3}}\times 0.1\times\frac{\sqrt{3}/2}{(s+0.5)^2+\left(\frac{\sqrt{3}}{2}\right)^2}$$

On taking inverse Laplace, $C(t) = L^{-1}[C(s)]$

$$= 1-e^{-t/2}\cos\frac{\sqrt{3}}{2}t-0.115\,e^{-t/2}\sin\frac{\sqrt{3}}{2}t$$

$$C(t) = 1-e^{-t/2}\times\left\{0.115\sin\frac{\sqrt{3}}{2}t+\cos\frac{\sqrt{3}}{2}t\right\}$$

$$s^2+2\xi\omega_n s+\omega_n^2 = s^2+s+1 \quad \text{(on comparing)}$$

$$\omega_n^2 = 1 \Rightarrow \omega_n = 1 \text{ rad/sec.}$$

and $\quad 2\xi\omega_n = 1 \Rightarrow \xi = 0.5$

3.4 Determine:

(i) time constant,

(ii) rise time,

(iii) peak time (t_p),

(iv) maximum overshoot and

(v) settling time(t_s) for the gain function given in (Q.No. 3.3).

[10 marks : 2008]

Solution:

By neglecting the effect of zero we can get,

$\xi = 0.5$, $\omega_n = 1$

(i) Time constant $= \dfrac{1}{\xi\omega_n} = 2$ sec

(ii) Rise time $= \dfrac{\pi-\tan^{-1}\frac{\sqrt{1-\xi^2}}{\xi}}{\omega_d} = 1 = \dfrac{\pi-\tan^{-1}\left(\frac{\sqrt{1-\xi^2}}{\xi}\right)}{\omega_n\sqrt{1-\xi^2}} = 2.42$ sec

(iii) Peak time $= \dfrac{\pi}{\omega_d} = \dfrac{\pi}{\omega_n\sqrt{1-\xi^2}} = 3.63$ sec

(iv) Maximum overshoot, $M_p = e^{-\xi\pi/\sqrt{1-\xi^2}} = 16.3\%$

(v) Settling time $= t_s = \dfrac{4}{\xi\omega_n} = 8$ sec.

3.5 The unit step response of a linear control system is shown in figure. Find the transfer function of a second order prototype system to model the system.

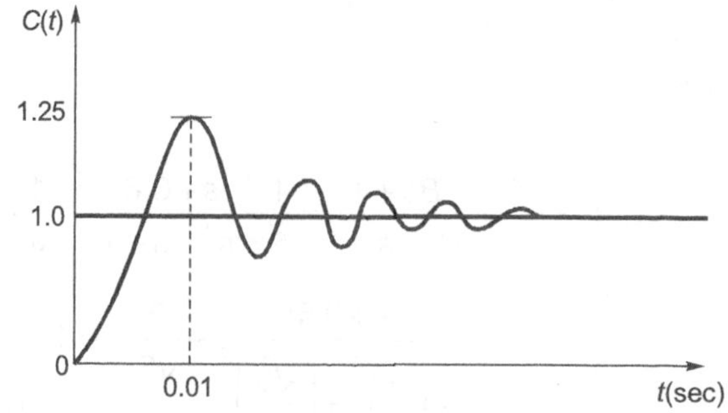

[10 marks : 2009]

Solution:

Maximum peak overshoot, $M_p = 0.25 = e^{-\frac{\xi\pi}{\sqrt{1-\xi^2}}}$

$\Rightarrow$ $e^{+\frac{\xi\pi}{\sqrt{1-\xi^2}}} = 4$

$\Rightarrow$ $\frac{\xi\pi}{\sqrt{1-\xi^2}} = ln\,4$ ...(*i*)

On solving equation (*i*), we get $\xi = 0.4$

Time for 1st peak $t_p = \frac{\pi}{\omega_d} = 0.01$

where, $\omega_d = \omega_n\sqrt{1-\xi^2}$

$$\omega_n\sqrt{1-\xi^2} = \frac{\pi}{0.01}$$

$$\omega_n = 342.77 \text{ rad/sec.}$$

Transfer function of the system $= \frac{\omega_n^2}{s^2 + 2\xi\omega_n s + \omega_n^2} = \frac{(342.77)^2}{s^2 + 2\times 0.4\times 342.77s + (342.77)^2}$

$$= \frac{(342.77)^2}{s^2 + 274.2s + (342.77)^2}$$

3.6 For a second order underdamped system, subjected to unit-step input, the time response shown first peak to be four times of the second overshoot. Determine the damping factor of the system and expected maximum overshoot.

[10 marks : 2010]

Solution:

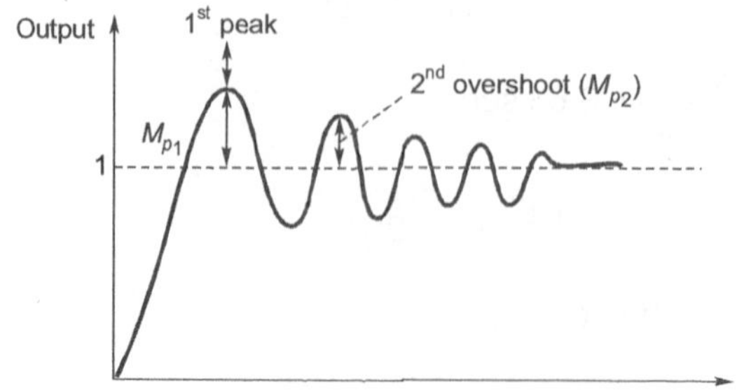

$$M_{p_1} = \text{Maximum overshoot (1}^{st}\text{ overshoot)} = e^{-\frac{\xi\pi}{\sqrt{1-\xi^2}}}$$

and $$M_{p_2} = \text{Second overshoot} = e^{\frac{-3\xi\pi}{\sqrt{1-\xi^2}}}$$

where, $$\xi = \text{damping factor}$$

$$\text{First peak} = 1 + M_{p1}$$

According to the problem,

$$\text{First peak} = 4 \times \text{second overshoot}$$

$$\Rightarrow \quad 1 + M_{p_1} = 4 M_{p_2}$$

$$\Rightarrow \quad 1 + e^{\frac{-\xi\pi}{\sqrt{1-\xi^2}}} = 4e^{\frac{-3\xi\pi}{\sqrt{1-\xi^2}}}$$

Assuming, $$x = e^{\frac{-\xi\pi}{\sqrt{1-\xi^2}}}$$

$$1 + x = 4x^3$$

$$\Rightarrow \quad 4x^3 - x - 1 = 0$$

$$x_1 = 0.76, \quad x_{2,3} = 0.38 \pm j0.429$$

x can not be complex quantity, hence $x = 0.76$

$$e^{\frac{-\xi\pi}{\sqrt{1-\xi^2}}} = 0.76$$

On solving the above equation, we get

$$\xi = \text{damping factor} = 0.087$$

$$\text{expected maximum overshoot} = \%M_p = e^{\frac{-\xi\pi}{\sqrt{1-\xi^2}}} \times 100$$

$$= e^{\frac{-0.087\times\pi}{\sqrt{1-(0.087)^2}}} \times 100 = 76\%$$

3.7 **For the system represented by a block diagram shown below, evaluate the closed-loop transfer function. Calculate damping factor, frequency of oscillation (if any), steady-state error if the input is unit ramp in θ_r.**

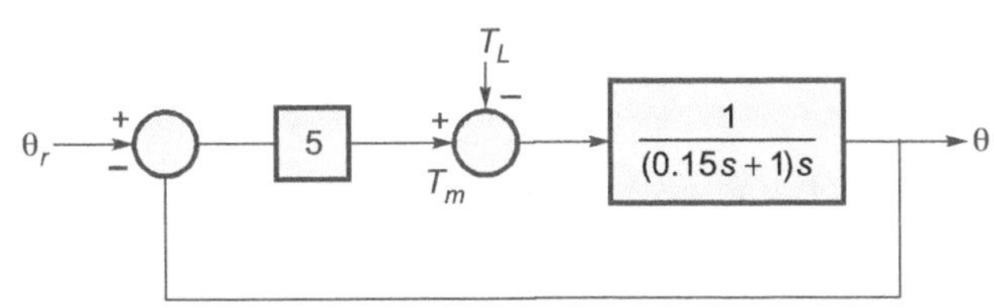

[10 marks : 2011]

Solution:

For finding closed loop transfer function $\frac{\theta(s)}{\theta_r(s)}$

T_L is assumed to be zero and the block diagram takes the form as shown

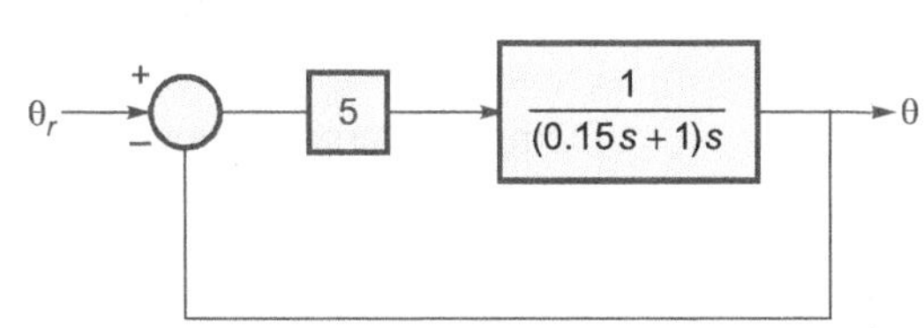

$$G(s) = \frac{5}{(0.15s+1)s} \text{ and } H(s) = 1$$

$$\frac{\theta(s)}{\theta_r(s)} = \frac{G(s)}{1+G(s)H(s)} = \frac{5/(0.15s+1)s}{1+\frac{5}{(0.15s+1)s}\cdot 1}$$

or $$\frac{\theta(s)}{\theta_r(s)} = \frac{5}{0.15s^2+s+5} = \frac{33.33}{s^2+6.678+33.33}$$

The characteristic equation is $s^2 + 6.67s + 33.33 = 0$

Comparing the above equation with $s^2 + 2\,\xi\omega_n s + \omega^2{}_n = 0$

we get,
$$\omega_n = \sqrt{33.33} = 5.77 \text{ rad/sec.}$$
$$2\xi\omega_n = 6.67$$
$$\Rightarrow \quad \xi = \frac{6.67}{2\times\omega_n} = \frac{6.67}{2\times 5.77} = 0.578 \text{ (damping factor)}$$
$$\text{damped natural frequency} = \omega_d = \omega_n\sqrt{1-\xi^2} = 4.71 \text{ rad/sec.}$$
$$E(s) = \frac{\theta_r(s)}{1+G(s)\,H(s)} \qquad \text{\{Error\}}$$
$$= \frac{\theta_r(s)}{1+\dfrac{5}{(0.15s+1)s}\cdot 1}$$

steady state error when $\theta_r(s) = \dfrac{1}{s^2}$

$$e_{ss} = \underset{s\to 0}{Lt}\,(sE(s)) = \underset{s\to 0}{Lt}\left[\frac{s\cdot\theta_r(s)}{1+\dfrac{5}{(0.15s+1)s}}\right]$$
$$= \underset{s\to 0}{Lt}\left[\frac{s\cdot 1/s^2}{1+\dfrac{5}{(0.15s+1)s}}\right] = \underset{s\to 0}{Lt}\left[\frac{1}{s+\dfrac{5}{(0.15s+1)}}\right]$$

(Steady state error) $\qquad e_{ss} = 0.2$

3.8 For a second-order system the location of poles is known to be –3 ± *j*7. Calculate peak time, % overshoot and approximate setting time for ±2% range.

[10 marks : 2011]

Solution:

For a second order system, the characteristic equation is $s^2 + 2\,\xi\omega_n s + \omega^2{}_n = 0$.
The roots of the above equation are given by

$$s_{1,\,2} = -\xi\omega_n + j\omega_n\sqrt{1-\xi^2} \qquad \text{...(i)}$$

on comparing the roots with the poles $s_{1,\,2} = -3 \pm j7$

we get,
$$\xi\omega_n = 3 \text{ and } \omega_n\sqrt{1-\xi^2} = 7$$
$$\frac{\xi}{\sqrt{1-\xi^2}} = \frac{3}{7}$$
$$\text{Damped natural frequency} = \omega_d = \omega_n\sqrt{1-\xi^2} = 7$$
$$\text{Peak time} = t_p = \frac{\pi}{\omega_d} = \frac{\pi}{7} = 0.448 \text{ sec.}$$

$$\%\text{overshoot} = e^{-\xi\pi/\sqrt{1-\xi^2}} = e^{-\left(\frac{3}{7}\pi\right)} = 0.26 = 26\%$$

$$\text{Setting time for } \pm 2\% \text{ range} = t_s = \frac{4}{\xi\omega_n} = \frac{4}{3} = 1.33 \text{ sec.}$$

3.9 A system is described in the below figure.

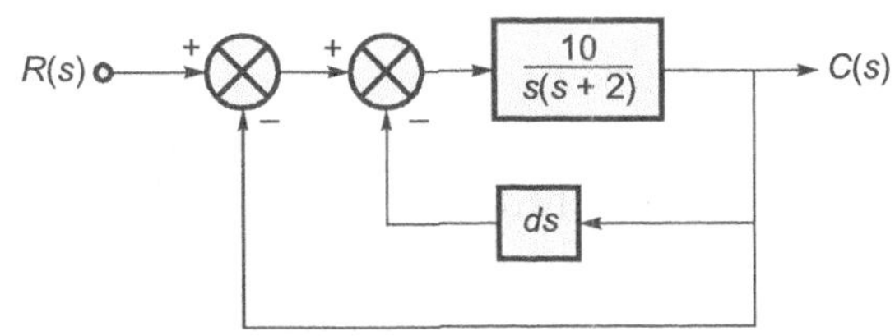

(i) In the absence of derivative feedback (i.e. d = 0) determine the damping ratio (δ), natural frequency (ω_n) and the steady state error resulting from a unit-ramp input.

(ii) Determine the derivative feedback constant (d) of which will increase the damping ratio of the system to 0.8. What is the steady state error to unit-ramp input with this setting of the derivative feedback constant.

(iii) By changing the forward gain of the amplifier, the steady state error of the system with derivative feedback to unit-ramp input is reduced to same value as in part (i) while the damping ratio is maintained at 0.8. Determine the value of amplifier gain K_A and the derivative feedback constant. You may use higher gain K_A in place of 10 (as given in the open loop transfer-function). Or you may use an additional amplifier of gain K_A between the two summing points without changing the value of 10 as given in the system.

[12 marks : 2012]

Solution:

(i) Characteristic equation, $1 + G(s)\,H(s) = 0$

$$s(s + 2) + 10 = 0$$
$$s^2 + 2s + 10 = 0$$

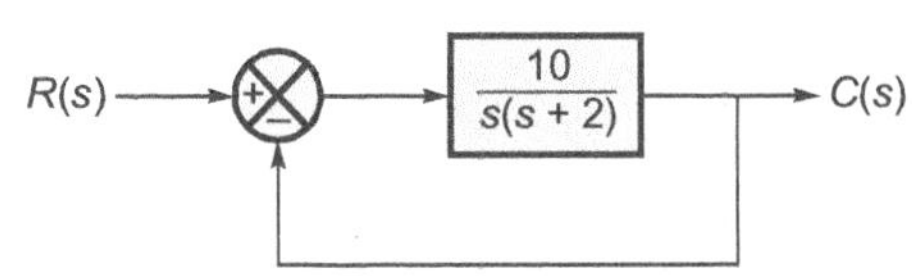

On comparing with standard equation

$$s^2 + 2\xi\omega_n + \omega_n^2 = 0$$

$$\Rightarrow \quad \omega_n^2 = 10 \text{ and } \xi\omega_n = 1$$

$$\Rightarrow \quad \omega_n = \sqrt{10} \text{ and } \xi = \frac{1}{\sqrt{10}}$$

The steady state error,

$$e_{ss} = \lim_{s\to 0} sE(s) = \lim_{s\to 0} \cdot \frac{s\cdot\frac{1}{s^2}}{1+\frac{10}{s(s+2)}} = \lim_{s\to 0} \frac{s(s+2)}{s(s^2+2s+10)} = \frac{2}{10} = \frac{1}{5}$$

(ii)
$$G_1(s) = \frac{\frac{10}{s(s+2)}}{1+ds\cdot\frac{10}{s(s+2)}} = \frac{1}{s}\cdot\frac{10}{(s+2)+10d} = \frac{10}{s[s+(10d+2)]}$$

Characteristic equation, $1 + G_1(s) = 0$

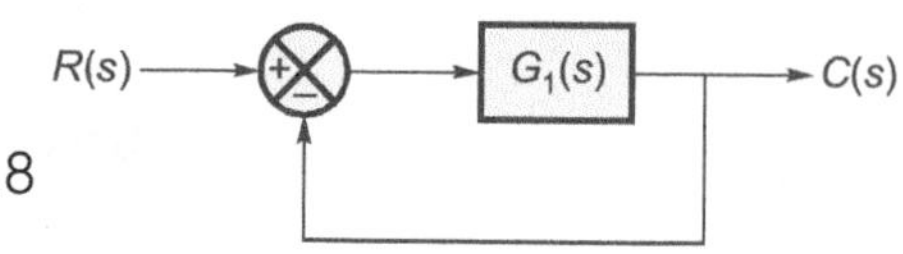

$$s^2 + (10d + 2)s + 10 = 0$$

$$\Rightarrow \quad \omega_n' = \sqrt{10} \quad \text{and} \quad \xi' = \frac{1}{2\sqrt{10}}(10d+2) = 0.8$$

$$\Rightarrow \quad 10d = 1.6\sqrt{10} - 2$$

$$d = 0.306$$

The steady state error

$$e_{ss} = \lim_{s \to 0} \frac{s \cdot \frac{1}{s^2}}{1 + \frac{10}{s(s+10d+2)}} = \lim_{s \to 0} \frac{(s+10d+2)}{s(s+10d+2)+10} = \frac{10d+2}{10} = \frac{5.06}{10} = 0.506$$

(iii) For forward gain K_A

$$G_1(s) = \frac{\frac{K_A}{s(s+2)}}{1 + ds\frac{K_A}{s(s+2)}} = \frac{K_A}{s(s+2) + dK_A s} = \frac{K_A}{s(s+2+dK_A)}$$

Characteristics equation,

$$1 + G_1(s) = 0$$

$$s^2 + s(2 + dK_A) + K_A = 0$$

$$\omega_n = \sqrt{K_A}, \; \xi = \frac{1}{2\sqrt{K_A}}(2 + dK_A) = 0.8$$

and

$$e_{ss} = \frac{1}{s} = \frac{2\xi}{\omega_n} = \frac{1.6}{\sqrt{K_A}}$$

$$\sqrt{K_A} = 8 \Rightarrow K_A = 64$$

$$0.8 = \frac{1}{2\sqrt{K_A}}(2 + dK_A)$$

$$0.8 = \frac{1}{2 \times 8}(2 + d \times 64) \Rightarrow 64d = \frac{54}{5}$$

$$d = 0.16875$$

3.10 Derive the expression for $c(t)$ (i.e. the output) for a second order system subject to a unit step input.

[5 marks : 2012]

Solution:

A general expression for the transfer function of a second order control system is given by

$$\frac{C(s)}{R(s)} = \frac{\omega_n^2}{s^2 + 2\xi\omega_n s + \omega_n^2}$$

As the input is an unit step function

$$r(t) = 1 \quad \text{and} \quad R(s) = \frac{1}{s}$$

$$\therefore \qquad C(s) = \frac{1}{s}\cdot\frac{\omega_n^2}{s^2+2\xi\omega_n s+\omega_n^2}$$

$$= \frac{1}{s}-\frac{s+2\xi\omega_n}{(s+\xi\omega_n)^2+\omega_d^2} \qquad \text{where, } \omega_d = \omega_n\sqrt{1-\xi^2}$$

$$= \frac{1}{s}-\frac{s+\xi\omega_n}{(s+\xi\omega_n)^2+\omega_d^2}-\frac{\xi\omega_n}{\omega_d}\cdot\frac{\omega_d}{(s+\xi\omega_n)^2+\omega_d^2}$$

Taking Laplace inverse on both sides.

$$C(t) = 1-e^{-\xi\omega_n t}\cdot\cos\omega_d t-\frac{\xi\omega_n}{\omega_d}\cdot e^{-\xi\omega_n t}\sin\omega_d t$$

$$C(t) = 1-\frac{e^{-\xi\omega_n t}}{\sqrt{1-\xi^2}}\cdot\sin(\omega_d t+\phi)$$

Where, $$\phi = \tan^{-1}\left(\frac{\sqrt{1-\xi^2}}{\xi}\right)$$

3.11 Derive the expression for generalised error series and also the generalised error series and also the generalised error coefficients for unity feedback system.

[5 marks : 2012]

Solution:

The error transfer function of a feedback control system is given by

$$\frac{E(s)}{R(s)} = \frac{1}{1+G(s)H(s)} = F_e(s) \text{ (say)}$$

$$\Rightarrow \qquad E(s) = F_e(s)\,R(s)$$

Using convolution theorem the inverse Laplace transform of $E(s)$ is

$$e(t) = f_e(t) * r(t-\tau) = \int_{-\infty}^{t} f_e(\tau)\cdot r(t-\tau)\,d\tau$$

where, $f_e(\tau) = \mathcal{L}^{-1} F_e(s)$

The function $r(t-\tau)$ is valid for $t \geq 0$ hence the lower limit of integral is changed from $-\infty$ to 0.

Using Taylor's series,

$$r(t-\tau) = r(t)-\tau r'(t)+\frac{\tau^2}{2!}r''(t)-\frac{\tau^3}{3!}r'''(t)\cdots$$

$$e(t) = \int_0^t f_e(\tau)\left\{r(t)-\tau r'(t)+\frac{\tau^2}{2!}r''(t)-\frac{\tau^3}{3!}r'''(t)\cdots\right\}d\tau$$

$$\lim_{t\to 0} e(t) = e_{ss} = r(t)\int_0^\infty f_e(\tau)d\tau - r'(t)\int_0^\infty \tau f_e(\tau)d\tau + r''(t)\int_0^\infty \frac{\tau^2}{2!} f_e(\tau)$$

Put, $$K_o = \int_0^\infty f_e(\tau)d\tau \;;\; K_1 = -\int_0^\infty t f_e(\tau)dt$$

$$K_2 = \int_0^\infty t^2 f_e(\tau)dt\cdots; \quad K_n = \int_0^\infty \tau^n f_e(\tau)d\tau$$

Therefore generalized error series for steady state error is

$$e_{ss} = K_o r(t) + K_1 r'(t) + \frac{K_2}{2!} r''(t) + \cdots + \frac{K_n}{n!} r^n(t)$$

The coefficients K_o, K_1, $K_2 \cdots K_n$ are termed as generalised error coefficient.

3.12 **Consider a negative unity feedback system with $G(s) = \dfrac{0.4s+1}{s(s+0.6)}$. Obtain peak overshoot, damped frequency of oscillation, settling time on 2% tolerance band, and response of the system to unit step input.**

[10 marks : 2013]

Solution:

Characteristic equation, $1 + G(s) H(s) = 0$

$$1 + \frac{0.4s+1}{(s)(s+0.6)} = 0$$

$$s^2 + s + 1 = 0$$

$$\Rightarrow \quad \omega_n = 1 \text{ and } \xi = 0.5$$

$$M_p = e^{\frac{-\pi\xi}{\sqrt{1-\xi^2}}} = e^{\frac{-\pi \times 0.5}{\sqrt{0.75}}} = 16.30\%$$

$$\omega_d = \omega_n\sqrt{1-\xi^2} = \sqrt{1-0.25} = 0.866 \text{ sec.}$$

$$\text{Settling time} = \frac{4}{\xi\omega_n} = 8 \text{ sec.}$$

Unit step response,

$$C(s) = G(s) H(s) = \frac{0.4s+1}{s^2(s+0.6)} = \frac{A}{s} + \frac{B}{s^2} + \frac{C}{s+0.6}$$

$$= \frac{(s^2+0.6s)A + (s+0.6)B + s^2C}{s^2(s+0.6)}$$

On comparing the coefficient of respective powers of s,

$$A + C = 0, \quad 0.6A + B = 0.4, \quad 0.6B = 1$$

$$A = -2.11, \quad B = 1.67, \quad C = 2.11$$

$$C(s) = -\frac{2.11}{s} + \frac{1.67}{s^2} + \frac{2.11}{s+0.6}$$

Taking inverse Laplace transformation,

We get, $C(t) = (-2.11 + 1.67t + 2.11e^{-0.6t})\, u(t)$

3.13 **Obtain the unit step response of a system whose impulse response $h(t) = u(t)$, where $u(t)$ = unit step input.**

[8 marks : 2014]

Solution:

Method-I:

Impulse response, $h(t) = u(t)$

$$\text{Unit step response} = \int_0^t u(t)\, dt = t\, u(t) = r(t)$$

Method-II:

Impulse response, $h(t) = u(t)$

$$\text{Transfer function} = \frac{1}{s}$$

$$\text{Step response} = \frac{1}{s} \times \frac{1}{s} = \frac{1}{s^2}$$

In time domain, Step response = $t\,u(t)$

3.14 Consider the feedback control system shown in figure given below:

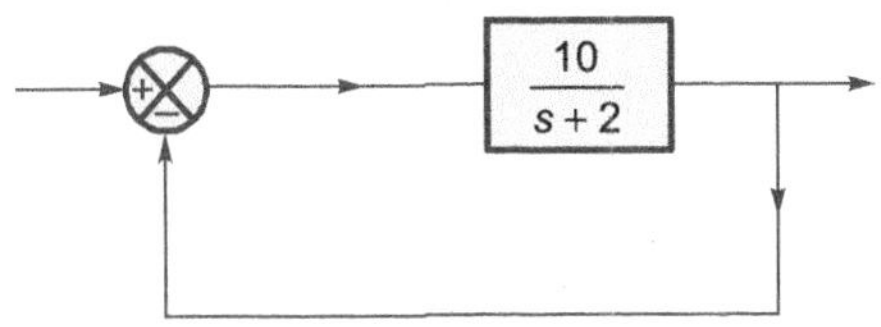

The above system is subjected to unit impulse input
(i) Obtain the expression for $c(t)$ and time constant.
(ii) If the feedback loop is opened, what would be $c(t)$ and the associated time constant ?
(iii) In which of the above two cases, the response would be faster?

[10 marks : 2015]

Solution:

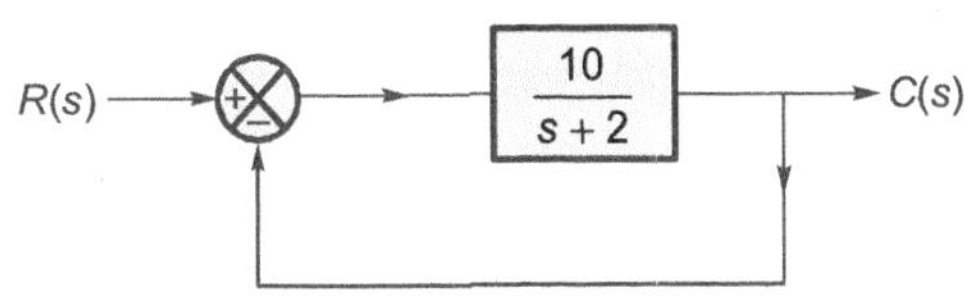

$R(s) = 1$

(i) For closed loop system

$$\text{Transfer function} = \frac{10}{s+12}$$

$$\because \quad \frac{C(s)}{R(s)} = \frac{10}{s+12}$$

For unit impulse input, $$C(s) = \frac{10}{s+12}$$

$$\text{Time response } c(t) = L^{-1}[C(s)]$$

$$c(t) = 10e^{-12t}u(t)$$

Here time constant $$\tau = \frac{1}{12} \text{ sec.}$$

(ii) For open loop system,

$$\text{Transfer function} = \frac{10}{s+2}$$

$$\frac{C(s)}{R(s)} = \frac{10}{s+2}$$

For unit impulse input, $R(s) = 1$

$$C(s) = \frac{10}{s+2}$$

$$\text{time response} \Rightarrow c(t) = L^{-1}\left[\frac{10}{s+2}\right] = 10\, e^{-2t}\, u(t)$$

and time constant $\Rightarrow \tau = \frac{1}{2}$ sec.

(iii) In above two cases, the time response is faster for closed loop system with time constant $\tau = \frac{1}{12}$ sec.

3.15 **The field of a dc servomotor is separately excited by means of a dc amplifier of gain K_A = 90. A voltage proportional to field current is now feedback negatively to the amplifier input as indicated in following figure. Determine the value of K so that field time constant is reduced to 4 milliseconds.**

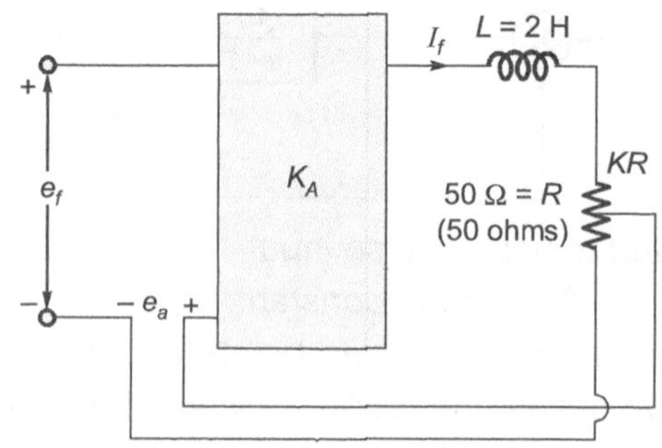

[10 marks : 2015]

Solution:

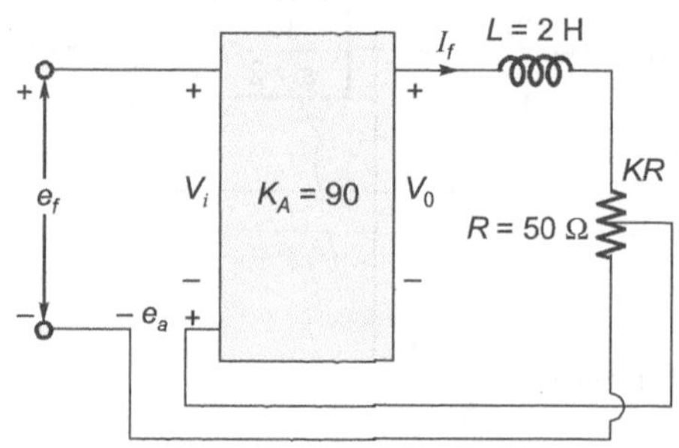

From the figure,
We can write,

$$e_a = I_f \cdot K \cdot R \quad \text{...(1)}$$

$$V_0 = I_f[KR + sL]$$

$$V_i = (e_f - e_a)$$

$$K_A = \frac{V_0}{V_i} = I_f \frac{[KR + sL]}{(e_f - e_a)}$$

$$\therefore \quad I_f = \frac{(e_f - e_a)K_A}{KR + sL} \quad \text{...(2)}$$

From equation (1) and (2),

$$I_f(KR + sL) = (e_f - I_f \cdot K \cdot R)K_A$$

$$I_f[KR + sL + K.K_A \cdot R] = e_f \cdot K_A$$

$$\frac{I_f}{e_f} = \frac{K_A}{R(K + K \cdot K_A) + sL}$$

$$\frac{I_f(s)}{e_f(s)} = \frac{K_A}{R(K + K \cdot K_A) + sL} \quad \text{...(3)}$$

From above transfer function, we can calculate time response and hence time constant,

$$\tau = \frac{L}{RK(1+K_A)}$$

But time constant given $t = 4 \times 10^{-3}$ sec.

So, $$\frac{L}{R(1+K \cdot K_A)} = 4 \times 10^{-3} \text{ sec} \quad \text{or} \quad \frac{2}{50(1+90K)} = 4 \times 10^{-3}$$

$$\Rightarrow \qquad K = \frac{1}{10}$$

3.16 For the circuit shown in figure below, let $R_1 = R_2$, $R_3 * C = 1/10$. Find the step response of the filter.

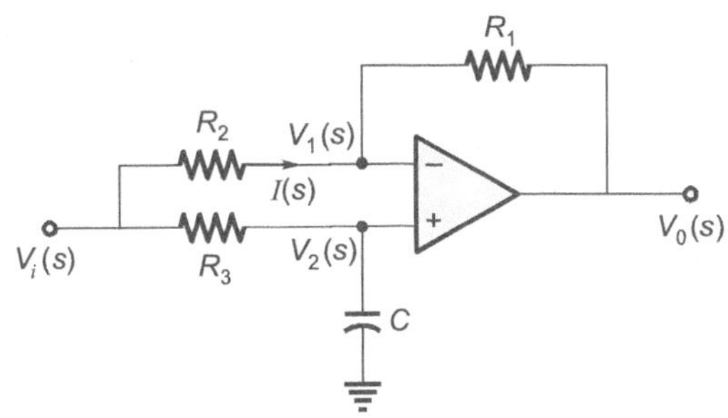

[10 marks : 2016]

Solution:

By superposition principle the output voltage,

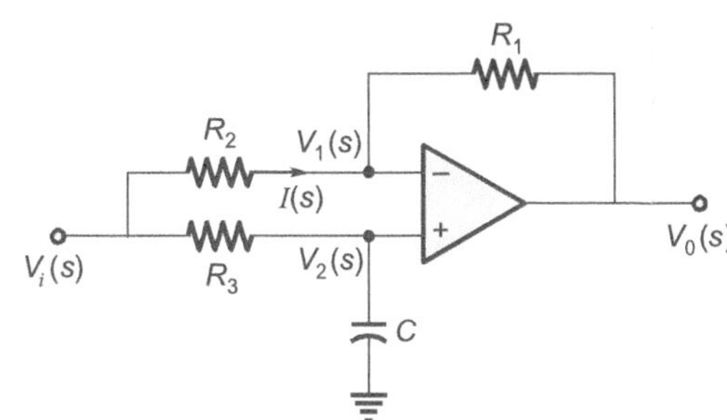

$$V_0(s) = -\frac{R_2}{R_1}[V_i(s)] + \frac{\left(1+\frac{R_2}{R_1}\right)}{(1+sCR_3)}V_i(s)$$

$$\frac{V_0(s)}{V_i(s)} = \left[-\frac{R_2}{R_1} + \frac{(1+R_2/R_1)}{1+sCR_3}\right]$$

$$\frac{V_0(s)}{V_i(s)} = \left[-1+\frac{2}{1+s/10}\right] \qquad \left[\because R_1 = R_2; R_3.C = \frac{1}{10}\right]$$

$$= \left[-1+\frac{20}{s+10}\right] = \left(\frac{-s+10}{s+10}\right)$$

$$\frac{V_0(s)}{V_i(s)} = \frac{(10-s)}{(s+10)}$$

$$V_0(s) = \frac{1}{s} \times \frac{(10-s)}{(10+s)} \qquad \left[\because V_i(s) = \frac{1}{s} \text{ (for unit step)}\right]$$

$$V_0(s) = \frac{1}{s} - \frac{2}{(s+10)}$$

Taking Laplace inverse to both sides:

$$V_0(t) = u(t) - 2e^{-10t}\,u(t)$$

3.17 The unit step response of a unity feedback system is $C(t) = 1 + e^{-4t} - 2e^{-2t}$.

Determine:

(i) the type and order of the system.

(ii) the static error constants of the system.

(iii) the open loop poles of the system.

[12 marks : 2017]

Solution:

Unit step response, $c(t) = 1 + e^{-4t} - 2e^{-2t}$

Taking Laplace transform, $C(s) = \frac{1}{s} + \frac{1}{s+4} - \frac{2}{s+2} = \frac{s^2+6s+8+s^2+2s-2s^2-8s}{s(s+4)(s+2)}$

$$C(s) = \frac{8}{s(s+4)(s+2)} = X(s)\,H(s)$$

$X(s)$ is Laplace transform of input which is unit step.

$$\therefore \quad X(s) = \frac{1}{s}, \quad H(s) = \frac{8}{(s+4)(s+2)}$$

$$H(s) = \frac{G(s)}{1+G(s)}$$

$\therefore$ Open loop transfer function $= \frac{8}{(s+4)(s+2)-8}$

$$G(s) = \frac{8}{s(s+6)}$$

(i) Type = 1, Order = 2

(ii) Positional error constant, $K_p = \underset{s\to 0}{Lt}\, G(s) = \underset{s\to 0}{Lt} \frac{8}{s(s+6)} = \infty$

Velocity error constant, $K_v = \underset{s\to 0}{Lt}\, sG(s) = \underset{s\to 0}{Lt}\, s \times \frac{8}{s(s+6)} = \frac{8}{6} = \frac{4}{3}$

Acceleration error constant, $K_a = \underset{s\to 0}{Lt}\, s^2 G(s) = \underset{s\to 0}{Lt}\, s^2 \times \frac{8}{s(s+6)} = 0$

(iii) Open-loop poles, $s = 0$, $s = -6$

3.18 Given a unity feedback system with $G(s) = \frac{K}{s(s+a)}$ as shown in the figure:

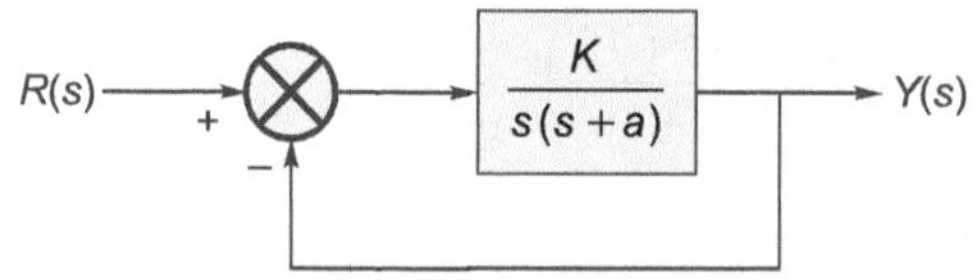

(i) Find the values of K and a, when the closed-loop system has $K_v = 100$ and admits 20% peak overshoot.

(ii) Find the values of K and a, when the closed-loop system has settling time (2% tolerance band) of 2 seconds and admits 10% peak overshoot.

[12 marks : 2018]

Solution:

(i) It is given that, $K_V = 100$ and $M_P = 20\%$

$$G(s) = \frac{K}{s(s+a)}$$

$$K_v = \lim_{s\to 0} sG(s)H(s) = \lim_{s\to 0} \frac{sK}{s(s+a)}$$

$$100 = \frac{K}{a}$$

$$K = 100\,a \qquad ...(1)$$

Let closed loop transfer function is,

$$\text{CLTF} = \frac{K}{s^2 + as + K}$$

Comparing it with standard form, we get,

$$2\xi\omega_n = a$$

$$2\xi\sqrt{K} = a$$

$$\xi = \frac{a}{2\sqrt{K}} \qquad ...(2)$$

$$M_p = e^{\frac{-\xi\pi}{\sqrt{1-\xi^2}}} = 0.2$$

$$\frac{-\xi\pi}{\sqrt{1-\xi^2}} = \ln(0.2)$$

$$2.5901(1-\xi^2) = \xi^2 9.8696$$

$$\xi = \sqrt{\frac{2.5901}{12.4597}} = 0.456$$

Putting this is equation (2),

$$0.456 \times 2 = \frac{a}{\sqrt{K}} \qquad ...(3)$$

Solving (1) and (3), $a = 83.17$, $K = 8317.44$

(ii) It is given that, $\tau_s = 2$ sec and $M_P = 10\%$

$$\tau_s = \frac{4}{\xi\omega_n} = 2 \text{ sec.}$$

$$\xi\omega_n = 2$$

$$M_P = e^{-\xi\pi/\sqrt{1-\xi^2}} = 0.1$$

$$-\frac{\xi\pi}{\sqrt{1-\xi^2}} = ln(0.1)$$

$$5.3019 = 15.1715\,\xi^2$$

$$\xi = 0.591$$

$$\omega_n = 3.384 \text{ rad/sec.}$$

$$\text{CLTF} = \frac{K}{s^2 + as + K}$$

$$\omega_n = \sqrt{K} = 3.384$$

$$K = 11.45$$

$$a = 2\xi\omega_n = 4$$

3.19 Show the permissible area for the poles of a second order system which must simultaneously meet the following criteria:

(i) Maximum percent overshoot $\leq 5\%$

(ii) Settling time for 2% criterion ≤ 500 ms

[12 marks : 2019]

Solution:

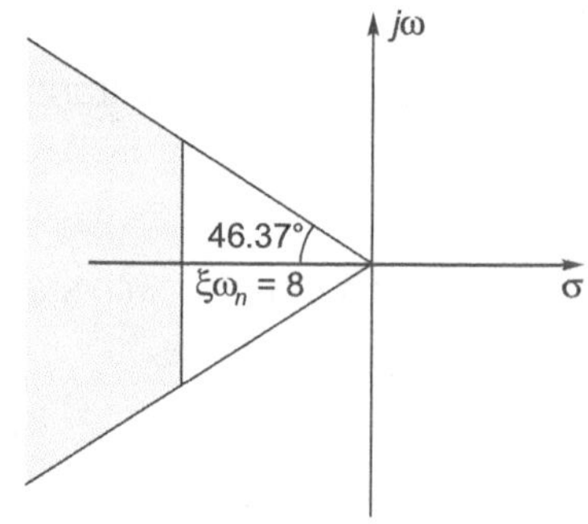

$$M_p \le 0.05$$

$$e^{\frac{-\xi\pi}{\sqrt{1-\xi^2}}} = 0.05$$

$$\frac{-\xi\pi}{\sqrt{1-\xi^2}} = ln\ 0.05$$

$$\xi = 0.69$$

$\Rightarrow$ $$\theta = \cos^{-1}(0.69) = 46.37°$$

$\therefore$ $$\xi \ge 0.69$$

$$t_s \le 500 \text{ ms}$$

$$\frac{4}{\xi\omega_n} \le 500 \text{ ms}$$

$$\xi\omega_n \ge 8$$

3.20 The transfer function of a linear system is given by

$$G(s) = \frac{10}{(s+1)(s+2)}$$

The sinusoidal steady-state response of the system to an input is given by

$$1 + \sin(t - 60°) + 5\sin(2t - 45°)$$

Determine the input.

[12 marks : 2019]

Solution:

Transfer function of system is,

$$G(s) = \frac{10}{(s+1)(s+2)}$$

$$A\sin(\omega_1 t + \phi_{input}) \to A|H(\omega_1)|\sin(\omega_1 t + \phi_{in} + \phi_H)$$

$$\phi_H = \angle H(\omega_1)$$

$$G(j\omega) = \frac{10}{(1+j\omega)(2+j\omega)}$$

At $\omega = 0$, $$G(j0) = \frac{10}{2} = 5$$

$$G_0 = 5\angle 0°$$

At $\omega = 1$ rad/s, $$G(j1) = \frac{10}{(1+j1)(2+j1)}$$

$$G_1\angle\phi_1 = 3.16\angle{-71.56°}$$

At $\omega = 2$ rad/s, $$G(j2) = \frac{10}{(1+j2)(2+j2)}$$

$$G_2\angle\phi_2 = 1.58\angle{-108.43°}$$

$$\text{Input} = \frac{1}{|G_0|} + \frac{1}{|G_1|}\sin(t - 60° - \phi_1) + \frac{5}{|G_2|}\sin(2t - 45° + \phi_2)$$

$$= \frac{1}{5} + \frac{1}{3.16}\sin(t - 60° + 71.56°) + \frac{5}{1.58}\sin(2t - 45° + 108.43°)$$

$$\text{Input} = 0.2 + 0.31\sin(t - 11.56°) + 3.16\sin(2t + 63.43°)$$

4. Concepts of Stability

4.1 The characteristic equation for a certain closed-loop digital control system is given as follows: $P(z) = 1 + 0.4z^{-1} - 0.69z^{-2} - 0.256z^{-3} + 0.32z^{-4} = 0$. Determine whether this system is stable or not using Jury's stability test.

[10 marks : 2004]

Solution:

$$P(z) = 1 + 0.4\,z^{-1} - 0.69\,z^{-2} - 0.256\,z^{-3} + 0.32\,z^{-4} = 0$$

$$\Rightarrow \quad P(z) = z^4 + 0.4\,z^3 - 0.69\,z^2 - 0.256\,z + 0.32$$

where, $n = 4$

Check for necessary condition:

$$P(1) = 1 + 0.4 - 0.69 - 0.256 + 0.32 = 0.774 > 0$$

$$(-1)^n P(-1) = (-1)^4 \times \{(-1)^4 + 0.4 \times (-1)^3 - 0.69 \times (-1)^2 - 0.256 \times (-1) + 0.32$$

$$= 0.486 > 0$$

Since, $P(1) > 0$ and $(-1)^n P(-1) > 0$, the necessary condition for stability are satisfied.

Check for sufficient condition:

where, $b_k = \begin{vmatrix} a_0 & a_{n-k} \\ a_n & a_k \end{vmatrix}$ for 3rd row $k = 0, 1.......(n-1)$

$c_k = \begin{vmatrix} b_0 & b_{n-1-k} \\ b_{n-1} & b_k \end{vmatrix}$ for 5th row $k = 0, 1........(n-2)$

Row	z^0	z^1	z^2	z^3	z^4
1	a_0	a_1	a_2	a_3	a_4
2	a_4	a_3	a_2	a_1	a_0
3	b_0	b_1	b_2	b_3	
4	b_3	b_2	b_1	b_0	
5	c_0	c_1	c_2		

$$P(z) = a_4 z^4 + a_3 z^3 + a_2 z^2 + a_1 z + a_0$$

Comparing the coefficients,

$a_4 = 1$; $a_3 = 0.4$; $a_2 = -0.69$; $a_1 = -0.256$ and $a_0 = 0.32$

Row	z^0	z^1	z^2	z^3	z^4
1	0.32	−0.256	−0.69	0.4	1
2	1	0.4	−0.69	−0.256	0.32
3	−0.8976	−0.48192	0.4692	0.394	
4	0.384	0.4692	−0.48192	−0.8976	
5	0.658	0.2523	−0.236		

Sufficient conditions for the system to be stable,

$$|a_0| < |a_n| \Rightarrow |a_0| < |a_4| \Rightarrow 0.32 < 1$$

$$|b_0| > |b_{n-1}| \Rightarrow |b_0| > |b_3| \Rightarrow 0.8976 > 0.384$$

$$|c_0| > |c_{n-2}| \Rightarrow |c_0| > |c_2| \Rightarrow 0.658 > 0.236$$

The necessary and sufficient condition for stability are satisfied, so system is stable.

4.2 Prove that for BIBO stability, the roots of the characteristic equation or the poles of the system transfer function cannot be located in the right half of s-plane or on the $j\omega$-axis.

[12 marks : 2005]

Solution:

A system with impulse response $m(\tau)$ is BIBO stable if and only if the impulse response is absolutely

integrable (i.e. $\int_0^\infty |Im(\tau)|d\tau$ is finite. This means that area under the absolute value curve of the impulse response $m(\tau)$ evaluated from $t = 0$ to $t = \infty$ must be finite.
The closed loop transfer function.

$$M(s) = \frac{A_1}{s+p_1} + \frac{A_2}{s+p_2} + \frac{A_3}{s+p_3} + \ldots\frac{A_n}{s+p_n}$$

The poles p_1, p_2, p_3 ... p_n may be at origin or lying on imaginary axis or lying on right or left half s-plane. The impulse response is given by inverse Laplace transform of $M(s)$. The inverse Laplace transform of each term of $M(s)$ depends on the location of poles. The impulse response of various terms of $M(s)$ are shown in table.

Table

Transfer function and location of roots on s-plane	**Impulse response (inverse Laplace transform and the sketch of time domain function)**
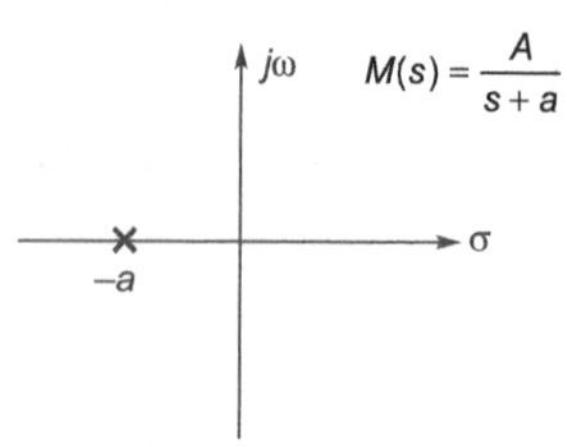 Root on negative real axis	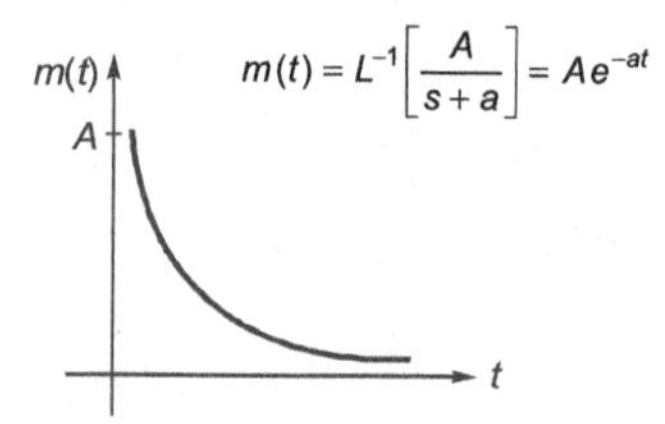 Response is exponentially decaying
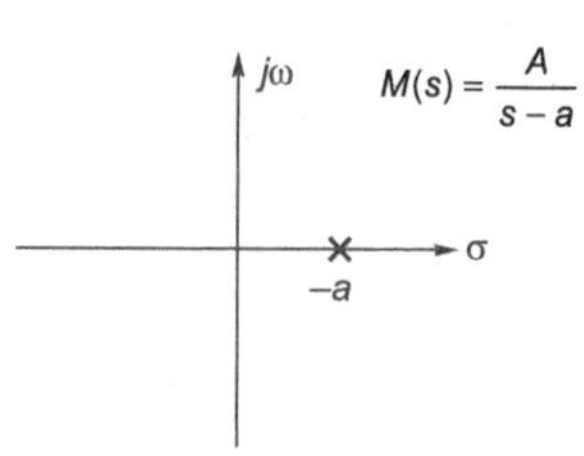 Root on positive real axis	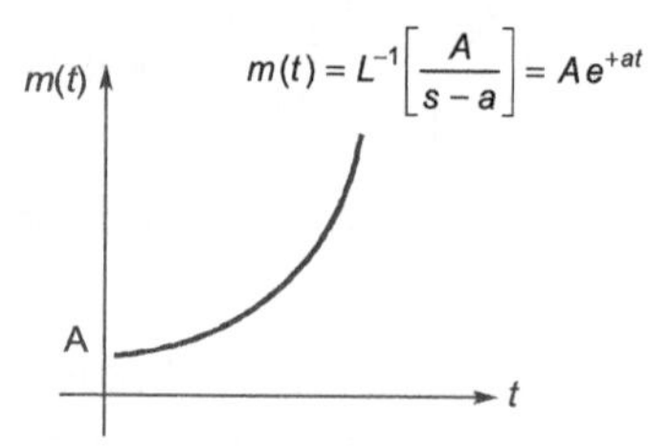 Response is exponentially increasing
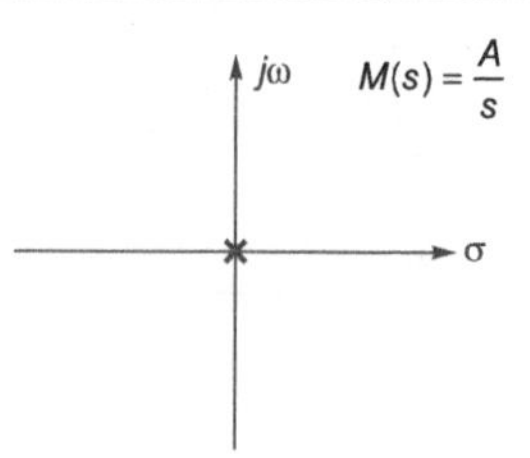 Single root at origin	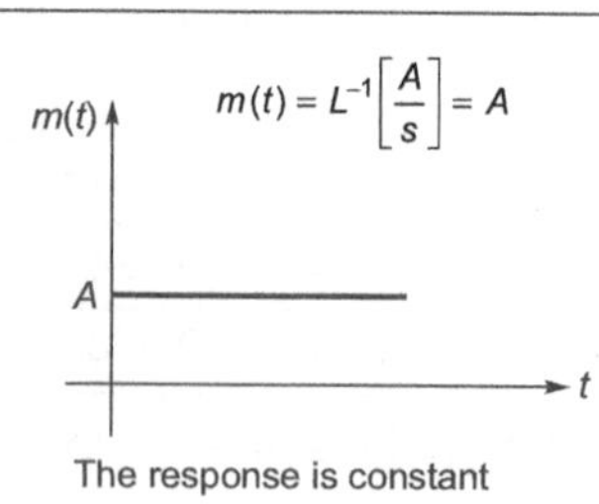 The response is constant
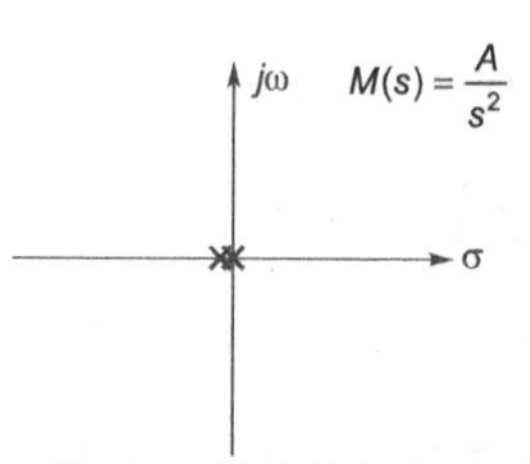 Double root at origin	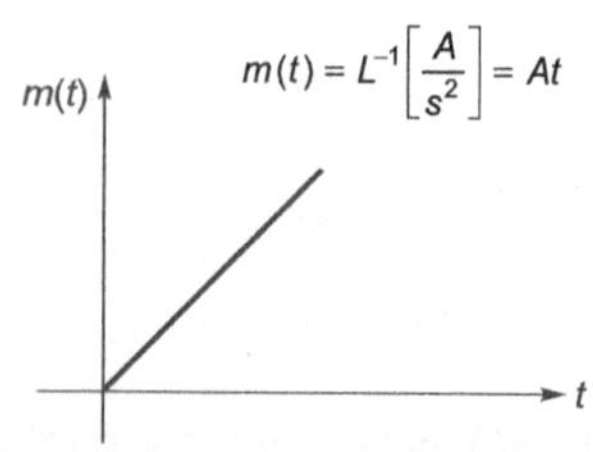 The response linearly increases with time

In summary the following three points may be stated regarding the stability of the system depending on the location of roots of characteristic equation.

(*i*) If all the roots of characteristic equation has negative real parts, then the system is stable.

(*ii*) If any root of the characteristic equation has a positive real or if there is a repeated root on the imaginary axis, then the system is unstable.

(*iii*) If the condition (*i*) is satisfied except for the presence of one or more non-repeated roots on the imaginary axis, then the system is limitedly or marginally stable.

4.3 **What are the methods for determining the stability of Linear Control system?**
A third order control system has the characteristic equation $s^3 + 3408.3s^2 + 1204000s + 1.5 \times 10^7 K = 0$. Find the value of K for which the system is marginally stable. For such a value of K determine the frequency of the undamped sinusoid in rad/sec of the zero input response.

[12 marks : 2006]

Solution:

The methods used for determining the stability of linear control system:

1. Routh Hurwitz criterion
2. Nyquist stability criterion
3. Using gain margin and phase margin
4. Root locus techniques

Constructing Routh-array, we have

s^3	1	1204000
s^2	3408.3	$1.5\times10^7 K$
s^1	$\dfrac{4.1\times10^9 - 1.5\times10^7 K}{3408.3}$	
s^0	$1.5\times10^7 K$	

For marginally stable system,

$$\frac{4.1\times10^9 - 1.5\times10^7 K}{3408.3} = 0$$

$$\therefore \qquad K = 273.57$$

Frequency of oscillation

$$\therefore \qquad 3408.3s^2 + 1.5 \times 10^7 K = 0$$

Put, $s = j\omega$ and $K = 273.57$

$$\Rightarrow \qquad -3408.3\,\omega^2 + 1.5 \times 10^7 \times 273.57$$

$$\omega = 1097.26 \text{ rad/sec.}$$

4.4 **A system has an open-loop transfer function of $\dfrac{10}{s(1+0.5s)(1+0.2s)}$ and is having feedback whose transfer function is $H(s) = (1 + Ts)$. What should be the value of T so that the closed-loop system operates stably?**

[10 marks : 2008]

Solution:

$$1 + G(s)\,H(s) = 0$$

$$\Rightarrow \qquad 1+\frac{10(1+Ts)}{s(1+0.5s)(1+0.2s)} = 0$$

$$\Rightarrow \qquad 0.1s^3 + 0.7s^2 + s + 10 + 10Ts = 0 \quad \rightarrow \text{Characteristic equation}$$

$$\Rightarrow \qquad s^3 + 7s^2 + (10 + 100T)s + 100 = 0$$

By Routh-Hurwitz criteria,

s^3	1	$10+100T$
s^2	7	100
s^1	$\dfrac{70+700T-100}{7}$	
s^0	100	

For stable system, we have

$$-30 + 700T \geq 0$$

$$700\,T \geq 30$$

$$T \geq \frac{30}{700}$$

4.5 For the feedback control system shown in figure find the range of K for the stability of closed loop system.

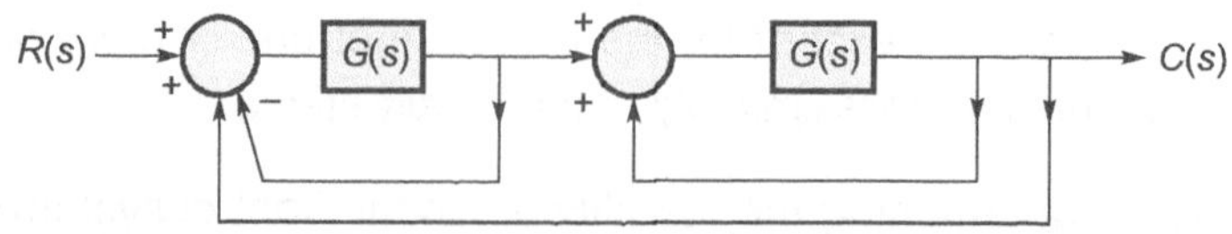

Given: $G(s) = \dfrac{K}{(s+4)(s+5)}$

[10 marks : 2009]

Solution:

By reducing the block diagram:

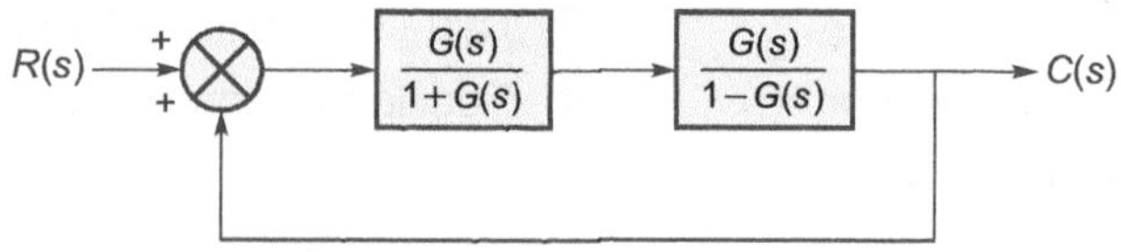

$$\frac{C(s)}{R(s)} = \frac{\dfrac{G(s)}{1+G(s)} \times \dfrac{G(s)}{1-G(s)}}{1-\left[\dfrac{G(s)}{1+G(s)}\right]\left[\dfrac{G(s)}{1-G(s)}\right]} = \frac{G^2(s)}{1-G^2(s)-G^2(s)} = \frac{G^2(s)}{1-2G^2(s)}$$

$$= \frac{K^2}{\left[(s+4)^2(s+5)^2\right]-2K^2} = \frac{K^2}{(s^2+8s+16)(s^2+10s+25)-2K^2}$$

$$= \frac{K^2}{s^4+10s^3+25s^2+8s^3+80s^2+200s+16s^2+160s+400-2K^2}$$

$$= \frac{K^2}{s^4+18s^3+121s^2+360s+400-2K^2}$$

By Routh criteria,

s^4	1	121	$400-2K^2$
s^3	18	360	
s^2	101	$400-2K^2$	
s^1	$\dfrac{101\times 360-(400-2K^2)18}{101}$		
s^0	$400-2K^2$		

Condition (I) for stability,

$$400 - 2K^2 > 0$$
$$400 > 2K^2$$
$$200 > K^2$$
$$K < \left|10\sqrt{2}\right|$$

Condition (II) for stability,

$101 \times 20 - 400 + 2K^2 > 0 \;\Rightarrow\; K^2 + 810 > 0$

$\therefore$ Both conditions are satisfied when $K < \left|10\sqrt{2}\right|$

4.6 For a controlled system shown in figure, determine the safe maximum gain, K_{cmax} of the controller and the steady state error due to only 0.3 unit-step disturbance input L, with K_C set to K_{cmax}.

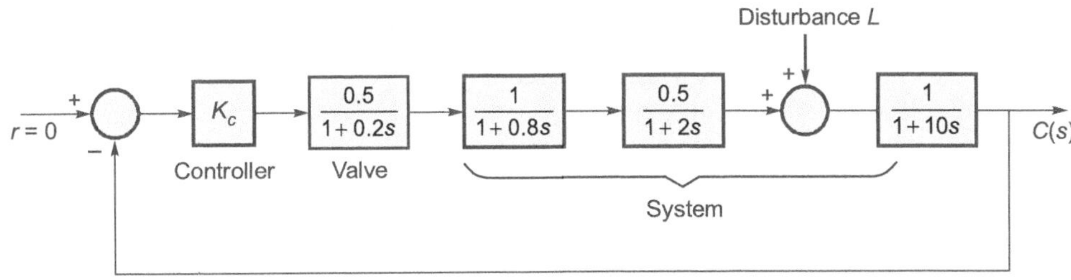

[10 marks : 2010]

Solution:

For determining the safe maximum gain, disturbance L is assumed to be zero. Hence the closed loop system is

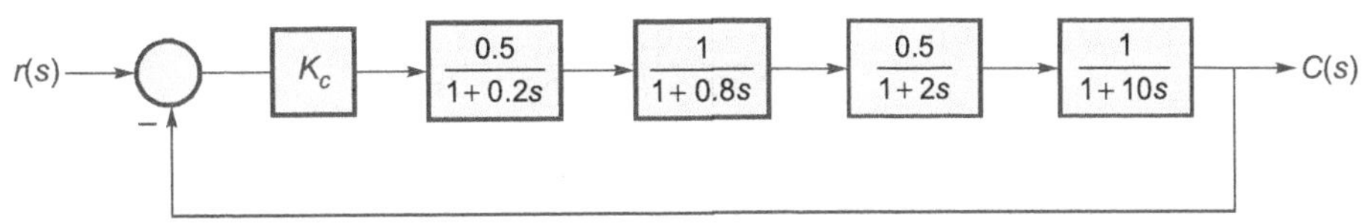

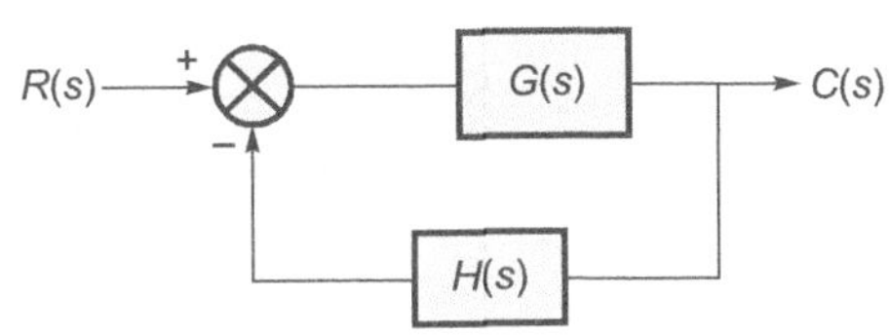

Transfer function of the system $T(s) = \dfrac{C(s)}{R(s)} = \dfrac{G}{1+G(s)H(s)}$

where, $H(s) = 1$ and $G(s) = \dfrac{K_C \times 0.5 \times 0.5}{(1+0.2s)(1+0.8s)(1+2s)(1+10s)}$

$$T(s) = \frac{0.25K_C/(1+0.2s)(1+10s)(1+0.8s)(1+2s)}{1+0.25K_C/(1+0.2s)(1+10s)(1+0.8s)(1+2s)}$$

$$\text{Characteristic equation} = (1+0.2s)(1+10s)(1+0.8s)(1+2s) + 0.25K_c$$
$$= 3.2s^4 + 21.92s^3 + 32.16s^2 + 13s + 1 + 0.25K_c$$

The Routh array is formed below,

s^4	3.2	32.16	$1 + 0.25K_c$
s^3	21.92	13	
s^2	30.26	$1+0.25K_c$	
s^1	$\dfrac{\{30.26 \times 13 - 21.92 \times (1+0.25K_c)\}}{30.26}$		
s^0	$1 + 0.25K_c$		

For the stability, sign of the elements in first column of Routh table should be same, in the above table the sign should be positive.

$$1 + 0.25\,K_c > 0$$

$$\Rightarrow \qquad K_c > -4 \text{ and } \frac{\{30.26 \times 13 - 21.92 \times (1 + 0.25\,K_c\}}{30.26} > 0$$

$$\Rightarrow \qquad 30.26 > 21.92\,(1 + 0.25\,K_c)$$

$$\Rightarrow \qquad 18 > 1 + 0.25\,K_c$$

$$\Rightarrow \qquad 17 > 0.25\,K_c$$

$$\Rightarrow \qquad 68 > K_c$$

$$-4 < K_c < 68 \quad \text{for stability}$$

Hence, $K_{cmax} = 68$

For finding steady-state error due to disturbance (L) of value 0.3 unit-step with $r(s) = 0$ and K_c set to K_{cmax}

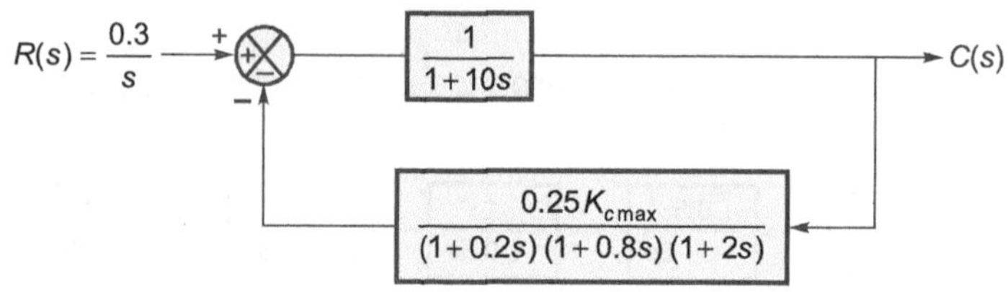

$$G(s) = \frac{1}{1+10s}$$

$$H(s) = \frac{0.25 \times K_{cmax}}{(1+0.2s)\,(1+0.8s)\,(1+2s)} = \frac{17}{(1+0.2s)\,(1+0.8s)\,(1+2s)}$$

$$E(s) = \frac{L(s)}{1+G(s)\,H(s)} \qquad \text{[Error]}$$

$$\text{Steady-state error} = e_{ss} = \underset{s\to 0}{Lt}\,[sE(s)]$$

$$e_{ss} = \underset{s\to 0}{Lt}\left[\frac{sL(s)}{1+G(s)H(s)}\right]$$

$$= \underset{s\to 0}{Lt}\left[\frac{s \times (0.3/s)}{1+\left(\dfrac{1}{1+10s}\right) \times \left\{\dfrac{17}{(1+0.2s)\,(1+0.8s)\,(1+2s)}\right\}}\right] = \frac{0.3}{1+17} = \frac{0.3}{18}$$

$$e_{ss} = 0.0167 \text{ (steady stable error)}$$

4.7 Determine the complete stability information by using Routh criteria for a unity feedback closed system modelled by a plant TF

$$G(s) = \frac{128}{s(s^7 + 3s^6 + 10s^5 + 24s^4 + 48s^3 + 96s^2 + 128s + 192)}$$

[10 marks : 2011]

Solution:

The characteristic equation of the system can be written as

$s^8 + 3s^7 + 10s^6 + 24s^5 + 48s^4 + 96s^3 + 128s^2 + 192s + 128 = 0$

The Routh table is formed below:

s^8	1	10	48	128	128
s^7	3	24	96	192	0

s^6	2	16	64	128	0	
s^5	0	0	0	0	0	Auxiliary equation
s^4						

- All the elements in the fourth row vanish and the application of Routh criterion fails. The situations occurs when the array has two consecutive rows having the same ratio of corresponding elements.
- The difficulty faced is overcome by forming an auxiliary equation using elements of the last row. The derivative of this auxiliary equation taken w.r.t. 's' and the coefficients of the differentiated equation are taken as the elements of the following row.
- The auxiliary equation is $A(s) = 2s^6 + 16s^4 + 64s^2 + 128$ and $\dfrac{dA(s)}{ds} = 12s^5 + 64s^3 + 128s$.
- The coefficients of the fourth row are thus 12, 64 and 128. The modified Routh array is given below:

s^8	1	10	48	128	128	
s^7	3	24	96	192	0	
s^6	2	16	64	128	0	
s^5	12	64	128	0	0	
s^4	5.33	42.67	128	0	0	
s^3	–32.06	–160.18	0	0	0	sign change
s^2	16.04	128	0	0	0	sign change
s^1	95.66	0	0	0	0	
s^0	128	0	0	0	0	

- As there are two sign changes in the first column, the system has two roots with positive real part indicating that the system is unstable.

4.8 The characteristic equation of a system is given by $s(s-1)(s^2+4s+20)+K(s+1)=0$. Find the range of K for which the system is stable.

[5 marks : 2012]

Solution:

$$s(s-1)(s^2+4s+20)+K(s+1) = 0$$
$$(s^2-s)(s^2+4s+20)+Ks+1 = 0$$
$$s^4+3s^3+16s^2+(K-20)s+1 = 0$$

Routh array:

$$\begin{array}{c|ccc} s^4 & 1 & 16 & 1 \\ s^3 & 3 & (K-20) & 0 \\ s^2 & \dfrac{68-K}{3} & 1 & \\ s^1 & \dfrac{(68-K)(K-20)-9}{68-K} & & \\ s^0 & 1 & & \end{array}$$

For system to be stable

$68 - K > 0$ and $(68 - K)(K - 20) > 9$

$\Rightarrow$ $K < 68$ and $K^2 - 88K + 1369 < 0$

$\Rightarrow$ $K < 68$ and $20.188 < K < 67.81$

$\Rightarrow$ $20.188 < K < 67.81$

4.9 A unity negative feedback control system has open loop transfer function $G(s) = \dfrac{K(s+1)}{s^3 + as^2 + 2s + 1}$.

Using Routh's criterion determine the value of 'K' and 'a' so that system oscillates at a frequency of 2 rad/sec.

[10 marks : 2013]

Solution:

Characteristic equation: $1 + G(s)H(s) = 0$

$$1 + \frac{K(s+1)}{(s^3 + as^2 + 2s + 1)} = 0$$

$$s^3 + as^2 + 2s + 1 + Ks + K = 0$$

$$s^3 + as^2 + (2 + K)s + 1 + K = 0$$

s^3	1	$2+K$
s^2	a	$1+K$
s^1	$\dfrac{(1+K) - a(2+K)}{a}$	0
s^0	$1+K$	

Auxiliary equation:

$$as^2 + (1 + K) = 0$$

$$s^2 + \frac{(1+K)}{a} = 0 \quad (\text{assuming } a \neq 0)$$

∵ System, oscillates at a frequency of 2 rad/sec.

So, $$\frac{1+K}{a} = 4$$

Also, $$\frac{(1+K) - a(2+K)}{a} = 0$$

$$a = \frac{(1+K)}{(2+K)}$$

$\Rightarrow$ $$\boxed{K = 2}$$

$\Rightarrow$ $$\boxed{a = \frac{3}{4}}$$

4.10 A unity feedback control system is characterised by openloop transfer function,

$$G(s) = \frac{K(s+13)}{s(s+3)(s+7)}$$

Using Routh's criteria, determine the value of gain 'K' for which system will be limitedly stable? Also, determine the closed loop poles for this value of 'K'.

[10 marks : 2015]

Solution:

Open loop transfer function, $$G(s) = \frac{K(s+13)}{s(s+3)(s+7)}$$

Characteristic equation:

$$1 + GH(s) = 0$$

$$s(s + 3)(s + 7) + K(s + 13) = 0$$

$$s^3 + 10s^2 + 21s + Ks + 13K = 0$$

Using Routh's criteria for stability,

s^3	1	$(21+K)$
s^2	10	$13K$
s	$\dfrac{10(21+K)-13K}{10}$	0
s^0	$13k$	

For the system to be marginally stable, $10(21 + K) - 13K = 0 \Rightarrow K = 70$

Now, closed loop transfer function,

$$CLTF = \frac{K(s+13)}{s^3+10s^2+(21+K)s+13K}$$

Putting $K = 70$;

$$CLTF = \frac{70(s+13)}{s^3+10s^2+91K+910}$$

Closed loop poles; $s = \pm j9.54; -10$

4.11 **Consider a third order control system with the following characteristic equation:**

$$s^3 + 3408.3\, s^2 + 1204000\, s + 1.5 \times 10^7 K = 0$$

Determine the value of K for which at least one root will lie on the $j\omega$ axis and none in the right half s-plane.

[10 marks : 2016]

Solution:

Characteristic equation;

$s^3 + 3408.3\, s^2 + 1204000\, s + 1.5 \times 10^7 K = 0$

Using Routh's array:

s^3	1	1204000
s^2	3408.3	1.5×10^7 K
s^1	$\dfrac{3408.3 \times 1204000 - 1.5 \times 10^7 . K}{3408.3}$	0
s^0	$1.5 \times 10^7 . K$	

For marginal stability or to get roots on $j\omega$ axis;

$$3408.3 \times 1.204 \times 10^6 - 1.5 \times 10^7 K = 0$$

or $$K = \frac{3408.3 \times 0.1204}{1.5} = 273.57$$

4.12 **An open-loop system $G(s) = \dfrac{1}{s^2(\tau s+1)}$ is placed in cascade with a proportional and derivative controller $K(s) = (1 + T_d s)$. If their unity feedback closed-loop system oscillates at a frequency of $\sqrt{2}$ rad/second, find the ranges/values of the system and controller parameters, i.e., ranges/values of K, T_d and τ.**

[12 marks : 2018]

Solution:

$$G(s) = \frac{K}{s^2(\tau s+1)}, \qquad K(s) = 1+\tau_d s$$

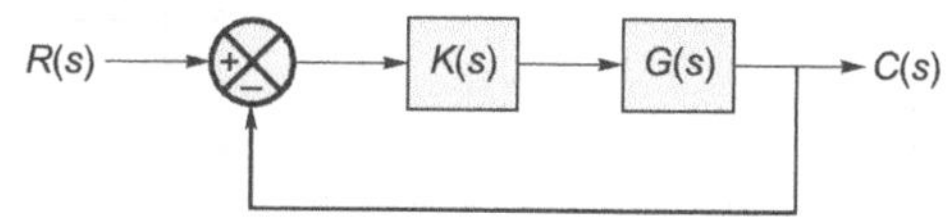

$$\text{CLTF} = \frac{K(1+\tau_d s)}{s^2(\tau s+1)+K(1+\tau_d s)}$$

Characteristic equation,

$$s^2(\tau s + 1) + K(1 + \tau_d s) = 0$$

$$\tau s^3 + s^2 + \tau_d Ks + K = 0$$

Let us from a Routh array,

When $\tau = \tau_d$, we get an auxiliary equation $A(s)$

$$\begin{array}{c|cc} s^3 & \tau & \tau_d K \\ s^2 & 1 & K \\ s^1 & \tau_d K - \tau K & \\ s^0 & K & \end{array}$$

$$A(s) = s^2 + K = 0$$

$$s^2 = -K$$

$$s = \pm j\sqrt{K}$$

$$\tau_d = \tau$$

System oscillates at $\sqrt{2}$ rad/sec.

So, on comparing $\sqrt{K} = \sqrt{2}$

$$K = 2$$

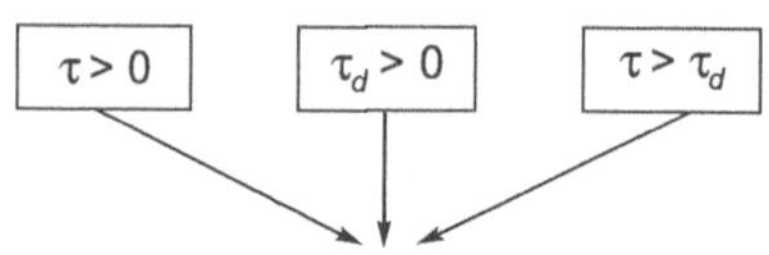

For system to be stable

4.13 For a unity feedback time delay system with open-loop transfer function, $G(s) = \dfrac{Ke^{-Ts}}{s(s+2)}$.

Calculate:

(i) the maximum tolerable value of delay, T, when $K = 1$;

(ii) phase margin when $K = \sqrt{5}$ and delay $T = 0.5$ seconds.

[20 marks : 2018]

Solution:

(i) $G(s) = \dfrac{Ke^{-Ts}}{s(s+2)}$, a unity feedback time delay system.

$$e^{-Ts} \approx (1 - Ts)$$

$$G(s) = \frac{(1-Ts)K}{s(s+2)}$$

The characteristic equation is,

$$s^2 + 2s + K - TsK = 0$$

$$s^2 + (2 - KT)\,s + K = 0$$

When, $K = 1$

$$s^2 + (2 - T)\,s + 1 = 0$$

$$\begin{array}{c|cc} s^2 & 1 & 1 \\ s^1 & 2-T & \\ s^0 & 1 & \end{array}$$

For system to be stable $2 - T > 0$

$$T < 2$$

The maximum tolerable value of $T = 2$.

(ii) When, $K = \sqrt{5}, \quad T = 0.5$

$$G(s) = \frac{\sqrt{5}(1-0.5s)}{s(s+2)}$$

$$G(j\omega) = \frac{\sqrt{5}(1-j0.5\omega)}{j\omega 2\left(1+j\frac{\omega}{2}\right)} = \frac{\sqrt{5}(1-j0.5\omega)}{j2\omega(1+j0.5\omega)}$$

$$|G(j\omega)| = \frac{\sqrt{5}}{2\omega} \qquad |G(j\omega)|_{\omega=\omega_{gc}} = 1$$

$$\frac{\sqrt{5}}{2\omega_{gc}} = 1 \qquad \omega_{gc} = \frac{\sqrt{5}}{2} = 1.118 \text{ rad/sec.}$$

$$\angle G(j\omega) = -90° - 2\tan^{-1}\left(\frac{\omega}{2}\right)$$

$$\angle G(j\omega)|_{\omega=\omega_{gc}} = -90° - 2\tan^{-1}\left(\frac{\omega_{gc}}{2}\right) = -148.412°$$

$$\text{Phase margin} = 180 + \angle G(j\omega)|_{\omega=\omega_{gc}} = 31.58°$$

4.14 The open loop transfer function of unity feedback control system is given by

$$G(s) = \frac{K}{s(s+a)(s+b)}, \quad 0 < a \le b$$

(i) Find the range of the gain constant K (> 0) for stability using Routh-Hurwitz criterion.

(ii) What type of control do you use if the system is required to have zero steady-state error for ramp input? Let 'A' be the parameter that can be varied in the introduced control. Find the range of 'K' for stability in terms of parameters a, b and A using Routh-Hurwitz criterion.

[20 marks : 2020]

Solution:

(i) Characteristic equation

$$1 + G(s).H(s) = 0$$

$$s(s^2 + (a+b)s + ab) + K = 0$$

$$s^3 + (a+b)s^2 + abs + K = 0$$

s^3	1	ab
s^2	$a+b$	K
s^1	$\frac{(a+b)ab-K}{a+b}$	
s^0	K	

For stability $K > 0$

and $(a+b)ab - K > 0$

$$(a+b)ab > K$$

$$K < (a+b)ab$$

$$\therefore \quad 0 < K < (a+b)ab$$

(ii) We need to use PI Controller to eliminate steady state error.

Let controller transfer function is $1+\frac{A}{s}$.

Characteristic equation is

$$1+\frac{(A+s)K}{s^2(s+a)(s+b)} = 0$$

$$s^4 + (a + b)s^3 + abs^2 + Ks + AK = 0$$

$$\begin{array}{c|ccc} s^4 & 1 & ab & AK \\ s^3 & (a+b) & K & \\ s^2 & \frac{(a+b)ab-K}{a+b} & AK & \\ s^1 & \frac{\left[\frac{(a+b)ab-K}{a+b}\right]K-(a+b)AK}{\frac{(a+b)ab-K}{a+b}} & & \\ s^0 & AK & & \end{array}$$

For the stability

$$\left[\frac{(a+b)ab-K}{a+b}-(a+b)A\right]K > 0$$

$$(a + b)ab - K - (a + b)^2A > 0$$

$$(a + b)ab - (a + b)^2A > K$$

$$K < (a + b)ab - (a + b)^2A$$

and $$\frac{(a+b)ab-K}{a+b} > 0$$

$$(a + b)ab > K$$

$$K < (a + b)ab$$

$\therefore$ $$K < (a + b)ab - (a + b)^2A$$

5. Root Locus Techniques

5.1 **A unity feedback control system has an open loop transfer function $G(s) = \frac{K(s+1)}{s(s-1)}$.**

Show that the root loci of complex roots are part of a circle with (–1, 0) as centre and radius = $\sqrt{2}$. Sketch the root locus with K as a variable parameter.

[10 marks : 2007]

Solution:

The characteristic equation of closed loop control system is, $1 + G(s) H(s) = 0$

The angle criterion for the root locus is

$$\angle G(s) = \pm 180°(2q + 1); \quad \text{where } q = 0, 1, 2$$

$$s = \sigma + j\omega$$

If we put the value of 's', we get,

$$\angle\frac{k(s+1)}{s(s-1)} = \angle\left[\frac{(\sigma+j\omega+1)}{(\sigma+j\omega)(\sigma+j\omega-1)}\right]$$

$$\tan^{-1}\frac{\omega}{\sigma+1}-\tan^{-1}\frac{\omega}{\sigma}-\tan^{-1}\frac{\omega}{\sigma-1} = -\pi$$

$$\pi+\tan^{-1}\frac{\omega}{\sigma+1} = \tan^{-1}\left(\frac{\omega}{\sigma}\right)+\tan^{-1}\left(\frac{\omega}{\sigma-1}\right)$$

Taking 'tan' on both sides,

$$\frac{\tan\pi+\dfrac{\omega}{\sigma+1}}{1-\tan\pi\left(\dfrac{\omega}{\sigma+1}\right)} = \frac{\dfrac{\omega}{\sigma}+\dfrac{\omega}{\sigma-1}}{1-\dfrac{\omega^2}{\sigma(\sigma-1)}}$$

$$\frac{\dfrac{\omega}{\sigma}+\dfrac{\omega}{\sigma-1}}{1-\dfrac{\omega^2}{\sigma(\sigma-1)}} = \frac{\omega}{\sigma+1} \qquad \text{[where } \tan\pi = 0]$$

$$\frac{(\sigma-1)+\sigma}{\sigma(\sigma-1)-\omega^2} = \frac{1}{\sigma+1}$$

$$\frac{2\sigma-1}{\sigma^2-\sigma-\omega^2} = \frac{1}{\sigma+1}$$

$$2\sigma^2-\sigma+2\sigma-1 = \sigma^2-\sigma-\omega^2$$

$$(\sigma^2+2\sigma+1)+\omega^2 = 2$$

$$\therefore \qquad (\sigma+1)^2+\omega^2 = 2 \qquad \ldots(i)$$

Equation (*i*) shows root locus in the s-plane; which is a circle with centre at (–1, 0) and radius $\sqrt{2}$.

$$G(s) = \frac{k(s+1)}{s(s-1)}$$

Open loop poles = 0, 1 $\quad n = 2$

Open loop zeros = –1 $\quad m = 1$

Number of branches to infinity $n - m = 2 - 1 = 1$

Characteristic equation,

$$1 + G(s) = 1+\frac{k(s+1)}{s(s-1)} = 0$$

$$\Rightarrow \qquad k = \frac{-s(s-1)}{(s+1)} = \frac{s-s^2}{s+1}$$

to find break away points, $\dfrac{dk}{ds} = 0$

$$\Rightarrow \qquad \frac{(1-2s)(s+1)-(s-s^2)}{(s+1)} = 0$$

$$s-2s^2+1-2s-s+s^2 = 0$$

$$\Rightarrow \qquad -s^2-2s+1 = 0$$

$$s = -2.414, 0.414$$

Characteristic equation,

$$\text{Numerator of } [1+G(s)] = 1+\frac{k(s+1)}{s(s-1)} = s(s-1)+k(s+1)$$

$$= s^2+(k-1)s+k$$

For intersection with $j\omega$-axis, the system is marginally stable. It implies that $k = 1$

$$s^2 + 1 = 0$$
$$s = \pm j1$$

Hence, root locus for the system.

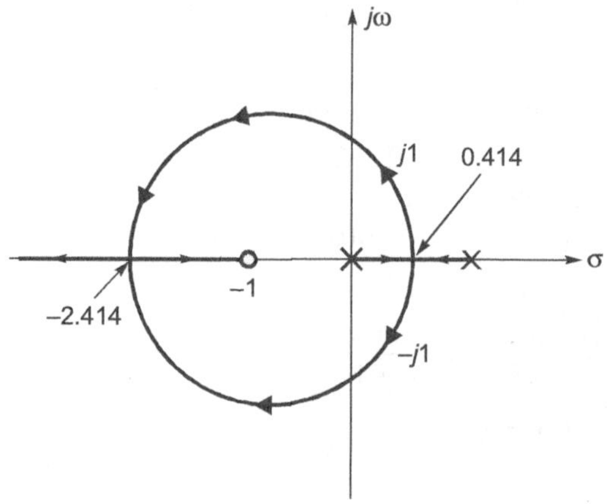

5.2 Draw the root loci of the system showing all the relevant point for open-loop transfer function of the system given by

$$G(s) = \frac{k}{s(s^2 + 4s + 8)}$$

[12 marks : 2008]

Solution:

$$\text{OLTF} = \frac{k}{s(s^2 + 4s + 8)}$$

Poles are at $s_1 = 0$ and $s_{2,3} = \dfrac{-4 \pm \sqrt{16-32}}{2} = -2 \pm j2$

There are 3 poles and no zero with root loci, all terminating at infinity.

$$\phi = \frac{(2q+1)180°}{P-Z} = 60°, 180°, 300° \text{ for } q = 0, 1, 2 \text{ (angle of asymptotes)}$$

$$\text{Centroid} = \frac{0 - 2 + j2 - 2 - j2}{3} = \frac{-4}{3} = -1.33$$

$$1 + \frac{k}{s(s^2 + 4s + 8)} = 0$$

$$\Rightarrow \quad k = -s(s^2 + 4s + 8) = -(s^3 + 4s^2 + 8s)$$

For break away points, $\dfrac{dk}{ds} = 0$

$$\Rightarrow \quad \frac{dk}{ds} = -(3s^2 + 8s + 8)$$

$$s_{1,2} = -\frac{8 \pm \sqrt{64 - 4 \times 8 \times 3}}{2 \times 3}$$

$$= -\frac{8 \pm \sqrt{64 - 96}}{6} = -1.33 + j0.943$$

As $\dfrac{dk}{ds}$ is imaginary, there is no breakaway point from the real axis.

Imaginary axis crossing:

$$\text{Characteristic equation} = s(s^2 + 4s + 8) + k$$
$$= s^3 + 4s^2 + 8s + k = 0$$

s^3	1	8
s^2	4	k
s^1	$\frac{32-k}{4}$	
s^0	k	

From Routh-Hurwitz Criteria:

For $k = 32$, the system is marginally stable and beyond $k = 32$ the system becomes unstable.

Hence, $\quad 4s^2 + k = 4s^2 + 32$

$$s = j2\sqrt{2} = j\omega$$
$$\omega = 2\sqrt{2} = 2.83$$

The root locus cuts the imaginary axis at $\pm j2.83$.

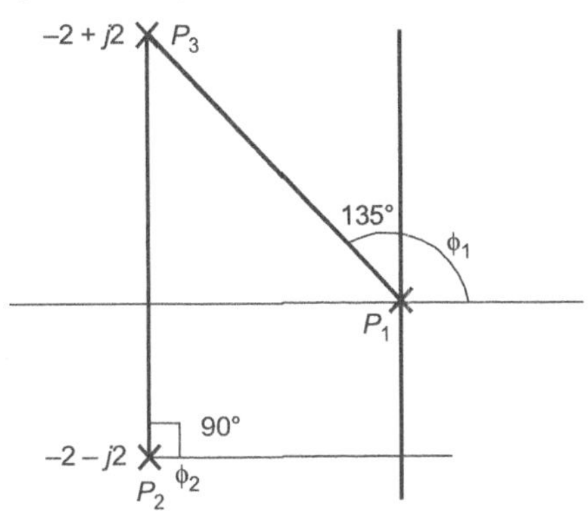

$$\phi_1 = 180° - \tan^{-1}\left(\frac{2}{2}\right) = 135°$$
$$\phi_2 = 90°$$
$$\Sigma\phi_p = \phi_1 + \phi_2 = 135° + 90° = 225°$$
$$\phi = \Sigma\phi_z - \Sigma\phi_p = 0 - 225° = -225°$$

Angle of departure, $\quad \phi_D = 180 + \phi = 180 - 225° = -45°$

Root locus of the given system:

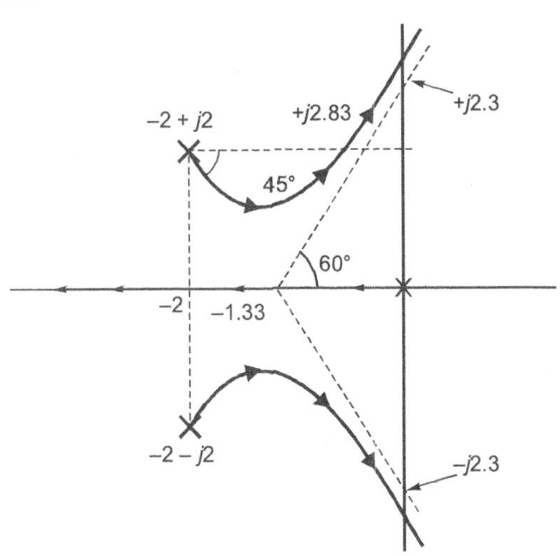

5.3 Given, $G(s)H(s) = \dfrac{K}{s(s+1)(s+4)}$, sketch the root locus of the system

(i) Determine the value of K for which the system is at the verge of instability.

(ii) For the damping ratio (δ) 0.34, determine the value of K and the gain margin (GM).

[10 marks : 2012]

Solution:

$$G(s)\,H(s) = \frac{K}{s(s+1)(s+4)}$$

Step-1: Number of open loop poles ; $P = 3$

Number of open loop zeros ; $Z = 0$

Number of branches terminating at infinity

$$= P - Z = 3$$

Step-2: Angle of asymptotes

$$\theta = \frac{(2q+1)180^\circ}{P-Z} \quad \text{where } q = 0, 1, 2$$

$$\theta_1 = \frac{180^\circ}{3} = 60^\circ$$

$$\theta_2 = \frac{3\times 180^\circ}{3} = 180^\circ$$

$$\theta_3 = \frac{5\times 180^\circ}{3} = 300^\circ$$

Step-3:

$$\text{Centroid} = \frac{\Sigma \text{ real part of open loop poles} - \Sigma \text{ real part of open loop zeros}}{P-Z}$$

$$= \frac{(-1-4)-(0)}{3-0} = -\frac{5}{3}$$

Step-4: Break away point

$$K + s(s^2 + 5s + 4) = 0$$

$$K = -s^3 - 5s^2 - 4s$$

$$\frac{dK}{ds} = -3s^2 - 10s - 4 = 0$$

$$3s^2 + 10s + 4 = 0$$

$$\Rightarrow \quad s_1, s_2 = -0.4648, -2.8685$$

Valid break-away point will be –0.4648

(i) Routh array table:

s^3	1	4
s^2	5	K
s^1	$\frac{20-K}{5}$	0
s^0	1	

For system to be stable,

$$20 - K > 0 \Rightarrow K < 20$$

For system to be marginally stable,

$$K = 20$$

$$A(s) = 5s^2 + 20 = 0$$

$$\Rightarrow \quad s = \pm 2j$$

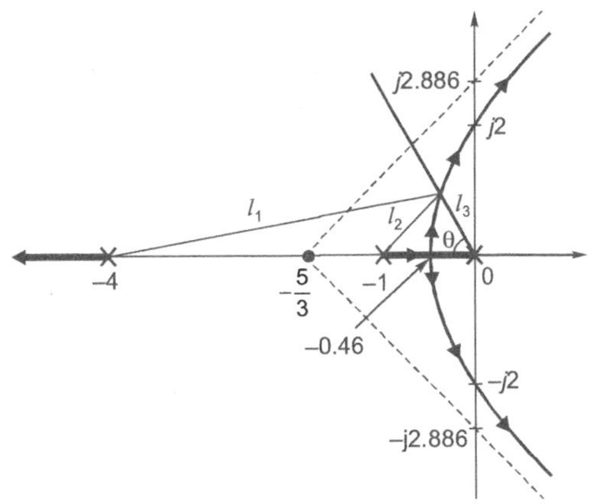

(ii) To find K,

$$\theta = \cos^{-1}\xi = \cos^{-1}(0.34) = 70.123^\circ$$

$$K = l_1 l_2 l_3$$

$$\text{Gain margin (GM)} = \frac{K\text{(Marginal stability)}}{K\text{ (desired)}}$$

5.4 The feedback control system has $G(s) = \dfrac{K(s+6)}{(s+4)}$ and an ideal integrator with unity gain in feedback path. Determine the following, with reference to Root locus technique:

(i) $K = 0$ and $K = \infty$ points on root loci

(ii) number of asymptotes

(iii) breakaway points, if any

[5 marks : 2013]

Solution:

$$G(s) = \frac{K(s+6)}{(s+4)} \qquad H(s) = \frac{1}{s} \qquad G(s)\,H(s) = \frac{K(s+6)}{s(s+4)}$$

(i) $K = 0$; represent the location of open loop poles i.e. $s = -4$ and $s = 0$ in the given case.
$K = \infty$ represent the open loop zero i.e. $s = -6$ and $s = -\infty$.

(ii) Number of asymptotes = number of open loop poles (P) – number of open loop zeros (Z)
$= (2-1) = 1$

(iii) Characteristic equation:

$$1 + \frac{K(s+6)}{(s)(s+4)} = 0 \Rightarrow K = \frac{-(s)(s+4)}{(s+6)}$$

For breakaway points, $\dfrac{dK}{ds} = 0$

$$\Rightarrow \left[\frac{(2s+4)(s+6) - (s^2+4s)}{(s+6)^2}\right] = 0$$

$$2s^2 + 16s + 24 - s^2 - 4s = 0$$

$$s^2 + 12s + 24 = 0$$

$$s = -2.536, \; -9.464$$

−2.536 ↑ Breakaway point; −9.464 ↑ Break in point

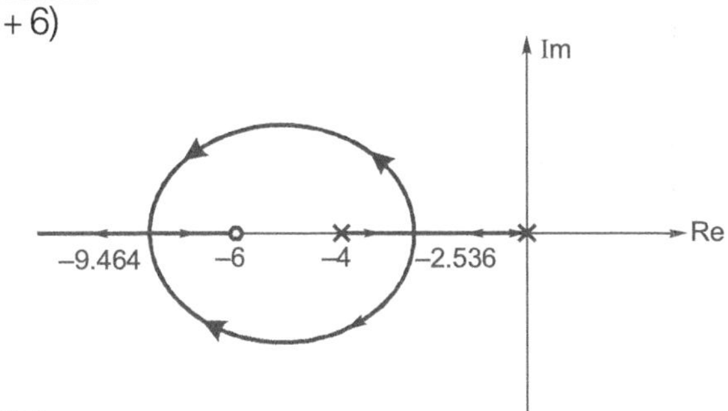

5.5 The system is described by $G(s) = \dfrac{K(s^2 + 6s + 10)}{s^2 + 2s + 10}$, $H(s) = 1$. Obtain $K = 0$, $K = \infty$ points in root-loci.

Show that the root -loci are arcs of a circle centred at origin with radius equal to $\sqrt{10}$.

[10 marks : 2015]

Solution:

$$G(s) = \frac{K(s^2 + 6s + 10)}{s^2 + 2s + 10}; \quad H(s) = 1$$

$$G(s)H(s) = \frac{K(s^2 + 6s + 10)}{s^2 + 2s + 10}$$

Characteristic equation, $1 + GH(s) = 0$; that will give poles of closed loop system.

$\therefore \quad s^2 + 2s + 10 + K(s^2 + 6s + 10) = 0$

or $\quad (s + 1 + 3j)(s + 1 - 3j) + K[(s + 3 + j)(s + 3 - j)] = 0$

for $\quad K \to 0; \quad \Rightarrow \quad (s + 1 + 3j)(s + 1 - 3j) = 0$

$\Rightarrow \quad s = -1 \pm 3j$; i.e., open loop poles

As $\quad K \to \infty; \quad \Rightarrow \quad (s + 3 + j)(s + 3 - j) = 0$

$\Rightarrow \quad s = -3 \pm j$; i.e., open loop zeros

For root locus, open loop poles, for $K \to 0; \quad \Rightarrow \quad s = -1 \pm j3$

open loop zeros, for $K \to \infty; \quad \Rightarrow \quad s = -3 \pm j$

Here, $n - m = 0$; Hence no asymptote and no root locus lie on real axis.

We require the angle of departure at poles and angle of arrival at zeros.

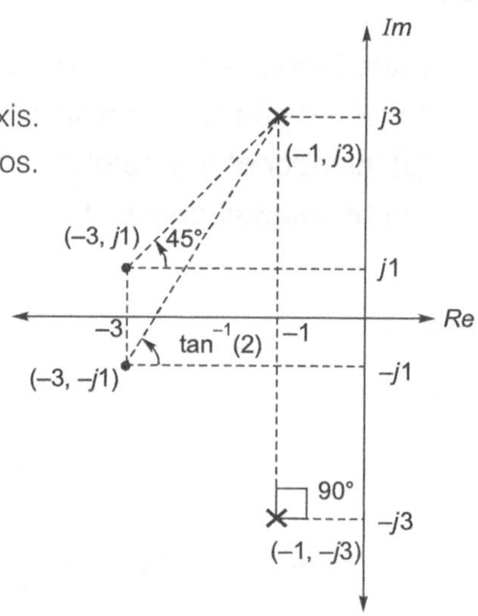

Angle of departure,
$$\phi_D = 180° + \phi$$
$$\phi = \Sigma\phi_z - \Sigma\phi_p$$
$$\phi = 45° + \tan^{-1}(2) - 90° = 18.43°$$
$$\phi_D = 180 + 18.43° = 198.43°$$

Similarly angle of arrival $\phi_A = 180° - \phi$ at zero $(-3, 1)$

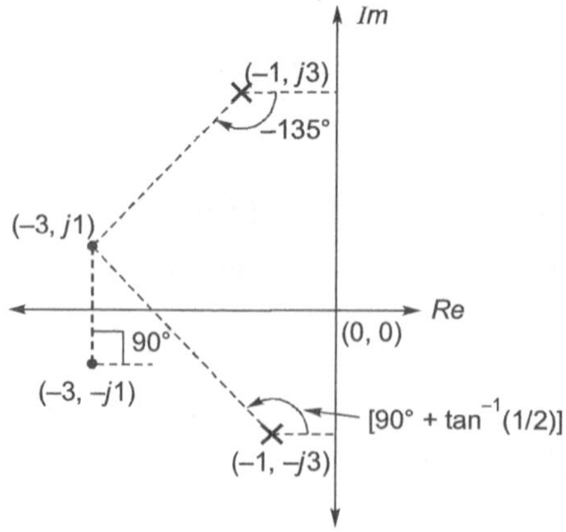

$$\begin{aligned}\phi &= \Sigma\phi_z - \Sigma\phi_p \\ &= 90 - [-135° + 90° + \tan^{-1}(1/2)] \\ &= 108.43°\end{aligned}$$

$$\phi_A = 71.57°$$

If we see the location of poles and zeros then distance from origin of both are same and thus the locus is the arc of a circle centred at origin (0, 0).

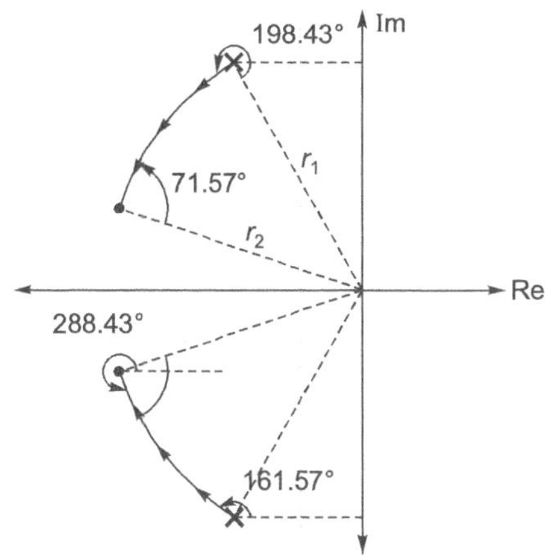

Here $$r_1 = r_2 = \sqrt{1^2+3^2} = \sqrt{10}$$

So the radius of arc = $\sqrt{10}$ unit.

Alternate solution:

$$G(s) = \frac{K(s^2+6s+10)}{s^2+2s+10} \text{ and } H(s) = 1$$

open loop transfer function,

$$G(s)\,H(s) = \frac{K(s^2+6s+10)}{s^2+2s+10}$$

Putting, $s = \sigma + j\omega$, on right hand side to get the root locus

$$G(\sigma+j\omega)\,H(\sigma+j\omega) = \frac{K[(\sigma+j\omega)^2+6(\sigma+j\omega)+10]}{[(\sigma+j\omega)^2+2(\sigma+j\omega)+10]}$$

For $GH(s)$ to be on root locus, by angle condition

$$\angle G(s)\,H(s) = (2q+1)\pi; \qquad \text{where, } q = 0, 1, 2, ...$$

or we can write; the imaginary part of $GH(s)$ must be zero.

Hence, $$G(\sigma+j\omega)\,H(\sigma+j\omega) = \frac{K[(\sigma^2-\omega^2+j2\sigma\omega)+6\sigma+j6\omega+10]}{[\sigma^2-\omega^2+j2\sigma\omega+2\sigma+j2\omega+10]}$$

or, $$= \frac{K[(\sigma^2-\omega^2+6\sigma+10)+j(2\sigma\omega+6\omega)]}{[\sigma^2-\omega^2+2\sigma+10)+j(2\sigma\omega+2\omega)]}$$

Relationalizing the above expression

$$= \frac{K[(\sigma^2-\omega^2+6\sigma+10)+j(2\sigma\omega+6\omega)][(\sigma^2-\omega^2+2\sigma+10)-j(2\sigma\omega+2\omega)]}{[(\sigma^2-\omega^2+2\sigma+10)^2+(2\sigma\omega+2\omega)^2]}$$

To make the imaginary terms equal to zero, we get

$$(\sigma^2-\omega^2+2\sigma+10)(2\sigma\omega+6\omega)-(\sigma^2-\omega^2+6\sigma+10)(2\sigma\omega+2\omega) = 0$$

or $$[(\sigma^2-\omega^2+2\sigma+10)(\sigma+3)-(\sigma^2-\omega^2+6\sigma+10)(\sigma+1)] = 0$$

or $$\sigma^3-\sigma\omega^2+2\sigma^2+10\sigma+3\sigma^2-3\omega^2+6\sigma+30 = \sigma^3-\sigma\omega^2+6\sigma^2+10\sigma+\sigma^2-\omega^2+6\sigma+10$$

or $$2\sigma^2+2\omega^2 = 20$$

or $$\sigma^2+\omega^2 = 10$$

Finally we can write,

$$(\sigma-0)^2+(\omega-0)^2 = (\sqrt{10})^2$$

which represent an equation of a circle having radius equal to $\sqrt{10}$ units and centre at (0, 0) i.e. origin.

Therefore the root loci is a part of circle centred at origin with radius equal to $\sqrt{10}$ units.

5.6 The open-loop transfer function of a unity feedback system is given as:

$$G(s)\,H(s) = \frac{4s+\alpha}{s(s^2+4s+9)}$$

Draw the root locus of the system when α varies from 0 to $+\infty$.

[20 marks : 2017]

Solution:

$$G(s)\,H(s) = \frac{4s+\alpha}{s(s^2+4s+9)}$$

Characteristic equation $= s(s^2 + 4s + 9) + 4s + \alpha = 0$

$$s^3 + 4s^2 + 13s + \alpha = 0$$

For $$G(s)\,H(s) = \frac{\alpha}{s(s^2+4s+13)}$$

Characteristic equation and roots will be the same.

Hence root locus will be same.

Open-loop poles $= s = 0,\ s = -2 \pm j3$

Part of root locus lying on real axis, LHS side of real axis

$$\text{Angle of asymptote} = \frac{180°(2k+1)}{P-Z},$$

$$k = 0, 1, - P - Z - 1 = 0, 1, 2$$

$$P = 3,\ Z = 0$$

$$= \frac{180°}{3}, \frac{180°\times 3}{3}, \frac{180°\times 5}{3}$$

$$= 60°, 180°, 300°$$

$$\text{Centroid} = \frac{\text{Sum of real part of poles} - \text{Sum of real part of zeroes}}{P-Z}$$

$$= \frac{0-2-2}{3} = -\frac{4}{3}$$

For break away points, $$\frac{d\alpha}{ds} = 0$$

$$1 + G(s)\,H(s) = 0$$

$$G(s)\,H(s) = -1$$

$$|G(s)\,H(s)| = 1$$

$$\alpha = s(s^2 + 4s + 13)$$

$$\frac{d\alpha}{ds} = s^2 + 4s + 13 + 2s^2 + 4s = 0$$

$$3s^2 + 8s + 13 = 0$$

$$s = \text{complex}$$

As root locus is symmetric about real axis and number of poles is 3.

Hence no break away points.

Angle of departure from $-2 + j3 = 180° -$ [(angle to the pole from other poles) − (angle to the pole from zeroes)]

Angle from, $s = -2 - j3 = 90°$

Angle from, $s = 0 = 123°$

Angle of departure from,

$$-2 + j3 = 180° - (123° + 90°)$$

$$= -33°$$

Similarly, angle of departure from $-2 - j3 = +147°$

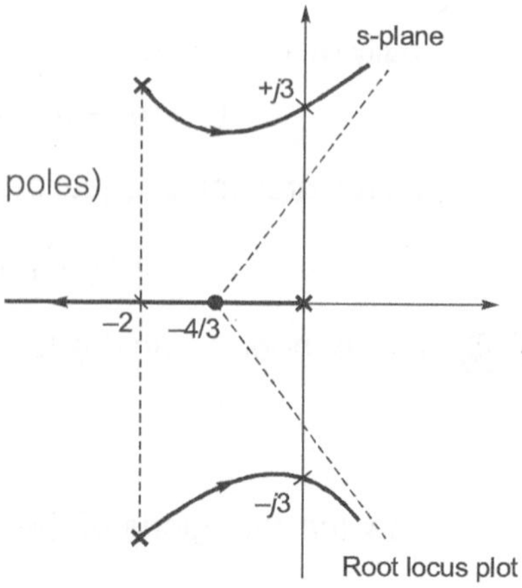

Root locus plot

5.7 For the system shown in the figure below, the step response of $G(s)$ is given by $(1.5 - 2e^{-t} + 0.5e^{-2t})$ $u(t)$ and $K(s)$ is the integral controller with $K(s) = \frac{K}{s}$. Sketch the approximate root locus of the closed-loop system poles as K varies from 0 to ∞. Also calculate the real part of poles when K becomes ∞:

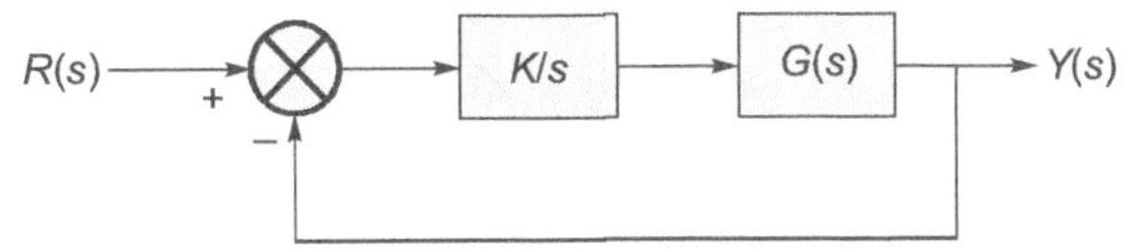

[20 marks : 2018]

Solution:

Sketch the root locus:

$$\text{Step response of } G(s) = s(t) = (1.5 - 2e^{-t} + 0.5e^{-2t})\,u(t)$$

$$G(s) = \frac{C(s)}{R(s)} \quad \text{for step input } R(s) = \frac{1}{s}$$

$$G(s) = \frac{\frac{1.5}{s} - \frac{2}{(s+1)} + \frac{0.5}{(s+2)}}{1/s}$$

$$= \frac{1.5(s^2+3s+2) - 2(s^2+2s) + 0.5(s^2+s)}{s(s+1)(s+2)\frac{1}{s}}$$

$$G(s) = \frac{(s+3)}{(s+1)(s+2)}$$

$$\text{OLTF} = \frac{K}{s}G(s) = \frac{K(s+3)}{s(s+1)(s+2)}$$

Let us sketch the root locus of the above system.

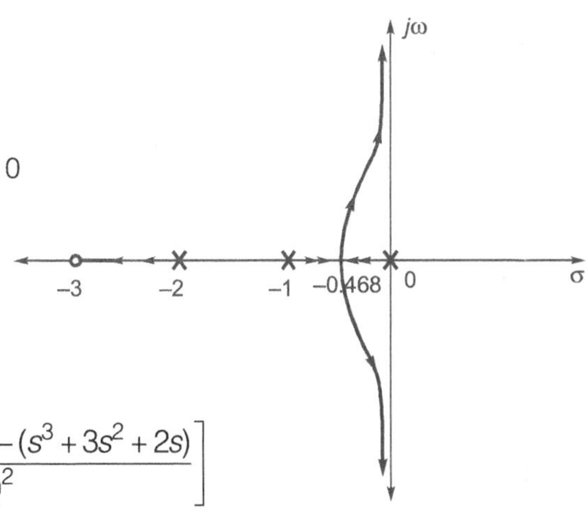

Centroid, $\sigma = \frac{(0)+(-1)+(-2)-(-3)}{P-Z} = 0$

CLTF: The characteristic equation is,

$$s(s^2 + 3s + 2) + K(s + 3) = 0$$

$$K = -\frac{(s^3+3s^2+2s)}{(s+3)}$$

$$\frac{dK}{ds} = -\left[\frac{(3s^2+6s+2)(s+3) - (s^3+3s^2+2s)}{(s+3)^2}\right]$$

Put, $\frac{dk}{ds} = 0$

$$3s^3 + 15s^2 + 20s + 6 = s^3 + 3s^2 + 2s$$

$$2s^3 + 12s^2 + 18s + 6 = 0$$

$$s^3 + 6s^2 + 9s + 3 = 0$$

$$s = \underset{\text{valid}}{-0.468}, \underset{\text{invalid}}{-3.879}, \underset{\text{invalid}}{-1.653}$$

Breakaway point is at $s = -0.468$

when, $K = \infty$

The real part of poles are (0, 0, −3).

5.8 The accompanying figure depicts the locus of closed loop poles of a system for $0 < K < \infty$. From the plot, determine the frequency with which the system is likely to exhibit sustained oscillation. Determine the value of K at which one of the closed loop poles lie at $s = -8$.

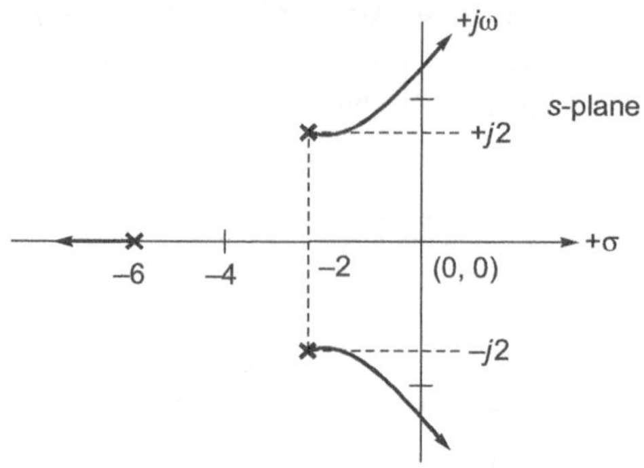

[12 marks : 2021]

Solution:

From the given RLD (Root Locus Diagram), the open loop gain transfer function is

$$GH = \frac{K}{(s+6)(s^2+4s+8)}$$

The characteristics equation is

$$q(s) = s^3 + 10s^2 + 32s + (48 + K) = 0$$

By using RH criterion

s^3	1	32
s^2	10	$48 + K$
s^1	$\frac{320-48-K}{10} = 0 \Rightarrow K = 272$	
s^0	$48 + K$	

The auxiliary equation :

$$A(s) = 10s^2 + 48 + 272 = 0$$

$$A(s) = 10s^2 + 320 = 0$$

$$A(s) = s^2 + 32 = 0$$

$$s = \pm j\sqrt{32} = \pm j5.65$$

$\therefore$ Frequency of oscillations = 5.65 rad/sec

To find K at $s = -8$

$$|GH|_{s=-8} = 1$$

$$\therefore \quad \left|\frac{K}{(-8+6)(64-32+8)}\right| = 1$$

$$\therefore \quad K = 80$$

5.9 The characteristic equation of a unity feedback (negative) system is given by $s^3 + 3ks^2 + (k+2)s + 4 = 0$.

(i) Determine the forward path transfer function $G(s)$.

(ii) Using Routh-Hurwitz criteria, find the range of k for which the system is stable.

[12 marks : 2022]

Solution:

(i) Characteristic equation

$$s^3 + 3Ks^2 + (K + 2)s + 4 = 0$$

$$s^3 + 3Ks^2 + Ks + 2s + 4 = 0$$

$$1 + \frac{K(3s^2 + s)}{s^3 + 2s + 4} = 0$$

Standard characteristic equation of a unity feedback (negative) system is given by

$$1 + G(s)H(s) = 0 \qquad \{H(s) = 1\}$$

On comparison, $G(s) = \dfrac{K(3s^2 + s)}{s^3 + 2s + 4}$

(ii) $CE = s^3 + 3Ks^2 + (K + 2)s + 4$

Routh-hurwitz Array is given by

s^3	1	$K+2$
s^2	$3K$	4
s	$\dfrac{3K(K+2)-4}{3K}$	0
s^0	4	

For system to be stable

$$\frac{3K(K+2) - 4 \times 1}{3K} > 0$$

$$3K^2 + 6K - 4 > 0$$

$$(K - 0.5)(K + 2.5) > 0$$

$$\therefore \quad K > 0.5$$

6. Frequency Response Analysis

6.1 The open loop transfer function of a unity feedback control system is given by the expression:

$$G(s) = \frac{K}{(s+2)(s+5)}$$

Draw the Nyquist plot of the closed loop system and comment upon the stability of the system.

[10 marks : 2001]

Solution:

On putting, $s = j\omega$

$$G(j\omega)H(j\omega) = \frac{K}{(j\omega+2)(j\omega+5)} = \frac{K(2-j\omega)\times(5-j\omega)}{(\omega^2+4)(\omega^2+25)}$$

$$= \frac{K(10 - 7(j\omega) - \omega^2)}{(\omega^2+4)(\omega^2+25)}$$

The plot will cut imaginary axis where real part of the equation is equal to zero.

$$\omega = \sqrt{10} \text{ rad/sec.}$$

Hence, Nyquist plot, P = number of open loop poles in the RHS of the s-plane.

The point $(-1 + j0)$ is not encircled by the Nyquist plot, therefore

$$N = 0 \text{ and } P = 0$$
$$N = P - Z_+$$
$$0 = 0 - Z_+$$
$$Z_+ = 0$$

As ($Z_+ = 0$), there are no roots of closed loop characteristics equation having positive real part, hence the closed-loop system is stable.

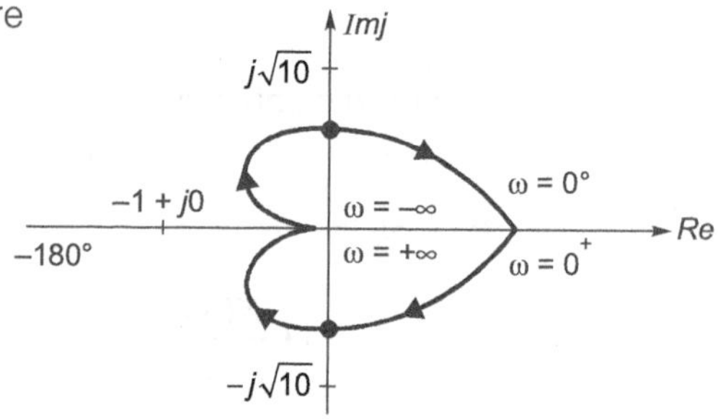

6.2 **From the asymptotic approximation plot of dB versus ω of a minimum phase system with real poles and zero shown in the below figure, determine the poles and zero of the system.**

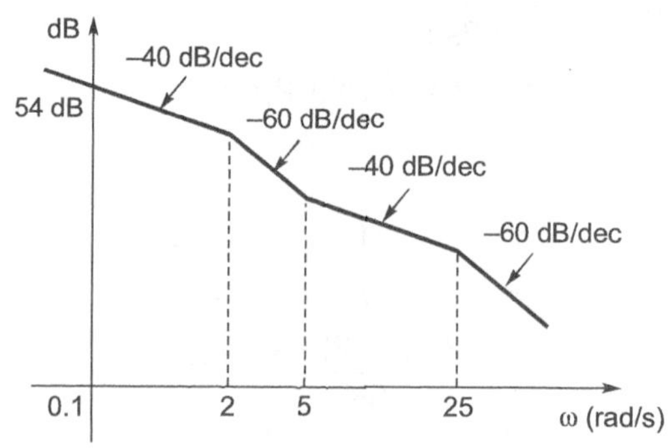

[10 marks : 2002]

Solution:

- Initially, there is a fall of 40 dB/dec upto 2. It implies that transfer function of the given system has two poles at origin.
- At corner frequency $\omega = 2$ rad/sec, the slope changes from –40 dB/dec to –60 dB/dec, then there is third pole at $\omega = 2$ rad/s.
- At corner frequency $\omega = 5$, slope changes from –60 dB/dec to –40 dB/sec. It implies that there is one zero at $\omega = 5$ rad/s.
- At $\omega = 25$ rad/s slope again changes from –40 dB/dec to –60 dB/dec. So, there is fourth pole at $\omega = 25$ rad/s.
- Let the gain of the system is K.
- From above analysis, the transfer function of the system is

$$T(s) = \frac{K\left(1+\frac{s}{5}\right)}{s^2\left(1+\frac{s}{2}\right)\left(1+\frac{s}{25}\right)} = \frac{10\,K\,(s+5)}{s^2(s+2)\,(s+25)} = \frac{50(s+5)}{s^2(s+2)\,(s+25)}$$

Hence, there is one zero at $s = -5$.

and poles at $s = -2, -25$ and double poles at origin.

At $\omega = 0.1$;

$$54 = -40 \log 0.1 + C$$
$$54 = 40 + C$$
$$C = 14$$
$$K = 10^{14/20} = 5$$

6.3 What are the different frequency response plots? Sketch the polar plot for the transfer function given below:

$$G(s) = \frac{100(s-5)}{s(s+10)}$$

[12 marks : 2003]

Solution:

The different frequency response plots are:

1. Bode plot
2. Nyquist plot
3. Nichol's chart
4. Polar plot

$$G(s) = \frac{100(s-5)}{s(s+10)}$$

Put, $s = j\omega$

$$\Rightarrow \quad G(j\omega) = \frac{100(j\omega-5)}{j\omega(j\omega+10)} \quad \ldots(i)$$

Rationalizing equation (i),

$$G(j\omega) = \frac{-j\,100(j\omega-5)\times(-j\omega+10)}{\omega(j\omega+10)\times(-j\omega+10)}$$

$$= \frac{-j\,100\left[\omega^2+15j\omega-50\right]}{\omega(\omega^2+100)} = \frac{100\left\{j(50-\omega^2)+15\,\omega\right\}}{\omega(\omega^2+100)}$$

Separating into real and imaging parts,

$$G(j\omega) = \frac{15\times100}{\omega^2+100} + j\frac{(50-\omega^2)\times100}{\omega(\omega^2+100)}$$

The real and imaginary parts $G(j\omega)$ for some values of ω are calculated in the following table.

ω	0	1	100	∞
Re $G(j\omega)$	0.15	14.85	0.1485	+0
Imj $G(j\omega)$	$+j\infty$	$j48.51$	$-j0.985$	$-j0$

- At $\omega = \sqrt{50} = 5\sqrt{2}$, the imaginary term is zero and plot crosses the real axis.
- On the basis of the above analysis, the polar plot of the transfer function is

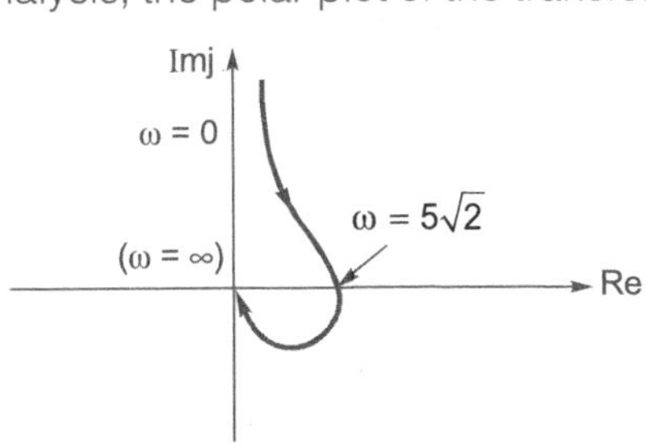

6.4 Define gain margin. Calculate the gain margin for the system for which

$$GH(s) = \frac{1}{s\left(1+\frac{s}{2}\right)\left(1+\frac{s}{10}\right)}$$

[10 marks : 2003]

Solution:

The gain margin is a factor by which the gain of a stable system is allowed to increase before the system reaches instability.

$$GH(s) = \frac{1}{s\left(1+\frac{s}{2}\right)\left(1+\frac{s}{10}\right)} = \frac{1}{s\left(\frac{2+s}{2}\right)\left(\frac{10+s}{10}\right)} = \frac{20}{s(s+2)(s+10)}$$

Put, $s = j\omega$

$$GH(j\omega) = \frac{20}{j\omega(j\omega+2)(j\omega+10)}$$

At (ω_{pc}), imaginary part of equation becomes zero.

$$= \frac{20}{j\omega\left[(j\omega)^2+10j\omega+2j\omega+20\right]} = \frac{20}{j\omega[-\omega^2+12j\omega+20]}$$

$$= \frac{20}{\left[-j\omega^3+12(j\omega)^2+20j\omega\right]} = \frac{12}{\left[-j\omega^3-12\omega^2+20j\omega\right]}$$

$$GH(j\omega) = \frac{20}{-12\omega^2+j(20\omega-\omega^3)}$$

At $\omega_{pc} = I_{mj}[GH(j\omega)] = 0$

$$20\,\omega_{pc} - \omega^3{}_{pc} = 0$$

$\Rightarrow$ $20\,\omega_{pc} = \omega^3{}_{pc}$

$\Rightarrow$ $\omega^2{}_{pc} = 20$

$\therefore$ $\omega_{pc} = 2\sqrt{5}$

$$GH(j\omega) = \frac{20}{\omega_{pc}\sqrt{\omega_{pc}^2+4}\sqrt{100+\omega_{pc}^2}}$$

$$x = \frac{20}{2\sqrt{5}\sqrt{20+4}\sqrt{100+20}} = \frac{20}{240}$$

(Gain margin) $G:M = \frac{1}{x} = \frac{240}{20} = 12$

$$GM = 20\log\left(\frac{1}{x}\right) = 20\log 12 = 21.58\text{ dB}$$

6.5 **Obtain the polar plot for a system whose characteristic equation is $s^3 + 3s^2 + 2s + 4 = 0$ and also obtain the Gain Margin.**

[10 marks : 2006]

Solution:

Given, $s^3 + 3s^2 + 2s + 4 = 0$ (characteristic equation)

or $1 + \frac{4}{s(s^2+3s+2)} = 0$

On comparing with $1 + G(s)\,H(s)$,

$$G(j\omega)\,H(s) = \frac{4}{s(s^2+3s+2)} = \frac{4}{s(s+1)\,(s+2)}$$

Put $s = j\omega$,

$$G(j\omega)\,H(j\omega) = \frac{4}{j\omega(j\omega+1)(j\omega+2)} = \frac{4(1-j\omega)(2-j\omega)}{j\omega(1+\omega^2)(4+\omega^2)}$$

$$= \frac{4[2-3j\omega+\omega^2]}{j\omega(1+\omega^2)(4+\omega^2)}$$

$$G(j\omega)\,H(j\omega) = -\frac{12}{(\omega^2+1)(\omega^2+4)} + \frac{4(\omega^2-2)j}{\omega(\omega^2+1)(\omega^2+4)}$$

The real and imaginary parts of $G(j\omega)\,H(j\omega)$ for some values of ω are calculated in the following table:

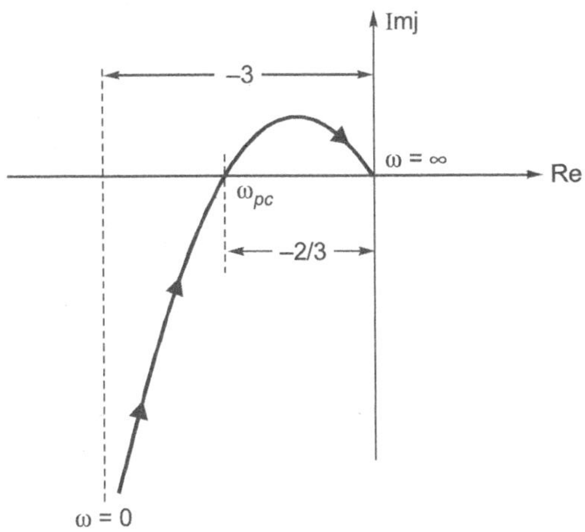

ω	0	$\sqrt{2}$	∞
$R/G(j\omega)\,H(j\omega)$	–3	–2/3	–0
$Imj\ Gs(j\omega)\,H(j\omega)$	$-j\infty$	0	$+j0$

at ω_{pc} (phase crossover frequency) imaginary part of $G(j\omega)\,H(j\omega)$ becomes zero.

$$\frac{4(\omega_{pc}^2-2)}{\omega_{pc}(\omega_{pc}^2+1)(\omega_{pc}^2+4)} = 0$$

$$\omega_{pc}^2 = 2 \Rightarrow \omega_{pc} = \sqrt{2} \text{ rad/sec.}$$

at $\omega_{pc} = \sqrt{2}$, magnitude of $G(j\omega)\,H(j\omega)$

$$x = |G(j\omega)H(j\omega)| = \frac{12}{(\omega_{pc}^2+1)(\omega_{pc}^2+4)} = \frac{12}{3\times 6} = \frac{2}{3}$$

$$\text{Gain margin} = 20\log\left(\frac{1}{x}\right) = 20\log\left(\frac{3}{2}\right) = 3.52 \text{ dB}$$

6.6 Consider $G(s)H(s) = \dfrac{5(s+3)}{s(s-1)}$. Sketch the complete Nyquist plot and then determine the stability of the closed loop system.

[10 marks : 2007]

Solution:

$$G(s)\,H(s) = \frac{5(s+3)}{s(s-1)}$$

Mapping of section C_1 $\omega \to 0^+$ to $+\infty$

Put, $s = j\omega$

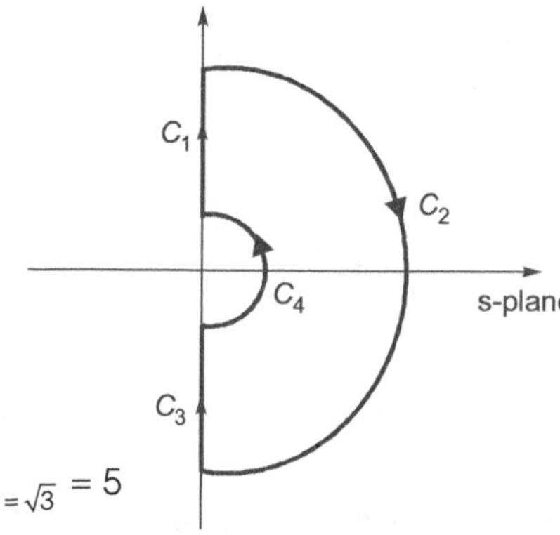

$$G(j\omega)H(j\omega) = \frac{5(j\omega+3)}{j\omega(j\omega-1)}$$

$$G(j\omega)H(j\omega) = \frac{5(j\omega+3)(-j\omega-1)}{j\omega(j\omega-1)(-j\omega-1)} = \frac{-5(-\omega^2+3j\omega+j\omega+3)}{j\omega(\omega^2+1)}$$

$$G(j\omega)H(j\omega) = \frac{-20}{(\omega^2+1)} - \frac{j5(\omega^2-3)}{\omega(\omega^2+1)}$$

The plot crosses the real axis at $\omega = \sqrt{3}$ magnitude of $|G(j\omega)H(j\omega)|_{\omega=\sqrt{3}} = 5$

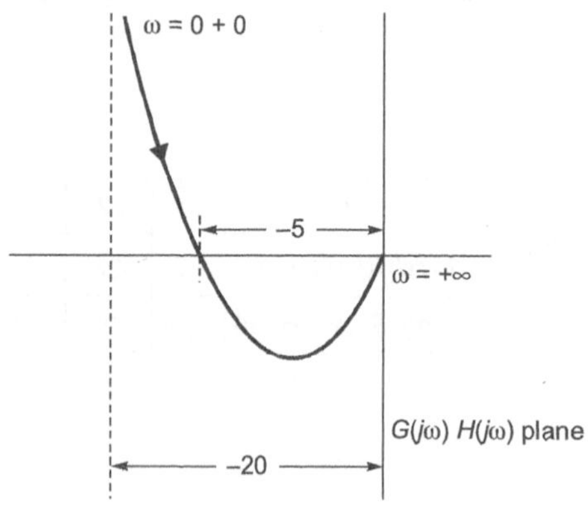

ω	0	$\sqrt{3}$	∞
$Re G(j\omega)H(j\omega)$	–20	–5	–0
$Imj\ G(j\omega)H(j\omega)$	$-j\infty$	0	$-j0$

Mapping of C_2:

$$s = \underset{R\to\infty}{Lt} Re^{j\theta} \quad \theta \to +\frac{\pi}{2} \text{ to } -\frac{\pi}{2}$$

$$G(s)H(s) = \underset{R\to\infty}{Lt} \frac{5(Re^{j\theta}+3)}{Re^{j\theta}\times(Re^{j\theta}-1)} = \underset{R\to\infty}{Lt} \frac{5}{Re^{j\theta}} = 0\ (origin)$$

Mapping of C_3:

Inverse polar plot.

Mapping of C_4:

$$s = \underset{R\to 0}{Lt} Re^{j\theta} \quad \theta \to -\frac{\pi}{2} \text{ to } \frac{\pi}{2}$$

$$G(s)H(s) = \frac{5\times(Re^{j\theta}+3)}{Re^{j\theta}\times(Re^{j\theta}-1)} = \underset{R\to 0}{Lt} -\frac{15}{Re^{j\theta}} = \infty \qquad \text{From}\left(-\frac{\pi}{2} \text{ to } \frac{\pi}{2}\right)$$

From the above analysis, Nyquist plot.

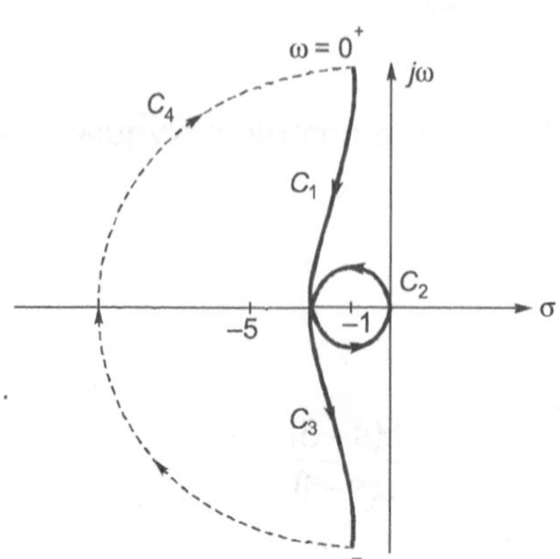

Number of encirclement of $(-1 + j0)$ $N = 1$ (anticlockwise)

Number of open loop poles in RHS of s-plane p = 1

Applying, $N = P - Z$

$$1 = 1 - Z \Rightarrow Z = 0$$

Number of closed loop poles in RHS of s-plane $Z = 0$

Hence the system is table.

6.7 **The transient response of a second order system when subjected to unit step input is found to have peak overshoot of 16.2 percent, occurring at time $t = \frac{\pi}{5\sqrt{3}}$ seconds. If this system is subjected to a sinusoidal input of 1 volt, determine (i) frequency of input at which amplitude of steady state response will have maximum value, (ii) maximum value of steady state output.**

[10 marks : 2007]

Solution:

For second order system, $M_p = e^{\frac{-\xi\pi}{\sqrt{1-\xi^2}}}$

$$e^{\frac{-\xi\pi}{\sqrt{1-\xi^2}}} = 0.162$$

$\therefore$ $\xi = 0.5$

Because of maximum overshoot occur at peak time

$$t_p = \frac{\pi}{\omega_d} = \frac{\pi}{5\sqrt{3}}$$

$$\omega_d = 5\sqrt{3} = \omega_n\sqrt{1-\xi^2} = \omega_n\sqrt{1-0.5^2}$$

$$\omega_n = 10 \text{ rad/sec}$$

For sinusoidal input, the frequency response is the steady state response (output)

So, Resonant frequency $(\omega_r) = \omega_n\sqrt{1-2\xi^2}$

$$= 10\sqrt{1-2\times 0.5^2} = 7.07 \text{ rad/sec}$$

And its resonant peak, $M_r = \frac{1}{2\xi\sqrt{1-\xi^2}} = 1.155$

6.8 **The asymptotic log – magnitude curve for open loop transfer function is sketched in figure below. Determine the transfer function.**

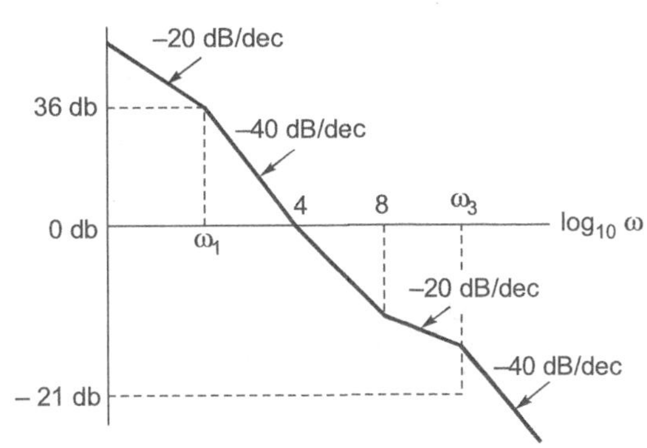

[10 marks : 2007]

Solution:

From above the bode plot,

The slope in between (ω_1 and 4) is –40 dB/dec.

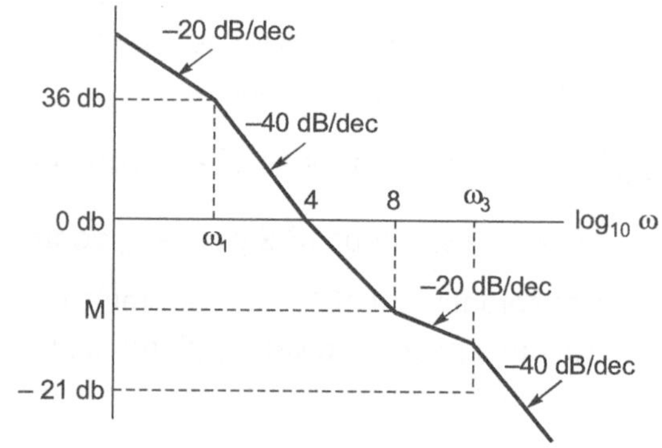

$$\therefore \quad -40 = \frac{0-36}{\log 4 - \log \omega_1}$$

$$\therefore \quad \omega_1 = 0.5 \text{ rad/sec}$$

The slope between (4 and 8) is (–40 dB/dec)

$$-40 = \frac{0-M}{\log 4 - \log 8}$$

$$\therefore \quad M = -12 \text{ dB}$$

The slope in between (8 and ω_3) is –20dB/dec

$$-20 = \frac{-12-(-21)}{\log 8 - \log \omega_3}$$

$$\therefore \quad \omega_3 = 22.547$$

For finding the value of (k)

$$20 \log k - 20 \log 0.5 = 36 \text{ dB}$$

$$\therefore \quad k = 31.54$$

From all the result,

$$\left(\frac{T}{F}\right) = \frac{(31.54)\left(1+\frac{s}{8}\right)}{s\left(1+\frac{s}{0.5}\right)\left(1+\frac{5}{22.55}\right)} = \frac{45\,(s+8)}{s(s+0.5)(s+22.55)}$$

6.9 The open-loop Bode plot of a third-order unity feedback system exhibits an initial slope of –20 dB/dec passing through 14 dB at ω = 1 rad/sec and also has simple corner frequencies at ω = 1 and ω = 4 rad/sec.

Determine:

(i) transfer function of the system and

(ii) gain cross-over frequency.

[10 marks : 2008]

Solution:

Slope in between (ω_1 = 1 and ω_2 = 4) is –40 dB/dec

$$\therefore \quad -40 = \frac{M-14}{\log 4 - \log 1}$$

$$\therefore \quad M \cong -10 \text{ dB}$$

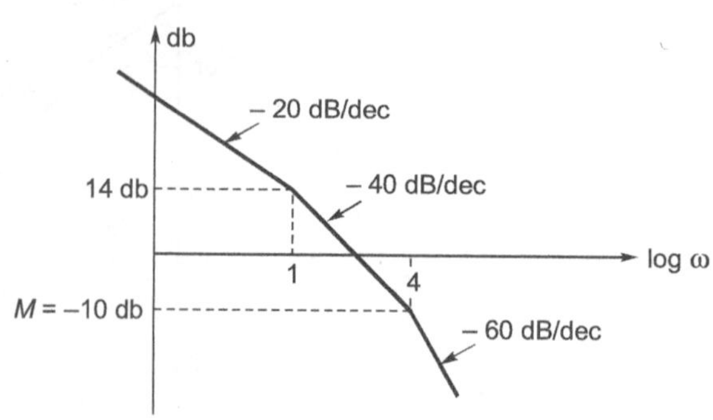

$$\text{Transfer function} = \frac{k}{s(s+1)\left(1+\frac{s}{4}\right)}$$

where, $20 \log k - 20 \log 1 = 14$ dB

$$\therefore \quad k \cong 5$$

$$\therefore \quad \text{Transfer function} = \frac{20}{s(s+1)(s+4)}$$

$$-40 = \frac{0-14}{\log \omega_{gc} - \log 1}$$

At gain cross over frequency, $\left|\frac{T}{F}\right| = 0$ db

$$\therefore \quad \log \omega_{gc} = 0.35$$

$$\therefore \quad \omega_{gc} = 2.238 \text{ rad/sec}$$

6.10 (i) The block diagram of a unity feedback control system is given in figure.

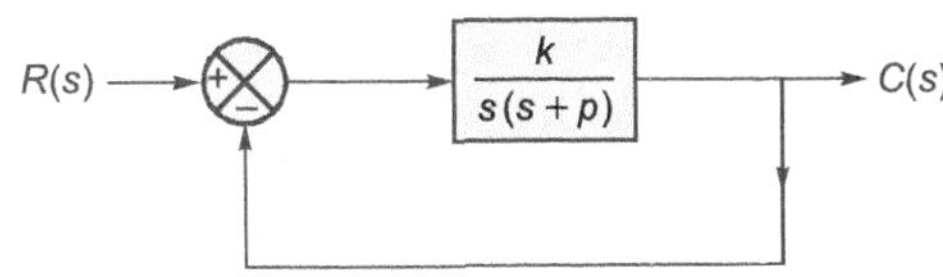

The parameters K and p are both greater than zero.

Determine the values of 'K' and 'p' to satisfy the following frequency domain specifications:

Resonant peak $M_p = 1.04$

Resonant frequency = 11.55 rad/sec.

(ii) For the figure, find the expression of the closed loop transfer function.

[12 +10 marks : 2009]

Solution:

(i)

$$\frac{C(s)}{R(s)} = \frac{k(s(s+p))}{1+\frac{k}{s(s+p)}\times 1} = \frac{k}{s(s+p)+k}$$

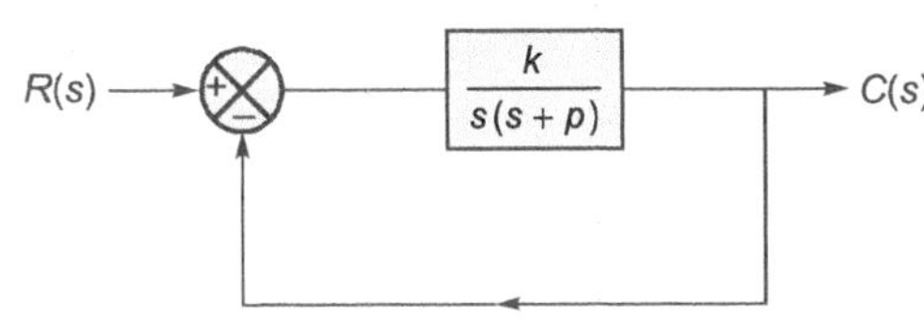

$$= \frac{k}{s^2+ps+k} = \frac{\omega_n^2}{s^2+2\xi\omega_n s+\omega_n^2}$$

On comparing $P = 2\xi\omega_n$ and $k = \omega^2{}_n$

Frequency specifications are given

$$\text{Resonant peak,} \quad M_p = 1.04 = \frac{1}{2\xi\sqrt{1-\xi^2}}$$

$$\text{and} \quad \text{Resonant frequency} = \omega_r = \omega_n\sqrt{1-2\xi^2}$$

$$\therefore \quad 2.08 = \frac{1}{\xi\sqrt{1-\xi^2}}$$

$$(2.08\,\xi)^2(1-\xi^2) = 1$$

$$4.3264\,\xi^2 - 4.3264\,\xi^4 = 1$$

$$\xi^2 = (0.3626, 0.6373)$$

$$\therefore \quad \xi = (0.6, 0.8)$$

$$11.55 = \omega_n\sqrt{1-2\times 0.3626}$$

$$\therefore \quad \omega_n = 22 \text{ and } \xi = 0.6$$

$$\text{If,} \quad \xi = 0.8$$

$$11.55 = \omega_n\sqrt{1-2\times 0.673} \quad \text{Imaginary quantity}$$

Hence, $\xi = 0.8$ is rejected.

$$k = \omega_n^2 = 22^2 = 484 \text{ and } p = 2\xi\omega_n = 2 \times 0.6 \times 22 = 26.4$$

(ii) From above figure,
$$\frac{C(s)}{R(s)} = \frac{484}{s^2 + 26.4s + 484}$$

6.11 The Nyquist plot of an all-pole second order open-loop system is shown in figure. Obtain the transfer function of the system.

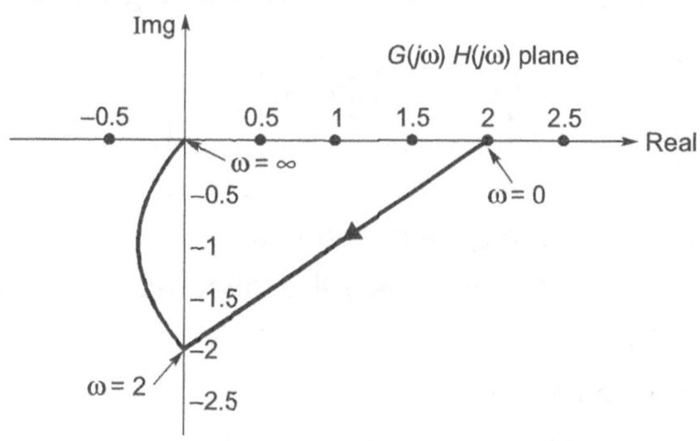

[12 marks : 2009]

Solution:

From the Nyquist-plot, we can conclude for an all pole second order system,

$$\text{Transfer function} = \left(\frac{T}{F}\right) = \frac{K}{(s+T_1)(s+T_2)} = \frac{K}{s^2 + (T_1+T_2)s + T_1T_2}$$

$$G(j\omega)\,H(j\omega) = \frac{K}{(j\omega + T_1)(j\omega + T_2)}$$

$$G(j\omega)\,H(j\omega)\big|_{\omega=0} = \frac{K}{T_1T_2} = 2$$

$$|G(j\omega)\,H(j\omega)| = \frac{K(-j\omega+T_1)(-j\omega+T_2)}{(\omega^2+T_1^2)(\omega^2+T_2^2)} = \frac{K\left[(-\omega^2+T_1T_2) - j\omega(T_1+T_2)\right]}{(\omega^2+T_1^2)(\omega^2+T_2^2)}$$

Next we consider, another point ($\omega = 2$) at imaginary line, real part of $G(j\omega)\,H(j\omega)$ is equal to zero.

$$-\omega^2 + T_1T_2 = 0$$

$$\therefore \quad T_1T_2 = \omega^2 = 4 \quad \ldots(i)$$

and
$$\frac{K}{T_1T_2} = 2$$

$$\therefore \quad K = 4 \times 2 = 8$$

The magnitude of the function,
$$-2 = \left.\frac{-K\omega(T_1+T_2)}{(\omega^2+T_1^2)(\omega^2+T_2^2)}\right|_{\omega=2}$$

$$2 = \frac{2(T_1+T_2)\times 8}{(4+T_1^2)(4+T_2^2)}$$

$$(4+T_1^2)(4+T_2^2) = 8(T_1+T_2)$$

$$16 + 4(T_1^2+T_2^2) + (T_1T_2)^2 = 8(T_1+T_2)$$

$$16 + 4\left[(T_1+T_2)^2 - 2T_1T_2\right] + 16 = 8(T_1+T_2)$$

$$32 + 4\left[(T_1+T_2)^2\right] - 8\times 4 = 8(T_1+T_2)$$

$$4(T_1 + T_2) = 8$$

$$\therefore \quad T_1 + T_2 = 2 \qquad \ldots(ii)$$

Both condition satisfied when, $\left(\dfrac{T}{F}\right) = \dfrac{8}{s^2 + 2s + 4}$

6.12 For the system shown in figure, find using Nyquist stability criterion the range of values of T so that closed-loop system is stable.

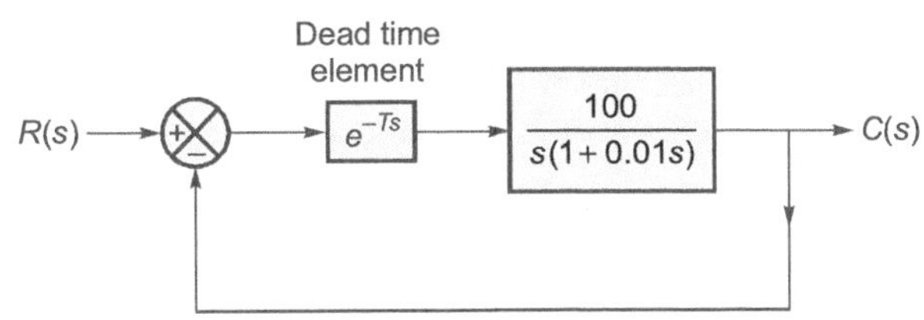

[10 marks : 2009]

Solution:

$$G(s) = \frac{e^{-Ts} \times 100}{s(1+0.01s)}$$

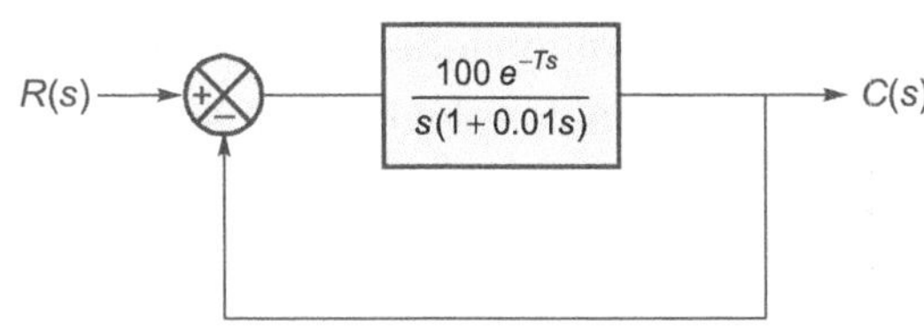

$$\therefore \quad G(j\omega) = \frac{e^{-j\omega T} \times 100}{j\omega(1+0.01 \times j\omega)}$$

where, $e^{-j\omega t} = \cos(\omega T) - j\sin(\omega T)$

$$\therefore \quad G(j\omega) = \frac{100[\cos(\omega T) - j\sin(\omega T)][1 - j\omega \times 0.01]x - j}{\omega(1+(0.01)^2\omega^2)}$$

$$= \frac{100[[-\cos(\omega T) \times 0.01 \times \omega - \sin\omega T]] - j[[\cos\omega T - \omega \times 0.01 \times \sin T\omega]]}{\omega\left[1+(0.01)^2\omega^2\right]}$$

For Nyquist plot,

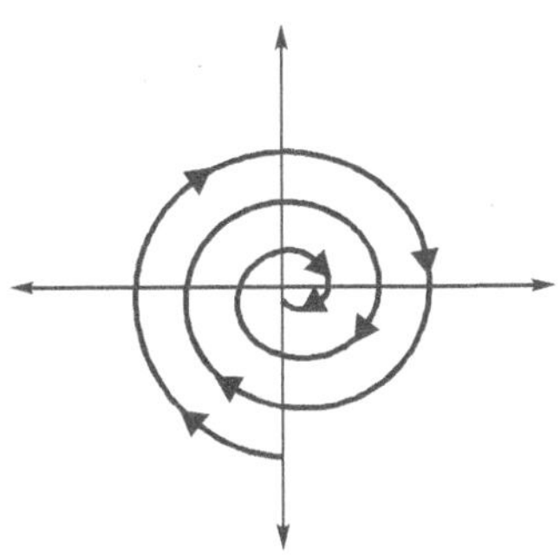

ω	0	∞
$\lvert M \rvert$	∞	0
$\angle$	-90	$-\infty$

From, Nyquist plot, we can seen that higher the values of (ω) the plot spirals round the origin. The intersection of $G(j\omega)$ plot with real axis is obtained equation imaginary part to zero.

$$\cos(\omega T) = \frac{\omega}{100} \times \sin T\omega \qquad \ldots(i)$$

and magnitude $|Gj\omega|$ at ($\omega = \omega_{pc}$) should be less than or equal to one for stability [Nyquist criteria]

$$|G(j\omega)|_{\omega_{pc}} = \frac{100[\sin\omega T + \omega \times 0.01 \times \cos\omega T]}{\omega(1+(0.01)^2\omega^2)}$$

Putting value of equation (*i*),

Then, $$\frac{100\left[\sin\omega T + \frac{\omega^2}{(100)^2}\sin\omega T\right]}{\omega(1+(0.01)^2\omega^2)} \le 1$$

$$\therefore \quad \frac{100(\sin\omega T)}{\omega} \le 1$$

$$\therefore \quad \sin\omega T \le \frac{\omega}{100}$$

$$\omega T \le \frac{\omega}{100} \qquad \text{[for smaller values } \sin\omega T \cong \omega T]$$

$$\therefore \quad T \le \frac{1}{100}$$

6.13 A system has transfer function $T(s) = \dfrac{s^2 - 2s + 1}{s^2 + 2s + 1}$.

Sketch the magnitude and phase responses of the system.
Sketch the polar-plot of $T(j\omega)$ as a function of ω.
Find poles and zeros of $T(s)$.

[12 marks : 2009]

Solution:

Poles of $T(s)$ = Double pole at –1
Zeros of $T(s)$ = Double zero at 1

$$T(s) = \frac{s^2 - 2s + 1}{s^2 + 2s + 1} = \frac{(s-1)^2}{(s+1)^2}$$

$$|T(j\omega)| = \frac{\sqrt{\omega^2 + 1^2} \times \sqrt{\omega^2 + 1^2}}{\sqrt{\omega^2 + 1^2} \times \sqrt{\omega^2 + 1^2}} = 1 \Rightarrow 20\log 1 = 0 \text{ dB}$$

$$\angle T(j\omega) = 2\tan^{-1}(-\omega) - 2\tan^{-1}(\omega) = -4\tan^{-1}(\omega)$$

Magnitude and phase plot,

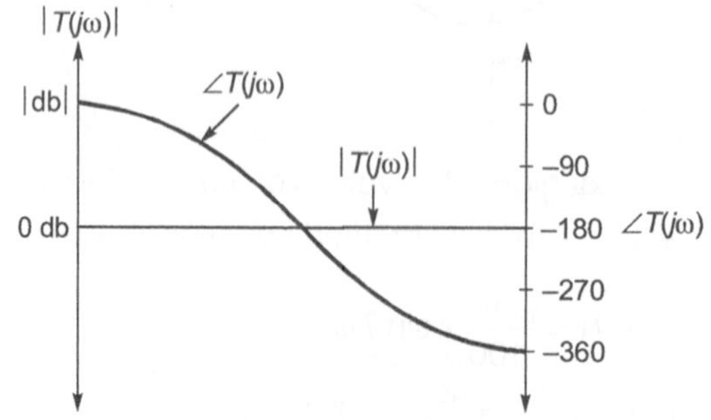

For polar plot $\omega \rightarrow (0 \rightarrow \infty)$

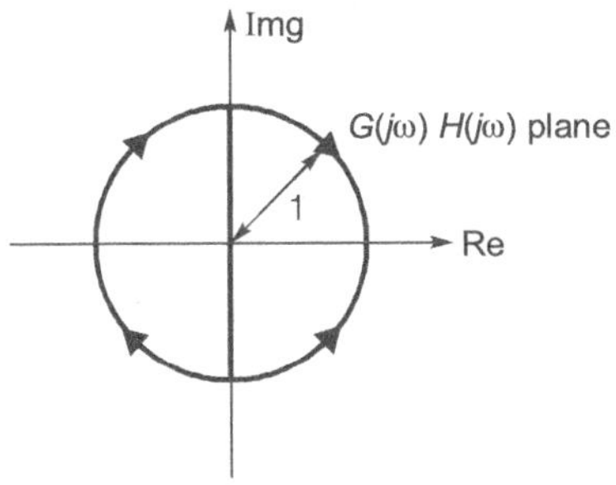

ω	0	1	∞
$\lvert T(j\omega)\rvert$	1	1	1
$\angle T(j\omega)$	0	–180	–360

6.14 Determine the safe maximum value of k for the unity feedback system, having open-loop transfer function,

$$G(s) = \frac{k(s+20)^2}{s^3}$$

Sketch the Nyquist plot with this value of k. Obtain the margins of stability and comment.

[10 marks : 2010]

Solution:

$$\text{Open Loop Transfer Function} = G(s) = \frac{k(s+20)^2}{s^3}$$

Put, $s = j\omega$

$$G(j\omega) = \frac{k(j\omega+20)^2}{(j\omega)^3}$$

$$\text{Magnitude of } G(j\omega) = M = |G(j\omega)| = \frac{k(\omega^2+400)}{\omega^3}$$

$$\text{Phase of } G(j\omega) = \phi = \angle G(j\omega) = -3\times 90° + 2\tan^{-1}\left(\frac{\omega}{20}\right)$$

$$= -270° + 2\tan^{-1}\left(\frac{\omega}{20}\right)$$

ω	0	20	∞
M	∞	$K/10$	0
ϕ	–270°	–180°	–90

From above table, phase of $G(j\omega)$ is –180° when ω = 20 rad/sec. It implies that the plot crosses the real axis at ω = 20 and magnitude is $k/10$.

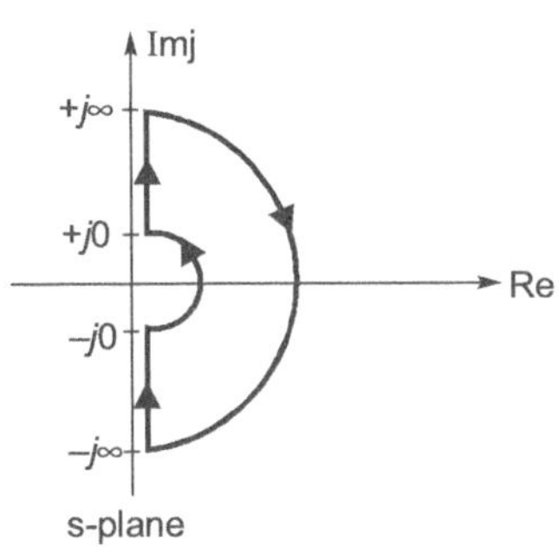

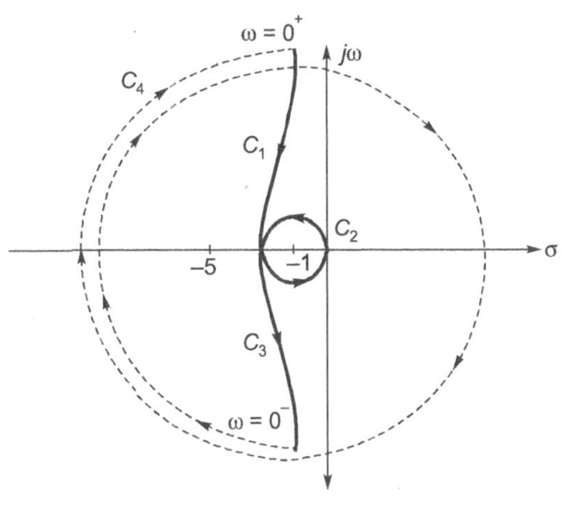

Number of open loop poles in RHS is s-plane $p = 0$

If $\frac{K}{10} = 1 \Rightarrow K_{mg} = 10$ $\quad N =$ Number of encirclement of $(-1 + j0) = 0$

$$K > 10$$

Applying, Nqyuist criteria $N = P - Z$

$$0 = 0 - Z$$

Number of closed loop poles in RHS of s-plane = 0.

Hence the system is stable for $K > 10$.

6.15 **For the system shown in the figure below, draw the Nyquist diagram and determine the margins of stability.**

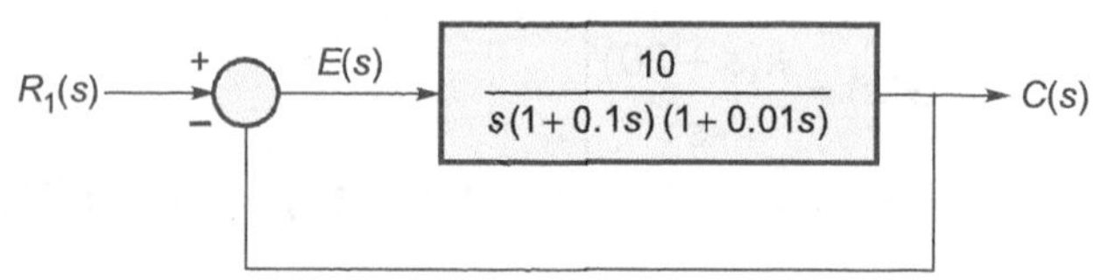

[10 marks : 2011]

Solution:

$$G(s) = \frac{10}{s(1+0.1\,s)\,(1+0.01\,s)} \quad \text{and} \quad H(s) = 1$$

$$G(s)\,H(s) = \frac{10}{s(1+0.1\,s)\,(1+0.01\,s)}$$

Put, $\quad s = j\omega$

$$\therefore \quad G(j\omega)\,H(j\omega) = \frac{10}{j\omega(1+j0.1\omega)+(1+j0.01\omega)} = \frac{-j10[(1-j0.1\omega)\,(1-j.001\omega)]}{\omega(1+0.1^2\,\omega^2)\,(1+0.01^2\,\omega^2)}$$

$$= \frac{10\left[-0.11\omega - j)\,(1-0.001\omega^2)\right]}{\omega(1+0.1^2\,\omega^2)\,(1+0.01^2\,\omega^2)} \quad \text{...(i)}$$

Separating equation (*i*) into real and imaginary parts

$$G(j\omega)\,H(j\omega) = \frac{-1.1}{(1+0.1^2\,\omega^2)\,(1+0.01^2\,\omega^2)} - \frac{j10(1-0.001\omega^2)}{\omega(1+0.1^2\,\omega^2)\times(1+0.01^2\,\omega^2)} \quad \text{...(ii)}$$

At $\omega = +0$, $\quad G(+j0)\,H(+j0) = -1.1 - j(\infty) = |\infty| \angle -\frac{\pi}{2} \quad$ ...(*iii*)

From equation (*i*) it is observed the Nyquist plot crosses the negative real axis and the value of ω at which this occurs is determined by equating the imaginary part of equation (*ii*) to zero

$$\frac{10(1-0.001\omega^2)}{\omega(1+0.1^2\,\omega^2)\,(1+0.01^2\,\omega^2)} = 0 \quad \text{...(iv)}$$

The solution of equation (*iv*) is

$$\omega = \frac{1}{\sqrt{0.001}} = 31.62 \text{ rad/sec.}$$

$$|G(j\omega)\,H(j\omega)|_{\omega=31.62} = \frac{-1.1}{(1+0.1^2\times 1000)\,(1+0.01^2\times 1000)}$$

$$= -0.091 \qquad \ldots(v)$$

At $\omega = +\infty$, $$G(j\infty)\,H(+j\infty) = -0 + j0 = |0|\angle\frac{\pi}{2} \qquad \ldots(vi)$$

In view equation (*iii*), (*v*) and (*vi*) the Nyquist plot is drawn. The plot for values of ω from $\omega = -\infty$ to $\omega = -0$ is shown by dotted lines. As the system is type-1, the plot is closed from $\omega = -0$ to $\omega = +0$ in the clockwise direction through an angle of π.

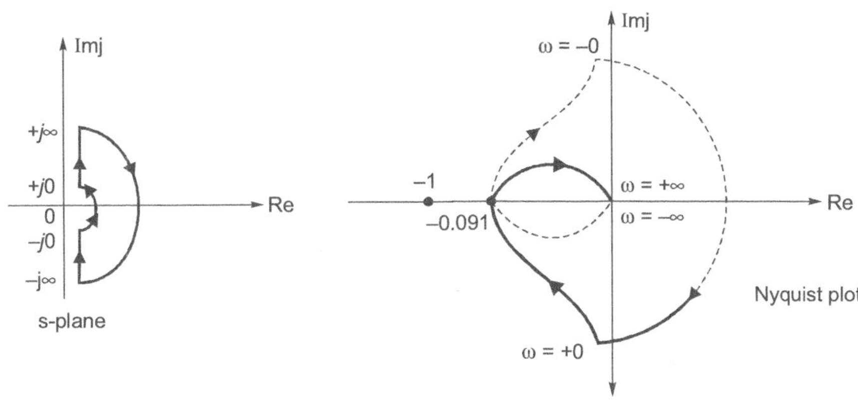

- The intersection of Nyquist plot with the real axis is –0.091 and the point (–1 + j0) is not encircled by the Nyquist plot and the closed loop system is stable (as $p_+ = 0$).

$$x = |G(j\omega)H(j\omega)| = 0.091$$

$$\text{Gain margin} = \frac{1}{x} = \frac{1}{0.91} = 11$$

$$Gm = 20\log\left(\frac{1}{x}\right) = 20.82 \text{ dB}$$

6.16 Sketch the complete Bode Plot of the unity feedback system whose open loop frequency function

$$G(j\omega) = \frac{10}{j\omega(0.1j\omega+1)\,(0.05\,j\omega+1)}$$

(i) Determine the Gain Margin and Phase Margin.

(ii) Find the open loop gain *K* for a Gain Margin of 20 dB.

[10 marks : 2012]

Solution:

$$G(j\omega) = \frac{10}{j\omega(0.1j\omega+1)\,(0.05\,j\omega+1)}$$

1. Corner frequencies are, $\omega_1 = \frac{1}{0.1} = 10$ rad/sec and $\omega_2 = \frac{1}{0.05} = 20$ rad/sec
2. The starting frequency of the Bode plot is taken as lower than ω_1 say the starting frequency is 1 rad/sec.
3. As the transfer is type 1, the initial part of Bode plot is –20 dB/decade and the intersection of the initial part of the plot with 0 dB axis occurs at $\omega = K$ i.e. at $\omega_1 = 10$. The initial slope continues till the lowest corner frequency $\omega = 10$ rad/sec is reached.

4. ω_1 = 10 rad/sec is due to term $\dfrac{1}{(1+j0\cdot 1\omega)}$, therefore, the slope after this frequency changes to –40 dB/decade and continues till the next corner frequency ω_2 = 20 rad/sec.

ω_2 = 20 rad/sec is due to term $\dfrac{1}{(1+j0.05\omega)}$, therefore, the slope after this frequency changes to –60 dB/decade and continues for frequencies greater than 20 rad/sec.

5.
$$\angle G(j\omega) = -90° - \tan^{-1}(0.1\omega) - \tan^{-1}(0.05\omega)$$

ω(rad/sec) =	1	10	20	30	40	50
$\angle G(j\omega)$ =	–98.57°	–161.56°	–198.43°	–217.87°	–229.4°	236.89°

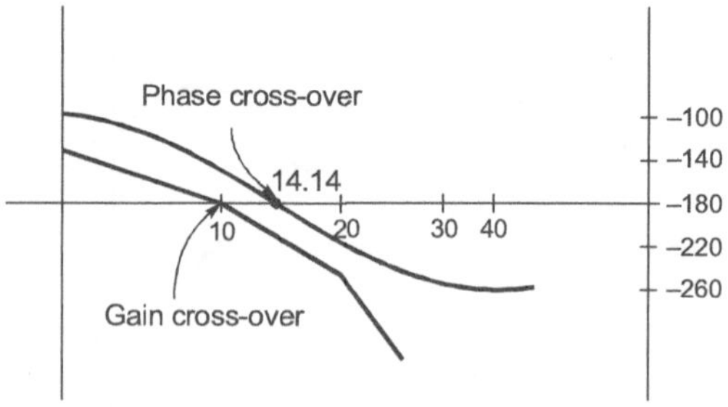

(i)
$$\text{Gain margin} = 20\log_{10}\frac{1}{\dfrac{10}{\left|j10\sqrt{2}(j\sqrt{2}+1)\left(\dfrac{j}{\sqrt{2}}+1\right)\right|}} = 20\log_{10}\frac{1}{\dfrac{10}{10\sqrt{2}\times\sqrt{3}\times\left(\dfrac{\sqrt{3}}{\sqrt{2}}\right)}}$$

$$= 20\log_{10}\left(\frac{1}{\dfrac{10}{30}}\right) = 20\log_{10}(3) = 9.542\text{ dB}$$

$$\text{Phase margin} = \angle GH + 180°$$
$$= -161.56° + 180° = 18.44°$$

(ii) If gain margin is 20 dB then

$$20 = 20\log_{10}\left(\frac{1}{X}\right)$$

$$\Rightarrow \quad X = 0.1 = |G(j\omega)|_{\omega=\omega_{pc}}$$

$$\therefore \quad \frac{K}{\sqrt{200}\left(\sqrt{1+(\sqrt{2})^2}\right)\left(\sqrt{1+\left(\dfrac{1}{\sqrt{2}}\right)^2}\right)} = 1$$

$$\Rightarrow \quad K = 3$$

6.17 The loop transfer function of a negative feedback control system is given by,

$$G(s)\,H(s) = \frac{K(1+s)}{s^2(1+0.316s)}$$

Determine analytically:
(i) Possible maximum phase margin and the frequency at which it occurs.
(ii) What should be the gain K for this phase margin?

[10 marks : 2013]

Solution:

(i) Given, loop transfer function is

$$G(s)\,H(s) = \frac{K(1+s)}{s^2(1+0.316s)}$$

$$\text{P.M.} = 180° + \angle G(s)H(s)\big|_{\omega=\omega_{gc}}$$

$$= 180° - 180° - \tan^{-1}\frac{0.316\,\omega_{gc}}{1} + \tan^{-1}\omega_{gc}$$

$$\text{P.M.} = \tan^{-1}\omega_{gc} - \tan^{-1}0.316\,\omega_{gc}$$

In order to find maximum phase margin,

$$\frac{d\,\text{P.M.}}{d\omega_{gc}} = \frac{1}{1+\omega_{gc}^2} - \frac{0.316}{1+(0.316\omega_{gc})^2} = 0$$

On solving,

$$\omega_{gc} = 1.8 \text{ rad/sec}$$

and $\quad$ P.M. at ω_{gc} = 1.8 rad/sec is maximum viz,

$$\text{P.M.} = \tan^{-1}1.8 - \tan^{-1}(0.316\times 1.8) = 31.31°$$

So, maximum phase margin is 31.31 at ω_{gc} = 1.8.

(ii) Gain crossover frequency is a frequency where system gain becomes 1

$$\frac{K\sqrt{1+\omega_{gc}^2}}{\omega_{gc}^2\left(\sqrt{1+(0.316\,\omega_{gc})^2}\right)} = 1$$

$$\frac{K\sqrt{1+(1.8)^2}}{(1.8)^2\sqrt{\left[(1+(0.316\times 1.8)^2\right]}} = 1$$

$$\Rightarrow \qquad K = 1.81$$

6.18 The block diagram of the system is shown in figure given below:

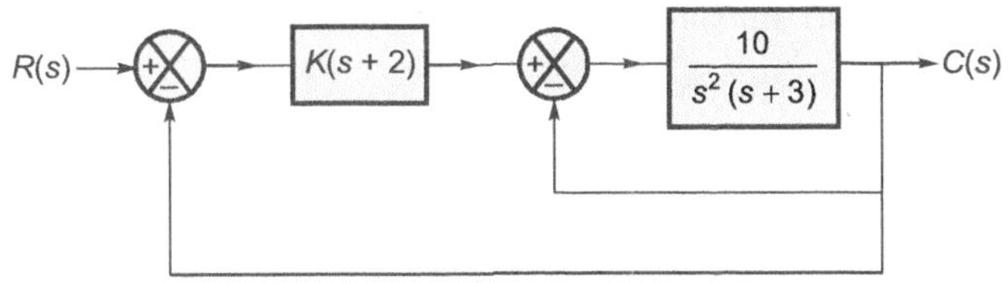

Obtain the phase crossover frequency.

[10 marks : 2015]

Solution:

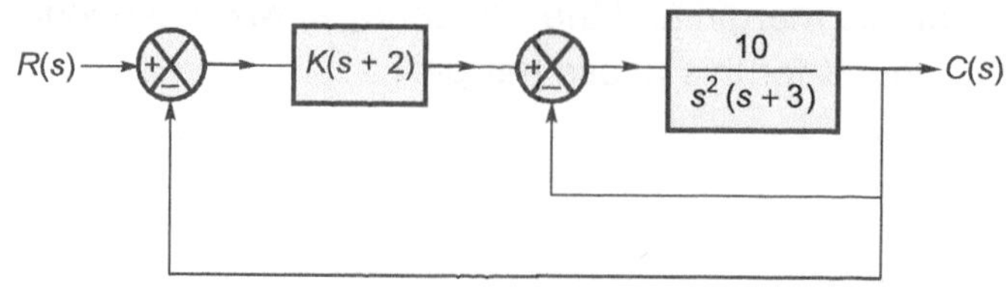

$$\text{Open loop transfer function} = \frac{10\,K(s+2)}{s^3+3s^2+10}$$

at phase cross frequency the phase of open loop transfer function must be –180°.
Hence at $s = j\omega$;

$$G(j\omega) = \frac{10\,K(2+j\omega)}{(10-3\omega^2)-j\omega^3}$$

$$\angle G(j\omega) = \tan^{-1}\left(\frac{\omega}{2}\right) - \tan^{-1}\left(\frac{\omega^3}{3\omega^2-10}\right)$$

At ω_{pc}, $\angle G(j\omega) = -180°$,

$$\tan^{-1}\left(\frac{\omega}{2}\right) - \tan^{-1}\left(\frac{\omega^3}{3\omega^2-10}\right) = -180°$$

$$\tan^{-1}\left[\frac{\frac{\omega}{2}-\frac{\omega^3}{3\omega^2-10}}{1+\frac{\omega^4}{2(3\omega^2-10)}}\right] = -180°$$

$\Rightarrow$ that gives;
$$\frac{\omega}{2}-\frac{\omega^3}{3\omega^2-10} = 0;$$

or
$$2\omega^2 = 3\omega^2 - 10;$$

$$\omega^2 = 10; \text{ or } \omega = \sqrt{10} \text{ rad/sec}$$

For proof check;

$$\angle G(s)\,(\text{at } \omega = \sqrt{10}) = \tan^{-1}\left(\frac{\sqrt{10}}{2}\right) - \tan^{-1}\left[\frac{10\sqrt{10}}{(30-10)}\right]$$

$$= \tan^{-1}\left(\frac{\sqrt{10}}{2}\right) - \tan^{-1}\left[\frac{\sqrt{10}}{2}\right] = -180°$$

6.19 Find the phase margin and gain margin of a feedback system with $G(s)H(s) = \frac{e^{-0.1s}}{s}$. Is the feedback system stable?

[12 marks : 2017]

Solution:

Given:
$$G(s)\,H(s) = \frac{e^{-0.1s}}{s}$$

Put, $s = j\omega$,

$$G(j\omega)\,H(j\omega) = \frac{e^{-j0.1\omega}}{j\omega}$$

or, $$G(j\omega)\,H(j\omega) = \frac{1}{\omega}\angle(-0.1\times 57.3^\circ \times \omega - 90^\circ)$$

For gain margin, we need to get phase cross-over frequency.

Then, at ω_{pc} (Phase cross-over frequency)

$$-0.1 \times 57.3^\circ \times \omega_{pc} - 90^\circ = -180^\circ$$

or, $$0.1 \times 57.3\,\omega_{pc} = 90^\circ$$

or, $$\omega_{pc} = 15.7 \text{ rad/sec}$$

Now, gain at ω_{PC}; $$M = \frac{1}{\omega_{PC}} = \frac{1}{15.7}$$

Gain margin, $$\text{G.M.} = 20\log\left(\frac{1}{M}\right) = 20\log(15.7)$$

$$= 23.92 \text{ dB}$$

For phase margin, we need to get gain cross-over frequency or at gain cross-over frequency (ω_{gc})

$$\frac{1}{\omega_{gc}} = 1 \text{ or } \omega_{gc} = 1 \text{ rad/sec}$$

Therefore, phase at ω_{gc}, $$\phi = -0.1 \times 57.3^\circ \times \omega_{gc} - 90^\circ$$

$$= -0.1 \times 57.3^\circ \times 1 - 90^\circ = -95.73^\circ$$

$$\text{Phase margin} = 180^\circ + \phi = 180^\circ - 95.73^\circ = 84.27^\circ$$

Comment : As both gain margin and phase margin are positive thus the given feedback system is stable for all frequencies.

6.20 **A feedback system is shown in the figure below. Using Nyquist stability criterion. Determine:**

(i) the number of closed-loop poles of the system in the right half s-plane.

(ii) the closed-loop stability of the system.

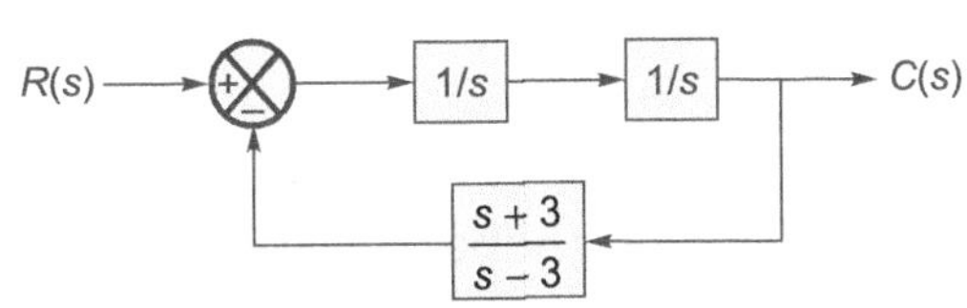

[20 marks : 2017]

Solution:

$$G(s) = \frac{1}{s^2}, \quad H(s) = \frac{(s+3)}{(s-3)}$$

$$G(s)\,H(s) = \frac{(s+3)}{s^2(s-3)}$$

P = Number of open-loop poles in RHS of s-plane.

Z = Number of closed-loop poles in RHS of s-plane.

N = Number of encirclements in anticlockwise direction of pt. $s = 1 \pm j0$

$$Z = N + P$$

Nyquist contour,

For C_4:

Put, $s = Re^{+j\theta}$

Mapping, $R \to \infty$ and θ varies from 90° to –90°

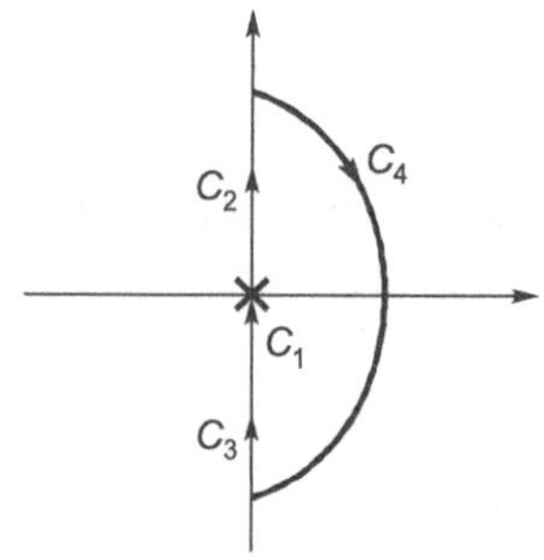

$$G(Re^{+j\theta})\,H(Re^{+j\theta}) = \frac{(Re^{j\theta}+3)}{R^2e^{2j\theta}(Re^{j\theta}-3)}$$

As, $R \to \infty$

$$\frac{Re^{j\theta}}{R^3e^{j3\theta}} = \frac{1}{R^2e^{j2\theta}} = 0\,e^{-j2\theta}$$

∴ A circle of radius = 0 from θ = –180° to 180°

For mapping C_1: Put $s = re^{j\theta}$

$r \to 0$, θ varies from –90° to 90°

$$G(re^{j\theta})\,H(re^{j\theta}) = \frac{(re^{j\theta}+3)}{r^2e^{j2\theta}(re^{j\theta}-3)}$$

As $r \to 0$,
$$= \frac{(3)}{r^2e^{+j2\theta}(-3)} = \infty\,e^{-j2\theta}$$

∴A circle of radius ∞ from θ = 180° to –180°

For mapping C_2:

	$\lvert M \rvert$	$\angle G(s)\,H(s)$
$\omega = 0$	∞	-2π
$\omega \to \infty$	0	$-\pi$

For C_3: Mirror image of C_2 on real axis.

∴ Number of encirclement in,

$$N = 1$$

Anticlockwise direction,

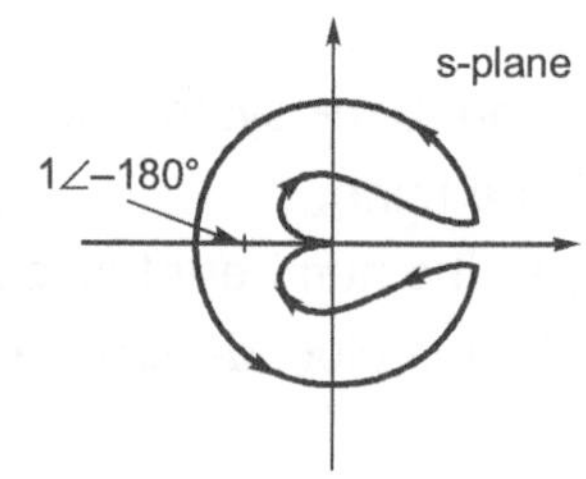

$$P = 1$$
$$Z = N + P$$
∴ $$Z = 2$$

Hence, two closed loop poles at RHS of s-plane system is unstable.

6.21 **The open-loop transfer function of a unity feedback system is given by**

$$G(s)\,H(s) = \frac{K}{(s+20)\,(s^2-2s+1)}$$

Use Nyquist stability criteria to find the range of K for closed-loop stability.

[20 marks : 2019]

Solution:

$$G(s)H(s) = \frac{k}{(s+20)\,(s-1)^2}$$

$$G(j\omega)H(j\omega) = \frac{k}{(20+j\omega)\,(-1+j\omega)^2}$$

$$|GH| = \frac{k}{\sqrt{400+\omega^2}\,(\omega^2+1)}$$

$$\angle GH = -360° + 2\tan^{-1}\omega - \tan^{-1}\frac{\omega}{20}$$

ω	|GH|	∠GH
0	$\frac{k}{20}$	–360°
∞	0	–270°

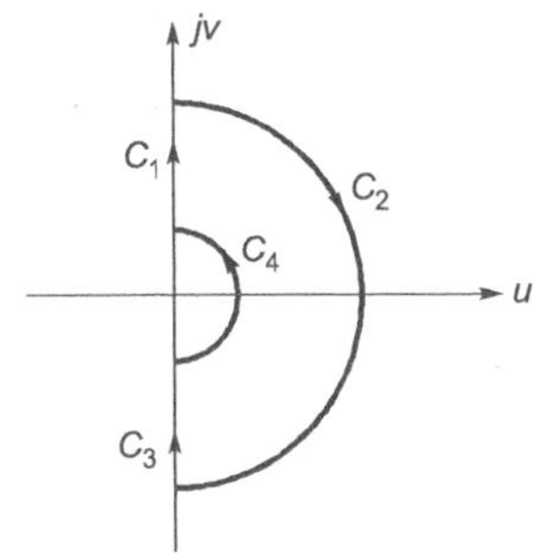

$$\angle GH = 90°$$

$$2\tan^{-1}\omega - \tan^{-1}\frac{\omega}{20} = 450°$$

$$\tan^{-1}\left(\frac{2\omega}{1-\omega^2}\right) - \tan^{-1}\frac{\omega}{20} = 450°$$

$$\tan^{-1}\left(\frac{40\omega - \omega + \omega^3}{20 - 20\omega^2 + 2\omega^2}\right) = 450°$$

$$\frac{39\omega + \omega^3}{20 - 18\omega^2} = \tan 90°$$

$$20 - \omega^2 \times 18 = 0$$

$$\omega = \sqrt{\frac{20}{18}} = 1.054 \text{ rad/ sec}$$

Contour:

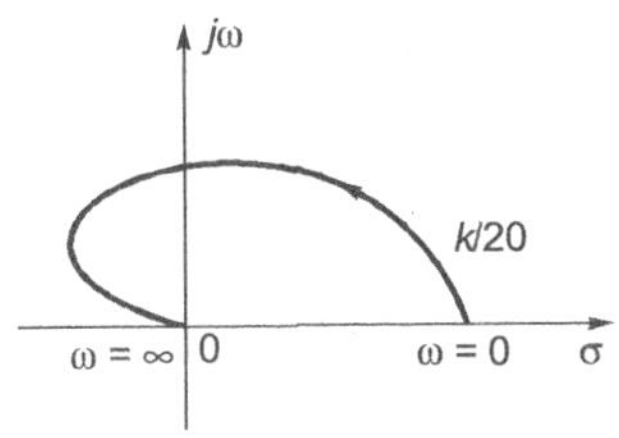

C_1: $s = j\omega$

C_3: $s = -j\omega$

Inverse polar plot:

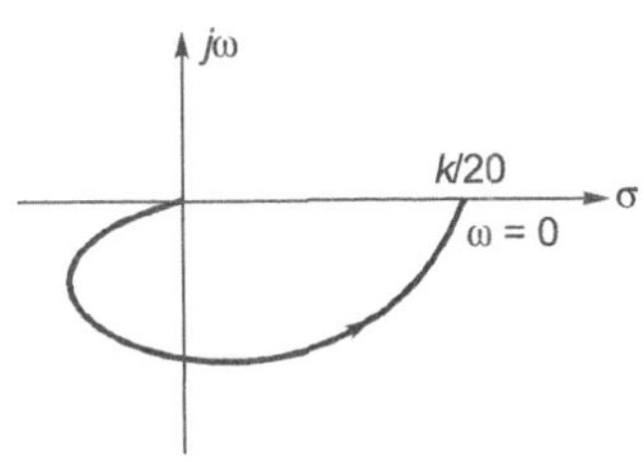

C_2: $S = \lim_{R\to\infty} Re^{j\theta}, \; \theta \to \left(\frac{\pi}{2} \to \frac{\pi}{2}\right)$

$$GH = \lim_{R\to\infty} \frac{k}{R^3 e^{j3\theta}} = \lim_{R\to\infty} \frac{k}{R^3} e^{-j3\theta}$$

$$= 0; \; -3\theta \to \left(\frac{3\pi}{2} \to \frac{-3\pi}{2}\right)$$

C_4: $S = \lim_{R\to 0} Re^{j\theta}, \; \theta \to \left(-\frac{\pi}{2} \to \frac{\pi}{2}\right)$

$$GH = \lim_{R\to\infty} \frac{k}{(Re^{j\theta}+20)\,(Re^{j\theta}+1)^2} = \frac{k}{20} e^{-j2\pi}$$

Nyquist plot:

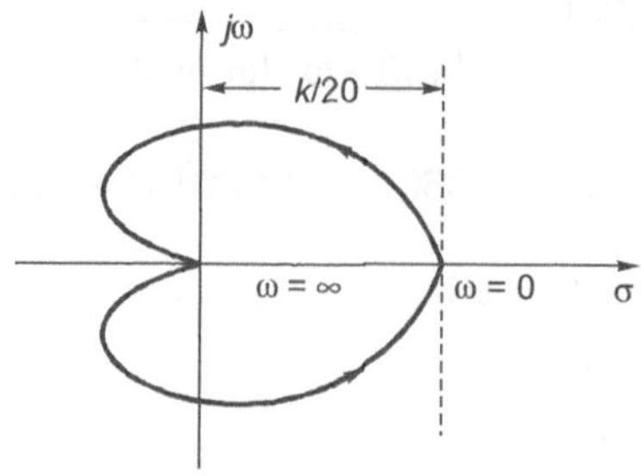

$$N = P - Z$$
$$P = 2$$
$$N = 2 - Z$$

For any value of k there is no encirclement of $(-1 + j0)$.

$\therefore$ $$N = 0$$
$$Z = 2$$

$\therefore$ For all values of k system in unstable.

6.22 A continuous LTIV system S with frequency response $H(j\Omega)$ is constructed by cascading two continuous-time LTIV systems with frequency response $H_1(j\Omega)$ and $H_2(j\Omega)$, respectively. Figures (a) and (b) show the straight-line approximations of Bode magnitude plots of $H_1(j\Omega)$ and $H(j\Omega)$, respectively. Find $H_2(j\Omega)$.

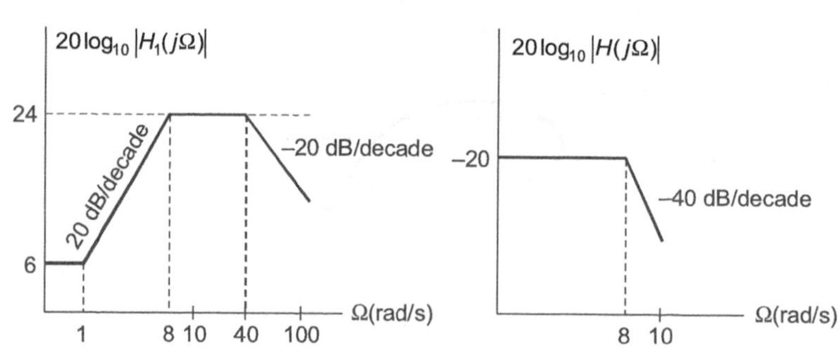

(a) (b)

[12 marks : 2020]

Solution:

$$H(j\Omega) = H_1(j\Omega) \cdot H_2(j\Omega)$$

$$H_2(j\Omega) = \frac{H(j\Omega)}{H_1(j\Omega)}$$

Forming $H(j\Omega)$:

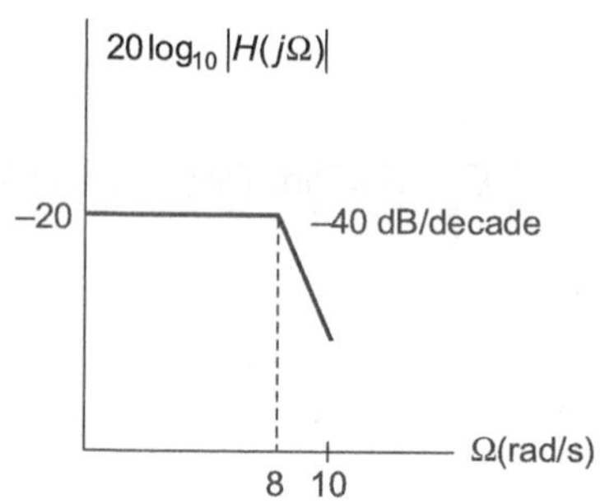

$$20 \log_{10} K = -20$$
$$\log_{10} K = -1$$
$$K = 10^{-1} = 0.1$$

and it has 2 poles at $s = -8$

$\therefore$ $$H_1(j\Omega) = \frac{0.1}{\left(1+\frac{s}{8}\right)^2} = \frac{0.1 \times 8^2}{(s+8)^2}$$

$$H_1(j\Omega) = \frac{6.4}{(s+8)^2}$$

Forming $H_1(j\Omega)$:

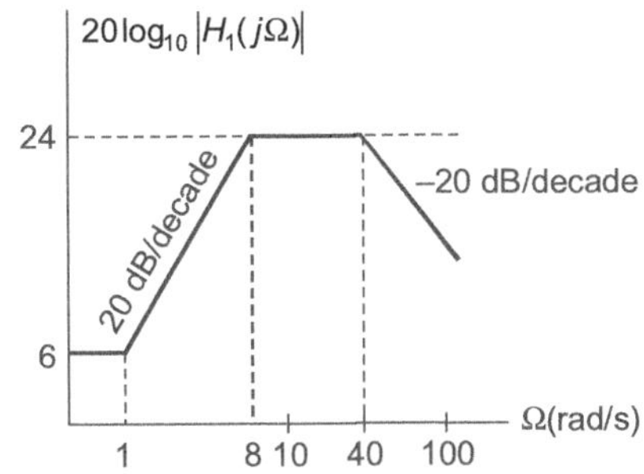

$$20 \log_{10} K = 6$$

$$\log_{10} K = \frac{6}{20}$$

$$K = (10)^{6/20} = 2$$

It has a zero at $s = -1$ and a pole at $s = -8$ and one more pole at $s = -40$

$$H_1(j\Omega) = \frac{2\left(\frac{s}{1}+1\right)}{\left(\frac{s}{8}+1\right)\left(\frac{s}{40}+1\right)} = \frac{2(s+1)\times 8\times 40}{(s+8)(s+40)}$$

$$H_1(j\Omega) = \frac{640(s+1)}{(s+8)(s+40)}$$

$$H_2(j\Omega) = \frac{H(j\Omega)}{H_1(j\Omega)} = \frac{\frac{6.4}{(s+8)^2}}{\frac{640(s+1)}{(s+8)(s+40)}}$$

$$H_2(j\Omega) = \frac{0.01(s+40)}{(s+8)(s+1)}$$

6.23 (i) From the Bode asymptotic magnitude plot of a minimum phase system, determine the open loop transfer function, What is the gain margin of resulting unity negative feedback closed loop system?

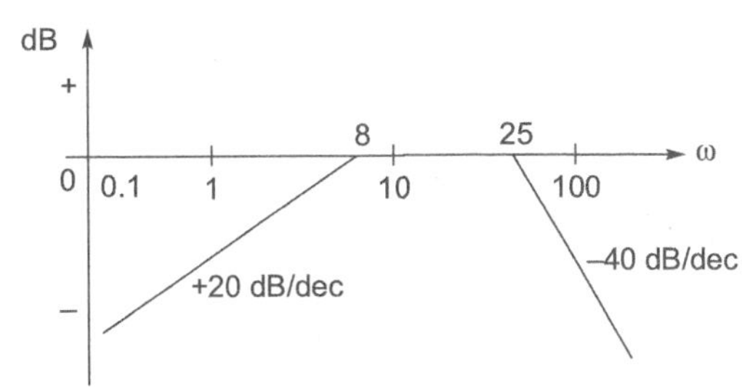

(ii) Given the open loop-transfer function:

$$G(s)H(s) = \frac{K}{(s+4)(s-8)}$$

Using Nyquist stability criteria, determine the condition for closed loop stability. Verify the result using Routh-Hurwitz test.

[10+10 = 20 marks : 2021]

Solution:

(i) Given bode plot has corner frequencies

$$\omega_1 = 8 \text{ rad/sec}$$
$$\omega_2 = 25 \text{ rad/sec}$$

$M_{dB} = 0$ at $\omega = 8$ rad/sec

$$M_{dB} = 20\log_{10}\omega + 20\log_{10}K$$
$$0 = 20\log_{10}8 + 20\log_{10}K$$

$\therefore$ $$K = 0.125$$

So, open loop transfer function

$$G(s)H(s) = \frac{Ks}{\left(\frac{s}{8}+1\right)\left(\frac{s}{25}+1\right)^2}$$

$$G(s)H(s) = \frac{0.125s}{\left(\frac{s}{8}+1\right)\left(\frac{s}{25}+1\right)^2}$$

Putting $s = j\omega$ in above equation

$$G(j\omega)H(j\omega) = \frac{0.125(j\omega)}{\left(\frac{j\omega}{8}+1\right)\left(\frac{j\omega}{25}+1\right)^2}$$

The angle condition

$$\angle G(j\omega)H(j\omega) = \phi = 90° - \tan^{-1}\left(\frac{\omega}{8}\right) - 2\tan^{-1}\left(\frac{\omega}{25}\right)$$

$$G(j\omega)H(j\omega) = \frac{0.125(j\omega)\left[1-\frac{j\omega}{8}\right]\left[1-\frac{j\omega}{25}\right]^2}{\left[1+\left(\frac{\omega}{8}\right)^2\right]\left[1+\left(\frac{\omega}{25}\right)^2\right]}$$

For phase cross over frequency,

$$I_{mg}[G(j\omega)H(j\omega)] = 0$$

$$G(j\omega)H(j\omega) = \frac{0.125\left[j\omega+\frac{\omega^2}{8}\right]\left[\frac{-\omega^2}{625}+1-\frac{2j\omega}{25}\right]}{\left[1+\left(\frac{\omega}{8}\right)^2\right]\left[1+\left(\frac{\omega}{25}\right)^2\right]}$$

$$\Rightarrow \quad \left(j\omega+\frac{\omega^2}{8}\right)\left(1-\frac{\omega^2}{625}-\frac{2j\omega}{25}\right) = j\omega - \frac{j\omega^3}{625} + \frac{2\omega^2}{25} + \frac{\omega^2}{8} - \frac{\omega^8}{5000} - \frac{2j\omega^3}{200}$$

$$I_{mg}[G(j\omega)H(j\omega)] = 0$$

$$\omega - \frac{\omega^3}{625} - \frac{2\omega^3}{200} = 0$$

$$\omega\left[-1+\omega^2\left(\frac{1}{625}+\frac{2}{200}\right)\right] = 0$$

$$\omega = 0$$

$$\omega = \sqrt{\frac{1}{0.0116}} = 9.2847 \text{ rad/sec}$$

ω	$\lvert G(j\omega)H(j\omega)\rvert$	$\angle G(j\omega)H(j\omega)$
0	0	90°
0.1	0.0124	88.82°
9.28	0.665	0°
15	0.64	–33.85°
100	0.058	–147.35°
1000	6.24×10^{-4}	–176.67
0	0	–180°

Nyquist plot of above system, taking gain as K.

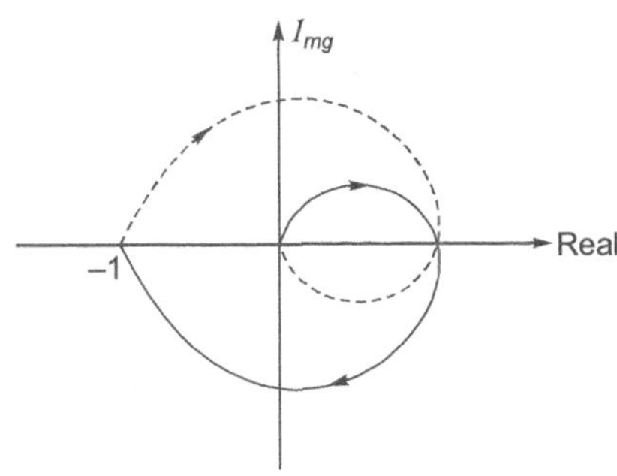

The system will be marginal stable for $0 < K < \infty$.

(ii) Given open loop transfer function

$$GH = \frac{K}{(s+4)(s-8)}$$

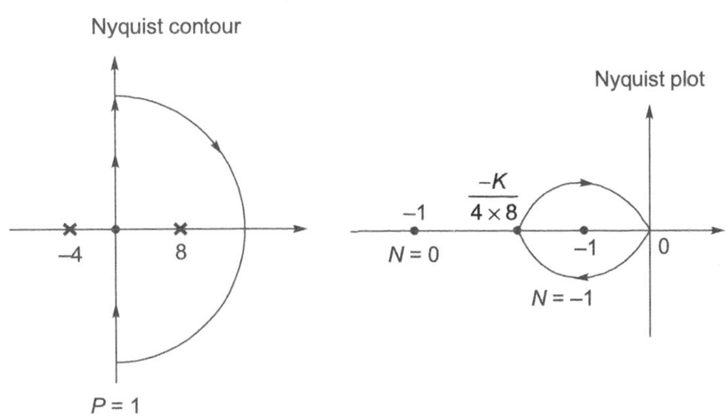

$$N = P - Z$$

$$P = 1$$

So, $\quad Z = N + 1$

For every case, $\quad Z \neq 0$

∴ In any case $N \neq P$

∴ CL system is unstable

Verification using R-H test:

$$q(s) = s^2 - 8s + 4s - 32 + K = 0$$
$$q(s) = s^2 - 4s + K - 32 = 0$$

s^2	1	$K - 32$
s^1	-4	
s^0	$K - 32$	

∴ unstable $\forall K$.

6.24 Forward path transfer function of a unity negative feedback system is $G(s) = \dfrac{25}{s(s+20)^2}$. Without drawing graph, analytically determine the gain margin.

[12 marks : 2021]

Solution:

Given open loop transfer function

$$GH = \frac{25}{s(s+20)^2}$$

$$GM = \frac{1}{M_{\text{at}\,\omega_{pc}}}$$

at $\omega_{pc} \Rightarrow \phi = -180°$

∴ Angle of GH ⇒ $$\phi = -90° - 2\tan^{-1}\left(\frac{\omega}{20}\right) = -180°$$

∴ By solving $$\omega_{pc} = 20 \text{ rad/sec}$$

$$M_{\text{at}\,\omega_{pc}} = \frac{25}{20\left(20^2 + 20^2\right)} = \frac{25}{20 \times 800} = \frac{1}{640}$$

∴ $$GM = 640$$

$$GM = 20 \log 640 = 56.12 \text{ dB}$$

6.25 The frequency response of a steady state gain already adjusted open loop transfer function is shown in the figure. Appropriately using the parameters highlighted in the figure, design a lag compensator to achieve a desired phase margin of +30° with a tolerance considered as 8°. Illustrate the design procedure clearly.

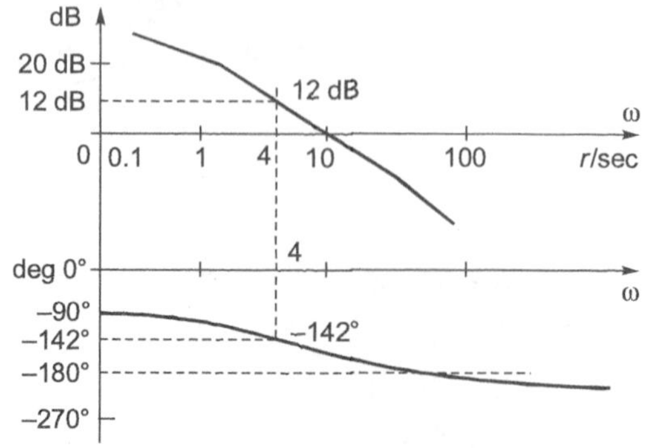

[12 marks : 2021]

Solution:

Let the transfer function of lag compensator be

$$G_c(s) = \frac{K(Ts+1)}{\alpha Ts+1}$$

From given Bode plot at $\omega = 4$; $M = 12$ dB

$$\phi = -142°$$

By adjusting K, M at $\omega = 4$ has to become 0 dB, such that ($\because$ 20 log 4 + 20 log K = 0)

$$\omega_{gc} = 4 \text{ rad/sec} \qquad (K = 0.25)$$

$\therefore$ $$\text{PM} = 180° - 142° = 38°$$

$\therefore$ $$K = 0.25$$

Desired phase margin, $$\text{PM} = 30°$$

$\therefore$ $$\phi_m = 30° - 38° - 8° = -16°$$

$\therefore$ $$\alpha = \frac{1-\sin\phi_m}{1+\sin\phi_m} = \frac{1+\sin 16°}{1-\sin 16°} = \frac{1.27}{0.73} = 1.76$$

At this frequency, $$\omega_{gc} = \omega_m = 4$$

$$M_m = 10\log_{10}\frac{1}{\alpha}\text{dB} = -2.45 \text{ dB}$$

$\therefore$ K further adjusted to 0.25 × 1.32

$\therefore$ $$K = 0.33$$

$$\omega_m = \frac{1}{T\sqrt{\alpha}}$$

$\Rightarrow$ $$T = \frac{1}{\omega_m\sqrt{\alpha}} = 0.19$$

$\therefore$ $$G_C(s) = \frac{0.33(0.19s+1)}{(0.33s+1)}$$

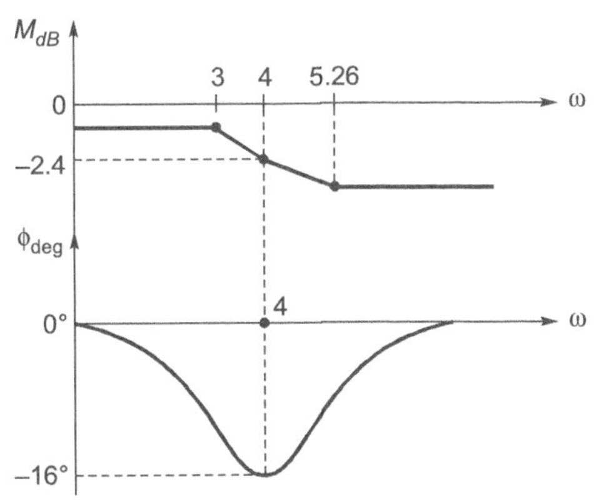

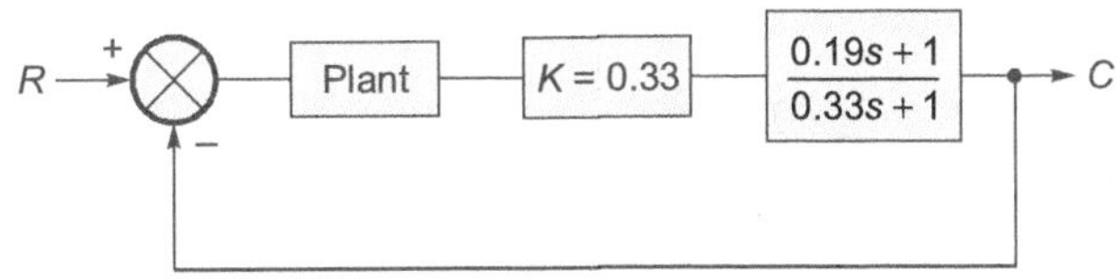

1. ω_{gc} of uncompensated system ≈ 10 rad/s
2. ω_{gc} of compensated system = 4 rad/s

6.26 The loop transfer function G(s)H(s) of a single-feedback-loop control system is given by

$$G(s)H(s) = \frac{K}{s^2(s+2)(s+10)}$$

Apply the Nyquist criterion and determine the value of K for the system to be stable. Also determine the gain margin if $K = 10$.

[20 marks : 2022]

Solution:

Given :
$$G(s)H(s) = \frac{K}{s^2(s+2)(s+10)}$$

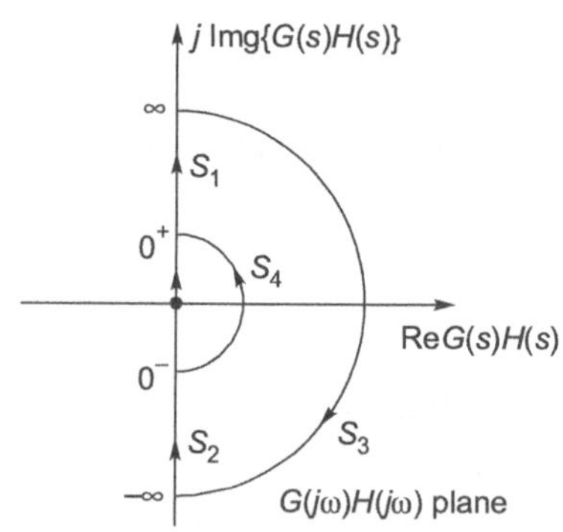

For s_1 :

$$G(j\omega)H(j\omega) = \frac{-K}{\omega^2(j\omega+2)(j\omega+10)}$$

$$= \frac{-K}{\omega^2}\left[\frac{1}{-\omega^2+12j\omega+20}\right]$$

$$G(j\omega)H(j\omega) = \frac{-K[(20-\omega^2)-12j\omega]}{\omega^2[(20\omega^2)^2+(12\omega)^2]}$$

$$= \frac{-K[20-\omega^2]}{\omega^2[(20-\omega^2)^2+(12\omega)^2]+\dfrac{j12K}{\omega[(20-\omega^2)^2+(12\omega)^2]}}$$

ω	0	1	2	5	∞
Re{$G(j\omega)H(j\omega)$}	∞	−0.037	-4.807×10^{-3}	5.513×10^{-5}	0
Img{$G(j\omega)H(j\omega)$}	∞	0.023	7.211×10^{-3}	6.62×10^{-4}	0

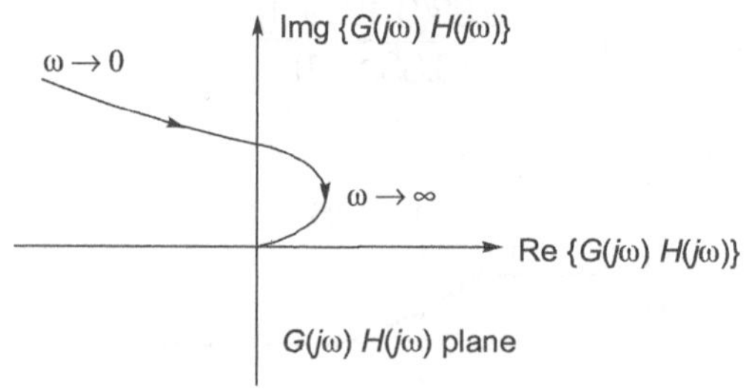

For s_2 : s_2 is mirror image of s_1.

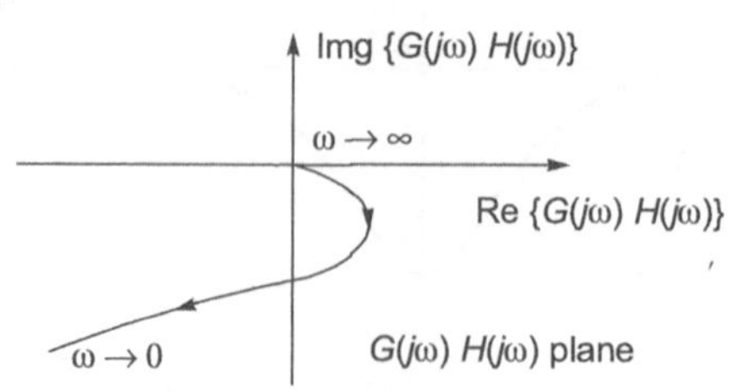

For s_3 :

$$s_3 = \lim_{\substack{R\to\infty \\ \theta\to\frac{\pi}{2}\text{to}-\frac{\pi}{2}}} Re^{j\theta}$$

$$G(s_3)H(s_3) = \frac{K}{s_3^2(s+2)(s+10)}$$

$$= 0.e^{-2\pi \text{ to } 2\pi}$$

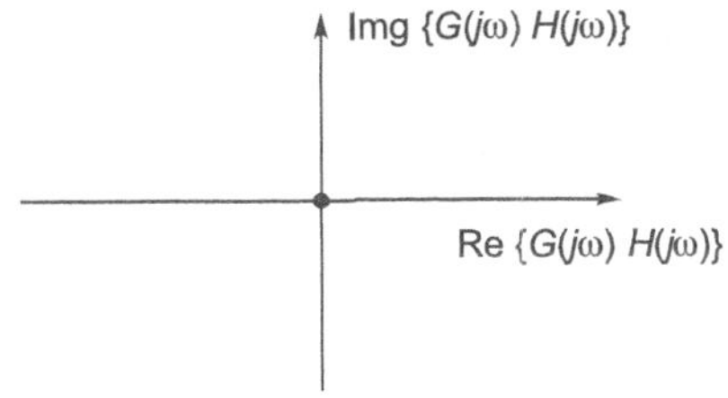

For s_4 :

$$s_4 = \lim_{\substack{R \to 0 \\ \theta \to -\frac{\pi}{2} \text{to} \frac{\pi}{2}}} Re^{j\theta}$$

$$\Rightarrow \quad G(s_4)H(s_4) = \frac{K}{s_4^2(s_4+2)(s_4+10)}$$

$$\Rightarrow \quad G(s_4)H(s_4) = \infty . e^{+\pi \text{ to } -\pi}$$

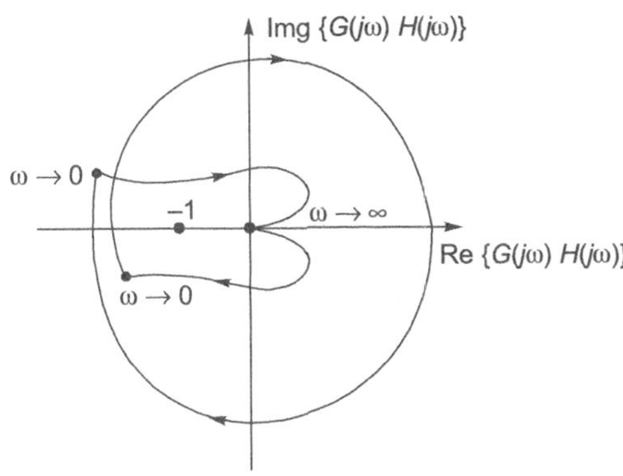

From Nyquist criteria,

Number of encirclements, $N = P - Z$

P is the open loop poles on R.H.S. of s-plane.

Z is the closed loop poles on R.H.S. of s-plane.

$$\Rightarrow \quad -2 = 0 - Z$$

As N is in clockwise direction,

$$\Rightarrow \quad Z = 2$$

Hence, the system is unstable.

For all values of K system is unstable.

Img$\{G(j\omega)H(j\omega)\}$ is not possible, hence gain margin is undefined.

6.27 A unity feedback control system has

$$G(s) = \frac{10 * K}{s\left(\frac{s}{2}+1\right)(s+10)}$$

(i) Find gain and phase margin for $K = 1$.

(ii) If a phase-lag element with transfer of $\frac{(1+2s)}{(1+5s)}$ is added in the forward path, find the new value of K to keep the same gain margin.

[20 marks : 2023]

Solution:

(i) Given OLTF is

$$G(s) = \frac{10K}{s\left(\frac{s}{2}+1\right)(s+10)}$$

For $K = 1$ (given)

We obtain, $$G(s) = \frac{20}{s(s+2)(s+10)}$$

For ω_{pc}, imaginary part would be zero on negative real axis.

$$G(-j\omega_{pc}) = \frac{20}{-j\omega_{pc}^3 - 12\omega_{pc}^2 + 20j\omega_{pc}}$$

$$= \frac{20}{-12\omega_{pc}^2 + j(20\omega_{pc} - \omega_{pc}^3)}$$

Putting imaginary part $[G(j\omega_{pc})] = 0$

$$\omega_{pc}(20 - \omega_{pc}^2) = 0$$

$$\omega_{pc} = 0, \ \sqrt{20} \text{ rad/sec}$$

Now, $$|G(j\omega_{pc})| = \left|\frac{20}{12 \times 20}\right|$$

Gain Margin, $$\text{G.M.} = \left|\frac{1}{G(j\omega_{pc})}\right|$$

$$\text{G.M.} = 12$$

$$\text{G.M. (dB)} = 20 \log 12$$

$$\text{G.M.} = 21.538 \text{ dB}$$

For ω_{gc} (gain cross over frequency)

$$|G(j\omega_{gc})| = 1$$

$$\left|\frac{20}{\omega\sqrt{\omega^2+4}\sqrt{\omega^2+100}}\right| = 1$$

$$400 = \omega^2(\omega^2 + 4)(\omega^2 + 100)$$

$$\omega^6 + 104\omega^4 + 400\omega^2 = 400$$

Assume : $\omega^2 = x$

$$x^3 + 104x^2 + 400x - 400 = 0$$

On solving,

$$x = -99.958, 0.822, -4.86$$

Valid, $$x = 0.822$$

$$\omega^2 = 0.822$$

$$\omega_{gc} = 0.906 \text{ rad/sec}$$

$$\angle G(\omega)\big|_{\omega=\omega_{gc}} = -90° - \tan^{-1}\frac{\omega_{gc}}{2} - \tan^{-1}\frac{\omega_{gc}}{10}$$

$$= -90° - \tan^{-1}\frac{0.906}{2} - \tan^{-1}\frac{0.906}{10}$$

$$\angle G(j\omega_{pc}) = -119.56$$

$$\text{P.M.} = 180° + \angle G(\omega_{gc})$$
$$= 180° + (-119.56)$$
$$\text{P.M.} = 60.434°$$

(ii) Open loop transfer function after adding phase lag element

$$G'(s) = \frac{(1+2s)}{(1+5s)} \times \frac{20k}{s(s+2)(s+10)}$$

$$G'(s) = \frac{20k(1+2s)}{s(1+5s)(s+2)(s+10)} \quad \text{...(1)}$$

∵ Gain margin is same as previous one.

So, G.M. = 21.538 (dB)

or G.M. = 12

For calculating ω_{PC},

$$\angle G'(j\omega) = -180°$$

$$-90° + \tan^{-1} 2\omega - \tan^{-1} 5\omega - \tan^{-1}\left(\frac{\omega}{2}\right) - \tan^{-1}\left(\frac{\omega}{10}\right) = -180°$$

$$\Rightarrow \tan^{-1}\left(\frac{2\omega - 5\omega}{1 + 2\omega \times 5\omega}\right) - \tan^{-1}\left(\frac{\frac{\omega}{2} + \frac{\omega}{10}}{1 - \frac{\omega}{2} \times \frac{\omega}{10}}\right) = -90°$$

$$\Rightarrow \tan^{-1}\left(\frac{-3\omega}{1 + 10\omega^2}\right) - \tan^{-1}\left(\frac{12\omega}{20 - \omega^2}\right) = -90°$$

$$\Rightarrow \quad \frac{\frac{3\omega}{1+10\omega^2} + \frac{12\omega}{20-\omega^2}}{1 - \left(\frac{3\omega}{1+10\omega^2}\right)\left(\frac{12\omega}{20-\omega^2}\right)} = \tan 90° = \frac{1}{0}$$

$$\Rightarrow \quad \left(\frac{3\omega}{1+10\omega^2}\right)\left(\frac{12\omega}{20-\omega^2}\right) = 1$$

$$\Rightarrow \quad 36\omega^2 = (1 + 10\omega^2)(20 - \omega^2)$$

$$\Rightarrow \quad 36\omega^2 = 20 - \omega^2 + 200\omega^2 - 10\omega^4$$

$$\Rightarrow \quad 10\omega^4 - 163\omega^2 - 20 = 0$$

$$\Rightarrow \quad \omega^2 = 16.42$$

$$\Rightarrow \quad \omega = 4.05$$

$$\therefore \quad \omega_{pc} = 4.05$$

$$\text{G.M.} = \frac{1}{|G'|_{\omega=\omega_{pc}}}$$

$$12 = \left|\frac{j\omega_{pc}(1 + 5j\omega_{pc})(j\omega_{pc} + 2)(j\omega_{pc} + 10)}{20k(1 + 2j\omega_{pc})}\right|$$

$$12 = \frac{1}{20k}\left|\frac{\omega_{pc}\sqrt{1+25\omega_{pc}^2}\ \sqrt{4+\omega_{pc}^2}\ \sqrt{100+\omega_{pc}^2}}{\sqrt{1+4\omega_{pc}^2}}\right|$$

$$12 = \frac{490.3}{20k}$$

$$k = 2.04$$

$\therefore$ At $k = 2.04$ gain margin is same as part (i).

7. Compensators and Controllers

7.1 The transfer function of a phase-lead controller is given as $G_C(s) = \frac{1+aTs}{1+Ts}, \sqrt{b^2-4ac}$ $a > 1$ and T is a constant depending on the circuit parameters.
Determine the maximum value of the phase lead which can be obtained from this controller.

[12 marks : 2005]

Solution:

For phase lead controller,

$$G_c(s) = \frac{1+aTs}{1+Ts} \Rightarrow \text{put } s = j\omega$$

$$G_c(j\omega) = \frac{1+jaT\omega}{1+jT\omega}$$

$$\phi = \angle G_c(j\omega) = \tan^{-1} a\omega T - \tan^{-1}\omega T$$

$$\therefore \quad \tan\phi = \frac{\omega T(a-1)}{1+a\omega^2 T^2} \quad \text{...}(i)$$

For getting maximum value of phase angle,

$$\frac{d\phi}{d\omega} = 0 \Rightarrow \frac{T(a-1)\times(1+a\omega^2T^2) - \omega T(a-1)\times(2a\omega T^2)}{(1+a\omega^2T^2)} = 0$$

$$\therefore \quad \omega_m = \frac{1}{T\sqrt{a}}$$

Putting ω_m in equation (*i*),

$$\tan\phi_m = \frac{a-1}{2\sqrt{a}} \text{ or } \phi_m = \tan^{-1}\left[\frac{a-1}{2\sqrt{a}}\right]$$

7.2 Draw a typical RC lag network. Why is it called a lag network? Comment on its effect on
(i) Gain cross-over frequency
(ii) Bandwidth
(iii) Signal to noise ratio.

[5 marks : 2013]

Solution:

RC Lag Network:

$$\text{T.F.} = \frac{V_o}{V_i} = \frac{R_2 + \frac{1}{Cs}}{R_1 + R_2 + \frac{1}{Cs}}$$

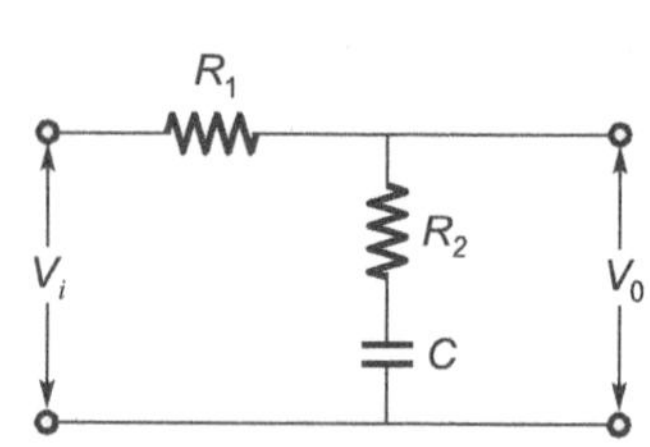

$$\frac{1+R_2Cs}{1+(R_1+R_2)Cs} = \frac{1+sT}{1+\beta Ts}$$

Where, $T = R_2C$ and $\beta = \frac{R_1+R_2}{R_2}$

It is called lag network because it adds negative phase shift in the system.

Effect on:

(1) Grain crossover frequency: Decreases

(2) Bandwidth: Decreases

(3) Signal to noise ratio: Increases

7.3 A closed loop system with unity feedback and having the forward loop transfer function as

$$G(s) = \frac{14.4}{s(1+0.1\,s)}$$

Modify the design using cascaded compensation to satisfy the optimum performance criterion, so that the transient response to unit step input reaches its final steady state value in minimum time without having any overshoot.

[20 marks : 2020]

Solution:

Let the controller be PD controller.

$$\text{Controller transfer function} = K_P + K_D s$$

$$\therefore \quad \text{Forward path transfer function} = \frac{14.4(K_P + K_D s)}{s(1+0.1s)}$$

$\therefore$ Characteristic equation is

$$s(1 + 0.1s) + 14.4K_P + 14.4K_D s = 0$$

$$0.1s^2 + s + 14.4K_D s + 14.4K_P = 0$$

$$0.1s^2 + (14.4K_D + 1)s + 14.4K_P = 0$$

$$s^2 + (144K_D + 10)s + 144K_P = 0$$

$$\omega_n = \sqrt{144K_P}$$

Let $K_P = 2$

$$\omega_n = \sqrt{288} = 12\sqrt{2} = 16.97$$

$$\therefore \quad 2\xi\omega_n = 144K_D + 10$$

as $\omega_n = 12\sqrt{2}$ rad/sec

$$\frac{2\omega_n - 10}{144} = K_D$$

$$\therefore \quad K_D = \frac{24\sqrt{2} - 10}{144} = 0.166$$

$\therefore$ Controller transfer function is $2 + 0.166s$.

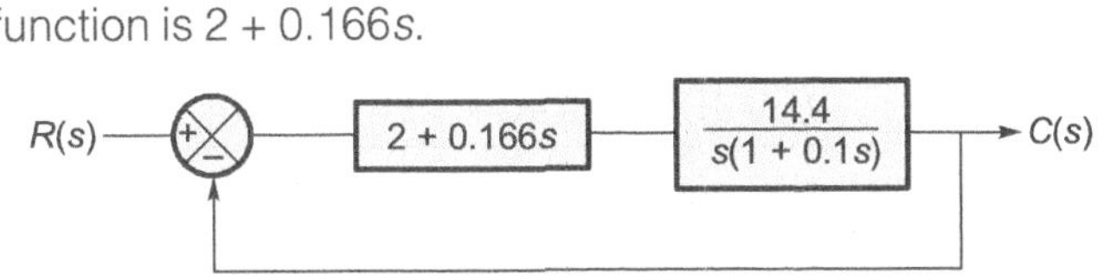

7.4 What are the advantages and limitations of Lead and Lag networks in a practical control system?

[12 marks : 2020]

Solution:

Advantages of Lead :

- Gain crossover frequency (ω_{gc}) increases hence bandwidth increases due to which speed increases.

- Phase becomes less lag hence phase margin increases due to which stability increases.
- Effect of resonance decreases due to which oscillations reduces.

Limitations :

- Due to increase in bandwidth, noise also increases.
- Steady state error cannot become zero.
- Ineffective if the type of a system is very high, in such case multistage compensator is preferred.

Advantages of Lag :

- Effect of noise decreases.
- Useful to reduce damping in heavily damped system.
- Steady state error can be reduced.

Limitations :

- Lag action causes less speed and stability hence recommended to be used in a system with good speeds and stability margins.
- If desired steady state error is zero then it cannot be achieved.

7.5 Design a PD controller for a unity feedback system whose open loop transfer function.

$$G(s)H(s) = \frac{10}{(s+1)(s+4)}$$

will have poles at $s = -4 \pm j4$.

[20 marks : 2023]

Solution:

Given open loop transfer function is :

$$G(s)H(s) = \frac{10}{(s+1)(s+4)}$$

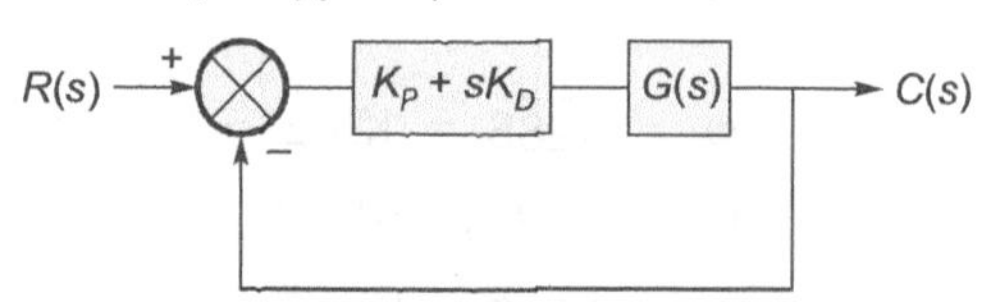

$$\frac{C(s)}{R(s)} = \frac{(K_P + sK_D)\cdot 10}{(s+1)(s+4) + (K_P + sK_D)\cdot 10}$$

Characteristic equation is,

$$s^2 + 5s + 4 + 10sK_D + 10K_P = 0$$

$$s^2 + s(5 + 10K_D) + 4 + 10K_P = 0$$

Poles will be :

$$s = \frac{-(5+10K_D) \pm \sqrt{(5+10K_D)^2 - 4(4+10K_P)}}{2}$$

Since given, $s = -4 \pm 4j$

On comparing,

$$\frac{-(5+10K_D)}{2} = -4$$

$$K_D = 0.3$$

$$\frac{\sqrt{(4(4+10K_P)-64)}}{2} = 4$$

$$4(4 + 10K_P) - 64 = 64$$

$$4 + 10K_P = \frac{128}{4}$$

$$K_P = 2.8$$

By using above data we can design a PD controller as :

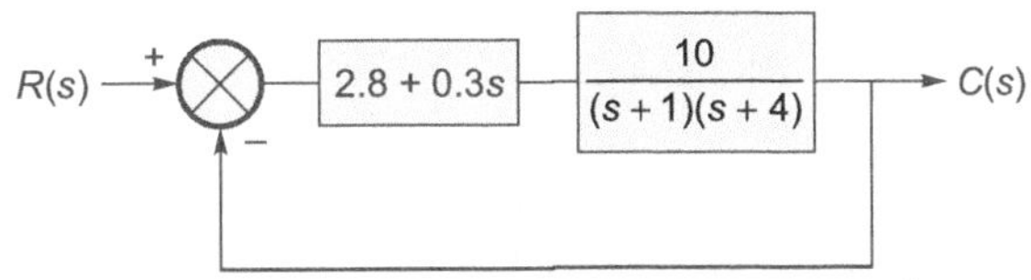

8. State Space Analysis

8.1 From the following state variable representation, determine the transfer function of the system.

$$\dot{x} = \begin{bmatrix} 0 & 1 & 0 \\ 0 & 0 & 1 \\ -40 & -44 & -14 \end{bmatrix} x + \begin{bmatrix} 0 \\ 1 \\ 0 \end{bmatrix} u$$

$$y = [0 \quad 1 \quad 0]x$$

[12 marks : 2002]

Solution:

For state variable representation,

$$\dot{x} = Ax + Bu \text{ and } y = Cx + Du$$

$$\left(\frac{T}{F}\right) = C(sI - A)^{-1} B + D$$

On comparing,

$$A = \begin{bmatrix} 0 & 1 & 0 \\ 0 & 1 & 0 \\ -40 & -44 & -14 \end{bmatrix} B = \begin{bmatrix} 0 \\ 1 \\ 0 \end{bmatrix} C = [0 \quad 10]$$

and D = null matrix

$$\therefore \qquad (sI - A) = \begin{bmatrix} s & -1 & 0 \\ 0 & s & -1 \\ 40 & 44 & s+14 \end{bmatrix} = B_1$$

For finding $(sI - A)^{-1}$

$$|B_1| = [s(s(s + 14) + 44) + 1(40)] = s^3 + 14s^2 + 44s + 40$$

$$B_{11} = (-1)^{1+1} [s(s + 14) + 44]$$

$$B_{12} = (-1)^3 [40]$$

$$B_{13} = (-1)^4 [0 - s \times 40]$$

$$B_{21} = (-1)^3 [-(s + 14) - 0]$$

$$B_{22} = s(s + 14)$$

$$B_{23} = -(44s + 40)$$

$$B_{31} = (-1)^4 \times 1$$

$$B_{32} = (-1)^5 [-s - 0]$$

$$B_{33} = s^2$$

$$B_1^{-1} = (sI - A)^{-1} = \frac{Adj\, B_1}{|B_1|} = \frac{\begin{bmatrix} s^2+14s+44 & s+14 & 1 \\ -40 & s(s+14) & s \\ -40s & -(44s+40) & s^2 \end{bmatrix}}{s^3+14s^2+44s+40}$$

$$\left(\frac{T}{F}\right) = C[sI - A]^{-1} B + D$$

$$\frac{T}{F} = [0\ 1\ 0]\,[sI - A]^{-1}\begin{bmatrix} 0 \\ 1 \\ 0 \end{bmatrix} = \frac{s(s+14)}{s^3+14s^2+44s+40}$$

8.2 A system is represented by

$$\dot{X} = AX + BU$$
$$Y = CX$$

All the states 'X' are available for measurement. Explain the procedure to design a state variable feedback to place the poles of the closed loop system at the eigenvalues of a matrix T.

[10 marks : 2003]

Solution:

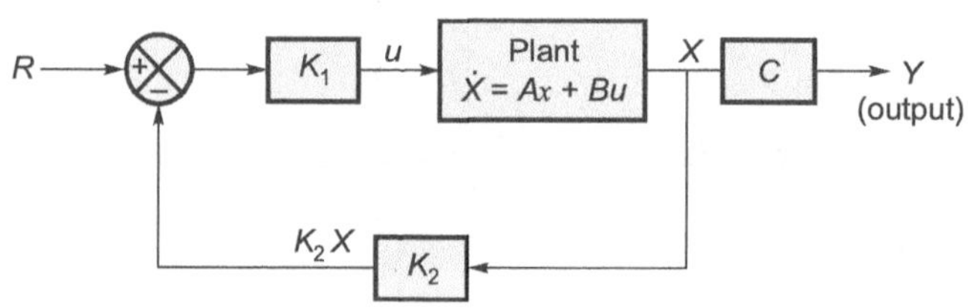

$$\dot{X} = AX + BU \quad \ldots(i)$$

This can be represented in the block diagram form with feedback compensation to some or all of the states as shown in the figure.

$$U = (R - K_2X) = K_1R - K_1K_2X \quad \ldots(ii)$$

Putting into equation (*i*),

$$\dot{X} = AX + B(K_1R - K_1K_2X)$$
$$= (A - BK_1K_2)\,X + BK_1R$$

so the effect of feedback is to modify the closed loop system matrix A to $(A - B\,K_1\,K_2)$. The closed loop characteristic polynomial is given by det $(sI - A)$.

The closed loop poles or eigen values are the roots of the above polynomial.

8.3 Write down the state equations and hence develop a state variable representation for the RLC network shown in figure below.

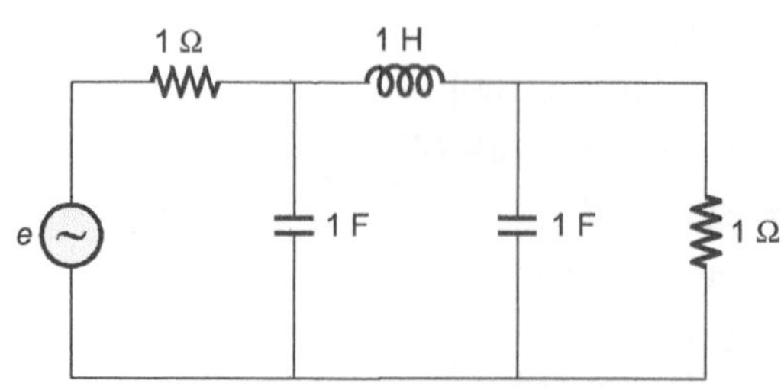

[10 marks : 2004]

Solution:

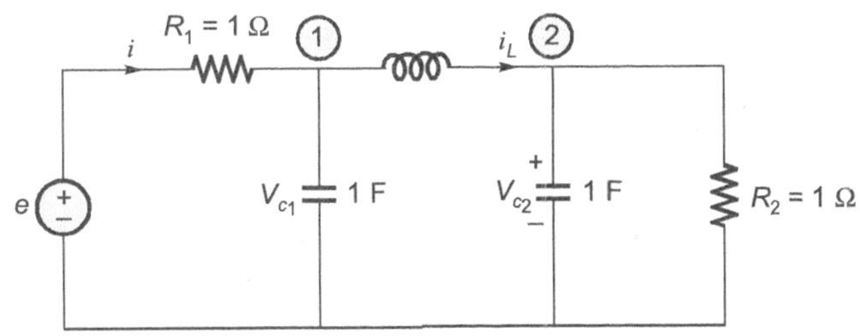

Let choose V_{c1}, V_{c2} and i_L as x_1, x_2 and x_3 as state variables.
From the circuit, applying KCL at node (1)

$$i = C\frac{dV_{c1}}{dt} i_L = \frac{e - V_{c1}}{R_1} \quad \text{...(i)}$$

and $$L\frac{di_L}{dt} = V_{c1} - V_{c2} \quad \text{...(ii)}$$

and $$i_L = C\frac{dV_{c2}}{dt} + \frac{V_{c2}}{R_2} \quad \text{...(iii)}$$

Putting the values and writing in state variables, we have

$$\dot{x}_1 + x_3 = e - x_1$$

or $$\dot{x}_1 = -x_1 - x_3 + e \quad \text{...(i)}$$

and $$\dot{x}_3 = x_1 - x_2 \quad \text{...(iii)}$$

and $$x_3 = u_2 + x_2$$

or $$u_2 = x_3 - x_2 \quad \text{...(ii)}$$

$$\therefore \quad \begin{bmatrix} \dot{x}_1 \\ \dot{x}_2 \\ \dot{x}_3 \end{bmatrix} = \begin{bmatrix} -1 & 0 & -1 \\ 0 & -1 & 1 \\ 1 & -1 & 0 \end{bmatrix} \begin{bmatrix} x_1 \\ x_2 \\ x_3 \end{bmatrix} + \begin{bmatrix} 1 \\ 0 \\ 0 \end{bmatrix} e$$

and output $$y = V_{c2} = x_2$$

$$y = [0\ 1\ 0] \begin{bmatrix} x_1 \\ x_2 \\ x_3 \end{bmatrix}$$

8.4 A system is described by the following state variable equations:

$$\begin{bmatrix} \dot{x}_1(t) \\ \dot{x}_2(t) \end{bmatrix} = \begin{bmatrix} -1 & 1 \\ 0 & -2 \end{bmatrix} \begin{bmatrix} x_1(t) \\ x_2(t) \end{bmatrix} + \begin{bmatrix} 1 \\ -1 \end{bmatrix} u(t),$$

where $u(t)$ is Unit step input and the output

$$y(t) = [1 \quad 1] \begin{bmatrix} x_1(t) \\ x_2(t) \end{bmatrix}$$

Determine $y(t)$, $t \geq 0$ when the initial values of the states at time $t = 0$ are $x_1(0) = x_2(0) = 1$.

[10 marks : 2005]

Solution:

$$\dot{x} = Ax + Bu$$

$$y = Cx \qquad U(s) = \frac{1}{s}$$

Here, $$A = \begin{bmatrix} -1 & 1 \\ 0 & -2 \end{bmatrix}, B = \begin{bmatrix} 1 \\ -1 \end{bmatrix}, C = [1 \;\; 1] \text{ and } X(0) = \begin{bmatrix} 1 \\ 1 \end{bmatrix}$$

$$[sI - A] = \begin{bmatrix} s+1 & -1 \\ 0 & s+2 \end{bmatrix} = \frac{\begin{bmatrix} s+1 & -1 \\ 0 & s+1 \end{bmatrix}}{(s+1)\;(s+2)}$$

$$y(t) = L^{-1}[Y(s)]$$

where, $$Y(s) = C\cdot[sI - A]^{-1} X(0) + C\cdot[sI - A]^{-1} \times B\cdot U(s)$$

$$Y(s) = C\cdot[sI - A]^{-1}\cdot\left\{\begin{bmatrix} 1 \\ 1 \end{bmatrix} + \begin{bmatrix} 1 \\ -1 \end{bmatrix} \times \left(\frac{1}{s}\right)\right\}$$

$$= C\cdot[sI - A]^{-1}\cdot\begin{bmatrix} 1 & + & 1/s \\ s & - & 1/s \end{bmatrix}$$

$$= [1 \;\; 1]\cdot\frac{\begin{bmatrix} s+2 & 1 \\ 0 & s+1 \end{bmatrix}}{(s+1)\,(s+2)}\cdot\begin{bmatrix} 1 & + & 1/s \\ 1 & - & 1/s \end{bmatrix} = [1 \;\; 1]\cdot\frac{\begin{bmatrix} (s+2)\left(1+\frac{1}{s}\right) + & \left(1-\frac{1}{s}\right) \\ (s+1) \qquad \times & \left(1-\frac{1}{s}\right) \end{bmatrix}}{(s+1)\,(s+2)}$$

$$= \frac{\left\{(s+2)\left(1+\frac{1}{s}\right) + \left(1-\frac{1}{s}\right) + (s+1)\left(1-\frac{1}{s}\right)\right\}}{(s+1)\,(s+2)}$$

$$= \frac{\left\{s+2+1+\frac{2}{s}+1-\frac{1}{s}+s+1-1-\frac{1}{s}\right\}}{(s+1)\,(s+2)}$$

$$= \frac{2s+4}{(s+1)\,(s+2)} = \frac{2(s+2)}{(s+1)\,(s+2)} = \frac{2}{s+1}$$

$$y(s) = \frac{2}{s+1}$$

$$y(t) = L^{-1}[Y(s)] = L^{-1}\left[\frac{2}{s+1}\right] = 2e^{-t}\,u(t)$$

8.5 What is meant by mathematical modelling of a physical system?

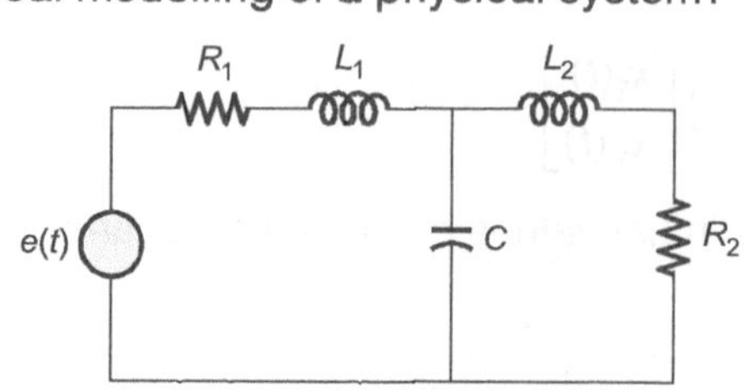

Obtain the state diagram for the network shown in the above figure. Write the state variable equation.
[12 marks : 2006]

Solution:

A control system, is a collection of physical objects connected together to serve an objective. The input output relations of various physical components of a system are governed by differential equations. The mathematical model of a system constitutes a set of differential equations. The response of output of the system can be studied by solving the differential equations for various input conditions.

Selecting the state variable as,

$$x_1(t) = i_1(t)$$
$$x_2(t) = i_2(t)$$
$$x_3(t) = V_c(t)$$

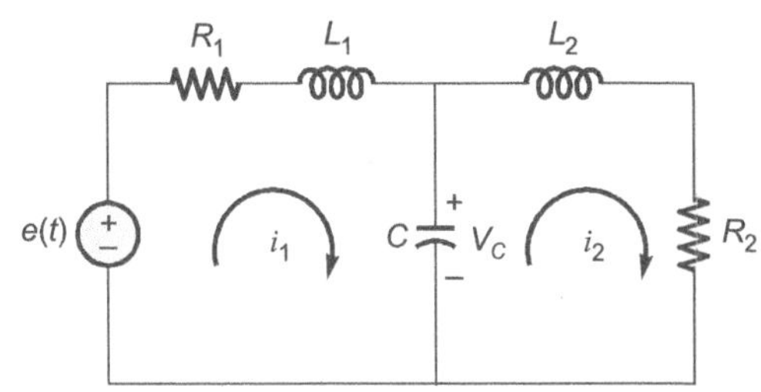

Writing KVL in Loop 1,

$$e(t) - R_1 i_1(t) - L_1\frac{di_1(t)}{dt} - V_c(t) = 0$$

$$\frac{di_1(t)}{dt} = -\frac{R_1}{L_1}i_1(t) - \frac{V_c(t)}{L_1} + e(t)$$

$$\Rightarrow \quad \dot{x}_1 = -\frac{R_1}{L_1}x_1 - \frac{x_3}{L_1} + \frac{e(t)}{L_1} \quad \ldots(i)$$

Writing KVL in Loop 2,

$$V_c(t) - L_2\frac{di_2(t)}{dt} - R_2 i_2(t) = 0$$

$$\Rightarrow \quad \frac{di_2(t)}{dt} = -\frac{R_2}{L_2}i_2(t) + \frac{V_c(t)}{L_2}$$

$$\Rightarrow \quad \dot{x}_2 = -\frac{R_2}{L_2}x_2 + \frac{x_3}{L_2} \quad \ldots(ii)$$

Writing KCL at node (a),

$$-i_1(t) + C\frac{dv_c(t)}{dt} + i_2(t) = 0$$

$$\Rightarrow \quad \frac{dv_c(t)}{dt} = \frac{i_1(t)}{C} - \frac{i_2(t)}{C}$$

$$\dot{x}_3 = \frac{x_1}{C} - \frac{x_2}{C} \quad \ldots(iii)$$

Equation (*i*), (*ii*) and *iii*) stable variable equations.

In matrix form

$$\begin{bmatrix}\dot{x}_1\\ \dot{x}_2\\ \dot{x}_3\end{bmatrix} = \begin{bmatrix}-\frac{R_1}{L_1} & 0 & -\frac{1}{L_1}\\ 0 & -\frac{R_2}{L_2} & \frac{1}{L_2}\\ \frac{1}{C} & -\frac{1}{C} & 0\end{bmatrix}\begin{bmatrix}x_1\\ x_2\\ x_3\end{bmatrix} + \begin{bmatrix}1/L_1\\ 0\\ 0\end{bmatrix}e(t)$$

State diagram:

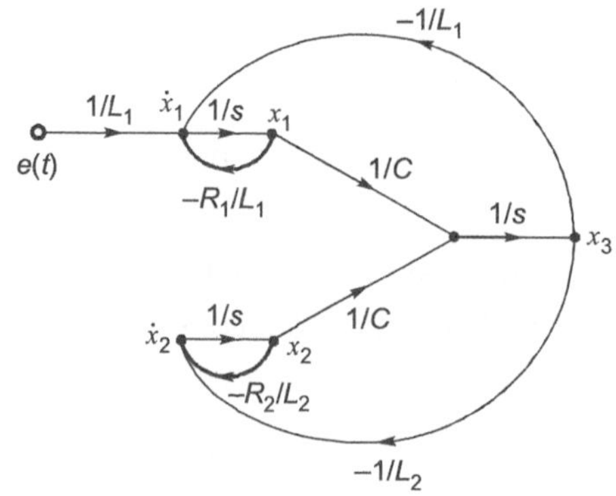

8.6 What is state variable feedback design? Explain how the poles of an original system can be shifted to another location say $-\lambda_1$ and $-\lambda_2$ for a second order system.

[10 marks : 2006]

Solution:

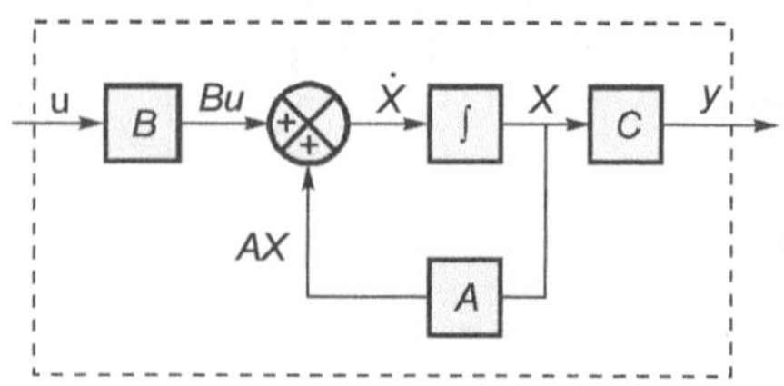

System without state feedback

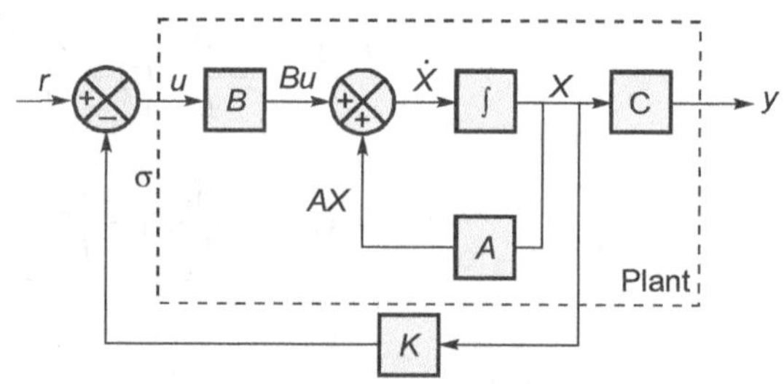

State variable feedback

$$\dot{X} = AX + Bu \quad ...(i)$$

$$y = CX \quad ...(ii)$$

Let,
r = System input when state variable feedback is employed.
σ = Feedback signal obtained from state variables
u = Plant input.

The feedback signal, σ is obtained from state feedback and it is related to the state variables by the equation,

$$\sigma = KX \quad ...(iii)$$

Where K = State feedback gain matrix of order $(1 \times n)$ and

$$K = (k_1\ k_2\ k_3\ ...k_n) \quad ...(iv)$$

In system employing state variable feedback, the plant input, u is the difference between system input, r and feedback input, σ.

∴ Plant input, $u = r - \sigma$ ...(*v*)

On substituting, $\sigma = KX$ in equation (*v*) we get,

$$u = r - KX \quad ...(vi)$$

The equation (*vi*) is called control law.

The state equation of the system with state variable feedback is obtained by substituting the expression for u, from equation (*vi*) in equation (*i*).

$$\therefore \quad \dot{X} = AX + Bu = AX + B(r - KX)$$
$$= AX + Br - BK\,X$$
$$= (A - BK)\,X + Br$$

Therefore, the state model of the system with state variable feedback is given by the following equations [equation (*vii*) and (*viii*)]

$\therefore$
$$\dot{X} = (A - BK)X + Br \quad ...(vii)$$
$$y = CX \quad ...(viii)$$
Where, $K = [k_1, k_2, k_3 \ldots k_n]$

and
$$r = u + KX$$
This design technique starts with the determination of desired closed-loop poles to satisfy transient response and/or frequency response requirements. By choosing an appropriate gain matrix, K for state feedback, it is possible to force the system to have closed loop poles at the desired locations, provided that the original system is completely state controllable. In this design technique it is assumed that all state variable are measurable and are available for feedback.

8.7 **For a system represented in state-space form, how can be corresponding transfer function model be obtained?**

[10 marks : 2010]

Solution:

The state equations of a system are given below:
$$\dot{x} = Ax + Bu \quad ...(i)$$
$$y = Cx + Du \quad ...(ii)$$
where, x is stable vector $(n \times 1)$

u is input (scaler)

y is output (scaler)

A is matrix $(n \times n)$

C is matrix $(1 \times n)$

D is scaler

Taking Laplace transform on both sides of equation (i) and (ii),
$$sX(s) - x(0) = AX(s) + Bu(s) \quad ...(iii)$$
$$Y(s) = CX(s) + Du(s) \quad ...(iv)$$
As per definition of transfer function $x(0) = 0$
$$sX(s) = AX(s) + Bu(s)$$
$$X(s) = (sI - A)^{-1} Bu(s) \quad ...(v)$$
Substituting (v) in equation (iv), the following equation is,
$$Y(s) = C(sI - A)^{-1} Bu(s) + Du(s)$$
$$Y(s) = [C(sI - A)^{-1} B + D] u(s)$$
The transfer matrix is $G(s) = \dfrac{Y(s)}{U(s)} = C(sI - A)^{-1} B + D$

8.8 **For the system given as:**
$$\dot{x} = \begin{bmatrix} 0 & 0 & -20 \\ 1 & 0 & -24 \\ 0 & 0 & -9 \end{bmatrix} x + \begin{bmatrix} 3 \\ 1 \\ 0 \end{bmatrix} u$$
$$y = [0 \;\; 0 \;\; 1] x$$
Obtain the transfer function. **[10 marks : 2010]**

Solution:
$$\text{Transfer function} = C(sI - A)^{-1} B + D$$

$$A = \begin{bmatrix} 0 & 0 & -20 \\ 1 & 0 & -24 \\ 0 & 1 & -9 \end{bmatrix} B = \begin{bmatrix} 3 \\ 1 \\ 0 \end{bmatrix} C = [0 \ 0 \ 1]$$

$$[sI - A] = \begin{bmatrix} s & 0 & 20 \\ -1 & s & 24 \\ 0 & -1 & s+9 \end{bmatrix}$$

$$[sI - A]^{-1} = \frac{Adj[sI - A]}{\det[sI - A]} = \frac{\begin{bmatrix} s^2+9s+24 & -20 & -20s \\ s+9 & s(s+9) & -(24s+20) \\ 1 & s & s^2 \end{bmatrix}}{s[s(s+9)+24]+20}$$

$$= \frac{\begin{bmatrix} s^2+9s+24 & -20 & -20s \\ s+9 & s(s+9) & -(24s+20) \\ 1 & s & s^2 \end{bmatrix}}{s^3+9s^2+24s+20}$$

$$\text{Transfer function} = C[sI - A]^{-1} B + D$$

$$\text{Transfer function} = [0 \ 0 \ 1] \frac{\begin{bmatrix} s^2+9s+24 & -20 & -20s \\ s+9 & s(s+9) & -(24s+20) \\ 1 & s & s^2 \end{bmatrix}}{(s^3+9s^2+24s+20)} \begin{bmatrix} 3 \\ 1 \\ 0 \end{bmatrix}$$

$$= \frac{\begin{bmatrix} 1 & s & s^2 \end{bmatrix}}{(s^3+9s^2+24+20)} \begin{bmatrix} 3 \\ 1 \\ 0 \end{bmatrix} = \frac{s+3}{(s^3+9s^2+24+20)}$$

8.9 **What is the property of invariance in state variable models?**

[10 marks : 2010]

Solution:

State equations of a system are

$$\frac{dx(t)}{dt} = Ax(t) + Bu(t) \quad \text{...(i)}$$

$$y(t) = Cx(t) + Du(t) \quad \text{...(ii)}$$

Let us consider that the equations are transformed into another set of equations of the same dimension by the following transformation

$$x(t) = P\overline{x}(t)$$

where P is non-singular $n \times n$ matrix, so

$$\overline{x}(t) = P^{-1}x(t) \quad \text{...(iii)}$$

The transformed state equations are written,

$$\frac{d\overline{x}(t)}{dt} = \overline{A}\overline{x}(t) + \overline{B}u(t) \quad \text{...(iv)}$$

$$\overline{y}(t) = \overline{C}\,\overline{x}(t) + \overline{D}\,u(t) \quad \text{...(v)}$$

Taking derivative of both sides of equation (*iii*),

$$\frac{d\bar{x}(t)}{dt} = P^{-1}\frac{dx(t)}{dt} = P^{-1}Ax(t) + P^{-1}Bu(t)$$

$$= P^{-1}AP\bar{x}(t) + P^{-1}Bu(t) \quad \text{...(vi)}$$

Comparing equation (*vi*) with equation (*iv*),

$$\bar{A} = P^{-1}AP \text{ and } \bar{B} = P^{-1}B \quad \text{...(vii)}$$

Using, equation (*iii*), equation (b) is written,

$$\bar{y}(t) = CPx(t) + \bar{D}u(t) \quad \text{...(viii)}$$

Comparing equation (*viii*) with equation (*ii*),

$$\bar{C} = CP \text{ and } \bar{D} = D$$

The transformation described is called a similarly transformation. One of the important properties of the similarly transformation is that characteristic equation, eigenvalues, eigenvectors and transfer functions are invariant under the transformation.

8.10 **For a system described by state-space model in controlled canonical form, explain the concept pole-placement design by state-variable feedback (SVFB) control approach.**

[10 marks : 2009]

Solution:

Refer (Q.No. 8.6).

8.11 **For the system specified below, design an SVFB controller such that the closed-loop poles of system are located at $s = -3 \pm j3$**

$$\dot{x} = \begin{bmatrix} 0 & 1 \\ 0 & 0 \end{bmatrix} x + \begin{bmatrix} 0 \\ 1 \end{bmatrix} u$$

[10 marks : 2010]

Solution:

To check controllability, $Q_c = [B \;\; AB]$

$$AB = \begin{bmatrix} 0 & 1 \\ 0 & 0 \end{bmatrix}\begin{bmatrix} 0 \\ 1 \end{bmatrix} = \begin{bmatrix} 1 \\ 0 \end{bmatrix}$$

$$Q_c = \begin{bmatrix} 0 & 1 \\ 1 & 0 \end{bmatrix} \neq 0$$

Hence, the system is controllable and SVFB design technique can be applied to this system.

For a second order system the feedback matrix K is of the form

$$K = [K_1 \;\; K_2]$$

The state equation for the closed loop system becomes

$$\dot{x} = (A - BK)x$$

$$= \left(\begin{bmatrix} 0 & 1 \\ 0 & 0 \end{bmatrix} - \begin{bmatrix} 0 \\ 1 \end{bmatrix}\begin{bmatrix} k_1 \\ k_2 \end{bmatrix}\right)x = \begin{bmatrix} 0 & 1 \\ -k_1 & -k_2 \end{bmatrix}x$$

The characteristic equation of the closed loop system is

$$|sI - (A - BK)| = \left|\begin{bmatrix} s & -1 \\ k_1 & s + k_2 \end{bmatrix}\right|$$

$$= s(s + k_2) + k_1 = s^2 + k_2 s + k_1 \qquad ...(i)$$

The closed loop poles of the system are needed at

$$s = -3 \pm 3$$

So, the desired characteristic equation is,

$$(s + 3 + j3)(s + 3 - j3) = s^2 + 6s + 18 \qquad ...(ii)$$

On comparing equation (*i*) with equation (*ii*),

$$k_1 = 18 \text{ and } k_2 = 6$$

Therefore, $$k = \begin{bmatrix} 18 \\ 6 \end{bmatrix}$$

8.12 **A system is represented by the following transfer function model**

$$G(s) = \frac{C(s)}{R(s)} = \frac{s+5}{(s+1)(s+2)(s+3)}$$

Obtained the state-space model for this system such that the system matrix is in diagonalized form. The choice of state variables needs to be clearly indicated.

[10 marks : 2011]

Solution:

$$G(s) = \frac{C(s)}{R(s)} = \frac{s+5}{(s+1)(s+2)(s+3)} = \frac{s+5}{s^3 + 6s^2 + 11s + 6}$$

$$= \frac{\frac{5}{s^3} + \frac{1}{s^2}}{1 + \frac{6}{s} + \frac{11}{s^2} + \frac{6}{s^3}} \qquad ...(i)$$

On the basis of equation (*i*), stable diagram is drawn, indicating state variables.

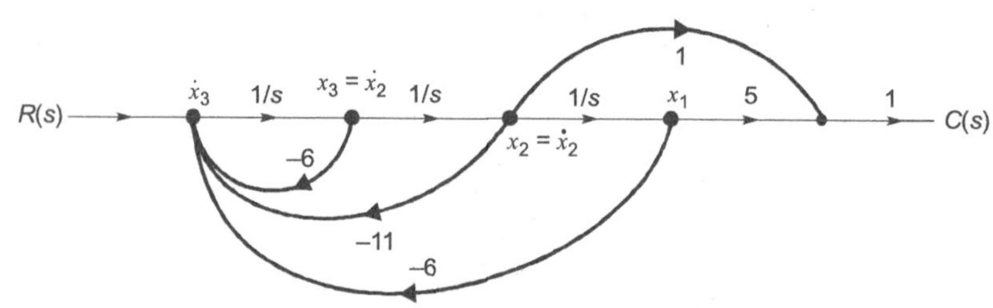

The output of each integrator is designated by state variable and thus the state equations are

$$\dot{x}_1 = x_2 \qquad (i)$$

$$\dot{x}_2 = x_3 \qquad ...(ii)$$

$$\dot{x}_3 = -6x_1 - 11x_2 - 6x_3 + r(t) \qquad ...(iii)$$

$$c = 5x_1 + x_2 \qquad ...(iv)$$

The matrix form of the state equations are

$$\begin{bmatrix} \dot{x}_1 \\ \dot{x}_2 \\ \dot{x}_3 \end{bmatrix} = \begin{bmatrix} 0 & 1 & 0 \\ 0 & 0 & 1 \\ -6 & -11 & -6 \end{bmatrix} \begin{bmatrix} x_1 \\ x_2 \\ x_3 \end{bmatrix} + \begin{bmatrix} 0 \\ 0 \\ 1 \end{bmatrix} r(t) \qquad ...(v)$$

$$c = \begin{bmatrix} 5 & 1 & 0 \end{bmatrix} \begin{bmatrix} x_1 \\ x_2 \\ x_3 \end{bmatrix} \qquad ...(vi)$$

above equation can be written as

$$\dot{x} = AX + Br \quad \text{...(vii)}$$

$$c = CX \quad \text{...(viii)}$$

where, $A = \begin{bmatrix} 0 & 1 & 0 \\ 0 & 0 & 1 \\ -6 & -11 & -6 \end{bmatrix}$ $B = \begin{bmatrix} 0 \\ 0 \\ 1 \end{bmatrix}$ and $C = [5 \quad 1 \quad 0]$

Matrix A is given in phase variable form, therefore Vandermonde's matrix is considered for diagonalization of matrix A.

The eigenvalues of matrix A are determined by solving following equation

$$|\lambda I - A| = \begin{bmatrix} \lambda & 0 & 0 \\ 0 & \lambda & 0 \\ 0 & 0 & \lambda \end{bmatrix} - \begin{bmatrix} 0 & 1 & 0 \\ 0 & 0 & 1 \\ -6 & -11 & -6 \end{bmatrix} = \begin{bmatrix} \lambda & -1 & 0 \\ 0 & \lambda & -1 \\ 6 & 11 & \lambda+6 \end{bmatrix}$$

$$= \lambda\,[\lambda\,(\lambda + 6) + 11] + 1 \cdot \{0 - (6)\} = \lambda^3 + 6\lambda^2 + 11\lambda + 6$$

$$= (\lambda + 1)\,(\lambda + 2)\,(\lambda + 3)$$

Thus, there distinct eigen values of matrix A are

$\lambda_1 = -1$, $\lambda_2 = -2$ and $\lambda = -3$

The Vandermonde's matrix is given by

$$P = \begin{bmatrix} 1 & 1 & 1 \\ \lambda_1 & \lambda_2 & \lambda_3 \\ \lambda_1^2 & \lambda_2^2 & \lambda_3^2 \end{bmatrix} = \begin{bmatrix} 1 & 1 & 1 \\ -1 & -2 & -3 \\ 1 & 4 & 9 \end{bmatrix}$$

The state equation for the system is given by

$$\dot{x} = AX + Br \quad \text{and} \quad c = CX$$

Put, $x = Pz$ in the above equation

$$\dot{P}z = APz + Br$$

$$\dot{z} = P^{-1}APz + P^{-1}Br$$

$$c = CPz$$

$$P^{-1} = \begin{bmatrix} 3 & 2.5 & 0.5 \\ -3 & -4 & -1 \\ 1 & 1.5 & 0.5 \end{bmatrix}$$

$$P^{-1}AP = \begin{bmatrix} 3 & 2.5 & 0.5 \\ -3 & -4 & -1 \\ 1 & 1.5 & 0.5 \end{bmatrix}\begin{bmatrix} 0 & 1 & 0 \\ 0 & 0 & 1 \\ -6 & -11 & -6 \end{bmatrix}\begin{bmatrix} 1 & 1 & 1 \\ -1 & -2 & -3 \\ 1 & 4 & 3 \end{bmatrix} = \begin{bmatrix} -1 & 0 & 0 \\ 0 & -2 & 0 \\ 0 & 0 & -3 \end{bmatrix}$$

$$P^{-1}B = \begin{bmatrix} 3 & 2.5 & 0.5 \\ -3 & -4 & -1 \\ 1 & 1.5 & 0.5 \end{bmatrix}\begin{bmatrix} 0 \\ 0 \\ 1 \end{bmatrix} = \begin{bmatrix} 0.5 \\ -1 \\ 0.5 \end{bmatrix}$$

$$CP = [5 \quad 1 \quad 0]\begin{bmatrix} 1 & 1 & 1 \\ -1 & -2 & -3 \\ 1 & 4 & 9 \end{bmatrix} = [4 \quad 3 \quad 2]$$

The state-space model for the system such that the system matrix is diagonalized form.

$$\begin{bmatrix} \dot{z}_1 \\ \dot{z}_2 \\ \dot{z}_3 \end{bmatrix} = \begin{bmatrix} -1 & 0 & 0 \\ 0 & -2 & 0 \\ 0 & 0 & -3 \end{bmatrix} \begin{bmatrix} z_1 \\ z_2 \\ z_3 \end{bmatrix} + \begin{bmatrix} 0.5 \\ -1 \\ 0.5 \end{bmatrix} r(t)$$

$$C = [4 \quad 3 \quad 2] \begin{bmatrix} z_1 \\ z_2 \\ z_3 \end{bmatrix}$$

8.13 A system is modelled by state-state model as

$$\dot{X} = \begin{bmatrix} -2 & 1 \\ 2 & -3 \end{bmatrix} X + \begin{bmatrix} 1 \\ -2 \end{bmatrix} U$$

$$Y = [1 \quad 0]\, X$$

Evaluate the state transition matrix and the autonomous response of the system with initial condition $x(0) = [1 \quad 2]^T$

[10 marks : 2011]

Solution:

$$A = \begin{bmatrix} -2 & 1 \\ 2 & -3 \end{bmatrix}; \quad B = \begin{bmatrix} 1 \\ -2 \end{bmatrix} \quad C = [1 \quad 0]$$

and

$$X(0) = \begin{bmatrix} 1 \\ 2 \end{bmatrix}$$

$$[sI - A] = \begin{bmatrix} s & 0 \\ 0 & s \end{bmatrix} - \begin{bmatrix} -2 & 1 \\ 2 & -3 \end{bmatrix} = \begin{bmatrix} s+2 & -1 \\ -2 & s+3 \end{bmatrix}$$

$$[sI - A]^{-1} = \frac{Adj\,[sI - A]}{|sI - A|} = \frac{\begin{bmatrix} s+3 & 1 \\ 2 & s+2 \end{bmatrix}}{(s+3)(s+2) - 2} = \frac{\begin{bmatrix} s+3 & 1 \\ 2 & s+2 \end{bmatrix}}{(s+1)(s+4)}$$

$$\phi(s) = [sI - A]^{-1} = \begin{bmatrix} \dfrac{s+3}{(s+1)(s+4)} & \dfrac{1}{(s+1)(s+4)} \\ \dfrac{2}{(s+1)(s+4)} & \dfrac{s+2}{(s+1)(s+4)} \end{bmatrix}$$

State transition matrix $= \phi(t) = L^{-1}[\phi(s)] = L^{-1}\{sI - A]^{-1}\}$

$$= L^{-1} \begin{bmatrix} \dfrac{s+3}{(s+1)(s+4)} & \dfrac{1}{(s+1)(s+4)} \\ \dfrac{2}{(s+1)(s+4)} & \dfrac{s+2}{(s+1)(s+4)} \end{bmatrix}$$

$$= L^{-1} \begin{bmatrix} \dfrac{1}{3}\left(\dfrac{2}{s+1} + \dfrac{1}{s+4}\right) & \dfrac{1}{3}\left(\dfrac{1}{s+1} - \dfrac{1}{s+4}\right) \\ \dfrac{2}{3}\left(\dfrac{1}{s+1} - \dfrac{1}{s+4}\right) & \dfrac{1}{3}\left(\dfrac{1}{s+1} + \dfrac{2}{s+4}\right) \end{bmatrix}$$

$$\text{State transition matrix } \phi(t) = \frac{1}{3}\begin{bmatrix} 2e^{-t}+e^{-4t} & e^{-t}-e^{-4t} \\ 2e^{-t}-2e^{-4t} & e^{-t}+2e^{-4t} \end{bmatrix}$$

Autonomous response of the system = $\phi(t) \times X(0)$

$$= \frac{1}{3}\begin{bmatrix} 2e^{-t}+e^{-4t} & e^{-t}-e^{-4t} \\ 2e^{-t}-2e^{-4t} & e^{-t}+2e^{-4t} \end{bmatrix}\begin{bmatrix} 1 \\ 2 \end{bmatrix} = \frac{1}{3}\begin{bmatrix} 2e^{-t}+e^{-4t} & + \ 2e^{-t}-2e^{-4t} \\ 2e^{-t}-2e^{-4t} & + \ 2e^{-t}+4e^{-4t} \end{bmatrix}$$

$$\text{Autonomous response of the system} = \frac{1}{3}\begin{bmatrix} 4e^{-t} - & e^{-4t} \\ 4e^{-t} + & 2e^{-4t} \end{bmatrix}$$

8.14 **A state variable description of a system is given by the matrix equation:**

$$\dot{X} = \begin{bmatrix} -1 & 0 \\ 1 & -2 \end{bmatrix} X + \begin{bmatrix} 1 \\ 0 \end{bmatrix} r(t), \; Y = [1 \;\; 1]\, X$$

Find:

(i) the transfer function $\dfrac{Y(s)}{R(s)}$

(ii) the eigen values of the system

(iii) the state transition matrix

(iv) prove the non-uniqueness of state variables in general.

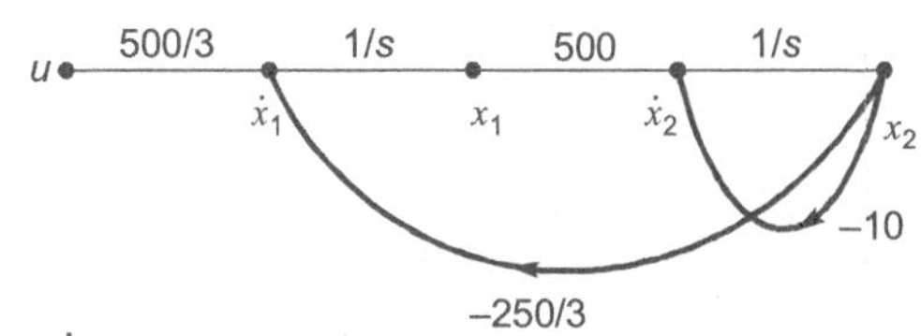

[12 marks : 2012]

Solution:

(i)

$$\dot{x} = Ax(t) + Br(t)$$

$$y(t) = Cx(t)$$

Taking Laplace transform on both sides

$$sX(s) = AX(s) + BR(s)$$

$$Y(s) = CX(s)$$

$$\Rightarrow \quad Y(s) = C(sI - A)^{-1}\, B\, R(s)$$

Therefore transfer matrix is $G(s) = \dfrac{Y(s)}{R(s)} = C(sI - A)^{-1}B$

$$G(s) = [1 \;\; 1]\left(\begin{bmatrix} s & 0 \\ 0 & s \end{bmatrix} - \begin{bmatrix} -1 & 0 \\ 1 & -2 \end{bmatrix}\right)^{-1}\begin{bmatrix} 1 \\ 0 \end{bmatrix}$$

$$= [1 \;\; 1]\begin{bmatrix} s+1 & 0 \\ -1 & s+2 \end{bmatrix}^{-1}\begin{bmatrix} 1 \\ 0 \end{bmatrix} = \frac{1}{(s+1)(s+2)}[1 \;\; 1]\begin{bmatrix} s+2 & 0 \\ 1 & s+1 \end{bmatrix}\begin{bmatrix} 1 \\ 0 \end{bmatrix}$$

$$= \frac{1}{(s+1)(s+2)}[1 \;\; 1]\begin{bmatrix} s+2 \\ 1 \end{bmatrix} = \frac{s+2}{(s+1)(s+2)} = \frac{1}{s+1}$$

(ii)

$$|\lambda I - A| = 0$$

$$\begin{vmatrix} \lambda+1 & 0 \\ -1 & \lambda+2 \end{vmatrix} = 0$$

$$(\lambda + 1)(\lambda + 2) = 0$$

$$\lambda = -1, -2$$

The two distinct eigen values are

$$\lambda_1 = -1, \quad \lambda_2 = -3$$

(iii) State transition matrix,

$$\phi(t) = \mathcal{L}^{-1}\left\{[sI - A]^{-1}\right\} = \mathcal{L}^{-1}\begin{bmatrix} \frac{1}{s+1} & 0 \\ \frac{1}{(s+1)(s+2)} & \frac{1}{s+2} \end{bmatrix} = \begin{bmatrix} e^{-t} & 0 \\ e^{-t} - e^{-2t} & e^{-2t} \end{bmatrix}$$

8.15 A feedback system has closed loop transfer function: $\dfrac{C(s)}{U(s)} = \dfrac{10(s+4)}{s(s+1)(s+3)}$

Obtain its canonical state model. Also write STM (State Transition Matrix) of canonical state model.

[10 marks : 2013]

Solution:

Canonical form is also known as partial fraction expansion form. In this parallel decomposition of a transfer function is a diagonal one.

$$\frac{C(s)}{U(s)} = \frac{A}{s} + \frac{B}{s+1} + \frac{C}{s+3}$$

Where, $\quad A = \dfrac{40}{3}, \quad B = -15, \quad C = \dfrac{5}{3}$

$$\frac{C(s)}{U(s)} = \frac{40/3}{s} + \frac{(-15)}{s+1} + \frac{5/3}{s+3}$$

The output of each integrator is assigned a state variable as shown in below drawn figure and the state equations are given as,

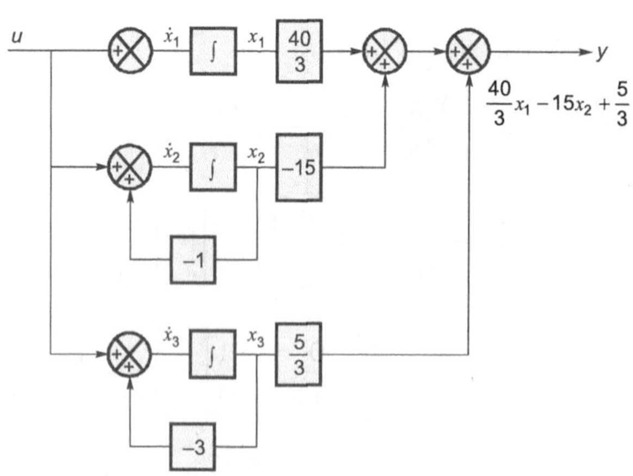

$$\dot{x}_1 = 0x_1 + 0x_2 + 0x_3 + u$$

$$\dot{x}_2 = 0x_1 - 1x_2 + 0x_3 + u$$

$$\dot{x}_3 = 0x_1 + 0x_2 - 3x_3 + u$$

The output equation is, $\quad y = \dfrac{40}{3}u_1 - 15x_2 + \dfrac{5}{3}x_3$

So, the canonical state model is given as,

$$\begin{bmatrix} \dot{x}_1 \\ \dot{x}_2 \\ \dot{x}_3 \end{bmatrix} = \begin{bmatrix} 0 & 0 & 0 \\ 0 & -1 & 0 \\ 0 & 0 & -3 \end{bmatrix} \begin{bmatrix} x_1 \\ x_2 \\ x_3 \end{bmatrix} + \begin{bmatrix} 1 \\ 1 \\ 1 \end{bmatrix} u$$

$$y = \begin{bmatrix} \frac{40}{3} & -15 & \frac{5}{3} \end{bmatrix} \begin{bmatrix} x_1 \\ x_2 \\ x_3 \end{bmatrix}$$

Comparing from standard equation we have

$$[A] = \begin{bmatrix} 0 & 0 & 0 \\ 0 & -1 & 0 \\ 0 & 0 & -3 \end{bmatrix}, \quad [B] = \begin{bmatrix} 1 \\ 1 \\ 1 \end{bmatrix}, \quad [C] = \begin{bmatrix} \frac{40}{3} & -15 & \frac{5}{3} \end{bmatrix}$$

Now, state transition matrix can be given as,

$$\phi(t) = \mathcal{L}^{-1}[sI - A]^{-1}$$

$$[sI - A] = \begin{bmatrix} s & 0 & 0 \\ 0 & s & 0 \\ 0 & 0 & s \end{bmatrix} - \begin{bmatrix} 0 & 0 & 0 \\ 0 & -1 & 0 \\ 0 & 0 & -3 \end{bmatrix} = \begin{bmatrix} s & 0 & 0 \\ 0 & s+1 & 0 \\ 0 & 0 & s+3 \end{bmatrix}$$

$$[sI - A]^{-1} = \frac{Adj\,[sI - A]}{|sI - A|} = \frac{\begin{bmatrix} (s+1)(s+3) & 0 & 0 \\ 0 & s(s+3) & 0 \\ 0 & 0 & s(s+1) \end{bmatrix}}{s(s+1)(s+3)} = \begin{bmatrix} \frac{1}{s} & 0 & 0 \\ 0 & \frac{1}{s+1} & 0 \\ 0 & 0 & \frac{1}{s+3} \end{bmatrix}$$

$$\phi(t) = \mathcal{L}^{-1}\left\{[sI - A]^{-1}\right\} = \begin{bmatrix} 1 & 0 & 0 \\ 0 & e^{-t} & 0 \\ 0 & 0 & e^{-3t} \end{bmatrix}$$

8.16 Consider the following matrix A:

$$A = \begin{bmatrix} 0 & 1 \\ 0 & -2 \end{bmatrix}$$

Compute state transition matrix e^{At}. [5 marks : 2016]

Solution:

$$A = \begin{bmatrix} 0 & 1 \\ 0 & -2 \end{bmatrix}$$

State transition matrix $\phi(t) = e^{At}$

or, $$\phi(t) = \mathcal{L}^{-1}[(sI - A)^{-1}]$$

$\therefore$ $$[sI - A] = \begin{bmatrix} s & -1 \\ 0 & s+2 \end{bmatrix}$$

$$[sI - A]^{-1} = \frac{1}{s(s+2)} \begin{bmatrix} s+2 & 1 \\ 0 & s \end{bmatrix}$$

$$\phi(t) = \mathcal{L}^{-1}\left[(sI - A)^{-1}\right] = \mathcal{L}^{-1}\begin{bmatrix} \frac{1}{s} & \frac{1}{s(s+2)} \\ 0 & \frac{1}{s+2} \end{bmatrix}$$

$$\phi(t) = \begin{bmatrix} e^{-t} & \frac{1}{2}\left(e^{-t} - e^{-2t}\right) \\ 0 & e^{-2t} \end{bmatrix}$$

8.17 Design a state feedback controller for the linear system described by the following equations:

$$3\dot{x}_1 + 250x_2 = 500u$$

$$\dot{x}_2 - 500x_1 + 10x_2 = 0$$

x_1 and x_2 are state variable and u is the input. Design specifications are 20% overshoot and setting time of 5 sec for a step input. Settling time is given for 2% tolerance band.

[20 marks : 2017]

Solution:

$$3\dot{x}_1 + 250x_2 = 500\text{ u}$$

$$\dot{x}_2 - 500x_1 + 10x_2 = 0$$

Settling time = 5s

Overshoot = 20%

$$0.2 = e^{-\xi\pi/\sqrt{1-\xi^2}}$$

$$\frac{\xi^2\pi^2}{1-\xi^2} = (In\,5)^2$$

$$\therefore \quad \xi = \frac{In5}{\sqrt{\pi^2 + (In5)^2}} = \frac{1.61}{3.53} = 0.456$$

$$\frac{4}{\xi\omega_n} = 5$$

$$\omega_n = \frac{4}{5\xi} = 1.75 \text{ rad/sec.}$$

Second order characteristic equation,

$$s^2 + 2\xi\omega_n s + \omega_n^2 = 0$$

$$s^2 + 1.5965 + 3.0625 = 0 \quad \text{...(i)}$$

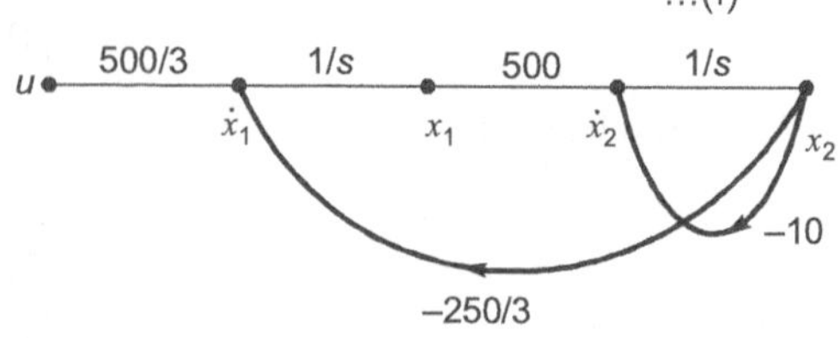

$$\dot{x}_1 = -\frac{250}{3}x_2 + \frac{500}{3}u$$

$$\dot{x}_2 = 500x_1 - 10x_2$$

Let, $k = [k_1 \;\; k_2]$ be state feedback matrix,

$$\dot{x}_1 = -\frac{500}{3}k_1 x_1 - \frac{250}{3}x_2 - \frac{500}{3}k_2 x_2$$

$$\dot{x}_2 = 500x_1 - 10x_2$$

$$\begin{bmatrix}\dot{x}_1\\ \dot{x}_2\end{bmatrix} = \begin{bmatrix}-\frac{500}{3}k_1 & -\frac{250}{3}-\frac{500}{3}k_2\\ 500 & -10\end{bmatrix}\begin{bmatrix}x_1\\ x_2\end{bmatrix}$$

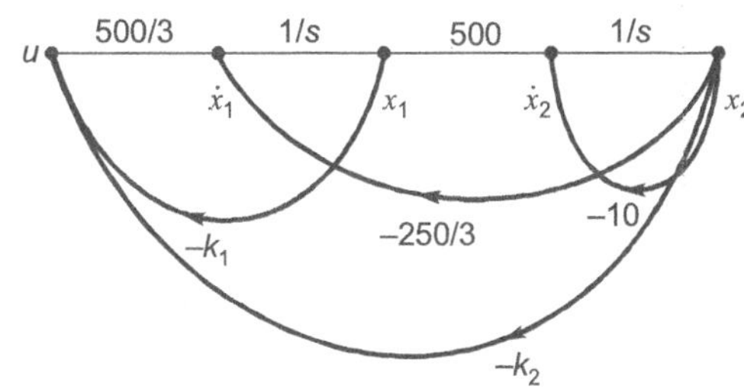

$$A = \begin{bmatrix}-\frac{500}{3}k_1 & -\frac{250}{3}-\frac{500}{3}k_2\\ 500 & -10\end{bmatrix}$$

$$[sI-A] = \begin{bmatrix}s+\frac{500}{3}k_1 & \frac{250}{3}+\frac{500}{3}k_2\\ -500 & s+10\end{bmatrix}$$

$$|sI-A| = \left(s+\frac{500}{3}k_1\right)(s+10)+500\left(\frac{250}{3}+\frac{500}{3}k_2\right)=0$$

Characteristic equation of required plant,

$$s^2+\left(10+\frac{500}{3}k_1\right)s+\frac{5000}{3}k_1+\frac{125000}{3}+\frac{250000}{3}k_2=0$$

Comparing this with (i), $10+\frac{500}{3}k_1 = 1.596$

$$\therefore \quad k_1 = -0.05$$

$$\frac{5000}{3}k_1+\frac{125000}{3}+\frac{250000}{3}k_2 = 3.0625$$

$$\therefore \quad k_2 = -0.5$$

8.18 **Given a system in state space representation as:**

$$\begin{bmatrix}\dot{x}_1\\ \dot{x}_2\end{bmatrix} = \begin{bmatrix}0 & 1\\ 0 & -3\end{bmatrix}\begin{bmatrix}x_1\\ x_2\end{bmatrix}+\begin{bmatrix}0\\ 1\end{bmatrix}u$$

$$y = [1 \quad 0]\begin{bmatrix}x_1\\ x_2\end{bmatrix}$$

(i) Check whether the system is observable or not.
(ii) Find the state transition matrix.
(iii) Design a state feedback controller to place closed-loop poles at $-1 \pm 2j$.

[20 marks : 2018]

Solution:

$$\begin{bmatrix}\dot{x}_1\\ \dot{x}_2\end{bmatrix} = \begin{bmatrix}0 & 1\\ 0 & -3\end{bmatrix}\begin{bmatrix}x_1\\ x_2\end{bmatrix}+\begin{bmatrix}0\\ 1\end{bmatrix}u$$

$$y = [1 \quad 0]\begin{bmatrix}x_1\\ x_2\end{bmatrix}$$

(i) $$A = \begin{bmatrix}0 & 1\\ 0 & -3\end{bmatrix}, \qquad C=[1 \quad 0]$$

$$A^T = \begin{bmatrix}0 & 0\\ 1 & -3\end{bmatrix}, \qquad C^T = \begin{bmatrix}1\\ 0\end{bmatrix}$$

$$A^T C^T = \begin{bmatrix} 0 \\ 1 \end{bmatrix}$$

The observability test matrix,

$$Q_0 = [C^T \quad A^T C^T]$$

$$Q_0 = \begin{bmatrix} 1 & 0 \\ 0 & 1 \end{bmatrix}$$

$$|Q_0| \neq 0 \qquad \text{(Since } |Q_0| \neq 0, \text{ the system is observable)}$$

(ii) State transition matrix, $\phi(t) = \mathcal{L}^{-1}[(sI - A)^{-1}]$

$$[sI - A] = \begin{bmatrix} s & -1 \\ 0 & s+3 \end{bmatrix}$$

$$[sI - A]^{-1} = \frac{1}{s(s+3)} \begin{bmatrix} s+3 & 1 \\ 0 & s \end{bmatrix} = \begin{bmatrix} \frac{1}{s} & \frac{1}{s(s+3)} \\ 0 & \frac{1}{s+3} \end{bmatrix}$$

Taking Laplace inverse,

$$\phi(t) = \begin{bmatrix} u(t) & \frac{1}{3}u(t) - \frac{1}{3}e^{-3t}u(t) \\ 0 & e^{-3t}u(t) \end{bmatrix}$$

(iii) State feed back controller design:

Such that closed loop poles are placed at $-1 \pm 2j$

The desired characteristic equation is,

$$(s + 1 + j2)(s + 1 - j2) = 0$$

$$s^2 + 2s + 5 = 0 \qquad \text{...(1)}$$

The characteristic equation using state variable feedback is

$$|sI - (A - BK)| = 0$$

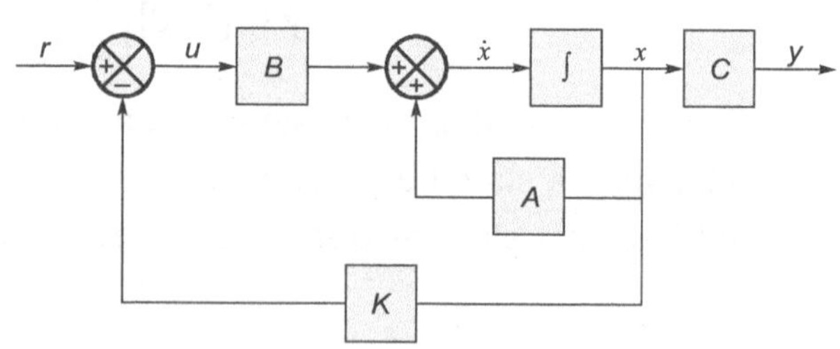

$$\left| \begin{bmatrix} s & 0 \\ 0 & s \end{bmatrix} - [A - BK] \right| = 0$$

$$[A - BK] = \begin{bmatrix} 0 & 1 \\ 0 & -3 \end{bmatrix} - \begin{bmatrix} 0 \\ 1 \end{bmatrix} [K_1 \quad K_2]$$

$$= \begin{bmatrix} 0 & 1 \\ -K_1 & -3 - K_2 \end{bmatrix}$$

$$|sI - (A - BK)| = 0$$

$$\left| \begin{bmatrix} s & -1 \\ K_1 & s + 3 + K_2 \end{bmatrix} \right| = 0$$

$$s^2 + 3s + K_2 s + K_1 = 0$$

$$s^2 + (3 + K_2)s + K_1 = 0 \qquad \text{...(2)}$$

Comparing (1) and (2), $K_1 = 5$, and $3 + K_2 = 2$

$$K_2 = -1$$

$$K = [5 \quad -1]$$

8.19 Check the controllability and observability of the system shown in the figure given below. u is the input and y is the output.

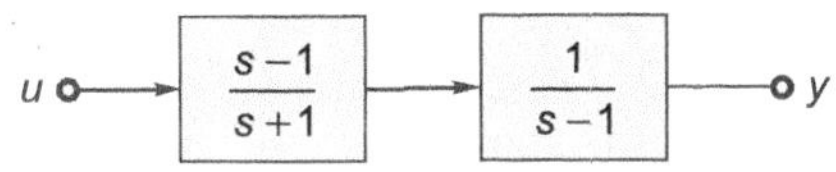

[20 marks : 2019]

Solution:

$$\text{T.F.} = \frac{s-1}{s^2-1}$$

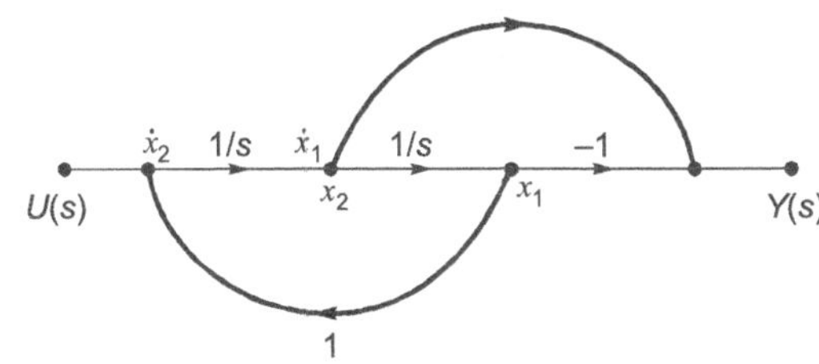

State model:

Controllable form,

$$X_0 = \begin{bmatrix} 0 & 1 \\ 1 & 0 \end{bmatrix} X + \begin{bmatrix} 0 \\ 1 \end{bmatrix} U$$

$$Y = [-1 \quad 1]\, X + [0]\, U$$

$$Q_C = \begin{bmatrix} 0 & 1 \\ 1 & 0 \end{bmatrix}; \quad |Q_C| \neq 0 \quad \therefore \text{ Controllable}$$

$$Q_0 = \begin{bmatrix} -1 & 1 \\ 1 & -1 \end{bmatrix}; \quad |Q_0| = 0 \quad \therefore \text{ Unobservable}$$

Statement:

Observable form,

$$X_0 = \begin{bmatrix} 0 & 1 \\ 1 & 0 \end{bmatrix} X + \begin{bmatrix} -1 \\ 1 \end{bmatrix} U$$

$$Y = [0 \quad 1]\, X + [0] U$$

$$Q_C = \begin{bmatrix} -1 & 1 \\ 1 & -1 \end{bmatrix}; \quad |Q_C| = 0 \quad \therefore \text{ Uncontrollable}$$

$$Q_0 = \begin{bmatrix} 0 & 1 \\ 1 & 0 \end{bmatrix}; \quad |Q_0| \neq 0 \quad \therefore \text{ Observable}$$

Conclusion: If pole-zero cancellation occurs then the system cannot be both controllable and observable.

8.20 The signal flow graph of a system relating output $y(t)$ to input $u(t)$ is shown in the figure. Represent the state variable model of the system. Determine its transfer function $\frac{y(s)}{u(s)}$ from the state model. Derive corresponding state transition matrix.

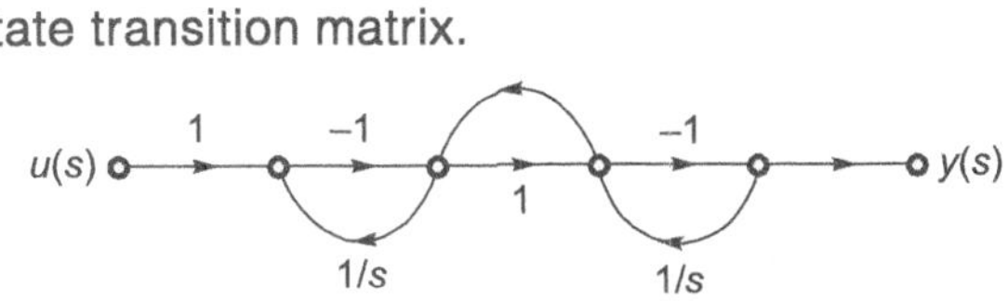

[20 marks : 2021]

Solution:

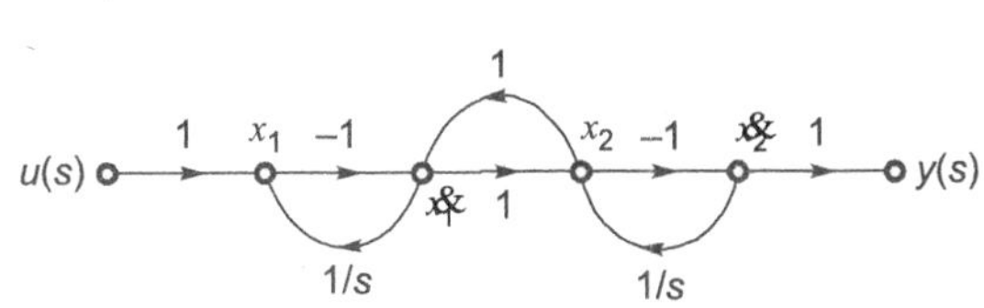

$$\dot{x}_1 = -x_1 + x_2 \; ; \qquad x_1 = x_1 + U$$

$\therefore$ $$\dot{x}_1 = -x_1 + x_2 - U$$

$$\dot{x}_2 = -x_2 \; ; \qquad x_2 = \dot{x}_1 + x_2$$

$\therefore$ $$\dot{x}_2 = x_1 - 2x_2 + U$$

$\therefore$ $$y = \dot{x}_2 = x_1 - 2x_2 + U$$

State model:

$$\dot{X} = \begin{bmatrix} -1 & 1 \\ 1 & -2 \end{bmatrix} X + \begin{bmatrix} -1 \\ 1 \end{bmatrix} U$$

$$Y = [1 \;\; -2]X + [1]U$$

$\Rightarrow$ $$TF = C[(sI - A)^{-1} B] + D = \frac{s^2}{s^2 + 3s + 1}$$

$\Rightarrow$ State transmission matrix, $$e^{At} = L^{-1}[(sI - A)^{-1}]$$

$\therefore$ $$e^{At} = \begin{bmatrix} 0.724e^{-0.385t} + 0.275e^{-2.615} & 0.448e^{-0.385t} - 0.448e^{2.615t} \\ 0.448e^{-0.385t} - 0.448e^{-2.615t} & 0.275e^{-0.385t} + 0.724e^{-2.615t} \end{bmatrix}$$

8.21 Consider a system described by the state model.

$$\dot{X} = \begin{bmatrix} -3 & 1 \\ -2 & 0 \end{bmatrix} X + \begin{bmatrix} 0 \\ 1 \end{bmatrix} u \; ; y = [1 \;\; 0]X$$

Design a control law $u = -KX$ so that the closed loop poles of the system occupy in s-plane at $-2 \pm j2$.

[8 marks : 2021]

Solution:

Given : $$\dot{X} = \begin{bmatrix} -3 & 1 \\ -2 & 0 \end{bmatrix} X + \begin{bmatrix} 0 \\ 1 \end{bmatrix} U \; ; \; Y = [1 \;\; 0]X$$

Using state variable feedback

$$U = -KX$$

Characteristic equation is

$$q(s) = |sI - (A - BK)| = 0$$

Where, $$K = [K_1 \;\; K_2]$$

$$BK = \begin{bmatrix} 0 \\ 1 \end{bmatrix} [K_1 \;\; K_2] = \begin{bmatrix} 0 & 0 \\ K_1 & K_2 \end{bmatrix}$$

$$A - BK = \begin{bmatrix} -3 & 1 \\ -2 & 0 \end{bmatrix} - \begin{bmatrix} 0 & 0 \\ K_1 & K_2 \end{bmatrix} = \begin{bmatrix} -3 & 1 \\ -2 - K_1 & -K_2 \end{bmatrix}$$

$$sI - [A - BK] = \begin{bmatrix} s+3 & -1 \\ 2+K_1 & s+K_2 \end{bmatrix}$$

$\therefore$ $$q(s) = |sI - (A - BK)| = s^2 + s(K_2 + 3) + 3K_2 + K_1 + 2 = 0$$

Desired, $$CLP = -2 \pm j2$$

$\therefore \qquad q(s) = s^2 + 4s + 8 = 0$

Upon comparing, $\qquad K_2 = 1\ ;\ K_1 = 3$

$\therefore \qquad K = [3 \quad 1]$

8.22 An LTI system is described by the following equations :

$$X = AX + Bx$$
$$y = CX + Dx$$

where
$$A = \begin{bmatrix} -2 & 0 & 0 & 0 \\ 0 & -1 & 0 & 0 \\ 0 & 0 & -5 & 0 \\ 0 & 0 & 0 & -3 \end{bmatrix};\ B = \begin{bmatrix} 1 \\ 1 \\ 0 \\ 0 \end{bmatrix};$$
$$C = [1 \quad 0 \quad 1 \quad 0];\ D = 0.$$

Draw the block diagram of the system and therefrom, identify the state variable(s) that are

(i) not controllable.

(ii) not observable.

(iii) neither controllable nor observable.

[12 marks : 2022]

Solution:

From given state model state and output equations can be written as

$$\dot{x}_1 = -2x_1 + U$$
$$\dot{x}_2 = -x_2 + U$$
$$\dot{x}_3 = -5x_3$$
$$\dot{x}_4 = -3x_4$$
$$y = x_1 + x_3$$

State diagram :

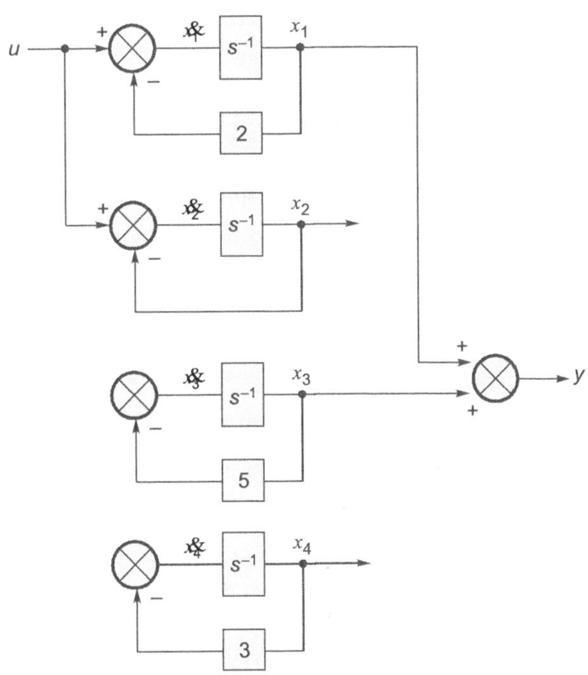

(i) State variable x_3 and x_4 are not controllable.
(ii) State variable x_2 and x_4 are unobservable.
(iii) State variable x_4 is uncontrollabel and unobservable.

8.23 Let the steady state velocity error be defined as the difference in velocity between input and output of the unity feedback system as time approaches infinity. Find the expression for the error in the velocity, $\dot{e}(\infty) = \dot{r}(\infty) - \dot{i}(\infty)$ and fill the following table for the error in velocity for different inputs in Type 0, 1, 2 system. Notations carry their usual meaning.

		Type		
		0	1	2
Input	Step			
	Ramp			
	Parabola			

[20 marks : 2022]

Solution:

$$\dot{e}(\infty) = \dot{r}(\infty) - \dot{i}(\infty) \text{ (given)}$$

$$e_{ss} = \text{Input} - \text{Output}$$

$e_{ss} \rightarrow$ Steady state error

$$e_{ss} = R(s) - R(s)\frac{G(s)}{1+G(s)} = \frac{R(s)}{1+G(s)}$$

(i) Position error constant (K_p). It is defined for unit step input.

$$\therefore \quad R(s) = \frac{1}{s}$$

$$e_{ss} = \lim_{s\to 0}\frac{sR(s)}{1+G(s)} = \lim_{s\to 0}\frac{s\times\frac{1}{s}}{1+G(s)}$$

$$\therefore \quad e_{ss} = \frac{1}{1+\lim_{s\to 0}G(s)} = \frac{1}{1+G(0)} = \frac{1}{1+K_p}$$

$$K_p = G(0) \rightarrow \text{Position error constant}$$

$\therefore$ For type 0 system, $e_{ss} = \dfrac{1}{1+K_p}$

Type 1 system, $K_p = \infty,\ e_{ss} = 0$

Type 2 system, $K_p = \infty,\ e_{ss} = 0$

(ii) Velocity error constant : It is defined for unit ramp input, i.e.,

$$R(s) = \frac{1}{s^2}$$

$$e_{ss} = \lim_{s\to 0}\frac{sR(s)}{1+G(s)} = \lim_{s\to 0}\frac{s\times\frac{1}{s^2}}{1+G(s)} = \lim_{s\to 0}\frac{1}{s+sG(s)}$$

$$= \frac{1}{\lim_{s \to 0} sG(s)} = \frac{1}{K_V}$$

$\therefore$ $K_V = \lim_{s \to 0} sG(s) \rightarrow$ Velocity error constant

For type 0, $K_V = 0,\ e_{ss} = \infty$

For type 1, $K_V = \text{finite},\ e_{ss} = \frac{1}{K_V}$

For type 2, $K_V = \infty,\ e_{ss} = 0$

(iii) Acceleration error constant : It is defined for unit parabolic input, i.e.,

$$R(s) = \frac{1}{s^3}$$

$$e_{ss} = \lim_{s \to 0} \frac{sR(s)}{1+G(s)} = \lim_{s \to 0} \frac{s \times \frac{1}{s^3}}{1+G(s)}$$

$$= \lim_{s \to 0} \frac{1}{s^2 + s^2G(s)} = \frac{1}{\lim_{s \to 0} s^2G(s)} = \frac{1}{K_a}$$

$\therefore$ $K_a = \lim_{s \to 0} s^2G(s) \rightarrow$ Acceleration error constant

For type 0, $K_a = 0,\ e_{ss} = \frac{1}{K_a} = \infty$

For type 1, $K_a = 0,\ e_{ss} = \frac{1}{K_a} = \infty$

For type 2, $K_a = \text{finite},\ e_{ss} = \frac{1}{K_a}$

Table for the error in velocity for different inputs in Type 0, 1, 2 system

		Type 0	Type 1	Type 2
Input	Step	$\frac{1}{1+K_p}$	0	0
	Ramp	∞	$\frac{1}{K_v}$	0
	Parabola	∞	∞	$\frac{1}{K_a}$

8.24 A certain system is described by

$$\begin{bmatrix} \dot{x}_1 \\ \dot{x}_2 \end{bmatrix} = \begin{bmatrix} -2 & 1 \\ -2 & 0 \end{bmatrix} \begin{bmatrix} x_1 \\ x_2 \end{bmatrix} + \begin{bmatrix} 1 \\ 3 \end{bmatrix} u(t);\quad y = \begin{bmatrix} 1 & 0 \end{bmatrix} \begin{bmatrix} x_1 \\ x_2 \end{bmatrix}$$

Determine the transformation matrix $[P]$ so that if $[x] = [P][Z]$; the state matrics $[\tilde{A}], [\tilde{B}], [\tilde{C}]$ and $[\tilde{D}]$ describing the dynamics of $[Z]$ are in control canonical form.

[20 marks : 2023]

Solution:

Given :

$$\begin{bmatrix} \dot{X}_1 \\ \dot{X}_2 \end{bmatrix} = \begin{bmatrix} -2 & 1 \\ -2 & 0 \end{bmatrix} \begin{bmatrix} X_1 \\ X_2 \end{bmatrix} + \begin{bmatrix} 1 \\ 3 \end{bmatrix} u(t)$$

$$y = [1 \quad 0]\begin{bmatrix} X_1 \\ X_2 \end{bmatrix}$$

$$A = \begin{bmatrix} -2 & 1 \\ -2 & 0 \end{bmatrix}, \; B = \begin{bmatrix} 1 \\ 3 \end{bmatrix}, \; C = [1 \quad 0], \; D = 0$$

The characteristic equation of A is

$$|sI - A| = \begin{bmatrix} s & 0 \\ 0 & s \end{bmatrix} - \begin{bmatrix} -2 & 1 \\ -2 & 0 \end{bmatrix}$$

$$|sI - A| = \begin{bmatrix} s+2 & -1 \\ 2 & s \end{bmatrix}$$

$$|sI - A| = s(s + 2) + 2$$

$$|sI - A| = s^2 + 2s + 2 \qquad \text{...(1)}$$

Thus, the coefficients of the characteristics equation are $a_0 = 2$, $a_1 = 2$.

$$M = \begin{bmatrix} a_1 & 1 \\ 1 & 0 \end{bmatrix} = \begin{bmatrix} 2 & 1 \\ 1 & 0 \end{bmatrix}$$

The controllability of matrix is

$$S = [B \quad AB] = \begin{bmatrix} 1 & 1 \\ 3 & -2 \end{bmatrix}$$

$$AB = \begin{bmatrix} -2 & 1 \\ -2 & 0 \end{bmatrix}\begin{bmatrix} 1 \\ 3 \end{bmatrix} = \begin{bmatrix} 1 \\ -2 \end{bmatrix}$$

Transformation matrix, $$P = SM = \begin{bmatrix} 1 & 1 \\ 3 & -2 \end{bmatrix}\begin{bmatrix} 2 & 1 \\ 1 & 0 \end{bmatrix}$$

$$P = \begin{bmatrix} 3 & 1 \\ 4 & 3 \end{bmatrix}$$

such that $[X] = [P]\;[Z]$

Thus, the control cannonical form is given by

$$[\bar{A}] = P^{-1}AP = \frac{1}{9-4}\begin{bmatrix} 3 & -1 \\ -4 & 3 \end{bmatrix}\begin{bmatrix} -2 & 1 \\ -2 & 0 \end{bmatrix}\begin{bmatrix} 3 & 1 \\ 4 & 3 \end{bmatrix}$$

$$= \frac{1}{5}\begin{bmatrix} 3 & -1 \\ -4 & 3 \end{bmatrix}\begin{bmatrix} -2 & 1 \\ -6 & -2 \end{bmatrix}$$

$$= \frac{1}{5}\begin{bmatrix} 0 & 5 \\ -10 & -10 \end{bmatrix} = \begin{bmatrix} 0 & 1 \\ -2 & -2 \end{bmatrix}$$

$$[\bar{B}] = P^{-1}B = \frac{1}{5}\begin{bmatrix} 3 & -1 \\ -4 & 3 \end{bmatrix}\begin{bmatrix} 1 \\ 3 \end{bmatrix}$$

$$= \frac{1}{5}\begin{bmatrix} 0 \\ 5 \end{bmatrix} = \begin{bmatrix} 0 \\ 1 \end{bmatrix}$$

$$[\bar{C}] = CP = [1 \quad 0]\begin{bmatrix} 3 & 1 \\ 4 & 3 \end{bmatrix} = [3 \quad 1]$$

$$[\bar{D}] = D = 0$$

■■■■

6 Electrical Machines

Revised Syllabus of ESE: *Single phase transformers, three phase transformers - connections, parallel operation, auto-transformer, energy conversion principles, DC machines-types, windings, generator characteristics, armature reaction and commutation, starting and speed control of motors, Induction motors - principles, types, performance characteristics, starting and speed control, Synchronous machines - performance, regulation, parallel operation of generators, motor starting, characteristics and applications, servo and stepper motors.*

1. Magnetic Circuits & Electromechanical Energy Conversion Systems

1.1 What are the no-load rotational losses in electrical machines? How can these be determined?

[7 marks : 2001]

Solution:

The mechanical loss and open circuit core loss combined together are caused by rotor rotation. Their sum is called as no-load rotational losses.

Mechanical Loss: This loss consists of bearing friction, brush friction and windage losses. The windage or wind friction loss includes the power required to circulate air through the machine and ventilating ducts and is approximately proportional to square of the speed.

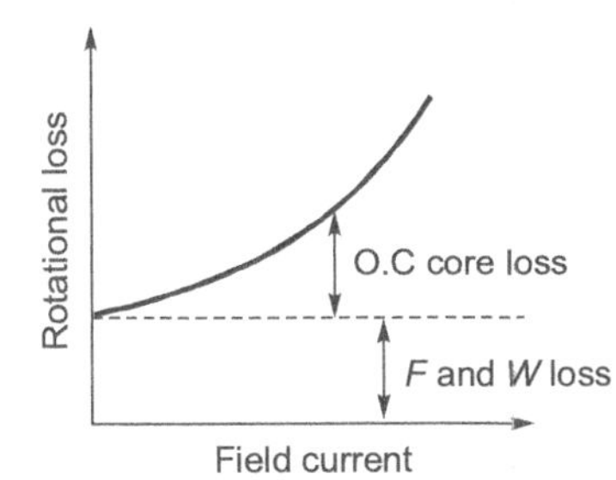

Open Circuit Core Loss: Consists of hysteresis and eddy current losses. These losses occur in case of stator and rotor carrying an alternating flux.

$$\text{Hysteresis loss } P_h = K_h f B_m^x$$

$$\text{Eddy current loss } P_e = K_e f^2 B_m^2$$

No load rotational losses can be determined by running the electrical machine as an unloaded motor at the rotor speed and with armature voltage equal to the normal generator emf. The total power input to the unloaded motor minus the no-load armature ohmic loss gives the magnitude of no-load rotational loss.

1.2 Which of the losses in rotating electrical machines are influenced by the magnitude of the flux, the load and square of the load?

Write a general expression for all the losses occurring in rotating electrical machines and prove that maximum efficiency occurs when losses proportional to square of current = constant losses.

[7 marks : 2001]

Solution:

(a) **Constant or Fixed Losses:** These losses are influenced by the magnitude of the flux. Under this no-load core loss, friction and windage loss.

(b) **Loss Proportional to Load Current:** Brush-contact loss occurs when current is to be conducted to, or from, the rotating part of the electrical machine through sliding contacts.

(c) **Losses Proportional to the Square of Load Current:** Resistance loss in various machine winding and stray load loss are proportional to the square of load current.

losses in rotating electrical machine may be written as $a + bI + cI^2$ and output or input as AVI where,

a = constant losses

bI = loss proportional to load current

A = Constant ($\sqrt{3} \times pf$ for 3-phase machines, pf for single phase machines and unity for d.c. machines)

V = machine voltage

Motor operation: Power input = AVI

$\therefore$ Efficiency, $$\eta = \frac{AVI - a - bI - cI^2}{AVI}$$

For constant voltage V,

$$\frac{d\eta}{dI} = \frac{(AV - b - 2cI)(AVI) - (AVI - a - bI - cI^2)(AV)}{(AVI)^2}$$

For efficiency to be maximum, $d\eta/dI$ must be equal to zero.

$\therefore$ $(AV - b - 2cI)(AVI) = (AVI - a - bI - cI^2)(AV)$

$\therefore$ $a = cI^2$

Generator operation: Power output = AVI

$\therefore$ Efficiency, $$\eta = \frac{AVI}{AVI + a + bI + cI^2}$$

For constant V, $$\frac{d\eta}{dI} = \frac{(AV)(AVI + a + bI + cI^2) - (AVI)(AV + b + 2cI)}{(AVI + a + bI + cI^2)^2}$$

For maximum efficiency,

$$\frac{d\eta}{dI} = 0$$

$\therefore$ $cI^2 = a$

[Losses proportional to square of current = constant losses].

1.3 The worst type of load on a supply system is

(a) rolling mill load (b) pumping load

(c) motors in paper mill (d) arc furnace load

[2 marks : 2002]

Solution: (d)

Option (d) is correct.

1.4 A coil wound on a magnetic core is excited by the following voltage sources:

(a) 100 V, 50 Hz (b) 110 V, 60 Hz

Compare the hysteresis losses and eddy-current losses with these two different sources. For hysteresis loss, consider steinmetz constant $n = 2$.

[8 marks : 2009]

Solution:

Hysteresis loss, $P_h = k_h f B_m^x$; Eddy current loss, $P_c = k_e f^2 B_m^2$

$$\frac{P_{h1}}{P_{h2}} = \frac{k_h f_1 B_{m_1}^2}{k_h f_2 B_{m_2}^2}$$

Given, $x = 2$
$$= \left(\frac{f_1}{f_2}\right)\left(\frac{V_1}{V_2}\cdot\frac{f_2}{f_1}\right)^2 = \left(\frac{50}{60}\right)\left(\frac{100}{110}\times\frac{60}{50}\right)^2$$

or,
$$\frac{P_{h1}}{P_{h2}} = 0.991$$

$$\frac{P_{e1}}{P_{e2}} = \frac{k_e f_1^2 B_{m_1}^2}{k_e f_2^2 B_{m_2}^2} = \left(\frac{50}{60}\right)^2\left(\frac{100}{110}\times\frac{60}{50}\right)^2 = 0.826$$

1.5 **The analysis of magnetic circuit is simplified by making an analogy between magnetic and d.c. resistive circuits, where in ϕ, the flux through the magnetic circuit is considered analogous to I, the current through the electric circuit, apart from analogies between other magnetic and electric circuit quantities. Identify differences between the two circuits in so far as through variables ϕ and I are concerned.**

[4 marks : 2009]

Solution:

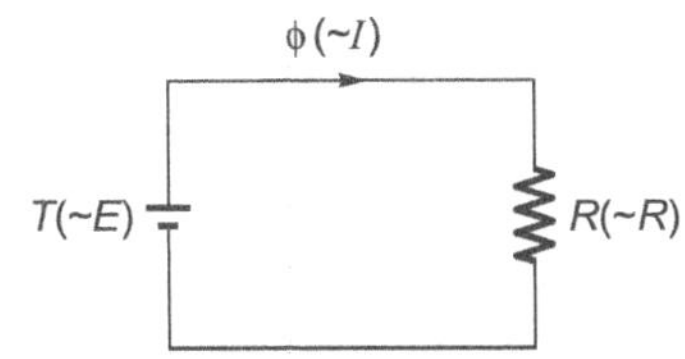

- The electrical circuit analog of the magnetic system is shown in figure, wherein (mmf) is analogous to E (emf) R_l (reluctance) is analogus to R (resistance) and ϕ(flux) is analogous to i (current).
- The analogy is not complete as
  (*i*) Magnetic reluctance is non-dissipative of energy unlike electric resistance.
  (*ii*) When τ is time-varying, the magnetic circuit still remains resistive as in figure while inductive effects are bound to appear in an electric circuit. This is because there is no establishment of magnetic flux.

1.6 **A full-pitched coil, having N turns rotates with an angular velocity of ω_r rad per sec in a field flux ϕ. Give an expression for the flux linkages with the coil as a function of time τ and derive therefrom an expression for the emf generated in this coil.**
Discuss nature of the two components of emf expression so obtained. Hence show that the speed voltage lags by 90° the flux that produces it.

[20 marks : 2012]

Solution:

The B-wave of a machine, assumed sinusoidal, is drawn as shown in figure below, and a single full-pitched coil (coil-side space separation π rad) is shown in cross-sectional form.

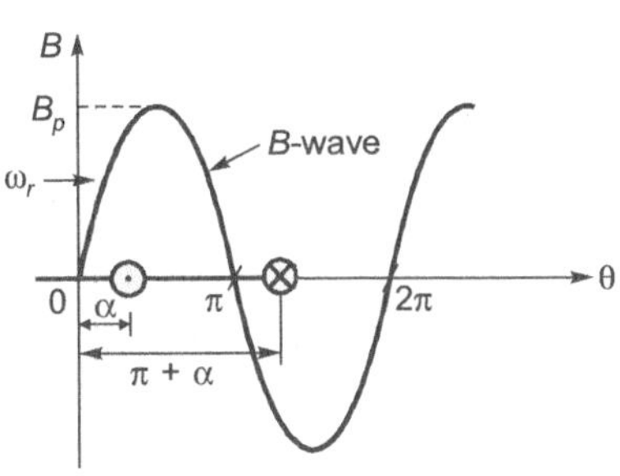

At any time t the coil has relatively moved by $\alpha = \omega_r t$ electrical rad to the right of the B-wave.

The B-wave can be expressed as
$$B = B_p \sin\theta$$
where, B_p = Peak flux density
$$\text{Mechanical angle } \theta_m = \frac{2}{P}\theta$$

Therefore, the flux ϕ linking the coil can be computed by integrating over the mechanical angle.
$$\phi = \int_{\frac{2\alpha}{P}}^{\frac{2(\pi+\alpha)}{P}} B_p \sin\left(\frac{P}{2}\theta_m\right) lr d\theta_m$$

where, l = Active coil-side length ; r = Mean radius of the stator at the air gap
$$\phi = \frac{2}{P}\int_{\alpha}^{(\pi+\alpha)} B_p lr \sin\theta d\theta = \frac{2}{P}\cdot 2B_p lr\cos\alpha = \frac{2}{P}\cdot 2B_p lr\cos\omega t$$
$$= \phi_m \cos\omega t \qquad ...(i)$$

Therefore, the flux linking the coil varies sinusoidally and has a maximum value of

$$\phi_m = \frac{4}{P} B_p lr \qquad \text{(flux/pole)}$$

at $\alpha = \omega t = 0$, which indeed is flux/pole.

The flux linkages of the coil at any time t are

$$\lambda = N\phi = N\phi_m \cos\omega t$$

where, N = Number of turns of the coil

Hence the coil induced emf is $e = -\dfrac{d\lambda}{dt} = N\phi_m \sin\omega t - N\dfrac{d\phi_m}{dt}\cos\omega t$

$N\phi_m\omega\sin\omega t$ is the speed voltage term, because it contains ω in it. The second term $N\dfrac{d\phi_m}{dt}\cos\omega t$ is the transformer voltage term because it involves time derivative.

Here field flux is time invariant, the transformer voltage term reduces to zero.

$$\therefore \quad e = N\phi_m\omega\sin\omega t$$

$$= N\phi_m\omega\cos\left(\omega t - \frac{\pi}{2}\right) \qquad \ldots(ii)$$

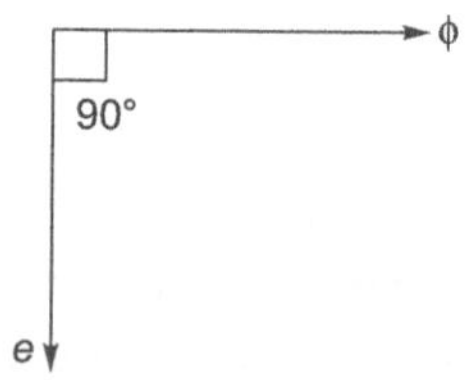

From equation (*i*) and (*ii*), it may be observed that the sinusoidally varying flux linking the coil leads the sinusoidally varying emf by 90°.

1.7 The self and mutual inductances of two coupled coils of an electromagnetic relay are given by

$$L_1 = \frac{2}{x},\ L_2 = \frac{3}{x} \text{ and } M = \frac{4}{x}$$

Over a certain displacement x in meters. Obtain the expression for force on armature as a function of time, if $i_1 = I_{m1}\sin\omega_1 t$ and $i_2 = I_{m2}\sin\omega_2 t$. Find the magnitude of average force in case (i) $\omega_1 \neq \omega_2$ and (ii) $\omega_1 = \omega_2$.

[20 marks : 2017]

Solution:

Given that: $L_1 = \dfrac{2}{x},\ L_2 = \dfrac{3}{x}$ and $M = \dfrac{4}{x}$

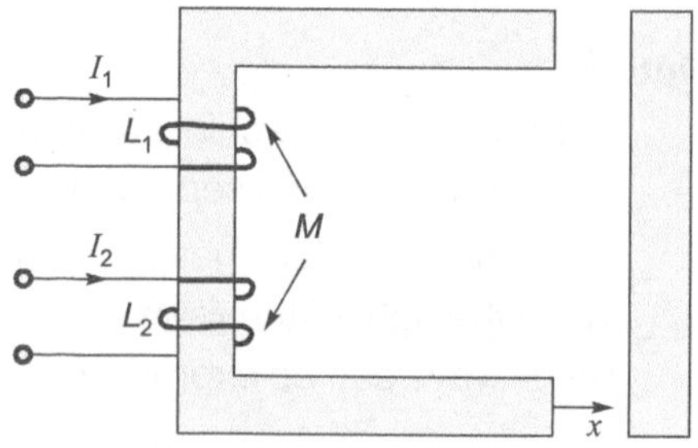

$$W_f' = \frac{1}{2}L_1 i_1^2 + M i_1 i_2 + \frac{1}{2}L_2 i_2^2$$

$$W_f' = \frac{1}{2}\cdot\frac{2}{x}i_1^2 + \frac{4}{x}i_1 i_2 + \frac{1}{2}\frac{3}{x}i_2^2 = \frac{i_1^2}{x} + \frac{4}{x}i_1 i_2 + \frac{3}{2x}i_2^2$$

$$F_f = \frac{\partial W_f'}{\partial x} = -\frac{i_1^2}{x^2} - \frac{4 i_1 i_2}{x_2} - \frac{3}{2x^2}i_2^2$$

$$= -\frac{1}{x^2}I_{m_1}^2\sin^2\omega_1 t - \frac{4}{x^2}(I_{m_1}\sin\omega_1 t)(I_{m_2}\sin\omega_2 t) - \frac{3}{2x^2}I_{m_2}^2\sin^2\omega_2 t$$

$$= -\frac{1}{x^2}I_{m_1}^2\left[\frac{1-\cos 2\omega_1 t}{2}\right] - \frac{4}{x^2}I_{m_1}I_{m_2}\left[\frac{\cos(\omega_1-\omega_2)t - \cos(\omega_1+\omega_2)t}{2}\right] - \frac{3}{2x^2}I_{m_2}^2\left[\frac{1-\cos 2\omega_2 t}{2}\right]$$

$$= -\frac{I_{m_1}^2}{2x^2} + \frac{I_{m_1}^2\cos 2\omega_1 t}{2x^2} - \frac{4}{2x^2}I_{m_1}I_{m2}\cos(\omega_1-\omega_2)t + \frac{4}{2x^2}I_{m_1}I_{m_2}\cos(\omega_1+\omega_2)t - \frac{3}{4x^2}I_{m_2}^2 + \frac{3}{4x^2}I_{m_2}^2\cos 2\omega_2 t$$

$$F_{f(\text{avg})} = \underset{T\to\infty}{Lt}\int_0^T F_f(t)\,dt$$

(i) If $\omega_1 \neq \omega_2$

$$F_{f(avg)} = -\frac{I_{m_1}^2}{2x^2} - \frac{3}{4x^2} I_{m_2}^2 \quad \text{(Minimum force)}$$

(ii) If $\omega_1 = \omega_2$

$$F_{f(avg)} = -\frac{1}{2x^2} I_{m_1}^2 - \frac{1}{2}\frac{4}{x^2} I_{m1} I_{m_2} - \frac{3}{4x^2} I_{m_2}^2 \quad \text{(Maximum force)}$$

1.8 For the electromechanical system shown below, the air-gap flux density under steady-state operating condition is given by

$$B(t) = B_m \sin\omega t$$

Find the instantaneous coil voltage and current along with force of magnetic field origin:

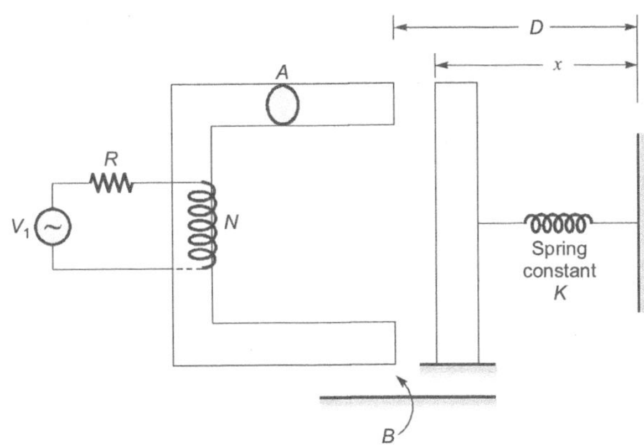

[20 marks : 2018]

Solution:

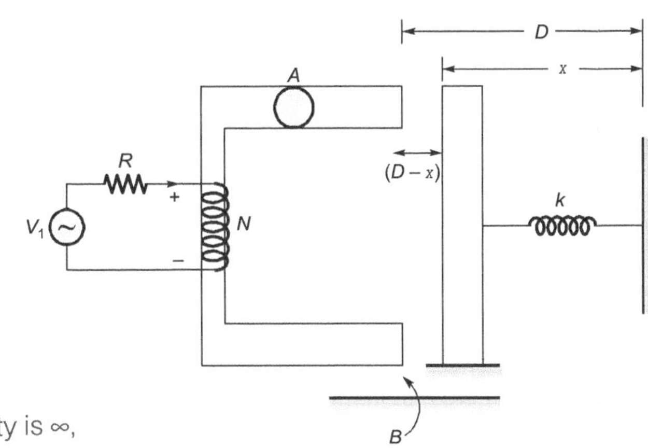

Instantaneous coil voltage in,

$$e_c = -N\frac{d\phi}{dt} = -N\frac{d(BA)}{dt}$$

$$= -NA\frac{d}{dt}(B_m \sin\omega t)$$

$$e_c = -NA\,\omega B_m \cos\omega t$$

$$V_1 = iR + e_c$$

$$i(t) = \frac{(V_1 + NB_m A\omega\cos\omega t)}{R}$$

Assuming the core body is ideal, then permeability is ∞,

Reluctance, $R_l = \dfrac{2(D-x)}{\mu_0 A}$

Self inductance of the configuration in

$$L(x) = \frac{N^2}{R_l} = \frac{N^2\mu_0 A}{2(D-x)}$$

Field energy stored in, $W_{fld}(i, x) = \dfrac{1}{2}L(x)i^2 = \dfrac{1}{2}\dfrac{N^2\mu_0 A}{2(D-x)}i^2$

$$W_{fld}(i, x) = \frac{N^2\mu_0 A}{4(D-x)}i^2$$

Magnetic force in given as, $f_e = \dfrac{dW_{fld}}{dx} = \dfrac{d}{dx}\left(\dfrac{N^2\mu_0 A}{4(D-x)}i^2\right)$

$$f_e = \frac{N^2\mu_0 A}{4(D-x)^2}i^2 = \frac{1}{4}\frac{N^2\mu_0 A}{(D-x)^2}i^2$$

$$MMF = Ni = H\times(D-x)\times 2$$

$$Ni = \frac{2B}{\mu_0}(D-x)$$

$$f_e = \frac{1}{4}\frac{\mu_0 A}{(D-x)^2}\left(\frac{2B}{\mu_0}(D-x)\right)^2$$

$$f_e = \frac{AB_m^2}{\mu_0}\sin^2\omega t$$

$$ff_e = \frac{AB_m^2\sin^2\omega t}{\mu_0}$$

Magnetic force in over come by force due the spring

$$f_e = kx$$

$$\frac{N^2}{4}\frac{\mu_0 A}{(D-x)^2}i^2 = kx$$

$$i^2 = \frac{4k(D-x)^2 x}{N^2\mu_0 A}$$

$$i = \frac{2(D-x)}{N}\sqrt{\frac{kx}{\mu_0 A}}$$

1.9 The magnetic circuit of a relay is shown in the figure. Calculate the energy that coil carries and the force on the armature of the relay when 3 Amp current flows in the coil. The air gap x is 2 cm, cross-section area of core is 50 cm^2 and the number of turns in the coil is 2000. Neglect the fringing effect and the reluctance of magnetic circuit in the core.

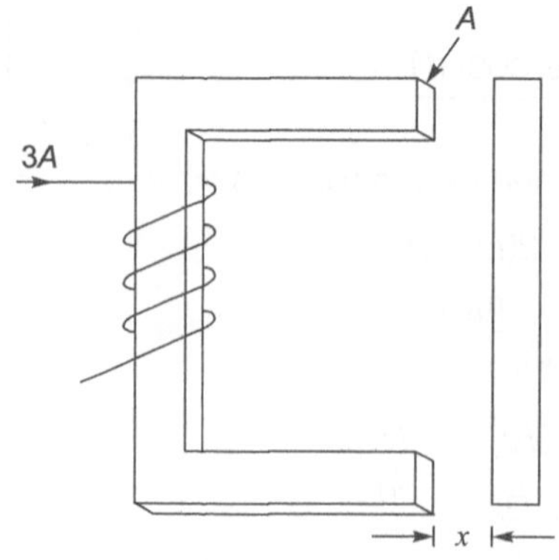

[20 marks : 2021]

Solution:

Given data : $i = 8$ A, $x = 2$ cm, $A = 50$ cm^2, $N = 2000$

To find :

(i) Energy stored in the coil

(ii) Force on the armature of the relay

(i) Since, no reluctance is offered by the core

$\therefore$ Reluctance, $R = \dfrac{2x}{\mu_o A}$ (2 is multiplied as there are two air gaps)

Hence, $$L = \frac{N^2}{R} = \frac{N^2}{2x}\mu_o A$$

$\Rightarrow$ $$L = \frac{(2000)^2 \times 4\pi \times 10^{-7} \times 50 \times 10^{-4}}{2 \times 2 \times 10^{-2}} = 0.6283$$

So, stored magnetic energy;

$$W = \frac{1}{2}LI^2 = \frac{1}{2} \times 0.6283 \times (3)^2$$
$$= 2.827 \text{ J}$$

(ii) Force on the armature of relay :

$$F = -\frac{1}{2}i^2\frac{dL}{dx} = \frac{1}{2}i^2 \cdot \frac{N^2\mu_o A}{2} \cdot \frac{1}{x^2}$$
$$= \frac{\mu_o N^2 A}{4x^2}i^2$$
$$F = \frac{4\pi \times 10^{-7} \times (2000)^2 \times 50 \times 10^{-4}}{4 \times (2 \times 10^{-2})^2} \times 9 = 141.37 \text{ N}$$

1.10 A star-delta transformer has delta side disconnected between A and D while supply is connected to the star side as shown in the Figure (a) below. An rms voltmeter between A and B reads 460 V under this condition. When A and D are connected, the same voltmeter between A and B reads 415 V. Find the voltage between A and D when they are disconnected.
Now the delta side is reconnected as star as shown in the Figure (b) with supply remaining the same on the other side. Find the voltages between P and N and between P and Q.
(Assume odd harmonics upto 7th order).

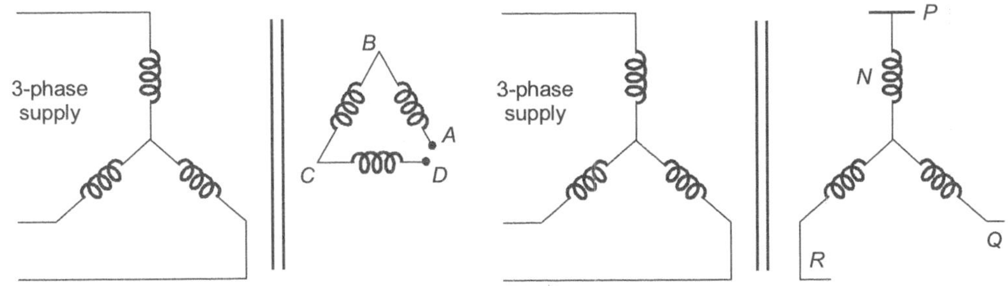

Figure (a) Figure (b)

[12 marks : 2022]

Solution:

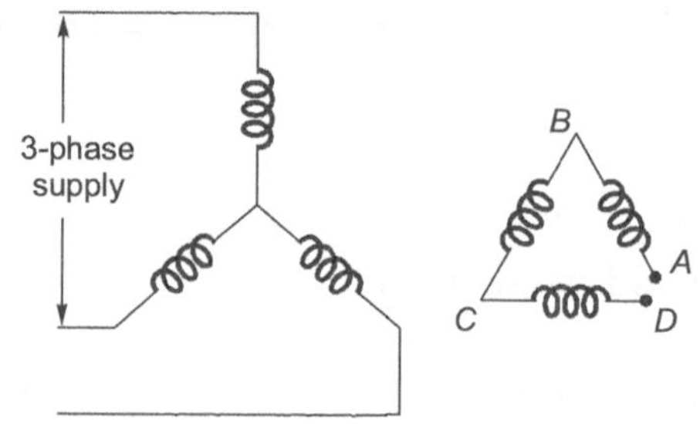

First case : *A* and *D* disconnected.

RMS voltmeter between *A* and *B* = 460 V when *A* and *D* are disconnected.

Δ is opened, so third harmonic voltage exist, along with fundamental, fifth and seventh.

$$\therefore \quad V_{AB} = \sqrt{E_1^2 + E_3^2 + E_5^2 + E_7^2} = 460 \text{ V}$$

$$\text{or,} \quad E_1^2 + E_3^2 + E_5^2 + E_7^2 = 460^2 \quad \text{...(1)}$$

Second case : When *A* and *D* are connected.

Δ is closed. So, third harmonic voltages will be eliminated due to closed delta.

Same voltmeter now records 415 V.

$$\therefore \quad V_{AB} = \sqrt{E_1^2 + E_5^2 + E_7^2} = 415 \text{ V}$$

$$\text{or} \quad E_1^2 + E_5^2 + E_7^2 = 415^2 \quad \text{...(2)}$$

By solving eqn. (1) and (2), we get E_3

$$\therefore \quad E_3 = 198.431 \text{ Volts}$$

Find voltage between *A* and *D* when they are disconnected which means imagine a voltmeter across *A* and *D*.

Delta is still opened.

Third harmonics do exist.

$$\therefore \quad V_{AD} = 3E_3$$

$$= 3(198.431) = 595.293 \text{ V}$$

If secondary is in Y. The connection is Y-Y ungrounded.

Third harmonics exist in phases but cancelled in lines.

$\therefore$ Voltage between *P* & *N* $\Rightarrow \sqrt{E_1^2 + E_3^2 + E_5^2 + E_7^2}$

Voltage between P & Q (lines) = $\sqrt{3} \times \sqrt{E_1^2 + E_5^2 + E_7^2}$

From (1) and (2) equations

$$V_{PN} = 460 \text{ V}$$

$$\text{and} \quad V_{PQ} = \sqrt{3} \times 415$$

$$= 718.8 \text{ V}$$

1.11 A toroidal core of mean length 15 cm and cross-sectional area 10 cm² has a uniformly distributed winding of 300 turns.

The B-H characteristic of the core can be assumed to be of rectangular form, as shown in the figure below. The coil is connected to a 100 V, 400 Hz supply. Determine the hysteresis loss in the core.

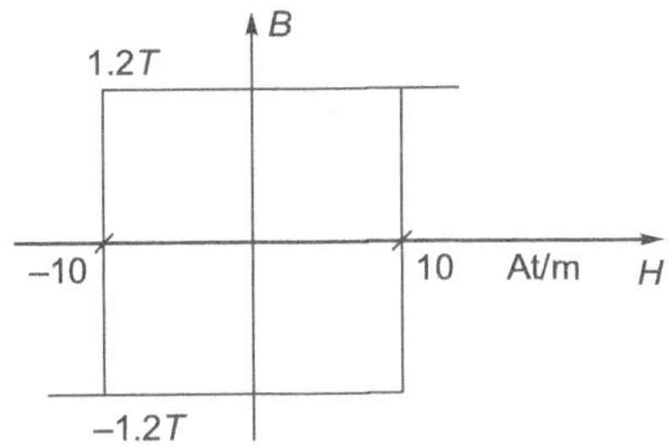

[12 marks : 2023]

Solution:

Hystersis energy density = Area under B-H curve

Hystersis energy density = $2.4 \times 20 = 48\ \text{J/m}^3$

Volume of toroidal core = Area × Mean length

$= 10 \times 10^{-4} \times 15 \times 10^{-2} = 150 \times 10^{-6}\ \text{m}^3$

Now, Hystersis energy loss, E = (Hystersis energy density) × (Volume of toroidal core)

$E = 48 \times 150 \times 10^{-6} = 7.2\ \text{mJ}$

Hystersis power loss, $P = \dfrac{E}{T} = E \times f = 7.2 \times 10^{-3} \times 400$

$P = 2.88$ Watts

2. Transformers

2.1 The hysteresis and eddy-current loss of 1-phase transformer working on 200 V, 50 Hz are P_h and P_e respectively. The percentage decrease in these losses when operated on a 160 V, 40 Hz supply would respectively be

(a) 32, 36
(b) 20, 36
(c) 25, 50
(d) 40, 80

[2 marks : 2001]

Solution:

Option (b) is correct.

Since $V/f \propto B_{mf}$ and hysteresis loss is $P_h = k_n f B_m^x$

then % decrease in hysteresis loss

$$= \frac{P_{h_1} - P_{h_2}}{P_{h_1}} \times 100 = \frac{f_2 \cdot B_{m_2}^x - f_1 B_{m_1}^x}{f_1 B_{m_1}^x} \times 100$$

$$= \left[1 - \frac{f_2}{f_1}\left(\frac{V_2}{V_1} \cdot \frac{f_1}{f_2}\right)^x\right] \times 100 = \left[1 - \frac{40}{50}\left(\frac{160}{200} \cdot \frac{50}{40}\right)^x\right] \times 100 = 20\%$$

Eddy current loss $= k_e f^2 B_m^{\ 2}$

% decrease in eddy current loss

$$= \frac{P_{e_1} - P_{e_2}}{P_{e_2}} \times 100 = \left[1 - \left(\frac{f_2}{f_1}\right)^2 \cdot \left(\frac{V_2}{V_1} \cdot \frac{f_1}{f_2}\right)^2\right] \times 100$$

$$= \left[1 - \left(\frac{40}{50}\right)^2 \cdot \left(\frac{160}{200} \cdot \frac{50}{40}\right)^2\right] \times 100 = 36\%$$

2.2 In a transformer core, third and fifth harmonic components of fluxes are respectively 10% and 4% of the fundamental flux. The third and fifth harmonic induced emfs in the winding, in terms of the fundamental induced emf are respectively.

(a) 30%, 20%
(b) 10%, 12%
(c) 50%, 20%
(d) 50%, 20%

[2 marks : 2001]

Solution:

$$E \propto f\phi$$

Option (d) is correct.

2.3 In transformer protection, harmonic restraint feature is incorporated to guard against

(a) magnetizing inrush current
(b) lightning
(c) overvoltage surges
(d) unbalanced operation

[2 marks : 2001]

Solution: (a)

Option (a) is correct.

2.4 A 2200/220 V, 1-phase transformer has maximum possible voltage regulation of 6% and it occurs at a p.f. of 0.3. Find the load voltage at full-load at p.f. of 0.8 lead.

[8 marks : 2001]

Solution:

Percentage voltage regulation at lagging p.f.,

$$\frac{E_2 - V_2}{E_2} = \left(\frac{I_2 r_{e_2}}{E_2}\cos\theta_2 + \frac{I_2 x_{e_2}}{E_2}\sin\theta_2\right)\times 100$$

For maximum voltage regulation,

$$\frac{d}{d\theta_2}\left(\frac{E_2 - V_2}{E_2}\right) = \frac{-I_2 r_{e_2}}{E_2}\sin\theta_2 + \frac{I_2 x_{e2}}{E_2}\cos\theta_2 = 0$$

or $$\tan\theta_2 = \frac{x_{e_2}}{r_{e_2}}$$

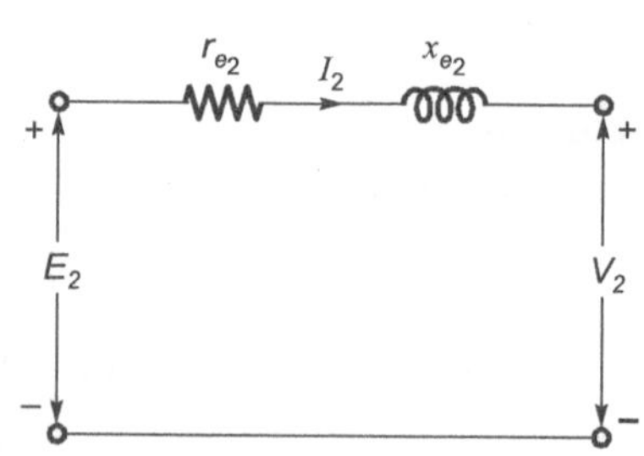

given, $$\cos\theta_2 = 0.3$$

$$\theta_2 = 72.54°$$

$$\tan\theta_2 = 3.179$$

$$\sin\theta_2 = 0.9539$$

$$x_{e2} = r_{e2} \times \tan\theta_2 = 3.179 \times r_{e2}$$

Given at, $$\phi = 72.54°$$

and $$\%\text{ regulation} = 6$$

$$6 = \left(\frac{I_2 r_{e_2}}{E_2}\cos\theta_2 + \frac{I_2 x_{e_2}}{E_2}\sin\theta_2\right)\times 100$$

$$6 = \left(\frac{I_2 r_{e_2}}{220}\times 0.3 + \frac{I_2(3.179\times r_{e_2})}{220}\times 0.9539\right)\times 100$$

$$13.2 = 3.3324\, I_2 r_{e_2}$$

$$I_2 r_{e_2} = 3.96$$

At leading p.f. of 0.8, the load voltage,

$$V_2 = E_2 - [I_2 r_{e_2}\cos\theta - I_2 x_{e_2}\sin\theta]$$

$$= 220 - [3.96 \times 0.8 - 3.179 \times 3.96 \times 0.6]$$

$$= 220 - [3.168 - 7.553] = 220 + 4.385$$

$$V_2 = 224.385 \text{ volt}$$

2.5 The efficiency at unity P.F of a 6600/384 V, 200 kVA single phase transformer is 98%, both at full load and at half full load. The P.F. at no load is 0.2 lagging and the full load regulation at a lagging P.F of 0.8 is 4%. Draw the equivalent circuit referred to *LV* side and insert all values.

[20 marks : 2002]

Solution:

$$\eta = 1 - \frac{\text{Losses}}{\text{Output} + \text{Losses}}$$

At full load,
$$0.98 = 1 - \frac{P_c + P_{sc}}{(2{,}00{,}000)(1) + P_c + P_{sc}}$$

or
$$P_c + P_{sc} = \frac{4000}{0.98} = 4081.63 \text{ W} \quad ...(i)$$

At half full load,
$$0.98 = 1 - \frac{P_c + \left(\frac{1}{2}\right)^2 P_{sc}}{\frac{1}{2}(2{,}00{,}000)(1) + P_c + \left(\frac{1}{2}\right)^2 P_{sc}}$$

or
$$P_c + \frac{1}{4}P_{sc} = \frac{2000}{0.98} = 2040.81 \text{ W} \quad ...(ii)$$

From equation (i) and (ii),
$$P_c = 1360.54 \text{ W}$$

and
$$P_{sc} = 2721.09 \text{ W}$$

$$\text{Voltage regulation at full load} = \epsilon_r \cos\theta_2 + \epsilon_x \sin\theta_2$$

or
$$0.04 = \epsilon_r \times 0.8 + \epsilon_x \times 0.6 \quad ...(iii)$$

Given,
$$\cos\theta_2 = 0.8$$
$$\sin\theta_2 = 0.6$$

$$\epsilon_r (r_e)_{p.u.} = \frac{\text{Ohmic loss at rated current}}{\text{Rated VA}} = \frac{2791.09}{200{,}000}$$

$$\therefore \quad \epsilon_r = 0.0136$$

Put the value of ϵ_r in equation (iii),
$$0.04 = 0.0136 \times 0.8 + \epsilon_x \times 0.6$$
$$\epsilon_x = 0.0485 \text{ p.u.}$$

$$r_{eL}(\Omega) = r_{e\,p.u.} \times \frac{(384)^2}{200{,}000} = \frac{0.0136 \times 147456}{200{,}000} = 0.010027\ \Omega$$

$$x_{eL}(\Omega) = \frac{0.0485 \times (384)^2}{200{,}000} = 0.035\ \Omega$$

$$R_{cL} = \frac{(V_L)^2}{P_c} = \frac{(384)^2}{1360.54} = 108.38\ \Omega$$

$$I_c = \frac{V_L}{R_{cL}} = \frac{384}{108.38} = 3.54 \text{ A}$$

$$I_c = I_e \cos\theta_0$$
$$3.54 = I_e \times 0.2$$
$$I_e = 17.7$$
$$I_m = I_e \sin\theta_0 = 17.7 \times 0.979 = 17.34\text{A}$$

$$X_{mL} = \frac{V_L}{I_m} = \frac{384}{17.34} = 22.14\ \Omega$$

Equivalent circuit referred to L.V side

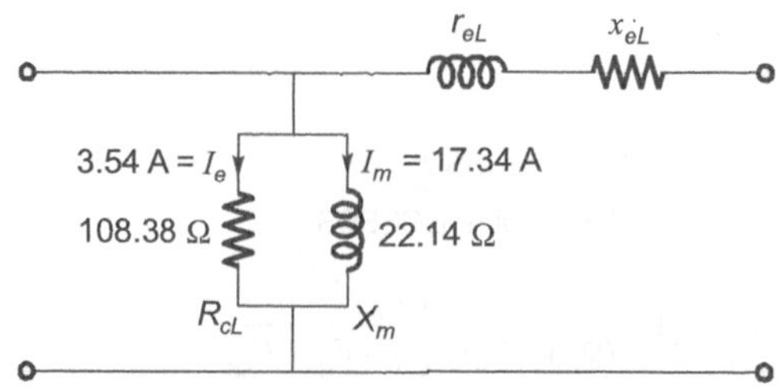

2.6 The low voltage winding of a 400/230 V single phase 50 Hz transformer is to be connected to a 25 Hz supply. In order to keep the magnetization current at the same level in both the cases the voltage at 25 Hz should be:

(a) 230 V (b) 460 V
(c) 115 V (d) 65 V [2 marks : 2003]

Solution: (c)

To keep the magnetizing current same, V/f should be same. Hence, option (c) is correct.

2.7 A 100 KVA transformer has its maximum efficiency of 98% at full load and unity p.f. during the day it is loaded as follows:

12 hrs — 20 kW at a p.f. of 0.5 lag
6 hrs — 20 kW at a p.f. of 0.9 lag
6 hrs — 20 kW at a p.f. of 0.8 lag

Calculate the "all day efficiency" of the transformer.

[16 marks : 2003]

Solution:

Given: $\eta_{max} = 0.98$ at full load i.e. $x = 1$ and unity p.f. ($\cos\phi = 1$)

$$\eta = \frac{x(\text{kVA})\cos\phi}{x(\text{kVA})\cos\phi + p_i + x^2 p_{cu}}$$

$p_{cu} \rightarrow$ Cu losses at full load

For η_{max}, $x^2 p_{cu} = p_i$; $x = 1$

$$\Rightarrow \quad p_{cu} = p_i$$

$$\eta_{max} = \frac{100\times 1}{100\times 1 + p_i + p_i}$$

$$\Rightarrow \quad 0.98 = \frac{100}{100 + 2p_i}$$

$$p_i = 1.02 \text{ kW always constant}$$

at full load i.e. 100 kVA cu loss = 1.02 kW

$$\eta_{\text{all day}} = \frac{\text{Output during 24 hours (kWh)}}{\text{kWh} + \text{losses during 24 hours}}$$

During 12 hours:

Load 20 kW at $\cos\phi = 0.5$ lag

$$\text{load kVA} = \frac{\text{kW}}{\cos\phi} = \frac{20}{0.5} = 40 \text{ kVA}$$

So transformer is loaded at,

(rated on full load) $x = \frac{40}{100} = 0.4$

$$P_{cu} = x^2 P_{cu,fl} = (0.4)^2 \times 1.02 = 0.1632 \text{ kW}$$

During 6 hours:

$$\text{load 20 kW at } \cos\phi = 0.9 \text{ lag}$$

$$\text{load kVA} = \frac{20}{0.9} = 22.22 \text{ KVA}$$

$$x = \frac{22.22}{100} = 0.2222$$

$$P_{cu} = x^2 P_{cu,fl} = (0.2222)^2 \times 1.02 = 0.0503 \text{ kW}$$

During 6 hours:

$$\text{load 20 kW at } pf \cos\phi = 0.8 \text{ lag}$$

$$\text{load kVA} = \frac{20}{0.8} = 25 \text{ kVA}$$

$$x = \frac{25}{100} = 0.25$$

$$P_{cu} = x^2 P_{cu,fl} = (0.25)^2 \times 1.02 = 0.0637 \text{ kW}$$

Total copper loss during the day,

$$= 0.1632 \times 12 + 0.0503 \times 6 + 0.0637 \times 6 = 2.6424 \text{ kWh}$$

Output during 24 hours:

$$= 20 \times 12 + 20 \times 6 + 20 \times 6 = 480 \text{ kWh}$$

$$\eta_{\text{all day}} = \frac{480}{480 + 1.02 \times 24 + 2.6424} = 0.9465 \quad \text{or} \quad \eta_{\text{all day}} = 94.65\%$$

2.8 A transformer is connected to a 1000 V, 50 Hz supply. The total core loss is 1000 W, of which 700 W are hysteresis and 300 W are eddy current loss. If the applied voltage is raised to 2000 V and the frequency to 100 Hz, find the new core loss.

[15 marks : 2004]

Solution:

Hysteresis loss, $P_h \propto f B^x \propto f\left(\frac{V}{f}\right)^x$

$$\frac{P_{h_1}}{P_{h_2}} = \frac{f_1}{f_2}\left(\frac{V_1}{V_2} \times \frac{f_2}{f_1}\right)^x$$

$$\frac{700}{P_{h_2}} = \frac{50}{100}\left(\frac{1000}{2000} \times \frac{100}{50}\right)^x$$

or $P_{h2} = \frac{700 \times 100}{50} = 1400 \text{ W}$

Eddy current loss, $P_e \propto B^2 f^2 \propto f^2\left(\frac{V}{f}\right)^2$

$$\frac{P_{e_1}}{P_{e_2}} = \left(\frac{f_1}{f_2}\right)^2\left(\frac{V_1}{V_2} \times \frac{f_2}{f_1}\right)^2$$

$$\frac{300}{p_{e_2}} = \left(\frac{50}{100}\right)^2 \left(\frac{1000}{2000} \times \frac{100}{50}\right)^2$$

$$p_{e2} = 300 \times 4 = 1200 \text{ W}$$

Total core loss, $p_c = p_{h2} + p_{e2} = 1400 + 1200 = 2600$ W

2.9 Derive the condition for maximum efficiency of a transformer. [15 marks : 2004]

Solution:

Condition for maximum efficiency

Efficiency, $$\eta = \frac{\text{Output power}}{\text{Input power}} = \frac{V_2 I_2 \cos\theta_2}{V_2 I_2 \cos\theta_2 + P_c + I_2^2 r_{e2}} \quad ...(i)$$

where, P_c = total core loss

$I_2^2 r_{e_2}$ = total ohmic losses

$V_2 I_2$ = output VA,

$\cos\theta_2$ = load p.f.

In above equation, P_c is constant and the load voltage V_2 remains practically constant. At a specified value of load p.f. $\cos\theta_2$, the efficiency will be maximum when $d\eta/dI_2 = 0$.

Therefore, $$\frac{d\eta}{dI_2} = \frac{[(V_2 I_2 \cos\theta_2 + P_c + I_2^2 r_{e_2})(V_2 \cos\theta_2) - (V_2 I_2 \cos\theta_2)(V_2 \cos\theta_2 + 2I_2 r_{e_2})]}{[V_2 I_2 \cos\theta_2 + P_c + I_2^2 r_{e_2}]^2}$$

For maximum efficiency,

$$\frac{d\eta}{dI_2} = 0$$

or $[V_2 I_2 \cos\theta_2 + P_c + I_2^2 r_{e2}](V_2 \cos\theta_2) = V_2 I_2 \cos\theta_2 (V_2 \cos\theta_2 + 2I_2 r_{e2})$

or $I_2^2 r_{e2} = P_c$

or [variable ohmic loss, $I_2^2 r_{e2}$ = constant core loss, P_c]

Hence the maximum efficiency occurs when the variable ohmic loss $I_2^2 r_{e2}$ is equal to the fixed core loss P_c.

2.10 The basic difference between the magnetizing current of a large capacity transformer and the magnetizing inrush current.

[5 marks : 2005]

Solution:

The magnetising current $(\bar{I}_m)$ is the component of exciting current $(\bar{I}_0)$, which is responsible for the production of flux. In the steady-state operation we assume V_1 and ϕ are both sinusoidal.

When the voltage V_1 is switched on to the transformer, the core flux and the corresponding exciting current undergo a transient before reaching steady-state values. The severity of the switching transient is related to the instant when the voltage wave is switched on; the worst condition being when the applied voltage has zero value at the instant of switching as shown below:

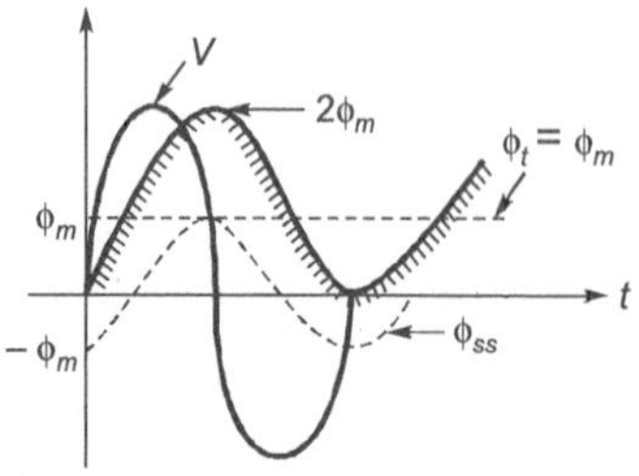

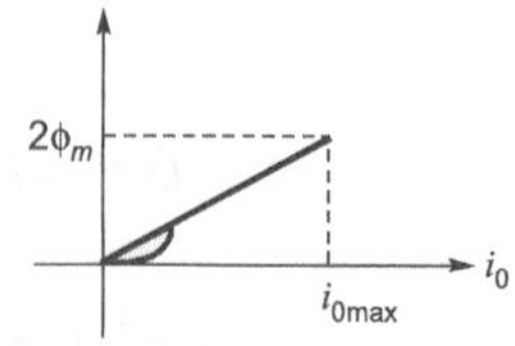

It is assumed here that the initial flux in the transformer at the instant of switching has zero value. It is seen from this figure that the steady-state value of flux demanded at this instant is ϕ_m, while the flux can only start with zero value (in the inductive circuit). If the circuit dissipation (core-loss) is assumed negligible, the flux transient will go through a maximum value of $2\phi_m$, a phenomenon called doubling effect. The corresponding exciting current will be very large as 100 times the normal exciting current. This transformer switching transient is referred to as the **inrush current.**

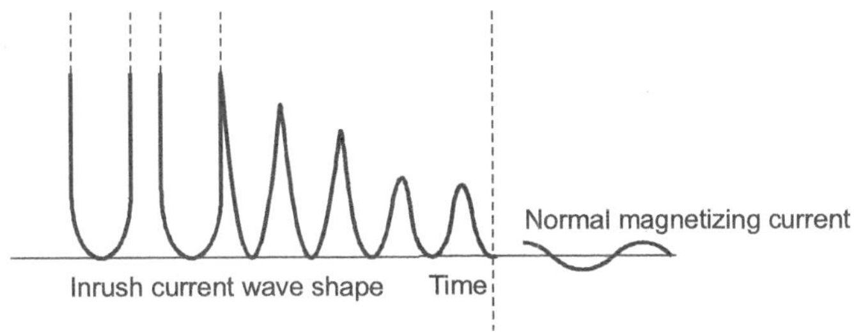

2.11 Calculate efficiency, voltage at the secondary terminals and primary input current when supplying full load secondary current at power factor (a) unity (b) 0.8 lag, for 4 kVA, 230/460V single phase transformer.

The following are test results:

Open circuit with 230 V applied to LV side – 0.6 A, 75 W

Short circuit with 20 V applied to HV side – 10 A, 60 W **[20 marks : 2005]**

Solution:

Open circuit test (primary side):

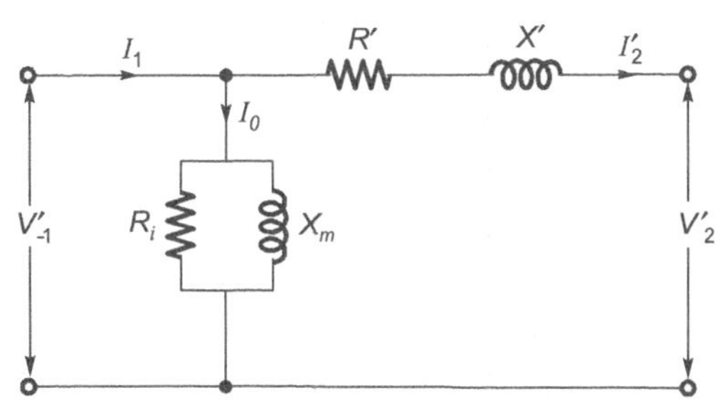

Referred to primary side

$$P_0 = V_0 I_0 \cos\theta_0$$

$$\Rightarrow \quad 75 = 230 \times 0.6 \times \cos\theta_0$$

$$\Rightarrow \quad \cos\theta_0 = 0.5434 \Rightarrow \theta_0 = 57.07°$$

$$\sin\theta_0 = 0.839$$

$$R_i = \frac{V_0^2}{P_0} = \frac{230^2}{75} = 705.33\ \Omega$$

$$I_m = I_0 \sin\theta_0 = 0.6 \times 0.839 = 0.5036 \text{ Amp.}$$

$$X_m = \frac{V_0}{I_m} = \frac{230}{0.5036} = 456.71\ \Omega$$

$$I_0 = 0.6\angle{-57.07°} \text{ Amp.}$$

Short circuit test (secondary side):

$$P_{sc} = I_{sc}^2 R$$

$$\Rightarrow \quad 60 = 10^2 \times R$$

$$\Rightarrow \quad R = 0.6\ \Omega$$

$$Z = \frac{V_{sc}}{I_{sc}} = \frac{20}{10} = 2$$

$$X = \sqrt{Z^2 - R^2} = 1.9\ \Omega$$

(a) Full load secondary current $= \dfrac{4 \times 10^3}{460} = 8.7$ Amp.

$$\text{Power factor} = \cos\phi = 1$$

$$\phi = 0°$$

Hence, $I_2 = 8.7\angle 0°$

Voltage at the secondary terminals, taking $V_2 = 460\angle 0°$ V as reference

$$E_2 = V_2 + I_2(R + jX)$$
$$= 460\angle 0° + 8.7\angle 0 \times (0.6 + j1.9)$$
$$= 465.51\angle 2.03° \text{ V}$$
$$|E_2| = 465.51 \text{ volts}$$

$$\text{Copper loss} = I_2^2 R = 8.7^2 \times 0.6 = 45.41 \text{ W}$$
$$\text{Iron loss} = 75 \text{ W}$$
$$\text{efficiency } \eta = \frac{\text{output}}{\text{output + losses}} \times 100 = \frac{4000 \times 1}{4000 \times 1 + 75 + 45.41} \times 100 = 97.07\%$$

Secondary current referred to primary,

$$I_2' = \frac{1}{\text{Voltage ratio}} \times I_2 = \frac{8.7\angle 0°}{\left(\frac{1}{2}\right)} = 17.4\angle 0° \text{ A}$$

E_2 referred to primary side,

$$E_2' = \frac{1}{2}E_2 = \frac{465.51\angle 2.03}{2} = 232.60\angle 2.03$$
$$I_0 = \frac{E_2'}{R_i} + \frac{E_2'}{jX_m} = \frac{232.60\angle 2.03}{705.33} + \frac{232.60\angle 2.03}{465.71\angle 90°}$$
$$I_0 = 0.598\angle -54.53° \text{ A}$$
$$\text{Input primary current} = I_0 + I_2'$$
$$= 0.598\angle -54.53 + 17.4\angle 0° = 17.75\angle -1.572 \text{ Amp.}$$

(b)

$$\text{Power factor} = \cos\phi = 0.8 \text{ lag}$$
$$\phi = 36.87° \text{ lag}$$
$$I_2 = 8.7\angle -36.87° \text{ A}$$

Voltage at the secondary terminals,

$$E_2 = V_2 + I_2(R + jX)$$
$$= 460\angle 0 + 8.7\angle -36.87° \times (0.6 + j1.9) = 474.20\angle 1.22 \text{ volts}$$
$$|E_2| = 474.20 \text{ volts}$$
$$\text{output} = \text{kVA} \cos\phi = 4000 \times 0.8 = 3200 \text{ W}$$
$$\text{efficiency} = \frac{3200}{3200 + 75 + 45.41} \times 100 = 96.37\%$$

Secondary current referred to primary side,

$$I_2' = 17.4\angle -36.87° \text{ Amp.}$$

E_2 referred to primary side,

$$E_2' = \frac{1}{2} \times E_2 = \frac{474.20\angle 1.22}{2} = 237.1\angle 1.22° \text{ V}$$
$$I_0 = \frac{E_2'}{R_i} + \frac{E_2'}{jX_m} = \frac{237.1\angle 1.22}{705.33} + \frac{237.1\angle 1.22}{465.71\angle 90°}$$
$$I_0 = 0.61\angle -55.34° \text{ Amp.}$$

Input primary current, $I_1 = I_0 + I_2'$

$$= 0.61\angle 59.34° + 17.4\angle -36.87° = 17.97\angle -37.48° \text{ Amp.}$$

2.12 Summarize the conditions for proper parallel operation of
(a) single-phase transformers
(b) 3-phase transformers [8 marks : 2005]

Solution:

The satisfactory and successful operation of transformers connected in parallel on both sides requires that they fulfill the following conditions:

(a) Single-phase transformers:

(*i*) The transformers must be connected properly as far as their polarity are concerned so that the net voltage around the local loop is zero. A wrong polarity connection results in a short circuit.

(*ii*) The transformers must have the same voltage ratio to avoid no-load circulating current when transformers are in parallel on both primary and secondary sides. Since the leakage impedance is low, even a small voltage difference can give rise to considerable no-load circulating current and extra I^2R loss.

(*iii*) There should exist only a limited disparity in the per-unit impedances (on their own base) of the transformers, otherwise a given active load is not proportionally shared by them.

(*iv*) The ratio of equivalent leakage reactance to equivalent resistance i.e. x_e/r_e should be same for all the transformers.

(b) **3-phase transformers:** Three-phase transformers must have zero relative phase displacement on the secondary sides and must be connected in a proper phase sequence. Only the transformers of the same phase group can be paralleled. For example, Y/Y and Y/Δ transformers cannot be paralleled, as their secondary voltages will have a phase difference of 30°.

2.13 **A 1500 kVA, 6.6/1.1 kV, 3-phase delta-star connected transformer has the following test result: S.C. test: (Instruments placed on h.v. side) 300 V, 131.21 A, 30 kW.**
Calculate its percentage resistance, percentage reactance drops, percentage efficiency and percentage regulation on full load at 0.8 power factor lagging. The iron loss during O.C. test with rated voltage supplied is 25 kW.

[14 marks : 2006]

Solution:

Short-circuit test is conducted on hv side i.e. delta side.

Hence,
$$V_{\text{phase}} = V_{l-l} = 300\text{ V}$$
$$I_{\text{phase}} = \frac{I_{l-l}}{\sqrt{3}} = \frac{131.21}{\sqrt{3}} = 75.75\text{ Amp.}$$
$$\text{Copper loss/phase} = \frac{30}{3} = 10\text{ kW}$$

Hence,
$$I^2_{phase} R_\Delta = 10 \times 10^3$$
$$R_\Delta = \frac{10 \times 10^3}{75.75^2} = 1.74\ \Omega$$
$$Z_\Delta = \frac{V_{phase}}{I_{phase}} = \frac{300}{75.75} = 3.96\ \Omega$$
$$X_\Delta = \sqrt{Z_\Delta^2 - R_\Delta^2} = \sqrt{3.96^2 - 1.74^2} = 3.55\ \Omega$$

Converting R_Δ, X_Δ into equivalent star R_Y, X_y
$$R_Y = \frac{R_\Delta}{3} = \frac{1.74}{3} = 0.58\ \Omega; \quad X_y = \frac{X_\Delta}{3} = \frac{3.58}{3} = 1.18$$

$$Z_{Base} = \left(\frac{(kV_B)^2}{MVA_B}\right) = \frac{6.6^2}{1.5} = 29.04\,\Omega$$

$$\text{Percentage resistance drop} = \in_r = \frac{R_Y}{Z_{Base}} = \frac{0.58}{29.04} = 0.0199 \text{ pu} = 1.99\%$$

$$\text{Percentage reactance drop} = \in_x = \frac{X_Y}{Z_{Base}} = \frac{1.18}{29.04} = 0.0406 \text{ pu} = 4.06\%$$

$$\cos\phi = 0.8 \text{ lagging}$$

$$\sin\phi = 0.6$$

$$\text{Percentage voltage regulation} = (\in_r \cos\phi + \in_x \sin\phi) \times 100$$

$$= (0.0199 \times 0.8 + 0.0406 \times 0.6) \times 100 = 4.028\%$$

$$\text{losses} = \text{copper loss} + \text{iron loss} = 30 + 25 = 55 \text{ kW}$$

$$\text{efficiency} = \frac{\text{output}}{\text{output} + \text{losses}} \times 100$$

$$= \frac{1500 \times 0.8}{1500 \times 0.8 + 55} \times 100 = 95.61\%$$

2.14 A iron cored transformer is working at a maximum flux density of 0.8 Web/m^2. Its core is replaced by silicon steel core, working at a maximum flux density of 1.2 Web/m^2. If the total flux is to remain the same, what is the reduction in volume expressed as a percentage of the original volume? The frequency and voltage per turn are the same in both cases.

(a) 33% (b) 9%
(c) 22% (d) 11%

[2 marks : 2007]

Solution:

$$\text{Voltage per turn} = 4.44\, f\phi_m = 4.44\, f B_m A$$

$$\Rightarrow \quad A \propto \frac{1}{B_m}$$

$$A_1 \propto \frac{1}{0.8} = 1.25$$

$$A_2 \propto \frac{1}{1.2} = 0.83$$

$$\%\text{ reduction in core volume} = \%\text{ reduction in core area}$$

$$= \left(\frac{1.25 - 0.83}{1.25}\right) \times 100 = 33\%$$

Hence, option (a) is correct.

2.15 A 3-phase load of 40 kW, 380 V having a p.f. of 0.8 (lagging) receives its power through a 3-phase auto transformer from a 3 phase 440 V 3-ϕ supply. The auto transformer is connected in star. The neutral is not grounded. Neglect exciting current and impedance of the transformer winding.

(a) Draw the diagram depicting the above situation.
(b) Calculate the currents entering the load from the auto transformer.
(c) Calculate the currents entering the transformer from the supply side.
(d) Show the currents flowing in the transformer winding along with directions.

[3 + 4 + 4 + 4 = 15 marks : 2007]

Solution:

(a)

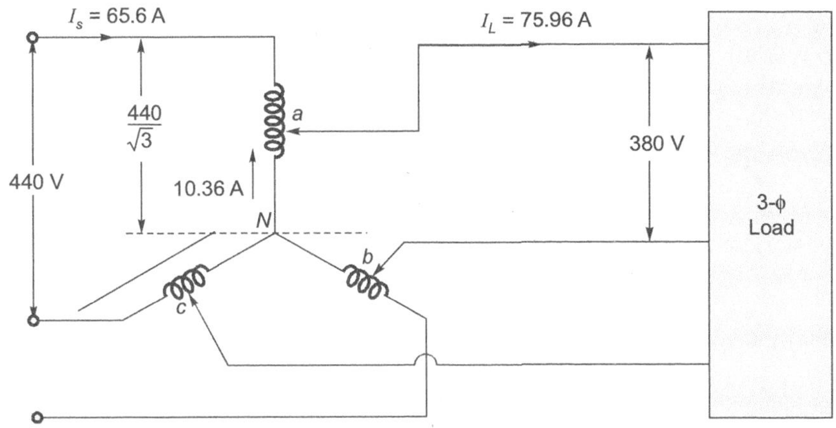

(b) The load current $I_L = \dfrac{40\times10^3}{\sqrt{3}\times380\times0.8} = 75.96$ Amp.

(c) Turn ratio $= \dfrac{440}{380} = \dfrac{V_s}{V_L} = \dfrac{I_L}{I_s}$

$$\Rightarrow \quad \frac{440}{380} = \frac{75.96}{I_s}$$

Supply current $= I_s = 65.6$ A

2.16 A 300 kVA, 11 kV/440 V, 50 Hz, 3-phase ΔY-transformer gave the following test results:
At rated voltage no load: 440 V, 21.1 A, 1.3 kW (*lv* side)
At rated current on short circuit: 630 V, 15.7 A, 3.08 kW (*hv* side)
Evaluate the rated loss, impedance voltage, per unit resistance and leakage reactance, efficiency and regulation on full load at 0.8 p.f. lagging.

[10 marks : 2008]

Solution:

Short-circuit test is conducted on h.v. side i.e. delta side.

Hence, $V_{phase} = V_{l-l} = 630$ V

$$I_{phase} = \frac{I_{l\text{-}l}}{\sqrt{3}} = \frac{15.7}{\sqrt{3}} = 9.064 \text{ Amp.}$$

Full load, Copper loss/phase $= \dfrac{3.08}{3}\times10^3 = 1026.67\ \Omega$

Hence, $(I_{phase})^2\times R_s = 1026.67$

$$R_s = \frac{1026.67}{(9.064)^2} = 12.5\ \Omega$$

$$Z_D = \frac{V_{phase}}{I_{phase}} = \frac{630}{9.064} = 69.50\ \Omega$$

$$X_D = \sqrt{Z_D^2 - R_D^2} = \sqrt{(69.5)^2-(12.5)^2} = 68.36\ \Omega$$

Converting Z_D, X_D and R_D into equivalent star Z_Y, X_Y and R_Y

$$Z_Y = \frac{Z_\Delta}{3} = \frac{69.50}{3} = 28.167\ \Omega\ ;$$

$$X_Y = \frac{68.36}{3} = 22.78\ \Omega \text{ and } R_Y = \frac{12.5}{3} = 4.167\ \Omega$$

$$Z_{Base}\,(h.v.\text{ side}) = \frac{(kV_B)^2}{(MVA_B)} = \frac{(11)^2}{(0.3)} = 403.34\ \Omega$$

$$\text{Impedance voltage} = \frac{Z_Y}{Z_{Base}} = \frac{28.167}{403.34} = 0.06983 \text{ pu}$$

$$\in_r = \text{Per unit resistance} = \frac{R_Y}{Z_{Base}} = \frac{4.167}{403.34} = 0.01033 \text{ pu}$$

$$\in_x = \text{Per unit reactance} = \frac{X_Y}{Z_{Base}} = \frac{22.78}{403.34} = 0.0564 \text{ pu}$$

$$\begin{aligned} \text{Voltage regulation} &= (\in_r \cos\phi + \in_x \sin\phi) \times 100 \\ &= (0.01033 \times 0.8 + 0.0564 \times 0.6) \times 100 \\ &= 4.21\% \end{aligned}$$

$$\begin{aligned} \text{Rated losses} &= \text{core loss + full load copper loss} \\ &= 1.3 + 3.08 \text{ kW} = 4.38 \text{ kW} \end{aligned}$$

$$\text{efficiency} = \eta = \left(\frac{\text{output}}{\text{output + losses}}\right) \times 100 = \left(\frac{300 \times 0.8}{300 \times 0.8 + 4.38}\right)$$

$$= 98.20\%$$

2.17 When a 2300/230 volts, 50 kVA, 50 Hz transformer is connected as an autotransformer to supply a 2300 V circuit from a 2530 V source, the kVA rating of the auto transformer will be

(a) 550 kVA (b) 500 kVA
(c) 450 kVA (d) 50 kVA

[2 marks : 2009]

Solution:

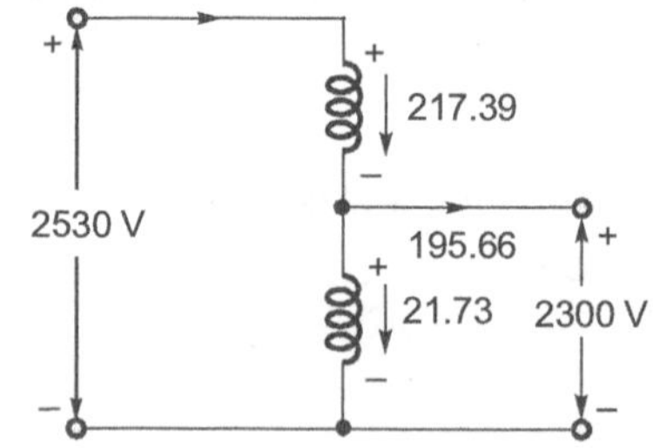

$$\text{Current in } LV \text{ winding} = \frac{50000}{230} = 217.39 \text{ A}$$

$$\text{Current in } HV \text{ winding} = \frac{50000}{2300} = 21.739 \text{ A}$$

$$\begin{aligned} \text{the kVA rating} &= 2530 \times 217.39 \\ &= 2300 \times 239.12 = 550 \text{ kV} \end{aligned}$$

Hence, option (a) is correct.

2.18 State and explain the conditions required for the successful parallel operation of single-phase transformers.

A single-phase load is supplied through a 34.5 kV feeder and 34.5/2.4 kV transformer. The feeder has an impedance of 50 + *j*80 ohms and the transformer has an equivalent impedance of 24 + *j*120 ohms referred to its high-voltage side. The load takes 260 kW at 2.3 kV and 0.866 lagging power factor.

(a) Find the voltage at the primary side of the transformer.
(b) Determine the voltage at the sending end of the feeder.
(c) Calculate the real and reactive power input at the sending end of the feeder.

[20 marks : 2009]

Solution:

The satisfactory and successful operation of transformers connected in parallel on both sides requires that they fulfil the following conditions:

(*i*) The transformers must be connected properly as far as their polarities are concerned so that the net voltage around the loop is zero. A wrong polarity connection results in a dead short circuit.

(*ii*) The voltage ratings and the voltage ratio of the transformers should be same to avoid no-load circulating current.

(*iii*) There should exist only a limited disparity in the per-unit impedances (on their own bases) of the transformers.

(*iv*) The ratio X/R should be same for all the transformers to avoid operation at different power factors.

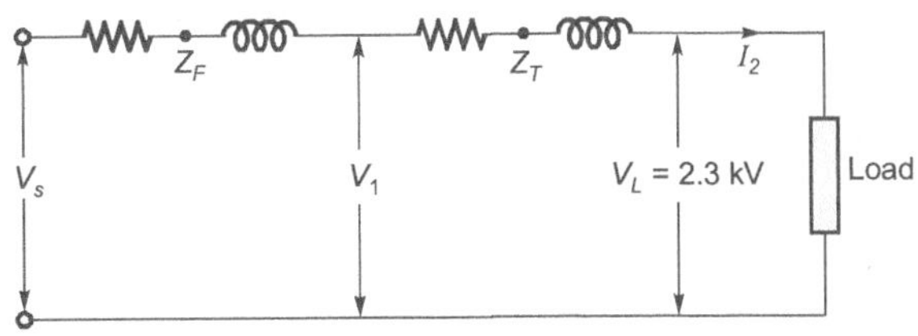

Voltage at the load side,

$$V_L = 2.3 \text{ kV} = 2300 \text{ V}$$

Taking V_L as the reference,

$$V_L = 2300\angle 0° \text{ V}$$

and Load current $$I_2 = \frac{260 \times 10^3}{2.3 \times 10^3 \times 0.866} = 130.53\angle -30° \text{ A} \quad \text{(Lagging pf)}$$

Feeder impedance referred to L.V. side

$$Z_F = (50 + j80) \times \left(\frac{2.4}{34.5}\right)^2 = (0.242 + j0.387)\ \Omega$$

Transformer impedance referred to *L.V.* side

$$Z_T = (24 + j120) \times \left(\frac{2.4}{34.5}\right)^2 = (0.116 + j0.580)\ \Omega$$

(a) Voltage at the primary side of the transformer,

$$V_1 = \text{Voltage ratio} \times (V_L + I_2 Z_T)$$

$$= \left(\frac{34.5}{2.4}\right) \times [2300\angle 0 + 130.53\angle -30° \times (0.116 + j0.582)]$$

$$= 33805\angle 1.41 \text{ V} = 33.8\angle 1.41 \text{ kV}$$

$$|V_1| = 33.8 \text{ kV}$$

Total impedance,

$$Z = Z_T + Z_F = (0.116 + j0.58) + (0.242 + j0.387)$$

$$= 0.358 + j0.967$$

(b) Voltage at the sending end of the feeder,

$$V_s = \text{Voltage ratio} \times (V_L + I_2 Z)$$

$$= \left(\frac{34.5}{2.4}\right) \times \{2300\angle 0° + 130.53\angle -30 \times (0.358 + j0.967)\}$$

$$= 34.573\angle 2.047° \text{ V} = 34.57\angle 2.047° \text{ kV}$$

$$|V_s| = 34.57 \text{ kV}$$

Active power loss $= (130.53)^2 \times 0.358 = 6100 \text{ W} = 6.1 \text{ kW}$

Reactive power loss $= (130.53)2 \times 0.967 = 16477 \text{ W} = 16.47 \text{ kW}$

Complex power at load end

$$= 260 + j260 \tan(\cos^{-1} 0.866)$$

$$= 260 + j150 \text{ kVA}$$

Complex power at sending end

$$= (260 + j150) + (6.1 + j16.47) = 266.1 + j166.47 \text{ kVA}$$

2.19 A two winding single phase transformer when connected either as a step down or step up autotransformer, under the assumptions of ignoring core loss, copper loss, magnetizing current and leakage reactance will have the maximum *VA* rating of the two winding transformer for a given *VA* rating of the two winding transformer having N_1 and N_2 primary and secondary turns respectively for

(a) $(N_1/N_2) << 1.0$ (b) $(N_1/N_2) = 1.0$

(c) (N_1/N_2) ; 1.0 but 1.0 (d) $(N_1/N_2) >> 1.0$

[5 marks : 2010]

Solution:

$$(VA)_{auto} = \left(\frac{a'}{a'-1}\right)(VA)_{TW}$$

where, $a' = N_1/N_2$

For $a' = N_1/N_2 = 1 \quad (VA)_{auto} >> (VA)_{TW}$

Hence, option (b) is correct.

2.20 A 6600 V/400 V/110 V star/star/mesh connected three-phase transformer has a magnetizing current of 5.5 A and balanced three-phase loads of 1000 kVA at 0.8 lag on secondary and 200 kVA, 0.5 leading power factor load on the tertiary. Find the primary current and power factor. Neglect losses.

[12 marks : 2011]

Solution:

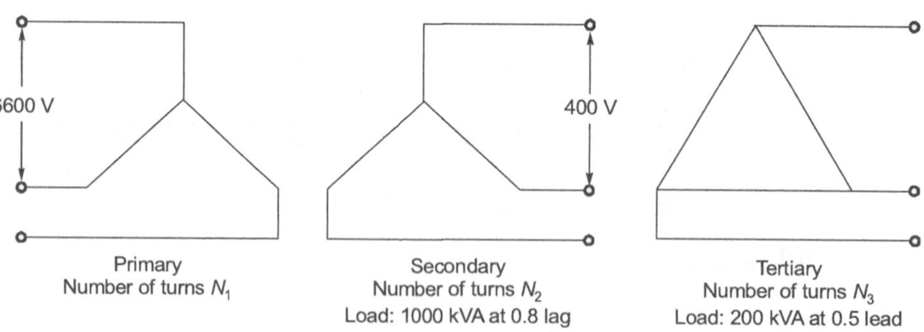

Turns ratio:

$$N_1 : N_2 : N_3 = \frac{6600}{\sqrt{3}} : \frac{400}{\sqrt{3}} : 110$$

Let, I_1, I_2 and I_3 be the phase currents in primary, secondary and tertiary windings.

$$I_3 \text{ (tertiary current per phase)} = \frac{\text{Power per phase}}{\text{Voltage per phase}}$$

$$= \frac{200 \times 10^3 / 3}{110} \angle 60° = 606.06 \angle 60° \text{ A}$$

Referred to primary, $I_3' = \left(\frac{N_3}{N_1}\right) I_3$

$$I_3' = \frac{110}{6600/\sqrt{3}} \times 606.06\angle 60° = 17.5\angle 60° \text{ A}$$

$$I_2 \text{(secondary current per phase)} = \frac{\text{Power per phase}}{\text{Voltage per phase}}$$

$$I_2 = \frac{1000 \times 10^3 / 3}{400/\sqrt{3}} \angle -36.87° = 1443.37\angle -36.87° \text{ A}$$

Referred to primary, $I'_2 = \left(\frac{N_2}{N_1}\right) I_2 = \left(\frac{400/\sqrt{3}}{6600/\sqrt{3}}\right) \times 1443.37\angle -36.87° \text{ A} = 87.47\angle -36.87° \text{ A}$

Magnetizing current lags the voltage by 90° as losses are neglected.

$$\text{Magnetizing current} = I_0 = 5.5\angle -90° \text{ A}$$

$$I_1 = \text{Primary current} = I_0 + I'_2 + I'_3$$

$$= 5.5\angle -90° + 87.47\angle -36.87° + 17.5\angle 60° = 89.62\angle -28.54 \text{ A}$$

$$|I_1| = 89.62 \text{ A}$$

and power factor $= \cos 28.54 = 0.878$ lagging.

Alternate Solution:

Power output on secondary $= 1000 \times 0.8 = 800$ kW

Power output on tertiary $= 200 \times 0.5 = 100$ kW

Total power output on secondary, 'S_2' $= 1000\angle \cos^{-1} 0.8$ kVA

Total power output on tertiary, 'S_3' $= 200\angle -\cos^{-1} 0.5$ kVA

Total magnetizing power of primary,

$$S_{mag} = \frac{\sqrt{3} \times 6600 \times 6.6\angle 90°}{1000} = 75.45\angle 90° \text{ kVA}$$

Now, total input power to primary,

$$\bar{S}_1 = \bar{S}_2 + \bar{S}_3 + \bar{S}_{mag}$$

$$= 1000\angle 36.86° + 200\angle -60° + 75.45\angle 90°$$

$$= 1024.586\angle 28.56° \text{ kVA}$$

$$\text{Input power factor} = \cos 28.56° \text{ lag}$$

$$= 0.8784 \text{ lag}$$

$$\bar{S}_1 = \sqrt{3} \times V_1 \times I_1$$

$$1024.586 = \sqrt{3} \times 6600 \times 10^3 \times I_1$$

Primary current, $I_1 = 89.628$ A

2.21 In open-circuit test on a 1-phase transformer, the ohmic losses are usually neglected in comparison with core loss. Justify.

[4 marks : 2012]

Solution:

The input power given by the wattmeter, shown in figure below, consists of core loss and ohmic loss. The exciting current being about 2 to 6 percent of the full load current, the ohmic loss in primary varies from 0.04 to 0.36 percent of the full load primary ohmic loss. Hence the ohmic loss during open circuit test is negligible in comparison with the normal core loss and the wattmeter reading can be taken as equal to transformer core loss.

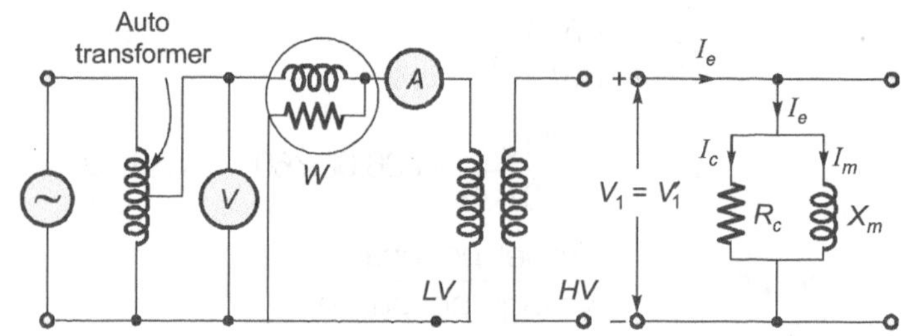

2.22 A single-phase transformer has voltage regulation of 6% and 6.6% for lagging power factors of 0.8 and 0.6 respectively. Full-load ohmic loss is equal to iron loss. Calculate (i) the lagging pf at which full-load voltage regulation is maximum and (ii) the full-load efficiency at unity power factor.

[8 marks : 2012]

Solution:

Per unit voltage regulation = $\varepsilon_r \cos\phi + \varepsilon_x \sin\phi$

For p.f. 0.8, $\varepsilon_r \times 0.8 + \varepsilon_x \times 0.6 = 0.06$

$$4\varepsilon_r + 3\varepsilon_x = 0.3 \quad ...(i)$$

For p.f. 0.6, $\varepsilon_r \times 0.6 + \varepsilon_x \times 0.8 = 0.066$

$$3\varepsilon_r + 4\varepsilon_x = 0.33 \quad ...(ii)$$

From equation (*i*) and (*ii*), $\varepsilon_r = 0.03$ and $\varepsilon_x = 0.06$

Condition for maximum voltage regulation,

$$\tan\phi' = \frac{\varepsilon_x}{\varepsilon_r} = \frac{0.06}{0.03} \Rightarrow \cos\phi' = 0.447 \text{ lagging}$$

$$\text{Efficiency, } \eta = \frac{\cos\phi}{\cos\phi + \dfrac{P_c}{V_2 I_2} + \dfrac{I_2^2 r_{e2}}{V_2 I_2}} = \frac{V_2 I_2}{V_2 I_2 + 2I_2^2 r_{e2}}$$

$$= \frac{V_2 I_2}{V_2 I_2 + 2\cdot\varepsilon_r V_2 I_2} = \frac{1}{1+2\times 0.03} = 0.9434$$

% efficiency = 94.34%

2.23 Three single phase transformers, each rated at 11 kVA, 220/440 V 50 Hz are connected to form a three phase step up, Y/D connection. The parameters of each transformers are

(220 V) Primary side: $r_1 = 39.5\ \text{m}\Omega$;
$x_1 = 61.5\ \text{m}\Omega$;
$R_c = 240\ \Omega$;
$x_\phi = 290\ \Omega$.

(440 V) Secondary side: $r_2 = 133.5\ \text{m}\Omega$;
$x_2 = 201\ \text{m}\Omega$

What will be power rating and efficiency of the transformer in Y/Δ-connection, when it delivers the rated load at rated voltage and 0.8 p.f. lagging?

[20 marks : 2013]

Solution:

$$\text{Primary side star equivalent voltage} = \left(\frac{220}{\sqrt{3}}\right) \text{V/phase}$$

$$\text{Secondary side star equivalent voltage} = 440 \text{ V/phase}$$

$$Z_{2\Delta} = (133.5 + j201)\ \text{M}\Omega$$

$$Z_{2Y} = \frac{(133.5 + j201)}{3} = (44.5 + j67)\ \text{M}\Omega$$

$$S_{load} = \sqrt{3} V_L \cdot I_L$$

$$I_L = \frac{3 \times 11 \times 10^3}{\sqrt{3} \times 440} \angle -\cos^{-1} 0.8 = 433.3\angle{-36.87}\ \text{A}$$

$$a = \frac{440}{(220/3)} = (2\sqrt{3})$$

Per phase equivalent circuit referred to primary side,

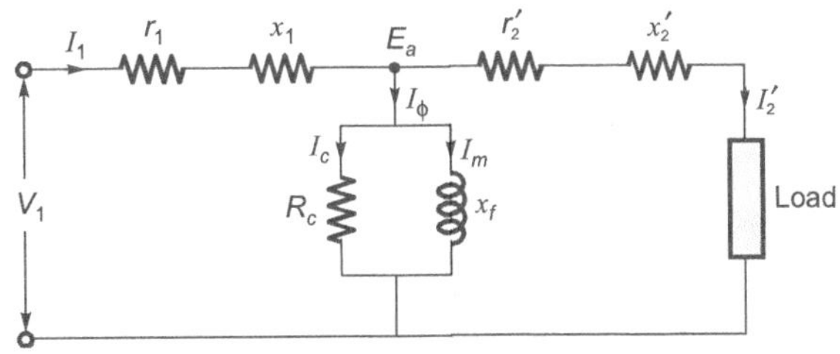

$$Z'_{2Y} = \frac{(44.5 + j67) \times 10^{-3}}{(2\sqrt{3})^2} = (3.71 + j5.583) \times 10^{-3}\ \Omega$$

$$I'_2 = \frac{(43.3\angle{-36.87})}{\sqrt{3}} \times 2\sqrt{3} = 86.6\angle{-36.87}\ \text{A}$$

$$E_2 = \frac{220}{\sqrt{3}} + (3.71 + j5.583) \times 10^{-3} \times 86.6\angle{-36.8^\circ}$$

$$E_2 = 127.56\angle 0.087\ \text{V}$$

$$I_0 = E_2\left(\frac{1}{240} + \frac{1}{j290}\right) = 0.689\angle{-39.52}\ \text{A}$$

$$I_1 = I_0 + I'_2 = 87.29\angle{-36.89}\ \text{A}$$

$$V_1 = E_2 + I_1 Z_1 = 127.56\angle 0.087 + 87.29\angle{-36.89}(0.0395 + j0.0615)$$

$$V_1 = 133.56\angle 1.037\ \text{V}$$

$$P_{in} = V_1 I_1 \cos\phi = 133.56 \times 87.29 \cos(1.037 + 36.89)$$

$$P_{in} = 9196.12\ \text{W}$$

$$P_{in}\text{(3-phase)} = 3 \times P_{in}\text{(1-phase)}$$

$$= 27.588\ \text{kW}$$

$$\eta = \frac{P_{out}}{P_{in}} \times 100 = \frac{33 \times 0.8}{27.588} \times 100 = 95.69\%$$

2.24 What are the conditions under which a transformer works at maximum efficiency? The maximum efficiency of a 50 KVA transformer is 97.4% and occurs at 90% of full load at UPF. Calculate efficiency at (*i*) full load, 0.8 pf and (*ii*) 1/2 full load, 0.9 pf.

[4 marks : 2014]

Solution:

Condition for maximum efficiency is variable loss = fixed loss

In case of transformer,

$$Cu \text{ loss} = \text{Iron loss}$$

or, $$P_{cu} = P_i \quad ...(1)$$

as given, $$\eta_{max} = \frac{x \times (\text{kVA}) \times \cos\phi}{x \times (\text{kVA}) \times \cos\phi + P_i + (P_{cu} = P_i)}$$

$$0.974 = \frac{0.9 \times 50 \times 1}{0.9 \times 50 \times 1 + 2P_i}$$

$$2\,P_i = \frac{0.9 \times 50}{0.974} - 0.9 \times 50$$

$$P_i = 0.6 \text{ kW}$$

From equation (1), $$P_{cu} = P_i = 0.6 \text{ kW}$$

At maximum efficiency,

$$x^2 \times (P_{cu})_{\text{full}} \text{ load} = P_i$$

so, $$(P_{cu})_{\text{full}} \text{ load} = \frac{0.6}{(0.9)^2} = 0.74 \text{ kW}$$

$$(P_{cu})_{\text{full}} \text{ load} = 0.74 \text{ kW}$$

(*i*) $$\eta_{\text{full load}} = \frac{50 \times 1 \times 0.8}{50 \times 1 \times 0.8 + 0.6 + 0.74} = 0.9675 \text{ or } 96.75\%$$

(*ii*) $$\eta_{1/2 \text{ full load}} = \frac{\frac{1}{2} \times 50 \times 0.9}{\frac{1}{2} \times 50 \times 0.9 + 0.6 + \left(\frac{1}{2}\right)^2 \times 0.74} = 0.96628 = 96.62\%$$

2.25 A 150 kVA, 2400/240 V transformer has the following parameters referred to the primary side: $R_1 = 0.5\ \Omega$ and $X_1 = 1.5\ \Omega$. The shunt magnetizing impedance is very large and can be neglected. At full load, the transformer delivers rated kVA at 0.85 lagging power factor and the secondary voltage is 240 V. Calculate:

(*i*) The voltage regulation

(*ii*) The efficiency assuming core losses to be 600 Ω.

[10 marks : 2014]

Solution:

Approximate equivalent circuit diagram referred to primary side is given below.

At full load,

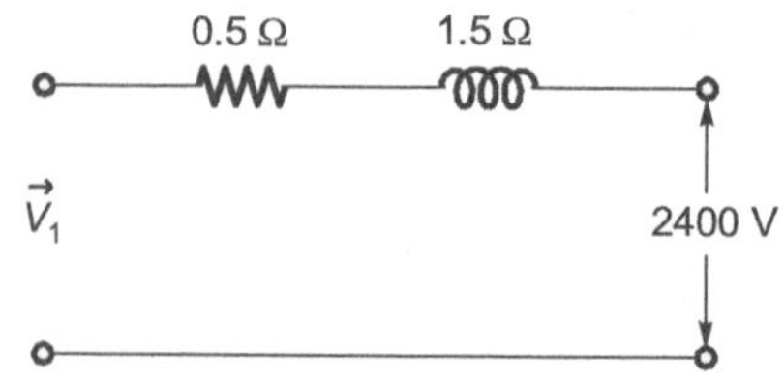

$$\text{Primary current} = \frac{150 \times 1000}{2400} = 62.5 \text{ A}$$

$$(\vec{I}_{\text{load}}) \text{ referred to primary} = \vec{I}_{\text{load}} = 62.5\angle{-\cos^{-1}(0.25)}$$

$$\vec{V}_1 = 2400\angle 0° + 62.5\angle{-31.78°} \times (0.5 + j1.5)$$

$$= 2476.74\angle 1.46 \text{ V}$$

(*i*) $$\text{Voltage regulation} = \frac{2476.74 - 2400}{2400} = 0.03197 \text{ or } 3.197\%$$

(*ii*) As given, core loss = 600 W

and Cu loss = $(62.5)^2 \times 0.5 = 1953.125$ watt

$$\eta_{\text{full load}} = \frac{150 \times 0.85}{150 \times 0.85 + (1953.125 + 600) \times 10^{-3}}$$

$$= \frac{150 \times 0.85}{150 \times 0.85 + 2.553} = 0.98036 = 98.036\%$$

2.26 A transformer has a maximum efficiency of 98% at $(3/4)^{th}$ of its full load at unity p.f. The iron losses equal 314 watts. Compute the efficiency of the transformer at 50% and 100% rated full load at the same power factor.

[10 marks : 2015]

Solution:

Let, output power at full load $= (P)_{fl}$

Cu losses at full load $= (P_{Cu})_{fl}$

at $3/4^{th}$ of full load maximum efficiency

so, $$\left(\frac{3}{4}\right)^2 \times (P_{Cu})_{fl} = P_i = 314 \text{ watt}$$

$$\Rightarrow \quad (P_{Cu})_{fl} = \frac{314 \times 16}{9} = 558.22 \text{ watt}$$

and $$0.98 = \frac{(P)_{fl} \times \frac{3}{4}}{(P)_{fl} \times \frac{3}{4} + 2 \times 314}$$

$$\Rightarrow \quad (P)_{fl} \times \frac{3}{4} \times 0.98 + 2 \times 314 \times 0.98 = (P)_{fl} \times \frac{3}{4}$$

$$\Rightarrow \quad (P)_{fl} \times \frac{3}{4}(1 - 0.98) = 2 \times 314 \times 0.98$$

$$\Rightarrow \quad (P)_{fl} = \frac{2 \times 314 \times 0.98 \times 4}{3 \times 0.02} = 41029.33 \text{ watt}$$

at 50% of rated full load, $$\eta = \frac{41029.33 \times \frac{1}{2}}{41029.33 \times \frac{1}{2} + 558.22 \times \frac{1}{4} + 314} \times 100 = 97.83\%$$

at 100% of rated full load, $$\eta = \frac{41029.33}{41029.33 + 558.22 + 314} \times 100 = 97.918\%$$

2.27 A single-phase, 25 kVA, 2300/230 V, 50 Hz distribution transformer has the following characteristics:

Core loss at full voltage = 250 W

Copper loss at half load = 300 W

(*i*) Determine the efficiency of the transformer when it delivers rated load current at 0.866 power factor lagging.

(*ii*) The transformer has the following (24-h) load cycle:

$\frac{1}{4}$ full load for 4 hours at 0.8 power factor

$\frac{1}{2}$ full load for 10 hours at 0.8 power factor

$\frac{3}{4}$ full load for 6 hours at 0.8 power factor

Full load for 4 hours at 0.9 power factor

Find the all-day efficiency.

[10 marks : 2016]

Solution:

(*i*) η at rated load, $\eta_{rated} = \dfrac{(VA)_{rated} \times pf}{(VA)_{rated}(pf) + losses}$

$$\text{Cu loss at half load} = 300 \text{ W}$$

$$\therefore \quad \text{Cu loss at F.L.} = 1200 \text{ W}$$

$$\eta = \frac{25000 \times 0.866}{25000 \times 0.866 + 250 + 1200}$$

$$= 0.9372 \text{ or } 93.72\%$$

(*ii*) Output for 24 hours in kWH

1/4 F.L at 0.8 P.F for 4 hrs.

$$\Rightarrow \quad \frac{1}{4}(25)(0.8) \times 4 = 20 \text{ kWH}$$

1/2 F.L at 0.8 P.f for 10 hrs

$$\Rightarrow \quad \frac{1}{2}(25)(0.8) \times 10 = 100 \text{ kWH}$$

3/4 F.L for 6 hrs at 0.8 PF

$$\Rightarrow \quad \frac{3}{4}(25)\,(0.8) \times 6 = 90 \text{ kWH}$$

Full load for 4 hrs at 0.9 kWH

$$\Rightarrow \quad (25)\,(0.9) \times 4 = 90 \text{ kWH}$$

$$\text{Total output for 24 hours} = 300 \text{ kWH}$$

$$\text{Iron loss for 24 hrs} = 250 \times 24 = 6 \text{ kWH}$$

$$\Rightarrow \quad \text{Cu loss at 1/4 F.L} = \left(\frac{1}{4}\right)^2 (1200) = 75 \text{ W}$$

For 4 hrs → 75 × 4 = 300 WH

$$\Rightarrow \quad \text{Cu loss at 1/2 F.L} = \left(\frac{1}{2}\right)^2 (1200) = 300 \text{ W}$$

For 10 hrs → 300 × 10 = 3000 WH

$$\Rightarrow \quad \text{Cu loss at 3/4 F.L} = \left(\frac{3}{4}\right)^2 (1200) = 675$$

For 6 hours → 675 × 6 = 4050 WH

$$\Rightarrow \quad \text{Cu loss at F.L} = 1200 \text{ W}$$

For 4 hours → 4800 WH

Total Cu loss for 24 hours = 12.150

$$\text{All day } \eta = \frac{\text{Output in kWH}}{\text{Out in kWH + core loss for 24 hrs + } Cu \text{ loss for 24 hrs}}$$

$$= \frac{300 \text{ kWH}}{300 \text{ kWH} + 6 \text{ kWH} + 12.15 \text{ kWH}}$$

$$\eta = \frac{300}{318.15} = 0.9429 = 94.29\%$$

2.28 A single-phase transformer has primary and secondary windings on each limb of the core. The cross-section of the magnetic core is 12 cm^2 and the length of the magnetic path is 50 cm. The core has a relative permeability of 20000. The primary and secondary windings have 500 and 1000 turns, respectively:

(i) If the primary winding is supplied with a current of 10 A, while the secondary winding is open-circuited, calculate the self-inductance L_{11} of the primary winding and the mutual inductance L_{12} between the two coils.

(ii) If the primary winding is de-energized, while the secondary winding is connected to a source from which it draws 8 A, calculate the self-inductance L_{22} of the secondary winding and the mutual inductance L_{21} between the two coils.

[4 marks : 2016]

Solution:

Reluctance of core 'S' $= \lambda/\mu_0 \mu_r A$

$$S = \frac{50 \times 10^{-2}}{12 \times 10^{-4} \times 4\pi \times 10^{-7} \times 20000} = 16587$$

(i) When primary is having 10 A, secondary open

$$\phi_1 = \frac{MMF \text{ of primary}}{S}$$

$$\phi_1 = \frac{N_1 I_1}{S} = \frac{500 \times 10}{16587} = 0.301 \text{ Wb}$$

$$L_{11} = \frac{N_1 \phi_1}{I_1} = \frac{500 \times 0.3}{10} = 15 \text{ H}$$

$$L_{12} = \frac{N_2 \phi_1}{I_1} = \frac{1000 \times 0.3}{10} = 30 \text{ H}$$

(ii) When secondary having 8 A, primary open,

$$\phi_2 = \frac{\text{MMF of secondary}}{S} = \frac{N_2 I_2}{S} = \frac{1000 \times 8}{16587} = 0.48 \text{ Wb}$$

$$L_{22} = \frac{N_2 \phi_2}{I_2} = \frac{1000 \times 0.48}{8} = 60.28 \text{ H}$$

$$L_{21} = \frac{N_1 \phi_2}{I_2} = \frac{500 \times 0.48}{8} = 30 \text{ H}$$

2.29 A single-phase transformer, having 1000 and 800 number of turns (weighing 80 kg of copper) in primary and secondary windings, is wound over hot-rolled steel core ($\mu_r = 6000$) of uniform cross-sectional area of 80 cm^2 weighing 100 kg. What will be the maximum primary voltage at 50 Hz that can be applied to primary winding which does not force the flux in core to exceed 1.2 T? What is the corresponding exciting current? If the core of this transformer is replaced by CRGO with maximum flux density, capability of 1.6 T, find the saving in core and wire material assuming volume density of both core materials to be approximately same and they have same core flux. Assume mean magnetic path length of 160 cm and $\mu_0 = 4\pi \times 10^{-7}$.

[20 marks : 2017]

Solution:

Given data: Turns ratio = 1000 T/800 T

Weight of copper = 80 kg

HRGO steel core, $\mu_r = 6000$

Area of core = 80 cm^2

Weight of core = 100 kg

$$B_{max} = 1.2\text{ T}$$

$$\text{Maximum voltage} = V_1 = \sqrt{2}\pi f B_{max} A_C N$$

$$= \sqrt{2}\times\pi\times 50\times 1.2\times 80\times 10^{-4}\times 1000$$

$$V_1 = 2132.58\text{ V}$$

$$\text{Reluctance of core} = R_C = \frac{1}{\mu_0\mu_r}\frac{l_c}{A_C}$$

$$= \frac{1}{4\pi\times 10^{-7}\times 6000}\times\frac{160\times 10^{-2}}{80\times 10^{-4}} = 26.525\times 10^3\text{ AT/Wb}$$

$$\text{No load current} = I = \frac{R\phi}{N} = \frac{R\times B\times A_C}{N}$$

$$= \frac{26.525\times 10^3\times 1.2\times 80\times 10^{-4}}{1000} = 0.2546\text{ A}$$

$$\text{Percentage saving in core} = \frac{\frac{1}{B_1}-\frac{1}{B_2}}{\frac{1}{B_1}}\times 100$$

Since, $\phi = BA_C = \text{constant}$

$$A_C \propto \frac{1}{B}$$

$$B_1 = 1.2\,T \text{ and } B_2 = 1.6\,T$$

$$= \frac{\frac{1}{1.2}-\frac{1}{1.6}}{\frac{1}{1.2}}\times 100 = 25\%$$

$$\text{Saving in core in kg} = 0.25\times 100 = 25\text{ kg}$$

$$\text{Percentage saving in Copper} = \frac{\sqrt{\frac{1}{B_1}}-\sqrt{\frac{1}{B_2}}}{\sqrt{\frac{1}{B_1}}}\times 100$$

Since, Circumference of core = Length of copper per turn

$$A_C = \text{side}^2$$

$$\text{side} = \sqrt{A_C}$$

$$A_C \propto \frac{1}{B}$$

$$\text{side} = \sqrt{\frac{1}{B}}$$

$$\%\text{ saving in Copper} = \frac{\sqrt{\frac{1}{1.2}}-\sqrt{\frac{1}{1.6}}}{\sqrt{\frac{1}{1.2}}}\times 100 = 13.39\%$$

$$\text{Saving of Copper in kg} = 0.1339\times 80 = 10.712\text{ kg}$$

2.30 An 11000/440 V, 50 Hz, 800 kVA transformer draws 7.5 kW when excited at normal voltage and frequency with secondary circuit open. At reduced voltage with full-load current, the transformer requires 1.42 kW input, when the secondary is short-circuited. Calculate the all-day efficiency, if the duty cycle of the transformer is as follows:

500 kW	0.8 p.f.	6 hours
700 kW	0.9 p.f.	4 hours
300 kW	0.95 p.f.	3 hours
No load	–	11 hours

[12 marks : 2017]

Solution:

Given that:

Full load output = 800 kVA

Iron loss, $P_i = 7.5$ kW

Full load copper loss, $P_{cu} = 1.42$ kW

For 6 hours:

Output kWh = 500 × 6 = 3000 kWh

Copper loss, $$P_{cu1} = 1.42\times\left(\frac{500/0.8}{800}\right)^2\times 6 = 5.20\text{ kWh}$$

For 4 hours:

Output kWh = 700 × 4 = 2800 kWh

Copper loss, $$P_{cu2} = 1.42\times\left(\frac{700/0.9}{800}\right)^2\times 4 = 5.369\text{ kWh}$$

For 3 hours:

Output kWh = 300 × 3 = 900 kWh

Copper loss, $$P_{cu3} = 1.42\times\left(\frac{300/0.95}{800}\right)^2\times 3 = 0.6638\text{ kWh}$$

All day output power = 3000 + 2800 + 900 = 6700 kWh

Iron loss for 24 hours = 7.5 × 24 = 180 kWh

Copper loss for 24 hours = $P_{cu1} + P_{cu2} + P_{cu3}$

= 5.20 + 5.369 + 0.6638 = 11.233 kWhr

All-day input = All day output + Iron loss + Copper loss

All-day efficiency, $$\eta = \frac{\text{All day output}}{\text{All day input}}\times 100 = \frac{6700}{6700+180+11.233}\times 100 = 97.225\%$$

2.31 Why is the waveshape of magnetizing current of a transformer non-linear? Explain the phenomenon of in-rush magnetizing current and derive its expression in terms of α, the angle of the voltage sinusoid at $t = 0$ and ϕ_r, the residual core flux at $t = 0$.

Use the graph sheet to show non-linearity of current from the assumed ϕ-i diagram of magnetic core of the transformer.

[20 marks : 2018]

Solution:

For linear magnetisation curve, the flux is proportional to magnetizing current and their waveforms are identical. In practise, the magnetic saturation and by hysteresis do occur and the waveforms of the flux and magnetizing current are different from each other.

Waveforms of magnetising current with hysteresis and magnetic flux:

When the flux is zero and rising as indicated by point o' the current is $o_a = o'b$. Therefore, point b lies on the exciting current waveform. When the flux is increasing and has attained a value as depicted by cd, the exciting current is equal to $of = cg$. For decreasing flux, as given by $c'd'$, the exciting current is $oj = c'g'$. In this manner, a sufficient number of points for the exciting current are obtained and a curve passing through them, gives the required waveform of the exciting current. Note that when the flux is increasing with time, use that portion of the hysteresis loop where the flux is also increasing. Same is true for decreasing value of flux.

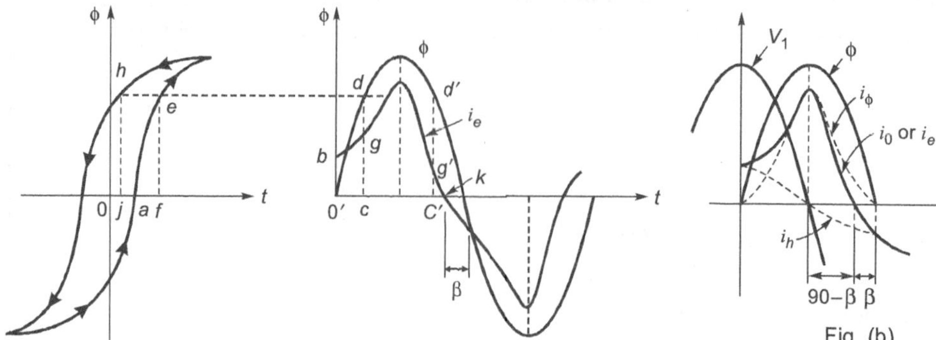

Fig. (a)

Fig. (b)

When the secondary side is open, the transformer takes only exciting (or no-load) current from the supply mains. Since the magnetizing component of current, 90° lagging the applied voltage V_1, is much larger than the core-loss component of current, the transformer at no load behaves almost like component of current, the transformer at no load behaves almost like a simple inductive reactor. As a result of it, the primary induced emf is equal and opposite to the applied voltage if small leakage impedance drop at no load is neglected. The waveforms of the applied voltage v_1 and the core flux ϕ, under steady-state conditions, are illustrated in figure (a). Note that at instant 1, v_1 is zero and ϕ is negative maximum and at instant 2, v_1 is positive maximum but flux ϕ is zero. For qualitative examination of inrush phenomena, constant flux-linkage theorem must be recalled. According to this theorem, the magnetic flux in an inductive circuit can't change suddenly, i.e. the flux just after closing the switch (i.e. at $t = 0^+$) must remain equal to the flux just before closing the switch (i.e. at $t = 0^-$).

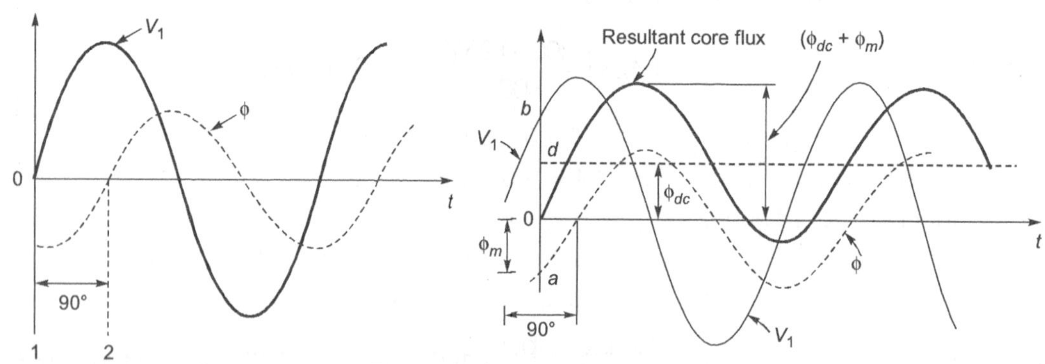

Fig. (a)

Fig. (b)

Consider an instant in between the two instants 1 and 2 as shown in figure. Here switching voltage *ob* demands a steady-state flux *oa*. But the flux just before closing the switch, i.e. at $t = 0^-$, is zero because v_1 is zero and it must remain zero at $t = 0+$ as per constant flux-linkage theorem. Therefore, when the transformer is energised at the instant shown in Fig. (b), a flux $\phi_{dc} = od = oa$ must be established in the transformer core so that resultant flux in the core at $t = 0^+$ remains zero. This flux ϕ_{dc} is called constant or *dc* flux and it remains constant in magnitude if primary-winding resistance r_1 is neglected. The *dc* flux adds to the steady-state alternating flux ϕ and the resultant core-flux wave becomes as shown by the thick curve in Fig. (b). Note that maximum value of the core flux is $\phi_{dc} + f_m$. Now consider instant 2, where the applied voltage v_1 is maximum positive and flux ϕ is zero. Here flux at both $t = 0 -$ and $t = 0 +$ is zero, therefore, $\phi_{dc} = 0$ and no transients take place. Core flux builds up as shown by curve ϕ in figure (a). This shows that when a transformer is switched on at the instant its applied voltage is at peak value, then core flux ϕ attains its steady-state value immediately after the primary is energised and therefore no transients appear.

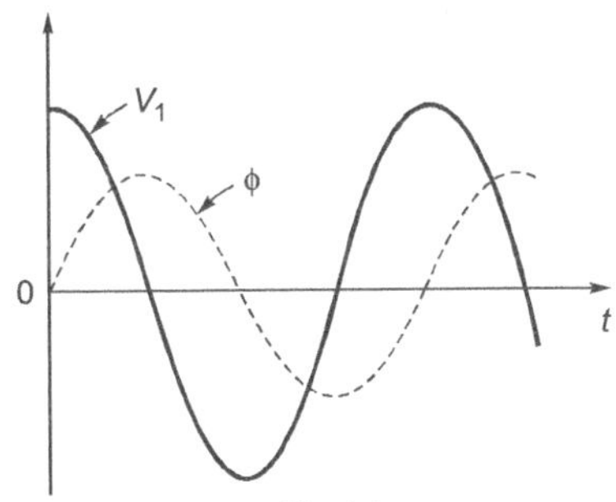

Fig. (a)

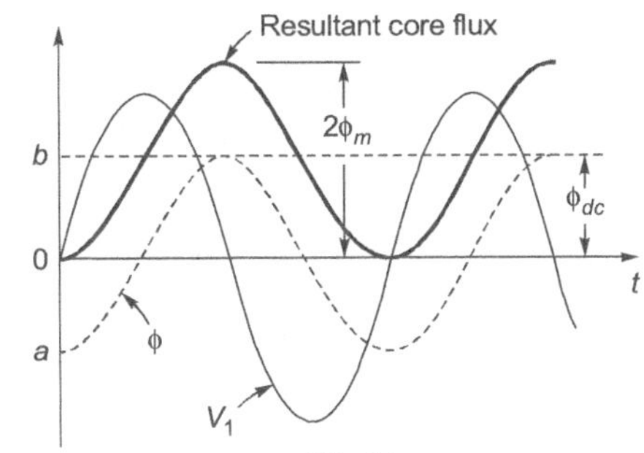

Fig. (b)

Now suppose there is residual magnetism $\phi_r = ob$ present in the transformer core. If the primary is switched on at the instant voltage is passing through zero and becoming positive as shown in figure, then flux at $t = 0^+$ must remain equal to ϕ_r (flux at $t = 0-$). This can happen only if there is established a constant flux $bc = \phi_{dc} = oa = \phi_m$. If primary resistance r_1 is neglected as before, then ϕ_r and ϕ_{dc} add to the steady-state alternating flux ϕ and the resultant core flux follows the thick curve as shown in figure. If time of closing the switch is considered at $t = 0$, then resultant core flux is given by $\phi_r + \phi_{dc} - \phi_m \cos \omega t = \phi_r + \phi_m(1 - \cos \omega t)$. After half a cycle from the instant of closing the switch, the core flux becomes equal to $\phi_r + 2\phi_m$ as shown. Actually, on account of the primary winding resistance r_1, both ϕ_{dc} and ϕ_r decay to zero with time and the core flux becomes a sine wave.

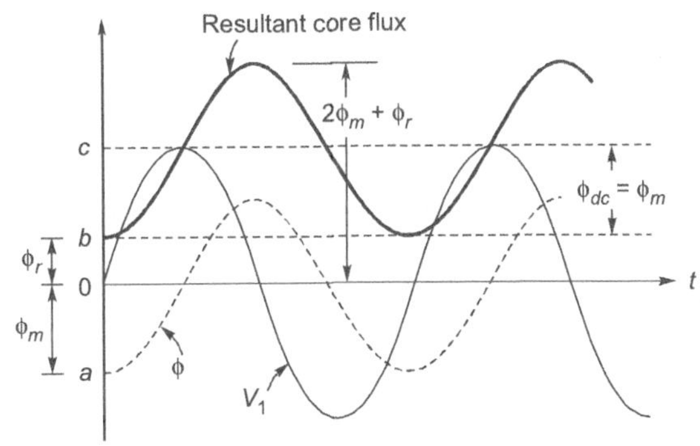

When voltage is switched on to the primary of an unloaded transformer, the e.m.f. equation for the primary circuit, as per Kirchhoff's voltage law, is given by

$$v_1 = V_{m1} \sin(\omega t + \theta_0)$$

$$= i_\phi r_1 + N_1 \frac{d\phi_t}{dt} \quad \text{...(i)}$$

Where, v_1 = primary applied voltage at the instant of closing the switch,

ϕ_t = core flux at any time t,

i_ϕ = magnetizing current (core-less component, being small, is neglected)

N_1 = primary turns,

V_{m1} = maximum value of the applied voltage wave,

and θ_0 = the angle which the voltage wave makes with the time origin as shown in figure

Assuming that the core flux ϕ_t links all the primary turns, then primary winding inductance L_1 is given by,

$$L_1 = \frac{N_1 \cdot \phi_t}{i_\phi}$$

The value of L_1 is not constant because of saturation in the transformer magnetization (B-H) curve, but here a linear relation between ϕ_t and i_ϕ is assumed.

$$\therefore \quad i_\phi = \frac{N_1 \cdot \phi_t}{L_1}$$

Substitution of this value of v_ϕ in equation (i) gives,

$$\frac{N_1 \cdot \phi_t}{L_1} r_1 + N \cdot \frac{d\phi_t}{dt} = V_{m1} \sin(\omega t + \theta_0)$$

or,
$$\left(\frac{r_1}{L_1} + P\right)\phi_t = \frac{V_{m1}}{N_1} \sin(\omega t + \theta_0) \quad \text{...(ii)}$$

Now solution of equation (ii) is given by,

$$\phi_t = \text{C.F.} + \text{P.I.}$$

C.F. The complementary function gives the transient part of the solution and is obtained from

$$\left(\frac{r_1}{L_1} + p\right)\phi_t = 0$$

From this,
$$P = -\frac{r_1}{L_1}$$

$\therefore$
$$\text{C.F.} = Ce^{-\frac{r_1}{L_1}t}$$

where C is a constant.

P.I. The particular integral gives the steady-state solution and is obtained by putting $p = j\omega$ in equation (ii),

$\therefore$
$$\text{P.I.} = \frac{V_{m1}}{N_1\sqrt{\left(\frac{r_1}{L_1}\right)^2 + \omega^2}} \sin\left(\omega t + \theta_0 - \tan^{-1}\frac{\omega L_1}{r_1}\right)$$

If $r_1 = 0$, then
$$\text{P.I.} = \frac{V_{m1}}{L_1\omega} \sin(\omega t + \theta_0 - \tan^{-1}\infty) = \phi_m \sin\left(\omega t + \theta_0 - \frac{\pi}{2}\right) = -\phi_m \cos(\omega t + \theta_0)$$

Therefore, the value of ϕ_t is given by,

$$\phi_1 = \text{C.F.} + \text{P.I.}$$

$$= Ce^{-\frac{r_1}{L_1}t} - \phi_m \cos(\omega t - \theta_0)$$

The value of constant C can be determined from the initial conditions. Now value of flux ϕ_t, at the instant of closing the switch, may be $\pm\phi_r$, where ϕ_r is the residual core flux.

$\therefore$ At time $t = 0$,
$$\phi_t = \pm\phi_r$$

and
$$\pm\phi_r = C - \phi_m \cos\theta_0$$

or,
$$C = \pm\phi_r + \phi_m \cos\theta_0$$

$\therefore$
$$\phi_t = (\phi_m \cos\phi_0 \pm \phi_r)e^{-\frac{r_1}{L_1}t_1} - \phi_m \cos(\omega t - \theta_0)$$

2.32 **The primary side of an ideal transformer (having 400 turns) in primary winding and 720 turns in secondary winding) is excited by a 1000 V, 50 Hz AC source. The secondary of the transformer is connected to a resistive load of 80 kW. There is one tapping in secondary winding at 480 turns and this tapping is supplying a pure inductive load of 100 kVA. Determine the primary current and its power factor.**

[12 marks : 2018]

Solution:

Given,
$$\vec{S}_2 = 80\angle 0° \text{ KVA}$$

$$\vec{S}_3 = 100\angle 90° \text{ KVA}$$

$$\vec{V}_1 = 1000 \text{ V}$$

Now applying the concept of complex power balance,

$$\vec{S}_1 = \vec{S}_2 + \vec{S}_3$$

$$\vec{S}_1 = (80 + j100) \text{ KVA}$$

$$\Rightarrow \quad \vec{V}_1 \vec{I}_1^* = (80\angle 0° + 100\angle 90°) \text{ KVA}$$

$$\vec{I}_1^* = \frac{(80 + j100) \times 10^3}{1000}$$

$$\vec{I}_1^* = 128.0625\angle 51.34° \text{ A}$$

$$\Rightarrow \quad \vec{I}_1 = 128.0625\angle -51.34° \text{ A}$$

$$\text{Primary power factor} = \cos(51.34°) \text{ lag} = 0.6247 \text{ lag}$$

2.33 A 1000 VA, 440/220 V single-phase two-winding transformer is connected as autotransformer to supply a load at 440 V from a supply voltage of 660 V ac mains. Draw the schematic diagram of the autotransformer with proper labelling. If the full load unity power factor (pf) efficiency of the two-winding transformer is 96.2%, what will be the full load efficiency of the autotransformer at 0.85 pf lagging? Also find the maximum primary and secondary currents of the autotransformer.

[20 marks : 2019]

Solution:

Given, 1000 VA, 440/220

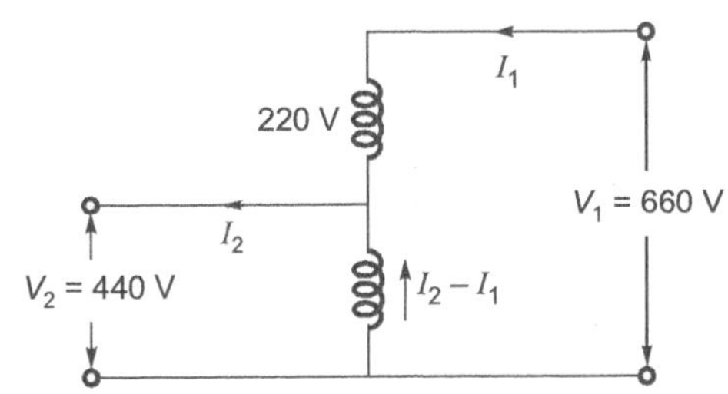

$$I_1 = \frac{1000}{220} = 4.545 \text{ A}$$

$$\Rightarrow \quad I_1 = 4.545 \text{ A}$$

$$\frac{-I_1 + I_2}{I_1} = \frac{V_1 - V_2}{V_1} = \frac{220}{440}$$

$$\Rightarrow \quad \frac{I_2}{I_1} - 1 = \frac{1}{2} \Rightarrow \frac{I_2}{I_1} = 1 + \frac{1}{2}$$

$$\Rightarrow \quad I_2 = \frac{3}{2} I_1$$

$$\Rightarrow \quad I_2 = \frac{3}{2} \times 4.545 = 6.8175 \text{ A}$$

As two winding transformer,

$$\eta_{TW} = \frac{1000}{1000 + P_L} = 0.962$$

$$\Rightarrow \quad P_L = \frac{1000}{0.962} - 1000 = 39.50 \text{ W}$$

$$\text{Auto transformer rating} = 3000 \text{ VA}$$

$$\eta_{auto} = \frac{3000 \times 0.85}{3000 \times 0.85 + 39.5} = 0.9847 \text{ or } 98.47\%$$

2.34 An unbalanced 2-ϕ, 1000 V, 50 Hz induction motor has unequal winding impedances, $Z_a = 3 + j2.7$ and $Z_b = 7 + j3\ \Omega$. This motor is supplied by Scott-connected transformer combination from a 3-ϕ, 11 kV system. Calculate phase currents I_a and I_b of the motor and line currents on 3-phase supply side.

[20 marks : 2019]

Solution:

$$\frac{N_1}{N_2} = \frac{11\times 1000}{1000} = 11$$

$$\therefore \quad \frac{\sqrt{3}}{2}\frac{N_1}{N_2} = \frac{11\sqrt{3}}{2} = 9.526$$

Motor currents are:

$$I_a = \frac{1000}{3+j2.7} \text{ and } I_b = \frac{1000}{7+j3}$$

$$I_a = 247.76\angle{-41.98°} \text{ A}$$

$$I_b = 131.31\angle{-23.198°} \text{ A}$$

Now currents on 3-phase side:

$$I_A = \frac{2}{\sqrt{3}}\left(\frac{N_2}{N_1}\right)\vec{I}_a = \frac{2}{\sqrt{3}}\times\frac{1}{11}\times 247.76\angle -41.98° \text{ A}$$

$$I_A = 26.008\angle{-41.98°} \text{ A}$$

$$\vec{I}_{BC} = \frac{N_2}{N_1}\vec{I}_b$$

$$\vec{I}_{BC} = \frac{131.31}{11}\angle -23.198°$$

$$= 11.937\angle{-23.198°} \text{ A}$$

$$\vec{I}_B = \vec{I}_{BC} - \frac{\vec{I}_A}{2}$$

$$\vec{I}_C = -\vec{I}_{BC} - \frac{\vec{I}_A}{2}$$

$$\Rightarrow \quad \vec{I}_B = 11.937\angle -23.198° - \frac{26.008}{2}\angle -41.98°$$

$$= 4.203\angle 71.91° \text{ A}$$

$$\vec{I}_C = -\vec{I}_{BC} - \frac{\vec{I}_A}{2} = 24.607\angle 147.005° \text{ A}$$

2.35 For a Scott connected transformer, prove that the number of turns on primary of the teaser transformer is $\frac{\sqrt{3}}{2}$ times the number of turns in primary of main transformer.

[12 marks : 2020]

Solution:

Scott connection is most common method of connecting two single phase transformer to perform a 3-ϕ to 2-ϕ conversion and vice-versa. Two transformers are connected electrically but not magnetically, one transformer is main transformer and other is known as teaser transformer.

Scott connection of transformers:

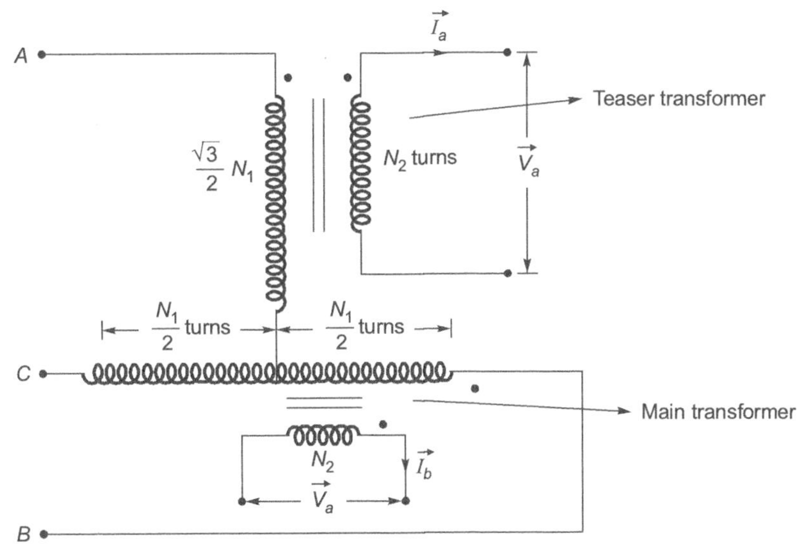

Frequently identical interchangeable transformers are used for the Scott connection, in which each transformer has primary winding of N_1 turns and is provided with tapping at 0.289 N_1, 0.5 N_1, 0.866 N_1.

Phasor diagram: The line voltages of the 3-ϕ system V_{AB}, V_{BC} and V_{CA}, which are balanced the same voltages are shown as a closed equilateral triangle in figure below.

$$|V_{AB}| = |V_{BC}| = |V_{CA}| = V_L \text{ (say)}$$

Let V_{BC} be taken as reference.

$$V_{BC} = V_L \angle 0°$$
$$V_{CA} = V_L \angle -120°$$
$$V_{AB} = V_L \angle +120°$$

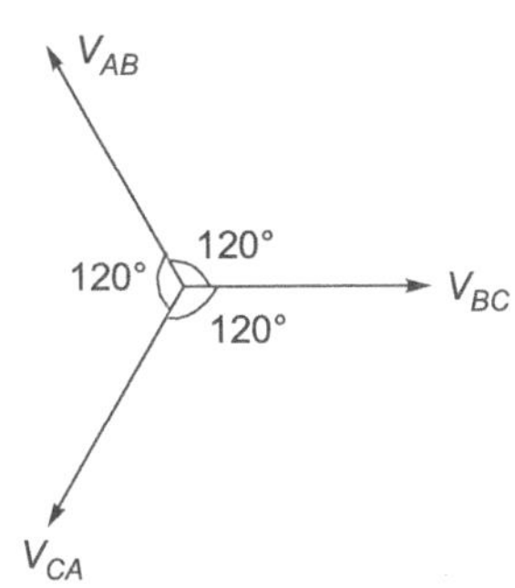

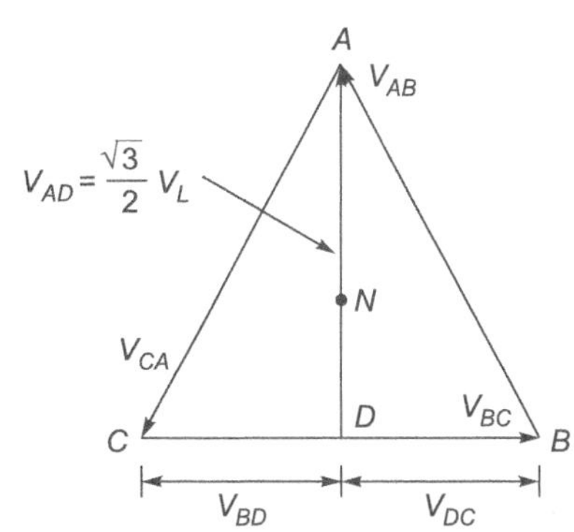

Voltages on transformer primary winding.

⇒ Since, D divides the primary BC of main transformer in two equal halves.

Number of turns in portion BD = Number of turns in portion DC = $\frac{N_1}{2}$.

Voltages V_{BD} and V_{DC} are equal. They are in phase with V_{BC},

$$V_{BC} = V_{DC} = \frac{1}{2} V_{BC}$$

$$= \frac{1}{2} V_L \angle 0° \text{ volts}$$

The voltage between A and D is,

$$V_{AD} = V_{AB} + V_{BD}$$

$$= V_L \angle 120° + \frac{V_L}{2}\angle 0°$$

$$V_{AD} = 0.866\ V_L \angle 90°$$

$$= \frac{\sqrt{3}}{2}\angle 90°$$

So teaser transformer has primary voltage rating $\frac{\sqrt{3}}{2}$ of the voltage rating of main transformer.

For the same flux in each transformer, voltage per turn should be the same. In order to keep voltage per turn same in primary of the main transformer and primary of teaser transformer, the number of turns in primary of the teaser, that is in portion AD should be equal to $\frac{\sqrt{3}}{2}N_1$.

So,
$$\frac{N_{\text{teaser}}}{N_{\text{main}}} = \frac{\sqrt{3}}{2}$$

N = Number of turns

2.36 A transformer of 150 kVA with 1% resistance and 4% leakage reactance is operating in parallel with another 300 kVA transformer having 1% resistance and 6% leakage reactance. The combination is delivering a load of 450 kVA at 400 V and unity power factor. Find the kVA loading on the 150 kVA transformer and the additional reactance to be connected in series with it to provide rated kVA loading on this transformer.

[12 marks : 2021]

Solution:

Given data is :

150 kVA transformer, $R = 1\%$,

$X = 4\%$

$\Rightarrow$ $Z_1 = (0.01 + j0.04)$

300 kVA transformer, $R = 1\%$,

$X = 6\% \Rightarrow Z_1 = (0.01 + j0.06)$

Load 450 kVA@400 V, upf

As R and X values are given in %, adjust them onto common/same base kVA,

Let common base kVA be 450 kVA

$\therefore$ $(Z_1)_{new} = (0.03 + j0.12)$

$(Z_2)_{new} = (0.015 + j0.09)$ Adjusted to common base kVA, 450 kVA

1. Load on 150 kVA transfer function,

$$S_1\angle\phi_1 = 450\angle 0° \times \frac{0.015 + j0.09}{0.03 + j0.12 + 0.015 + j0.09} = 191.17 \text{ kVA}$$

2. Additional reactance (X) required to make S_1 rated kVA i.e., 150 kVA

$$150\angle 0° = 450\angle 0° \times \left[\frac{0.015 + j0.09}{(0.015 + j0.09) + (0.03 + j(0.12 + X))}\right]$$

By solving we get $X = 0.06$ p.u.

$$\text{p.u.} = \frac{\text{Actual}}{\text{Base}} = \text{Actual} = (\text{p.u.}) \times \text{base}$$

$$Z_{base} = \frac{V^2}{V_A} = \frac{400^2}{450 \times 10^3} = 0.3555\ \Omega$$

∴ Additional reactance to be added will be

$$X_{actual} = \frac{0.06}{3} \times 0.3555\,\Omega = 7.07\ \text{m}\Omega$$

2.37 **A 10 KVA, 50 Hz single-phase transformer has a maximum efficiency of 97% at rated frequency and rated voltage while delivering 90% of rated load at 0.8 p.f. lag. The same transformer shows maximum efficiency of 96% at same load when supplied from a 35 Hz source at rated voltage. Find (i) the hysteresis and core losses of the transformer under rated condition and (ii) efficiency of the transformer at rated voltage and rated load at 0.8 pf lag.**
(Assume no stray losses and a Steinmetz constant of 2.0 for the core)

[20 marks : 2021]

Solution:

Given data :

10 KVA, 50 Hz, $\eta_{max} = 0.97$ at rated voltage and frequency

at 90% rated load, 0.8 p.f. lagging

$$\therefore \quad 0.97 = \frac{0.9(10 \times 10^3)(0.8)}{0.9 \times 10 \times 10^3 \times 0.8 + P_{i1} + P_{i1}} \quad \text{...(i)}$$

With same transformer, $\eta_{max} = 0.96$ at same load

If $f = 35$ Hz at rated V

$$0.96 = \frac{0.9(10 \times 10^3)(0.8)}{0.9 \times (10 \times 10^3) \times (0.8) + P_{i2} + P_{i2}} \quad \text{...(ii)}$$

From equation (i) and (ii), we get P_{i1} and P_{i2}

$$P_{i1} = 111.34 \text{ W at rated } V \text{ and } f = 50 \text{ Hz}$$

$$P_{i1} = 144 \text{ W at rated } V \text{ and } f = 35 \text{ Hz}$$

V/f not constant, so B_m not constant

We know,

Eddy current loss, $P_e \propto B_m^2 f^2$, $P_h = B_m^x f$ $\quad (\because \text{Given } x = 2)$

Hysteresis loss, $P_h \propto B_m^2 f$

$$\therefore \quad P_e \propto \frac{V^2}{f^2} \cdot f^2 \qquad \left(\because B_m = \frac{V}{f}\right)$$

$$\Rightarrow \quad P_e \propto V^2$$

$$P_h \propto \frac{V^2}{f^2} \cdot f$$

$\Rightarrow$ For hysteresis loss, $P_h \propto \dfrac{V^2}{f}$

$$P_e = K_1 V^2 \quad \because \text{ Voltage is constant}$$

$$P_h = K_2 \frac{V^2}{f}$$

$$P_e = K_1 \text{ and } P_h = \frac{K_2}{f}$$

$$P_i = P_e + P_h$$

$$P_{i1} = K_1 + \frac{K_2}{f_1}$$

$$\Rightarrow \quad 111.34 = K_1 + \frac{K_2}{50} \quad \text{(from } P_{i1} = 111.34\text{) ...(iii)}$$

$$P_{i2} = K_1 + \frac{K_2}{f_2}$$

$$\Rightarrow \quad 144 = K_1 + \frac{K_2}{35} \quad \text{(from } P_{i2} = 144\text{) ...(iv)}$$

By solving (iii) and (iv),

$$K_1 = 35.133,$$
$$K_2 = 3810.34$$

(i) P_h at rated frequency and voltage

$$\Rightarrow \quad P_h = \frac{K_2}{f_1} = \frac{3810.34}{50}$$

$$\therefore \quad P_h = 76.2 \text{ W}$$

P_i at rated V, f

$$\Rightarrow \quad P_e = K_1 = 35.133 \text{ W}$$

Total core loss,

$$\Rightarrow \quad P_i = P_e + P_h = 111.34 \text{ W}$$

(ii) η at rated load 0.8 p.f. lagg, rated V, f

$$\eta = \frac{1 \times (10 \times 10^3)(0.8)}{1 \times 10 \times 10^3 \times 0.8 + P_i + P_{cu}}$$

Where, P_i : Iron loss at rated $V \forall f$

P_{cu} : Full load Cu loss

From equation (i) conditions :

If fraction of load at max η is 0.9 $\rightarrow (0.9)^2 (P_{cu}) = P_i$

$\therefore$ Full load *Cu* loss $P_{cu} = \frac{P_i}{0.9^2} = \frac{111.34}{0.9^2} = 137.45$ W

$$\eta = \frac{1 \times 10 \times 10^3 \times 0.8}{1 \times 10 \times 10^3 \times 0.8 + 111.34 + 137.457}$$

$$= \frac{8000}{8248.797} = 0.9698 \text{ or } 96.98\%$$

2.38 **The efficiency of a 10 kVA, 110/220 V, 50 Hz, single phase transformer is 96% at three-fourth of full load at 0.8 pf leading and 96.5% at full load upf.**

Determine the :
(i) constant loss "P_i".
(ii) maximum efficiency at upf.

[12 marks : 2022]

Solution:

(i) $S = 10$ kVA, $f = 50$ Hz

Let constant loss = P_i, Copper loss = P_{Cu}

Case I : Efficiency, $\eta = 96\%,\ x = \frac{3}{4}$ of full-load

Power factor = 0.8

$$\text{Efficiency, } \eta = \frac{xS \times Pf}{Pf \times xS + P_i + x^2 P_{Cu}}$$

$$0.96 = \frac{\frac{3}{4} \times 10 \times 0.8}{0.8 \times \frac{3}{4} \times 10 + P_i + \left(\frac{3}{4}\right)^2 \times P_{Cu}}$$

$$P_i + \frac{9}{16} P_{Cu} = 0.25 \qquad \text{...(i)}$$

Case II : Efficiency, $\eta = 96.5\%,\ x = 1$ (full-load)

Power factor = 1

$$0.965 = \frac{1 \times 10 \times 1}{1 \times 1 \times 10 + P_i + 1^2 \times P_{Cu}}$$

$$P_i + P_{Cu} = 0.3626 \qquad \text{...(ii)}$$

Now, solve eqn. (i) and eqn. (ii)

$$P_i = 0.10522 \text{ kW} = 105.22 \text{ W}$$

$$P_{Cu} = 0.25737 \text{ kW} = 257.37 \text{ W}$$

Hence, constant loss, $P_i = 105.22$ W

(ii) For maximum efficiency

Constant loss = Copper loss

$$Pi = x^2 P_{Cu} \qquad (x \rightarrow \%\text{ load at which maximum efficiency occur})$$

$$105.22 = x^2 \times 257.37$$

$$x = \sqrt{\frac{105.22}{257.37}} = 0.6393$$

So, maximum efficiency occur at 63.93% of full-load

Power factor = 1

$$\eta_{max} = \frac{10 \times 0.6393 \times 1}{10 \times 0.6393 \times 1 + 2 \times 0.10522} = 96.813\%$$

2.39 A 25 kVA, 2500 V/250 V two winding transformer is to be used as autotransformer with a source voltage of 2500 V. Find the maximum power that can be supplied by the autotransformer to load at unity power factor. Find the conducted and transformed power under this condition.
Also find the efficiency of the autotransformer at unity power factor and maximum output power condition if the efficiency of the single phase transformer at half load, 0.8 pf lag and rated voltage is 90%. Assume the no load losses for the single phase transformer as 500 W.

[20 marks : 2022]

Solution:

Given : Rated kVA, $S = 25 \text{ kVA}$

Voltage rating, $\frac{V_1}{V_2} = \frac{2500 \text{ V}}{250 \text{ V}}$

Power factor, $\cos\phi = 1$

Current on 250 V side, $I_2 = \frac{S}{V_2 \cos\phi} \text{A}$

$\Rightarrow \quad I_2 = \frac{25000}{250 \times 1} \text{A}$

$\Rightarrow \quad I_2 = 100 \text{ A}$

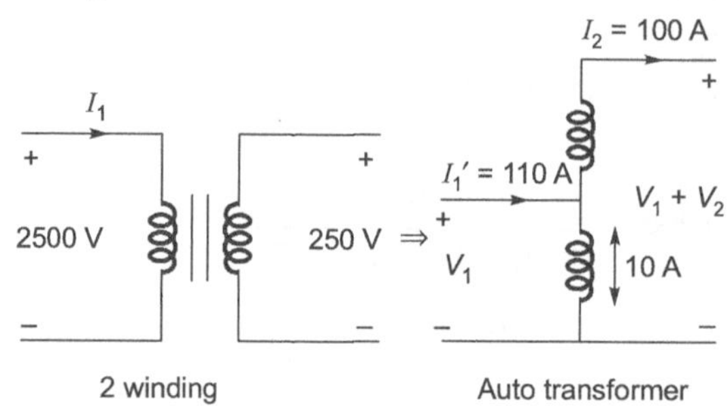

Current on primary side, $I_1 = \frac{S}{V_1 \cos\phi} \Rightarrow I_1 = \frac{25000}{2500} \Rightarrow I_1 = 10 \text{ A}$

Total power supplied at unity power factor,

$$P_T = (2500 + 250) \times 100$$
$$P_T = 2750 \times 100$$
$$P_T = 275 \text{ kW}$$

$$I_1' = \frac{P_T}{V_1} \Rightarrow I_1' = \frac{275000}{2500} \text{A} \Rightarrow I_1' = 110 \text{ A}$$

Induction power transfer, $P_I = 2500 \times 10$

$P_I = 25 \text{ kW at u.p.f.}$

Conductive power transfer, $P_C = P_T - P_I$

$\Rightarrow \quad P_C = 250 \text{ kW at u.p.f.}$

Efficiency of 2 winding transformer at power factor 0.8 lag at half load,

$$\eta = 90\% \Rightarrow 0.9 = \frac{2.5 \times 0.8 \times 1000 \times 0.5}{0.5 \times 25 \times 1000 \times 0.8 + P_L}$$

where, P_L is losses. $P_L = 1111.111 \text{ W}$

$$P_L = \frac{1}{4} P_{Cu} + P_i$$

where P_{Cu} is full load copper loss and P_i is no load loss.

$$P_i = 500 \text{ W (given)}$$

$$\Rightarrow \quad P_{Cu} = 2444.44 \text{ W}$$

The losses in 2 winding transformer and auto-transformer are same.

So, efficiency of auto-transformer,

$$\eta_a = \frac{275000}{275000 + P_{Cu} + P_i} \times 100\%$$

$$\Rightarrow \quad \eta_a = 98.94\%$$

2.40 **The maximum efficiency of a 500 KVA, 3300/500 V, 50 Hz single-phase transformer is 97% and occurs at $\frac{3}{4}$ full load, unity power factor. If the impedance is 10%, find the voltage regulation at full load, power factor 0.8 leading.**

[12 marks : 2023]

Solution:

$\therefore$ We know that,
$$\%\eta = \frac{x \times (\text{kVA})\cos\phi}{(\text{kVA})\cos\phi + P_i + x^2 P_{Cu}}$$

where,
$$x = \text{fraction of full load}$$

$$0.97 = \frac{0.75 \times 500 \times 1}{0.75 \times 500 \times 1 + 2P_i}$$

$$363.75 + 1.94P_i = 375$$

$$\Rightarrow \quad P_i = 5.7989 \simeq 5.8 \text{ kW}$$

According to maximum, $\eta\ x^2 P_{Cu} = P_i$

$$0.75^2(P_{Cu}) = 5.7989$$

$$\therefore \quad P_{Cu} = \frac{5.7989}{0.75^2} = 10.309 \text{ kW}$$

$$\%R = \% \text{ Cu loss}$$

$$\Rightarrow \quad \frac{10.309}{500} \times 100 = 0.0206$$

$$\%R = 2.06\%$$

$$\%Z = 10\%$$

$$\therefore \quad \%X = \sqrt{10^2 - 2.06^2} = 9.7855\%$$

V.R. (FL) 0.8 p.f. lead $\Rightarrow \%R \cos\phi - \% \times \sin\phi$

$$= 2.06 \times 0.8 - 9.7855 \times 0.6$$

$$= 1.648 - 5.87131 = -4.22\%$$

So, required V.R. is –4.22%.

2.41 **Two identical 250 KVA, 230/460 volt transformers are connected in open delta to supply a balanced 3-phase star connected load at 460 volt and at a power factor of 0.8 lagging.**

Answer the following :

(i) Draw the phasor diagram of the open-delta condition.

(ii) Find the maximum secondary line current without overloading the transformers.

(iii) Find the real power delivered by each transformer and the total real power delivered.

(iv) Find the primary line currents.

(v) If a similar transformer is now added to complete the Δ, find the percentage increase in real power that can be supplied. Assume that the load voltage and power factor remain unchanged at 460 volt and 0.8 lagging, respectively.

[20 marks : 2023]

Solution:

Given : Two 250 kVA, 230/460 V, V-V

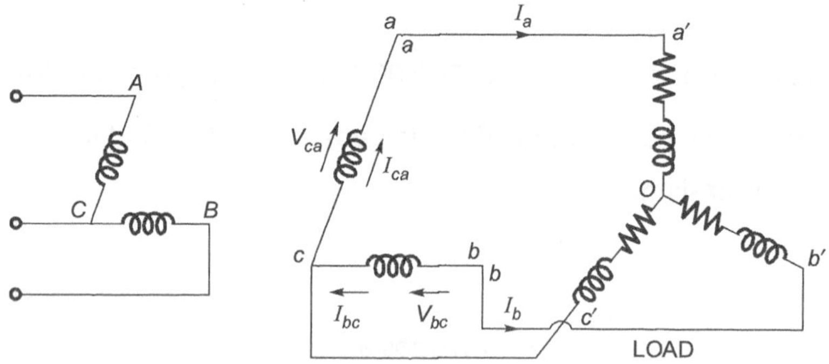

(i) To draw phasor diagram :

Applying KVL at loop : $Caa'oC'C$

KVL at loop : $bCC'ob'b$

$$V_{ca} = V_{a'o} + V_{oc'} = V_{a'o} + (-V_{c'o})$$

$$V_{bc} = V_{c'o} + V_{ob'} = V_{c'o} + (-V_{b'o})$$

KCL at a, $\quad I_{ca} = I_a$

KCL at b, $\quad I_{bc} = -I_b$

Required phasor diagram of open delta condition :

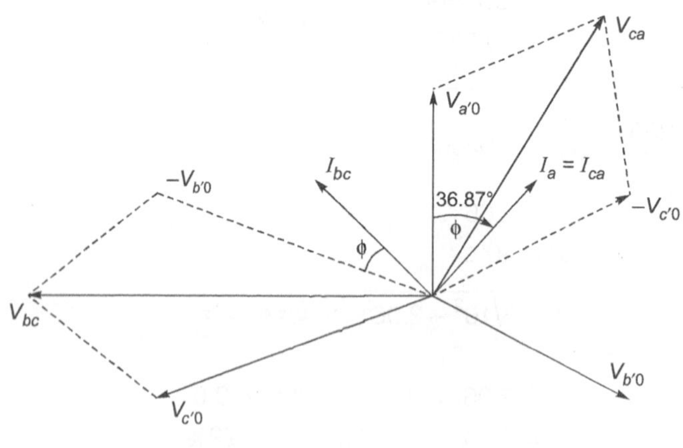

I_{ca} laggs V_{ca} by an angle of 6.87°.

∴ p.f. is cos (6.87) lagg 0.9928 lagg.

I_{bc} laggs V_{bc} by an angle of 66.87°.

∴ P.f. is cos(66.87) lags = 0.3928 lagg.

(ii) V-V Correction Capacity is :

$$2 \times 250 \times 0.866 = 433 \text{ kVA}$$

∴ Load on V-V must be 433 kVA (not to overload)

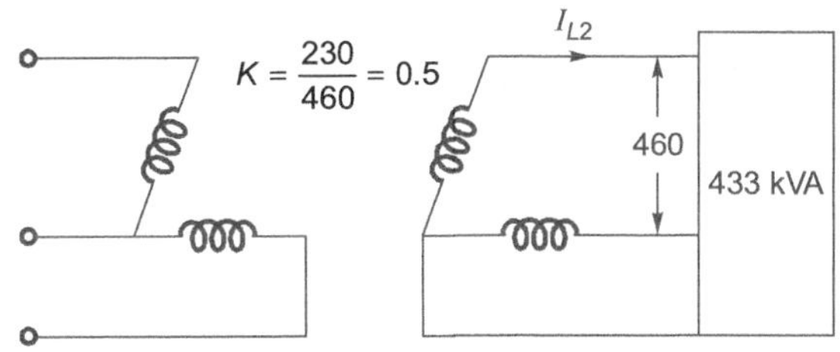

$$\sqrt{3}V_{L2}I_{L2} = 433 \text{ kVA}$$

$$\sqrt{3} \times 460 \times I_{L2} = 433 \times 10^3$$

$$\therefore \quad I_{L2} = 543.478 \text{ A} = I_{ph2}$$

$$I_{ph1} = \frac{I_{ph2}}{K} = 1086.956 \text{ A}$$

$$I_{ph1} = I_{L1} = 1086.956 \text{ A}$$

Maximum sec. line current without overloading is 543.478 A.

(iii) Real power delivered by each T/F

T/F 1 : $460 \times 543.478\angle 6.87°$

$$= 248204.9 + j29904.239$$

T/F 2 : $460 \times 543.478\angle 66.87°$

$$= 98204.623 + j227903.875$$

Total real power supplied is

248204.9 + 98204.523 = 346409.523 W

or 346.409 kW

(iv) Primary line current is done in (ii).

$$I_{L1} = I_{ph1} = 1086.956 \text{ A}$$

(v) If another 250 kVA T/F is added.

Total capacity is 3 × 250 = 750 kVA

Load can be 750 kVA, at 0.8 pf lagg.

Real power is : $\cos\phi = \frac{P}{S}$

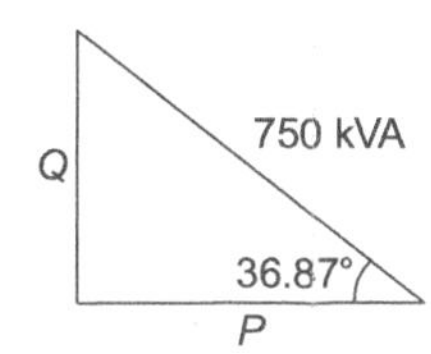

$$0.8 = \frac{P}{750}$$

$$\therefore \quad P = 600 \text{ kW}$$

V-V supplying 346.409 kW.

Δ-Δ supplying 600 kW.

$$\% \text{ Increase} = \frac{600 - 346.409}{346.409} \times 100 = 73.2\%$$

3. Direct Current Machines

3.1 Explain the effect of armature reaction on the main field flux by using the developed view of armature-current sheet and poles of a d.c. machine. Hence, outline the bad effects of armature reaction. Discuss how the resultant flux density waveform obtained above gets modified with the use of interpoles.

[18 marks : 2001]

Solution:

The armature mmf produces two undesirable effects on the main field flux and these are,

(a) net reduction in the main field flux per pole.

(b) distortion of the main field flux wave along the air-gap periphery.

Reduction in the main flux per pole reduces the generated voltage and torque, where as the distortion of the main-field flux influences the limits of successful commutation in d.c. machines.

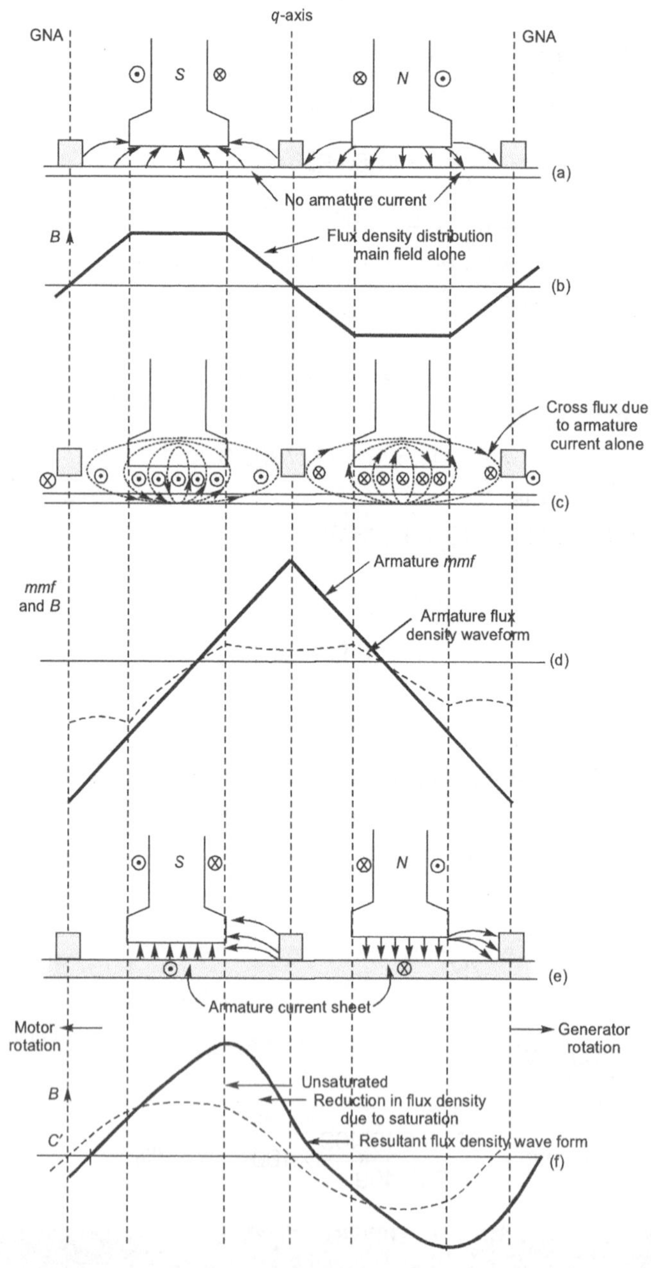

Use of Interpoles to modified flux density waveform: The effect of armature reaction in the interpolar zone can be overcome by interpoles, placed in between the main poles. With interpoles, in the interpolar zone, the armature cross flux is neutralized and in addition some flux is produced three. This additional flux in the interpolar zone induces rotational emf in the commulator coil in such direction as to oppose the reactance voltage. If this rotational emf due to the additional interpolar flux is equal and opposite to the reactance emf, then the resultant emf in the commulator coil would be zero and therefore zero current in the coil which amounts to sparkles commutation. The magnetic axis of interpole winding is in line with the quadrature axis. Interpole winding is connected in series with armature so that interpole mmf is able to neutralize the effect of armature mmf in the interpolar zone at all levels of load current not exceeding the safe limit.

3.2 **Consider the following statements regarding the speed control of d.c. motors:**

1. **Ward-Leonard method is suitable for constant torque drives.**
2. **Ward-Leonard method is suitable for constant power drives.**
3. **Field-control method facilitates speed control below base speed.**
4. **Armature-resistance control method is more efficient than Ward-Leonard method.**
5. **Field control method is suitable for constant-torque drives.**
6. **Armature-resistance control method is suitable for constant torque drive.**

From these, the correct answer is

(a) 1, 2, 6 **(b) 1, 2, 5**
(c) 1, 6, 2 **(d) 1, 2, 4**

[2 marks : 2001]

Solution: (a)

Option (a) is correct.

3.3 **Why does the external characteristic of a d.c. shunt generator turn back as it is overloaded?**

[4 marks : 2001]

Solution:

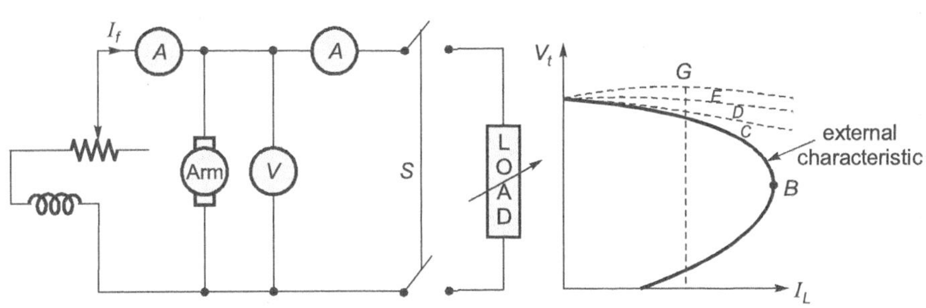

As the load resistance is decreased (load current increased), the terminal voltage drops until point B is reached. If load resistance is further decreased, the load current increases momentarily. This momentary increase in load current, produces more armature reaction thus causing a reduction in the terminal voltage and field current. The net reduction in terminal voltage and field current. The net reduction in terminal voltage is so large that the load current decreases and the external characteristic turn back.

3.4 **A 500 V, 25 HP, DC shunt motor takes a current of 2.4 A while running light loaded. The field and armature resistances are 650 ohms and 0.57 ohm, respectively. Calculate the full-load efficiency, assuming a brush drop of 2 V.**

[10 marks : 2002]

Solution:

Given, 500 V; 25 HP; $r_f = 650\ \Omega$; $r_a = 0.57\ \Omega$

$$I_f = \frac{500}{650} = 0.77 \text{ amp.}$$

At no load, $$I_{a0} = I_{L0} - I_f$$

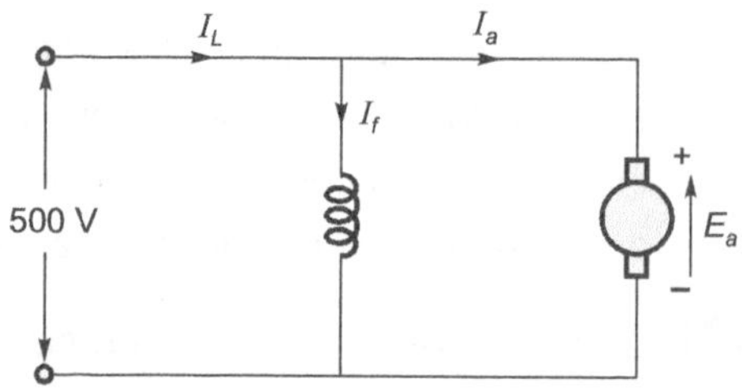

$$= 2.4 - 0.77 = 1.63 \text{ amp.}$$

$$\text{Constant losses} = V_t \cdot I_{L0} - I_{a0}^2 \times r_a - V_b \cdot I_{a0}$$
$$= 500 \times 2.4 - (1.63)^2 \times 0.57 - 2 \times 1.63$$
$$= 1195.23 \text{ Watt}$$

Now at full-load, $E_b I_a = 25 \times 746$ (power output)

$$\text{Power input} = \text{Power output} + \text{total losses}$$
$$500(I_a + 0.77) = 25 \times 746 + V_b I_a + \text{constant losses} + I_a^2(0.57)$$
$$385 + 498\, I_a = 19845.23 + I_a^2\,(0.57)$$

or $$I_a^2 - 873\, I_a + 34140.75 = 0$$

$$\therefore \quad I_a = \frac{873 \pm \sqrt{(873)^2 - 4 \times 34140.75}}{2}$$
$$I_a = 831.96 \text{ A}; 41.04 \text{ A} \quad \text{(discarded)}$$
$$\text{Input} = V_t(I_a + I_f) = 500\,(41.04 + 0.77)$$
$$= 20905 \text{ Watt}$$
$$\text{Efficiency} = \frac{\text{Output}}{\text{Input}} \times 100 = \frac{25 \times 746}{20905} \times 100 = 89.21\%$$

3.5 Why is the starting current high in a DC motor? Explain the working of a four-point starter for a DC machine.

[10 marks : 2002]

Solution:

At the time of starting, the motor speed is zero, therefore, counter emf $E_a (= k_a \phi \omega_m)$ is also zero. Consequently for the armature circuit, the voltage equation is $V_t = 0 + I_a r_a$ for shunt motor and $V_t = 0 + I_a(r_a + r_s)$ for both series and compound motors. With rated applied voltage the starting armature current is, therefore, V_t/r_a for shunt motor and $V_t/(r_a + r_s)$ for both series and compound motors. Since the resistances r_a and $(r_a + r_s)$ are much smaller, the motor draws large starting armature current from the supply mains.

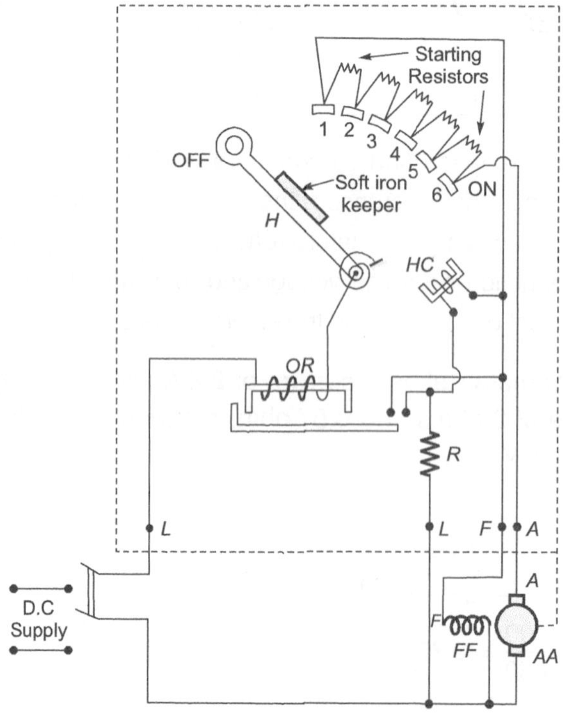

Working for four-point starter: The four-point starter is used when wide range of speed by shunt field control is required.

Under normal running conditions with starter handle in the ON position, the holding coil HC is in series with the starting resistance and an additional resistance *R* as shown in figure.

The function of resistance *R* is to prevent short circuit of the supply mains, in case the overload release OR operates, when HC gets short circuited by OR, the current through R is limited by its own resistance and starting resistance.

When the motor is at rest starter handle H is kept in the off position. The starting resistance is connected between contact studs 1, 2, 3.......6. For starting the motor, the handle is rotated to come in contact with stud 1. As soon as handle *H* touches stud 1, the shunt field and holding coil HC get connected in series across the supply, whereas the armature gets connected in series with the entire starting resistance. Since the current begin to flow in both the field and armature windings, the motor starts rotating. After the armature has picked up sufficient speed, the handle *H* is moved to stud 2, thereby cutting out the resistance between stud 1 and 2. Movement of the handle is continued slowly fill the soft iron keeper touches the holding magnet.

3.6 A series motor of resistance 1.0 Ω between the terminals runs at 1000 rpm of 220 V with a current of 15 A. Find the speed at which it will run when connected in series with a 4.5 ohms resistance and taking a current of 10 A at the same supply voltage. Assume linear magnetization characteristic.

[15 marks : 2003]

Solution:

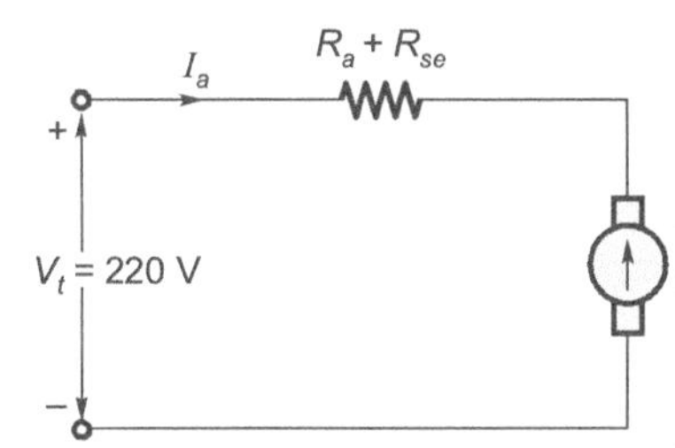

Given, $\phi \propto I_a$

or, $\phi = K_{se} I_a$

$$E = k_n \phi N$$

$$R_a + R_{se} = 1\ \Omega$$

$$N = 1000 \text{ rpm}$$

$$V = 220 \text{ V},$$

$$I = I_{se} = I_a = 15 \text{ A}$$

$$E = V - I(R_a + R_{se}) = 220 - 15 \times 1$$

$$E = 205 \text{ V}$$

$\therefore$ $E = k_n k_{se} I_a N$

$$k_n k_{se} = \frac{E}{I_a N} = \frac{205}{15 \times 1000}$$

$$k_n k_{se} = 13.67 \times 10^{-3} \text{ V/Amp-rpm}$$

Condition, $R_{ext} = 4.5\ \Omega,\ I = 10 \text{ A},\ N = ?$

$$E = V - I(R_a + R_{se} + R_{ext}) = 220 - 10\,[1 + 4.5]$$

$$= 165 \text{ volt}$$

Speed, $$N = \frac{E}{k_n k_{se} I_a} = \frac{165}{13.67 \times 10^{-3} \times 10} = 1207 \text{ rpm}$$

3.7 Discuss briefly the different methods used for electrical braking of dc motors.

[10 marks : 2003]

Solution:

Electrical Braking: There are three kinds of electric braking:

(a) Rheostatic or dynamic braking

(b) Plugging and

(c) Regenerative braking

(a) Rheostatic or Dynamic Braking (Shunt Motor):

Figure (a) shows the rheostatic braking in which armature of the shunt motor is disconnected from the supply and it is connected across a variable resistance R. The field winding is kept undisturbed and this braking is controlled by varying the series resistance R. This method uses the generator action in a motor to bring it to rest.

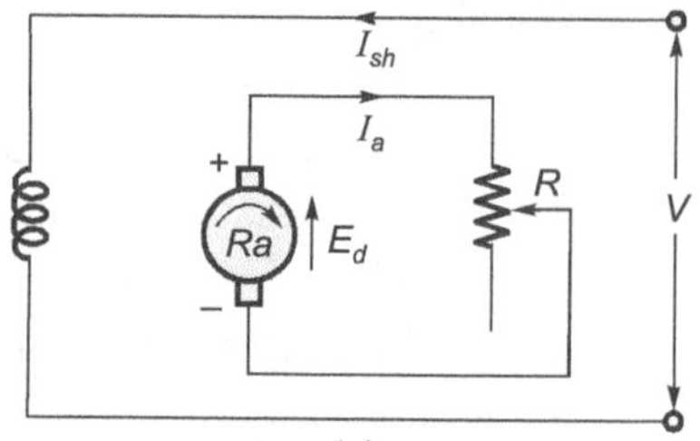

(a)

Rheostatic Braking (Series Motor):

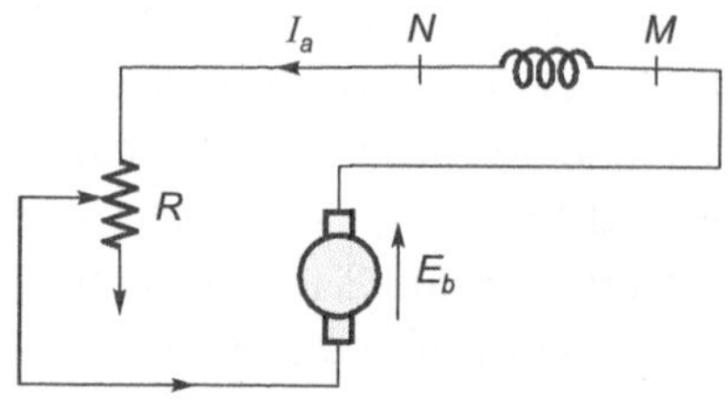

Figure shows the rheostatic braking of DC series motor. In this method the motor is disconnected from supply. The field connection is reversed and the motor is connected through a variable resistance R.

(b) Plugging or Reverse Braking (Shunt Motor):

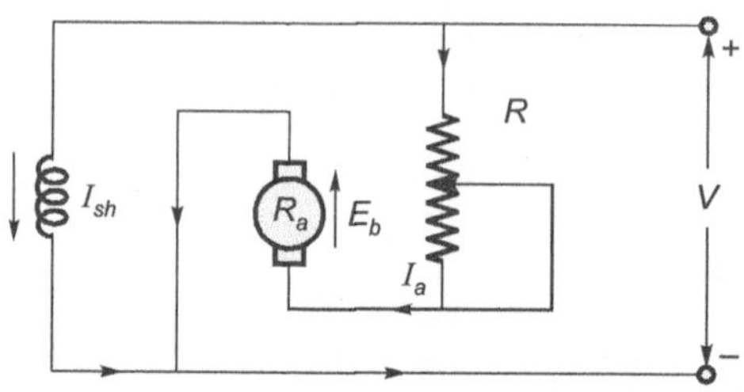

Figure shows plugging or reverse braking. In this method, the armature terminals are reversed to rotate the motor in reverse direction and the applied voltage V and the back emf E_b start acting in the same direction. To limit the armature current, a resistance is inserted in series with the armature during reversing the armature. The kinetic energy of the system is dissipated in the armature and braking resistances.

Plugging or Reverse Current Braking (Series Motor):

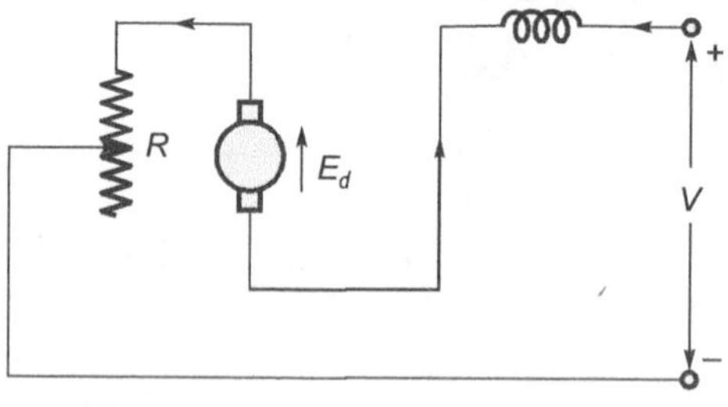

It is similar to that of shunt motor.

(c) Regenerative Braking (Shunt Motor):

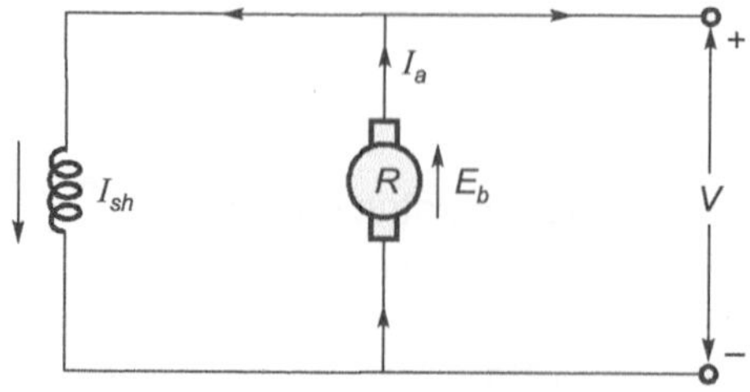

In regenerative braking, E_b is greater than V. Figure shows regenerative braking. The direction of I_a and the armature torque T_B are reversed. Most of the braking energy is returned to the supply. Regenerative braking is used for downgrade motion of an electric train. The kinetic energy of the system is dissipated in the armature and braking resistance.

3.8 **A dc motor develops the max mechanical power when, the armature current is such that**
(a) the back-emf is equal to 3/4th of the applied emf.
(b) the back emf is equal to one half of the applied emf.
(c) The back emf is equal to 1/4th of the applied emf.
(d) the back emf is equal to 2/3 of the applied emf.

[2 marks : 2004]

Solution:

The back emf is equal to one half of the applied emf. Hence, option (b) is correct.

3.9 **Why is DC series motor highly variable speed motor?** [4 marks : 2004]

Solution:

In dc series motor, if saturation and armature reaction are neglected, then main flux ϕ is directly proportional to armature current I_a. Therefore, $\phi = CI_a$ where C is any constant.

$$E_a = k_a \phi \omega_m = V_t - I_a(r_a + r_s)$$

$$\omega_m = \frac{V_t}{k_a\phi} - \frac{I_a(r_a + r_s)}{k_a\phi} = \frac{V_t}{k_a C I_a} - \frac{(r_a + r_s)}{k_a C}$$

From above, since speed depend upon inversely to current so at no load speed of the series motor becomes dangerously high due to small no load current.

So, we can say that d.c. series motor is highly variable speed motor.

3.10 **A series generator of total resistance 0.5 ohm is running at 1000 rpm and delivering 5 kW at a terminal potential difference of 100 V. If the speed is raised to 1500 rpm and the power is adjusted to 8 kW, find the new current and terminal voltage. Assume that the M/C is working on the straight portion of the characteristic such that the flux is proportional to the current and the emf generated is proportional to product of flux and speed.**

[15 marks : 2004]

Solution:

Given: $\phi \propto I$ or $\phi = k_{se} I$ and $E \propto \phi \,.\, w$ or $E = k_n \phi N$

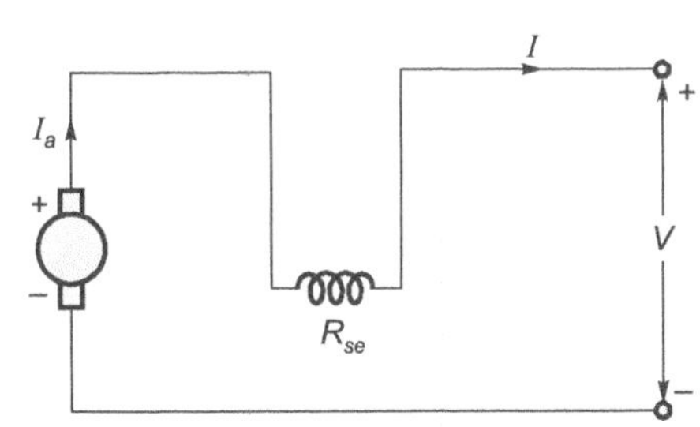

$$I_a = I_{se} = I$$

$$R_a + R_{se} = 0.5\ \Omega$$

$$N = 1000 \text{ rpm},$$

$$P = 5 \text{ kW},$$

$$V = 100 \text{ V}$$

If speed is changed – $N = 1500$ rpm, $P = 8$ kW

Given, $\phi = k_{se} I_a$, $k_{se} \rightarrow$ constant

Power delivered, $P = VI$

$$5 \times 10^3 = 100 \times I$$

$$I = 50 \text{ A}$$

Generated emf, $E = V + I_a(R_a + R_{se})$

$$E = 100 + 50 \times 0.5$$

$$E = 125 \text{ V}$$

$$\because \quad E = \frac{\phi ZN}{60} \times \frac{P}{A} = k_n \phi N = k_n k_{se} IN$$

$$k_n k_{se} = \frac{E}{IN} = \frac{125}{50 \times 1000} = 2.5 \times 10^{-3} \text{ V/A-rpm}$$

Now speed is raised, $N = 1500$ rpm

$$P = 8 \times 10^3 \text{ W}$$

$$E = k_n k_{se} IN = 2.5 \times 10^{-3} \times I \times 1500 = 3.75 I$$

$$P = VI = [E - I(R_a + R_{se})] \cdot I$$

$$8 \times 10^3 = [3.75 I - 0.5 I] \cdot I$$

$$I = 49.6$$

$$E = 3.75 \times 49.6 = 186$$

$$V = E - I(R_a + R_{se}) = 3.75 \times 49.6 - 49.6 \times 0.5 = 161.2 \text{ V}$$

3.11 A shunt wound motor runs at 500 RPM on a 200 V supply. $R_a = 0.5\ \Omega$, the current drawn is 30 A in addition to field current. What resistance must be placed in series with the armature in order that the speed may be reduced to 300 rpm, the current in the armature remaining same? If the load is changed so that the inserted resistance, the armature current reduces to 15 A, what will be the speed?

[10 marks : 2004]

Solution:

$$E = V - I_a R_a = 200 - 30 \times 0.5 = 185 \text{ V}$$

$$k_n \phi = \frac{E}{N} = \frac{185}{500} = 0.37 \text{ V/rpm}$$

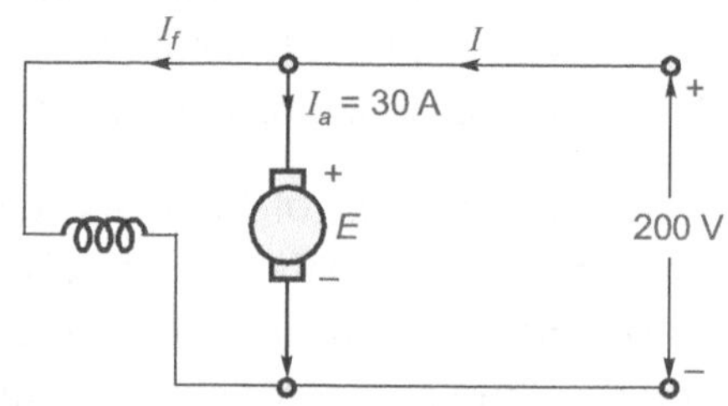

For, $N' = 300$ rpm,

$$R_{ext} = ?$$

$$I_a = 30$$

$$E' = k_n \phi N' = 0.37 \times 300 = 111 \text{ V}$$

$$111 = 200 - 30(0.5 + R_{ext})$$

$$R_{ext} = 2.46\ \Omega$$

$$I_a = 15 \text{ A},$$

$$R_a = 0.5\ \Omega,$$

$$R_{ext} = 2.46\ \Omega$$

$$E = V - I_a(R_a + R_{ext})$$

$$E = 200 - 15(0.5 + 2.46) = 155.5 \text{ V}$$

Speed, $$N = \frac{E}{k_n \phi} = \frac{155.5}{0.37} = 420 \text{ rpm}$$

3.12 A 220 V d.c. compound generator has resistance of the armature, shunt and series windings as 0.1 ohm, 50 ohm and 0.06 ohm respectively. The load current is 100 A at 220 V. Find the induced emf and armature current when the machine is connected as a

(a) long shunt

(b) short shunt

(c) how will the ampere/turn of the series winding will change if in (a) a diverter resistance of 0.1 ohm be connected in parallel with series winding? Ignore armature reaction.

[12 marks : 2005]

Solution:

(a) $V = 220$ V; $R_a = 0.1\ \Omega$; $R_f = 50\ \Omega$; $R_{se} = 0.06\ \Omega$ {long shunt}

$$I_f = \frac{220}{50} = 4.4\text{ A}$$

Load current, $I_l = I - I_f = 100$ A

$$I = 100 + 4.4 = 104.4\text{ A}$$

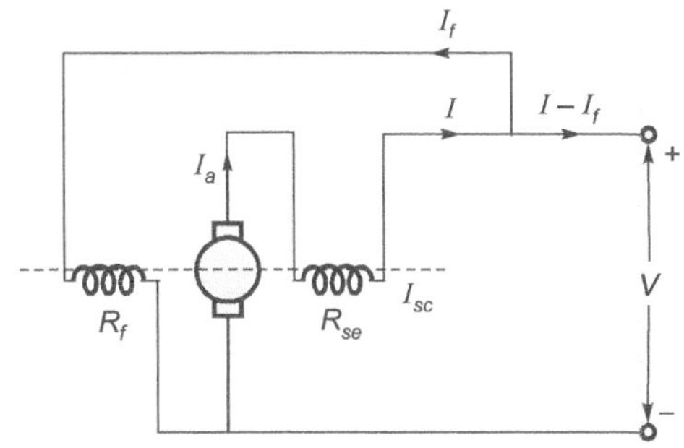

This current flows through armature as well as series field winding, hence

$$I = I_{se} = I_a$$

induced emf in the armature,

$$E = V + I(R_a + R_{se})$$
$$= 220 + 104.4(0.1 + 0.06) = 236.7\text{ V}$$

(b) $V = 220$ V; $R_a = 0.1\ \Omega$; $R_f = 50\ \Omega$; $R_{se} = 0.06\ \Omega$ {short shunt}

Load, $I = 100\text{ A} = I_{se}$

Voltage across shunt field and armature,

$$V_1 = V + I_{se} \times R_{se} = 220 + 100 \times 0.06 = 226$$

$$I_f = \frac{V_1}{R_f} = \frac{226}{50} = 4.52\text{ A}$$

Armature current,

$$I_a = I + I_f = 100 + 4.52 = 104.52\text{ A}$$
$$E = V_1 + I_aR_a = 226 + 104.52 \times 0.1$$
$$= 236.452\text{ V}$$

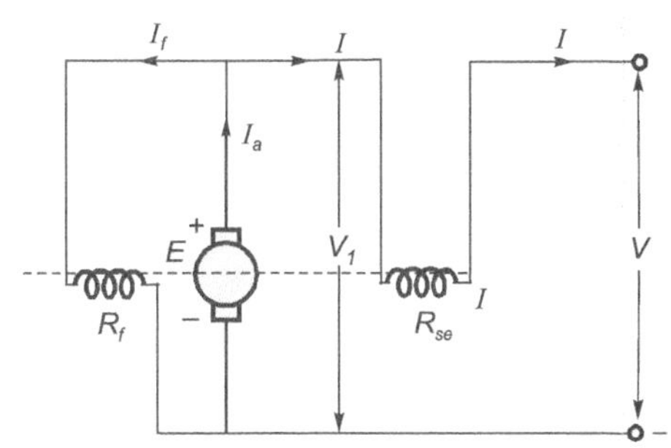

(c) Series field A.*T*s are proportional to series field current.

$$\text{Series field current with diverter} = \frac{0.1}{0.1+0.06}I = 0.625I$$

Where, I = total current through series field winding and diverter resistance

$$\therefore \text{ \% reduction in series field AT} = \frac{I - 0.625I}{I} \times 100 = 37.5\%$$

3.13 A 220 V D.C. machine has an armature resistance 1 Ω. If the full-load current is 20 A, the difference in induced voltage when the machine is running as a motor, and as a generator is

(a) 20 V (b) 0 V
(c) 40 V (d) 60 V

[2 marks : 2006]

Solution:

$E_g = V + I_aR_a$; E_g = generator induced voltage

V = terminal voltage of the machine

$E_m = V - I_aR_a$; E_m = motor induced voltage

Difference in induced voltage,

$$E_g - E_m = (V + I_aR_a) - (V - I_aR_a)$$
$$= 2\,I_aR_a = 2 \times 20 \times 1$$
$$= 40\text{ V}$$

Hence, option (c) is correct.

3.14 With connection diagrams for both shunt and separately excited D.C. generator, draw important characteristic of these generators.

[6 marks : 2006]

Solution:

Separately-excited Generators: These generators are used when a wide range of output voltage is required.

1. **No-load Characteristic:** This characteristic gives the variation of armature generated emf E_a with field current I_f, for zero armature current and constant speed.

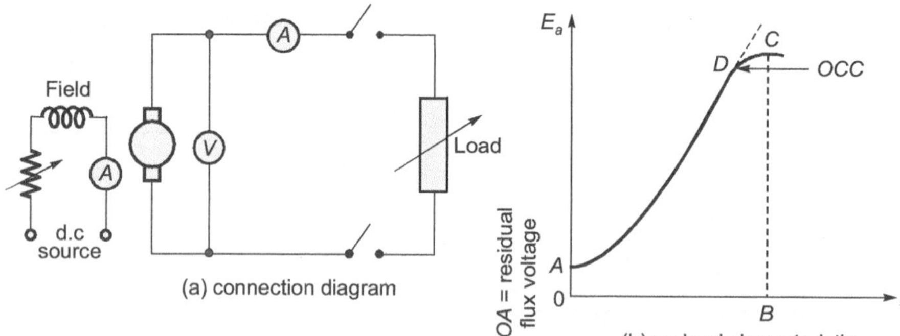

(a) connection diagram

(b) no load characteristic

2. **Load Characteristic:** This characteristic gives the relationship between the terminal voltage V_t and field current I_f for constant I_a and speed.

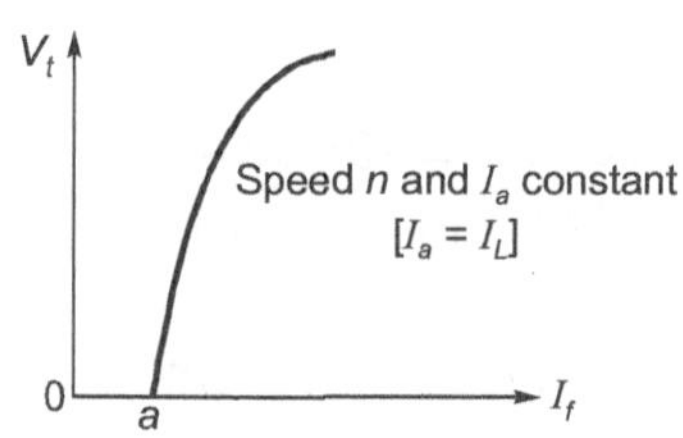

3. **External Characteristic or (Volt Ampere Characteristic):** This characteristic gives the variation of armature terminal voltage V_t with load current I_L for constant speed and fixed field current.

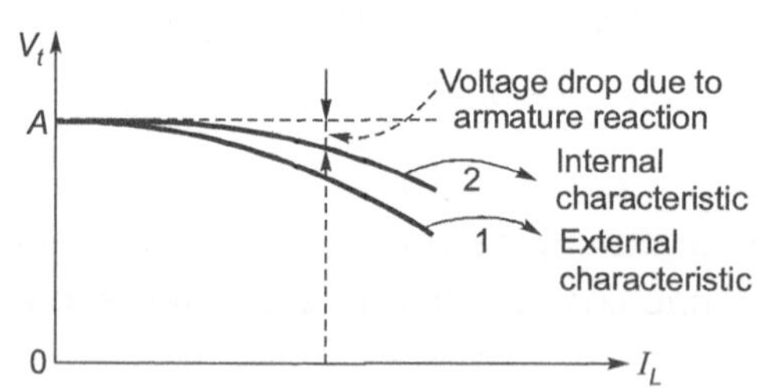

Shunt Generator: These generators are most frequently employed, because no separate source for excitation is required. However the load current must be below the maximum current for avoiding large dips in the terminal voltage.

Connection Diagram:

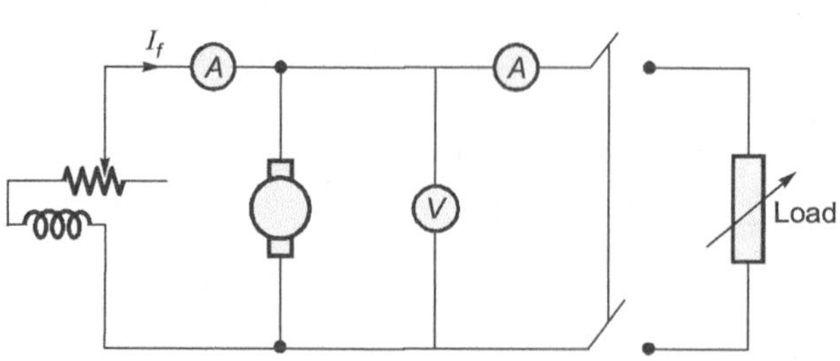

1. **No-load Characteristic:** In case of shunt generator small amount of current (1 to 3% of rated current) flowing in the armature of the shunt generator has negligible effect on the main flux.

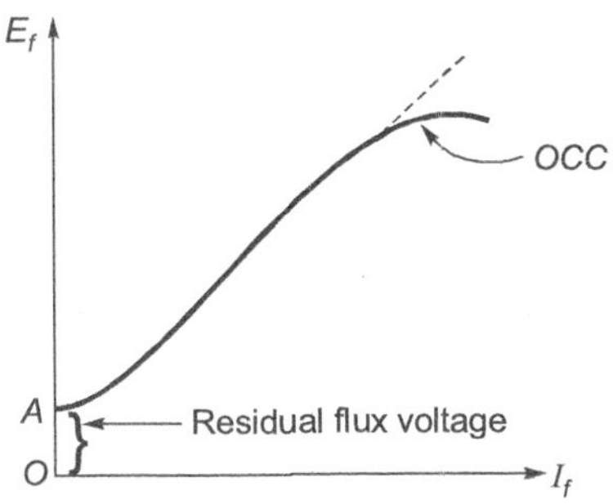

2. **Load Characteristic:** The load characteristic obtained for separate and shunt excitation is same. The slight difference is due to different armature current.

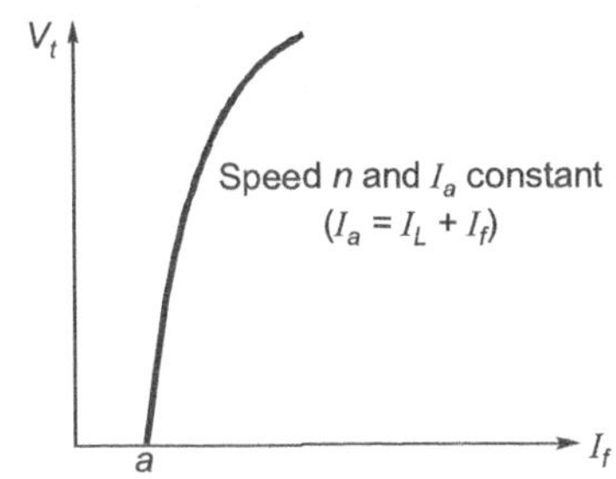

3. **External Characteristic:** A plot of terminal voltage and local current I_L, with preset value of field current and speed gives external characteristic.

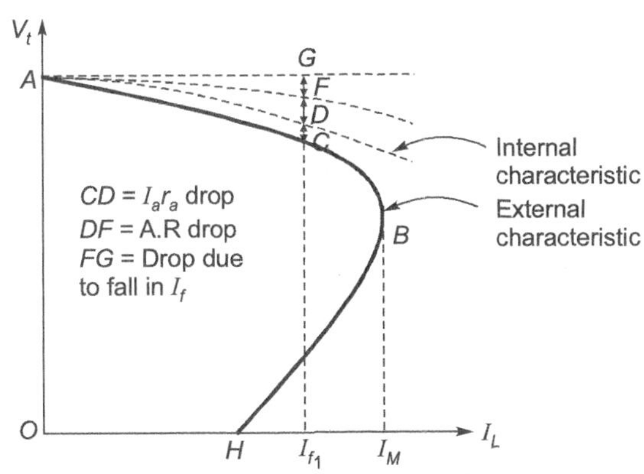

4. **Armature Characteristic:** Shunt generator armature characteristic is obtained by running it as a separately excited generator.

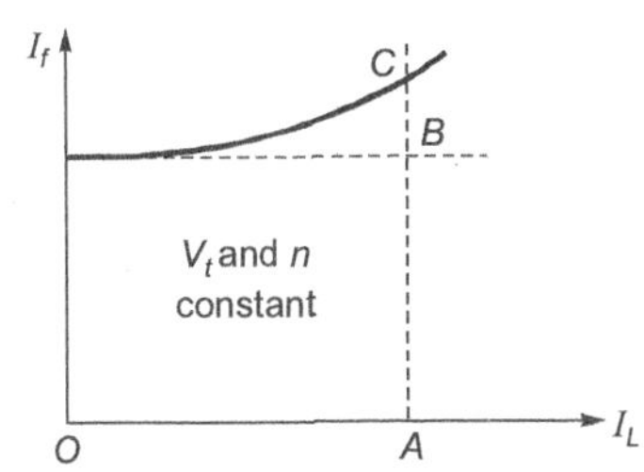

This characteristic can be employed for calculating the number of series turns for any degree of compounding, in d.c. machine.

3.15 What happens to the speed when the flux is reduced by 10% in a 200 V d.c.? Shunt motor having an armature resistance of 0.2 ohm carrying a current of 50 Amps and running at 960 rpm prior to weakening of field. The total torque may be assumed constant. Neglect losses

(a) 1250 rpm (b) 1066 rpm
(c) 920 rpm (d) 576 rpm [2 marks : 2007]

Solution: (b)

$$T = k\phi n = \text{constant}$$

$$T_1 = T_2$$

$$\Rightarrow \quad K\phi_1 n_1 = k\phi_2 n_2$$

$$\phi_1 960 = 0.90\,\phi_1 n_2$$

$$n_2 = \frac{960}{0.9} = 1066 \text{ rpm}$$

Hence, option (b) is correct.

3.16 Describe the meaning of "armature reaction". How does it affect the performance of a D.C. generator? How can the performance be improved with regard to the above?

[4 marks : 2007]

Solution:

Armature Reaction: When the armature of a d.c. machine carries current, the distributed armature winding produces its own mmf (distributed) known as armature reaction. The machine air-gap is now acted upon by the resultant mmf distribution caused by simultaneous action of the field ampere-turns ($A\,T_f$) and armature ampere-turns ($A\,T_a$). As a result the air-gap flux density gets distorted as compared to the flat-topped (trapezoidal) wave with quarterwave symmetry when the armature did not carry any current.

The effect of armature mmf

1. net reduction in the main field flux per pole.
2. distortion of the main field flux wave along the air-gap periphery.

This reduction in flux causes a decrease in the generator terminal voltage.

The cross-magnetizing effect of armature mmf can be minimised at the design and construction stage of a d.c. machine. Various methods of mitigating the effects of armature reaction:

(a) **High-reluctance Pole Tips:** If the reluctance of the pole tips is increased, then the magnitude of armature cross flux is reduced and the distortion of the resultant flux density wave is minimised.

(b) **Reduction in Armature Flux:** Another constructional technique of reducing the armature cross flux is to create more reluctance in the path of armature flux without reducing the main field flux. This is achieved by using field-pole laminations having several rectangular holes punched in them.

(c) **Strong Main-field Flux:** During the design of a d.c. machine, it should be ensured that the main field mmf is sufficiently strong in comparison with full-load armature mmf.

(d) **Interpoles:** The effect of armature reaction in the interpolar zone can be overcome by inter poles, placed in between the main poles.

(e) **Compensating Winding:** The effect of armature reaction under the pole shoes can be limited by using compensating winding. This winding is embedded in slots cut in the pole faces of the d.c. machine.

3.17 A 230 V, D.C. Machine has R_a = 0.3 W and R_{sh} = 160 Ω respectively. It is running as a motor on NO LOAD at 1000 RPM taking an armature current of 3.3 A rated voltage. When the motor is run on FULL LOAD at rated voltage, the line current has a value of 40 Amps. Calculate the speed and torque developed for this condition, assuming that armature reaction weakens the no load flux by 4%.

[10 marks : 2007]

Solution:

In a d.c. motor, $I_L = I_a + I_f$

Shunt field current, $I_f = \dfrac{230}{160} = 1.44\text{ A}$ (Constant)

At no load, $I_{a0} = 3.3\text{ A}$ (Given)

$$E_{a0} = 230 - 0.3 \times 3.3 = 229\text{ V}$$

$$n_0 = 1000\text{ RPM}$$

$$E_{a0} = K_a'\,\phi\, n_0$$

or $229 = K_a'\,\phi \times 1000$ ...(*i*)

On load, $I_{a1} = 40 - 1.44 = 38.56\text{ A}$

$$E_{a1} = 230 - 0.3 \times 38.56 = 218.43\text{ V} \quad \text{...(ii)}$$

Flux/pole, $\phi_1 = 0.96\,\phi$

$$E_{a1} = K_a'\,\phi_1\, n_1$$

$$218.43 = K_a' \times 0.96\,\phi\, n_1 \quad \text{...(iii)}$$

Dividing equation (*iii*) by equation (*i*), $\dfrac{218.43}{229} = \dfrac{0.96\,n_1}{1000}$

$$n_1 = 993.58\text{ RPM}$$

$$T_1\,\omega_1 = E_{a_1} I_{a_1}$$

$$\frac{2\pi \times 993.58}{60} T_1 = 218.43 \times 38.56$$

$$T_1 = 80.95\text{ Nm}$$

3.18 Armature reaction in a d.c. shunt generator, running at full load with the brushes not shifted from the geometrical neutral plane and saturation neglected, is

(a) absent
(b) cross-magnetising
(c) de-magnetising
(d) magnetising

[2 marks : 2008]

Solution: (b)

Option (b) is correct.

3.19 Describe how to evaluate hysteresis and eddy current losses experimentally for a shunt d.c. generator. A d.c. shunt motor rated at 250 V, 10 kW, 1500 rpm has a full load efficiency of 80%. Its field and armature resistances are 110 ohm and 0.25 ohm respectively. Find the value of the resistance to be inserted in series with the armature and the power lost in the armature circuit to reduce the speed to 1200 rpm if the load torque is independent of the speed.

[12 marks : 2008]

Solution:

To evaluate hysteresis and eddy current losses, swinburners test is performed on shunt D.C. generator. The machine is run as D.C. shunt motor at no-load at rated speed. Field current is adjusted to a rated value. The power absorbed by the motor during test is equal to no-load losses which include hysteresis, eddy current and windage losses.

$R_f = 110\ \Omega$, $R_a = 0.25\ \Omega$

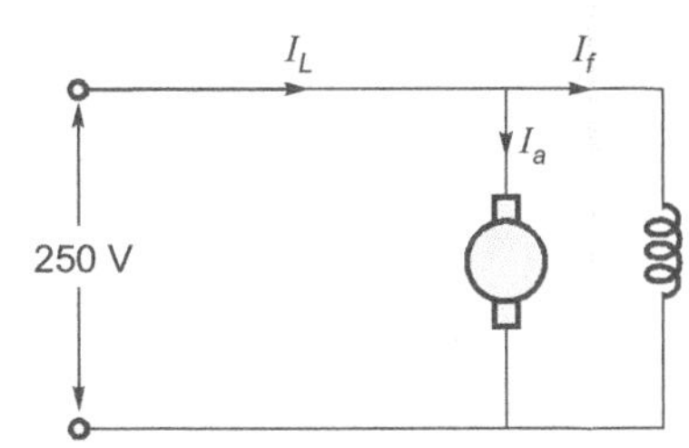

$$I_f = \frac{250}{110} = 2.27\text{ A}$$

$$P_{out} = 10\text{ kW}$$

$$I_a = 50 - I_f = 47.73\text{ A}$$

Now, $E_a = V_t - I_a \times R_a$

$$= 250 - 47.73 \times 0.25 = 238.068 \text{ V}$$

Since, $P_{rotational} = E_{a_1} \times I_{a_1} - P_{out}$

$$= 238.068 \times 47.73 - 10000$$

$$= 1362.37 \text{ W} \quad \text{(Treated as constant)}$$

Now, when $N = 1200$ rpm, T_{shaft} = constant (as T_{load} = constant)

Since load torque is constant,

$$P_{out} = T_{load} \times \omega_m$$

or, $P_{out} \;\alpha\; \omega_m$

$$\frac{P_{out(2)}}{P_{out(1)}} = \frac{N_2}{N_1};$$

$$P_{out(2)} = 10000 \times \frac{1200}{1500} = 8000 \text{ W}$$

Now, Power at armature $= P_{out} + P_{rotational}$

$$= 8000 + 1362.37 = 9362.37 \text{ W}$$

and as we know, $E_a = K\phi\omega$ or $E_a \propto N$

then, $\frac{E_{a_2}}{E_{a_1}} = \frac{N_2}{N_1}$

or, $\frac{E_{a_2}}{238.062} = \frac{1200}{1500} = 0.8$

$$E_{a_2} = 0.8 \times 238.062 = 190.454 \text{ V}$$

$\because$ $P_{arm.} = E_{a_2} \times I_{a_2} = 9362.37$

$\Rightarrow$ $I_{a_2} = \frac{9362.37}{190.454} = 49.16 \text{ A}$

$\because$ $E_{a_2} = V_t - I_{a_2}(R_a + R_{ext})$

$$190.454 = 250 - 49.16\,(0.25 + R_{ext})$$

Solving we get, $R_{ext} = 0.96135\ \Omega$

Power lost in armature circuit $= (R_a + R_{ext}) \times I_{a_2}^2$

$$= (1.211) \times (49.16)^2 = 2926.63 \text{ W} = 2.9266 \text{ kW}$$

3.20 **The terminal voltage of a d.c. shunt motor is halved and the load torque is varied as the square of the speed, the field flux remaining constant, consequently the armature current would be approximately,**

(a) constant **(b) halved**

(c) one-fourth of the normal value **(d) twice the normal value** **[2 marks : 2009]**

Solution: (c)

Load torque $T_L \propto n^2$

Electromagnetic torque, $T_e = k_a \phi I_a$,

ϕ = constant

Under steady state, $T_e = T_L$

$$I_a \propto n^2 \quad \quad ...(i)$$

$$E = V_t - I_a r_a = k_a \phi n \quad \quad ...(ii)$$

From (*i*) and (*ii*) the armature current would be approximately one fourth of the normal value, option (c).

3.21 Identify various losses that occur in the shunt d.c. machine. A d.c. machine is connected across a 240 V line. It rotates at 1200 rpm and is generating 230 volts. The armature current is 40 amperes.

(a) Is the machine functioning as a generator or as a motor?

(b) Find the resistance of the armature circuit.

(c) Determine the electromagnetic torque.

(d) If the load is thrown off, what will be the generated voltage and the speed of the machine, assuming that there is negligible effect of armature reaction?

[12 marks : 2009]

Solution:

(a) Here generating voltage 230 less than terminal voltage 240, so the machine work as motor.

(b)
$$V_t = E_a + I_a r_a$$
$$240 = 230 + I_a r_a$$
$$10 = 40 \times r_a$$
$$r_a = 0.25\ \Omega$$

(c) The electromagnetic torque,

$$T_e = \frac{E_a . I_a}{\omega_m} = \frac{E_a . I_a}{\frac{2\pi n}{60}}$$

or
$$T_e = \frac{230 \times 40 \times 60}{2 \times \pi \times 1200} = 73.21 \text{ N-m}$$

(d) If the load is thrown off, the generated voltage is equal to the terminal voltage i.e., 240 volts.

$$E_{a0} = K_a' \phi N_0$$

$$\frac{230}{240} = \frac{1200}{N_0} \Rightarrow N_0 = 1252 \text{ rpm}$$

Various Losses Occurs in the d.c. Shunt Machine:

(a) No-load Rotational Loss: This loss is made up of two losses, namely

(*i*) the iron loss at working flux and speed and

(*ii*) the mechanical loss, i.e. friction and windage losses at the operating speed.

(b) I^2R Loss:

(*i*) Armature circuit loss $I_a^2 r_a$: Where r_a includes the resistances of brush contacts, armature winding interpole winding and compensating winding, if present.

(*ii*) Field ohmic loss $V_f I_f$: This loss includes the field-rheostat loss.

(c) Stray Load Losses: These are produced by

(*i*) the distortion of the air-gap flux due to the armature reaction and

(*ii*) the currents in the commutated coil.

3.22 Improved commutation in d.c. machines can not be achieved by

(a) use of interpoles

(b) using brushes of higher resistivity

(c) increasing reactance voltage

(d) decreasing reactance voltage

[2 marks : 2010]

Solution: (c)

Increased reactance voltage will further delay the commutation. Hence, option (c) is correct.

3.23 Explain the various methods of speed control of d.c. series motors including the case when two identical d.c. series motors are available.

A 4 pole d.c. series wound motor takes 20 A from 250 V d.c. supply to run at 600 rpm when all the four field coils are in series. If the load torque increases as the square of speed, find the speed and the input current when the field coils are connected in two parallel groups of two coils in series each. Assume the flux is proportional to the current and ignore losses.

[5 marks : 2010]

Solution:

As we know speed $= n = K_N \frac{E_a}{\phi} = K_N\left(\frac{V - I_a R_a}{\phi}\right)$. This equation gives us two methods of effecting speed changes i.e. the variation of field excitation I_f and that of terminal voltage, V.

1. **Diverter field control:**

   A diverter resistor is connected across the field winding. By varying R_d the field current and hence the field ampere-turns can be varied and desired speed can be obtained.

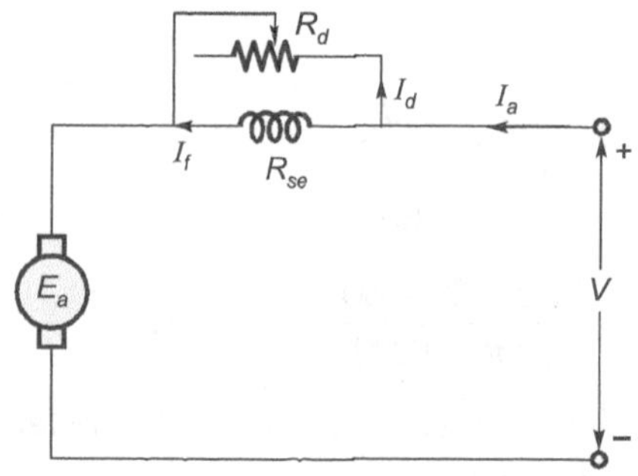

2. **Tapped-field control:**

   Here the field ampere turns are adjusted in steps by varying the number of turns included in the circuit.

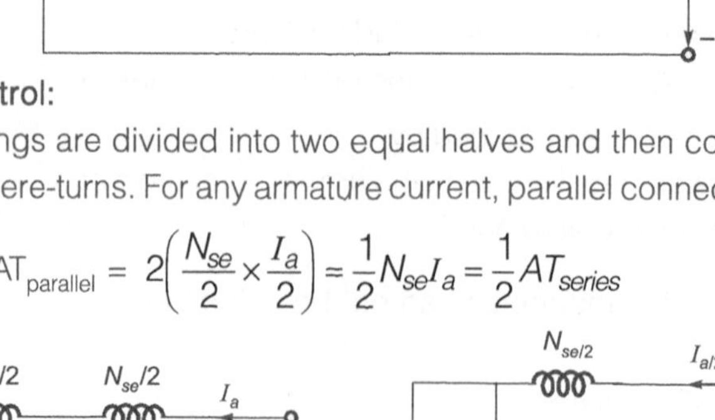

3. **Series-parallel control:**

   Here the field windings are divided into two equal halves and then connected in series or parallel to control the field ampere-turns. For any armature current, parallel connection of half-windings gives,

$$AT_{parallel} = 2\left(\frac{N_{se}}{2} \times \frac{I_a}{2}\right) = \frac{1}{2} N_{se} I_a = \frac{1}{2} AT_{series}$$

4. Series-parallel control of two identical motors:

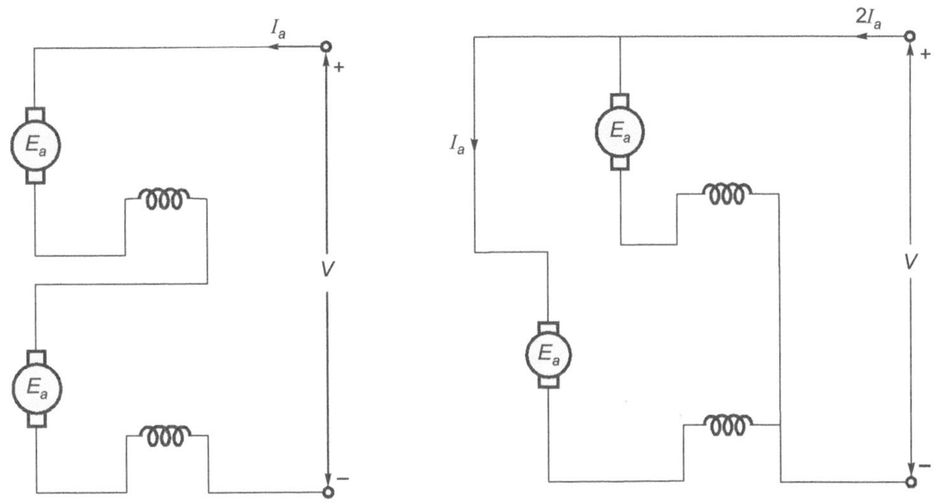

(a) Series connection (b) Parallel connection

Here two identical motors are coupled together mechanically to a common load. Two speeds at constant torque are possible in this method one by connecting the motors armature in series and the other by connecting them in parallel as shown in figure. When connected in series, the terminal voltage across each motor is $V/2$ whereas when they are connected in parallel it is V. Thus armature control of speed is achieved.

Numerical:

Electromagnetic torque $T_e \propto \phi I_a$ and load torque $T_L \propto n^2$

under steady state conditions,

$$T_L = T_e \Rightarrow n^2 \propto \phi I_a$$

If I_{a_1} is the armature current when four field coils are connected in series, then

$$n_1^2 \propto \phi_1 I_{a_0}$$

or $$n_1^2 \propto \phi_1 I_{a_1} \text{ as } \phi_1 \propto I_{a_1}$$

If I_{a_2} is the armature current when four field coils are connected in two parallel groups, then

$$n_2^2 \propto \phi_2 I_{a_2}$$

or $$n_2^2 \propto \left(\frac{I_{a_2}}{2}\right) I_{a_2} \propto \frac{I_{a2}^2}{2} \text{ as } \phi_2 \propto \frac{I_{a_2}}{2}$$

$\therefore$ $$\left(\frac{n_1}{n_2}\right)^2 = \frac{I_{a_1}^2}{I_{a_2}^2/2}$$

$$\left(\frac{600}{n_2}\right)^2 = 2\times\left(\frac{20}{I_{a_2}}\right)^2$$

$\Rightarrow$ $$n_2 = 21.21 I_{a_2} \quad ...(i)$$

Counter emf with all the four coils in series,

$$E_{as} = V_t - I_{a_1}(r_a + r_s) \propto n_1\phi_1 \propto n_1 I_{a_1}$$

and with the four coils in two parallel groups,

$$E_{ap} = V_t - I_{a_2}\left(r_a + \frac{r_s}{2}\right) \propto n_2\phi_2 \propto n_2 \times \left(\frac{I_{a_2}}{2}\right)$$

$$\frac{E_{as}}{E_{ap}} = \frac{n_1 I_{a_1}}{n_2(I_{a2}/2)}$$

Since, r_a and r_s are not given and losses are ignored

$$E_{as} = E_{ap} = V_t = 250 \text{ V}$$

$$\frac{250}{250} = \frac{n_1 I_{a_1}}{n_2(I_{a2}/2)}$$

$$\Rightarrow \quad n_2 I_{a_2} = 2n_1 I_{a_1}$$

$$\Rightarrow \quad (21.21 I_{a_2}) I_{a_2} = 2 \times 600 \times 20$$

$$I_{a_2} = 33.63 \text{ Amp.}$$

and $$n_2 = 21.21 \times 33.63 = 713.3 \text{ rpm}$$

3.24 What are the various conditions which have to be fulfilled before a shunt excited d.c. generator will generate rated voltage across the armature terminals?

[5 marks : 2010]

Solution:

A shunt excited d.c. generator may fail to self-excite for any of the following reason:

1. Residual magnetism is absent. This difficulty can be overcome by exciting the field winding from a separate d.c. source for a few seconds with the armature at rest.
2. The field connection to the armature is such that the induced emf due to the residual magnetism tends to destroy the residual magnetism. This condition can be remedied by reversing the field connection to the armature.
3. The field circuit resistance is more than the critical value. For critical resistance R_f-line coincides with the linear portion of the magnetization curve.
4. Speed is less than critical speed. At critical speed, the open-circuit characteristic (*OCC*) is tangential to the R_f-line.

3.25 Explain the different methods of electrical braking of d.c. motors and compare their advantages and disadvantages.

[5 marks : 2010]

Solution:

There are three methods of electrical braking:

(i) plugging or counter current
(ii) dynamics or rheostatic and
(iii) regenerative

(i) Plugging:

- This involves the sudden reversal of the connections of either the field or armature winding during motor operation but it is a common practice to reverse the armature connections.
- A strong braking torque is achieved by maintaining the supply voltage to the armature with connection reversed. The effective armature voltage ($E_a + V$) is initially ≈ 2 V, so that a limiting braking resistor (may be a starting resistor) must be brought into the circuit.
- The kinetic energy of the moving system is dissipated in the armature and braking resistances. The supply must be switched off close to zero speed (unless the intention is to run the motor in the reverse direction). The large initial current and the resultant high mechanical stress the application of plugging to small motor only.

(ii) Dynamic Braking:

- The armature is disconnected from the supply and then a braking resistor R_b is immediately connected across it. The motor acts as a generator, driven by the stored kinetic energy dissipating power in R_s. This is a simple method of bringing a motor nearly to a stand-still. The field circuit is left connected to the supply.
- The only danger is that if the supply fails, braking also fails.

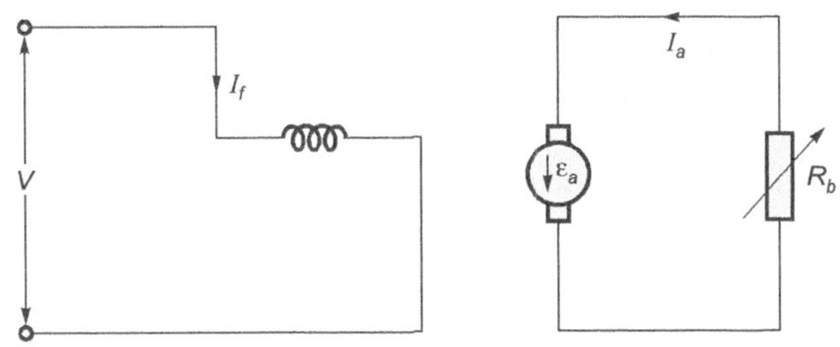

- If the field is left connected across the armature, the initially the braking torque is the same but starts falling sharply with speed and the problem arises once the speed falls below the critical value for self-excitation.

(iii) Regenerative Braking:

- In this method most of the braking energy is returned to the supply and is used specially where the duly cycle requires the braking or slowing of the machine more frequently and is most useful in holding a descending load of high potential energy at a constant speed.
- The condition for regeneration is that the rotational emf is more than the applied voltage so that the current is reversed and the mode of operation changes from motoring to generating.
- Regeneration is possible with a shunt and a separately excited motors and with compound motors with weak series compounding.
- The method needs a supply capable of accepting the generated power without undue rise of the terminal voltage.

3.26 **The purpose of providing dummy coils in the armature of a DC machine is to**

(i) increase voltage induced

(ii) decrease the armature resistance

(iii) provide mechanical balance for the rotor

(iv) reduce the copper loss

[12 marks : 2011]

Solution:

(iii) provide mechanical balance for the rotor.

3.27 **Why is armature control superior to field control scheme in the case of a DC shunt motor?**

[12 marks : 2011]

Solution:

Armature control is superior to field control scheme, due to following reasons:

(*i*) It provides a constant-torque drive. In the shunt motor case by keeping the field current at maximum value full motor torque can be obtained at full-load armature current at all speeds.

(*ii*) Since the main field ampere-turns are maintained at a large value, flux density distortion caused by armature reaction is limited.

(*iii*) Unlike field control scheme, speed reversal can be easily implemented here.

3.28 **Explain No Voltage Release (NVR) and Over Load Release (OLR) coils provided in a DC motor starter.**

[12 marks : 2011]

Solution:

The holding coil (HC) is also called no-volt release coil and has the following functions:

- In case of power failure, electromagnet (HC) gets demagnetized and the spiral spring brings the handle back to its off position. If during the power failure, the handle fails to return to off position, the motor might be damaged in case the power is restored because then there would be no starting resistance in the armature circuit.
- If the shunt field becomes open circuited accidently, HC gets demagnetized and the starter handle is returned by spring pull to the off position. In case the starter handle is not released the speed starts increasing with the decaying of the field flux. The small residual flux will result in dangerously high speeds.

  Another protective device OR, known as the overload release is provided in series with the armature circuit. This OR is a small electromagnet. In case the armature current exceeds a preset value due to overload OR becomes more strong and attracts to movable soft iron pivoted at one end. As the soft iron is attached, two terminals of the no-volt release HC gets short circuited. In this manner, HC gets demagntized and the starter arm is pulled back to the off position, by the spiral spring thus the motor is thus automatically disconnected from the mains in case of overload.

3.29 **A 400 V shunt motor draws 30 A while supplying the rated load at a speed of 120 rad/sec. The armature resistance is 1.0 ohm and the field winding resistance is 250 ohms. Determine the external resistance that must be inserted in series with the armature circuit so that armature current has not exceed 150% of its rated value when the motor is plugged. Find the braking torque at the instant of plugging.**

[12 marks : 2011]

Solution:

$V_t = 400$ V, $I_L = 30$ A, $R_a = 1\ \Omega$

Before plugging:

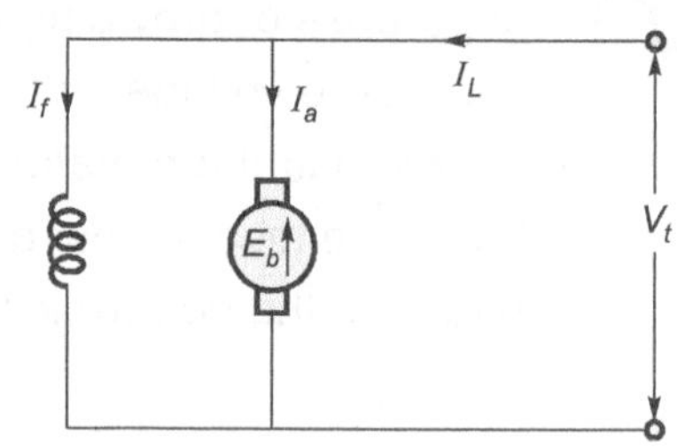

$$I_L = 30 \text{ A}$$

$$I_f = \frac{400}{250} = 1.6 \text{ A}$$

$$I_a = I_L - I_f = 30 - 1.6$$

$$= 28.4 \text{ A (rated current)}$$

Back emf.
$$E_b = V_t - I_a R_a$$

$$= 400 - 28.4 \times 1 = 371.6 \text{ V}$$

In plugging, the armature of the motor is reversed.

Total resistance in the armature circuit during plugging

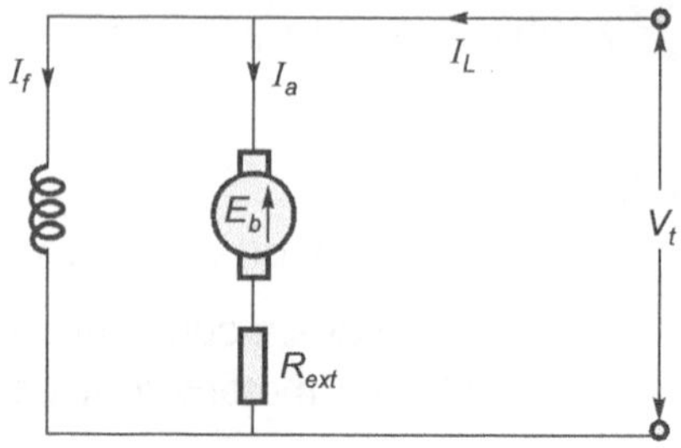

$$R_b = R_{ext} + R_a$$

At the instant of plugging,

$$I_a = 1.5 \times 28.4 = 42.6 \text{ A}$$

$$V_t - I_a R_b + E_b = 0$$

$$\Rightarrow \quad R_b = \frac{V_t + E_b}{I_a} = \frac{400 + 371.6}{42.6}$$

$$\Rightarrow \quad R_{ext} + R_a = 18.11\ \Omega$$

The external resistor that must be inserted

$$R_{ext} = 18.11 - R_a$$
$$= 18.11 - 1 = 17.11\ \Omega$$

Plugging torque $= T_{plug} = \frac{E_b I_a}{\omega} = \frac{371.6 \times 42.6}{120} = 131.92$ N-m

Load torque, $T_{load} = K\phi I_a$

$\because$ $K\phi = \frac{E}{\omega} = \frac{371.6}{120}$

$$T_{load} = \frac{371.6}{120} \times 28.4 = 87.94 \text{ N-m}$$

Braking torque, $T_{braking} = T_{plugging} + T_{load} = 131.92 + 87.94 = 219.86$ N-m

3.30 **A 240 V dc shunt motor has a torque constant of 5 Nm/A and its armature circuit resistance is 0.5 Ω. At what speed in rad/sec and in rpm should the motor be driven so as to obtain regenerative braking torque of 250 Nm?**

[4 marks : 2012]

Solution:

Given, $V = 240$ V, Torque constant, $K = 5$ Nm/A

$$T = KI$$
$$250 = 5 \times I \Rightarrow I = 50 \text{ A}$$

In regenerative braking, direction of current I_a will reverse imposing torque which is opposite to the direction of rotation.

$\therefore$ $E_b = V - (-I_a)\, r_a = 240 + 50 \times 0.5 = 265$ V

$$E = K\omega_m$$
$$265 = 5\,\omega_m$$
$$\omega_m = 53 \text{ rad/sec} = \frac{53 \times 60}{2\pi} \text{ rpm} = 506.11 \text{ rpm}$$

3.31 **A 400-V dc shunt motor, with an armature resistance of 0.2 Ω, runs at 1000 rpm and takes an armature current of 60 A. If the field flux is suddenly increased by 20%, obtain, at this instant, new values of armature current and the torque in terms of initial torque.**

What is the operating mode of dc shunt machine under these conditions? State the assumption made, if any.

[7 marks : 2012]

Solution:

Initial counter emf, $E_a = V_t - I_a r_a = V_t - I_a r_a$

$$= 400 - 60 \times 0.2 = 388 \text{ V}$$

With a sudden increase in field flux by 20%, the speed remains at 1000 rpm due to motor inertia, therefore, the new counter emf becomes

$$E_a' = 388 \times 1.2 = 465.6$$

$\therefore$ The new value of armature current

$$I_a' = \frac{(400 - 465.6)}{2} = -328 \text{ A}$$

Since the armature current is now negative, the machine acts momentarily as a generator and feeds the power to the supply, at the expense of its kinetic energy.

$$\text{New armature current} = \frac{328}{60}\text{(initial current of 60 A)}$$

and the corresponding torque $= \left(\frac{\text{new current}}{\text{initial current}} \times \frac{\text{new flux}}{\text{initial flux}}\right) \times \text{(initial torque)}$

$$= \frac{328}{60} \times 1.2 \times \text{(initial torque)} = 6.56 \text{ (initial torque)}$$

3.32 A 220 V DC shunt motor takes 20 A at full load running at 2500 rpm. The armature resistance is 0.4 Ω and shunt field resistance of 176 Ω. The machine is converted into a long shunt differentially compound motor by augmenting an additional series field winding with 0.1 Ω resistance. There is a 11% change in the total flux when compound motor develops the same torque. Assume rotational losses to be constant under all loading conditions.
[Note: Given question is incomplete. But it can be assumed that speed of long shunted differentially compound motor with the given conditions can be asked.]

[4 marks : 2013]

Solution:

Case-1:

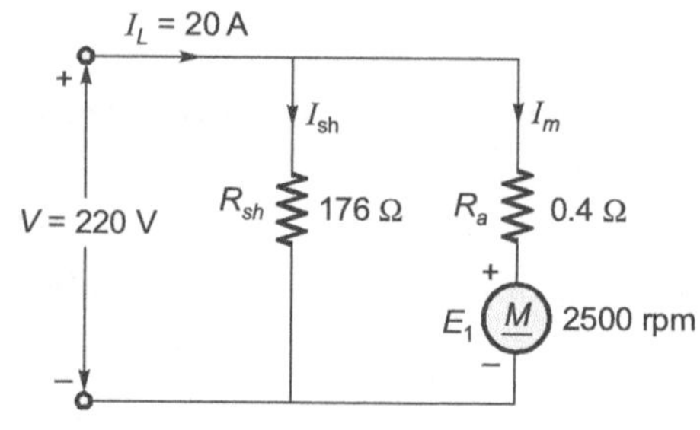

$$I_{sh} = \frac{V}{R_{sh}} = \frac{220}{176} = 1.25\ A$$

$$I_M = I_L - I_{sh}$$
$$= 20 - 1.25 = 18.75 \text{ A}$$
$$E_1 = V - I_m R_a$$
$$= 220 - 18.75 \times 0.4$$
$$= 212.5 \text{ V}$$

Case-2:

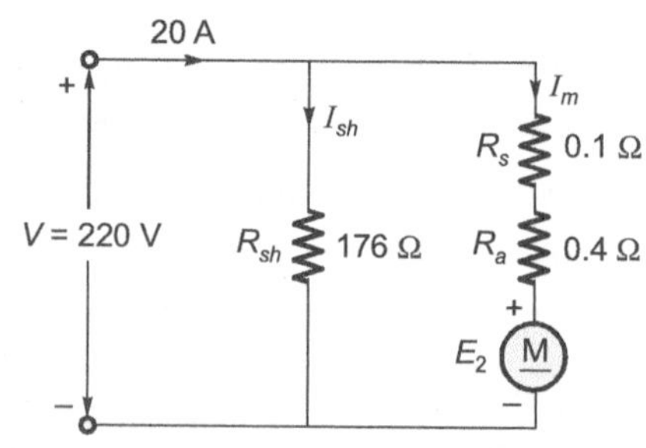

$$E_2 = V - I_m(R_a + R_s)$$
$$= 220 - 18.75 \times (0.1 + 0.4)$$
$$= 210.6 \text{ V}$$
$$E \propto \phi N$$
$$\frac{E_1}{E_2} = \frac{\phi_1 N_1}{\phi_2 N_2}$$
$$N_2 = \frac{210.6 \times 2500\,\phi_1}{212.5 \times (0.89\,\phi_1)} = 2784.2 \text{ rpm} \qquad (\phi_2 = 0.89\,\phi_1)$$

3.33 Two DC series motors with different air gaps but otherwise identical run at 700 and 750 rpm respectively, when taking 50 A at 500 V. The total resistance of each motor is 0.36 Ω. If the motors are now mechanically coupled and connected in series electrically to a 500 V DC supply and together takes 50 A current. Calculate the speed at which the coupled set will run.

[10 marks : 2013]

Solution:

$$E_{a_1} = E_{a_2} = V - R_a I_a$$
$$= 500 - (0.36)(50) = 482 \text{ V}$$

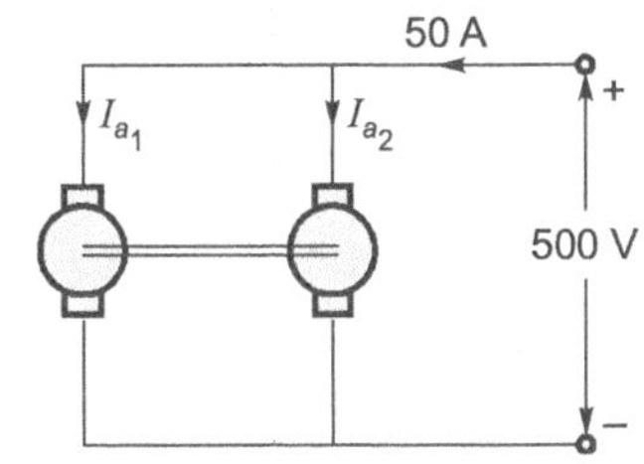

$$N_{m_1} = 700 \text{ rpm}$$

$$N_{m_2} = 750 \text{ rpm}$$

$\because$ $$E_{a_1} = K\phi_1 N_{m_1}$$

and $$E_{a_2} = K\phi_2 N_{m_2}$$

$\because$ $$E_{a_1} = E_{a_2}$$

then, $$\frac{\phi_1}{\phi_2} = \frac{N_{m_2}}{N_{m_1}}$$

or $$\frac{\phi_1}{\phi_2} = \frac{750}{700} = \frac{15}{14} \quad \text{...(i)}$$

when two motors are connected in series and mechanically coupled.

$$E_{a_1} + E_{a_2} = 500 - 50\,(0.72)$$

$$E_{a_1} + E_{a_2} = 464 \text{ V} \quad \text{...(ii)}$$

Since, $$N_{m_1} = N_{m_2} = N_m$$ (For mechanical coupled motors)

then, $$\frac{E_{a_2}}{E_{a_1}} = \frac{\phi_2}{\phi_1} = \frac{14}{15}$$ [(From equation (i)]

or, $$E_{a_2} = \frac{14}{15}E_{a_1}$$

From equation (ii), $$E_{a_1} + \frac{14}{15}E_{a_1} = 464$$

$\Rightarrow$ $$E_{a_1} = 240 \text{ V}$$

Comparing with data of separate operation for machine (i),

$$E_{a_1} = K\phi\, N_{m_1}$$

or, $$\frac{E'_{a_1}}{E''_{a_1}} = \frac{N'_{m_1}}{N''_{m_1}}$$

$$\frac{240}{482} = \frac{N}{700}$$

$$N = 348.55 \text{ rpm}$$

Similar result can be obtained from machine 2.

If, $$E'_{a_2} = 224$$

or, $$\frac{224}{482} = \frac{N}{750}$$

$$N = 348.55 \text{ rpm}$$

3.34 The poles to the dc machine are laminated even though the field winding current is dc. Explain why?
[4 marks : 2014]

Solution:

In dc, the core losses occurs mainly in the armature iron, it is because the armature in dc-machine is subjected to alternating flux as it rotates under the effect of main field poles. With the slotted armature passing across the field poles, the flux density wave pulsates in magnitude, slot is under the middle of field pole and the flux density is AB. With the relative motion between armature and field poles, too may come under the middle of pole, under this condition, airgap flux density is $A'B'$.The field mmf is same in both these figures. Here $A'B' > AB$, as the airgap length along the middle of pole is less in Figure (b) than in Figure (a). These pulsations in flux density wave arising from slot openings cause losses in the field iron, particularly in the pole faces (or pole shoes). This loss in the pole shoes occurring due to relative motion between field poles and slotted armature is referred to as pulsation loss. In order to reduce this loss, pole shoes in dc machine are laminated.

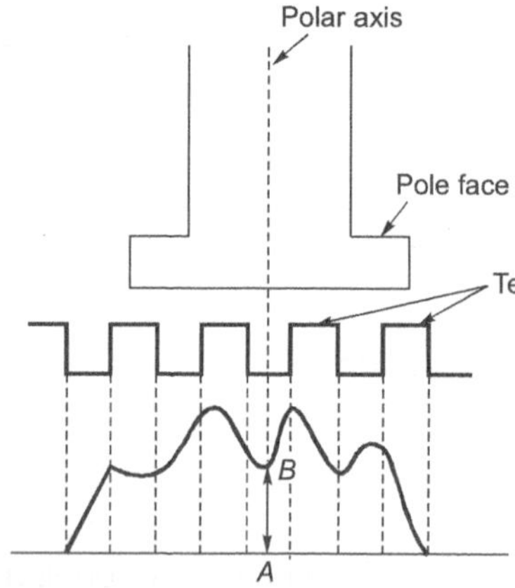

Fig. (a)

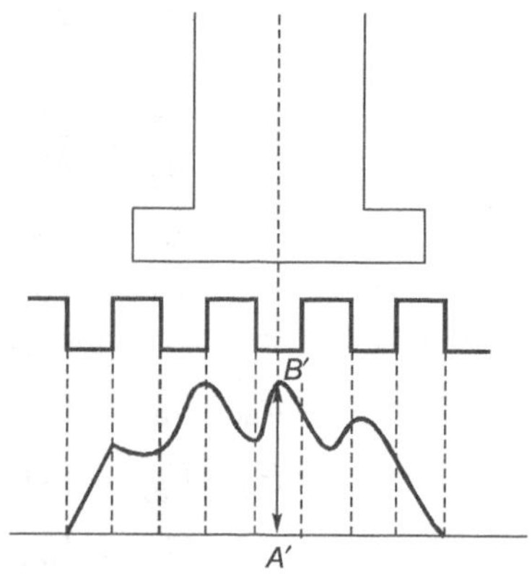

Fig. (b)

3.35 A 37.3 kW dc motor has a full load speed of 1145 rpm. The armature current at full load is 75 A and the friction, windage and core-losses are 8000 W. If the flux in each pole of the motor is reduced to 60% of its rated value and armature current is 75 A, what is the electromagnet torque developed by the motor?

[4 marks : 2015]

Solution:

Developed power, $P_d = E_b I_a = (37.3 + 8)$ kW

$P_d = 45.3$ kW

and, $P_d \propto E_b \propto \phi$ $[I_a = \text{constant}]$

$$\frac{P_{d_1}}{P_{d_2}} = \frac{E_{b_1} I_{a_1}}{E_{b_2} I_{a_2}}$$

$$\Rightarrow \quad \frac{45.3}{P_{d_2}} = \frac{E_{b_1} \times 75}{0.6 E_{b_1} \times 75} = \frac{1}{0.6}$$

$$\Rightarrow \quad P_{d_2} = 27.18 \text{ kW}$$

and $$T_d = \frac{27.18 \times 10^3 \times 60}{2\pi \times (1145)} = 226.68 \text{ N-m}$$

Developed Torque $= T_d = 226.68$ N-m

3.36 A dc shunt generator is developing rated terminal voltage at some speed. Answer the following with a brief explanation:

(i) the direction of rotation is reversed.
(ii) in addition to the reversal of direction, the residual magnetism is also reversed.
(iii) only the field winding terminals of the original machine are interchanged.
(iv) only the residual magnetism of the original machine is reversed.
(v) both the direction of rotation and field winding connections of th original machine are reversed?

[4 marks : 2016]

Solution:

(i) No build up (Since residual flux gets destroyed)
(ii) No build up (Residual flux gets cancelled)
(iii) No build up (Φ_R gets cancelled)
(iv) Build up voltage at appositive / negative polarity.
(v) Build up voltage at negative polarity.

3.37 A 240 V series motor takes 40 A when giving its rated output at 1500 rpm. Its resistance is 0.3 Ω. Find what resistance must be added to obtain rated torque at (a) starting, and (b) at 1000 rpm.

[4 marks : 2016]

Solution:

As torque remains same, I_a same in both cases.

(a) Starting $\rightarrow E_b = 0$

$$\therefore \quad E_b = V - I_a (R_a + R_{ext} + R_{se})$$

$$0 = 240 - 40 (0.3 + R_{ext})$$

$$\therefore \quad R_{ext} = 5.7\ \Omega$$

(b)

$$\frac{N_2}{N_1} = \frac{E_{b2}}{E_{b1}} \times \frac{I_{a1}}{I_{a2}} \qquad \left(\begin{matrix}\phi \propto I_a \\ I_{a2} = I_{a1}\end{matrix}\right)$$

$$\therefore \quad \frac{1000}{1500} = \frac{E_{b2}}{240 - 40(0.3)}$$

$$\therefore \quad E_{b2} = 152 \text{ volts}$$

$$\therefore \quad E_{b2} = 240 - 40 (0.3 \times R_{ext})$$

$$= 152 \text{ volts}$$

$$\therefore \quad R_{ext} = 1.9\ \Omega$$

3.38 A 220 V, 7 hp dc series motor is mechanically coupled to a fan. It draws 25 A and runs at 300 rpm when connected to rated supply. The torque required by the fan is proportional to the square of the speed. The resistance of armature and field windings are 0.6 Ω and 0.4 Ω, respectively. Neglect armature reaction and rotational loss:

(i) Determine the power delivered to the fan and the torque developed by the machine.
(ii) The speed is to be reduced to 200 rpm by inserting a resistance R_s in the armature circuit. Determine the value of this resistance and the power delivered to the fan.

[10 marks : 2016]

Solution:

(i)

$$V = 220,$$

$$R_a = 0.6\ \Omega,$$

$$R_{se} = 0.4\ \Omega,$$

$$I_a = 25 \text{ A}$$

$$E_b = V - I_a (R_a + R_{se})$$

$$= 220 - 25 (0.6 + 0.4)$$

$$\therefore \quad E_b = 195 \text{ volts}$$

$$\text{Power developed} = E_b I_a = 195 \times 25 = 4875 \text{ W}$$

$\because$ No rotational loss $\rightarrow$ Power developed = delivered

$$\text{Torque developed} = T = \frac{60}{2\pi N} P$$

$$\therefore \quad T = \frac{60}{2\pi(300)} 4875 = 155.25 \text{ N-m}$$

(ii) Given: $T \propto N^2$

speed reduced to 200 rpm

$$\therefore \quad \frac{T_2}{T_1} = \left(\frac{N_2}{N_1}\right)^2$$

Series motor:

$$\therefore \quad T \propto I_a^2$$

$$\therefore \quad \left(\frac{I_{a2}}{I_{a1}}\right)^2 = \left(\frac{N_2}{N_1}\right)^2 \Rightarrow I_{a2}^2 = \left(\frac{N_2}{N_1}\right)^2 I_{a1}^2$$

$$\therefore \quad I_{a2}^2 = \left(\frac{200}{300}\right)^2 (25)^2 = 16.67 \text{ A}$$

$$\frac{N_2}{N_1} = \frac{E_{b2}}{E_{b1}} \times \frac{\phi_1}{\phi_2} \Rightarrow \frac{N_2}{N_1} = \frac{E_{b2}}{E_{b1}} \times \frac{I_{a1}}{I_{a2}}$$

$$\therefore \quad \frac{200}{300} = \frac{E_{b2}}{195} \times \frac{25}{16.67}$$

$$\therefore \quad E_{b2} = 86.684 \text{ volts}$$

$$E_{b2} = V - I_{a2}(R_a + R_{se} + R_{ext})$$

$$\therefore \quad 86.684 = 220 - 16.67\,(0.6 + 0.4 + R_{ext})$$

$$\therefore \quad R_{ext} = 7\ \Omega$$

$$\therefore \quad \text{Power delivered} = E_{b2} \cdot I_{a2}$$

$$= 86.684 \times 16.67 = 1445 \text{ Watts}$$

3.39 A shunt motor is connected to a constant d.c. voltage source and it drives a constant load torque. Determine the effect of back emf E_a on speed as a function of flux, when $E_a < \frac{V_t}{2}$ and $E_a > \frac{V_t}{2}$.

[20 marks : 2017]

Solution:

We know that,

$$E_b = k\phi\omega_m \qquad \text{...(i)}$$

$$E_b = V - I_a R_a \qquad \text{...(ii)}$$

$$T = k\phi I_a \qquad \text{...(iii)}$$

From equation (i) and (ii),

$$k\phi\omega_m = V - I_a R_a$$

$$\omega_m = \frac{V - I_a R_a}{k\phi}$$

By substituting,

$$I_a = \frac{T}{k\phi} \qquad \text{(From equation (iii))}$$

$$\omega_m = \frac{V}{k\phi} - \frac{T R_a}{k^2\phi^2}$$

Differentiating ω_m with respect to ϕ

Case (i):

$$\frac{d\omega_m}{d\phi} > 0$$

$$-\frac{V}{k\phi^2} + \frac{2T R_a}{k^2\phi^3} > 0$$

Again putting,

$$T = k\phi I_a$$

$$-\frac{V}{k\phi^2}+\frac{2I_a R_a}{k\phi^2} > 0$$

$$2I_a R_a > V$$

$$2V-2E_b > V$$

$$E_b < \frac{V}{2}$$

$\therefore$ when $E_b < \frac{V_t}{2}$ speed of the motor increases with rise in flux.

Case (ii):

$$\frac{d\omega_m}{d\phi} < 0$$

$$-\frac{V}{k\phi^2}+\frac{2TR_a}{k^2\phi^3} < 0$$

Putting, $T = k\phi I_a$

$$-\frac{V}{k\phi^2}+\frac{2I_a R_a}{k\phi^2} < 0$$

$$2I_a R_a < V$$

$$V-E_b < \frac{V}{2}$$

$$E_b > \frac{V}{2}$$

$\therefore$ when $E_b > \frac{V_t}{2}$ speed of the motor decreases with rise in flux.

3.40 **A 20 kW, 500 V DC shunt motor (having 90% full-load efficiency) has 40% armature copper losses of its full-load losses. Calculate the resistance values of a 4-section starter suitable for limiting starting current between 120% to 200% of full-load current. Assume field resistance of 250 Ω.**

[20 marks : 2018]

Solution:

Given, Full load output = 20 kW at 500 V

$$\eta = 90\%$$

$\therefore$ $$\text{Input} = \frac{20000}{0.9} = 22222\text{ W}$$

$\therefore$ $$\text{Losses} = \text{Input} - \text{Output} = 2222\text{ W}$$

and as armature copper losses are 40% of full load losses

$$\text{Armature copper losses} = 0.4 \times 2222 = 888.8\text{ W}$$

$$\text{Full load line current} = \frac{22222}{500} = 44.4\text{ Amp}$$

$$\text{Field current} = \frac{500}{250} = 2\text{ A}$$

Full load armature current, $I_a = I_L - I_f = 42.4$ Amp

$$\text{Armature resistance} = \frac{888.8}{(42.4)^2} = 0.49\ \Omega$$

Starting current refers to line current,

Minimum starting line current = 1.2 × 44.4 = 53.3 A

Minimum starting armature current = 53.3 – 2 = 51.3 A

Maximum starting line current = 2 × 44.4 = 88.8 A

∴ Maximum starting armature current = 88.8 – 2 = 86.8 A

A starter having 4 sections is as follows:

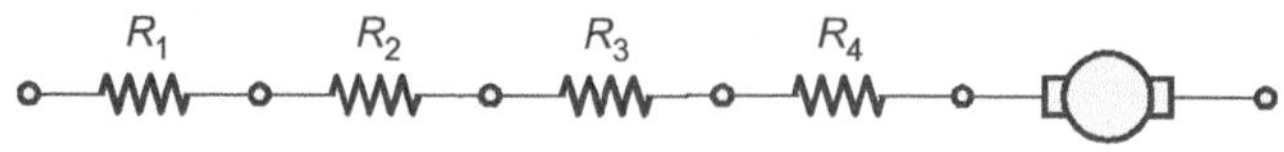

$$K = \frac{I_{a2}}{I_{a1}} = \frac{51.3}{86.8} = 0.591$$

Also, $$\frac{500}{R_{total}} = 86.8$$

⇒ $$R_{total} = 5.76\ \Omega$$

We know, $$R_1 = R_{total}(1 - K) = 5.76(1 - 0.591) = 2.356\ \Omega$$

$$R_2 = KR_1 = 0.591 \times 2.356 = 1.392\ \Omega$$

$$R_3 = K^2R_1 = 0.8229\ \Omega$$

$$R_4 = K^3R_1 = 0.486\ \Omega$$

3.41 A 400 V DC shunt motor has armature and field resistance of 0.2 Ω and 200 Ω respectively. It draws a current of 6 A on no-load and 70 A on full-load. If its no-load and full-load speeds are the same, determine the field weakening due to load current as percentage of no-load flux.

[20 marks : 2020]

Solution:

Given that, $V_t = 400$ V DC

Armature resistance, $(r_a) = 0.2\ \Omega$

Field resistance, $(r_{fL}) = 200\ \Omega$

No load speed = Full load speed

$N_{NL} = N_{fL}$

Let field flux at no-load = ϕ_{NL} Wb

and field flux at full load = ϕ_{fL} Wb

Back emf at no-load = $E_{b(NL)}$

Back emf at full load = $E_{b(FL)}$

Armature current at full load = $I_{a(FL)}$

Armature current at no-load = $I_{a(NL)}$

Electrical equivalent circuit of given shunt motor is

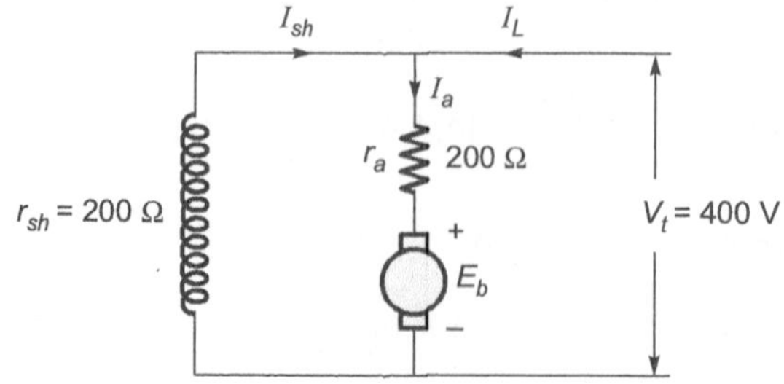

At no load, armature current is $I_{a(NL)}$

$$I_{a(NL)} = I_{L(NL)} - I_{sh}$$

$$I_{a(NL)} = 6 - \frac{400}{200} = 4 \text{ amp}$$

Back emf of motor, at no load = $E_{b(NL)}$

$$E_{b(NL)} = V_t - I_{a(NL)} \cdot r_a$$

$$E_{b(NL)} = 400 - 4 \times 0.2 = 399.2 \text{ volts}$$

At full load, armature current is = $I_{a(FL)}$

$$I_{a(FL)} = I_{L(fL)} - I_{sh}$$

$$I_{a(FL)} = 70 - \frac{400}{200} = 68 \text{ amp}$$

Back emf of motor, at full load = $E_{b(FL)}$

$$E_{b(FL)} = V_t - I_{a(FL)} \cdot r_a$$

$$E_{b(FL)} = 400 - 68 \times 0.2 = 386.40 \text{ volts}$$

⇒ As we know that back emf is directly proportional to speed and flux of motor $E_b \alpha N \cdot \phi$

$$\frac{E_{b(FL)}}{E_{b(NL)}} = \frac{N_{fL} \cdot \phi_{fL}}{N_{NL} \cdot \phi_{NL}}$$

$$\phi_{fL} = \frac{386.40}{399.20} \times \phi_{NL} \qquad [\because N_{fL} = N_{NL}]$$

$$\phi_{fL} = 0.9679 \, \phi_{fL}$$

$$\text{Reduction in load flux} = \frac{\phi_{FL} - \phi_{NL}}{\phi_{NL}} = \frac{0.9679 - 1}{1}$$

Percentage reduction in flux = –0.0320 × 100% = –3.20%

So as the DC shunt motor loaded from no load to full load, by keeping the speed constant, it's field will be weak due to load current. For given motor, % reduction in field is 3.20%.

3.42 A 220 V, 8-pole, 4.5 kW, 1100 rpm, lap connected dc generator has 1200 conductors. Each conductor has a resistance of 100 mΩ. The generator is run at half rated speed and is delivering rated current to load. Find the induced emf and corresponding terminal voltage under this condition, Assume constant field flux and no magnetic saturation of the machine during operation.

[12 marks : 2021]

Solution:

Given : 220 V, 8-pole, 4.5 kW, 1100 rpm, lap DC generator

Total number of conductors, Z = 1200, each conductor resistance = 100 mΩ

If resistance per conductor is 'x' Ω

No. of conductors = Z

No. of parallel paths = A

Resistance of Armature (R)

$$R_a = \frac{xZ}{A^2} = \frac{100 \times 10^{-3} \times 1200}{8^2} = 1.875 \Omega$$

Given :

Rated output of generator = 4.5 kW

$$\therefore \qquad \text{Rated current} = I = \frac{4500}{220} = 20.4545 \text{ A}$$

At rated speed, rated load and rated terminal voltage (V)

$$E_{g1} = V + I_a R_a = 220 + 20.4545(1.875) = 258.35 \text{ V}$$

Generator runs at half rated speed, but rated 'I_a'

$$E_g \propto N$$

Since ϕ is constant

$$E_{g2} = \frac{N_2}{N_1} \times E_{g1} = \frac{N_1/2}{N_1} \times 258.35 \text{ V} = 129.175 \text{ V}$$

$$V_2 = E_{g2} - I_a R_a = 129.175 - 20.4545\,(1.875)$$
$$= 90.82 \text{ V}$$

3.43 **A 240 V shunt motor takes a current of 3.5 A on no load. The armature resistance is of 0.4 Ω, and shunt field resistance of 160 Ω when motor operates at full load. It takes 24 A and runs at 2400 rpm when the motor is converted to long shunt compound type by adding a field winding of 0.1 Ω. There is a change of 10% in the total flux, when the compound motor develops the same torque. Determine the power developed and speed of the motor when it is connected as**

(i) a cumulative compound motor.

(ii) a differential compound motor.

[20 marks : 2022]

Solution:

At full load, $I_L = 24 \text{ A}, N = 2400$

$$I_{sh} = \frac{V}{R_{sh}} = \frac{240}{160} = 1.5 \text{ A}$$

$$I_a = I_L - I_{sh} = 22.5 \text{ A}$$

$$E_b = 240 - 22.5(0.4) = 231 \text{ V}$$

(i) It is mentioned that shunt became long shunt cumulative with change in flux 10%. Considering cumulative flux increased by 10%.

So, $\phi_2 = 1.1\phi_1$

Mentioned same torque, $T \propto \phi I_a$

$$\therefore \quad \phi_1 I_{a1} = \phi_2 I_{a2}$$

$$I_{a2} = \frac{\phi_1}{\phi_2} I_{a1} = \frac{\phi_1}{1.1\phi_1} 22.5$$

$$I_{a2} = 20.454 \text{ A}$$

$$\therefore \quad E_{b2} = V - I_{a2}(R_a + R_{se})$$
$$= 240 - 20.454(0.4 + 0.1) = 229.77 \text{ V}$$

$$\frac{N_2}{N_1} = \frac{E_{b2}}{E_{b1}} \times \frac{\phi_1}{\phi_2}$$

$$\frac{N_2}{2400} = \frac{229.77}{231} \times \frac{\phi_1}{1.1\phi_1}$$

$$\therefore \quad N_2 = 2170.2 \text{ rpm}$$

Power developed : $E_{b2} I_{a2} = 229.77 \times 20.454$

$$= 4699.7 \text{ W}$$

(ii) Considering differentially compounded flux change given 10%.

So $\phi_2 = 0.9\phi_1$

Torque is same given

$\therefore$ $\phi_1 I_{a1} = \phi_2 I_{a2}$

$$I_{a2} = \frac{\phi_1}{0.9\phi_1} \times 22.5 = 25 \text{ A}$$

$$E_{b2} = V - I_{a2}(R_a + R_{se}) = 240 - 25(0.4 + 0.1)$$
$$= 227.5 \text{ V}$$

$$\frac{N_2}{N_1} = \frac{E_{b2}}{E_{b1}} \times \frac{\phi_1}{\phi_2}$$

$$\frac{N_2}{2400} = \frac{227.5}{231} \times \frac{\phi_1}{0.9\phi_1}$$

$$N_2 = 2626.26 \text{ rpm}$$

Power developed : $E_{b2} \times I_{a2} = 227.5 \times 25$
$= 5687.5 \text{ W}$

3.44 **A dc motor is mechanically connected to a constant torque load. When the armature is connected to a 120 volt dc supply, it draws an armature current of 10 amperes and runs at 1800 rpm. The armature resistance is R_a = 0.1 Ω. Accidentally, the field circuit breaks and the flux drops to the residual flux, which is only 5% of the original flux.**

(i) Determine the value of the armature current immediately after the field circuit breaks (i.e. before the speed has had time to change from 1800 rpm).

(ii) Determine the hypothetical final speed of the motor after the field circuit breaks.

Neglect the inductance of the armature circuit.

[20 marks : 2023]

Solution:

$$V = 120 \text{ V}, I_a = 10 \text{ A}, R_a = 0.1\ \Omega, N = 1800$$
$$\phi_2 = 0.05\ \phi_1, (\phi \text{ reduced by } 95\%)$$

(i) I_a when field circuit breaks immediately before speed change from 1800 rpm.

$$E_b = V - I_a R_a$$
$$= 120 - 10(0.1) = 119 \text{ V}$$

$E_b \propto \phi N$, when $\phi \downarrow 95\%$, N : Constant

E_b also drops to 95% instantly.

(OR) If flux is 5% of original, E_b also same.

$\therefore$ $E_{b2} = 0.05 E_{b1} = 5.95 \text{ V}$

Value of armature current immediately after the field circuit breaks

$$I_{a2} = \frac{V - E_b}{R_a} = \frac{120 - 5.95}{0.1} = 1140.5 \text{ A}$$

(ii) Final speed (Hypothetically)

Given constant torque : $T \propto \phi I_a$

To maintain torque constant I_{a2} should be :

$$\frac{T_2}{T_1} = \frac{\phi_2}{\phi_1} \cdot \frac{I_{a2}}{I_{a1}}$$

$$\Rightarrow \quad 1 = \frac{0.05\phi_1}{\phi_1} \cdot \frac{I_{a2}}{10}$$

$$\Rightarrow \quad I_{a2} = 200 \text{ A}$$

For $I_{a2} = 200$ A, $\quad E_{b2} = V - I_{a2}R_a$

$$E_{b2} = 120 - 200(0.1) = 100 \text{ V}$$

$$\frac{N_2}{N_1} = \frac{E_{b2}}{E_{b1}} \times \frac{\phi_1}{\phi_2}$$

$$\Rightarrow \quad \frac{N_2}{1800} = \frac{100}{119} \times \frac{\phi_1}{0.05\phi_1}$$

Speed after the field circuit breaks

$$N_2 = 30252.1 \text{ rpm}$$

4. Synchronous Machines

4.1 A star-connected alternator is synchronized with an infinite bus of 11 kV; its steam input is then increased till its output power is 15 MW. Now when its excitation emf is increased to 130%, the synchronous machine starts operating at p.f. of 0.8 lagging. Compute the synchronous reactance of the machine. Neglect armature resistance. Determine the power factor, load angle and armature current of the machine before the excitation emf is increased.

[16 marks : 2001]

Solution:

From the figure,

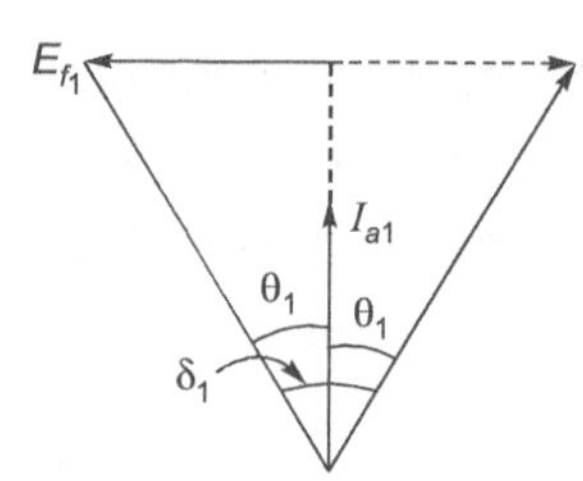

$$E_{f_1} = V_t \text{ and } \delta_1 = 2\theta_1$$

Given, $$\frac{E_{f_1}V_t \sin\delta_1}{X_s} = \frac{15}{3}$$

$$\left(\frac{11}{\sqrt{3}}\right)^2 \cdot \frac{\sin\delta_1}{X_s} = 5$$

$$\frac{\sin\delta_1}{X_s} = 0.123$$

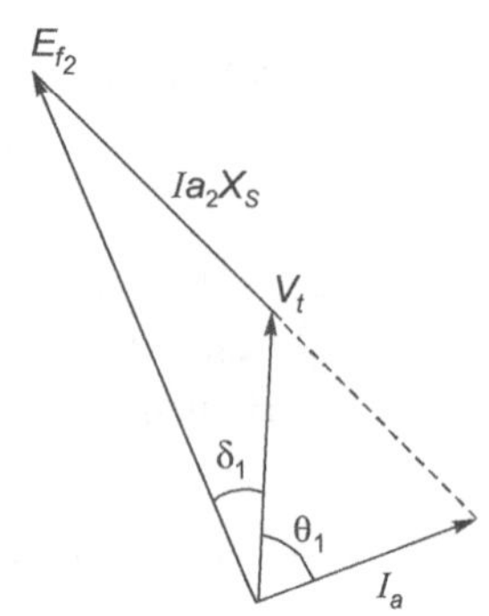

Now, when excitation increases to 130%, then phasor diagram

$$E_{f_2} = 1.3\ E_{f_1};\ \theta = \cos^{-1} 0.8 = 37°$$

From the phasor, $$E_{f_2} = [(V_t \cos\theta_1)^2 + (V_t \sin\theta_1 + I_{a_2} X_s)^2]^{1/2}$$

Given, $$15 \times 10^6 = \sqrt{3} \times 11 \times \cos\theta \times I_{a_2} \times 10^3$$

$$I_{a_2} = 984 \text{ amp}$$

$$\therefore \quad \left[\left(\frac{11}{\sqrt{3}} \times 0.8\right)^2 + \left(\frac{11}{\sqrt{3}} \times 0.6 + 0.984X_s\right)^2\right]^{1/2} = 1.3 \times \frac{11}{\sqrt{3}}$$

$$25.81 + \left(\frac{11}{\sqrt{3}} \times 0.6 + 0.984X_s\right)^2 = 68.163$$

$$\frac{11\times0.6}{\sqrt{3}}+0.984X_s = \sqrt{42.353}$$

$$X_s = 2.74\ \Omega$$

Then,

$$\sin\delta = 0.123\times2.74$$

$$\delta = 19.70°$$

Then initial power factor,

$$\cos\theta = \cos(\delta/2) = 0.985 \text{ (leading)}$$

4.2 **Why synchronous motors have no starting torque of their own?**

[4 marks : 2002]

Solution:

In case of three-phase synchronous motor, electromagnetic torque is given by

$T_e \propto$ (stator field strength) (rotor field strength) sin δ

where δ = torque angle between stator poles and rotor poles with the rotor stationary, when 3-phase supply is given to stator, a rotating magnetic field is set up. As a result, the torque angle between rotating stator poles and stationary rotor poles varies with time. Let this angle δ as a function of time be expressed as $\delta = \omega t$, then

Torque $\propto$ (stator field strength) (rotor field strength) sinωt. The torque given by above expression varies sinusoidally with time. Its value reverse during each half cycle, average value of this torque over a complete cycle is zero. Thus a synchronous motor has no self-starting torque.

4.3 **A cylindrical rotor hydro-generator is feeding an active power of 0.25 p.u. into a large network bus which is held at 1.0 p.u. voltage. The generator is overexcited with an induced voltage of 1.5 p.u. The synchronous impedance of the generator and the connecting link are j0.725 p.u./phase and j0.11 p.u./phase respectively. Calculate the percent change in reactive power output measured at the network bus in each of the following cases:**

(a) If the turbine torque is increased by 100%, keeping the excitation of the generator constant.

(b) If the turbine torque is held constant at the initial value but the excitation is increased by 20% (neglect saturation).

[20 marks : 2002]

Solution:

For cylindrical rotor hydro-generator,
Assuming $R_a = 0$,

$$P_{out} = \frac{E_f V_t}{X_s}\sin\delta$$

$$Q_{out} = \frac{(E_f\cos\delta - V_t)V_t}{X_s}$$

$V_t = 1$ pu, $X_s = j0.725 + j0.11 = j0.835$ pu

$E_{f_1} = 1.5$ pu, $P_{out_1} = 0.25$

$$P_{out1} = \frac{E_{f_1}V_t}{X_s}\sin\delta_1$$

$$\Rightarrow \quad 0.25 = \frac{1.5\times1}{0.835}\times\sin\delta_1 \quad\Rightarrow\quad \delta_1 \simeq 8°$$

$$Q_{out1} = \frac{(E_{f_1}\cos\delta_1 - V_t)V_t}{X_s} = \frac{(1.5\cos 8° - 1)\times 1}{0.835} = 0.5818$$

(a) 100% increase in torque means 100% increase in real power

$$P_{out2} = 0.5\,\text{pu} = \frac{E_{f_1}V_t}{X_s}\sin\delta_2$$

$$\Rightarrow \quad 0.5 = \frac{1.5\times 1}{0.835}\sin\delta_2 \Rightarrow \delta_2 = 16.16°$$

$$Q_{out2} = \frac{(E_{f_1}\cos\delta_2 - V_t)V_t}{X_s} = \frac{(1.5\cos 16.16 - 1)\times(1)}{0.835} = 0.5278$$

$$\%\text{ change in } Q_{out} = \frac{Q_{out_2} - Q_{out_1}}{Q_{out_1}}\times 100$$

$$= \frac{0.5278 - 0.5818}{0.5818}\times 100 = -9.28\%$$

(b)

$$P_{out3} = 0.25 \qquad \{\text{turbine torque is constant}\}$$

$$E_{f3} = 1.2\times E_{f_1} = 1.2\times 1.5 = 1.8$$

$$P_{out3} = \frac{E_{f_3}V_t}{X_s}\sin\delta_3$$

$$\Rightarrow \quad 0.25 = \frac{1.8\times 1}{0.835}\sin\delta_3 \Rightarrow \delta_3 = 6.66°$$

$$Q_{out3} = \frac{(E_{f_3}\cos\delta_1 - V_t)V_t}{X_s} = \frac{(1.8\cos 6.66 - 1)\times(1)}{0.835} = 0.9435$$

$$\%\text{ change in } Q_{out} = \frac{Q_{out_3} - Q_{out_1}}{Q_{out_1}}\times 100$$

$$= \frac{0.9435 - 0.5818}{0.5818}\times 100 = 62.16\%$$

4.4 A 3-phase synchronous motor has

(a) High starting torque
(b) No starting torque
(c) Low starting torque
(d) Low starting current

[2 marks : 2003]

Solution: (b)

Option (b) is correct.

4.5 Explain the following: Synchronous impedance of an alternator.

[4 marks : 2003]

Solution:

Synchronous impedance of an alternator: In the short-circuit test, entire emf E_f is consumed in circulating the short-circuit current I_{sc}, through the synchronous impedance Z_s. Therefore,

$$Z_s = \frac{E_f}{I_{sc}} = \frac{\text{Open circuit terminal voltage for certain field current}}{\text{Short-circuit current for the same field current}}$$

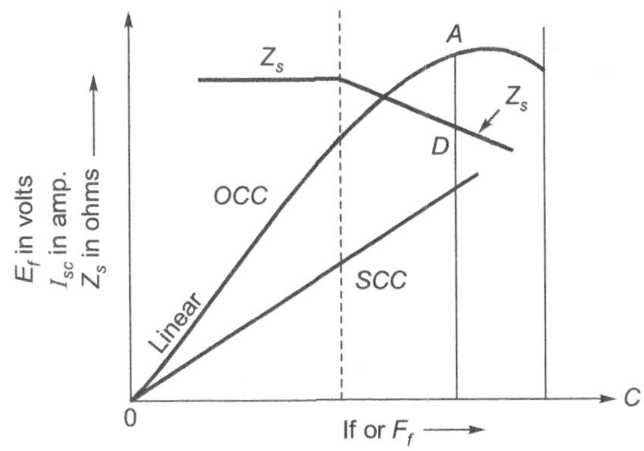

If there were no saturation, Z_s would be constant. Actually Z_s is variable and it decreases with the on set of saturation in the *OCC*.

By mathematically,

$$Z_s = \sqrt{r_a^2 + X_s^2}$$

$$X_s = \text{Synchronous reactance}$$

4.6 Find the synchronous impedance and reactance of a single-phase alternator in which a given field current produces an armature current of 250 A, on short-circuit and a generated emf of 1500 V on open-circuit. The armature resistance is 2.0 ohms. Calculate the terminal potential difference when a load of 250 A at 6.6 kV at a lagging p.f. of 0.8 is switched off

[15 marks : 2003]

Solution:

Synchronous impedance,

$$Z_s = \frac{E_f}{I_{sc}} = \frac{1500}{250} = 6\ \Omega$$

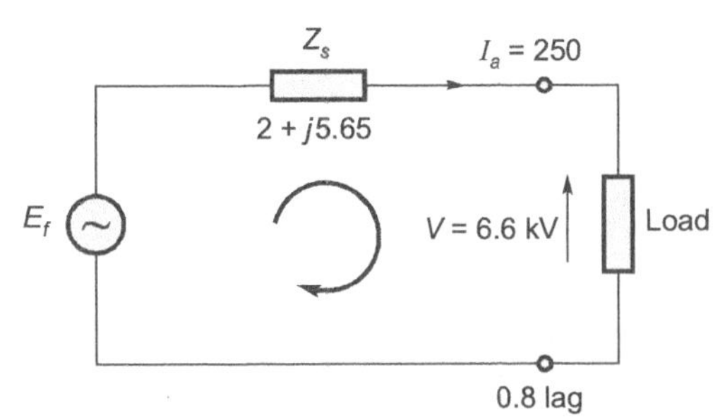

$$Z_s = \sqrt{X_s^2 + r_a^2}$$

Synchronous reactance,

$$X_s = \sqrt{Z_s^2 - r_a^2} = \sqrt{(6)^2 - (2)^2}$$

or $\quad X_s = 5.656\ \Omega$

$$\bar{V} = 6.6 \times 10^3 \angle 0^\circ$$

$$I_a = 250 \text{ A}$$

Load p.f. $\quad \cos\phi = 0.8$ lag

$$\bar{I}_a = 250\angle{-36.9}$$

$$Z_s = 2 + j5.65 = 5.99\ \angle 70.5^\circ$$

$$\bar{E} = \bar{V} + \bar{I}_a\bar{Z}_s = 6600\ \angle 0^\circ + 250\ \angle{-36.9^\circ} \times 5.99\ \angle 70.5^\circ$$

$$\bar{E} = 7.89\ \angle 6.03 \text{ kV}$$

Terminal voltage if load is switched off,

$$V_t = E_f = 7.89 \text{ kV}$$

4.7 Which type of alternator is used in hydro-electric power stations?

(a) Non-salient pole alternator (b) Turbo generator

(c) Salient pole alternator (d) Steam turbine alternator [2 marks : 2004]

Solution: (c)

Option (c) is correct.

4.8 An alternator has an armature resistance of 0.3 Ω and leakage reactance of 1.22 Ω. The alternator supplies 100 A current to a feeder of resistance 1.5 Ω and reactance 2.0 Ω. The voltage at the far end of the feeder is 3000 V. The load current having a p.f. of 0.8 lagging with respect to this voltage. Find the terminal voltage of alternator and the emf generated. [10 marks : 2004]

Solution:

Assuming 3-ϕ alternator,

$$V = \frac{3000}{\sqrt{3}} \angle 0^\circ$$

$$I = 100\angle -36.9^\circ$$

$$\bar{V}_t = \bar{V} + \bar{I}(R_f + jX_f)$$

V_t = terminal voltage of the alternator

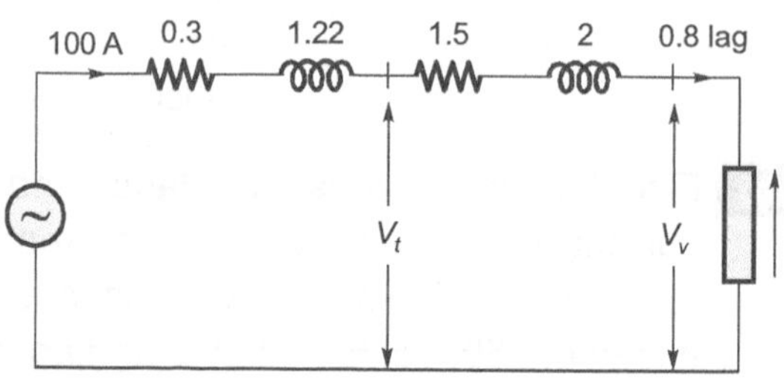

$$\bar{V}_t = \frac{3000}{\sqrt{3}} + 100\angle -36.9^\circ(1.5 + j2)$$

$$\bar{V}_t = 1973.32\angle 2.03$$

$$\bar{V}_{t(l-l)} = 1973.32 \times \sqrt{3}$$

$$\bar{V}_{t(l-l)} = 3417.89 \text{ V}$$

$$\bar{E} = \bar{V} + \bar{I}_a[(R_a + R_f) + j(X_s + X_f)] \quad \text{or} \quad \bar{E} = \bar{V}_t + \bar{I}_a(R_a + jX_s)$$

$$\bar{E} = 1973.32\angle 2.03 + (0.3 + j1.22)\,100\angle -36.9^\circ = 2074.71\angle 4.130$$

$$\bar{E}_{(l-l)} = 2074.71 \times \sqrt{3} = 3593.50 \text{ V}$$

4.9 A 3-phase synchronous generator with constant steam input supplies power to an infinite bus at a lagging power factor. If the excitation increases.

(a) Both power angle and power factor decreases.

(b) Both power angle and power factor increases.

(c) The power angle decreases while power factor increases.

(d) The power angle increases while power factor decreases. [2 marks : 2005]

Solution:

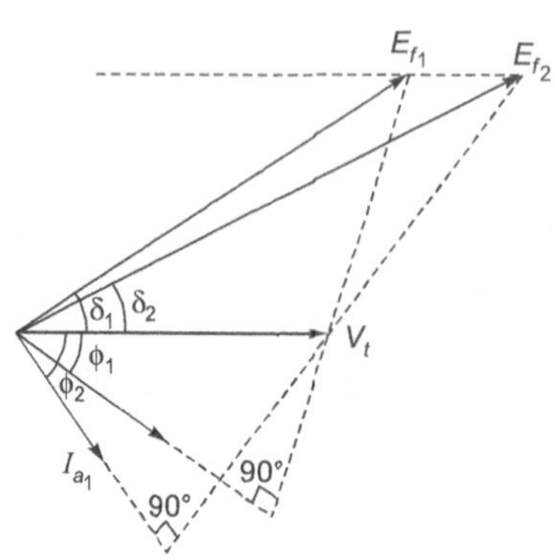

Both power angle and power factor decreases. Hence, option (a) is correct.

4.10 A synchronous generator supplies rated power at 0.8 p.f. lagging. Its resistance and synchronous reactance are 0.01 and 1.0 p.u. Calculate the terminal voltage if the open-circuit voltage is 2.1 p.u. What is the minimum allowable excitation voltage?

[14 marks : 2005]

Solution:

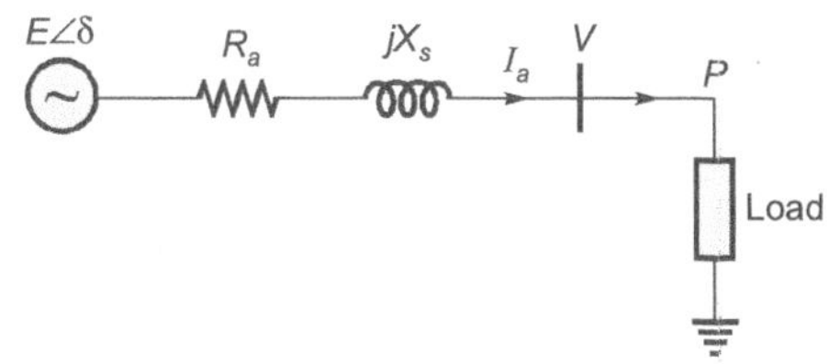

Load p.f. $\cos\phi = 0.8$ lag

$R_a = 0.01$ p.u.

$X_s = 1.0$ p.u.

$E = 2.1$ p.u.

$E^2 = (V\cos\phi + I_aR_a)^2 + (V\sin\phi + I_aX_S)^2$

Let, $I_a = 1$ p.u.

$(2.1)^2 = (V \times 0.8 + 1 \times 0.01)^2 + (V \times 0.6 + 1 \times 1)^2$

$4.41 = 0.64\,V^2 + 1 \times 10^{-4} + 1.6 \times 10^{-2}\,V + 0.36\,V^2 + 1 + 1.2\,V$

$3.4099 = V^2 + 1.216\,V$

or $V^2 + 1.216\,V - 3.4099 = 0$

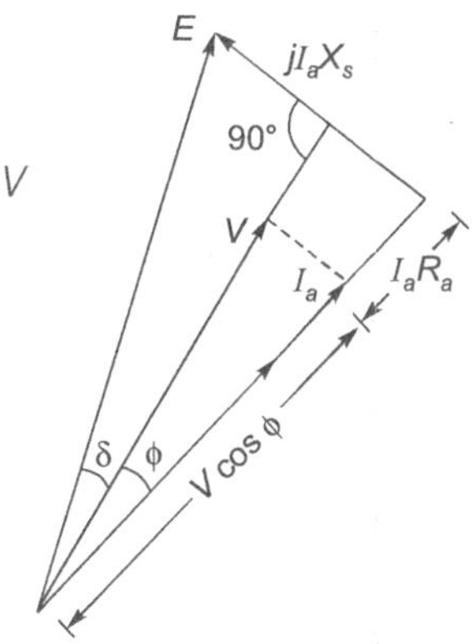

or $$V = \frac{-1.216 \pm \sqrt{(1.216)^2 + 4(3.4099)}}{2}$$

$$= \frac{-1.216 \pm 3.888}{2}$$

$V = 1.336$ V, -2.552 V (left)

Terminal voltage, $V = 1.336$ volt

For the minimum excitation voltage:

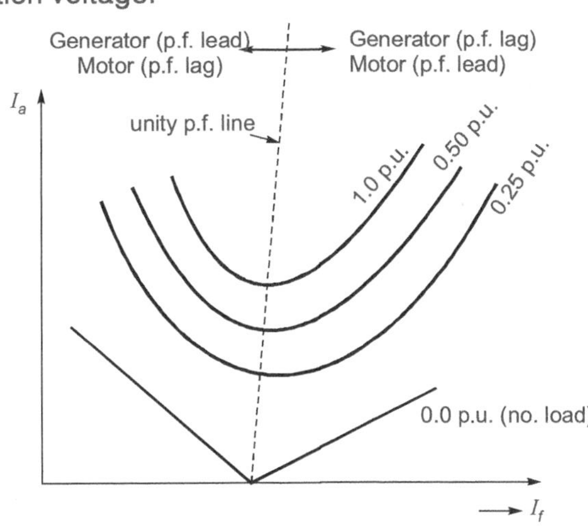

For $I_a = 1$ p.u.,

E_{min} if p.f. leading $\cos\phi = 0$,

$\sin\phi = 1$

$E^2_{min} = (1.336 \times 0 + 1 \times 0.01)^2 + (1.336 \times 1 - 1 \times 1)^2$

$E_{min} = 0.3361$ volt

Note: For upf, $E_f^2 = (V_t + I_a r_a)^2 + (I_a X_s)^2$

4.11 A star-connected 3-phase alternator delivers a 3-phase star connected load at a power factor of 0.8 lagging. A wire connects the load and the alternator. The terminal voltage at no-load is 2500 V, and at full-load of 1460 kW it is 2200 V. Determine the terminal voltage when it delivers a 3-phase star-connected load having a resistance of 6 W and reactance 8 W per phase respectively. Assume constant current and field excitation.

[14 marks : 2006]

Solution:

$$V_{\text{no load}} = 2500 \text{ V}$$
$$V_{\text{at load}} = 2200 \text{ V}$$
$$\text{load} = 1460 \text{ kW at 0.8 power factor}$$

$\therefore$
$$1460 \times 10^3 = \sqrt{3} \times 2200 \times I \times 0.8$$
$$I = 478.9 \text{ A}$$

For synchronous reactance X_s

$$\frac{2500}{\sqrt{3}} = \sqrt{\left(\frac{2200}{\sqrt{3}} \times 0.8\right)^2 + \left(\frac{2200}{\sqrt{3}} \times 0.6 + 478.9\, X_s\right)^2}$$
$$X_s = 0.54\ \Omega$$

For terminal voltage when load $(6 + j8)\ \Omega$ connected,

$$I = \frac{\frac{2500}{\sqrt{3}}}{6 + j(8 + 0.54)} = 138.3 \angle{-54.9°} \text{ A}$$

$$Z_L = 6 + j8\ \Omega$$
$$|V_{Ph}| = |I Z_L|$$
$$= 138.3\angle{-54.9} \times (6 + j8) = 1383\angle{-1.77} \text{ V}$$

Terminal voltage,
$$V_t = \sqrt{3} \times 1383 = 2395.4 \text{ V}$$

4.12 Two alternator working in parallel supply a lighting load of 3000 kW and a motor load aggregating to 5000 kW at a p.f. of 0.72. One machine is loaded upto 5000 kW at 0.8 p.f. lagging. What is the load and power factor of the other machine?

[14 marks : 2006]

Solution:

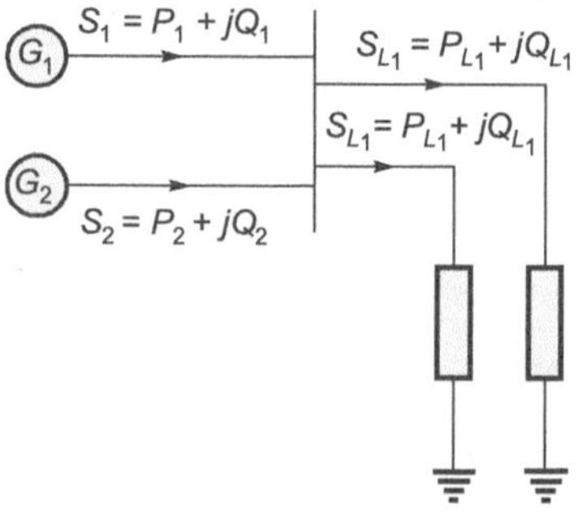

Given,
$$P_{L2} = 5 \text{ MW}$$
$$\cos\phi = 0.72$$

$\because$
$$P_{L_2} = S_{L_2} \cos\phi$$
$$S_{L_2} = \frac{5}{0.72} = 6.94 \text{ MVA}$$
$$Q_{L_2} = S_{L_2} . \sin\phi$$
$$= 6.94 \times \sin(\cos^{-1} 0.72) = 4.816 \text{ MVAR}$$

Given,
$$P_{L_1} = 3 \text{ MW}$$
$$\cos\phi = 1$$

$\therefore$
$$S_{L_1} = 3 \text{ MW}$$
$$Q_{L_1} = 0$$

Given,
$$P_1 = 5 \text{ MW}$$
$$\cos\phi = 0.8$$
$$S_1 = \frac{5}{0.8} = 6.25 \text{ MVA}$$
$$Q_1 = S_1 \sin\phi = 6.25 \times 0.6 = 3.75 \text{ MVAR}$$

$\because$
$$P_1 + P_2 = P_{L_1} + P_{L_2}$$

$$\therefore \quad 5 + P_2 = 3 + 5$$
$$P_2 = 3 \text{ MW}$$
$$\because \quad Q_1 + Q_2 = Q_{L_1} + Q_{L_2}$$
$$3.75 + Q_2 = 0 + 4.81$$
$$Q_2 = 1.06 \text{ MVAR}$$
$$\tan\phi = \frac{Q_2}{P_2} = \frac{1.06}{3} = 0.35$$
$$\text{Power factor } \cos\phi = 0.94$$

Second machine loaded upto 3 MW at 0.94 lag p.f.

4.13 **What are the methods of starting of synchronous motors?**

[4 marks : 2006]

Solution:

Since synchronous motors are not self-starting inherently, we should have some means for starting synchronous motors.

The methods are given below:

1. **Induction Motor Start:** Damper windings, consisting of copper bronze bars embedded in slots in the pole faces and short-circuited at both ends are usually provided in synchronous motors which serve not only to damp out oscillations during hunting but are also suitably designed as a squirrel-cage winding for starting purposes. If the rotor reaches near synchronous speed, the field circuit is suddenly energised and the rotor and stator fields interlock each other.
2. **Auxiliary Motor Start:** Using an auxiliary motor, the synchronous motor is first run as an alternator and is synchronised with the three-phase bus-bars. After synchronisation, supply to auxiliary motor is cut, and the alternator is made to run as synchronous motor drawing power from three-phases AC mains.
3. **Using Resistor in the Field Circuit:** Instead of leaving the field circuit open during starting of synchronous motor, it can be short-circuited and can be used as a damper winding. When an additional resistance of value 100 times that of the field resistance, is inserted in series with the field, the starting torque will be large. The field resistance is reduced as the motor accelerates until it becomes three to four times that of field itself. This method can be used in machines where large starting torque are required.
4. **Super Synchronous Start:** The armature is not rigidly bolted to the bed-plates as in an ordinary motor. It is capable of rotating about the rotor shaft. But under normal conditions, it is held stationary by a brake band surrounding the frame of the armature core. The rotor is mechanically coupled to load. The brake band on stator is released and when line voltage is impressed on armature terminals, the stator will try to rotate. When the armature reaches near-synchronous speed, the rotor field is excited and the machine pulls into synchronism.

4.14 **Calculate the rms value of the induced emf per phase of a 10 pole, three phase, 50 Hz alternator with 2 slots per pole per phase and 4 conductors per slot in two layers. The coil span is 150°. The flux per pole is 0.12 Wb.**

[8 marks : 2006]

Solution:

$$\text{Total number of conductors} = 2 \times 10 \times 3 \times 4 = 240$$
$$\text{Total number of turns} = \frac{240}{2} = 120$$
$$\text{Number of turns/phase} = \frac{120}{3} = 40 = T_{phase}$$

$$\text{Coil span} = 150°$$

$$\text{Chording angle} = 180° - \text{coil span} = 180 - 150° = 30°$$

$$\alpha = 30°$$

$$\text{Chording factor} = K_p = \cos\frac{\alpha}{2} = \cos 15° = 0.966$$

m = number of slots/pole/phase = 2

β = angle between adjacent slots

$$= \frac{180°}{\text{Number of slots/pole}} = \frac{180°}{m \times \text{phase}} = \frac{180°}{2\times 3} = 30°$$

$$\text{Distribution factor} = K_d = \frac{\sin\left(\frac{m\beta}{2}\right)}{m\sin\left(\frac{\beta}{2}\right)} = \frac{\sin\left(\frac{2\times 30}{2}\right)}{2\times\sin\left(\frac{30}{2}\right)} = 0.966$$

Rms value of the induced emf $E_{RMS} = 4.44 \times f \times \phi \times K_P \times K_D \times T_{phase}$

$$E_{RMS} = 4.44 \times 50 \times 0.12 \times 0.966 \times 0.966 \times 40$$

$$= 994.37 \text{ volts/phase}$$

4.15 A 8 pole alternator runs at 750 RPM. It supplies power to a 6 pole induction motor which has a full load slip of 3%. The full load speed of the motor is

(a) 1050 rpm (b) 970 rpm
(c) 960 rpm (d) 1250 rpm

[2 marks : 2007]

Solution:

$P = 8$, $N_8 = 750$ rpm, $f = \frac{N_s P}{120} = \frac{750\times 8}{120} = 50\text{ Hz}$ (supply frequency)

for inductor motor, $N_s = \frac{120f}{P} = \frac{120\times 50}{6} = 1000\text{ rpm}$

$$N = (1 - s)N_s = (1 - 0.03) \times 1000 = 970 \text{ rpm}$$

Hence, option (d) is correct.

4.16 A 500 KVA, 1100 V, 50 Hz Y connected 3-phase alternator has stator resistance of 0.1 ohm/phase and synchronous impedance of 1.5 ohm/phase. The alternator is supplying full load at unity power factor. The induced emf per phase for this condition is

(a) 769 V (b) 832 V
(c) 692 V (d) 935 V

[2 marks : 2007]

Solution:

$$I_a = \frac{500\times 10^3}{\sqrt{3}\times 1.1\times 10^3} = 262.43 \text{ amp}$$

$$E_a = \frac{V_t}{\sqrt{3}} + I_a(r_a + jX_s) = \frac{1100}{\sqrt{3}} + 262.43(0.1 + j1.5) = 769 \text{ V}$$

Hence, option (a) is correct.

4.17 Explain the choice of synchronous machine on the basis of the generating station.

[4 marks : 2007]

Solution:

A synchronous generator is universally employed for the generation of three-phase power at all generating stations. The largest-sized electrical machines are polyphase synchronous generators.

The constructional features of the two types of synchronous machine are:

1. Cylindrical rotor type 2. Salient pole type

The cylindrical-rotor synchronous generator are called turbo generators or turbo-alternators and are mainly used as steam turbine driven alternators. A cylindrical-rotor synchronous machine is characterised by long core length and small diameter so as to limit the centrifugal forces developed in the high speed rotor. The salient-pole construction is the most suitable for multipolar slow-speed water-turbine generators. That is why salient-pole synchronous generators are called hydro-generators. Most of the synchronous motors are of the salient-pole type. A salient-pole synchronous machine has small core length and large diameter so that large number of field poles can be accommodated on the rotor periphery.

4.18 Describe with all relevant circuit diagrams and graphs, the method of determining the regulations of a 3-phase alternator using ZPF method. Compare the results of this method with EMF and MMF Methods.
[10 + 5 marks : 2007]

Solution:

- This method is based on the separation of armature leakage reactance drop and the armature reaction effects. Hence it gives more accurate results. The experimental data required is (*i*) no load curve and (*ii*) full load zero power factor curves.
- It is the curve of terminal voltage against excitation when armature is delivering full load current at zero power factor.
- The reduction in voltage due to armature reaction is found from above and voltage drop due to armature leakage reactance X_L (also called potier reactance) is found from both. By combining these two, E_r can be calculated. It should be noted that if we vertically and to V the drop due to resistance and leakage reactance X_L, we get E_r. The zero power factor lagging curve can be obtained.
  (a) If a similar machine is available which may be driven at no-load as synchronous motor at practically zero p.f.
  (b) By loading the arlternator with pure reactors.
  (c) By connecting the alternator to a 3-ϕ line with ammeters and wattmeters connected for measuring current and power and by so adjusting the field current that we get full load armature current with zero wattmeter reading.

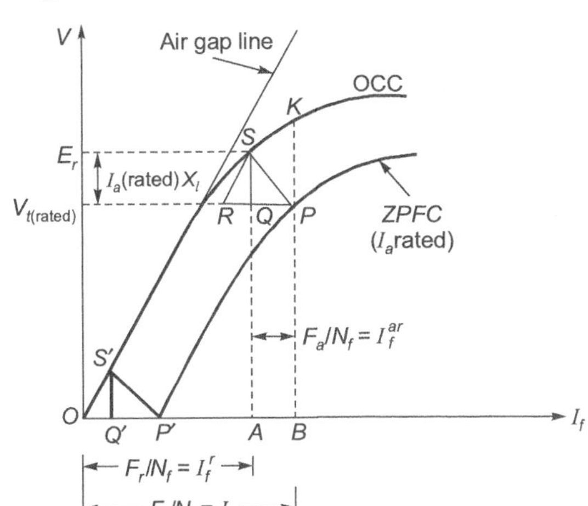

From the *SC* test $I_{SC} = I_a$(rated) which locates *P′* on I_f- axis such that $OP' = I_f^{SC}$

- From the ZPF test at V_t(rated) and I_a(rated) locate the point *P* such that $OB = I_f^{zpf}$.
- From *P* draw a line parallel to I_f- axis and locate *R* such that *RP* = *OP′*.
- From *R* draw the line parallel to the air-gap line which locates point *S* on *OCC*.
- From *S* draw *SQ* perpendicular to *RP*.
- $PQ = I_f^{ar}; X_l = \dfrac{SQ(\text{to scale})}{\sqrt{3}\, I_a(\text{rated})}$

$$\% \text{ Regulation} = \left(\frac{E_r - V}{V}\right) \times 100$$

Comparison of results with mmf and emf method:

- In the emf method, the phasor diagram involving voltages is used, whereas in mmf method, the phasor diagram involving mmf is used. For the zpf method, the emf are handled as voltages and the mmf as field ampere turns or field ampere.
- emf method gives higher value of voltage regulation.
  mmf method gives lower value of voltage regulation.
  zpf method gives accurate value of voltage regulation.

4.19 **A 3.75 MVA, 10 kV, 3-phase, 50 Hz, 10 pole low speed hydrogenerator has 144 slots containing a two-layer diamond winding with 5 conductors per coil side in each slot. The coil span is 12 slot pitches. The flux per pole is 0.116 Wb. Calculate the phase emf.**

[9 marks : 2008]

Solution:

Slots per pole per phase,
$$q = \frac{144/3}{10} = \frac{24}{5} = 4.8$$

Angular slot pitch,
$$\gamma = \frac{10 \times 180}{144} = \frac{25}{2} = 12.5$$

$$\text{Coil span} = 12\gamma = 12 \times \frac{25}{2} = 150°$$

Chording angle,
$$\epsilon = (\text{one pole pitch}) - (\text{coil span}) = 180° - 150° = 30°$$

$$k_d = \frac{\sin\left(\frac{q\gamma}{2}\right)}{q\sin\left(\frac{\gamma}{2}\right)} = \frac{\sin\left(\frac{4.8 \times 12.5}{2}\right)}{4.8\sin\left(\frac{12.5}{2}\right)} = 0.9568$$

$$k_p = \cos\frac{\epsilon}{2} = \cos 15° = 0.965$$

$$\text{Number of turns per phase} = N_{ph} = \frac{144 \times 5}{3} = 240$$

$$E_p = \sqrt{2} \cdot \pi \cdot f \cdot k_d \cdot k_p \cdot N_{ph} \cdot \phi$$

$$E_p = \sqrt{2} \times \pi \times 50 \times 0.9568 \times 0.966 \times 240 \times 0.116 = 5716.13 \text{ V}$$

4.20 **Why are the windings of synchronous generators of 3-phase distributed over slots per phase and are short pitched? Find expression for k_d and k_p.**

[9 marks : 2008]

Solution:

The advantages of distributing the winding in slots are:

1. reduction of the harmonics in the generated emf wave, thus making it approach a sine wave.
2. full utilisation of the armature iron and copper.
3. adding rigidity and mechanical strength to the winding.
4. the flux ϕ linking the coil,

$$\phi = \frac{4}{P} B_p l_r \text{ (flux/pole)}$$

From above equation the flux/pole is limited by the machine dimensions and the peak flux which cannot exceed a specified value dictated by saturation characteristic of iron. Therefore, for indicating an emf of an appropriate value in a practical machine a large number of coil turns are needed and it is not possible to accommodate all these in a single slot pair. So in 3-phase windings of synchronous generators distributed over slots per phase.

Expression fo k_d: Let 2-pole 3-phase machine with $m = 3$. The angle between adjacent slots is

$$\gamma = \frac{\pi P}{S} \text{ elect. rad.}$$

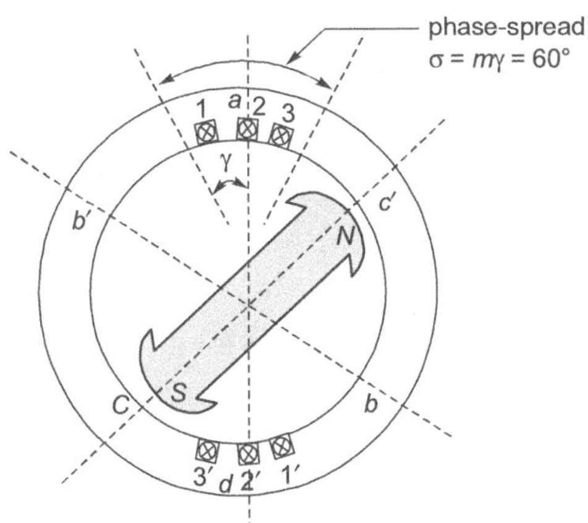

(a) Synchronous generator with distributed winding

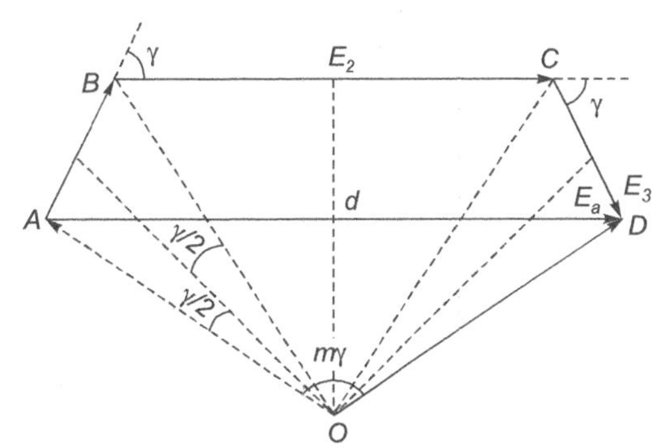

(b) Phasor diagram of coil emf's to yield phase voltage

The winding of phase a in this machine has three coil (11′, 22′ and 33′) which are placed in three slot-pairs distributed in space with an angular separation of γ elect. rad. The total angle $\sigma = m\gamma$ occupied by the phase winding along the armature periphery is called the phase spread. Such a winding is referred to as the distributed winding. Since the machine is always wound with identical coils, the sinusoidal emfs induced in coils 11′, 22′ and 33′ have the same rms value (E) but have a progressive time phase difference of γ because these coils are uniformly distributed in space. These coils are series connected to yield the phase voltage E_a which is the phasor sum of the coil emf's as shown in figure (b). From the figure because of distribution, the rms phase voltage is less than the algebraic sum of the rms coil voltages. This reduction ratio called the breadth factor (also distribution factor). From figure (b), the coil emf phasors from sides of a regular polygon, the centre of whose circumscribing circle is constructionally located in the diagram.

The phase voltage E_a is given by the resultant phasor [AD in figure (b)].

$$k_b = \frac{AD}{3AB} \quad \text{or} \quad \frac{AD}{m\,AB} \text{ (in general)}$$

From the geometry of figure (b),

$$AB = 2\,OA \sin \gamma/2$$

$$AD = 2\,OA \sin \gamma m/2$$

$$\therefore \qquad k_b = \frac{\sin m\gamma/2}{m \sin \gamma/2} < 1 \text{ for } m > 1$$

where, $$\gamma = \frac{180}{\text{slots per pole}} \text{ Elect. degrees}$$

Advantage of Short Pitch Winding are:

1. Reduction in the copper for overhang. This results in less cost of the machine.
2. Reduction of harmonics in the generated emf wave, thereby rendering the output emf wave almost a sine wave.

Expression for Pitch Factor:

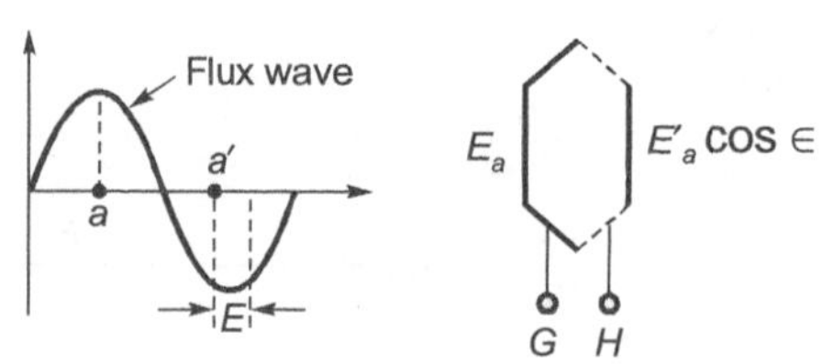

(a)

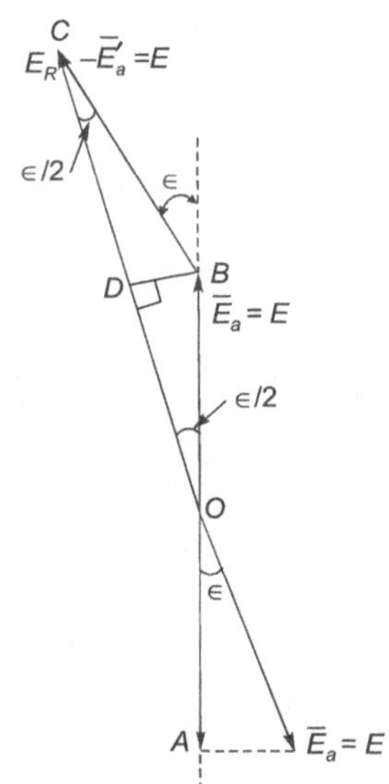

(b)

Figure (a) shows the short pitch coil and figure (b) shows the emf induced in the coil sides *a* and *a′* in phasor form. So the resultant emf E_R across the coil-ends 6, *H* is

$$\bar{E}_R = \bar{E}_a - \bar{E}'_a$$

From figure (b), In triangle *OBC*,

$$\angle OBC = 180 - \epsilon$$

$$\therefore \qquad \angle OBD = \frac{1}{2}\,|\angle OBC| = 90 - \frac{\epsilon}{2}$$

Since, $$\angle BOD = 90°$$

$$\angle DOB = \frac{\epsilon}{2} = \angle BCD$$

The resultant voltage E_R from figure (b) is,

$$E_R = OC = OD + DC$$

$$= OB \cos\frac{\epsilon}{2} + CB \cos\frac{\epsilon}{2} = 2E \cos\frac{\epsilon}{2}$$

The pitch factor is defined as the ratio of resultant emf of a chorded coil to the resultant emf had the same coil being full pitched, symbol k_p. Thus,

$$k_p = \frac{\text{Resultant emf of a chorded coil}}{\text{Resultant emf of a full-pitched coil}}$$

$$k_p = \frac{2E\cos\frac{\epsilon}{2}}{2E} = \cos\frac{\epsilon}{2}$$

The chording angle is $\epsilon°$ for fundamental flux wave and for nth space field harmonic, the chording angle becomes $n\epsilon°$ electrical. Therefore, the pitch factor for n^{th} harmonic is,

$$k_{pn} = \cos\frac{n\epsilon}{2}$$

4.21 **Draw the open-circuit characteristic and short circuit characteristic of synchronous machine, and show the variation of synchronous impedance, Z_s, with the field current, I_f. Explain the nature of variation of Z_s.**
A 3-phase, Y-connected synchronous generator rated at 10 kVA and 230 V has a synchronous reactance of 1.2 ohms per phase and an armature resistance of 0.5 ohms per phase. Calculate the following:
(a) The % voltage regulation at full load with 0.8 lagging power factor.
(b) The power factor of the load such that the voltage regulation is zero on full load.
[20 marks : 2009]

Solution:

Figure shows the open-circuit and short-circuit characteristic of synchronous machine and also the variation of synchronous impedance Z_s with field current I_f.

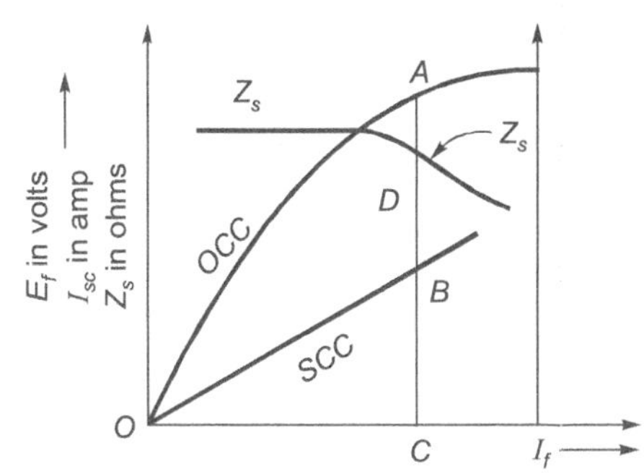

It is seen from the figure that for a field current of OC amperes,

$$Z_s \text{ in ohms} = CD = \frac{\text{AC in volts}}{\text{BC in amperes}}$$

If there were no saturation, Z_s would be constant. Actually Z_s is variable and it decreases with the onset of saturation in the OCC.

Numerical: Given that, 3-phase, Y-connected 10 kVA and 230 V synchronous generator, with X_s = 1.2 ohms/phase, R_a = 0.5 ohm/phase. We have to calculate:

(a) % voltage regulation at full load with 0.8 lagging power factor.

$$I_a \text{ per phase} = \frac{10 \times 10^3}{\sqrt{3} \times 230} = 25.1 \text{ Amp}$$

$$\cos\phi = 0.8;$$
$$\sin\phi = 0.6$$

$$V_t \text{ per phase} = \frac{230}{\sqrt{3}} = 132.79 \text{ volt}$$

$$E_f = \sqrt{(V_t\cos\phi + I_aR_a)^2 + (V_t\sin\phi + I_aX_s)^2}$$

$$= \sqrt{(132.79 \times 0.8 + 25.1 \times 0.5)^2 + (132.79 \times 0.6 + 25.1 \times 1.2)^2}$$

$$E_f = 161.75 \text{ volts}$$

$$\% \text{ voltage regulation} = \frac{E_f - V_t}{V_t} \times 100\% = \frac{161.75 - 132.79}{132.79} \times 100\%$$

$$\% \text{ V. R.} = 21.8\%$$

(b) Let $\cos\phi$ be the power factor at which V.R. becomes zero. The *p.f.* must be leading,

$$E_f^2 = (V_t \cos\phi + I_a R_a)^2 + (V_t \sin\phi - I_a X_s)^2$$

$$= V_t^2 + 2\,V_t I_a (R_a \cos\phi - X_s \sin\phi) + I_a^2 (R_a^2 + X_s^2)$$

For $V.R. = \text{Zero}$, $E_f = V_t = 132.79$ volt

$\therefore$ $$(132.79)^2 = (132.79)^2 + 2 \times 132.79 \times 25.1\,(0.5 \times \cos\phi - 1.2 \sin\phi) + (25.1)^2 [(0.5)^2 + (1.2)^2]$$

or $$0.5 \cos\phi - 1.2 \sin\phi = 0.1597$$

or $$a \sin(\phi - \theta) = 0.1597$$

where, $$a = 1.3 \quad \text{and} \quad \theta = 22.62°$$

$\therefore$ $$1.3 \sin(\phi - 22.62°) = 0.1597$$

$$\sin(\phi - 22.62°) = 0.1228$$

$$\phi - 22.62° = 7.053 \quad \text{or} \quad \phi = 29.67°$$

$$\cos\phi = 0.8688 \text{ (lead)}$$

4.22 **A 3-phase synchronous generator is excited by d.c. field to give rated voltage at its terminals on no load when a sudden short (symmetric) circuit occurs at the terminals.**

Show the typical plots of three armature phase and field current and also show the typical plot of the a.c. component of short circuit current in both actual and semi logarithmic plot identifying different operational conditions.

Draw the approximate equivalent circuits of the synchronous generators for x_d'', x_d' and x_d in terms of leakage, demagnetising field and damper winding reactances.

Define direct axis transient open circuit time constant T_{d0}'.

[5 marks : 2010]

Solution:

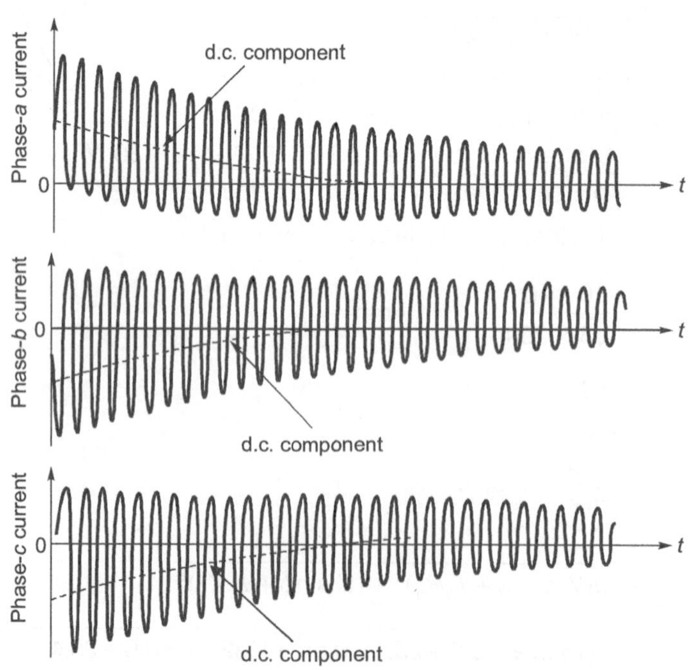

Short-circuit current waves forms in the three-phases of a synchronous generator

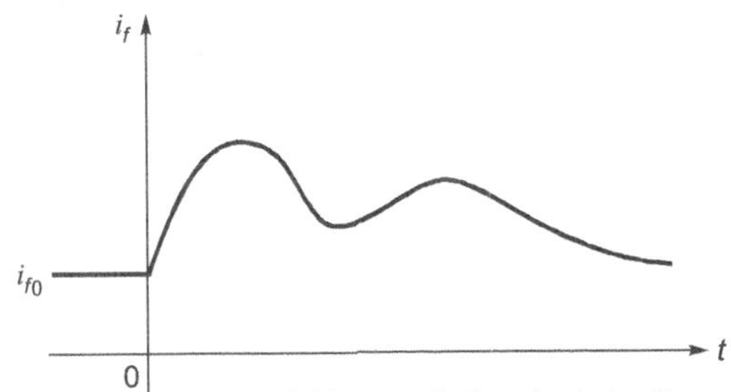

Plot of field current after short-circuit

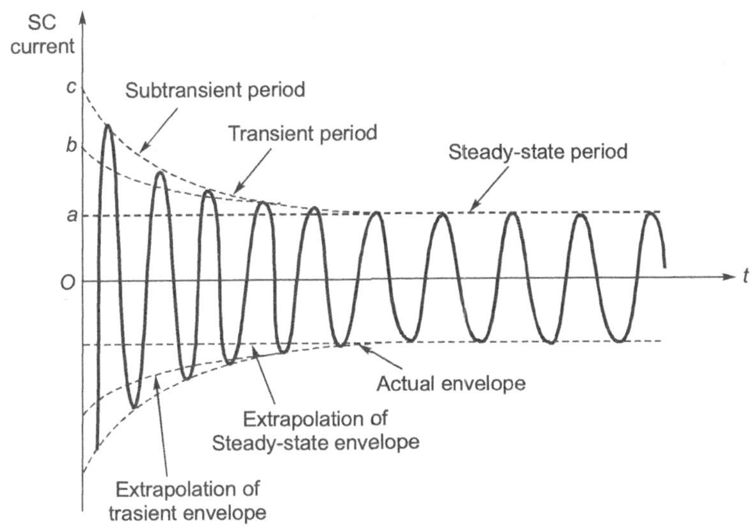

Symmetric short circuit in synchronous generator

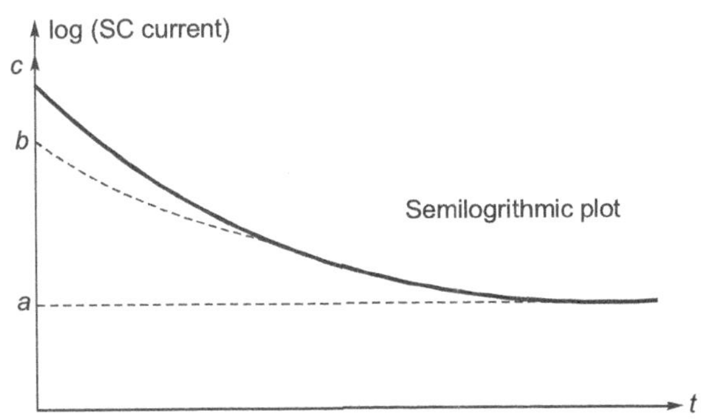

Let,

x_l = leakage reactance

x_a = armature reactance

x_f = demagnetizing field reactance

x_{dw} = damper winding reactance

$x_d = x_l + x_a$ = synchronous reactance

$x'_d = x_l + x_f || x_a$ = direct axis transient reactance

$x''_d = x_l + x_f || x_{aw} || x_a$ = direct axis subtransient reactance

(a) Steady state short circuit model of a synchronous machine.

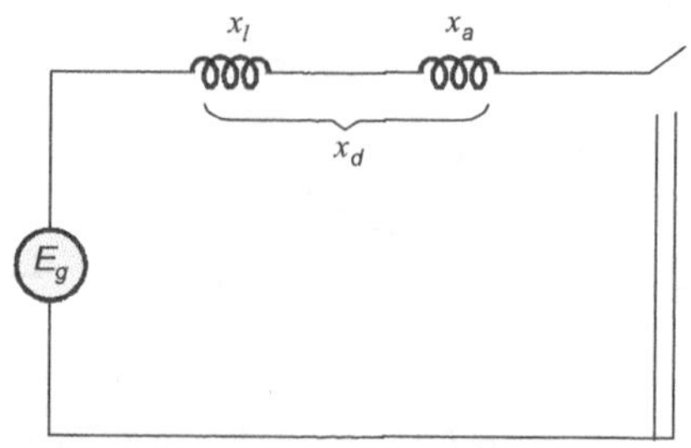

(b) Approximate circuit model during transient period of short circuit.

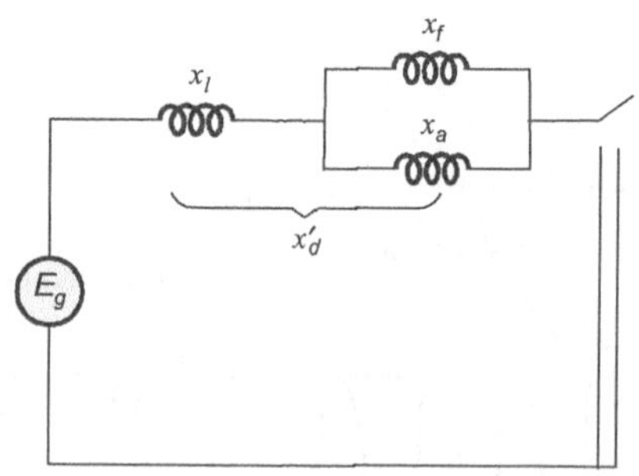

(c) Approximate circuit model during subtransient period of short circuit.

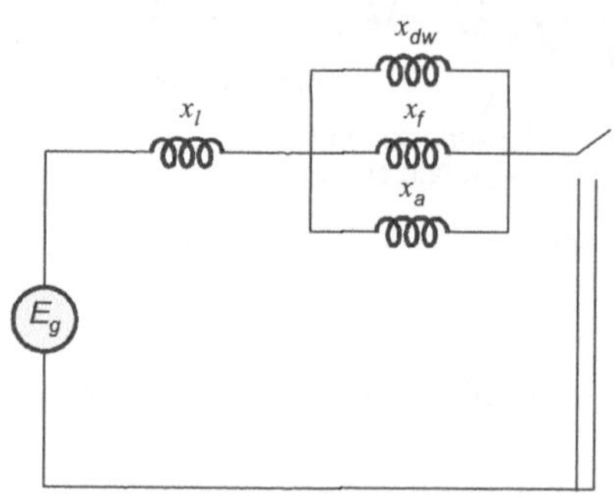

Direct axis transient open circuit time constant T_{d0}' :

It is time required, following a sudden change in operating conditions, for the slowly changing component of the open circuit armature voltage which is due to direct-axis flux, to decrease to $1/e$, that is 0.368 of its initial value the machine running at rated speed.

4.23 What is 'Hunting' in synchronous machines and what are its effects? Does it occur in synchronous generators only or in synchronous motors also? How is it reduced in salient pole synchronous generators and in turbo alternators? Formulate analytically the dynamic of hunting in case of round rotor synchronous generators and identity when hunting may lead to operational instability?

[5 marks : 2010]

Solution:

The synchronous machine oscillates about the operating point, due to:

1. a sudden change in load.
2. a fault in the supply system.
3. a load or write containing harmonic torques.
4. a sudden change in field current.

This oscillatory behaviour of the synchronous machines is known as hunting.

The effects of hunting are as follows:

- It produces severe mechanical stress and fatigue in the shaft.
- It causes great surges in current and power flow.
- It increases machine losses and thus the temperature rise of the machine.
- Hunting occurs in both synchronous generators and synchronous motors.
- To minimize hunting to a tolerable level, damping must be introduced in the machines. Additional damping is provided in the salient pole synchronous machine by means of damper bars located in the main poles of the machine and short-circuited through round rings at both ends. As the rotor oscillates the damper bars have a relative movement with respect to the air-gap flux pattern which causes induction of emf and flow of currents in these bars. The torque created by the bar currents as per lenz's law always opposes the relative motion.
- Damping windings are not used on turbo generators. But the solid steel rotor cores of such machines, provide path for eddy currents, especially in the quadrature axis, where the iron may form an equivalent rotor circuit, thus producing the same effects as those of damper bars.
- Under steady state conditions,

$$P_e = P_m$$

where, P_e = electrical power output of the machine

P_m = mechanical power input to the machine

- If this power balance is disturbed, the machine undergoes electromechanical dynamics,

$$\text{Accelerating Power} = P_a = P_m - P_e$$

- In the absence of losses this power is absorbed in accelerating the rotor inertia,

$$P_m - P_e = \frac{1}{2} I\alpha'$$

where, I = moment of inertia of rotor

α' = rotor acceleration

- If powers are expressed in MW

$$P_m - P_e = M \propto = M\frac{d^2\theta}{dt^2} \qquad \ldots(i)$$

where, $\propto = \dfrac{d^2\theta}{dt^2}$ = rotor acceleration in elect. deg/s

M = Inertia constant in MJs/elect. deg.

- $$\delta = -\omega_s t$$

where, ω_s = synchronous speed in electr. deg/s

δ = rotor angular displacement from the synchronous rotating reference frame

- Taking the second derivative,

$$\frac{d^2\delta}{dt^2} = \frac{d^2\theta}{dt^2}$$

Equation (*i*) becomes,

$$P_m - P_e = M\frac{d^2\delta}{dt^2}$$

where, $P_e = P_{emax} \sin\delta$

$$\Rightarrow \quad P_m - P_{e,\max} \sin\delta = M\frac{d^2\delta}{dt^2} \text{ (swing equation)} \qquad \ldots(ii)$$

- Under steady conditions,

$$P_{m0} = P_{e,\max} \sin\delta_0$$

- With the mechanical input power remaining constant at P_{m0}, let the angle δ be distributed from δ_0 to $\delta_0 + \Delta\delta$.

Then, $$P_e = P_{e,max} \sin(\delta_0 + \Delta\delta) \approx P_{e,max} \sin\delta_0 + \left(\frac{\partial P_e}{\partial \delta}\right)_0 \Delta\delta$$

or, $$P_{e0} + \Delta P_e = P_{e,max} \sin\delta_0 + \left(\frac{\partial P_e}{\partial \delta}\right)_0 \Delta\delta \text{ or } \Delta P_e = \left(\frac{\partial P_e}{\partial \delta}\right)_0 \Delta\delta$$

Now, equation (*ii*) becomes, $$-\Delta P_e = -\left(\frac{\partial P_e}{\partial \delta}\right)_0 \Delta\delta = M\frac{d^2(\delta_0 + \Delta\delta)}{dt^2}$$

or, $$M\frac{d^2\Delta\delta}{dt^2} + \left(\frac{\partial P_e}{\partial \delta}\right)_0 \Delta\delta = 0$$

or, $$\left[MP^2 + \left(\frac{\partial P_e}{\partial \delta}\right)_0\right]\Delta\delta = 0 \quad \text{...(iii)}$$

- The incremental change $\Delta\delta = \delta - \delta_0$ is governed by the linear second-order differential equation (iii) whose characterise roots are

$$P = \pm\left[\frac{-(\partial P_e/\partial\delta)_0}{M}\right]^{1/2} \quad \text{...(iv)}$$

Now, $$\left(\frac{\partial P_e}{\partial \delta}\right)_0 = P_{e,max} \cos\delta_0$$

- $\left(\frac{\partial P_e}{\partial \delta}\right)_0 > 0$ for $\delta < 90°$, i.e. in the stable operating zone of the machine, the roots of the characteristic equation (iii), are a complex conjugate pair indicating sinusoidal oscillatory behaviour about the operating point (P_{e0}, δ_0).

4.24 An industrial load of 4000 kW is supplied at 11 kV, the power factor being 0.8 lagging. A synchronous motor is required to meet an additional load of 1500 HP(1103.25 kW) and the same time to raise the resultant power factor to 0.95 lagging. Determine the kVA capacity of the motor and the power factor at which it must operate. Take the efficiency of the motor as 80%.

[12 marks : 2011]

Solution:

Let, P_1 and Q_1 be the active and reactive power requirements of the industrial load.

So, $P_1 = 400$ kW and $Q_1 = P_1 \tan(\cos^{-1} 0.8)$

$$= 4000 \times \tan(36.87) = 3000 \text{ kVAR}$$

Let P_e and Q_2 be the active and reactive power requirement of the synchronous motor.

$$P_2 = \frac{\text{Output of synchronous motor}}{\text{efficiency}}$$

$$= \frac{1103.25}{0.8} = 1379.06 \text{ kW}$$

Let P_T and Q_T, be the total active and reactive power requirements of the system.

$$P_T = P_1 + P_2 = 4000 + 1379.06 = 5379.06 \text{ kW}$$

$$Q_T = Q_1 + Q_2$$

Resultant power factor $= \cos\phi_2 = 0.95$

$$\Rightarrow \quad \phi_2 = 18.195°$$

$$\tan\phi_2 = \frac{Q_T}{P_T}$$

$$\Rightarrow \quad Q_T = 0.328 \times 5379.06 = 1764.33 \text{ kVAR}$$

$$\Rightarrow \quad Q_1 + Q_2 = 1764.33$$

$$Q_2 = 1764.33 - Q_1 = 1764.43 - 3000$$

$$= -1235.67 \text{ kVAR}$$

Negative value of Q_2 indicates that synchronous motor supplies reactive power

$$\tan\phi_3 = \frac{Q_2}{P_2} = \frac{1235.67}{1379.06} = 0.896$$

$$\text{Power factor of the motor} = 0.744 \text{ leading}$$

$$\text{kVA capacity of the motor} = \sqrt{P_2^2 + Q_2^2} = \sqrt{1379.06^2 + 1235.67^2}$$

$$= 1851.67 \text{ kVA}$$

4.25 **A salient pole alternator has $X_d = 1.4$, $X_q = 1.0$ and $r_a = 0$. If this alternator delivers rated kVA at unity p.f. and at rated voltage, find its power angle and excitation voltage.**

[4 marks : 2012]

Solution:

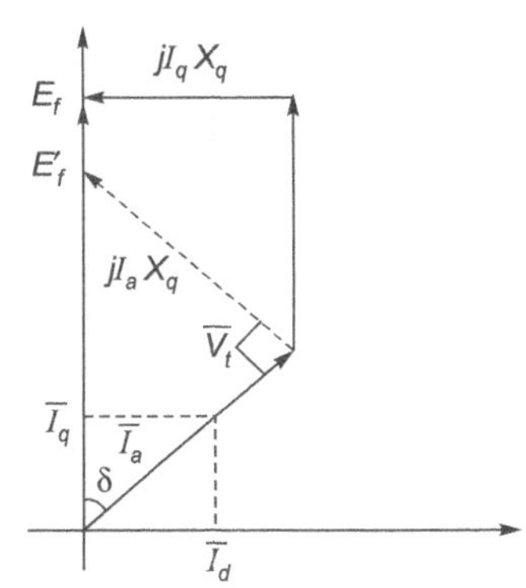

As, $\quad r_a = 0$

$$\bar{E}_f = \bar{V}_t + j\bar{I}_d X_d + j\bar{I}_q X_q$$

Given, $\quad \bar{V}_t = 1\angle 0°$

$$\bar{I}_a = 1\angle 0°$$

$$\bar{E}'_f = \bar{V}_t + j\bar{I}_a X_q$$

$$= 1\angle 0° + j0.1\angle 0° \times 1 = 1 + j = \sqrt{2}\angle 45°$$

$\therefore \quad \delta = 45°$

$$I_d = I_a \sin\delta = 1 \times \frac{1}{\sqrt{2}} = 0.707$$

and $\quad I_q = I_a \cos\delta = 0.707$

$$E_f = E'_f + I_d(X_d - X_q) = 1.414 + 0.707(1.4 - 1) = 1.697\angle 45° \text{ p.u.}$$

4.26 **A 3-ϕ, 7 MVA, 11 kV, ⅄-connected alternator is synchronized with infinite bus at rated voltage. Now the steam input to the machine set is increased till the synchronous machine begin to operate at a load angle 40°. Synchronous machine has synchronous impedance (0 + j12 Ω). Calculate the power factor, armature current and output real power and reactive power delivered to the ∞ bus under these condition. Draw phasor diagrams at (i) load angle = 40° and (ii) no reactive power flows.**

[10 marks : 2012]

Solution:

$\because$ At synchronization:

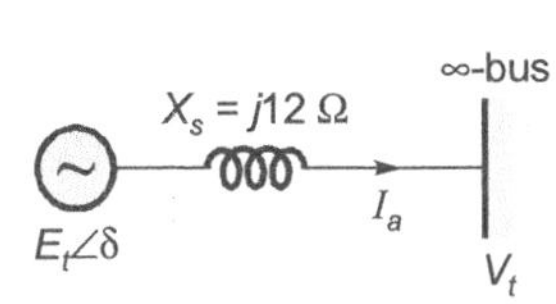

$$|E_f| = |V_t|$$

$$\because \quad V_t = \frac{11}{\sqrt{3}} \text{ kV per phase}, \quad \delta = 40°$$

$\because \quad \bar{E}_f = \bar{V}_t + jXs \cdot I_a$

$$I_a = \frac{\bar{E}_f - \bar{V}_t}{X_s} = \frac{\frac{11}{\sqrt{3}}\angle 40^\circ - \frac{11}{\sqrt{3}}\angle 0^\circ}{j12} = 0.362\angle 20^\circ \text{ kA}$$

$\because$ Power factor = cos20° leading = 0.9397 leading

Total power output = $\bar{S}_{out} = \sqrt{3} V \cdot I_a^*$

$$\bar{S}_{out} = \sqrt{3} \times 11 \times 10^3 \angle 0^\circ \times 362\angle -20^\circ$$

$= (6.481 - j2.36)$ MVA

where, $P = 6.481$ MW

and $Q = 2.36$ MVAR leading

$\because$ P = constant

$VI_a \cos\phi$ = constant

or $I_a \cos\phi$ = constant

$$I_{a_2} \cos\phi_2 = I_{a_1} \cos\phi_1$$

$\Rightarrow \quad I_{a_2} \times 1.0 = 362 \times \cos 20^\circ = 340.17$ A

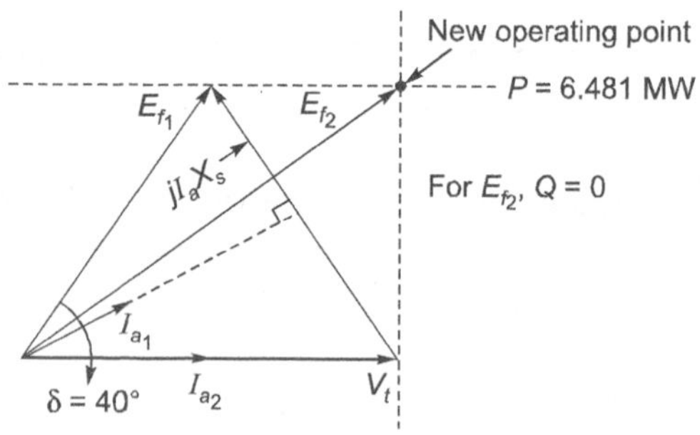

Now, $$\bar{E}_{f_2} = \frac{11}{\sqrt{3}}\angle 0^\circ + j0.34017\angle 0^\circ \times 12$$

$= 7.55\angle 32.73^\circ$ kV (L-N)

or, $\bar{E}_{f_2} = 13.076$ kV (L-L)

4.27 A generator is supplying 2000 MW to an infinite bus via a transmission line of reactance 0.1 p.u. The base MVA is 1000 MVA and both terminal voltage and infinite bus voltage are at 1 p.u. Find the reactive power supplied by the machine to the infinite bus.

[4 marks : 2013]

Solution:

$$P = \frac{E_f V_t}{X_s} \sin\delta = \frac{2000 \text{ MW}}{1000 \text{ MVA}} = 2 \text{ p.u.}$$

$$2 = \frac{1 \times 1}{0.1} \sin\delta$$

$\Rightarrow \quad \sin\delta = 0.2$

$\Rightarrow \quad \delta = 11.54^\circ$

$$Q = \frac{V}{X_s}(E_f \cos\delta - V) = \frac{1}{0.1}[1.0 \times \cos(11.54^\circ) - 1] = -0.202 \text{ p.u.}$$

$$Q = -0.202 \times 1000 \text{ MVAR} = -202.147 \text{ MVAR}$$

4.28 A 44 MVA, 10.5 kV, 50 Hz, Y-connected three phase salient pole synchronous generator has $x_d = 1.83\ \Omega$ and $x_q = 1.21\ \Omega$. It delivers the rated load at 0.8 pf lagging. The armature resistance is negligible determine the power developed by the generator and % voltage regulation.

[10 marks : 2013]

Solution:

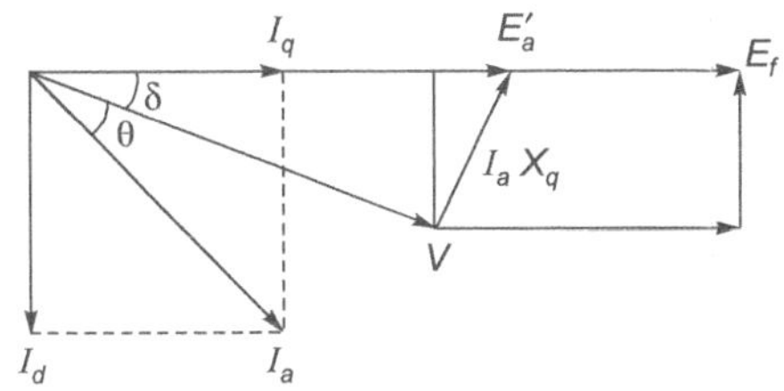

$$I_a = \frac{44\times10^6}{\sqrt{3}\times10.5\times10^3} = 2419.37\angle-36.87°\text{ A}$$

$$E'_a = V + jI_aX_q$$

$$E'_a = \frac{10500}{\sqrt{3}} + j(1.21)(2419.37\angle-36.87°)$$

$$E'_a = 8161.857\angle16.67°\text{ V}$$

$$I_d = (2419.37)\sin(36.87° + 16.67°) = 1945.83\text{ A}$$

$$|E_f| = |E'_a| + |I_d(X_d - X_q)|$$

$$= (8161.857) + (1945.83)(1.83 - 1.21) = 9368.272$$

$$\Rightarrow \quad E_f = 9368.272\angle16.67°\text{ V}$$

$$\text{Voltage regulation} = \frac{9368.273 - \frac{10500}{\sqrt{3}}}{\frac{10500}{\sqrt{3}}}\times100 = 54.53\%$$

$$\text{Power developed} = \text{Output power} \qquad [\because R_a = 0]$$

$$= S\cos\phi = 44\times0.8 = 35.2\text{ MW}$$

4.29 Explain with phasor diagram as to why in an alternator under short circuit conditions core losses reduce very much.

[4 marks : 2014]

Solution:

Under short circuit condition, the magnitude of current is very high and the armature reaction effect due to thin current is completely demagnetizing (ideally).

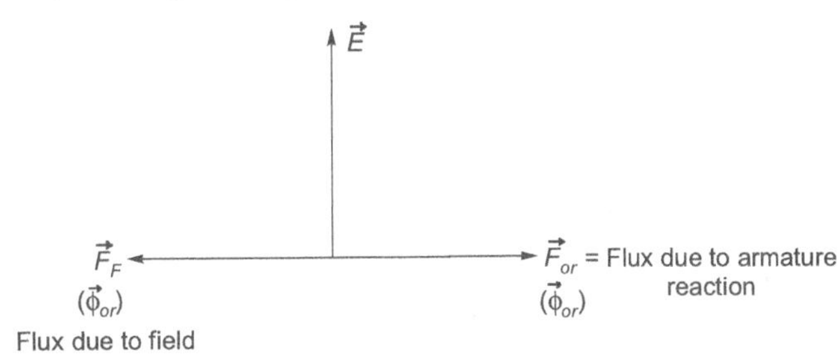

So, net flux in air gap is very less.

As the flux is very less, the core loss becomes very loss.

4.30 A cylindrical rotor synchronous motor having negligible armature, resistance is connected to an infinite bus and is operating at no load at normal excitation. What will happen if the excitation of the motor is (*i*) increased and (*ii*) decreased? Explain with help of phasor diagram.

[4 marks : 2014]

Solution:

No load: $(\delta = 0)$

$$P = \frac{EV}{X}\sin\delta = 0 = VI_a\cos\phi$$

$$\Rightarrow \quad I_a\cos\phi = 0$$

Under normal excitation:

$$I_a = 0$$

$$\Rightarrow \quad I_a \cos\phi = 0$$

$$\Rightarrow \quad I_a = 0$$

Over excitation (i.e.) excitation is increased:

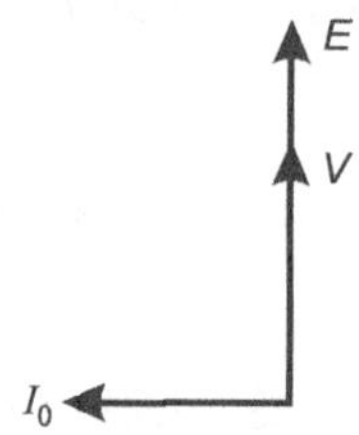

Since, it is overexcited, no-load current leads the excitation voltage (E) by 90°.

Over excitation (or) excitation is decreased:

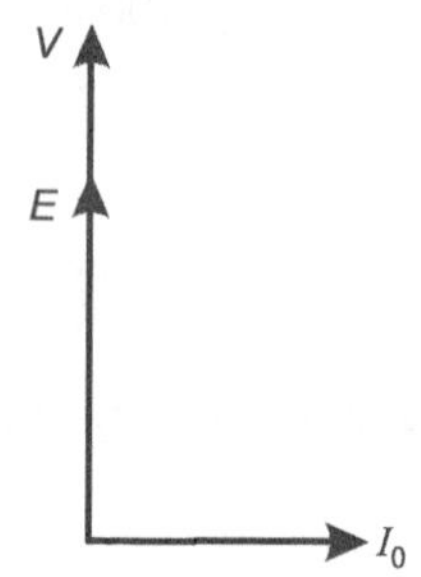

4.31 A 75 MVA, 13.8 kV, three-phase, eight-pole, 60 Hz salient pole synchronous machine has the following d-axis and q-axis reactances: $X_d = 1.0$ pu and $X_q = 0.6$ pu. The synchronous generator is delivering rated MVA at rated voltage and 0.866 power factor lagging. Choose a power base of 75 MVA and voltage base of 13.8 kV.

(*i*) Draw the phasor diagram of the machine.

(*ii*) Compute the excitation voltage E_f.

(*iii*) If the machine is connected to 3-phase system having 1.0 pu voltage, find the maximum power that generator can deliver.

[15 marks : 2014]

Solution:

Phasor diagram,

$$\phi = \cos^{-1}(0.866) = 30°$$

$$X_q = 0.6 \text{ pu}, X_d = 1 \text{ pu}$$

(*i*)

$$(\vec{V}_t)_{pu} = \frac{13.8}{13.8} = 1\angle 0°$$

$$(\vec{I}_a) = 1\angle{-30°}$$

$$\vec{E}_f' = \vec{V}_t + j\vec{I}_a X_q$$

$$= 1\angle 0 + j1\angle{-30°} \times 0.6$$

$$\vec{E}_f' = 1.4\angle 21.786$$

$$\vec{E}_f' = 1.4, \delta = 21.78°, E_f \text{ leads } V_t.$$

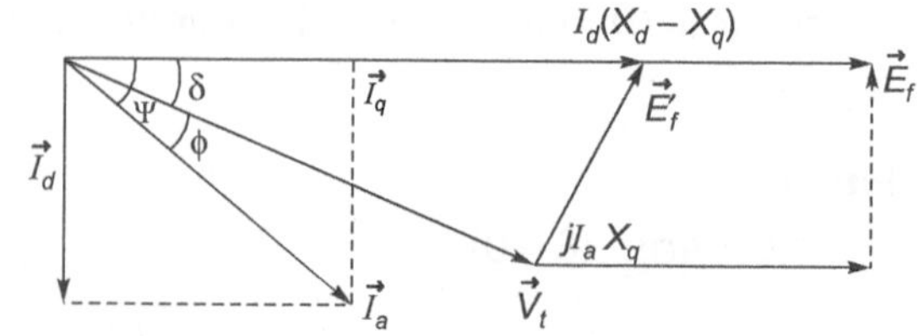

$$\Psi = \phi + \delta = 30° + 21.78° = 51.78°$$

$$I_d = I_a \sin\Psi = 1 \times 0.7856 = 0.7856$$

$$I_q = I_a \cos\Psi = 1 \times 0.6186 = 0.6186$$

(*ii*)
$$E_f = E_f' + I_d(X_d - X_q)$$

$$= 1.4 + 0.7856\,(1 - 0.6) = 1.7142 \text{ pu}$$

or
$$E_f = 13.8 \times 1.7142 = 23.65 \text{ kV}$$

(*iii*)
$$P = \frac{VE_f}{X_d}\sin\delta + \frac{V^2}{2}\left[\frac{1}{X_q} - \frac{1}{X_d}\right]\sin 2\delta$$

$$= \frac{1 \times 1.714}{1}\sin\delta + \frac{(1)^2}{2}\left[\frac{1}{0.6} - \frac{1}{1}\right]\sin 2\delta = 1.714 \sin\delta + \frac{1}{2} \times \frac{4}{6}\sin 2\delta$$

$$= 1.714 \sin\delta + 0.33 \sin 2\delta$$

For P_{max},
$$\frac{dP}{d\delta} = 0$$

$$\frac{dP}{d\delta} = 1.714 \cos\delta + 0.33 \times 2 \times \cos 2\delta$$

$$\Rightarrow \quad 1.714 \cos\delta + 0.66\,(2\cos 2\delta - 1) = 0$$

$$\Rightarrow \quad 1.714 \cos\delta + 1.32 \cos 2\delta - 0.66 = 0$$

$$\Rightarrow \quad 1.32 \cos 2\delta + 1.714 \cos\delta - 0.66 = 0$$

$$\cos\delta = 0.31, -1.609 \text{ (neglecting if)}$$

$$\boxed{\delta = 71.94}$$

$$P_{max} = 1.714 \sin(71.94) + 0.33 \sin(2 \times 71.94)$$

$$= 1.8240 \text{ pu or } 75 \times 1.8240 = 136.80 \text{ MW}$$

4.32 A 208 V, 45 kVA, 0.8 pf leading D connected 50 Hz synchronous machine has a synchronous reactance of 2.5 Ω and a negligible armature resistance. Its friction and windage losses are 1.5 kW, and its core losses are 1.0 kW. Initially, the shaft is supplying a 15 hp load, and the motor's power factor is 0.80 leading.

(*i*) Draw the phasor diagram of the motor and find the line current and line-line voltage.

(*ii*) If the shaft load is increased to 30 hp, fund the new values of line current and line-line voltage and draw the phasor diagram.

[15 marks : 2014]

Solution:

At 15 hp load,

$$\text{Total input power} = P_{01p} + P_{fn} + P_{\text{core coil}}$$

As, $R_a \approx 0$, $P_{cu} \approx 0$

(*i*) Total input power = $(15 \times 746 + 1.5 \times 10^3 + 1 \times 10^3)$ watts = 13690 watts

$$\text{Line current} = \frac{13690}{\sqrt{3} \times 208 \times 0.8}$$

$$I_2 = 47.499 \approx 48 \text{ A}$$

$$\text{Phase current} = \frac{48}{\sqrt{3}} \text{ A} = 27.42 \text{ A}$$

From the diagram given below,

$$\vec{E}_f = \vec{V} - j\vec{I}_a X_s$$

$$= 208\angle 0° - j2.5 \times 27.42\angle \cos^{-1} 0.8$$

$$\vec{E}_f = 255.09\angle -12.41° \text{ V}$$

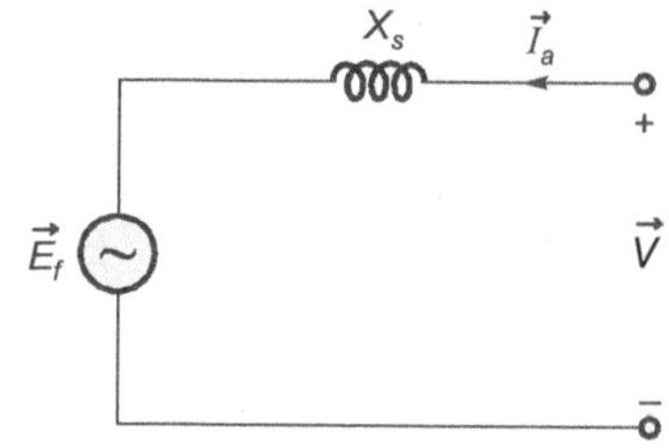

Phasor diagram,

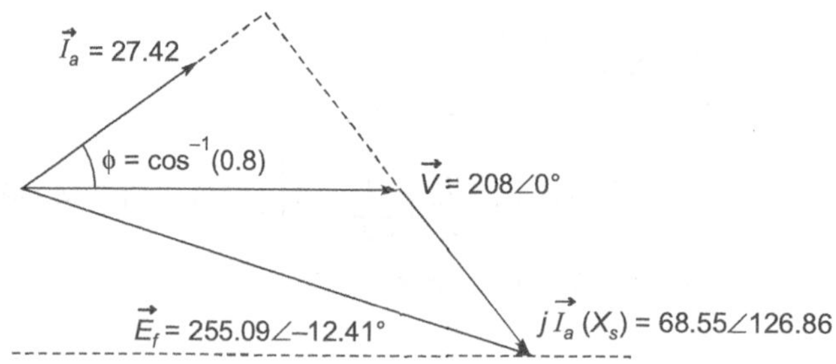

(*ii*) If shaft load is 30 hp

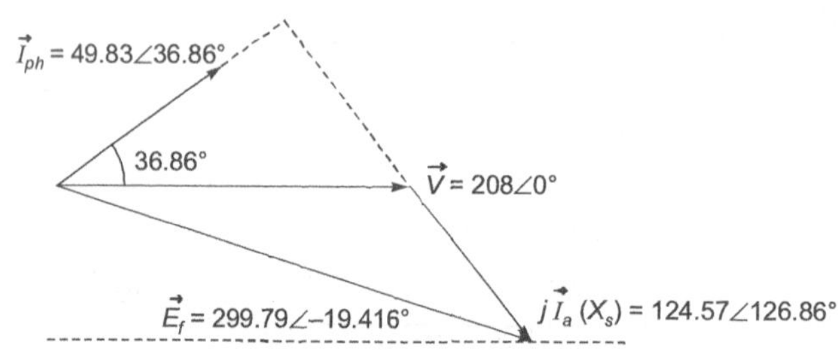

$$P_{\text{input}} = (30 \times 746 + 1.5 \times 10^3 + 1 \times 10^3) \text{ kW}$$
$$= 24880 \text{ kW}$$

$$I_L = \frac{24880}{\sqrt{3} \times 208 \times 0.8} = 86.32 \text{ A}$$

$$I_{pn} = \frac{86.32}{\sqrt{3}} = 49.83 \text{ A}$$

and,
$$\vec{E}_f = \vec{V} - j\vec{I}_a(X_s) = 208\,(0 - j)\,(49.83\angle \cos^{-1}(0.8))\,(2.5)$$

$$\vec{E}_f = 299.79\angle -19.416° \text{ V}$$

4.33 **A 3-phase, 4-pole alternator is to be synchronized to an infinite bus of frequency 50 Hz. Three synchronizing lamps L_1, L_2 and L_3 are connected between the phases RYB and RBY of the alternator and the bus bar respectively. Determine the sequence in which the lamps will become dark and the frequency of lamps becoming dark if the speed of incoming generator is (i) 1490 rpm (ii) 1510 rpm. In which case synchronizing switch should be closed and why?**

[15 marks : 2015]

Solution:

3-ϕ, 4 pole machine, infinite bus frequency is 50 Hz

$$N_s = \frac{120 \times 50}{4} = 1500 \text{ rpm}$$

(i) Incoming generator speed is 1490 rpm

As the incoming generator is slower than 1500 rpm.

So, sequence is $L_1 - L_2 - L_3$

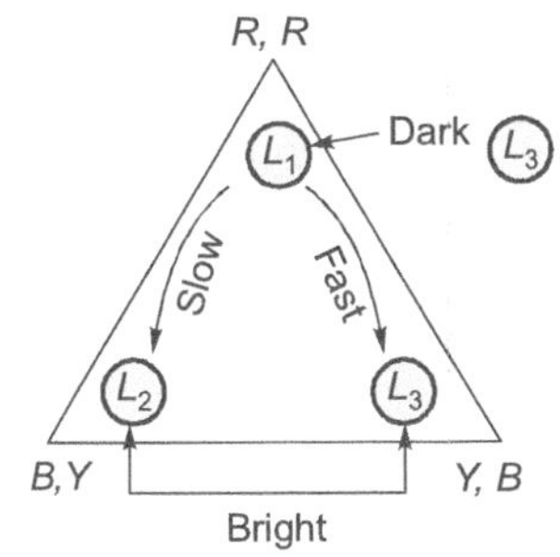

$$\text{Relative frequency} = \left[\frac{1500 - 1490}{1500}\right] \times 50 = 0.333 \text{ cycles/sec.}$$

(ii) Incoming generator speed is 1510 rpm.

As the incoming generator is faster than 1500 rpm.

So, sequence is $L_1 - L_3 - L_2$

$$\text{Relative frequency} = \left[\frac{1500 - 1510}{1500}\right] \times 50 = 0.333 \text{ cycles/sec.}$$

In second case speed is more than 1500 rpm so synchronizing switch should be closed because it will give power to the system.

4.34 **A manufacturing plant uses 100 kVA at 0.6 p.f. lagging under normal operation. A synchronous motor is added to the system to improve the overall power factor. The power required by the synchronous motor is 10 kW. Determine the overall power factor when the synchronous motor operates at 0.5 p.f. leading. What must be the power factor of the motor to improve the overall power factor to 0.9 lagging?**

[15 marks : 2015]

Solution:

As shown in the power triangle given below:

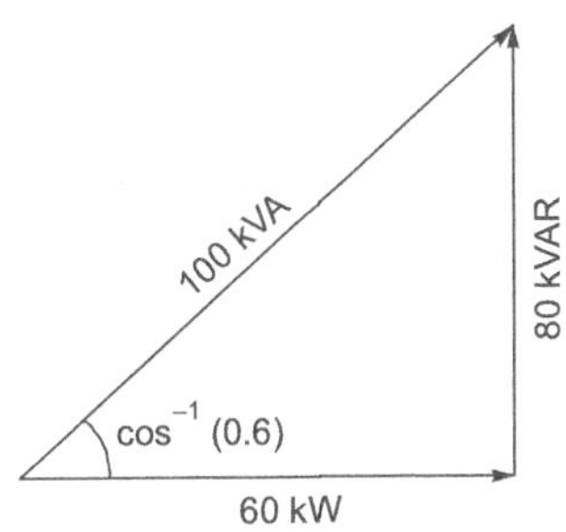

Plant reactive power demand = 80 MVAR

Now, synchronous motor is added to improve the overall power factor.

Power required by the synchronous motor = 10 kW and operating p.f. = 0.5 p.f. leading

So,

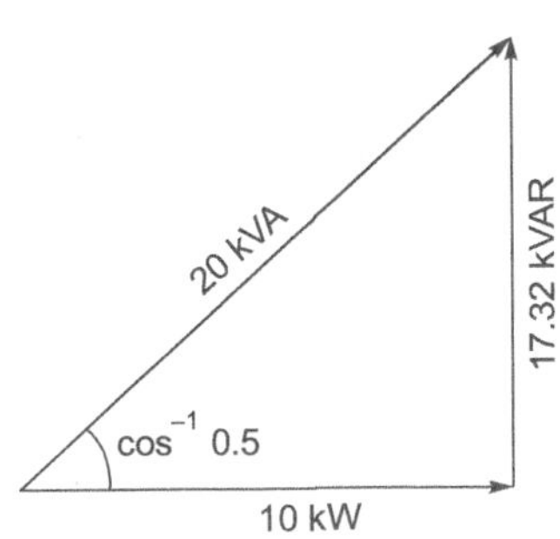

kVAR supplied by motor = 17.32 kVAR

overall reactive power of system after addition of motor = (80 – 17.32) kVAR = 62.68 kVAR

and, overall active power of system (plant + motor) = (60 + 10) kW = 70 kW

So,

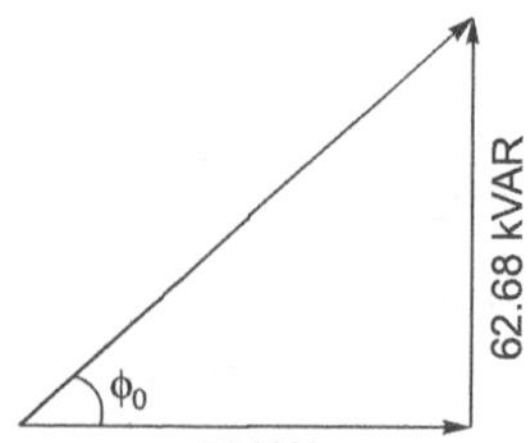

$$\phi_0 = \phi_{overall} = \tan^{-1}\left(\frac{62.68}{70}\right) = 41.842°$$

$$\text{overall p.f.} = \cos\phi_0 = 0.745 \text{ lagging}$$

Now, if overall p.f. 0.9 lagging is required then,

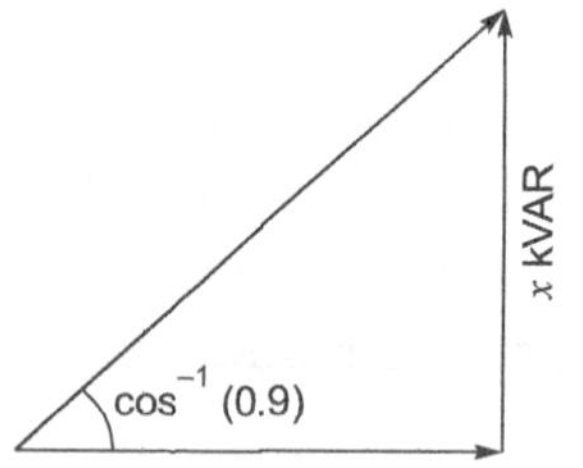

From above power triangle,

$$\tan[\cos^{-1}(0.9)] = \frac{x}{70}$$

$\Rightarrow$ Reactive power of system = 33.90 kVAR

Initial reactive power = 80 kVAR

So, reactive power supplied by motor = (80 – 33.90) KVAR = 46.1 kVAR

Now, Power triangle of motor is shown in figure,

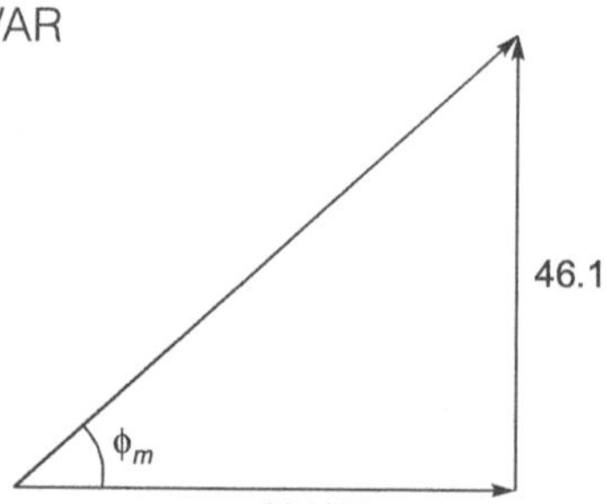

$$\phi_{motor} = \tan^{-1}\left(\frac{46.1}{10}\right) = 77.76°$$

and, $\cos\phi_{motor} = 0.212$ p.f. leading

Note: Synchronous motor in overexcited case takes leading p.f. current. So, it can be said that takes leading KVAR or gives lagging KVAR to compensate reactive power demand.

Hence, improve p.f. of system.

4.35 Two synchronous generators are operating in parallel and supplying a load of 2.5 MW at 0.8 pF lagging. Generator '1' has no-load frequency of 51.5 Hz and a slope (S_{P1}) of 1 MW/Hz. Generator '2' has a no-load frequency of 51 Hz and a slope (S_{P2}) of 0.8 MW/Hz.

(i) At what frequency is this system operating, and how much power is shared by each of the two generators?

(ii) What will be the system frequency and generated powers, if the governor set point on G_2 is increased by 0.5 Hz?

(iii) How can the load be transferred from Generator '1' to Generator '2' without changing the system frequency?

[10 marks : 2015]

Solution:

Generator 1,

$$\text{No load frequency} = 51.5 \text{ Hz}$$

$$(S_{p_1}) = \frac{1 \text{MW}}{\text{Hz}}$$

Generator 2,

$$\text{No load frequency} = 51 \text{ Hz}$$

$$(S_{p_2}) = \frac{0.8 \text{ MW}}{\text{Hz}}$$

(i) Generator 1, $\tan\phi_1 = \dfrac{51.5 - f}{x} = 1$

$\Rightarrow \quad 51.5 - f = x$

$\Rightarrow \quad x + f = 51.5 \quad \text{...(1)}$

Generator 2, $\tan\phi_2 = \dfrac{51 - f}{2.5 - x} = \dfrac{1}{0.8}$

$\Rightarrow \quad 51 \times 0.8 - 0.8 \times f = 2.5 - x$

$\Rightarrow \quad x - 0.8f = -38.3 \quad \text{...(2)}$

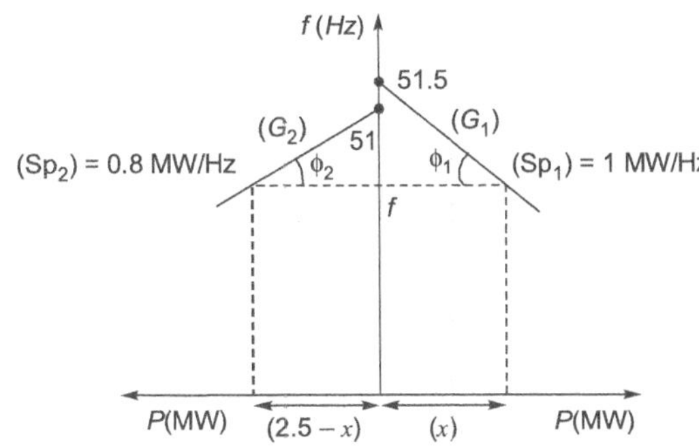

Solving (1) and (2),

$$x = 1.61 \text{ MW}$$

$$y = 49.89 \text{ Hz}$$

$$\text{Frequency of operation} = 49.89 \text{ Hz}$$

$$\text{Power supplied by } G_1 = 1.611 \text{ MW}$$

$$\text{Power supplied by } G_2 = (2.5 - 1.61) = 0.89 \text{ MW}$$

(ii) After increased governor set point to 0.5 Hz

Generator 1, $\tan\phi_1 = \dfrac{51.5 - f}{y} = 1$

$\Rightarrow \quad y + f = 51.5 \quad \text{...(1)}$

Generator 2,

$$\tan\phi_2 = \frac{51.5 - f}{2.5 - y} = \frac{1}{0.8}$$

$\Rightarrow \quad 51.5 \times 0.8 - 0.8f = 2.5 - y$

$\Rightarrow \quad y - 0.8f = -38.7 \quad \text{...(2)}$

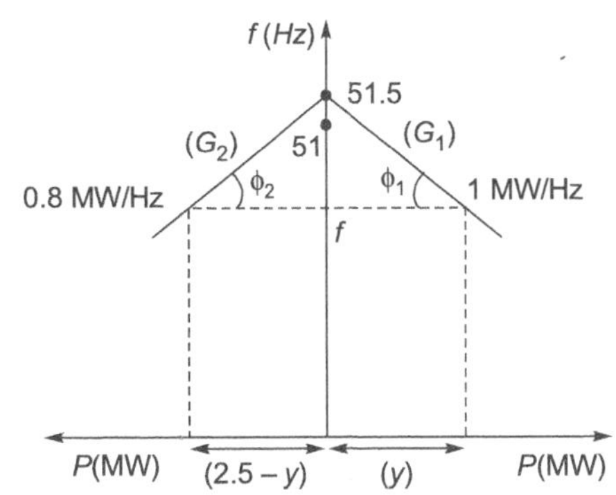

Solving equation (1) and (2),

$$y = 1.39 \text{ MW}$$

$$f = 50.11 \text{ Hz}$$

$$\text{System frequency} = 50.11 \text{ Hz}$$

Power generated by equation (1),

$$P_{G1} = 1.39 \text{ MW}$$

$$P_{G2} = 1.11 \text{ MW}$$

(iii) For the load transfer from generator '1' to generator '2' without changing system frequency, generator '1' must be operating at no load at frequency $f = 50.11$ Hz as shown in characteristics.

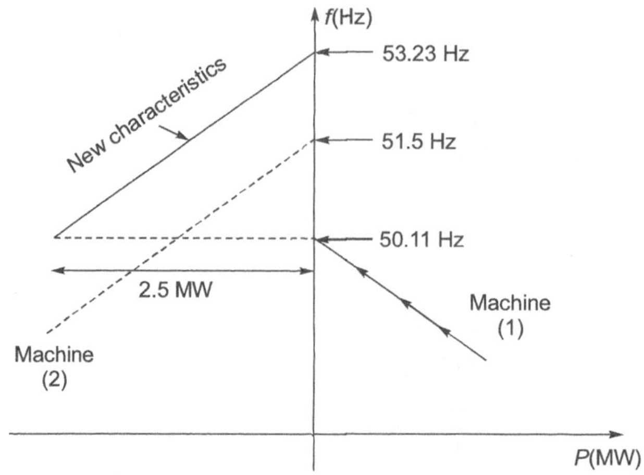

Whereas for generator '2' the total load = 2.5 MW operating at $f = 50.11$ Hz

Now the no load frequency of generator '2'; f_{0_2}

$$\because \qquad 0.8 = \frac{2.5}{f_{0_2} - 50.11} = 53.235 \text{ Hz}$$

Therefore, generator '2' no load frequency increases from 51.50 Hz to 53.23 Hz by 1.735 Hz and generator '1' no load frequency lower from 51.50 Hz to 50.11 Hz by 1.39 Hz.

4.36 Draw the V-curve of a salient pole synchronous motor operating at no-load. What do you mean by normal excitation? Explain physically why the motor operates at leading power factor under over-excitation.

[4 marks : 2016]

Solution:

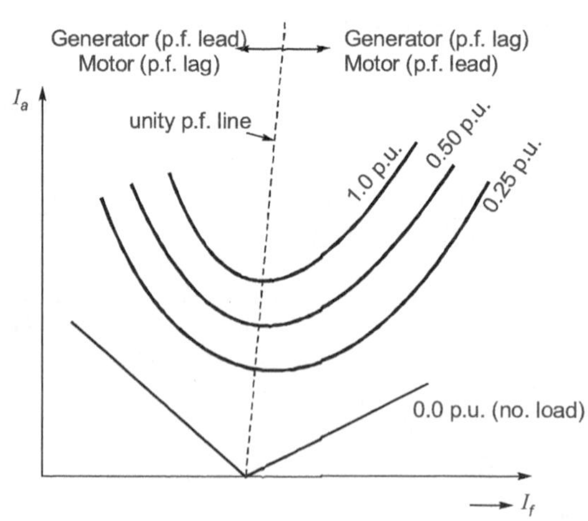

For Generator:

When, $\quad E_f \cos\delta = V \Rightarrow Q_{out} = 0$

$\therefore$ operating at unity p.f. then generator is normally excited.

For Motor:

When $E_f \cos\delta = V$, then motor is normally excited then $Q_{in} = 0$

$\therefore$ operating at unity p.f.

4.37 A 25 kVA, 230 V, three-phase four-pole, 50 Hz, wye-connected synchronous generator has a synchronous reactance of 1.5 W /phase and negligible stator resistance. The generator is connected to an infinite bus of 230 V, 50 Hz.

(i) Determine the excitation voltage when the machine is delivering rated kVA at 0.8 power factor lagging.

(ii) The field excitation is increased by 20% without changing the prime mover power output. Find the armature current, power factor and reactive power supplied by the machine.

(iii) With the field excitation current as in part (i), the input power from the prime mover is increased very slowly. What is the steady state limit? Determine the stator current, power factor and reactive power.

[20 marks : 2016]

Solution:

25 kVA, 230 V, $X_s = 1.5\ \Omega/\text{ph}$

Considering 230 V as a line voltage.

$$\sqrt{3} V_l I_l = 25000$$

$$\Rightarrow \quad I_l = \frac{25000}{\sqrt{3} \times 230}$$

$$\therefore \quad I_l = 62.757 \text{ A} \Rightarrow 62.76 \text{ A}$$

$$V_{ph} = \frac{230}{\sqrt{3}} = 132.8 \text{ V}$$

(i)
$$E_{ph} = V_{ph} + I_a R_a + j I_a X_s$$

$$V_{ph} = 132.8 \text{ V},$$

$$I_a \angle -\phi = 62.76 \angle -36.86^\circ \text{ A}$$

$$X_s = 1.5\ \Omega$$

$$\therefore \quad E_{ph} = 203.716 \angle 21.6965^\circ \text{ V}$$

$$\therefore \quad \delta = 21.7^\circ$$

(ii) Excitation increased by 20%

$$\therefore \quad E_1 \sin \delta_1 = E_2 \sin \delta_2$$

$$E_1 = 203.7 \text{ V}$$

$$\delta_1 = 21.7^\circ$$

$$E_2 = 203.7 \times 1.2 = 244.44 \text{ volts}$$

$$\therefore \quad \sin \delta_2 = \frac{203.7 \times \sin(21.7)}{244.44} = 0.308$$

$$\therefore \quad \delta_2 = 17.95^\circ$$

$$\therefore \quad I_2 = \frac{E_2 \angle \delta_2 - V}{jX_s} = \frac{244.44 \angle 17.95^\circ - 132.8^\circ}{j1.5} = 83.33 \angle -53^\circ \text{ A}$$

$$\text{Reactive power per phase} = \left[\frac{E_2 V}{X_s} \cos \delta_2 - \frac{V^2}{X_s} \right]$$

$$\therefore \quad Q = \frac{244.44 \times 132.5}{1.5} \cos(17.95) - \frac{(132.8)^2}{1.5} = 8784 \text{ VAR}$$

For 3-phase $Q_{3\text{-}\phi} = 26.352$ kVAR [Q can also be calculated for $\sqrt{3} V_l I_l \sin\phi$]

(iii) Steady state limit:

$$P_{max} = \frac{3E_{ph}V_{ph}}{X_s}(\sin 90°)$$

$$\therefore \quad P_{max} = \frac{3\times 203.716\times 132.8}{1.5} = 54.1 \text{ kW}$$

Current corresponding to maximum power,

$$I_{max} = \sqrt{\frac{V^2+E^2-2VE\cos\theta}{Z_s}} = \sqrt{\frac{(132.8)^2+(203.716)^2}{1.5}} = 198.55 \text{ A}$$

$$\therefore \quad \text{kVA output} = \sqrt{3}V_l I_l = \sqrt{3}\times 230\times 198.55 = 79.1 \text{kVA}$$

$$\text{p.f.} = \frac{\text{kW}}{\text{kVA}} = \frac{54.1}{79.1} = 0.6839 \text{ leading} \qquad (\because \text{ max output})$$

4.38 **A salient-pole synchronous motor (with negligible armature resistance and X_d = 23.2 Ω and X_q = 14.5 Ω/phase) can support a maximum load of 563 kW without field excitation. This motor is now excited with nominal field current and the motor is loaded with a load torque of 3.82 kN-m. If the motor draws armature current at 0.8 power factor (leading), determine excitation emf and corresponding power angle (δ).**

[12 marks : 2019]

Solution:

According to given condition there will be only reluctance power and for it to maximum δ = 45°.

$$\therefore \quad \frac{563\times 10^3}{3} = \frac{V^2}{2\times 23.2\times 14.5}(23.2-14.5)$$

On solving, $V_{ph} = 3809.57$ V

Now, $P' = T\times\omega_s = 3.82\times 10^3\times\frac{2\pi\times 1000}{60}$

Note: Here any data pertaining to speed is not given but it is impossible to solve the question without speed hence assume N_s = 1000 rpm.

$\therefore \quad P' = 400.02$ kW

Now, $P' = \sqrt{3}VI\cos\phi$

$\Rightarrow \quad 400.02\times 10^3 = \sqrt{3}\times 6.6\times 1000\times I_a\times 0.8$

$\Rightarrow \quad I_a = 43.73$

$$\tan\Psi = \frac{V\sin\phi + I_aX_q}{V\cos\phi - I_aR_a}$$

$\Psi = 43.77°$

$\therefore \quad \delta = \Psi - \phi = 43.77 - 36.86 = 6.91°$

$E = V\cos\delta - I_dX_d$

$= 3809\cos(6.91°) - 30.25(23.2)$

$= 3080.25$ V

4.39 **Draw phasor diagram of an over-excited salient-pole synchronous motor having armature resistance R_a, d and q-axis reactances X_d and X_q respectively. Also prove, for lagging power factor,**

$$\tan(\phi-\delta) = \frac{V_t\sin\phi - I_aX_q}{V_t\cos\phi - I_aR_a}$$

where V_t is the terminal voltage applied to motor, ϕ being the power factor angle, δ is power angle and I_a is armature current.

[12 marks : 2019]

Solution:

Phasor diagram of over excited salient pole synchronous motor:

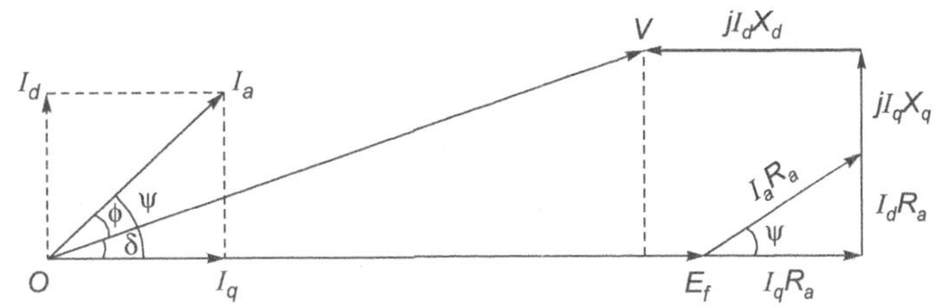

For lagging power factor:

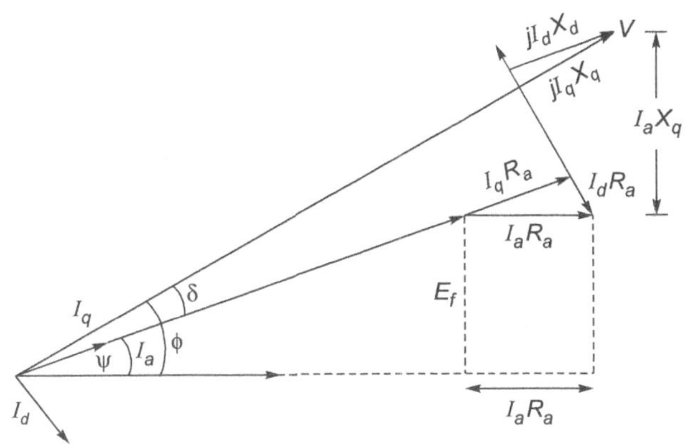

From above figure:

$$\tan \psi = \frac{V_t \sin\phi - I_a X_q}{V_t \cos\phi - I_a R_a}$$

4.40 A salient pole star connected alternator is connected to infinite bus operating at 1.0 p.u. voltage. The alternator has $X_d = 0.75$ p.u. and $X_q = 0.5$ p.u. on per phase basis. It is delivering 1.0 p.u. power to the infinite bus at 0.8 p.f. lag. Calculate (i) the load angle and excitation voltage under this condition, (ii) the maximum power that can be delivered by the alternator with same excitation and the corresponding load angle, (iii) the armature current and p.f. under maximum power condition, and (iv) the theoretical value of maximum power that the alternator can deliver when its field circuit is suddenly disconnected due to fault.

[20 marks : 2020]

Solution:

Given, $V = 1$ pu, $P = 1$ pu

$$\cos\phi = 0.8,\ \phi = 36.86$$

$$I_a = \frac{P}{V\cos\phi} = \frac{1}{1\times 0.8} = 1.25 \text{ pu}$$

(i)

$$\tan \psi = \frac{V\sin\phi + I_a X_a}{V\cos\phi + I_a R_a} = \frac{1\times 0.6 + 1.25\times 0.5}{0.8}$$

$$\psi = \tan^{-1}(1.53125) = 56.853°$$

As we know

Load angle $(\delta) = 56.853 - 36.86 = 19.98°$ $[\because \delta = \psi - \phi]$

$$I_q = I_a \cos\psi = 1.25 \times \cos(56.85) = 0.6835$$

$$I_d = I_a \sin\psi = 1.25 \sin(56.85) = 1.045$$

Excitation voltage, $E = V\cos\delta + I_q R_a + I_d X_d$

$$E = 1 \times \cos(19.98) + 1.0465 \times 0.75$$

$$= 1.724 \text{ pu}$$

(ii)
$$P = \frac{E \cdot V}{X_d}\sin\delta + \frac{V^2}{2}\left[\frac{1}{X_q} - \frac{1}{X_d}\right] \cdot \sin 2\delta$$

$$P = \frac{1.724 \times 1}{0.75}\sin\delta + \frac{1}{2} \times \frac{2}{3}\sin 2\delta$$

$$P = 2.2986 \sin\delta + 0.33 \sin 2\delta \quad \text{...(i)}$$

For maximum power, $\frac{dP}{d\delta} = 0$

$$\frac{dP}{d\delta} = 2.2986\cos\delta + 0.66\cos 2\delta = 0$$

$\Rightarrow$ $\delta = 75.46°$

So maximum power delivered by salient pole generator at load angle $(\delta) = 75.46°$.

$$P_{max} = 2.2986 \sin 75.46° + 0.33 \sin(2 \times 75.46°)$$

$$P_{max} = 2.3853 \text{ pu}$$

(iii)
$$Q = \frac{V \cdot E}{X_d}\cos\delta - \frac{V^2}{2X_d X_q}\left[(X_d + X_q) - (X_d + X_q)\cos 2\delta\right]$$

Relative power (Q) under maximum power delivered condition.

$$Q = \frac{1.724}{0.75}\cos(75.37) - \frac{1}{2 \times 0.5 \times 0.75}[1.25 - 0.25\cos(2 \times 75.37)]$$

$$Q = 0.5805 - 1.9574$$

$$Q = -1.3769 \text{ pu}$$

Power factor under maximum power delivering condition.

$$\cos\phi = \cos\left[\tan^{-1}\left(\frac{Q}{P}\right)\right] = \cos\left[\tan^{-1}\left(\frac{-1.3769}{2.387}\right)\right]$$

$$\cos\phi = 0.866 \text{ leading}$$

Armature current under maximum power delivering condition is

$$P = V_t \cdot I_a \cos\phi$$

$$I_a = \frac{2.387}{1 \times 0.866} = 2.7556 \text{ pu}$$

(iv) When excitation (E) is removed in generator, then generator will able to deliver reluctance power only and reluctance power will be maximum corresponds to $\delta = 45°$.

$$P_{max}\big/_{E=0} = \frac{V_t^2}{2}\left[\frac{1}{X_q} - \frac{1}{X_d}\right]$$

$$P_{max}\big/_{E=0} = \frac{1}{2}\left[\frac{2}{3}\right] = \frac{1}{3} \text{ pu}$$

4.41 A 15 kW, 400 V, 3-phase, star connected synchronous motor has synchronous impedance of 0.4 + *j*4 Ω. Find the motor excitation voltage for full load output at 0.866 leading power factor. Take the armature efficiency of 95%.

[20 marks : 2020]

Solution:

Given that, Rated power, $P_o = 15$ kW

$$\vec{Z}_s = (0.4 + j4)\Omega$$

Line to line voltage, $\vec{V}_t = 400$ V

Power factor $= \cos\phi = 0.866$ lead

$$\phi = 30°$$

$$\eta = 0.95$$

$$P_{in} = \frac{P_{out}}{\eta} = \frac{15}{0.95} = 15.7894 \text{ kW}$$

As we know, $P_{in} = \sqrt{3}\cdot V_L \cdot I_L \cos\phi$

$$\vec{I}_L = \frac{15789.40}{\sqrt{3}\times 400\times 0.866} = 26.316\angle\cos^{-1}(0.866) = 26.316\angle 30° \text{ A}$$

Excitation voltage for given motor is $= \vec{E}_f$

$$\vec{E}_f = \vec{V}_t - \bar{I}_a\bar{Z}_s$$

$$= \frac{400}{\sqrt{3}}\angle 0 - (26.31\angle 30°)(0.4 + j4)$$

$$\vec{E}_f = 290.90 \angle -19.35 \text{ V } [L - N]$$

$$\vec{E}_f = 503.85 \angle -19.35 \text{ V } [L - L]$$

4.42 A three-phase, 6-pole, 50 Hz salient pole alternator is directly connected to 3500 V, 3-phase supply mains to deliver power. It has $X_d = 8.0\ \Omega$, $X_q = 6.0\ \Omega$ on per phase basis. The excitation is so adjusted to achieve an equivalent per phase internal generated voltage of 1500 V at a load angle of 15 degrees. Find the delivered power, armature current and power factor under this condition. Now the alternator is made to deliver maximum power under the same value of excitation voltage. Find the new value of load angle and delivered power under this situation.

[20 marks : 2021]

Solution:

Given :

Line voltage, $V = 3500$ (L-L),

$X_d = 8\ \Omega$,

$$X_q = 6\ \Omega$$

Excitation voltage, $\vec{E}_f = 1500\angle 15°\text{ V} = 2598\angle 15°\text{ V [L-L]}$

Now, active power delivered by alternator

$$P = \frac{E_f V_t}{X_d}\sin\delta + \frac{V_t^2}{2}\left(\frac{1}{X_L} - \frac{1}{X_d}\right)\sin 2\delta$$

$$P = \frac{2598 \times 3500}{8}\sin(15°) + \frac{(3500)^2}{2}\left[\frac{1}{6} - \frac{1}{8}\right]\sin(30°)$$

$$P_{out} = 421.784\text{ kW}$$

Reactive power delivered by generator

$$Q_{out} = \frac{E_f \cdot V_t}{X_d}\cos\delta - \frac{V_t^2}{2X_d X_q}\left[(X_q + X_d) - (X_d - X_q)\cos 2\delta\right]$$

$$Q_{out} = \frac{2598 \times 3500}{8}\cos(15°) - \frac{(3500)^2}{2\times 8\times 6}(14 - 2\cos 30°)$$

$$= -467.55\text{ kVAR}$$

Q_{out} is negative so alternator is working at leading power factor.

$$\text{Apparent power, } S = \sqrt{P^2 + Q^2} = \sqrt{(421.784)^2 + (467.55)^2} = 629.68\text{ kVA}$$

As we know, apparent power is given as

$$S = \sqrt{3}V_L I_a$$

Armature current, $I_a = \dfrac{629.68 \times 10^3}{\sqrt{3} \times 3500} = 103.87\text{ Amp}$

Power factor, $\cos\phi = \dfrac{P}{\sqrt{3}V_L I_a} = \dfrac{421.784 \times 10^3}{\sqrt{3} \times 3500 \times 103.87} = 0.67\text{ leading}$

So, $P = 421.784\text{ kW}$

$$I_a = 103.87\text{ A}$$

$$\cos\phi = 0.67\text{ leading}$$

Now, $E_f = \text{constant} = 2598\text{ V}$

$$P = \frac{3500 \times 2598}{8}\sin\delta + \frac{(3500)^2}{8}\left[\frac{1}{6} - \frac{1}{8}\right]\sin 2\delta$$

$$= 1136.625\sin\delta + 255.208\sin 2\delta \quad \text{...(i)}$$

For maximum power, $\dfrac{dP}{d\delta} = 1136.625\cos\delta + 255.208 \times 2\cos 2\delta = 0$

By solving, $\delta = 69.90°$

Power angle of alternator under maximum power delivering condition

On substituting, $\delta = 69.90°$ in equation (i),

$$P = 1136.625\sin(69.90°) + 255.208\sin(2 \times 69.90°)$$

$$P_{max} = 1232.12\text{ kW}$$

$$\delta_{max} = 69.90°$$

$$P_{max} = 1232.12\text{ kW}$$

4.43 A 6.6 kV star-connected synchronous motor has synchronous impedance $Z_s = (2 + j10)\ \Omega$ per phase. Its excitation is so adjusted that for an input power of 500 kW, the motor pf is 0.7 leading. Now the motor is connected in parallel with a load drawing 1000 kW power at 0.8 pf lag while its input power is changed to 600 kW with same excitation as above.

Find :

(i) the new load angle of the motor.

(ii) the total input power factor for the load and synchronous motor combination.

[20 marks : 2022]

Solution:

Given : $V_t = 6.6$ kV

$Z_s = (2 + j10)\ \Omega$/Ph

Y-connected synchronous motor.

(i) Given : $P_{in} = 500$ kW, $\cos\phi = 0.7$ leading

$\phi = -45.57°$

As we know,

$$P_{in} = \sqrt{3}V_L I_L \cos\phi$$

Input line current of motor,

$$\vec{I}_a = \frac{P_{in}}{\sqrt{3}\times V_L \cos\phi}$$

$$= \frac{500}{\sqrt{3}\times 6.6\times 0.7} = 62.48\angle 45.57° \text{ A}$$

Excitation emf of motor is given as,

$$\vec{E}_f = \vec{V}_t - \vec{Z}_s\vec{I}_a$$

$$= \frac{6600}{\sqrt{3}}\angle 0° - (2+j10)(62.48\angle 45.57°)$$

$$= 4202.34\angle -7.19° \text{ Volt (per phase)}$$

$$\vec{E}_f = \sqrt{3}\times 4202.34\angle -7.19°$$

$$= 7278.65\angle -7.19° \text{ V (line to line)}$$

Now motor input power changed to 600 kW

$P_{in} = 600$ kW

$|E_f| = 7278.65$ Volts

Now,
$$P_{in} = \frac{V_t^2}{Z_s}\cos\theta_s - \frac{E_f\cdot V_t}{Z_s}\cos(Q_s+\delta)$$

where, δ = new load angle

$$600 = \frac{6.6^2\times 10^3}{10.198}\cos(78.70°) - \frac{7278.65\times 6.6}{10.198}\cos(78.70+\delta)$$

$$\frac{7278.65\times 6.6}{10.198}\cos(78.70+\delta) = 836.96 - 600 = 236.96$$

$$\cos(78.70+\delta) = 0.05$$

New power angle, $\delta = \cos^{-1}(0.05) - 78.70° = 8.42°$

Therefore, $E_f\angle-\delta = 7278.65\angle-8.42°$ Volts (line to line)

(ii) From part (i)

$$\vec{E}_f = 7278.65\angle-8.42° \text{ Volts}$$

Motor input current, $\vec{I}_a = \dfrac{\vec{V}_t - \vec{E}_f}{\vec{Z}_s}$

$$\vec{I}_a = \frac{6600\angle 0° - 7278.65\angle -8.42°}{(2+j10)\sqrt{3}}$$

$$= 119.94\angle 40.70° \text{ A}$$

New power factor of motor,

$$\cos\phi = \cos(40.69°) = 0.7582 \text{ leading}$$

Total input power of system

$$\vec{s}_{in} = \vec{s}_L + \vec{s}_M$$

$$= 1250\angle 36.86° + 791.34\angle-40.69°$$

$$\vec{s}_{in} = 1617.16\angle 8.316° \text{ kVA}$$

Therefore, power factor of overall system is

$$\cos\phi = \cos(8.136°) = 0.9894 \text{ lagging}$$

5. Three Phase Induction Machine

5.1 **What are the terms air-gap power, internal mechanical power developed and shaft power? How are these terms related with each other?**

[4 marks : 2001]

Solution:

Air gap power (P_g): The power that is transferred from the stator to the rotor via the air-gap magnetic field, is known as the Air-gap power (P_g)

$$P_g = \frac{3I_2'^2 R_2'}{s}$$

Subtracting the rotor copper loss from Air-gap power (P_g) gives the internal mechanical power developed (P_m)

$$P_m = P_g - 3I_2'^2 R_2'^2 = \frac{3I_2'^2 R_2'^2}{s} - 3I_2'^2 R_2$$

$$= 3I_2'^2 R_2'\left(\frac{1}{s} - 1\right) = (1-s)P_g$$

The internal mechanical power developed (P_m) is three times the electrical power absorbed in resistance $R_2'\left(\frac{1}{s} - 1\right)$.

Shaft power (P_{sh}) is the power available at shaft after subtracting mechanical losses from P_m.

$$P_{sh} = P_m - \text{mechanical losses}$$

5.2 Explain how the desirable features of high-starting torque and low-operating slip are obtained in a double cage polyphase induction motor. A double-cage motor has stand still impedance of 1 + *j*1 Ω and 0.3 + *j*5 Ω for its two cage. Compare the relative torques of the two cages (a) at stand still and (b) at a slip of 0.5.

[12 marks : 2001]

Solution:

A double-cage polyphase induction motor consists of two layers of bars short-circuited by end rings. The upper bars have a smaller cross-sectional area than the lower bars and consequently a higher resistance and low reactance because much lower leakage flux linking to the upper bars. And simultaneously lower bars have low resistance and high reactance. Therefore, in the starting, the current is mainly confined to the outer cage with a consequent decrease in starting current and an increase in starting torque. Under running condition the reactance difference between the two cages evens out because of low frequency of rotor currents such that these act to conduct current in proportion to their dc resistances and as a group present a low resistance rotor to the air-gap flux giving an excellent running performance. Two types of double cage rotor constructions are available.

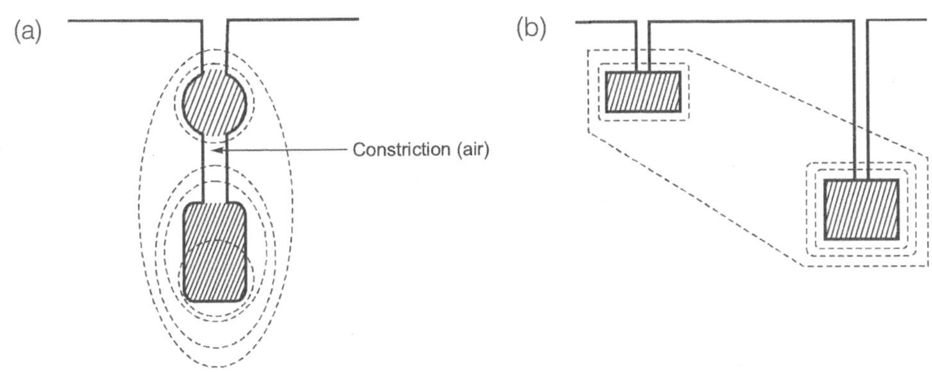

Approximate circuit model of double-cage induction motor,

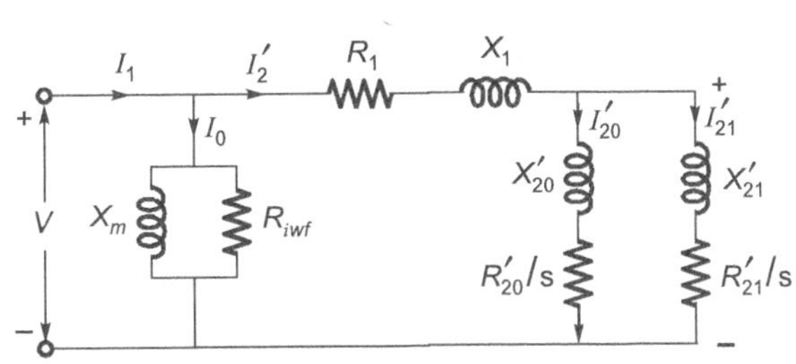

Torque-slip characteristic,

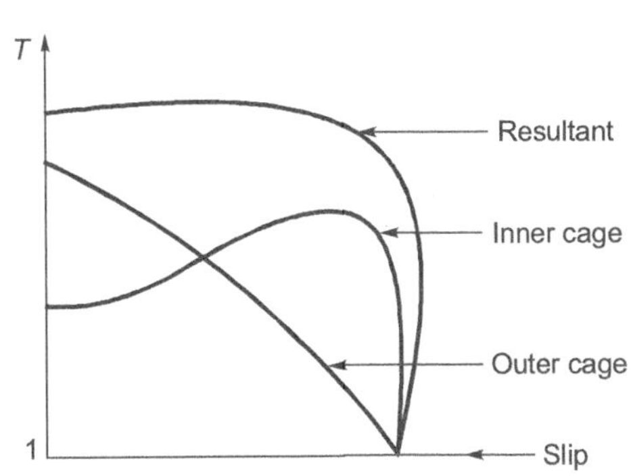

Given standstill impedances,

$$\text{outer cage} = 1 + j1\ \Omega$$
$$\text{inner cage} = 0.3 + j5\ \Omega$$

(a) At stand still $s = 1$

$$T_s = \frac{3}{\omega_s}\cdot\frac{V'^2 R_2}{R_2^2 + X_2^2} \quad \text{(as seen on the rotor side)}$$

Where, V' = rotor induced emf

Substituting values,

$$T_{si} = \frac{3}{\omega_s}\cdot\frac{V'^2(0.3)}{(0.3)^2+(5)^2}$$

$$T_{so} = \frac{3}{\omega_s}\cdot\frac{V'^2(1)}{(1)^2+(1)^2}$$

$$\frac{T_{so}}{T_{si}} = \frac{(0.3)^2+(5)^2}{(1)^2+(1)^2}\times\frac{1}{0.3} = 41.82$$

(b)

$$T = \frac{3}{\omega_s}\times\frac{V'^2(R_2/s)}{(R_2/s)^2 + X_2^2}$$

Given, $s = 0.05$

$$T_{si} = \frac{3}{\omega}\times\frac{V'^2(0.3/0.05)}{(0.3/0.05)^2+(5)^2}$$

$$T_{so} = \frac{3}{\omega_s}\times\frac{V'^2(1/0.05)}{(1/0.05)^2+1}$$

$$\frac{T_{so}}{T_{si}} = \frac{(6)^2+(5)^2}{(20)^2+(1)^2}\times\frac{1}{0.3} = 0.507$$

5.3 The speed of an induction motor is controlled by controlling its supply frequency. If the speed of the machine is reduced by reducing the frequency by 50% of the rated frequency, to keep the flux in the machine constant, the motor voltage compared to rated voltage must be

(a) increase by 25% (b) increase by 50%
(c) decrease by 50% (d) decrease by 25% [2 marks : 2002]

Solution:

Given, ϕ = constant means $\frac{V}{f}$ = constant

Option (c) is correct.

5.4 For the purpose of starting an induction motor, a Y/Δ switch is equivalent to an auto-transformer of ratio.

(a) 33.3% (b) 57.7%
(c) 73.2% (d) 100% [2 marks : 2002]

Solution:

Star-delta starting reduces the starting torque to one-third that obtainable by direct-delta starting and also the starting line current to one-third. It just acts like auto transformer starting with $x = \frac{1}{\sqrt{3}}\times 100 = 57.7\%$.

Hence, option (b) 57.7% is correct.

5.5 A squirrel-cage induction motor has a starting current of six times the full-load current at a slip of 0.04. Calculate the line current and starting torque in p.u. of full load values for the following methods of starting.

(a) Direct switching

(b) Auto-transformer starting with motor current limited to 2.0 p.u.

(c) Star-Delta starting

[10 marks : 2002]

Solution:

Given, $I_{sc} = 6 \times I_{fl}$ at $s = 0.04$

(a) $I_{st}\text{(line current)} = I_{sc} = 6I_{fl} = 6 \text{ pu}$

Starting torque in p.u. of full-load value

or $$\frac{T_{st}}{T_{fl}} = \left(\frac{I_s}{I_{fl}}\right)^2 \times 0.04 = 36 \times 0.04 = 1.44 \text{ p.u.}$$

$\Rightarrow$ $T_{st} = 1.44 \text{ pu}$

(b) $I_{st}\text{(motor)} = x \cdot I_{sc} = 2I_{fl}$

and $I_{sc} = 6 \cdot I_{fl}$

then $x = \frac{1}{3}$

Line current, $$I_{st}\text{(line)} = x(x\, I_{sc}) = x^2 I_{sc} = \frac{1}{9} \cdot 6 \cdot I_{fl}$$

$$I_s\text{(line)}_{\text{p.u.}} = \frac{I_s\text{(line)}}{I_{fl}} = \frac{2}{3} = 0.67 \text{ pu}$$

Starting torque in p.u. of full-load torque,

$$\frac{T_s}{T_{fl}} = x^2 \left(\frac{I_{sc}}{I_{fl}}\right)^2 s_{fl} = \frac{1}{9} \times 36 \times 0.04 = 0.16 \text{ (p.u.)}$$

$\Rightarrow$ $T_{st} = 0.16 \text{ pu}$

(c) Starting line current,

$$I_{st} = \sqrt{3} I_{sc} = \sqrt{3}.6 I_{fl} \text{ (direct-delta starting)}$$

$$\frac{I_{st}(\Delta)}{I_{fl}} = 6\sqrt{3} = 10.392 \text{ p.u.}$$

In Y-starting line (phase current)

$$I_{st}(Y) = \frac{I_{sc}}{\sqrt{3}}$$

$$\frac{I_{st}(Y)}{I_{fl}} = \frac{6}{\sqrt{3}} = 3.45 \text{ p.u.}$$

$$\frac{T_s}{T_{fl}} = \frac{1}{3} \cdot \left(\frac{I_{sc}}{I_{fl}}\right)^2 \cdot s_{fl} = \frac{1}{3} \cdot (6)^2 \times 0.04 = 0.48 \text{ p.u.}$$

I_{st} = starting phase-current delta

5.6 A 3-phase induction motor draws 1000 kVA at a p.f. of 0.8 lag. A synchronous condenser is connected in parallel to draw an additional 750 kVA at a p.f. of 0.6 lead. The p.f. of the total load supplied by the mains is

(a) unity (b) 0.707 lead

(c) 0.6 lag (d) zero [2 marks : 2003]

Solution: (a)

Reactive power drawn by induction motor

$$Q_1 = -1000 \times 0.6 = -600 \text{ kVA}$$

Reactive power supplied by condenser,

$$Q_s = +750 \times \sin(\cos^{-1} 0.6) = 600 \text{ kVA}$$

Total power, $Q = Q_I + Q_s = 0$ kVA (unity pf)

So, the option (a) is correct.

5.7 A 1200 V, 50 Hz star connected induction motor has a star connected slipring rotor with a transformation ratio of 3.75. The rotor resistance per phase is 0.016 ohm and leakage inductance of 0.8 mH/phase. Neglect stator impedance. Find:

(a) rotor starting current per phase with slip ring short circuited,

(b) the rotor p.f. at starting,

(c) the external resistance per phase required to obtain a starting current of 125 A in the stator,

(d) the rotor current of 4% slip and,

(e) rotor p.f. at 4% slip. [16 marks : 2003]

Solution:

$$\text{Phase voltage} = \frac{1200}{\sqrt{3}} = 692.82 \text{ V}$$

Per phase equivalent circuit,

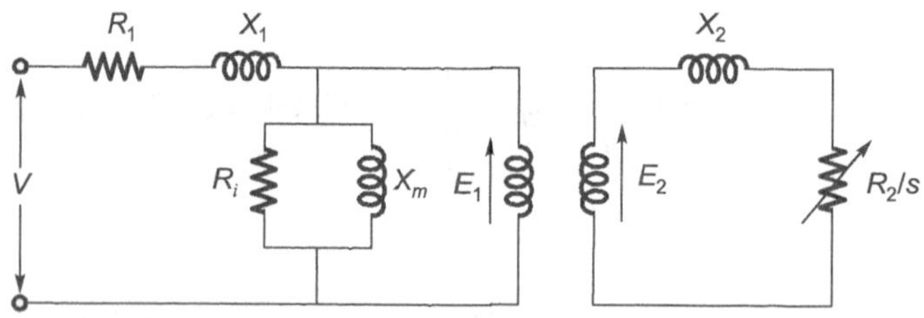

Neglect stator impedance,

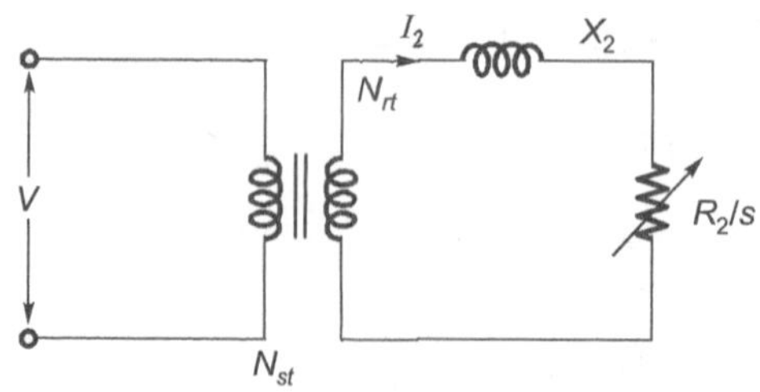

Transformation ratio $\frac{N_{st}}{N_{rt}} = 3.75$ (given)

equivalent circuit refer to stator side,

$$R_2' = \frac{R_2}{(N_{rt}/N_{st})^2} = (3.75)^2 \times 0.016\ \Omega$$

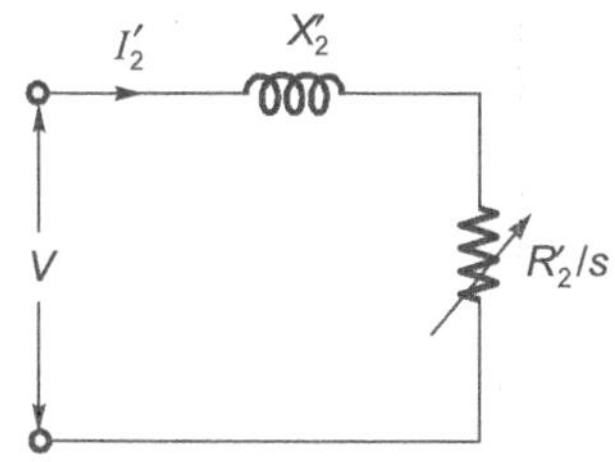

$$R_2' = 0.225\ \Omega$$

$$X_2 = 2\pi f L$$

$$= 2 \times 3.14 \times 50 \times 0.8 \times 10^{-3}$$

$$X_2 = 0.251\ \Omega$$

$$X_2' = 3.53\ \Omega$$

(a) Slip ring short-circuited i.e. no external resistance in rotor circuit at starting $s = 1$

$$I'_{2(st)} = \frac{V}{R_2' + jX_2'} = \frac{\frac{1.2\times10^3}{\sqrt{3}}\angle 0^\circ}{0.225 + j3.53}$$

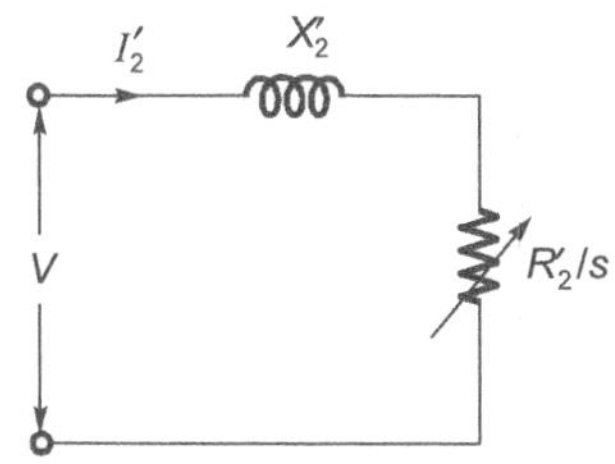

$$I'_{2(st)} = 195.87\underline{|-86.35}$$

$$|I'_{2(st)}| = 195.87\text{ A}$$

$$I_2' = \frac{N_{rt}}{N_{st}} \times I_2$$

$$I_2 = I_2' \times \frac{N_{st}}{N_{rt}}$$

$$I_2 = 195.87 \times 3.75 = 734.5\text{ A}$$

(b) Rotor p.f. at starting, $s = 1$

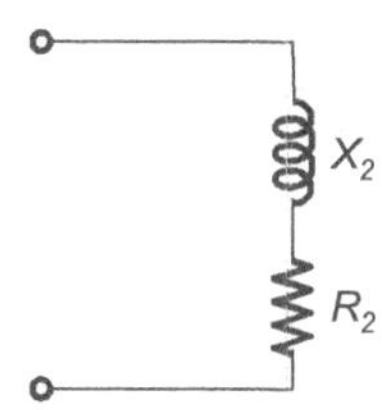

$$\tan\phi = \frac{x_2}{R_2}$$

$$\cos(86.35) = 0.064\text{ lag}$$

(c) Let, $R_{21} = R_2 + R_{ext}$

Starting current on stator side,

$$I_2' = 125\text{ A}$$

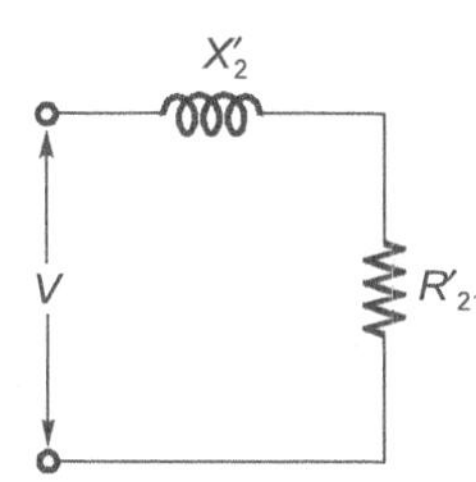

$$\bar{I}_2' = \frac{V}{R_{21}' + jX_2'}$$

$$I_2' = \frac{V}{\sqrt{R_{21}'^2 + X_2'^2}}$$

$$125 = \frac{\frac{1.2\times10^3}{\sqrt{3}}}{\sqrt{(R_{21}')^2 + (3.53)^2}}$$

$$R_{21}'v = 4.27\ \Omega$$

$$R_{21} = \frac{4.27}{(3.75)^2} = 0.304\ \Omega$$

$$R_{ext} = 0.304 - 0.016 = 0.288\ \Omega \quad \textbf{Ans.}$$

(d) The rotor current of 4% slip,

$$I_2' = \frac{V}{\frac{R_2'}{s} + jX_2'} = \frac{\frac{1200}{\sqrt{3}}\angle 0^\circ}{\frac{0.225}{0.04} + j3.53} = \frac{\frac{1200}{\sqrt{3}}}{5.625 + j3.53}$$

$$I_2' = 104.32\angle{-32.1^\circ}$$

(e) Rotor p.f. at 4% slip

$$\text{Rotor current} = 104.32 \times 3.75$$
$$= 391.2\text{ A}$$
$$\text{p.f.} = \cos(32.1^\circ)$$
$$= 0.847 \text{ lag.}$$

5.8 Discuss the relative merits and demerits of single cage and double cage induction motors

[8 marks : 2003]

Solution:

S.No.		Single cage	Double cage
1.	Starting performance	As compare to double cage rotor single cage have less starting torque so at starting less heating loss occur.	A double cage motor develops higher starting torque for low starting current and its rotor heating loss is more.
2.	Full-load performance	Full load slip is higher than double cage rotor. It has higher efficiency.	Slip and efficiency is lower than the single cage rotor.
3.	Torque slip characteristic	It is not fesible in a single cage induction motor.	Wide range of torque-slip characteristic is obtained.

5.9 A star connected squirrel-cage induction motor has following parameters and rating; $R_s = 2\ \Omega$, $R_v' = 3\ \Omega$, $X_s = X_v' = 3.5\ \Omega$
$V = 400$ V, 50 Hz, 1380 RPM. It is driven by a voltage source inverter which gives constant V/f control to IM. If the inverter frequency is variable from 10% of rated frequency to base frequency, calculate:
(a) frequency for a speed of 1000 RPM and full load torque.
(b) torque for a frequency of 35 Hz and speed of 950 RPM.

[15 marks : 2004]

Solution:

Given, constant V/f,

$$V = \frac{400}{\sqrt{3}};$$
$$f = 50\text{ Hz}$$
$$\frac{V}{f} = \frac{400}{\sqrt{3} \times 50}$$

or $$\frac{V}{f} = 4.6$$

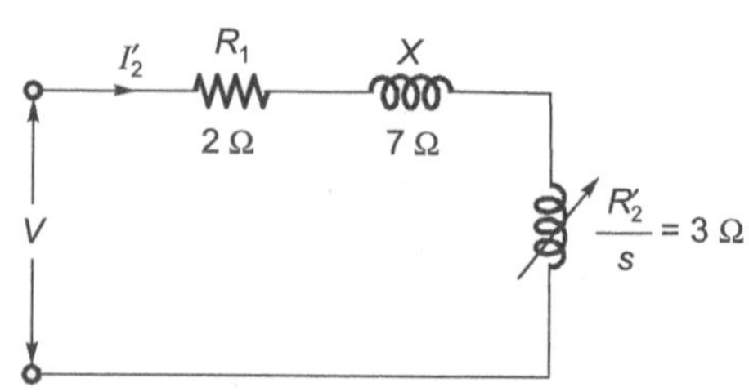

and frequency 10% to rated means $5 \to 50$ Hz

At $$V = \frac{400}{\sqrt{3}};$$

$$f = 50\text{ Hz}$$ $\left(\text{From } \frac{6000}{P}\right)$

$\because$ $$N_r = 1380\text{ rpm};$$
$$N_s = 1500\text{ rpm};$$
$$p = 4$$

$$\omega_s = \frac{2\pi N_s}{60} = \frac{2\times\pi\times 1500}{60} = 157 \text{ rad/sec}$$

$$S_{fl} = \frac{N_s - N_r}{N_s} = \frac{1500-1380}{1500} = 0.08$$

Full load torque,

$$T_{fl} = \frac{3}{\omega_s}\cdot\frac{V^2\cdot R_2'/S_{fl}}{\left(R_1+\frac{R_2'}{S_{fl}}\right)+x^2} = \frac{3}{157}\cdot\frac{\left(\frac{400}{\sqrt{3}}\right)^2\times\frac{3}{0.08}}{\left(2+\frac{3}{0.08}\right)^2+(7)^2}$$

$$T_{fl} = 23.5 \text{ Nm}$$

(a) $f = ?$

$$\frac{V}{f} = 4.6$$

$$N_r = 1000 \text{ rpm}$$

$$T_{fl} = 23.5$$

$$\omega_s = \frac{2\pi\times N_s}{60} = \frac{2\pi}{60}\times\frac{120f}{4}$$

$$\omega_s = \pi f$$

$$X = 2\pi f L = \frac{f}{50}\times(2\pi\times 50\times L)$$

$\therefore$
$$X_{50\text{ Hz}} = 2\pi\times 50\times L = 7$$

or
$$X = \frac{7f}{50}$$

$$S_{fl} = \frac{\omega_s-\omega_r}{\omega_s} = 1-\frac{104.7}{\pi f} = 1-\frac{33.3}{\pi f}$$

$$23.5 = \frac{3}{\pi f}\times\frac{(4.6f)^2\dfrac{3}{\left(1-\frac{33.3}{f}\right)}}{\left[2+\left(\dfrac{3}{1-\frac{33.3}{f}}\right)\right]^2+\left(\frac{7f}{50}\right)^2}$$

For full load i.e. low slip region.

$$\left(R_1+\frac{R_2'}{S}\right)^2 + X^2 \cong \left(\frac{R_2'}{S}\right)^2$$

i.e.,
$$23.5 \cong \frac{3}{\pi f}\cdot\frac{(4.6f)^2\left(\dfrac{3}{1-\frac{33.3}{f}}\right)}{\left(\dfrac{3}{1-\frac{33.3}{f}}\right)^2} \quad \text{or} \quad 23.5 = \frac{3}{\pi}\cdot(4.6)^2\left(\frac{f-33.3}{3}\right)$$

$$f = 36.78 \text{ Hz}$$

(b) Torque for a frequency of 35 Hz and speed of 950 rpm.

$$N_r = 950;\quad N_s = 1050$$

$\therefore$
$$S = \frac{1050-950}{1050} = 0.09$$

$$T = \frac{3}{\omega_S} \cdot \frac{V^2}{\left(R_1 + \frac{R_2'}{S}\right)^2 + (X_1 + X_2')^2} \cdot \frac{R_2'}{S_{f1}}$$

$$\omega_s = \frac{2\pi N_s}{60} = \frac{2\pi \times 1050}{60} = 109.95 \text{ rad/sec.}$$

$$\frac{V}{f} = 4.6 \text{ constant}$$

$$\therefore \quad V = 4.6 \times 35 = 161 \text{ V}$$

$$X = \frac{35}{50} \times 7 = 4.9 \qquad \left(\because X = \frac{7f}{50}\right)$$

$$T = \frac{3}{109.25} \frac{(161)^2 \times \frac{3}{0.09}}{\left(2 + \frac{3}{0.09}\right)^2 + (4.9)^2} = 19.39 \text{ Nm}$$

5.10 For a slip ring induction motor, if the rotor resistance is increased, then
(a) starting torque and efficiency increase.
(b) starting torque decreases but efficiency increases.
(c) starting torque increases but efficiency decreases.
(d) starting torque and efficiency decreases. [2 marks : 2005]

Solution: (c)

5.11 From the short circuit test on a 50 H.P. 440 V, 50 Hz, 6 pole star connected, 3-phase induction motor, the following data were obtained:

$$V = 230 \text{ V}, \quad I = 140 \text{ A}; \quad \cos\phi = 0.35 \text{ (line values)}$$

The motor drives a load having a constant torque of 300 N-m. Estimate the maximum percentage reduction in the supply voltage possible before the motor stalls. Assume that the copper losses are equally divided between the stator and the rotor. Neglect magnetization current.

[14 marks : 2005]

Solution:

$$V_{sc} = \frac{230}{\sqrt{3}} V; \quad I_{sc} = 140 \text{ A}; \quad \cos\phi_{sc} = 0.35,$$

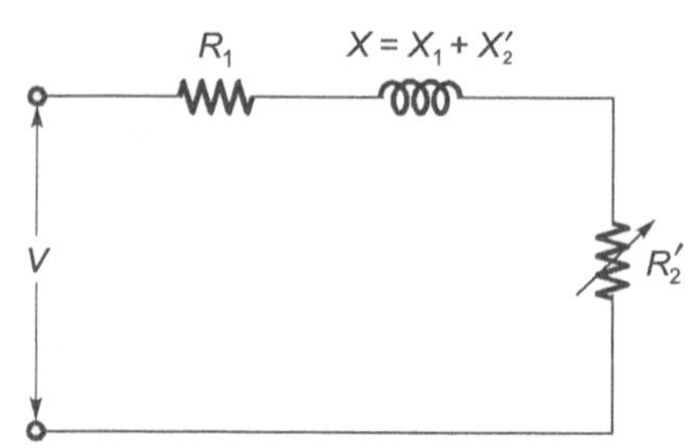

Per phase, $P_{sc} = V_{sc} I_{sc} \cos\phi$

$$= \frac{230}{\sqrt{3}} \times 140 \times 0.35 = 6.5 \text{ kW}$$

or, $P_{sc} = I_{SC}^2 R$

$$R = \frac{6.5 \times 10^3}{(140)^2} = 0.331\ \Omega$$

$$R_1 + R_2' = 0.331\ \Omega$$

$$R_1 = R_2' = 0.165\ \Omega$$

$$Z_{sc} = \frac{V_{sc}}{I_{sc}} = \frac{230/\sqrt{3}}{140} = 0.948\ \Omega$$

$$X = \sqrt{Z_{sc}^2 - R_0^2} = 0.8885\ \Omega$$

$$X_1 + X_2' = X = 0.8885\ \Omega$$

$$X_1 = X_2' = 0.4442\ \Omega$$

At V_0, $T_L = T_{max}$

If supply voltage < V_0, the motor comes to stall,

$$T_L = T_{max} = \frac{3}{\omega_s} \cdot \frac{0.5\,V_0^2}{R_1 + \sqrt{R_1^2 + X^2}}$$

As $N_s = \frac{120\text{ f}}{\text{P}} = 1000\text{ rpm}$

$$\therefore \quad 300 = \frac{3}{\frac{2\pi \times 1000}{60}} \times \frac{0.5V_0^2}{0.165 + \sqrt{(0.165)^2 + (0.8885)^2}}$$

$$V_0 = 149.6$$

Actual, $V = \frac{440}{\sqrt{3}} = 254\text{ volt}$

$$\%\text{ reduction} = \frac{V - V_0}{V} \times 100 = \frac{254 - 149.6}{254} \times 100 = 41.10\%$$

5.12 Name the chief methods of speed control of a 3-phase induction motor. Explain briefly one of the most modern methods of speed control of an induction motor namely (*V/f*) control.

[12 marks : 2005]

Solution:

Methods of controlling the speed of the induction motor can be visualized by consideration of the speed equation

$$n = (1 - s)\,n_s \qquad \ldots(i)$$

From this equation, there are two basic ways of speed control,

(a) Slip-control for fixed synchronous speed.

(b) Control of synchronous speed.

Since, $n_s = \frac{120f}{p}$

There are two ways to control, synchronous speed-control of supply frequency and control of stator poles. The later method gives a step control as poles can be changed in multiple of two, pole changing is carried out in a squirrel-cage motor only and that too for two steps.

Speed control of an induction motor by V/f control: The synchronous speed of the induction motor can be controlled in a stepless way over a wide range by changing the supply frequency.

The resultant air-gap flux per pole is,

$$\phi_r = \frac{1}{4.44\,K_{w_1} N_{ph1}} \cdot \left(\frac{V}{f}\right) \qquad \ldots(ii)$$

Therefore, in order to avoid saturation in stator and rotor cores which cause sharp increase in magnetization current, the flux ϕ_r must be kept constant as f is varied. To achieve this, from equation (*i*) that when f is varied, V must also be varied such that (V/f) remains constant. Variable (V, f) supply from constant (V, f) supply can be arranged by the converter-inverter arrangement shown in figure below which employs SCR circuitry.

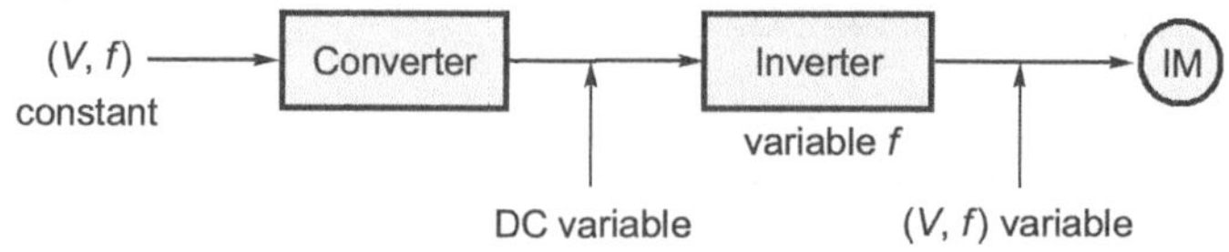

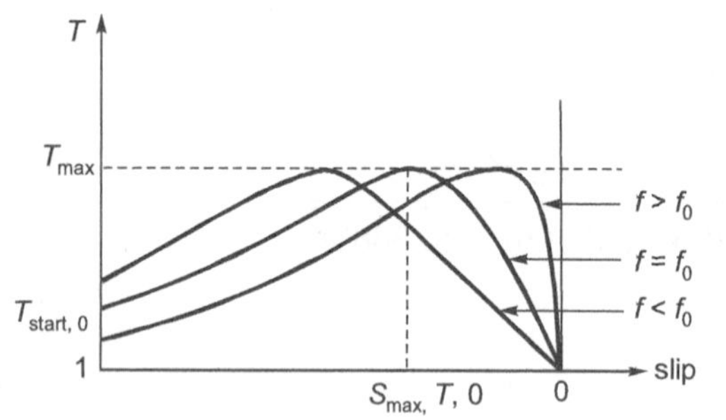

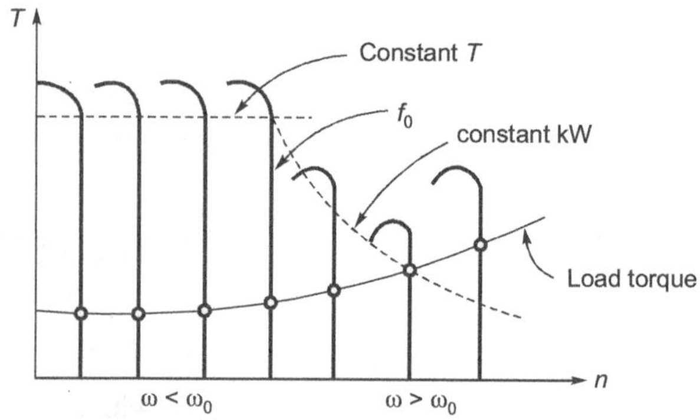

Torque-slip characteristics; variable f, constant (V/f)

5.13 A 4-pole, 50 Hz, 3-phase induction motor has blocked rotor reactance per phase which is four times the rotor resistance per phase. The speed at which maximum torque develops is

(a) 1125 rpm (b) 1500 rpm
(c) 1050 rpm (d) 1210 rpm

[2 marks : 2006]

Solution: (a)

For maximum torque,

$$s_{max} = \frac{R}{X} = \frac{1}{4} = 0.25$$

Synchronous speed, $$n_s = \frac{120f}{P} = \frac{120 \times 50}{4} = 1500 \text{ rpm}$$

$$\text{Speed at maximum torque} = (1 - s_{max})\, n_s = (1 - 0.25) \times 1500 = 1125 \text{ rpm}$$

Hence, option (a) is correct.

5.14 Derive the following for the 3-phase induction motor due to interaction of rotor and stator fields:

(a) Torque developed
(b) Starting torque
(c) Condition for maximum torque
(d) Effect of change in supply voltage on starting torque
(e) Effect of change in supply voltage on torque and slip
(f) Full load torque and maximum torque.

[12 marks : 2006]

Solution:

(a) Torque Developed:

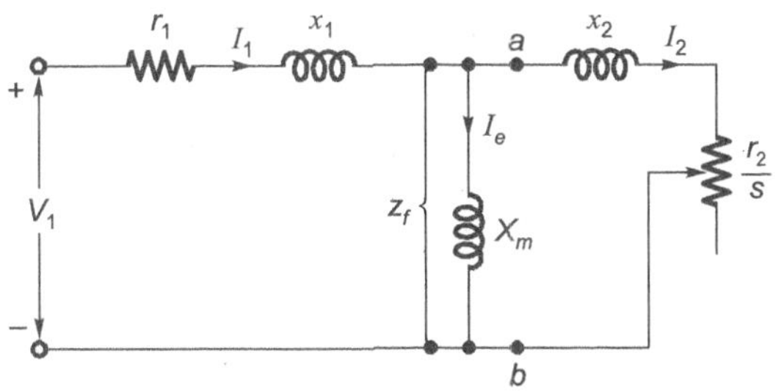

Induction motor equivalent circuit without core loss

Applying Thevenin's theorem, taking two points *a* and *b*.

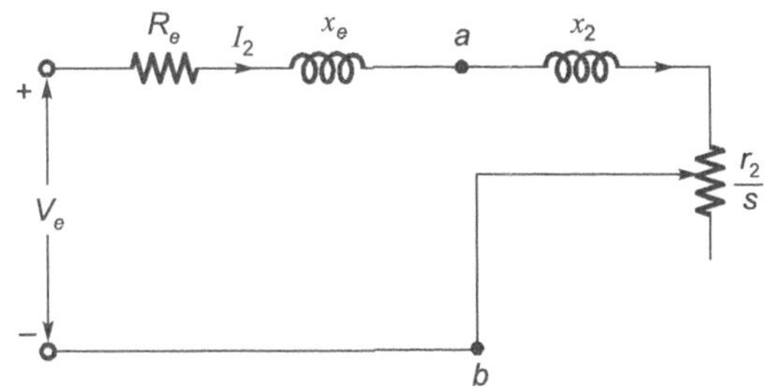

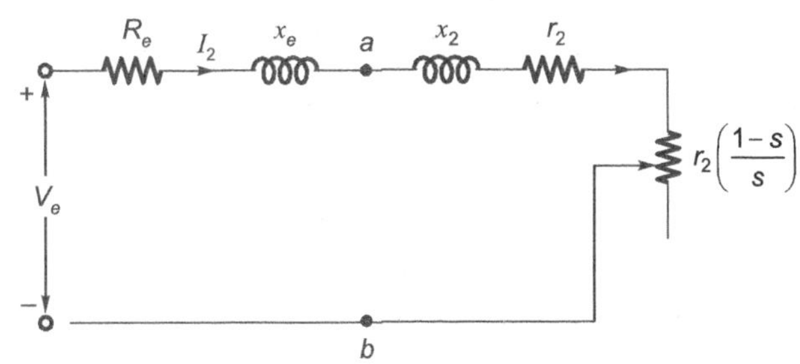

Thevenin's equivalent circuit of an induction motor

$$\overline{V}_e = \frac{V_1(jX_m)}{r_1 + j(x_1 + X_m)}$$

and
$$\overline{Z}_e = \frac{(r_1 + jx_1)(jX_m)}{r_1 + j(x_1 + X_m)}$$

For most induction motors, $(x_1 + X_m)$ is much greater than r_1. In view of this r_1 can be neglected.

$\therefore$
$$V_e = \frac{V_1(jX_m)}{j(x_1 + X_m)} = \frac{V_1 X_m}{X_1}$$

and
$$\overline{Z}_e = R_e + jX_e = \frac{r_1 X_m}{x_1 + X_m} + j\frac{x_1 X_m}{x_1 + X_m}$$

$$\overline{Z}_e = \frac{r_1 X_m}{X_1} + j\frac{x_1 X_m}{X_1}$$

Here, $X_1 = x_1 + X_m$, is the stator self reactance per phase.

From equivalent circuit, rotor current

$$\overline{I}_2 = \frac{\overline{V}_e}{\left(R_e + \frac{r_2}{s}\right) + j(x_2 + X_e)}$$

$\because$ Electromagnetic torque,

$$T_e = \frac{3}{\omega_s} \cdot \frac{I_2^2 r_2}{s} \text{ Nm}$$

$$\therefore \quad T_e = \frac{3}{\omega_s} \cdot \frac{V_e^2}{\left(R_e + \frac{r_2}{s}\right)^2 + (x_2 + X_e)^2} \cdot \frac{r_2}{s} \text{ Nm} \quad \ldots(i)$$

(b) Starting Torque: At starting, slip $s = 1.00$

From equation (i) starting torque.

$$T_{e,st} = \frac{3}{\omega_s} \cdot \frac{V_e^2}{(R_e + r_2)^2 + (x_2 + X_e)^2} \cdot r_2 \text{ Nm}$$

(c) Condition for Maximum Torque: This is also referred to as stalling torque, pullout torque or breakdown torque T_{em}.

$$\therefore \quad T_e = \frac{3}{\omega_s} \cdot \frac{I_2^2 r_2}{s}$$

From above equation maximum torque occur when $I_2^2 \cdot (r_2/s)$ is maximum, i.e. when power delivered to r_2/s is maximum. By maximum power transfer theorem r_2/s will be maximum when impedance r_2/s becomes equal to the magnitude of impedance seen by r_2/s towards the voltage source V_e, i.e. when

$$\frac{r_2}{s_{mT}} = \sqrt{R_e^2 + (X_e + x_2)^2} = \sqrt{R_e^2 + X^2}$$

where $X = x_2 + X_e$

Thus the slip s_{mT} at which maximum torque occur is given by

$$s_{mT} = \frac{r_2}{\sqrt{R_e^2 + X^2}}$$

Substitution of $\frac{r_2}{s_{mT}}$ in place of $\frac{r_2}{s}$ in equation (i) gives maximum torque T_{em} as

or
$$T_{em} = \frac{3}{\omega_s} \cdot \frac{V_e^2}{2\left[R_e + \sqrt{R_e^2 + X^2}\right]}$$

(d) Effect of Change in Supply Voltage on Starting Torque: Starting torque is proportional to the square of the stator voltage V_1.

(e) Effect of Change in Supply Voltage on Torque and Slip:

$$T \propto s V^2$$

(f) Full Load Torque and Maximum Torque:

$$T_{fl} = \frac{3}{\omega_s} \cdot \frac{V_e^2}{\left(R_e + \frac{r_2}{s_{fl}}\right)^2 + (X_e + x_2)^2} \cdot \frac{r_2}{s_{fl}}$$

5.15 Why do you use Double Cage Induction Motor? Explain disadvantages if any. [4 marks : 2007]

Solution:

A rotor design, which though more expensive gives still better starting and running performance than the deep-bar design, is the double-cage rotor. The squirrel-cage winding in this design consists of two layers of bars short-circuited by end rings. The upper bars have a smaller cross-sectional area than the lower bars and consequently a higher resistance. The slots accommodating the two sets of bars are joined by a constriction which also shows the slot leakage flux pattern for the double cage rotor. By arguments similar to those presented for the deep-bar rotor construction, it is seen that the upper bars have a much lower leakage flux linkage and therefore a much lower reactance. Furthermore, the self-leakage flux linking the upper/lower bars can be controlled by the dimension of the air constriction. The constriction is also necessary because of the fact that in its absence the main flux will return via the iron path between the two slots thereby "missing" the inner bars which then would not contribute to torque development.

It is found that the outer cage has high resistance and low reactance while the inner cage has low resistance and high reactance. Therefore, in the starting the current is mainly confined to the outer cage with a consequent decrease in starting current and an increase in starting torque. Under running condition the reactance difference between the two cages evens out because of low frequency of rotor current such that these act to conduct current in proportion to their d.c. resistances and as a group present a low-resistance rotor to the air-gap flux giving an excellent running performance.

Disadvantage: Rotor design is more expensive.

5.16 The speed of a slip ring three phase induction motor can be controlled from the rotor side by

(a) changing the supply voltage
(b) changing the supply frequency
(c) rheostatic control
(d) changing the number of poles

[2 marks : 2008]

Solution: (c)

Option (c) is correct.

5.17 A 4-pole, 400 V, 10 kW slip ring 3-phase induction motor has rotor resistance = 0.16 ohm per phase and standstill reactance = 0.27 ohm per phase. The voltage across the slip rings at standstill is 141 V per phase. The motor develops a torque of 62.4 Nm at a slip of s = 0.035 and rotor current of 31.1 A. Find the magnitude and phase of emf to be injected to the rotor circuit so that the motor runs at s = 0.02 and develops the same torque.

[10 marks : 2008]

Solution:

$$I_2 = \frac{E_2}{\sqrt{(r_2/s)^2 + x_2^2}}$$

$$31.1 = \frac{E_2}{\sqrt{(0.16/0.035)^2 + (0.27)^2}}$$

$$E_2 = 142.41 \text{ V}$$

$$\theta_2 = \tan^{-1}\frac{s\,x_2}{r_2} = \tan^{-1}\frac{0.035 \times 0.27}{0.16} = 3.38$$

$$T_e = \frac{1}{\omega_s}\cdot\frac{I_2^2 r_2}{s} \Rightarrow T_e \propto \frac{I_2^2}{s}$$

$$\Rightarrow \quad \frac{I_2^2}{0.02} = \frac{(31.1)^2}{0.035} \Rightarrow I_2 = 23.51 \text{ A}$$

For current 23.51 A induced emf E_2'

$$23.51 = \frac{E_2'}{\sqrt{(0.16/0.02)^2 + (0.27)^2}}$$

$$E_2' = 188.18 \text{ V}$$

$$\theta_2' = \tan^{-1}\frac{0.02 \times 0.27}{0.16} = 1.93$$

$$\text{injected emf} = 188.18\angle 1.93° - 142.41\angle 3.38°$$
$$= 45.95\angle -2.56° \text{ V}$$

5.18 **With the help of a neat diagram, explain the steps for the construction of circle diagram of a 3-phase induction motor on the basis of data for its no load and block rotor tests. Show the output and torque lines assuming equal copper losses in the stator and the rotor. Further, identify the starting torque and indicate how (a) power factor (b) slip (c) efficiency can be computed for a given point of operation on the circle diagram.**

[20 marks : 2008]

Solution:

Due to variation of load, slip changes. From figure 1, if the winding impedance changes while the reactance remains same, the resistance varies. The locus of the current for different loading conditions is a semi-circle having diameter (V_P/X_{02}) = ($V_P/X_1 + X_2'$). If the diameter of the line is known, the semicircle can be drawn after locating the no-load current (I_{OP}) and blocked rotor current (I_{SC}) corresponding to the rated applied voltage to the stator.

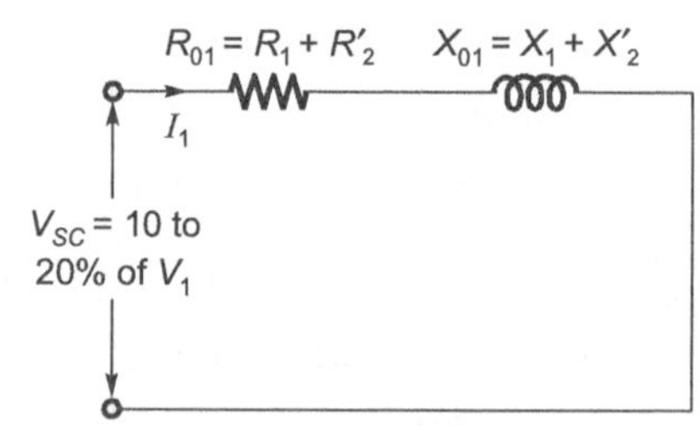

(a) Equivalent circuit of Induction motor during blocked rotor test

Now,
$$I_{SC} = \frac{I_{fl} \times V_P}{V_{SC}}$$

where I_{fl} is the full-load phase current.

Figure (b) shows the circle diagram for a 3-ϕ induction motor. From origin O, a vertical line is drawn representing the axis of phase voltage (V_P). The vectors OA and OB are drawn representing I_{OP} and I_{SC} respectively. I_{OP} and I_{SC} lag the phase voltage V_P by an angle ϕ_0 and ϕ_{SC} respectively. The line AB is joined which forms the chord of the semicircle. A perpendicular bisector of the line AB is drawn which cuts the extended horizontal line drawn from A at C. A semicircle is drawn with C as centre and CA as radius which forms the locus of the semicircle.

A perpendicular is drawn from B which meets the extended AC at D. BD is divided as follows:

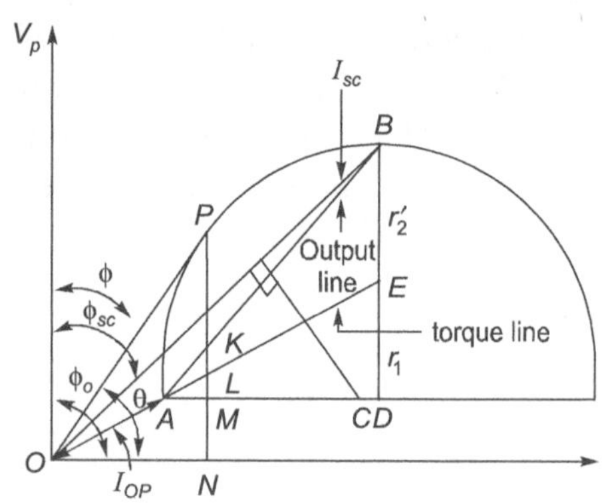

(b) Circle diagram of a 3-ϕ induction motor

$$\frac{BE}{ED} = \frac{\text{Rotor current loss per phase}}{\text{Stator current loss per phase}}$$

The line AE is joined. Let the input stator current per phase be OP at a power factor angle ϕ for a given load condition. A perpendicular is drawn from M which cuts extended AC at N. The input power per phase = $V_P \times OP \cos\phi = V_P \times NP$.

Since V_P remains constant the power input to a certain scale in N_P which can be calculated from current scale.

Therefore, we can write the following:

The power input = NP | The power output = KP

Rotor current loss = LK | Stator current loss = ML

and No-load losses = NM

Therefore,
$$\text{percentage efficiency} = \frac{KP}{NP} \times 100\%$$

$$\text{The percentage slip} = \frac{\text{Rotor copper loss}}{\text{Rotor input}} = \frac{I_2^2 R_2}{P_2} = \frac{LK}{LP} \times 100$$

$$\text{The torque} = LP \text{ syn. Watt/phase}$$

To get the maximum quantities, let us consider figure (c). At point F maximum output occurs because at this point the tangent is parallel to the output line *AB*. To locate F a line is drawn from *C* to *F* such that it is perpendicular to *AB*. From point *F* a vertical line is drawn such that it cuts the output line at the point *G*. *GF* gives the maximum output. Maximum torque occurs at the point *H* where the tangent is parallel to the torque line. To locate *H* a line is drawn from *C* to *H* such that it is perpendicular to *AE*. From *H* a vertical line is drawn which cuts the torque line at *I*. *HI* gives the maximum torque. At point *J*, tangent is horizontal and *JK* gives the maximum input power. The induction motor will be unstable at *J* because the point *J* is beyond *H*.

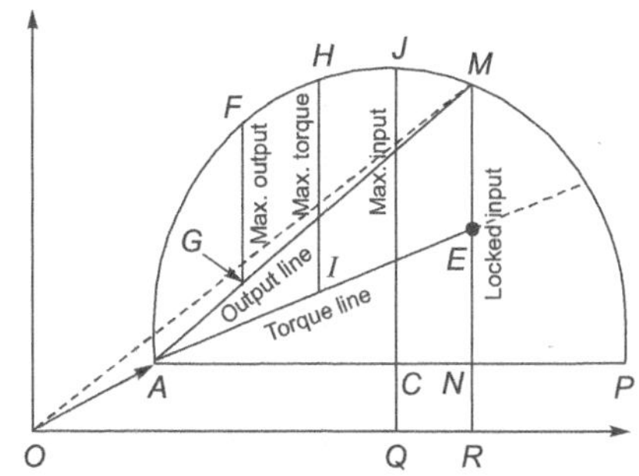

(c) Maximum to quantities

5.19 **Give methods for starting of 3-phase squirrel-cage induction motors.**
A 3-phase, 400 V, 100 kW, 50 Hz, 6-pole induction motor operates at 3% slip at full load. Determine the following:

(a) The speed of the motor and its direction relative to the rotating magnetic field.
(b) The rotor frequency.
(c) The speed of the stator field.
(d) The speed of the air-gap field.
(e) The speed of the rotor field relative to stator rotating field.

Solution:

There are primarily two methods of starting squirrel-cage induction motors:

1. full-voltage starting, and
2. reduced-voltage starting.

The full-voltage starting consists of *DOL* starting, only reduced voltage starting is the most popular method of starting three-phase squirrel-cage induction motors and consists of

1. stator impedance starting
2. auto-transformer starting and
3. star-delta starting.

Numerical:

Given, 400 V, 100 KW, 50 Hz, 6 pole IM, slip = 3% or 0.03

(a) The speed of the motor,

$$N_s = \frac{120f}{P} = \frac{120 \times 50}{6} = 1000 \text{ rpm}$$

$$N_r = (1 - s)N_s = 0.97 \times 1000 = 970 \text{ rpm}$$

Forward field direction.

(b) The rotor frequency, $f = sf_1 = 0.03 \times 50 = 1.5$ Hz

(c) Speed of the stator field = N_s = 1000 rpm

(d) The speed of the air-gap field = N_s = 1000 rpm

(e) The speed of rotor field relative to stator rotating field = zero.

5.20 **Explain the various methods of starting large induction motors with wound rotors and compare their values of starting torques.**

[5 marks : 2010]

Solution:

The methods used for starting squirrel cage motors can also be employed for starting wound-rotor motors. Some of the methods are:

1. **Stator-impedance starting:**

   Inclusion of resistors or inductors in the three lines feeding the stator of the induction motor reduces the stator terminal voltage to xV of the rated voltage V.

$$I_s = xI_{sC} \quad \text{and} \quad \frac{T_s}{T_{fl}} = x^2\left(\frac{I_{sC}}{I_{fl}}\right)^2 s_{fl}$$

   Thus, while the starting reduces by a fraction of x of the rated-voltage starting current (I_{sC}), the starting torque is reduced by a fraction x^2 of that obtainable with direct switching.

2. **Auto transformer starting:**

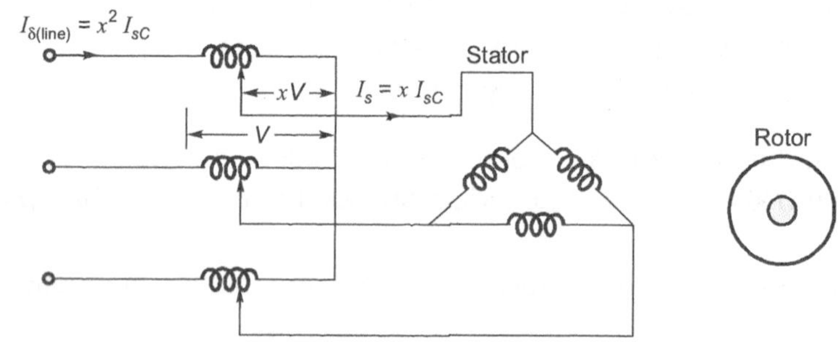

- If the voltage is reduced to a fraction x of the rated voltage V, the motor starting current is $I_s = x\,I_{sC}$.
- The current drawn from the supply is

$$I_{s(\text{Line})} = x(x\,I_{sC}) = x^2 I_{sC}$$

and

$$\frac{T_s}{T_{fl}} = x^2\left(\frac{I_{sC}}{I_{fl}}\right)^2 s_{fl}$$

- While the starting torque is reduced to a fraction x^2 of that obtainable by direct starting, the starting line current is also reduced by the same fraction.

3. **Star-delta starting:**

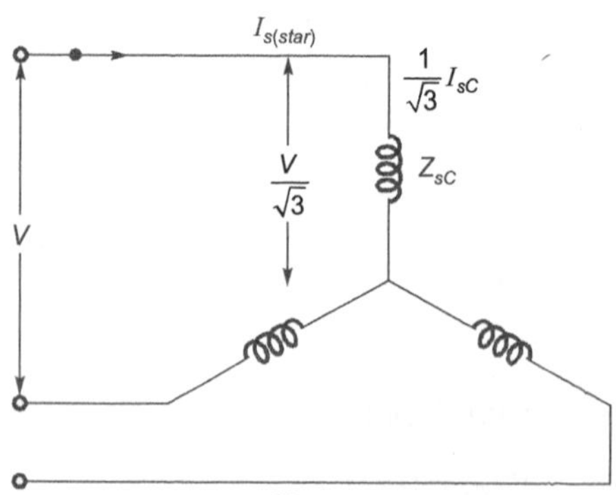

Star

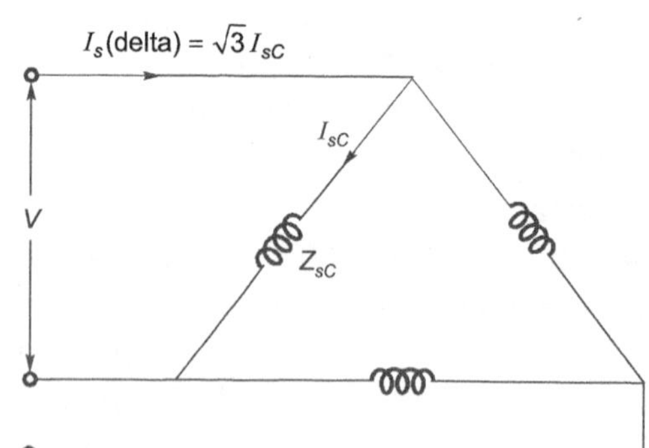

- The motor designed for delta running is started across full-line voltage by connecting the phases in star

$$\frac{I_{s(star)}}{I_{s(delta)}} = \frac{1}{3} \quad \text{and} \quad \frac{T_{s(star)}}{T_{fl}} = \frac{1}{3}\left(\frac{I_{sC}}{I_{fl}}\right)^2 fl$$

  Thus star-delta starting reduces the starting torque to one-third that obtainable by direct-delta starting and also the starting line current to one-third.
- The above methods are usually used for wound rotor induction motors because the advantages of wound-rotor induction motors cannot be fully realized.

The simplest and cheapest method of starting is by means of added rotor resistance and is explained below:

The addition of external resistance in the rotor circuit of a motor

(*i*) decreases its starting current.

(*ii*) increases its starting torque.

(*iii*) improves its starting power factor.

$$T_s = \frac{3}{\omega_s}\frac{V_2(R_2' + R_{ext}')}{(R_2' + R_{ext}')^2 + X_2'} \quad \text{and} \quad I = \frac{V}{\sqrt{(R_2' + R_{ext}')^2 + X_2'^2}}$$

- By a suitable choice of R'_{ext}, the starting current and torque can be both adjusted to desirable levels. Since the maximum starting torque achievable is much more than the full-load torque.

5.21 **A 4-pole, 50 Hz, 3-phase induction motor delivers a shaft torque of 110 N-m at full load and running at 950 rpm. Calculate:**

(i) rotor copper loss (ii) power input to the rotor (iii) the mechanical losses account for 100 W.

[12 marks : 2011]

Solution:

$$\text{Synchronous speed} = N_s^2 = \frac{120f}{P}$$

$$\Rightarrow \quad N_s^2 = \frac{120 \times 50}{4} = 1500 \text{ rpm}$$

$$\text{Rotor speed} = N = 950 \text{ rpm}$$

$$\text{Slip} = \frac{N_s - N}{N_s} = \frac{1500 - 950}{1500} = 0.367$$

$$\omega = \frac{2\pi N}{60} = 99.48 \text{ rad/sec.}$$

$$\text{Shaft torque} = 110 \text{ N-m}$$

Net mechanical output or shaft power = Shaft torque × Rotor speed (rad/sec.)

$$P_8 = 110 \times 99.48 = 10942 \text{ W} = 10.942 \text{ kW}$$

Gross mechanical output of the rotor = Shaft power + Mechanical losses

$$= 10.942 + 0.1 = 11.042 \text{ kW}$$

Power input to the rotor = Air gap power = P_G

As we know that,

Gross mechanical output of the rotor = $(1 - s)\, P_G$

$$(1 - s)\, P_G = 11.042 \text{ kW}$$

$$\text{Power input to the rotor} = \frac{11.042}{1 - 0.367} = 17.443 \text{ kW}$$

$$\text{Rotor copper loss} = sP_G = 0.367 \times 17.443 = 6.40 \text{ kW}$$

5.22 **If an induction motor is operating at 60% of its synchronous speed, the maximum efficiency under ideal conditions (theoretically possible) is**

(a) 100% **(b) 40%**

(c) 50% **(d) 60%**

[12 marks : 2011]

Solution: (d)

$$s = 0.4$$

$$\text{Ideal efficiency} = \frac{1-s}{1} = \frac{1-0.4}{1} = 0.6$$

5.23 If stator impedance of a three-phase induction motor is neglected, show from its equivalent circuit that maximum torque T_{em} per phase is given by

$$T_{em} = \frac{1}{\omega_s} \cdot \frac{V_1^2}{2X_2}$$

and hence show that, $$\frac{T_e}{T_{em}} = \frac{2}{\dfrac{s_{mT}}{s} + \dfrac{s}{s_{mT}}}$$

where s is any slip and s_{mT} = slip at which maximum torque occurs. [8 marks : 2012]

Solution:

Equivalent circuit without stator impedance,

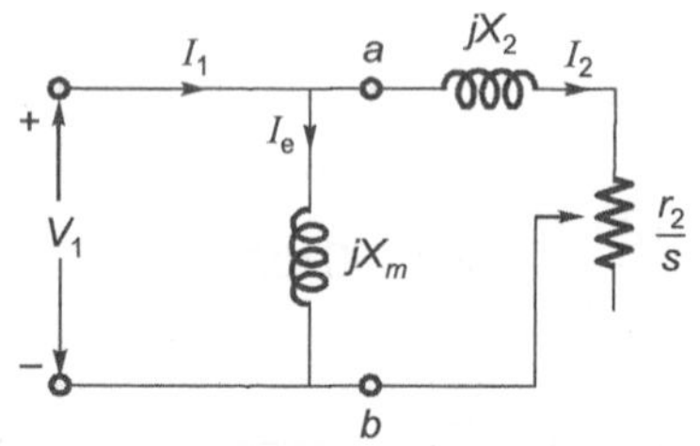

Induction motor equivalent circuit

By applying Thevenins theorem across ab

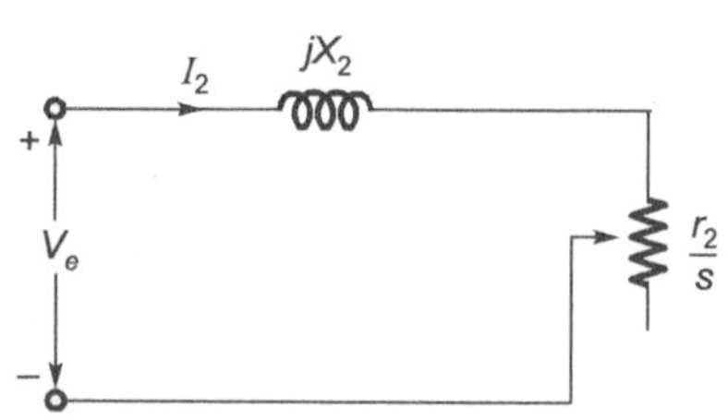

$$V_e = V_1$$

$$\therefore \qquad I_2 = \frac{V_1}{\dfrac{r_2}{s} + jX_2}$$

Total torque, $$T_e = \frac{m}{\omega_s} = \frac{V_1^2}{\left(\dfrac{r_2}{s}\right)^2 + (x_2)^2} \cdot \frac{r_2}{s}$$

where, m = number of stator phases

From the maximum power transfer theorem, the torque will be maximum when impedance r_2/s becomes equal to the magnitude of impedance seen by r_2/s towards the voltage source v_e.

$$\frac{r_2}{s_{mT}} = x_2 \Rightarrow s_{mT} = \frac{r_2}{x_2}$$

Maximum torque, $$T_{em} = \frac{mV_1^2}{\omega_s} \frac{1}{(x_2)^2 + (x_2)^2} \cdot (x_2) = \frac{mV_1^2}{2\omega_s x_2}$$

$$\frac{T_e}{T_{em}} = \frac{m}{\omega_s} \cdot \frac{V_1^2}{\left(\dfrac{r_2}{s}\right)^2 + x_2^2} \cdot \frac{r_2}{s} \times \frac{2\omega_s x_2}{mV_1^2} = \frac{\dfrac{r_2}{s}}{\left(\dfrac{r_2}{s}\right)^2 + x_2^2} \times 2x_2$$

$$\frac{T_e}{T_{em}} = \frac{\frac{r_2}{s}}{\left(\frac{r_2}{s}\right)^2 + \left(\frac{r_2}{s_{mT}}\right)^2} \cdot 2 \times \frac{r_2}{s_{mT}} \qquad \left(\text{as } x_2 = \frac{r_2}{s_{mT}}\right)$$

$$= \frac{\frac{2}{s}}{\frac{1}{s^2} + \frac{1}{s_{mT}^2}} \times \frac{1}{s_{mT}} = \frac{2}{\frac{s_{mT}}{s} + \frac{s}{s_{mT}}}$$

5.24 **For the rotor circuit of a 3-phase induction motor, show that locus of the tip of rotor-current phasor I_2 is a circle with diameter equal to E_2/x_2. Symbols have their usual meaning.**

[6 marks : 2012]

Solution:

The rotor circuit voltage in phasor form

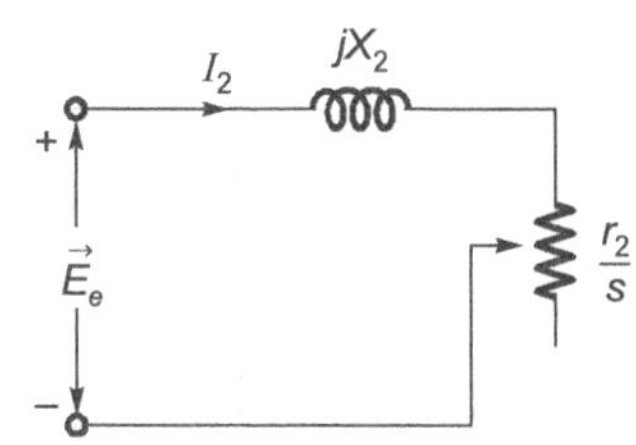

$$\bar{E}_2 = \bar{I}_2 \frac{r_2}{s} + j\bar{I}_2 x_2$$

or

$$\frac{\bar{E}_2}{jx_2} = \bar{I}_2 + \bar{I}_2 \frac{\frac{r_2}{s}}{jx_2}$$

or

$$-j\frac{\bar{E}_2}{x_2} = \bar{I}_2 - j\bar{I}_2 \frac{r_2}{sx_2}$$

In above equation denotes constant current; $-j\frac{E_2}{x_2}$ implies that this current lags E_2 by 90°.

The phasor diagram shows that the tip of rotor current makes a circle with diameter $\frac{E_2}{x_2}$.

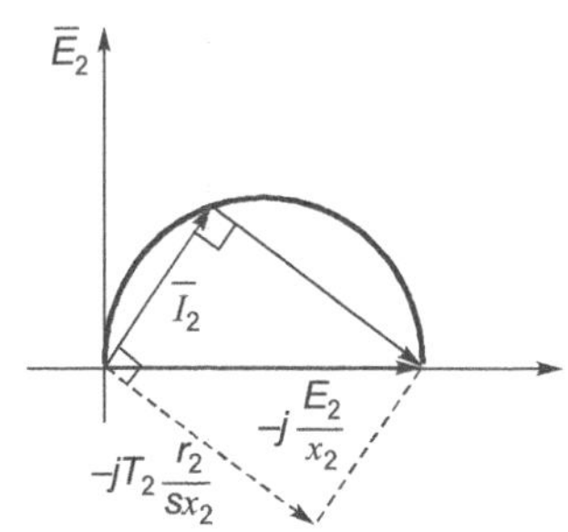

5.25 **Discuss briefly various speed control techniques for induction motors (both squirrel cage and wound rotor types).**

[10 marks : 2013]

Solution:

Speed control of Induction Motor:

The rotor speed of an induction motor is given by

$$N_r = \frac{120\,f}{P}(1 - s)$$

From above, it is seen that speed can be changed by a change in frequency f, number of poles P or slip s.

Stator voltage control:

if

$$V \to xV$$
$$x < 1$$
$$T \to x^2 T$$

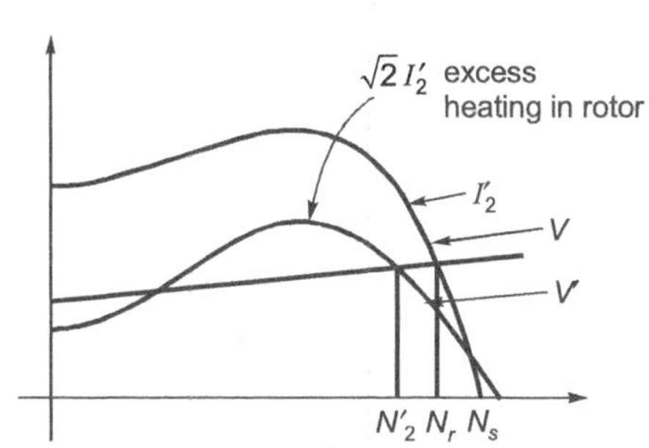

at low slip,

$$T \simeq \frac{3}{\omega_s} \frac{V^2}{(R_2'/s)} \simeq \frac{3}{\omega_s} \cdot \frac{V^2 s}{R_2'}$$

$$V \rightarrow V', \; s \rightarrow s'$$

Rotor resistance control: (only for SRIM):

$$R_2' = R_{20}' + R_{ext} \text{ wide range of speed control}$$

- The only disadvantage of this method is that, the slip power is to be wasted in external resistor. So efficiency is poor however, if slip power is return to the supply, efficiency is improve that scheme is called slip power recovery scheme.

Frequency Control:

$$\phi\downarrow \propto \frac{V}{\uparrow f}$$

if $f\uparrow = \phi\downarrow$, Torque developed $\downarrow$

$$T\downarrow = \frac{3}{\omega_s} \frac{V^2 (R_2'/s)}{\left(R_1 + \frac{R_2'}{s}\right) + \uparrow x^2}$$

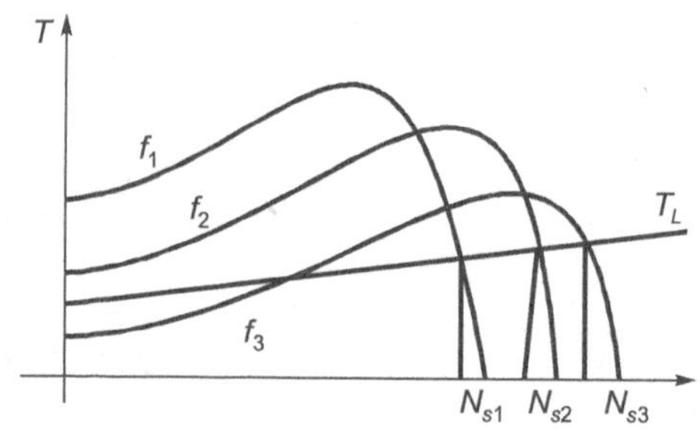

i.e. $\phi \propto \frac{V}{f}$ = constant

$$\left.\begin{array}{l}\phi \rightarrow \text{constant} \\ T \rightarrow \text{constant}\end{array}\right\}$$

***V/f* Control:**

$$\phi_r \propto \frac{V}{f} \Rightarrow \text{constant}$$

Nominal voltage V_0 is rated nominal frequency f_0

$$\frac{V}{f} = \frac{V_0}{f_0}$$

$$\boxed{V = \left(\frac{f}{f_0}\right) V_0}$$

Speed, $\omega_s = \frac{4\pi f}{P}$

$$\omega_{s_0} = \frac{4\pi f_o}{P}$$

$$\frac{\omega_s}{\omega_{s_0}} = \frac{f}{f_o} \Rightarrow \boxed{\omega_s = \frac{f}{f_o}\omega_{s_0}}$$

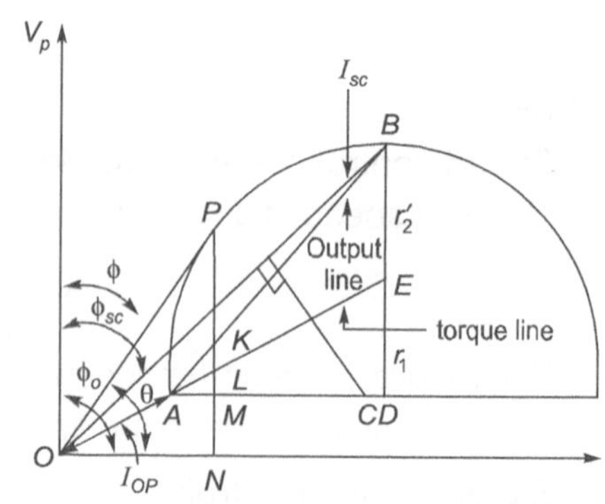

(b) Circle diagram of a 3-ϕ induction motor

if $f > f_0$

$$V = V_0$$

$$\phi_r \downarrow \propto V_0 / f\uparrow$$

5.26 A 400 V, Y-connected, 3 phase, 6 pole 50 Hz wound rotor induction has following parameters referred to the stator $r_1 = r_2' = 1\,\Omega$; $x_1 = x_2' = 2\,\Omega$. Stator to rotor turns ratio = 2.3.

(i) For regenerative braking at what speed the motor will hold an overhauling torque of 100 Nm.

(ii) For plugging operation the initial full load speed is 950 rpm. the motor is braked by inserting additional resistance in the rotor circuit during plugging so as to reduce the braking current to 1.5 times its full load current. Compute the external resistance and initial braking torque.

[20 marks : 2013]

Solution:

(i) 400 V, Y-connected, 3-ϕ, 6-P, 50 Hz

$$r_1 = r_2' = 1\ \Omega, \qquad x_1 = x_2' = 2\ \Omega$$

$$\text{Stator to rotor turns ratio} = 2.3$$

$$Z = (r_s + jx_s) + \left(\frac{r_r}{s} + jx_r\right)$$

$$Z = \left(1 + \frac{1}{s}\right) + (4j)$$

$$P = (3)(I_2)^2 \cdot \left(\frac{r_2'}{s}\right)$$

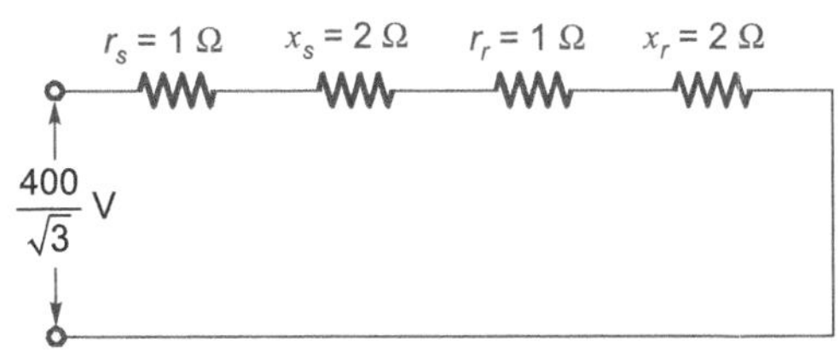

$$P = (3)\left(\frac{V}{\sqrt{\left(1+\frac{1}{s}\right)^2 + (4)^2}}\right)^2 \cdot \left(\frac{1}{s}\right)$$

$$T = \frac{(3)}{(\omega_m)}\left(\frac{V}{\sqrt{\left(1+\frac{1}{s}\right)^2 + 16}}\right)^2 \cdot \left(\frac{1}{s}\right)$$

For regenerative braking:

The overhauling torque = –100 N-m

From torque slip relation:

$$-100 = \frac{3}{\omega_{sm}} \times \frac{(231)^2 \times \frac{1}{s}}{\left(1+\frac{1}{s}\right)^2 + 16} \quad \text{or} \quad -100 = \frac{3}{104.7} \times \frac{(231)^2 \times \frac{1}{s}}{\left(1+\frac{1}{s}\right)^2 + 16}$$

or,
$$\frac{-100 \times 104.7}{3 \times 231^2} = \frac{1}{s\left[\left\{1 + \frac{1}{s^2} + 2s\right\} + 16\right]}$$

or,
$$s\left\{s + \frac{1}{s^2} + \frac{2}{s} + 16\right\} = -15.28$$

$$s + \frac{1}{s} + 2 + 16s = -15.28$$

$$17s^2 + 17.28s + 1 = 0$$

Solving we get: $s = -0.0616$ (accepted); -0.95 (rejected)

For
$$s = -0.0616$$
$$N_r = 1000 + (1000 \times 0.0616)$$
$$\cong 1061 \text{ rpm}$$

(ii) **For Plugging:**

Current before plugging at full load;

$$I'_{2(FL)} = \frac{(400/\sqrt{3})^2 \angle 0^\circ}{\left(1+\frac{1}{0.05}\right)+j4} \qquad [\because s_{FL} = 0.05]$$

$$I'_{2(FL)} = 10.8\angle{-10.78^\circ} \text{ A}$$

Now, full load torque;

$$T_{FL} = \frac{3}{\omega_{sm}} \times \frac{I'^2_{2FL}}{s_{FL}} = \frac{3}{104.7} \times \frac{(10.8)^2}{0.05} = 66.87 \text{ N-m}$$

Now after plugging, field is reversed so,

new slip,
$$s_{\text{plugging}} = 2 - s_{FL} = 1.95$$
$$I_{\text{plugging}} = 1.5 \times I_{FL} = 1.5 \times 10.8 = 16.2 \text{ A}$$
$$= \frac{V}{\sqrt{\left\{1+\frac{R'_{2ext}+R'_2}{s_{\text{plugging}}}\right\}^2 + X'^2_2}}$$

Now,
$$16.2 = \frac{231}{\sqrt{\left\{1+\frac{1+R'_{2ext}}{1.95}\right\}^2 + 4^2}}$$

or,
$$203.21 - 16 = \left(1+\frac{1+R'^2_{2ext}}{1.95}\right)^2$$

After solving, we get
$$R'_{2ext} = 23.73\ \Omega$$

or
$$R_{2(ext)} = \frac{23.73}{a^2} = \frac{23.73}{(2.3)^2} = 4.485\ \Omega$$

$\because$
$$T_{\text{braking}} = T_{\text{load}} + T_{\text{plugging}}$$

and
$$T_{\text{plugging}} = \frac{3}{104.7} \times (16.2)^2 \times \left(\frac{24.73}{1.95}\right) = 95.37 \text{ N-m}$$

Now,
$$T_{\text{braking}} = 95.37 + 66.87 = 162.24 \text{ N-m}$$

5.27 **A 3-phase, 4-pole slip ring induction motor is connected to 3-phase, 50 Hz supply from the motor side through slip rings and the stator terminals are shorted. The machine is found to be running at 1440 rpm. Determine:**

(i) The frequency of stator current.

(ii) The speed of rotor magnetic field with respect to rotor and its direction w.r.t. direction of rotation of rotor.

(iii) The speed of stator magnetic field with respect to and its direction w.r.t. direction of rotation of rotor.

(iv) The speed of stator magnetic field with respect to rotor magnetic field.

[4 marks : 2014]

Solution:

$$N_s = \frac{120f}{P} = \frac{120 \times 50}{4} = 1500 \text{ rpm}$$

(i) Frequency of stator current = 50 Hz

(ii) Speed of rotor magnetic field w.r.t. rotor = $(N_s - N)$ = 1500 – 1440 = 60 rpm rotor magnetic field is in the same direction of rotor.

(iii) Speed of stator magnetic field w.r.t. stator = $N_s - N$ = 1500 – 1440 = 60 rpm stator magnetic field is in the same direction of stator.

(iv) Speed of stator magnetic field w.r.t. rotor

Magnetic field = zero

5.28 A 3-phase, 4-pole slip ring induction machine is connected to a 3-phase, 50 Hz supply. If the rotor terminals are shorted, the machine runs in clockwise direction seen from one end. Now the rotor terminals are opened and the machine is made to run with the help of a prime mover. What will be the frequency of the voltage across the slip rings, if

(i) the machine is not running?

(ii) the machine is rotating at a speed of 1500 rpm in clockwise direction?

(iii) the machine is rotating at a speed of 1450 rpm in anti-clockwise direction?

(iv) the machine is rotating at a speed of 1550 rpm in clockwise direction?

[4 marks : 2016]

Solution:

(i) $\because$ $s = 1$

Rotor frequency, $F = 50$ Hz

(ii) $\because$ $s = 0,$

Rotor frequency, $s = 0, \quad sF = 0$ (as $E_2 = 0$)

(iii) $$s = \frac{N_s - (-N)}{N_s} = \frac{1500 + 1450}{1500} = 1.967$$

$\therefore$ Rotor frequency, $sF = 98.33$ Hz

(iv) $$s = \frac{1500 - 1550}{1500} = -0.033$$

$\therefore$ Rotor frequency $= sF = 1.67$ Hz

5.29 On a short circuit test, a 12-pole, 3-phase, 50 Hz induction motor with an equivalent standstill rotor resistance equal to the stator resistance took 250 A, and 100 kW. Find the starting torque developed.

[4 marks : 2016]

Solution:

$$T_g = \frac{3 \times 60}{2\pi N_s} \frac{I_2^2 R_2}{s}$$

$$T_{st} = \frac{3 \times 60}{2\pi N_s} I_{st}^2 R_2$$

$$N_s = \frac{120 \times 50}{12} = 500 \text{ rpm}$$

Given, $3I_{st}^2(R_1 + R_2') = 100$ kW

$\therefore$ $R_1 + R_2' = 0.533\ \Omega$

Given, $R_1 = R_2'$

$\therefore$ $R_2' = 0.27\ \Omega$

$$\therefore \quad T_{st} = \frac{3\times 60}{2\pi(500)}(250)^2(0.27) = 955.41 \text{ N-m}$$

5.30 A three-phase, 25 hp, 230 V, 50 Hz, induction motor draws 60 A from the source at 0.866 lagging power factor. The motor losses include the following:

Stator copper loss P_{cus} = 850 W
Magnetic core loss P_{core} = 450 W
Rotor copper loss P_{cur} = 1050 W
Rotational loss P_{rot} = 500 W

Determine the following:

(i) Air-gap power P_{ag} (ii) Slip s
(iii) Mechanical power developed (iv) Output power
(v) Efficiency of the motor

[10 marks : 2016]

Solution:

$$\text{Input of motor} = \sqrt{3}V_l I_l \cos\phi$$
$$= \sqrt{3}\times 230\times 60\times 0.866$$
$$= 20700 \text{ watts}$$
$$\text{Stator output} = \text{Input} - \text{stator copper loss} - \text{core loss}$$
$$= 20700 - 850 - 450$$
$$= 19400 \text{ watts}$$

(i) $$\text{Stator output} = \text{Rotor input}$$
$$= \text{Airgap power} = 19400 \text{ watts}$$

(ii) $$\text{Rotor copper loss} = \text{Stator rotor input}$$

$$\Rightarrow \quad S = \frac{\text{Rotor copper loss}}{\text{Rotor input}}$$

$$\therefore \quad S = \frac{1050}{19400} = 0.054$$

(iii) $$\text{Mechanical power developed} = (1-s) \quad \text{Rotor input} = (1-0.054)(19400)$$
$$= 18352.4 \text{ watts}$$

(iv) $$\text{Output power} = 18352.4 - \text{Rotor loss}$$
$$= 17852.4$$

(v) $$\eta = \frac{17852.4}{20700} = \frac{\text{output}}{\text{input}} = 86.24\%$$

5.31 A 10 kW, 400 V, 50 Hz, 4-pole delta connected squirrel cage induction motor is excited by 90 V with blocked rotor. The machine consumes 1350 watts and draws 35 A from a.c. mains. The d.c. resistance of stator winding per phase is 0.6 Ω. Assuming effective a.c. resistance per phase to be 1.2 times the d.c. value, compute the starting torque for direct on line starting. Assume $x_2 << X_m$.

[12 marks : 2017]

Solution:

Given:

Blocked rotor condition: $s = 1$, $V_{BR} = 90$ V, $I_{BR} = 35$ A, $W_{BR} = 1350$ Watts

Starting condition: $s = 1$, for direct online starting.

Therefore adjusting all above values as if the blocked rotor test is conducted at rated voltage

$$\left.\begin{aligned} V_{BR} &\rightarrow I_{BR} \\ V_{\text{rated}} &\rightarrow I_{SC} \end{aligned}\right\}$$

$$\therefore \qquad I_{SC} = \frac{400 \times 35}{90} = 155.55 \text{ A}$$

$$\left.\begin{aligned} I_{BR}^2 &\rightarrow W_{BR} \\ I_{SC}^2 &\rightarrow W_{SC} \end{aligned}\right\}$$

$$\therefore \qquad W_{SC} = \frac{(155.55)^2 \times (1350)}{(35)^2} = 26664.76 \text{ W}$$

$$\text{Stator copper losses for } I_{SC} = 3\left(\frac{I_{SC}}{\sqrt{3}}\right)^2 \cdot R_1$$

$$= 3 \times \left(\frac{155.55}{\sqrt{3}}\right)^2 (1.2 \times 0.6) = 17420.97 \text{ W}$$

W_{SC} = Stator and Rotor copper losses (For V_{rated} or I_{SC})

Stator output = Rotor input = Stator input – Stator losses

Neglecting stator core losses in blocked condition,

Rotor input = 26664.76 – 17420.97 = 9243.79 W

$$T_{st} = \frac{60}{2\pi N_s}$$

$$\text{Rotor power input} = \frac{60}{2\pi \times 1500} \times 9243.79$$

$$T_{st} = 58.85 \text{ N-m}$$

5.32 Develop an expression for torque of a 3-phase induction motor from first principles and show that,

$$\frac{T_{dm}}{T_{fl}} = \frac{1}{2}\frac{\beta^2 + S_{fl}^2}{\beta S_{fl}}$$

where, $\beta = R_2/X_2$, T_{dm} and T_{fl} are breakdown and full-load torque respectively, S_{fl} is the value of slip at full-load torque.

[20 marks : 2017]

Solution:

The torque of an induction motor, being due to interaction of the rotor and stator fields, depends on the strength of those field and the phase relation between them.

Thus torque developed by the rotor of an induction motor is directly proportional to

1. Rotor current, I_2
2. Stator flux per pole, ϕ
3. Power factor of the rotor circuit, $\cos\phi_2$

i.e. torque, $T \propto \phi I_2 \cos\phi_2$

Since rotor emf per phase at standstill, $E_2 \propto \phi$

So, torque developed, $T \propto E_2 I_2 \cos\phi_2$

or, $T = kE_2 I_2 \cos\phi_2$ (where k is any constant)

Equivalent circuit without stator impedance,

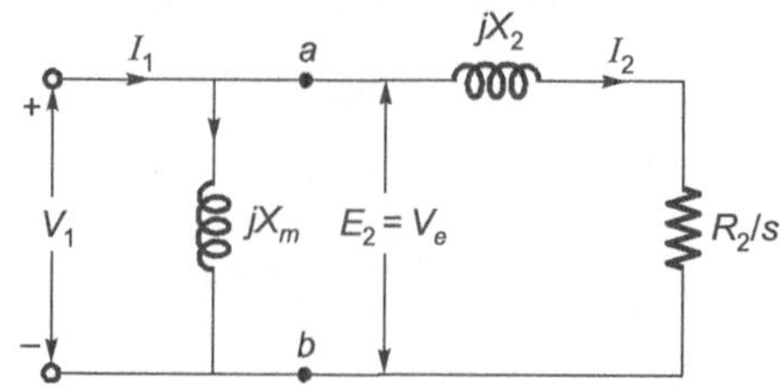

By applying Thevenin theorem across ab

$$V_e = E_2 = V_1$$

and
$$I_2 = \frac{V_1}{\frac{R_2}{s} + jX_2}$$

Full load, torque develop,
$$T_{fl} = \frac{3}{\omega_s} \cdot \frac{V_1^2}{\left(\frac{R_2}{S_{fl}}\right)^2 + (X_2)^2} \cdot \frac{R_2}{S_{fl}} \quad \text{...(i)}$$

($S_{fl} \rightarrow$ slip at full load)

From the maximum power transfer theorem, the torque, with be maximum when impedance, R_2/s becomes equal to the magnitude of impedances seen by R_2/s towards the voltage source V_e,

i.e., $\frac{R_2}{X_2} = X_2$

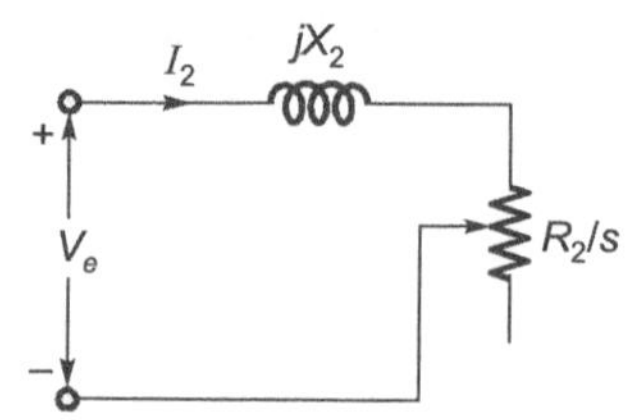

or,
$$S_{m,T} = \frac{R_2}{X_2} = \beta$$

Maximum torque or breakdown torque,

$$T_{dm} = \frac{3V_1^2 \cdot X_2}{\omega_s[(X_2)^2 + (X_2)^2]} = \frac{3V_1^2}{2\omega_s X_2} \quad \text{...(ii)}$$

From equation (i) and (ii), we get

$$\frac{T_{dm}}{T_{fl}} = \frac{\frac{3V_1^2}{2\omega_s X_2}}{\frac{3V_1^2 R_2}{\omega_s\left[\left(\frac{R_2}{S_{fl}}\right)^2 + X_2^2\right] S_{fl}}} = \frac{(R_2/S_{fl})^2 + (X_2)^2}{2 \cdot \frac{R_2}{S_{fl}} \cdot X_2}$$

$$= \frac{\left(\frac{R_2}{S_{fl}}\right)^2 + \left(\frac{R_2}{\beta}\right)^2}{2\left(\frac{R_2}{S_{fl}}\right) \cdot \left(\frac{R_2}{\beta}\right)} = \frac{\left(\frac{1}{S_{fl}}\right)^2 + \left(\frac{1}{\beta}\right)^2}{2\left(\frac{1}{S_{fl}}\right)\left(\frac{1}{\beta}\right)}$$

$$\frac{T_{dm}}{T_{fl}} = \frac{\beta^2 + S_{fl}^2}{2S_{fl} \cdot \beta} = \frac{1}{2} \cdot \frac{\beta^2 + S_{fl}^2}{\beta \cdot S_{fl}}$$

5.33 A 3-phase, 6-pole, 460 V, 50 Hz induction generator operate at 480 V. The generator has its rated output power of 20 kW. It is driven by a turbine at a speed of 1015 rpm. The generator has the following electrical parameters:

$$R_1 = 0.2\ \Omega,\ R_2 = 0.15\ \Omega,\ R_{sh} = 320\ \Omega$$
$$X_1 = 1.2\ \Omega,\ X_2 = 1.29\ \Omega,\ X_M = 42\ \Omega$$

Find the active power delivered by the generator and reactive power it requires from the system to operate.

[20 marks : 2018]

Solution:

Given, $R_1 = 0.2\ \Omega,\ R_2 = 0.15\ \Omega,\ R_{sh} = 320\ \Omega$

$X_1 = 1.2\ \Omega,\ X_2 = 1.29\ \Omega,\ X_M = 42\ \Omega$

Number of poles = 6

Frequency, $f = 50$ Hz

Output power = 20 kW,

$N_r = 1015$ rpm

$$N_s = \frac{120 \times 50}{6} = 1000 \text{ rpm}$$

Terminal voltage line, $V = 480$ V

$$\therefore \quad \text{Phase voltage} = \frac{480}{\sqrt{3}} = 277.12 \text{ V}$$

$$\text{Slip,} \quad s = \frac{N_s - N_r}{N_s} = \frac{1000 - 1015}{1000} = -0.015$$

Note: Negative value of slip indicates it is operating in generating mode.

$$\frac{R_2}{s} = \frac{0.15}{-0.015} = -10\ \Omega$$

Equivalent circuit,

$$Z_{XY} = (-10 + j1.29) \parallel (320) \parallel j42 = (-9.155 + j3.5)\ \Omega$$

$$Z_i = 0.2 + j1.2 - 9.155 + j3.5 = (-8.955 + j4.7)\ \Omega$$

$$Z_i = 10.11\angle 152.2^\circ\ \Omega$$

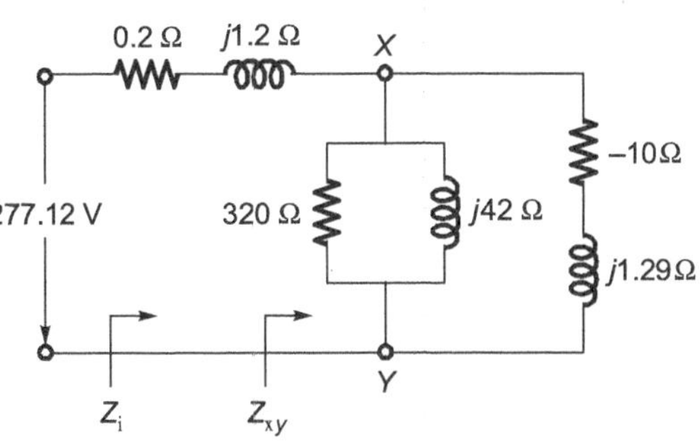

$$I_1 = \frac{V_{ph}}{Z_{total}} = \frac{277.12\angle 0^\circ}{10.11\angle 152.3^\circ}$$

$$I_1 = 27.39\angle -152.3^\circ \text{ A}$$

$$\text{Active power } (P) = \sqrt{3} \times V_L \times I_L \times \cos\phi$$

$$= \sqrt{3} \times 480 \times 27.39 \times \cos(152.3)$$

$$= -20161.84 \text{ W} = -20.161 \text{ kW}$$

$$\text{Reactive power} = P \tan\phi$$

$$= 10585.20 \text{ VAR} = 10.585 \text{ kVAR}$$

5.34 A 400 V, 50 Hz, 6-pole, 960 rpm, Y-connected induction motor has the following parameters per phase referred to stator:

$$r_1 = 0.4\ \Omega;\ r_2' = 0.2\ \Omega;\ x_1 = x_2' = 1.5\ \Omega;\ X_m = 30\ \Omega$$

The motor is controlled by a variable frequency inverter at a constant flux of rated value for operation below synchronous speed, while in super-synchronous operation region flux is weakened by keeping voltage constant at rated value. Assume straight line for torque vs. slip characteristics for slip $s < s_m$ (motor region) and $s > s_m'$ (generator region). The connected load on the shaft is constant torque type.

Calculate the inverter frequency and current drawn by the stator when torque on the shaft is half-rated while motoring at 500 rpm.

[20 marks : 2018]

Solution:

For straight line torque Vs slip characteristic,

$$T = \frac{sV^2}{\omega_{sm}R_2}$$

For constant flux, $V \propto f$

$\therefore$ $T \propto sf$

$$T_2 = \frac{1}{2}T_{rated}$$

$$N_{sr} = \frac{120f}{P} = \frac{120 \times 50}{6} = 1000 \text{ rpm}$$

$$s_{fr} = \left(\frac{N_s - N}{N_s}\right) = \left(\frac{1000 - 960}{1000}\right) = 0.04$$

$$\frac{T_2}{T_{rated}} = \frac{1}{2}$$

$$\frac{s_2 f_2}{s_{fr} f_r} = \frac{1}{2}$$

$$s_2 f_2 = \left(\frac{0.04 \times 50}{2}\right) = 1$$

$$f_2 = \frac{N_{s_2}P}{120} = \frac{N_{s2} \times 6}{120} = \frac{N_{s2}}{20}$$

$\therefore$

$$\frac{s_2 N_{s2}}{20} = 1$$

$$s_2 N_{s2} = 20$$

$$N_{s2} - N = sN_{s2}$$

$$N_{s2} = 20 + 500 = 520 \text{ rpm}$$

$$f_2 = \frac{N_{s2}}{20} = \frac{520}{20} = 26 \text{ Hz}$$

$$I_2 = \frac{sV_2}{R_2}$$

$$V_2 = V_1 \times \frac{f_2}{f_1} = 400 \times \frac{26}{50} = 208 \text{ V}$$

$$s_2 = \frac{20}{N_{s2}} = \frac{20}{250} = 0.0385$$

$$I_2 = \frac{0.0385}{0.2} \times \frac{208}{\sqrt{3}} = 23.094 \text{ A}$$

5.35 Draw and elaborate (with appropriate mathematical justification) the graphical locus of induction motor (voltage, current and power) for a complete range of slip from approximate equivalent circuit model. Justify its circular nature for naming it as circle diagram of induction motor.

Also, state and explain with the help of the circle diagram, how to obtain rotor/stator copper losses, torque and slip at any arbitrary point on circle diagram.

[20 marks : 2019]

Solution:

As load varies, the slip changes and hence as seen from the equivalent circuit, the winding impedance changes, viz. the reactance remaining same, the resistance varies. It can be shown that the locus of current for different loading conditions is a semicircle, the diameter of which is given by

$$\frac{V_p}{x_2} = \frac{V_p}{x_2 + x_2'}$$

Knowing the diameter line, the semicircle can be drawn locating two points on the semicircle, viz, no-load current I_{op} and blocked rotor current I_{sc} that corresponds to the rated applied voltage to the stator.

$$I_{sc} = \frac{I_p V_p}{C_{sc}}$$

Figure shows the circle diagram for a 3-phase induction motor. Draw a vertical line from the origin 'O' representing the axis of phase voltage, V_p. Draw vectors *OA* and *OB* with magnitudes I_{op} and I_{sc} lagging the phase voltage vector V_p an angle ϕ_o and ϕ_{sc}, respectively. Join *AB* forming chord on the semicircle. Draw the perpendicular bisector of the line *AB* and let it cut the horizontal line drawn from *A* to *C*. With '*C*' as centre and *CA* as radius, draw a semicircle which forms the locus of the load current.

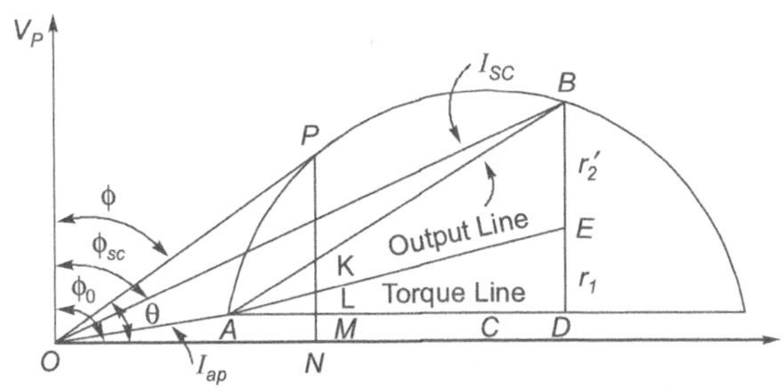

Circle diagram of 3-phase induction motor

Predetermination of characteristics from the circle diagram : Draw a perpendicular from '*B*' to meet the diameter at '*D*'. Divide *BD* in the following ratio,

$$\frac{BE}{ED} = \frac{\text{Rotor current loss / phase}}{\text{Stator current loss / phase}} = \frac{I_2'^2 r_2'}{I_2'^2 r_1}$$

and join *AE*.

For a given loading condition, let the input stator current per phase be '*OP*' at a power factor angle ϕ, lagging. Draw a perpendicular from '*P*' to meet the horizontal line drawn from origin '*O*' at '*N*'.

Then, the power input/phase = $V_P \times$ OP cos ϕ = $V_P \times NP$

As V_p is constant, *NP* represents the power input to certain scale (which can be calculated from the current scale).

Accordingly,
the power input = NP
the power output = KP
rotor current loss = LK
stator current loss = ML
no-load losses = NM

From the above,

$$\text{the percentage efficiency} = \frac{KP}{NP} \times 100\%$$

the torque = *LP* synchronous watts/phase

5.36 **A 440 V, 50 HZ, 6-pole Y-connected induction motor has following parameters per phase referred to the stator:**

$$R_s = R_r' = 0.3\ \Omega,\ X_s = X_r' = 1.0\ \Omega \text{ and } X_m = 40\ \Omega$$

The nominal full load slip is 0.05.
The motor is to be braked by plugging from its initial full load condition. Determine initial braking torque without braking resistor (R_B).
Also find the value of R_B so that braking current is limited to 1.5 times the full load current. What will be the corresponding breaking torque as a ratio of full load torque? Note: Assume braking resistor R_B is connected to rotor circuit.

[20 marks : 2019]

Solution:

(i) Given: $R_S = R_r' = 0.3$ W ; $X_S = X_r' = 1.0$ W ; $s_{fL} = 0.05$

Full load current,
$$I_{rf'} = \frac{440/\sqrt{3}}{\sqrt{\left(0.3+\frac{0.3}{0.05}\right)^2+(1+1)^2}} = 38.43 \text{ A}$$

Full load torque,
$$T_{fL} = \frac{3\times(38.43)^2\times 0.3}{0.05\times 104.72} = 253.85 \text{ Nm}$$

In plugging, slip, $s_b = 2 - s_f = 2 - 0.05 = 1.95$

Initial braking current,
$$I_r' = \frac{440/\sqrt{3}}{\sqrt{\left(0.3+\frac{0.3}{1.95}\right)^2+(1+1)^2}} = 123.86 \text{ A}$$

Initial braking torque,
$$T = \frac{3\times(123.86)^2\times 1}{104.72\times 1.95} = 225.38 \text{ Nm}$$

(ii) With an external resistance R_e in rotor,

$$I_r' = \frac{V}{\sqrt{\left(R_s+\left(\frac{R_r'+R_e'}{2-s}\right)\right)^2+(X_s+X_r')^2}}$$

or
$$1.5\times 38.43 = \frac{440/\sqrt{3}}{\sqrt{\left(0.3+\left(\frac{0.3+R_e'}{1.95}\right)\right)^2+4}}$$

$$\Rightarrow \quad \left(0.3+\left(\frac{0.3+R_e'}{1.95}\right)\right)^2+4 = 19.42$$

$$\frac{0.3+R_e'}{1.95} = 3.6268$$

$$R_e' = 6.772\ \Omega$$

As stator to turns ratio is not given hence,

$$R_e' = R_e = 6.772\ \Omega$$

$$T = \frac{3\times(1.5\times 38.43)^2\times 6.772}{1.95\times 104.72} = 330.595 \text{ Nm}$$

$$\frac{T}{T_f} = \frac{330.595}{253.85} = 1.302$$

5.37 Consider a three-phase induction motor with the following parameters :

Number of poles	: 4
Supply frequency	: 50 Hz
Full load supply	: 1470 rpm
Rotor resistance	: 0.12 Ω
Standstill reactance	: 1.12 Ω

Find :

(i) Slip for maximum torque.

(ii) Ratio of maximum torque to full load torque.

[4 + 8 = 12 marks : 2020]

Solution:

Given,

$$P = 4$$
$$f = 50 \text{ Hz}$$
$$N_r = 1470 \text{ rpm}$$
$$r_1' = 0.12\ \Omega$$
$$r_2' = 1.12\ \Omega$$

$\Rightarrow$ Synchronous speed of motor $= N_s = \dfrac{120f}{P} = \dfrac{120\times 50}{4} = 1500$ rpm

$$\text{Full load slip } S_{fl} = \frac{N_s - N_r}{N_s} = \frac{1500-1470}{1500} = 0.02$$

(i) Slip at maximum torque is given by

$$s_{MT} = \frac{r_2'}{x_2'} \qquad [\because \text{ When stator impedance is ignored}]$$

$$s_{MT} = \frac{0.12}{1.12} = 0.1071$$

(ii) Full load torque of induction motor is given as

$$T_{fL} = \frac{3}{\omega_s}\cdot\frac{V_{ph}^2\cdot\dfrac{r_2'}{s_{fl}}}{\left(\dfrac{r_2'}{s_{fl}}\right)^2+(x_2')^2} \qquad \text{...(i)}$$

Maximum torque of induction motor is given as

$$T_{\max} = \frac{3}{\omega_s}\cdot\frac{V_{ph}^2}{(2x_2')} \qquad \text{...(ii)}$$

On dividing equation (ii) by equation (i)

$$\frac{T_{\max}}{T_{fL}} = \frac{\dfrac{3}{\omega_s}\cdot\dfrac{V_{ph}^2}{(2x_2')}}{\dfrac{3}{\omega_s}\cdot\dfrac{V_{ph}^2\cdot\dfrac{r_2'}{s_{fl}}}{\left(\dfrac{r_2'}{s_{fl}}\right)^2+(x_2')^2}}$$

$$\frac{T_{max}}{T_{fL}} = \frac{\left(\frac{r_2'}{s_{fl}}\right)^2 + (x_2')^2}{2x_2' \cdot \frac{r_2'}{s_{fl}}}$$

On solving

$$\frac{T_{max}}{T_{fL}} = \frac{(s_{fl})^2 + (s_{MT})^2}{2 \cdot s_{fl} \cdot s_{MT}} = \frac{(0.02)^2 + (0.1071)^2}{2 \times 0.1071 \times 0.02}$$

$$\frac{T_{max}}{T_{fL}} = 2.77$$

5.38 A 50 Hz, 3-phase induction motor has a slip of 0.2 for maximum torque, when operated on rated frequency and rated voltage. If the motor is run on 60 Hz supply with application of rated voltage, find the ratio of

(i) Starting currents

(ii) Starting torques

(iii) Maximum torques

with respective values at 50 Hz.

Neglect the stator impedance.

[7+7+6 = 20 marks : 2020]

Solution:

Given, $f = 50$ Hz, 3-ϕ

$S_{mT} = 0.2$

Now machine made to operate on 60 Hz.

(i) Starting current of induction motor is given as

$$I_{st} = \frac{V_{ph}}{\sqrt{(r_2')^2 + (x_2')^2}} \quad [\because \text{ stator impedance is ignored}]$$

$$\frac{I_{st}(60\text{ Hz})}{I_{st}(50\text{ Hz})} = \frac{\sqrt{(r_2')^2 + (x_2')^2}}{\sqrt{(r_2')^2 + (x_2'')^2}} \quad [x_2'' = \text{impedance at 60 Hz}]$$

$$[x_2'' = 1.2x_2']$$

$$= \frac{\sqrt{1 + \left(\frac{x_2'}{r_2'}\right)^2}}{\sqrt{1 + \left(\frac{1.2x_2'}{r_2'}\right)^2}}$$

$$\frac{I_{st}(60\text{ Hz})}{I_{st}(50\text{ Hz})} = \frac{\sqrt{26}}{\sqrt{1+36}} = \sqrt{\frac{26}{37}} \quad \left[S_{mT} = \frac{r_2'}{x_2'} = 0.2, \Rightarrow \frac{x_2'}{r_2'} = 5\right]$$

Ratio of starting currents,

$$\frac{I_{st}(60\text{ Hz})}{I_{st}(50\text{ Hz})} = 0.8382 \quad \text{...(i)}$$

(ii) Starting torque of induction motor at 60 Hz w.r.t. starting torque of induction motor at 50 Hz

$$T_{st} = \frac{3I_{st}^2 r_2'}{\omega_s} = \frac{3}{\omega_2}\frac{V_{PL}^2}{\left(r_2'^2 + x_2'^2\right)} \cdot r_2'$$

$$\frac{T_{st}(60\text{ Hz})}{T_{st}(50\text{ Hz})} = \frac{\dfrac{3}{\omega_s'}\dfrac{V_{ph}^2}{\left(r_2''^2 + x_2''^2\right)} \cdot r_2'}{\dfrac{3}{\omega_s}\dfrac{V_{ph}^2}{\left(r_2'^2 + x_2'^2\right)} \cdot r_2'}$$

Where, $\omega_s \rightarrow$ angular synchronous speed at 50 Hz

$\omega_s' \rightarrow$ angular synchronous speed at 60 Hz

Ratio of starting torques,

$$\frac{T_{st}(60\text{ Hz})}{T_{st}(50\text{ Hz})} = \frac{\omega_s\left(r_2'^2 + x_2'^2\right)}{\omega_s'\left(r_2'^2 + x_2''^2\right)}$$

$$= \frac{50(1+5^2)}{60\left[1+(1.2\times 5)^2\right]} = \frac{50\times 26}{60\times 37} = 0.5856$$

(ii) Maximum torque at 60 Hz w.r.t 50 Hz

$$T_{max} = \frac{3V_{ph}^2}{2\omega_s x_2'}$$

Ratio of maximum torques

$$\frac{T_{max}(60\text{ Hz})}{T_{max}(50\text{ Hz})} = \frac{\dfrac{3V_{ph}^2}{2\omega_s' x_2''}}{\dfrac{3V_{ph}^2}{2\omega_s x_2'}} = \frac{\omega_s x_2'}{\omega_s' x_2''}$$

$$= \frac{50\times 50}{60\times 60} = \frac{25}{36} = 0.695$$

5.39 An induction motor of 1.5 kW, 3-phase, 415 V, 50 11/, 1440 rpm is to undergo blocked rotor and no load tests. The motor is located away from the supply panel and the per phase impedance of the connecting cable is (5 + *j* 2.5)Ω. The metering is done at the panel end. The motor draws 0.7 A current and takes 150 W Input power under no load condition at rated voltage. For blocked rotor condition, it draws a current of 2.5 A and takes input power of 250 W when 75 V (L - L) is applied from the panel. Calculate the machine equivalent circuit parameter referred to stator side.

(Assume equal distribution of resistance and leakage reactance between rotor and stator, negligible rotation losses and star connected stator of the machine.)

[20 marks : 2021]

Solution:

Under open circuit condition, stator impedance of motor winding can be neglected,

Now,

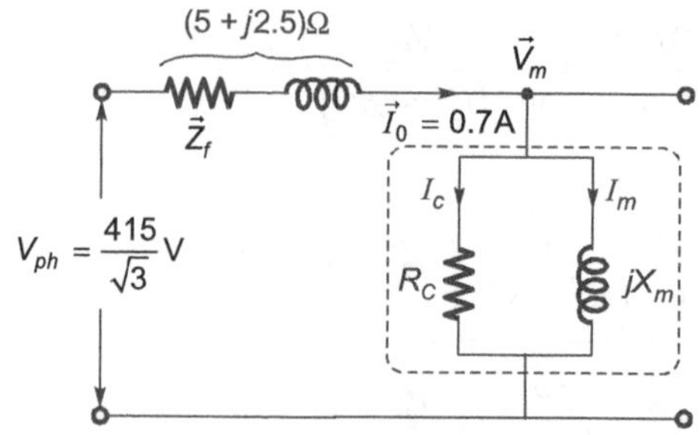

At no-load power test, the no load power (PNL) = 150 W

$$P = \sqrt{3}V_L I_L \cos\phi_0 = 150$$

$$\cos\phi_0 = \frac{150}{\sqrt{3}\times 415\times 0.7} = 0.298 \text{ lagging}$$

$$\phi_0 = 72.65°$$

$$\vec{V}_m = V-(5+j2.5)\vec{I}$$

$$= \frac{415}{\sqrt{3}}\angle 0° - (5+j2.5)\times 0.7\angle -72.65°$$

$$\vec{V}_m = 236.90\angle 0.6917 \text{ V}$$

Also,
$$\frac{V_m^2}{R_C} = 150-(0.7)^2\times 5$$

Equivalent resistance of core loss,

$$R_C = \frac{(236.90)^2}{147.55} = 380.35\ \Omega$$

Core loss current,
$$\vec{I}_c = \frac{\vec{V}_m}{R_c} = \frac{236.90\angle 0.6917}{380.35} = 0.6228\angle 0.6917° \text{ A}$$

Magnetising current,
$$\vec{I}_m = \vec{I}_0 - \vec{I}_c$$

$$= 0.7\angle -72.65° - 0.6228\angle 0.6917°$$

$$\vec{I}_m = 0.7924\angle -121.49$$

Magnetising reactance,
$$X_m = \left|\frac{V_m}{I_m}\right| = \frac{236.90}{0.7924} = 298.96\ \Omega$$

Now, under blocked rotor test, no-load current of motor can be neglected because of reduced supply voltage, I_0 will be negligible as compared to full load current

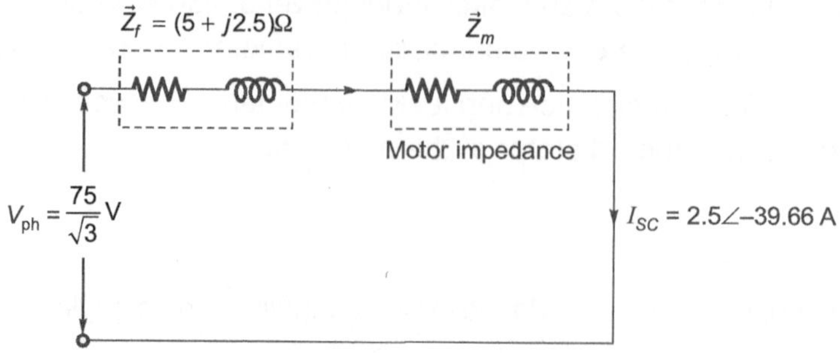

Power factor of motor under blocked rotor condition,

$$\cos\phi = \frac{250}{\sqrt{3}\times 75\times 2.5} = 0.7698 \text{ lag}$$

$$\phi = 39.66°$$

Total impedance,
$$\vec{Z}_T = \vec{Z}_f + \vec{Z}_m$$

$$\vec{Z}_T = \frac{\vec{V}}{I_{sc}} = \frac{\left(\frac{75}{\sqrt{3}}\right)}{2.5\angle -39.66°} = 17.32\angle 36.66\ \Omega$$

$$= (13.90 + j10.34)\ \Omega$$

Motor winding impedance,

$$\vec{Z}_m = \vec{Z}_T - \vec{Z}_f$$

$$= (13.90 + j10.34) - (5 + j2.5)$$

$$\vec{Z}_m = (8.90 + j7.84)\ \Omega/\text{ph}$$

Since winding impedance is equally distributed between rotor and stator,

$$\vec{Z}_{\text{stator}} = \frac{\vec{Z}_m}{2} = (4.45 + j3.92)\Omega/\text{ph}$$

$$\vec{Z}_{\text{rotor}} = \frac{\vec{Z}_m}{2} = (4.45 + j3.92)\Omega/\text{ph}$$

Now, the equivalent circuit of motor is

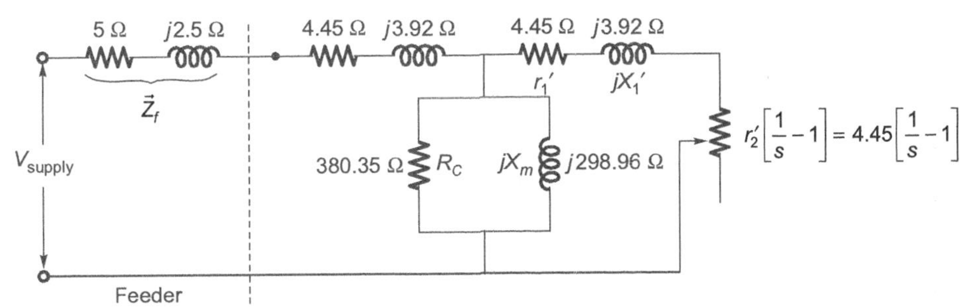

5.40 A 415 V, 4-pole, 3-phase. 50 Hz, 1440 rpm induction motor has per phase Standstill rotor resistance and reactances of 0.4 Ω and 1.3 Ω respectively at rated frequency. Find torque at rated Speed and the ratios of starting torque to maximum torque and rated torque to maximum torque. Now, the motor is supplied from a source of 40 Hz at 20% reduced voltage. Find the operating slip at rated torque and the new ratios of rated torque to maximum torque and starting torque to maximum torque. (Assume no saturation and negligible stator impedances)

[20 marks : 2021]

Solution:

Given data :

415 V, 4-pole, 50 Hz, 1440 rpm, I.M.

$$R_2 = 0.4\ \Omega,$$

$$X_2 = 1.3\ \Omega \text{ (per ph) @ rated frequency}$$

Find $T_f \rightarrow$ Torque at rated speed 1440

Full load slip, $$S_f = \frac{1500-1440}{1500} = 0.04$$

Find $\frac{T_{st}}{T_{max}}$ and $\frac{T_f}{T_{max}}$

As we know, $$\frac{T_{st}}{T_{max}} = \frac{2s_m}{s_m^2+1}$$

$$\frac{T_f}{T_{max}} = \frac{2s_f\, s_m}{s_f^2+s_m^2}$$

Maximum torque will occur at slip,

$$s_m = \frac{R_2}{X_2} \approx \frac{0.4}{1.3} = 0.3077$$

$$\frac{T_{st}}{T_{max}} = \frac{2\times 0.3077}{(0.3077)^2+1} = \frac{0.6154}{1.094679} = 0.5621$$

$$\frac{T_f}{T_{max}} = \frac{2\times 0.04\times 0.3077}{(0.04)^2+(0.3077)^2} = \frac{0.024616}{0.0962} = 0.2556$$

Next, motor supplied from 40 Hz source and 20% reduced voltage [V/f ratio is constant] f reduced by 20%, V reduced by 20% B_m constant and slip speed remaining constant in such case.
For new frequency 40 Hz,

$$N_{S2} = \frac{120\times 40}{4} = 1200 \text{ rpm}$$

$$X \propto f$$

$\Rightarrow$ New rotor reactance at 40 Hz,

$$X_2 = \frac{40}{50}\times 1.3 = 1.04\ \Omega$$

New slip at maximum torque,

$$S_m = \frac{R_2}{X_{2new}} = \frac{0.4}{1.04} = 0.3846$$

New S_f is calculated from condition $S\,N_s$ is constant in V/f control at same torque

S_1 $$S_1 \cdot N_{S1} = S_2 N_{S2}$$

$\Rightarrow$ $$S_2 = \frac{S_1 N_{S1}}{N_{S2}}$$

$$S_2 = \frac{0.04\times 1500}{1200} = 0.05$$

New operating slip at rated torque $S_2 = 0.05$

$$\frac{T_f}{T_{max}} = \frac{2\times(0.05)(0.3846)}{(0.05)^2+(0.3846)^2} = 0.255$$

$$= \frac{2\times 0.3846}{0.3846^2+1} = 0.67$$

5.41 Draw the Speed-Torque characteristics of a three-phase induction motor. A 3-phase, 50 Hz, 400 V, 8-pole, star-connected induction motor has the following circuit parameters referred to stator side in an exact equivalent circuit model :

$R_1 = 0.21\ \Omega$, $R_2' = 0.32\ \Omega$, $X_1 + X_2' = 4.8\ \Omega$, $R_i = 138\ \Omega$, $X_m = 18.1\ \Omega$

Assuming $X_1 = X_2'$ and slip $S = 4\%$, find the

(i) total impedance seen from stator side (per-phase).

(ii) input line current.

(iii) input power drawn.

(iv) gross mechanical power developed.

(v) gross torque developed.

[20 marks : 2022]

Solution:

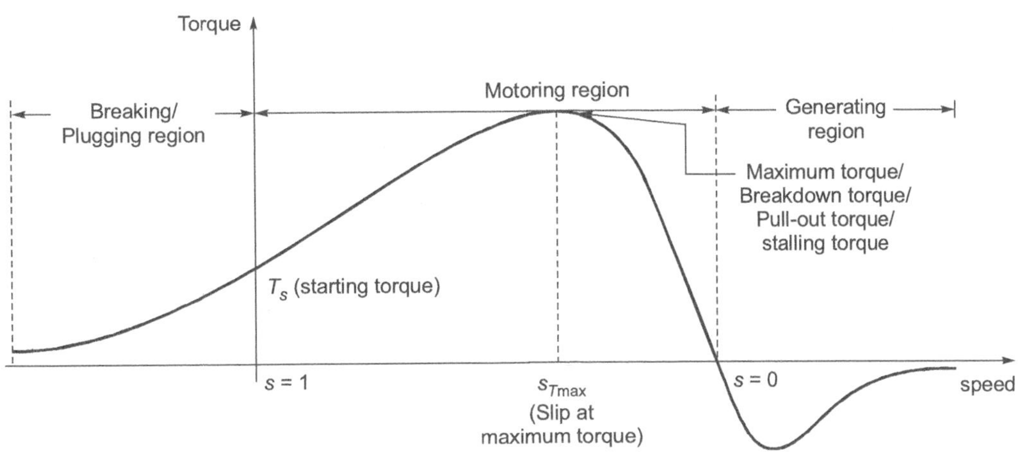

Given : Parameter of 3-ϕ induction motor

$$R_1 = 0.21\ \Omega$$
$$X_1 + X_2' = 4.8\ \Omega$$
$$X_m = 18.1\ \Omega$$
$$R_2' = 0.32\ \Omega$$
$$R_i = 138\ \Omega$$
$$\text{Slips, } s = 4\% = 0.04$$

and $X_1 = X_2'$

frequency, $f = 50$ Hz

Number of poles, $P = 8$

Supply voltage, $V = 400$ V

As $X_1 = X_2'$ ⇒ $X_1 = X_2' = 2.4\ \Omega$

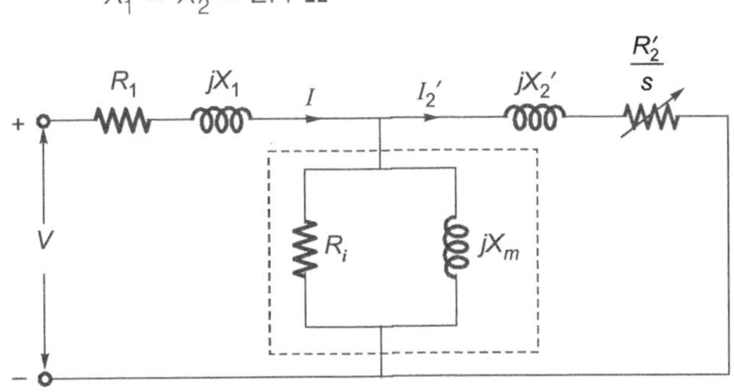

(i) Total impedance, $Z = R_1 + jX_1 + \left[R_i \parallel jX_m \parallel \left(\frac{R_2'}{s} + jX_2'\right)\right]$

$\Rightarrow$ $Z = 0.21 + 2.4j + \left[138 \parallel 18.1j \parallel \left(\frac{0.32}{0.04} + j2.4\right)\right]$

$Z = (5.5335 + 6.3144j)\ \Omega$

$\Rightarrow$ $Z = 8.396\angle 48.771°\ \Omega$

(ii) Input line current, $I = \frac{V}{\sqrt{3}Z}$ A

$I = 27.506\angle{-48.771}$ Å

(iii) Input power drawn,

$P = \text{Re}\left\{\sqrt{3}VI^*\right\}$

$P = \text{Re}\{12559.887 + j14332.38\}$

$P = 12.56$ kW

(iv) Net impedance of shunt branch,

$Z_i = (138 \parallel 18.1j)\ \Omega$

$\Rightarrow$ $Z_i = (2.334 + 17.794j)\ \Omega$

$\Rightarrow$ $Z_i = 17.9463\angle 82.528°\ \Omega$

So, by current division, $I_2' = I \times \frac{Z_i}{Z_i + 8 + 2.4j}$

$I_2' = 21.761\angle{-29.143}$ A

So, Air gap power, $P_g = 3|I_2'|^2\left(\frac{R_2'}{s}\right)$

$P_g = 11.365$ kW

Gross mechanical power developed,

$P_d = P_g(1 - s)$

$P_d = 10.910$ kW

(v) Gross torque developed, $T_d = \frac{P_d}{\frac{2\pi N_s}{60}(1-s)}$

$\Rightarrow$ $T_d = \frac{P_g \times 60}{2\pi N_s}$

Synchronous speed, $N_s = \frac{120f}{P} \Rightarrow N_s = \frac{120 \times 50}{8}$

$\Rightarrow$ $N_s = 750$ rpm

$T_d = 144.704$ Nm

5.42 A 3-phase, star-connected, 4-pole, 415 V, 50 Hz induction motor has equivalent circuit parameters of $R_s = 1.1\ \Omega$, $R_r = 0.9\ \Omega$, $X_{ls} = X_{lr} = 2.7\ \Omega$ and $X_m = 67\ \Omega$, all referred from stator side. The motor is driving a load whose torque is proportional to square of speed. For a load torque of 35 N-m the speed is 1440 rpm in the load characteristics. The motor is supplied from a three phase PWM inverter and the speed control is achieved through voltage control method. Now, if the motor speed is to be brought down to 1250 rpm, find the

(i) load torque.
(ii) inverter applied voltage.
(iii) motor input current and power factor.
(iv) motor input power.
(v) motor developed output power.
(Assume negligibel no load losses and no input harmonics to the motor).

[20 marks : 2022]

Solution:

$$R_s = 1.1\ \Omega,\ R_r = 0.9\ \Omega,\ X_{ls} = X_{lr} = 2.7\ \Omega$$
$$X_m = 67\ \Omega$$
$$V_{LL} = 415\ \text{V},\ f = 50\ \text{Hz},\ P = 4$$
$$N_S = \frac{120 \times 50}{4} = 1500\ \text{rpm}$$

For load-torque = 35 N-m, $N = 1440$ rpm

$$\text{Torque} \propto N^2$$

(i)
$$\frac{T_1}{T_2} = \frac{N_1^2}{N_2^2}$$
$$\frac{35}{T_2} = \frac{(1440)^2}{(1250)^2}$$
$$T_2 = 26.373\ \text{N-m}$$
$$N_2 = 1250$$
$$s = \frac{1500 - 1250}{1500} = 0.166$$

(ii)
$$\text{Load torque} = \frac{3V_{Ph}^2}{\omega_s\left[\left(r_1 + \frac{r_2'}{5}\right)^2 + (X_1 + X_2')^2\right]} \times \frac{r_2'}{s}$$

$$26.373 = \frac{3 \times V_{ph}^2}{\frac{2 \times 3.14 \times 1500}{60}\left[\left(1.1 + \frac{0.9}{0.1666}\right)^2 + (2.7 + 2.7)^2\right]} \times \frac{0.9}{0.1666}$$

Fundamental rms voltage of inverter

$$V_{Ph} = 135.098\ \text{V (per phase)}$$
$$V_{L\text{-}L} = \sqrt{3} \times 135.098 = 233.997\ \text{V}$$

(iii)
$$I = I_m + I_1$$
$$= \frac{135.098}{j67} + \frac{135.098}{\left(1.1 + \frac{0.9}{0.166}\right) + j(2 \times 2.7)}$$
$$= 17.311\angle -44.77^\circ$$

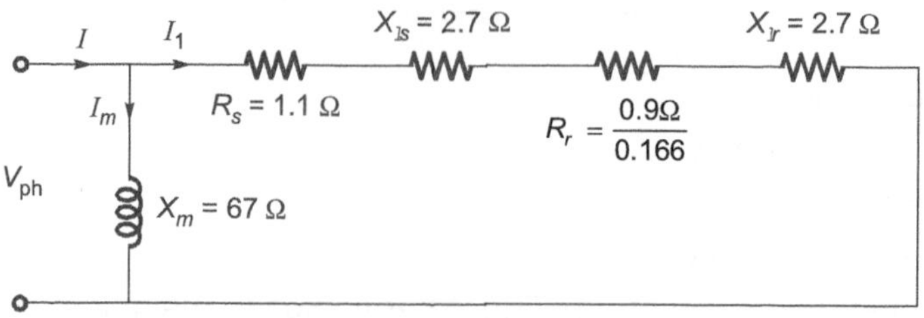

Input current, $I = 17.311$ A

$$\text{Power factor} = \cos 44.77^\circ = 0.709 \text{ (lagging)}$$

(iv) $$\text{Motor input power} = \sqrt{3} \times V_{LL} \times I \times Pf$$

$$3 = \sqrt{3} \times 233.997 \times 17.311 \times 0.709 = 4974.384 \text{ W}$$

(v) $$I_1 = \frac{135.098}{\left(1.1 + \frac{0.9}{0.166}\right) + j(2 \times 2.7)} = 15.955\angle{-39.624^\circ}$$

Motor developed output power

$$= 3I_1^2 R_r \left(\frac{1}{s} - 1\right)$$

$$= 3 \times 15.955^2 \times 0.9 \left(\frac{1}{0.166} - 1\right)$$

$$= 3453.149 \text{ W}$$

5.43 A 3-phase, 440 V, 50 Hz, four pole wound rotor induction motor develops full load torque at a slip of 0.04 (i.e. 4%) when the slip rings are short circuited. The maximum torque it can develop is 2.5 per unit. The stator leakage impedance is negligible. The rotor resistance measured between two slip rings is 0.5 Ω.

(i) Determine the speed of the motor at maximum torque. Derive the formula used.
(ii) Determine the starting torque in per unit. (Full load torque is one per unit torque).
(iii) Determine the value of resistance to be added to each phase of the rotor circuit so that maximum torque is developed at the starting condition.
(iv) Determine the speed at full-load torque with the added rotor resistance of part (iii).

[20 marks : 2023]

Solution:

Given : 440 V, 4-pole, 50 Hz, N_s = 1500 rpm, S_F = 0.04, T_{max} = 2.5 pu

$$\therefore \quad T_{max} = 2.5 T_f$$

$$R_2 = \frac{0.5}{2} = 0.25 \ \Omega \text{ per phase}$$

(i) **Speed of motor at max torque**

Slip at which max torque occurs :

Torque relation neglecting stator impedance :

$$T_1 = \frac{3\times 60}{2\pi N_s}\cdot\frac{SE_2^2R_2}{R_2^2+(SX_2)^2}$$

For a constant V and F

$$T \propto \frac{SR_2}{R_2^2+(SX_2)^2}$$

Let $T = \frac{1}{Y}$

where $$Y \propto \frac{R_2^2+(SX_2)^2}{SR_2}$$

If T to be maximum, Y must be minimum.

According to maximum-minimum theorem,

$$\frac{dy}{ds} = 0$$

$$Y \propto \frac{R_2}{S}+\frac{SX_2^2}{R_2}$$

$$\frac{dy}{ds} = 0\left|\frac{-R_2}{S^2}+\frac{X_2^2}{R_2}\right. = 0$$

$$R_2^2 = (SX_2)^2 \text{ or } R_2 = SX_2$$

or $$S_{mT} = \frac{R_2}{X_2}$$

The above slip is the slip at which maximum torque occurs.

For given question : $S_f = 0.04$

$$\frac{T_{max}}{T_f} = 2.5 \text{ or } \frac{T_f}{T_{max}} = \frac{1}{2.5}$$

$$\frac{T_f}{T_{max}} = \frac{2S_fS_m}{S_m^2+S_f^2} = \frac{1}{2.5}$$

$$\frac{2\times 0.04\times S_m}{S_m^2+(0.04)^2} = \frac{1}{2.5}$$

$$0.2S_m = S_m^2 + 0.0016$$

$$S_m^2 - 0.2S_m + 0.0016 = 0$$

By solving, $S_m = 0.191$

$\therefore$ Speed at which Max torque occurs

$$N_m = N_s(1 - S_m) = 1500(1 - 0.191)$$

$$N_m = 1213.5 \text{ rpm}$$

(ii) $$\frac{T_{st}}{T_f} = ?;\quad T_{st} \text{ in p.u.} = ?$$

$$\frac{T_{st}}{T_{max}} = \frac{2S_m}{S_m^2+1}$$

$$= \frac{2\times 0.191}{0.191^2+1} = 0.3685$$

$$\frac{\frac{T_{st}}{T_{max}}}{\frac{T_f}{T_{max}}} = \frac{T_{st}}{T_f} = \frac{0.3685}{\frac{1}{2.5}}$$

$$= 0.921 \text{ p.u.}$$

(iii)

$$S_m = \frac{R_2}{X_2} = 0.191$$

$$\therefore \quad X_2 = \frac{R_2}{0.191} = \frac{0.25}{0.191}$$

$$= 1.3089\ \Omega$$

For maximum T_{st} :

$$R_2 + R_{ext} = X_2$$

$$\therefore \quad R_{ext} = X_2 - R_2$$

$$= 1.3089 - 0.25 = 1.0589\ \Omega$$

(iv) If 1.0589 Ω is added to rotor then total R_2 = 1.3089 Ω

$$T_f \propto \frac{S}{R_2}$$ For same full load 'T'

$$S \propto R_2$$

$$\therefore \quad \frac{S_2}{S_1} = \frac{R_2 + R_{ext}}{R_2}$$

$$\frac{S_2}{0.04} = \frac{1.3089}{0.25}$$

$$S_2 = \frac{1.3089}{0.25} \times 0.04 = 0.2094$$

$$\therefore \quad N_2 = N_{S2}(1 - S_2)$$

$$= 1500(1 - 0.2094)$$

Required rotor speed after adding the resistance in rotor,

$$N_2 = 1185.9 \text{ rpm}$$

6. Fractional Kilowatt Motors (Special Machines)

6.1 Why is it advantageous to use double revolving field theory for determining the running performance of a single-phase induction motor?

Draw torque-speed characteristics of a single-phase induction motor based on double-revolving field theory and discuss about the magnitude of torque at zero speed and synchronous speed.

Sketch waveform of rotor current under normal running conditions of the single-phase induction motor.

[12 marks : 2001]

Solution:

Under stationary rotor condition ($n = 0$, i.e. $s = 1$), the two rotating fields slip past the rotor at the same slip, $s = 1$, and inducing equal currents in the squirrel-cage rotor. The two rotating fields have the same strength and produce equal and opposite torques resulting in net starting torque of zero value. Further, the two rotating fields induce a resultant emf in the stator which balances the applied voltage assuming low leakage impedance of the stator winding.

If, however, the rotor is made to run at speed n in the direction of the forward field, the two slip are now s and $(2 - s)$. For normal operation $(2 - s) >> s$ and as a consequence the backward field induced rotor currents are much larger than at stand still and have a lower power factor. The corresponding opposing rotor mmf in presence of the stator impedance, causes the backward field to be greatly reduced in strength. On the other hand, the low-slip forward rotating field induces smaller currents of a higher power factor in the rotor than at standstill. This leads to great enhancement in the forward flux wave.

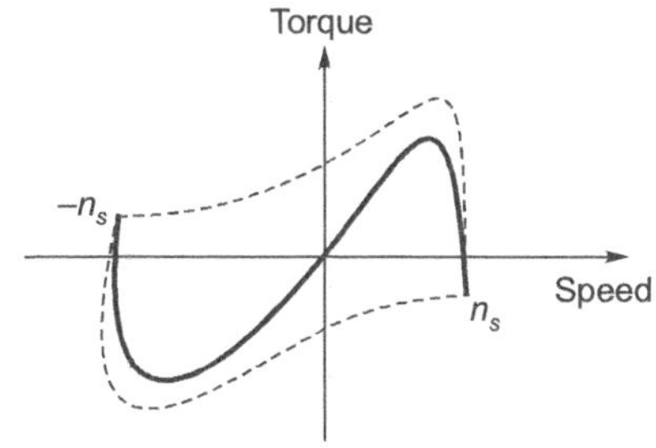

Torque-speed characteristic of single-winding 1-ϕ motor

This reduction in the backward field and strengthening of the forward field is slip-dependent and the difference increases as slip s (with respect to the forward field) reduces or the rotor speed in the forward direction becomes close to the synchronous speed, infact, at near about the synchronous speed, the forward field may be several times the backward field. As a result there is a net running torque. The two fields together must always induces the stator winding emf to balance the applied voltage. The complete torque-speed characteristic as the sum of the two (forward and backward) torque-speed characteristics is drawn in figure.

6.2 **Using double revolving field theory explain the working of a single-phase induction motor.**
[10 marks : 2002]

Solution:

Figure gives the schematic diagram of a single-phase induction motor with one stator winding and a squirrel-cage rotor. The winding is distributed in space so that the space fundamental of mmf is the most dominant component of the actual mmf distribution. The space harmonics of mmf, as in the case of a 3-phase induction motor, would then be ignored. When the winding carries a sinusoidal current, it produces a sinusoidally space-distributed mmf whose peak values pulsates with time.

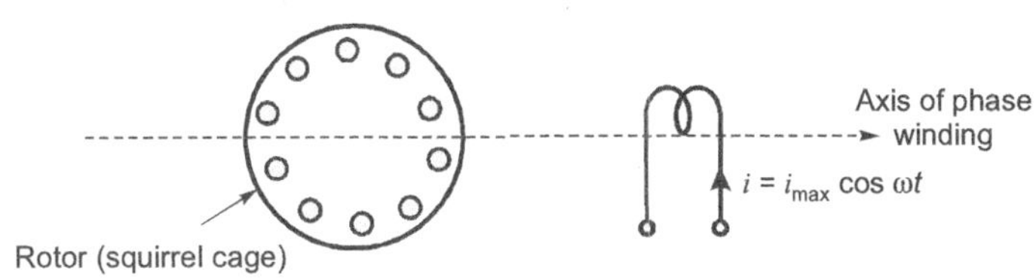

As seen from the axis of the winding, the mmf at any time t is

$$F = F_{peak} \cos \theta \quad \text{...}(i)$$

where θ is the angle measured from the winding axis

Now, $$F_{peak} = F_{max} \cos \omega t \quad \text{...}(ii)$$

So that the mmf has both space and time distribution expressed as

$$F = F_{max} \cos \theta \cos \omega t \quad \text{...}(iii)$$

This equation can be trigonometrically manipulated into the form

$$F = (1/2)F_{max} \cos(\theta - \omega t) + (1/2)F_{max} \cos(\theta + \omega t) \quad \text{...}(iv)$$

equation (*iv*) shows, a pulsating single-phase field can be considered as superposition of two rotating fields rotating at synchronous speed is opposite direction.

$(1/2)F_{max} \cos(\theta - \omega t)$; the forward rotating field, F_f.

$(1/2)F_{max} \cos(\theta + \omega t)$; the backward rotating field, F_b.

The forward and backward rotating fields along with the rotor which is rotating at speed n in the direction of the forward field have slip s and $(2 - s)$ respectively. Under stationary rotor condition, the two rotating field slip past the rotor at the same slip $s = 1$, and inducing equal currents in the squirrel-cage rotor. The two rotating fields have the same strength and produce equal and opposite torques resulting is net starting torque of zero value.

If however, the rotor is made to run at speed n in the direction of the forward field, the two slips are now s and $(2-s)$. For normal operation $(2-s) >> s$ and as a consequence the backward field induced rotor currents are much larger than at stand still and have a lower power factor. The corresponding opposing rotor mmf, in presence of the stator impedance, causes the backward field to be greatly reduced in strength. On the other hand, the low-slip forward rotating field induces smaller currents of a higher power factor in the rotor than at stand still. This lead to great enhancement in the forward flux wave. This reduction in the backward field and strengthening of the forward field is slip-dependent and the difference increases as slip reduces or the rotor speed in the forward direction becomes close to the synchronous speed.

6.3 **Give the reasons why a single-phase induction-motor has poorer performance as compared to a 3-phase induction motor.**

[5 marks : 2009]

Solution:

In a 3-ϕ induction motor the maximum torque is independent of the rotor resistance, while the slip at which it occurs increases with the rotor resistance. No such neat result is possible in a 1-ϕ induction motor as the backward rotating field thereby reducing the forward torque. As a result the maximum torque in a 1-ϕ induction motor reduces as the motor resistance is increases. As a consequence of the presence of the backward field, the performance of a 1-ϕ motor for the same frame size. It has a lower maximum torque at higher slip and greater losses. Further, it has greater volt-ampere and wait input because of their consumption in the backward rotating field. Even the stator copper-losses are higher in a 1-ϕ motor as a single winding is required to carry all the current. All this results in lower efficiency and higher temperature rise for 1-ϕ motors. For a given power and speed rating, a 1-ϕ motor must therefore have a larger frame size than a 3-ϕ motor.

6.4 **Classify 1-phase induction motors by the methods of starting and compare their performance and mention typical application areas. A 230 V, 6 pole, 50 Hz, 375 Watt single phase induction motor has the following parameters at standstill.**

$r_1 = 11.4$ ohm $x_1 = 14.3$ ohm $x_0 = 275$ ohm

$r'_2 = 13.8$ ohm $x'_2 = 14.3$ ohm Ignore R_0

Find the input current, power and power factor when the motor is operating at $s = 0.06$.

[5 marks : 2010]

Solution:

Single-phase induction motor is classified based on their method of starting.

1. **Resistance split-phase motor:** It has a low starting current and moderate starting torque. It is used for easily started loads and typical applications include fans, saws, grinders, blowers, centrifugal pumps, washing machines etc.
2. **Capacitor-start motor:** This motor has a high starting torque and therefore is used for hard starting loads such as compressors, conveyors, pumps, certain machine tools, refrigeration and air conditioning equipment etc.
3. **Permanent capacitor motor:** It has a high starting torque but slightly lower than that of the capacitor-start motor as a result of the compromise between starting and running performances and the capacitor cost. Because of the permanent capacitor it has a better running power factor and efficiency and a quieter and smoother operation. It is used for both easy and hard to start loads. In fact in modern practical ceiling fans, air-circulators and blowers use this type of motor.
4. **Two value capacitor motor:** It combines the advantages of capacitor-start and permanent capacitor motors and is used for hard to start loads. At the same time it gives a high power factor and efficiency under running conditions. Typical applications are refrigerators, compressors and stockers.

5. **Shaded-pole motor:** It is a cheep motor with a low starting torque and low power factor and efficiency during running. It is commonly used for fans of all kinds (particularly table fans), humidifiers, vending machines, photocopying machine, advertising displays.

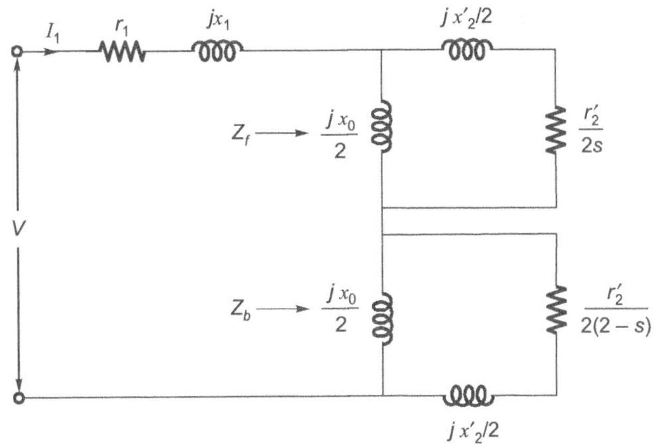

$$Z_f = \left(\frac{jX_0}{2}\right) \bigg\| \left(\frac{r_2'}{2s} + j\frac{x_2'}{2}\right) = \left(j\frac{275}{2}\right) \bigg\| \left(\frac{13.8}{2\times 0.06} + j\frac{14.3}{2}\right)$$

$\Rightarrow$ $$Z_f = 85.75\angle 42.04\ \Omega$$

$$Z_b = \left(\frac{jX_0}{2}\right) \bigg\| \left(\frac{r_2'}{2(2-s)} + j\frac{x_2'}{2}\right) = \left(j\frac{275}{2}\right) \bigg\| \left(\frac{13.8}{2\times(2-0.06)} + j\frac{14.3}{2}\right)$$

$$= 7.58\angle 64.96^\circ\ \Omega$$

Taking supply voltage as the reference,

$$V = 230\angle 0^\circ\ \text{V}$$

$$\text{Input current} = I = \frac{V}{(r_1 + jX_1) + Z_f + Z_b}$$

$\Rightarrow$ $$I = \frac{230\angle 0^\circ}{(11.4 + j14.3) + 85.75\angle 42.04^\circ + 7.58\angle 64.96^\circ} = 2.07\angle -45.10^\circ\ \text{Amp.}$$

Input power factor

$\Rightarrow$ $$\cos\phi = \cos(45.10^\circ) = 0.7058 \quad \text{(lagging)}$$

$$\text{Input power} = VI\cos\phi = 230 \times 2.07 \times 0.7058 = 336.03\ \text{Watts}$$

6.5 Explain, with the help of motor sketch and phasor diagram, how rotating magnetic field is produced in a single-phase shaded-pole motor. Discuss the direction of rotor rotation.

[7 marks : 2012]

Solution:

The figure shown below gives the schematic diagram of a shaded-pole motor. The main winding flux ϕ_m is alternating in nature, it therefore induces emf $\bar{E}_{sc}$ in the shading coil by transformer action as shown in figure given below. The magnitude of the ring current I_{sc} and its angle of lag behind E_{sc}, depends upon the impedance of the short-circuited shading coil. The current I_{sc} produce shading coil flux ϕ_{sc} in phase with it. Now, the shaded pole carries both ϕ_m and ϕ_{sc}, so that their phasor sum give the total flux ϕ_{sp} in the shaded pole. Since main pole flux ϕ_m and shaded-pole flux ϕ_{sp} are having time phase displacement, a rotating field is produced giving rise to a starting torque.

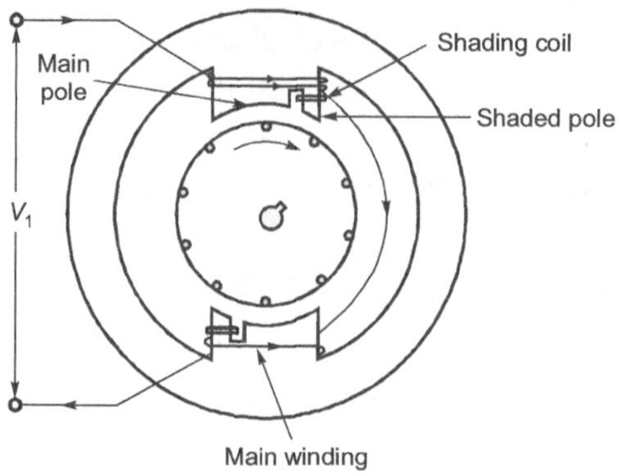

The main pole flux leads the shaded-pole flux, ϕ_m reaches maximum first and a little time latter, the shaded pole flux ϕ_{sp} also reaches maximum i.e. the rotating flux always rotates from unshaded pole to shaded pole.

6.6 A 240 V, 50 Hz, 2 pole universal motor operates at a speed of 10000 rpm on full load and draws a current of 7.12 A at 0.92 lagging power factor. The motor parameters are $r_a = 6.34\ \Omega$; $x_a = 9.62\ \Omega$; $r_s = 4.89\ \Omega$; $X_s = 3.6\ \Omega$. Calculate efficiency of the motor if rotational losses are 60 W.

[4 marks : 2013]

Solution:

$$P_c = I^2(r_a + r_s)$$
$$= (7.12)^2 \times (6.34 + 4.89) = 569.30 \text{ W}$$
$$P_o = VI\cos\phi = 240 \times 7.12 \times 0.92 = 1572.096 \text{ W}$$
$$\eta = \frac{P_o}{P_o + \text{losses}} = \frac{1572.096}{1572.096 + 569.30 + 60} \times 100\% = 71.41\%$$

6.7 Draw neat phasor diagrams and T-s characteristics of single phase capacitor run, capacitor start-capacitor run, capacitor start motors. Compare their performance on the basis of these characteristics.

[10 marks : 2013]

Solution:

Capacitor Start Motor: Capacitors are used to improve the starting and running performance of the single phase induction motors. The capacitor-start motor is identical to a split-phase motor except that starting winding has as many turns as the main winding. More over a capacitor C is connected in series with the starting winding.

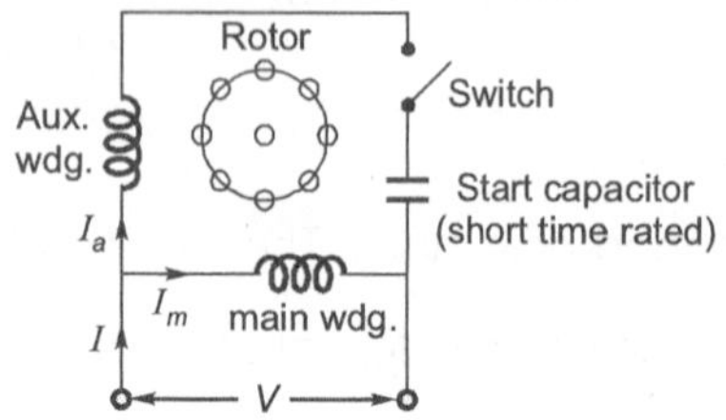

Fig. (a)
Schematic diagram

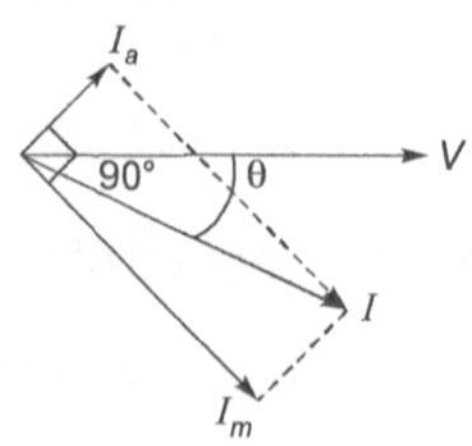

Fig. (b)
Phasor diagram

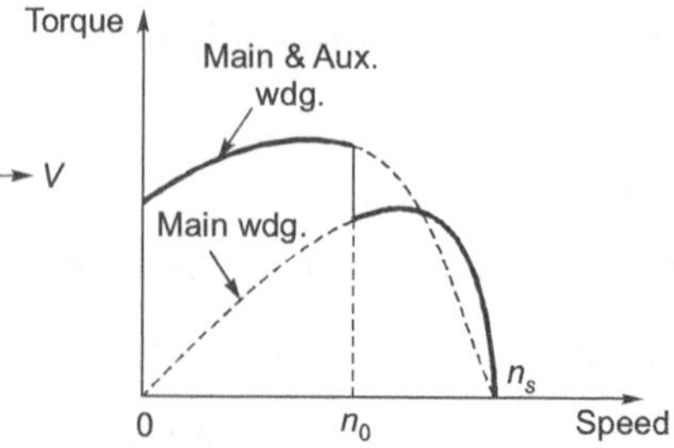

Fig. (c)
Torque-speed charateristic

The value of capacitor is so chosen that I_a leads I_m by about 90° so that the starting torque is maximum for certain value of I_a and I_m. Again, the starting winding is opened by the centrifugal switch when the motor attains about 75% of synchronous speed. The motor then operates as a single phase induction motor and continues to accelerate till it reaches the normal speed.

Characteristics:

1. Although starting characteristics of a capacitor-start motor are better than those of a split-phase motor both machine possess the same running characteristics because the main windings are identical.
2. The phase angle between two currents is about 90° compared to about 25° in a split-phase motor consequently, for the same starting torque, the current in the starting winding is only about half that in a split phase motor. Therefore, the starting winding of a capacitor start motor heats up less quickly and is well suited to application involving either frequent or prolonged starting periods.
3. Capacitor-start motors are used where high starting torque is required and where high starting period may be long. The power rating of such motor lies between 120 W and 0.75 kW.

Capacitor Run:

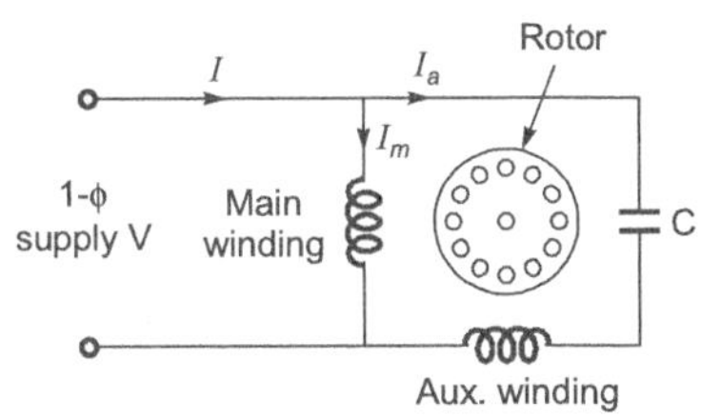

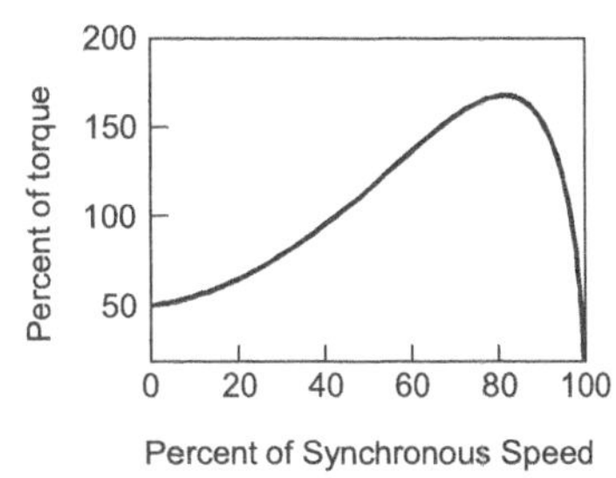

In this motor, the capacitor that connected in series with the auxiliary winding is not cut out after starting and is left in circuit all the time. This simplifies the construction and decreases the cost because the centrifugal and decreases the cost because the centrifugal switch is not needed. The power factor, torque pulsation and efficiency are also improved because the motor runs as a two-phase motor. The motor runs more quietly. The capacitor value is of the order of 20-50 μF and because it operates continuously, it is an ac paper oil type. The capacitor is compromise between the best starting and running value and therefore starting torque is sacrificed.

Characteristics:

1. These motor are used where the required starting torque is low such as air-moving equipment i.e. fan, blower and voltage regulators and also oil burners where quite operation is particularly desirable.

Capacitor-Start-Capacitor Run:

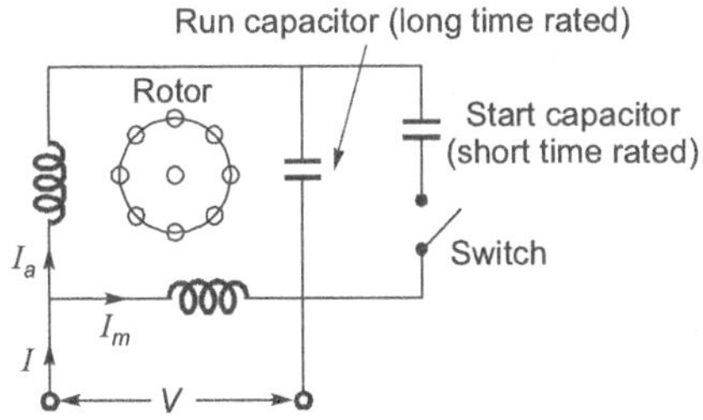

Fig. (a) : Schematic Diagram

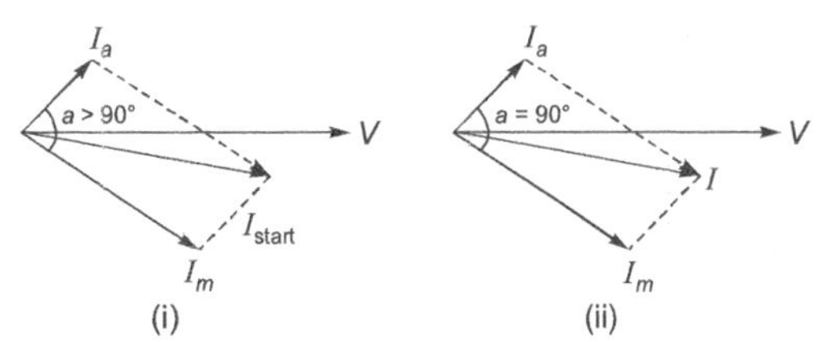

Fig. (b) : Phasor Diagram

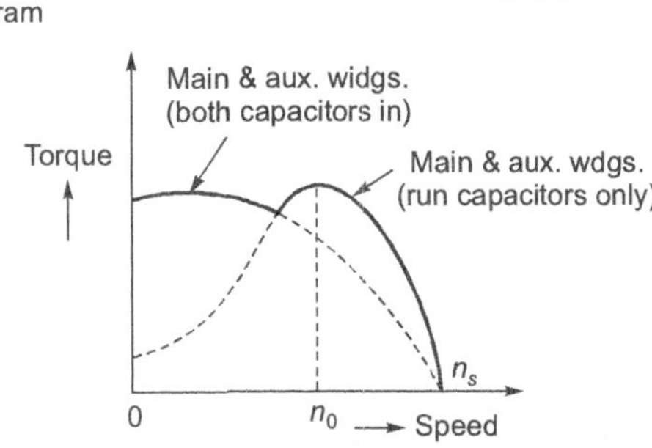

Fig. (c) : Torque-speed characteristic

Two capacitor one for starting and one for running theoretically, optimum starting and running performance can be achieved by having two capacitors.

The starting capacitor is larger in value and is of ac electrolytic type. The running capacitor permanently connected in series with the starting winding, is of smaller value and is of the paper oil type.

Characteristics:

1. Ability to start heavy loads.
2. Extremely quite operation.
3. Higher efficiency and power factor.
4. Ability to develop 25% overload capacity. Hence such motors are ideally suited where load requirements are severe as in the case of compressors and conveyors etc.

6.8 In a 4-pole, 50 Hz single-phase induction motor, the power absorbed by the forward and backward fields are respectively 200 W and 21 W at a motor speed of 1440 rpm. The no-load rotational loss is 41 W. Compute the shaft torque at the above speed.

[4 marks : 2015]

Solution:

Method-1:

$$N = 1440 \text{ rpm}, \; s = \frac{1500-1440}{1500} = 0.04$$

$$\omega_m = 150.79 \text{ rad/sec}$$

Air gap power for forward field = $P_{gf} = 200$ watt

Air gap power for backward field = $P_{gb} = 21$ watt

Rotational loss = 41 watt

Rotor copper-loss corresponding to forward field = sP_{gf}

Rotor copper-loss corresponding to backward field = $(2-s)P_{gb}$

Total rotor copper loss = $sP_{gf} + (2-s)P_{gb}$

Electrical power converted to gross mechanical form is

$$P_m = (1-s)\,\omega_s T = \omega_m T = (1-s)\,(P_{gf} - P_{gb})$$

it can be also written as,

$$P_m = (1-s)\,P_{gf} + [1-(2-s)]P_{gb}$$

or,

$$P_m = (1-0.04)\times 200 + [1-(2-0.04)]\times 21$$

$$P_m = 192 + (-20.16) = 171.84 \text{ watt}$$

$$P_{shaft} = P_m - P_{rot.loss} = (171.84-41) \text{ watt} = 130.84 \text{ watt.}$$

$$T_{shaft} = \frac{P_{shaft}}{\omega_m} = \frac{130.84}{150.79} = 0.8676 \text{ Nm}$$

Method-2:

$$\omega_m = 150.79 \text{ rad/sec}$$

$$T_{fwd} = \frac{P_{gf}}{\omega_s} = \frac{200}{157.08} = 1.2732$$

$$T_{bwd} = \frac{P_{gb}}{\omega_s} = \frac{21}{157.08} = 0.1337$$

Net developed torque = $T_{fwd} - T_{bwd} = 1.2732 - 0.1337 = 1.1395$ Nm

Mech. power developed = $T_{net} \times \omega_m$

$$P_{dev} = 1.1395 \times 150.79 = 171.825 \text{ Watt}$$

$$P_{shaft} = P_{dev} - P_{rotational\ loss} = 171.825 - 41 = 130.825 \text{ Watt}$$

$$T_{shaft} = \frac{P_{shaft}}{\omega_m} = \frac{130.825}{150.79} = 0.8676 \text{ Nm}$$

■■■■

7 Power Systems

Revised Syllabus of ESE: *Basic power generation concepts, steam, gas and water turbines, transmission line models and performance, cable performance, insulation, corona and radio interference, power factor correction, symmetrical components, fault analysis, principles of protection systems, basics of solid state relays and digital protection; Circuit breakers, Radial and ring-main distribution systems, Matrix representation of power systems, load flow analysis, voltage control and economic operation, System stability concepts, Swing curves and equal area criterion. HVDC transmission and FACTS concepts, Concepts of power system dynamics, distributed generation, solar and wind power, smart grid concepts, environmental implications, fundamentals of power economics.*

1. Generating Power Stations

1.1 Draw a labelled schematic diagram of a typical thermal power station. How do you compare thermal plants with hydro electric plants from the economic point of view?

[15 marks : 2002]

Solution:

Schematic Diagram of a Typical Steam Power Station:

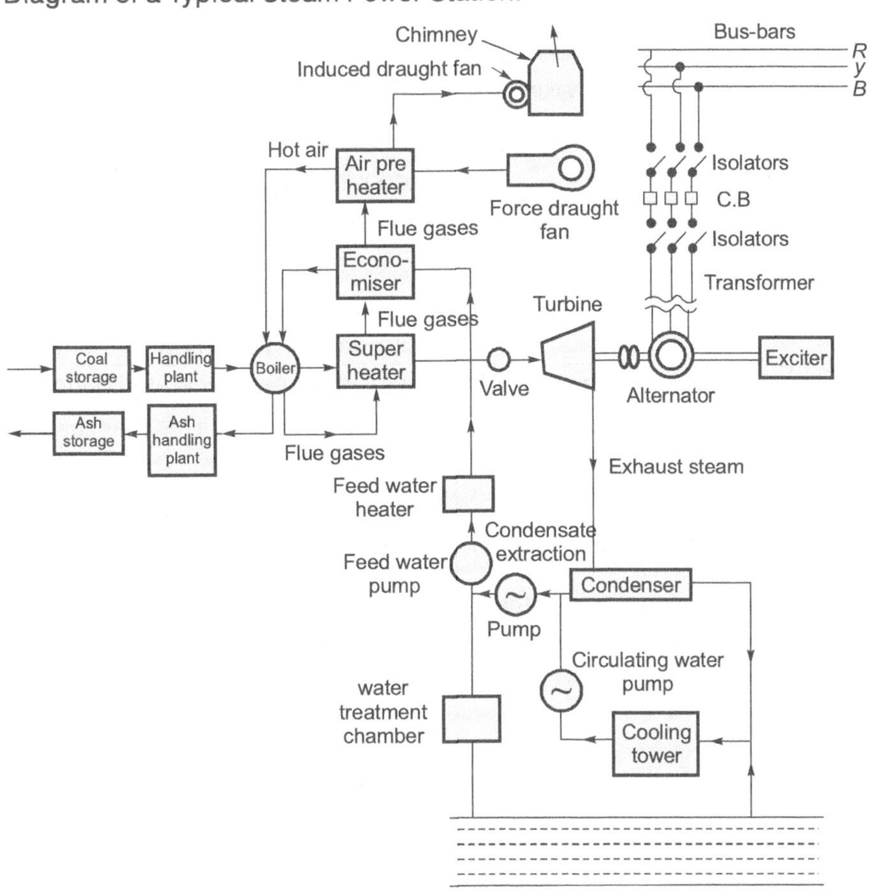

Comparison of Steam Power Plant with Hydroelectric Power Plant:

Item	Steam Power Plant	Hydroelectric Power Plant
1. Initial cost (approximate) per kW in rupees	Initial cost is lower than those of hydroelectric and nuclear power plant (1000 to 1500).	Initial cost is very high because of dam construction and excavation work (1500 to 4000).
2. Running cost	Higher than hydroelectric and nuclear plant because of the requirement of huge amount of coal.	Practically nil because not fuel is required.
3. Cost of fuel	Maximum because huge amount of coal is transported to the plant site.	Practically nil.
4. Maintenance cost	Quite high as skilled operating staff is required.	Quite low.
5. Transmission and distribution cost	Quite low as these are generally located near the load centres.	Quite high as these are located quite away from the 10%.
6. Fixed cost per annum (interest) on capital	13%	10%

1.2 Define the following:

(a) Diversity factor

(b) Load factor

(c) Plant capacity factor

(d) Plant use factor

[10 marks : 2004]

Solution:

(a) **Diversity Factor:** Diversity factor is defined as the ratio of the sum of individual maximum demand to the simultaneous maximum demand of the whole group of consumers.

$$\text{Diversity factor} = \frac{\text{Sum of individual maximum demands}}{\text{Simultaneous maximum demand of the consumers}}$$

(b) **Load Factor:**

$$\text{Load Factor} = \frac{\text{Average load}}{\text{Maximum load}} = \frac{\text{Energy consumed during a period}}{\text{Maximum demand} \times \text{time under consideration}}$$

(c) **Plant Capacity Factor:** The plant capacity factor gives an idea about the reserve capacity requirements of a power station. It is defined as

$$\text{Plant capacity factor} = \frac{\text{Acutal energy generated}}{\text{Maximum energy that could have been generated during the period}}$$

(d) **Plant Use Factor:** Another factor which affects the cost of energy is the plant use factor and is defined as

$$\text{Plant use factor} = \frac{\text{Annual energy generated}}{(\text{Capacity of plant}) \times (\text{No. of hours plant is actually in operation during the year})}$$

1.3 **What are pumped storage plants? Describe with neat sketches the principle of operation of such a plant. Also, discuss the role of the plant in a large interconnected power system.**

[10 marks : 2008]

Solution:

Pumped Storage Plant: Pumped storage plants are an special type of power plant which work as ordinary hydro power plants for part of the time and when such plants are not producing power, they can be used as pumping stations which pump water from tail race to the head race. During this time, these plants utilize power available from the grid to run the pumping set.

Thus, pumped storage plants can operate only if these plants are interconnected in a large grid.

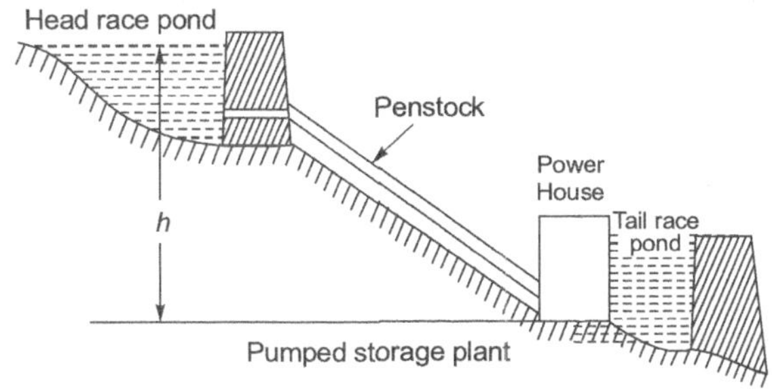

Principle of Operation: The pumped storage plant is consists of two ponds, one at high level and other at low level with power house near the low level pond. The two ponds are connected through a penstock.

It is an igneous way of conserving the limited water resources on the one hand and balancing the load on the distribution system, on the other hand. The plant operate as a source of electrical energy during system peak hours and as a sink during off-peak hours.

Role of the Plant in a Large Interconnected Power System:

(a) **Increased Reliability of Supply:** In the event of power failure at one station, the system can be fed from the other station. Generation in a hydrostation is greatly affected by river flow, storage available, floods and droughts. Forced outages at steam, station depends on efficient working of boilers, turbines and all the associated auxiliary plants. Forced outgages as well as scheduled outages can be easily met in an interconnected system.

(b) **Reduction in Total Installed Capacity:** The amount of such reduction depends on the characteristics of the interconnected system and the desired degree of service reliability. In case of isolated operation of power stations, reserve would have to be maintained separately in each power station. Similarly spinning reserve required in a power system is reduced.

(c) **Economic Operations:** Various methods of loading the generator units in the most economical way with interconnection should be studied. Savings derived from reduction in spinning reserve and economic loading of the generator units can be calculated. This ultimately reduces the total capital and running costs to a minimum.

2. Performance of Transmission Lines, Line Parameters and Corona

2.1 In an untransposed three-phase transmission line

(a) The sequence network do not have mutual coupling.

(b) A positive sequence current may cause a negative sequence voltage drop.

(c) The sequence impedance matrix is diagonal. [2 marks : 2002]

Solution: (b)

Option (b) is correct.

2.2 How does the use of bundle conductors reduce corona loss in an EHV line? [4 marks : 2002]

Solution:

A bundle conductor is a conductor made up of two or more sub-conductors and is used as one phase conductor. The reactance of the bundle conductors is reduced because the self GMD of the conductors is increased,

$$L = 2\times10^{-7} \ln\left(\frac{D_m}{D_{sA}}\right) \text{H/m}$$

By bundling the conductors the self GMD of the conductors is increased thereby; the critical disruptive voltage is increased and hence corona loss is reduced.

2.3 The Thevenin's equivalent impedance of a busbar in a three-phase 400 kV system is 0.20 p.u. at a base of 500 MVA. Calculate the reactive power needed to (a) boost the voltage by 5 kV at the busbar (b) reduce the voltage by 4 kV at the busbar. What equipment is needed in each case?

[10 marks : 2002]

Solution:

$$\Delta V = \frac{QX}{V}$$

$$X = \frac{0.2 \times 400^2}{500} = 64\ \Omega$$

(a) For boosting the voltage by 5 kV,

$$5000 = \frac{Q \times 64}{400 \times 1000}$$

or $Q = 31.25$ MVAR injected

For voltage boost up static shunt capacitor is used.

(b) To reduce voltage by 4 kV,

$$4000 = \frac{Q \times 64}{400 \times 1000}$$

or $Q = 25$ MVAR extracted

Voltage reduction is achieved by using reactor.

2.4 The surge impedance of a 400 kV, 100 km transmission line is 300 ohms. For a 200 km length the line surge impedance will be

(a) 300 ohms (b) 150 ohms
(c) 600 ohms (d) 400 ohms

[2 marks : 2005]

Solution:

Surge impedance does not depend on the line length. Hence, Option (a) is correct.

2.5 Explain: Surge impedance loading of transmission line. [5 marks : 2005]

Solution:

Surge Impedance Loading (SIL): A transmission line may be considered as generating capacitive reactive voltamperes in its shunt capacitance and consuming inductive voltampers in its series inductance.

The load at which the inductive and capacitive reactive voltampers are equal and opposite is called surge impedance loading (SIL) or natural load of the line.

Capacitive voltampere generated by the line

$$= \frac{V^2}{X_C} = V^2 \omega C/\text{phase}$$

Here, X_C = Shunt capacitive reactance per phase

Inductive reactive voltampers absorbed by the line = $I^2 X_L = I^2 \omega L$ per phase.

Here, X_L = Series inductive reactance per phase under natural load conditions,

$$V^2 \omega C = I^2 \omega L$$

$$\frac{V}{I} = \sqrt{\frac{L}{C}} = Z_0 = \text{SIL}$$

The surge impedance load of a line may also be defined as the power delivered by it to a purely resistance load equal to its surge impedance. The SIL, gives definite meaning to the terms lightly loaded or fully loaded lines.

2.6 Assume that the equations between the sending end voltage and current with the corresponding receiving end voltage and current in terms of *A, B, C, D* constants of a long transmission line are known, derive equations for sending end and receiving end power.

[10 marks : 2005]

Solution:

Single transmission line (2-mode/2-bus system) is shown in figure.

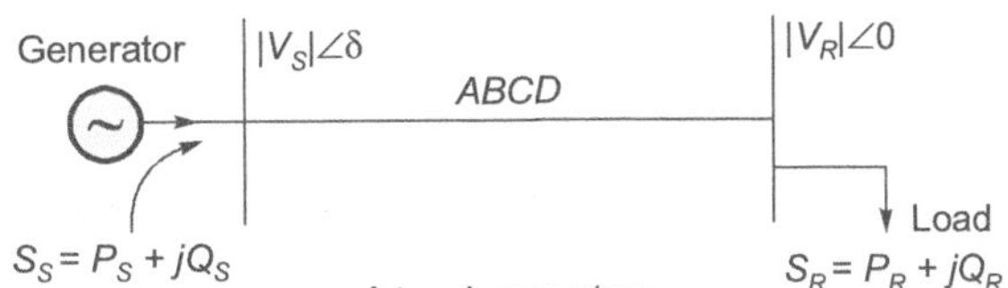

A two-bus system

Let us take the receiving-end voltage as a reference phasor ($V_R = |V_R|\angle 0°$) and let the sending-end voltage lead it by an angle δ ($V_S = |V_S|\angle\delta$). The angle δ is known as torque angle.

The complex power leaving the receiving-end and entering the sending end of the transmission line can be expressed as (on per phase basis)

$$S_R = P_R + jQ_R = V_R I_R^* \quad \text{...}(i)$$

$$S_S = P_S + jQ_S = V_s I_S^* \quad \text{...}(ii)$$

Receiving-end and sending-end currents can, however be expressed in terms of receiving-end sending-end voltages. By rearranging,

$$\begin{bmatrix} V_S \\ I_S \end{bmatrix} = \begin{bmatrix} A & B \\ C & D \end{bmatrix} \begin{bmatrix} V_R \\ I_R \end{bmatrix}$$

and $\quad AD - BC = 1$

$$I_R = \frac{1}{B}V_S - \frac{A}{B}V_R \quad \text{...}(iii)$$

$$I_S = \frac{D}{B}V_S - \frac{1}{B}V_R \quad \text{...}(iv)$$

Let *A, B, C, D* the transmission line constants, be written as,

$$A = |A|\angle\alpha,$$
$$B = |B|\angle\beta,$$
$$D = |D|\angle\alpha \text{ (since } A = D)$$

Therefore we can write,

$$I_R = \left|\frac{1}{B}\right||V_S|\angle(\delta-\beta) - \left|\frac{A}{B}\right||V_r|\angle(\alpha-\beta)$$

$$I_S = \left|\frac{D}{B}\right||V_s|\angle(\alpha+\delta-\beta) - \left|\frac{1}{B}\right||V_R|\angle(-\beta)$$

Substituting for I_R in equation (*i*) we get

$$S_R = |V_R|\angle 0\left[\left|\frac{1}{B}\right||V_S|\angle(\beta-\delta) - \left|\frac{A}{B}\right||V_R|\angle(\beta-\alpha)\right]$$

$$= \frac{|V_S||V_R|}{|B|}\angle(\beta-\delta) - \left|\frac{A}{B}\right||V_R|^2\angle(\beta-\alpha) \quad \text{...}(v)$$

Similarly,

$$S_S = \left|\frac{D}{B}\right||V_s|^2\angle(\beta-\alpha) - \frac{|V_s||V_R|}{|B|}\angle(\beta+\delta) \quad \text{...}(vi)$$

If equation (v) is expressed in real and imaginary parts, we can write the real and reactive powers at the receiving-end as

$$P_R = \frac{|V_S||V_R|}{|B|}\cos(\beta-\delta) - \left|\frac{A}{B}\right||V_R|^2\cos(\beta-\alpha) \quad ...(vii)$$

$$Q_R = \frac{|V_S||V_R|}{|B|}\sin(\beta-\delta) - \left|\frac{A}{B}\right||V_R|^2\sin(\beta-\alpha) \quad ...(viii)$$

Similarly, the real and reactive powers at sending-end are,

$$P_S = \left|\frac{D}{B}\right||V_S|^2\cos(\beta-\alpha) - \frac{|V_S||V_R|}{|B|}\cos(\beta+\delta) \quad ...(ix)$$

$$Q_S = \left|\frac{D}{B}\right||V_S|^2\sin(\beta-\alpha) - \frac{|V_S||V_R|}{|B|}\sin(\beta+\delta) \quad ...(x)$$

2.7 What do you understand by Ferranti effect? Determine the sending end voltage and efficiency by π-method of a line, given resistance of line (R = 0.2 × 120 = 24 Ω), inductive reactance (X_L = 48.98 Ω) and capacitance reactance (C = 1.2 μF). The line delivers 40 MW at 132 kV and 0.8 p.f. lagging.

[14 marks : 2006]

Solution:

Ferranti effect: When a long line is operating under no load or light load condition, the receiving end voltage is greater than the sending end voltage. This is known as Ferranti-effect.

If the reactive power generated at a point is more than the reactive power absorbed, the voltage at that point becomes higher than the normal value and vice-versa. The inductive reactance of the line is a sink for the reactive power whereas the shunt capacitance generate reactive power.

The SIL gives definite meaning to the terms lightly loaded or full loaded lines. If the loading is less than SIL the reactive power generated is more than absorbed, therefore the receiving end voltage is greater than the sending end voltage. This explains, the phenomenon due to Ferranti effect.

Receiving end voltage,

$$V_{r(l-l)} = 132 \text{ kV}$$

$$V_r(l-n) = \frac{132}{\sqrt{3}} = 76.21 \text{kV}$$

$$I_l = \frac{P}{\sqrt{3}\times V_r(l-l)\times pF} = \frac{40\times10^6}{\sqrt{3}\times132\times10^3\times0.8}$$

$$= 218.7 \text{ Amp.}$$

Taking, V_r as the reference,

$$I_l = 218.7\angle{-36.87^\circ}$$

$$I_c = j\omega C\times V_r = 2\pi f\times C\times V_r\angle 90^\circ$$

$$= j\times2\times\pi\times50\times0.6\times10^{-6}\times76.21\times10^3\angle90^\circ = 14.36\angle90^\circ$$

$$I_R = I_l + I_c = 218.7\angle{-36.87} + 14.36\angle90^\circ = 210.39\angle{-33.73}$$

$$V_s = V_r + I_Q\times(R+jX_L)$$

$$= 76.21 + 210.39\angle{-33.73}\times(24+j48.98)\times10^{-3} \text{ kV}$$

$$= 86.32\angle3.83 \text{ kV}$$

Sending end line to line voltage,

$$V_s(l-l) = V_s\times\sqrt{3} = 149.51 \text{kV}$$

Power at receiving end $P_R = 40$ MW

$$\text{Losses} = 3 \times I_R^2 \times R$$
$$= 3 \times (210.39)^2 \times 24 \times 10^{-6} \text{ MW} = 3.187 \text{ MW}$$

Power at sending end,

$$P_s = P_R + \text{Losses} = 40 + 3.187 = 43.187$$

$$\text{Efficiency} = \eta = \frac{P_R}{P_s} \times 100 = 92.62\%$$

2.8 **Using the distributed parameter form of transmission line model, obtain the equations for V_s and I_s, in terms of V_R, I_R, line resistance/km, r, line inductance per km, l, conductance per km, g, capacitance per km, C, propagation constant, gamma γ and characteristic impedance, Z_C.**

[15 marks : 2007]

Solution:

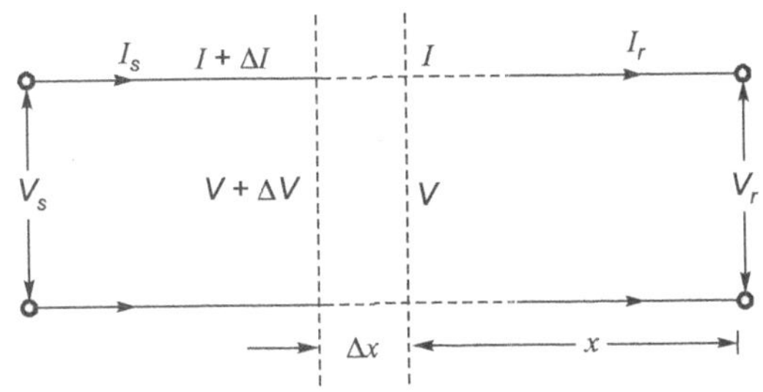

Let,
z = series impedance per unit length
y = shunt admittance per unit length
l = length of the line
$Z = zl$ = total series impedance
$Y = yl$ = total shunt admittance

Let the receiving end as the reference for measuring distances. Take an elemental length dx of the line at a distance of x from the receiving end. Let the voltage and current at a distance x are V and I and at a distance $x + dx$, $V + \Delta V$ and $I + \Delta I$ respectively,

$$\left.\begin{aligned} \Delta V &= Iz\,\Delta x \\ \Delta I &= Vy\,\Delta x \end{aligned}\right\} \quad \ldots(i)$$

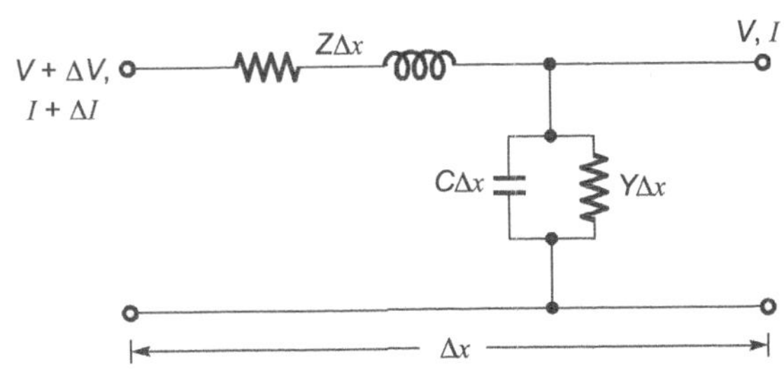

From equation (*i*),

$$\left.\begin{aligned} \frac{\Delta V}{\Delta x} &= Iz \\ \frac{\Delta I}{\Delta x} &= Vy \end{aligned}\right\} \quad \ldots(ii)$$

Which is the limit when $\Delta x \to 0$ reduce to

$$\frac{dV}{dx} = Iz \quad ...(iii)$$

$$\frac{dI}{dx} = Vy \quad ...(iv)$$

Differentiating equation (*iii*), we get

$$\frac{d^2V}{dx^2} = z\frac{dI}{dx} = z.y.V$$

or

$$\frac{d^2V}{dx^2} - zyV = 0 \quad ...(v)$$

The solution of this equation is

$$V = A\exp(\sqrt{yz}.x) + \beta\exp.(-\sqrt{yz}.x) \quad ...(vi)$$

Now, from equations (*iii*) and (*vi*) let

$$Z_C = \sqrt{\frac{z}{y}}$$

and

$$\gamma = \sqrt{yz} = \alpha + j\beta \quad ...(vii)$$

where Z_c is known as characteristic impedance and γ the propagation constant.

The equation (*vi*) and (*vii*) are rewritten as

$$V = Ae^{\gamma x} + Be^{-\gamma x} \quad ...(viii)$$

$$I = \frac{1}{Z_c}(Ae^{\gamma x} - Be^{-\gamma x}) \quad ...(ix)$$

Two constants are to be determined, hence two boundary conditions should be known. As the receiving end voltage and current are known

$\therefore$ At

$$x = 0,$$
$$V = V_r$$
$$I = I_r$$

Substituting these values in equation (*viii*) and (*ix*)

$$V_r = A + B$$

$$I_r = \frac{1}{Z_c}(A - B)$$

$$A = \frac{V_r + I_rZ_C}{2} \text{ and } B = \frac{V_r - I_rZ_C}{2}$$

Substituting the values of A and B in equation (*viii*) and (*ix*), we obtain

$$V = \frac{V_r + I_rZ_C}{2}e^{\gamma x} + V_r - \frac{I_rZ_C}{2}e^{-\gamma x} \quad ...(x)$$

$$I = \frac{1}{Z_C}\left[\frac{V_r + I_rZ_C}{2}e^{\gamma x} - \frac{V_r - I_rZ_C}{2}e^{-\gamma x}\right] \quad ...(xi)$$

The above equation can be rearranged as

$$V = V_r\frac{e^{\gamma x} + e^{-\gamma x}}{2} + I_rZ_C\frac{e^{\gamma x} - e^{-\gamma x}}{2}$$

$$V = V_r \cos h\gamma x + I_r Z_c \sin h\gamma x \quad ...(xii)$$

and $$I = \frac{1}{Z_c}\left[V_r\frac{e^{\gamma x}-e^{-\gamma x}}{2} + I_r Z_c \frac{e^{\gamma x}+e^{-\gamma x}}{2}\right]$$

$$I = \frac{V_r}{Z_c}\sin h\gamma x + I_r \cos h\gamma x \qquad \ldots(xiii)$$

Rewriting these equations for $x = l$, where $V = V_s$ and $I = I_s$

$$V_s = V_r \cos h\gamma l + I_r Z_c \sin h\gamma l$$

$$I_s = V_r\frac{\sin h\gamma l}{Z_c} + I_r \cos h\gamma l$$

2.9 There are 6 conductors in a Double circuit transmission line. Each conductor has a radius of 12 mm. The 6 conductors are arranged horizontally. The centre to centre distance between all the conductors is 2 m. The sequence of conductors are from left to right as follows: *a*, *b*, *c*, *a′*, *b′*, *c′*. Calculate the inductance per km per phase of this system.

[10 marks : 2007]

Solution:

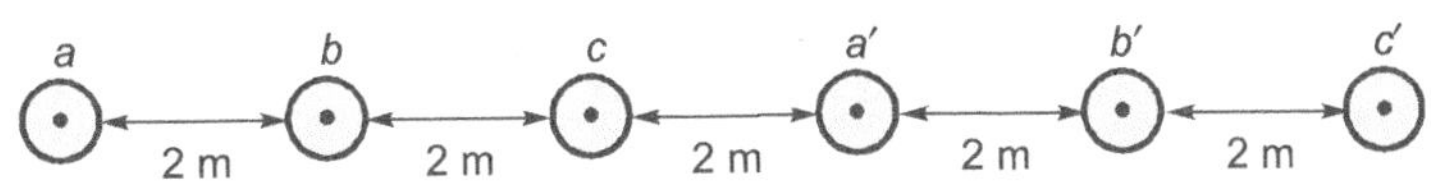

$$GMD_1 = (2 \times 4 \times 8 \times 10)^{1/4} = (640)^{1/4} = 5.03$$

Similarly, $$GMD_2 = (2 \times 2 \times 4 \times 8)^{1/4} = (128)^{1/4} = 3.36$$

and $$GMD_3 = (4 \times 2 \times 2 \times 4)^{1/4} = (64)^{1/4} = 2.83$$

Equivalent, $$GMD = \sqrt[3]{GMD_1 \times GMD_2 \times GMD_3}$$

The equivalent, $$GMD = \{(5.03) \times (3.36) \times (2.83)\}^{1/3} = 3.63$$

$$GMR_1 = \text{Self } GMD_1 = \sqrt{r' \times D_{aa'}} = \sqrt{0.7788 \times r \times D_{aa'}}$$

$$= \sqrt{0.7788 \times 6 \times 12 \times 10^{-3}} = 0.237$$

Similarly, $$GMR_2 = \sqrt{0.7788 \times 6 \times 12 \times 10^{-3}} = 0.237$$

and $$GMR_3 = \sqrt{.7788 \times 6 \times 12 \times 10^{-3}} = 0.237$$

The equivalent,

$$GMR = (0.237 \times 0.237 \times 0.237)^{1/3} = 0.237$$

$$\text{Inductance per phase} = 2 \times 10^{-7} ln\frac{GMD}{GMR} = 2 \times 10^{-7} ln\frac{3.63}{0.237}$$

$$= 5.458 \times 10^{-7} \text{ Henry/m}$$

$$= 5.458 \times 10^{-4} \text{ Henry/km} = 0.5458 \text{ mH/km}$$

2.10 A 3-phase 50 Hz transmission line has resistance, inductance and capacitance per phase of 10 ohms, 0.1 H and 0.9 μF respectively and delivers at a load of 35 MW at 132 kV and 0.8 p.f. lag. Determine the efficiency and regulation of the line using nominal-*T* method.

[20 marks : 2008]

Solution:

$R = 10\ \Omega$ and $X_L = j\omega L = j \times 2 \times \pi \times 50 \times 0.1 = 31.4$ and $C = 0.9\ \mu F$

Hence, $$Z = R + jX_L = 10 + j31.4\ \Omega$$

$$Y = j\omega C = j \times 2\pi \times 50 \times 0.9 \times 10^{-6} = j0.282 \times 10^{-3}\ S$$

Nominal T-model,

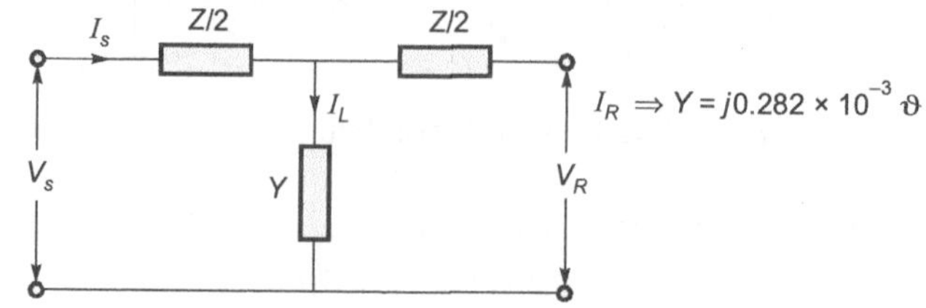

⇓

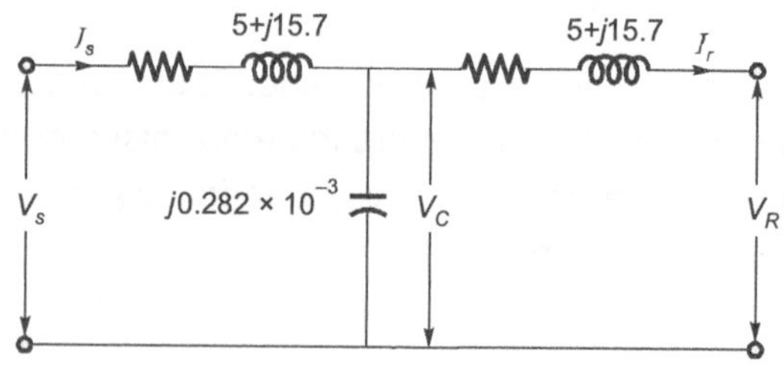

$$I_R = \text{load current} = \frac{35\times10^3}{\sqrt{3}\times132\times0.8} = 191.35 \text{ amp.}$$

$$\text{p.f.} = 0.8$$

Taking, V_r as the reference voltage,

$$V_R = \frac{132}{\sqrt{3}}\angle 0° = 76.21\angle 0° \text{ kV}$$

$$I_R = 191.35\angle{-36.87} \text{ A}$$

Voltage, $$V_C = V_R + I_R \times \frac{Z}{2}$$

$$= 76.21 + 191.35\angle{-36.87} \times (5 + j15.7) \times 10^{-3} = 78.8\angle 1.33° \text{ kV}$$

Current, $$I_C = YV_C$$

$$= j0.282 \times 10^{-3} \times 78.8\angle 1.33 \times 10^{-3} = 22.22\angle 91.33° \text{ Amp.}$$

Sending end current,

$$I_s = I_R + I_C = 91.35\angle{-36.87°} + 22.22\angle 91.33°$$

$$\Rightarrow \quad I_s = 178.46\angle{-31.25} \text{ A}$$

Sending end voltage,

$$V_s = V_C + \frac{Z}{2} \times I_s$$

$$V_s = 78.8\angle 1.33 + 178.46\angle{-31.25} \times (5 \times j15.7) \times 10^{-3}$$

$$\Rightarrow \quad V_s = 81.08\angle 2.65 \text{ kV}$$

$$V_R' = \frac{V_s}{A} = \frac{81.08\angle 2.65}{0.9955\angle 0.0811} = 81.44\angle 2.5689°$$

$$A = 1 + \frac{YZ}{2} = 1 + \frac{(j0.282\times10^{-3})(10+j31.4)}{2} = 0.9955\angle 0.0811°$$

$$\text{Regulation of the line} = \frac{V_R' - V_R}{V_R} \times 100 = \frac{81.44 - 76.21}{76.21} \times 100 = 6.8626\%$$

$$\text{Lines losses} = 3\times\left[I_s^2 \times \frac{R}{2} + I_R^2 \times \frac{R}{2}\right] = 3 \times [(178.46)^2 \times 5 + (191.35)^2 \times 5] \times 10^{-6} \text{ MW} = 1.027 \text{ MW}$$

Efficiency, $$\eta = \frac{35}{35 + 1.027} \times 100 = 97.15\%$$

2.11 The surge impedance of a 3-phase 400 kV transmission line is 400 Ω. The surge impedance loading (SIL) is

(a) 400 MW (b) 1600 MW
(c) 400 kW (d) 200 MW [2 marks : 2009]

Solution: (a)

$$\text{SIL} = \frac{(400\text{ kV})^2}{400\,\Omega} = 400\text{ MW}$$

Option (a) is correct.

2.12 A 50 Hz, 3-phase transmission line is 200 km long. It has a total series impedance of 35 + *j*140 Ω and shunt admittance of 930 × $10^{-6}\angle 90$ J. It delivers 40 MW power at 220 kV with 0.9 power factor lagging. Find the magnitude of the sending-end voltage. Consider nominal-π model of the line.

[20 marks : 2009]

Solution:

Total series impedance of the line,

$$Z = 35 + j140\ \Omega$$

Shunt admittance,

$$Y = 930\times10^{-6}\angle 90°\ \mho$$

$$\frac{Y}{2} = 465\times10^{-6}\angle 90°\ \mho$$

$$I_R = \frac{40\times10^3}{\sqrt{3}\times220\times0.9} = 116.6\text{ amp.}$$

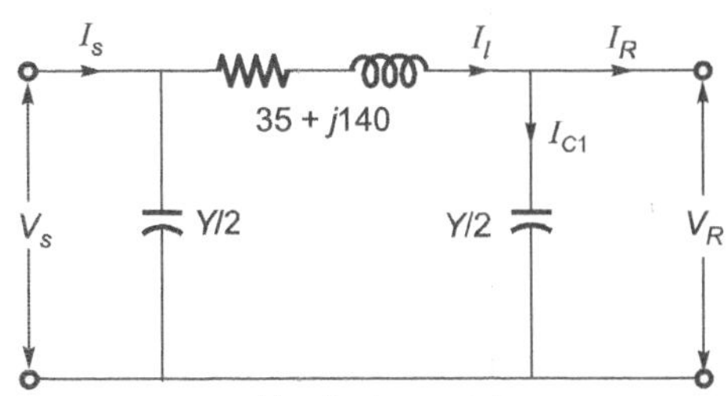

Nominal-π model

Taking V_R as the reference,

$$V_R = \frac{220}{\sqrt{3}}\angle 0° = 127\angle 0°$$

$$I_R = 116.6\angle{-25.84°}\text{ amp.}$$

$$I_{C_1}p = \frac{Y}{2}\times V_Rp = 465\times10^{-6}\angle 90°\times127\times10^3\angle 0 = 56.055\angle 90°\text{ amp.}$$

$$I_l = I_R + I_{C_1}p$$

$$= 116.6\angle{-25.84} + 59.055\angle 90° = 105.26\angle 4.48°\text{ amp.}$$

$$V_s = V_R + I_l\times Z$$

$$= 127\angle 0° + 105.26\angle 4.48°\times(35+j140)\times10^{-3} = 130.38\angle 6.6°\text{ kV}$$

$$V_{s(l-l)}p = 130.38\sqrt{3} = 225.82\text{ kV}$$

2.13 A 220 kV, 3-phase transmission line is 470 km long. The resistance per phase is 0.15 Ω per km and the inductance per phase is 1.5923 mH per km. The line is supplying a 3-phase load of 381 MVA at 0.8 power factor lagging. Find:

(i) the voltage and power at the sending end of the line.
(ii) the voltage regulation and efficiency of the line. [15 marks : 2010]

Solution:

(i) Length of the line = 40 km

Resistance/phase of the line $R_L = 0.15\times40 = 6\ \Omega$

Inductance/phase of the line $L = 1.5923\text{ mH}\times40 = 63.629\text{ mH}$

Assumption:

The line is operating at 50 Hz. Inductive reactance of the line,

$$X_L = \omega L = 2\pi f\times L$$

$$X_L = (2\pi\,50)\times(63.629)\times10^{-3} = 20\ \Omega$$

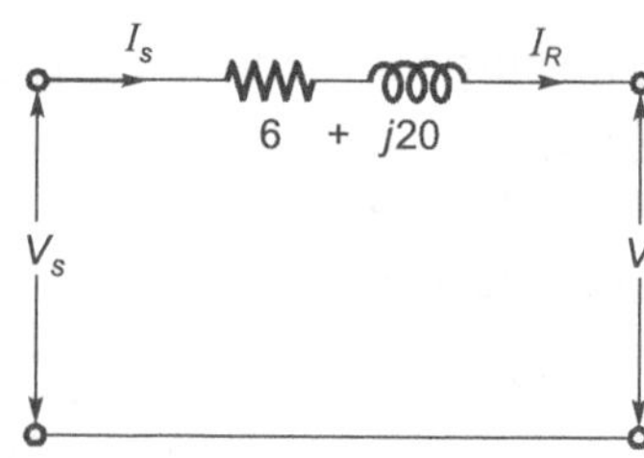

Impedance of the line,

$$Z_L = R_L + jX_L = 6 + j20$$

Receiving end voltage, $V_R = 220$ kV = 127 kV (phase voltage)

Load current, $$I_R = \frac{381 \times 10^3}{\sqrt{3} \times 220} = 999.86 \text{ amp.}$$

Assuming V_R as the reference,

$$V_R = 127\angle 0^\circ \text{ kV}$$

and $$I_R = 999.86\angle -36.87^\circ \text{ amp.}$$ {as p.f. = 0.8 lagging}

$$V_s = V_R + I_R Z_L$$
$$= 127 + (999.86\angle -36.87) \times (6 + j20) \times 10^{-3} \text{ kV}$$

$\Rightarrow$ $$V_s = 144.33\angle 4.92 \text{ kV}$$

and $$I_s = I_R = 999.86\angle -36.87^\circ$$

angle between V_s and I_s, $\phi_s = 4.92 - (-36.87) = 41.8^\circ$

$$V_s = 144.33 \times \sqrt{3} \text{ kV} \approx 250 \text{ kV (line to line)}$$

$$P_s = \text{Power at sending end}$$
$$= \sqrt{3} \times V_s(l-l) \times I_s \times \cos\phi_s$$
$$= \sqrt{3} \times 250 \times 999.86 \times \cos 41.8^\circ \times 10^{-3} \text{ MW} \approx 322.8 \text{ MW}$$

(ii) $$\text{Voltage regulation} = \frac{|V_{R(\text{no load})}| - |V_{R(\text{full load})}|}{|V_{R(\text{full load})}|} \times 100$$

$$V_{R(\text{no load})} = V_s = 250 \text{ kV}$$
$$V_{R(\text{full load})} = 220 \text{ kV}$$

$$\text{Voltage regulation} = \left(\frac{250 - 220}{220}\right) \times 100 = 13.63\%$$

$$\text{Receiving end power} = P_R = 381 \times 0.8 = 304.8 \text{ MW}$$

$$\text{Efficiency} = \frac{P_R}{P_s} \times 100 = \frac{304.8}{322.8} \times 100 = 94.42\%$$

2.14 A 3-phase double circuit line is arranged as shown below:

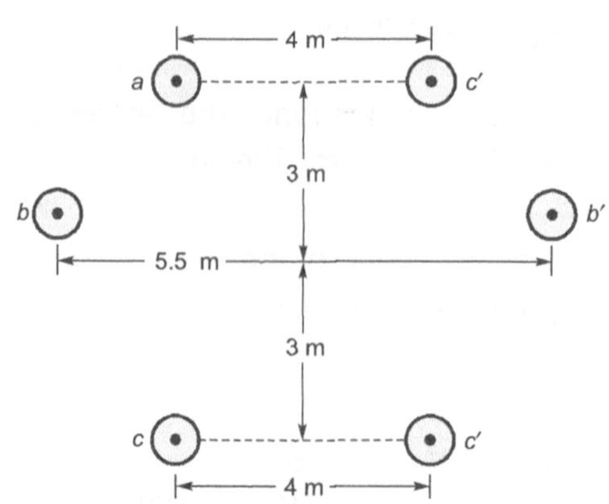

The conductors are transposed. The radius of each conductor is 0.75 cm. Phase sequence is *ABC*. Find the inductance per phase per km.

[10 marks : 2011]

Solution:

Radius of each conductor = r = 0.75 cm

Self GMD of each conductor = 0.7788 × 0.75 cm = 0.5841 cm = 0.00584 m

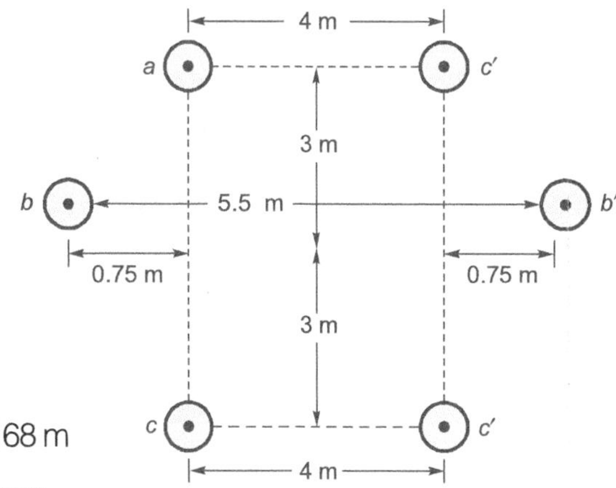

$$D_{bc} = D_{ab} = \sqrt{3^2 + 0.75^2} = 3.092 \text{ m}$$

$$D_{ab'}' = \sqrt{3^2 + 4.75^2} = 5.618 \text{ m}$$

$$D_{aa'}' = \sqrt{6^2 + 4^2} = 7.211 \text{m}$$

$$D_{m_3} = \sqrt[4]{D_{ac}\, D_{ac'}\, D_{a'c}\, D_{a'c'}}$$

$$= \sqrt[4]{6 \times 4 \times 4 \times 6} = 4.898 \text{ m}$$

$$D_{m_1} = D_{m_2} = \sqrt[4]{3.092 \times 3.092 \times 5.618 \times 5.618} = 4.168 \text{ m}$$

$$D_m = \sqrt[3]{D_{m_1} D_{m_2} D_{m_3}} = \sqrt[3]{4.168 \times 4.168 \times 4.898} = 4.398 \text{ m}$$

Self GMD of each phase,

$$D_{s_1} = \sqrt{0.00584 \times 7.211} = 0.2052\, m = D_{s_3}$$

$$D_{s_2} = \sqrt{0.00584 \times 5.5} = 0.179 \text{ m}$$

$$D_s = \sqrt[3]{D_{s_1} D_{s_2} D_{s_3}} = \sqrt[3]{0.2052 \times 0.179 \times 0.2052} = 0.196 \text{ m}$$

$$\text{Inductance} = 2 \times 10^{-4} ln\left(\frac{D_m}{D_s}\right) \text{H/km/phase}$$

$$= 2 \times 10^{-4} ln\left(\frac{4.398}{0.196}\right) \text{H/km/phase}$$

$$= 0.622 \text{ mH/km/phase}$$

2.15 Starting from fundamentals, derive the equations for sending end voltage and sending end current for a long transmission line. Use the distributed parameter form of representation of the long line. Obtain the A, B, C, D parameters of the line.

[10 marks : 2011]

Solution:

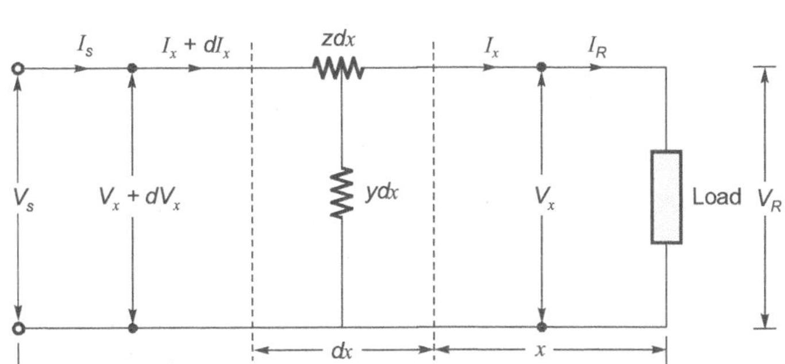

Let dx be an elemental section of the line at a distance x from the receiving end having a series impedance zdx and a shunt admittance ydx. The rise in voltage to neutral over the elemental section in the direction of increasing x is dVx.

We can write the following differential relationship across the elemental section:

$$dV_x = I_x z dx \text{ or } \frac{dV_x}{dx} = zI_x \quad ...(i)$$

$$dI_x = V_x y dx \text{ or } \frac{dI_x}{dx} = yV_x \quad ...(ii)$$

Differentiating equation (*i*) with respect to x, we obtain,

$$\frac{d^2V_x}{dx^2} = z\frac{dI_x}{dx}$$

Substituting the value of $\frac{dI_x}{dx}$ from equation (*ii*), we get

$$\frac{d^2V_x}{dx^2} = yzV_x \quad ...(iii)$$

This is a linear differential equation whose general solution can be written as follows:

$$V_x = C_1 e^{rx} + C_2 e^{-rx} \quad ...(iv)$$

where, $r = \sqrt{yz}$ ...(*v*)

and C_1 and C_2 are arbitrary constants to be evaluated.
Differential equation (*iv*) with respect to x

$$\frac{dV_x}{dx} = C_1 r e^{rx} - C_2 r e^{-rx} = zI_x$$

$$I_x = \frac{C_1}{Z_c}e^{rx} - \frac{C_2}{Z_c}e^{-rx} \quad ...(vi)$$

where, $Z_c = \left(\frac{z}{y}\right)^{1/2}$ ...(*vii*)

The constants C_1 and C_2 may be evaluated by using the end conditions, i.e. when $x = 0$, $V_x = V_R$ and $I_x = I_R$.
Substituting these values in equation (*v*) and (*vi*) gives,

$$V_R = C_1 + C_2$$

$$I_R = \frac{1}{Z_c}(C_1 - C_2)$$

which upon solving yields, $C_1 = \frac{1}{2}(V_R + Z_c I_R)$

$$C_2 = \frac{1}{2}(V_R - Z_c I_R)$$

with C_1 and C_2 as determined above, equation (iv) and (v) yield the solution for V_x and I_x as

$$V_x = \left(\frac{V_R + Z_c I_R}{2}\right)e^{rx} + \left(\frac{V_R - Z_c I_R}{2}\right)e^{-rx} \quad ...(viii)$$

$$I_x = \left(\frac{V_R / Z_c + I_R}{2}\right)e^{rx} - \left(\frac{V_R / Z_c - I_R}{2}\right)e^{-rx}$$

Here, Z_c = characteristic impedance of the line
r = propagation constant

Rearranging equation (*viii*), we get

$$V_x = V_R\left(\frac{e^{rx}+e^{-rx}}{2}\right)+I_R Z_c\left(\frac{e^{rx}-e^{-rx}}{2}\right)$$

$$I_x = V_R\frac{1}{Z_c}\left(\frac{e^{rx}-e^{-rx}}{2}\right)+I_R\left(\frac{e^{rx}+e^{-rx}}{2}\right)$$

These can be rewritten after introducing hyperbolic functions, as

$$V_x = V_R \cosh rx + I_R Z_c \sinh rx \quad \text{...(ix)}$$

$$I_x = I_r \cosh rx + V_R\frac{1}{Z_c}\sinh rx$$

when, $x = l$, $V_x = V_s$, $I_x = I_s$

$$V_s = V_R \cosh rl + I_R Z_c \sinh rl \quad \text{...(x)}$$

$$I_s = V_R\frac{1}{Z_c}\sinh rl + I_R \cosh rl \quad \text{...(xi)}$$

Expression (*x*) and (*xi*) represent the equations for sending end voltage (V_s) and sending and current (Is).

$$\begin{bmatrix} V_s \\ I_s \end{bmatrix} = \begin{bmatrix} \cosh rl & Z_c \sinh rl \\ \dfrac{\sinh rl}{Z_c} & \cosh rl \end{bmatrix}\begin{bmatrix} V_R \\ I_R \end{bmatrix} \quad \text{...(xii)}$$

Comparing equation (*xii*) we get,

$$\begin{bmatrix} V_s \\ I_s \end{bmatrix} = \begin{bmatrix} A & B \\ C & D \end{bmatrix}\begin{bmatrix} V_R \\ I_R \end{bmatrix}$$

We get,

$$A = D = \cosh rl$$

$$B = Z_c \sinh rl$$

$$C = \frac{1}{Z_c}\sinh rl$$

2.16 **A 60 Hz, 3-phase transmission line is 200 km long. It has a total series impedance of 35 + *j*140 Ω and a shunt admittance of 930 × 10⁻⁶∠90° S. It delivers 40 MW at 220 kV and 0.9 power factor lagging.**
(*i*) Determine the voltage, current, and power factor at the sending end of the line.
(*ii*) Find the voltage regulation and efficiency of the line.

[15 marks : 2014]

Solution:

(*i*) Phase voltage at receiving end,

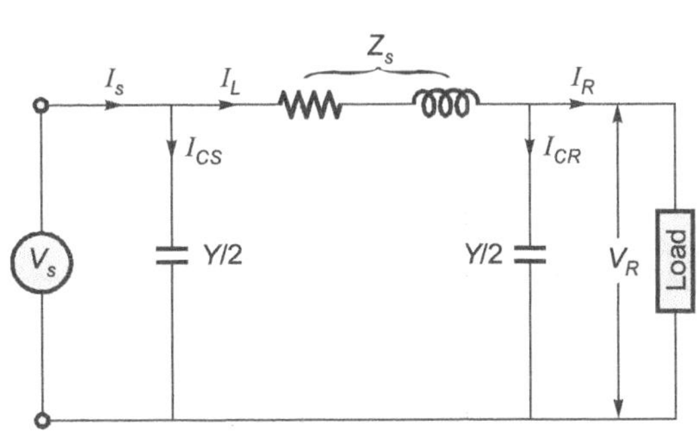

$$V_R = \frac{220}{\sqrt{3}} = 127 \text{ kV or } 127{,}000 \text{ V}$$

Receiving end power factor = $\cos\phi_R = 0.9$ lag

$$\phi_R = \cos^{-1}(0.9) = 25.84°$$

Receiving end current,

$$I_R = \frac{\text{load supplied in MW} \times 10^6}{\sqrt{3}\times V_{RL}\times\cos\phi_R}$$

$$= \frac{40\times10^6}{\sqrt{3}\times220\times10^3\times0.9} = 116.6364 \text{ A}$$

Series impedance of line,

$$Z = (35 + j140) = 144.3\angle 75.96°\ \Omega$$

Shunt admittance, $Y = 930 \times 10^{-6}\angle 90° s$

Taking phase voltage at receiving end, V_R as reference phasor, we have

$$V_R = 127{,}000\angle 0° \text{ volts}$$

Receiving end current,

$$I_R = 116.6364\angle -25.84° \text{ A} = (104.97 - j50.84) \text{ A}$$

Charging current at receiving end,

$$I_{CR} = \frac{1}{2} Y V_R$$

$$= \frac{1}{2} \times 930 \times 10^{-6}\angle 90° \times 127{,}000\angle 0°$$

$$I_{CR} = j59.005 \text{ A} = 59.055\angle 90° \text{ A}$$

Line current, $I_L = I_R + I_{CR} = (104.97 - j50.84) + (0 + j59.055)$

$$I_L = (104.97 + j8.215) = 105.3\angle 4.47° \text{ A}$$

Sending end phase voltage,

$$V_S = V_R + I_L \cdot Z$$

$$= 127{,}000\angle 0° + 105.3\angle 4.47° \times 144.3\angle 75.96° = 130389\angle 6.59° \text{ V}$$

Sending end line voltage,

$$V_{SL} = \sqrt{3} \times 130389 = 225 \text{ kV}$$

Charging current at sending end is,

$$I_{CS} = \frac{1}{2} Y V_s = \frac{1}{2} \times 930 \times 10^{-6}\angle 90° \times 130389\angle 6.59°$$

$$I_{CS} = 60.63\angle 96.59° \text{ A}$$

Sending end current,

$$I_S = I_L + I_{CS}$$

$$= 105.3\angle 4.47° + 60.63\angle 96.59°$$

$$I_S = 119.54\angle 34.92° \text{ A}$$

Sending end power factor angle,

$$\phi_s = 6.59° - (34.92°) = -28.33$$

$$\cos\phi_s = 0.8802 \text{ leading}$$

(ii) The voltage regulation,

$$\%\ V\text{regulation} = \frac{V_{SL} - V_{RL}}{V_{RL}} \times 100 = \frac{225 - 220}{220} \times 100 = 2.27\%$$

$$\eta = \left(\frac{\text{Output}}{\text{Input}}\right) \times 100 = \left(\frac{40 \times 10^6}{3 \times 130389 \times 119.54 \times 0.8802}\right) = 97.18\%$$

2.17 Discuss the physical significance of Surge Impedance and Surge Impedance Loading.

[2 marks : 2015]

Solution:

A transmission line may be considered as generating capacitive reactive volt amperes in shunt capacitance and consuming (absorbing) inductive reactive voltamperes in its series inductance. The load at which the inductive and capacitive reactive voltamperes are equal and opposite, called the surge impedance load (SIL) or natural load of the line.

Let,
V = Phase voltage at the receiving end
I = Phase current
L = Series inductance per phase
X_L = Series inductive reactance per phase
X_C = Shunt capacitive reactance per phase.
Z_0 = Surge impedance per phase

Capacitive voltamperes (VAr) generated in the line $= \dfrac{V^2}{X_C} = V^2\omega c$ per phase

Inductive reactive voltamperes (VAr) absorbed by the line $= I^2X_L = I^2\omega L$ per phase

Under natural load conditions

$$V^2\omega C = I^2\omega L$$

$$\frac{V}{I} = \sqrt{\frac{L}{C}} = Z_0$$

At this load the voltage V and current I are in the same phase at all points along the line.

Under such conditions the line is terminated in its surge impedance Z_0 which is purely resistive. When a line is terminated in its surge impedance Z_0 the power delivered by it is called the natural loading or surge impedance loading (SIL).

Surge impedance loading of a line may be defined as the power delivered by it to a purely resistive load equal to its surge impedance.

If P_0 is its natural loading $(\text{SIL})_{1\phi}$ of the line per phase

$$(\text{SIL})_{1\phi} = P_0 = V_P I_P \cos\phi$$

Since, the load is purely resistive.

$$\cos\phi = 1$$

$$P_0 = V_P I_P = V_P\frac{V_P}{Z_0} = \frac{V_P^2}{Z_0} \text{ W/phase}$$

$$(\text{SIL})_{3\phi} = \frac{(KV_L)^2}{Z_0} \text{ MW}$$

2.18 **A three-phase, 50 Hz completely transposed transmission line has the following constants:**
Resistance per mile per phase = 0.25 Ω
Inductance per mile per phase = 2.0 mH
Capacitance per mile per phase = 0.014 μF
The transmission line is 60 miles long, and line-to-line voltage at the receiving end is 132 kV. The load connected at the receiving end is 70000 kW at 0.8 power factor lagging. Using T-model of the line,
(i) Determine the current and the line-to-line voltage at the sending end.
(ii) Find the voltage regulation.
(iii) Calculate the real and reactive power at the sending end.
(iv) Find the efficiency of the transmission line. **[10 marks : 2016]**

Solution:

Given data:
f = 50 Hz, R = 0.25 Ω/miles/phase
L = 2 mH/miles/phase, C = 0.014 μF/miles/phase
l = 60 miles, V_R = 132 kV
P_R = 70 MW $\cos\phi$ = 0.8 lag

Using 'T' modes:

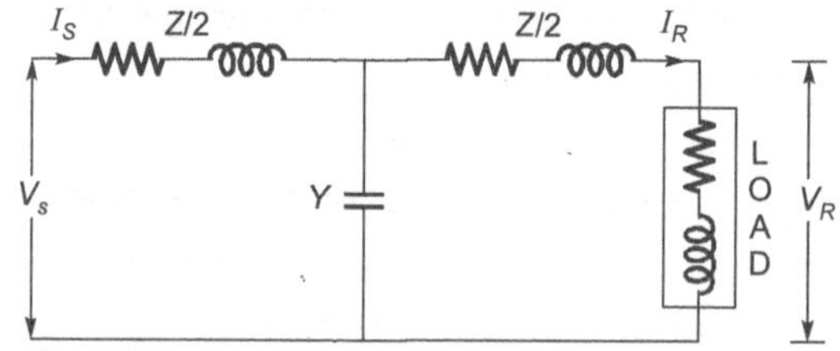

$$Z = (R + j\omega L)\, l$$
$$= [0.25 + j(2\pi \times 50 \times 2 \times 10^{-3})] \times 60 = 40.57\angle 68.3° \ \Omega$$
$$Y = j\omega Cl = j(2\pi \times 50 \times 0.014 \times 10^{-6}) \times 60$$
$$= j0.264 \times 10^{-3} \ \mho$$

ABCD parameters:

$$A = D = 1 + \frac{YZ}{2}$$
$$= 1 + \left(\frac{0.269 \times 10^{-3}\angle 90° \times 40.57\angle 68.3°}{2}\right) = 0.995\angle 0.116°$$
$$B = Z\left(1 + \frac{YZ}{4}\right)$$
$$= 40.57\angle 60.83°\left[1 + \frac{40.57\angle 60.83° \times 0.269 \sin^{-3}\angle 90°}{4}\right]$$
$$B = 40.55\angle 60.98° \ \Omega$$
$$C = Y = 0.269 \times 10^{-3}\angle 90° \ \mho$$

From the given P_R

$$|I_R| = \frac{P_R}{\sqrt{3}V_R \cos\phi_R} = \frac{70 \times 10^6}{\sqrt{3} \times 132 \times 10^3 \times 0.8} = 382.71 \text{ A}$$
$$\phi_R = \cos^{-1} 0.8 = 36.86°$$
$$I_R = 382.71\angle -36.86° \text{ A}$$

(i) (a)
$$V_S = A V_R + B I_R$$
$$= \sqrt{3}\left[0.995\angle 0.166° \times \frac{132 \times 10^3}{\sqrt{3}} + 40.55\angle 60.98° \times 382.71\angle -36.86°\right]$$
$$V_S = 156.277\angle 4.13° \text{ kV}$$

(b)
$$I_S = CV_R + DI_R$$
$$= \left[\left(0.269 \times 10^{-3}\angle 90° \times \frac{132 \times 10^3}{\sqrt{3}}\right) + (0.995\angle 0.116° \times 382.71\angle -36.86°)\right]$$
$$I_S = 368.89\angle -34.19° \text{ A}$$

(ii)
$$\% V_{REG} = \frac{\left|\frac{V_S}{A}\right| - |V_R|}{|V_R|} \times 100 = \frac{\frac{156.277}{0.995} - 132}{132} \times 100$$
$$\% V_{REG} = 18.98\%$$

(iii)
$$P_S = \sqrt{3}|V_s I_s|\cos\phi_s$$
$$= \sqrt{3} \times 156.277 \times 10^3 \times 368.89 \times \cos(34.19° + 4.13°)$$
$$P_S = 78.33 \text{ MW}$$
$$Q_s = P_s.\tan\phi_s = \sqrt{3}|V_s I_s|\sin\phi_s$$

$$= \sqrt{3} \times 156.277 \times 10^3 \times 368.89 \times \sin(34.19° + 4.13°)$$

$$Q_s = 61.91 \text{ MVAR}$$

(iv)
$$\%\,\eta = \frac{P_R}{P_S} \times 100 = \frac{70}{78.33} \times 100 = 89.36\%$$

2.19 The per phase parameters of 50 Hz, 100 km long, 3-phase transmission line are R = 10 Ω, L = 111.7 mH, C = 0.9954 μF. The transmission line delivers 20 MW at a power factor of 0.8 lagging and 66 kV to a balanced load. Calculate the sending end voltage, efficiency and regulation using nominal-T representation.

[12 marks : 2017]

Solution:

Given that:

Resistance of line per phase, $R = 10\ \Omega$

Inductive reactance of line per phase,

$$X = 2\pi f L = 2\pi \times 50 \times 111.7 \times 10^{-3}$$
$$= 35.09\ \Omega$$

Capacitive susceptance of line per phase,

$$Y = 2\pi f C$$
$$Y = 2\pi \times 50 \times 0.9954 \times 10^{-6}$$
$$= 3.127 \times 10^{-4}\ \text{S}$$

Line impedance, $Z = (10 + j35.09)\ \Omega = 36.487\angle 74.093°\ \Omega$

Load power factor, $\cos\phi = 0.80$

Phase angle = 36.87° (lagging)

Receiving end line voltage, V_{RL} = 66 kV or 66000 V

Receiving end phase voltage, $V_R = \frac{66000}{\sqrt{3}} = 38105\ \text{V}$

Load current, $I_R = \frac{20 \times 10^6}{\sqrt{3} \times 66000 \times 0.8} = 218.7\ \text{A}$

Now, using T-method and taking receiving end voltage as reference phasor,

$$V_R = 38105\angle 0°\ \text{V}$$

and
$$I_R = 218.7\angle -36.87°\ \text{A}$$

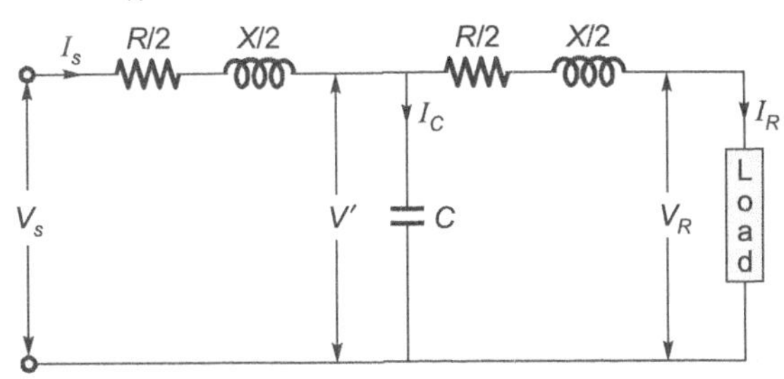

Phase voltage across condenser,

$$V' = V_R + I_R \frac{Z}{2}$$

$$V' = (38105\angle 0°) + \left[(218.7\angle -36.87°)\left(\frac{36.487\angle 74.093°}{2}\right)\right]$$

$$= (41282.07 + j2413.537) = 41352.562\angle 3.346°\ \text{V}$$

Charging current, $I_C = V'Y = (41352.562\angle 3.346°)\,(j3.127 \times 10^{-4})$

$$= (-0.7547 + j12.909) = 12.931\angle 93.346° \text{ A}$$

Sending end current, $I_S = I_R + I_C$

$$I_S = 218.7\angle -36.87° + 12.931\angle 93.346°$$
$$= (174.205 - j118.3114) = 210.5825\angle -34.1824° \text{ A}$$

Sending end voltage, $V_S = V' + I_S \frac{Z}{2}$

$$V_S = 41352.562\angle 3.346° + (210.5825\angle -34.1824°) \times \left(\frac{36.487\angle 74.093°}{2}\right)$$
$$= (44228.8773 + j4878.406) = 44497.106\angle 6.294° \text{ V}$$

Sending end line voltage, $V_{SL} = \sqrt{3} \times 44497.106$

$$= 77071.25 \text{ V or } 77.0712 \text{ kV}$$

Line efficiency,

$$\eta = \frac{\sqrt{3} V_{RL} I_{RL} \cos\phi_R}{\sqrt{3} V_{SL} I_{SL} \cos\phi_S} \text{ or } \frac{P_L}{\sqrt{3} V_{SL} I_{SL} \cos\phi_S}$$

$$= \frac{20 \times 10^6}{\sqrt{3} \times 77071.25 \times 210.5825 \times \cos[6.294° - (-34.1824°)]} \times 100$$

$$= 93.5312\%$$

$$\text{Voltage regulation} = \frac{V_{SL} - V_{RL}}{V_{RL}} \times 100$$

$$= \frac{77.0712 - 66}{66} \times 100 = 16.7745\%$$

2.20 (i) **Differentiate between characteristic impedance and surge impedance of a line. What do you mean by Surge Impedance Loading (SIL) of a transmission line?**

(ii) **A three-phase, 50 Hz transmission line is 400 km long. The voltage at the sending end is 220 kV. The line parameters are: $r = 0.125$ ohm/km, $x = 0.4$ ohm/km and $y = 2.8 \times 10^{-6}$ mho/km. Find the sending end current and receiving end voltage when there is no load on the line. Make a comment on the value of receiving end voltage.**

[20 marks : 2018]

Solution:

(i) Characteristic Impedance (Z_c):

Characteristic impedance of a line is the ratio of amplitudes of voltage and current of a single wave propagating along the line,

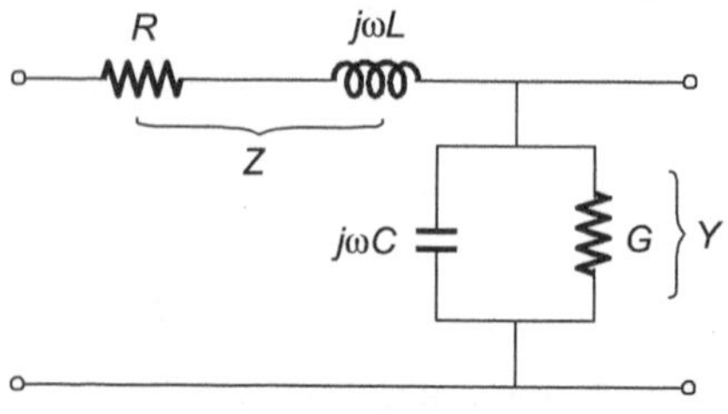

$$Z_c = \frac{V}{I} = \sqrt{\frac{Z}{y}}$$

where,

$$Z = R + j\omega L$$
$$Y = G + j\omega C$$

Surge Impedance (Z_s):

When the reactive VARs supplied by the line are equal to reactive VARs absorbed, the impedance offered by the line in such case is called surge impedance of the line

$$I^2 \omega L = V^2 \omega C$$

$$\frac{V}{I} = \sqrt{\frac{L}{C}} = Z_s$$

Surge Impedance Loading (SIL):

The loading condition in which the VARs absorbed by the line are equal to VARs generated by the line is called surge impedance loading of the line.

Under SIL the voltage throughout the length of the transmission line is same.

Surge impedance loading of a transmission line is the power transmitted to a purely resistive load equal to the surge impedance of the line.

$$\text{SIL} = \frac{V^2}{Z_s}\text{ MW}$$

(ii) Length of the line, $l = 400$ km, $f = 50$ Hz, sending end voltage, $V_s = 220$ kV

$$Z = (r + jx)\times l$$
$$= (0.125 + j0.4) \times 400 = (50 + j160)\ \Omega$$
$$Y = j2.8 \times 10^{-6} \times 400 = j1.12 \times 10^{-3}\ \mho$$
$$\gamma l = \sqrt{YZ} = \sqrt{j1.12\times10^{-3}\times(50+j160)}$$
$$= \sqrt{0.1877\angle 81.325^\circ} = 0.4332\angle 81.325^\circ$$
$$\gamma l = (\alpha l + j\beta l)$$
$$= (0.0653 + j0.4282)$$
$$Z_c = \sqrt{\frac{Z}{Y}} = \sqrt{\frac{50+j160}{j1.12\times10^{-3}}} = \sqrt{149670.13}\angle\left(\frac{-17.35^\circ}{2}\right)$$

Characteristic impedance of line,

$$Z_c = 386.87\angle -8.68^\circ\ \Omega$$
$$\alpha l = 0.0654$$
$$\beta l = 0.4282\times\frac{180}{\pi} = 24.53^\circ$$
$$\cosh\gamma l = \cosh(\alpha l + j\beta l)$$
$$\cosh\gamma l = \cosh\alpha l\cos\beta l + j\sinh\alpha l\sin\beta l$$
$$= \cosh(0.0654)\cos(24.53^\circ) + j\sinh(0.0654)\sin(24.53^\circ)$$
$$= 0.9121\angle 1.7^\circ$$
$$\sinh\gamma l = \sinh(\alpha l + j\beta l)$$
$$\sinh\gamma l = \sinh\alpha l\cos\beta l + j\cosh\alpha l\sin\beta l$$
$$= \sinh(0.0654)\cos(24.53^\circ) + j\cosh(0.0654)\sin(24.53^\circ)$$
$$= 0.4202\angle 81.86^\circ$$

At no load,

$$I_R = 0$$
$$V_S = \cosh\gamma l\, V_{R0}$$
$$V_s = 0.9121\angle 1.7^\circ \times V_{R0}$$
$$V_{R0} = \frac{220}{0.9121\angle 1.7^\circ}$$

No load receiving end voltage, $V_{Ro} = 241.2\angle -1.7^\circ$ kV $(L-L)$

Sending end current, $I_s = \dfrac{\sinh\gamma l}{Z_c}\times V_{R_0}$

$$= \frac{0.4203\angle 81.86^\circ}{386.87\angle -8.68^\circ}\times\frac{241.2}{\sqrt{3}}\angle -1.7^\circ\times10^3$$
$$I_s = 151.25\angle 88.84^\circ\text{ A}$$

Effect of line capacitance causes the no load receiving end voltage to be more than the sending end voltage. It becomes more pronounce as the length increases.

2.21 A 220 kV three-phase transmission line is 90 km long. The resistance is 0.1 Ω/km and the inductance is 1.0 mH/km. Use the short transmission line model to find:

(i) Voltage at the sending end, and

(ii) Voltage regulation at the sending end.

[12 marks : 2019]

Solution:

Note: Data regarding load is not given hence.

Assume: P_L = 10 MW at unity power factor

Given,

$$V_R = 220 \text{ kV}$$

$$Z = [0.1 + j(2\pi \times 50 \times 1 \times 10^{-3})] \times 90$$

$$= 29.672\angle 72.34°\ \Omega$$

$$I_R = \frac{10\times 10^6}{\sqrt{3}\times 220\times 10^3} = 26.24 \text{ A}$$

$$\bar{V}_s = \bar{V}_R + \bar{I}Z_R$$

$$= \frac{220}{\sqrt{3}}\times 10^3 + 26.24\times 29.672\angle 72.34°$$

$$\bar{V}_s = 127.2554\angle 0.334 \text{ kV phase}$$

$$\left|\vec{V}_{sL}\right| = 127.255\times\sqrt{3} = 220.412 \text{ kV line}$$

(ii) Voltage regulation,

$$|VR| = \frac{|V_s|-|V_R|}{|V_R|} = \left(\frac{220.412-220}{220}\right)\times 100 = 0.187\%$$

2.22 A three-phase equilateral transmission line has a total corona loss of 55 kW at 110 kV and 100 kW at 114 kV. What is the disruptive critical voltage between lines ? What is the corona loss at 120 kV?

[12 marks : 2020]

Solution:

Three phase corona power loss

$$P_c = 3\times\frac{244}{\delta}(f+25)\sqrt{\frac{r}{d}}(V_{Ph}-V_{do})^2\times 10^{-5} \text{ kW/h}$$

As air density factor, δ, supply frequency *f*, radius of conductor *r* and conductor spacing same.

$$P_c \propto (V_{Ph}-V_{do})^2$$

So,

$$\frac{P_{c1}}{P_{c2}} = \frac{(V_{ph1}-V_{do})^2}{(V_{ph2}-V_{do})^2}$$

$$\frac{55}{100} = \frac{\left(\frac{110}{\sqrt{3}}-V_{do}\right)^2}{\left(\frac{114}{\sqrt{3}}-V_{do}\right)^2} = \frac{(63.50-V_{do})^2}{(65.81-V_{do})^2}$$

$$0.7416 = \frac{63.50-V_{do}}{65.81-V_{do}}$$

$$(0.7416)(65.81-V_{do}) = (63.5-V_{do})$$

$$48.806-0.7416V_{do} = 63.5-V_{do}$$

$$0.2584V_{do} = 14.693$$

$$V_{do} = 56.861 \text{ kV}$$

For corona loss at 120 kV

As $$P_c \propto \left(\frac{120}{\sqrt{3}} - V_{do}\right)^2 \propto (69.282 - V_{do})^2$$

$$\frac{P_c}{55} = \frac{(69.282 - V_{do})^2}{(63.50 - V_{do})^2}$$

Using $$V_{do} = 56.861 \text{ kV}$$

$$\frac{P_c}{55} = \left[\frac{69.282 - 56.861}{63.50 - 56.861}\right]^2 = \left(\frac{12.421}{6.639}\right)^2$$

Corona loss, $$P_c = 192.5176 \text{ kW}$$

Disruptive critical voltage between lines

$$= \sqrt{3}V_{do} = \sqrt{3} \times 56.861 \text{ kV} = 98.486 \text{ kV}$$

2.23 A three-phase, 50 Hz transmission line has a span of 250 km. It supplies a balanced load of 25 MVA at 0.8 lagging power factor. The receiving end load voltage is 132 kV. The line conductors are spaced equilaterally 3 m apart. The conductor resistance is 0.11 ohm/km and its effective diameter is 1.6 cm, Using the nominal-*T* method, find sending end voltage and current, Also determine the voltage regulation at receiving end of transmission line.

[20 marks : 2021]

Solution:

Given : Line length, $$L = 250 \text{ km}$$

$$V_R = 132 \text{ V}$$

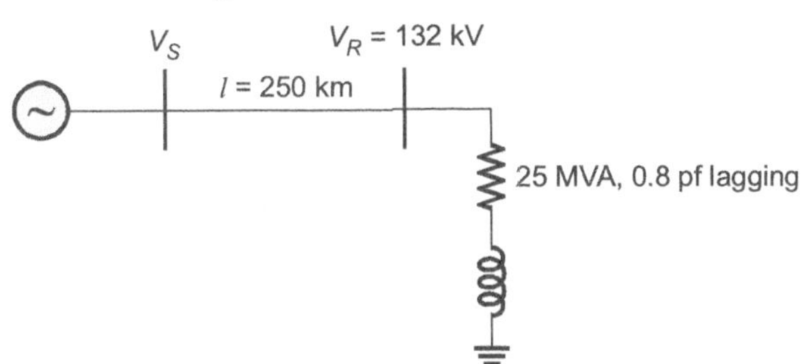

Conductor resistance, $$R_1 = 0.11\ \Omega\text{/km/ph}$$

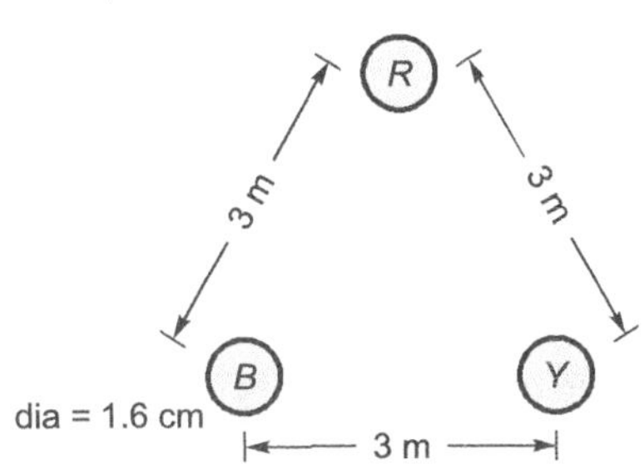

Inductance per phase, $$L_{ph} = 2 \times 10^{-7} \ln\left(\frac{D}{r'}\right) = 2 \times 10^{-7} \ln \frac{3}{\left(\frac{1.6}{2} \times 10^{-2} \times 0.7788\right)}$$

Capacitance per phase,
$$C_{ph} = \frac{2\pi \in_0 \in_r}{\ln\left(\frac{D}{r}\right)} = \frac{2\pi \times 8.854 \times 10^{-12} \times 1}{\ln\left(\frac{3}{\frac{1.6}{2} \times 10^{-2}}\right)} = 9.386 \times 10^{-12} \text{ F/m}$$

$$= 9.386 \text{ nF/km/ph}$$

Nominal T-network, the equivalent circuit can be drawn as,

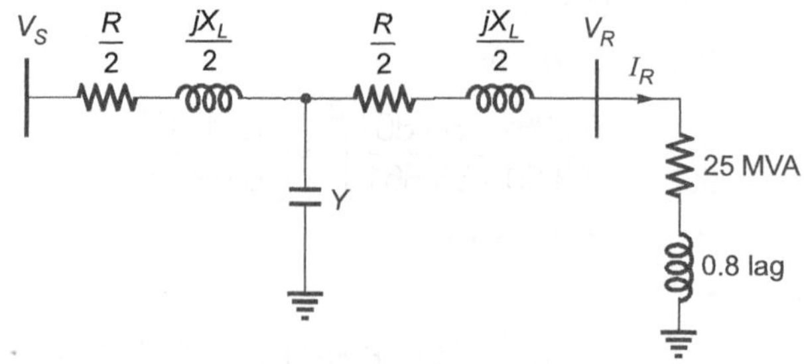

In lumped parameter,
Total impedance,

$$Z = (R + j\omega L) \times L$$
$$= [0.11 \times j(2\pi \times 50 \times 1.235 \times 10^{-3})] \times 250$$
$$= 27.5 + j97\ \Omega = 100.819\angle 74.14°\ \Omega/\text{ph}$$

Total admittance,

$$Y = j\omega C l$$
$$= j(2\pi \times 50 \times 9.386 \times 10^{-9}) \times 250$$
$$= 7.371 \times 10^{-4}\angle 90°\ \mho/\text{ph}$$

For nominal T-network

$$A = D = \left(1 + \frac{YZ}{2}\right)$$
$$= 1 + \frac{(7.371 \times 10^{-4}\angle 90°)(100.819\angle 74.14°)}{2} = 0.964\angle 0.6°$$
$$B = Z\left[1 + \frac{YZ}{4}\right]$$

$\Rightarrow$
$$B = 100.819\angle 74.17°\left[1 + \frac{7.371 \times 10^{-4}\angle 90° \times 100.819\angle 74.17°}{4}\right]$$
$$B = 98.98\angle 74.45°\ \Omega$$

$\Rightarrow$
$$C = Y = 7.371 \times 10^{-4}\angle 90°\ \mho$$

Receiving end current,

$$|I_R| = \frac{S_R}{\sqrt{3} \cdot V_R} = \frac{25 \times 10^6}{\sqrt{3} \times 132 \times 10^3} = 109.346 \text{ A}$$
$$\bar{I}_R = 109.346\angle -\cos^{-1} 0.8 = 109.346\angle -36.86° \text{ A}$$

1. The sending end voltage (V_s)

$$V_{sph} = A\frac{\bar{V}_{RL}}{\sqrt{3}} + B \cdot \bar{I}_R$$

$$V_{sph} = 0.964\angle 0.6^\circ \times \frac{132 \times 10^3}{\sqrt{3}} + 98.98\angle 74.45^\circ \times 109.346\angle -36.86^\circ$$

$$V_{sph} = 82.41\angle 5.13^\circ \text{ kV/ph [L-N]}$$

$$V_{SL} = \sqrt{3} \times 91.89\angle 8.8^\circ$$

$$= 142.74\angle 5.13^\circ \text{ kV [L-L] (sending end voltage line to line)}$$

2. Sending end current :

$$I_{Sph} = I_{SL} = \frac{C\bar{V}_{RL}}{\sqrt{3}} + D \cdot \bar{I}_R$$

$$= 7.371 \times 10^{-4}\angle 90^\circ \times \frac{132}{\sqrt{3}} \times 10^3 + (0.964\angle 0.6^\circ) \times 109.346\angle -36.86^\circ$$

$$= 85.219\angle -4.15^\circ \text{ A}$$

3.

$$\% V_{reg} = \frac{\left|\frac{V_{SL}}{A}\right| - |V_{RL}|}{|V_{RL}|} \times 100$$

$$\text{Regulation } \% V_{reg} = \frac{\frac{142.74}{0.964} - 132}{132} \times 100 = 12.10\%$$

2.24 **(i) A single phase overhead transmission line of 50 km length is to be designed with copper conductor of 5.04 cm diameter. It is expected to have a maximum line reactance of 31.4 Ω. Determine the optimal spacing between the conductors.**

(ii) Discuss the impact on line reactance if the conductors in the above case are replaced by stranded bundle conductors of the same outer diameter and line spacing. Assume an ACSR conductor with 6 conductors of Aluminium of 1.68 cm diameter each around one central steel conductor for your analysis.

[6+6 = 12 marks : 2021]

Solution:

(i) Given data is :

Copper conductor,

$$l = 50 \text{ km}$$

$$\text{Dia} = 5.04 \text{ cm},$$

$$\text{Radius, } r = \frac{5.04}{2} = 2.52 \text{ cm}$$

$$\text{Line reactance, } X_L = (2\pi f L)l = 31.4\ \Omega$$

$$\text{Inductance, } L = \frac{31.4}{2\pi \times 50 \times 50 \times 10^3} = 2 \times 10^{-6} \text{ H/m}$$

$$L = 2 \times 10^{-7} \ln\left(\frac{d}{r}\right) = 2 \times 10^{-6} \text{ H/m}$$

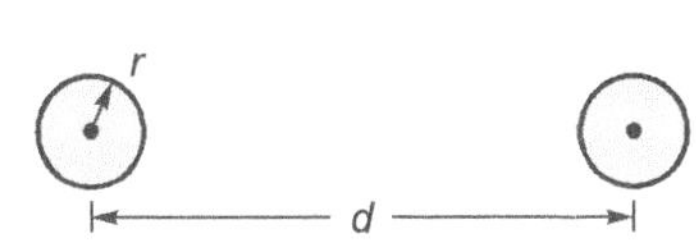

For copper assumed single conductor hence $r' \approx r$ is considered

$$2 \times 10^{-7} \ln\left(\frac{d}{2.52 \times 10^{-2}}\right) = 2 \times 10^{-6}$$

$$d = 555.066 \text{ m (which is not practical)}$$

(ii) ACSR - 7 stranded :

$\Rightarrow$ Dia of each strand = 1.68 cm

We know,

$$D = (2x - 1)\text{dia}$$
$$= (2 \times 2 - 1) \times 1.68 \times 10^{-2}$$
$$= 0.0504 \text{ m}$$

So, radius of whole ASCR system

$$r = \frac{D}{2} = 0.0252 \text{ m}$$

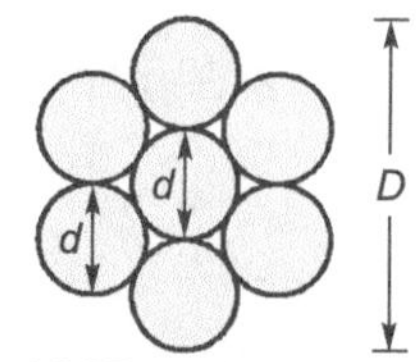

ACSR conductors

Inductance of ASCR conductors,

$$L_{ACSR} = 2\times 10^{-7} \ln\left(\frac{d}{0.7788\times r}\right)$$
$$= 2\times 10^{-7} \ln\frac{555.066}{(0.7788\times 0.0252)}$$
$$L_{ASCR} = 2.05 \times 10^{-6} \text{ H/m}$$

So, we know reactance can be given as

$$X_L = (2\pi fL)\times l$$
$$= 2\pi \times 50 \times 2.05 \times 10^{-6} \times 50 \times 10^3$$
$$\text{Reactance, } X_L = 32.20\ \Omega$$

2.25 (i) **What do you mean by Tuned Power Lines? A 3-phase, 50 Hz, 500 kV, lossless transmission line is 600 km long. The line inductance is 1 mH/km/phase and capacitance is 10 nF/km/phase. Determine the phase constant β, surge impedance Z_c, velocity of propagation v, and line wavelength λ.**

(ii) **A 200 km long, 50 Hz, 3-phase transmission line has a total series impedance of 40 + *j*125 Ω and shunt admittance of 10^{-3} ℧. It is feeding to a load of 62.5 MVA at 220 kV with 0.8 pf lagging. Find the sending end voltage, current and power factor using nominal π-method.**

[10 + 10 marks : 2022]

Solution:

(i) A tuned line is where the receiving-end voltage and current are numerically equal to the corresponding sending-end values so that there is no voltage drop on load.

$$V_{L\text{-}L} = 500 \text{ kV}$$
$$f = 50 \text{ Hz}$$
$$L = 1 \text{ mH/km/phase}$$
$$C = 10 \text{ nF/km/phase}$$

Surge impedance,

$$Z_C = \sqrt{\frac{L}{C}}$$
$$= \sqrt{\frac{1\times 10^{-3}}{10\times 10^{-9}}} = 316.22\ \Omega$$

Velocity of propagation,

$$V = \frac{1}{\sqrt{LC}}$$
$$= \frac{1}{\sqrt{1\times 10^{-3}\times 10\times 10^{-9}}}$$

$$= 3.162 \times 10^5 \text{ km/sec}$$

Line wavelength, $\lambda = \dfrac{V}{f}$

$$= \frac{3.162 \times 10^5}{50}$$

$$= 6324.55 \text{ km}$$

Phase constant, $\beta = \dfrac{2\pi}{\lambda}$ rad/km

$$= \frac{2\pi}{6324.55} \text{ rad/km}$$

$$= 9.929 \times 10^{-4} \text{ rad/km}$$

(ii) Given that $Z = 40 + j125$

$$Y = j10^{-3} \text{ ℧}$$

$$V_s = AV_R + BI_R$$

$$I_S = CV_R + DI_R$$

$$V_R = \frac{220}{\sqrt{3}} = 127 \text{ kV} \quad \text{(Phase)}$$

$$I_R = \frac{62.5 \times 10^3}{\sqrt{3} \times 220} = 164 \text{ A}$$

$$\phi_R = \cos^{-1}(0.8) = 36.86°$$

A, B, C, D for nominal π can be calculated as

$$A = D = 1 + \frac{YZ}{2}$$

$$= 1 + \frac{j10^{-3}(40 + j125)}{2} = 0.9377\angle 1.22°$$

$$B = Z = 40 + j125 = 131.24\angle 72.25°$$

$$C = \left(1 + \frac{YZ}{4}\right)Y$$

$$= \left(1 + \frac{j10^{-3}(40 + j125)}{4}\right) j10^{-3}$$

$$= 96.88 \times 10^{-5}\angle 90.59°$$

$$V_s = 0.9377\angle 1.22 \times 127 \times 10^3\angle 0° + 131.24\angle 72.25° \times 164\angle -36.86°$$

$$= 137.42\angle 6.2°$$

$$I_s = 96.88 \times 10^{-5}\angle 90.59° \times 127 \times 10^3\angle 0° + 0.9377\angle 1.22 \times 164\angle -36.86°$$

$$= 128.13\angle 15.1°$$

$$\phi_s = 15.1° - 6.2° = 8.9°$$

$$\text{P.F.} = \cos\phi_s = \cos 8.9° = 0.987 \text{ lead}$$

2.26 A three phase overhead transmission line in delta configuration is operating at 400 kV between phases at 50 Hz. The overall conductor diameter is 5.0 cm each. Find the allowable minimum spacing between the conductors to avoid corona loss under fair weather condition.

Also find the corona loss under stormy weather condition where the disruptive critical voltage reduces by 20%.
(Assume air density factor of 0.95, irregularity factor of 0.85 and disruptive critical voltage of 450 kV (L-L) under fair weather condition).

[12 marks : 2022]

Solution:

Given : Supply voltage, $V = 400\text{ kV}$ (Δ-connected)

Critical disruptive voltage, $V_C = 450\text{ kV}$

Air density factor, $\delta = 0.95$

Irregularity factor, $M = 0.85$

As Corona loss $\propto (V - V_C)^2$ ...(1)

Diameter of conductor, $D = 5.0\text{ cm}$

Radius, $r = 2.5\text{ cm}$

Frequency, $f = 50\text{ Hz}$

And breakdown strength of air, $g = 21.1\text{ kV/cm (rms)}$

So, $$V_C = Mg\delta_r \ln\left(\frac{d}{r}\right)$$

where d is the distance between the conductor.

So, minimum distance for no corona loss is

when $$V_C = \frac{V}{\sqrt{3}} \quad \text{(from (1))}$$

$$\Rightarrow \quad \frac{400}{\sqrt{3}} = 0.85 \times 21.1 \times 0.95 \times 2.5 \times \ln\left(\frac{d}{2.5}\right)$$

$$\Rightarrow \quad d = 5.6565\text{ m}$$

If critical disruptive voltage reduces by 20%,

i.e., $$V_{C1} = 450 \times (1 - 0.2)$$
$$V_{C1} = 360\text{ kV}$$

Corona Power loss, $$P_L = 242.2 \times 10^{-5} \times \frac{f+25}{\delta} \times \sqrt{\frac{r}{d}} \times (V_{Ph} - V_C)^2 \text{ kW/km/Phase}$$

$$= 242.2 \times 10^{-5} \times \frac{50+25}{0.95} \times \sqrt{\frac{2.5}{565.65}} \times (230.94 - 207.84)^2 \text{ kW/km/Phase}$$

$$= 6.783\text{ kW/km/Phase}$$

2.27 Calculate the inductance and capacitance of the single-circuit, two-bundle conductor, 200 km long line as shown below. The diameter of each conductor is 5 cm.

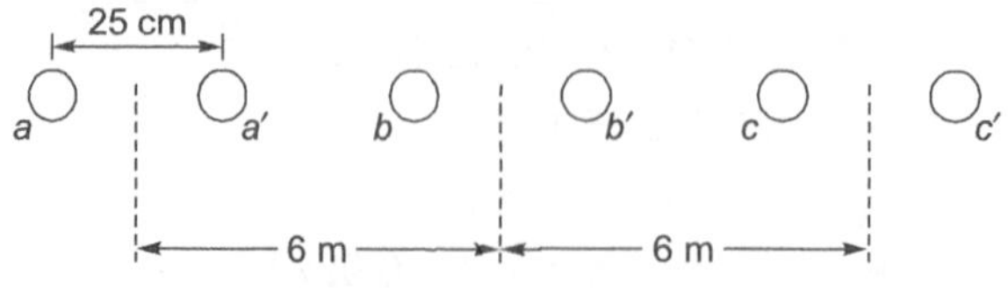

[12 marks : 2023]

Solution:

For bundle conductors,

$$L = 2\times10^{-7}\ln\frac{D_m}{D_s}\ \text{H/m}$$

$$C = \frac{2\pi\epsilon_o}{\ln\frac{D_m}{D_s}}\ \text{F/m}$$

Here, $D_m = 3\sqrt{d_1d_2d_3} = 3\sqrt{6\times6\times12} = 7.56$ m

The diameter, $D = 5$ cm

$$r = \frac{D}{2} = 2.5\ \text{cm}$$

$$D_s \text{ for inductance} = \sqrt[4]{DaaDaa'Da'aDa'a'}$$

$$Daa = Da'a' = 0.7788 \times 2.5 = 1.947$$

$$Da'a = Daa' = 25$$

$$D_s = \sqrt[4]{1.947\times25\times25\times1.947} = 6.976\ \text{cm}$$

$$L = 2\times10^{-7}\ln\frac{756}{6.976} = 9.37\times10^{-7}\ \text{H/m}$$

For 200 km length, $L = 200 \times 10^3 \times 9.37 \times 10^{-7} = 0.1874$ H

$$D_s \text{ for capacitor} = \sqrt[4]{DaaDaa'Da'aDa'a'}$$

Here, $Daa = Da'a' = 2.5$ cm

$$Daa' = Da'a = 25\ \text{cm}$$

$$D_s = \sqrt[4]{2.5\times25\times25\times2.5} = 7.9\ \text{cm}$$

$$C = \frac{2\pi\epsilon_o}{\ln\frac{D_m}{n_s}} = \frac{2\pi\times8.854\times10^{-12}}{\ln\frac{756}{7.9}} = 12.2\times10^{-12}\ \text{F/m}$$

For 200 km, $C = 200 \times 10^3 \times 12.2 \times 10^{-12} = 2.44\ \mu$F

2.28 A 250 km long, three-phase, 50 Hz, transmission line has the following line constants :

$$A = D = 0.9\angle1°,\quad B = 120\angle72°,\quad C = 0.001\angle90°\ \Omega$$

The sending end voltage is 230 kV.
Find:
(i) Line charging current
(ii) Maximum active power that can be transferred at 220 kV and also the corresponding reactive power.

[20 marks : 2023]

Solution:

$$A = D = 0.9\angle1°$$

$$B = 120\angle72°$$

$$C = 0.001\angle90°$$

$$V_s = 230\ \text{kV},\ l = 250\ \text{km}$$

(i) Line charging current, $I_c = VY$

In main lines Y is C parameter

$$I_c = \frac{230\times10^3}{\sqrt{3}}\times0.001 = 132.8\ \text{Amp}$$

(ii) We know that, $P_{R,\max} = \frac{V_S V_R}{B} - \left|\frac{A}{B}\right| |V_R^2| \cos(\theta - \alpha)$

$$V_S|_{Ph} = \frac{230}{\sqrt{3}} = 132.8 \text{ kV}$$

$$V_R|_{Ph} = \frac{220}{\sqrt{3}} = 127 \text{ kV}$$

$$P_{R,\max} = \frac{132.8 \times 127}{120} - \frac{0.9}{120}(127)^2 \cos(72 - 1)$$

$$= 101.163 \text{ MW/ph}$$

For 3-ϕ, $P_{R,\max} = 303.5$ MW

$$\text{R.P. at } P_{R,\max} = -\left(\frac{A}{B}\right) V_R^2 \sin(\theta - \alpha)$$

$$= -\frac{0.9}{120}(127)^2 \sin(72 - 1) = -114.38 \text{ MVAR/ph}$$

For 3-ϕ = 343.13 MVAR to be injected.

3. Compensation Techniques, Voltage Profile Control & Load Frequency Control

3.1 The voltage of a particular bus is regulated by controlling the

(a) active power of the bus (b) reactive power of the bus

(c) phase angle (d) phase angle and reactive power

[2 marks : 2001]

Solution: (b)

Reactive power of the bus.

If the reactive power generated is greater than consumed, the voltage goes up and vice-versa.

3.2 Why shunt capacitors are preferred over series capacitors for improvement of power factor in distribution system?

[4 marks : 2002]

Solution:

- Series capacitor compensation reduces the series impedance of the line which causes voltage drop and is the most important factor in finding the maximum power transmission capability of a line.
  When series compensation is used, these are chances of sustained over voltages to the ground the series capacitor terminals. This over voltage can be the power limiting criterion at high degree of compensation.
- The shunt capacitors are used across an inductive load so as to provide part of the reactive VARs required by the load to keep the voltage within desirable limits.
- For the same voltage boost, the reactive power capacity of a shunt capacitor is greater than that of a series capacitor. The shunt capacitor improves the pf of the load while the series capacitor has hardly any impact on the pf.
- Series capacitors are more effective for long lines for improvement of system scarcity.

3.3 Two 200 MVA alternators operate in parallel. The frequency drops in the first machine from 50 Hz at no load to 48 Hz at full load, whereas in case of the other machine, the frequency drops from 50 Hz to 47 Hz under the same conditions.

(a) How the two machines will share a total load of 300 MW?

(b) Determine the maximum load at unity power factor which can be delivered by the two machines without overloading any of them.

[13 marks : 2003]

Solution:

(a) From the information given in the question, for machine 1

$$f_1 = \frac{48-50}{200}P_1 + 50$$

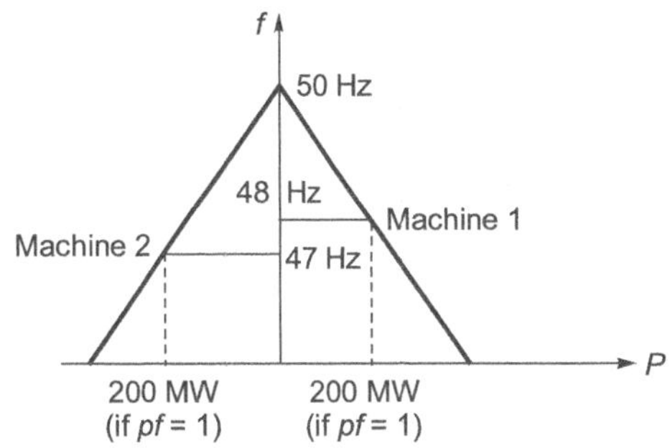

and for machine 2,

$$f_2 = \frac{47-50}{200}P_2 + 50$$

and $P_1 + P_2 = 300$ MW ...(*i*)

as the two alternators working in parallel,

$$f_1 = f_2$$

$$\left(\frac{48-50}{200}\right)P_1 + 50 = \left(\frac{47-50}{200}\right)P_2 + 50$$

$$2P_1 = 3P_2 \qquad ...(ii)$$

On solving equation (*i*) and (*ii*),

$$P_1 = 180 \text{ MW and } P_2 = 120 \text{ MW}$$

(b) At unity power factor rating of the machine = 200 MW

Assuming machine 2 works on maximum load of 200 MW, $P_2 = 200$ MW

From equation (*ii*), $P_1 = 300$ MW

so machines 1 will be overloaded.

If machine 1 works on maximum load of 200 MW, $P_1 = 200$ MW

From equation (*ii*), $P_2 = 133.33$ MW

Machine 2 is not overloaded.

Hence, $P_1 = 200$ MW, $P_2 = 133.33$ MW

Total load = 333.333 MW

3.4 A power system has a total load of 1260 MW at 50 Hz. The load varies 1.5% for every 1% change in frequency. Find the steady state frequency deviation when a 60 MW load is suddenly tripped. The speed regulation parameter $R = 0.0025$ Hz per MW.

[10 marks : 2010]

Solution:

Steady state frequency deviation, $$\Delta f = -\left(\frac{1}{B+\left(\frac{1}{R}\right)}\right)\Delta P_D$$

where, ΔP_D = Change in load

$\Rightarrow$ ΔP_D = –60 MW (as load is reduced)

R = 0.0025 Hz/MW

$$B = \frac{\left(\frac{\partial P_D}{\partial f}\right)}{P_r} \text{ pu MW/unit change in frequency}$$

$$\Rightarrow \quad B = \frac{\partial P_D}{\partial f} \text{ MW/unit change in frequency}$$

$$\Rightarrow \quad B = \frac{1.5\% \text{ of } 1250}{1\% \text{ of } 50} = \frac{1.5 \times 1250}{1 \times 50} = 37.5 \text{ MW/Hz}$$

$$\Delta f = -\left(\frac{1}{B + \left(\frac{1}{R}\right)}\right) \Delta P_D \text{ Hz}$$

$$\Rightarrow \quad \Delta f = -\left\{\frac{1}{37.5 + \frac{1}{0.0025}}\right\} \times (-60) \text{ Hz} = 0.137 \text{ Hz}$$

3.5 **In a power system, how is the receiving end voltage controlled?** [4 marks : 2012]

Solution:

The receiving end voltage, in power system, can be controlled by using

- Shunt capacitors
- Series capacitors
- Synchronous transformers
- Boster transformers

The first three methods are categorised as reactive var injection method.

For an isolated small system, the voltage control is done by adjusting the excitation of the generator at the sending end. The larger the reactive power required by the load the more is the excitation to be provided at the sending end.

3.6 **A 3-phase, 50 Hz transmission line at 11 kV delivers a load of 1000 kW at 0.8 pF (lagging) over 10 kms. Calculate the line current, receiving end voltage and efficiency of transmission. Resistance and reactance of each line conductor may be assumed to be 0.5 Ω/km and 0.56 Ω/km respectively.**

[10 marks : 2012]

Solution:

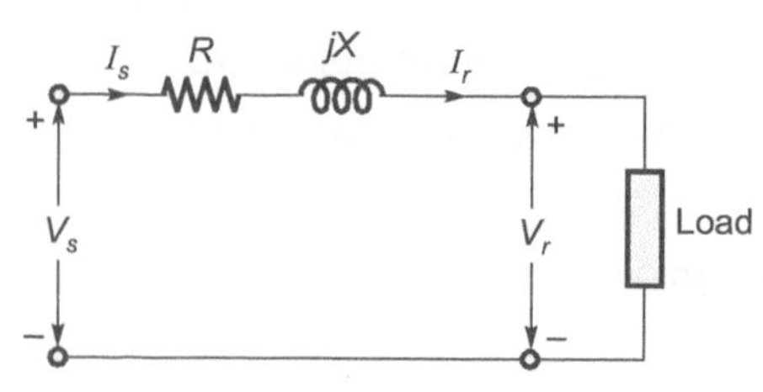

$$V_s = \frac{11000}{\sqrt{3}} = 6351 \text{ V}$$

$$I_r = \frac{1000 \times 10^3}{3 \times V_r \times 0.8} = \frac{416.67 \times 10^3}{V_r}$$

$$V_s = V_r + I_r R \cos\phi_r + I_r \times \sin\phi_r$$

$$6351 = V_r + \frac{416.67 \times 10^3}{V_r}[5 \times 0.8 + 5.6 \times 0.6]$$

$$6351 = V_r + \frac{3066.67 \times 10^3}{V_r}$$

$$V_r^2 - 6351 V_r + 3066.67 \times 10^3 = 0$$

$$V_r = 5824.5 \text{ V} \quad \text{or} \quad 526.5 \text{ V}$$

V_r cannot be 526.5 V.

Therefore, $\quad V_r = 5824.5 \text{ V}$

$$\text{Line current} = \frac{416.67 \times 10^3}{5824.5} = 71.5\text{ A}$$

$$\text{Receiving end line voltage} = \frac{\sqrt{3} \times 5824.5}{1000} = 10.09\text{ kV}$$

$$\text{Efficiency} = \frac{\text{Power delivered at the receiving end}}{\text{Power sent at the sending end}}$$

$$= \frac{10}{10 + 3\left[(71.5)^2 \times 5\right]} \times 100 = 90.3\%$$

3.7 **Differentiate between load-frequency control and economic dispatch control.** **[5 marks : 2012]**

Solution:

The presence of an integral controller aids us to attain better dynamic response with zero steady state deviation in frequency whenever there is a variation in load. This variation in load also disturbs the an economic dispatch of load. Hence, in addition to an integral controller, an economic dispatch controller should also be provided for satisfactory operation of the power system. The block diagram of a load frequency control with economic dispatch control is shown in figure.

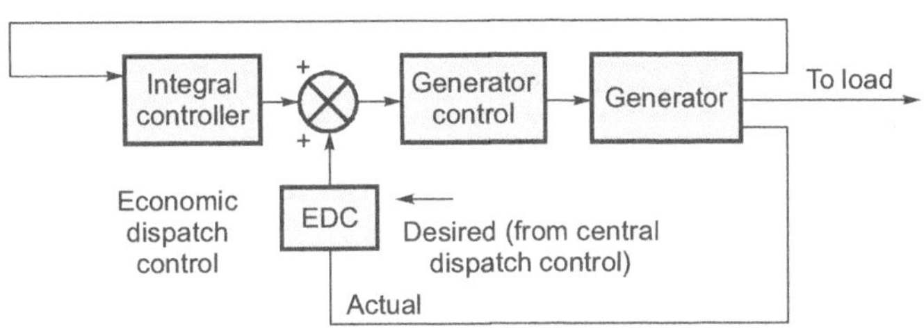

Block diagram of LFC with EDC

As shown in the block diagram, if there is any variation in load, the load frequency controller, which is fast-acting (within zero seconds) responds and actualises the speed changer (generator control) accordingly. The economic dispatch controller, which is slow acting (one minute), responds to the load change together with die input from the central dispatch control and an error signal is generated. This error signal together with the error signal generated by integral controller actualises the speed changer.

Since the load frequency controller is fast acting and economic dispatch controller is slow acting, the power system may operate with *EDC* error only for few seconds before the *EDC* generates a command signal

3.8 **A 1000 MW control area-1 is interconnected with control area-2. The 1000 MW area has the system parameters as follows:**

$$R = 2\text{ Hz/p.u. MW}$$

Damping coefficient = 0.01 p.u. MW/Hz and $\Delta P_{D_1} = 0.01\text{ p.u. MW}$

Area-2 has the same parameters of the 5000 MW base. Compute the static frequency drop and static tie-line power. Consider 5000 MW as base.

[10 marks : 2015]

Solution:

Given data:

Area-1: Speed Regulation (R_1) = 2 Hz/pu MW

Damping coefficient (β_1) = 0.01 pu MW/Hz

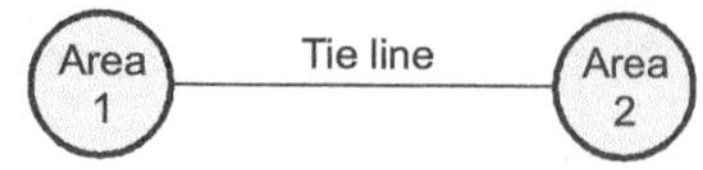

$$\Delta P_{D_1} = 0.01 \text{ pu MW}$$

$$\text{Capacity of power } P_1 = 1000 \text{ MW}$$

Area-2:

$$\text{Speed Regulation } (R_2) = 2 \text{ Hz/pu MW}$$

$$\text{Damping coefficient } (\beta_2) = 0.01 \text{ pu MW/Hz}$$

$$\Delta P_{D_2} = 0.01 \text{ pu MW}$$

$$\text{Capacity of power } P_2 = 5000 \text{ MW}$$

As per new base:

Area-2:

$$R_2 = 2 \text{ Hz/pu MW}$$

$$\beta_2 = 0.01 \text{ pu MW/Hz}$$

$$\Delta P_{D_2} = 0.01 \text{ pu MW}$$

$$P_2 = 5000 \text{ MW}$$

Area-1:

$$R_{new} = R_{old} \times \frac{P_{new}}{P_{old}}$$

$$R_{new} = 2 \times \frac{5000}{1000} = 10 = \text{Hz/pu MW} = R_1$$

$$\beta_1 = 0.01 \text{ pu MW/Hz}$$

$$\Delta P_{D_{1(new)}} = \Delta P_{D_{1(old)}} \times \frac{P_{old}}{P_{new}} = 0.01 \times \frac{1000}{5000}$$

$$\Delta P_{D_{1(new)}} = 2 \times 10^{-3} \text{ pu MW}$$

$$a_{12} = \frac{P_1}{P_2} = \frac{1000}{5000} = \frac{1}{5} = 0.2$$

(*i*) Steady state frequency (or) Static frequency drop = (Δf)

$$\boxed{\Delta f = \frac{-(a_{12}\Delta P_{D_1} + \Delta P_{D_2})}{\beta_2 + a_{12}\beta_1}}$$

where,

$$\beta_1 = \beta_1 + \frac{1}{R_1} = 0.01 + \frac{1}{10} = 0.11$$

$$\beta_2 = \beta_2 + \frac{1}{R_2} = 0.01 + \frac{1}{2} = 0.51$$

Substituting in the above formula,

$$\Delta f = \frac{-(0.2 \times 2 \times 10^{-3} + 0.01)}{0.51 + 0.2 \times 0.11} = -0.0195 \text{ pu Hz}$$

For 50 Hz $\Rightarrow$ $\Delta f = -0.0195 \times 50 = -0.975$ Hz

(*ii*) Static tie line power,

$$\Delta P_{Tie} = \frac{\beta_1(\Delta P_{D_2}) - \beta_2(\Delta P_{D_1})}{(\beta_2 + a_{12}\beta_1)}$$

$$= \frac{0.11 \times 0.01 - 0.51 \times 2 \times 10^{-3}}{0.51 + 0.2 \times 0.11} = 1.503 \times 10^{-4} \text{ pu MW}$$

For 5000 MW of base,

$$\Delta P_{Tie} = 1.503 \times 10^{-4} \times 5000$$

$$= 0.7515 \text{ MW}$$

4. Distribution Systems, Cables and Insulators

4.1 For a certain industrial organisation the maximum and minimum power demands are 50 MW and 10 MW respectively. Its load duration curve can be approximated as shown in Fig. below. The hydro power available at the time of minimum regulated flow is just sufficient to take a peak load of 60 MWh per day. Further, it is observed that it will be economical to pump water from fail race to the reservoir tank by utilizing the steam power plant during off peak periods and thus running the station at 100 percent load factor. If the efficiency of the steam electric conversion is 60%, calculate the maximum capacity of each type of plant.

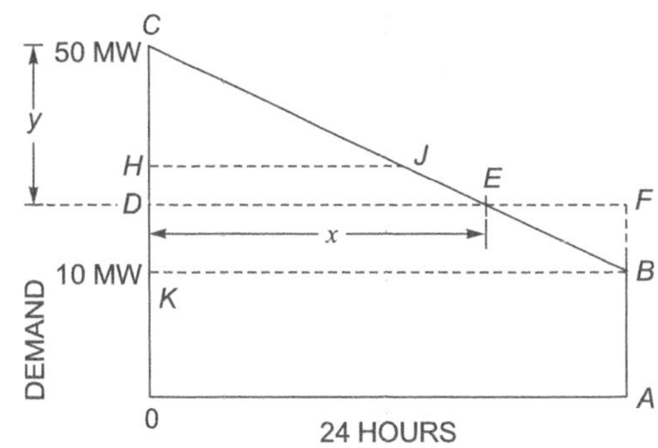

Load duration curve

[14 marks : 2006]

Solution:

OCBA represents the load duration curve for the combined system as shown in figure. The total maximum demand (i.e. 50 MW) is represented by *OC*, whereas the minimum demand (i.e. 10 MW) is represented by *OD*.

Let, *OD* = Capacity of steam plant

DC = Capacity of hydro plant

Area *CHJ* = The energy available from hydro plant in the low flow period

Area *EFB* = The off-peak period energy available from steam plant

The energy of hydro plant is represented by area *HDEJ* and available from reservoir has been supplied by steam power plant represented by area *FBE*. As steam electric conversion is 60%.

$$\therefore \quad \text{Area } HDEJ = 0.6 \times \text{Area } FBE \quad \ldots(i)$$

$$\text{But,} \quad \text{Area } HDEJ = \text{Area } CDE - \text{Area } CHJ = \frac{1}{2}xy - 60 \text{ MW}$$

$$\text{Now,} \quad \text{Area } FBE = \frac{1}{2} \times EF \times FB = \left[\frac{1}{2}(24-x)\ (40{,}000-y)\right]$$

Put in equation (*i*),

$$\frac{1}{2}xy - 60{,}000 = 0.6\left[\frac{1}{2}(24-x)(40{,}000-y)\right]$$

$$\text{or} \quad 0.5\,xy - 60{,}000 = 0.6\left[\frac{1}{2}(9{,}60{,}000 - 24y - 40{,}000x + xy)\right]$$

$$\text{or} \quad 0.5\,xy - 60{,}000 = 288{,}000 - 7.2y - 12000x + 0.3xy$$

$$\text{or } 0.2\,xy + 12000\,x + 7.2y - 3{,}48{,}000 = 0 \quad \ldots(ii)$$

From similar triangles *CDF* and *CKB*, we get,

$$\frac{y}{40{,}000} = \frac{x}{24}$$

$$\therefore \quad y = \frac{40{,}000x}{24} \quad \ldots(iii)$$

Putting, $y = \dfrac{40{,}000x}{24}$ from equation (*iii*) in equation (*ii*), we get

$$333\,x^2 + 24000x - 3{,}48{,}000 = 0$$

or $$x^2 + 72x - 1045 = 0$$

$$\therefore \quad x = \frac{-72 \pm \sqrt{5184 + 4180}}{2} = \frac{-72 \pm 96.77}{2} = 12.38$$

Other root is rejected as it is negative.

∴ Capacity of the hydro plant is

$$y(= DC) = \frac{40{,}000 \times 12.38}{24} = 20.63 \text{ MW}$$

Capacity of steam plant = 60 MW – 20.63 MW = 39.367 MW

4.2 **Figure shows a small industrial distribution system. The power system supplies power at constant voltage of 480 V, and the impedance of the distribution lines is negligible. Load 1 is a Δ-connected load with a phase impedance of 10∠30° Ω, and load 2 is a Y-connected load with a phase impedance of 5∠–36.87° Ω.**

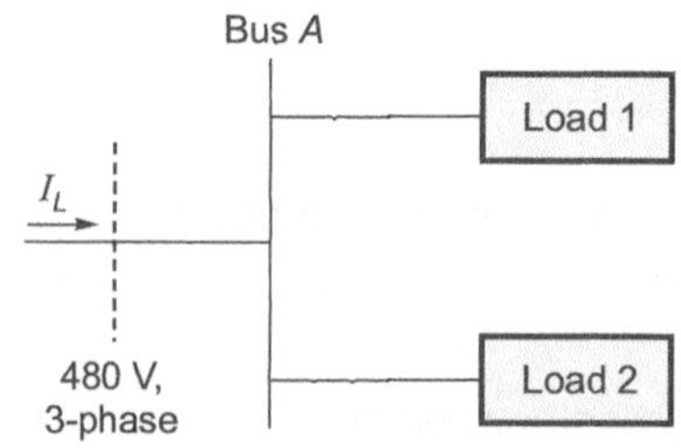

(i) Find the overall power factor of the distribution system.

(ii) Find the total current supplied to the distribution system.

[15 marks : 2014]

Solution:

Load 1 is a Δ-connected load with a phase impedance of 10∠30° Ω.

Load 2 is a Y-connected load with a phase impedance of 5∠–36.87° Ω.

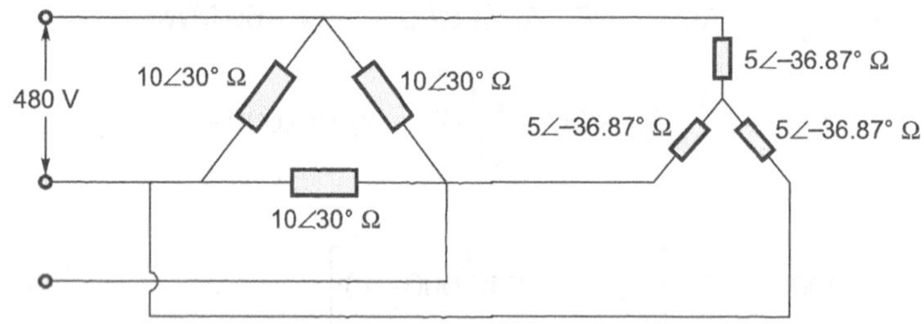

Transforming delta load to star,

$$\bar{Z}_{star} = \frac{\bar{Z}_{delta}}{3} = \frac{10\angle 30^\circ}{3} = 3.33\angle 30^\circ \ \Omega$$

Since, impedances of loads are balanced. So, we go for single phase circuit representation.

$$\bar{I}_{ph} = \bar{I}_1 + \bar{I}_2$$

$$= \frac{277.13}{3.33\angle 30^\circ} + \frac{277.13}{5\angle -36.87^\circ}$$

$$= 83.22\angle -30^\circ + 55.426\angle 36.84^\circ$$

$$\bar{I}_{ph} = 116.7107\angle -4.108^\circ \text{ A}$$

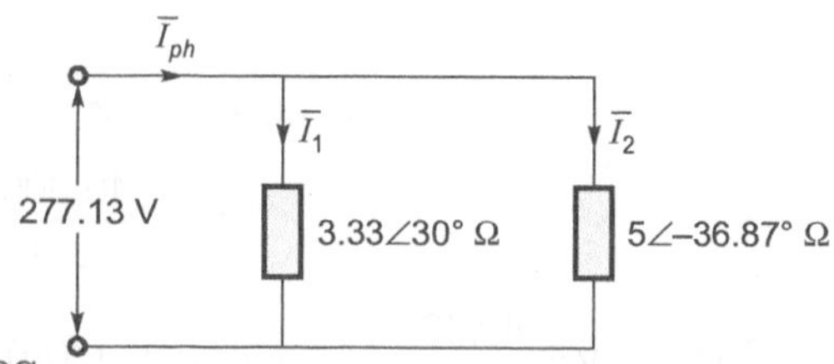

(*i*) The overall power factor = cosϕ = cos(4.108°) = 0.9974 lag

(*ii*) The total current supplied to the distribution system = 116.7107 A

4.3 Show how a string of insulators be protected against damage when a flash over occurs. Each line of a 3-phase system is suspended by a string of three similar insulators. If the voltage across the line unit is 10 kV, determine the line voltage of the system. Assume that the shunt capacitance between each insulator and the earthed metalwork of the tower is one-tenth of the capacitance of the insulation itself.

[10 marks : 2014]

Solution:

When a flash over occurs in a line then huge currents will flow through the line. The huge voltage across the string of the insulators will occur. This huge voltage will be distributed across each insulator. In such a way that the insulator which is nearer to power conductor will have maximum stress or voltage and decreases as we go away from the conductor. The insulators can withstand the voltages until it does not cross the puncher voltage.

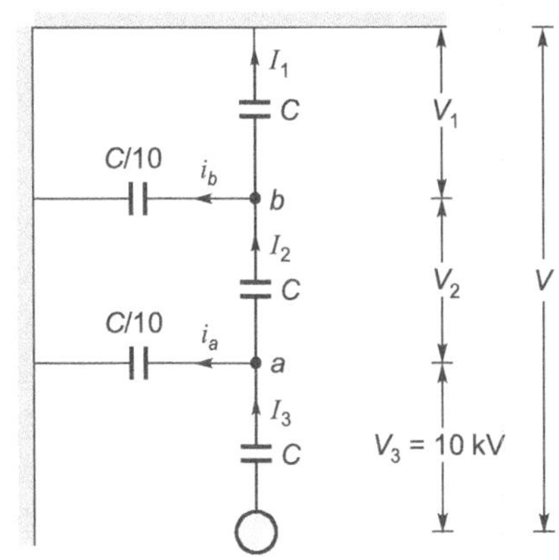

Applying KCL at node '*a*' as

$$I_3 = I_2 + i_a$$

$$V_3\omega C = V_2\omega C + (V_1 + V_2)\frac{\omega C}{10}$$

$$V_3 = \frac{10\,V_2 + (V_1 + V_2)}{10}$$

$$10\,V_3 = 11\,V_2 + V_1$$

$$V_1 + 11\,V_2 = 100000 \quad \text{...(1)}$$

Applying KCL at node '*b*',

$$I_2 = I_1 + i_b$$

$$V_2\omega C = V_1\omega C + V_1\frac{\omega C}{10}$$

$$10\,V_2 = 10\,V_1 + V_1 = 11\,V_1$$

$$V_1 = \frac{10}{11}V_2$$

$$V_1 = 0.9090\,V_2 \quad \text{...(2)}$$

Substituting equation (2) in equation (1),

$$0.9090\,V_2 + 11\,V_2 = 100000$$

$$11.9090\,V_2 = 100000$$

$$V_2 = \frac{100000}{11.9090} = 8397.01\text{ V}$$

$$V_1 = 0.9090\,V_2 = 0.9090 \times 8397.01$$

$$= 87632.88\text{ V}$$

$$V = V_1 + V_2 + V_3$$

$$= 7632.88 + 8397.01 + 10000$$

$$= 26029.89 \simeq 26.02\text{ kV}$$

4.4 A single-phase distributor has loop resistance of 0.3 Ω and a reactance of 0.4 Ω. The far end of the distributor has a load current of 80 A and power factor of 0.8 lagging at 220 V. The mid-point *M* of the distributor has a load current of 50 A at power factor of 0.707 lagging with reference to voltage *M*. Calculate the sending end voltage and power factor.

[15 marks : 2014]

Solution:

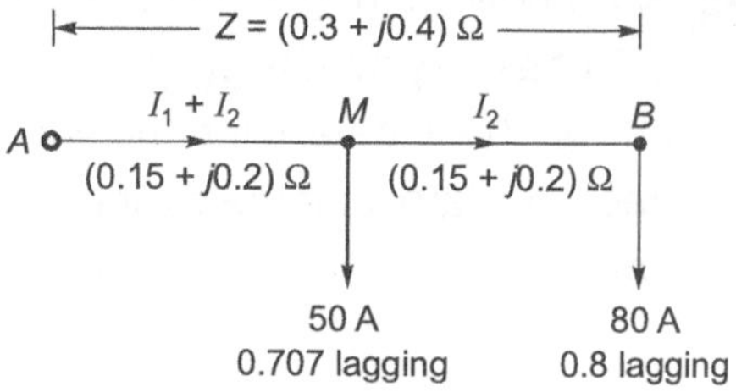

As M is the mid-point of the line, the impedance of the section AM is equal to the MB.

$$Z_{AM} = \frac{0.3 + j0.4}{2} = (0.15 + j0.2)\ \Omega$$

Current through section MB is = 80(0.8 – j0.6)

$$I_2 = I_{MB} = (64 - j48)\ A$$

Current through section AM $= I_1 + I_2$

$$= 50(0.707 - j0.707) + (64 - j48)$$

$$= (99.35 - j83.55)\ A$$

Voltage drop in section MB is, $V_{MB} = I_{MB}(Z_{MB}) = (64 - j48)(0.15 + j0.2)$

$$V_{MB} = (19.2 + j5.6)\ V$$

Voltage drop at M, $V_M = V_{MB} + V_B = (19.2 + j5.6) + (220 + j0) = (239.2 + j5.6)\ V$

Voltage drop in section AM, $V_{AM} = (I_1 + I_2)\, Z_{AM}$

$$= (99.35 - j83.35)(0.15 + j0.2)$$

$$V_{AM} = (31.57 + j7.36)\ V$$

Voltage at sending end is, $V_A = V_{AM} + V_M$

$$= (31.57 + j7.36) + (239.2 + j5.6)$$

$$= (270.77 + j12.96)\ V = 271.07\angle 2.74°\ V$$

Current through A is $129.68\angle{-40°}$ A

so, sending end power factor is cos(42.74°) = 0.734 lagging

4.5 **A total load of 10000 kW at 33 kV and power factor 0.8 lagging is delivered to a substation by two 3-phase feeders connected in parallel. One of the cables has a resistance of 1.5 Ω for each conductor and a reactance of 1.4 Ω per phase and delivers 6000 kW at a power factor of 0.75 lagging. Calculate the corresponding values of resistance and reactance of the second cable.**

[10 Marks : 2016]

Solution:

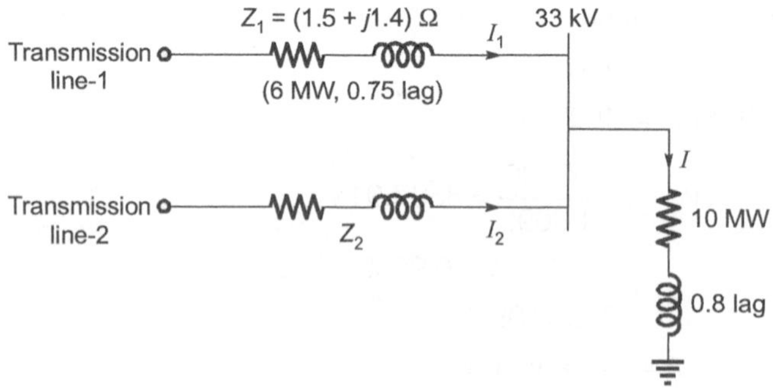

From the given network: $|I| = \frac{P_R}{\sqrt{3}V_R\cos\phi} = \frac{10\times10^6}{\sqrt{3}\times33\times10^3\times0.8} = 218.7\ \text{A}$

$\cos\phi = 0.8 \Rightarrow \phi = 36.86°$, $I = 218.7\angle{-36.86°}$ A

Transmission line-1 carries: $P_1 = 6$ MW, $\cos\phi_1 = 0.75$ lag, $\phi_1 = 41.4°$

$$|I_1| = \frac{P_1}{\sqrt{3}V_R\cos\phi} = \frac{6\times10^6}{\sqrt{3}\times33\times10^3\times0.75} = 140\ \text{A}$$

$$I_1 = 140\angle{-41.4°}\ \text{A}$$

By using current division rule,

$$I_1 = I \cdot \frac{Z_2}{(Z_1 + Z_2)}$$

$$Z_2 = \frac{Z_1}{\left(\frac{I}{I_1} - 1\right)} = \frac{(1.5 + j1.4)}{\left(\frac{218.7\angle -36.86^\circ}{140\angle -41.4^\circ}\right)} = (3.096 + j1.825)\ \Omega$$

$\therefore$ Impedance of transmission line-2 = $(3.096 + j1.825)\ \Omega$

4.6 **Define string efficiency with reference to a suspension insulator assembly. Explain how this efficiency can be raised by the introduction of guard rings.**
Each of the three insulators forming a string has a self-capacitance of C farads. The shunting capacitance of the connecting metal work of each insulator is 0.2 C to earth and 0.1 C to the line. A guard ring increases the capacitance to the line of the metal work of the lowest insulator to 0.3 C. Calculate the string efficiency of this arrangement (i) with the guard ring, and (ii) without the guard ring.

[10 Marks : 2016]

Solution:

Without guard ring:

At node A:

$$I_2 + i_x = I_1 + i_1$$

$$V_2 \omega C + (V_2 + V_3)\, \omega(0.1\text{ C}) = V_1 \omega C + V_1 \omega(0.1\text{ C})$$

$$1.2\, V_1 - 1.1 V_2 - 0.1\, V_3 = 0 \quad \text{...(i)}$$

At node B:

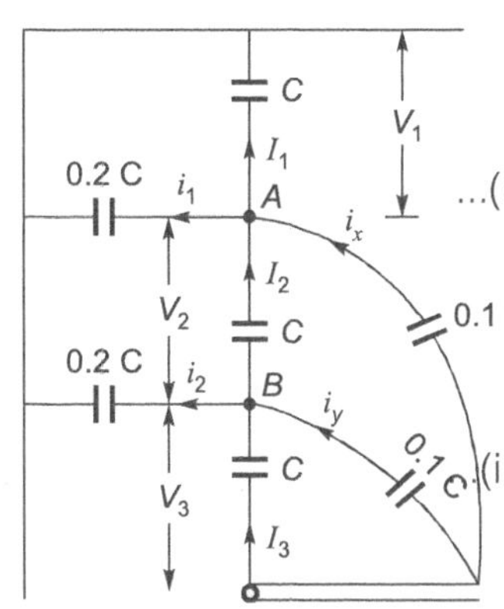

$$I_3 + i_y = I_2 + i_2$$

$$V_3\omega C + V_3(0.1\, \omega C) = (V_1 + V_2)\, 0.2\, \omega C + V_2\omega C$$

$$0.2\, V_1 + 1.2\, V_2 - 1.1\, V_3 = 0 \quad \text{...(ii)}$$

Divide (i) and (ii) with V_3,

$$\frac{1.2\, V_1}{0.1 V_3} - \frac{1.1 V_2}{0.1 V_3} = 1$$

$$12\frac{V_1}{V_3} - 11\frac{V_2}{V_3} = 1 \quad \text{(iii)}$$

Equation (ii),

$$0.2\frac{V_1}{V_3} + \frac{1.2 V_2}{V_3} = 1.1$$

$$2\frac{V_1}{V_3} + 12\frac{V_2}{V_3} = 11 \quad \text{...(iv)}$$

Let,

$$\frac{V_1}{V_3} = x$$

$$\frac{V_2}{V_3} = y$$

$$V_2 = 0.783\, V_3, \quad \text{...(v)}$$

$$V_1 = 0.801\, V_3 \quad \text{...(vi)}$$

Substitute (v) and (vi) in

$$V = V_1 + V_2 + V_3$$

$$V = 2.584\, V_3$$

$$\Rightarrow \qquad \%\text{string } \eta = \frac{V}{3V_3} \times 100 = \frac{2.584}{3} \times 100$$

$$\%\eta = 86.1\%$$

(i) With guard ring:

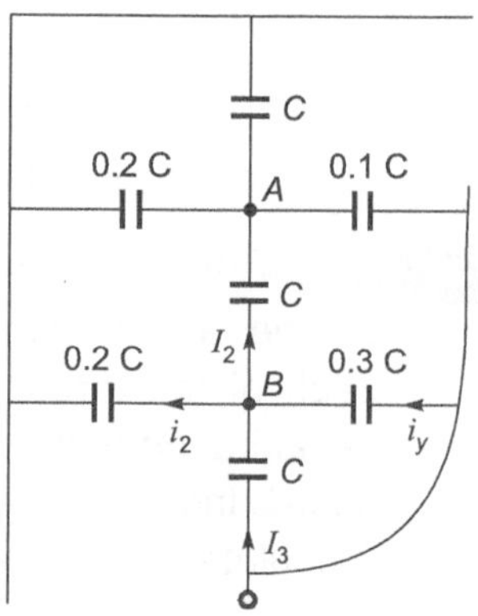

With guard ring node A equation is not changed.

i.e., $12\ V_1 - 1.1\ V_2 - 0.1\ V_3 = 0$

or, $$12\frac{V_1}{V_3} - 11\frac{V_2}{V_3} = 1 \qquad \text{...(i)}$$

At node B: $I_3 + i_y = I_2 + i_2$

$$\Rightarrow \quad V_3\omega C + V_3(0.3\,\omega C) = (V_1 + V_2)\,0.2\,\omega C + V_2\omega C$$

$$0.2\ V_1 + 1.2\ V_2 - 1.3\ V_3 = 0$$

$$0.2\frac{V_1}{V_3} + 1.2\frac{V_2}{V_3} = 1.3$$

$$2\frac{V_1}{V_3} + 12\frac{V_2}{V_3} = 13 \qquad \text{...(ii)}$$

By solving (i) and (ii), $\frac{V_1}{V_3} = 0.9337, \quad \frac{V_2}{V_3} = 0.9277$

Substitute these values in

$$V = V_1 + V_2 + V_3$$

$$V = V_3 + 0.9277\ V_3 + 0.9337\ V_3 = 2.86\ V_3$$

$$\%\eta = \frac{V}{3V_3} \times 100 = \frac{2.86}{3} \times 100$$

$$\text{String } \eta = 95.4\%$$

Hence, with guard ring string efficiency increased.

4.7 **Determine the currents supplied to ring mains shown in the figure below from A to B, when $V_A = V_B$ and $V_B = V_A + 6$ volts:**

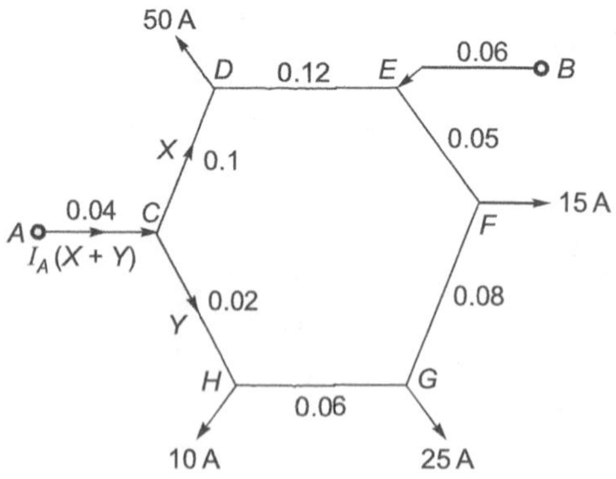

[20 marks : 2017]

Solution:

Path-1:

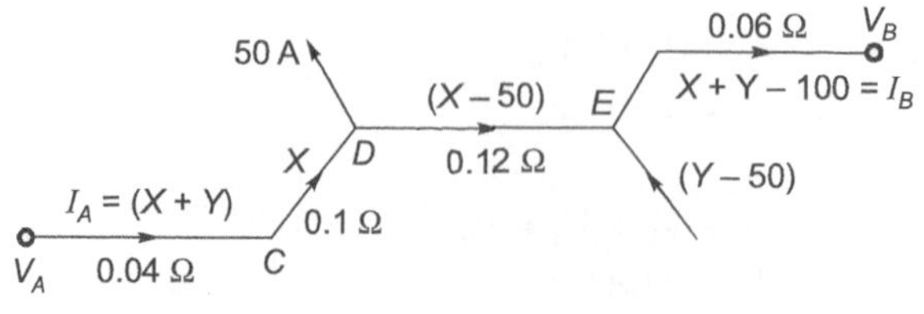

$$V_A - V_B = (X+Y)\,0.04 + (0.1X) + (X-50)\,0.12 + (X+Y-100)\,0.06$$

$$V_A - V_B = 0.32X + 0.1Y - 12 \qquad \text{...(i)}$$

Path-2:

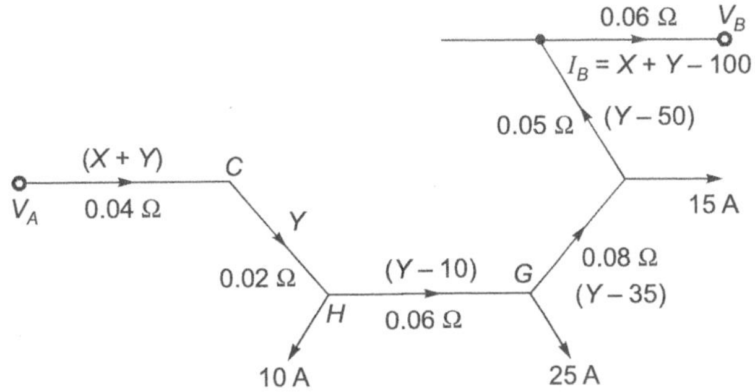

$$V_A - V_B = (X+Y)\,0.04 + 0.02Y + (Y-10)\,0.06 + (Y-35)\,0.08 + (Y-50)\,0.05 + (X+Y-100)\,0.06$$

$$V_A - V_B = 0.1X + 0.31Y - 11.9 \qquad \text{...(ii)}$$

Case-I: If, $V_A = V_B$

$$0.32X + 0.1Y = 12$$
$$0.1X + 0.31Y = 11.9$$
$$X = 28.3632$$
$$Y = 29.2376$$
$$I_A = (X+Y)$$
$$= 28.3632 + 29.2376 = 57.6 \text{ A}$$
$$I_B = X + Y - 100$$
$$I_B = 57.6 - 100 = -42.4 \text{ A}$$

Case-II: If, $V_B = V_A + 6$

$$V_A - V_A - 6 = 0.32X + 0.1Y - 12$$
$$V_A - V_A - 6 = 0.1X + 0.31Y - 11.9$$
$$32X + 0.1Y = 6$$
$$0.1X + 0.31Y = 5.9$$
$$X = 14.2376; \quad Y = 14.4394$$
$$I_A = X + Y$$
$$= 14.2376 + 14.4394 = 28.677 \text{ A}$$
$$I_B = X + Y - 100 = -71.323 \text{ A}$$

4.8 An electric train running between two stations *A* and *B*, 10 km apart and maintained at voltages 550 V and 500 V respectively, draws a constant current of 600 A. The resistance for both go and return conductors is 0.04 Ω/km. Find the point of minimum potential between the stations, the voltage at that point and currents drawn from both the stations at that point.

[12 marks : 2018]

Solution:

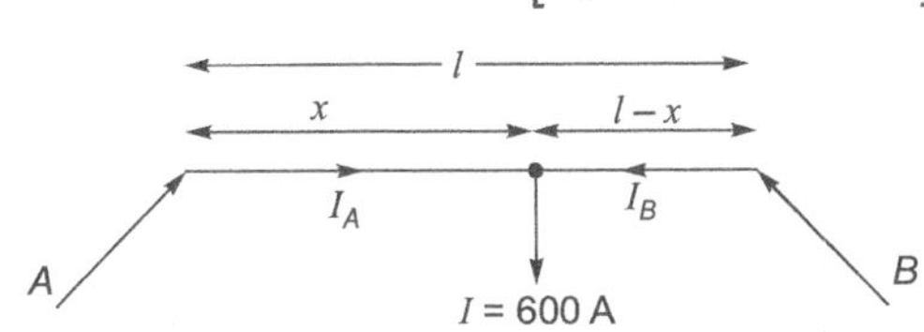

Given, $V_A = 550$ V, $V_B = 500$ V

Distance between two stations is (l) = 10 km

Current drawn by train = 600 A

Let x be the point of minium potential.

$\therefore$ $V_x = V_A - I_A r . x = 550 - I_A(0.04x)$ ...(i)

Also, $V_x = V_B - I_B r(l-x)$

$= 500 - (600 - I_A)(0.04)(l - x)$

$$= 500 - (600 - I_A)(0.4 - 0.04x) \quad ...(ii)$$

From equation (i) and (ii),

$$550 - I_A(0.04x) = 500 - (600 - I_A)(0.4 - 0.04x)$$

$$I_A = (290 - 24x)\,2.5$$

From equation (i),

$$V_x = 550 - I_A(0.04x)$$

$$= 550 - (0.04x)(290 - 24x)\,2.5$$

$$V_x = 550 - 29x + 2.4x^2$$

To get minimum value, $\frac{dV_x}{dx} = 0$

$\Rightarrow$ $-29 + 4.8x = 0$

$\Rightarrow$ $x = 6.04$ km

$\therefore$ $V_x = 550 - 29 \times 6.04 + 2.4 \times 6.04^2 = 462.396$ V

$$I_A = (290 - 24 \times 6.04)\,2.5 = 362.6 \text{ A}$$

$$I_B = 600 - I_A = 237.4 \text{ A}$$

4.9 **(i) What do you mean by grading of cables? What are the methods of grading?**

(ii) Derive the condition for minimum value of gradient at the surface of the conductor.

(iii) Determine the economic overall diameter of a single-core cable metal sheathed for a working voltage of 75 kV, if the dielectric strength of the insulating material is 60 kV/cm.

[20 marks : 2018]

Solution:

(i) Grading of cable means providing the multiple homogenous or heterogenous layer of insulation in a cable so that uniform dielectric stress can be maintained which minimises the usage of insulation for a given radius and operating voltage.

Methods:

- **Capacitive grading:** In this , two or more insulating materials are used. Materials with larger permittivity are kept nearer to the conductor.
- **Intersheath grading:** In this a homogenous dielectric is separated into two or more layers by this at appropriate potential by providing tapping in the auxiliary autotransformer such that maximum stress at all the layers are equal.

(ii) Gradient at the distance x form the centre of the conductor within the material in given by,

$$g = \frac{q}{2\pi \in x} \text{ V/m}$$

Let r be the radius of conductor and R be overall radius.

Potential is given as $V = -\int E.dl$

$$V = -\int_R^r \frac{q}{2\pi \in x} dx$$

$$V = -\frac{q}{2\pi \in} ln\, x \Big|_R^r$$

$$V = \frac{q}{2\pi \in} ln\left(\frac{R}{r}\right) V$$

$$\therefore \quad g = \frac{V}{x ln(R/r)} \text{ V/m}$$

At surface i.e. $x = r$

$$g_{max} = \frac{V}{r\,ln(R/r)} \text{ V/m}$$

For minimum value of gradient at surface,

$$\frac{dg_{max}}{dr} = 0$$

$$\frac{d}{dr}\left(\frac{V}{r\ln(R/r)}\right) = 0$$

$$\Rightarrow \quad -V\left[ln\frac{R}{r} + r \times \frac{1}{(R/r)} \times \left(-\frac{R}{r^2}\right)\right] = 0$$

$$\Rightarrow \quad ln\left(\frac{R}{r}\right) = 1$$

$$\Rightarrow \quad \frac{R}{r} = e$$

$$r = \left(\frac{R}{e}\right)$$

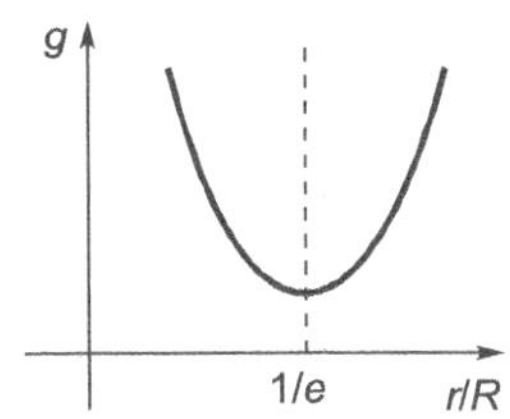

(iii) For economic over all diameter

$$R = re$$

Given, $V = 75$ kV; $g = 60$ kV/cm

$$g = \frac{V}{r}$$

$$r = \frac{V}{g} = \frac{75}{60} = 1.25 \text{ cm}$$

Overall diameter, $D = 2R = 2re = 6.796$ cm

5. Fault Analysis

5.1 **List the advantages of using per-unit values in power system calculations.** [8 marks : 2001]

Solution:

Advantages of per-unit system in power system:

(a) In a large interconnected power system with various voltage levels and various capacity equipments it has been found quite convenient to work with per-unit (pu.) system for quantities for analysis purposes rather than in absolute values of quantities.

(b) With p.u system there is less chance of making mistake in phase and line voltages, single phase or three phase quantities.

(c) The p.u. impedance of the transformer is same whether referred on to primary or secondary side of the transformer which is not in case of when considering absolute value of these impedances.

(d) The parameters of transformers as well as rotating machines lie roughly in the same range of numerical values irrespective of their ratings if expressed in per unit of their ratings; correctness of analysis becomes immediately obvious in this system.

5.2 **A 100 MVA, 33 kV, 3-phase generator has a subtransient reactance of 15%. The generator is connected to the motors through transmission line and transformers as shown in figure given below. The motors have rated inputs of 30 MVA, 20 MVA and 50 MVA at 30 kV with 18% subtransient reactance.**

The three phase transformers are rated at 100 MVA, 33 kV (Δ)/110 kV (λ) with leakage reactance of 9%. The line has a reactance of 50 ohms. Selecting the generator ratings as base quantities. Obtain the p.u. reactance diagram of the system.

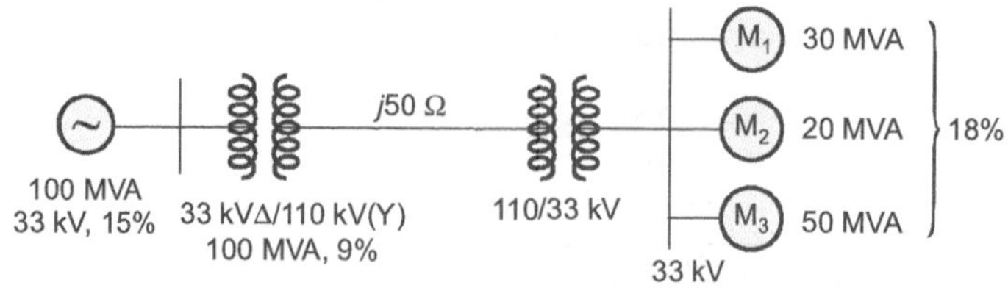

[10 marks : 2001]

Solution:

Taking generator's ratings as base values,

$$(MVA)_b = 100 \text{ MVA}; \quad (kV)_b = 33 \text{ kV}$$

$$\text{pu reactance of the generator} = j0.15 \text{ pu}$$

As the ratings of the transformers are 100 MVA, 33 kV

$$\text{pu reactance of the transformers} = j0.09 \text{ pu}$$

The base value of the line, $(kV)_{b\,(\text{line})} = 33 \times \left(\frac{110}{33}\right) = 110 \text{ kV}$

and in the motor circuit, $(kV)_{b\,(\text{motor})} = 110 \times \left(\frac{33}{110}\right) = 33 \text{ kV}$

pu reactance of the transmission line,

$$X_{pu\,(\text{line})} = j50 \times \frac{100}{(110)^2} = j0.4132 \text{ pu} \qquad \left[Z_{pu} = Z_{actual} \times \frac{(MVA)_b}{(kV_b)^2}\right]$$

As we know,

$$Z_{pu\,(\text{new})} = Z_{pu(old)} \times \frac{(MVA)_{b(new)}}{(MVA)_{b(old)}} \times \left[\frac{(kV)_{b(old)}}{(kV)_{b(new)}}\right]^2$$

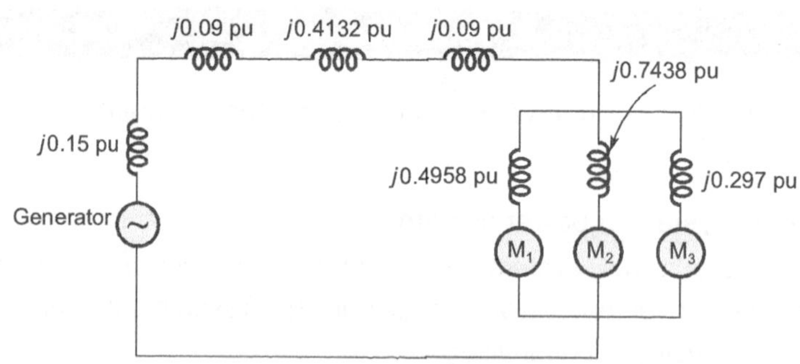

pu reactance diagram of the system

Motor-1:

$$X_{pu\,(m_1)} = j0.18 \times \left(\frac{100}{30}\right) \times \left(\frac{30}{33}\right)^2 = j0.4958\ pu$$

Motor-2:

$$X_{pu\,(m_2)} = j0.18 \times \left(\frac{100}{20}\right) \times \left(\frac{30}{33}\right)^2 = j0.7438 \text{ pu}$$

Motor-3:

$$X_{pu\,(m_3)} = j0.18 \times \left(\frac{100}{50}\right) \times \left(\frac{30}{33}\right)^2 = j0.2975 \text{ pu}$$

5.3 **A 50 MVA, 11 kV, 3-phase alternator was subjected to different types of faults. The fault current were 3-phase fault = 1870 A; Line to line fault = 2590 A; Single line to ground fault = 4130 A. The alternator is solidly grounded. Find the p.u. values of three sequence reactances of the alternator**

[10 marks : 2001]

Solution:

Here the alternator is solidly grounded this means that the value of $Z_n = 0$.

Let X_1, X_2 and X_0 be the positive, negative and zero sequence network reactances respectively of the alternator.

For 3-phase fault, Fault current = $\frac{E_{ph}}{X_1}$ (magnitude)

$$\text{or} \qquad 1870 = \frac{11000/\sqrt{3}}{X_1}$$

$$X_1 = \frac{11000}{\sqrt{3} \times 1870} = 3.396\ \Omega$$

$$\text{For line-line fault we have, Fault current} = \frac{\sqrt{3}\,E_{ph}}{X_1 + X_2}$$

$$\text{or} \qquad 2590 = \frac{\sqrt{3} \times 11000/\sqrt{3}}{X_1 + X_2}$$

$$\text{or} \qquad X_1 + X_2 = \frac{11000}{2590} = 4.247\ \Omega$$

$$X_2 = 4.247 - 3.396 = 0.851\ \Omega$$

For line-to-ground fault, we have,

$$\text{Fault current} = \frac{3E_{ph}}{X_1 + X_2 + X_0} \quad \text{or} \quad 4130 = \frac{3 \times 11000/\sqrt{3}}{X_1 + X_2 + X_0}$$

$$\text{or} \qquad X_1 + X_2 + X_0 = \frac{\sqrt{3} \times 11000}{4130}$$

$$\text{or} \qquad X_0 = 0.366\ \Omega$$

Assuming 50 MVA and 11 kV as base values

$$\text{Base impedance} = Z_b = \frac{(kV)_b^2}{(MVA)_b} = \frac{11^2}{50} = 2.42\ \Omega$$

$$X_{0\,(pu)} = \frac{X_0\,\Omega}{Z_B} = \frac{0.366}{2.42} = 0.151 \text{ p.u.}$$

$$X_{1\,(pu)} = \frac{X_1\,\Omega}{Z_b} = \frac{3.396}{2.42} = 1.403 \text{ p.u.}$$

$$X_{2\,(pu)} = \frac{X_2\,\Omega}{Z_b} = \frac{0.851}{2.42} = 0.352 \text{ p.u.}$$

5.4 **Derive an expression for total complex power in a 3-phase system in terms of symmetrical components of voltages and currents.**

[10 marks : 2001]

Solution:

Reference phasors V_{a1}, V_{a2} and V_{a0}.

$$V_a = V_{a1} + V_{a2} + V_{a0}$$
$$V_b = \alpha^2 V_{a1} + \alpha V_{a2} + V_{a0}$$
$$V_c = \alpha V_{a1} + \alpha^2 V_{a2} + V_{a0}$$

$$\begin{bmatrix} V_a \\ V_b \\ V_c \end{bmatrix} = \begin{bmatrix} 1 & 1 & 1 \\ \alpha^2 & \alpha & 1 \\ \alpha & \alpha^2 & 1 \end{bmatrix} \begin{bmatrix} V_{a1} \\ V_{a2} \\ V_{a0} \end{bmatrix}$$

or $$V_p = AV_s$$

where, $$V_p = \begin{bmatrix} V_a \\ V_b \\ V_c \end{bmatrix} \text{ and } V_s = \begin{bmatrix} V_{a1} \\ V_{a2} \\ V_{a0} \end{bmatrix}$$

or $$V_s = A^{-1} V_p$$

and $$A^{-1} = \frac{1}{3} \begin{bmatrix} 1 & \alpha & \alpha^2 \\ 1 & \alpha^2 & \alpha \\ 1 & 1 & 1 \end{bmatrix}$$

$\therefore$ $$V_{a1} = \frac{1}{3}[V_a + \alpha V_b + \alpha^2 V_c]$$

$$V_{a2} = \frac{1}{3}[V_a + \alpha^2 V_b + \alpha V_c]$$

$$V_{a0} = \frac{1}{3}[V_a + V_b + V_c]$$

Similarly for a set of currents, $I_p = AI_s$ and $I_s = A^{-1} I_p$

Total complex power in a three phase circuit,

$$S = V_p^T I_p^* = V_a I_a^* + V_b I_b^* + V_c I_c^*$$

or $$S = [AV_s]^T [AI_s]^* = V_s^T A^T A^* I_s^*$$

Consider, $$A^T A^* = \begin{bmatrix} 1 & \alpha^2 & \alpha \\ 1 & \alpha & \alpha^2 \\ 1 & 1 & 1 \end{bmatrix} \begin{bmatrix} 1 & 1 & 1 \\ \alpha & \alpha^2 & 1 \\ \alpha^2 & \alpha & 1 \end{bmatrix} = 3 \begin{bmatrix} 1 & 0 & 0 \\ 0 & 1 & 0 \\ 0 & 0 & 1 \end{bmatrix}$$

$$A^T A^* = 3U$$

$\therefore$ $$S = 3V_s^T U I_s^* = 3V_s^T I_s^* = 3V_{a1} I_{a1}^* + 3V_{a2} I_{a2}^* + 3V_{a0} I_{a0}^*$$

= Sum of symmetrical components of powers

5.5 Draw the zero sequence equivalent circuits of 3-phase transformers with the following connections of the windings:

(a) Δ / Δ

(b) Δ / Y

(c) 

(d) 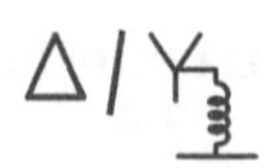

(e) Y / Y

(f) 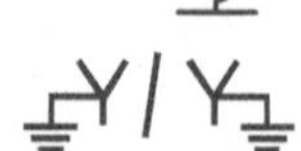

[10 marks : 2001]

Solution:

Connection | Zero Sequence Equivalent Circuit

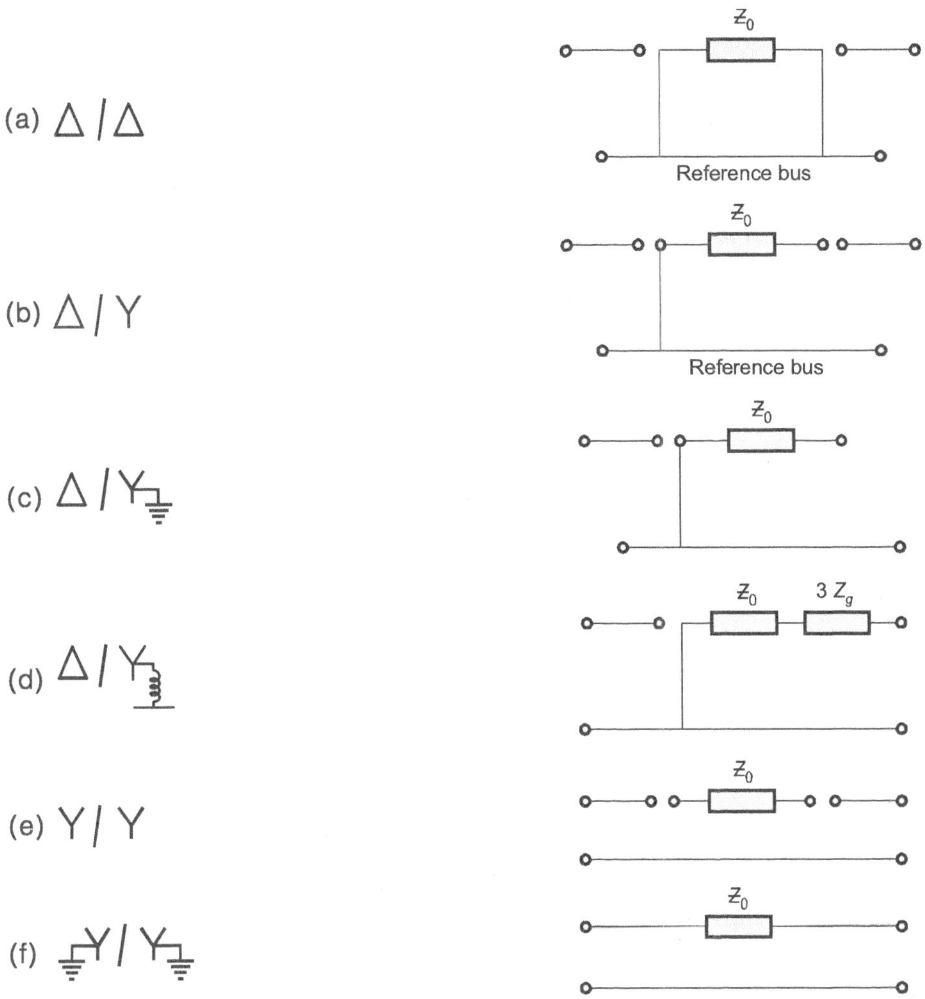

5.6 Two identical 11 kV, 50 MVA, 3-phase alternators are connected in parallel and supply a substation by a feeder having an impedance of $(0.4 + j0.7)$ ohm to positive and negative sequence currents and $(0.7 + j3.0)$ ohm to zero sequence current. The positive, negative and zero sequence reactances of each of the generators are 0.6 ohm, 0.4 ohm and 0.2 ohm respectively. Both machines have their neutrals earthed through resistances of 0.2 ohm. Calculate the potential of the alternator neutral with respect to earth, if an earth fault occurs simultaneously on the blue and yellow phases of the substation. Neglect prefault power and generator resistances.

[15 marks : 2002]

Solution:

For synchronous generators,

$$X_1\,(\text{pu}) = \frac{0.6 \times 50}{(11)^2} = 0.248 \text{ p.u.}$$

$$X_2\,(\text{pu}) = \frac{0.4 \times 50}{(11)^2} = 0.165 \text{ p.u.}$$

$$X_0\,(\text{pu}) = \frac{0.2 \times 50}{(11)^2} = 0.083 \text{ p.u.}$$

For feeder,

$$X_1 = X_2 = \frac{(0.4 + j0.7) \times 50}{(11)^2}$$

$$= 0.165 + j0.289 \text{ p.u.}$$

$$X_0 = \frac{(0.7 + j3.0) \times 50}{(11)^2} = 0.289 + j1.239 \text{ p.u.}$$

Two identical generator operator in parallel, hence

$$X_{1\,eq} = \frac{0.248}{2} j + 0.165 + 0.289j = 0.165 + 0.413j$$

$$X_{2eq} = \frac{0.165}{2} j + 0.165 + 0.289j = 0.165 + j0.3715$$

$$X_{0eq} = \frac{j0.083 + 3R_g}{2} + 0.289 + 1.239j$$

$$= \frac{j0.083 + 3 \times 0.0826}{2} + 0.289 + 1.239j = 0.413 + 1.281j$$

For L-L-G fault

Assuming prefault voltage E_a to be 1 pu,

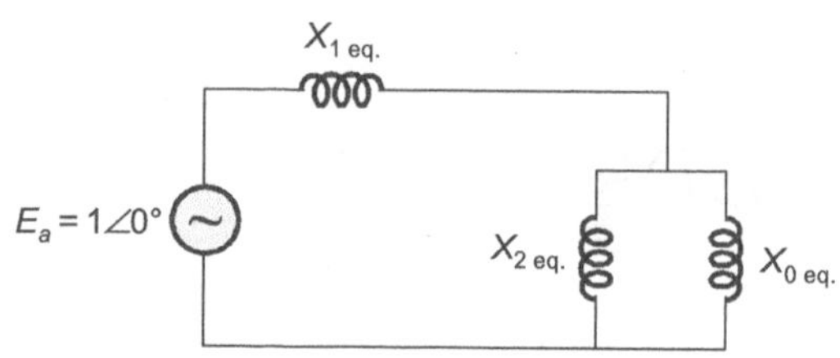

$$I_{a1} = \frac{E_a}{X_{1eq} + \dfrac{X_{2eq} \times X_{0eq}}{X_{2eq} + X_{0eq}}}$$

$$= \frac{1}{(0.165 + 0.413j) + \dfrac{(0.165 + 0.372j)(0.413 + 1.281j)}{(0.165 + 0.372j) + (0.413 + 1.281j)}}$$

$$= 0.496 - 1.223j \text{ p.u.}$$

$$I_{a0} = \frac{E_a - I_{a1} X_{1eq}}{X_{0eq}}$$

$$= \frac{1 - (0.496 - 1.223j)(0.165 + 0.413j)}{0.413 + 1.281j} = 0.092 - 0.291j \text{ p.u.}$$

$\therefore$ I_{a0} in each generator,

$$I_{a0} = 0.046 - 0.146j$$

Potential of alternator neutral with respect to earth $3I_{a0}X_0$

$$= 3 \times (0.048 - 0.146j) \times (0.0826) = (0.011 - 0.036j) \text{ p.u.}$$

Potential of alternator neutral with respect to earth in volt

$$= (0.011 - 0.036j) \times 11000 = 121 - j396 = 414 \angle -73° \text{ volts}$$

5.7 An alternator (star connected) is connected to Delta-Star transformer with star neutral. On the star side of the transformer a single-line-to-ground fault occurs. This is equivalent to

(a) A line-to-ground fault on the generator side of the transformer.

(b) A line-to-line fault on the generator side of the transformer.

(c) A 3-phase fault on the generator side of the transformer.

(d) A single-line-to-ground fault on the generator side of the transformer.

[2 marks : 2003]

Solution:

For a single line to ground fault, all the three sequence currents are present. But, due to delta connection of the transformer, generator feeds only positive and negative sequence currents, but can not feed zero sequence current which is also absent in line to line fault. So it is equivalent to a line to line fault on the generator side of the transformer. Hence option (b) is correct.

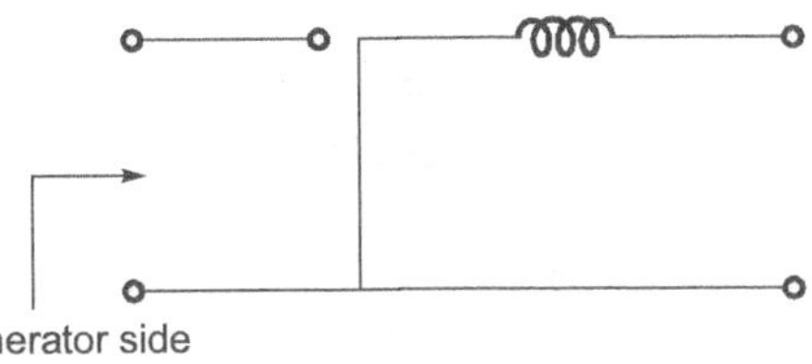

5.8 **A 20 MVA, 33 kV, 3-phase alternator is subjected to different types of shout-circuits and the following are the values of fault current.**

3-phase short circuit = 319 A

Single line-to-ground fault = 659 A

Line-to-line fault = 435 A

Determine the positive, negative and zero sequence reactances of the generator in per unit and in ohms. Neglect resistive part.

[12 marks : 2003]

Solution:

Let X_1, X_2 and X be the positive, negative and zero sequence reactances respectively of the alternator.

For 3-phase fault, fault current = $\dfrac{E_{ph}}{X_1}$ (magnitude)

or $$319 = \frac{33000/\sqrt{3}}{X_1} \text{ or } X_1 = 59.725 \text{ ohm}$$

For single line-to-ground fault, we have

$$\text{Fault current} = \frac{3E_{ph}}{X_1 + X_2 + X_0} \text{ (magnitude)}$$

or $$659 = \frac{3 \times 33000/\sqrt{3}}{X_1 + X_2 + X_0}$$

or $$X_1 + X_2 + X_0 = 86.733 \text{ ohm}$$

$\therefore$ $$X_0 = 86.733 - X_1 - X_2$$

$$= 86.733 - 59.725 - X_2$$

$$X_0 = 27 - X_2$$

For line-to-line fault, we have

$$\text{Fault current} = \frac{\sqrt{3}E_{ph}}{X_1 + X_2} \text{ (magnitude)}$$

or $$435 = \frac{\sqrt{3} \times 33000/\sqrt{3}}{X_1 + X_2}$$

or $$X_1 + X_2 = 75.862 \text{ ohm}$$

$\therefore$ $$X_2 = 75.862 - 59.725 = 16.137 \text{ ohm}$$

$\therefore$ $$X_0 = 27 - 16.137 = 10.863 \text{ ohm}$$

In terms of per-unit value,

Base impedance, $$Z_b = \frac{(KV_b)^2}{(MVA_b)} = \frac{(33)^2}{(20)} = 54.45 \text{ ohm}$$

$$X_{0\,(\text{p.u.})} = \frac{X_0\,\Omega}{Z_b} = \frac{10.863}{54.45} = 0.1995 \text{ p.u.}$$

$$X_{1\,(\text{p.u.})} = \frac{X_1\,\Omega}{Z_b} = \frac{59.725}{54.45} = 1.0968 \text{ p.u.}$$

$$X_{2\,(\text{p.u.})} = \frac{X_2\,\Omega}{Z_b} = \frac{16.137}{54.45} = 0.2963 \text{ p.u.}$$

5.9 The per unit impedance $Z_{(pu)}$ in a 3-phase system is

(a) $\dfrac{Z_{(\text{ohms})} \times (MVA)_B}{(KV)_B^2}$ (b) $\dfrac{Z_{(\text{ohms})} \times (kV)_B^2}{(MVA)_B}$

(c) $\dfrac{1000 \times (kV)_B}{\sqrt{3}\, I_B}$ (d) $\dfrac{1000 \times (kV)_B}{I_B \times 10^6}$

[2 marks : 2004]

Solution: (a)

Option (a) is correct.

5.10 A synchronous generator and motor are rated as 30,000 kVA, 13.2 kV, and both have subtransient reactance of 20%. The line connecting them has a reactance of 10% on the base of machine rating. The motor is drawing 20,000 kW at 0.8 p.f. leading and terminal voltage of 12.8 kV when a symmetrical three phase fault occurs at the motor terminals. Find the subtransient current in the generator, motor and fault by using the internal voltage of the machine.

[30 marks : 2004]

Solution:

Loaded as motor 20 MW at 0.8 p.f. leading at terminal voltage 12.8 kV.

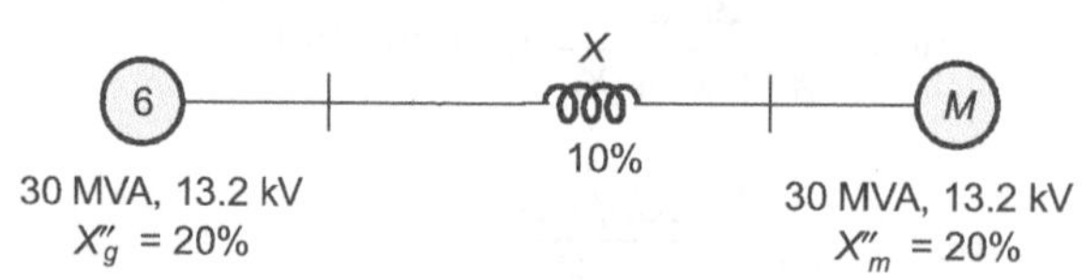

$$MVA_{(\text{BASE})} = 30$$
$$kV_{(\text{BASE})} = 13.2$$

Per unit reactance diagram,

$$(kA)_B = \frac{30}{\sqrt{3} \times 13.2} = 1.312 \text{ kA}$$

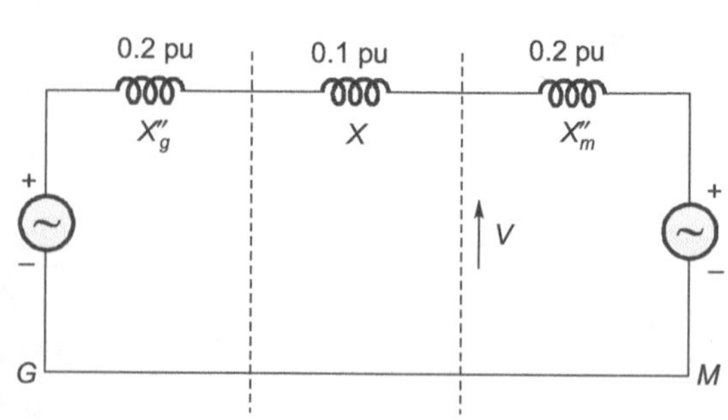

$$\text{Motor taking power in p.u.} = \frac{20}{30} = 0.67 \text{ p.u.}$$

$$\text{Terminal voltage } V = \frac{12.8}{13.2} = 0.96 \text{ p.u.}$$

$$P_{\text{p.u.}} = V_{\text{p.u.}} \times I_{\text{p.u.}} \times \cos\phi$$
$$0.67 = 0.96 \times I_{\text{p.u.}} \times 0.8$$
$$I_{\text{p.u.}} = 0.87$$
$$\cos\phi = 0.8 \text{ leading}$$

$\therefore \quad \bar{I}_0 = 0.87\angle 36.9°$ pu

Taking terminal voltage as the reference,

$$\bar{V}_0 = 0.96\angle 0° \text{ pu}$$

Generator:

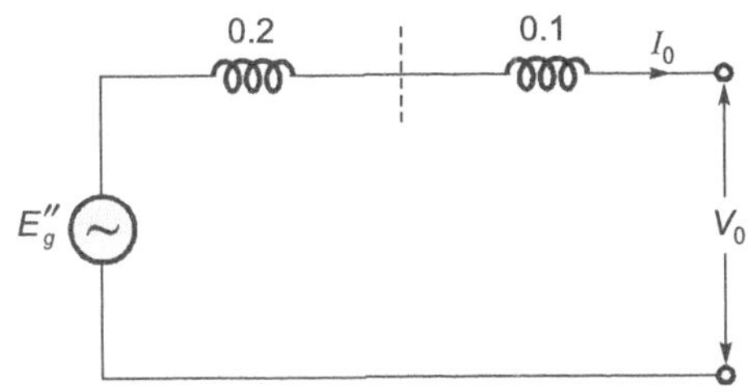

e.m.f. behind subtransient reactance,

$$E_g'' = V_0 + j(0.2 + 0.1)\, I_0 = 0.96\angle 0° + j0.3 \times 0.87\angle 36.9$$
$$= 0.96\angle 0° + 0.261\angle 126.9 = 0.82\angle 14.5° \text{ pu}$$

Motor,

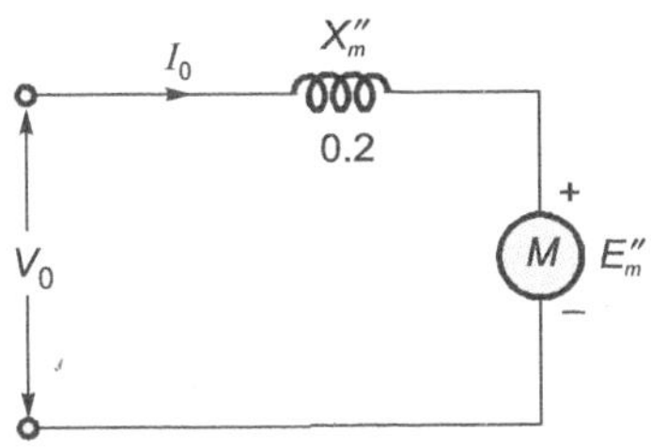

Back e.m.f. behind subtransient reactance

$$E_m'' = V_0 - jX_m''\, I_0$$
$$= 0.96\angle 0° - j0.2 \times 0.87\angle +36.9$$
$$= 1.07\angle -7.5° \text{ pu}$$

3-ϕ fault at motor terminals

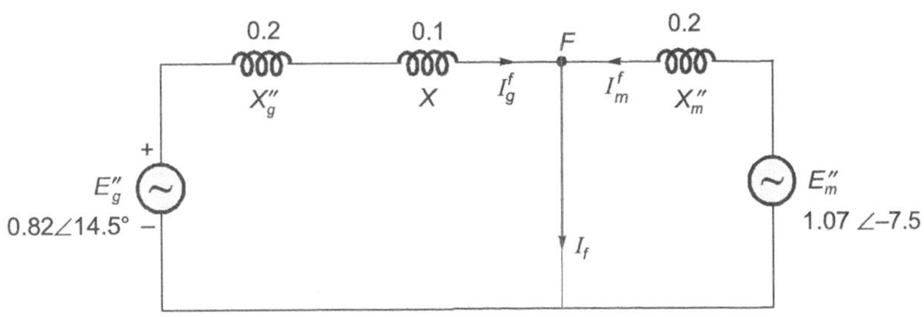

$$I_g^f = \frac{E_g''}{j(X_g'' + X)} = \frac{0.82\angle 14.5}{j(0.2 + 0.1)} = 2.76\angle -75.5 \text{ pu}$$

$$I_m^f = \frac{E_m''}{jX_m''} = \frac{1.07\angle -7.50}{j0.2} = 5.35\angle -97.5 \text{ pu}$$

$$I_F^f = I_g^f + I_m^f = 7.976\angle -90.052 \text{ pu}$$

$$(KA)_B = \frac{(MVA)_B}{\sqrt{3}(kV)_B} = \frac{30}{\sqrt{3} \times 13.2} = 1.31$$

$$|I_g^f| = 2.76 \text{ p.u} = 2.76 \times 1.31 = 3.62 \text{ kA}$$

$$|I_m^f| = 5.35 \text{ p.u.} = 5.35 \times 1.31 = 7 \text{ kA}$$

$$|I_F^f| = 7.976 \text{ p.u.} = 7.976 \times 1.31 = 10.44 \text{ kA}$$

5.11 Two 11 kV, 20 MVA, three phase, star connected generators operate in parallel. The +ve, –ve and zero sequence reactances of each being respectively $j0.18$, $j0.15$, $j0.10$ p.u. The star point of one of the generator is isolated and that of the other is earthed through a 2 W resistor. A single line-to-ground fault occurs at the terminals of one of the generators.

Estimate:

(a) the fault current

(b) current in grounding resistor and

(c) voltage across the grounding resistor

[15 marks : 2004]

Solution:

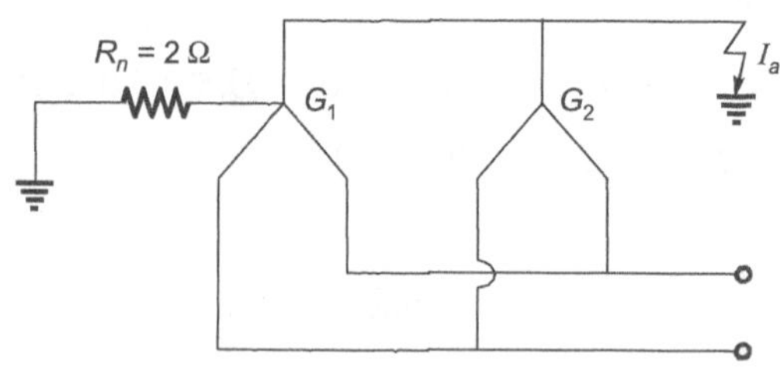

Note: All values are given in per unit.

Since the two identical generators operate in parallel,

$$X_{1eq} = \frac{j0.18}{2} = j0.09, \qquad R_n = 2 \times \frac{20}{11^2} = \frac{40}{121}$$

$$X_{2eq} = \frac{j0.25}{2} = j0.075$$

Since the star point of the second generator is isolated, its zero sequence reactance does not come into picture.

Therefore, $$Z_{0eq} = j0.10 + 3R_n = j0.10 + 3 \times \frac{2 \times 20}{(11)^2} = 0.99 + j0.1$$

For an LG fault,

I_f (fault current for LG fault)

$$= I_a = 3I_{a1} = \frac{3E_a}{X_{1eq} + X_{2eq} + Z_{0eq}}$$

(a) $$I_f = \frac{3 \times 1}{j0.09 + j0.075 + j0.1 + 0.99} = \frac{3}{0.99 + j0.265} = 2.827 - j0.756$$

(b) Current in the grounding resistor

$$I_f = 2.827 - j0.756 = 2.926\angle{-14.97}$$

$$|I_f| = 2.926 \times \frac{20}{\sqrt{3} \times 11} = 3.07 \text{ kA}$$

(c) Voltage across grounding resistor = $R_n \times I_f$

$$= \frac{40}{121}(2.827 - j0.756)$$

$$= 0.932 - j0.249 = 0.965 \times \frac{11}{\sqrt{3}} = 6.13 \text{ kV}$$

5.12 Obtain the per unit reactance diagram of the power system shown below:

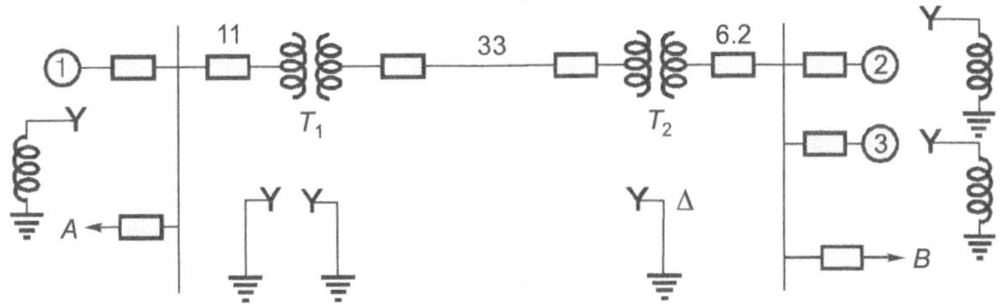

Specifications of the system components are:

Generator 1: 30 MVA, 10.5 kV, $X'' = 1.6\ \Omega$

Generator 2: 15 MVA, 6.6 kV, $X'' = 1.2\ \Omega$

Generator 3: 25 MVA, 6.6 kV, $X'' = 0.56\ \Omega$

Transformer T_1: 15 MVA, 33/11 kV,

$X = 15.2$ ohms/phase on high tension side

Transformer T_2: 15 MVA, 33/6.2 kV,

$X = 16$ ohms/phase on high tension side

Transmission line 20.5 ohms/phase

Load A 40 MW, 11 kV 0.9 P.F. lag

Load B 40 MW, 6.6 kV 0.5 P.F lag

[15 marks : 2004]

Solution:

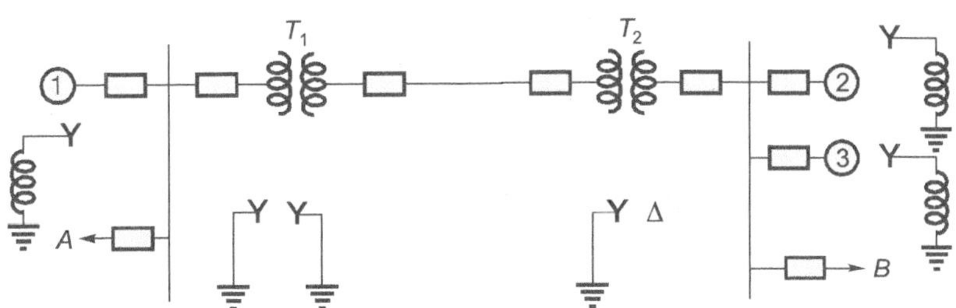

Let, $(MVA)_{base} = 30$ MVA

$(kV)_{base} = 33$ kV on the transmission line

So $(kV)_{base}$ in the circuit of generator 1 is 11 kV and that in the circuits of generator 2 and 3 is 6.2 kV.

$$Z_{pu} = Z_{actual} \times \frac{(MVA)_{base}}{(kV)^2_{base}}$$

Transmission line:

$$X_{line} = 20.5 \times \frac{30}{33^2} = 0.564$$

Transformer T_1:

$$X_{T1} = 15.2 \times \frac{30}{33^2} = 0.418$$

Transformer T_2:

$$X_{T2} = 16 \times \frac{30}{33^2} = 0.44$$

Generator G_1:

$$X_{G2} = 1.6 \times \frac{30}{11^2} = 0.396$$

Generator G_2:

$$X_{G_2} = 1.2\times\frac{30}{6.2^2} = 0.936$$

Generator G_3:

$$X_{G_3} = 0.56\times\frac{30}{6.2^2} = 0.437$$

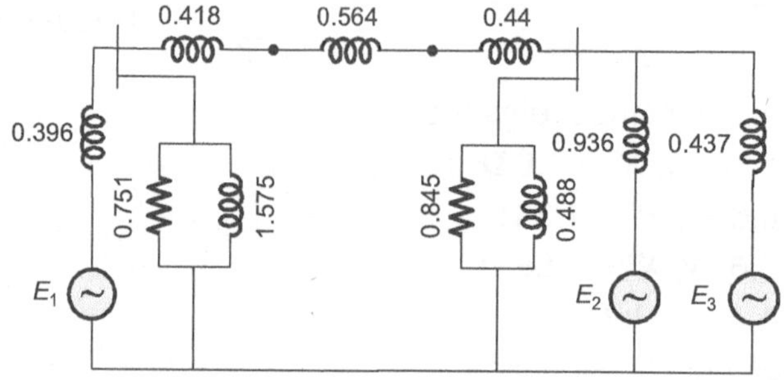

For Load A,

$$V = \frac{11}{11} = 1\text{pu} \qquad P = \frac{40}{30} = 1.33$$

$$\cos\phi = 0.9\text{ lag} \qquad \sin\phi = 0.43$$

$$Q_{pu} = P_{pu}\times\frac{\sin\phi}{\cos\phi} = 0.635$$

$$R_{pu} = \frac{V_{pu}^2}{P_{pu}} = \frac{1^2}{1.33} = 0.751$$

$$X_{pu} = \frac{V_{pu}^2}{Q_{pu}} = 1.575$$

For Load B,

$$V = \frac{6.6}{6.2} = 1.06 \qquad P = \frac{40}{30} = 1.33$$

$$\cos\phi = 0.5\text{ lag} \qquad \sin\phi = 0.866$$

$$Q_{pu} = P_{pu}\times\frac{\sin\phi}{\cos\phi} = 2.30$$

$$R_{pu} = \frac{V_{pu}^2}{P_{pu}} = \frac{1.06^2}{1.33} = 0.845$$

$$X_{pu} = \frac{V_{pu}^2}{Q_{pu}} = \frac{1.06^2}{2.3} = 0.488$$

5.13 A symmetrical 3-phase short-circuit-occurs on the 22 kV bus bars of the circuit shown as a one-line diagram in the above figure. Calculate the fault current and the fault apparent power.

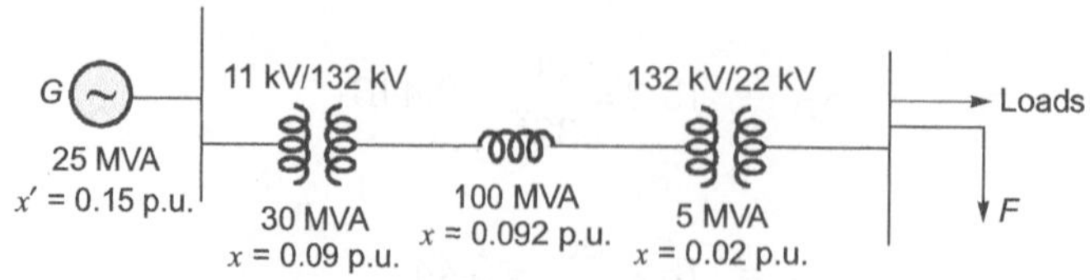

[10 marks : 2005]

Solution:

Let the $(kV)_B$ of the generator is = 11

$(kV)_B$ of the line is = 132

$(kV)_B$ of the load is = 22

$(MVA)_B$ = 100

Generator:

$$X_{p.u.} = 0.15 \times \frac{100}{25} \times \left(\frac{11}{11}\right)^2 = 0.6 \text{ p.u.}$$

Transformer T_1:

$$X_{p.u.} = 0.09 \times \frac{100}{30} \times \left(\frac{11}{11}\right)^2 = 0.3 \text{ p.u.}$$

Transformer T_2:

$$X_{p.u.} = 0.02 \times \frac{100}{5} \times \left(\frac{11}{11}\right)^2 = 0.4 \text{ p.u.}$$

Transmission Line TL:

$$X_{p.u.} = 0.092 \text{ pu}$$

Assuming prefault voltage of the generator to be $1\angle 0°$ pu.

The per unit reactance diagram is,

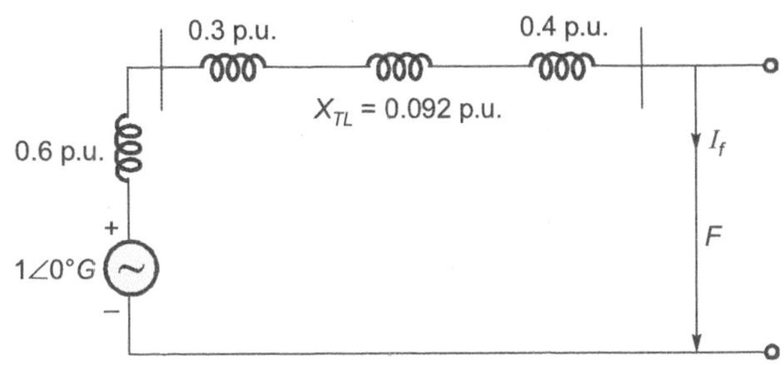

$$I^f = \frac{1\angle 0°}{j(0.3 + 0.092 + 0.4 + 0.6)}$$

$$= \frac{1\angle 0°}{j1.392} = 0.718 \angle -90°$$

$$|I^f| = 0.718 \text{ p.u.}$$

$$\text{Fault } VA = V_0 I^f = 1 \times 0.718 \text{ p.u.}$$

$$= 0.718 \times 100 = 71.8 \text{ MVA}$$

$$(kA)_B = \frac{100}{\sqrt{3} \times 22} = 2.62 \text{ kA}$$

$$|I^f| = 2.620 \times 0.718 = 1.88 \text{ kA}$$

5.14 **Two generating stations having short-circuit capacities of 1200 MVA and 800 MVA respectively and operating at 11 kV are linked by an interconnected cable having a reactance of 0.5 ohm per phase. Determine the short-circuit capacity of each station.**

[14 marks : 2006]

Solution:

Assuming base MVA as 1200, the percent reactance of one generating station is 100% and that of the other is

$$\frac{1200}{800} \times 100 = 150\%$$

The % reactance of the cable is

$$\frac{0.5 \times 1200}{11 \times 11} \times 100 = 496\%$$

When a 3-phase fault takes place of 1200 MVA capacity plant the equivalent circuit will be as follows:

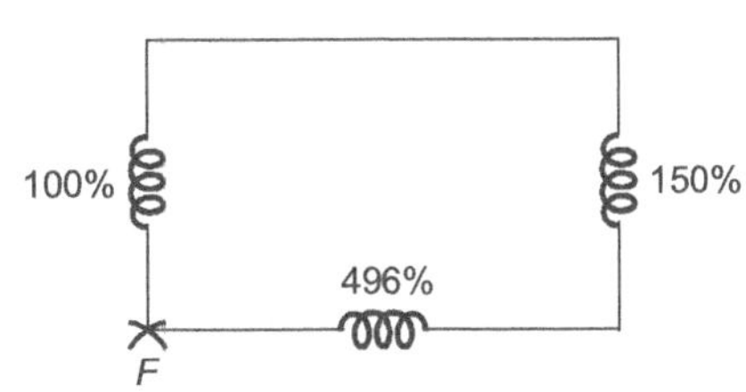

When the fault is at F, fault impedance between F and the neutral bus will be 86.59%.

∴ The short-circuit MVA of this bus will be

$$\frac{1200}{86.59} \times 100 = 1386 \text{ MVA}$$

For fault at the other station – The equivalent fault impedance between F and neutral bus will be -119.84%.

∴ The short-circuit MVA will be

$$\frac{1200}{119.84} \times 100 = 1001 \text{ MVA}$$

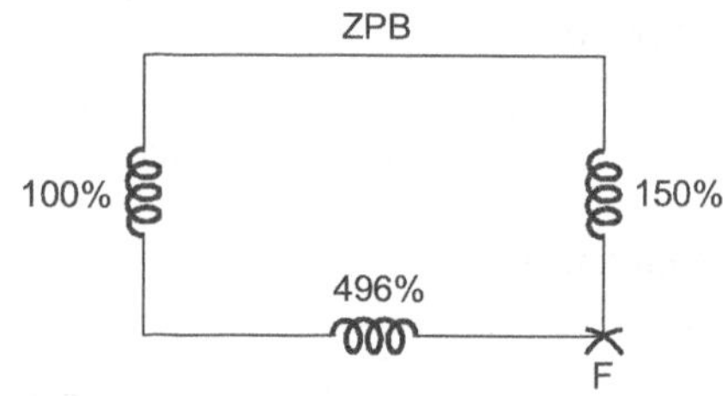

5.15 Draw the positive sequence, negative sequence and zero sequence Impedance networks for the below 3-phase transformer connections.

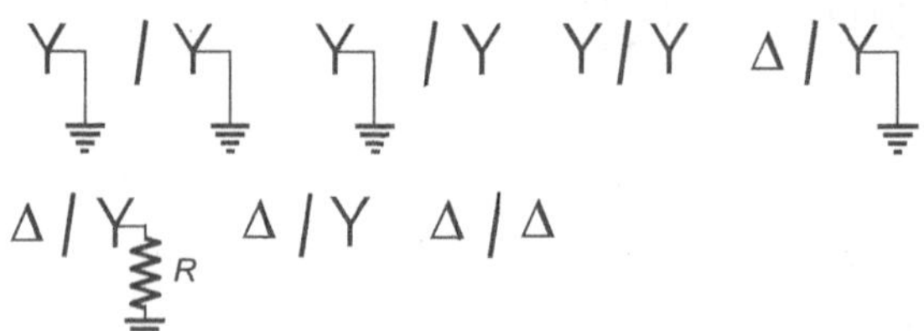

[7 × 2 = 14 marks : 2007]

Solution:

Zero sequence equivalent circuit of transformers,

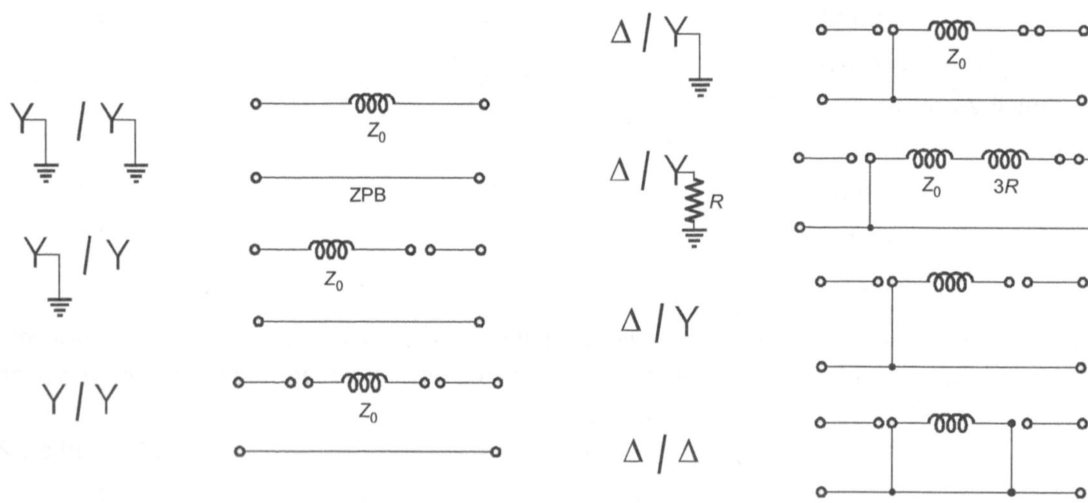

5.16 A 3-phase generator is rated 7500 kVA and 13.8 kV. It has $X''_d = 9\%$, $X'_d = 15\%$, $X_d = 100\%$. This generator is connected to a 3-phase transformer (step up) through a 3-phase circuit breaker which has a speed of 5 cycles. The generator is operating on NO LOAD and at rated voltage. Under this condition, a 3-phase fault occurs between the breaker and the transformer.

Calculate:

(a) Sustained short circuit current in the C.B.
(b) Initial symmetrical RMS current in the breaker.
(c) Maximum possible D.C. component of short circuit current in the C.B.
(d) Momentary current rating of C.B.
(e) Current to be interrupted by the breaker.
(f) Interrupting kVA.

[1 + 5 × 2 = 11 marks : 2007]

Solution:

(a) Since the steady state reactance 100%

∴ The steady state short circuit kVA = 7500 kVA

$$\text{Short circuit MVA} = \frac{\text{Rated MVA} \times 100}{\%\text{ Reactance}}$$

∴ Steady state short circuit current = $\frac{7500}{\sqrt{3} \times 13.8}$ = 313.77 amps.

(b) The initial symmetrical rms current is the current corresponding to sub-transient state where the % reactance is 9.

∴ $$\text{Short circuit MVA} = \frac{7.5}{9} \times 100 = 83.33 \text{ MVA}$$

Initial symmetrical rms,

∴ $$\text{Current} = \frac{83.33 \times 1000}{\sqrt{3} \times 13.8} = 3486.41 \text{ amps. (rms)}$$

(c) The maximum possible d.c. component

= peak value of the subtransient current

= $\sqrt{2} \times 3486.41$ = 4930.52 amps.

(d) Momentary current rating = 1.6 × 3486.41 = 5578.26 amps.

(e) Since it is a 5-cycle breaker the current to be interrupted by the breaker

= 1.1 × Symmetrical breaking current

= 1.1 × 3486.41 = 3835.05 amps.

(f) The interrupting kVA = $\sqrt{3} \times 13.8 \times 3835.05$ = 91666.54 kVA

5.17 A 3-phase generator is rated 25 MVA, 13.2 kV and X''_d = 0.20 p.u.; X_2 = 0.30 p.u. and X_0 = 0.10 p.u. The neutral is solidly grounded. A line-to-line fault occurs on phases B and C of the generator. Calculate:

(a) I_b in amps (b) I_c in amps
(c) V_{AB} in volts (d) V_{BC} in volts
(e) V_{CA} in Volts

[7 marks : 2007]

Solution:

The sequence network for L-L fault is shown in figure. Since the zero sequence network is absent, assuming $(1 + j0.0)$ prefault per unit voltage.

$$I_{a1} = \frac{E_a}{Z_1 + Z_2} = \frac{1 + j0.0}{j0.20 + j0.30} = -2j$$

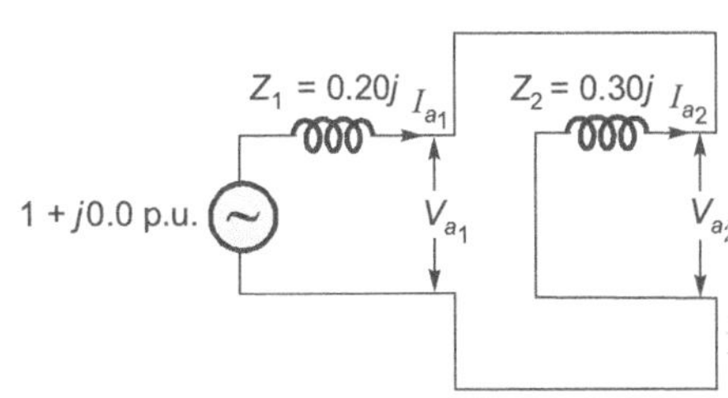

Sequence network

Now for a L-L fault,

$$I_{a1} = -I_{a2} = -2j$$

∴ $$I_{a2} = 2j$$

and $$I_{a0} = 0$$

∴ $$I_b = -I_c,$$

and $$I_b = I_{b1} + I_{b2} + I_{b0} = I_{b1} + I_{b2}$$

$$= \lambda^2 I_{a1} + \lambda I_{a2}$$

where, $$\lambda = 1\angle 120° = (-0.5 - j0.866)(-2j) + (-0.5 + j0.866)(2j)$$

$$= -3.464 \text{ p.u.}$$

$$\text{Now base current} = \frac{25 \times 1000}{\sqrt{3} \times 13.2} = 1093 \text{ ampere}$$

$$\therefore \quad \text{Fault current} = 1093 \times 3.464 = 3786.15 \text{ ampere}$$

$$\therefore \quad |I_b| = |I_c| = 3786.15 \text{ ampere}$$

For line-to-line voltages,

$$V_{a1} = E_a - I_{a1} Z_1 = 1 + j0.0 - (-2j)(j0.20) = 0.6 \text{ p.u.}$$

Similarly, $V_{a2} = -I_{a2} Z_2 = (-2j)(0.30j) = 0.6$ p.u.

i.e., $V_{a1} = V_{a2} = 0.6$ p.u.

$$V_a = V_{a1} + V_{a2} + V_{a0} = V_{a1} + V_{a2} = 2 \times 0.6 = 1.2 \text{ p.u.}$$

$$V_b = \lambda^2 V_{a1} + \lambda V_{a2}$$

$$= (-0.5 - j0.866)(0.6) + (-0.5 + j0.866)(0.6) = -0.6$$

and $V_b = V_c = -0.6$

Line voltage, $V_{ab} = V_a - V_b = 1.2 + 0.6 = 1.8$ p.u.

$$V_{ac} = V_a - V_c = 1.2 + 0.6 = 1.8 \text{ p.u.}$$

and $V_{bc} = V_b - V_c = 0.0$ p.u.

For line-to-line voltages,

$$V_{ab} = 1.8 \times \frac{13.2}{\sqrt{3}} = 13.72 \text{ kV}$$

$$V_{ac} = 1.8 \times \frac{13.2}{\sqrt{3}} = 13.72 \text{ kV}$$

$$V_{bc} = 0.0 \text{ kV}$$

5.18 One-line diagram of a small power system is given below. Draw the zero-sequence network.

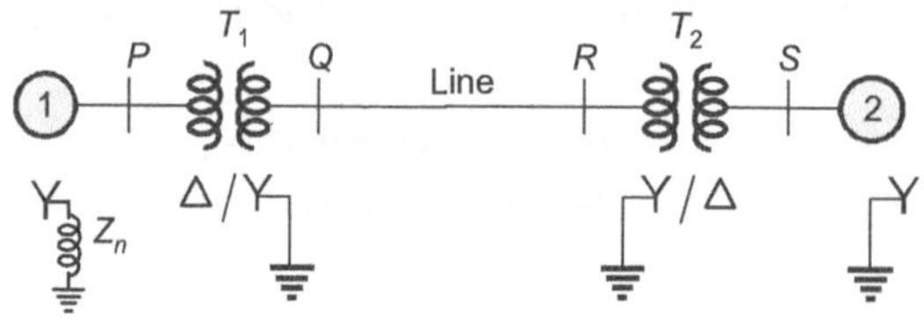

The zero-sequence reactances of the various components are denoted as follows:
Generator 1 = X_{10}; Line = X_{L0}; Generator 2 = X_{20}; Transformer $T_1 = X_{t10}$; Transformer $T_2 = X_{t20}$

[4 marks : 2009]

Solution:

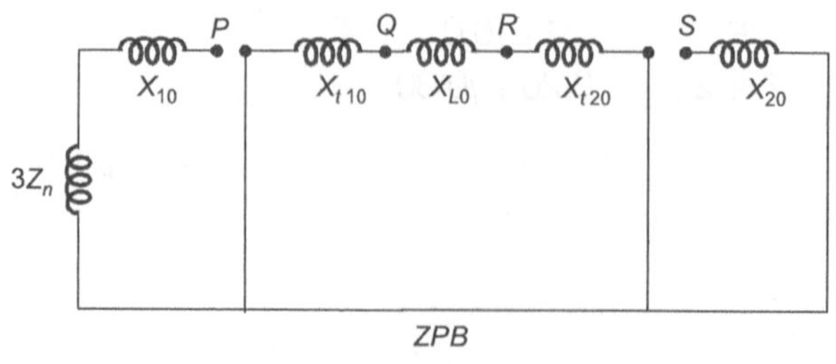

5.19 A 3-phase, 50 Hz generator is rated at 500 MVA, 20 kV with $X_d'' = 0.2$ per unit. It supplies purely resistive load of 400 MW at 20 kV. The load is connected directly across the terminals of the generator. If all the three phases of the load are short circuited simultaneously, find the initial symmetrical rms current in the generator in per unit on a base of 500 MVA, 20 kV.

[5 marks : 2009]

Solution:

Taking,
$$(MVA)_B = 500 \text{ MVA}$$
$$(kV)_B = 20 \text{ kV}$$

pu reactance of the generator $X_d'' = j0.2$ pu

$$P_L = \text{Load} = 400 \text{ MW}$$

$$\Rightarrow \quad P_L = \frac{400}{500} = 0.8 \text{ pu}$$

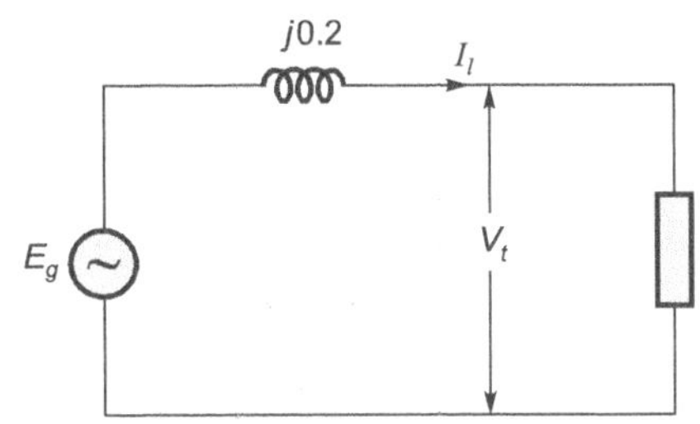

$$\text{Terminal voltage} = V_t = 20 \text{ kV or } V_t = \frac{20}{20} = 1 \text{ pu}$$

$$\text{Pre-fault current,} \quad I_l = \frac{P_L}{V_t} = \frac{0.8}{1} = 0.8\ pu$$

$$I_l = 0.8\angle 0 \quad \text{Load being resistive}$$

$$E_g = V_t + jX_d'' I_l = 1 + j0.2 \times 0.8$$
$$= 1 + j0.16 \text{ pu} = 1.0127\angle 9.09$$

Short circuit at the terminal of the load

$$I_{BL} = \frac{E_g}{jX_d''} = \frac{1.0127\angle 9.09°}{j0.2} = 5.06\angle -80.91° \text{ pu}$$

$$|I_{sc}| = 5.06 \text{ pu}$$

$$\text{Base current} = (kA)_B = \frac{500 \times 10^3}{\sqrt{3} \times 20} = 14.43 \text{ kA}$$

$$|I_{sc}| = 5.06 \times 14.43 = 73 \text{ kA}$$

5.20 The one line diagram of a simple power system is given below. The transformation ratio of the step-up transformer is 11/220 kV. The base MVA = 100 and base kV = 11 on the generator side. The base kV on the transmission side is

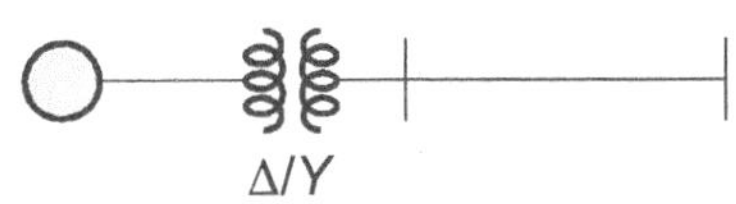

(a) 11 kV
(b) 220 kV
(c) $220\sqrt{3}$ kV
(d) $\sqrt{3} \times 220$ kV

[2 marks : 2010]

Solution: (b)

$$\text{Base kV on the transmission side} = (\text{Base kV on the generator side}) \times \frac{220}{11} = 11 \times \left(\frac{220}{11}\right) = 220 \text{ kV}$$

Hence option (b) 220 kV is correct.

5.21 Determine the positive-sequence component of the three current $I_a = 10\angle 0°$ A, $I_b = 10\angle 230°$ A and $I_c = 10\angle 130°$ A.

[4 marks : 2010]

Solution:

As we know,

$$\begin{bmatrix} I_{a_0} \\ I_{a_1} \\ I_{a_2} \end{bmatrix} = \frac{1}{3} \times \begin{bmatrix} 1 & 1 & 1 \\ 1 & \alpha & \alpha^2 \\ 1 & \alpha^2 & \alpha \end{bmatrix} \begin{bmatrix} I_a \\ I_b \\ I_c \end{bmatrix}$$

where, operator $\alpha = 1\angle 120° \Rightarrow \alpha^2 = 1\angle 240°$

Only positive-sequence components I_{a_1}, I_{b_1} and I_{c_1} are to be calculated,

$$I_{a_1} = \frac{1}{3}\times\left[I_a + \alpha I_b + \alpha^2 I_c\right]$$

where,

$$I_a = 10\angle 0° \text{ A}$$
$$I_b = 10\angle 230° \text{ A}$$
$$I_c = 10\angle 130° \text{ A}$$

$$I_{a_1} = \frac{1}{3}\times[10\angle 0° + (1\angle 120°)\times(10\angle 230°) + (1\angle 240°)\times(10\angle 130°)$$

$$I_{a_1} = 9.89\angle 0° \text{ A}$$

as we know, $I_{b_1} = \alpha^2 I_{a_1} = (1\angle 240°)\times(9.89\angle 0°) = 9.89\angle 240° \text{ A}$

and $I_{c_1} = \alpha I_{a_1} = (1\angle 120°)\times(9.89\angle 0°) = 9.89\angle 120° \text{ A}$

Hence,

$$I_{a_1} = 9.89\angle 0° \text{ A}$$
$$I_{b_1} = 9.89\angle 240° \text{ A}$$
$$I_{c_1} = 9.89\angle 120° \text{ A}$$

5.22 A synchronous generator is rated 20 MVA, 13.8 kV. It has $X_1 = 0.25$ pu. $X_2 = 0.35$ pu and $X_0 = 0.10$ pu. The neutral is solidly grounded. The machine is on no-load and is operating at rated voltage when a D-L-G fault occurs at its terminals. Find the subtransient current in all the phases and the fault (all in amps.) and the line-to-line voltages in all the phases (in kV).

[10 marks : 2011]

Solution:

$$\text{Base MVA} = (\text{MVA})_B = 20 \text{ MVA}$$
$$\text{Base kV} = (\text{kV})_B = 13.8 \text{ kV}$$

Base current, $$I_B = \frac{(\text{MVA})_B}{\sqrt{3}\times(\text{kV})_B} = \frac{20\times 10^3}{\sqrt{3}\times 13.8} = 836.74 \text{ amps.}$$

$X_1 = 0.25$ pu; $X_2 = 0.35$ pu and $X_0 = 0.10$ pu

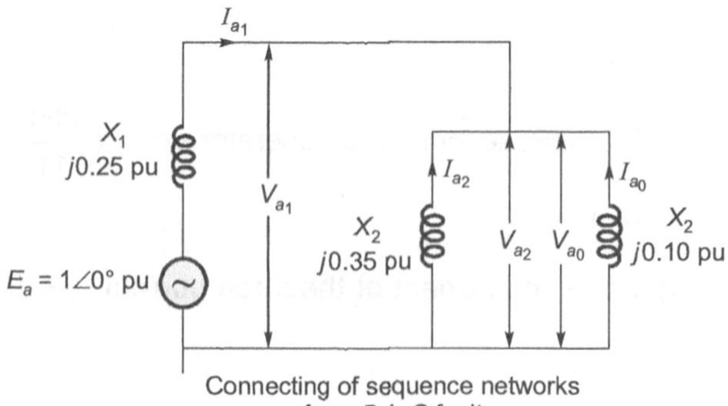

Connecting of sequence networks for a *D-L-G* fault

$$I_{a_1} = \frac{E_a}{X_1 + X_2||X_0} = \frac{1\angle 0°}{j0.25 + j0.35||j0.10} = -j3.051\text{pu}$$

$$I_{a_2} = -I_{a_1}\times\left(\frac{X_0}{X_2 + X_6}\right) = -(-j3.051)\times\left(\frac{j0.10}{j0.35 + j0.10}\right) = j0.678\text{pu}$$

$$I_{a_0} = -I_{a_1} \times \left(\frac{X_2}{X_2 + X_0} \right) = -(-j3.051) \times \left(\frac{j0.35}{j0.35 + j0.1} \right) = j2.373 \text{ pu}$$

$$\text{Fault current} = I_f = 3I_{a_0} = 3 \times j2.373 = j7.119 \text{ pu} = 7.119\angle 90° \text{ pu}$$

As we know, current in different phases are

$$I_a = I_{a_0} + I_{a_1} + I_{a_2} = j2.373 - j3.051 + j0.678 = 0$$

$$\alpha = 1\angle 120°$$

$$I_b = I_{a_0} + \alpha^2 I_{a_1} + \alpha I_{a_2}$$
$$= j2.373 + (1\angle 120)^2 \times (-j3.051) + 1\angle 120 \times j0.678$$
$$= 4.80\angle 132.21° \text{ pu}$$

$$I_c = I_{a_0} + \alpha I_{a_1} + \alpha^2 I_{a_2}$$
$$= j2.373 + 1\angle 120° \times (-j3.051) + (1\angle 120)^2 \times j.678$$
$$= 4.806\angle 47.78° \text{ pu}$$

Values of calculated currents in ampere.

$$\text{Actual current} = \text{Base current} \times \text{Current in pu}$$
$$I_a = 0$$
$$I_b = 836.74 \times 4.806\angle 47.78° = 4021.37\angle 132.21° \text{ amp.}$$
$$I_c = 836.74 \times 4.806\angle 47.78° = 4021.37\angle 47.78° \text{ amp}$$
$$I_f = 836.74 \times 7.119\angle 90° = 5956.75\angle 90° \text{ amp.}$$

From figure,

$$V_{a_0} = V_{a_2} = V_{a_1} = E_a - I_{a_1} \times X_1$$
$$= 1\angle 0° - (-j3.051) \times (j0.25) = 0.2373 \text{ pu}$$

As we know,
$$V_a = V_{a_0} + V_{a_1} + V_{a_2}$$
$$= 3 \times V_{a_1} = 3 \times 0.2373 = 0.7119 \text{ pu}$$

$$1 + \alpha + \alpha^2 = 0$$

$$V_b = V_{a_0} + \alpha^2 V_{a_1} + \alpha V_{a_2} = V_{a_1}(1 + \alpha^2 + \alpha) = 0$$

$$V_c = V_{a_0} + \alpha V_{a_1} + \alpha^2 V_{a_2} = V_{a_1}(1 + \alpha + \alpha^2) = 0$$

Line to line voltages in pu,

$$V_{ab} = V_a - V_b = 0.7119 - 0 = 0.7719\angle 0°$$
$$V_{bc} = V_b - V_c = 0$$
$$V_{ca} = V_c - V_a = 0 - 0.7119$$
$$= 0.7119\angle 180° \text{ pu}$$

$$\text{Voltage in kV} = \text{Base voltage} \times \text{Voltage in pu}$$
$$V_{ab} = 13.8 \times 0.7119\angle 0 = 9.824\angle 0° \text{ kV}$$
$$V_{bc} = 0$$
$$V_{ca} = 13.8 \times 0.7119\angle 180° = 9.824\angle 180° \text{ kV}$$

5.23 Draw the zero sequence network of the transformer connections shown below:

[10 marks : 2011]

Solution:

(a) 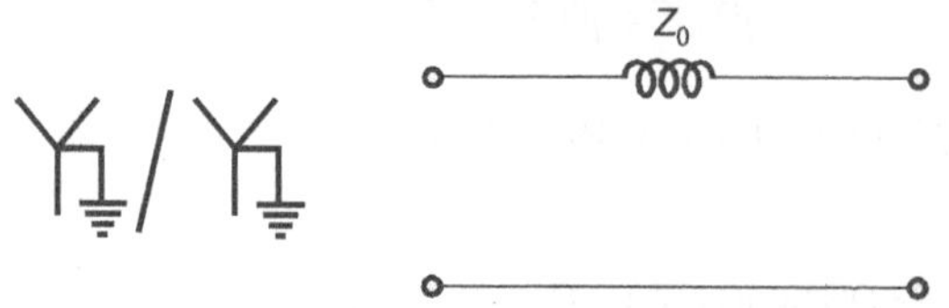

(b) 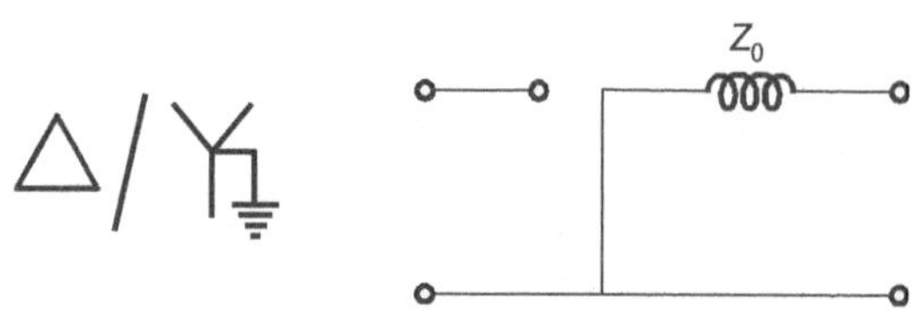

(c) 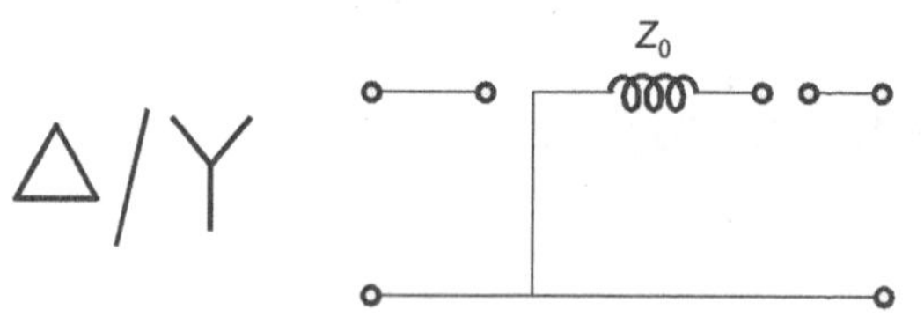

(d) 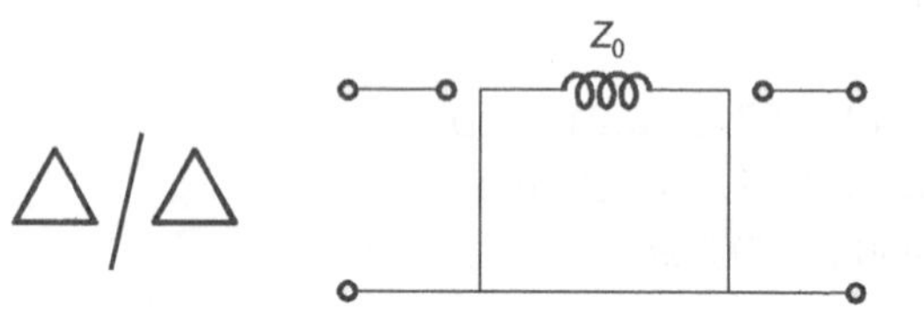

5.24 Show from the first principles that the power consumed in a 3-phase load can be computed from the symmetrical components, provided the currents and voltages are known.

[10 marks : 2012]

Solution:

The relation between unsymmetric phasor V_a, V_b, V_c and symmetrical components V_{a0}, V_{a1}, V_{a2}

$$[V_{012}] = [A]^{-1}[V_{abc}] \quad \text{or} \quad [V_{abc}] = [A][V_{012}]$$

where,
$$[A]^{-1} = \frac{1}{3}\begin{bmatrix} 1 & 1 & 1 \\ 1 & a & a^2 \\ 1 & a^2 & a \end{bmatrix} \quad \text{and} \quad [A] = \begin{bmatrix} 1 & 1 & 1 \\ 1 & a^2 & a \\ 1 & a & a^2 \end{bmatrix}$$

For currents, $[I_{012}] = [A]^{-1}[I_{abc}]$ or $[I_{abc}] = [A][I_{012}]$

The total complex power in a 3-phase circuit is

$$S = V_a I_c^* + V_b I_b^* + V_c I_c^* = [V_a \quad V_b \quad V_c]\begin{bmatrix} I_a \\ I_b \\ I_c \end{bmatrix}^*$$

$$S = [V_{abc}]^T [I_{abc}]^* = [A\,V_{012}]^T [A\,I_{012}]^*$$

$$S = [V_{012}]^T [A]^T [A]^* [I_{012}]^* \qquad \left(\text{as } [AV_{012}]^T = [V_{012}]^T [A]^T\right)$$

$$= 3[V_{012}]^T [I_{012}]^* \qquad \left(\text{as } [A]^T [A]^* = 3I\right)$$

Hence, the power can be computed from symmetrical component if the symmetrical components of voltage and currents are known.

5.25 A 20 MVA, 11 kV, star-connected generator has positive, negative and zero sequence reactances of 25%, 35% and 10% respectively. The neutral is earthed through reactance of 8%. When the generator is unloaded, a short circuit occurs between two lines. Calculate the fault currents in all the phases and voltages assuming that the fault point is grounded.

[10 marks : 2014]

Solution:

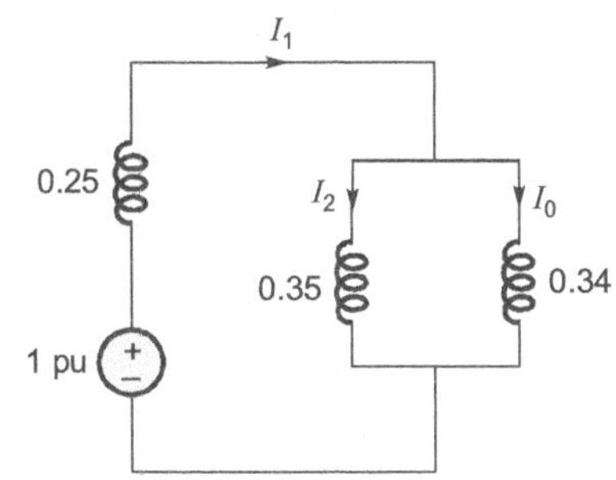

The type of fault here is double line to ground fault,

Total zero sequence impedance

$$= Z_0 = 3Z_n + Z_0 g$$

$$= (3 \times 0.08) + 0.10 = 0.34$$

Hence, the negative sequence impedance and zero sequence impedance are in parallel, the equivalent impedance is

$$\frac{0.35 \times 0.34}{0.35 + 0.34} = 0.172$$

$\therefore$ I_1 = Positive sequence current

$$= \frac{1}{0.25 + 0.172}$$

$$I_1 = 2.369 \text{ pu}$$

According to current division rule,

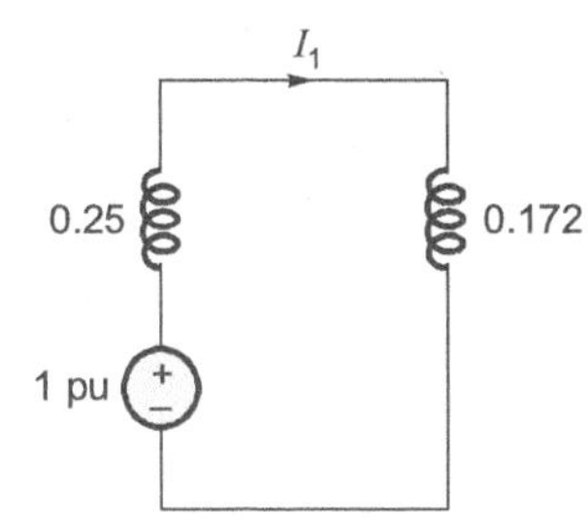

$$I_2 = I_1 \times \frac{0.34}{0.34 + 0.35} = 1.167 \text{ pu}$$

$$I_0 = I_1 \times \frac{0.35}{0.35 + 0.34} = 1.20 \text{ pu}$$

$$\begin{bmatrix} I_a \\ I_b \\ I_c \end{bmatrix} = \begin{bmatrix} 1 & 1 & 1 \\ 1 & a^2 & a \\ 1 & a & a^2 \end{bmatrix} \begin{bmatrix} I_0 \\ I_1 \\ I_2 \end{bmatrix} = \begin{bmatrix} 1 & 1 & 1 \\ 1 & 1\angle 240^\circ & 1\angle 120^\circ \\ 1 & 1\angle 120^\circ & 1\angle 240^\circ \end{bmatrix} \begin{bmatrix} 1.2 \\ 2.369 \\ 1.167 \end{bmatrix}$$

$$\begin{bmatrix} I_a \\ I_b \\ I_c \end{bmatrix} = \begin{bmatrix} 4.736 \\ 1.18\angle -118.6^\circ \\ 1.18\angle 118.6^\circ \end{bmatrix} \text{pu}$$

$$V_0 = I_0 Z_0 = 1.20(0.34) = 0.408 \text{ pu}$$

$$V_1 = I_1 Z_1 = 2.369\,(0.25) = 0.5922 \text{ pu}$$

$$V_2 = I_2 Z_2 = 1.167\,(0.35) = 0.408 \text{ pu}$$

$$\begin{bmatrix} V_a \\ V_b \\ V_c \end{bmatrix} = \begin{bmatrix} 1 & 1 & 1 \\ 1 & a^2 & a \\ 1 & a & a^2 \end{bmatrix} \begin{bmatrix} V_0 \\ V_1 \\ V_2 \end{bmatrix} = \begin{bmatrix} 1 & 1 & 1 \\ 1 & 1\angle 240^\circ & 1\angle 120^\circ \\ 1 & 1\angle 120^\circ & 1\angle 240^\circ \end{bmatrix} \begin{bmatrix} 0.408 \\ 0.5922 \\ 0.408 \end{bmatrix}$$

$$\begin{bmatrix} V_a \\ V_b \\ V_c \end{bmatrix} = \begin{bmatrix} 1.4082 \\ 0.1842\angle -120^\circ \\ 0.1842\angle 120^\circ \end{bmatrix} \text{pu}$$

5.26 What do you understand by infinite line and infinite bus? [2 marks : 2015]

Solution:

Infinite line: A transmission line of finite length (lossless or lossy) that is terminated at one end with a impedance equal to the characteristic impedance appears to the source like a infinitely long transmission line and produces no reflections.

Voltage reflection coefficients $(\rho_v) = 0$

Voltage transmission coefficient $(T_v) = 1 + T_v = 1$

At this condition: $\boxed{V_S = V_L}$

V_S = source voltage, V_L = load voltage

Infinite Bus: A system Bus of constant voltage and constant frequency regardless of the load is called infinite busbar system or simply infinite bus. The characteristics of an infinite bus are as follows:

(a) The terminal voltage remains constant, because the incoming machine is too small to increase or decrease it.

(b) The frequency remains constant, because the system inertia is too large to enable the incoming machine to alter the frequency of the system.

(c) The synchronous impedance is very small since the system has a large number of alternators in parallel.

5.27 **A 3-phase transmission line, operating at 33 kV and having a resistance and reactance of 6 Ω and 21 Ω respectively, is connected to the generating station bus-bars through a 3000 kVA step-up transformer which has a reactance of 5%. Three alternators are connected to the bus-bar, two alternators are of 10000 kVA with a reactance of 15% and the third alternator is of 5000 kVA with a reactance of 10%. Calculate the kVA at the short-circuit fault between the phases occurring (i) at the high voltage terminals of the transformer, and (ii) at the load end of the transmission line.**

[10 marks : 2016]

Solution:

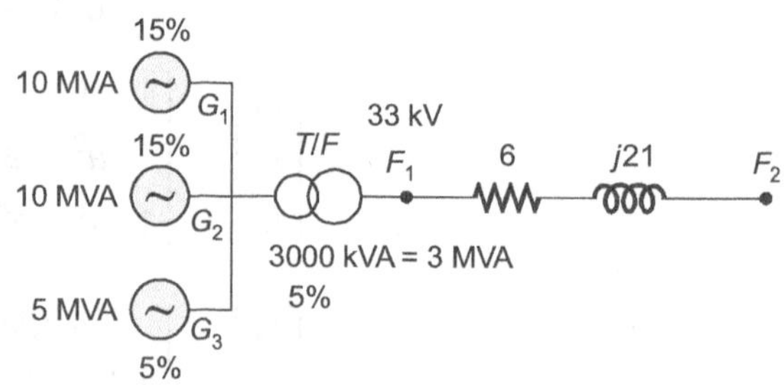

Select common MVA = 10 MVA,

For $G_1 = G_2$

$\Rightarrow \quad X = 15\% = 0.15$ pu

$$G_3 = X_n = X_0 \times \frac{(\text{MVA})_n}{(\text{MVA})_0} \times \left(\frac{\text{kV}_A}{\text{kV}_n}\right)^2$$

$$= 5 \times \frac{10}{5} \times \frac{1}{1} = 10\% = 0.1 \text{ p.u}$$

Transformer: $$X_n = 5 \times \frac{10}{3} \times \left(\frac{1}{1}\right)^2 = 16.67\% = 0.1667 \text{ p.u.}$$

$$Z_{pu} = \frac{Z_\Omega (\text{MVA})_b}{(\text{kV})^2} = \frac{(6 + j21) \times 10}{(33)^2}$$

$$Z_{pu} = (0.055 + j0.193) \text{ p.u.}$$

Reactance diagram:

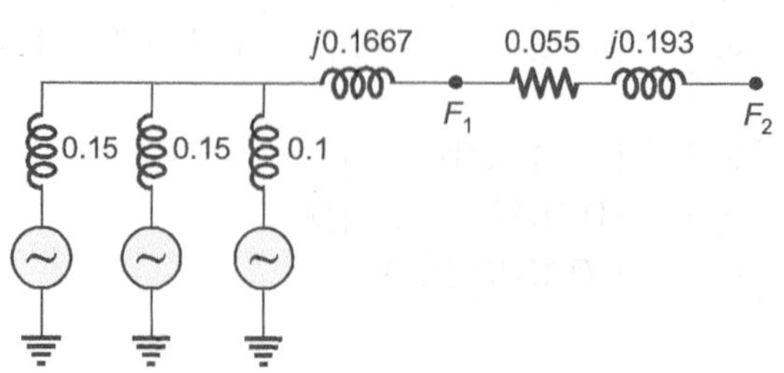

(i) For fault at F_1:

$$Z_{Th} = (0.15 \| 0.15 \| 0.1) + 0.1667 = j0.2095 \text{ p.u.}$$

$$(MVA)_{sc} = \left|\frac{(MVA)_b}{Z_{Th}}\right| = \left|\frac{10}{0.2095}\right|$$

$$(MVA)_{sc} = 47.71 \text{ MVA}$$

(ii) Fault at F_2:

$$Z_{Th} = j0.2095 + 0.055 + j0.193 = 0.4062\angle 82°$$

$$(MVA)_{sc} = \frac{(MVA)_b}{Z_{Th}} = \frac{10}{0.4062\angle 82°} = 24.61 \text{ MVA}$$

5.28 **(i) Under what condition a single line-to-ground fault at the terminals of a generator can be more severe than a 3-phase symmetrical fault at the same location?**

(ii) A 3-phase power system is represented by one-line diagram as shown in the figure below:

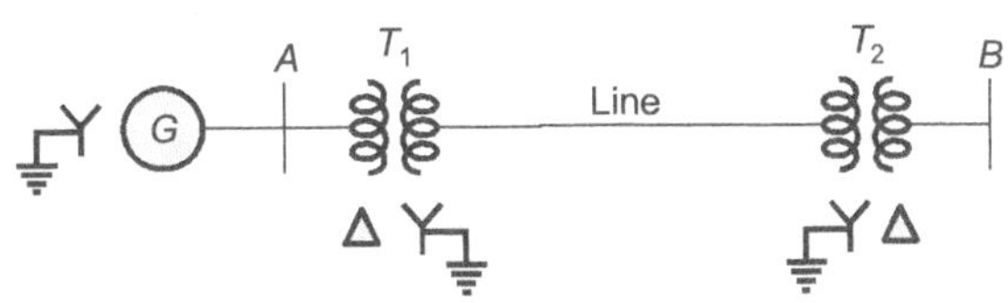

The ratings of the equipments are the following:

Generator (G): 15 MVA, 6.6 kV, X_1 = 15%, X_2 = 10%

Transformers: 15 MVA, 6.6 kV delta/33 kV star, $X_1 = X_2 = X_0$ = 6%

Line reactance: $X_1 = X_2 = 2\ \Omega$ and $X_0 = 6\ \Omega$

Find the fault current for a ground fault on one of the bus bars at *B*.

[20 marks : 2018]

Solution:

(i) Fault current in line to ground fault is given as,

$$I_{FLG} = \frac{3V_{th}}{(x_1 + x_2 + x_0 + 3z_n)}$$

where V_{th} is the thevenin voltage at fault location and x_1, x_2, x_0 are positive, negative, zero sequence impedance at fault location and Z_n in the neutral impedance.

Fault current in 3-ϕ fault is given as,

$$I_{f3\text{-}\phi} = \frac{V_{th}}{x_1}$$

For fault current in LG fault to be more severe.

$$I_{fLG} > I_{f3\text{-}\phi}$$

$$\frac{3V_{th}}{(x_1 + x_2 + x_0 + 3z_n)} > \frac{V_{th}}{x_1}$$

$$\Rightarrow \quad 3x_1 > (x_1 + x_2 + x_0 + 3z_n)$$

$$\Rightarrow \quad z_n < \frac{1}{3}(2x_1 - x_2 - x_0)$$

If,

$$x_1 = x_2$$

Then, $$z_n < \frac{1}{3}(x_1 - x_0)$$

The above condition makes the LG fault current it more severe.

(ii)

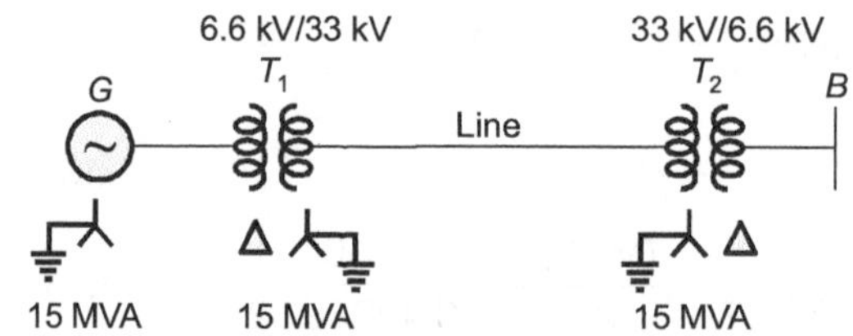

Positive sequence network:

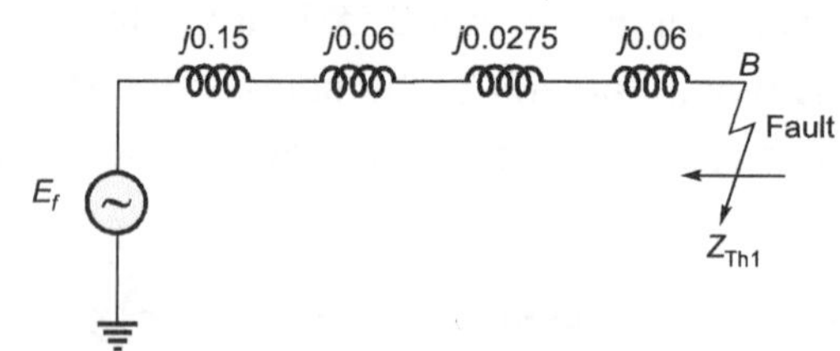

For Transmission line, $X_1 = X_2 = 2\ \Omega,\ S_b = 15\text{ MVA},\ V_b = 33\text{ kV}$

$$X_{p.u.} = X_{ohmic} \times \frac{\text{MVA}_b}{(\text{kV})^2}$$

In per unit, $$X_1 = X_2 = \frac{2 \times 15}{(33)^2} = 0.0275\text{ p.u.}$$

$$X_0 = 6\ \Omega$$

Zero sequence reactance of transmission line,

$$(X_0)_{p.u.} = \frac{6 \times 15}{(33)^2} = 0.0826\text{ p.u.}$$

Positive sequence Thevenin impedance:

$$Z_{Th1} = j(0.15 + 0.06 + 0.0275 + 0.06)$$
$$= j0.2975\text{ p.u.}$$

Negative sequence network:

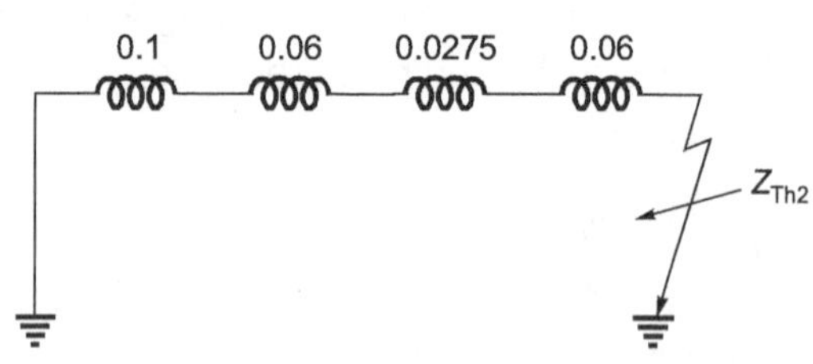

$$Z_{Th2} = j(0.10 + 0.06 + 0.0275 + 0.06)$$
$$= j0.2475\text{p.u.}$$

Zero sequence network:

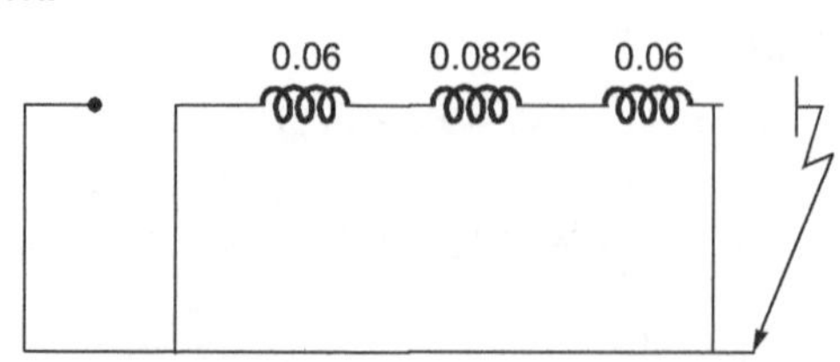

Z_0 = zero sequence reactance is infinite because of open circuit.

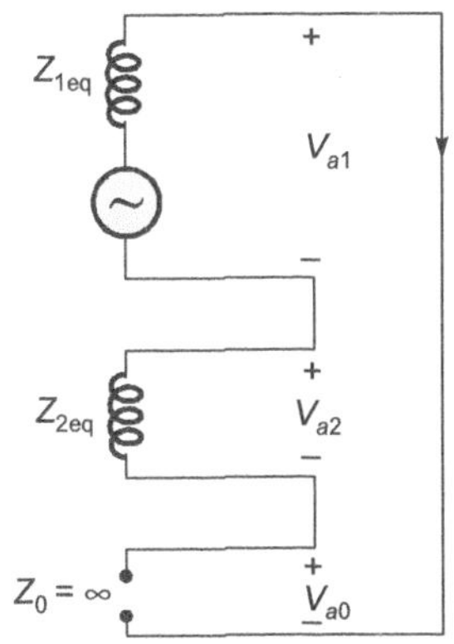

∴ The fault current is = 0

5.29 A 25 MVA, 13.8 kV generator with $X_d'' = 15\%$ is connected through a 25 MVA, 13.8/6.9 kV transformer with leakage reactance of 10% to a bus which supplies four identical motors as shown in the figure. The sub-transient reactance X_d'' of each motor is 20% on base of 5 MVA, 6.9 kV. Find:

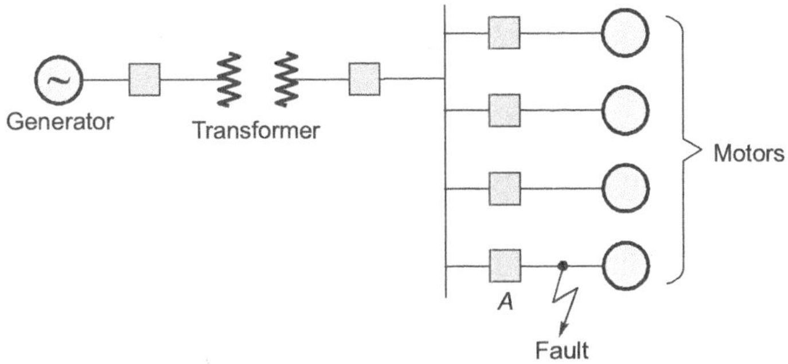

(i) The sub-transient current in the fault.
(ii) The sub-transient current in breaker A.

[20 marks : 2019]

Solution:

(i) Let, Base MVA = 25 MVA

For generator base voltage = 13.8 kV

For motors base voltage = 6.9 kV

Generator G: X''_{dg} p.u. = $j0.15$ p.u.

Each motor, X''_{dm} p.u. = $j0.2 \times \frac{25}{5} = j1.0$ p.u.

Transformer, $X_{T\,p.u.}$ = j0.10 p.u.

Reactance diagram:

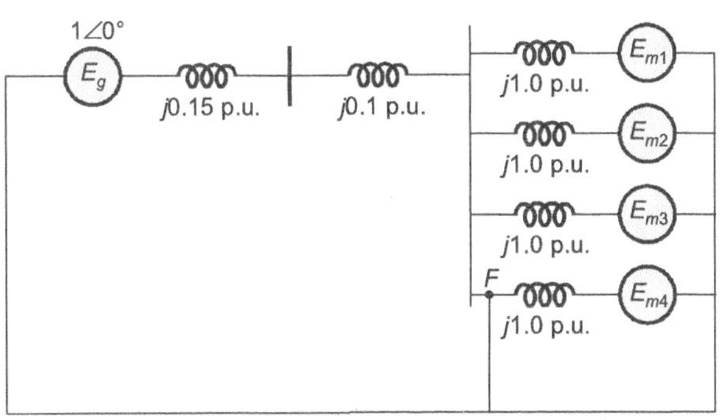

$$X_{eq\,p.u.} = \frac{\frac{j1.0}{4} \times 0.25}{\frac{j1.0}{4} + j0.25} = j0.125 \text{ p.u.}$$

The p.u. subtransient fault current,

$$I_{fp.u.} = \frac{1.0}{j0.125} = -j8 \text{ p.u.}$$

Base current,

$$I_b \text{ in 6.9 kV circuit} = \frac{(\text{MVA})_b \times 10^3}{\sqrt{3} \times (\text{kV})_b} = \frac{25 \times 10^3}{\sqrt{3} \times 6.9} = 2091.84 \text{ A}$$

$$I_f = I_{fp.u.} \times I_b$$
$$= 8 \times 2091.84 = 16734.79$$

(ii) For subtransient current in breaker A,

$$|I''_{CA}| = \frac{1\angle 0^\circ}{j0.25} + \frac{3 \times 1\angle 0^\circ}{j1.0} = 7.0 \text{ p.u.}$$

$$|I''_{CA}| = 7 \times 2091.84 = 14642.88 \text{ A}$$

5.30 Two 11 kV, 30 MVA, three-phase synchronous generators operate in parallel supplying a substation through a feeder having an impedance of (0.6 + j0.8) ohms to positive and negative sequence currents and (1.0 + j2.6) ohms to zero sequence currents. Each generator has X_1 = 0.8 ohms, X_2 = 0.5 ohms and X_0 = 0.2 ohms and has its neutral grounded through a reactance of 0.2 ohms. Evaluate the fault currents in each line and the potential above earth attained by the generator neutrals, consequent to simultaneous occurrence of earth fault on the Y and B phases at the sub-station.

[20 marks : 2020]

Solution:

Let the base MVA be 30 MVA and base kV, 11 kV.

For synchronous generators.

Per unit positive sequence reactance

$$X_1 = j0.8 \times \frac{30}{(11)^2} = j0.1983 \text{ p.u.}$$

Per unit negative sequence reactance

$$X_2 = j0.5 \times \frac{30}{(11)^2} = j0.1239 \text{ p.u.}$$

Per unit zero sequence reactance

$$X_0 = j0.2 \times \frac{30}{(11)^2} = j0.0495 \text{ p.u.}$$

For feeder,

$$X_1 = X_2 = (0.6 + j0.8) \times \frac{30}{(11)^2} = 0.2479(0.6 + j0.8)$$
$$= 0.14874 + 0.19832j \text{ p.u.}$$

$$X_0 = (1 + j2.6) \times \frac{30}{(11)^2} = 0.2479(1 + j2.6)$$

$$= 0.2479 + 0.646j \text{ p.u.}$$

Grounding reactance, $R_G = 0.2 \times \dfrac{30}{(11)^2} = j0.04958$ p.u.

As both generator (identical) operate in parallel

$$X_{1eff} = j\frac{0.1983}{2} + 0.14874 + j0.19832$$
$$= j0.09915 + 0.14874 + j0.19832$$
$$= 0.14874 + j0.29747 \text{ p.u.}$$

$$X_{2eff} = j\frac{0.1239}{2} + 0.14874 + j0.19832$$
$$= j0.06195 + 0.14874 + j0.19832 = 0.299\angle 60.25^\circ \text{ p.u.}$$

$$X_{0eff} = j\frac{0.04958 + (3 \times j0.04958)}{2} + 0.2479 + j(0.6446)$$
$$= 0.2479 + j0.74376 \text{ p.u.} = 0.784\angle 71.56^\circ \text{ p.u.}$$

For LLG fault on generator terminals

Assuming pre-fault voltage E_a be $1\angle 0^\circ$ p.u.

$$I_{a1} = \frac{E_a}{X_{1eff} + \dfrac{X_{2eff} \times X_{0eff}}{X_{2eff} + X_{0eff}}} \text{ p.u.}$$

$$I_{a1} = \frac{1\angle 0^\circ}{(0.14874 + j0.29747) + \dfrac{(0.14874 + j0.26027)(0.2479 + j0.74376)}{0.14874 + j0.26027 + 0.2479 + j0.74376}} \text{ p.u.}$$

$$= 1.81723\angle -63.4109 \text{ p.u.}$$

$$I_{a0} = -\left(\frac{E_a - I_{a1}X_{1eff}}{X_{0eff}}\right)$$
$$= -\left(\frac{1 - (0.84132 - j1.62609) \times (0.14874 + j0.19832)}{0.32227 + j0.66935}\right)$$
$$= -0.4135 + j0.62613 \text{ p.u.}$$
$$= -0.504\angle -71.598^\circ \text{ p.u.}$$

I_{a0} for each generator

$$\frac{0.504\angle -71.598}{2} = -0.252\angle -71.598 \text{ p.u.}$$

Potential of alternator neutral w.r.t. ground

$$= 3 \times I_{a0} \text{ per generator} \times R_G$$
$$= 3 \times (-0.252\angle -71.598) \times j0.04958$$
$$= 0.03075 - j0.04656$$
$$= -3.7428 \times 10^{-3}\angle 18.4^\circ \text{ p.u.}$$

Potential of alternator neutral w.r.t. ground

$$-3.7428 \times 10^{-2}\angle 18.4^\circ \times \frac{11000}{\sqrt{3}} = -237.69\angle 18.4^\circ \text{ V}$$

$$I_{R2} = I_{R1} - I_{R0}$$
$$I_{a2} = -1.320\angle -60.294^\circ \text{ p.u.}$$

The sequence current in each generator will be

$$I_{g0} = \frac{I_{a0}}{2} = -0.252\angle -71.598°$$

$$I_{g1} = \frac{I_{a1}}{2} = 0.908615\angle -63.4109°$$

$$I_{g2} = \frac{I_{a2}}{2} = -0.66\angle -60.294°$$

$$\begin{bmatrix} I_{af=0} \\ I_{bf} \\ I_{cf} \end{bmatrix} = \begin{bmatrix} 1 & 1 & 1 \\ 1 & \alpha^2 & \alpha \\ 1 & \alpha & \alpha^2 \end{bmatrix} \begin{bmatrix} I_{af}^{(0)} \\ I_{af}^{(1)} \\ I_{af}^{(2)} \end{bmatrix}$$

$$I_{bf} = I_{af}^{(0)} + \alpha^2 I_{af}^{(1)} + \alpha I_{af}^{(2)}$$

$$= -0.252\angle -71.598° + 1\angle 240°(0.908615\angle -63.4109°)$$
$$+ 1\angle 120°(-0.66\angle -60.294°)$$
$$= -0.252\angle -71.598° + 0.90861\angle 176.5891 - 0.66\angle 59.706°)$$
$$= 1.3481\angle -168.156° \text{ p.u.}$$

$$I_{cf} = -0.252\angle -71.598° + (1\angle 120°) \times (0.908615\angle -63.4109°)$$
$$+ (1\angle 240°) \times (-0.66\angle -60.294°)$$
$$= -0.252\angle -71.598° + 0.908615\angle 56.589° - (0.66\angle -179.706°)$$
$$= 1.4684\angle 42.61° \text{ p.u.}$$

$$I_{bf\,(actual)} = 2122.707\angle -168.156° \text{ A},$$
$$I_{cf\,(actual)} = 2312.13\angle 42.61° \text{ A}$$

5.31 A 100 MVA, 20 kV, 50 Hz three-phase generator is connected to a 100 MVA 20/400 kV three-phase transformer. The machine has the following per unit reactances and time constants:

$$X_d'' = 0.15 \text{ p.u.} \qquad \tau_d'' = 0.035 \text{ sec}$$
$$X_d' = 0.25 \text{ p.u.} \qquad \tau_d' = 0.5 \text{ sec}$$
$$X_d = 1.25 \text{ p.u.} \qquad \tau_d = 0.3 \text{ sec}$$

The transformer reactance in 0.25 per unit, The generator is operating at the rated voltage and no-load when a three phase short-circuit occurs at the secondary terminals of the transformer. Find the subtransient transient and the steady state short circuit currents in per unit and actual amperes on both sides of the transformer.

[20 marks : 2021]

Solution:

Let base is 100 MVA, 20 kV at generator side. So, base current on LV side of transformer,

$$(I_b)_{LV} = \frac{100 \times 10^3}{\sqrt{3} \times 20} = 2886.75 \text{ A}$$

Base current on HV side of transformer

$$(I_b)_{HV} = \frac{100 \times 10^3}{\sqrt{3} \times 400} = 144.337 \text{ A}$$

Subtransient symmetrical fault current,

$$I_f''(\text{rms}) = \frac{E_g}{X_d'' + X_{tr}} = \frac{1}{j0.15 + j0.25} = 2.5\angle -90° \text{ p.u.}$$

Actual current on HV side,

$$(I^2_{HV})_f = 2.5 \times 144.337 = 360.842 \text{ A}$$

$$\text{Actual current on LV side} = 2.5 \times 2886.75$$

$$(I^2_{LV})_f = 7216.875 \text{ A}$$

Transient symmetrical fault current,

$$I'_f(\text{rms}) = \frac{E_g}{X'_d + X_{tr}} = \frac{1}{j0.25 + j0.25} = 2\angle{-90^\circ} \text{ p.u.}$$

Transient symmetrical fault currents,

$$\text{Actual current (HV side)} = 2 \times 144.337 = 288.674 \text{ A}$$

$$\text{Actual current (LV side)} = 2 \times 2886.75$$

$$I'_{f(LV)} = 5773.5 \text{ A}$$

Steady state current (rms), $$I_s = \frac{E_g}{X_d + X_{tr}} = \frac{1}{j1.25 + j0.25} = 0.667\angle{-90^\circ} \text{ p.u.}$$

Actual steady state short circuit current,

At HV side $$(I_f)_{HV} = 0.667 \times 144.337 = 96.272 \text{ A}$$

At LV side $$(I_f)_{LV} = 0.667 \times 2886.75 = 1925.462 \text{ A}$$

5.32 **The positive, negative and zero sequence reactances of a 25 MVA, 13.2 kV synchronous generator are 0.3 pu, 0.2 pu and 0.1 pu respectively. The generator is star connected and neutral is solidly grounded. When it is unloaded, find the fault current and line-line voltages when a fault of**

(i) Line-line occurs,

(ii) Double line to ground occurs.

[20 marks : 2023]

Solution:

Given : $Z_1 = j0.3$ pu; $Z_2 = j0.2$ pu; $Z_0 = j0.1$ pu

$G = 25$ MVA; $V = 13.2$ kV

Y = Current generation, Solid grounded neutral

Base current, $$I_b = \frac{25 \times 10^3}{\sqrt{3} \times 13.2} = 1.09(10)^3 = 1093.5 \text{ A}$$

(i) L-L form $$I_f = -j\sqrt{3}I_{a1}$$

$$I_{a1} = \frac{E_a}{Z_1 + Z_2} = \frac{1.0}{j0.3 + j0.2} = -j2.0$$

Hence, fault current, $$I_f = -j\sqrt{3}(-j2.0) \times 1093.5 = 3787.88 \text{ A}$$

(ii) For LLG fault, $$I_f = 3I_{ao}$$

$$I_{ao} = \frac{I_o Z_1 - E_a}{Z_o}$$

$$I_{a1} = \frac{E_a}{Z_1 + Z_2 \parallel Z_0}$$

$$I_{a1} = \frac{1.0}{j0.3 + j0.2 \,||\, j0.1} = -j2.727$$

$$I_{a0} = \frac{(-j2.727)(j0.3) - 1.0}{j0.1} = j1.818$$

Hence, fault current, $I_f = 3I_{a0} = 3 \times 1.818 \times 1093.5$

$= 5964$ Amp

6. Load Flow Studies

6.1 Why is one of the buses taken as slack bus in load flow studies? [4 marks : 2001]

Solution:

In a power system there are mainly two types of buses: load and generator buses. For these buses we have specified the real power P injections. Now $\sum_{i=1}^{n} P_i$ = real power loss P_L.

Where P_i is the power injection at the buses, which is taken as positive for generator buses and in negative for load buses. The losses remain unknown until the load flow solution is complete.

It is for this reason that generally one of the generator buses is made to take the additional real power to supply transmission losses. That is why this type of bus is also known as the slack or swing bus. At this bus, the voltage magnitude V and phase angle δ are specified whereas real and reactive power P_G and Q_G are obtained through the load flow solution.

6.2 Draw the reactance diagram of the system whose bus admittance matrix in given below. First, second, third and fourth rows refer to the buses 1, 2, 3, 4 respectively

$$Y_{bus} = j\begin{bmatrix} -3.78 & 1.25 & 2.50 & 0 \\ 1.25 & -3.42 & 1.11 & 1.00 \\ 2.50 & 1.11 & -4.89 & 1.25 \\ 0 & 1.00 & 1.25 & -2.31 \end{bmatrix}$$

[12 marks : 2001]

Solution:

We know that, $Y_{ik} = -y_{ik}$

when, $i \neq k$

and $z_{ik} = \dfrac{1}{y_{ik}}$

$$Y_{12} = -y_{12} = j1.25 = Y_{21}$$

$\therefore$ $y_{12} = -j1.25$

$$Z_{12} = \frac{1}{y_{12}} = -\frac{1}{j1.25} = j0.8$$

and $Y_{13} = -y_{13} = j2.5$

$\therefore$ $Z_{13} = -\dfrac{1}{j2.5} = j0.4$

$\therefore$ $Y_{14} = -y_{14} = 0$

$\therefore \quad Z_{14} = \infty$

It means that these is no line between bus 1 and bus 4.

$$Y_{23} = -y_{23} = j1.11$$

$$Z_{23} = -\frac{1}{j1.11} = j0.9$$

$$Y_{24} = -y_{24} = j1.00$$

$$\therefore \quad y_{24} = -j1.00$$

$$Z_{24} = -\frac{1}{j1.00} = j1.00$$

$$Y_{34} = -y_{34} = j1.25$$

$$\therefore \quad Z_{34} = -\frac{1}{j1.25} = j\,0.8$$

The reactance diagram is given is below.

The row shown below are column reminder indicates the shunt element.

Here $j(-3.78 + 1.25 + 2.5 + 0) = j0.03$. The negative sign indicates inductor, similarly for all buses.

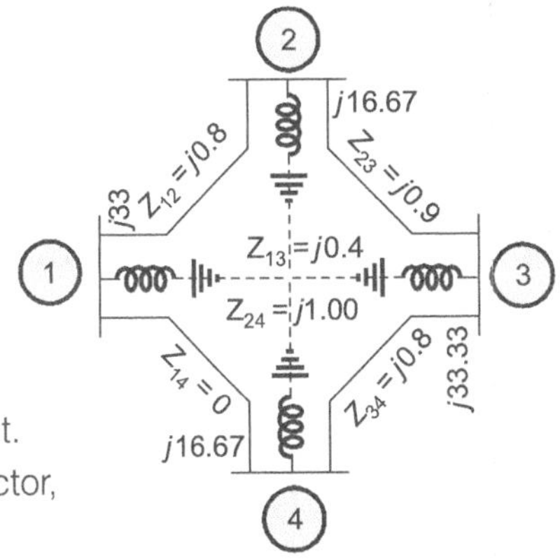

6.3 Y_{BUS} as used in load flow study, and Z_{BUS} as used for short circuit study are:

(a) the same

(b) inverse of each other

(c) are not related to each other [2 marks : 2003]

Solution: (b)

Option (b) is correct.

6.4 In load flow studies of a power system, a voltage control bus is specified by:

(a) Real power and reactive power

(b) Reactive power and voltage magnitude

(c) Voltage and voltage phase angle

(d) Real power and voltage magnitude [2 marks : 2006]

Solution: (d)

Option (d) is correct.

6.5 Consider the network shown in figure. The bus numbers and impedances are marked. Determine the bus impedance matrix of the network.

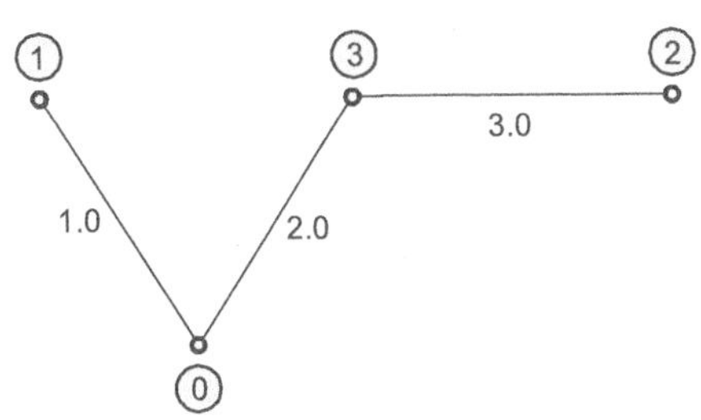

[4 marks : 2008]

Solution:

Step-1

Add branch $Z_{10} = 1$ (from bus 1 to bus 0)

$$Z_{BUS} = [1]$$

Step-2

Add branch $Z_{30} = 2$ {from bus 2 (new) to bus 0}

$$Z_{BUS(new)} = \begin{bmatrix} Z_{BUS(old)} \\ \hline Z_{30} \end{bmatrix}$$

$$Z_{BUS(old)} = [1]$$

$$Z_{BUS(new)} = \begin{array}{c} \\ 1 \\ 3 \end{array}\begin{array}{c} \begin{matrix} 1 & 3 \end{matrix} \\ \begin{bmatrix} 1 & 0 \\ 0 & 2 \end{bmatrix} \end{array}$$

Step-3

Add branch $Z_{23} = 3$ {from bus 2 (new) to bus 3 (old)}

$$Z_{BUS(new)} = \left[\begin{array}{c|c} & Z_{ij} \\ & Z_{2j} \\ Z_{BUS(old)} & \vdots \\ & Z_{nj} \\ \hline Z_{j1}\ Z_{j2} \cdots Z_{jn} & Z_{jj} + Z_b \end{array}\right]$$

$Z_b = 3;\ j = 3$

$$[Z_{31}\ \ Z_{33}] = [0\ \ 2]$$

$$\begin{bmatrix} Z_{13} \\ Z_{23} \end{bmatrix} = \begin{bmatrix} 0 \\ 2 \end{bmatrix}$$

$$Z_{BUS(old)} = \begin{array}{c} \\ 1 \\ 3 \end{array}\begin{array}{c} \begin{matrix} 1 & 3 \end{matrix} \\ \begin{bmatrix} 1 & 0 \\ 0 & 2 \end{bmatrix} \end{array}$$

$$Z_{j1} = Z_{33} = 2$$

$$j = 3$$

$$Z_{BUS(new)} = \begin{array}{c} \\ 1 \\ 3 \\ 2 \end{array}\begin{array}{c} \begin{matrix} 1 & 3 & 2 \end{matrix} \\ \left[\begin{array}{cc|c} 1 & 0 & 0 \\ 0 & 2 & 2 \\ \hline 0 & 2 & 3+2 \end{array}\right] \end{array} = \begin{array}{c} \\ 1 \\ 3 \\ 2 \end{array}\begin{array}{c} \begin{matrix} 1 & 3 & 2 \end{matrix} \\ \begin{bmatrix} 1 & 0 & 0 \\ 0 & 2 & 2 \\ 0 & 2 & 5 \end{bmatrix} \end{array}$$

On rearranging the above bus impedance matrix,

$$Z_{BUS} = \begin{array}{c} \\ 1 \\ 2 \\ 3 \end{array}\begin{array}{c} \begin{matrix} 1 & 2 & 3 \end{matrix} \\ \begin{bmatrix} 1 & 0 & 0 \\ 0 & 5 & 2 \\ 0 & 2 & 2 \end{bmatrix} \end{array}$$

Alternative method:

$$V_1 = 1.0\, I,$$

$$V_2 = 2.0(I_2 + I_3)\, 3.0\, I_2$$

$$= 5I_2 + 2.0I_3$$

$$V_3 = 2.0(I_2 + I_3) = 2.0\, I_2 + 2.0\, I_3$$

$$\begin{bmatrix} V_1 \\ V_2 \\ V_3 \end{bmatrix} = \begin{bmatrix} 1.0 & 0.0 & 0.0 \\ 0.0 & 5.0 & 2.0 \\ 0.0 & 2.0 & 2.0 \end{bmatrix}\begin{bmatrix} I_1 \\ I_2 \\ I_3 \end{bmatrix}$$

6.6 Explain algorithm for solution of Load Flow problem using Newton Raphson method when the system consists of all types of buses (Flow chart not required).

[15 marks : 2008]

Solution:

Algorithm for Solution of Load Flow Problem:

1. Assume a suitable solution for all buses except the slack bus.

   Let, $V_p = 1 + j0.0$

   For, $P = 1, 2, ..., n \; P \neq S, \; V_S = a + j0.0$

2. Set convergence criterion = $\in$ i.e. if the largest of absolute of the residues exceeds $\in$ the process is repeated, otherwise it is terminated.
3. Set iteration count $K = 0$.
4. Set bus count $P = 1$.
5. Check if P is a slack bus. If yes, go to step 10.
6. Calculate the real and reactive powers P_p and Q_p respectively using equations

$$P_p = \sum_{g=1}^{n}\{e_p(e_g G_{pg} + f_g B_{pg})\} + \{f_p(f_g G_{pg} - e_g B_{pg})\}$$

$$Q_p = \sum_{g=1}^{n}\{f_p(e_g G_{pg} + f_g B_{pg})\} - \{e_p(f_g G_{pg} - e_g B_{pg})\}$$

   where, $Y_{pg} = G_{pg} - jB_{pg}$

   and $V_p = e_p + jf_p$

7. Evaluate: $\Delta P_p^k = P_{sp} - P_p^k$
8. Check if the bus in the question is a generator bus. If yes, compare the Q_p^k with the limits. If it exceeds the limit, fix the reactive power generation to the corresponding limits. If it exceeds the limit, fix the reactive power generation to the corresponding limit and treat the bus as a load bus for that iteration and go to next step. If the lower limit is violated set $Q_{psp} = Q_p$ min. If the limit is not violated evaluate the voltage residue

$$|\Delta V_p|^2 = |V_p|^2_{s\,pec} - |V_p^k|2$$

   and go to step 10.

9. Evaluate: $\Delta Q_p^k = Q_{ps} - Q_p^k$
10. Advance the bus count by 1, i.e. $P = P + 1$ and check if all the buses have been accounted. If not go to step 5.
11. Determine the largest of the absolute value of the residue.
12. If the largest of the absolute value of the residue is less than $\in$, go to step 17.
13. Evaluate elements for Jacobian matrix.
14. Calculate voltage increments Δe_p^k and Δf_p^k
15. Calculate new bus voltages,

$$e_p^{k+1} = e_p^k + \Delta e_p^k \quad \text{and} \quad f_p^{k+1} = f_p^k + \Delta f_p^k.$$

   Evaluate cos δ and sin δ of all voltages.

16. Advance iteration count $k = k + 1$ and goto step 4.
17. Evaluate bus and line powers and print the result.

6.7 **Explain gauss-seidel iterative method for solving load flow equations.**

[20 marks : 2009]

Solution:

The bus voltage equations can also be solved by the gauss-seidel method. In this method the new calculated voltage V_i^{k+1} immediately replace V_i^k and is used in the solution of the subsequent equations.

The general load flow equation resultant from gauss-seidal method will be

$$V_p^{k+1} = \frac{1}{Y_{pp}}\left[\frac{P_p - jQ_p}{(V_p^k)^*} - \sum_{q=1}^{p-1} Y_{pq}V_q^{k+1} - \sum_{q=p+1}^{n} Y_{pq}V_q^k\right] \quad \text{...}(i)$$

Before we proceed to solve these equation (*i*) the following point must be kept in mind:

1. The voltages and admittances are complex quantities.
2. In load buses P and Q are known quantities whereas in voltage controlled bus only P is known and Q is not known. Therefore, for solving equation corresponding to a voltage controlled bus Q must first be calculated and is given as

$$Q_p = \sum_{q=1}^{n}\{f_p(e_g g_{pq} + f_q B_{pq})\} - \{e_p(f_q gpq - e_q B_{pq})\} \quad \text{...}(ii)$$

where, $Y_{pq} = G_{pq} - jB_{pq}$

and $V_p = e_p + jf_p$

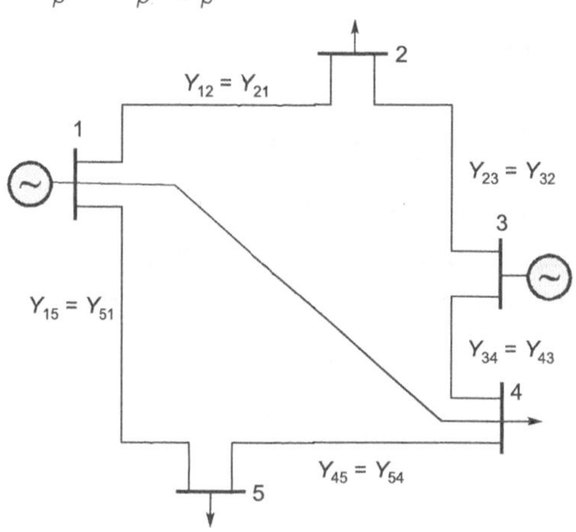

After Q at the voltage controlled bus has been calculated, it should be checked whether this value violates the reactive power generation at the bus i.e. whether it is less than the minimum reactive power generation permissible (because of stability problem) or it is more than the maximum reactive power generation permissible (because of rotor heating). If it violates, the voltage controlled bus is made to act as a load bus for that iteration only and the reactive power to be substituted in the expression for that iteration will correspond to the limit it has violated, i.e. if it is less than Q_{min}, the value to be substituted will be Q_{min}. If the calculated value of Q lies within the limits, this value of Q will be substituted in the expression.

If the value of Q for a generator bus is calculated after assuming magnitude equal to $|V|_{sp}$, for that bus and phase angle corresponding to the value in that iteration and if Q so obtained violates the limit, the value of voltage should be taken corresponding to the voltage in that iteration and not V_{sp}. Otherwise the voltage should correspond to specified voltage and phase angle as in that iteration.

3. The number of nonlinear equation is $(n-1)$, where n is the number of buses in the system.

The following is Gauss-seidel iterative procedure for solving equation:

1. Assume a flat voltage profile $1 + j0.0$ for all nodal voltages except the slack bus 1. Assume a suitable value of $\in$ the convergence criterion i.e. if the absolute value of the maximum change in voltage between any two consecutive iterations is less than a prespecified tolerance $\in$, the convergence is achieved and the iterative procedure is terminated.
   (a) Set iteration count $k = 0$
   (b) Set bus count $p = 1$
   (c) Check for slack bus, if it is a slack bus, go to step 4(a), otherwise go to next step.
2. Check which of the buses are voltage controlled and which are load buses. For voltage controlled buses go to next statement otherwise go to step 4.
3. Replace the value of the voltage magnitude of voltage controlled bus in that iteration by the specified value. Keep the phase angle same as in that iteration. Calculate Q for the generator bus. If Q lies within the lower and upper bounds calculate the term $(P - jQ)/V$ for this bus. Repeat this for all voltage controlled buses and calculate this term and substitute this term $(P - jQ)/V$ in the load flow equation corresponding to the voltage controlled bus. Calculate the new value of voltage for the bus. If there are more than one generator buses, the voltage magnitude of that bus only is replaced by its specified value, while calculating P and Q of a particular bus. The voltage of other generator buses will be corresponding value in that iteration.
4. For bus P evaluate V_p^{k+1} from equation (i) and change in voltage

$$\Delta V_p^k = V_p^{k+1} - V_p^k$$

   4 (a) Advance the bus count by 1 and check if all the buses have been taken into account. If yes, go to next step, otherwise go to step 1(c).
5. Find out the largest of the absolute value of the change in voltage. If this is less than a prespecified tolerance move on to next step, otherwise go back to step 2.
6. Calculate the injected power and the line flows using the nodal voltages.

The process of convergence due to G-S method is slow i.e. it requires a large number of iterations before a solution is obtained. The process of convergence can be speeded up if the voltage correction during consecutive iteration is modified to

$$V_{p(acc)}^{k+1} = V_p^k + a(V_p^{k+1} - V_p^k)$$

where α is known as acceleration factor and is a real number. A suitable value of α for a particular system can be obtained by running trial load flows. $\alpha = 1.6$ is a general recommended value for most of the systems. However, a wrong selection of α may result in slower convergence and sometimes even result in divergence from the solution.

6.8 **The bus impedance matrix of four-bus network with values in per unit is**

$$Z_{BUS} = \begin{bmatrix} 0.15 & 0.08 & 0.04 & 0.07 \\ 0.08 & 0.15 & 0.06 & 0.09 \\ 0.04 & 0.06 & 0.13 & 0.05 \\ 0.07 & 0.09 & 0.05 & 0.12 \end{bmatrix}$$

Generators are connected to buses 1 and 2 and their sub-transient reactances were included when finding Z_{BUS}. Find the sub-transient current in the fault for a three phase fault on bus 4 neglecting pre-fault current.

Assume the voltage at the fault is 1.0 per unit before the fault occurs. Find also the per unit current from generator 2 whose subtransient reactance is 0.2 per unit.

[10 marks : 2010]

Solution:

$$\text{Fault current } I_r^f = \frac{V_r^0}{Z_{rr} + Z_f}$$

Fault occurs at bus 4, so $r = 4$

$$V_r^0\big|_{r=4} = V_4^0 = 1\angle 0° \qquad \text{(Given)}$$

$$Z_{rr}\big|_{r=4} = Z_{44} = j0.12$$

$$Z^f = 0$$

so fault current, $$I_4^f = \frac{V_4^0}{Z_{44}} = \frac{1\angle 0}{j0.12} = -j8.33\, pu$$

Voltage of bus 1, $$V_i^f = E_i - Z_{ir} I_r^f$$

Voltage at bus 2,

so, $$i = 2 \text{ and } r = 4$$

$$Z_{24} = j0.09 \text{ and } I_4^f = -j8.33 \text{ pu}$$

$E_2 = 1\angle 0°$ {prefault current is zero},

so, $$V_2^f = E_2 - Z_{24} I_2^f$$

$$= 1\angle 0 - (j0.09) \times (-j8.33) = 0.2503 \text{ pu}$$

$$X''_{G2} = j0.2 \text{ (subjected reactance of generator 2)}$$

$$I_{G2}^f = \text{Current from generator 2}$$

$$= \frac{E_2 - V_2^f}{X''_{G2}} = \frac{1 - 0.2503}{j0.2}$$

$$I_{G2}^f = -j3.7485 \text{ pu}$$

6.9 The one line-diagram of a simple three-bus power system with generator at bus 1 is given below. The line impedances are marked in per unit on 100 MVA base. The voltages obtained by performing load flow are:

$V_1 = 1.05\angle 0°$ pu; $V_2 = 0.98183\angle -3.5035°$ pu; $V_3 = 1.00125\angle -2.8628°$ pu

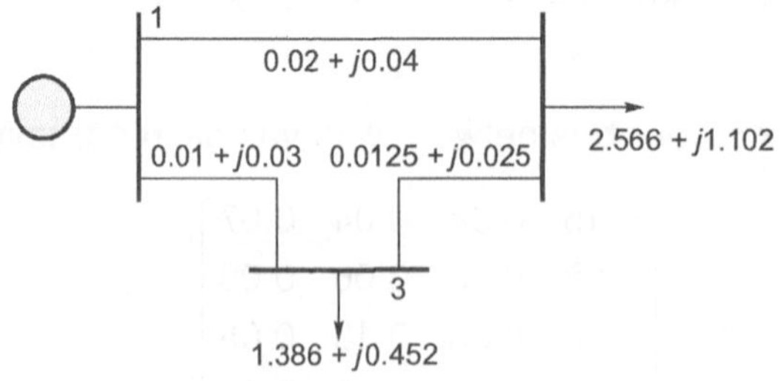

Determine:

(i) Slack bus power

(ii) Complex power flow on line 1 – 2 [15 marks : 2010]

Solution:

$|V_1| = 1.05, |V_2| = 0.98183$ and $|V_3| = 1.00125$

$\delta_1 = 0°, \delta_2 = 3.5035°$ and $\delta_3 = -2.8624°$

Let, $$Z_{12} = 0.02 + j0.04,\ Z_{13} = 0.01 + j0.03 \text{ and } Z_{23} = 0.0125 + j0.025$$

$$y_{12} = \frac{1}{Z_{12}} = \frac{1}{0.02 + j0.04} = 22.36\angle -63.43°$$

$$y_{13} = \frac{1}{Z_{13}} = \frac{1}{0.01+ j0.03} = 31.62\angle -71.56°$$

$$y_{23} = \frac{1}{Z_{23}} = \frac{1}{0.0125+ j0.025} = 35.77\angle -63.43°$$

$$Y_{BUS} = \begin{bmatrix} Y_{11} & Y_{12} & Y_{13} \\ Y_{21} & Y_{22} & Y_{23} \\ Y_{31} & Y_{32} & Y_{33} \end{bmatrix}$$

Now, elements of Y_{BUS},

$$Y_{11} = y_{12} + y_{13} = 22.36\angle{-63.43°} + 31.62\angle{-71.56°} = 53.84\angle{-68.2}$$
$$Y_{22} = y_{12} + y_{23} = 22.36\angle{-63.43°} + 35.77\angle{-63.43°} = 58.13\angle{-63.43}$$
$$Y_{33} = y_{13} + y_{23} = 31.62\angle{-71.56} + 35.77\angle{-63.43°} = 67.22\angle{-67.24}$$
$$Y_{12} = Y_{21} = -y_{12} = -22.36\angle{-63.43°} = 22.36\angle 116.57°$$
$$Y_{13} = Y_{31} = -y_{31} = -31.62\angle{-71.56} = 31.62\angle 108.44$$
$$Y_{23} = Y_{32} = -y_{23} = -35.77\angle{-63.43} = 35.77\angle 116.57$$

Now, power injected as i^{th} bus,

$$P_i = |V_i|\sum_{k=1}^{n}|V_R||Y_{ik}|\cos(\theta_{ik} + \delta_k - \delta_i)$$

$$\theta_i = -|V_i|\sum_{k=1}^{n}|V_k||Y_{ik}|\sin(\theta_{ik} + \delta_k - \delta_i)$$

(i) $i = 1$, slack-bus power,

$$P_1 = |V_1|\{|V_1||Y_{11}|\cos(\theta_{11} + \delta_1 - \delta_1) + |V_2||Y_2|\cos(\theta_{12} + \delta_2 - \delta_1) + |V_3||Y_{13}|\cos(\theta_{13} + \delta_3 - \delta_1)\}$$

$$P_1 = 1.05 \times \{1.05 \times 53.84 \times \cos(-68.2) + 0.98183 \times 22.36 \times \cos(116.57 + (-3.5035) - 0) + 1.00125 \times 31.62 \times \cos(108.44 + (-2.8624) - 0)\} = 4.082 \text{ pu}$$

$$Q_1 = -|V_1| \times \{|V_1||Y_{11}|\sin(\theta_{11} + \delta_1 - \delta_1) + |V_2||Y_{12}|\sin(\theta_{12} + \delta_2 - \delta_1) + |V_3||Y_{13}|\sin(\theta_{13} + \delta_3 - \delta_1)\}$$

$$= -1.05 \times \{1.05 \times 53.84 \times \sin(-68.2) + 0.98183 \times 22.36 \times \sin(116.57 + (-3.5035) - 0)) + 1.00125 \times 31.62 \times \sin(108.44 + (-2.8624) - 0)\}$$

$$= 1.883 \text{ pu}$$

Slack Bus Power $= S_1 = P_1 + jQ_1$

$= 4.082 + j1.883$ pu

(ii) MVA base = 100 MVA

$S_1 = 408.2 + j188.3$ MVA

Complex power flow on line 1-2,

$$S_{12} = V_1 I_{12}^*$$

where,
$$I_{12} = \frac{V_1 - V_2}{Z_{ik}}$$

or
$$I_{12} = \frac{(1.05\angle 0°) - (0.98183\angle -3.5035°)}{0.02 + j0.04} = 2.061\angle{-22.83°}$$

$$S_{12} = V_1 I_{12}^* = 1.05\angle 0° \times \{2.061\angle -22.83°\}$$

$$= 2.164\angle 22.83° \text{ pu} = 1.994 + j0.839 \text{ pu}$$

$$\text{MVA base} = 100$$

$$S_{12} = 199.4 + j83.9 \text{ MVA}$$

6.10 The figure shows single line diagram of a power system with generators at buses 1 and 3. The voltage at bus-1 is $1.05\angle 0°$ p.u. and at bus-3, $|V| = 1.04$ p.u. Line impedances are in p.u. and the line charging susceptances are neglected. Obtain the state vector after one iteration using Fast Decoupled Load Flow.

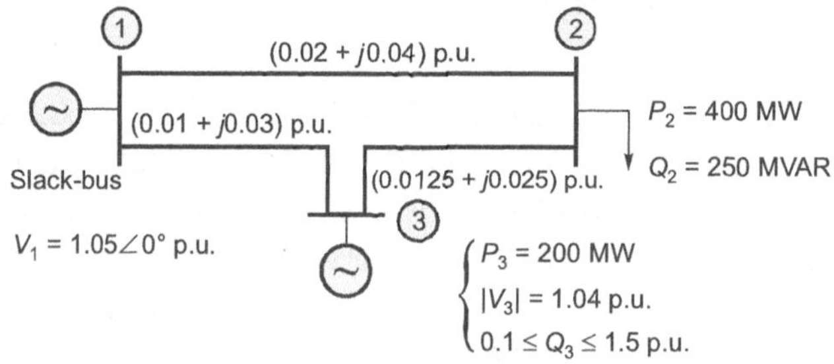

[10 marks : 2015]

Solution:

Single line diagram:

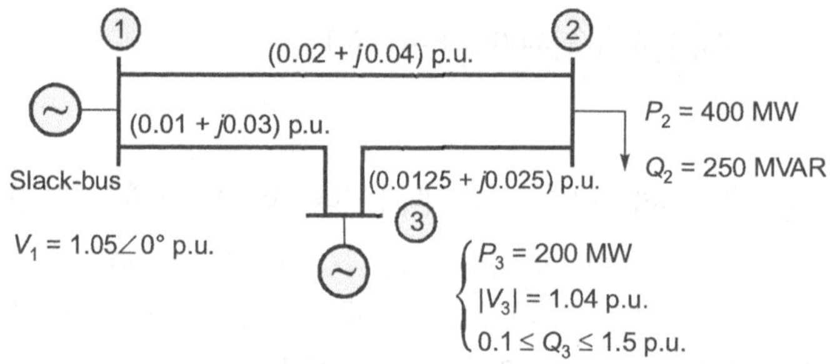

From given figure

Bus 1 : Slack bus

2 : PQ bus (load bus)

3 : PV bus

From the given line impedances convert in to admittances.

$$\frac{1}{0.02 + j0.04} = (10 - j20) \text{ p.u.};$$

$$\frac{1}{0.01 + j0.03} = (10 - j30) \text{ p.u.}$$

$$\frac{1}{0.0125 + j0.025} = (16 - j32) \text{ p.u.}$$

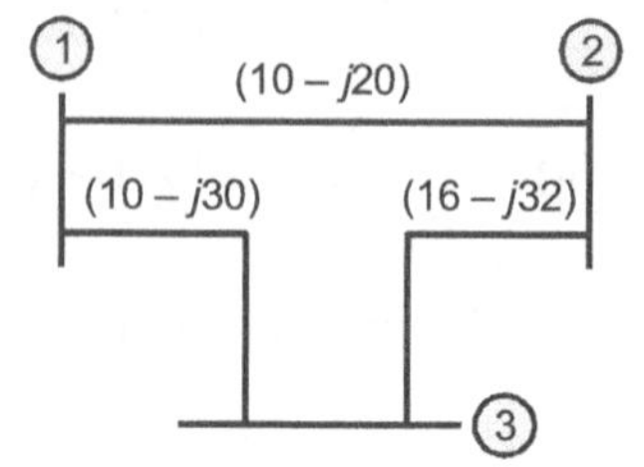

$$[Y_{BUS}] = \begin{bmatrix} (20 - j50) & -(10 - j20) & -(10 - j30) \\ -(10 - j20) & (26 - j52) & -(16 - j32) \\ -(10 - j30) & -(16 - j32) & (26 - j62) \end{bmatrix} \text{p.u.}$$

Initial voltages are

$$V_1 = 1.05\angle 0^\circ$$

$$V_2 = 1\angle 0^\circ \quad \text{(Assumed)}$$

$$|V_3| = 1.04$$

$$V_3 = 1.04\angle 0^\circ \quad \text{(Angle assumed)}$$

Unknown parameters are $|V_2|\angle\delta_2$ and $\angle\delta_3$

By using fast decoupled method,

$$\begin{bmatrix} \dfrac{\Delta P_2}{|V_2|} \\ \dfrac{\Delta P_3}{|V_3|} \end{bmatrix} = \begin{bmatrix} -B_{22} & -B_{23} \\ -B_{32} & -B_{33} \end{bmatrix} \begin{bmatrix} \Delta\delta_2 \\ \Delta\delta_3 \end{bmatrix} \quad ...(1)$$

$$\left[\frac{\Delta Q_2}{|V_2|}\right] = [-B_{22}][\Delta|V_2|] \quad ...(2)$$

where, $\left.\begin{matrix} B_{22} = -52, & B_{23} = 32 \\ B_{32} = 32, & B_{33} = -62 \end{matrix}\right\}$ from Y-Bus matrix

$$\Delta P_2 = P_{2S} - P_{2C}^{(0)}; \quad \Delta P_3 = P_{3S} - P_{3C}^{(0)}; \quad \Delta Q_2 = Q_{2S} - Q_{2C}^{(0)}$$

$$\begin{aligned} P_{2C}^{(0)} &= G_{22}\left|V_2^2\right| + |V_1||V_2|(G_{12}\cos\delta_{12} + B_{12}\sin\delta_{12}) + |V_2||V_3|(G_{23}\cos\delta_{23} + B_{23}\sin\delta_{23}) \\ &= 26\times 1^2 + 1.05\times 1\times(-10\cos(0) + 20\sin(0)) + 1\times 1.04\times(-16\cos(0) + 32\sin(0)) \\ &= -1.14 \end{aligned}$$

$$\begin{aligned} P_{3C}^{(0)} &= G_{33}|V_3|^2 + |V_1||V_3|(G_{13}\cos\delta_{13} + B_{13}\sin\delta_{13}) + |V_2||V_3|(G_{23}\cos\delta_{23} + B_{23}\sin\delta_{23}) \\ &= 26\times 1.04 + 1.05\times 1.04(-10) + 1\times 1.04\times(-16) = -0.52 \text{ pu} \end{aligned}$$

$$\begin{aligned} Q_{2C}^{(0)} &= -B_{22}\left|V_2^2\right| + |V_1||V_2|(G_{12}(\sin\delta_{12}) - B_{12}\cos\delta_{12}) + |V_2||V_3|(G_{23}\sin\delta_{23} + B_{23}\cos\delta_{23}) \\ &= -(-52)\times 1 + (1.05)(1)[-20] + 1\times 1.04\times(-32) \\ &= -2.28 \text{ pu} \end{aligned}$$

Assume base MVA = S_b = 100 MVA

$$P_{2S} = 400 \text{ MW}; \quad Q_{2S} = 250 \text{ MVAR}$$

$$S_{2S} = \frac{(P_{2S} + jQ_2S)}{S_b} = \frac{(400 + j250)}{100} = (4 + j2.5) \text{ pu}$$

$$P_{3S} = 200 \text{ MW}, \quad P_{3S} = \frac{200}{100} = 2 \text{ pu}$$

$$\Delta P_2 = P_{2S} - P_{2C} = 4 + 1.14 = 5.14 \text{ pu.}$$

$$\Delta P_3 = P_{3S} - P_{3C}^{(0)} = 2 - (-0.52) = 2.52 \text{ pu}$$

$$\Delta Q_2 = Q_{2S} - Q_{2C}^{(0)} = 2.5 - (-2.28) = 4.78 \text{ pu}$$

By using fast decoupled matrix (1),

$$\begin{bmatrix} \dfrac{5.14}{1} \\ \dfrac{2.52}{1.04} \end{bmatrix} = \begin{bmatrix} -(-52) & -32 \\ -32 & -(-62) \end{bmatrix} \begin{bmatrix} \Delta\delta_2 \\ \Delta\delta_3 \end{bmatrix}$$

$$\begin{bmatrix}\Delta\delta_2\\ \Delta\delta_3\end{bmatrix} = \begin{bmatrix}52 & -32\\ -32 & 62\end{bmatrix}^{-1}\begin{bmatrix}5.14\\ 2.42\end{bmatrix} = \begin{bmatrix}0.028 & 0.0145\\ 0.0145 & 0.023\end{bmatrix}_{2\times2}\begin{bmatrix}5.14\\ 2.42\end{bmatrix}_{2\times1}$$

$$\begin{bmatrix}\Delta\delta_2\\ \Delta\delta_3\end{bmatrix} = \begin{bmatrix}0.18\\ 0.13164\end{bmatrix}$$

$$\Delta\delta_2 = 0.18°$$
$$\Delta\delta_3 = 0.13164°$$

From equation (2),
$$\left[\frac{\Delta Q_2}{|V_2|}\right] = [-B_{22}][\Delta|V_2|]$$

$$\left[\frac{4.78}{1}\right] = [-(-52)][\Delta|V_2|]$$

$$\Delta|V_2| = 0.09192$$

At the end of first Iteration,

$$V_3\angle\delta_3 = 1.04\angle 0.13164°$$

$$V_2\angle\delta_2 = 2.09192\angle 0.18°$$

6.11 For the power system shown in the following figure, the bus admittance matrix Y_{bus} is given by

$$Y_{bus} = \begin{bmatrix}3.0-j9.0 & -2.0+j6.0 & -1.0+j3.0\\ -2.0+j6.0 & 2.5-j7.5 & -0.5+j1.5\\ -1.0+j3.0 & -0.5+j1.5 & 1.5-j4.5\end{bmatrix}$$

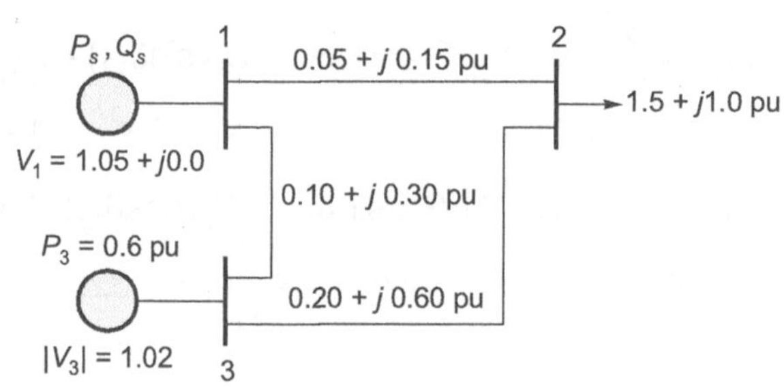

The per-unit bus voltages and power injections are also given in the figure.

(i) For each bus k, specify the bus type, and determine which of the variable V_k, d_k, P_k, and Q_k, are input data and which are unknown.

(ii) Assume an initial estimate of $V_2 = 1.0\angle 0°$, and $\delta_3 = 0°$, and calculate the bus real and reactive power mismatches to be used in the first iteration of the Newton-Raphson power flow method.

(iii) Set up the linearized system of equations that are solved at each iteration.

[10 marks : 2016]

Solution:

(i)

Bus No.	Bus type	Specified	unspecified
1	Slack Bus	$\|V_1\|, \delta_1$	P_1, Q_1
2	*PQ* Bus	P_2, Q_2	$\|V_2\|, \delta_2$
3	*PV* Bus	$P_3, \|V_3\|$	Q_3, δ_3

(ii)
$$P_{2\,specified} = (0-1.5) = -1.5 \text{ pu}$$
$$Q_{2\,specified} = (0-1) = -1 \text{ pu}$$

$$P_{3\,specified} = (0.6 - 0) = 0.6 \text{ pu}$$

$$P_2(|V_2|, \delta_2, \delta_3) = |y_{21}||V_1||V_2|\cos(y_{21} + \delta_1 - \delta_2) + |y_{22}||V_2|^2 \cos y_{22} + |y_{23}||V_2||V_3|\cos(Y_{23} + \delta_3 - \delta_2)$$

P_2 corresponding to initial guess

$$P_2(|V_2|^{(0)}, \delta_2^{(0)}, \delta_3^{(0)}) = 6.32 \times 1.05 \times 1 \cos(108.43° + 0 - 0) + 7.9 \times 1^2 \times \cos(-71.56) + 1.58 \times 1 \times 1.02 \cos(108.43 + 0 - 0)$$

$$P_2(|V_2|^{(0)}, \delta_2^{(0)}, \delta_3^{(0)}) = -0.108$$

Mismatch in P_2 corresponding to initial guess

$$\Delta P_2^{(0)} = P_{2\,specified} - P_2(|V_2|^{(0)}, \delta_2^{(0)}, \delta_3^{(0)})$$

$$= -1.5 - (-0.108) = -1.392$$

Similarly,

$$P_3(|V_2|, \delta_2, \delta_3) = |y_{31}||V_1||V_3|\cos(y_{31} + \delta_1 - \delta_3) + |y_{32}||V_2||V_3|\cos(y_{32} + \delta_2 - \delta_3) + |y_{33}||V_3|^2 \cos(y_{33})$$

P_3 corresponding to initial guess

$$P_3(|V_2|^{(0)}, \delta_2^{(0)}, \delta_3^{(0)}) = 3.16 \times 1.05 \times 1.02 \cos(108.43 + 0 - 0) + 1.58 \times 1 \times 1.02 \cos(108.43 + 0 - 0) + 4.74 \times 1.02^2 \cos(-71.56) = -0.019$$

Mismatch in P_3 corresponding to initial guess

$$\Delta P_3^{(0)} = P_{3\,specified} - P_3(|V_2|^{(0)}, \delta_2^{(0)}, \delta_3^{(0)})$$

$$= 0.6 - (-0.019) = 0.619 \text{ p.u}$$

$$Q_2(|V_2|, \delta_2, \delta_3) = -\left[|y_{21}||V_1||V_2|\sin(y_{21} + \delta_1 - \delta_2) + |V_2|^2 \sin y_{22} + |y_{23}||V_2||V_3|\sin(y_{23} + \delta_3 - \delta_2)\right]$$

Q_2 corresponding to initial guess

$$Q_2(|V_2°|, \delta_2°, \delta_3°) = -[6.32 \times 1.05 \times 1 \sin(108.43° + 0 - 0) + 7.9 \times 1^2 \times \sin(-71.56) + 1.58 \times 1 \times 1.02 \sin(108.43° + 0 - 0)]$$

$$= -0.329 \text{ p.u.}$$

Mismatch in Q_2 corresponding to initial guess

$$\Delta Q_2^{(0)} = Q_{2\,specified} - Q_2(|V_2|^0, \delta_2^{(0)}, \delta_3^{(0)})$$

$$= -1 - (-0.329) = -0.671$$

Mismatch matrix, $$\begin{bmatrix} \Delta P_2^{(0)} \\ \Delta P_3^{(0)} \\ \Delta Q_2^{(0)} \end{bmatrix} = \begin{bmatrix} -1.392 \\ 0.619 \\ -0.671 \end{bmatrix}$$

(iii) Equation to be solved in each iteration,

$$\begin{bmatrix} \frac{\partial P_2}{\partial \delta_2} & \frac{\partial P_2}{\partial \delta_3} & \frac{\partial P_2}{\partial |V_2|} \\ \frac{\partial P_3}{\partial \delta_2} & \frac{\partial P_3}{\partial \delta_3} & \frac{\partial P_3}{\partial |V_2|} \\ \frac{\partial Q_2}{\partial \delta_2} & \frac{\partial Q_2}{\partial \delta_3} & \frac{\partial Q_2}{\partial |V_2|} \end{bmatrix} \begin{bmatrix} \Delta \delta_2 \\ \Delta \delta_3 \\ \Delta |V_2| \end{bmatrix} = \begin{bmatrix} \Delta P_2 \\ \Delta P_3 \\ \Delta Q_2 \end{bmatrix}$$

Jacobian matrix

6.12 For a simple four-bus system, the line admittances are given below:

Bus code	Admittance
1 - 2	2 - *j*8
1 - 3	1 – *j*4
2 - 3	0.666 – *j*2.664
2 - 4	1 – *j*4
3 - 4	2 – *j*8

The schedule of active and reactive power is given below:

Bus	P_i	Q_i	V_i	Remarks
1	–	–	1.04	Slack
2	0.5	0.2	–	*PQ*
3	0.4	0.3	–	*PQ*
4	0.3	0.1	–	*PQ*

Assuming a flat voltage start, determine the voltage at the end of first iteration using Gauss-Seidel method. Take α = 1.6 (α is acceleration factor).

[20 marks : 2017]

Solution:

$$Y_{11} = y_{12} + y_{13} = (2 - j8) + (1 - j4) = (3 - j12)$$
$$Y_{21} = Y_{12} = -y_{12} = (-2 + j8)$$
$$Y_{31} = Y_{13} = -y_{13} = (-1 + j4)$$
$$Y_{41} = Y_{14} = 0$$
$$Y_{22} = y_{12} + y_{23} + y_{24}$$
$$= (2 - j8) + (0.666 - j2.664) + (1 - j4) = (3.666 - j14.664)$$
$$Y_{32} = Y_{23} = -y_{23} = (-0.666 + j2.664)$$
$$Y_{42} = Y_{24} = -y_{24} = (-1 + j4)$$
$$Y_{33} = y_{13} + y_{23} + y_{34}$$
$$= (1 - j4) + (0.666 - j2.664) + (2 - j8) = (3.666 - j14.664)$$
$$Y_{43} = Y_{34} = -y_{34} = (-2 + j8)$$
$$Y_{44} = y_{42} + y_{43}$$
$$= (1 - j4) + (2 - j8) = (3 - j12)$$

Thus, the admittance matrix,

$$Y_{BUS} = \begin{bmatrix} 3-j12 & -2+j18 & -1+j4 & 0 \\ -2+j8 & 3.666-j14.664 & -0.666+j2.664 & -1+j4 \\ -1+j4 & -0.666+j2.664 & 3.666-j14.664 & -2+j8 \\ 0 & -1+j4 & -2+j8 & 3-j12 \end{bmatrix}$$

The power for generator bus are taken as positive while the power for load buses are taken as negative.

Initial value, $V_1^{(0)} = 1.04\angle 0°, V_2^0 = V_3^0 = V_4^0 = 1.0$

For the given system,

$$V_2^{(1)} = \frac{1}{y_{22}}\left[\frac{P_2 - jQ_2}{V_2^*} - Y_{21}V_1^{(0)} - Y_{23}V_3^{(0)} - Y_{21}V_4^{(0)}\right]$$

$$= \frac{1}{(3.666 - j14.664)}\left[\frac{-0.5 + j0.2}{1 - j0} - (-2 + j8)\times 1.04 - (-0.666 + j2.664)(1 + j0) - (-1 + j4)(1 + j0)\right]$$

$$= \frac{1}{(3.666 - j14.664)}[-0.5 + j0.2 + 2.08 - j8.32 + 0.666 - j2.664 + 1 - j4]$$

$$V_2^1 = \frac{3.246 - j14.784}{3.666 - j14.664} = 1.00096 - j0.02888 = 1.0014\angle{-1.653°}$$

$$V'_{2(acce)} = (1 + j0) + 1.6[(1.00096 - j0.02888) - (1 + j0) = 1.00154 - j0.046208 = 1.0026\angle{-2.6416°}$$

Now, $$V_3^{(1)} = \frac{1}{Y_{33}}\left[\frac{P_3 - jQ_3}{V_3^*} - Y_{31}V_1^{(0)} - Y_{32}V_2^{(1)} - Y_{34}V_4^{(0)}\right]$$

$$= \frac{1}{(3.666 - j14.664)}\left[\frac{-0.4 + j0.3}{(1 - 0 - j0.0)} - (-1 + j4) \times 1.04 - (-0.666 + j2.664)(1.00154 - j0.046208) - (-2 + j8)(1 + j0)\right]$$

$$= \frac{1}{(3.666 - j14.664)}[-0.4 + j0.3 + 1.04 - j4.16 + 0.54393 - j2.69888 + 2 - j8]$$

$$V_3^{(1)} = \frac{3.18393 - j14.55888}{3.666 - j14.664} = (0.99216 - j0.03114)$$

$$V_{3(acce)}^1 = (1 + j0) + 1.6[(0.99216 - j0.03114) - (1 + j0) = (0.98746 - j0.049824) = 0.988712\angle{-2.8885°}$$

and $$V_4^1 = \frac{1}{Y_{44}}\left[\frac{P_4 - jQ_4}{V_4^*} - Y_{42}V_2^{(1)} - Y_{43}V_3^{(1)}\right]$$

$$= \frac{1}{(3 - j12)}\left[\frac{-0.3 + j0.1}{1 - j0} - (-1 + j4)(1.00154 - j0.046208) - (-2 + j8)(0.98746 - j0.049824)\right]$$

$$= \frac{1}{(3 - j12)}[-0.3 + j0.1 + 0.816708 - j4.05237 + 1.57633 - j7.99933]$$

$$V_4^{(1)} = \frac{2.09304 - j11.9517}{3 - j12} = 0.97843 - j0.070187$$

$$V_{4(acce)}^{(1)} = (1 + j0) + 1.6[(0.97843 - j0.070187) - (1 + j0)]$$

$$= 0.965488 - j0.112992 = 0.971997\angle{-6.634456°}\text{ V}$$

6.13 The figure below shows single line diagram of a power system with generators at bus-1 and bus-3. The voltage at bus-1 is $1.05\angle 0°$ p.u. and at bus-3, $|V| = 1.04$ p.u. Line impedances are in p.u. and line charging suseptances are neglected. Obtain state vector using Fast Decoupled Load Flow (FDLF) for one iteration.

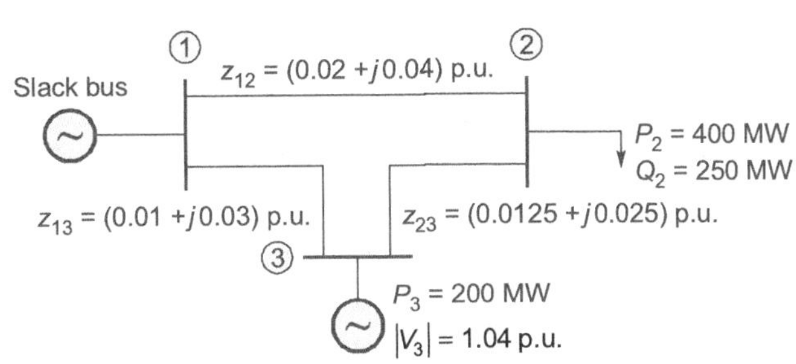

[20 marks : 2020]

Solution:

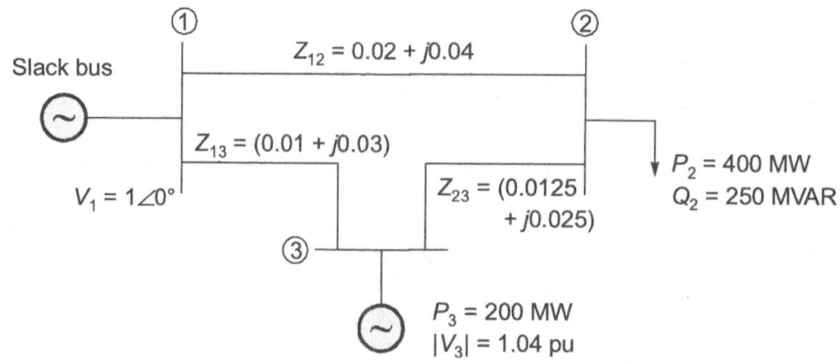

$$Y_{12} = \frac{1}{Z_{12}} = 10 - 20j$$

$$Y_{13} = \frac{1}{(0.01 + j0.013)} = 10 - 30j$$

$$Y_{23} = \frac{1}{(0.0125 + j0.025)} = 16 - j32$$

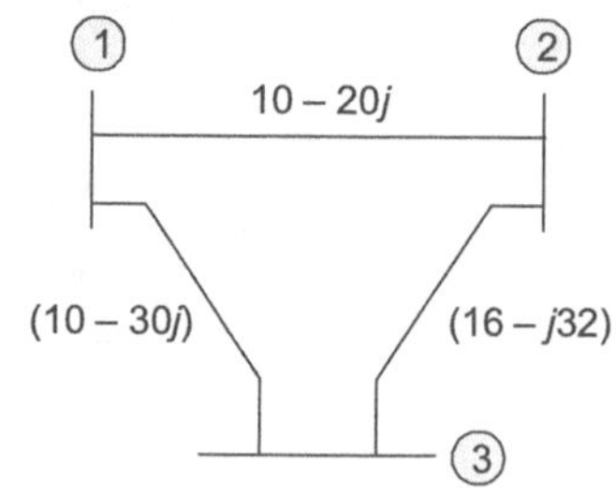

$$Y_{Bus} = \begin{bmatrix} 20 - j50 & (-10 + j20) & (-10 + j30) \\ -10 + j20 & (26 - j52) & (-16 + j32) \\ (-10 + j30) & (-16 + j32) & (26 - j62) \end{bmatrix}$$

$$= \begin{bmatrix} 53.85\angle -68.195^\circ & 22.36\angle 116.566^\circ & 31.622\angle 108.44^\circ \\ 22.36\angle 116.566^\circ & 58.37\angle -63.434^\circ & 35.777\angle 116.566^\circ \\ 31.622\angle 108.44^\circ & 35.777\angle 116.566^\circ & 67.230\angle -67.246^\circ \end{bmatrix}$$

Bus 2 is *PQ* Bus required to calculate $|V_2| \angle \delta_2$

Bus 3 is *PV* Bus required to calculate δ_3, Q_3

$$B' = \begin{bmatrix} -52 & 32 \\ 32 & -62 \end{bmatrix}$$

The inverse of the above matrix is

$$[B']^{-1} = \begin{bmatrix} -0.028182 & -0.014545 \\ -0.014545 & -0.023636 \end{bmatrix}$$

From the expressions for real power at bus 2 and 3 and the reactive power at bus 2 are

$P_2 = |V_2||V_1||Y_{21}| \cos(\theta_{21} - \delta_2 + \delta_1) + |V_2^2||Y_{22}| \cos \theta_{22} + |V_2||V_3||Y_{23}| \cos(\theta_{23} - \delta_2 + \delta_3)$

$P_3 = |V_3||V_1||Y_{31}| \cos(\theta_{31} - \delta_3 + \delta_1) + |V_3||V_2||Y_{32}| \cos (\theta_{32} - \delta_3 + \delta_2) + |V_3^2|||Y_{33}| \cos \theta_{33}$

$Q_2 = -|V_2||V_1||Y_{21}| \sin(\theta_{21} - \delta_2 + \delta_1) - |V_2^2||Y_{22}| \sin \theta_{22} - |V_2||V_3||Y_{23}| \sin(\theta_{23} - \delta_2 + \delta_3)$

The load and generation expressed in per units are

$$S_2^{sch} = -\frac{(400 + j250)}{100} = -4.0 - j2.5 \text{ p.u.}$$

$$P_3^{sch} = \frac{200}{100} = 2.0 \text{ p.u.}$$

The slack bus voltage is $V_1 = 1.05\angle 0$ p.u. and the bus 3 voltage magnitude is $|V_3| = 1.04$ pu. Starting with an initial estimate of $|V_2^{(0)}| = 1.0$, $\delta_2^{(0)} = 0.0$, and $\delta_3^{(0)} = 0.0$, the power residuals are computed from the equation.

$$\Delta P_2^{(0)} = P_2^{sch} - P_2^{(0)} = -4.0 - (-1.14) = -2.86$$

$$\Delta P_3^{(0)} = P_3^{sch} - P_3^{(0)} = 2.0 - (0.5616) = 1.4384$$

$$\Delta Q_2^{(0)} = Q_2^{sch} - Q_2^{(0)} = -2.5 - (-2.28) = -0.22$$

$$\begin{bmatrix} \Delta\delta_2^{(0)} \\ \Delta\delta_3^{(0)} \end{bmatrix} = -\begin{bmatrix} -0.028182 & -0.014545 \\ -0.014545 & -0.023636 \end{bmatrix} \begin{bmatrix} \dfrac{-2.8600}{1.0} \\ \dfrac{1.4384}{1.04} \end{bmatrix}$$

$$\begin{bmatrix} \Delta\delta_2^{(0)} \\ \Delta\delta_3^{(0)} \end{bmatrix} = \begin{bmatrix} -0.060483 \\ -0.008909 \end{bmatrix}$$

Since bus 3 is a regulated bus, the corresponding row and column of B' are eliminated and we get

$$B'' = [-52]$$

$$\Delta|V_2| = \left[\frac{-1}{52}\right]\left[\frac{-0.22}{1.0}\right] = -0.0042308$$

The new bus voltages in the first iteration are

$$\delta_2^{(1)} = 0 + (-0.060483) = -0.060483 \text{ rad}$$

$$\delta_3^{(1)} = 0 + (-0.008909) = -0.008909 \text{ rad}$$

$$|V_2^{(1)}| = 1 + (-0.0042308) = 0.995769 \text{ p.u.}$$

6.14 Why are the load flow studies necessary in power system?
For a 3-bus system as shown in figure (data are given in table), construct the Y-bus.

Bus	Impedance Z_{in} (pu)	Line charging $y'_{ik}/2$ (pu)
1 - 2	0.02 + j0.06	j0.03
1 - 3	0.08 + j0.24	j0.025
2 - 3	0.06 + j0.18	j0.02

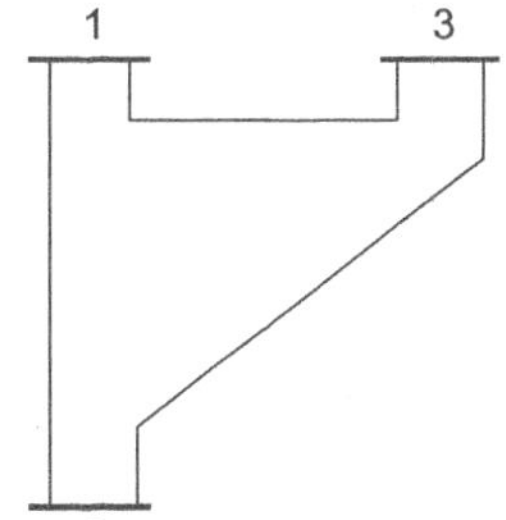

[20 marks : 2022]

Solution:

Load flow studies are one of the most important aspects of power system planning and operation. The load flow gives us the sinusoidal steady state of the entire system – voltages, real and reactive power generated and absorbed and line losses.

Significance of load flow analysis in power system are as follows :

- We can obtain the voltage magnitudes and angles at each bus in the steady state. This is rather important as the magnitudes of the bus voltages are required to be held within a specified limit. Once the bus voltage magnitudes and their angles are computed using the load flow, the real and reactive power flow through each line can be computed.
- Also based on the difference between power flow in the sending and receiving ends, the losses in a particular line can also be computed.
- From the line flow we can also determine the over and under load conditions.
- The load flow study of a power system is essential to decide the best operation of existing system and for planning the future expansion of the system.

- It helps in designing a new power system network.
- It helps in system loss minimization and transformer tap setting for economic operation.

As per the data, the equivalent network is

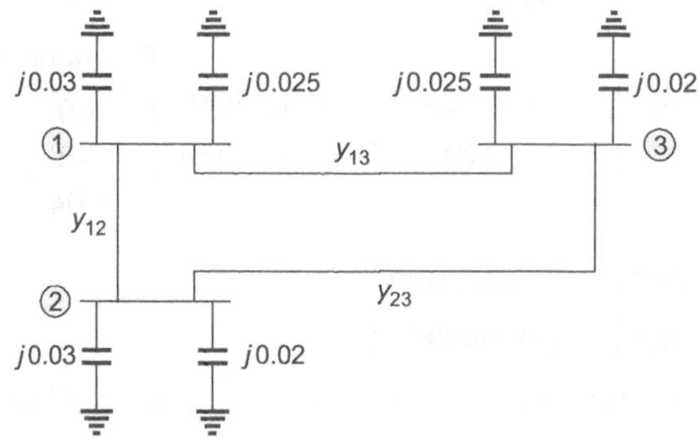

$$y_{12} = \frac{1}{z_{12}} = \frac{1}{0.02 + j0.06} = \frac{0.02 - j0.06}{(0.02)^2 + (0.06)^2} = 5 - j15$$

$$y_{13} = \frac{1}{z_{13}} = \frac{1}{0.08 + j0.24} = \frac{0.08 - j0.24}{(0.08)^2 + (0.24)^2} = 1.25 - j3.75$$

$$y_{23} = \frac{1}{z_{23}} = \frac{1}{0.06 + j0.18} = \frac{0.06 - j0.18}{(0.06)^2 + (0.18)^2} = 1.67 - j5.0$$

$$Y_{BUS} = \begin{bmatrix} Y_{11} & Y_{12} & Y_{13} \\ Y_{21} & Y_{22} & Y_{23} \\ Y_{31} & Y_{32} & Y_{33} \end{bmatrix}$$

$$= \begin{bmatrix} y_{12} + y_{13} + j0.03 + j0.025 & -y_{12} & -y_{13} \\ -y_{12} & y_{12} + y_{23} + j0.03 + j0.02 & -y_{23} \\ -y_{13} & -y_{23} & y_{13} + y_{23} + j0.025 + j0.02 \end{bmatrix}$$

$$= \begin{bmatrix} 6.25 - j18.695 & -5.0 + j15 & -1.25 + j3.75 \\ -5.0 + j15 & 6.67 - j19.95 & -1.67 + j5.0 \\ -1.25 + j3.75 & -1.67 + j5.0 & 2.92 - j8.705 \end{bmatrix}$$

7. Power System Stability

7.1 Using equal area criterion, derive the expression for critical clearing angle for a system having a generator feeding a large system through a double circuit transmission line. When fault occurs at middle of one of the lines.

[10 marks : 2001]

Solution:

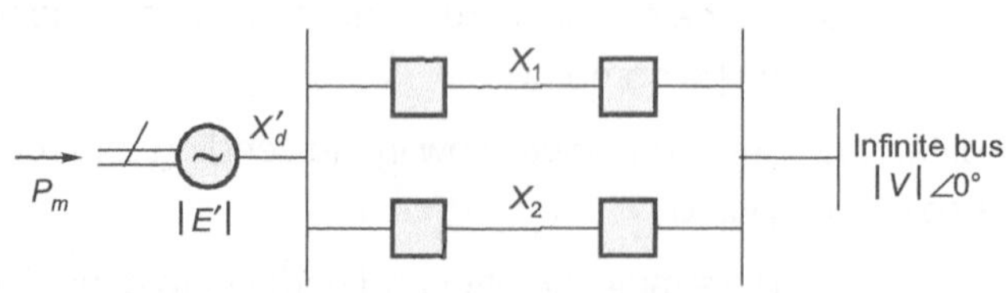

It is assumed that fault occurs away from the line ends. (say in the middle of a line).

Before the occurrence of a fault, the power angle curve is given by,

$$P_{e_I} = \frac{|E'||V|}{X'_d + X_1||X_2} \sin\delta = P_{\max_1} \sin\delta$$

Circuit model of the system during fault is shown below:

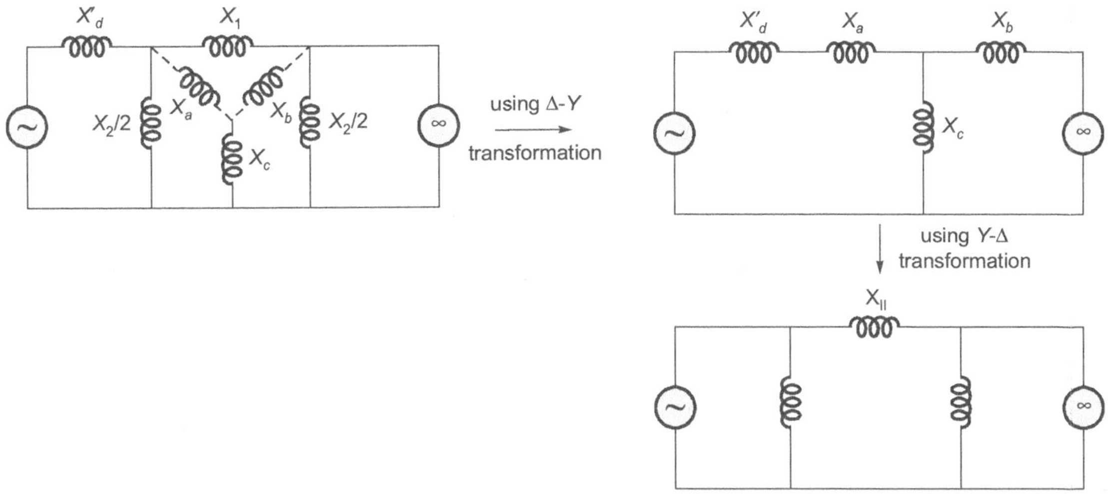

The power angle curve during fault is given by,

$$P_{e_{II}} = \frac{|E'||V|}{X_{\text{II}}} \sin\delta = P_{\max_{\text{II}}} \sin\delta$$

The circuit breaker at the two ends of the faulted line open at time t_L (corresponding to angle δ_c), disconnecting the faulted line. The power flow is now via the healthy line, with power angle curve

$$P_{e_{III}} = \frac{|E||V|}{X'_d + X_1} \sin\delta = P_{\max_{\text{III}}} \sin\delta$$

A_1 = Accelerating area

A_2 = Deaccelerating area

According to equal area criterion,

$$A_1 = A_2$$

$$A_1 = \int_{\delta_0}^{\delta_{cr}} (P_m - P_{e_{\text{II}}})\, d\delta$$

$$A_2 = \int_{\delta_{cr}}^{\delta_{\max}} (P_{e_{\text{III}}} - P_m)\, d\delta$$

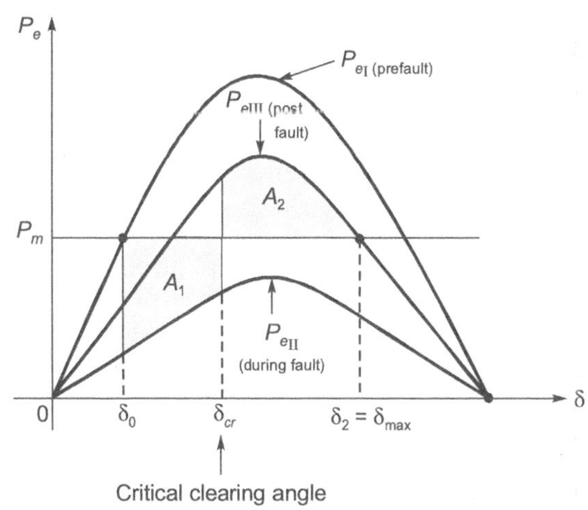

where, $$\delta_{\max} = \pi - \sin^{-1}\left(\frac{P_m}{P_{\max_{\text{II}}}}\right)$$

$$\int_{\delta_0}^{\delta_{cr}} (P_m - P_{\max_{\text{II}}} \sin\delta)\, d\delta = \int_{\delta_{cr}}^{\delta_{\max}} (P_{\max_{\text{III}}} \sin\delta - P_m)\, d\delta$$

$$\Rightarrow \quad P_m(\delta_{cr} - \delta_0) - P_{\max_{\text{II}}}(\cos\delta_0 - \cos\delta_{cr}) = P_{\max_{\text{III}}}(\cos\delta_{cr} - \cos\delta_{\max}) - P_m(\delta_{\max} - \delta_{cr})$$

$$\Rightarrow \quad \delta_{cr} = \cos^{-1}\left[\frac{P_m(\delta_{\max} - \delta_0) - P_{\max_{\text{II}}} \cos\delta_0 + P_{\max_{\text{III}}} \cos\delta_{\max}}{P_{\max_{\text{III}}} - P_{\max_{\text{II}}}}\right]$$

and angles are in radian.

7.2 A large generator is delivering 1.0 p.u. power to an infinite bus through a transmission network. The maximum powers which can be transferred for pre-fault, fault and post-fault conditions are 1.8 p.u., 0.4 p.u. and 1.3 p.u. respectively. Find critical clearing angle.

[10 marks : 2001]

Solution:

Given,
$$P_{\max I} = 1.8 \text{ p.u.}$$
$$P_{\max II} = 0.4 \text{ p.u.}$$
and
$$P_{\max III} = 1.3 \text{ p.u.}$$
$$P_m = 1.0 \text{ p.u. (initial loading)}$$

$$\delta_0 = \sin^{-1}\left(\frac{P_m}{P_{\max_I}}\right) = \sin^{-1}\left(\frac{1.0}{1.8}\right) = 33.75° = 0.59 \text{ rad}$$

$$\delta_{max} = \pi - \sin^{-1}\left(\frac{P_m}{P_{\max III}}\right) = \pi - \sin^{-1}\left(\frac{1}{1.3}\right) = \pi \sin^{-1}\left(\frac{1}{1.3}\right)$$
$$= 129.71° = 2.26 \text{ radians}$$

We know that,

$$\cos\delta_{cr} = \frac{P_m(\delta_{max} - \delta_0) - P_{\max_{II}}\cos\delta_0 + P_{\max_{III}}\cos\delta_{max}}{P_{\max_{III}} - P_{\max_{II}}}$$

$$= \frac{1.0(2.26 - 0.59) - 0.4\cos 33.75° + 1.3\cos 129.71°}{1.3 - 0.4} = 0.564$$

$$\therefore \quad \delta_{cr} = 55.66°$$

7.3 The power systems are operated with power angle around

(a) 10° (b) 30°
(c) 70° (d) 80°

[2 marks : 2005]

Solution:

Option (b) is correct.

7.4 A 90 MVA, 11 kV water wheel generator has an inertia constant $H = 3$. The stored energy in the rotor at synchronous speed is

(a) 40 kJ (b) 270 kJ
(c) 270 MJ (d) 40 MJ

[2 marks : 2005]

Solution:

$$G = 90 \text{ MVA}$$

Stored energy in the rotor $= GH = 90 \times 3 = 270$ MJ

Option (c) is correct.

7.5 A 50 Hz two pole turbo alternator rated 50 MVA, 13.2 kV has an inertia constant $H = 5.0$ MJ/MVA. Determine the kinetic energy stored in the rotor at synchronous speed. Determine the acceleration if the input less the rotational losses is 65000 HP and the electrical power developed is 40 MW. If the acceleration computed for the generator is constant for a period of 10 cycles, determine the change in torque angle in that period and the r.p.m. at the end of 10 cycles. Assume that the generator is synchronised with a large system and has no accelerating torque before the 10 cycles period begins.

[18 marks : 2005]

Solution:

(a) Since, $$H = \frac{\text{Stored energy in mega joules}}{\text{Machine rating in MVA}}$$

∴ K.E. stored in the rotor in mega joules

$$= H \times \text{machine rating in MVA}$$
$$= 5 \times 50 = 250 \text{ Mega joules}$$

(b) The accelerating power = Mechanical power input – Electrical power output

$$P_a = P_i - P_G = 65000 \times 0.735 - 40000 = 7775 \text{ kW} = 7.775 \text{ MW}$$

Now the acceleration is

$$\frac{d^2\delta}{dt^2} = \frac{P_a}{M} = \frac{7.775}{M}$$

$$M = \frac{GH}{\pi f} = \frac{50 \times 5}{\pi \times 50} = 1.591 \text{ megajoules-sec/radian}$$

$$\frac{d^2\delta}{dt^2} = \frac{7.775}{1.591} = 4.886 \text{ rad/sec}^2$$

$$= 4.886 \times \frac{180}{\pi} \approx 280 \text{ elect} - \text{degree/sec}^2$$

(c) Again using swing equation,

$$\frac{d^2\delta}{dt^2} = \frac{P_a}{M} = \text{Constant} = 4.886 \text{ rad/sec}^2$$

On multiplying with sides by $\frac{2d\delta}{dt} \times dt$

$$\frac{2d\delta}{dt} \times \frac{d^2\delta}{dt^2} \times dt = 2 \times 4.886 \times \frac{d\delta 2}{dt} \times dt$$

On integrating both sides,

$$\left(\frac{d\delta}{dt}\right)^2 = 9.772\,\delta + A$$

Since at $t = 0$, $\frac{d\delta}{dt} = 0;\ A = 0$

$$\therefore \quad \frac{d\delta}{dt} = \sqrt{9.772} \times \sqrt{\delta} \quad \text{or} \quad \frac{d\delta}{\sqrt{\delta}} = \sqrt{9.772}\, dt$$

$$\delta^{-1/2} d\delta = 3.126\, dt$$

$$2\delta^{1/2} = 3.126\, t$$

$$\delta^{1/2} = 1.563\, t$$

$$\delta = 2.443 \times t^2$$

Now, $$t = \frac{10}{50} = 0.2 \text{ sec (time taken for 10 cycles)}$$

$$\delta = 2.442 \times 0.04 = 0.09768 \text{ radians}$$
$$= 5.5966 \text{ electrical degrees}$$

Now, $$\frac{d\delta}{dt} = 3.129\sqrt{\delta}$$

$$= 3.126 \times \sqrt{0.09768} = 0.9769 \text{ elect-rad/sec}$$

Since, there are 2 poles,

$$\omega_e = \left(\frac{P}{2}\right)\omega_m$$

$$\left(\frac{d\delta}{dt}\right)_m = 0.9769 \text{ mechanical-rad/sec}$$

$$\left(\frac{d\delta}{dt}\right)_m = \frac{0.9769}{2\pi}\times 60 = 9.328 \text{ rpm}$$

Synchronous speed,

$$N_S = \frac{120f}{P} = \frac{120\times 50}{2} = 3000 \text{ r.p.m.}$$

Rotor speed at the end of 10 cycles = 3000 + 9.328 = 3009.328 rpm.

7.6 **A two-machine power system delivers a load of 25 MW at 0.8 p.f. lag and has a double circuit. The system reactance is 150 percent on 100 MVA base. A sudden symmetrical line-to-ground fault occurs in one of the circuits which reduced the power supplied to 40% which is subsequently cleared by simultaneous action of the circuit breakers on both sides of the faulted line. Calculated in the electrical degrees the "critical clearing angle". Assume that during fault conditions the system reactance attains such a value that the maximum power becomes 30% of the normal maximum value, when the faulty line is isolated the maximum power of the system is 60% of the normal maximum power.**

[14 marks : 2006]

Solution:

Let the three power angle curves be represented as:

$P_{e_I} = P_m \sin\delta$ before the fault

$P_{e_{II}} = r_1 P_m \sin\delta$ during the fault

$P_{e_{III}} = r_2 P_m \sin\delta$ after the fault

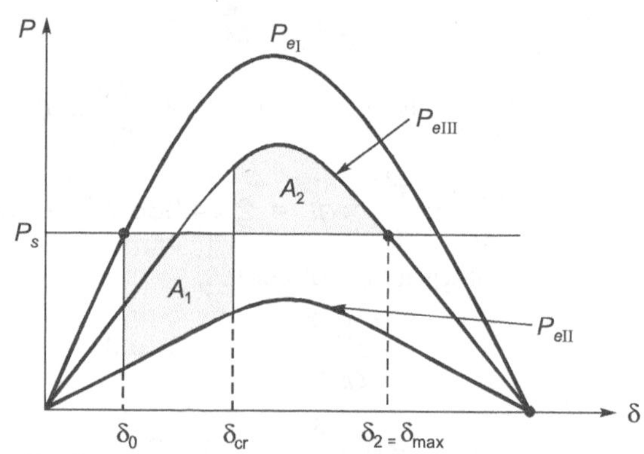

For transient stability limit,

According equal area criterion,

$$A_1 = A_2$$

where, $P_s = P_m \sin\delta_0$

$$A_1 = \int_{\delta_0}^{\delta_c}(P_s - P_{e_{II}})d\delta = \int_{\delta_0}^{\delta_c}(P_m\sin\delta_0 - r_1P_m\sin\delta)\,d\delta$$

$$= P_m\sin\delta_0\times(\delta_c-\delta_0) - r_1\,P_m\{\cos\delta_0-\cos\delta_c\} \quad \text{...(i)}$$

$$A_2 = \int_{\delta_c}^{\delta_m}(P_{e_{III}} - P_s)d\delta = \int_{\delta_c}^{\delta_m}(r_2P_m\sin\delta - P_m\sin\delta_0)d\delta$$

$$= r_2\,P_m\times\{\cos\delta_c-\cos\delta_m\} - P_m\sin\delta_0\{\delta_m-\delta_c\} \quad \text{...(ii)}$$

On equating equation (i) and (ii),

$$P_m\sin\delta_0\times(\delta_c-\delta_0) - r_1\,P_m\times\{\cos\delta_0-\cos\delta_c\} = r_2\,P_m\times\{\cos\delta_c-\cos\delta_m\} - P_m\sin\delta_0\times\{\delta_m-\delta_c\}$$

On simplifying, the equation,

$$\cos\delta_c = \frac{(\delta_m-\delta_0)\sin\delta_0 - r_1\cos\delta_0 + r_2\cos\delta_m}{r_2 - r_1}$$

Given, $r_1 = 0.3$ and $r_2 = 0.6$

Base MVA = 100 MVA

Power supplied, $P_s = \dfrac{25}{0.8 \times 100} = 0.3125$

System reactance = 1.5 pu

So, Maximum power $= P_m = \dfrac{1}{1.15} = 0.6666$ pu

$$P_s = P_m \sin\delta_0$$

$$\Rightarrow \quad \sin\delta_0 = \frac{P_s}{P_m} = \frac{0.3125}{0.6666} = 0.4688$$

$$\delta_0 = 27.95\,° \text{ or } 0.488 \text{ radian}$$

$$\delta_m = \pi - \sin^{-1}\left(\frac{P_s}{P_{eIII}}\right) = \pi - \sin^{-1}\left(\frac{P_m \sin\delta_0}{r_2 P_m}\right) = \pi - \sin^{1}\left(\frac{\sin\delta_0}{r_2}\right)$$

$$= 128.617\,° \text{ or } 2.245 \text{ radian}$$

As we know, $\cos\delta_c = \dfrac{(\delta_m - \delta_0)\sin\delta_0 - r_1\cos\delta_0 + r_2\cos\delta_m}{r_2 - r_1}$

On putting values of δ_m, δ_0, r_2 and r_1 in above equation

$$\cos\delta_c = \frac{(2.245 - 0.4688) \times 0.4688 - 0.3 \times \cos 27.95° + 0.6 \times \cos 128.617°}{(0.6 - 0.3)} = 0.613$$

$$\delta_c = \cos^{-1}(0.613)$$

Critical clearing angle = 52.19°

7.7 **A 50 Hz synchronous generator is connected to an infinite bus through a line. The p.u. reactances of the generator and the line are $j0.3$ p.u. and $j0.2$ p.u. respectively. The generator no load voltage is 1.1 p.u. and that of the infinite Bus is 1.0 p.u. The inertia constant of the generator is 3 MW-sec/MVA.**

(a) If the generator is loaded to 60% of its maximum power transfer capacity and small perturbation is given, calculate resulting natural frequency of oscillations.

(b) If the generator is loaded to 75% of its maximum power transfer capacity and a small perturbation is given, calculate the new natural frequency of oscillations.

[12 marks : 2007]

Solution:

Since the system is operating initially under steady state condition, a small perturbation in power will make the rotor oscillation. The natural frequency of oscillation is given by,

$$f_n = \left\{\left(\frac{\partial P_e}{\partial \delta}\right)\delta_0 / M\right\}^{\frac{1}{2}} \text{ rad/sec}$$

(a) 60% Loading:

Now, $\dfrac{\partial P_e}{\partial \delta} = \dfrac{V_1 V_2}{X}\cos\delta = \dfrac{1.1 \times 1}{0.5}\cos\delta_0$

$$= \frac{1.1 \times 1}{0.5} \times 0.8 \qquad \left[\text{since, } \sin\delta_0 = \frac{0.6}{1} = 0.6\right] = 1.76$$

$$M = \frac{GH}{\pi f} = \frac{1 \times 3}{50\pi}$$

$$\therefore \quad f_n = \left(\frac{1.76}{3} \times 50\pi\right)^{\frac{1}{2}} \text{ rad/sec} = 9.6 \text{ rad/sec} = 1.53 \text{ Hz}$$

(b) 75% Loading:

$$\sin \delta_0 = 0.75 \text{ or } \delta_0 = 0.848 \text{ rad}$$

$$\left.\frac{\partial P_e}{\partial \delta}\right|_{\delta_0} = \frac{1.1 \times 1.0}{0.5} \times 0.6614$$

$$\therefore \quad f_n = \left(\frac{1.455}{3} \times 50\pi\right)^{\frac{1}{2}} = 8.726 \text{ rad/sec} = 1.39 \text{ Hz}$$

7.8 Define and derive swing equation for a finite machine connected to an infinite bus. Discuss the applications in the study of power system stability.

[10 marks : 2008]

Solution:

Swing Equation: The equation describing the relative motion of rotor (load angle δ) with respect to the stator field as a function of time is known as swing equation.

Derivation. Let T_s represents the shaft torque and T_e the electromagnetic torque and if these are assumed positive for a generator, the net torque causing acceleration is:

$$T_a = T_s - T_e \quad \text{...}(i)$$

A similar relation holds good,

$$P_a = P_s - P_e \quad \text{...}(ii)$$

where, P_a is the accelerating power, since a synchronous machine is a rotating body, the laws of motion apply to this also,

$$P_a = T_a \omega \quad \text{...}(iii)$$

$$\omega = \frac{2\pi n_s}{60}, \text{ is the angular velocity in mechanical radians/sec.}$$

$$\therefore \quad P_a = T_a \omega = I \alpha \omega = M \alpha \quad \text{...}(iv)$$

where, M = angular momentum in Joule-sec/electrical radian

α = acceleration in mechanical rad/sec^2

The acceleration α can be expressed in terms of the angular position of the rotor as

$$\alpha = \frac{d^2\theta}{dt^2} \quad \text{...}(v)$$

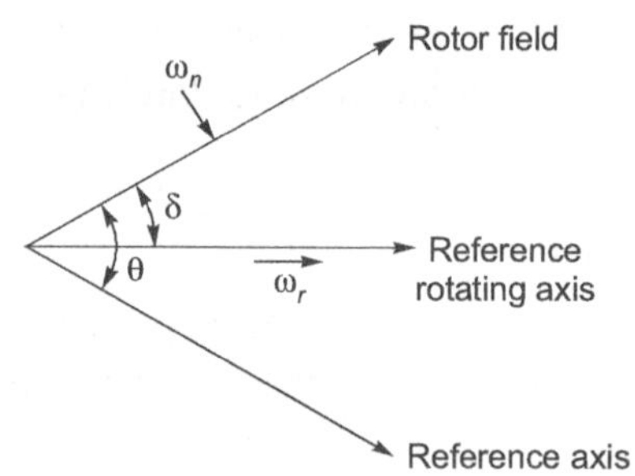

The angle θ changes continuously w.r.t. time when a sudden change occurs in the system. The value of θ is given by,

$$\theta = \omega_r t + \delta \quad \text{...}(vi)$$

where ω_r is the angular velocity of the reference synchronously rotating axis and δ is the angular displacement in electrical degree from the synchronously rotating reference axis.

Taking the derivative of equation

$$\frac{d\theta}{dt} = \omega_r + \frac{d\delta}{dt} \quad \text{...}(vii)$$

and

$$\frac{d^2\theta}{dt^2} = \frac{d^2\delta}{dt^2} \quad \text{...}(viii)$$

or

$$M\alpha = P_a \Rightarrow M\frac{d^2\delta}{dt^2} = P_a = P_s - P_e \quad \text{...Swing equation}$$

Application of Swing Equation in the Study of Power System Stability: The dynamics of the system can be described by swing equation which is non-linear. In case the changes are small, these equation can be linearized around the initial operating point.

Consider a system consisting of a generator connected to an infinite bus bar through a lossless network shown below figure with initial operating point on the power angle curve as (P_0, δ_0).

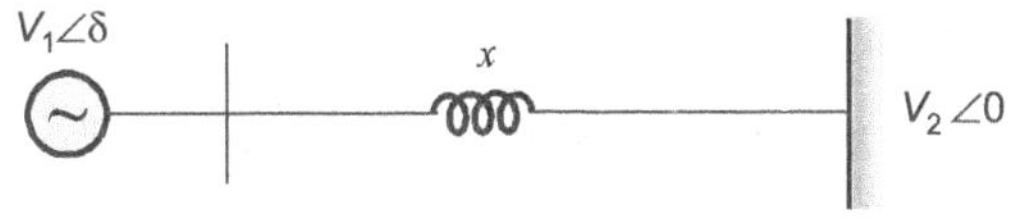

Finite machine connected to an infinite bus

Say the load is changed (increased) by ΔP, as a result of which the load angle changes by $\Delta\delta$ and the swing equation can be linearized around the point (P_0, δ_0) and is given as,

$$M\frac{d^2\Delta\delta}{dt^2} = P_i - P_e = P_i - (P_0 + \Delta P) = -\Delta P$$

$$= -\left(\frac{\partial P}{\partial \delta}\right)\Bigg|_{\delta_0} \Delta\delta \qquad ...(i)$$

Now let, $\frac{d}{dt} = P$ equation (*i*) reduces to

$$MP^2\Delta\delta + \frac{\partial P}{\partial \delta}\Bigg|_{\delta_0} .\Delta\delta = 0$$

or

$$\left(MP^2 + \frac{\partial P}{\partial \delta}\Bigg|_{\delta_0}\right)\Delta\delta = 0 \qquad ...(ii)$$

Equation (*ii*) is the characteristic equation with the two roots.

$$P = \pm\left(\frac{(-\delta P/\partial\delta)\delta_0}{M}\right)^{1/2} \qquad ...(iii)$$

Case 1: When $\partial P/\partial\delta$ is positive $\delta < (\pi/2)$, the two roots are pure imaginary and conjugate, the rotor motion is oscillatory and undamped around δ_0 and the system is stable.

Case 2: When $\partial P/\partial\delta$ is negative $\delta > (\pi/2)$, then the both roots are real, one positive and other negative respectively and hence the system is unstable.

Case 3: When $\partial P/\partial\delta = 0$, $\delta = 90°$, the system is critically stable.

7.9 A 50 Hz, 3-phase generator is supplying 60% of P_{max} to an infinite bus through a reactive network. A fault occurs which increases the reactance of the network between the generator internal voltage and the infinite bus by 400%. When the fault is cleared, the maximum power that can be delivered is 80% of the original maximum value. Determine the critical clearing angle for the condition described.

[20 marks : 2009]

Solution:

Let P_m be the maximum power that can be delivered.

$$P_m \sin\delta_0 = 0.6\, P_m = P_s$$

or $\delta_0 = 36.86° = 0.643$ radian

During fault the reactance is 400% of the, value before the fault

$\therefore$ $r_1 = 0.25$ $\qquad [x_2 = 4x$ and $P_m \propto 1/x]$

and $r_2 = 0.80$ (given)

The critical clearing angle δ_c is given by

$$\delta_c = \cos^{-1}\frac{(P_s/P_m)(\delta_m - \delta_0) + r_2\cos\delta_m - r_1\cos\delta_0}{r_2 - r_1} \qquad ...(i)$$

$$\therefore \qquad \delta_m = \pi - \sin^{-1}\left(\frac{P_s}{0.8P_m}\right) = \pi - \sin^{-1}\left(\frac{0.6P_m}{0.8P_m}\right) = 2.293 \text{ radian} = 131.4°$$

Substituting these value in equation (*i*),

$$\delta_c = \cos^{-1}\frac{0.6(2.293-0.643)-0.80\times0.661-0.25\times0.800}{0.55}$$

$$= \cos^{-1}0.475 = 61.64°$$

7.10 The single line diagram of a three-phase power system is given below. The generator is delivering 1.0 per unit power to the infinite bus. The pre-fault power angle equation is $P_e = 2.10\sin\delta$. Calculate the critical clearing angle and critical clearing time when the system is subjected to a 3-phase fault at point P (i.e. sending end of the short-line). The fault is cleared by opening the circuit breaker 5. The inertia constant $H = 50$ MJ/MVA.

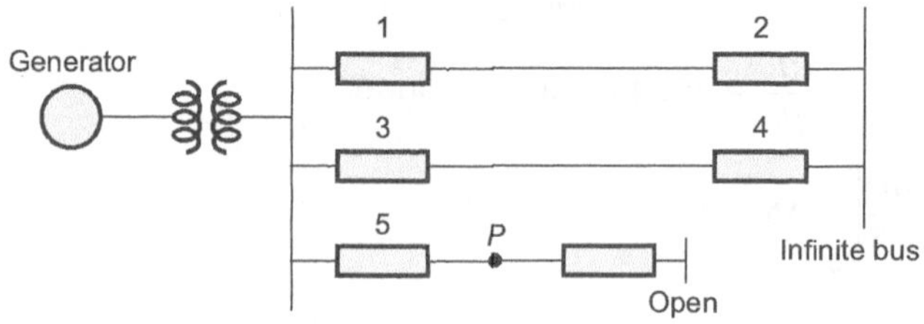

[15 marks : 2010]

Solution:

If a three-phase fault occurs at the point P the electrical output of the generator instantly reduces to zero

$$P_e = P_{max}\sin\delta = 2.10\sin\delta$$

Given, $P_m = 1$ pu

Before fault, $P_m = P_e = 2.10\sin\delta_0$

$$1 = 2.10\sin\delta_0$$

$$\sin\delta_0 = 1/2.10$$

$$\Rightarrow \delta_0 = 28.43$$

$$\delta_{max} = 2.645 \text{ rad or } 151.56°$$

A_1 = Accelerating area

$$= \int_{\delta_0}^{\delta_{cr}}(P_m - 0)d\delta = \int_{\delta_0}^{\delta_{cr}}P_m\,d\delta \qquad ...(i)$$

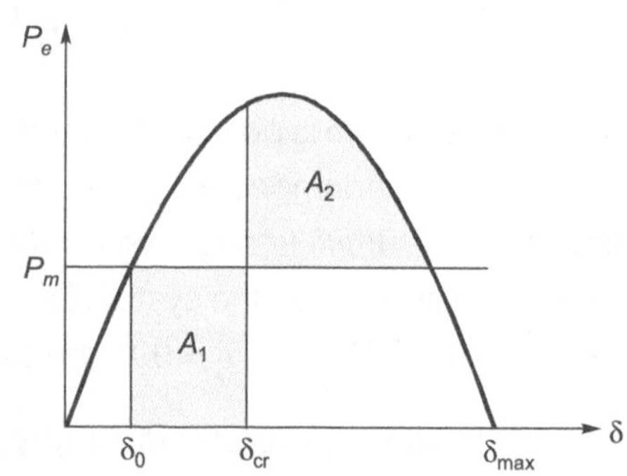

Critical clearing angle

$$= \int_{\delta_0}^{\delta_{cr}}(P_e - P_m)d\delta = \int_{\delta_{cr}}^{\delta_{max}}(P_{max}\sin\delta - P_m)d\delta = \int_{\delta_{cr}}^{\delta_{max}}(2.1\sin\delta - P_m)d\delta \qquad ...(ii)$$

According to equal area criterion, $A_1 = A_2$

$$\int_{\delta_0}^{\delta_{cr}}P_m\,d\delta = \int_{\delta_{cr}}^{\delta_{max}}(2.1\sin\delta - P_m)d\delta$$

$$\Rightarrow \quad P_m(\delta_{cr}-\delta_0) = 2.1\times(\cos\delta_{cr}-\cos\delta_{max}) - P_m(\delta_{max}-\delta_{cr})$$

$$\Rightarrow \quad P_m(\delta_{max}-\delta_0) = 2.1\times\{\cos\delta_{cr}-\cos\delta_{max})$$

$$1\times(2.645-0.496\} = 2.1\times\{\cos\delta_{cr}-\cos151.56°\}$$

$$\Rightarrow \quad \cos\delta_{cr} = 0.144$$

$\Rightarrow$ Critical clearing angle $\delta_{cr} = \cos^{-1}(0.144) = 81.72°$

Swing equation, $$M\left(\frac{d^2\delta}{dt^2}\right) = P_m - P_e$$

$P_e = 0$, during fault,

and $$M = \frac{H}{\pi f} \text{ in pu system}$$

$$\Rightarrow \quad \frac{d^2\delta}{dt^2} = \left(\frac{\pi f}{H}\right) \times P_m$$

On integrating twice,

$$\delta = \left(\frac{\pi f}{2H}\right) \times P_m t^2 + \delta_0 \Rightarrow \delta_{cr} = \left(\frac{\pi f P_m}{2H}\right) t_{cr}^2 + \delta_0$$

$$t_{cr} = \left[\frac{2H(\delta_{cr} - \delta_0)}{\pi f P_m}\right]^{1/2} = \left[\frac{2 \times 5 \times (1.426 - 0.496)}{\pi \times 50 \times 1}\right]^{1/2} = 0.243 \text{ sec.}$$

7.11 **Sketch typical swing curves for a synchronous machine:**

(i) showing that the machine is stable after a disturbance

(ii) showing that the machine is unstable after a disturbance.

[10 marks : 2011]

Solution:

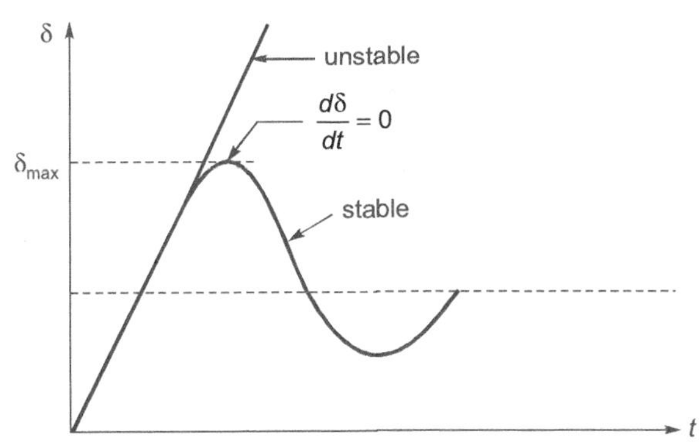

- If the system is unstable continues to increase indefinitely with time and the machine loses synchronism.
- On the other hand, if the system is stable, $\delta(t)$ performs oscillations, (non-sinusoidal) whose amplitude decreases in actual practice because of damping terms.

7.12 **Define steady-state stability and stability limit with the half of *P-S* characteristic. What are the techniques available to improve steady-state stability?**

[4 marks : 2012]

Solution:

The steady state stability is the stability of the system under conditions of gradual or relatively slow change in load.

Consider a cylindrical rotor synchronous generator connected to infinite bus operating at constant speed with constant field current and no saturation, as shown in figure given below:

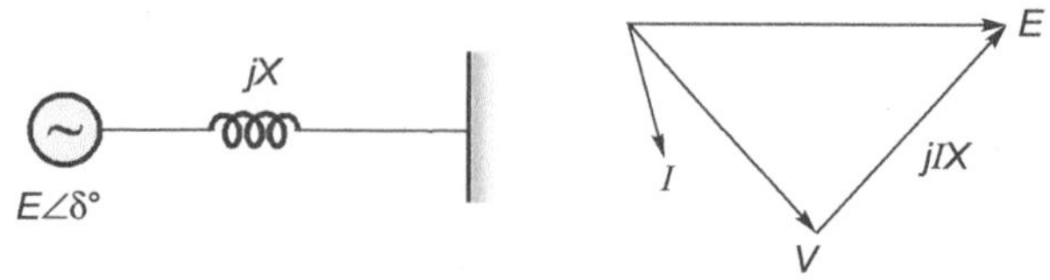

The power output of machine,

$$P = \frac{EV}{X}\sin\delta$$

The maximum power output for fixed E and V

$$P_{max} = \frac{EV}{X}$$

This is termed the pull-out power of a synchronous generator against an infinite bus at constant field excitation. Since any attempt to increase the power output further will result in a loss of synchronism.

Steady state stability limit

The maximum power which a generator can deliver depends upon the field excitation of the generator.

If the change in excitation is assumed to be initiated immediately following the change in load, the stability limit under such conditions may be termed dynamic stability limit. In general dynamic limit will be higher than the steady state stability limit.

The steady state limit can be improved by

- increasing the excitation of a generator or motor so that emfs are increased and consequently the maximum power transferred increases.
- reducing the transfer reactance.

7.13 A synchronous generator is connected to an infinite bus with power supply at 0.45 pu of maximum capacity. Find the critical clearing angle for the fault to be cleared if it is known that the reactance of generator and line becomes four times of prefault value. The maximum power deliverable after clearing of a fault is 70% of the original maximum value. Use equal area criterion to obtain solution.

[6 marks : 2012]

Solution:

Let P_m be the maximum power that can delivered.

$$P_{max}\sin\delta_o = 0.45\,P_{max}$$

$$\Rightarrow \quad \delta_o = 26.74° = 0.47 \text{ rad.}$$

$$\gamma_1 = \frac{1}{4} = 0.25, \quad \gamma_2 = 0.7$$

$$\gamma_2 P_{max}\sin\delta_{max} = P_m$$

and $$\frac{P_m}{P_{max}} = 0.45 \quad \text{(given)}$$

$$\sin\delta_{max} = \frac{0.45}{0.7}$$

$$\Rightarrow \quad \delta_{max} = 180° - 40° = 140° = 2.44 \text{ rad.}$$

$$\cos\delta_{cr} = \frac{0.45(2.44 - 0.47) + 0.7\cos 140° - 0.25\cos 26.74°}{0.7 - 0.25}$$

$$= \frac{0.8865 - 0.536 - 0.2233}{0.45} = 0.283$$

$$\delta_{cr} = 73.58°$$

7.14 A 500 MVA, 20 kV, 60 Hz, 4-pole synchronous generator is connected to an infinite bus through a purely reactive network. The generator has an inertia constant H = 60 MJ/MVA and is delivering power of 1.0 pu to the infinite bus at steady state. The maximum power that can be delivered is 2.5 p.u. A fault occurs that reduces the generator output to zero. Determine the

(*i*) angular acceleration

(*ii*) speed in rpm at the end of 15 cycles.

[10 marks : 2014]

Solution:

(*i*)

$$P_e = P_m = 1 \text{ pu}$$

$$P_{max} = 2.5 \text{ pu}$$

$$\frac{Md^2\delta}{dt^2} = P_m - P_e$$

$P_e = 0,$ $\quad P_m = 1$ pu

$$\therefore \quad \frac{Md^2\delta}{dt^2} = P_m$$

where, $\quad M = \frac{GH}{\pi f}$ or $\boxed{M_{pu} = \frac{H}{\pi f}}$

$$M_{pu} = \frac{6}{\pi \times 60} = 0.031 \text{ MJ-s/elec. rad}$$

$$\frac{d^2\delta}{dt^2} = \alpha = \text{angular acceleration}$$

$$M_{pu} \times \alpha = P_{m(pu)}$$

$$0.031 \times \alpha = 1$$

$$\alpha = 32.26 \text{ elec. rad/s}^2$$

(*ii*)

$$\frac{Md^2\delta}{dt^2} = P_m$$

Integrating on both sides,

$$M\frac{d\delta}{dt} = P_m t$$

$$\frac{d\delta}{dt} = \frac{P_m t}{M} \qquad \left[\because t = \frac{15}{60} \text{ sec.}\right]$$

$$= \frac{1 \times 0.25}{0.031} = 8.064 \text{ rad/sec.}$$

Speed in rpm at the end of 15 cycles is = N_s + (8.064) rad/s

Converting 8.064 rad/s in to rpm

$$8.064 \times 60 = 483.84 \text{ rad/m}$$

One revolution is equal to 2π radians and the machine is of four pole so, for every two pole it completes electrical 360°

$$= \frac{483.84}{2\pi \times 2} = \frac{77}{2} \text{ revolutions/min}$$

$$\therefore \quad N_s + \frac{77}{2} \text{ revolutions/min} = \frac{120 \times 60}{4} + \frac{77}{2}$$

Speed at the end of 15 cycles = 1838.5 rpm

7.15 A power system to which a generator is to be connected at a certain bus may be represented by the Thevenin's voltage $E_{th} = 0.9\angle 0°$ p.u. in series with $Z_{th} = 0.25\angle 90°$ p.u. When connected to the system, E_g of the generator is $1.4\angle 30°$ p.u. Synchronous reactance of the generator on the system base is 1.0 p.u.

(i) Find the bus voltage V_t and real power (P) and reactive power (Q) transferred to the system at the bus.

(ii) If the bus voltage is to be raised to $|V_t| = 1{\cdot}0$ p.u. for the same P transferred to the system, find the value of E_g required and the value of Q transferred to the system at the same bus. Assume all the other system emf's are unchanged in magnitude and angle, that is, Thevenin's voltage and impedance are constant.

[15 marks : 2015]

Solution:

(i)

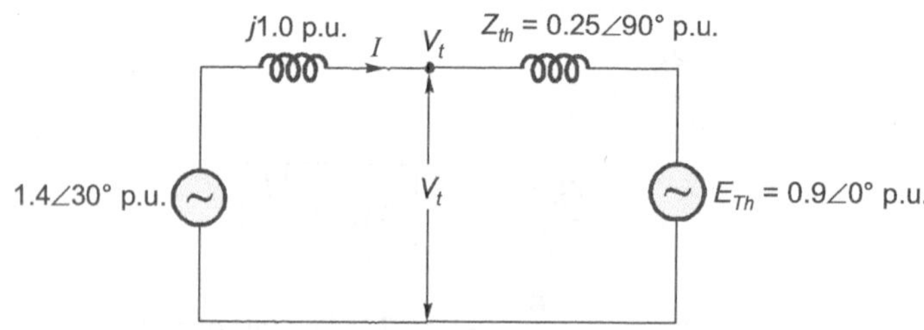

$$\Rightarrow \quad \frac{V_t - 1.4\angle 30°}{j1} + \frac{V_t - 0.9\angle 0°}{j0.25} = 0$$

$$\Rightarrow \quad V_t\left[\frac{1}{j1} + \frac{1}{j0.25}\right] = \frac{1.4\angle 30°}{j1} + \frac{0.9\angle 0°}{j0.25}$$

$$\Rightarrow \quad V_t = \frac{4.863\angle -81.723°}{5\angle -90°} = 0.9726\angle 8.277°$$

Power transferred to the system at the bus,

$$S = V_t I^*$$

$$S = [0.9726\angle 8.277]\left[\frac{0.9726\angle 8.277 - 0.9\angle 0°}{j0.25}\right]^*$$

$$S = [0.9726\angle 8.277]\,[0.6132\angle -24.04]^*$$

$$S = 0.504 + 0.3188\,j$$

Active power = 0.504 p.u.

Reactive power = 0.3188 p.u.

(ii)

$$V_t = 1\angle\delta$$

$$P = \frac{V_t \times 0.9 \sin\delta}{0.25} = 0.5038$$

$$\delta = 8.04°$$

$$I = \frac{1\angle 8.04° - 0.9\angle 0°}{(0.25j)} = 0.6656\angle -32.8°$$

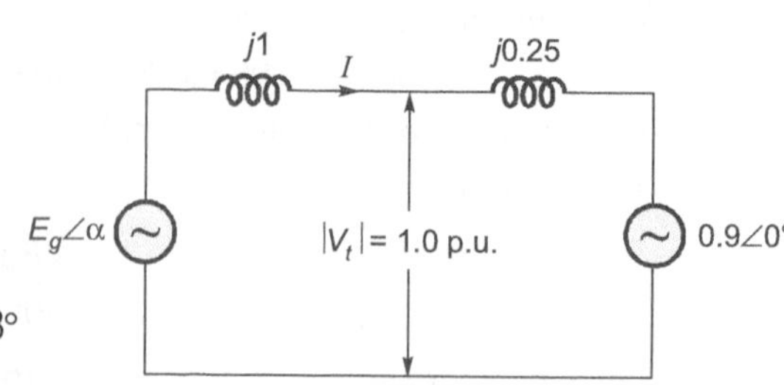

$$E_g\angle\alpha = V_t\angle\delta + \vec{I}(j1) = 1\angle 8.04° + (0.6656\angle -32.8°)(j1)$$

$$E_g\angle\alpha = 1.52\angle 27.373°$$

$$Q = \frac{EV}{X}\cos\alpha - \frac{V^2}{X} = \frac{[1.52\times 1\times \cos(27.37°)-1]}{0.25} = 1.399 \text{ pu.}$$

$$|E_g| = 1.52 \text{ p.u.}$$

$$\alpha = 27.373°$$

$$Q = 1.399 \text{ p.u.}$$

7.16 A three-phase power system consists of a synchronous machine connected through a lossless double circuit transmission line to an infinite bus-bar. A fault occurs on the transmission line. The maximum power transfer to the system is 5.0 p.u. during pre-fault condition and immediately prior to the instant of the fault, the power transfer is 2.5 p.u. The power angle curves during the fault and post-fault conditions have peak values of 2 p.u. and 4 p.u. respectively. Determine the permissible increase in the angular displacement, between the voltages at the two ends of the system beyond which the circuit breakers could not clear the fault in time for the system to remain in synchronism.

[10 marks : 2015]

Solution:

Given that,

$$P_{max} = 5 \text{ p.u.} = (P_{max})_I$$

$$P_{m_0} = 2.5$$

$$P_{m_0} = P_{max}\sin\delta_0$$

$$2.5 = 5\sin\delta_0$$

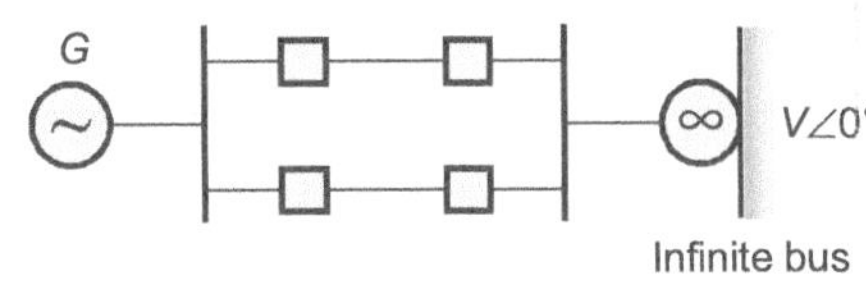

$$\delta_0 = \sin^{-1}\left(\frac{2.5}{5}\right) = 30° \text{ (or) } 0.5236 \text{ rad}$$

and (P_m) during fault = 2 p.u.

$$\gamma_1 = \frac{(P_{max})\text{ during fault}}{(P_{max})\text{ before fault}} = \frac{(P_{max})_{II}}{(P_{max})_I}$$

$$\gamma_1 = \frac{2}{5} = 0.4$$

$$\gamma_2 = \frac{(P_{max})\text{ after fault}}{(P_{max})\text{ before fault}} = \frac{(P_{max})_{III}}{(P_{max})_I}$$

$$= \frac{4}{5} = 0.8$$

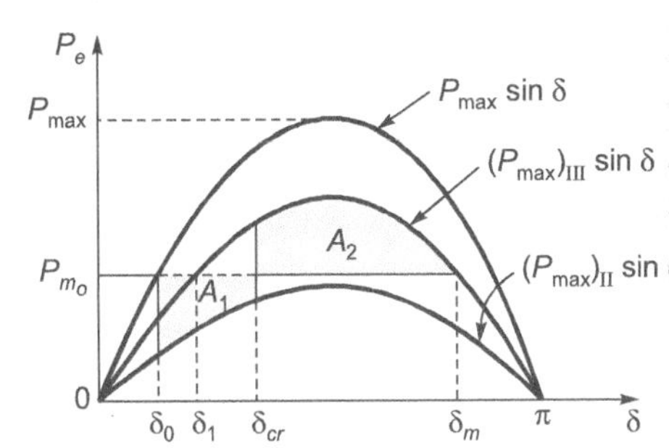

$$\delta_1 = \sin^{-1}\left[\frac{P_{m_0}}{P_{max\,III}}\right] = \sin^{-1}\left[\frac{2.5}{4}\right]$$

$$\delta_1 = 38.6822°\text{(or) } 0.6751 \text{ rad}$$

and

$$\delta_m = \pi - \delta_1 = \pi - 0.6751$$

$$\delta_m = 2.4664 \text{ rad}$$

We know that,

$$\delta_{cr} = \cos^{-1}\left[\frac{(\delta_m-\delta_0)\sin\delta_0 + \gamma_2\cos\delta_m - \gamma_1\cos\delta_0}{(\gamma_2-\gamma_1)}\right] = 1.5695 \text{ rad or } 89.92°$$

7.17 A 500 MVA, 20 kV, 50 Hz, four-pole synchronous generator is connected to an infinite bus through a purely inductive network. The generator has an inertia constant H = 6.0 MJ/MVA and is delivering power of 1.0 p.u. to the infinite bus at steady-state. The maximum power that can be delivered is 2.5 p.u. A fault occurs that reduces the generator output power to zero.

(i) Find the angular acceleration.
(ii) Find the speed in rpm at the end of 15 cycles.
(iii) Find the change in angle d at the end of 15 cycles.

[15 Marks : 2016]

Solution:

Given data: $S = 500$ MVA, $V = 20$ kV, $f = 50$ Hz, $P = 4$ poles, $H = 6$ MJ/MVA, $P_m = 1$ p.u., $P_{max} = 2.5$ p.u.

Due to fault, $P_e = 0$

From the swing equation,

$$M \cdot \frac{d^2\delta}{dt^2} = P_a = (P_m - P_e)$$

where,

$$M = \frac{HS}{180f}$$

$$M_{p.u.} = \frac{H}{180f}$$

$$\Rightarrow \quad \frac{6}{180 \times 50} = 6.66 \times 10^{-4} \text{ MJsec/elec. degree}$$

(i) Angular acceleration:

$$\alpha_e = \frac{d^2\delta}{dt^2} = \frac{P_a}{M} = \frac{P_m - P_e}{M} = \frac{1-0}{6.66 \times 10^{-4}} = 1500 \text{ elec.degree/sec}^2$$

$$\alpha_m = 1500 \times \left(\frac{2}{p}\right) = 1500 \times \frac{2}{4} = 750 \text{ elec. degree/sec}^2$$

$$\alpha_m = 750 \times \frac{60}{360} = 125 \text{ rpm/sec}$$

(ii)

$$t = 15 \text{ cycles} = \frac{15}{50} = 0.3 \text{ sec.}$$

$$N_s = \frac{120f}{p} = \frac{120 \times 50}{4} = 1500 \text{ rpm}$$

Speed at the end of 15 cycles = 0.3 sec

$$N = 1500 + 125 \times 0.3 = 1537.5 \text{ rpm}$$

(iii) Load angle δ at the end of 15 cycles. From swing equation integrate twice,

$$\delta = \frac{P_a \cdot t^2}{2M} = \frac{1 \times (0.3)^2}{2 \times 6.66 \times 10^{-4}} = 67.56°$$

7.18 A synchronous generator, capable of developing 500 MW of power, operates at a power angle of 8°. By how much can the input shaft power be increased suddenly without loss of stability?

[20 marks : 2017]

Solution:

Given: $P_{max} = 500$ MW

$$\delta_0 = 8° = 0.1396 \text{ radians}$$

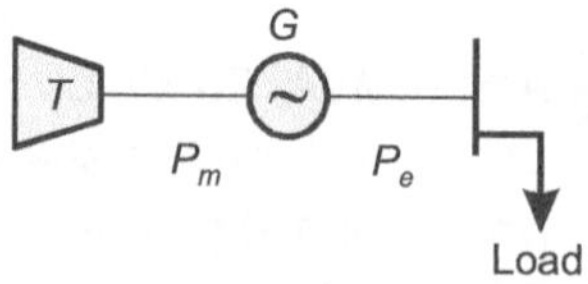

By using equal area criteria for generator without loosing synchronism

For change in mechanical input power.

$$A_1 = A_2$$

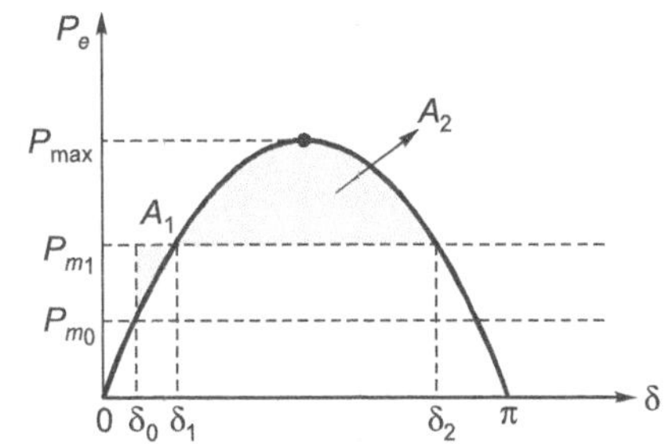

$$\int_{\delta_0}^{\delta_1} (P_{m_1} - P_{max} \sin\delta)\, d\delta = \int_{\delta_1}^{\delta_2} (P_{max} \sin\delta - P_{m_1})\, d\delta$$

By solving integration,

$$(\cos\delta_2 - \cos\delta_0) + \sin\delta_1(\delta_2 - \delta_0) = 0 \qquad \text{...(i)}$$

where, $\sin\delta_1 = \dfrac{P_{m_1}}{P_{max}}$

For maximum input power to be stable,

$$\delta_2 = \pi - \delta_1$$

Substituting in equation (i),

$$(\pi - \delta_1 - \delta_0) \sin\delta_1 - \cos\delta_1 - \cos\delta_0 = 0$$

$$\delta_0 = 0.1396 \text{ rad}$$

$$(3.0019 - \delta_1) \sin\delta_1 - \cos\delta_1 - 0.9902 = 0$$

Calculating δ_1 by using Newton Raphson method.

Let, $\delta_1^0 = 0.8$ radians (Initial value)

$$x_2 = x_1 - \frac{f(x_1)}{f'(x_1)}$$

$$f'(\delta_1) = \frac{d}{d\delta_1}(3 \sin\delta_1 - \delta_1 \sin\delta_1 - \cos\delta_1 - 0.99)$$

$$f'(\delta_1) = 3 \cos\delta_1 - \delta_1 \cos\delta_1$$

$$\delta_1^1 = \delta_1^0 - \frac{f(\delta_1^0)}{f'(\delta_1^0)}$$

$$\delta_1^1 = 0.8 - \frac{(-0.1085)}{1.5327} = 0.8707$$

$$\delta_1^2 = 0.8707 - \frac{-5.8450 \times 10^{-3}}{1.37188} = 0.8749$$

$\therefore$ Value of δ_1 converges at, $\delta_1 = 0.8749 \text{ rad} = 50.128°$

$$P_{m_1} = P_{max} \sin\delta_1$$

$$= 500 \sin(50.128°) = 383.74 \text{ MW}$$

$\therefore$ Maximum input power can be applied without loosing synchronism is,

$$P_{m_1} = 383.74 \text{ MW}$$

7.19 A 50 Hz, 4-pole turbogenerator rated 500 MVA, 22 kV has an inertia constant of 7.5 MJ/MVA. Find:

(i) Rotor acceleration, if the input to the generator is suddenly raised to 400 MW for an electrical load of 350 MW.

(ii) The speed of rotor is rpm, if the rotor acceleration calculated in part (i) is constant for a period of 10 cycles.

(iii) The change in torque angle δ in elect. degrees.

[20 marks : 2019]

Solution:

Given: $P = 4$, $G = 500$ MVA, 22 kV, $H = 7.5$ MJ/MVA

(i) $P_{accelerating} = 400 - 350 = 50$ MW

By using swing equation,

$$M\frac{d^2\delta}{dt^2} = P_a$$

$$\alpha = \frac{P_a}{M}$$

$$M = \frac{GH}{180f} = \frac{500\times 7.5}{180\times 50} = 0.4166 \text{ MJ/elec.degree}$$

$$\alpha = \frac{50}{0.4166} = 120 \text{ elec.degree/s}^2$$

(ii) $$\alpha = \frac{120}{2} = \text{mechanical degree/s}^2$$

$$= 60 \text{ mech. degree/s}^2$$

$$\alpha = \frac{60\times 60}{360} = 10$$

$$\text{Change in speed} = \Delta N = \alpha t$$

$$= 10 \times t$$

$$t = 10 \times 0.2 = 2 \text{ rpm}$$

$\therefore$ Speed at the end of 10 cycles $= N + \Delta N = 1500 + 2 = 1502$ rpm

(iii) New torque angle, $\delta = \delta_0 + \Delta\delta$

Change in torque angle, $\Delta\delta = \frac{1}{2}\cdot\alpha\cdot t^2 = \frac{1}{2}\times 10\times(0.2)^2 = 0.2°$

7.20 A generator is connected by a double line to an infinite bus, the voltage of which is $V = 1$ pu as shown in the figure. Per unit values of reactances and voltages are indicated in the figure. A three-phase short-circuit occur at the point P. The circuit breakers A and B open simultaneously and remain open. The mechanical power supplied to the generator before the fault is $P_m = 1$ pu.

(i) Determine the electrical powers P_{e1}, P_{e2} and P_{e3} before, during and post the fault.

(ii) Draw on the same graph, power angle curves for P_{e1}, P_{e2} and P_{e3}.

(iii) Calculate the angles δ_0, δ_1 and δ_{max} where δ_0 is the initial power angle, δ_1 is the post fault power angle and δ_{max} is the maximum power angle.

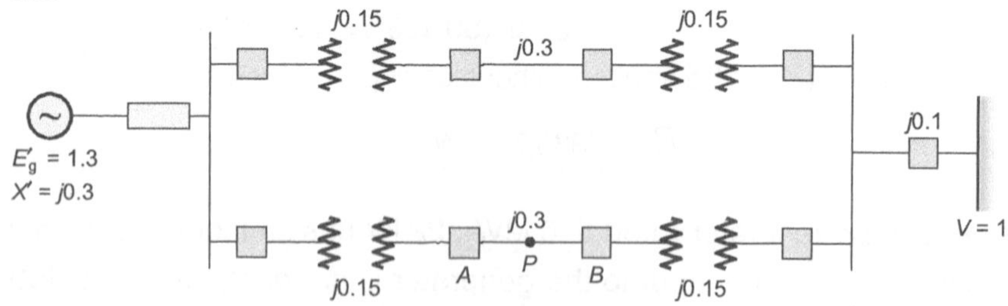

[20 marks : 2019]

Solution:

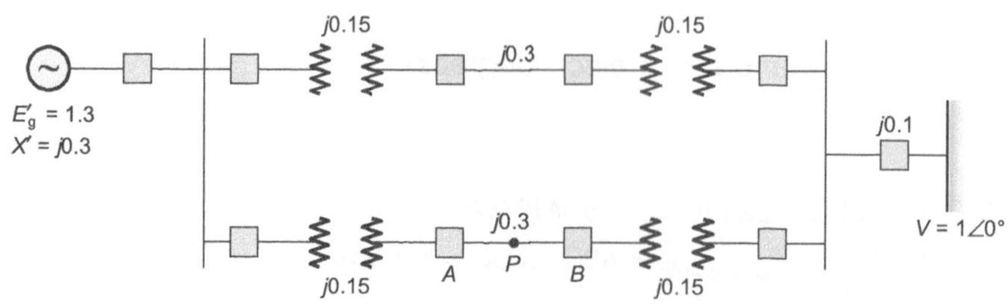

Prefault condition:

$$X = j0.3 + j0.1 + \left(\frac{j0.15 + j0.3 + j0.15}{2}\right) = j0.7 \text{ p.u.}$$

Hence,
$$P_{e1\,max} = \frac{1.3 \times 1}{0.7} = 1.8571 \text{ p.u.}$$

During fault:

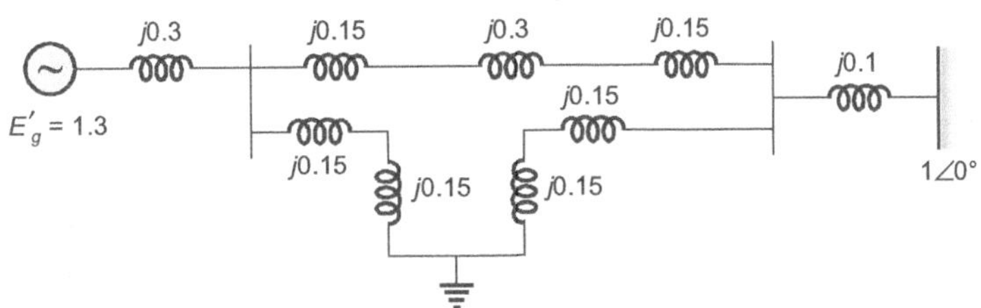

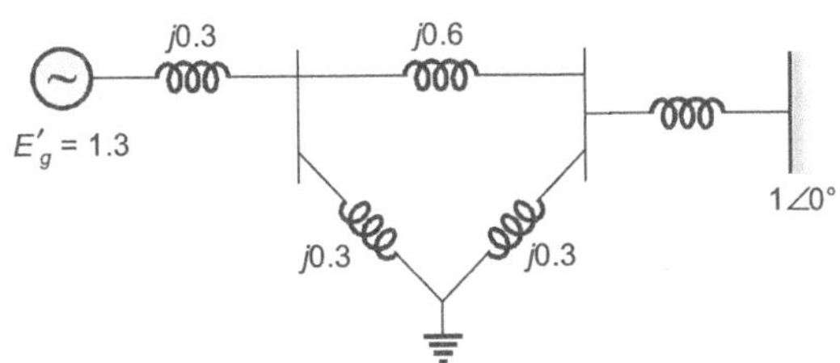

Applying Δ to ⅄ transformation,

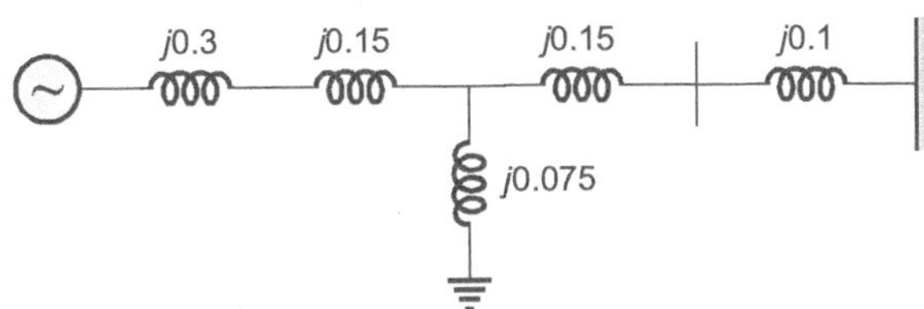

Again ⅄ to Δ,

$$X = j0.45 + j0.25 + \frac{j0.45 \times 0.25}{j0.075} = j2.2 \text{ p.u.}$$

$\therefore$
$$P_{e2\,max} = \frac{1.3 \times 1}{2.2} = 0.59 \text{ p.u.}$$

Post fault:

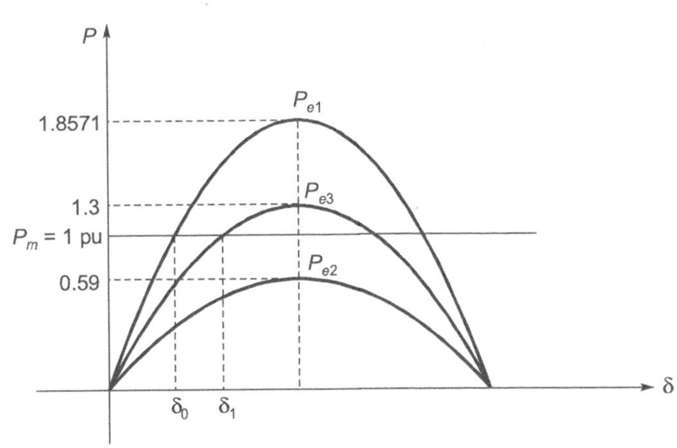

One line should be isolated,

$$X = j0.3 + j0.1 + j0.15 + j0.3 + j0.15$$

$$= j1.0 \text{ p.u.}$$

$$P_{e3\max} = \frac{1.3 \times 1}{1} = 1.3 \text{ p.u.}$$

For δ_0:

$$P_{e1} = P_m$$

$\Rightarrow$ $$1 = 1.8571 \sin\delta_0$$

$\Rightarrow$ $$\delta_0 = \sin^{-1}\left[\frac{1}{1.8571}\right] = 32.58°$$

For δ_1:

$$1 = 1.3 \sin\delta_2$$

$$\delta_1 = \sin^{-1}\left(\frac{1}{1.3}\right) = 50.284°$$

$$\delta_{max} = 180° - 50.284° = 129.715°$$

7.21 A synchronous machine is connected to an infinite bus through a transformer and a double circuit line shown in the figure. The infinite bus voltage is $V = 1.0\angle 0°$ p.u. The direct axis transient reactance of the machine is 0.20 p.u., the transformer reactance is 0.10 p.u. and the reactance of each of the transmission lines is 0.4 p.u., all to a base of the rating of the synchronous machine. Initially the machine is delivering 0.8 p.u. power with a terminal voltage of 1.05 p.u. The inertia constant $H = 5$ MJ/MVA. All resistances are neglected. Determine the equation of motion of the machine rotor.

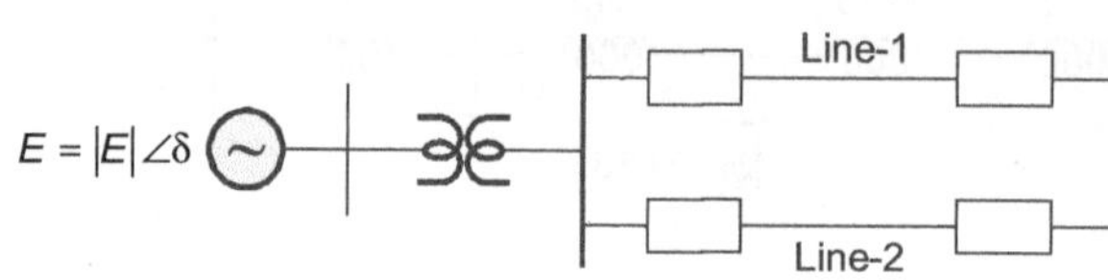

[20 marks : 2020]

Solution:

For given power system :

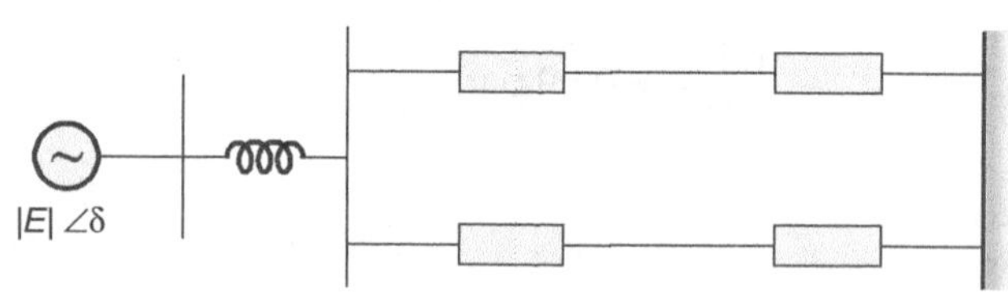

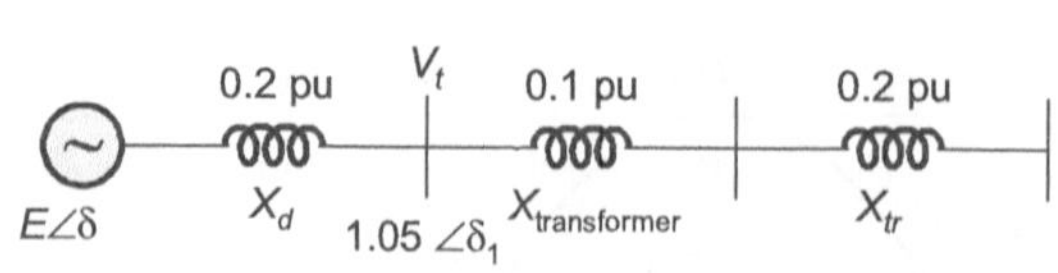

Using power relation

$$\frac{V_t V \sin\delta_1}{X} = 0.8$$

$$\frac{1(1.05)\sin\delta_1}{0.3} = 0.8 \text{ or } \delta_1 = \sin^{-1} 0.2285 = 13.21°$$

Now using voltage equation

$$I_a = \frac{1.05\angle 13.21° - 1\angle 0°}{0.3j} = 0.803\angle -5.289° \text{ p.u.}$$

$$E = 1.05\angle 13.21 + 0.803\angle{-5.23} \times 0.2\angle 90°$$
$$E = 1.111\angle 21.086° \text{ p.u.}$$
$$\delta = 21.086°$$

$$M\frac{d^2\delta}{dt^2} = P_m - P_e \quad \text{...(swing equation)}$$

where
$$P_e = \frac{EV\sin\delta}{X_{eq}} = \frac{1.11 \times 1\sin\delta}{0.5} = 2.222 \sin\delta$$

$$M = \frac{SH}{\pi f} = \frac{1 \times 5}{\pi \times 50} = 0.0318$$

$$0.0318\frac{d^2\delta}{dt^2} = 0.8 - 2.222\sin\delta$$

7.22 For a system shown in the figure, a three phase fault occurs at point P, which is followed by simultaneous opening of the circuit breakers R_1 and R_2.

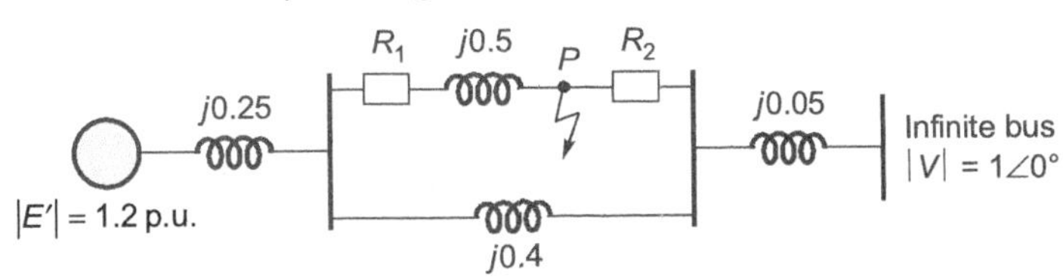

If the generator was delivering 1.0 p.u power prior to fault, find the power angle δ in pre-fault condition and the maximum permissible angle δ_{max} post-fault after clearing by removing the faulted line by breakers.

[12 marks : 2021]

Solution:

With reference to figure, three separate power angle curves are involved,

I. Normal operation (prefault)

$$X_I = 0.25 + \frac{0.5 \times 0.4}{0.5 + 0.4} + 0.05 = 0.522 \text{ p.u.}$$

$$P_{eI} = \frac{|E'||V|}{X_1}\sin\delta = \frac{1.2 \times 1}{0.522}\sin\delta = 2.3 \sin\delta$$

II. During fault :

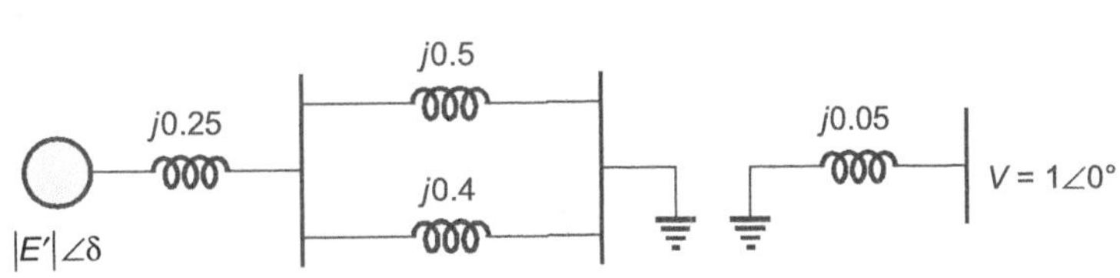

Pre-fault operating power angle is given by

$$1.0 = 2.3 \sin\delta_0$$

or,
$$\delta_0 = 25.8° = 0.45 \text{ radians}$$

During fault it is clear that no power is transferred during fault i.e., fault is near to bus bar

$$P_{e\,II} = 0$$

III. Post fault operation (fault cleared by opening the faulted line)

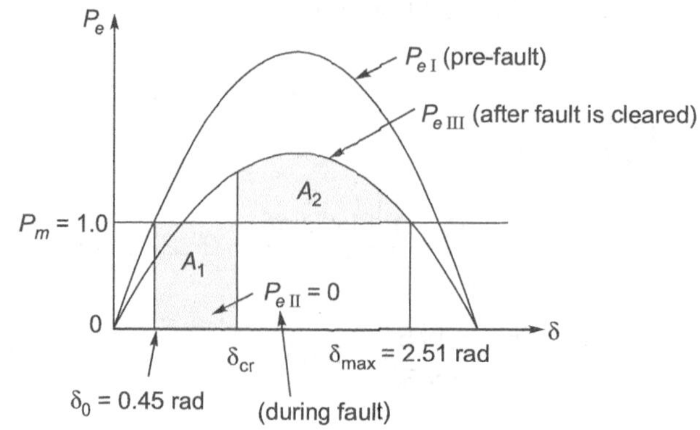

$$X_{III} = 0.25 + 0.4 + 0.05 = 0.7$$

$$P_{e\,III} = \frac{1.2 \times 1.0}{0.7} \sin\delta$$

$$= 1.712 \sin \delta$$

The maximum permissible angle δ_{max} for area $A_1 = A_2$ is given by

$$\delta_{max} = \pi - \sin^{-1}\frac{1}{1.714}$$

$$= 2.51 \text{ radian} = 143.81°$$

7.23 **What do you mean by the steady state stability limit of a power system? Find the steady state power limit of a power system consisting of a generator with equivalent reactance of 0.5 pu, connected to an infinite bus through a series reactance of 0.1 pu. The terminal voltage of the generaor is held at 1.2 pu and the infinite bus voltage at 1.0 pu.**

[20 marks : 2022]

Solution:

Steady state stability is defined as the ability of an electric power system to maintain synchronism between machines within the system and an external tie line following a small and slow disturbance.

So, steady state stability limit refers to the maximum power which can be transferred without loss of stability.

Given : Generation reactance, $\chi_g = 0.5$ pu

Service reactance of line, $\chi_2 = 0.1$ pu

Terminal voltage of generator, $V_b = 1.2$ pu

Infinite bus voltage, $V = 1.0$ pu

Let the generator voltage be '$E_g\angle\delta°$, then

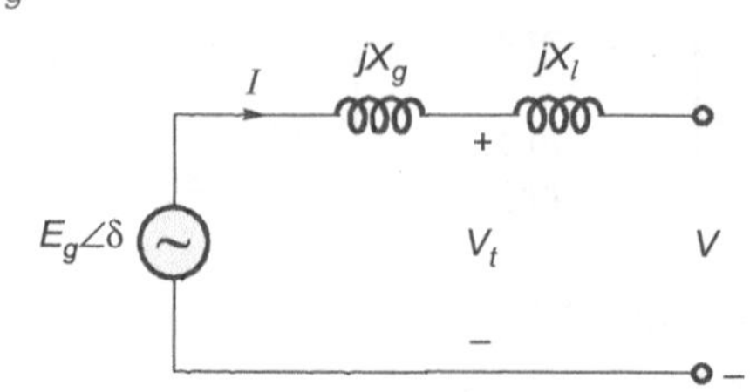

Current flowing, $I = \dfrac{E_g\angle 90° - V}{jX_g + jX_l} = \dfrac{V_t\angle\theta - V}{jX_l}$

Let $V_l = 1.2\angle\theta$

So, $$I = \frac{1.2\angle\theta - 1}{0.1j}$$

$\Rightarrow$ $$E_g = 1.2\angle\theta + j0.5\left[\frac{1.2\angle\theta - 1}{0.1j}\right]$$

$\Rightarrow$ $$E_g = 1.2\angle\theta + 6\angle\theta - 5$$
$$= 7.2\angle\theta - 5$$
$$= 7.2\cos\theta - 5 + j7.2\sin\theta$$

As for steady state limit, $\delta = 90°$

So, $$\text{Re}\{E_g\} = 0 \Rightarrow 7.2\cos\theta - 5 = 0$$

$\Rightarrow$ $$\cos\theta = \frac{5}{7.2} \Rightarrow \theta = 46.017°$$

So, $$E_g = 7.2\angle 46.017 - 5$$

$\Rightarrow$ $$|E_g| = 5.1807 \text{ pu}$$

So, steady state limit, $$\text{SSSL} = \frac{|E_g|\,|V|}{|(X_g) + jX_l|}$$
$$\text{SSSL} = 8.6346 \text{ pu}$$

7.24 For a single machine infinite bus shown below, if δ_c is the critical clearing angle for a three-phase short circuit 'F', prove that the clearing time 't_c' of the circuit breaker CB must satisfy the following:

$$t_c \le \sqrt{\frac{2H(\delta_c - \delta_0)}{\pi f P_i}}$$

where P_i is the mechanical power input,
δ_0 is the initial power angle,
f is the frequency and

H is the machine inertia constant and is given by $H = \frac{\pi f}{G} J\left(\frac{2}{P}\right)^2 \omega_e \times 10^{-6}$

J is moment of inertia of rotor (kg-m^2),
ω_c is synchronous speed in electrical rad/sec
G is three-phase MVA rating (base) of machine

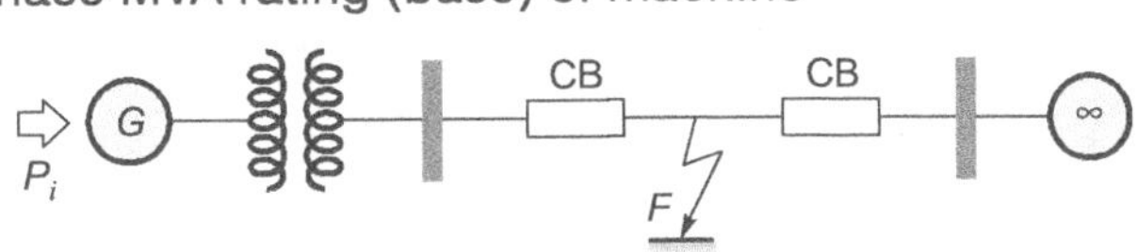

Also express the relation of δ_{cr} with δ_o, δ_{cr} is the critical clearing angle and corresponding critical clearing time.

[20 marks : 2023]

Solution:

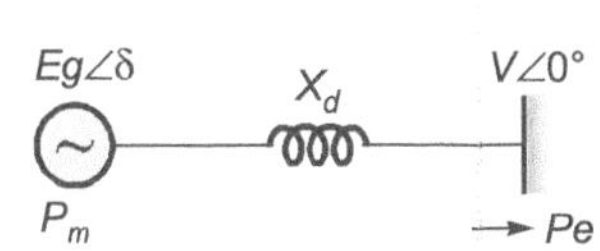

For single machine infinite bus system

$$M\frac{d^2\delta}{dt} = P_a = P_m - P_e$$

Here, $$M = \frac{GH}{\pi f}$$

Machine inertia constant, $H = M\cdot\frac{\pi f}{G} = \frac{\pi f}{G}J\left(\frac{2}{P}\right)^2 \omega_c \times 10^{-6}$

The above equation can be solved for δ as

$$\delta = \delta_o + \frac{P_a}{2M}t^2$$

if $\delta \to \delta_{cr}$, $t \to t_{cr}$, $P_a = P_m - P_e$

$$\delta_{cr} = \delta_o + \frac{(P_m - P_e)}{2M}t_{cr}^2$$

Critical clearing time, $t_{cr} = \left[\frac{(\delta_{cr} - \delta_o)2M}{(P_m - P_e)}\right]^{1/2}$

As 3-ϕ fault is occured at point F, $P_e = 0.0$.

$$t_{cr} = \left[\frac{(\delta_{cr} - \delta_o)}{P_m}\cdot 2\frac{GH}{\pi f}\right]^{1/2}$$

As 3-ϕ fault accelerates the machine more, the clearance line should be less than this, i.e., $t_c < \left[\frac{(\delta_{cr} - \delta_o)}{P_m}\cdot\frac{2GH}{\pi f}\right]^{1/2}$. (Proved).

8. Switchgear and Protection

8.1 A 3-phase circuit breaker is rated at 2000 MVA, 33 kV, its making current will be

(a) 40 kA (b) 50 kA
(c) 70 kA (d) 90 kA

[2 marks : 2001]

Solution: (d)

$$\text{Breaking current} = \frac{2000}{\sqrt{3} \times 33} = 34.99 \text{ kA}$$

$$\text{Making current} = 2.55 \times 34.99$$

$$= 89.22 \text{ kA} \cong 90 \text{ kA}$$

$$\text{Rating of C.B.} = \sqrt{3} \times \text{Line voltage} \times \text{Breaking current}$$

$$\text{Making current} = 2.55 \times \text{Breaking current}$$

Hence, option (d) is correct.

8.2 Explain the following terms referred to a circuit breaker:

(a) Symmetrical breaking current (b) Asymmetrical breaking current
(c) RRRV (d) Making current
(e) Breaking capacity

[15 marks : 2002]

Solution:

(a) **Symmetrical Breaking Current:** It is the rms value of a.c. component of the current in the pole at the instant of contact separation.

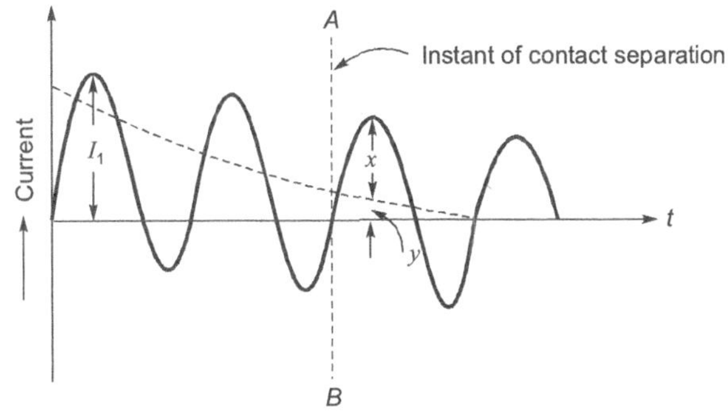

The symmetrical breaking current is given by $x/\sqrt{2}$ amp.

(b) **Asymmetrical Breaking Current:** It is the rms value of the total current comprising the a.c. and d.c. components of the current in the pole at the instant of contact separation

$$I_{sym} = \sqrt{\left[\left(\frac{x}{\sqrt{2}}\right)^2 + y^2\right]}$$

(c) **Rate of Rise of Restriking Voltage (RRRV):**

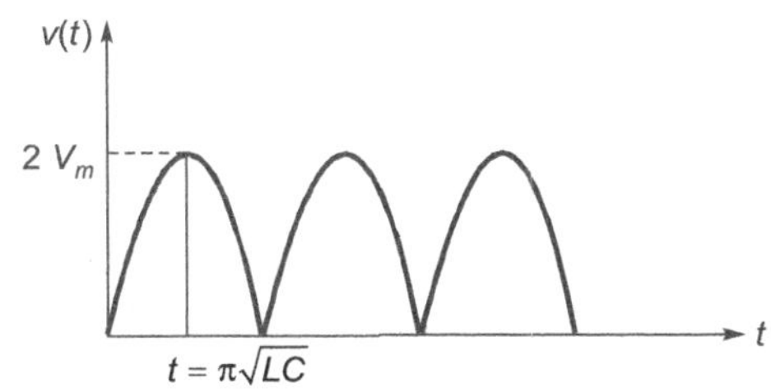

Restriking voltage across breaker contacts

$$\text{The average } RRRV = \frac{\text{Peak value of restriking voltage}}{\text{Time taken to reach to peak value}} = \frac{2V_m}{\pi\sqrt{LC}}$$

The ionization at current zero depends upon the voltage appearing between the contacts. This voltage is known as restriking voltage which depends upon the power factor and other factors of the circuit like the inductance and capacitance. The expression for voltage is given by (for a loss less system)

$$v = V\left(1 - \cos\frac{t}{\sqrt{LC}}\right)$$

where v = restriking voltage at any instant t, V the value of voltage at the instant of interruption and L and C are the series inductance and shunt capacitance upto the fault point

$$\therefore \text{ RRRV,} \quad \frac{dv}{dt} = \frac{V_m}{\sqrt{LC}}\sin\frac{t}{\sqrt{LC}}$$

$$\text{This is maximum when,} \quad \frac{t}{\sqrt{LC}} = \frac{\pi}{2} \text{ or } t = \frac{\pi}{2}\sqrt{LC}$$

and the value is $\frac{V_m}{\sqrt{LC}}$.

(d) **Making Current:** The making current is the peak value of the maximum current loop, including d.c. component, in any phase during the first cycle of current when the C.B. is closed. The maximum force in any phase is a function of the square of the maximum instantaneous current occurring in that phase on closing. It is therefore, the practice to specify making current in terms of peak value rather than in terms of rms value.

(e) **Breaking Capacity:** The breaking capacity of a breaker is the product of the breaking current and the recovery voltage.

8.3 **(a) Discuss the general principle of operation of a generator differential protection scheme. Give the 3-phase connection of the biased scheme.**

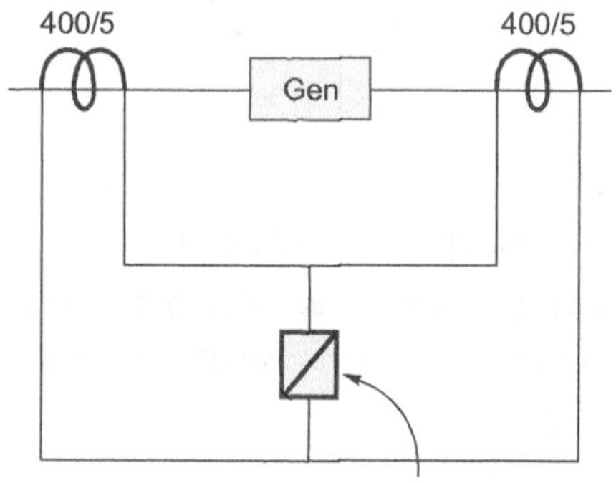

100 mA differential relay

(b) The scheme shown below is used for protection of the generator winding by an ordinary differential relay, having a minimum pick up current of 100 mA. The CTs on the grounded neutral and the live ends have actual ratios of 79 and 81 respectively though their nominal ratios are same. Show that the differential relay will trip even when the generator is delivering, full load current of (400 + *j*0.0) A, to the bus and there is no fault in the differential zone.

(c) To over come the defect in the question (b) a percentage differential relay having the same minimum pick up current of 100 mA and 20% slope was used. Drawing the slope characteristic of the relay. Show that the undesired tripping has been avoided.

[7 + 5 + 6 = 18 marks : 2003]

Solution:

(a) **General Principle of Operation of a Generator Differential Protection Scheme:**

In this system of protection, currents at the two ends of the protected sections are compared. Under normal operating conditions, these currents are equal but may become unequal on the occurrence of a fault in the protected section. The difference of the currents under fault conditions is arranged to pass though the operating coil of the relay. The relay then closes its contacts to isolate protected section from the system. This form of protection is also known as Merz – Price circulating current scheme.

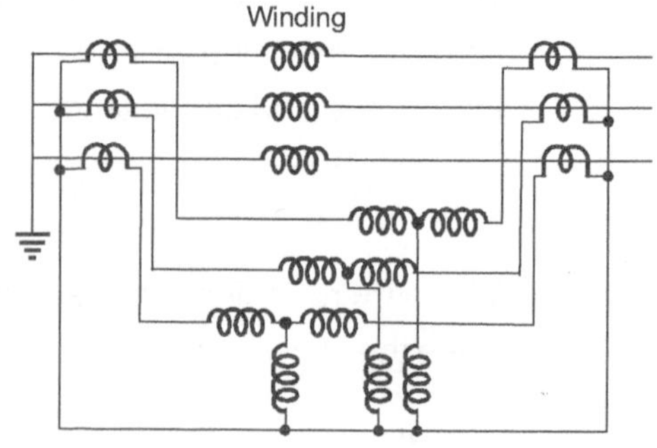

Stator protection Y grounded alternator

It is the general practice to provide differential protection for generators above 10 MVA. This form of protection is most suited and should be used if justified economically.

If all the six terminals of a star connected 3-ϕ generator are available, the scheme of percentage differential relay shown in figure below is provided.

It can be seen that for an external fault the relay does not operate and for an internal fault it does operate. In case the generator is delta connected, shown in figure below gives the scheme of percentage differential protection.

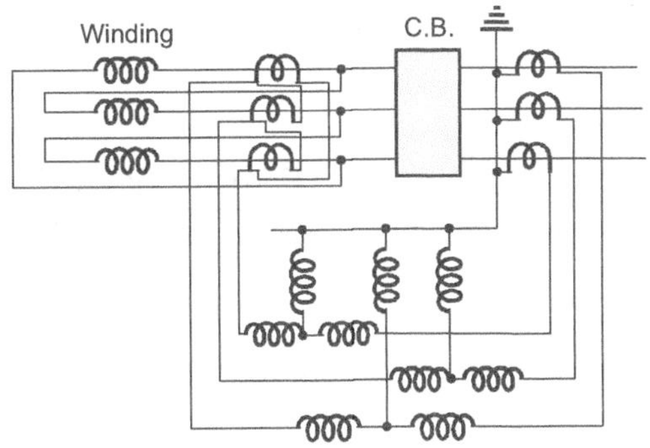

Stator protection Δ connected alternator

It can be seen again that for an external line-to-line fault, the relays do not operate whereas for an internal fault they will operate.

(b) Current Through The Differential Relay:

$$I_0 = I_1 - I_2 = \left(\frac{400}{79} - \frac{400}{81}\right) A$$

$$= 0.125 \text{ A} = 125 \text{ mA}$$

As $I_0 > 100$ mA, the relay will operate even when no fault in differential zone.

(c) The current in operating coil = 125 mA

The average current through the restraining coil

$$= \frac{I_1 + I_2}{2} = \left(\frac{400}{79} + \frac{400}{81}\right) = \frac{1}{2} = 5 \text{ Amp.}$$

with 20% slope; the operating current

$$= 0.20 \times 5 + I_{min} \text{ (pick up)} = (0.20 \times 5 + 100 \times 10^{-3}) \text{ A}$$

$$= 1.10 \text{ Amp.}$$

Since the current in operating coil is 125 mA, the relay will not operate and undesired tripping is avoided.

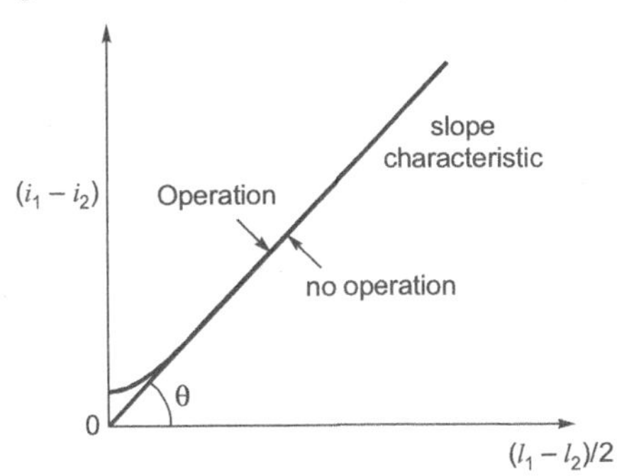

8.4 A fault current of 2000 A is passing on the primary side of a 400/5 C.T. on the secondary side of the C.T., an inverse-time over current relay is connected whose plug setting is set at 50%. The plug setting multiplier will be

(a) 25 (b) 50

(c) 10 (d) 30

[2 marks : 2003]

Solution: (c)

The pick up value of the relay is 5 Amps but since the relay setting is 50%, therefore, the operating current of the relay is,

$$5 \times \frac{50}{100} = 2.5 \text{ Amp.}$$

The plug setting multiplier of the relay is,

$$\text{PSM} = \frac{\text{Secondary current}}{\text{Relay current setting}} = \frac{\text{Primary current (fault current)}}{\text{Relay current setting} \times \text{C.T. ratio}} = \frac{2000}{2.5 \times 80} = 10$$

So the option (c) is correct.

8.5 Discuss the merits and demerits of a vacuum circuit breaker for low voltage applications.

[10 marks : 2003]

Solution:

Merits of a Vacuum Circuit Breaker:

1. Because of the short gap and excellent recovery characteristics of vacuum breakers, they can be used where the switching frequency is high and required to be reliable.
2. For low fault interrupting capacities the cost is low as compared to other interrupting devices.
3. The vacuum switches can be used for capacitor switching which is a very difficult task using oil circuit breakers.
4. They can be used along with static over current relays and gives an overall clearance time of less than 40 m-sec on phase-to-phase fault.
5. They can interrupt any current (fault). The outstanding feature of a *VCB* is that it can break any heavy fault current perfectly just before the contacts reach the definite open position.
6. Less maintenance requirement.
7. Better than air or oil *C.B.* when voltages are high and current to be interrupted is less.

Demerits:

Contacts get roughened after use and thus dielectric strength decreases.

Cost is higher than SF_6 circuit breakers.

8.6 The stability of arc in vacuum depends on

(a) the contact material only

(b) the contact material and its vapour pressure

(c) the circuit parameters only

(d) the combination of (b) and (c)

[2 marks : 2005]

Solution: (d)

Option (d) is correct.

8.7 For protection of parallel feeders fed from one end, the relay require are:

(a) Non-directional relay at the source end and directional relay at the load end.

(b) Non-directional relays at both ends.

(c) Directional relays at source end and non-directional relays at load end.

(d) Directional relays at both ends

[2 marks : 2005]

Solution:

Option (a) is correct.

8.8 Explain: A loss of excitation relay used for alternator protection.

[5 marks : 2005]

Solution:

Loss of Excitation Relay: Very large alternator cannot be allowed to run asynchronously for long as the relative motion between the stator field and the rotor induces large currents in the rotor body and, therefore, there is high rate of heating of the rotor surfaces and the loss of excitation scheme is arranged to trip after certain time delay.

The protection scheme uses an offset Mho relay operated from ac current and voltage at the generator terminals.

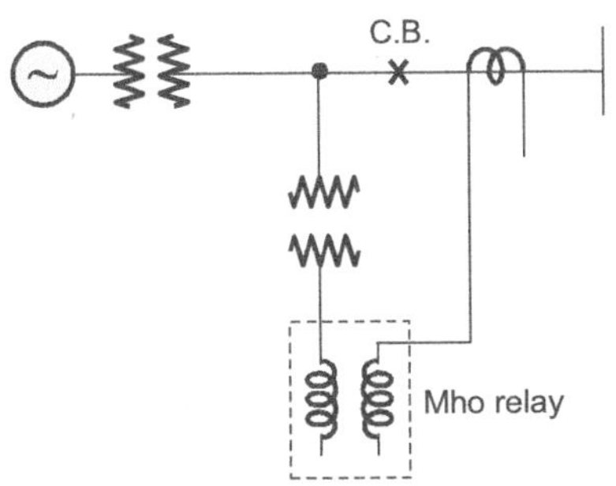

(a) Relay connections for loss of excitation

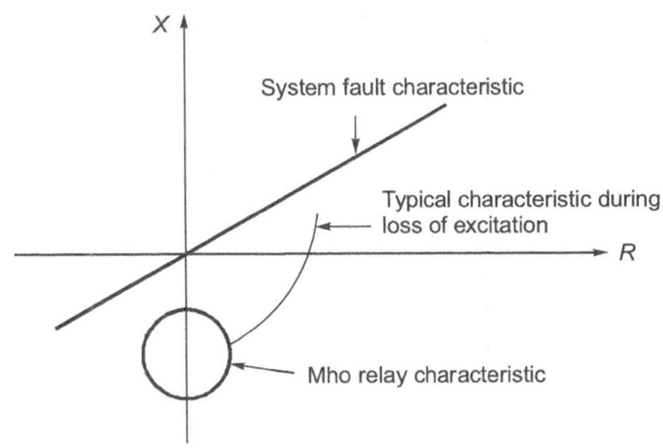

(b) Loss of excitation characteristic

The relay setting is so arranged that the relay operates whenever the excitation goes below a certain value and the machine starts running asynchronously. Figure (a) shows the relay connection and figure (b) shows the various characteristics on $R-X$ diagrams. It is seen that the impedance as seen by the relay during loss of excitation will swing into the relay characteristics and thus the relay will operate. The loci of impedance for system fault and for power swings is also shown in figure (b) and it can be seen that for these condition the relay will not operate.

8.9 Explain with necessary diagram the phenomena of current chopping in an air blast circuit breaker. How this problem can be rectified by using resistance switching? Why mostly air blast circuit breakers are susceptible to current chopping?

[12 marks : 2005]

Solution:

Current chopping in air blast circuit breaker: It is the phenomena of current interruption before the natural current zero is reached. This results in the production of high voltage transient across the contacts of the circuit breaker. Consider the figure (*i*), suppose the arc current is i when it is chopped down to zero value as shown by point a in figure (*ii*). As the chop occurs at current i, therefore, the energy stored in inductance is $Li^2/2$. This energy will transferred to the capacitance C, charging the latter to a prospective voltage e is given by:

$$\frac{1}{2}Li^2 = \frac{Ce^2}{2}$$

or

$$e = i\sqrt{\frac{L}{C}} \text{ volts} \quad ...(i)$$

The prospective voltage e is very high as compared to the dielectric strength gained by the gap so that the breaker restrikes. As the de-ionising force is still in action, therefore, chop occurs again but the arc current this time is smaller than the previous case. This induces a lower prospective voltage to re-ignite the arc.

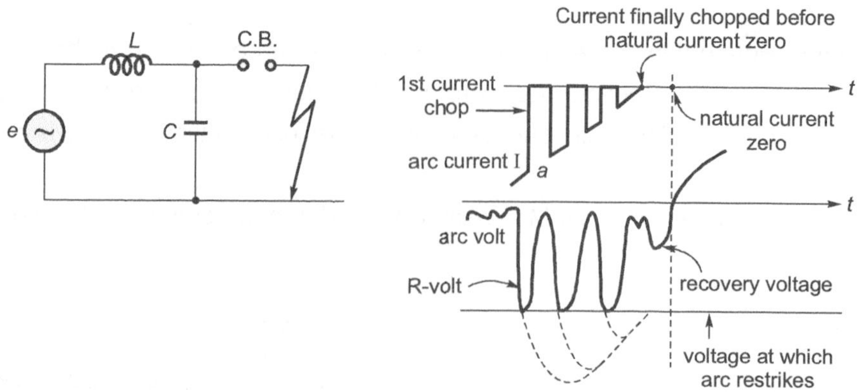

In fact, several chops may occur until a low enough current is interrupted which produces insufficient induced voltage to the restrike across the breaker gap. Consequently, the final interruption of current takes place.

Resistance Switching: The excessive voltage surge during circuit interruption can be prevented by the use of shunt resistance and connected across the circuit breaker contacts as shown in figure below. This is known as resistance switching.

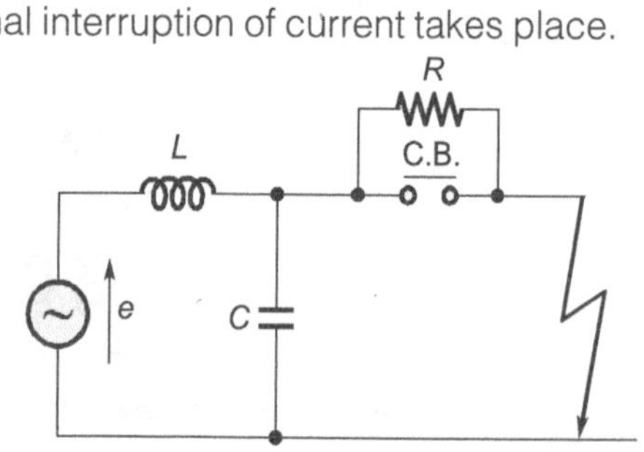

From the figure, when a fault occurs, the contacts of the circuit breaker are opened and an arc is stuck between the contacts. Since the contacts are shunted by resistance R, a part of arc currents flow through this resistance. This results in the decrease of arc current and an increase in the rate of de-ionisation of the arc-path.

Consequently, the arc resistance is increased. The increased arc resistance leads to a further increase in current through shunt resistance. This process continues, the arc current becomes so small that it fails to maintain the arc. Now, the arc is extinguished and circuit current is interrupted.

The shunt resistor also helps in limiting the oscillatory growth of re-striking voltage. It can be proved mathematically that natural frequency of oscillation of the circuit shown in figure,

$$f_n = \frac{1}{2\pi}\sqrt{\frac{1}{LC} - \frac{1}{4R^2C^2}}$$

The effect of shunt resistance R is to prevent the oscillatory growth of re-striking voltage and cause it to grow exponentially upto recovery voltage.

This is being most effective when the value of R is so chosen that the circuit is critically damped R for critical damping $= 0.5\sqrt{L/C}$. R should always be less than this value.

Reason for the air-blast circuit breaker susceptible to current chopping: Current chopping mainly occurs in air-blast circuit breakers because they retain the same extinguishing power irrespective of the magnitude of the current to be interrupted. When breaking low currents (e.g. transformer magnetising current) with such breakers, the powerful de-ionising effect of air-blast causes the current fall abruptly to zero well before the natural current zero is reached.

8.10 Explain with necessary diagram the principle of operation of a distance protection scheme. How a 3-zone stepped units help to achieve fast discrimination? How many units are required for a complete protection scheme? How the CTs and VTs associated with these relays are connected to a 3-phase transmission line? Indicate the reasons of mode of connections of CTs and VTs in such a way.

[18 marks : 2005]

Solution:

Distance Protection: Whenever over current relaying is found slow or is not selective distance protection be used. Since the fault currents depends upon the generating capacity and system configuration, the distance relays are preferred to the over current relays.

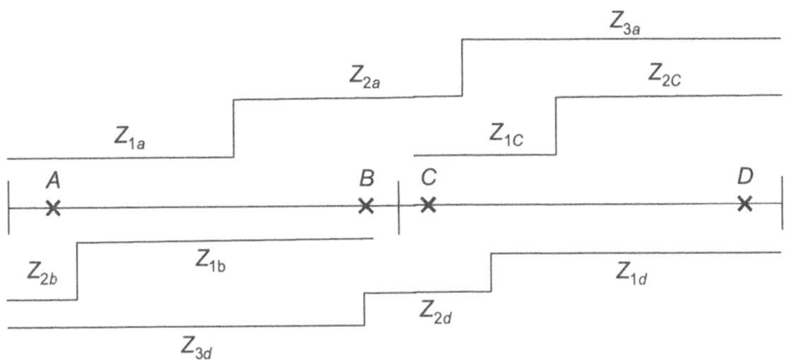

3-zone protection

The protection scheme is divided in three zones. The first zone Z_{1a} is extended only upto 80% and not 100% length of the line as the relay impedance measurement will not be very accurate towards the end of the line especially when the current is offset. 80% of the line *AB* and is a high speed zone. No intentional time lag is provided for this zone. Second zone Z_{2a} for relay at *A* covers remaining 20% length of the line *AB* and 20% of the adjoining line. In case of an arcing fault in section *AB* which adds to the impedance of the line as seen by the relay at *A*, the adjustment is such that the relay at *A* will see that impedance in second zone and will operate. This is why the second zone is extended into the adjoining line. The operating time of the second zone is normally about 0.2 to 0.5 seconds. The third zone unit at *A* will provides back up protection for fault in the line *CD*. The delay time for the third zone is usually 0.4 to 1.00 sec.

In case the feeder is being fed from both the ends and say the fault takes place in the second zone of the line *AB* (20% of the line *AB*), the relay at *B* will operate instantaneously (because it lies in the first zone of *BA*) whereas the fault lies in the second zone of the relay at *A*. This is undesirable from stability point of view and it is desirable to avoid this delay. This is made possible when the relay at *B* gives an intertrip signal to the relay at *A* in order to trip the breaker quickly rather than waiting for zone-2 tripping.

Correction of CT and VT:

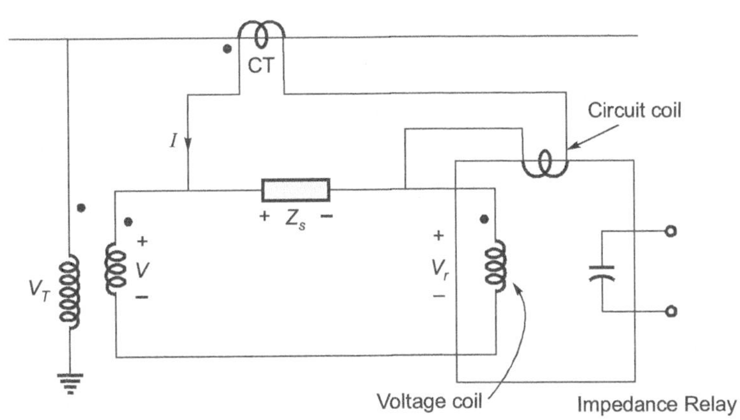

- Impedance relay are also called distance relay as line impedance is proportional to distance and are non-directional relays and therefore need a directional relay with them.

General relay equation, $\theta = K_1|I|^2 - K_2|V|^2 + K_4$

I is sensed by CT and V is sensed by VT, here $K_4 = 0$

- $$\frac{|V|}{|I|} = |Z| < \left(\frac{K}{K_2}\right)^{1/2}$$

$|V|$ prevents relay operation, so it is the restraining quantity of this relay.
$|I|$ tries to operate it, so it is the operating quantity of this relay.

8.11 Which of the following circuit breakers is generally used in railway electrification?

(a) Air blast circuit breaker
(b) Minimum oil circuit breaker
(c) Bulk oil circuit breaker
(d) SF6 circuit breaker

[2 marks : 2006]

Solution:

Option (a) is correct.

8.12 A 100/1 A bar primary current transformer supplies an over current relay setting at 50% pick up and it has a burden of 2 VA. Determine the knee point voltage and cross section of the core if the CT has 50 turns on its secondary and the fault current is 15 times the relay setting. Assume the flux density as 1.4 Wb/m^2 and frequency = 50 Hz.

[4 marks : 2006]

Solution:

The operating current of the relay = 1 × 0.50 = 0.5 Amp

$$\text{The secondary voltage} = \frac{2\text{ VA}}{0.5} = 4 \text{ volts}$$

The CT secondary voltage when current is 15 times the relay setting = 15 × 4 = 60 volts. The knee voltage must be slightly greater than 60 volts.

Now $$E = 4.44\, B_m A f N$$

$$\therefore \quad A = \frac{60}{4.44 \times 1.4 \times 50 \times 50}$$

or, $$A = 3.86 \times 10^{-3} \text{ sq. m or } A = 38.6 \text{ sq. cms}$$

8.13 The making capacity of a circuit breaker is

(a) less than the asymmetrical breaking capacity of the breaker.
(b) greater than the asymmetrical breaking capacity of the breaker.
(c) equal to the symmetrical breaking capacity of the breaker.
(d) equal to the asymmetrical breaking capacity.

[2 marks : 2007]

Solution:

Option (b) is correct.

8.14 Describe with suitable diagrams how the stator winding of a 3-phase alternator is protected from:

(a) Earth faults on the stator winding
(b) Unbalanced current in the stator winding
(c) Earth fault on the rotor winding
(d) Overloading of alternator

[4 × 3 = 12 marks : 2007]

Solution:

(a) **Earth Faults on the Stator Winding:** If the star point is not available because it is made inside the generator and if it is grounded through some low impedance, percentage differential relaying for ground faults only can be provided. This protection is known as earth fault protection. For an external fault, the current cannot flow through the operating coil and hence the relay does not operate.

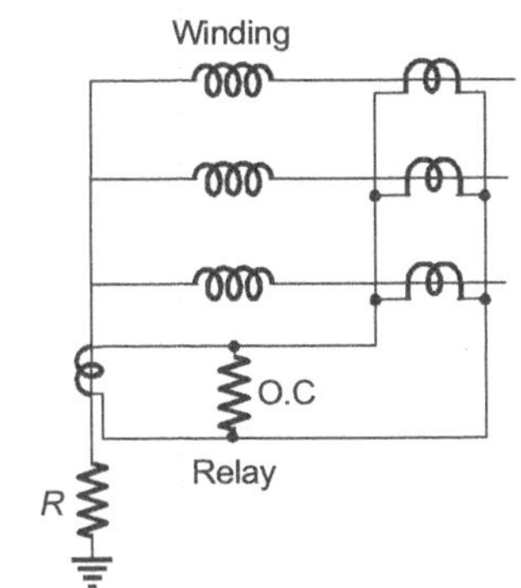

For an internal fault, the current will flow only through the C.T in the neutral and not in the winding C.Ts. Therefore, the current will flow through the operating coil and the relay will operate.

(b) **Unbalanced Currents in the Stator Winding:** The unbalanced loading results in circulation of negative sequence currents in the stator winding which gives rise to a rotating magnetic field. The protection of alternators against negative phase sequence currents. Shown in figure below:

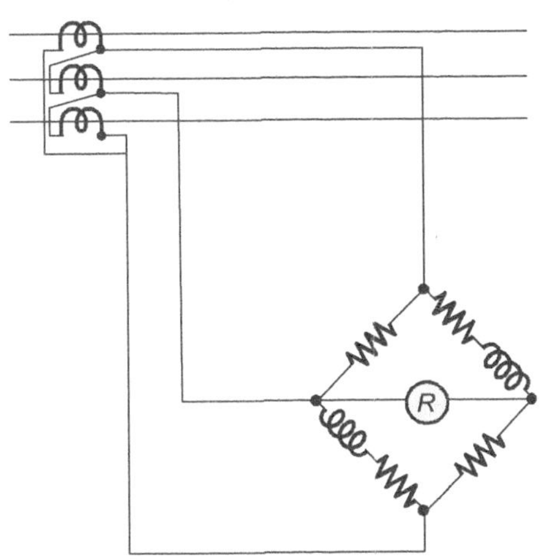

Negative sequence relay

The relay is connected to trip the generator main breaker. Sometimes an auxiliary alarm relay is provided which gives warning when the maximum continuous permissible negative phase sequence current is exceeded. The relay normally used is an IDMT relay.

(c) **Earth Fault on the Rotor Winding:** Figure shown below shows the modern method of protecting the rotor against earth faults or open circuits. A small power supply is connected to the positive pole of the field circuit. A fault detecting relay and a high resistance to limit the current are connected in series with this circuit. A fault at any point on the field circuit will pass a current of sufficient magnitude through the relay to cause operation. The earth fault relays are instantaneous and are connected to the alarm circuit for indication as a single ground fault does not require immediate attention to the set.

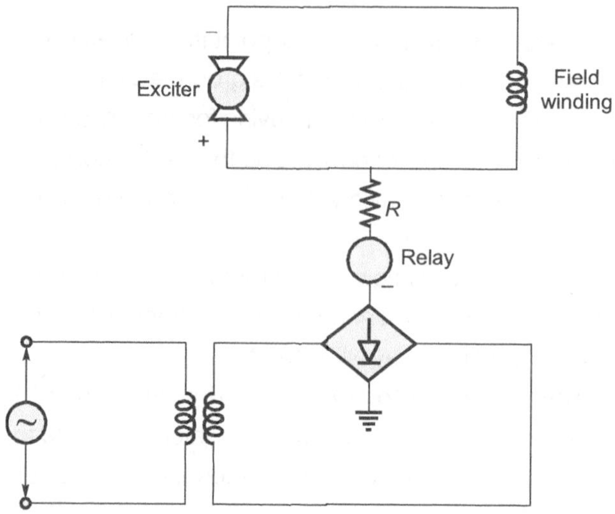

Rotor earth fault detection

(d) **Overloading of Alternator:** The overload operation of the alternator results in overheating of the stator winding. Normally an overcurrent relay with time delay adjustment should serve the purpose. But because the temperature of the winding not only depends upon the overloading but also on the state of the cooling system, if the cooling system fails, the temperature of the stator winding may reach dangerous values even though the alternator is not fully loaded. Also, if an overcurrent relay is used, it has got to be discriminated with respect to other overcurrent relays on the system. Since we are using this relay at the source, it will be the slowest in operation and hence poses a serious problem to the stator windings. The most reliable method will, therefore, be one which senses the temperature of the winding and depending upon the temperature gives an operating signal. The temperature detector coils in the form of thermistors or thermocouples are embedded at various points in the stator winding to give an indication of the temperature condition.

Generators rated below about 50 MW are not provided with temperature detecting devices for overload protection. They are provided with thermal relays which use bimetallic strips are matched with the heating and cooling characteristics of the machine to be protected. The thermal relay will also not respond to overheating due to failure of the cooling system.

8.15 The chances of arc interruption in subsequent current zeros

(a) increase in case of ABCB but decreases in OCB.

(b) decreases in case of ABCB but increases in OCB.

(c) decreases in both cases.

(d) increase in both case.

[2 marks : 2008]

Solution:

Option (b) is correct.

8.16 Explain how an arc is initiated and sustained in an oil circuit breaker (CB) when the CB contacts separate. Also explain the terms: Restriking voltage, Recovery voltage, Rate of rise of Restriking voltage (RRRV).

[15 marks : 2008]

Solution:

Initiation of an Arc in Oil Circuit Breaker: Initially when the contacts just begin to separate the magnitude of current is very large, but the contact resistance being very small, a small voltage appears across them. But the distance of separation being very small, a large voltage gradient is set up which is good enough to cause ionization of the particles between the contacts. Also it is known that with the copper contacts which are generally used for the circuit breakers very little thermal ionization can occurs at temperature below the melting point. For effective field emission the voltage gradient required is 10^6 V/cm. From this arc is initiated by the field emission rather than the thermal ionization. This high voltage gradient exists only for a fraction of a microsecond. But in this short period a large number of electrons would have been liberated from the cathode and these electrons while reaching anode, on their way would have collided with the atoms and molecules of the gases. Thus each emitted electron tends to create others and these in turn derive energy from the field and multiply. In short, the work done by the initially emitted electrons enables the discharge to be maintained. Finally, if the current is high, the discharge attains the form of an arc having a temperature high enough for thermal ionization, which results in lower voltage gradient. This an arc is initiated due to field effect and then maintained due to thermal ionization.

The arc can be interrupted if the contact gap could be deionized. The process of deionization is possible in the following ways:

(a) High pressure

(b) Forced convection and turbulence

(c) Arc splitting

Restriking Voltage: The transient voltage which appears across the breaker contacts at the instant of arc extinction is known as the restriking voltage.

Recovery Voltage: The power frequency r.m.s voltage that appears across the breaker contacts after the transient oscillations die out and final extinction of arc has resulted in all the poles is called the recovery voltage.

Rate of Rise of Restriking Voltage (RRRV): It is the slope of steepest tangent to the restriking voltage curve. It is expressed in volts per microsecond.

The average,
$$\text{RRRV} = \frac{\text{Peak value of restriking voltage}}{\text{Time taken to reach to peak value}} = \frac{2V_m}{\pi\sqrt{LC}}$$

or
$$v = V_m\left(1 - \cos\frac{t}{\sqrt{LC}}\right)$$

The RRRV is given by,
$$\frac{dv}{dt} = \frac{V_m}{\sqrt{LC}}\sin\frac{t}{\sqrt{LC}}$$

The rate at which the restriking voltage rises is, important in the arc extinction process because the ionization process will depend upon this rate.

8.17 **A 3-phase 66 kV/11 kV star/delta transformer is protected by Merz-price protection scheme. The CTs on the LT side have a ratio of 420/5 amp. Determine the CT ratio on the HT side. Also explain why biasing is provided in percentage differential scheme of protection.**

[10 marks : 2008]

Solution:

Since the L.T. side is delta connected, the CTs on that side will be star connected. Therefore, if 420 amps is the line current, the ET secondary current is 5 amps. The line current on the star side of the power transformer will be

$$420 \times \frac{11}{66} = 70 \text{ amps.}$$

The CTs on the star side are delta connected and the current required on the relay side of the CT is 5 amps. Therefore, the current in the CT secondary (phase current) is $5/\sqrt{3}$ amps.

∴ The CT ratio on the HT side will be 70 : $5/\sqrt{3}$.

Reason to provide biasing in percentage differential scheme of protection: In differential protection the two CTs used were identical. But in practice this is not true. Current transformers of the type normally used do not transform their current so accurately under transient conditions especially. This is true because the short circuit current is offset, i.e. it contains dc components. Suppose the two CTs under normal conditions differ in their magnetic properties slightly in terms of different amounts of residual magnetism or in terms of unequal burden on the two CTs one of the CTs will saturate earlier during short circuit currents (offset current) and thus the two CTs will transform their primary current differently even for a through fault conditions. This effect is more pronounced especially when the scheme is used for the protection of power transformers. To accommodate these features, biasing is provided in percentage differential scheme of protection.

8.18 **A single-phase equivalent circuit for studying the transient recovery voltage when a CB clears a fault is given below. Compute average value of rate of rise of restriking voltage (RRRV).**

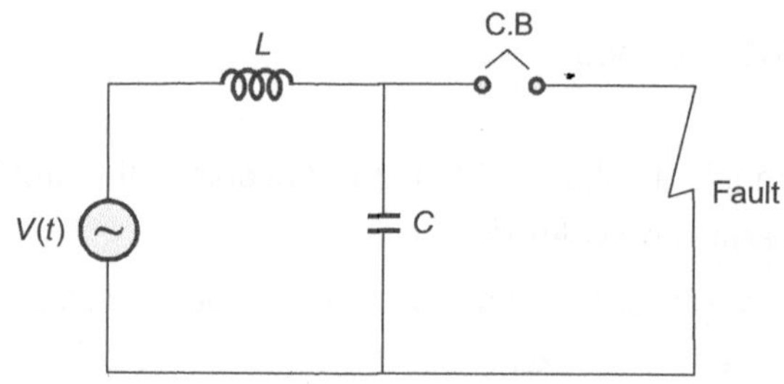

$V(t)$ = 11000 cos 314t volts
L = 1 mH
C = 400 pF

[10 marks : 2009]

Solution:

$$\text{RRRV} = \frac{2V_m}{\pi\sqrt{LC}}$$

Given, $V_m = 11000$

$$\therefore \quad \text{RRRV} = \frac{2 \times 11000}{\pi\sqrt{1 \times 10^{-3} \times 400 \times 10^{-12}}}$$

$$= 1.107 \times 10^{10} \text{ volts}$$

$$= 11.07 \text{ kV}/\mu\text{-sec}$$

8.19 Draw a neat circuit diagram of Merz-Price per cent differential protection scheme for a 3-phase Δ-Y connected transformer.

[5 marks : 2010]

Solution:

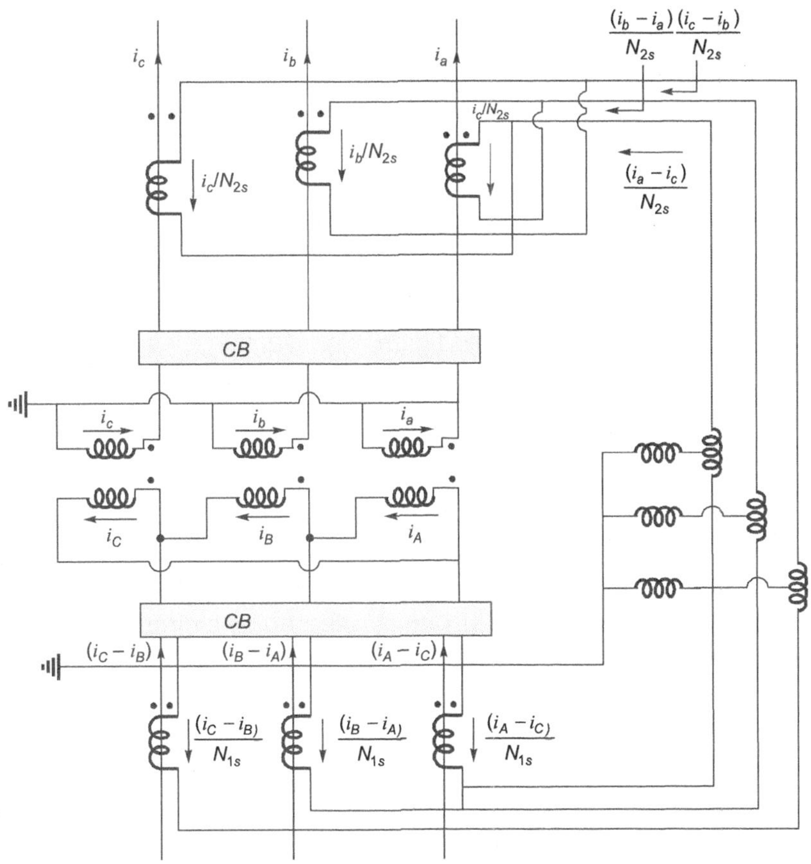

8.20 A ring feeder with five sections and fed at one point is to be protected using directional over current (DOC) relays and over current (OC) relays with suitable time grading. Explain the working of the scheme. Show the location of DOC's and OC's and their time of operation. Assume a time grading of 5 ms between the relays. The fastest relays needs 5 ms for it to operate.

[10 marks : 2011]

Solution:

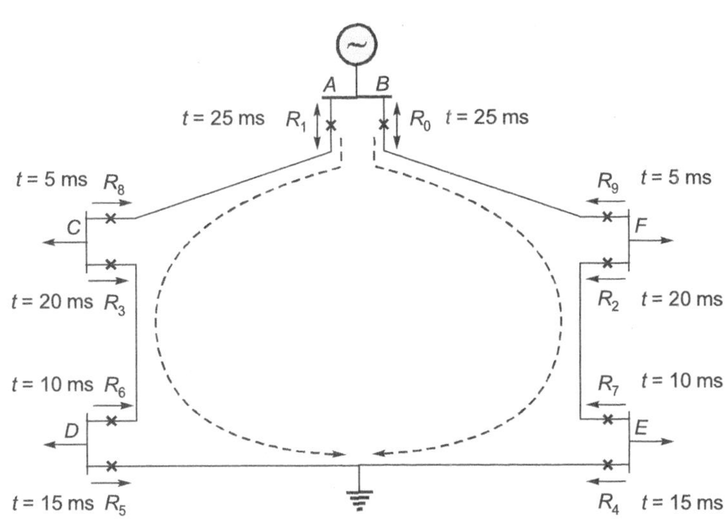

Fig. (a): Ring feeder with five sections and fed at one point

- Relays R_0 and R_1 are non-directional over current relay and relays R_2, R_3, R_4, R_5, R_6, R_7, R_8 and R_9 are directional over current relays. Hence total 2 non-directional over current and 8 over directional current relays and required for the scheme.

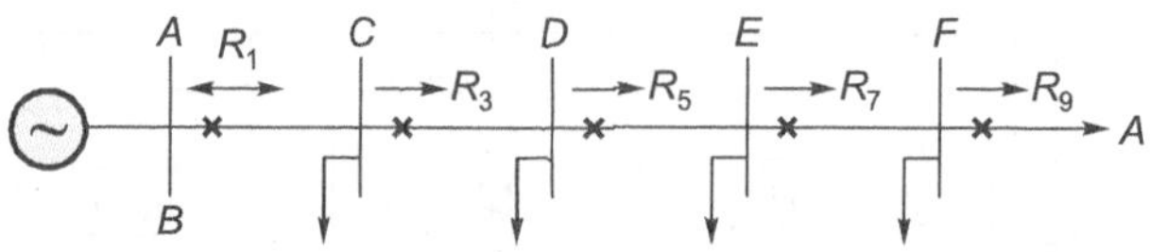

Fig. (b): Ring opened at B and spread

- Relay R_9 which is farthest from source require minimum time (5 ms) to operate. There is time grading of 5 ms between the relays. Relay R_1 which is nearest to source takes maximum time (25 ms).
- Consider a fault in the section *DE*, shown in figure (a) with dotted lines. The relays R_1, R_3, R_5, R_0, R_2 and R_4 will start moving. Among R_1, R_3 and R_5, Relay R_5 has minimum time (15 ms) and it will operate first. The relays R_1 and R_3 will reset as the fault current ceases to flow through these relays.
- Among relays R_0, R_2 and R_4, relay R_4 has minimum time (15 ms) therefore relay R_4 will operate first, and the relays R_0 and R_2 will reset.
- As relays R_4 and R_5 operate during the fault in section *DE*, the section *DE* gets isolated.

8.21 **In a power system power is supplied to a short-line through transformer connected to bus-bar. If a line-to-ground fault occurs on one of the lines and is cleared by a circuit breaker close to transformer (on line side), derive the expression for restriking voltage and its natural frequency.**

[5 marks : 2012]

Solution:

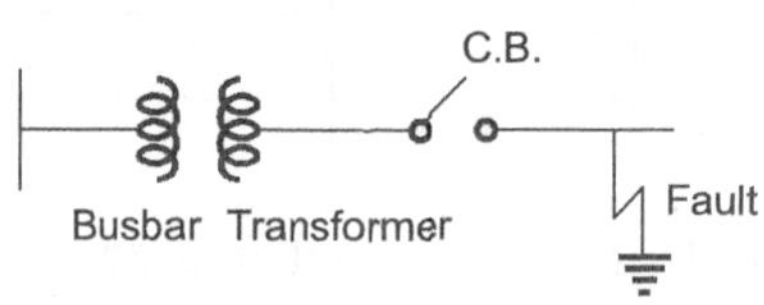

The equivalent electric circuit for analysis of restriking voltage is shown below:

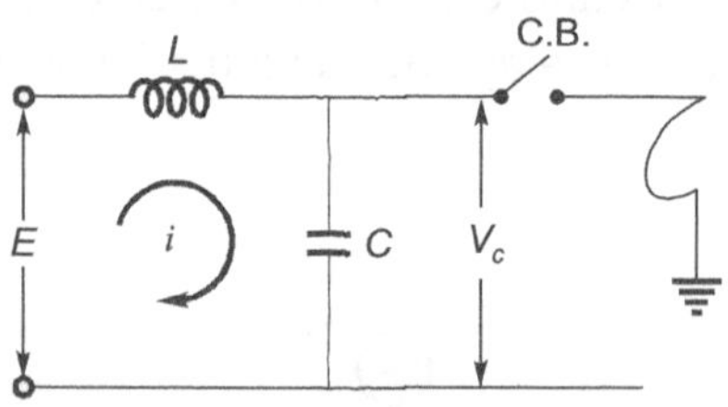

In above circuit *L* and *C* are the inductance and capacitance per phase of the system.

When the circuit breaker (C.B.) is closed, the short circuit current flows through *R*, *L* and the contacts of the C.B., the capacitance being short-circuited by the fault.

When the C.B. contacts are opened and the arc is extinguished, the current i is diverted through capacitance *C*, resulting in a transient condition.

The inductance and capacitance forms a series oscillatory circuit. The voltage across capacitance is called restriking voltage.

$$E = L\frac{di}{dt} + \frac{1}{C}\int i\,dt \qquad \ldots(i)$$

$$\frac{di}{dt} = \frac{d^2q}{dt} = \frac{d^2}{dt^2}(Cv_c) = C\frac{d^2v_c}{dt^2}$$

and

$$\int\frac{i\,dt}{C} = \frac{q}{C} = v_c$$

The equation (i) becomes,

$$LC\frac{d^2v_c}{dt^2}+v_c = E$$

By taking Laplace transform on both side.

$$LC\, s^2\, v_c(s) + v_c(s) = \frac{E}{s}$$

$$v_c(s)\left[LCs^2+1\right] = \frac{E}{s}$$

$$v_c(s) = \frac{E}{LC\cdot s\left(s^2+\frac{1}{LC}\right)}$$

Therefore natural frequency, $\omega_n = \frac{1}{\sqrt{LC}}$ or $f_n = \frac{1}{2\pi\sqrt{LC}}$

Taking inverse Laplace transform,

$$v_c(t) = E(1-\cos\omega_n t) = \text{Restriking voltage}$$

8.22 **A 220 kV circuit breaker is used to protect a transmission line. During a fault due to short circuit the demagnetization effect of armature reaction brought down voltage to 95% of rated voltage, pf had been 0.5 lagging and natural frequency of oscillation was observed to be 20 kHz. Calculate maximum restriking voltage and average RRRV for both grounded and undergrounded faults.**

[10 marks : 2012]

Solution:

$$f_n = 20\text{ kHz}$$

The restriking voltage, $v_c = E(1-\cos\omega_n t)$

The maximum value of restriking voltage = $2\,E_{peak}$

$$= 2\times\frac{220}{\sqrt{3}}\times\sqrt{2}\times0.95\times\sin\phi = 341.3\times\frac{\sqrt{3}}{2} = 295.57\text{ V}$$

The maximum value of RRRV = $\omega_n\, E_{peak}$

$$= 2\pi\times20\times10^3\times\frac{220}{\sqrt{3}}\times\sqrt{2}\times0.95\times1000\times\frac{\sqrt{3}}{2}\text{ V/sec.}$$

$$= 18.57\text{ kV/}\mu\text{ sec}$$

8.23 **Explain the principle of operation of sulphur-hexafluoride circuit breakers with neat figures and list advantages.**

[5 marks : 2012]

Solution:

Sulphur hexafluoride (SF_6) has good dielectric strength and excellent arc quenching property. It is an inert, nontoxic, nonflammable and heavy gas.

When a free electron comes in collision with a neutral gas molecule, the electron is absorbed by the neutral gas molecule and a negative ion is formed. As the negative ions so formed are heavy they do not attain sufficient energy to contribute to ionisation of the gas. This property gives a good dielectric property.

The gas has an excellent property of recombination after the removal of the source which energizes the arc. This gives an excellent arc quenching property.

The circuit breaker shown below is a puffer-type SF_6 circuit breaker. In this, gas is compressed by moving cylinder system and is released through a nozzle to quench the arc.

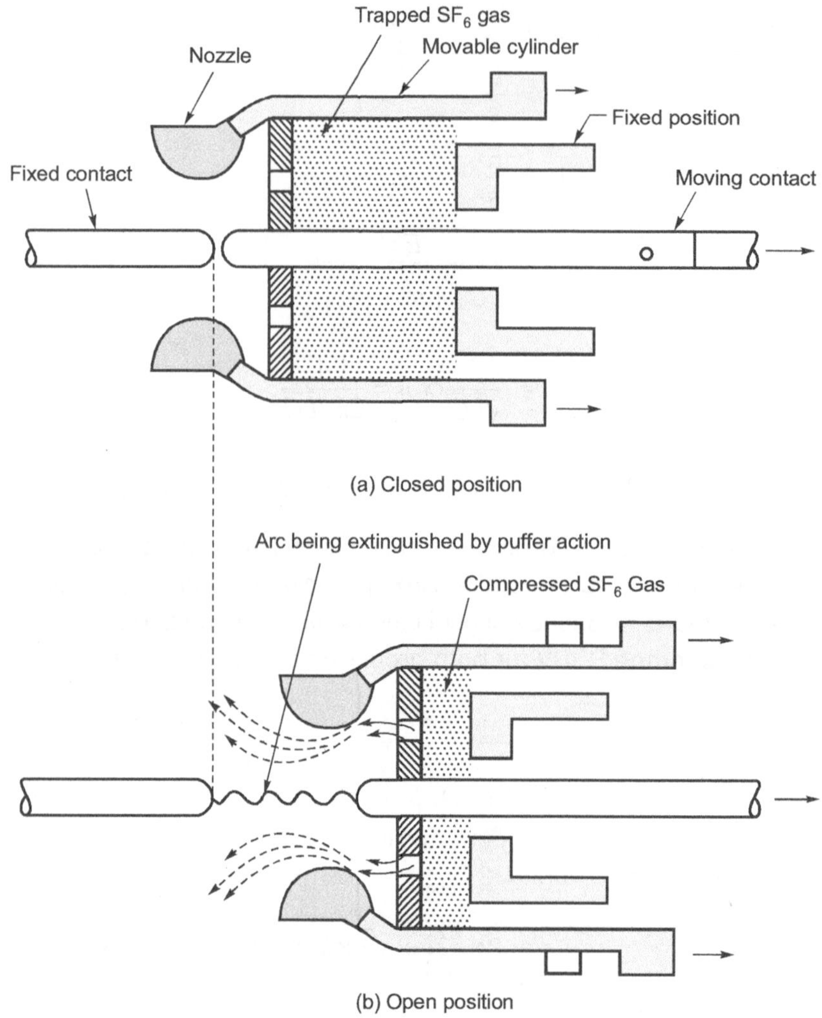

Puffer-type SF_6 circuit breaker

Advantages:

- Excellent arc quenching property.
- Good dielectric strength.
- Manufactured in the voltage range 3.6 kV to 765 kV.
- Problem of current chopping is minimized.
- Electric clearances are very much reduced due to high dielectric strength.

8.24 **What is a low inductive current chopping problem in circuit breakers and how it is overcome to have smooth decay of restriking voltage?**

[5 marks : 2012]

Solution:

When low inductive current is being interrupted and the arc quenching force of the circuit breaker is more than necessary to interrupt a low magnitude of current, the current will be interrupted before its natural zero instant. In such a situation, the energy stored in the magnetic field appears in the form of high voltage across the stray capacitance, which will cause restriking of the arc.

$$\frac{1}{2}Li^2 = \frac{1}{2}Cv^2$$

$$\therefore \qquad V = i\sqrt{\frac{L}{C}}$$

If v is more than the withstanding capacity of the gap between the contacts, the arc appears again. Since the quenching force is more, the current is again chopped. This phenomena continues till the value of v becomes less than the withstanding capacity of the gap.

Therefore the interruption of capacitance current produces high voltage transients across the gap of the circuit breaker.

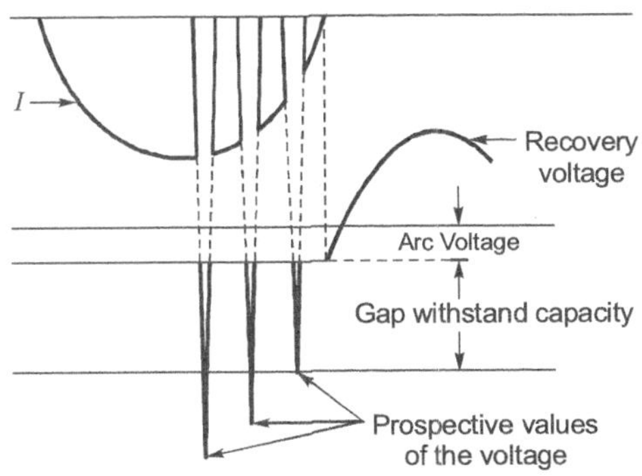

This problem is practically solved by using air blast circuit breakers or multibreak breakers.

8.25 **In a 132 kV system, the phase-to-ground capacitance is 0.01 μF and the inductance is 4 H. Calculate the voltage appearing across the electrodes of CB if a magnetizing current at 5 amperes is interrupted. Calculate the critical resistance to be connected, to eliminate restriking.**

[5 marks : 2012]

Solution:

$$L = 4\text{ H},\ C = 0.01\ \mu\text{F} = 10^{-8}\text{ F}$$

$$i = 5\text{ A}$$

Voltage appearing across the electrodes of circuit breaker

$$V = i\sqrt{\frac{L}{C}} = 5\sqrt{\frac{4}{10^{-8}}} = 5 \times 2 \times 10^4\text{ V} = 100\text{ kV}$$

The value of resistance to be used across space.

$$R = \frac{1}{2}\sqrt{\frac{L}{C}} = \frac{1}{2}\sqrt{\frac{4}{10^{-8}}} = 10^4\ \Omega = 10\text{ k}\Omega$$

8.26 **Draw the connections and explain the operation of a differential (relay) protection of a 3-phase Δ-Y transformer.**

[5 marks : 2012]

Solution:

The percentage differential protection or Merzpize protection gives the protection against phase to phase faults and phase to ground faults to the power transformers. The principle of such a protection scheme is the comparison of the currents entering and leaving the ends of a transformer. In ⅄-Δ transformer, the primary is star (⅄) connected and secondary is delta (Δ) connected. Hence to compensate for the phase differences, the C.T. secondaries on primary side must be connected in delta while the C.T. secondaries on delta side must be connected in star. The star point of the 3-ϕ transformer primary as well as the star connected C.T. secondaries must be grounded.

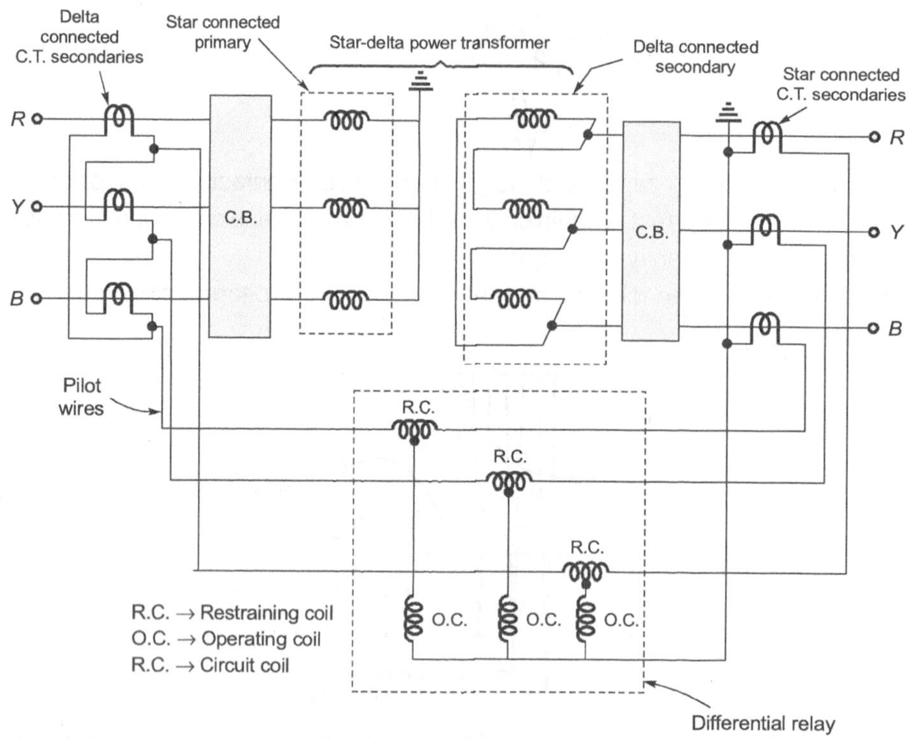

Merz-Price protection for star-delta power transformer

8.27 A 50 MVA, 132/66 kV, λ-Δ transformer is protected by differential protection. Draw a connection diagram and calculate the suitable C.T. ratio.

[10 marks : 2012]

Solution:

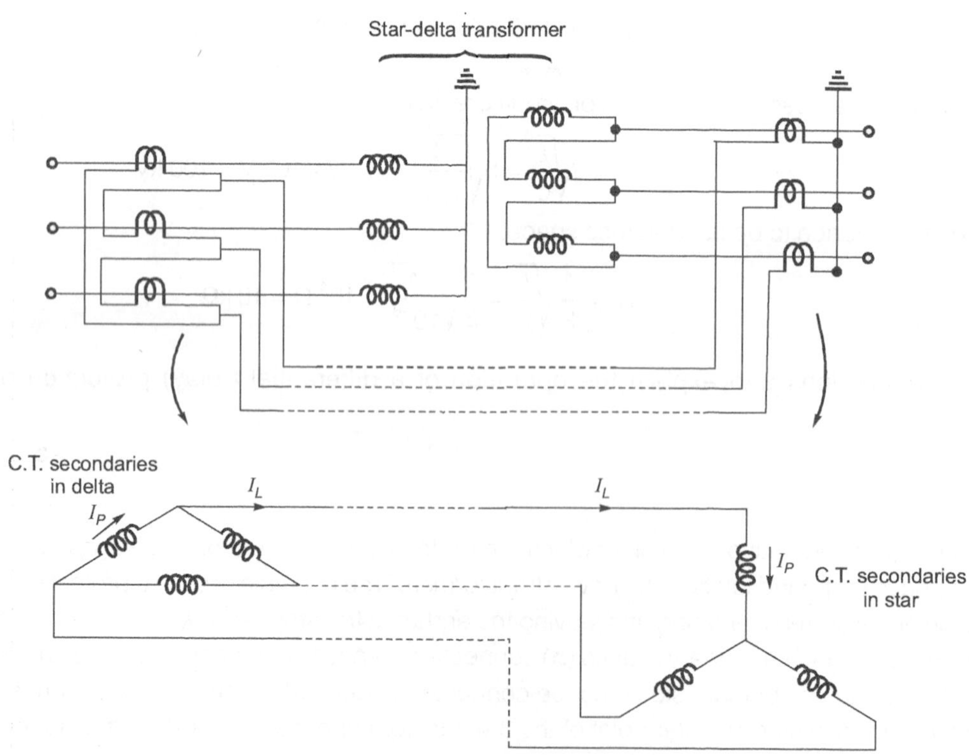

On primary side which is 132 kV side, let the current be 300 A and CT ratio is 500/5 A the secondary phase current of CT, on primary side

$$I_p = \frac{5}{500} \times 300 = 3\text{ A}$$

$$\therefore \quad I_L = \sqrt{3} I_p = 3\sqrt{3}\text{ A} \qquad \text{(delta connected CTs)}$$

The same current flows through the star connected C.T. secondaries. Hence each secondary of C.T. on the secondary side of transformer carries a current of $3\sqrt{3}A$.

The apparent power on both sides must be same.

$$\sqrt{3} V_{L1} I_{L1} = \sqrt{3} V_{L2} I_{L2}$$

$$\therefore \quad \sqrt{3} \times 132 \times 300 = \sqrt{3} \times 66 \times I_{L2}$$

$$\therefore \quad I_{L2} = 600\text{ A}$$

Thus each primary of C.T. connected in star on LV side carries a current of 600 A. While each secondary carries current of $3\sqrt{3}$ A

$$\text{CT ratio on 66 kV side} = \frac{600}{3\sqrt{3}} = \frac{200}{\sqrt{3}} = 115.47:1 \text{ required C.T. ratio on L.V. side.}$$

8.28 **What is the problem with load encroachment in case of distance protection through mho relay?**
[4 marks : 2013]

Solution:

Load Encroachment Problem:

The mal-operation of zone 3 impedance relays with mho-characteristics is a factor for causing cascading failures. This mal-operation could be due to the increase of the load level to the limit that the relay interprets the system voltage and current into an impedance that its value appears to the relay as if it is a fault while it is not, e.g. load encroachment.

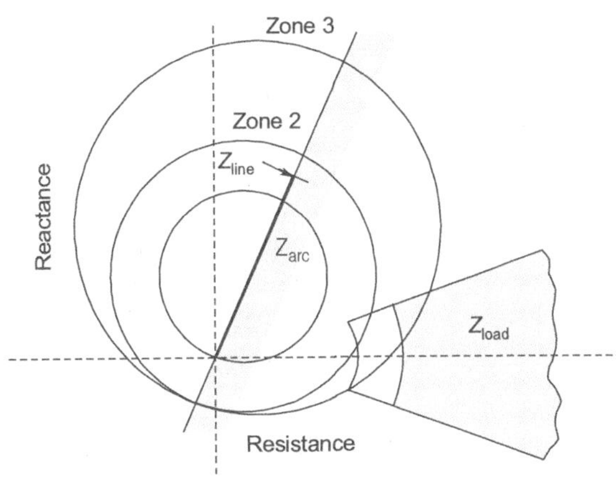

Encroachment of Load into Zone 3

Although the line characteristics are far from the load characteristics, it is not possible to set zone 3 setting to take into account only the line characteristics because it has to accommodate for the existence of fault resistance.

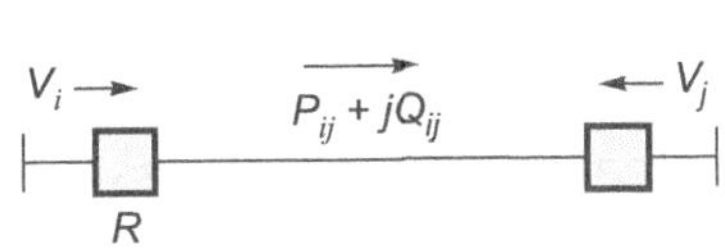

Power flow on transmission line

The apparent impedance seen by the relay R for the steady state positive sequence model of a transmission line is given by,

$$Z_R = \frac{|V_i|^2}{P_{ij} - jQ_{ij}} = \frac{|V_i|^2}{P_{ij}^2 + Q_{ij}^2}(P_{ij} + jQ_{ij})$$

The following conclusions can be derived from the equation:

- Quadrant of Z_R in the R-X plane correspond to the quadrant of apparent power S_{ij} in $P_{ij} - Q_{ij}$ plane.
- The apparent impedance seen by the relay is proportional to square of the magnitude of bus voltage.
- The apparent impedance seen by the relay is inversely proportional to the apparent power flowing on the line.
- During peak load conditions, these effects will reduce the apparent impedance seen by the relay to a small value to fall within Z_2 or Z_3 characteristic.
- Then the relay will pick up and trip the circuit after its time dial setting requirements are met and the relay is said to trip on load encroachment.

8.29 **Where and why do we use negative sequence relay in a power system?** [4 marks : 2013]

Solution:

Negative Phase Sequence of Phase Unbalance Relay:

Whenever there is an unbalanced circuit, the unbalanced currents will have a negative phase sequence component. A negative phase sequence (or phase unbalance) relay is essentially provided for the protection of generators and motors against unbalanced loading that may arise due to phase-to-phase faults.

Essentially such a relay has a filter circuit which is responsive only to the negative sequence components. Since small magnitude over-current can cause dangerous conditions, it becomes necessary to have low setting of such relays. Although, an earth relay can also provide the desired protection but only in case when there is a fault between any phase and earth. For phase-to-phase faults an earth relay cannot provide necessary protection and hence negative phase sequence relay is required.

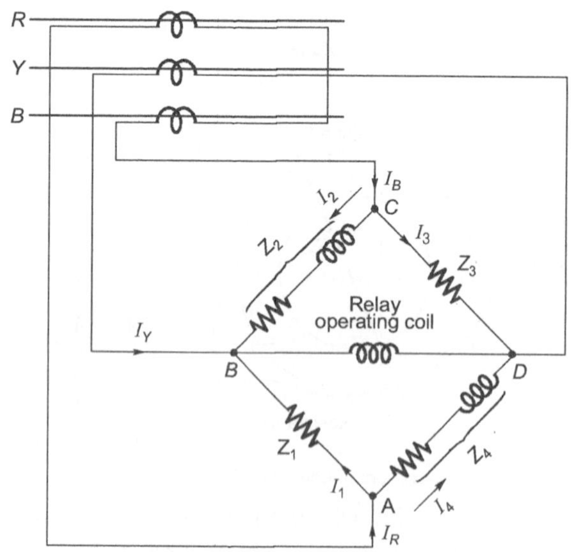

Negative Sequence Relay

8.30 **For the case of opening a lightly loaded long transmission line through a CB, explain and specify what can be the maximum voltage that can remain across the transmission line after opening of the CB?**

[10 marks : 2013]

Solution:

A long transmission line draws a substantial quantity of charging current. If a lightly loaded long transmission line is open circuited, the voltage at receiving end may become greater than voltage at sending end. This is known as Ferranti effect and is due to the voltage drop across the line inductance being in phase with the sending end voltage. Therefore both capacitance and inductance are responsible to produce this phenomenon. The capacitance and charging current is negligible in short line but significant in medium line and appreciable in long line. The effect of the line capacitance is to cause the no-load receiving end voltage to be more than the sending end voltage. The effect becomes more pronounced as the line length increases.

A simple explanation of the Ferranti effect on an approximate basis can be advanced by lumping the inductance and capacitance parameters of the line. The capacitor is lumped at the receiving end of the line

$$I_s = \frac{V_S}{\left(\frac{1}{j\omega Cl} + j\omega Ll\right)}$$

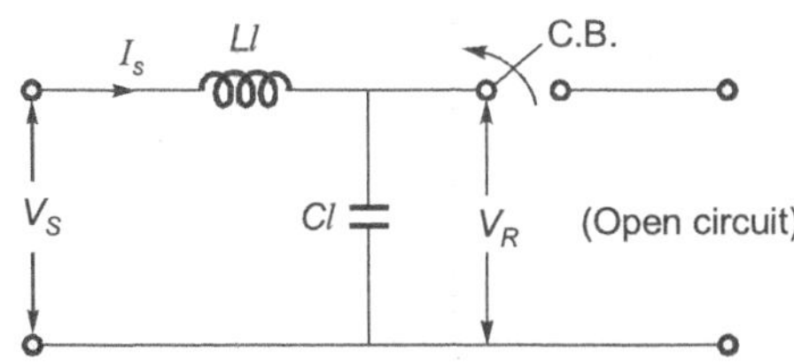

where, C is capacitance per unit length of line,
L is inductance per unit length of line,
and l is length of line

Since C is small compared to L, ωLl can be neglected in comparison to $\frac{1}{\omega Cl}$, thus

$$I_S \approx jV_S\,\omega Cl$$

Now, V_R(receiving end voltage) $= V_S - I_s\,(j\omega Ll)$

$$V_R = V_S + V_S\omega^2 CLl^2 = V_S(1 + \omega^2 CLl^2)$$

This much of maximum voltage can remain across the transmission line after opening of the C.B.

8.31 **Discuss about the three zone protection of EHV transmission line.** [10 marks : 2013]

Solution:

For achieving coordination between primary and backup protection, 3-zone distance relays are employed. Further because the impedance to fault as seen from the line end is entirely different for phase and ground faults, a separate set of distance relays must be employed for recognizing these faults.

Setting Impedance Relays: The underlying basis of impedance setting being the same in either direction, it is explained with reference to one direction only (left to right in Fig. (a)).

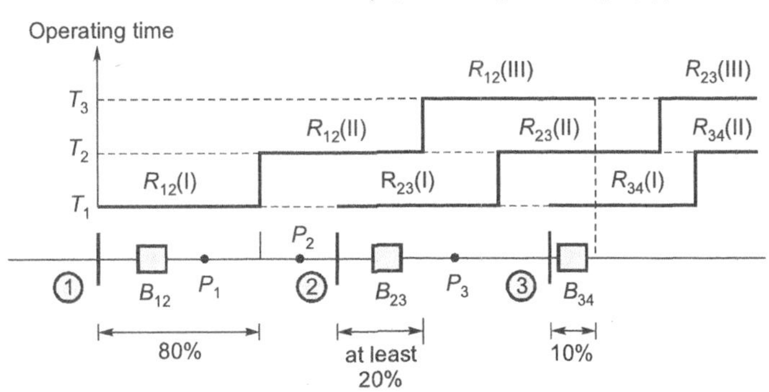

Fig. (a) Setting of Impedance Relays

Consider the setting of the first zone impedance of relay R_{12}. If in an attempt to cover the whole line the impedance Z_1 is set the full impedance of the line 1-2, this relay (R_{12}) will not be able to distinguish between faults at P_2 and P_3 either side of the bus 2, as the impedance-to-fault for faults at either of these points is the same. To overcome this problem, the zone-*I* (operating time T_1, instantaneous) impedance of the relay (R_{12}) is set to operate upto 80% of the line impedance ($Z_1 = 0.8\ Z_{12}$) as shown in the figure. The remaining 20% of the line is afforded protection by the zone-II of R_{12} with operating time T_2 (i.e. with a time delay of ($T_2 - T_1$)).

Thus in the direction left-to-right, only 80% of the line has fast (instantaneous) protection. The zone-I of R_{23} is set similarly. To provide backup protection to R_{23}, the zone-II of R_{12} must extend to at least 20% of the line 2-3 ($Z_2 = Z_{12} + 0.2\ Z_{23}$). In order not to clash with the zone-II of R_{23}, the zone-II of R_{12} cannot fully back protect the line 2-3. The remaining portion of the line 2-3 is back-protected by the zone-III (operating time T_3 with time delay ($T_3 - T_1$) of R_{12}, which must extend a little beyond the bus 3, say 10% ($Z_3 = Z_{12} + Z_{23} + 0.1\ Z_{34}$)). Relays in the other direction are set similarly. It must be observed here that only middle 60% of any line is fast protected while the remaining 40% is fast protected from one end, and slow (T_2) protected from the other end. When multiple lines emanate from a bus as shown in Fig. (b), the zone-II of R_{12} must extend to 20% of the shortest line and its zone-III must extend just beyond the longest line (line 2-4 in Fig. (b)) in order to fully back-protect all the line (lines 2-3 and 2-4). This is illustrated by the zone setting diagram of Fig. (c).

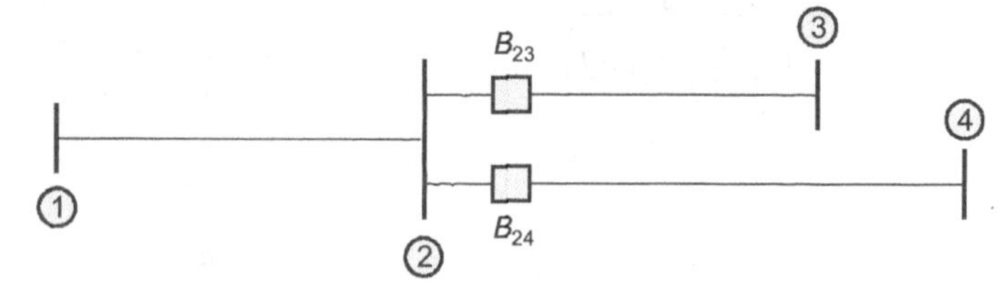

Fig. (b) Multiple lines outgoing from a bus

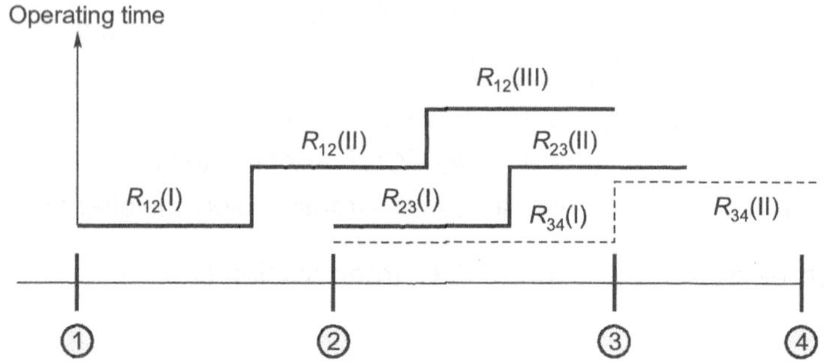

Fig. (c) Zone setting of relays

8.32 **Differentiate between type tests and routine tests. What are the different tests carried out to prove the ability of circuit breaker?**

[10 marks : 2015]

Solution:

There are two types of tests of circuit breakers namely routine tests and type tests. Routine tests are performed on every piece of circuit breaker in the premises of the manufacturer. The purpose of the routine tests is to confirm the proper functioning of a circuit breaker. Type tests are performed in a high voltage laboratory, such tests are performed on sample piece of circuit breaker of each type confirm their characteristics and rated capacities according to their design. These tests are not performed on every piece of circuit breaker. A few important type test, such as breaking capacity, making capacity, short time current rating come in the category of short circuit testing of circuit breakers.

1. Direct Testing	2. Indirect Testing
(a) Test for breaking capacity. (b) Test for making capacity. (c) Duty cycle test (d) Short-time current test	(a) Unit testing (b) Unit testing

Direct testing: In direct testing, the circuit breaker in test under the condition which actually exist on power systems. It is subjected to restriking voltage which is expected in practical situation.

Test for breaking capacity:

During this test following measurement are taken.

1. Symmetrical breaking current
2. Asymmetrical breaking current
3. Recovery voltage
4. Frequency of oscillation and RRRv

The circuit breaker must be capable of breaking all current up to its rated capacity.

Test for Making capacity: This measured the rated making current, i.e., the peak value of the first major loop of the short circuit current wave.

Duty cycle test:

The following duty cycle tests are performed.

1. B–3–B–3–B test are performed at 10%, 30% and 60% of the rated symmetrical breaking capacity.
2. B–3–MB–3–MB

   This test can also be performed as two separate tests

   (a) M–3–M make test

   (b) B–3–B–3–B break test

Short time current test: The rated short time current is passed through the circuit breaker under test for a specific short duration (1 second or 3 second) and current as measured by taking an oscillograph of the current wave.

Indirect test:

Unit testing: Generally, high voltage circuit breaker are designed with several are interrupter unit in series. Each unit can be tested separately. From the test of one unit the capacity of the complete breaker can be determined.

Synthetic testing: In this testing, there are two sources of power supply for the testing, a current source a voltage source. The current source is a high current, low voltage source. It supplies short circuit current during the test. The voltage source is a high voltage, low current source. It provides restriking and recovery voltage.

8.33 **Two relays R_1 and R_2 are connected in two sections of a feeder as shown in the following figure. CTs are of the ratio 1000/5. The plug setting of relay R_1 is 100% and of R_2 is 125%. The operating time characteristics of the relay is given in the following table:**

Operating time characteristics for TMS = 1						
PSM	2	4	5	8	10	20
Operating time (seconds)	10	5	4	3	2.8	2.4

The time multiplier setting of the relay R_1 is 0.3. The time grading scheme has a discriminative margin of 0.5 s between the relays. A three-phase short-circuit at F results in a fault current of 5000 A. Find the actual operating time of R_1 and R_2. What is the time multiplier setting (TMS) of R_2?

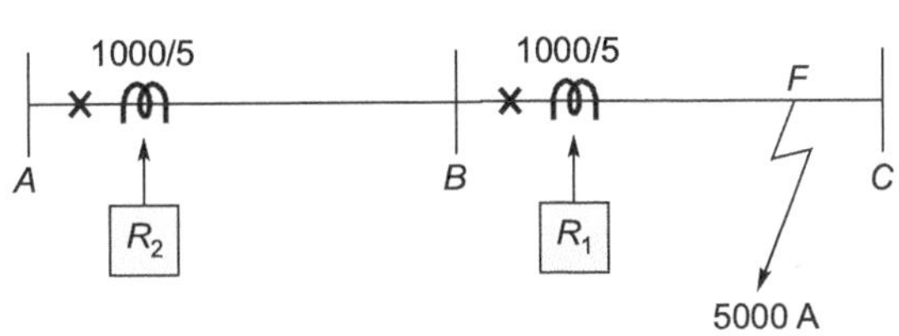

[12 marks : 2018]

Solution:

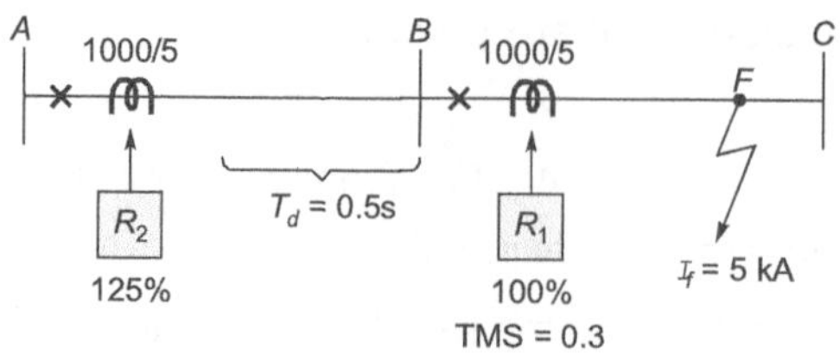

$$I_{\text{pick up}} = \text{Plug setting} \times \text{C.T. secondary current}$$

$$\text{PSM} = \text{Plug setting multiplier}$$

$$= \frac{I_f}{I_{PK} \times \text{C.T. ratio}}$$

$$T_s = T_P + T_d$$

= Primary relay time + Time delay between primary and backup relay

T = Time of operation of any relay

= Time multiplier settling (TMS) × Time calculated from IDMT characteristics corresponding to PSM.

	R_1	R_2
I_{PK}	1 × 5 = 5 A	1.25 × 5 = 6.25 A
PSM	$\dfrac{5000}{5\times\dfrac{1000}{5}} = 5$	$\dfrac{5000}{6.25\times\dfrac{1000}{5}} = 4$
T	0.3 × 4 = 1.2 sec.	1.2 + 0.5 = 1.7 sec.
TMS	0.3	$\dfrac{1.7}{5} = 0.34$

Actual operating time of R_1 = 1.2 sec.

Actual operation time of R_2 = 1.7 sec.

TMS of R_2 = 0.34

8.34 **(i) In case of a circuit breaker, define the terms 'restriking voltage' and 'RRRV', and express their maximum values in terms of system voltage.**

(ii) Which circuit breaker is preferred for voltages 132 kV and above?

(iii) In a 132 kV system, the reactance per phase up to the location of circuit breaker is 5 Ω and capacitance to earth is 0.03 μF. Calculate the maximum value of restriking voltage, the maximum value of RRRV and frequency of transient oscillation.

[20 marks : 2018]

Solution:

(i) **Restriking voltage:** At the instant of arc extinction, an LC transient occurs including the generator inductance and stray capacitance causing high frequency damped oscillations. This voltage appearing across the circuit-breaker is known as restriking voltage.

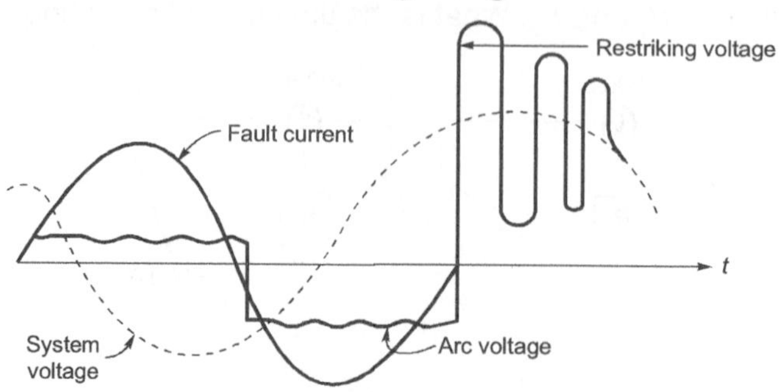

RRRV: It is the rate of rise of restriking voltage which appears across the circuit breaker.

For an instant $e = E_m \sin\omega t$,

$$V_B(s) = \frac{\frac{1}{sC}}{\left(\frac{1}{sC} + sL\right)} \times \left(\frac{E_m}{s}\right) = \frac{E_m}{s(s^2LC+1)}$$

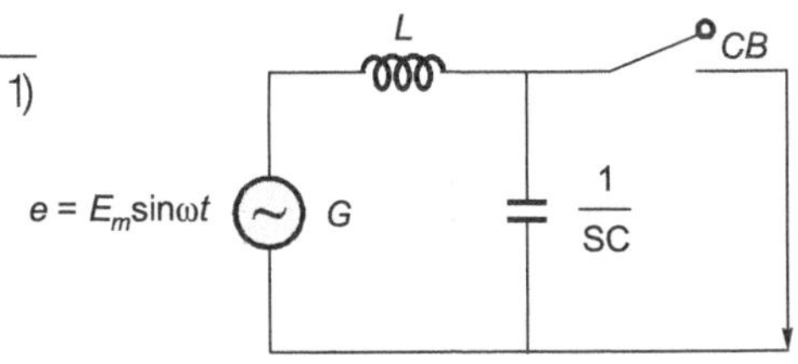

$$V_B(s) = E_m\left[\frac{1}{s} - \frac{s}{s^2 + 1/LC}\right]$$

Take inverse L.T, $V_B(t) = E_m\left(1 - \cos\frac{1}{\sqrt{LC}}\right)\text{kV} = E_m(1 - \cos\omega t)\text{ kV}$

Maximum restriking voltage occurs at,

$$\omega t = \pi$$

$$V_{B\max} = 2E_m$$

$$\text{RRRV} = \frac{dV_B}{dt} = E_m\left(\frac{1}{\sqrt{LC}}\sin\omega t\right)$$

$$\text{RRRV} = \frac{E_m}{\sqrt{LC}}\sin\omega t\text{ kV/sec}$$

$$\text{RRRV}_{\max} = \frac{E_m}{\sqrt{LC}}\text{ kV/sec}$$

(ii) SF_6 circuit breaker is preferred for voltages 132 kV and above because of the following reasons.

(a) **High dielectric strength:** SF_6 has high electronegativity so it absorbs the free e^- in space avoids the possibility of electron avalanche and therefore give rise the high dielectric strength.

(b) **Effective arc quenching:** SF_6 has unique property of after the source emerging the spark is removed. This makes SF_6 100 times effective as air in arc quarching.

(c) **High RRRV rating:** Due to lower thermal time constant of SF_6, for the same operating voltage frequency of mains is 100 times as to air, and RRRV ∝ Natural frequency (f_n), therefore it can withstand severe RRRV. Thus most suitable for short line faults without suitabling resistors and can interrupt capacitive current without restriking.

(d) **Excellent heat transfer capability:** Because of its high 'molecular weight with its low gaseous viscosity enables it transfer heat by convection more effectively.

(e) It requires low pressure at which SF_6 is stored and used.

(iii)
$$E_m = \frac{132\sqrt{2}}{\sqrt{3}} = 107.78\text{ kV/phase}$$

Max restriking voltage,

$$TR\,V_{\max} = 2\,E_m = 2 \times 107.78 = 215.56\text{ kV}$$

$$L = \left(\frac{X_L}{\omega}\right) = \frac{5}{100\pi} = 15.915\text{ mH}$$

$$RRR\,V_{\max} = \frac{Em}{\sqrt{LC}}$$

$$RRR\,V_{\max} = \frac{107.78}{\sqrt{15.915 \times 10^{-3} \times 0.03 \times 10^{-6}}}$$

$$= 4932.581\text{ kV/sec}$$

$$f_n = \frac{1}{2\pi\sqrt{LC}}$$

$$f_n = \frac{1}{2\pi\sqrt{15.915\times10^{-3}\times0.03\times10^{-6}}}$$

$$= 7283.769 \text{ Hz} = 7.283 \text{ kHz}$$

8.35 Draw the wiring diagram showing currents for power and relaying circuit used for protecting a transformer of the rating 25 MVA, 220 Y/13.8 Δ kV, X = 10%. The transformer has a short-term overload capacity of 30 MVA. You are required to use CTs with common turns ratios such as 50/5 A, 100/5 A, 150/5 A, ..., 1000/5 A, 1200/5 A. If needed, auxiliary CT of adequate turns ratio may be used.

[20 marks : 2019]

Solution:

Power transformer (over load of 30 MVA)

$$S = \sqrt{3}V_1I_1 = \sqrt{3}V_2I_2$$

$$30\times10^6 = \sqrt{3}\times220\times10^3\times I_1$$

$$= \sqrt{3}\times13.8\times10^3\times I_2$$

$$I_1 = 78.72 \text{ A},\qquad I_2 = 1255.10 \text{ A}$$

From the CT ranges given,

For CT_2 select: 1400 A/5 A

Pilot wire [Secondary of CT_2] $\Rightarrow i_2 \Rightarrow \dfrac{1255.10}{(1400/5)} = 4.4825$ A

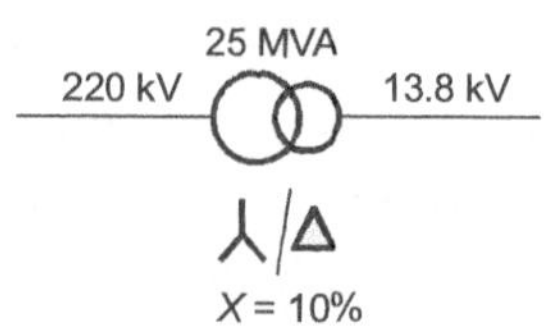

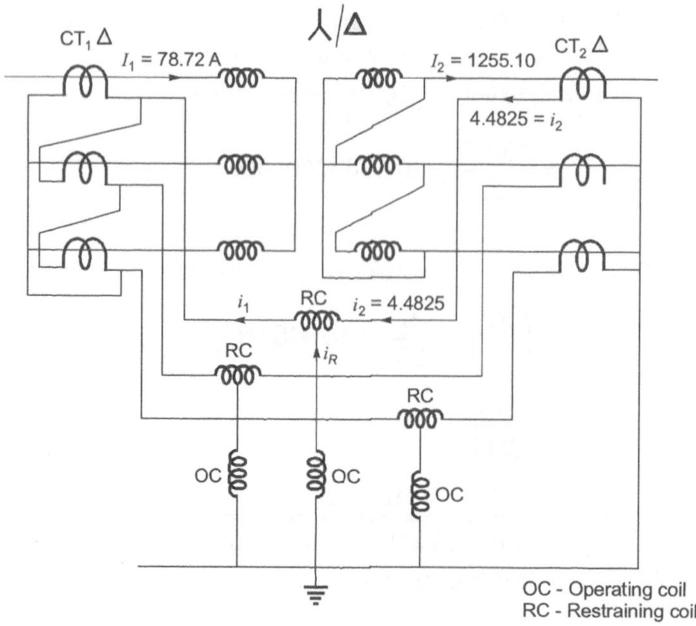

Case-(i):

If, $i_1 = 4.4825 \Rightarrow i_R = i_1 - i_2 = 0$

$$CT_2 \text{ secondary current} \Rightarrow \frac{4.4825}{\sqrt{3}} = 2.5879 \text{ A}$$

$$CT_1 \text{ primary current} = I_1 = 78.72 \text{ A}$$

$$\text{Required CT ratio is } \frac{78.72}{2.5879} = \frac{78.72}{\left(\frac{4.4825}{\sqrt{3}}\right)} \text{ A}$$

Case-(ii):

The above rating is not available. So we have to use 100 A/5 A CT on the primary side of power transformer.

With CT_1 100 A/5 A

$$CT_1 \text{ secondary current} = \frac{78.72}{100/5} = 3.936 \text{ A}$$

Pilot wire current, $i_1 = 3.936 \times \sqrt{3} = 6.81735 \text{ A}$

$$i_R = i_1 - i_2$$

$\Rightarrow$ 6.81735 – 4.4825 $= 2.3348$ A

For avoiding relay maloperation: % difference relay has to be used with slope of

$$k\left(\frac{i_1 + i_2}{2}\right) \geq i_R$$

$$k \geq \frac{i_R}{\left(\frac{i_1 + i_2}{2}\right)}$$

$$k \geq \frac{2.3348}{\left(\frac{6.818735 + 4.4825}{2}\right)}$$

$$k \geq 0.4132$$

$$k \geq 41.32\%$$

Minimum % setting required for % differential relay.

9. Optimal Power System Operation

9.1 **The fuel inputs of plants 1 and 2 are given as**

$$F_1 = 0.2 P_1^2 + 40 P_1 + 120 \text{ Rs/hr.}$$

$$F_1 = 0.25 P_2^2 + 30 P_2 + 150 \text{ Rs/hr.}$$

Determine the economic operating schedule and the corresponding cost of generation if the maximum and minimum loading of each machine is 100 MW and 25 MW, the demand is 180 MW and transmission losses are neglected. If the load is equally shared by both units, determine the saving obtained by loading the units as per incremental cost.

[13 marks : 2003]

Solution:

(a) Given,

$$F_1 = 0.2 P_1^2 + 40 P_1 + 120 \text{ Rs/hr.}$$

$$F_2 = 0.25 P_2^2 + 30 P_2 + 150 \text{ Rs/hr.}$$

The incremental production cost of both the units are,

$$\frac{dF_1}{dP_1} = 0.4\,P_1 + 40 \text{ Rs/MW hr.} \quad ...(i)$$

and

$$\frac{dF_2}{dP_2} = 0.5\,P_2 + 30 \text{ Rs/MW hr.} \quad ...(ii)$$

Now for economic operation of the units,

$$\frac{dF_1}{dP_1} = \frac{dF_2}{dP_2}$$

i.e.,

$$0.4\,P_1 + 40 = 0.5\,P_2 + 30$$

$$0.4\,P_1 - 0.5\,P_2 = -10$$

and

$$P_1 + P_2 = 180 \text{ MW}$$

or

$$P_1 = \frac{80}{0.9} = 88.89 \text{ MW}$$

$$P_2 = 91.11 \text{ MW}$$

Now cost of generation $= F_1 + F_2$

$$F_1 = 0.2(88.89)^2 + 40(88.89) + 120$$

$$= 5255.88 \text{ Rs/hr.}$$

$$F_2 = 0.25(91.11)^2 + 30(91.11) + 150$$

$$= 4958.55 \text{ Rs/hr.}$$

$$\text{Total cost} = F_1 + F_2 = 10214.43 \text{ Rs/hr.}$$

For $25 < P_1,\quad P_2 < 100$ MW

Both P_1 and P_2 lying within minimum and maximum limits of each plant.

Economic load sharing, $P_1 = 88.89$ MW

$P_2 = 91.11$ MW

(b) Cost:

If, $P_1 = 88.89$ MW

and $P_2 = 91.11$ MW

$$F_1 = 5255.88 \text{ Rs/hr.}$$

$$F_2 = 4958.55 \text{ Rs/hr.}$$

$$F = F_1 + F_2 = 10214.43 \text{ Rs/hr.}$$

If load shared equally:

$$P_1 = P_2 = 90 \text{ MW}$$

$$F_1 = 0.2\,(90)^2 + 40\,(90) + 120 = 5340 \text{ Rs/hr.}$$

$$F_2 = 0.25\,(90)^2 + 30\,(90) + 150 = 4875 \text{ Rs/hr.}$$

Total cost, $F_1 + F_2 = 10215$ Rs/hr.

$$\text{Saving} = 10215 - 10214.43 = 0.57 \text{ Rs/hr.}$$

9.2 What are the objectives of 'optimal scheduling of hydro-thermal units?

[4 marks : 2012]

Solution:

Hydrothermal scheduling of a power system is concerned with thermal unit commitment and dispatch, the hourly generation of hydro units.

The objective is to minimize the total operating cost of thermal units over a period of upto one weak, subject to system-wide demand and reserve requirements and individual unit constraints.

9.3 A system consists of two plants connected by a transmission line. The only load is located at plant 2. When 200 MW is transmitted from plant 1 to plant 2 power loss in the line is 16 MW. Find the required generation for each plant and the power received by the load when λ for the system is \$12.50/MW-hr. Assume that the incremental fuel costs can be approximated to be

$$\frac{dF_1}{dP_1} = 0.010P_1 + 8.5 \text{ \$ / MWh}; \quad \frac{dF_2}{dP_2} = 0.015P_2 + 9.5 \text{ \$ / MWh}$$

[20 marks : 2013]

Solution:

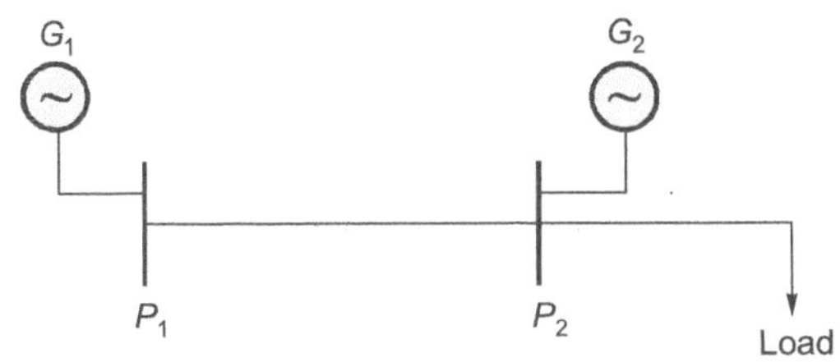

$$B_{11} = \frac{P_L}{P_1^2} = \frac{16}{(200)^2} = 4\times10^{-4}$$

$$\lambda = \frac{dF_1}{dP_1} \times \text{Penalty factor}$$

$$12.50 = (0.010P_1 + 8.5)\frac{1}{(1-2B_{11}P_1)}$$

$$12.50 - 12.5 \times 2 \times 4 \times 10^{-4} P_1 = 0.010 P_1 + 8.5$$

$$P_1 = 200 \text{ MW}$$

Similarly,
$$12.50 = \frac{dF_2}{dP_2} \times L_2$$

$$12.50 = 0.015 P_2 + 9.5$$

$$P_2 = 200 \text{ MW}$$

$$P_{gen} = P_1 + P_2 = 200 + 200 = 400 \text{ MW}$$

$$P_L = B_{11}P_1^2 = 4\times10^{-4}\times200^2 = 16 \text{ MW}$$

$$P_{load} = P_{gen} - P_L = 400 - 16 = 384 \text{ MW}$$

9.4 Distinguish between unit commitment and economic load dispatch. [2 marks : 2015]

Solution:

Unit Commitment:

Unit Commitment is used to suggest sufficient number of generating units with sufficient generating capacity to meet a given load economically with sufficient reserve capacity to meet any abnormal, operating conditions like failure of one of generators i.e. to commit generating capacity to obtain reliable and economic supply of given load.

Following methods are used for unit commitment problem:

1. Priority list
2. Dynamic programming
3. Lagrange Multiplier

Economic Load Dispatch:

Economic Load Dispatch involves the solution of two different problems.

1. Unit commitment or predispatch problems where in it is required to select optimally out of the available generating stations to operate, to meet the expected load and provide a specific margin of operating reserve over a specified time.
2. The online economic dispatch where it is required to distribute the load among the generating units actually paralleled with the system so that minimizing the cost of energy.

9.5 A system consists of two plants connected by a transmission line and a load is at power plant-2 as shown in the figure. Data for the loss equation consists of the information that 200 MW transmitted from Plant-1 to the load results in transmission loss of 20 MW. Find the optimum generation schedule considering transmission losses to supply a load of 204.41 MW. Also evaluate the amount of financial loss that may be incurred if at the time of scheduling transmission losses are not coordinated. The incremental fuel cost characteristics of plant-1 and plant-2 are given by

$$\frac{df_1}{dP_1} = 0.025\,P_1 + 14 \quad ₹/\text{MW-hr}$$

$$\frac{df_2}{dP_2} = 0.05\,P_2 + 16 \quad ₹/\text{MW-hr}$$

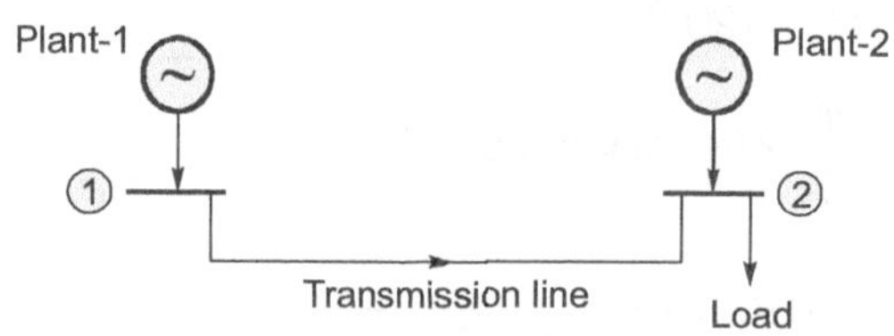

[20 marks : 2020]

Solution:

As load is not present at bus-1 so transmission loss is independent of plant 2 generation. So B_{12} and B_{22} are zero.

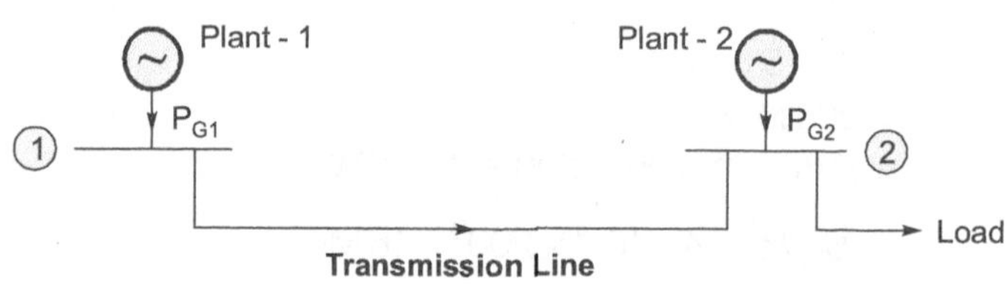

Power loss due to flow of 200 MW from bus (1) to bus (2) is 20 MW.

$$20 = B_{11}(200)^2$$

$$B_{11} = 5 \times 10^{-4}\ \text{MW}^{-1}$$

$$P_L = 5\times10^{-4}P_{G1}^2$$

and $$\frac{\partial P_L}{\delta P_{G2}} = 0$$

Penalty factor for plant 1,

$$L_1 = \frac{1}{1-\dfrac{\delta P_L}{\delta P_{G1}}} = \frac{1}{1-10\times10^{-4}P_{G1}}$$

Penalty factor for plant 2,

$$L_2 = \frac{1}{1-0} = 1$$

Now for optimum scheduling

$$IC_1L_1 = IC_2L_2 = \lambda$$

$$\frac{(0.025P_{G1}+14)}{1-10^{-3}P_{G1}} = (0.05P_{G2} + 16) \times 1$$

$$P_D = P_{G1} + P_{G2} - P_L$$

$$204.41 = P_{G1} + P_{G2} - 5 \times 10^{-4}\,P_{G1}^2$$

$$P_{G2} = 204.41 + 5 \times 10^{-4}P_{G1}^2 - P_{G1}$$

$$\frac{(0.025P_{G1}+14)}{(1-10^{-3}P_{G1})} = 0.05[204.41 + 5 \times 10^{-4}P_{G1}^2 - P_{G1}] + 16$$

$$\frac{(0.025P_{G1}+14)}{1-0.001P_{G1}} = [10.2205 + 2.5 \times 10^{-5}P_{G1}^2 - 0.05P_{G1} + 16]$$

$$0.025P_{G1} + 14 = [26.2205 + 2.5 \times 10^{-5}P_{G1}^2 - 0.05P_{G1}] \times [1 - 0.001P_{G1}]$$

$$2.5 \times 10^{-8} P_{G1}^3 + 7.5 \times 10^{-5}P_{G1}^2 - 0.10122P_{G1} + 12.2205 = 0$$

$$P_{G1} = 134.801 \text{ MW}$$

$$P_L = 9.08552 \text{ MW}$$

$$P_{G2} = 78.6945 \text{ MW}$$

Cost function of each generation plant can be given as :

$$C_1 = 0.025\frac{P_{G1}^2}{2} + 14P_{G1} + K_1$$

$$C_2 = 0.05\frac{P_{G2}^2}{2} + 16P_{G2} + K_2$$

Using values of P_{G1} and P_{G2}, we get

$$C_1 = 2114.355 + K_1$$

$$C_2 = 1413.932 + K_2$$

$$\text{Total investment cost} = 2114.355 + K_1 + 1413.932 + K_2$$

$$= 3528.287 + K_1 + K_2$$

Without considering the losses

$$P_{G1} + P_{G2} = 204.41 \quad \text{...(1)}$$

$$\frac{dF_1}{dP_{G1}} = \frac{dF_2}{dP_{G2}}$$

$$0.025P_{G1} + 14 = 0.05P_{G2} + 16$$

$$0.025P_{G1} - 0.05P_{G2} = 2$$

$$P_{G1} = 162.94 \text{ MW}$$

$$P_{G2} = 41.47 \text{ MW}$$

Also,

$$C_1 = \frac{0.025}{2}P_{G1}^2 + 14P_{G1} + K_1 = 2613.028 + K_1$$

$$C_2 = \frac{0.05}{2}P_{G2}^2 + 16P_{G2} + K_2 = 706.514 + K_2$$

$$\text{Total Cost} = 3319.542 + K_1 + K_2$$

$$\text{Financial Loss} = (3528.287 + K_1 + K_2) - (3319.542 + K_1 + K_2)$$

$$= 208.745 \text{ Rs./hr.}$$

9.6 The incremental fuel cost for a generating plant having two units are

$$IC_1 = 20 + 0.1P_1 \quad ₹\text{/MWhr}$$

$$IC_2 = 15 + 0.012P_2 \quad ₹\text{/MWhr}$$

If the total demand P_D = 200 MW, determine the division of load between the units for the most economical operation.

[12 marks : 2023]

Solution:

Given incremental fuel cost is,

$$I_{C1} = 0.1P_1 + 20 \text{ Rs/MW hr}$$

$$I_{C2} = 0.12P_2 + 15 \text{ Rs/MW hr}$$

For the total load as 200 MW, give ELD

In general, $P_G = P_1 + P_2 = P_D + P_L$

Here there are no losses, so

$$P_G = P_1 + P_2 = P_D$$

i.e., $P_1 + P_2 = 200$ ...(1)

For economic load dispath losses,

$$I_{C1} = I_{C2}$$

$$0.1P_1 + 20 = 0.12P_2 + 15$$

$$0.1P_1 - 0.12P_2 = -5$$

$$10P_1 - 12P_2 = -500 \quad \text{...(2)}$$

By solving (1) and (2)

Required load shared by generating plant is,

$$P_1 = 86.34 \text{ MW}$$

$$P_2 = 113.64 \text{ MW}$$

10. HVDC Transmission, FACTS and Recent Trends in Power Systems

10.1 Compare EHV AC and HVDC options for an integrated power network. [10 marks : 2002]

Solution:

As compared to EHV AC, HVDC has following advantages and disadvantages.

Advantages:

1. HVDC systems are economical for long distance bulk power transmission by overhead lines (reduced tower costs).
2. There is greater power per conductor and simpler line construction.
3. Ground return is possible.
4. There is no charging current and skin effect.
5. The voltage regulation problem is much less serious for DC, since only the IR drop is involved (IX = 0). For the same reason steady-state stability is no longer a major problem.
6. There is easy reversibility and controllability of power flow through a DC link.
7. The DC line is an asynchronous link and it can interconnect two rigid systems operating at different frequencies.
8. Each conductor can be operated as an independent circuit.
9. Smaller amount of right of way and narrower tower are required.
10. AC line requires more insulation between the tower and conductors as well as greater clearance above the earth as compared to DC line.
11. Line losses are smaller.
12. No reactive compensation of DC line is required.
13. Corona loss, radio interference and audible emissions are less as compared to AC.

Disadvantages:

1. The systems are costly since installation of complicated converters and DC switchgear is expensive.
2. Converters require considerable reactive power.
3. Harmonics are generated which require filters.
4. Lack of HVDC circuit breakers hampers network operation.
5. There is nothing like DC transformers which can change the voltage level. Voltage transformation has to be provided on the AC sides of the system.

6. Reactive power required by the load is to be supplied locally as no reactive power can be transmitted over a DC link.
7. Pollution affects DC more than AC. More frequency clearing of insulators is required.

10.2 Give a neat sketch of a 12-pulse bipolar HVDC station indicating the position of various equipment. Give the uses and limitations of each equipment.

[15 marks : 2003]

Solution:

A 12-pulse converter, has two 6 pulse converters in series. One 6 pulse converter is with converter transformer connected in star-delta and the other with star-star. The phase shift between secondary 3-phase AC voltage waveforms of two transformers is 30°. The triggering pulse to valves of two 6-pulse converters are staggered to get 12-pulse DC wave form. Thus a 12-pulse DC wave form in obtained with 360°/12 = 30° phase shift between consecutive pulses is obtained.

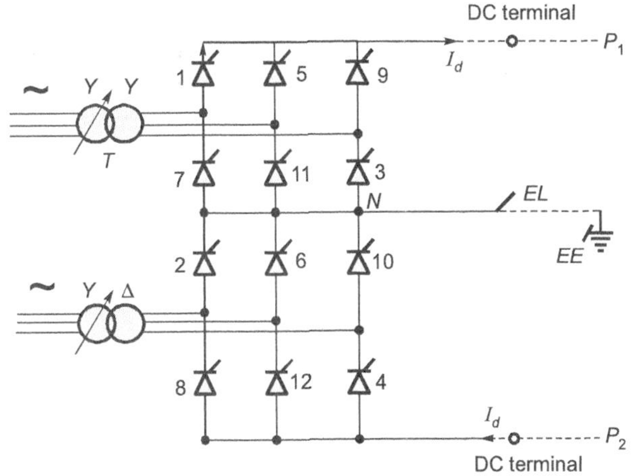

12 pulse converter bridge

A large DC smoothing reactor (0.2 $H \rightarrow 1$ H) is necessary on DC side of each pole to smoothen the DC current waveform. Each pole in a terminal substation has one 12-pulse converter bridge.

Configuration of a Bipolar 2 Terminal DC System:

(a) **Converter Transformer (*T*):** are connected between converter values and the AC bus. These are specially designed as they have a DC voltage component coming from valve side. They are either single phase units or 3-ϕ units with either two windings type or three winding type.

(b) **Valves (*V*):** are made-up of series connected thyristors. Valves are connected in bridge formation. Valves transfer power from AC to DC and vice-versa. Valves are usually water cooled.

(c) **Smoothing Reactor (*R*):** is necessary for converter operation and for smoothing the DC current. Smoothing reactor is generally oil cooled.

(d) **Electrode Line (*EL*):** Connects the midpoint of converters with a distant earth electrode (*E*). The earth electrode is located 5 to 20 Km away from HVDC substation so as to prevent galvanic corrosion of station earth-mat.

(e) **AC Harmonic Filter (*AF*):** Cover a large area under AC yard. These filters are composed of resistor banks, reactors, capacitor banks. They eliminate the AC harmonics arising out of the converter operation.

(f) **Shunt Compensation (*C*):** is provided by shunt capacitors. They supply reactive power schemes, AC filters capacitor provide shunt compensation also.

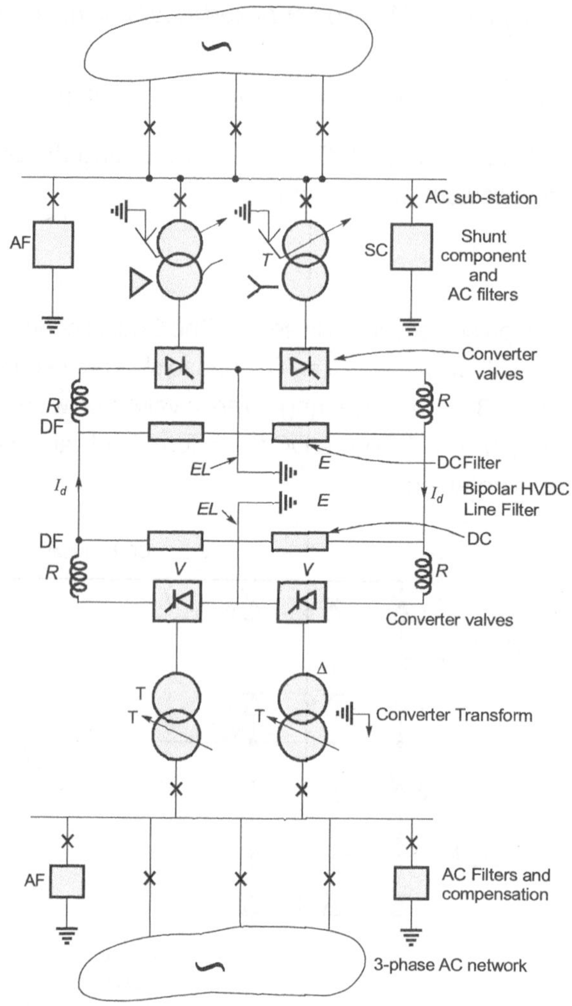

10.3 In H.V.D.C. converter station equipment using thyristors it is necessary to use a large number of thyristors in series because

(a) current rating of thyristors are low.

(b) voltage rating of thyristors are low.

(c) thyristors always fail to an internal open circuit.

(d) none of the above

[2 marks : 2003]

Solution: (b)

Option (b) is correct.

10.4 In a 3-phase bridge rectifier circuit for HVDC transmission, the ratio of output dc voltage to input ac voltage is

(a) 0.5 (b) 1.0

(c) $\sqrt{3}$ (d) 2

[2 marks : 2004]

Solution: (d)

Option (d), For a given alternating voltage the output direct voltage is doubled as the two anodes conducts simultaneously.

10.5 **Why is DC used for high voltage transmission of electric power?** [4 marks : 2004]

Solution:

As compared to EHV AC, HVDC has following advantages and disadvantages.

Advantages:

1. HVDC systems are economical for long distance bulk power transmission by overhead lines (reduced tower costs).
2. There is greater power per conductor and simpler line construction.
3. Ground return is possible.
4. There is no charging current and skin effect.
5. The voltage regulation problem is much less serious for DC, since only the IR drop is involved ($IX = 0$). For the same reason steady-state stability is no longer a major problem.
6. There is easy reversibility and controllability of power flow through a DC link.
7. The DC line is an asynchronous link and it can interconnect two rigid systems operating at different frequencies.
8. Each conductor can be operated as an independent circuit.
9. Smaller amount of right of way and narrower tower are required.
10. AC line requires more insulation between the tower and conductors as well as greater clearance above the earth as compared to DC line.
11. Line losses are smaller.
12. No reactive compensation of DC line is required.
13. Corona loss, radio interference and audible emissions are less as compared to AC.

10.6 **Explain with necessary diagrams the different kinds of HVDC links used in HVDC systems. Also explain the relative advantages and disadvantages of using these links. What are the precautions needed for series and parallel connection of thyristors to construct a HVDC system?**

[12 marks : 2005]

Solution:

Kinds of dc links:

(a) Bipolar System:

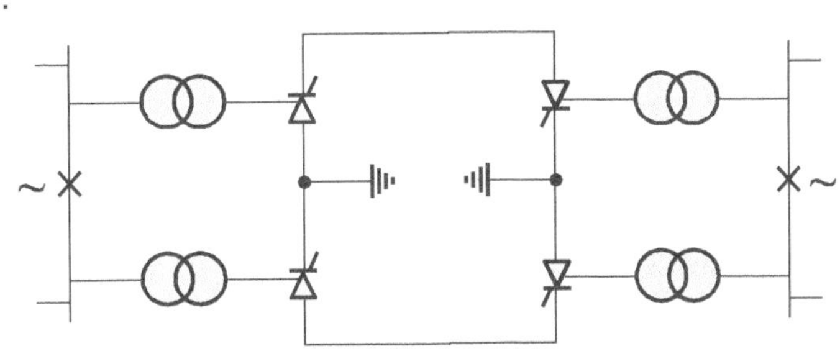

Configuration:

(*i*) Two poles, one positive with respect to earth and other negative.
(*ii*) Pole includes substation pole and transmission line pole.
(*iii*) The midpoint of bipoles in each terminal is earthed via an electrode line and an earth electrode.
(*iv*) Earth electrodes located about 5 to 25 km away from terminals.

Remarks:

(*i*) Normal mode of operation: Bipolar, with power flow through line conductors and negligible current through earth.
(*ii*) During fault on a pole the mode is changed to monopolar with reduced power flow through one pole and return earth.

(b) Monopolar System:

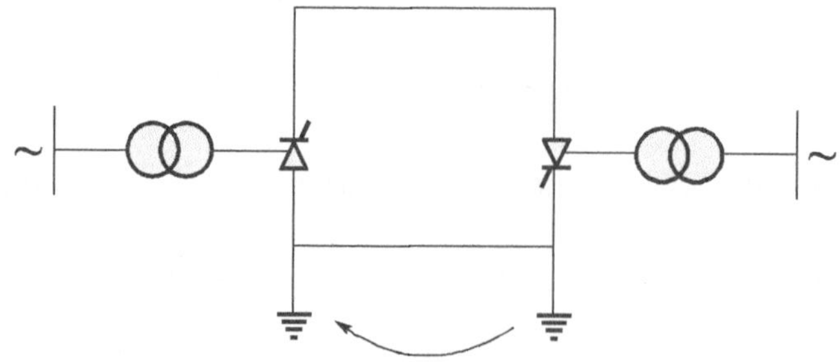

Configuration:

(*i*) One pole and return earth

(*ii*) Earthing of pole via electrode line and earth electrode.

(*iii*) Earth electrode located away from terminal substation.

(*iv*) The pole is normally negative with respect to earth as the corona loss as well as radio interference are reduced.

Remarks:

(*i*) Power rating almost half of the rating of bipolar system.

(*ii*) Used for HVDC submarine cables.

(*iii*) Recent HVDC projects are all bipolar and earlier monopolar systems are being extended to bipolar.

(c) Homopolar System:

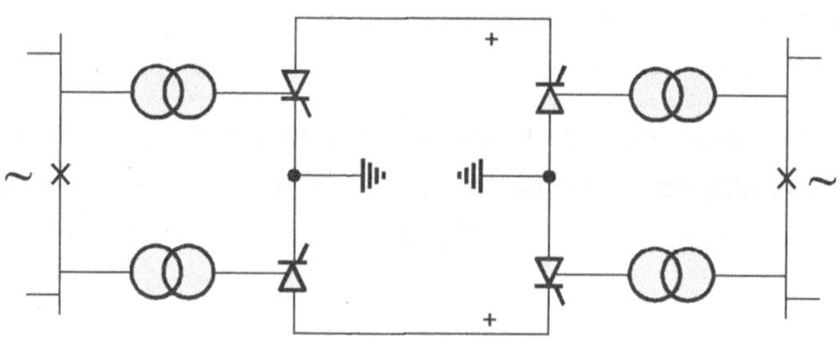

Configuration:

Two poles of same polarity and return earth.

Remarks:

This system was used earlier for combination of cable and overhead transmission.

Precautions needed for series and parallel connection of thyristors to construct a HVDC system: In case of HVDC transmission, the voltage and current levels are so high that a single thyristor cannot meet these requirements. Under such circumstances, it is essential to use more than one thyristors in parallel to obtain increased current requirements and in series to achieve higher voltages.

Parallel Connections: When thyristors are connected in parallel the current sharing between them may not be equal. The thyristor with lower dynamic resistance will take more current resulting in further reduction in resistance and further increasing the flow of current through it. The process is cumulative till the thyristor gives way. For parallel operation of thyristor it is desirable that the finger voltage of various devices should be same, the latching current level of all the devices is such that when gate pulse is applied all of them will turn on and remain on when the gate pulse is removed. Also the holding current of various devices should not differ much. In order to nullify the difference in characteristic of thyristors due to slightly different turn-on time, finger voltage, holding current, latching current etc. which results in unequal current sharing, it is desirable to insert suitable value of inductance in each thyristor circuit.

Series connection of thyristors: In order to obtain higher dc voltage for HVDC transmission, two or more than two thyristors are to be connected in series. In case, the thyristors have different leakage resistances, the thyristors with high leakage resistance will have large voltage drop across it. Higher resistance of equal values are connected across the thyristors.

10.7 HVDC monopolar link uses

(a) one conductor usually of negative polarity.

(b) one conductor usually of positive polarity.

(c) two conductors, one of positive and the other of negative polarity.

(d) two conductors both of negative polarity.

[2 marks : 2009]

Solution: (a)

The line is normally operating with negative polarity as the corona loss and the radio interference are reduced. Option (a) is correct.

10.8 What are the types of HVDC transmission system applications?

[10 marks : 2010]

Solution:

(a) Monopolar Link:

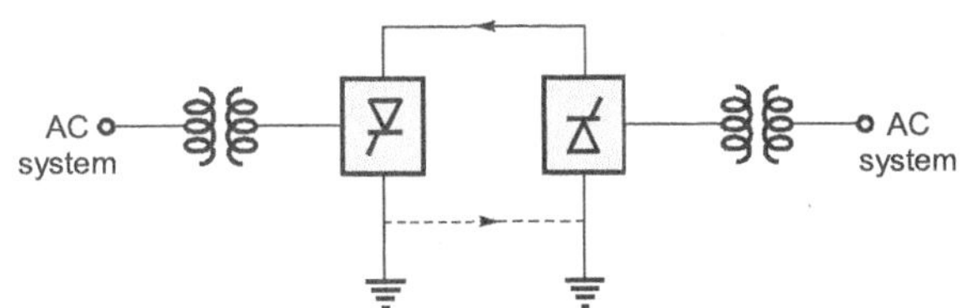

- It has only one energised conductor normally of negative polarity and uses ground or sea water as the as the return path.
- The negative polarity is preferred on overhead lines due to lesser radio interference.

(b) Bipolar Link:

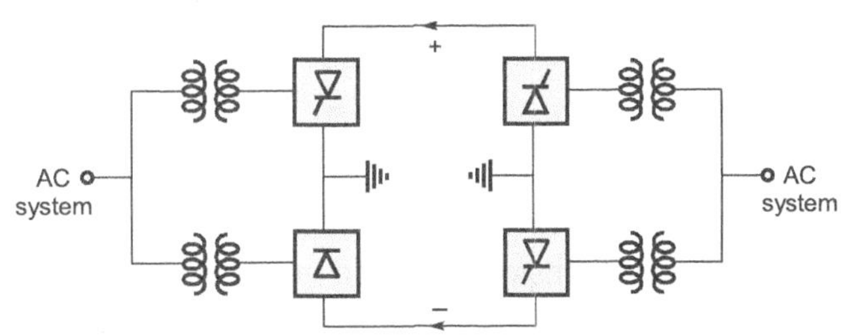

- The link has two conductors, one positive and the other negative potential of the same magnitude.
- At each terminal, two conductors of equal rated voltages are connected in series on the DC side.
- The neutral points are grounded, at one or both ends. If both the neutrals are grounded, the two poles operate independently.
- If one conductor has a fault, the other conductor can supply half the rated load.

(c) Homopolar Link:

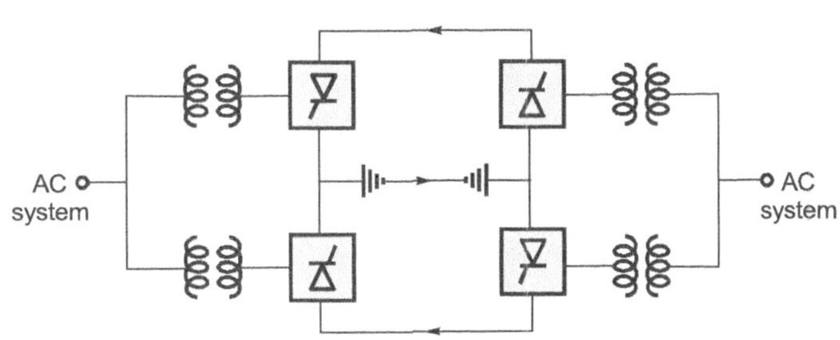

- A homopolar link has two or more conductors all having the same polarity (usually negative), and it always operated with ground as the return.
- If one of the conductors develops a fault, the converter equipment can be reconnected, so that the healthy conductor (with some overload capacity) can supply more than 50% of the rated power.

10.9 **Explain the working of a thyristor-controlled reactor-fixed capacitor** [8 marks : 2012]

Solution:

Basically, the Thyristor Controlled Reactor(TCR) only provides continuously controllable reactive power in the lagging power-factor range. To extend the dynamic controllable range to the leading power-factor domain, a fixed-capacitor bank is shunt-connected with the TCR. The TCR MVA is rated larger than the fixed capacitor to compensate the capacitive MVA and provide net inductive-reactive power should a lagging power-factor operation be desired. The fixed-capacitor banks which is usually connected in a star configuration are split into more than one 3-phase group.

Each capacitor contains a small tuning inductor connected in series and tunes the branch to act as a filter for a specific harmonic order. For instance, one capacitor group is tuned to the 5th harmonic and another to the 7th harmonic, whereas another group is designed to act as a high-pass filter. At fundamental frequency, the tuning reactors slightly reduce the net MVA rating of the fixed capacitors.

An FC–TCR is usually connected to the high-voltage power system by means of a step-down coupling transformer, as shown in figure. By dimensioning the ratings of the TCR and the capacitor, respectively, the production and absorption ranges can be selected according to the system requirements.

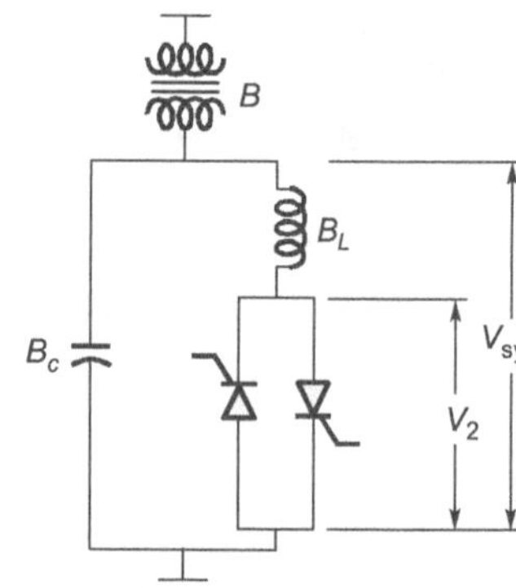

An FC-TCR with a step-down transformer

10.10 **A capacitor is connected across an ac regulator feeding inductor (TCR). Input is at 230 V, 50 Hz and inductive reactance (X_L) = 10 Ω; capacitive reactance (X_C) = 10 Ω. Calculate the net VAR supplied by the circuit at α = 135°.**

[10 marks : 2013]

Solution:

The given circuit is a Thyristor-controlled series capacitor (TCSC). The TCSC consists of the series-compensating capacitor shunted by a thyristor controlled reactor (TCR). Varying the delay angle a can vary the inductive impedance of the TCR.

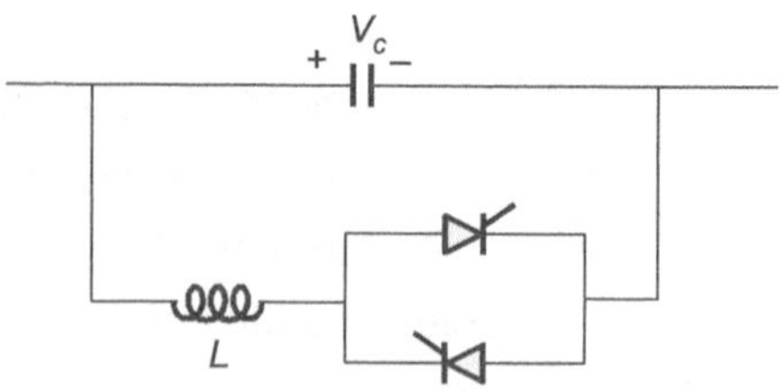

$$X_L(\alpha) = X_L \frac{\pi}{\pi - 2\alpha - \sin 2\alpha}$$

$$= 10\frac{\pi}{\pi - 4.71 + 1} = -55.31$$

$$X_T(\alpha) = \frac{X_C X_L(\alpha)}{X_L(\alpha) - X_C} = \frac{10 \times (-55.31)}{-55.31 - 10} = 8.4688\ \Omega$$

The effective impedance of TCSC is given by,

$$Z_T = jX_T = j8.4688\ \Omega$$

Degree of compensation, $\gamma = \dfrac{X_C}{X_L + X_C} = \dfrac{10}{10+10} = 0.5$

Total VAR supplied by circuit is given as,

$$Q = \frac{2V^2}{X_T} \times \frac{\gamma}{(1-\gamma)^2}(1-\cos\alpha)$$

$$= \frac{2\times(230)^2}{8.4688}\times\frac{0.5}{0.5\times0.5}\times(1-\cos 135°)$$

$$= 12492.9\times\frac{1}{0.5}\times 1.707 = 42.65 \text{ kVAR}$$

10.11 Compare point-to-point HVDC links and back-to-back HVDC links and mention their applications.

[2 marks : 2015]

Solution:

Point-to-Point:

- The links connected between two points of a single AC system (or) Two separate AC systems are commonly known as point-to-point HVDC links.
  (Preferrably with a Transmission network between them)
- In this, we can use Multiterminal links (more than '2' AC Network can be interconnected asynchronously)
  *The stability of multiterminal point to point HVDC interconnection is high.

Applications:

- Point to point (two terminal) HVDC links involving lines are bipolar but with monopolar operation used specifically under uncertainity (or) emergency situations.
- Normally designed to provide maximum independence between poles to avoid Bipolar.

Back-to-Back:

- It provides interconnection between two adjacent systems through converter station without any transmission line.
- HVDC inverter and rectifier are installed in same station in back-to-back coupling.

Applications:

- Mainly used for asynchronous ties.
- Designed for monopolar (or) bipolar operation with a different number of valve groups per pole depends on purpose of interconnection and desired reliability.
- Mainly used to control the power and stabilize the system. Connected with two different frequencies system.

10.12 (i) What is Smart Grid?
(ii) Compared to Supervisory Control And Data Acquisition (SCADA) system, what are the advantages of Phasor Measurement Unit (PMU)?
(iii) Explain operation of PMU with a neat diagram.

[4+4+4 = 12 marks : 2020]

Solution:

Smart grid:

A smart grid is an electrical grid which includes a variety of operational and energy measures including smart meters, smart appliances, renewable energy resources, and energy efficiency resources. Electronic power conditioning and control of the production and distribution of electricity are important aspects of the smart grid.

Characteristics of a Smart Grid:

- Increased use of digital information and controls technology to improve reliability, security, and efficiency of the electric grid.
- Dynamic optimization of grid operations and resources, with full cyber-security.
- Deployment and integration of distributed resources and generation, including renewable resources.
- Development and incorporation of demand response, demand-side resources, and energy- efficiency resources.

- Deployment of smart' technologies (real-time, automated, interactive technologies that optimize the physical operation of appliances and consumer devices) for metering, communications concerning grid operations and status, and distribution automation.
- Integration of smart' appliances and consumer devices.
- Deployment and integration of advanced electricity storage and peak-shaving technologies, including plug-in electric and hybrid electric vehicles, and thermal storage air conditioning.
- Provision to consumers of timely information and control options.
- Development of standards for communication and interoperability of appliances and equipment connected to the electric grid, including the infrastructure serving the grid.
- Identification and lowering of unreasonable or unnecessary barriers to adoption of smart grid technologies, practices, and services."

Phasor measurement units (PMUs) measure current and voltage by amplitude and phase at selected stations of the transmission system. The high precision time synchronization (via GPS) allows comparing measured values (synchrophasors) from different substations far apart and drawing conclusions as to the system state and dynamic events such as power swing conditions.

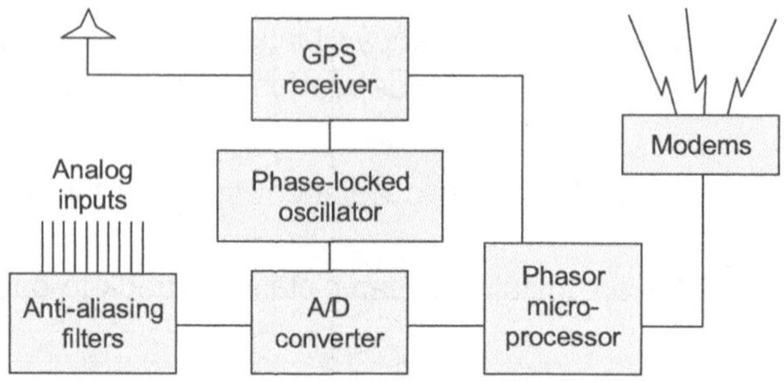

Block Diagram of PMU

Advantages of PMUs over SCADA system :

- Phasor measurement units (PMUs), produce accurate time stamped measurements of voltage and current magnitude as well as phasor angles.

  They also report the status of breakers with timestamps synchronized to those of the measurements. Because PMUs calculate synchrophasors with respect to a global angle reference, the number of critical measurements is less than when the state estimator uses SCADA measurements.
- Another advantage of using PMU measurements for state estimation, was that the angle measurements are made directly, thus reducing the errors introduced by inaccuracies in network parameters. The SCADA system measurements of voltage angles must be calculated using measurements of voltage, measurements of active power, reactive power measurements, network parameters, and a reference angle. Quality of results depends heavily on network quality parameters which are not always precise.

  Therefore, PMU measurements provides more direct and more precise than traditional SCADA measurements, because PMU measurements do not depend on network parameters.
- One of the major advantages of using synchrophasors is the ability to provide coherent data from different parts of the network. System operators and engineers require knowing the trends of voltage phase angle differences among coherent groups of generators and major interconnections to monitor the stability of the system. The phase angle difference also provides knowledge to the system operators on the available power transfer margin. We cannot obtain precise high resolution voltage phase angle differences using SCADA based measurements.
- Synchronized phasor measurements offer solutions to a number of vexing protection problems. These include the protection of series compensated lines, protection of multiterminal lines, and the inability to satisfactorily set out-of-step relays. In many situations the reliable measurement of a remote

voltage or current on the same reference as local variables has made a substantial improvement in protection functions possible. In some examples communication of such measurements from one end of a protected line to the other is all that is required while in others communication across large distances is necessary.

11. Power System Transients

11.1 **Two long overhead transmission lines *A* and *B* having surge impedances of 400 W and 420 W respectively are connected by a short underground cable *C* of surge impedance 50 ohms. A rectangular surge of magnitude 100 kV and of infinite length travels along *A* towards the cable *C*. Find out the surge voltage which is transmitted into the cable at the junction of *A* and *C* when the first reflected wave from the junction of *C* and *B* reaches the former junction.**

[15 marks : 2002]

Solution:

Let, $Z_A = 400\ \Omega$, $Z_B = 420\ \Omega$, $Z_C = 50\ \Omega$, $V_s = 100$ kV

At junction *A*, *C* refracted wave

$$V_t = V_s \times \left(\frac{2Z_C}{Z_A + Z_C}\right) = 100 \times \frac{2\times 50}{400+50} = 22.22 \text{ kV}$$

At junction *BC* reflection coefficient,

$$r_{BC} = \frac{Z_B - Z_C}{Z_B + Z_C} = \frac{420-50}{420+50} = 0.7872$$

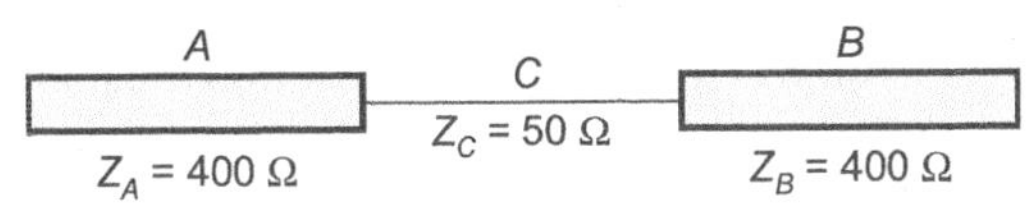

Magnitude of reflected wave at junction *B*, *C*

$$V_{r_{BC}} = V_t \times r_{BC} = 22.22 \times 0.7872 = 17.49 \text{ kV}$$

Reflection coefficient at junction *A*, *C*

$$r_{AC} = \frac{Z_A - Z_C}{Z_A + Z_C} = \frac{400-50}{400+50} = 0.777$$

Reflected wave at junction *A*, *C*

$$V_{r_{AC}} = V_{r_{BC}} \times r_{AC}$$

$$= 17.49 \times 0.777 = 13.59 \text{ kV}$$

Total surge voltage transmitted into cable

$$= V_t + V_{r_{AC}}$$

$$= 22.22 + 13.59 = 35.81 \text{ kV}$$

11.2 **A surge of 100 kV travelling in a line of natural impedance 600 ohms arrives at a junction with two lines of impedances 800 ohms and 200 ohms respectively. Find the surge voltages and currents transmitted into each branch line. Derive the equation you are using.**

[16 marks : 2007]

Solution:

A voltage wave *V* is travelling over the line with surge impedance Z_1 as shown in figure.

When it reaches the junction, it looks a change in impedance and therefore, suffers reflection and refraction.

Let V_2'', I_2'' and V_3'', I_3'' be the voltages and currents in the lines having surge impedances Z_2 and Z_3 respectively. Since Z_2 and Z_3 form a parallel path as far as the surge wave is concerned, $V_2'' = V_3'' = V''$.

Therefore, the following relations hold good:

$$V + V' = V''$$

$$I = \frac{V}{Z_1} \quad \text{and} \quad I' = -\frac{V'}{Z_1}$$

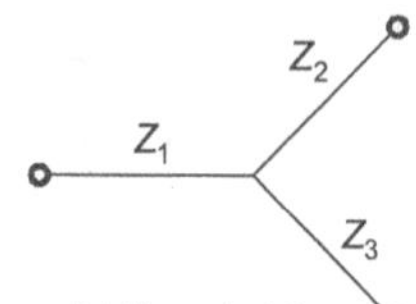

A bifurcated line

and $$I_2'' = \frac{V''}{Z_2} \quad \text{and} \quad I_3'' = \frac{V''}{Z_3}$$

and $$I + I' = I_2'' + I_3'' \qquad ...(i)$$

Substituting in equation (*i*) the values of currents,

$$\frac{V}{Z_1} - \frac{V'}{Z_1} = \frac{V''}{Z_2} + \frac{V''}{Z_3}$$

Substituting for, $$V' = V'' - V$$

$$\frac{V}{Z_1} - \frac{V'' - V}{Z_1} = \frac{V''}{Z_2} + \frac{V''}{Z_3}$$

or $$\frac{2V}{Z_1} = V''\left[\frac{1}{Z_1} + \frac{1}{Z_2} + \frac{1}{Z_3}\right]$$

$$V'' = \frac{2V/Z_1}{\frac{1}{Z_1} + \frac{1}{Z_2} + \frac{1}{Z_3}}$$

The various natural impedances are: $Z_1 = 600\ \Omega$, $Z_2 = 800\ \Omega$, $Z_3 = 200\ \Omega$. The surge magnitude is 100 kV. The surge as it reaches the joint suffers reflection and here the two lines are in parallel; therefore, the transmitted voltage will have the same magnitude and is given by

$$E'' = \frac{2E/Z_1}{\frac{1}{Z_1} + \frac{1}{Z_2} + \frac{1}{Z_3}} = \frac{2 \times 100/600}{\frac{1}{600} + \frac{1}{800} + \frac{1}{200}}$$

$$= \frac{0.333}{(1.67 + 1.25 + 5.0) \times 10^{-3}} = 42.04 \text{ kV}$$

The transmitted current in line, $$I_2 = \frac{42.04 \times 1000}{800} = 52.55 \text{ amps.}$$

The transmitted current in line, $$I_3 = \frac{42.04 \times 1000}{200} = 210.2 \text{ amps.}$$

11.3 A surge of 10 kV magnitude travels along a cable towards its junction with an overhead line. The inductance and capacitance of the cable and overhead line are respectively 0.3 mH, 0.4 μF and 1.5 mH, 0.012 μF per km. Find the voltage rise at the junction due to the surge.

[10 marks : 2009]

Solution:

In this problem the surge travels from the cable towards the overhead line and hence there will be positive voltage reflection at the junction

$$V = 10 \text{ kV}$$

The natural impedance of the cable

$$Z_1 = \sqrt{\frac{0.3 \times 10^{-3}}{0.4 \times 10^{-6}}} = 27.38$$

The natural impedance of the line, $$Z_2 = \sqrt{\frac{1.5 \times 10^{-3}}{0.012 \times 10^{-6}}} = 353.55\ \Omega$$

The voltage rise at the junction is the voltage transmitted into the overhead line as the voltage is zero before the surge reaches the junction

$$E'' = V\times\left(\frac{2Z_2}{Z_1+Z_2}\right) = 10\times\left(\frac{2\times 353.55}{27.38+353.55}\right) = 18.56 \text{ kV}$$

11.4 **A surge of 10 kV travels along a cable towards its junction with an overhead line. The surge impedances of the cable and the line are 50 Ω and 450 Ω, respectively. The surge voltage transmitted into the line is**

(a) 18.0 kV **(b) 4.0 kV**

(c) 20.0 kV **(d) 2.0 kV**

[2 marks : 2010]

Solution: (a)

$$V_s = 10 \text{ kV}$$

$$Z_c = 50\ \Omega \text{ and } Z_l = 450\ \Omega$$

$$\text{Surge voltage} = 2V_s\times\left(\frac{Z_l}{Z_c+Z_l}\right) = 2\times 10\left(\frac{450}{50+450}\right) kVp = 18 \text{ kV}$$

Hence, option (a) 18.0 kV is correct.

11.5 **(i) A surge of 100 kV is incident on a line having a surge impedance of 400 ohms. It meets a cable having a surge impedance of 40 ohms. Derive expression for the transmitted voltage and reflected voltage and compute their values.**

(ii) Explain the practical importance of this situation.

[10 marks : 2011]

Solution:

(i)

Z_1 = surge impedance of the line

Z_2 = surge impedance of the cable

v_i, i_i = incident wave pair

v_r, i_r = reflected wave pair

v_t, i_t = transmitted wave pair

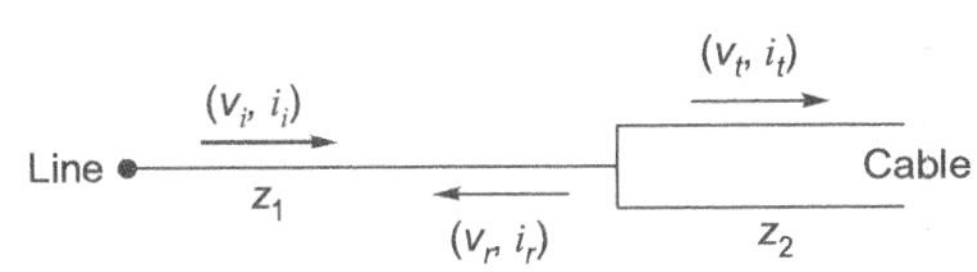

Applying the Kirchhoff's voltage and current laws at the junction

$$v_i + v_r = v_t \quad ...(i)$$

$$i_i + i_r = i_t \quad ...(ii)$$

$$i_i = \frac{v_i}{Z_1};\ i_r = -\frac{v_r}{Z_1} \text{ and } i_t = \frac{v_t}{Z_2}$$

Putting the above expressions in equation (*ii*), we get

$$\frac{v_i}{Z_1} - \frac{v_r}{Z_1} = \frac{v_t}{Z_2} \quad ...(iii)$$

From equation (*i*) and (*iii*), we get

$$v_r = \left(\frac{Z_2 - Z_1}{Z_2 + Z_1}\right)v_i \quad ...(iv)$$

and

$$v_t = \left(\frac{2Z_2}{Z_2 + Z_1}\right)v_i \quad ...(v)$$

Given: $V_i = 100$ kV, $Z_2 = 40\ \Omega$ and $Z_1 = 400\ \Omega$

$$\text{Transmitted voltage} = V_t = \left(\frac{2Z_2}{Z_2 + Z_1}\right)V_i = \left(\frac{2\times 40}{400+40}\right)\times 100 = 18.18\text{ kV}$$

$$\text{Reflected voltage} = V_r = \left(\frac{Z_2 - Z_1}{Z_2 + Z_1}\right)V_i = \left(\frac{40-400}{40+400}\right)\times 100 = -81.81\text{ kV}$$

(ii) With these values it can be seen that the voltage entering the cable will be 18.18% of the incident voltage. It is for this reason that an overhead line is terminated near a station by connecting the station equipment to the overhead line through a short length of underground cable. Besides the reduction in the magnitude of the voltage wave, the steepness is also reduced because of the capacitance of the cable. The reduction in steepness is very important because this is one of the factors for reducing the voltage distribution along the windings of the equipment.

11.6 For the below circuit find the voltage at the receiving end just before 5*T* where *T* is the time taken by the voltage wave to travel the length of the line.

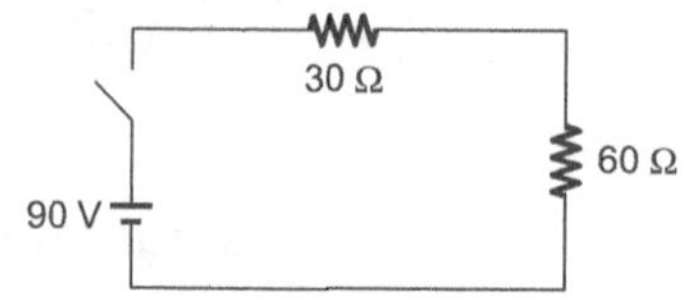

[10 marks : 2013]

Solution:

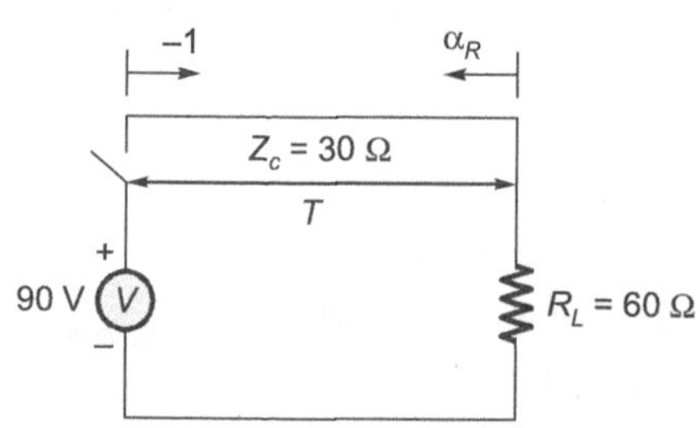

In order to keep track of the multiplicity of the successive reflection at the discontinuities in the system, Bewley has devised a time-space diagram. In the lattice diagram two axis are established, a horizontal one scaled in distance along the system and vertical one scaled in time.

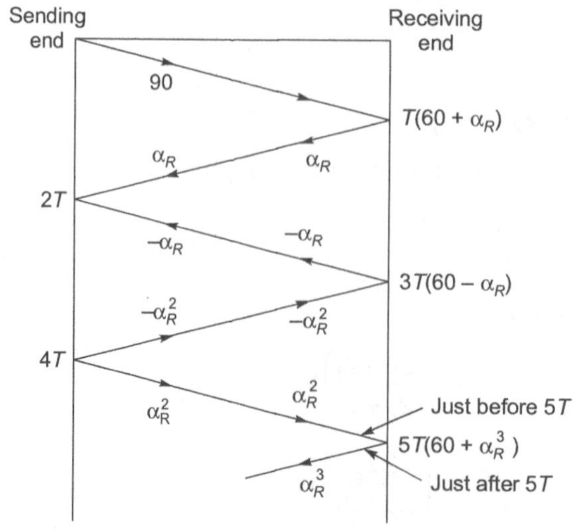

A d.c. generator of 90 V is switched ON to a line of characteristic impedance $Z_c = 30\ \Omega$, with a load resistance $R_L = 60\ \Omega$ at its receiving end. The reflection coefficient at the receiving end is

$$\alpha_R = \frac{R_L - Z_C}{R_L + Z_C} = \frac{60-30}{60+30} = 0.33$$

Voltage impressed on the line can be given by voltage divider rule,

$$V = 90 \times \left(\frac{60}{30+60}\right) = 60 \text{ V}$$

Now voltage at receiving end can be given as (just before $5T$)

$$V_R = (60+\alpha_R) - (\alpha_R + \alpha_R^2) + \alpha_R^2$$

$$V_R = 60 + \alpha_R - \alpha_R - \alpha_R^2 + \alpha_R^2 = 60 \text{ volt}$$

■■■■

8 Power Electronics and Drives

Revised Syllabus of ESE: *Semiconductor power diodes, transistors, thyristors, triacs, GTOs, MOSFETs and IGBTs - static characteristics and principles of operation, triggering circuits, phase control rectifiers, bridge converters - fully controlled and half controlled, principles of choppers and inverters, basis concepts of adjustable speed dc and ac drives, DC-DC switched mode converters, DC-AC switched mode converters, resonant converters, high frequency inductors and transformers, power supplies.*

---

1. Power Semiconductor Devices

1.1 Describe the turn-off process in a GTO with relevant voltage and current waveforms. Enumerate the advantages and disadvantages of a GTO as compared to a conventional thyristor.

[12 marks : 2001]

Solution:

Before the initiation of turn-off process, a GTO carries a steady current I_a. This figure shows a typical turn-off dynamic characteristic for a GTO. The total turn off time t_q is subdivided into three different periods; namely the storage period (t_s), the fall period (t_f) and the tail period (t_t). In other words,

$$t_q = t_s + t_f + t_t$$

Initiation of turn-off process starts as soon as negative gate current begins to flow after $t = 0$. The rate of rise of this gate current depends upon the gate circuit inductance and the gate voltage applied. During the storage period, anode current I_a and anode voltage (equal to on-state voltage drop) remain constant. Termination of the storage period is indicated by a fall in I_a and rise in V_a.

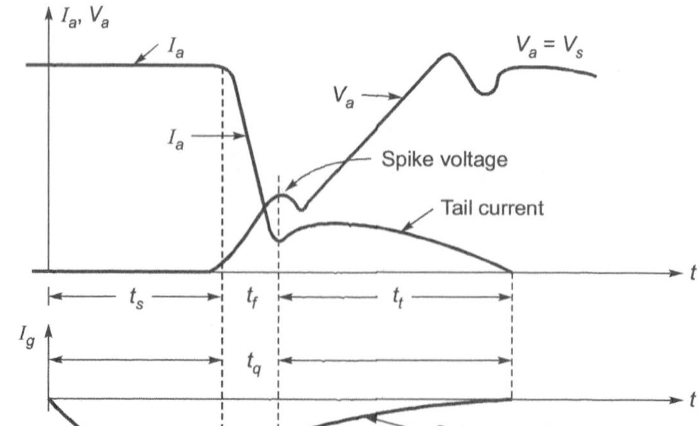

During t_s, excess charges, i.e. holes in p-base are removed by negative gate current and the centre junction comes out of saturation. In other words, during storage time t_s, the negative gate current rises to a particular value and prepares the GTO for turning-off (or commutation) by flushing out of the stored carriers. After t_s, anode current begins to fall rapidly and anode voltage starts rising. As shown in figure, the anode current falls to a certain value and then abruptly changes its rate of fall. Interval during which anode current falls rapidly is the fall time t_f, is of the order of 1 μsec. The fall period t_f is measured from the instant gate current is maximum negative to the instant anode current falls to its tail current.

At the time $t = t_s + t_f$, there is a spike in voltage due to abrupt current change. After t_f, anode current I_a and anode voltage V_a keep moving towards their turn-off values for a time t_t called tail time. After t_t, anode current reaches zero value.

A GTO has the following disadvantage as compared to a conventional thyristor:

(i) Magnitude of latching and holding currents is more in a GTO.

(ii) On state voltage drop and the associated loss is more in a GTO.

(iii) Due to the multicathode structure of GTO, triggering gate current is higher than that required for a conventional SCR.

(iv) Gate drive circuit losses are more

(v) Its reverse-voltage blocking capability is less than its forward-voltage blocking capability. But this is no disadvantage so far as inverter circuits are concerned.

Inspite of all these demerits, GTO has the following advantages over an SCR:

(i) GTO has faster switching speed.

(ii) Its surge current capability is comparable with an-SCR.

(iii) It has more *di*/*dt* rating at turn-on.

(iv) GTO circuit configuration has lower size and weight as compared to SCR circuit unit.

(v) GTO unit has higher efficiency because an increase gate-drive power loss and on-state loss is more than compensated by the elimination of forced commutation losses.

(vi) GTO unit has reduced acoustical electromagnetic noise due to elimination of commutation chokes.

1.2 What is a GTO? Discuss its advantages over a normal thyristor. Discuss the advantage of a GTO over bipolar transistor in low power applications.

[8 marks : 2003]

Solution:

GTO is pnpn device, can be turned on like an ordinary thyristor by a pulse of positive gate current, but it can be turned off easily by a negative gate pulse of appropriate amplitude.

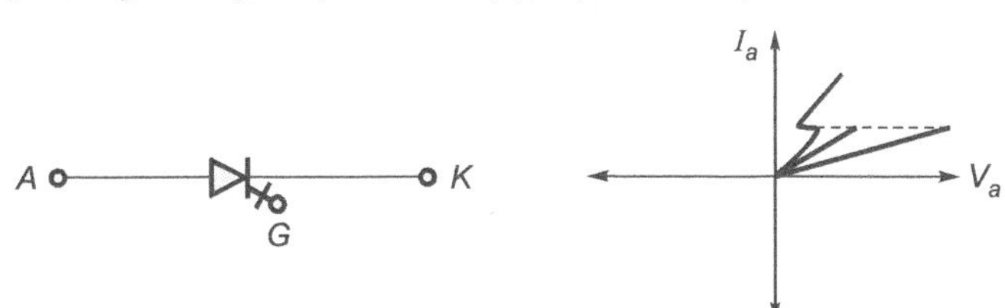

GTO

1. GTO has faster switching speed.
2. Its surge current capability is comparable with an SCR.
3. It has more di/dt rating at turn-on.
4. GTO unit has higher efficiency due to the elimination of forced commutation losses.
5. GTO has reduced acoustical and electromagnetic noise due to elimination of commutation chokes.
6. GTO circuit configuration has lower size and weight as compared to thyristor circuit unit.
   - In BJT switching, lateral current flow is the basic limiting factor in BJT performance. It causes lateral voltage drop which leads to emitter current crowding, which causes decrease in current gain. Excessive current crowding causes second breakdown and destruction of the device.

- Turning off of BJT should be done in a controlled manner of negative base current to avoid excessive stored charge which may cause long turn off time and large power dissipation. These problems are avoided in a GTO in low power applications.

1.3 **What is an Unijunction transistor? Draw a basic UJT pulse trigger circuit with typical waveforms and explain its operation.**

[8 marks : 2003]

Solution:

An UJT is made up of an n-type silicon (si) base to which p-type emitter is embedded. It has three terminals the emitter (E), base one B_1 and base two B_2 between bases B_1 and B_2, the Unijunction behave like ordinary resistance.

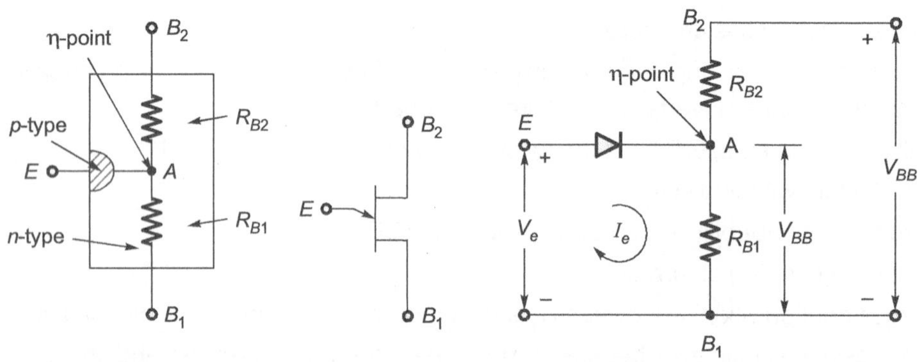

Basic structure of UJT Symbolic representation Equivalent circuit

In figure (a), when source voltage V_{BB} is applied, capacitor C begins to charge through R exponentially towards V_{BB}. During this charging, emitter circuit of UJT is an open circuit.

The capacitor voltage v_c, equal to emitter voltage v_e, is given by

$$v_C = v_e = V_{BB}(1 - e^{-t/RC})$$

The time constant of the charge circuit is τ_1 = RC.

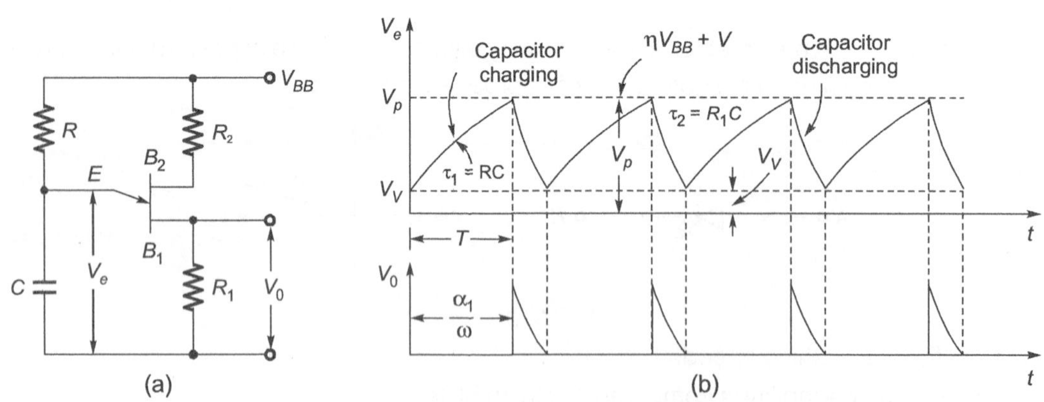

Fig. (2) UJT oscillator (a) Connection diagram and (b) Voltage waveforms

When this emitter voltage v_e (or v_c) reaches the peak-point voltage V_p (= η V_{BB} + V_D), the Unijunction between $E - B_1$ breaks down. As a result, UJT turns on and capacitor C rapidly discharge through low resistance R_1 with a time constant $\tau_2 = R_1 C$. Here τ_2 is much smaller than τ_1. When the emitter voltage decays to the valley-point voltage V_v, UJT turns off. The time T required for capacitor C to charge from initial voltage V_v to peak-point voltage V_p, through large resistance R, can be obtained as under:

$$V_p = \eta V_{BB} + V_D = V_v + V_{BB}(1 - e^{-t/RC})$$

Assuming, $V_D = V_v,\ \eta = (1 - e^{-t/RC})$

$$T = \frac{1}{f} = RC\ln\left(\frac{1}{1-\eta}\right)$$

In case T is taken as the time period of output pulse duration (neglecting small discharge time), then the value of firing angle α_1 is given by

$$\alpha_1 = \omega T = \omega RC\ln\frac{1}{1-\eta}$$

where 'ω' is the angular frequency of UJT oscillator.

1.4 If the turn-on time of a SCR is 7-micro sec., an ideal gate trigger pulse should have
(a) short rise-time and pulse width of 8 μsec.
(b) short rise-time and pulse width of 4 μsec.
(c) high rise-time with pulse width of 4 μsec.
(d) high rise-time with pulse width of 8 μsec.

[2 marks : 2004]

Solution: (a)

An ideal gate trigger should have short rise time and pulse width of should be greater than turn on time of a SCR.

1.5 Two thyristors *A* and *B* have rated gate-current of 100 mA and 2 A respectively
(a) *B* is GTO and *A* is conventional SCR.
(b) *A* is GTO and *B* is conventional SCR.
(c) Thyristor *A* may operate as transistor.
(d) None of the above

[2 marks : 2004]

Solution: (a)

Due to multi cathode structure of GTO, triggering gate current is higher than that required for a conventional SCR.

1.6 Draw the symbols and characteristics of the following devices:
(i) Diode, (ii) Thyristor,
(iii) GTO, (iv) Triac and
(v) IGBT

[10 marks : 2005]

Solution:

Device	Symbol	Characteristics
(i) Diode	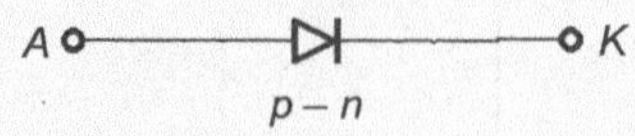	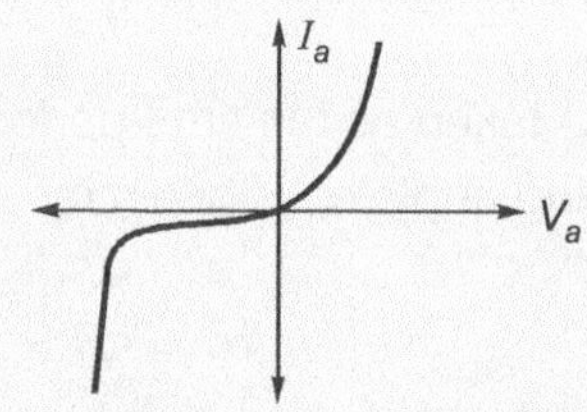
(ii) Thyristor	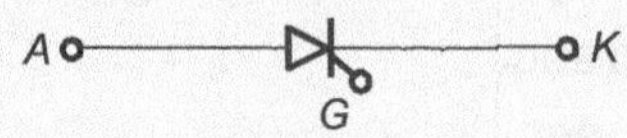	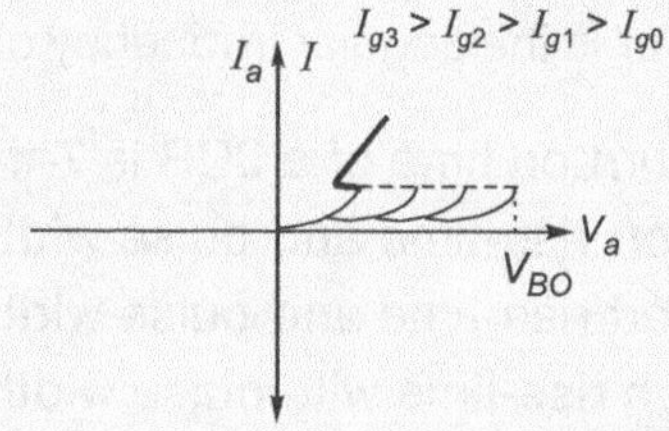
(iii) GTO	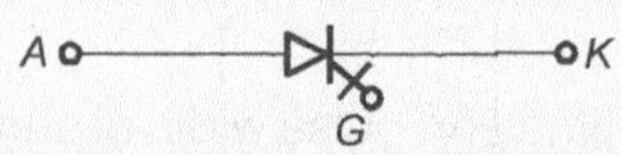	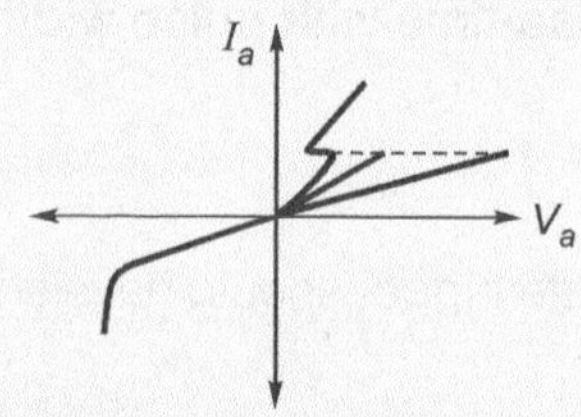
(iv) Triac	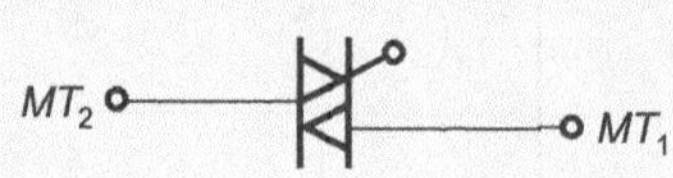	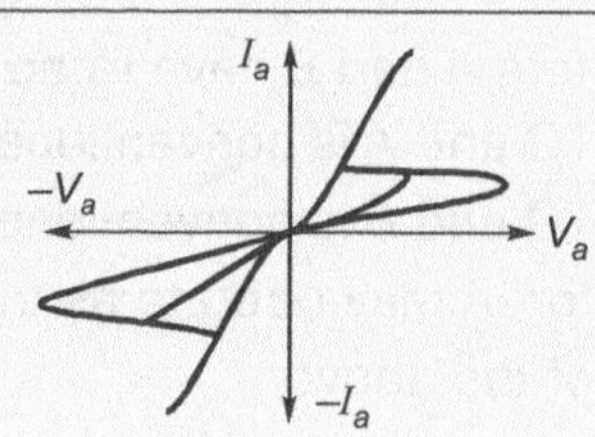
(v) IGBT	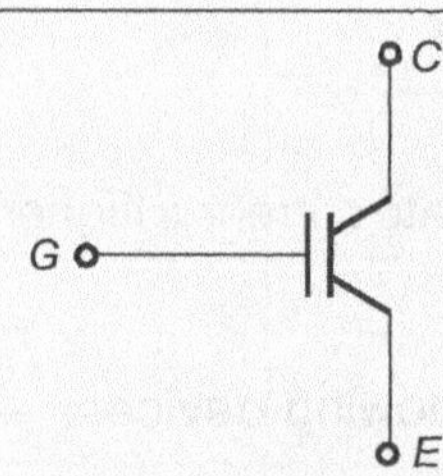	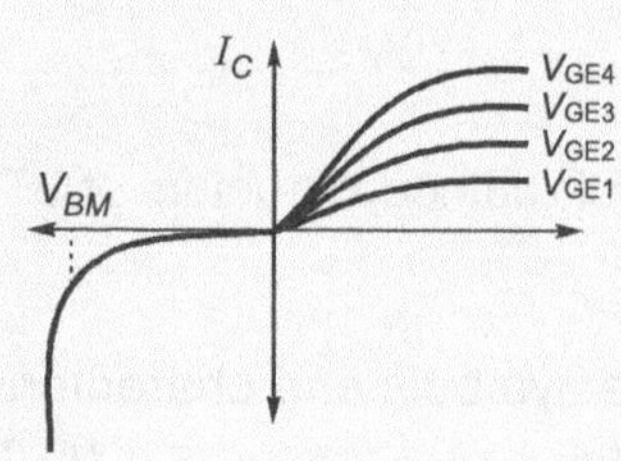

1.7 In ac applications, a different of harmonics is needed. The total harmonic ratio (THR) is given by:

(a) $\sqrt{\dfrac{f_{rms}^2 - f_{1rms}^2}{f_{rms}}}$ (b) $\sqrt{\dfrac{f_{rms}^2 - f_{1rms}^2}{f_{1\,rms}^2}}$

(c) $\sqrt{\dfrac{f_{1\,rms}^2 - f_{rms}}{f_{rms}}}$ (d) $\sqrt{\dfrac{f_{1rms}^2 - f_{rms}}{f_{1\,rms}}}$

[2 marks : 2006]

Solution: (b)

$$\text{Total harmonic distortion} = \sqrt{\left(\frac{f_{(rms)\,\text{harmonic}}}{f_{1\,(rms)}}\right)^2 - 1}$$

1.8 Point out the differences between latching current and hold current for the thyristor. What do you understand by string efficiency related to thyristors? For a thyristor, maximum junction temperature is 125° C. The thermal resistances for thyristor-sink combination are $\theta_{jc} = 0.16$ and $\theta_{cs} = 0.08°$ C/W. For a heat sink temperature of 70° C compute the total average power loss in the thyristor sink combination. In case the heat sink is brought down to 60° C by forced cooling, find the percentage increase in the device rating.

[14 marks : 2006]

Solution:

Latching current: The minimum value of anode current which the thyristor must attain during turn-on process to maintain conduction even after the removal of gate pulse is called latching current.

(i) **Holding current:** It is defined as the minimum value of anode current below which it must fall for turning off the thyristor.

In general latching current > holding current.

String efficiency is a term that is used for measuring the degree of utilization of SCR in a string.

(ii) String efficiency = $\dfrac{\text{Actual voltage (series) or current (parallel) rating of the whole string}}{\text{No. of SCR's in the string} \times \text{individual voltage or current rating of one SCR}}$

Series operation of SCR's:

$$\eta_s = \frac{V_1 + V_2}{2V_1} \qquad \boxed{V_1 > V_2}$$

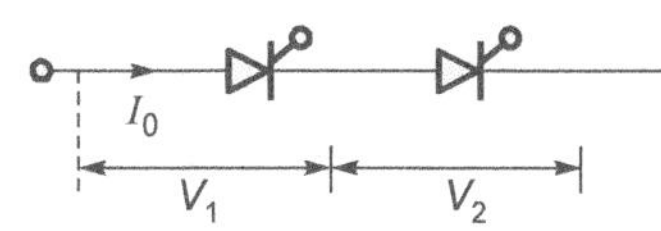

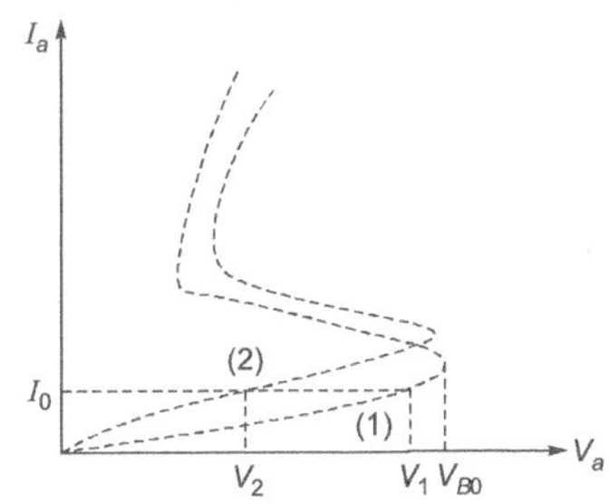

Parallel Operation of SCR's:

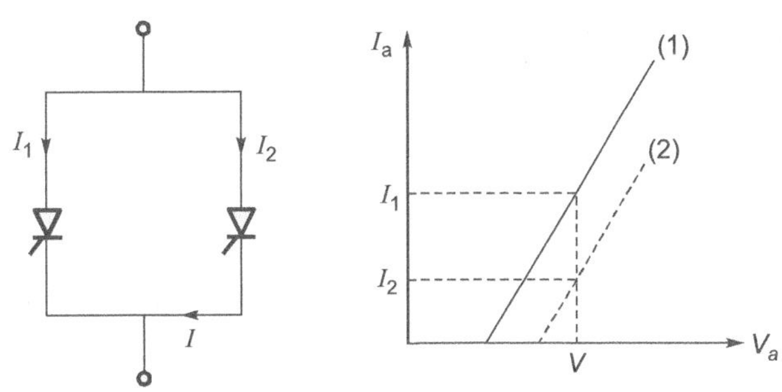

$$\text{String efficiency} = \frac{I_1 + I_2}{2I_1} \qquad \boxed{I_1 > I_2}$$

(iii) From the equivalent circuit,

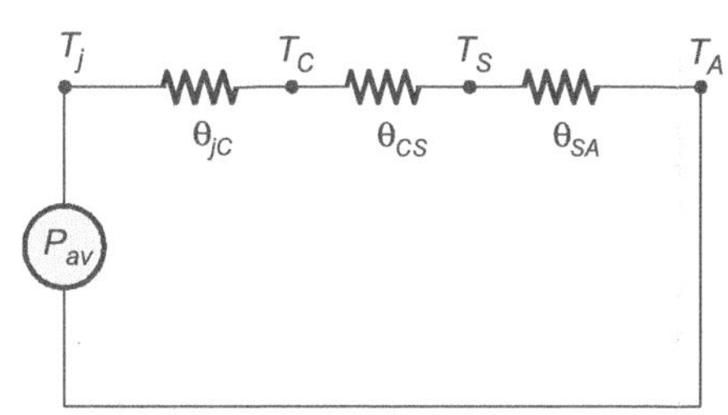

$$T_j = T_s + P_{av}(\theta_{jC} + \theta_{CS})$$

$$\therefore \qquad P_{av1} = \frac{125 - 70}{0.16 + 0.08} = 229.17 \text{ W}$$

Thus total power loss in the thyristor-sink combination is 229.17 W with improved cooling.

$$P_{av2} = \frac{125-60}{0.24} = 270.83 \text{ W}$$

Thyristor rating is proportional to the square root of average power loss.

$$\text{\% increase in thyristor rating} = \frac{\sqrt{270.83}-\sqrt{229.17}}{\sqrt{229.17}} \times 100 = 8.71$$

1.9 **Compare GTO thyristor with conventional thyristor and give merits and demerits. Why is a GTO thyristor preferred over SCR in chopper and inverter circuits?**

[4 marks : 2008]

Solution:

Disadvantage of GTO compared to conventional thyristor:

1. Magnitude of latching and holding currents is more in a GTO.
2. On state voltage drop and the associated loss is more in a GTO.
3. Due to multi cathode structure of GTO, Gate current is higher.
4. GTO has its reverse blocking capability less than its forward voltage blocking capability.
5. Gate drive circuit losses are more.

Advantage of GTO over conventional thyristor:

1. GTO has faster switching speed.
2. It's surge current capability is comparable with an SCR.
3. It has more di/dt rating at turn-on.
4. It's circuit configuration has lower size and weight.
5. It has higher efficiency due to the elimination of forced commutation losses.
6. GTO unit has reduced electromagnetic noise due to elimination of commutation chokes.
   Due to its faster switching speed and its elimination of forced commutation losses, mainly we use it in inverter and chopper circuits.

1.10 **As a consequence of low internal generation in a GTO, it has**

(a) **an increased latching current value**
(b) **an increased holding and latching currents**
(c) **both increased holding and latching currents**
(d) **increased holding current and decreased latching current**

[2 marks : 2009]

Solution: (b)

As a consequences of internal generation in a GTO it has an increased holding and latching current.

1.11 **In figure, the source voltage is 100 V and the load resistance is 10 ohm. The SCR can withstand a *dV/dt* value of 50 V/ms. If the snubber discharge current must be limited to 2 A, find the value of the snubber resistor and capacitor.**

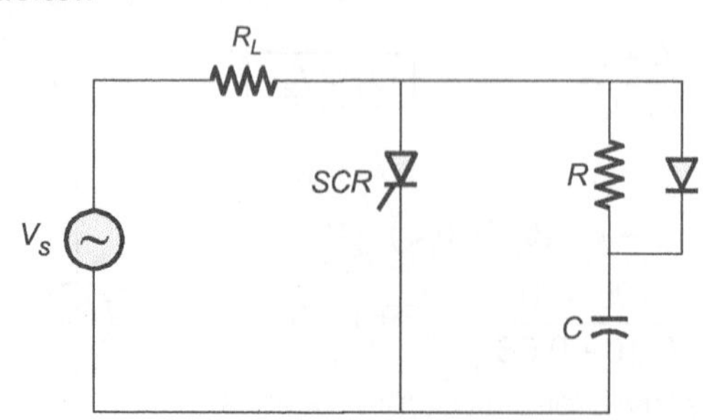

[2 marks : 2011]

Solution:

Capacitor C will charge upto maximum voltage of the ac source through load resistor R_L and discharge through resistor R.

$$\text{Discharge current} = I_d = \frac{V_m}{R} = \frac{\sqrt{2}V_s}{R}$$

$$I_d = 2\text{ A}$$

$$R = \frac{\sqrt{2}V_s}{I_d} = \frac{\sqrt{2}\times 100}{2} = 70.71\,\Omega$$

$$\left(\frac{dV}{dt}\right)_{max} = \frac{0.632\,V_m}{R_L C}$$

$$\Rightarrow \quad C = \frac{0.632\times\sqrt{2}\times 100}{10\times 50} = 0.178\,\mu\text{F}$$

1.12 Explain the switching characteristics of power MOSFET. [5 marks : 2011]

Solution:

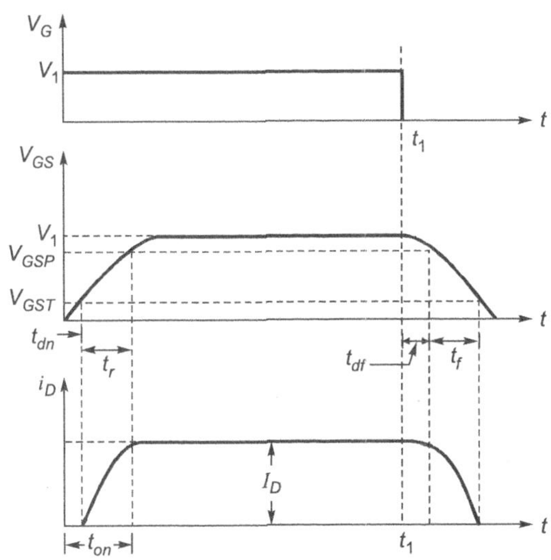

- The switching characteristics of a power MOSFET are influenced to a large extent by the internal capacitance of the device and the internal impedance of the gate drive circuit. At turn-on, there is an initial delay t_{dn} during which input capacitance charges to gate threshold voltage V_{GST}. Here t_{dn} is called turn-on delay time.
- There is further delay t_r, called rise time, during which gate voltage rises to V_{GSP}, a voltage sufficient to drive the MOSFET into on state. During t_r, drain current rises from zero to full-on current I_D. Thus, the total turn on time is $t_{on} = t_{dn} + t_r$. The turn-on time can be reduced by using low-impedance gate-drive source.
- As MOSFET is a majority carrier device, turn-off proves is initiated soon after removal of gate voltage at time t_1. Time turn-off delay time, t_{df}, is the time during which input capacitance discharges from overdrive gate voltage V_1 to V_{GSP}. The full time, t_f, is the time during which, input capacitance discharges from V_{GSP} to threshold voltage. During t_f, drain current falls from I_D to zero. So when $V_{GS} \le V_{GST}$, PMOSFET turn-off is complete.

1.13 Determine the diffusion capacitance due to holes in a Ge diode when the forward biased current is I = 26 mA. Given that mean life time of holes, τ = 20 μ sec at T = 300°K.

[4 marks : 2011]

Solution:

Given that, $I_f = 26\text{ mA} = 26 \times 10^{-3}\text{ A}$

Mean life time of holes $\tau = 20\ \mu\text{sec} = 20 \times 10^{-6}\text{ sec}$

$T = 300°\text{ K}$

We know that C_D(diffusion capacitance) = $\tau.g$

where, τ — is mean carrier life time

g — dynamic conduction

and equal to $$g = \frac{I_f}{\eta V_T}$$

where η utility factor and for G_e diode $\eta = 1$

$$V_T = 26\text{ mV at }300°\text{ K}$$
$$V_T = 26 \times 10^{-3}\text{ V}$$

$$\therefore \quad C_D = \frac{\tau.I_f}{\eta V_T}$$

Putting the corresponding value we get

$$C_D = \frac{20\times10^{-6}\times26\times10^{-3}}{1\times26\times10^{-3}} = 20 \times 10^{-6}\text{ F} = 20\ \mu\text{F}$$

1.14 Give one example for each of the following:

1. **Uncontrolled turn-on and off.**
2. **Controlled turn-on and uncontrolled turn-off.**
3. **Controlled turn-on and off.**
4. **Continuous gate signal requirement.**
5. **Pulse gate requirement.**
6. **Unipolar voltage capability.**
7. **Bidirectional current capability.**
8. **Unidirectional current capability.** **[8 marks : 2012]**

Solution:

1. Uncontrolled turn-on and off — (Power diode)
2. Controlled turn-on and uncontrolled turn off — (SCR)
3. Controlled turn-on and off — (IGTB)
4. Continuous gate signal requirement — (BJT)
5. Pulse gate requirement — (GTO)
6. Unipolar voltage capability — (MOSFET)
7. Bidirectional current capability — (TRIAC)
8. Unidirectional current capability — (GTO)

SCR — Silicon controlled rectifier

IGBT — Insulated gate bipolar transistor

GTO — Gate turn-off thyristor

1.15 Explain in detail different power losses in semiconductor power devices. **[16 marks : 2012]**

Solution:

The power-generated in the junction region of a thyristor in a normal operation consists of the following components of dissipation:

1. Forward-conduction
2. Turn-off or commutation
3. Turn-on switching
4. Forward and Reverse blocking
5. Gate pulse triggering

1. **Forward Conduction Loss:** The average anode current multiplied by the forward voltage drop across the SCR is the average power dissipated in the thyristor. ON state conduction losses are the major source of junction heating for normal duty cycle and power-frequencies. figure shown below illustrates the variation of the ON state average conduction loss in watts with the average current in amperes for various conduction angles for operation on from 50 Hz to 400 Hz. This type of information is generally supplied by the manufacturer. The curve marked d.c. is applicable for continuous direct-current These curves are based on the current waveform which is the remainder of the half-sine wave which results when delayed angle triggering is used in a single phase resistive load circuit. These power curves are integrated product of the instantaneous anode current and ON state voltage drop. This integration can be performed graphically or analytically for conduction angles other than those listed, using the ON state voltage-current characteristic curves for the specific device. In the line commutated converters and a.c. regulator circuits, the forward conduction loss is the major source of junction heating.

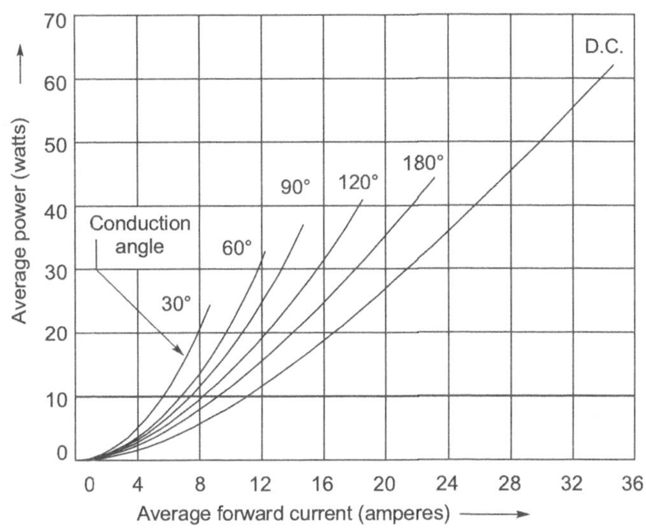

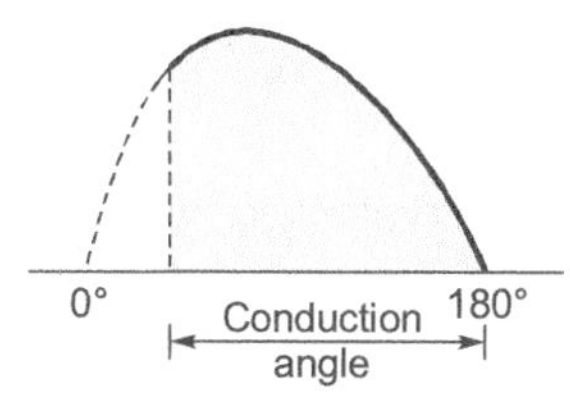

Average forward power dissipation for sinusoidal current waveform

2. **Turn-on Losses:** Since the switching process takes a finite time, there is a relatively high voltage across the thyristor while a current flows. Therefore, this loss is rather higher than the turn-off loss. For example, by the time the current has reached 90 per cent of its final value, there may still be 10 percent of the supply voltage across the device. Accordingly, appreciable power may be dissipated during this turn-on interval. Above 400 Hz switching, additional circuitry is used to reduce the switching losses or else some derating of the normal forward current is made to allow for the extra dissipation.
3. **Turn-off Losses:** The turn-off power losses arises during the time of decay of reverse current, according to the product of the instantaneous values of reverse current and reverse voltage, may reach high peak values up to several kilowatts. It is possible during rapid turn-off for the reverse current to rise to a value comparable to the forward current. When the thyristor impedance starts to increase, dissipation occurs as the current falls and the reverse voltage builds up. To limit the rate of change of current at turn-off and hence the energy to be dissipated, circuit inductance is used. This also limits the rate of rise of forward current which is an advantage but the inductance can give rise to high reverse voltage transients during turn-off. In high frequency inverters, where the thyristors arc switched ON and OFF several times in each supply cycle, the turn-on and turn-off losses may also have to be taken into consideration while selecting the device ratings since the switching loss may constitute a significant portion of the total loss.
4. **Forward and Reverse Blocking Losses:** As mentioned in the previous section, a thyristor has different regions of operation. In the forward blocking region, anode is made positive with respect to cathode and the anode current is the small forward leakage current Therefore, the forward blocking power loss is the

integration of product of the forward blocking voltage and forward leakage current. Similarly, reverse power loss occurs in reverse blocking region. The forward power loss is generally small compared to the conduction-loss.

5. **Gate Power Loss:** The gate power loss is the mean power loss due to gate current between the gate and main terminals. Gate losses are negligible for pulse types of triggering signals. Losses may become more significant for gate signals with a high duty cycle.

1.16 **Explain the requirements for an SCR to be triggered by a gate pulse.** [4 marks : 2012]

Solution:

Requirements for an SCR to be triggered by a gate pulse.

- SCR should be forward bias mode.
- A positive gate voltage between gate and cathode.
- The gate pulse width should be chosen to ensure that anode current rises above the latching current.

1.17 **A three phase diode rectifier connected to 415 V line to line source and feed a resistive load of 25 Ω. Assume drawl of balanced quasi square waveform currents in the three phases, the distortion factor given to be 3/π. Compute power drawn at fundamental frequency from mains.**

[4 marks : 2013]

Solution:

Given, $V_{LL} = 415\text{ V}, \quad R = 25\ \Omega$

For given distortion factor 3/π, power drawn at fundamental frequency from main is given by

$$P = \frac{2V_m I_d}{\pi}\cos\alpha$$

Since, it is a diode rectifier so $\alpha = 0$

$$\Rightarrow \quad P = \frac{2V_m I_d}{\pi}$$

where $$V_m = \sqrt{\frac{2}{3}}V_{LL} = \sqrt{\frac{2}{3}}\times 415 = 338.85\text{ V}$$

and $$I_d = \frac{3\sqrt{3}}{\pi R}\cdot V_m = \frac{3\sqrt{3}}{\pi\times 25}\times 338.85 = 22.418$$

$$P = \frac{2\times 338.85\times 22.418}{\pi} = 4836.00\text{ Watt}$$

1.18 **A thyristor string is formed by series and parallel connection of thyristors. The voltage and current ratings of the string are 11 kV, 4 kA respectively. The thyristor to be employed has voltage and current ratings of 1.7 kV, 1 kA. The string efficiency is 90% for both series and parallel combinations. If the maximum blocking current is 15 mA and maximum charge storage (Q_{max}) is 24 micro Coulombs (μC), calculate the value of resistance and capacitance of equalizer circuit.** [4 marks : 2013]

Solution:

$$\text{Number of series branches} = \frac{\text{Whole string rating}}{n\times\text{rating of a SCR}} = \frac{11\text{kV}}{0.9\times 1.7\text{kV}} = 7.19$$

So, 7 SCRs are not sufficient ⇒ 8 SCRs are required.

$$R = \frac{nV_b - V_m}{(n-1)I} = \frac{8\times 1.7 - 11}{7\times 15} = 24.76\text{ k}\Omega$$

$$C = \frac{(n-1)\,Q_{max}}{nV_b - V_m} = \frac{(7)\,(24\times 10^{-6})}{8\times 1.7 - 11} = 64.6\text{ nF}$$

1.19 The reverse recovery time of a diode is t_{rr} = 6 ms, and the rate of fall of the diode current di/dt = 10 A/ms. If the softness factor SF = 0.5.

(i) Find the storage charge Q_{RR},

(ii) Find the peak reverse current I_{RR}, and

(iii) Draw the labelled reverse recovery characteristics. [12 marks : 2019]

Solution:

(i)

$$SF = \frac{t_b}{t_a} = 0.5 = \frac{1}{2}$$

$$t_a = 2t_b$$

$$t_{rr} = t_a + t_b = 6$$

$$3t_b = 6$$

$$t_b = 2\ \mu s;\quad t_a = 4\ \mu s$$

$$\frac{di}{dt} = \frac{I_{RM}}{t_a}$$

$$I_{RM} = 4 \times 10 = 40\ A$$

$$Q_{RR} = \frac{1}{2} \times I_{RM} \times t_{rr} = \frac{1}{2} \times 40 \times 6 = 120\ \mu C$$

(ii)

$$\frac{di}{dt} = \frac{I_{RM}}{t_a}$$

$$I_{RM} = 4 \times 10 = 40\ A$$

(iii)

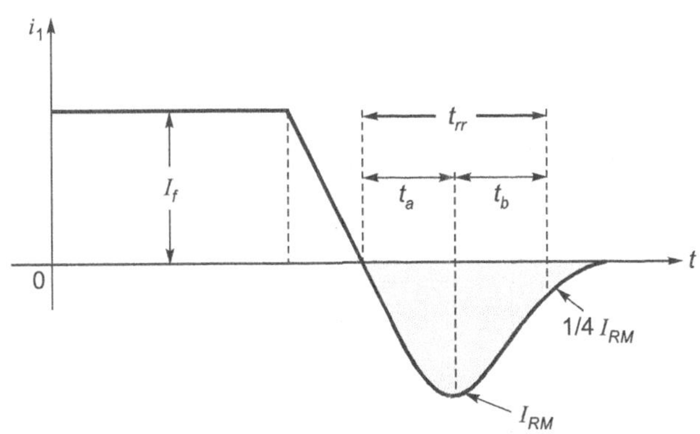

1.20 A thyristor is having the I-V characteristic as given in the figure below. It is used in a half wave rectifier circuit with resistive load operating at α = 30° and carrying a peak load current of 100 A. Determine the average conduction loss in the thyristor.

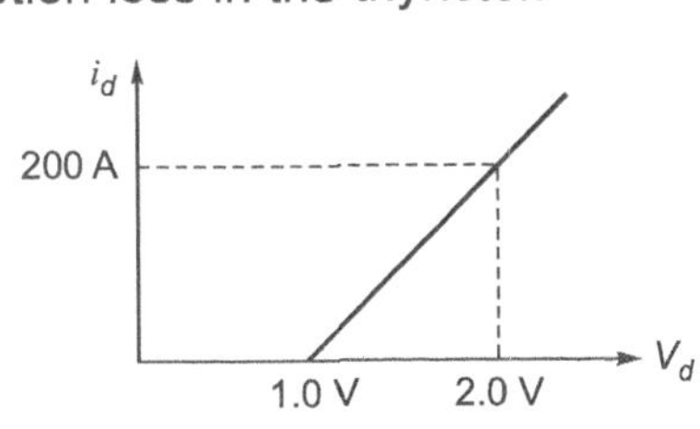

[12 marks : 2020]

Solution:

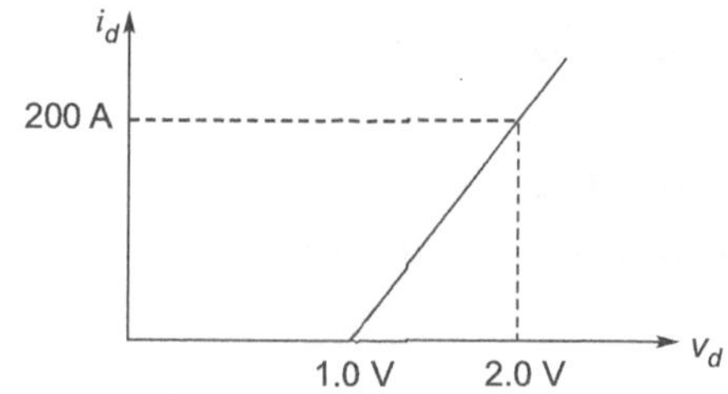

Equivalent conduction circuit for thyristor is

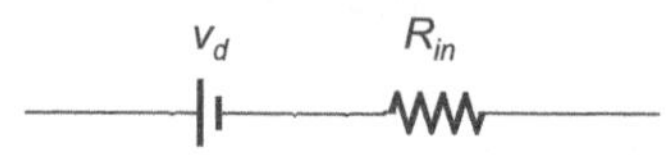

Now $$R_{in} = \frac{2-1}{200} = \frac{1}{200}\Omega = 5\text{ m}\Omega$$

$$V_f = 1 \text{ volt}$$

Now, $$I_{peak} = 100 \text{ A}, \alpha = 30°$$

For half wave rectifier and resistive load

$$I_{dc} = \frac{I_{peak}}{2\pi}(1+\cos\alpha) = 29.698 \text{ A}$$

$$I_{rms} = \frac{I_{peak}}{2\sqrt{\pi}}\left[(\pi-\alpha)+\frac{1}{2}\sin 2\alpha\right]^{\frac{1}{2}}$$

$$= \frac{100}{2\sqrt{\pi}}\left[\left(\pi-\frac{\pi}{6}\right)+\frac{1}{2}\sin 60°\right]^{\frac{1}{2}} = 49.273 \text{ A}$$

$$\text{Average power loss} = I_{dc} \times V_f + I^2_{rms}R_{in}$$

$$= 29.698\times 1+\frac{(49.273)^2}{200}$$

$$= 41.8371 \text{ W}$$

1.21 In the figure below, the transisotr Q is operating at 10 kHz and 40% duty ratio. If the transistor has on-state voltage drop of 1 V and $t_{on} = t_{off} = 5$ μs, find its total losses during the operation.
(Assume linear rise and fall characteristics of the voltage and currents in the device during switching).

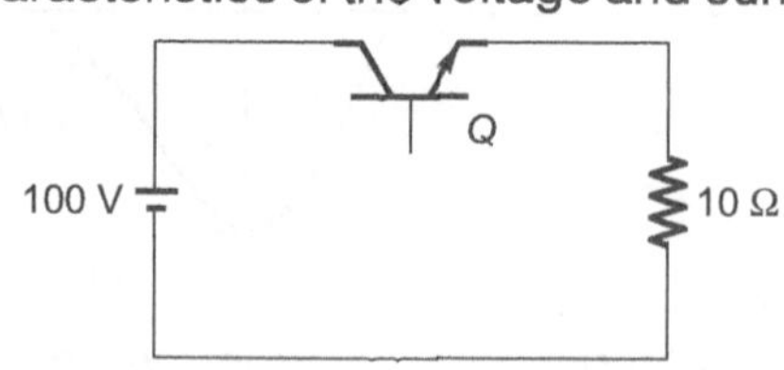

[12 marks : 2022]

Solution:

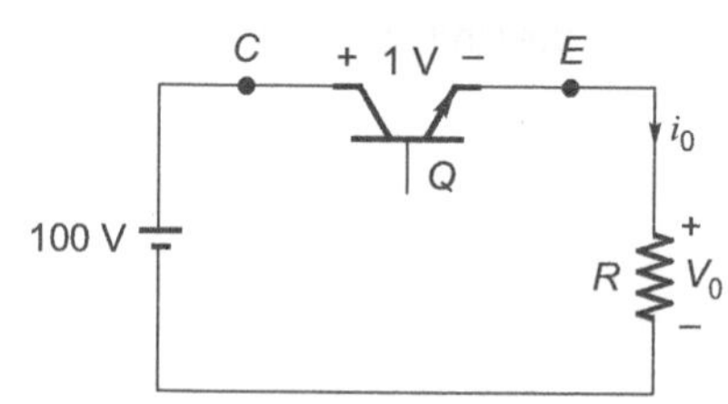

$$t_{ON} = t_{OFF} = 5 \text{ μsec}$$

BJT → ON (Ideal), $$i_o = \frac{V_o}{R} = \frac{V_s}{R} = \frac{100}{10} = 10 \text{ A}$$

Considering V-drop : $$i_o = \frac{V_s - V_{drop}}{R}$$

$$i_o = \frac{100-1}{10}$$

$$= \frac{99}{10}$$

$$i_o = 9.9 \text{ A}$$

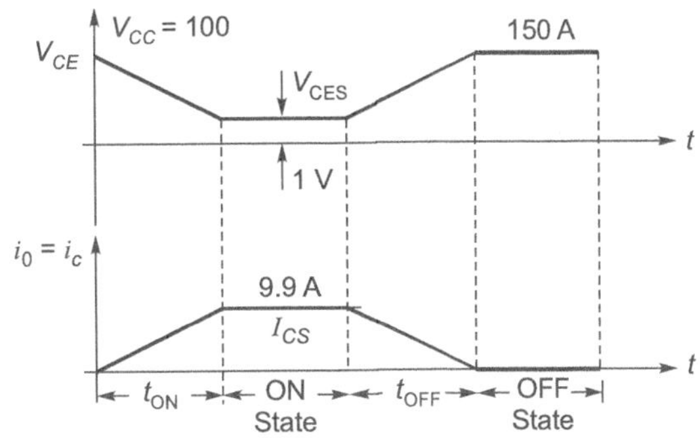

t_{ON} **process :**

$$i_C = \frac{I_{CS}}{t_{ON}} \cdot t$$

$$V_{CE} = -\left(\frac{V_{CC} - V_{CES}}{t_{ON}}\right)t + V_{CC}$$

Average power loss during t_{ON} process

$$= \frac{1}{T}\int_0^{t_{ON}} V_{CE} \cdot i_C \cdot dt$$

$$= \frac{1}{T}\int_0^{t_{ON}} \left[-\left(\frac{V_{CC} - V_{CES}}{t_{ON}}\right)t + V_{CC}\right] \cdot \left(\frac{I_{CS}}{t_{ON}} \cdot t\right) dt$$

$$- f \cdot I_{CS} \cdot t_{ON}\left[\frac{V_{CC}}{2} - \frac{V_{CC} - V_{CES}}{3}\right]$$

$$= 10 \times 10^3 \times 9.9 \times 5 \times 10^{-6}\left[\frac{100}{2} - \frac{100 - 1}{3}\right]$$

$$= 8.415 \text{ W}$$

t_{OFF} **process :**

Average power loss during t_{OFF} process

$$= \frac{1}{T}\int_0^{t_{OFF}} V_{CE} \cdot i_C \cdot dt$$

$$= \frac{1}{T}\int_0^{t_{OFF}} \left[\left(\frac{V_{CC} - V_{CES}}{t_{OFF}}\right) \cdot t + V_{CES}\right] \cdot \left[\frac{-I_{CS}}{t_{OFF}} \cdot t + I_{CS}\right] dt$$

$$\simeq f \cdot t_{OFF} \cdot \frac{I_{CS}}{6}(V_{CC} - V_{CES})$$

$$= 10 \times 10^3 \times 5 \times 10^{-6} \times \frac{9.9}{6}(100 - 1)$$

$$= 8.1675 \text{ W}$$

On State :

$$V_{CE} = 1\text{ V}, i_C = 9.9\text{ A}$$

Duty ratio :

$$\alpha = \frac{T_{ON}}{T}$$

$$\alpha = T_{ON}.f$$

$$\therefore \quad T_{ON} = \frac{\alpha}{f} = \frac{0.4}{10.10^3}$$

$$T_{ON} = 40\ \mu s$$

∴ Average power loss during ON state

P_{Avg} (On state) :

$$P_{Avg}\text{(On State)} = \frac{1}{T}\int_0^{T_{ON}} V_{CE}\cdot i_C \cdot dt$$

$$= f\int_0^{T_{ON}} 1\times 9.9\times dt$$

$$= f.T_{ON}.9.9$$

$$= 10\times 10^3 \times 40\times 10^{-6}\times 9.9$$

$$= 3.96\text{ W}$$

$$P_{Avg}\text{(OFF State)} = \frac{1}{T}\int_0^{T_{OFF}} V_{CE}\cdot i_C dt$$

$$= 0$$

∴ Total average power loss

$$= P_{Avg}(t_{ON\ process}) + P_{Avg}\text{(ON state)} + P_{Avg}(t_{OFF\ process}) + P_{Avg}\text{(OFF state)}$$

$$= 8.415\text{ W} + 3.96\text{ W} + 8.1675 + 0$$

$$= 20.54\text{ W}$$

1.22 For the figure shown below, the transistor 'Q' is excited by a pulse of duration 't_1' with a periodicity of $\frac{1}{T}$.

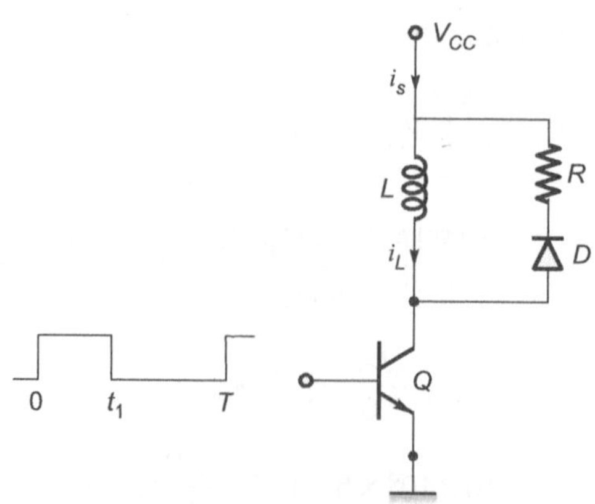

(i) Draw the current waveforms of 'i_s' and 'i_L'.

(ii) Expression for absorbed average power by resistor 'R' in the circuit.

Assume $\frac{L}{R}$ ratio to be too small in comparison to 'T'.

(iii) Expression for $i_L(t)$, the current through inductor 'L'.

[20 marks : 2023]

Solution:

Given circuit is :

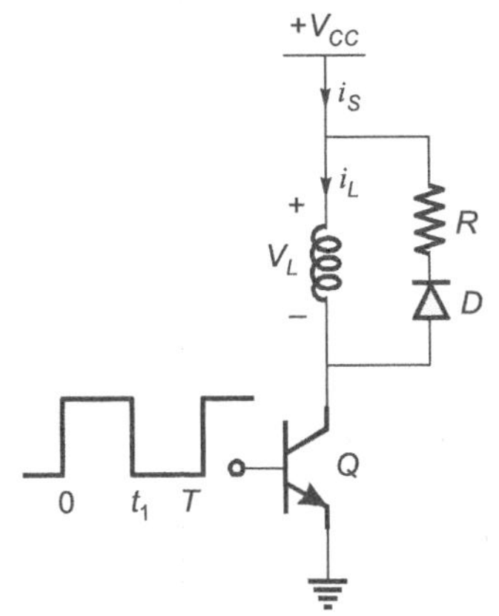

(I) $0 \le t \le t_1$:

$Q \rightarrow$ ON :

$$\therefore \quad V_L = V_{CC}$$

$$L \cdot \frac{di_L}{dt} = V_{CC}$$

$$\int di_L = \frac{V_{CC}}{L} \int dt$$

$$i_L = \frac{V_{CC}}{L} t + K$$

At $t = 0$, $\quad i_L = 0 \quad \therefore K = 0$

(i) $\quad i_S = i_L = \frac{V_{CC}}{L} \cdot t$

$$I_{mx} = \frac{V_{CC}}{L} \cdot t_1$$

(II) $t_1 \le t \le T$: $[0 \le t' \le (T - t_1)]$

$Q \rightarrow$ OFF :

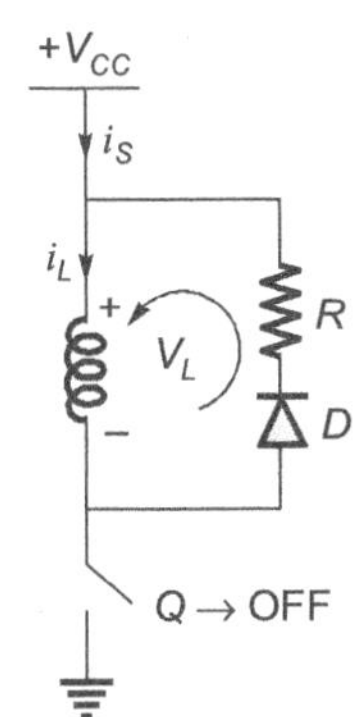

$$\because \quad i_s = 0, \ \tau = \frac{L}{R}$$

$$i_L = K_i e^{-t'/\tau}$$

(i) Required current expression is,

$$i_L = I_{mx} \cdot e^{-\frac{t'}{\tau}} = \frac{V_{CC}}{L} \cdot t_1 e^{\frac{-t'}{\tau}}$$

$$V_L = L \cdot \frac{di_L}{dt} = L \cdot \frac{d}{dt}\left(I_{mx} \cdot e^{-\frac{t'}{\tau}}\right)$$

$$V_L = L \cdot I_{mx} - \frac{1}{\tau} e^{\frac{-t'}{\tau}}$$

$$V_L = \frac{-LI_{mx}}{\tau} \cdot e^{\frac{-t'}{\tau}}$$

Required waveform of i_s and i_L :

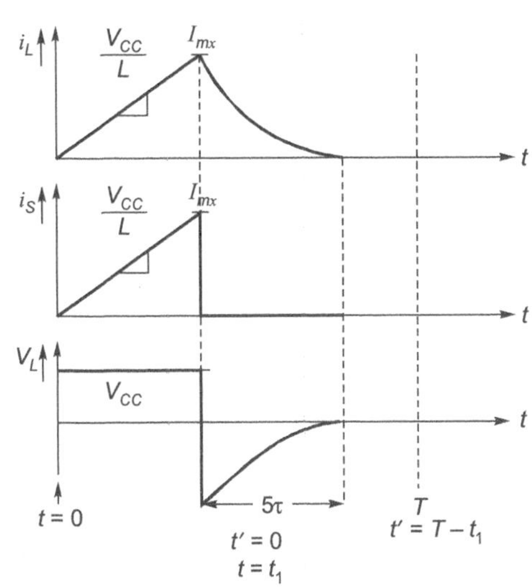

At $t = t_1$, energy stored in inductance

$$E = \frac{1}{2} L I_{mx}^2$$

$\therefore$ During the interval : $t_1 \le t \le T; \quad 0 \le t' \le (T - t_1)$

$\frac{1}{2} L I_m^2 \Rightarrow$ Energy dissipated in resistor

$$\therefore \quad P_{avg} = \frac{1}{T} \times \text{Energy dissipated in resistor}$$

$$= \frac{1}{T} \times \frac{1}{2} L I_{mx}^2$$

$$P_{avg} = \frac{1}{T} \cdot \frac{1}{2} \cdot L \left(\frac{V_{CC}}{L} t_1 \right)^2$$

(ii) Hence, absorbed power in resistor R is

$$P_{avg} = \frac{V_{CC}^2 t_1^2}{2T \cdot L}$$

2. Diode Rectifiers

2.1 In a full wave rectifier circuit with centre-tap transformer, independently of the filter used, the peak inverse voltage across each diode is equal to

(i) V_m (ii) $2V_m$

(iii) $\frac{V_m}{2}$ (iv) $\frac{V_m}{\sqrt{2}}$

where V_m is the maximum transformer voltage measured from the midpoint (centre-tap) to either end.

[2 marks : 2011]

Solution:

In case of centre-tap transformer the peak inverse voltage across each diode = 2 V_m.

So (ii) is correct option.

2.2 A single-phase uncontrolled diode bridge rectifier is used to charge a battery of V_B volts. A small inductance L is connected in series with the battery to limit the charging current. The source voltage is V_s of frequency ω. Draw the output voltage, load current and inductor voltage waveforms. Derive the expression for charging current.

[10 marks : 2016]

Solution:

$\theta_1 \le \omega t \le \beta$

KVL : $D_1 D_2 \rightarrow$ ON

$$-V_S + V_L + V_B = 0$$

$$V_L = V_S - V_B$$

$$V_L = V_m \cdot \sin \omega t - V_B$$

$$L\frac{di_L}{dt} = V_m \sin\omega t - V_B$$

$$\int di_L = \frac{1}{L}\int [V_m \sin\omega t - V_B].dt$$

$$i_L = \frac{-V_m}{\omega L}\cos\omega t - \frac{V_B \cdot t}{L} + K$$

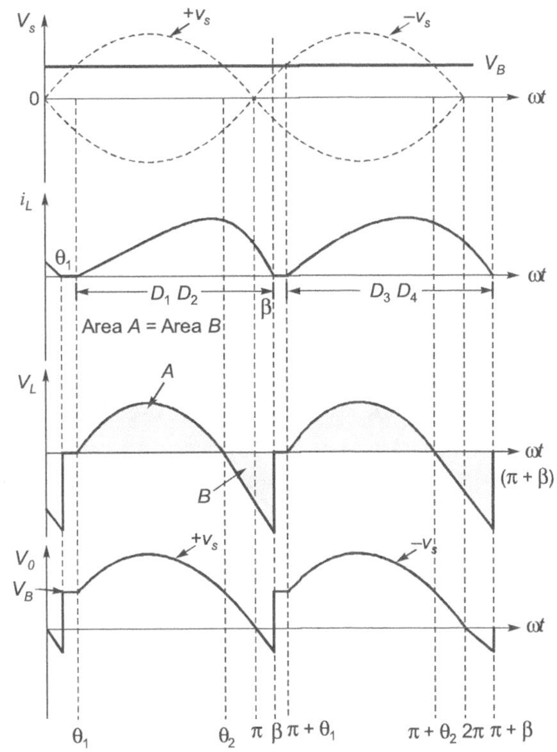

Use initial conditions to find K.

At $\omega t = \theta_1$, $i_L = 0$

$$0 = \frac{-V_m}{\omega L}\cos\theta_1 - \frac{V_B \cdot \theta_1}{\omega L} + K$$

$$K = \frac{1}{\omega L}[V_m \cos\theta_1 + V_B\theta_1]$$

$$I_{L\text{avg}} = \frac{1}{\pi}\int_{\theta_1}^{\beta} i_L . d(\omega t)$$

2.3 **Determine the ripple factor, form factor and utilization factor for a single-phase diode bridge rectifier supplying a purely resistive load.**

[12 marks : 2017]

Solution:

Single-phase diode bridge rectifier:

When 'a' is positive with respect to 'b' diode D_1, D_2 conduct together so that output voltage is V_{ab}. Each of the diodes D_3 and D_4 is subjected to a reverse voltage of V_s.

When 'b' is positive with respect to 'a', diodes D_3, D_4 conduct together and output voltage is V_{ba}. Each of the two diodes D_1 and D_2 experience a reverse voltage of V_s.

Average value of output voltage, $$V_0 = \frac{1}{\pi}\int_0^{\pi} V_m \sin\omega t \, d(\omega t) = \frac{2V_m}{\pi}$$

Average output current, $$I_0 = \frac{V_0}{R}$$

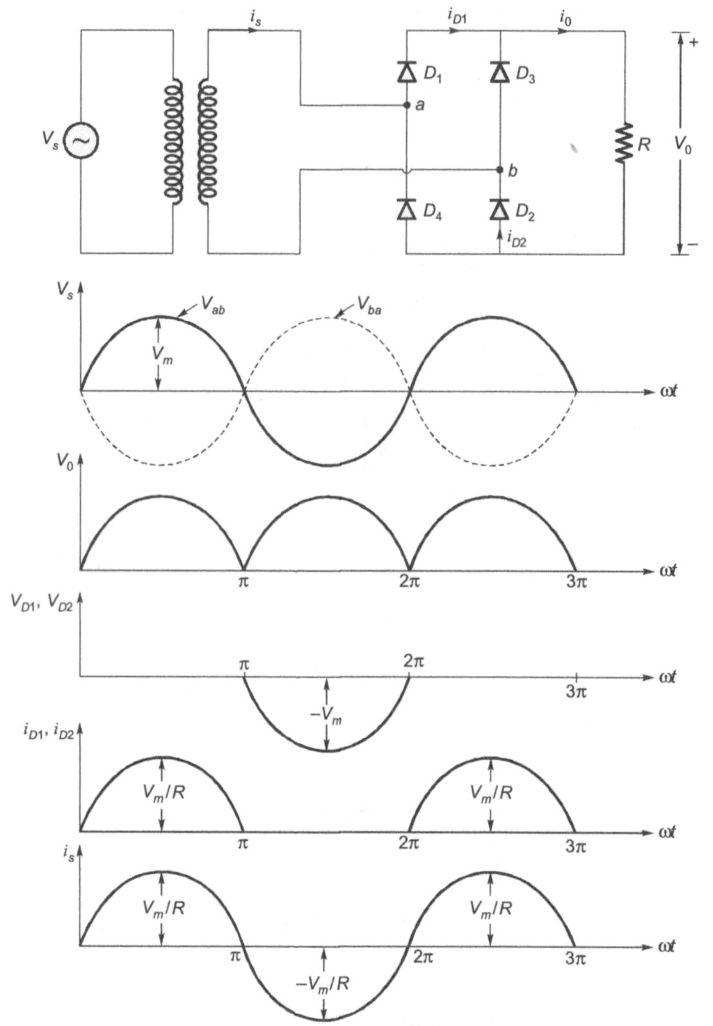

Rms value of output voltage, $V_{or} = \left[\frac{1}{\pi}\int_0^{\pi} V_m^2 \sin^2 \omega t \, d(\omega t)\right]^{1/2} = \frac{V_m}{\sqrt{2}} = V_s$

Rms value of load current, $I_{or} = \frac{V_s}{R}$

Form factor, $FF = \frac{V_{or}}{V_0} = \frac{V_m/\sqrt{2}}{2V_m/\pi} = \frac{\pi}{2\sqrt{2}} = 1.11$

Ripple voltage, $V_r = \sqrt{V_{or}^2 - V_0^2} = \left[\left(\frac{V_m}{\sqrt{2}}\right)^2 - \left(\frac{2V_m}{\pi}\right)^2\right]^{1/2} = 0.30776\, V_m$

Voltage ripple factor, $VRF = \frac{V_r}{V_0} = \frac{0.30776\, V_m}{2V_m/\pi} = 0.4834$

Transformer utilization factor, $TUF = \frac{P_{dc}}{VA \text{ rating of transformer}}$

Rms value of source voltage, $V_s = \frac{V_m}{\sqrt{2}}$

Rms value of source current, $I_s = \frac{I_m}{\sqrt{2}}$

$$\text{VA rating of transformer} = V_s I_s = \frac{V_m}{\sqrt{2}} \cdot \frac{I_m}{\sqrt{2}} = \frac{V_m I_m}{2}$$

$$P_{dc} = V_0 I_0 = \frac{2V_m}{\pi} \cdot \frac{2I_m}{\pi} = \left(\frac{2}{\pi}\right)^2 \cdot V_m I_m$$

So,
$$TUF = \frac{P_{dc}}{\text{VA rating of transformer}} = \frac{\frac{4}{\pi^2} V_m I_m}{V_m I_m / 2} = \frac{8}{\pi^2} = 0.81057$$

3. Phase Controlled Rectifiers

3.1 In a 3-phase semi converter, for firing angle equal to 120° and extinction angle equal to 110°, each SCR and free-wheeling diode conduct, respectively for

(a) 60°, 50°
(b) 30°, 60°
(c) 60°, 10°
(d) 30°, 50°

[2 marks : 2001]

Solution:

For 3-ϕ semiconductor, for (α = 120°), thyristor and diode conducts for 60° only. As extinction angle is equal to 110°, free wheeling diode conducts for 50° only. Hence, option (a) is correct.

3.2 A single-phase semiconverter feeds RLE load such that load current is constant for a firing angle of 30°. Sketch waveforms for source voltage V_s, load voltage V_0, load current I_0, source current I_s, one thyristor current and free-wheeling diode current for firing angle α = 30°. Prove that input power factor for the semiconverter for α = 90° is 0.63662. [14 marks : 2001]

Solution:

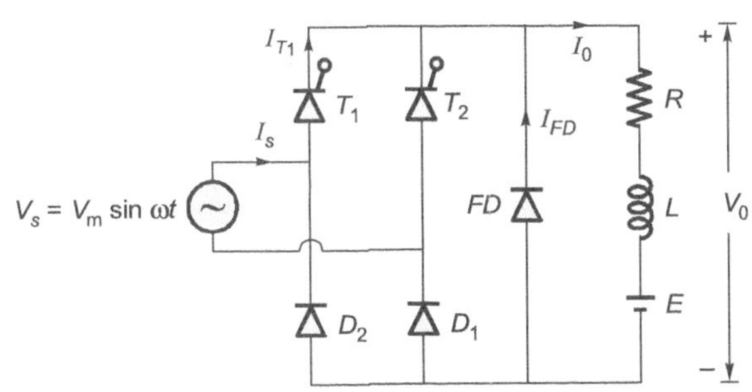

A single-phase semiconverter

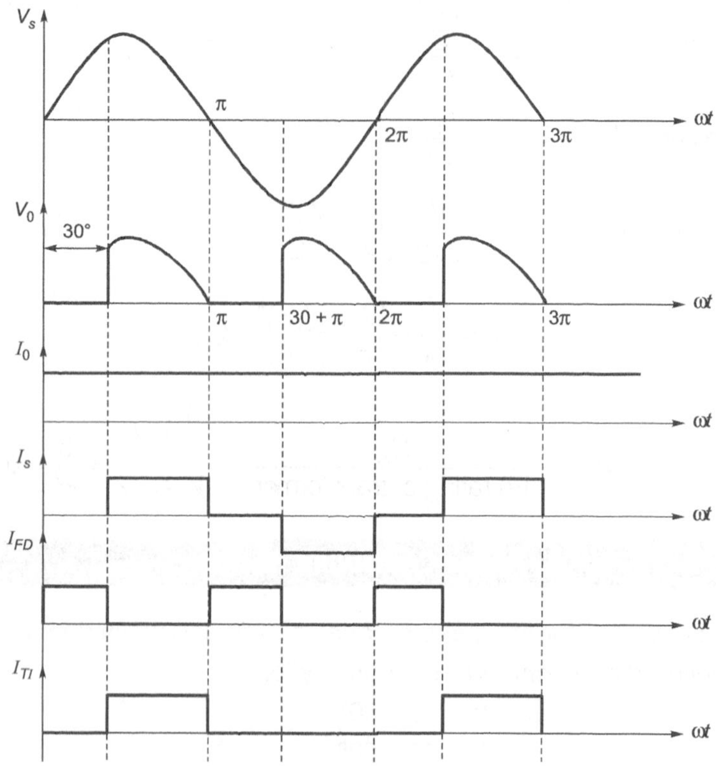

For single phase semiconverter, average output voltage

$$V_0 = V_t = \frac{V_m}{\pi}(1+\cos\alpha)$$

R.M.S. value of source current $I_{sr} = I_0\sqrt{\frac{\pi-\alpha}{\pi}}$

and input power factor for ($\alpha = 90°$)

$$\text{Input power factor} = \frac{V_t \times I_0}{V_s \times I_{sr}} = \frac{\frac{V_m}{\pi}[1+\cos 90]\times I_0}{\left(\frac{V_m}{\sqrt{2}}\right)\times\sqrt{\frac{\pi/2}{\pi}}\times I_0} = \frac{2}{\pi} = 0.63662$$

3.3 **Why input power factor of a single-phase half-controlled bridge-rectifier is higher than that for a fully-controlled bridge-rectifier supplying an RL load for the same firing angle?**

[4 marks : 2002]

Solution:

Input power factor of 1-ϕ half-bridge rectifier is higher than that for a fully-controlled bridge-rectifier of RL load for the same firing angle because some energy is returned by the inductor to source in a fully-controlled bridge rectifier. So net power delivered to load will decrease.

where,

$$\text{Power factor of input supply} = \frac{\text{Supplied power to load}}{\text{Source volt ampere}}$$

For a 1-ϕ full-bridge converter, during the interval π to (π + α) or (π to β) 'V_s' is negative and 'I_s' is positive. So energy stored in L is returned to the supply while in case 1-ϕ half-controlled converter energy stored in L is delivered to R through the free wheeling diode (FD).

3.4 A DC battery is charged through a resistor R as shown in the figure.

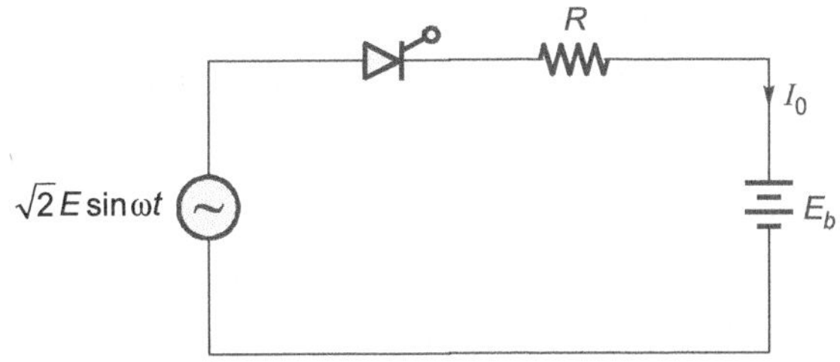

Derive an expression for the average charging current in terms of source voltage E, back e.m.f. E_b and resistance R. The SCR is fired continuously. If E = 220 V(r.m.s.), E_b = 100 (DC) and R = 10 ohms, calculate:

(i) Battery charging current

(ii) Power supplied to the battery [20 marks : 2002]

Solution:

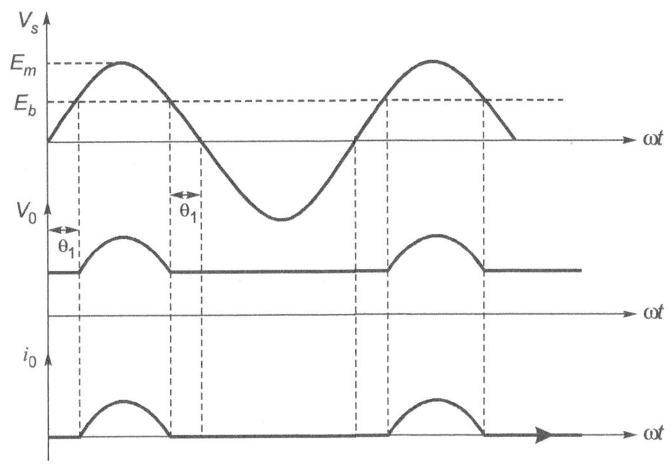

The voltage equation is,

$$E_m \sin\omega t = E_b + i_0 R$$

$$i_0 = \frac{E_m \sin\omega t - E_b}{R}$$

SCR is turned on when $E_m \sin\theta_1 = E_b$ and is turned off when $E_m \sin\theta_2 = E_b$

where, $\theta_2 = \pi - \theta_1$

The charging current of the battery is equal to average value of the output current.

where, $$i_0 = \begin{cases} \dfrac{E_m \sin\omega t - E_b}{R}, & \theta_1 < \theta < \pi - \theta_1 \\ 0, & \text{else} \end{cases} \qquad (\because E_m = \sqrt{2}E)$$

$\therefore$ $$\text{Average current} = I_{0(\text{av})} = \frac{1}{2\pi}\int_0^{2\pi} i_0 \, d\theta = \frac{1}{2\pi R}\int_{\theta_1}^{\pi-\theta_1} (E_m \sin\omega t - E_b) d\theta$$

$$= \frac{1}{2\pi R}\left[2E_m \cos\theta_1 - E_b(\pi - 2\theta_1)\right] = \frac{1}{2\pi \times 10}\left[2\times\sqrt{2}\times 220 \times \cos\theta_1 - 100(\pi - 2\theta_1)\right]$$

where $$\theta_1 = \sin^{-1}\left(\frac{100}{\sqrt{2}\times 220}\right) = 18.75° = 0.327 \text{ rad}$$

$\therefore$ $$I_{\text{av.}} = 5.42 \text{ A}$$

The power supplied to battery = $E \times I_{\text{av.}}$ = 100 × 5.42 = 542 W

3.5 A single phase semiconverter (using two SCR's and two diodes) is supplying dc voltage to a *RL* load. A free wheeling diode is connected across the load. Find expressions for the average and rms load voltages in terms of firing angle a. Also define input power factor.

[15 marks : 2004]

Solution:

During the interval α to π, T_1 and D_1 conducts and ac source delivers energy to the load circuit. This energy is partially stored in inductance *L* and partially dissipated as heat in *R*. During the free wheeling period π to $(\pi + \alpha)$, energy stored in inductance is recovered and dissipated in *R*.

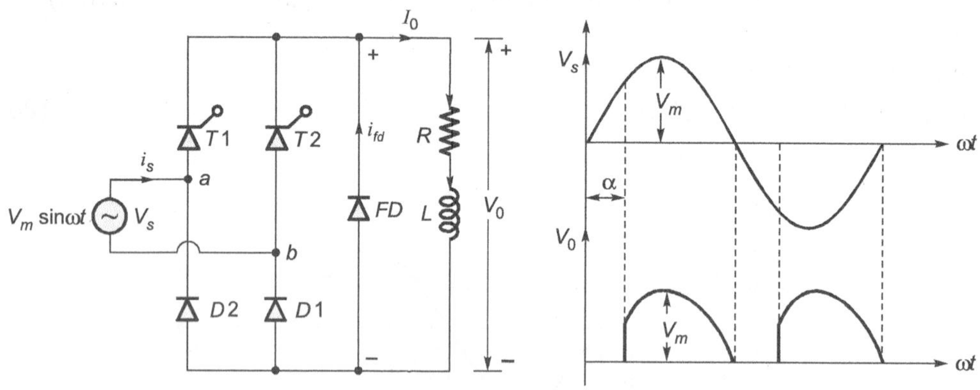

The average load voltage, $$V_0 = \frac{1}{\pi}\int_{\alpha}^{\pi} V_m \sin\omega t \cdot d(\omega t) = \frac{V_m}{\pi}(1+\cos\alpha)$$

The rms load voltage, $$V_{or}^2 = \frac{1}{\pi}\int_{\alpha}^{\pi} V_m^2 \sin^2 \omega t \cdot d(\omega t) = \frac{V_m^2}{2\pi}\left[\left|\omega t - \frac{\sin 2\omega t}{2}\right|_{\alpha}^{\pi}\right] = \frac{V_s^2}{\pi}\left[(\pi-\alpha) + \frac{\sin 2\alpha}{2}\right]$$

$$V_{or} = V_s\left[\frac{1}{\pi}\left\{(\pi-\alpha) + \frac{\sin 2\alpha}{2}\right\}\right]^{1/2}$$

$$\text{Output power} = V_0 I_0 = \frac{V_m}{\pi}(1+\cos\alpha)\, I_0$$

Assuming I_0 to be ripple free,

$$\text{rms input current} = I_{or} = \sqrt{\frac{\pi-\alpha}{\pi}} \cdot I_0$$

$$\text{Input power factor} = \frac{\text{Output power}}{\text{Input VA}} = \frac{V_0 I_0}{V_{or} I_{or}}$$

$$= \frac{\frac{V_m}{\pi}(1+\cos\alpha)\cdot I_0}{V_s \cdot \sqrt{\frac{\pi-\alpha}{\pi}} \cdot I_0}$$

$$= \frac{\frac{\sqrt{2}\cdot V_s}{\pi}(1+\cos\alpha)}{V_s \cdot \sqrt{\frac{\pi-\alpha}{\pi}}} = \left[\frac{2}{\pi(\pi-\alpha)}\right]^{1/2}(1+\cos\alpha)$$

3.6 A single-phase semiconverter is operated from a 50 Hz, 240 V ac source. If a resistive load of 100 ohm is connected at the dc terminals of the converter and the average output voltage is 25% of the maximum possible average output voltage, calculate the firing delay angle and the average and r.m.s. load currents.

[10 marks : 2004]

Solution:

The average output voltage of 1-ϕ semiconverter

$$V_0 = \frac{V_m}{\pi}(1+\cos\alpha)$$

Maximum possible value of $V_0 = \frac{2V_m}{\pi}$ for $\alpha = 0$

$$0.25\times\left(\frac{2V_m}{\pi}\right) = \frac{V_m}{\pi}(1+\cos\alpha)$$

$$1+\cos\alpha = 0.5$$

$$\Rightarrow \quad \cos\alpha = -0.5$$

$$\alpha = 120°$$

Average load current, $$I_0 = \frac{V_0}{R} = \frac{V_m}{\pi R}(1+\cos\alpha) = \frac{\sqrt{2}V_s}{\pi R}(1+\cos\alpha)$$

$$= \frac{\sqrt{2}\times 240}{\pi\times 100}\times(1+\cos 120°) = 0.54 \text{ Amp.}$$

Rms load current $$= I_{or} = \frac{V_{or}}{R} = \frac{V_s}{R}\left[\frac{1}{\pi}\left\{(\pi-\alpha)+\frac{\sin 2\alpha}{2}\right\}\right]^{1/2}$$

$$= \frac{240}{100}\times\left[\frac{1}{\pi}\times\left\{\left(\pi-\frac{2\pi}{3}\right)+\frac{\sin 240}{2}\right\}\right]^{1/2} = 1.06 \text{ Amp.}$$

3.7 A single-phase thyristor converter with a resistive load is shown below. Supply voltage V_S is sinusoidal at a fixed frequency.

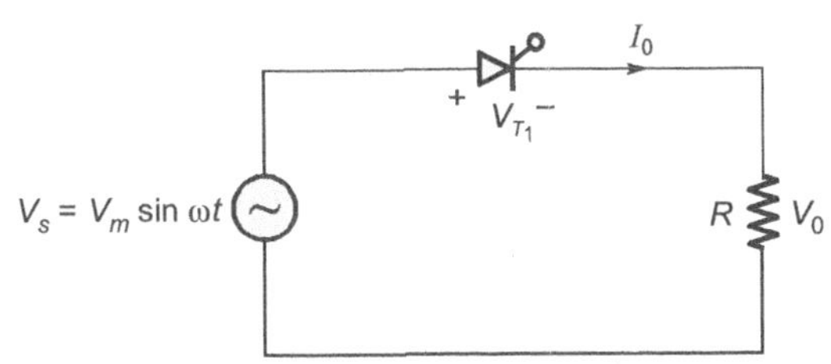

(i) Draw the waveforms of V_S, V_0 and V_{T_1} at the firing angle α = 45°. Neglect current.

(ii) If the supply voltage is 230 V (rms) at 50 Hz, calculate for α = 45° and R = 100 ohms.

(a) Average output voltage and current.

(b) R.M.S. value of supply current.

(c) Ripple factor.

Derive the formula used.

[20 marks : 2005]

Solution:

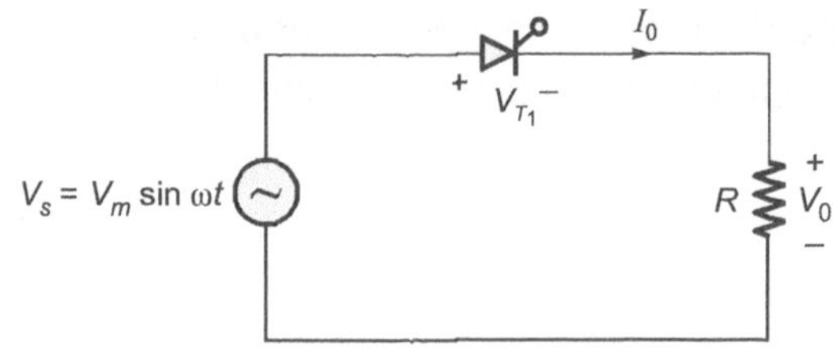

(i)

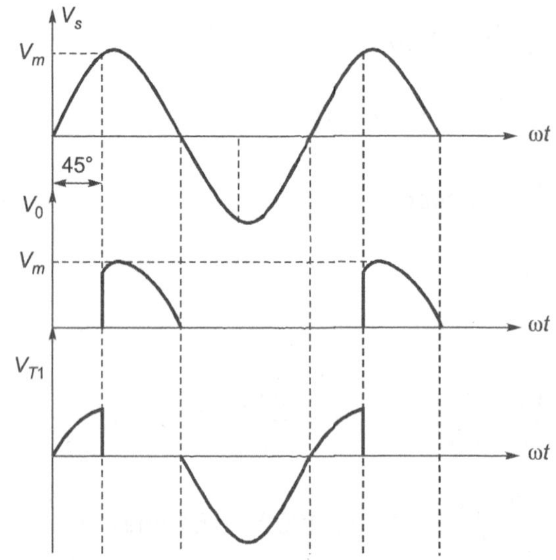

(ii) (a)

$$V_{0(avg)} = \frac{1}{2\pi}\int_{\alpha}^{\pi} V_m \sin \omega t \, d(\omega t)$$

$$V_{0(avg)} = \frac{V_m}{2\pi}(1+\cos\alpha) = \frac{\sqrt{2}\times 230}{2\times\pi}(1+\cos 45°) = 88.37 \text{ volts}$$

$$I_{0(avg)} = \frac{V_{0(avg.)}}{R} = \frac{88.37}{100} = 0.88 \text{ amp.}$$

(b)

$$V_{0(rms)} = \left[\frac{1}{2\pi}\int V_m^2 \sin^2 \omega t \, d(\omega t)\right]^{1/2} = \frac{V_m}{2\sqrt{\pi}}\left[(\pi-\alpha)+\frac{1}{2}\times\sin 2\alpha\right]^{1/2}$$

$$= \frac{230\times\sqrt{2}}{2\times\sqrt{\pi}}\left[\left(\pi-\frac{\pi}{4}\right)+\frac{1}{2}\times\sin 2\times 45°\right]^{1/2} = 155.1 \text{ Volts}$$

$$I_{0(rms)} = \frac{V_{0(rms)}}{R} = \frac{155.1}{100} = 1.55 \text{ amp.}$$

(c)

$$\text{Ripple factor} = \frac{\sqrt{V_{0(rms)}^2 - V_{0(av)}^2}}{V_{0(av)}} = 1.44$$

3.8 A semiconverter is connected to a 240 V, 50 Hz supply. The load current I_a can be assumed to be continuous and its ripple current is negligible. Calculate the harmonic factor of input current for $\alpha = \pi/2$. Derive all the relevant formulae used using Fourier series analysis. Obtain also expressions for r.m.s. value of supply current and r.m.s. value of fundamental current in terms of I_a and α.

[20 marks : 2005]

Solution:

1-ϕ semiconverter circuit is shown in figure (a).

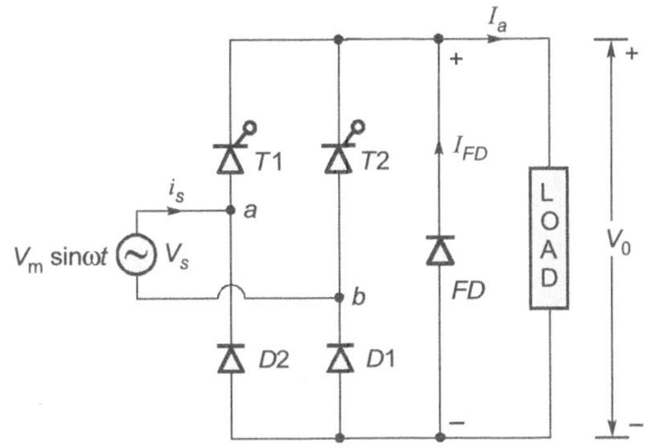

(a)

- The load current is assumed to be continuous and ripple free.
- The various waveforms V_s, V_0, I_a and I_s are shown in figure (b).

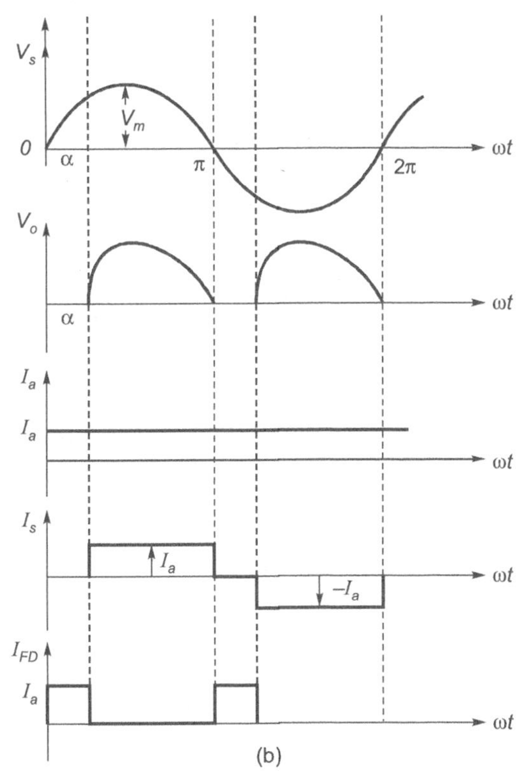

(b)

- The instantaneous input current $i_s(t)$ can be expressed in Fourier series as:

$$i_s(t) = a_0 + \sum_{n=1,2,3}^{\infty} (a_n \cos n\omega t + b_n \sin n\omega t)$$

where,
$$a_0 = \frac{1}{2\pi}\int_0^{2\pi} i_s(t) d(\omega t)$$

$$a_n = \frac{1}{\pi}\int_0^{2\pi} i_s(t)\cdot \cos n\omega t \cdot d(\omega t) \quad \text{and} \quad b_n = \frac{1}{\pi}\int_0^{2\pi} i_s(t)\cdot \sin n\omega t\cdot d(\omega t)$$

$$a_0 = \frac{1}{2\pi}\left[\int_{\alpha}^{\pi} i_a \cdot d(\omega t) - \int_{\pi+\alpha}^{2\pi} I_a \cdot d(\omega t)\right] = 0$$

$$a_n = \frac{1}{\pi}\left[\int_{\alpha}^{\pi} i_a \cos n\omega t \cdot d(\omega t) - \int_{\pi+\alpha}^{2\pi} I_a \cos n\omega t \cdot d(\omega t)\right]$$

$$= \frac{I_a}{n\pi}\left[\left|\sin n\omega t\right|_{\alpha}^{\pi}\right] - \left[\left|\sin n\omega t\right|_{n+\alpha}^{2\pi}\right]$$

$$= -\frac{2I_a}{n\pi}\sin n\alpha \text{ .... for } n = 1, 3, 5 \text{ ....}$$

$$= 0 \text{ .... for } n = 2, 4, 6 \text{ ....}$$

$$b_n = \frac{1}{\pi}\left[\int_{\alpha}^{\pi} I_a \sin n\omega t \cdot d(\omega t) - \int_{n+\alpha}^{2\pi} I_a \sin n\omega t \cdot d(\omega t)\right]$$

$$= \frac{2I_a}{n\pi}(1+\cos n\alpha) \text{ .... for } n = 1, 3, 5 \text{ ....}$$

$$= 0 \text{ .... for } n = 2, 4, 6$$

$$C_n = \left[\left(-\frac{2I_a}{n\pi}\sin n\alpha\right)^2 + \left(\frac{2I_a}{n\pi}(1+\cos n\alpha)\right)^2\right]^{1/2} = \frac{2\sqrt{2}I_a}{n\pi}(1+\cos n\alpha)^{1/2}$$

as we know, $1 + \cos\theta = 2\cos^2\frac{n\theta}{2}$

$$C_n = \frac{2\sqrt{2}I_a}{n\pi}\left[2\cos^2\frac{n\alpha}{2}\right]^{1/2} = \frac{4I_a}{n\pi}\cos\frac{n\alpha}{2}$$

$$\theta_n = \tan^{-1}\left(\frac{a_n}{b_n}\right) = \tan^{-1}\left[-\frac{\sin n\alpha}{1+\cos n\alpha}\right] = \tan^{-1}\left[-\frac{2\sin\frac{n\alpha}{2}\cdot\cos\frac{n\alpha}{2}}{2\cos^2\frac{n\alpha}{2}}\right] = -\frac{n\alpha}{2}$$

Hence, $$i_s(t) = \sum_{n=1,3,5}^{\infty}\frac{4I_a}{n\pi}\cos\frac{n\alpha}{2}\cdot\sin\left(n\omega t - \frac{n\alpha}{2}\right)$$

Rms value of nth harmonic input current,

$$I_{sn} = \frac{4I_a}{\sqrt{2}\,n\pi}\cos\frac{n\alpha}{2} = \frac{2\sqrt{2}}{n\pi}I_a\cdot\cos\frac{n\alpha}{2}$$

Hence, Rms value of the fundamental current,

$$I_{sl} = \frac{2\sqrt{2}}{n\pi}I_a\cdot\cos\frac{\alpha}{2} \quad \text{for} \quad n = 1$$

Rms value of total input current,

$$I_s = \left[\frac{I_a^2(\pi-\alpha)}{\pi}\right]^{1/2} = I_a\left[\frac{\pi-\alpha}{\pi}\right]^{1/2}$$

$$\text{CDF} = \frac{I_{sl}}{I_s} = \left(\frac{2\sqrt{2}}{\pi}I_a\cos\frac{\alpha}{2}\right)\times\left(\frac{\sqrt{\pi}}{I_a\sqrt{\pi-\alpha}}\right) = \frac{2\sqrt{2}\cos\frac{\alpha}{2}}{\sqrt{\pi(\pi-\alpha)}}$$

$$\text{Harmonic factor} = \left[\frac{1}{CDF^2} - 1\right]^{1/2} = \left[\frac{\pi(\pi - \alpha)}{8\cos^2\frac{\alpha}{2}} - 1\right]^{1/2} = \left[\frac{\pi(\pi - \alpha)}{4(1 + \cos\alpha)} - 1\right]^{1/2}$$

Hence, harmonic factor of input current for $\alpha = n/2$

$$= \left[\frac{\pi(\pi - \pi/2)}{4(1 + \cos\pi/2)} - 1\right]^{1/2} = 0.4834$$

3.9 **Draw the circuit diagram of a single-phase semi converter and derive an expression for the average voltage across the load in terms of supply voltage and firing angle α. Explain the semi converter operation and show the waveforms for the input voltage, output voltage and current through different diodes and thyristors.**

[18 marks : 2005]

Solution:

- A single-phase semiconverter bridge with two thyristors and three diodes is shown in figure. The two thyristors are *T*1, *T*2; the two diodes are *D*1, *D*2; the third diode connected across load is freewheeling diode FD. The load is of RLE type as for the full converter bridge. Various voltage and current waveforms for this converter are shown in (b), where load current is assumed continuous over the working range.

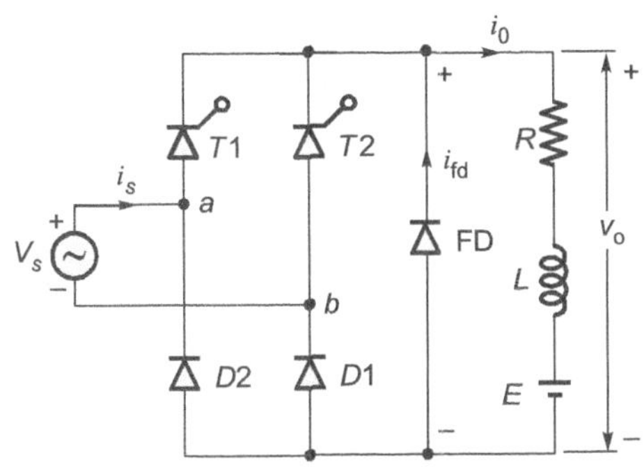

(a) Single-phase semiconverter

- After $\omega t = 0$, thyristor *T*1 is forward biased only when source voltage $V_m \sin\omega t$ exceeds *E*. Thus, *T*1 is triggered at a firing angle delay α such that $V_m \sin\alpha > E$. With T1 on, load gets connected to source through *T*1 and *D*1 for the period $\omega t = \alpha$ to π, load current i_0 flows through RLE, *D*1, source and *T*1 and the load terminal voltage v_0 is of the same waveshape as the ac source voltage v_s. Soon after $\omega t = \pi$, load voltage v_0 tends to reverse as the ac source voltage changes polarity. The load or output, current i_0 is transferred from *T*1, *D*1 to FD. As SCR *T*1 is reverse biased at $\omega t = \pi + \alpha$ through FD, *T*1 is turned off at $\omega t = \pi + \alpha$. The load terminals are short circuited through FD, therefore load, or output, voltage v_0 is zero during $\pi < \omega t < (\pi + \alpha)$. After $\omega t = \pi$, during the negative half cycle, *T*2 will be forward biased only when source voltage is more than *E*. At $\omega t = (\pi + \alpha)$, source voltage exceeds *E*, *T*2 is therefore triggered. Soon after $(\pi + \alpha)$, FD is reverse biased and is therefore turned off; load current now shifts from FD to *T*2, *D*2. At $\omega t = 2\pi$, FD is again forward biased and output current i_0 is transferred from *T*2, *D*2 to FD as explained before. The source current i_s is positive from α to π when *T*1, *D*1 conduct and is negative from $(\pi + \alpha)$ to 2π when *T*2, *D*2 conduct, see figure.
- During the interval α to π, *T*1 and *D*1 conduct and ac source delivers energy to the load circuit. This energy is partially stored in inductance *L*, partially stored as electric energy in load-circuit emf *E* and partially dissipated at heat in *R*. During the freewheeling period π to $(\pi + \alpha)$, energy stored in inductance is recovered and is partially dissipated in *R* and partially added to the energy stored in load emf *E*. No energy is fed back to the source during freewheeling period.

For semiconverter, the average output voltage V_0, from figure (b), is given by

$$V_0 = \frac{1}{\pi}\int_{\alpha}^{\pi} V_m \sin\omega t \cdot d(\omega t) = \frac{V_m}{\pi}(1+\cos\alpha)$$

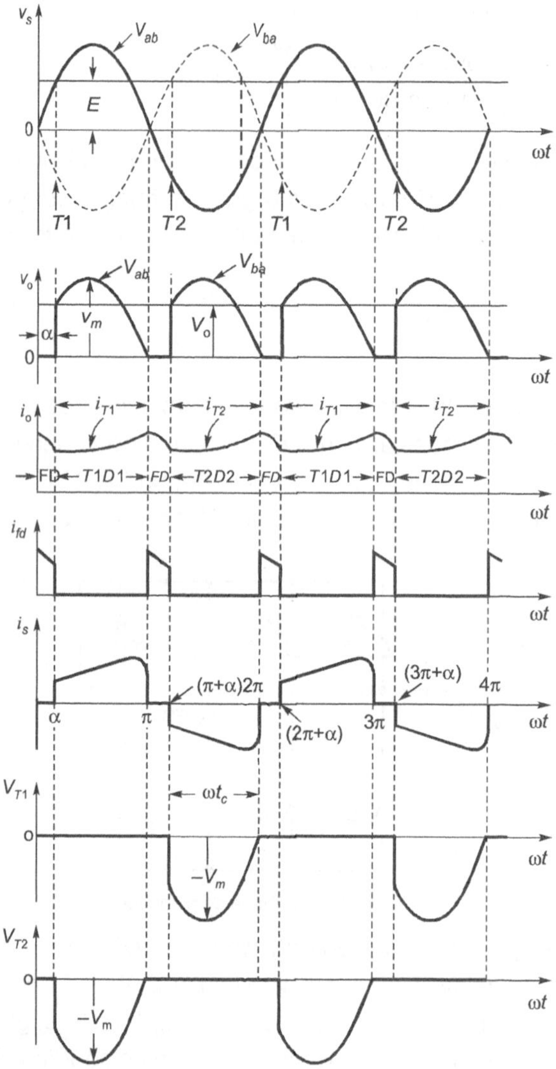

(b) Voltage and current waveforms for continuous load current

3.10 A 230 V, 50 Hz one pulse SCR controlled converter is triggered at firing angle of 40° and the load current extinguishes at an angle of 120°. Find the circuit turn off time, average output voltage and the average load current for R = 5 ohms and L = 2 mH.

[12 marks : 2007]

Solution:

Half wave rectifier with (RL) load,

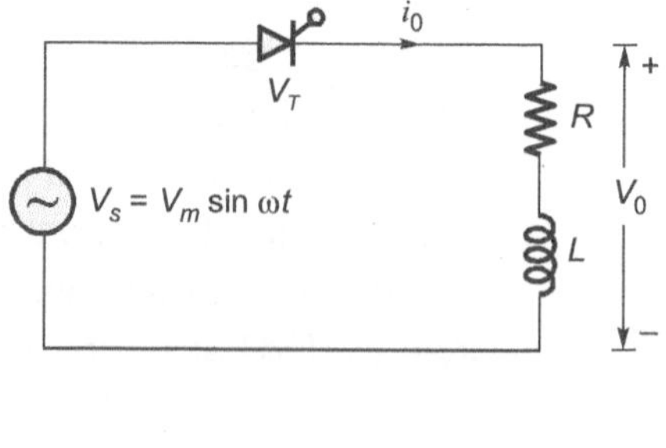

$$\text{Circuit turn-off time} = t_c = \frac{2\pi-\beta}{\omega} = \frac{(360°-120°)\pi}{180\times 2\pi\times 50}$$

$$= 13.33 \text{ m-sec}$$

$$\text{Average output voltage} = V_0 = \frac{V_m}{2\pi}[\cos\alpha - \cos\beta]$$

$$= \frac{\sqrt{2}\times 230}{2\pi}[\cos 40° - \cos 120°] = 65.54 \text{ volts}$$

and $\text{Average load current} = I_0 = \frac{V_0}{R} = \frac{65.54}{5} = 13.10 \text{ Amps}$

3.11 **A three-phase full converter is supplying a purely resistive load at 300 V d.c. for 0° firing angle. The output voltage for 90° firing angle would be**

(a) 0 V (b) 40 V
(c) 50 V (d) 100 V

[2 marks : 2008]

Solution:

Average output voltage of 3-ϕ full converter,

$$V_0 = \frac{3\,V_{ml}}{\pi}\cos\alpha \quad \text{for} \quad 0 < \alpha < \pi/3$$

For $\alpha = 30°, V_0 = 300$

$$V_0 = \frac{3\,V_{ml}}{\pi}\cos$$

$$300 = \frac{3\,V_{ml}}{\pi} \quad \text{...}(i)$$

Average output voltage of 3-ϕ full converter, for $\frac{\pi}{3} < \alpha < \frac{2\pi}{3}$

$$V_0 = \frac{3V_{ml}}{\pi}\left[1+\cos\left(\alpha+\frac{\pi}{3}\right)\right] = 300\times\left[1+\cos\left(\frac{\pi}{2}+\frac{\pi}{3}\right)\right] = 40.19 \text{ volts}$$

Hence, option (b) 40 volts is correct.

3.12 **A three-phase full converters is supplying a resistive load. Show that the average output voltage of the converter is given by**

$$V_0 = \frac{3\,V_{ml}}{\pi}\cos\alpha \text{ for } 0 < \alpha < \frac{\pi}{3}$$

and $$V_0 = \frac{3\,V_{ml}}{\pi}\left[1+\cos\left(\alpha+\frac{\pi}{3}\right)\right] \text{for } \frac{\pi}{3} < \alpha < \frac{2\pi}{3}$$

where V_{ml} = **Maximum value of line voltage.**

Also plot the output voltage waveform for $\alpha = \frac{\pi}{2}$**, for the same converter.**

[15 marks : 2008]

Solution:

Average output voltage can be obtained by finding the dashed area abcd over periodic cycle with 00′ as the origin at the maximum value of V_{ab}, V_0 is given by

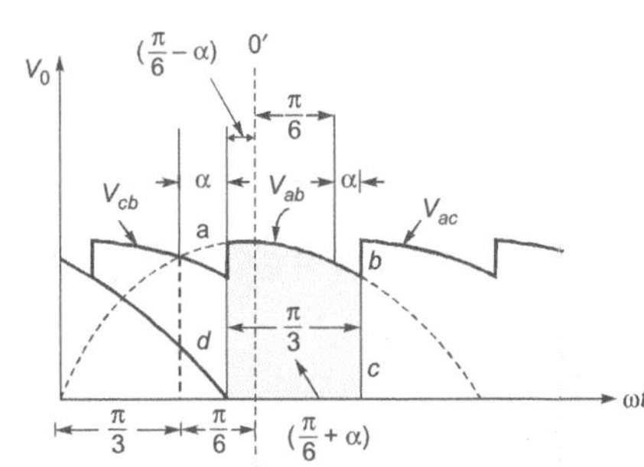

$$V_0 = \frac{3}{\pi}\int_{-\left(\frac{\pi}{6}-\alpha\right)}^{\left(\frac{\pi}{6}+\alpha\right)} V_{ml}\cos\omega t(d\omega t)$$

$$= \frac{3V_{ml}}{\pi}\left[\sin\left(\alpha+\frac{\pi}{6}\right)+\sin\left(\alpha-\frac{\pi}{6}\right)\right] = \frac{3\,V_{ml}}{\pi}\cos\alpha$$

For $\alpha > \pi/3$

$$V_0 = \frac{3}{\pi}\int_{-\left(\frac{\pi}{6}-\alpha\right)}^{\pi/2} V_{ml}\cos\omega t\cdot d\omega t$$

$$= \frac{3}{\pi}\left[V_{ml}\sin\omega t\right]_{-\left(\frac{\pi}{6}-\alpha\right)}^{\pi/2} = \frac{3V_{ml}}{\pi}\left(1+\cos\left(\alpha+\frac{\pi}{3}\right)\right)$$

3.13 A single-phase full converter is connected to an AC supply of 330 sin314t volts. It operates at a firing angle $\alpha = \frac{\pi}{4}$. The load current is maintained constant at 5 A and the load voltage is 140 V. Calculate: (i) Source inductance (ii) Angle of overlap and (iii) the load resistance. Derive the formula used.

[15 marks : 2008]

Solution:

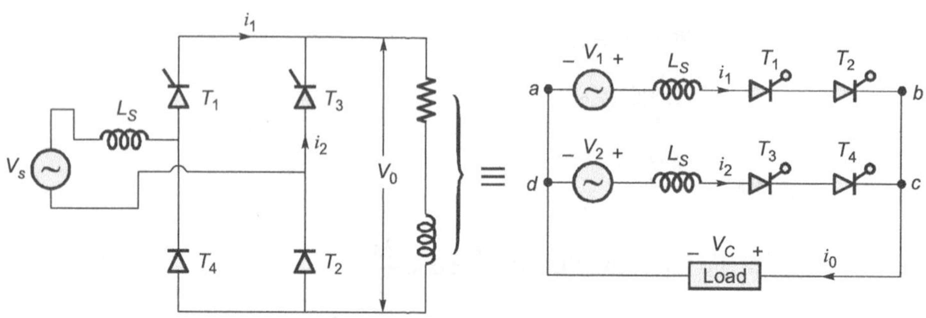

1-ϕ full converter with source inductance L

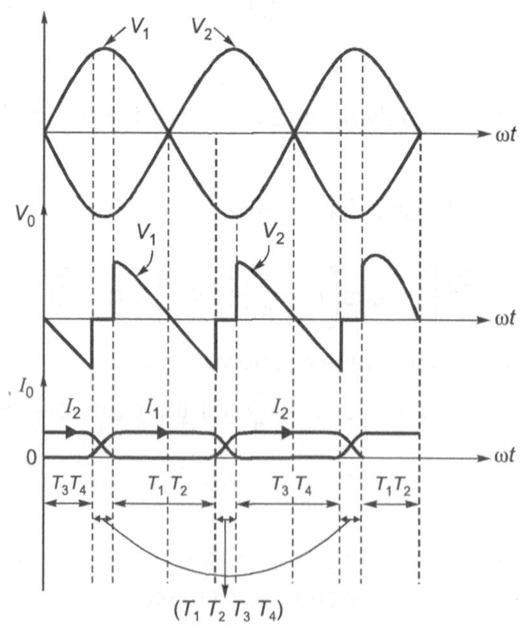

From the equivalent circuit, applying KVL in loop 'abcd' gives

$$V_1 - L_S\frac{di_1}{dt} = V_2 - L_S\frac{di_2}{dt}$$

$$V_1 - V_2 = L_S\left(\frac{di_1}{dt}-\frac{di_2}{dt}\right)$$

If $\quad V_1 = V_m \sin \omega t$ then,

$$V_2 = -V_m \sin \omega t$$

$$\therefore \quad L_S\left(\frac{di_1}{dt} - \frac{di_2}{dt}\right) = 2V_m \sin \omega t$$

As the load assumed constant throughout, $i_1 + i_2 = I_0$

$$\frac{di_1}{dt} - \frac{di_2}{dt} = 0$$

$$\frac{di_1}{dt} - \frac{di_2}{dt} = \frac{2V_m}{L_s} \sin\omega t$$

Addition of equation gives,

$$\frac{di_1}{dt} = \frac{V_m}{L_s} \sin\omega t$$

Load current 'i_1' through thyristor pair T_1, T_2 build up from zero to (I_0) during the overlap angle μ at ($\omega t = \alpha$) at $\omega t = \alpha$, $\quad i_1 = 0$ and at $\omega t = (\alpha + \mu)$, $i_1 = I_0$

$$\int_0^{I_0} i_1 = \frac{V_m}{L_s} \int_{\alpha/\omega}^{(\alpha+\mu)/\omega} \sin\omega t \cdot dt \Rightarrow I_0 = \frac{-V_m}{\omega L_s}\left[\cos\alpha - \cos(\alpha+\mu)\right] \quad ...(i)$$

and average voltage (output),

$$V_0 = \frac{V_m}{\pi} \int_{\alpha+\mu}^{(\alpha+\pi)} \sin \omega t \, d(\omega t) = \frac{V_m}{\pi}\left[\cos(\alpha+\mu) + \cos\alpha\right] \quad ...(ii)$$

$$\therefore \quad V_0 = \frac{2V_m}{\pi}\cos\alpha - \frac{\omega L_s}{\pi} I_0 \text{ or } V_0 = \frac{2V_m}{\pi}\cos(\alpha+\mu) + \frac{\omega L_s}{\pi} I_0$$

Here, $\quad V_m = 330$ V, $\omega = 314$, $\alpha = \dfrac{\pi}{4}$

$I_0 = 5$ A, $V_0(av) = 140$ V

(*i*) $$V_0 = \frac{1}{\pi}\left[2 \times 330 \times \cos\left(\frac{\pi}{4}\right) - 314 \times L_s \times 5\right] = 140 \therefore L_S = 17.113 \text{ mH}$$

(*ii*) $$I_0 = \frac{V_m}{\omega L_s}\left[\cos\alpha - \cos(\alpha+\mu)\right]$$

$$5 = \frac{330}{314 \times 0.017113}\left[\cos\frac{\pi}{4} - \cos\left(\frac{\pi}{4} + \mu\right)\right]$$

$$\therefore \quad \mu = 6.267°$$

(*iii*) The average voltage across the output resistance.

$$V_0 = I_0 R$$

$$\Rightarrow \quad R = \frac{V_0}{I_0} = \frac{140}{5} = 28\ \Omega$$

3.14 A d.c. battery is charged through a resistor R as shown in the below figure. Derive an expression for the average value of charging current in terms of E_m, E_b, R. Assume that the SCR is fixed in every cycle.

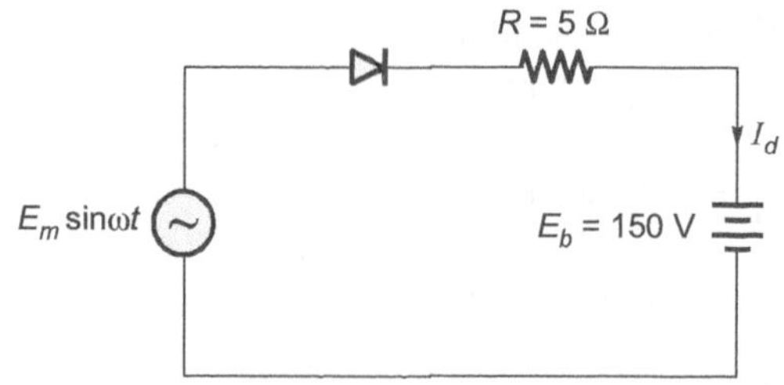

(i) For an a.c. supply voltage of 230 V, 50 Hz, find the value of average charging current.
(ii) Find average power supplied to the battery and that dissipated in the resistance.
(iii) Calculate the power factor at the supply. (Neglect SCR drop).

[3 + 5 + 5 + 5 marks : 2010]

Solution:

For the circuit, the voltage equation is

$$E_m \sin\omega t = E_b + i_0 R$$

$$\Rightarrow \quad i_0 = \frac{E_m \sin\omega t - E_b}{R}$$

SCR is turned on when $E_m \sin\theta_1 = E_b$

and is turned $\theta_2 = \pi - \theta_1$.

Average value of charging current

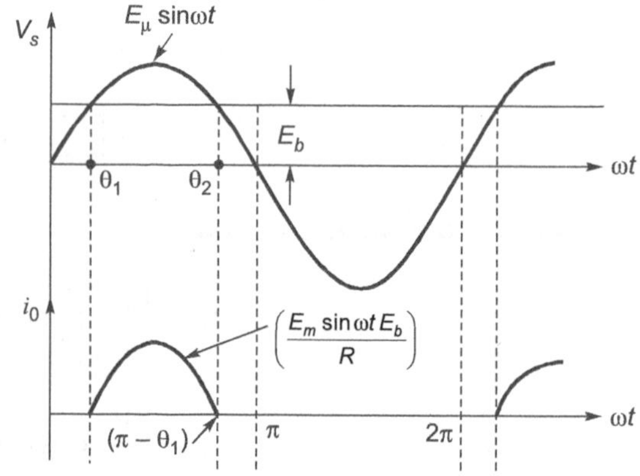

$$I_d = \frac{1}{2\pi R}\left[\int_{\theta_1}^{\pi-\theta_1}(E_m \sin\omega t - E_b)\, d(\omega t)\right]$$

$$= \frac{1}{2\pi R}\left[2E_m \cos\theta_1 - E_b(\pi - 2\theta_1)\right]$$

For $\quad E_m = \sqrt{2}\times 230$ and $R = 5\ \Omega$

Here, $\quad \theta_1 = \sin^{-1}\left(\frac{E_b}{E_m}\right) = \sin^{-1}\left(\frac{150}{\sqrt{2}\times 230}\right)$

$$= 27.46° = 0.48 \text{ rad.}$$

$$I_d = \left(\frac{1}{2\times\pi\times 5}\right)\times\left[2\times\sqrt{2}\times 230\times\cos 27.46 - 150\times(\pi - 2\times 0.48)\right]$$

$$= 7.958 \text{ amp.}$$

Power supplied to the battery = $E_b I_d$ = 150 × 7.958 = 1193.7 Watts

Rms value of the charging current,

$$I_{dr} = \left[\frac{1}{2\pi R^2}\left\{(E_s^2 + E_b^2)\times(\pi - 2\theta_1) + E_s^2 \sin 2\theta_1 - 4E_m E_b \cos\theta_1\right\}\right]^{1/2}$$

$$= 14.84 \text{ amp.}$$

Here Es is rms value of supply voltage,

$$E_s = \frac{E_m}{\sqrt{2}}$$

Power dissipated in resistor R

$$= I_{dr}^2 \times R = (14.84)^2 \times 5$$

$$= 1101.128 \text{ W}$$

Rms value of input current

$$I_{sr} = I_{dr} = 14.84$$

$$\text{Supply p.f.} = \frac{\text{Output power}}{\text{Input power}} = \frac{E_b I_d + I_{dr}^2 R}{E_s I_{sr}}$$

$$= \frac{1193.7 + 1101.128}{230 \times 14.84} = 0.6723 \text{ lagging}$$

3.15 A freewheeling diode in a phase controlled converter:

(a) decreases the possibility of discontinuous conduction in the load.

(b) increase the possibility of discontinuous conduction.

(c) improves the power factor.

(d) causes additional reactive power requirement. [2 marks : 2010]

Solution: (c)

3.16 A single-phase semiconverter using two SCRs and two diodes is supplying d.c. voltage to RLE (Resistance, Inductance, Battery) load. A free wheeling diode is connected across the load. Draw the circuit diagram of the semiconverter and show the region of converter operation. Draw waveforms for the input voltage, output voltage, input current and current through the SCRs and diodes. Derive expressions for average output voltage and rms output voltage. (Assume highly inductive load). [10 marks : 2010]

Solution:

Regions of Converter Operation:

- $0 < \omega t < a$, FD conducts.
- $\alpha < \omega t < \pi$, $T_1 D_1$ conduct.
- $\pi < \omega t < \pi + \alpha$, FD conducts.
- $\pi + \alpha < \omega t < 2\pi$, $T_2 D_2$ conduct.
- When $T_1 D_1$ and $T_2 D_2$ conduct output voltage follows input voltage.
- When FD conducts, output voltage is zero.
- For semiconverter, the average output voltage,

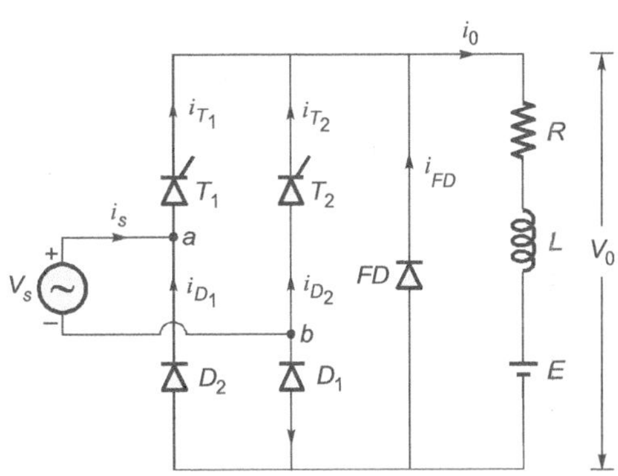

Circuit diagram of the semiconverter

$$V_0 = \frac{1}{\pi}\int_\alpha^\pi V_m \sin\omega t \cdot d(\omega t) = \frac{V_m}{\pi}(1+\cos\alpha)$$

- Rms value of output voltage,

$$V_{or}^2 = \frac{1}{\pi}\int_\alpha^\pi V_m^2 \sin^2\omega t \cdot d(\omega t) = \frac{V_m^2}{2\pi}\left[\left|\omega t - \frac{\sin 2\omega t}{2}\right|_\alpha^\pi\right]$$

$$= \frac{V_s^2}{\pi}\left[(\pi - \alpha) + \frac{\sin 2\alpha}{2}\right]$$

$$V_{or} = V_s\left[\frac{1}{\pi}\left\{(\pi - \alpha) + \frac{\sin 2\alpha}{2}\right\}\right]^{1/2}$$

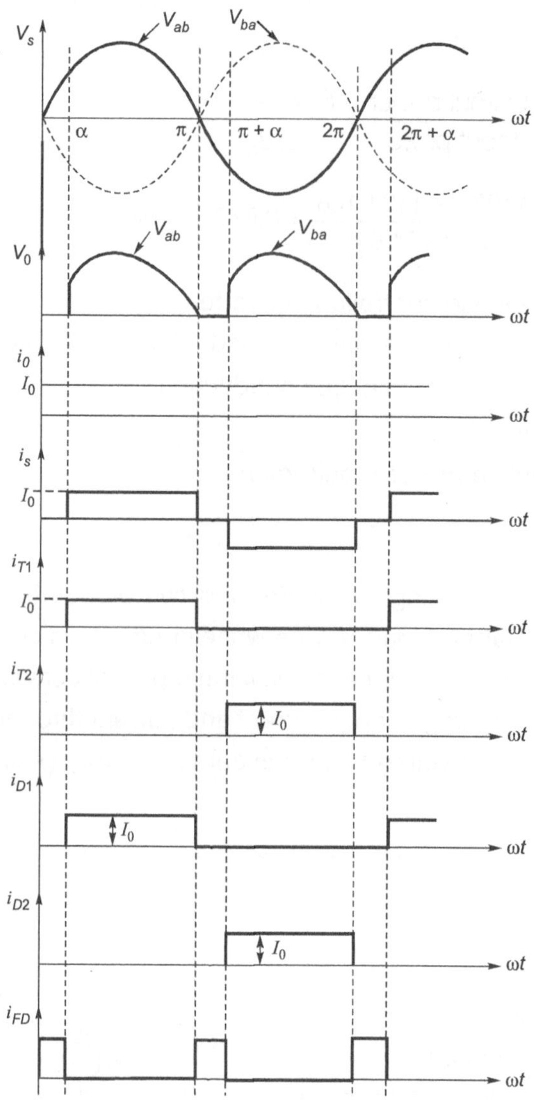

3.17 Adding an inductance L in series and a free wheeling diode (FWD) in parallel to the load circuit of an SCR-converter has several advantages. Enumerate the advantages of the load inductance and free wheeling diode.

[10 marks : 2010]

Solution:

- Current through an inductance L can not change instantaneously, hence an inductance L in series with the load circuit does not allow load current to fall to zero and prevents discontinuous operation of the SCR converter.

  The load performance deteriorates if load current becomes discontinuous. Using inductance of very high value results into almost constant and ripple free load current.
- The advantages of using free wheeling diode are:
  1. Input pf is improved.
  2. Load current waveform is improved and as a result load performance is better.
  3. As energy stored in L is transferred to R during the free wheeling period, overall converter efficiency improves.

4. Free wheeling diode prevents the load voltage V_0 from becoming negative.

- All the above advantages of using free wheeling diode are due to fact that, the energy stored in inductor is delivered to load resistance R through The FD when V_0 is negative and i_0 is positive. In the absence of FD, that energy is returned to the supply resulting into lower power factor.

3.18 In a phase controlled circuit using a 1-phase, 230 V, 50 Hz supply the triggering angle is adjusted to 30° in both half cycles of a resistive load. Calculate the r.m.s. value of the output voltage.

[5 marks : 2011]

Solution:

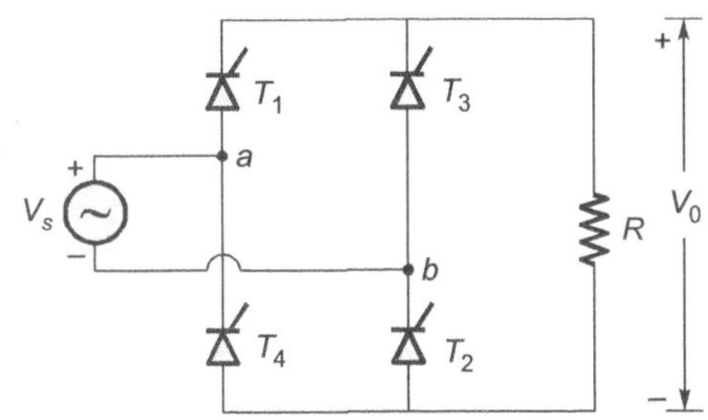

Single-phase full converter with resistive load

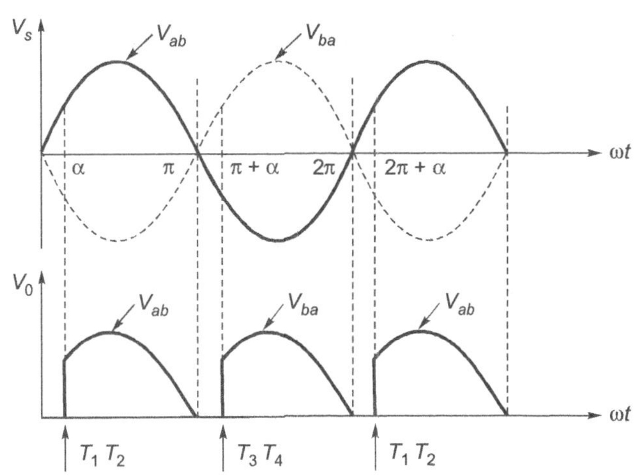

Let, V_{or} = r.m.s. output voltage and $V_s = V_m \sin\omega t$

$$V_{or}^2 = \frac{1}{\pi}\int_{\alpha}^{\pi} V_m^2 \sin^2 \omega t \cdot d(\omega t) = \frac{V_m^2}{2\pi}\left|\omega t - \frac{\sin 2\omega t}{2}\right|_{\alpha}^{\pi}$$

$$V_{or} = \frac{V_m}{\sqrt{2}}\left[\frac{1}{\pi}\left\{(\pi - \alpha) + \frac{\sin 2\alpha}{2}\right\}\right]^{1/2}$$

For $$V_m = 230 \times \sqrt{2}\,V \text{ and } \alpha = 30° = \frac{\pi}{6}$$

$$V_{or} = \frac{230\sqrt{2}}{\sqrt{2}}\left[\frac{1}{\pi}\left\{\left(\pi - \frac{\pi}{6}\right) + \frac{\sin 60}{2}\right\}\right]^{1/2}$$

$$= 226.66 \text{ V (rms value of output voltage)}$$

3.19 Show that a fully controlled 1-phase AD-DC bridge converter can operate in two quadrants.

[5 marks : 2011]

Solution:

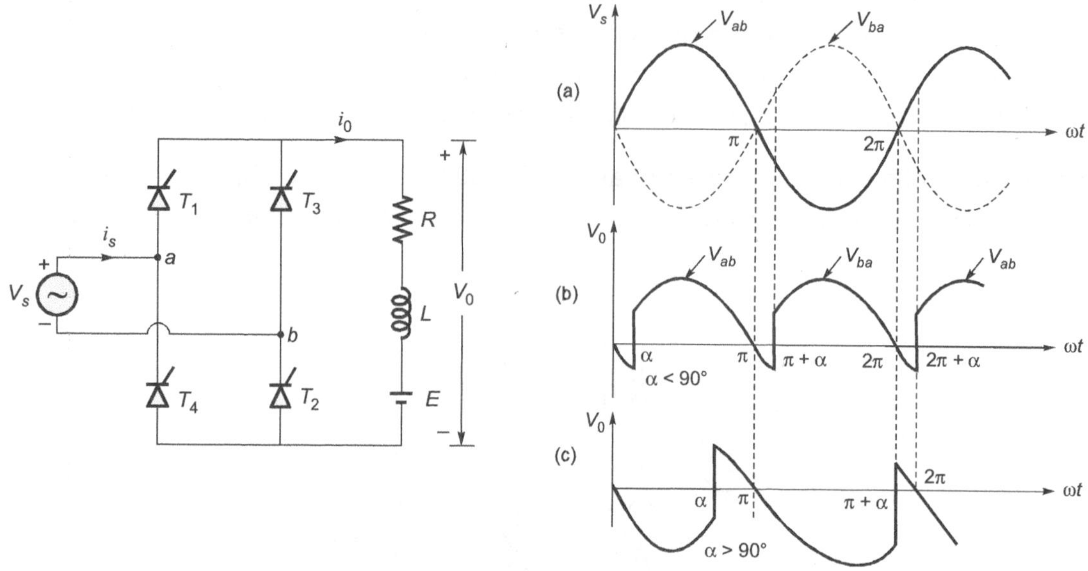

- Average value of output voltage $V_0 = \frac{2V_m}{\pi}\cos\alpha$.
- In figure (b), $\alpha < 90°$, V_0 is positive, and net power flow is from ac source to dc load. This mode of operation is converter operation.
- In figure (c), $\alpha > 90°$, V_0 is negative. If load circuit emf E is reversed, this source E will feed power back to ac supply. This mode of operation is called line-commuted inverter.

3.20 **State the different forced commutation methods used for improving the power factor in controlled AC-DC rectifiers.**

[4 marks : 2012]

Solution:

In forced commutation, the commutating components L and C do not carry load current continuously. In this commutation method, forward current of the thyristor is forced to zero by external circuitry called commutation circuit.

Forced commutation methods are:

- Resonant-pulse commutation (or class B commutation).
- Complementary commutation (or class C commutation).
- Impulse commutation (or class D commutation).

3.21 **A thyristors connected in series with inductive load (resistance = 0) is triggered at an angle α in each positive half cycle. Draw the load voltage and load current. Derive the expression for load current. Comment on power flow.**

[4 marks : 2014]

Solution:

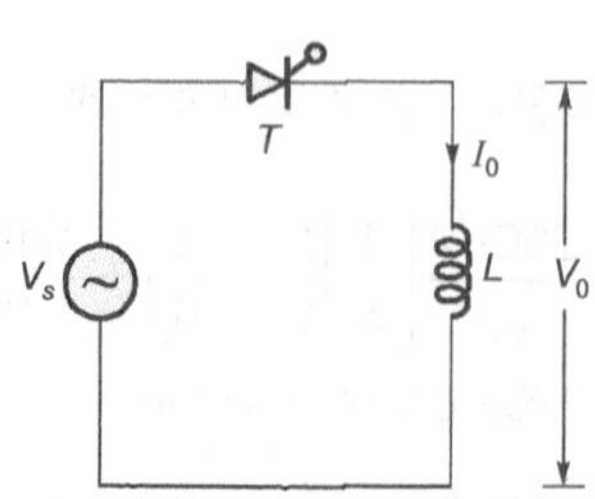

The output waveforms of the circuit are as follows.

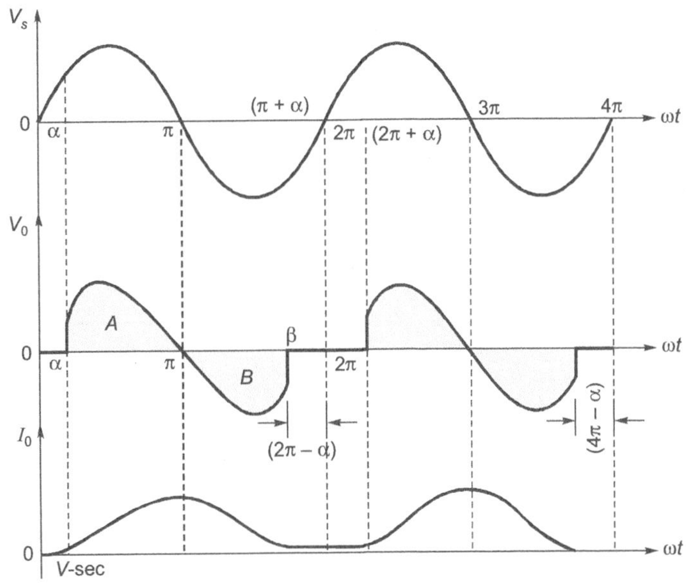

The area A is equal to B

$$V_m \sin\omega t = L\frac{di}{dt}$$

$$\frac{di}{dt} = \frac{V_m}{L}\sin\omega t$$

$$\int_0^i di = \frac{V_m}{\omega L}\int_\alpha^{\omega t}\sin\omega t\, d(\omega t)$$

$$i = \frac{V_m}{\omega L}(\cos\alpha - \cos\beta)$$

At extinction angle 'β' the current is zero.

$$0 = \frac{V_m}{\omega L}(\cos\alpha - \cos\beta)$$

$$\cos\alpha = \cos\beta$$

$$\therefore \quad \beta = 2\pi n \pm \alpha$$

$$\beta = 2\pi - \alpha$$

3.22 "With highly inductive load a fully controlled converter works as an inverter whenever the delay angle is more than 90°". Is it true or false? Explain with the help or waveforms.

[4 marks : 2014]

Solution:

Yes, the statement is true.

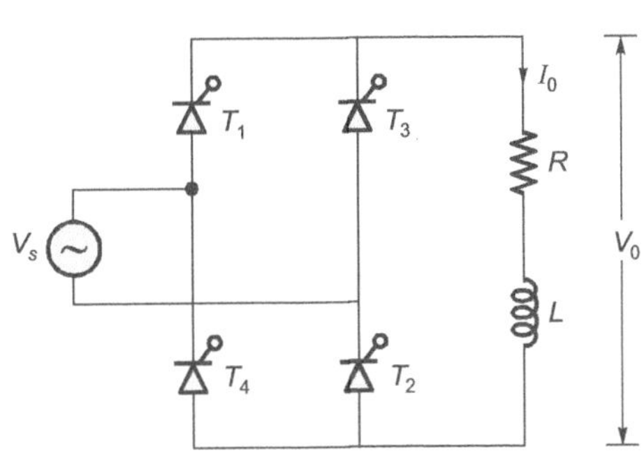

The output waveforms of this circuit are as shown below.

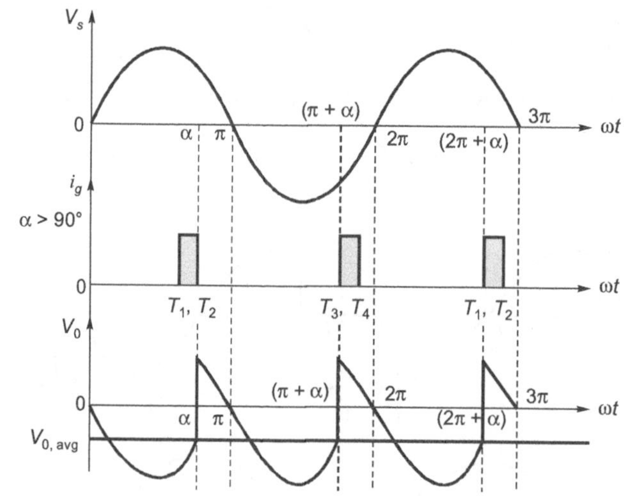

In the statement it is mentioned that the load is highly inductive in nature. So, $T = \frac{L}{R}$ the time constant is increased. The average output voltage is less than zero.

$\therefore$ The circuit behaves as inverter whenever delay angle is more than 90°.

3.23 **A single-phase 2-pulse mid-point converter triggered at a firing angle of 120°, operates in inverter mode. The load inductance is such that current is discontinuous in nature. Draw output voltage, source current and thyristor voltage waveforms.**

[10 marks : 2014]

Solution:

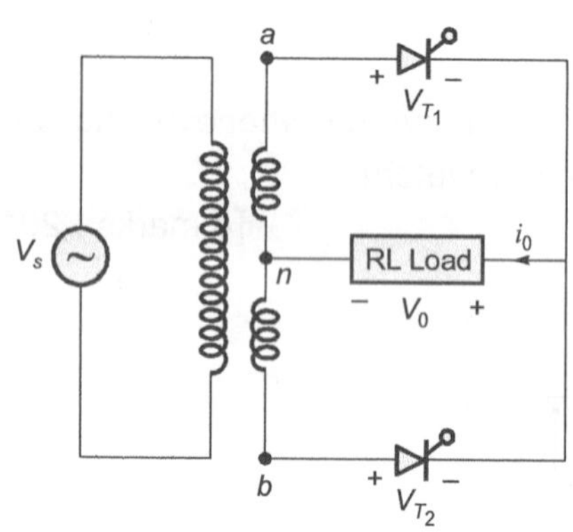

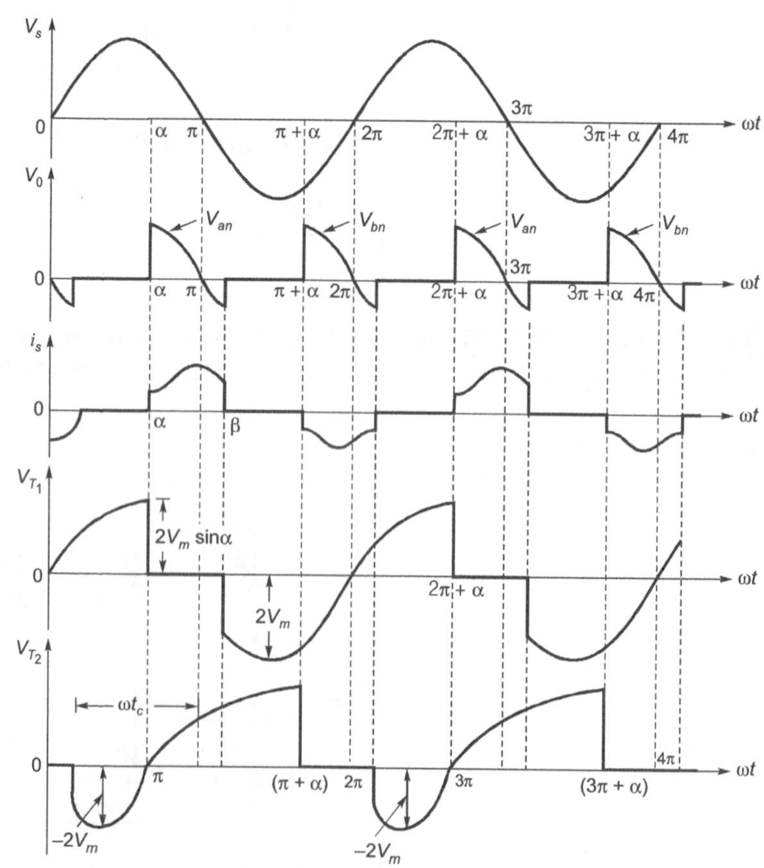

3.24 A single-phase fully controlled bridge converter is used to control the speed of a separately excited dc motor. A reactor of 50 mH is connected in the armature circuit. The converter is connected to 220 V, 50 Hz supply and is operated at a firing angle (α) of 90°. The back emf of the motor is 180 V. Draw the output voltage waveform of the converter and determine the peak value of current drawn. Neglect the resistance and reactance of dc machine armature.

[15 marks : 2015]

Solution:

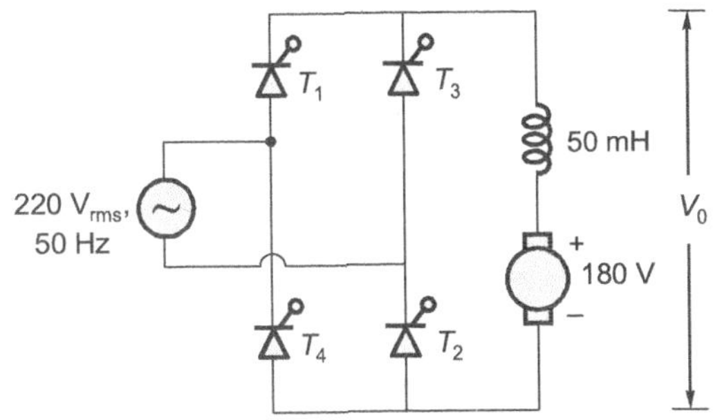

Output waveforms:

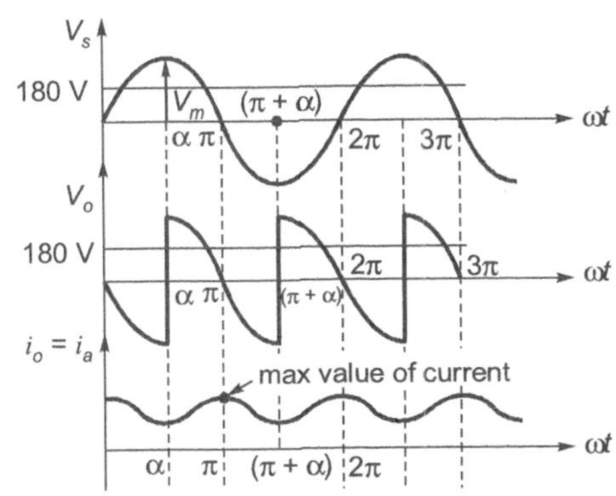

When thyristors T_1 and T_2 are ON then the circuit is

By KVL:

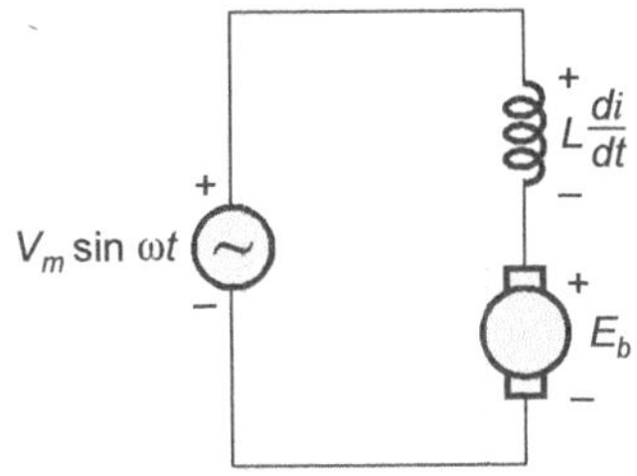

$$V_m \sin \omega t = L\frac{di}{dt} + E_b$$

$$L\frac{di}{dt} = V_m \sin \omega t - E_b$$

$$di = \left(\frac{V_m \sin\omega t - E_b}{L}\right) dt$$

Integrating on both sides,

$$i(t) = \frac{-V_m \cos\omega t}{\omega L} - \frac{E_b}{L}t + K$$

At $\omega t = \alpha$

$$i = 0$$

$$0 = -\frac{180}{50 \times 10^{-3}}(0.005) + K$$

$$\left[\because \omega t = \frac{\pi}{2} \quad t = \frac{\pi}{4\pi f} = \frac{1}{4f} = 5\,\text{ms}\right]$$

$$K = 18$$

The maximum value of current is obtained at $\omega t = \pi$

$$i(\pi) = -\frac{V_m}{\omega L}\cos\pi - \frac{180}{50\times10^{-3}}(0.01)+18 \qquad \left[\because\ \omega t = \pi \quad t = \frac{\pi}{2\pi f} = \frac{1}{2f} = 0.01\text{ s}\right]$$

$$= \frac{220\sqrt{2}}{5\pi} - 18$$

Maximum value of current drawn is

$$i_{max} = 1.8069\text{ A}$$

3.25 **A single-phase fully controlled converter feeding power to RL load is triggered at a firing angle of 120°. Draw output voltage, output current and input source current waveforms. Explain the flow of power in the circuit.**

[4 marks : 2016]

Solution:

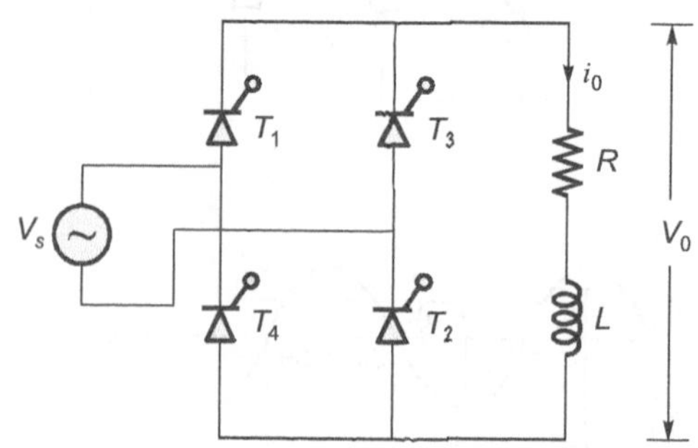

Output waveforms:

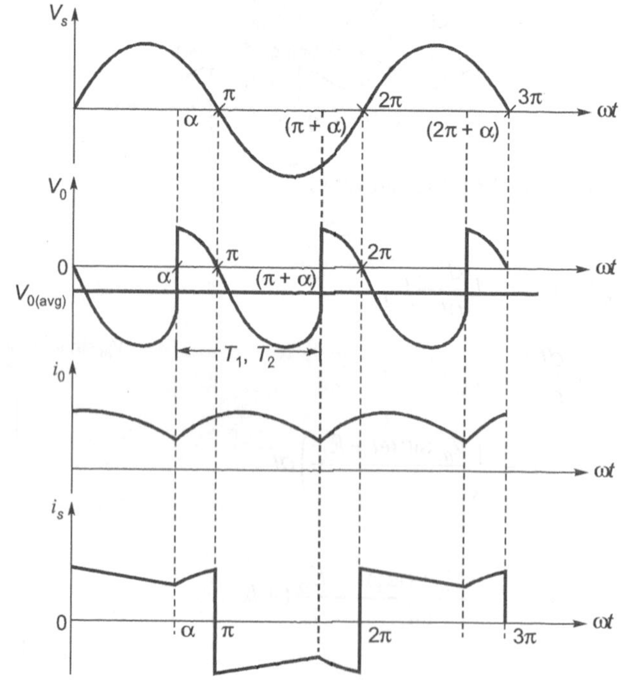

Firing angle, $\alpha > 90°$

Average output voltage, $V_0 = \frac{2V_m}{\pi}\cos\alpha$, is a negative value

$$P = (-V_0)\,I_0$$

Power is supplied from dc to ac, i.e. load to source.

3.26 A three-phase, three-pulse, half-wave controlled rectifier a supplying an R-L load, where $L \rightarrow \infty$. A freewheeling diode is also connected across this load. Determine the fundamental displacement factor and distortion factor for this converter as a function of firing angle α and hence determine the power factor of the converter.

[20 marks : 2017]

Solution:

The given circuit is a three-phase three-pulse converter.

Case-I: $\alpha \le \frac{\pi}{6}$, free wheeling diode will not conduct

$$i_R = I_0 \quad \text{when } T_1 \text{ is ON}$$

$$i_R = 0 \quad \text{when } T_1 \text{ OFF}$$

$$i_R = a_1 \cos\omega t + b_1 \sin\omega t$$

$$a_1 = \frac{1}{\pi}\int_0^{2\pi} f(\omega t)\cdot\cos\omega t\cdot d(\omega t)$$

$$= \frac{1}{\pi}\int_{\frac{\pi}{6}+\alpha}^{\frac{5\pi}{6}+\alpha} I_0 \cos\omega t\cdot d(\omega t) \quad \left[\because T_{ON} \text{ from} \left(\frac{\pi}{6}+\alpha\right) \text{ to} \left(\frac{5\pi}{6}+\alpha\right)\right]$$

$$a_1 = \frac{\sqrt{3}I_0}{\pi}\sin\alpha$$

$$b_1 = \frac{1}{\pi}\int_{\frac{\pi}{6}+\alpha}^{\frac{5\pi}{6}+\alpha} I_0 \sin\omega t\cdot d(\omega t) = \frac{\sqrt{3}I_0}{\pi}\cos\alpha$$

$$c_1 = \sqrt{a_1^2 + b_1^2} = \frac{\sqrt{3}I_0}{\pi}$$

$$\phi_1 = \tan^{-1}\left(\frac{a_1}{b_1}\right) = \alpha$$

$$i_{R_1} = c_1 \sin(\omega t + \phi_1) = \frac{\sqrt{3}I_0}{\pi}\sin(\omega t + \alpha)$$

Fundamental displacement factor = FDF = $\cos\phi_1 = \cos\alpha$

$$\text{Distortion factor} = g = \frac{I_{R_1\,\text{rms}}}{I_{R\text{rms}}} = \frac{\frac{\sqrt{3}I_0}{\sqrt{2}\pi}}{I_0/\sqrt{3}} = \frac{3}{\sqrt{2}\pi}$$

$$\text{Power factor} = \frac{3}{\sqrt{2}\pi}\cos\alpha$$

Case-II: $\alpha > \frac{\pi}{6}$ freewheeling diode will conduct

T_1 will conduct from $\left(\frac{\pi}{6}+\alpha\right)$ to π

$$i_{R_1} = a_1 \cos\omega t + b_1 \sin\omega t$$

$$a_1 = \frac{1}{\pi}\int_{\frac{\pi}{6}+\alpha}^{\pi} I_0 \cos\omega t \cdot d(\omega t) = -\frac{I_0}{\pi}\sin\left(\frac{\pi}{6}+\alpha\right)$$

$$b_1 = \frac{1}{\pi}\int_{\frac{\pi}{6}+\alpha}^{\pi} I_0 \sin\omega t \cdot d(\omega t) = \frac{I_0}{\pi}\left[1+\cos\left(\frac{\pi}{6}+\alpha\right)\right]$$

$$c_1 = \sqrt{a_1^2 + b_1^2}$$

$$= \frac{I_0}{\pi}\sqrt{\sin^2\left(\frac{\pi}{6}+\alpha\right) + \left[1+\cos\left(\frac{\pi}{6}+\alpha\right)\right]^2}$$

$$= \frac{2I_0}{\pi}\cos\left(\frac{\pi}{12}+\frac{\alpha}{2}\right)$$

$$I_{R_{1(\text{rms})}} = \frac{\sqrt{2}I_0}{\pi}\cos\left(\frac{\pi}{12}+\frac{\alpha}{2}\right)$$

$$\phi_1 = \tan^{-1}\left(\frac{a_1}{b_1}\right) = \tan^{-1}\left(-\tan\left(\frac{\frac{\pi}{6}+\alpha}{2}\right)\right) = -\left(\frac{\frac{\pi}{6}+\alpha}{2}\right)$$

$$\text{FDF} = \cos\phi_1 = \cos\left(\frac{\pi}{12}+\frac{\alpha}{2}\right)$$

$$\text{Distortion factor} = \frac{I_{S_1}}{I_S} = \frac{\frac{\sqrt{2}I_0}{\pi}\cos\left(\frac{\pi}{12}+\frac{\alpha}{2}\right)}{I_O \times \sqrt{\frac{\frac{5\pi}{6}-\alpha}{2\pi}}}$$

$$\text{Digital factor} = \frac{2\cos\left(\frac{\alpha}{2}+\frac{\pi}{12}\right)}{\sqrt{\pi\left(\frac{5\pi}{6}-\alpha\right)}}$$

$$\text{Power factor} = \frac{2\cos^2\left(\frac{\alpha}{2}+\frac{\pi}{12}\right)}{\sqrt{\pi\left(\frac{5\pi}{6}-\alpha\right)}}$$

3.27 A full controlled full wave bridge AC/DC converter is fed from a single-phase, 230 V, 50 Hz supply, and is in turn feeding to an R-L load (R = 10 Ω and L = 100 mH). The firing angle α = 60°. Investigate whether load current remains continuous or not. Compute rms load current considering only the dominant harmonic, and determine the power absorbed by the load. Also compute voltage ripple factor.

[20 marks : 2018]

Solution:

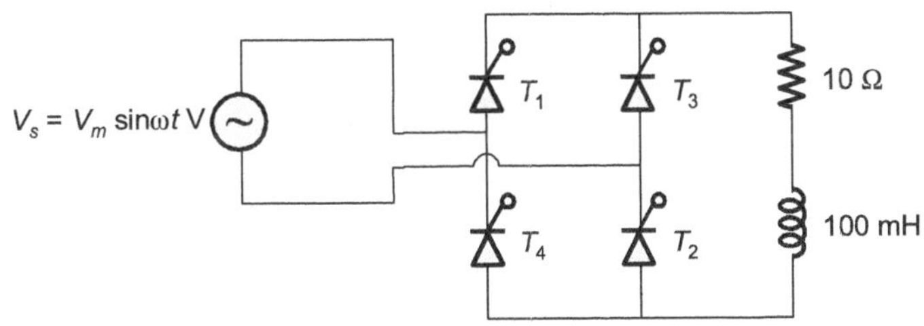

$$\phi = \tan^{-1}\left(\frac{\omega L}{R}\right) = \tan^{-1}\left(\frac{2\pi \times 50 \times 100 \times 10^{-3}}{10}\right) = 72.34°$$

$$i_0(t) = \frac{V_m}{Z}\sin(\omega t - \phi) + Ae^{-Rt/L} \quad ...(i)$$

At $\omega t = \alpha$, then, $i_0(t) = 0$

$$0 = \frac{V_m}{Z}\sin(\alpha - \phi) + A.e^{-R\alpha/\omega L}$$

$$A = \frac{-\frac{V_m}{Z}\sin(\alpha - \phi)}{e^{\frac{-R\alpha}{\omega L}}}$$

$$A = \frac{-V_m}{Z}\sin(\alpha - \phi).e^{\frac{R\alpha}{\omega L}} \quad ...(ii)$$

Substituting equation (ii) in equation (i),

$$i_0(t) = \frac{V_m}{Z}\sin(\omega t - \phi) - \frac{V_m}{Z}\sin(\alpha - \phi).e^{\frac{R\alpha}{\omega L}}.e^{\frac{-Rt}{L}}$$

$$i_0(t) = \frac{V_m}{Z}\left[\sin(\omega t - \phi) + \sin(\phi - \alpha).e^{-\frac{R}{\omega L}(\omega t - \alpha)}\right]$$

At $\omega t = \beta$ the value of $i_0(t) = 0$

$$0 = \sin(\beta - \phi) + \sin(\phi - \alpha).e^{\frac{-R}{\omega L}(\beta - \alpha)}$$

$$0 = \sin(\beta - 1.2626) + \sin(0.2154)\, e^{-0.3183(\beta - 1.0472)}$$

Solving the above transdental equation we obtain $\beta = 4.476$ radians

$$\beta = 256.45°$$

$$\beta > \pi + \alpha$$

∴ The load current is continuous.

Average output voltage, $$V_0 = \frac{2V_m}{\pi}\cos\alpha$$

$$V_0 = \frac{2\sqrt{2} \times 230}{\pi}\cos 60° = 103.536 \text{ V}$$

$$I_0 = \frac{V_0}{R} = \frac{103.536}{10} = 10.354 \text{ A}$$

By Fourier Analysis, $$a_n = \frac{2}{\pi}\int_{\alpha}^{\pi+\alpha} V_m \sin\omega t \cos n\omega t \, d\omega t$$

$$a_2 = \frac{2}{\pi}\int_{\alpha}^{\pi+\alpha} \frac{V_m}{2}.2\sin\omega t\cos 2\omega t(d\omega t)$$

$$= \frac{2V_m}{\pi}\left[\frac{\cos 3\alpha}{3} - \cos\alpha\right] = -172.56$$

$$b_n = \frac{2}{\pi}\int_{\alpha}^{\pi+\alpha} V_m \sin\omega t \sin n\omega t\,(d\omega t)$$

$$= \frac{V_m}{\pi}\int_{\alpha}^{\pi+\alpha} [\cos\omega t - \cos 3(\omega t)]d\omega t$$

$$b_2 = \frac{2\sqrt{2}\times 230}{\pi}\left[\frac{\sin 3\alpha}{3} - \sin\alpha\right] = -179.33$$

$$V_2 = \sqrt{a_2^2 + b_2^2} = \sqrt{(172.56)^2 + (179.33)^2} = 248.87 \text{ V}$$

$$Z_2 = 10 + j2\,(2\pi\, 50 \times 100 \times 10^{-3}) = 63.62\angle 80.96° \ \Omega$$

$$I_2 = \frac{248.87}{63.62} = 3.912 \text{ A}$$

$$I_{rms} = \sqrt{I_0^2 + \left(\frac{I_2}{\sqrt{2}}\right)^2} = \sqrt{10.354^2 + \left(\frac{3.912}{\sqrt{2}}\right)^2} = 10.717 \text{ A}$$

Power consumed by the load,

$$P = I_{orms}^2 R = (10.717)^2 \times 10 = 1148.54 \text{ W}$$

Voltage ripple factor,

$$\text{VRF} = \frac{\sqrt{\left(\frac{V_m}{\sqrt{2}}\right)^2 - \left(\frac{2V_m}{\pi}\cos\alpha\right)^2}}{\frac{2V_m}{\pi}\cos\alpha} = \frac{\sqrt{230^2 - (103.536)^2}}{103.536} = 1.98$$

3.28 A single-phase thyristor controlled bridge rectifier is supplying a dc load of 1 kW. A 1.5 kVA isolation transformer with a source side voltage rating of 120 V at 50 Hz is used. It has total leakage reactance of 8% based on its rating. The source voltage of nominally 115 V is in the range of ±10%. Assuming load current is nearly constant, find:

(i) The minimum turns ratio of the transformer, if the dc load voltage is to be regulated at constant value of 100 V,

(ii) The reduction in average load voltage due to commutation, and

(iii) The value of firing angle α when the source voltage is 115 + 10% V.

[20 Marks : 2019]

Solution:

$$P_0 = 1000 \text{ W}$$

$$Z_b = \frac{\text{kV}^2}{\text{MVA}} = \frac{120^2}{1500} = 9.6 \ \Omega$$

$$X_{Ls} = 0.08 \times 9.6$$

$$\omega L_s = 0.768 \ \Omega$$

$$L_s = 2.445 \text{ mH}$$

(i) Let 'a' be the turns ratio,

$$a = \frac{V_P}{V_s}$$

$$P_0 = 100 \times I_0 = 1000$$

$$I_0 = 10 \text{ A}$$

For minimum turns ratio $\alpha = 0$,

and $V_P = 115 \times 0.9 = 103.5$ V

$$V_0 = \frac{2\sqrt{2}}{\pi} V_s - \Delta V_0 = \frac{0.9 V_P}{a} - \left(\frac{4f L_s I_0}{a^2}\right)$$

$$\frac{0.9 \times 103.5}{a} - \frac{4 \times 50 \times 2.445 \times 10^{-3} \times 10}{a^2} = 100$$

$$\frac{93.15}{a} - \frac{4.89}{a^2} = 100$$

$$100a^2 - 93.15a + 4.89 = 0$$

$$a = 0.876, 0.0558$$

Possible value, $a = 0.876$

(ii) $$\Delta V_{d0} = \frac{4fL_s I_0}{a^2} = \frac{(4 \times 2.445 \times 10^{-3} \times 10 \times 50)}{0.876^2} = \frac{4.89}{0.876^2}$$

$$\Delta V_{d0} = 6.372 \text{ V}$$

(iii) $$V_P = 115 \times 1.1 = 126.5 \text{ V}$$

$$V_0 = \frac{0.9}{a} V_P \cos\alpha - \Delta V_0$$

$$\frac{0.9}{0.876} \times 126.5 \cos\alpha - 6.372 = 100$$

$$\cos\alpha = 0.8154$$

$$\alpha = 35.07°$$

3.29 A PV panel is connected with a single phase fully controlled converter as shown in the circuit below. The panel is supplying a current of 5 A and generated power is 1000 W. The series inductance in the circuit is large to make the current flat and continuous. Find (i) the triggering angle of the thyristor bridge, (ii) output voltage at rectifier terminal and (iii) input power factor.

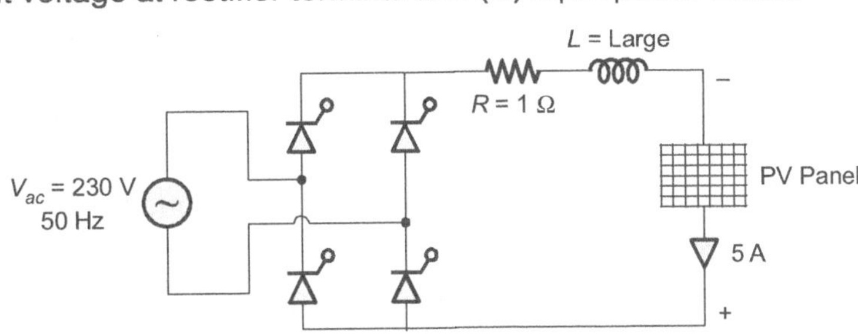

[12 marks : 2020]

Solution:

Given converter simplified layout,

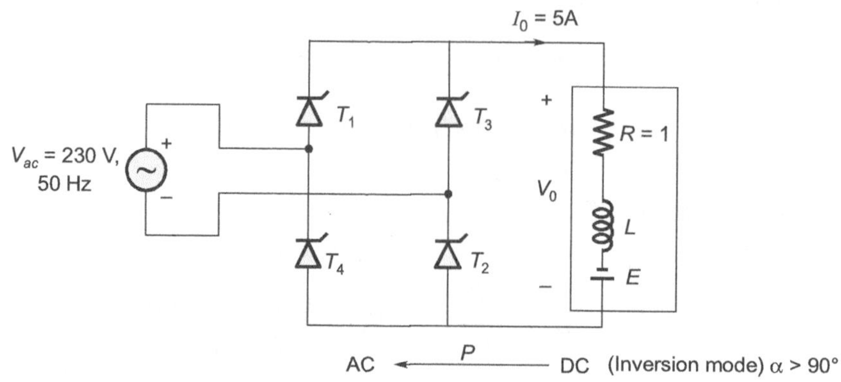

Generated power in the panel (solar cell)

$$EI_o = 1000 \text{ W}$$

$$E = \frac{1000}{I_o} = \frac{1000}{5} = 200 \text{ V}$$

$$V_o = -E + I_oR$$

$$\frac{2V_M}{\pi}\cos\alpha = -200 + (5 \times 1) = -195 \text{ V}$$

$$\frac{2.230\sqrt{2}}{\pi}\cdot\cos\alpha = -195$$

$$\cos\alpha = \frac{-195}{650.54} = -0.941698$$

(i) Triggering angle, $\alpha = 160.338°$

(ii) Output voltage, $V_o = -195$ V

(iii) Input power factor, $PF = g.FDF$

$$PF = 0.9\cos\alpha$$

$$= 0.9\cos(160.3350)$$

$$PF = -0.8475 \text{ lag}$$

3.30 A 3-phase half-controlled rectifier with free-wheeling diode is supplying a separately excited DC motor for speed control purpose. The AC input to the converter is 415 V, 3-phase, 50 Hz. The motor parameters are :

$$V = 220 \text{ V DC}, \; P = 10.5 \text{ kW}$$

Rated speed = 1100 rpm,

Armature resistance, $r_a = 0.4\ \Omega$

The field current is kept constant at rated value. The motor is operated at rated speed delivering half rated torque.

(i) Find motor terminal voltage and triggering angle of thyristor bridge.

(ii) Find the speed of the motor if one of the input phases to the converter is out due to fault and the triggering angle is kept as before with same load torque.

(iii) Also find the new triggering angle if the motor speed is to be maintained at rated value with same load torque.

(Neglect losses in the machine)

[20 marks : 2020]

Solution:

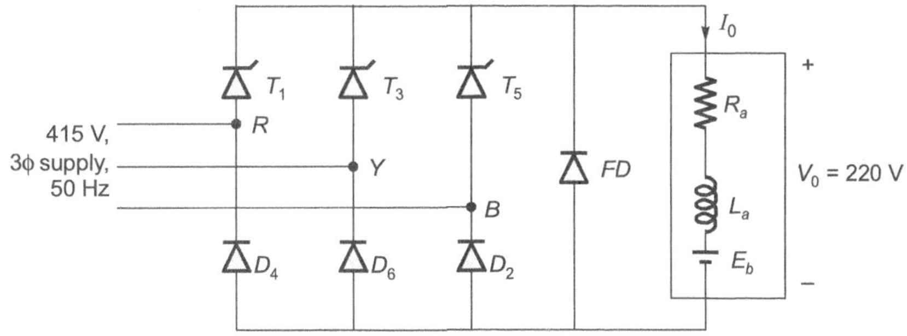

$$P_o = 10.5 \text{ kW}$$
$$N_r = 1100 \text{ rpm}$$
$$R_a = 0.4\ \Omega$$

Motor operated at rated speed and half the rated torque.

$$P_o = V_o I_o$$
$$10.5 \times 10^3 = 220 \times I_o$$

$$\text{Average current, } I_o = \frac{10.5\times10^3}{220} = 47.7 \text{ A}$$

At rated values,

$$V_o = E_b + I_o R_a$$
$$220 = K_m \cdot \frac{2\pi N_r}{60} + I_o R_a$$
$$220 = K_m \cdot \frac{2\pi\times1100}{60} + (47.7\times0.4)$$
$$K_m = \frac{201\times60}{2\pi\times1100}$$
$$K_m = 1.745 \text{ V.s/rad}$$

At half the rated torque, $$I_o = \frac{I_{oRated}}{2} = \frac{47.7}{2}$$
$$I_o = 23.85 \text{ A}$$

(i) $$V_o = E_b + I_o R_a$$

Terminal voltage of motor,

$$V_o = K_m \cdot \frac{2\pi N_r}{60} + I_o R_a$$
$$V_o = 1.745\times\frac{2\pi\times1100}{60} + (23.85\times0.4) = 210.54 \text{ V}$$
$$\frac{3V_{mL}}{2\pi}(1+\cos\alpha) = 210.54$$
$$\frac{3\times415\sqrt{2}}{2\pi}(1+\cos\alpha) = 210.54$$
$$1+\cos\alpha = \frac{1322.86}{1760.695} = 0.751$$
$$\cos\alpha = -0.24867$$

Triggering angle of bridge,

$$\alpha = 104.41°$$

(ii)

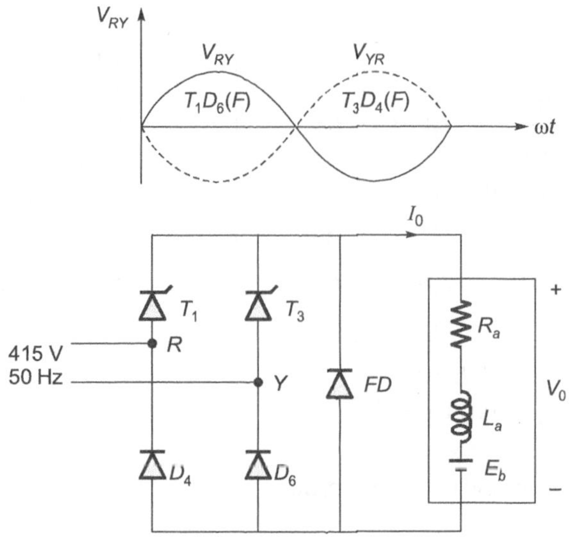

Now it works like single phase half controlled rectifier.

Using average voltage relation,

$$V_o = \frac{V_{mL}}{\pi}(1+\cos\alpha)$$

$$V_o = \frac{415\sqrt{2}}{\pi}(1+\cos 104.41) = 140.324 \text{ volts}$$

$$V_o = E_b + I_o R_a$$

$$V_o = K_m \frac{2\pi N}{60} + (23.85 \times 0.4)$$

$$140.324 = 1.745 \times \frac{2\pi N}{60} + 9.54$$

$$130.778 = 1.745 \times \frac{2\pi}{60} \text{N}$$

$$\therefore \quad N = \frac{130.778 \times 60}{1.745 \times 2\pi}$$

$$N = 716.061 \text{ rpm}$$

(iii) $\alpha = ?$

$$N = N_r = 1100 \text{ rpm}$$

$$V_o = E_b + I_o R_a$$

$$\frac{V_{mL}}{\pi}(1+\cos\alpha) = K_m \cdot \frac{2\pi N_r}{60} + I_o R_a$$

$$\frac{415\sqrt{2}}{\pi}(1+\cos\alpha) = 1.745 \times \frac{2\pi \cdot 1100}{60} + (23.85 \times 0.4)$$

$$186.815(1 + \cos\alpha) = 201 + 9.54$$

$$1 + \cos\alpha = \frac{210.549}{186.815} = 1.127$$

$$\cos\alpha = 0.127$$

$$\alpha = 82.7°$$

3.31 For the circuit shown in the figure,

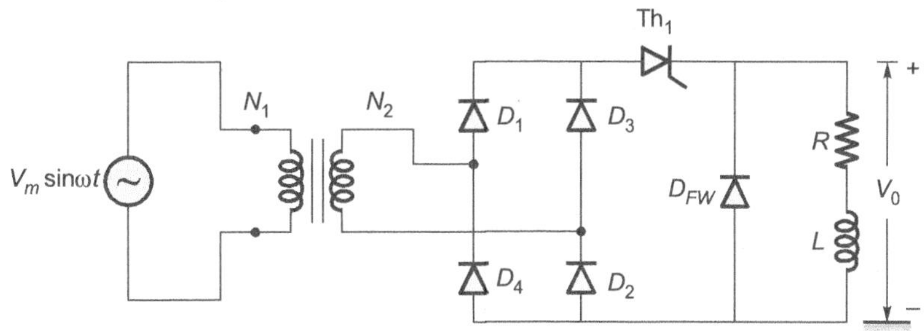

(i) Draw the output voltage $V_{0(+)}$ waveform.

(ii) Obtain the expression of $V_{0,\,av}$ i.e., average output voltage.

(iii) Discuss limitation and application area.

Assume thyristors are fired at α with $2f_s$ frequency, where $f_s = \omega/2\pi$ and ω is the synchronous supply frequency.

[12 marks : 2021]

Solution:

(i)

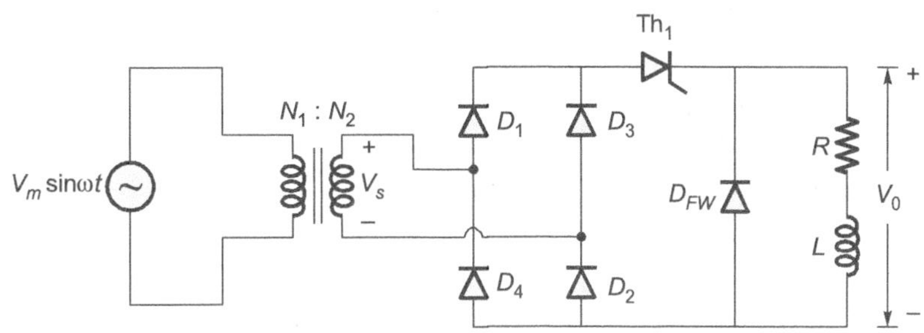

⇒ Secondary voltage of transformer

$$V_s = (V_m \sin\omega t) \times \frac{N_2}{N_1} = V_{m_s} \sin\omega t \qquad \left[\because V_{m_s} = \frac{V_m N_2}{N_1}\right]$$

- The given circuit is very much similar to a standard single phase semiconverter bridge where the load is RL load.
- Here in the circuit the following two cases are possible.
  1. Continuous conduction case
  2. Discontinuous conduction case

Case-I : Here the load current is assumed continuous over the working range.

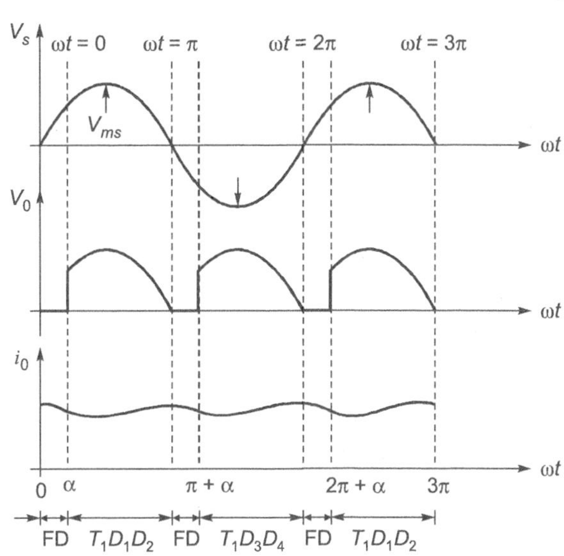

- For semiconverter, the average output voltage V_0, is given by

$$V_{0\,\text{avg}} = \frac{1}{\pi}\int_0^{\pi} V_{m_s} \sin\omega t \cdot d\omega t = \frac{V_{m_s}}{\pi}(1+\cos\alpha)$$

- Here the load current is assumed to be discontinuous current, means load current builds up from zero, rises to a maximum and then decays to zero at ($\beta > \pi$).

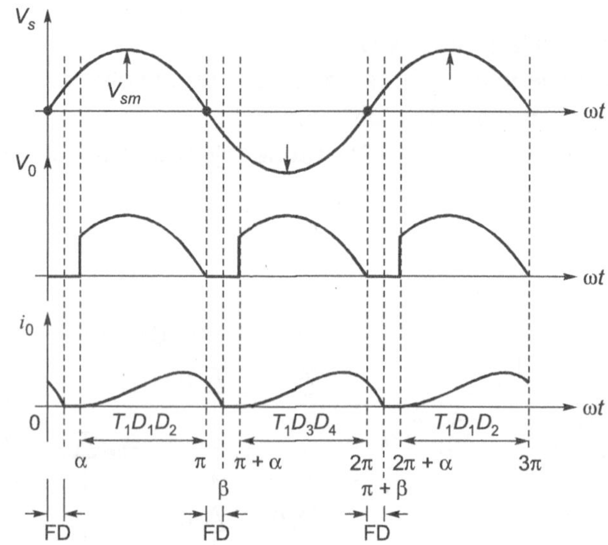

(ii) The average output voltage,

$$V_{0,\,\text{avg}} = \frac{1}{\pi}\int_0^{\pi} V_{m_s} \sin\omega t \cdot d\omega t = \frac{V_{m_s}}{\pi}(1+\cos\alpha) \qquad \left(\because V_{m_s} = V_m \times \frac{N_2}{N_1}\right)$$

(iii) **Limitation :** After the thyristor (Th_1) stops conducting during freewheeling period, reverse voltage is not applied across the thyristor, so commutation problem is there.

Application : It is used in speed control of a DC motor i.e. a DC electric drive.

3.32 A single phase full bridge fully controlled converter is supplying a battery at 100 V for charging application. The converter is connected to 240 V, 50 Hz AC supply. The interconnecting inductor between converter and battery is very large to make the load current flat, continuous and ripple free at 10 A. The inductor has a resistance of 1.5 Ω. Find the

(i) operating triggering angle.

(ii) average and rms values of converter output voltage.

(iii) power supplied to the battery.

(iv) converter input power.

(v) input power factor and displacement factor.

(vi) thyristor rms current.

Draw source current, thyristor current and output voltage waveforms of the converter.

Assume a conduction voltage drop of 1.5 V for each thyristor.

[20 marks : 2022]

Solution:

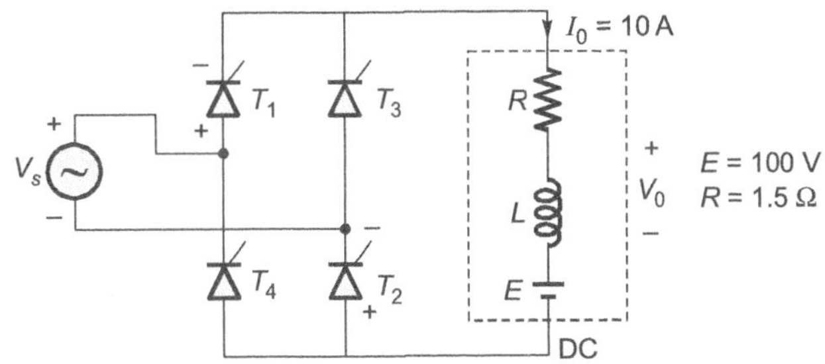

(i) $T_1 T_2 \rightarrow$ ON : KVL : Consider drop of T_1 and T_2

$$-v_s + 1.5 + v_o + 1.5 = 0$$

$$v_o = v_s - 3V$$

$$v_o = V_m \cdot \sin \omega t - 3$$

$$V_o = \frac{1}{T}\int_{\alpha}^{\pi+\alpha} (V_M \sin\omega t - 3) d(\omega t)$$

$$V_o = \frac{1}{\pi}\int_{\alpha}^{\pi+\alpha} (V_M \sin\omega t - 3) d(\omega t)$$

$$= \frac{2V_M}{\pi}\cos\alpha - \frac{3}{\pi}\int_{\alpha}^{\pi+\alpha} d(\omega t)$$

$$= \frac{2V_M}{\pi}\cos\alpha - \frac{3}{\pi}(\omega t)_a^{\pi+\alpha}$$

$$V_o = \frac{2V_m}{\pi}\cos\alpha - 3$$

$$V_o = E + I_o R$$

$$= 100 + (10 \times 1.5)$$

$$V_o = 115\ V$$

$$\frac{2V_m}{\pi}\cos\alpha - 3 = 115$$

$$\frac{2\times 240\sqrt{2}}{\pi}\cos\alpha = 118$$

$$\cos\alpha = 0.546$$

$$\alpha = 56.89^\circ$$

Operating triggering angle, α = 56.9°

(ii) Average value of converter output voltage

$$V_o = 115\ V$$

$T_1 T_2 \rightarrow$ ON : Total voltage drop of Thyristor

$$= V_T = 1.5 + 1.5 = 3\ V$$

$$V_{or} = \left[\frac{1}{\pi}\int_{\alpha}^{\pi+\alpha} (V_m \sin\omega t - V_T)^2 d(\omega t)\right]^{1/2}$$

$$V_{or} = \left[\frac{1}{\pi}\left\{\int_{\alpha}^{\pi+\alpha} V_m^2 \sin^2 \omega t d(\omega t) + \int_{\alpha}^{\pi+\alpha} -2V_m \sin\omega t \cdot V_T d(\omega t) + \int_{\alpha}^{\pi+\alpha} V_T^2 d(\omega t)\right\}\right]^{1/2}$$

$$V_{or} = \left[\frac{1}{\pi}\left\{\left(\frac{V_m^2}{2}+V_T^2\right)\pi - 2V_mV_T\cos\alpha\right\}\right]^{1/2}$$

$$V_{or} = \left[\frac{1}{\pi}\{(240^2+3^2)\pi - 2.240\sqrt{2}\cdot 3\cos 56.89\}\right]^{1/2}$$

rms value of converter output voltage

$$V_{or} = 238.54\text{ V}$$

(iii) Power supplied to battery

$$= EI = 100 \times 10 = 1000\text{ W}$$

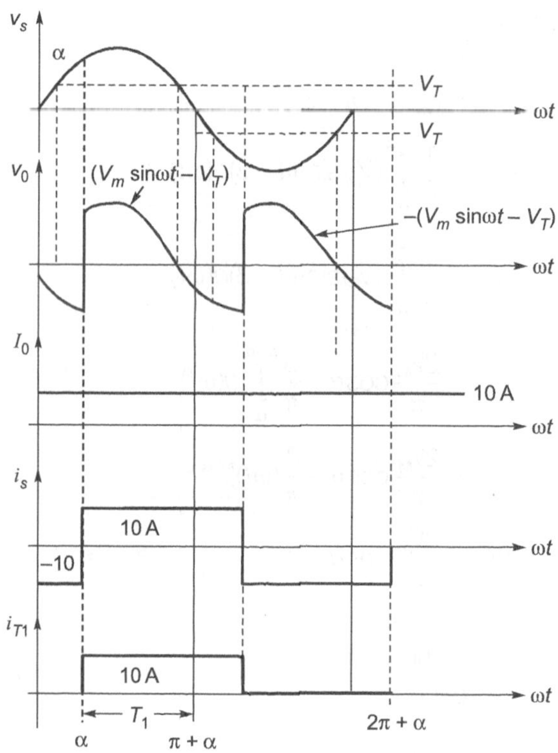

(iv) Converter input power

$$P_{in} = P_1 = V_{sr}I_{s1}\cos\phi_1 = 240\cdot\frac{2\sqrt{2}}{\pi}I_o\cos\alpha$$

$$= 240\left(\frac{2\sqrt{2}}{\pi}\cdot 10\right)\cos(56.89)$$

$$= 1{,}179.89\text{ W}$$

(v) Input power factor, $\quad PF = g.FDF = 0.9\cos\alpha$

$$= 0.9 \times \cos(56.89) = 0.4916$$

Displacement factor,

$$FDF = \cos\alpha = \cos(56.89)$$

$$FDF = 0.546$$

(vi) Thyristor rms current,

$$(I_T)_{rms} = I\left(\frac{\pi}{2\pi}\right)^{1/2} = \frac{I_o}{\sqrt{2}} = \frac{10}{\sqrt{2}} = 7.07\text{ A}$$

3.33 For a Class-D Commutation circuit shown below, calculate : (i) peak current through Main and Auxiliary thyristor; (ii) turn-off time(s) for Main and Auxiliary thyristors

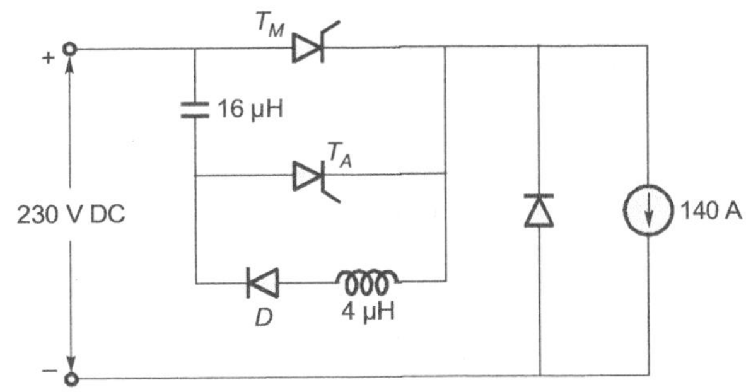

where T_M is main thyristor and T_A is Auxiliary thyristor. [12 marks : 2023]

Solution:

Class D - Commutation Circuit :

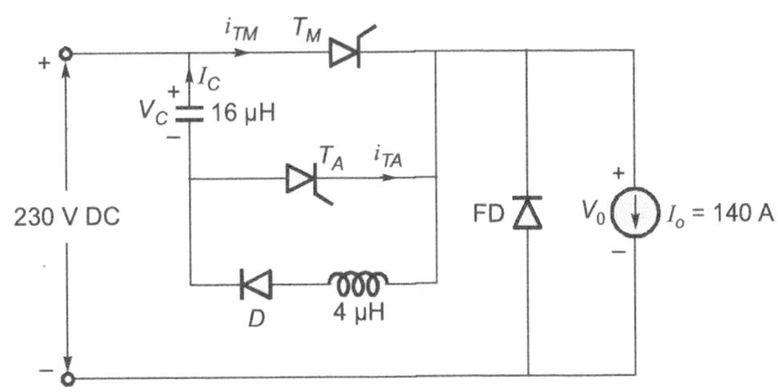

Required waveform is :

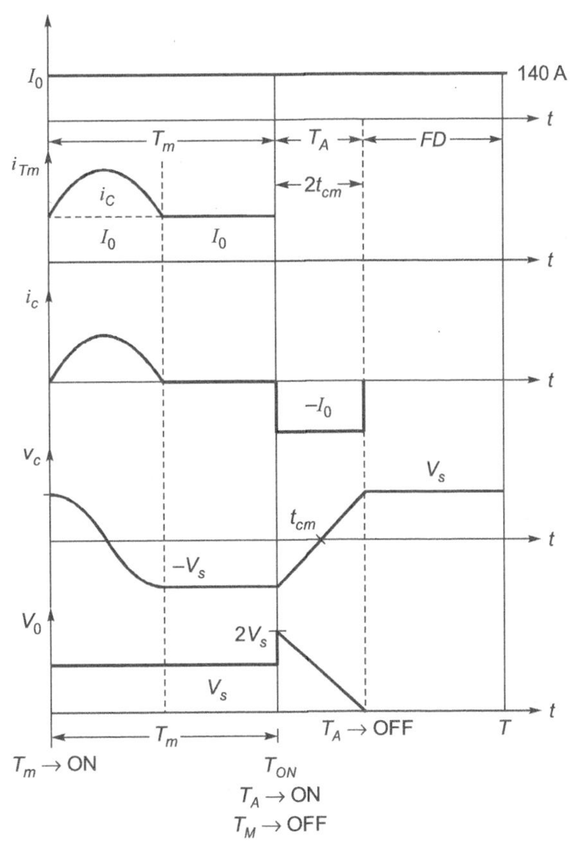

(i) Peak current through main thyristor,

$$(i_{TM})_{Peak} = I_o + I_P$$

$$= I_o + V_s\sqrt{\frac{C}{L}}$$

$$= 140 + 230\sqrt{\frac{16\ \mu F}{4\ \mu H}}$$

$$= 140 + (230 \times 2)$$

Peak current through auxiliary thyristor is 600 A

$$(i_{TA})_{Peak} = I_o = 140 \text{ A}$$

(ii) Circuit turn OFF time of Main Thyristor

$$t_{cm} = \frac{C}{I_o}V_s$$

$$= \frac{16.10^{-6}}{140} \times 230$$

$$t_{cm} = 26.28\ \mu S$$

Circuit turn OFF time of T_A is,

$$t_{CA} = \frac{\pi}{2}\sqrt{LC} = \frac{\pi}{2}\sqrt{4.10^{-6} \times 16.10^{-6}}$$

$$= 12.56\ \mu S$$

3.34 A half-wave uncontrolled rectifier circuit is fed from ac source with source inductance 'L_s'. It is driving a dc load at a constant current I_d as shown in figure below,

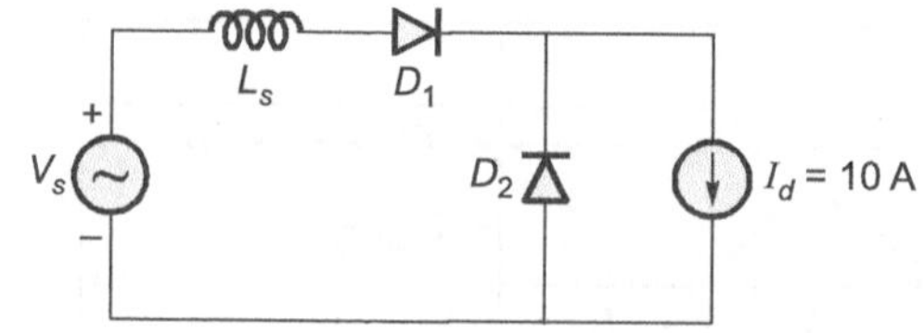

Calculate average output voltage V_d, average power P_d commutation overlap angle μ and plot the waveform of source current i_s, if

(i) V_s = 310 sin(314*t*) and L_s = 0.

(ii) V_s = 310 sin(314*t*) and L_s = 5 mH.

(iii) V_s is a square wave of 310 V and 50 Hz with a source inductance L_s = 5 mH.

[20 marks : 2023]

Solution:

Given circuit is :

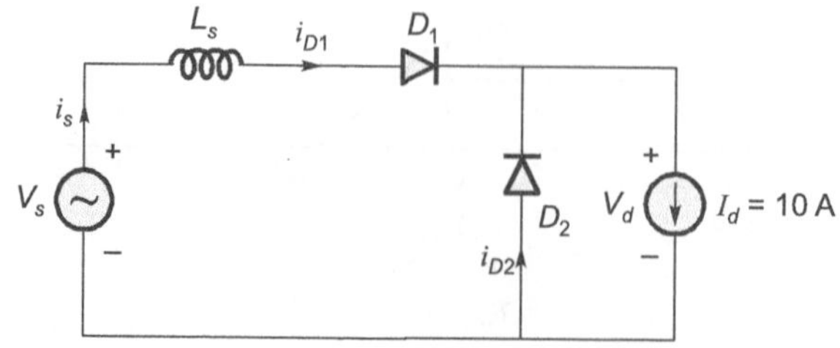

(i) Required waveform when V_s = 310 sin(314t) and L_s = 0

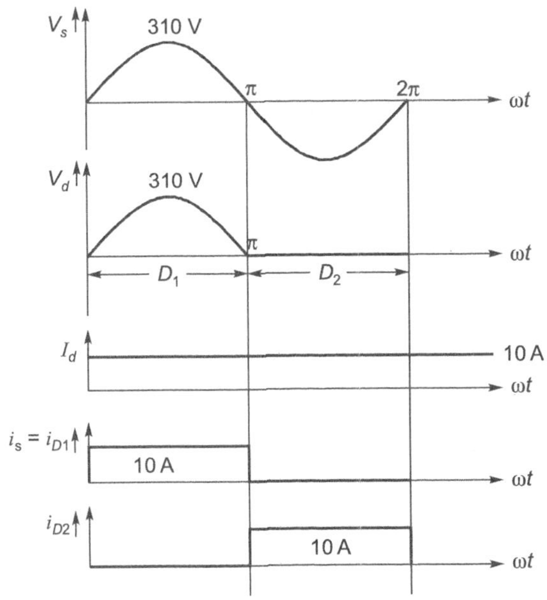

Average output voltage,

$$V_{d,avg} = \frac{1}{2\pi}\int_0^{\pi} V_m \sin\omega t \cdot d(\omega t) = \frac{V_m}{\pi} = \frac{310}{\pi} = 98.67 \text{ V}$$

Average output power, $P_d = V_d \cdot I_d = 98.676 \times 10$
$= 986.76$ W

Commutation angle, $\mu = 0$

$\because$ $L_s = 0$

(ii) Required waveform when V_s = 310 sin(314t) and L_s = 5 mH

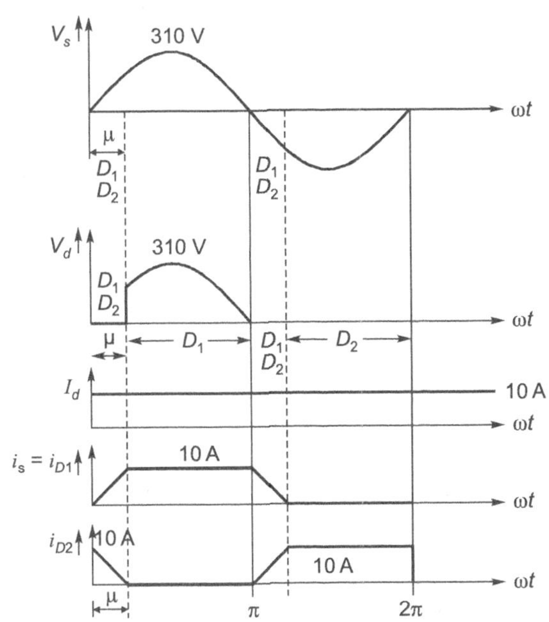

$$V_d = \frac{1}{2\pi}\int_0^{\pi} V_m \sin\omega t \cdot d(\omega t)$$

Average output voltage, $V_d = \frac{V_m}{2\pi}[1+\cos\mu] = \frac{310}{2\pi}[1+\cos(18.31)]$

$= 96.178$ V

Average output power, $P_d = V_d I_d$

$= 96.178 \times 10$

$= 961.78$ W

During overlap angle,

$$V_s = V_L$$

$$V_m \sin \omega t = L_s \frac{di_s}{dt}$$

$$di_s = \frac{V_m \sin\omega t}{L_s} dt$$

$$V_m \sin \omega t\, dt = L_s\, di_s$$

$$\int_0^{\mu} V_m \sin\omega t d(\omega t) = \omega L_s \int_0^{I_d} di_s$$

$$V_m[1 - \cos \mu] = \omega L_s I_d$$

$$1 - \cos \mu = \frac{\omega L_s I_d}{V_m}$$

$$\cos \mu = 1 - \frac{314 \times 5.10^{-3} \times 10}{310}$$

$$\mu = 18.31°$$

(iii)

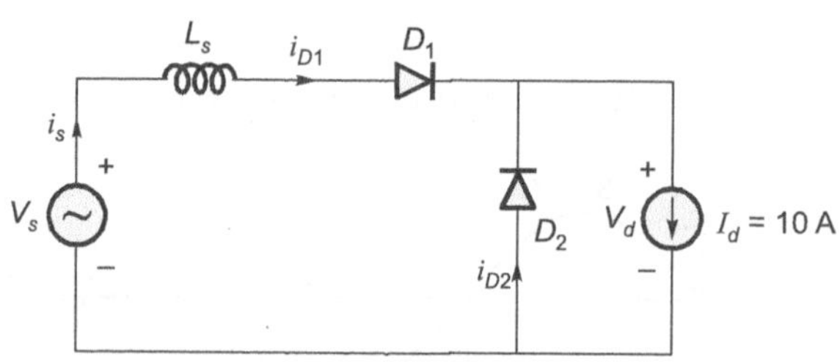

Required waveform when V_s is a square waveform.

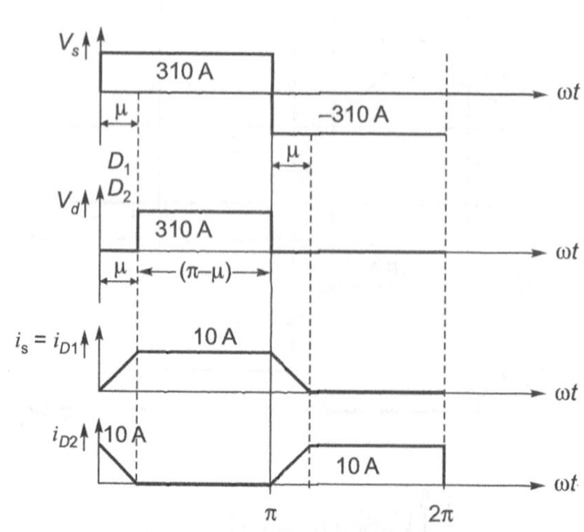

During overlap period : $D_1D_2 \rightarrow$ ON

$$\therefore \quad V_s = L_s \frac{di_s}{dt}$$

$$\omega = 2\pi.50$$

$$\omega = 100\pi$$

$$V_s.dt = L_s di_s$$

$$\int_0^{\mu} V_s d(\omega t) = \omega L_s \int_0^{I_d} di_s$$

$$V_s\mu = \omega L_s I_d$$

$$\mu = \frac{\omega L_s I_d}{V_s} = \frac{100\pi \times 5.10^{-3} \times 10}{310}$$

$$\mu = 0.0506 \text{ rad}$$

$$\mu = 2.9°$$

Average output voltage, $V_d = V_s\left(\frac{\pi - \mu}{2\pi}\right) = V_s\left(\frac{180° - \mu°}{360°}\right)$

$$= 310\left(\frac{180° - 2.9°}{360°}\right) = 152.5 \text{ V}$$

Average output power, $P_d = V_d I_d = 152.5 \times 10 = 1525$ W

4. Choppers

4.1 A step-down chopper operates from d.c. voltage source V_s and feeds a d.c. motor armature with counter e.m.f. E_b. From oscilloscopic traces, it is found that the current increases for on-time t_r (= T_{on}), falls to zero over time t_f and remains zero for time t_0 (off-period = $t_f + t_0 = T_{off}$) in every chopping cycle. Then the average voltage across the motor would be

(a) $\dfrac{V_s \cdot T_r}{(t_r + t_f + t_0)}$ (b) $\dfrac{V_s \cdot t_r + E_b \cdot t_f}{(t_r + t_f + t_0)}$

(c) $\dfrac{V_s \cdot t_r + E_b \cdot t_0}{(t_r + t_f + t_0)}$ (d) $\dfrac{V_s \cdot t_r + E_b(t_f + t_0)}{(t_r + t_f + t_0)}$ [2 marks : 2001]

Solution:

From the figure we can conclude that,

$$V_0(\text{av}) = \frac{V_s \times t_r + E_b \times t_0}{(t_r + t_f + t_0)}$$

Hence, option (c) is correct.

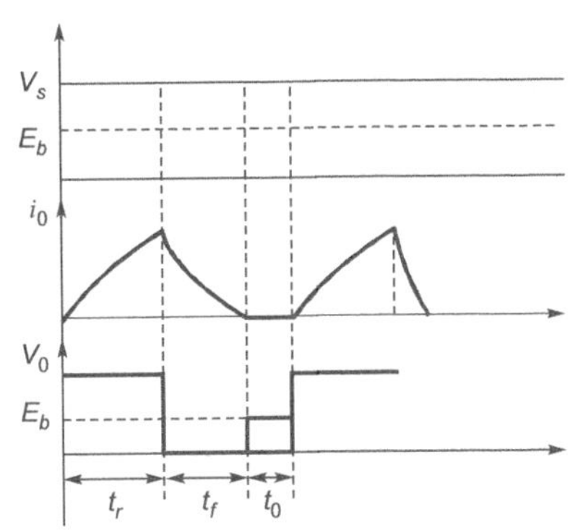

4.2 What is d.c. chopper? Discuss with necessary circuit diagrams the principle of operation of a
(i) step down chopper, (ii) step-up chopper.
Give comments on chopping frequency.

[12 marks : 2003]

Solution:

A d.c. chopper is a static device that converts fixed d.c. input voltage to a variable d.c. output voltage directly. Actually a step down chopper is a high speed on/off semiconductor switch. It connects source to load and disconnects the load from source at a fast speed. In this manner, a chopped load voltage as shown in Fig. (b) is obtained from a constant dc supply of magnitude V_s. In Fig. (a) chopper is represented by a switch SW inside a dotted rectangle, which may be turned-on or turned-off as desired.

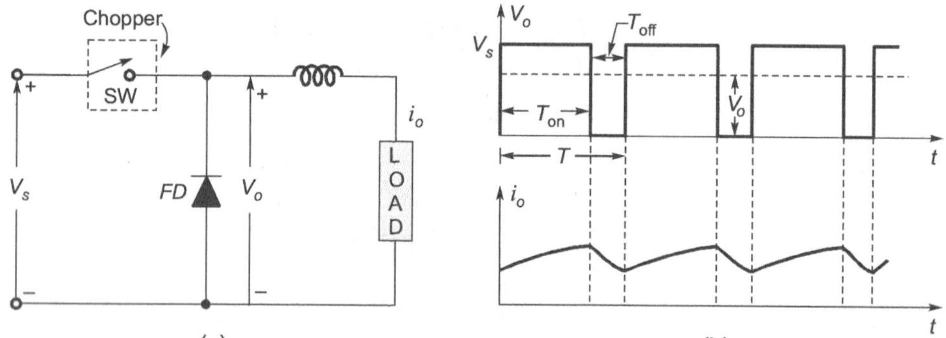

(a) (b)

Fig. (a) Elementary chopper circuit and (b) output voltage current waveforms

During the period T_{on}, chopper is on and load voltage is equal to source voltage V_s. During the interval T_{off}, chopper is off, load current flows through the freewheeling diode FD. As a result, load terminals are short circuited by FD and load voltage is therefore zero during T_{off}. In this manner a chopped dc voltage is produced at the load terminals. The load current as shown in Fig. (b) is continuous. From Fig. (b), average load voltage V_0 is given by

$$V_0 = \frac{T_{on}}{T_{on} + T_{off}} V_s = \frac{T_{on}}{T} V_0 = \alpha V_s \quad \text{...}(i)$$

where, T_{on} = on-time; T_{off} = off-time

$T = T_{on} + T_{off}$ = chopping period

$\alpha = \frac{T_{on}}{T}$ = duty cycle

Thus load voltage can be controlled by varying duty cycle α. Equation (i) shows that load voltage is independent of load current. Equation (i) can also be written as

$$V_0 = f \times T_{on} \cdot V_s \quad \text{where, } f = \frac{1}{T} = \text{chopping frequency}$$

Step-up Choppers

For the chopper configuration of Fig. (a). Average output voltage V_0 greater than input voltage V_s can be obtained by a chopper called step-up chopper. Fig. illustrates an elementary form of a step-up chopper.

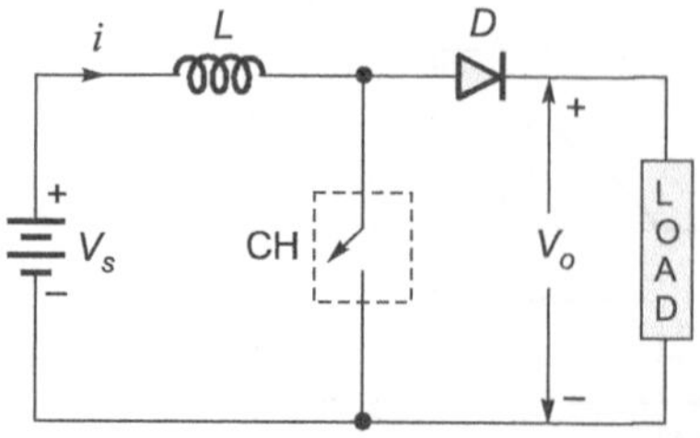

(a) Step-up chopper

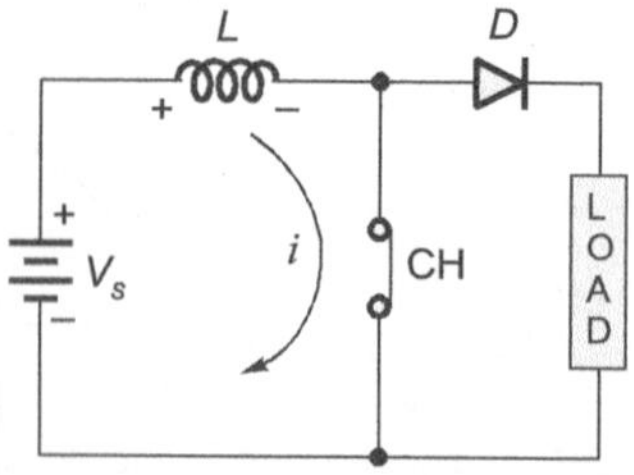

(b) L stores energy

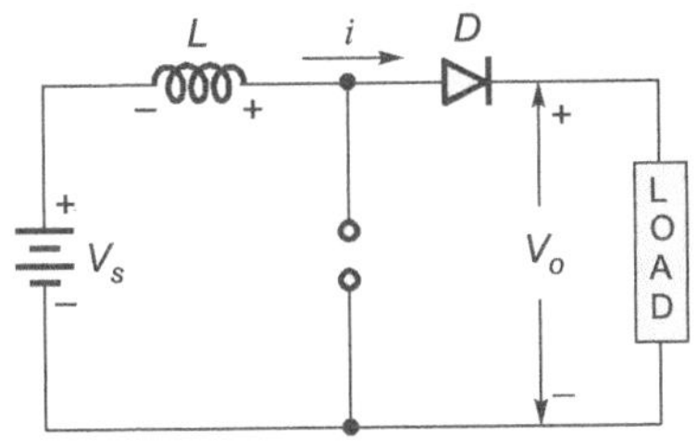

(c) $L \cdot di/dt$ is added to V_s

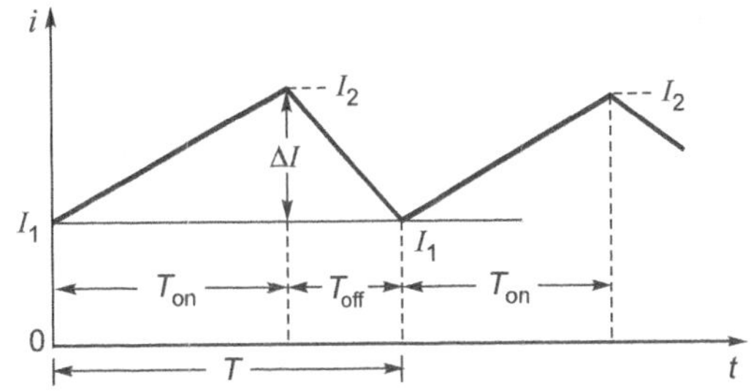

(d) Current waveform

In this chopper, a large inductor L in series with source voltage V_s is essential as shown in Fig. (a). When the chopper CH is on, the closed current path is as shown in Fig. (b) and inductor stores energy during T_{on} period. When the chopper CH is off, as the inductor current cannot die down instantaneously, this current is forced to flow through the diode and load for a time T_{off}, Fig. (c). As a result, voltage across the load, given by $V_0 = V_s + L(di/dt)$, exceeds the source voltage V_s. In this manner, the circuit of Fig.(a) acts as a step-up chopper and the energy stored in L is released to the load.

When CH is on, current through the load would increase from I_1 to I_2 as shown in Fig. (d). When CH is off, current would fall from I_2 to I_1. With CH on, source voltage is applied to L i.e. $v_L = V_s$. When CH is off, KCL for Fig. (c) gives $v_L - V_0 + V_s = 0$, or $v_L = V_0 - V_s$. Here v_L = voltage across L. Assuming linear variation of output current, the energy input to inductor from the source, during the period T_{on}, is

$$W_{in} = \text{(voltage across } L\text{) (average current through } L\text{) } T_{on}$$

$$= V_s \cdot \left(\frac{I_1 + I_2}{2}\right) T_{on} \qquad ...(i)$$

During the time T_{off}, when chopper is off, the energy released by inductor to the load is

$$W_{off} = \text{(voltage across } L\text{) (average current through } L\text{) } T_{off}$$

$$= (V_0 - V_s)\left(\frac{I_1 + I_2}{2}\right) \cdot T_{off} \qquad ...(ii)$$

Considering the system to be lossless, these two energies given by Eq.. (*i*) and (*ii*) will be equal

$$\therefore \quad V_s\left(\frac{I_1 + I_2}{2}\right) T_{on} = (V_0 - V_s)\left(\frac{I_1 + I_2}{2}\right) \cdot T_{off}$$

$$V_0 = V_s \frac{T}{T - T_{on}}$$

$$= V_s \frac{1}{1 - \alpha} \qquad ...(iii)$$

Output voltage depends upon α that can be controlled by varying frequency. There are two schemes:

(i) Constant frequency and

(ii) Variable frequency for having such control.

Constant frequency scheme is better than variable frequency scheme. In constant frequency scheme, T_{on} can not be reduced to zero for most of the commutation circuits used in choppers. As such, low range of α control is not possible in this scheme.

4.3 Explain how dc input voltage *V* can be stepped-up to get 2 V at the load terminals using a dc to dc chopper.

[15 marks : 2004]

Solution:

Basic circuit of step-up chopper,

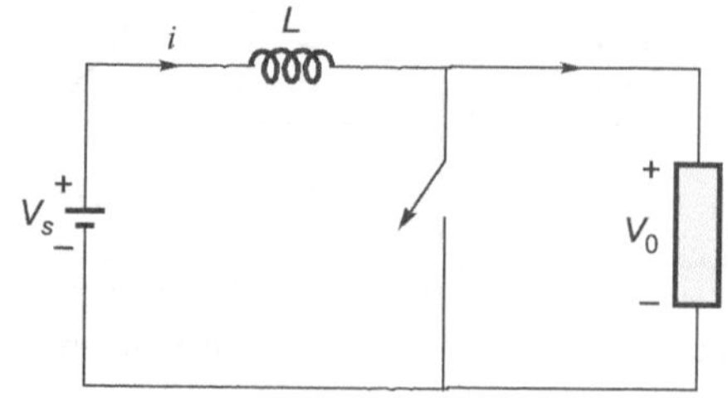

On the time of (T_{ON}),

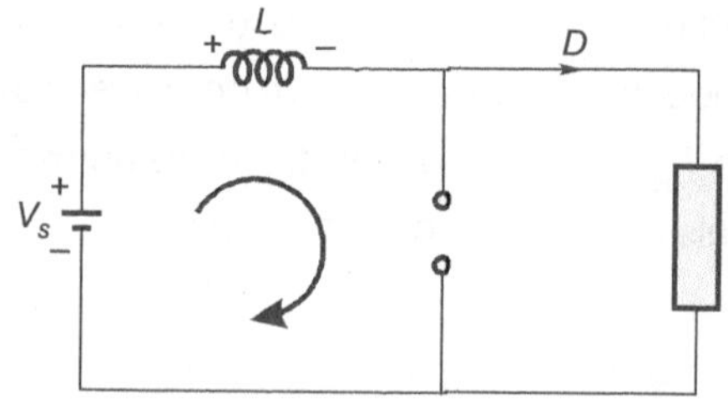

On the time of (T_{off}),

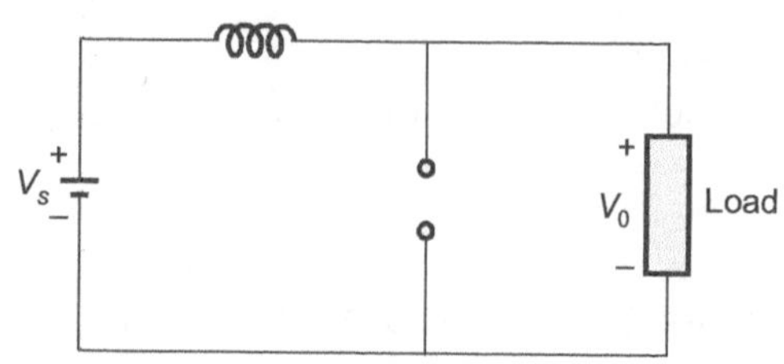

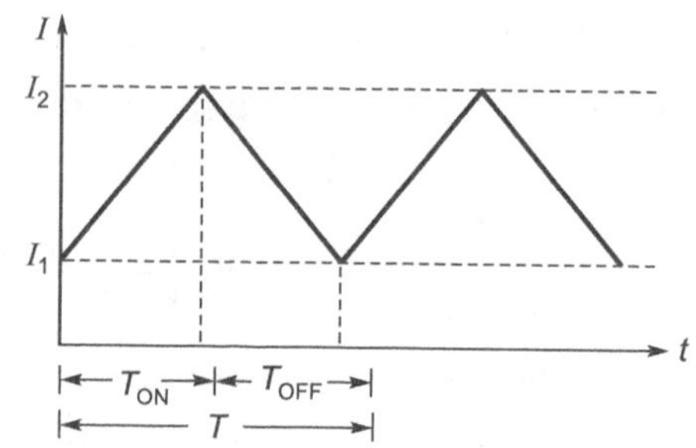

During period T_{ON}, the energy given to inductor from source is,

$$W_{ON} = V_s\left(\frac{I_1+I_2}{2}\right)T_{ON}$$

and during period 'T_{OFF}' the energy release by inductor to the load is

$$W_{OFF} = (V_0 - V_s)\left(\frac{I_1+I_2}{2}\right)T_{OFF}$$

Considering the system to be lossless,

$$V_s\left(\frac{I_1+I_2}{2}\right)T_{ON} = (V_0 - V_s)\left(\frac{I_1+I_2}{2}\right)T_{OFF}$$

$$V_0 = V_s \cdot \frac{T}{T - T_{ON}} = \frac{V_s}{1-\delta}$$

If, $V_s = V,\ V_0 = 2\text{ V (given)}$

Thus, $$(1-\delta) = \frac{V}{2\text{ V}}$$

$\therefore$ $$\delta = \frac{1}{2}$$

Thus for a duty cycle $\frac{1}{2}$ by having $T_{ON} = T_{OFF}$ the voltage can be stepped from $\frac{1}{2}$V to 2 V.

4.4 A step-up chopper has load voltage of 600 V and is supplied from a constant input dc source of 200 V. If the OFF-time of the chopper is 50-μsec., compute the ON time of the chopper. Also compute the ON time for the same frequency, if the desired output voltage is 300 V.

[10 marks : 2004]

Solution:

For a step up chopper, $V_0 = \dfrac{V_s}{1-\delta}$

$$\therefore \quad 600 = \frac{200}{1-\delta}$$

$$\therefore \quad \delta = \frac{2}{3}$$

$$\therefore \quad \delta = \frac{T_{ON}}{T} = \frac{2}{3} = \frac{T - T_{OFF}}{T}$$

$$\therefore \quad T_{OFF} = \frac{T}{3}$$

$$\therefore \quad T = 3 \times 50\ \mu\text{ sec} = 150\ \mu\text{ sec}$$

and $T_{ON} = T - T_{OFF} = 100\ \mu\text{sec}$

Now if desired output voltage is (300 V), then

$$V_0 = 300 = \frac{V_s}{1-\delta} = \frac{200}{1-\delta}$$

$$\therefore \quad \delta = \frac{1}{3}$$

$$\therefore \quad T_{ON} = \frac{T}{3} = \frac{150\ \mu\text{sec}}{3} = 50\ \mu\text{ sec}$$

4.5 (i) With proper diagrams, explain the working of a step up chopper.

(ii) A step up chopper has input voltage of 220 V and output voltage of 660 V. If the non-conducting time of thyristor-chopper is 100 μ secs, compute the pulse width of the output voltage. If the pulse width is halved, for constant frequency operation, find the new output voltage.

[6 + 6 = 12 marks : 2007]

Solution:

(i)

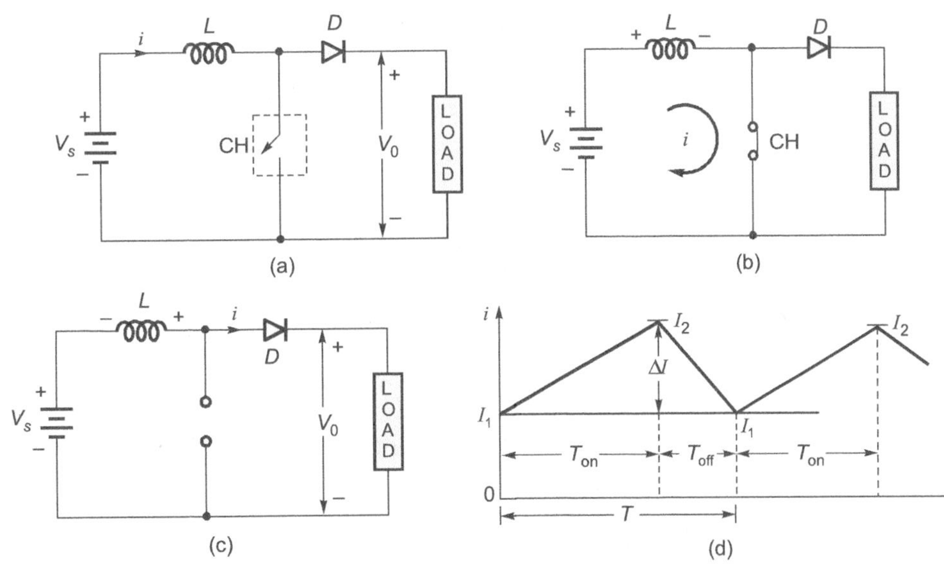

(a) Step-up chopper, (b) L stores energy and (c) $L \cdot di/dt$ is added to V_s (d) current waveform

In this chopper, a large inductor L in series with source voltage V_s is essential as shown in Fig. (a). When the chopper CH is on, the closed current path is as shown in Fig. (b) and inductor stores energy during T_{on} period. When the chopper CH is off, as the inductor current cannot die down instantaneously, this current is forced to flow through the diode and load for a time T_{off}, Fig. (c). As a result, voltage across the load, given by $V_0 = V_s + L(di/dt)$, exceeds the source voltage V_s. In this manner, the circuit of Fig. (a) acts as a step-up chopper and the energy stored in L is released to the load.

When CH is on, current through the load would increase from I_1 to I_2 as shown in Fig. (d). When CH is off, current would fall from I_2 to I_1. With CH on, source voltage is applied to L i.e. $v_L = V_s$. When CH is off, KCL for Fig. (c) gives $v_L - V_0 + V_s = 0$, or $v_L = V_0 - V_s$. Here v_L = voltage across L. Assuming linear variation of output current, the energy input to inductor from the source, during the period T_{on}, is

$$W_{in} = \text{(voltage across } L\text{) (average current through } L\text{) } T_{on}$$

$$= V_s \cdot \left(\frac{I_1 + I_2}{2}\right) T_{on} \qquad ...(i)$$

During the time T_{off}, when chopper is off, the energy released by inductor to the load is

$$W_{off} = \text{(voltage across } L\text{) (average current through } L\text{)} T_{off}$$

$$= (V_0 - V_s)\left(\frac{I_1 + I_2}{2}\right) \cdot T_{off} \qquad ...(ii)$$

Considering the system to be lossless, these two energies given by Eqs. (*i*) and (*ii*) will be equal

$$\therefore \quad V_s\left(\frac{I_1 + I_2}{2}\right) T_{on} = (V_0 - V_s)\left(\frac{I_1 + I_2}{2}\right) \cdot T_{off}$$

$$V_0 = V_s \frac{T}{T - T_{on}} = V_s \frac{1}{1 - \alpha} \qquad ...(iii)$$

It is seen from equation (iii) that average voltage across the load can be stepped up by varying the duty cycle. If chopper of Fig. (a) is always off, $\alpha = 0$ and $V_0 = V_s$. If this chopper is always on, $\alpha = 1$ and $V_0 = \infty$ (infinity). In practice, chopper is turned on and off so that α is variable and the required step-up average output voltage, more than source voltage, is obtained.

(ii) Using, $$V_0 = V_s \cdot \frac{1}{1 - \alpha}$$

$$660 = 220 \frac{1}{1 - \alpha} \quad \text{or } \alpha = \frac{2}{3} = \frac{T_{on}}{T}$$

$$\therefore \quad T_{on} = \frac{2}{3}T \text{ and } T_{off} = T - T_{on} = \frac{1}{3}T$$

$$\frac{1}{3}T = 100\ \mu\text{s (given)}$$

$$\therefore \quad T = 300\ \mu\text{s and } T_{on} = \frac{2}{3} \times 300 = 200\ \mu\text{s (pulse width)}$$

When pulse width is halved, $T_{on} = \frac{1}{2} \times 200 = 100\ \mu\text{s}$

For constant frequency operation,

$$T = 300\ \mu\text{s} ;\ T_{off} = T - T_{on} = 200\ \mu\text{s}\ \alpha = \frac{T_{on}}{T} = \frac{100}{300} = \frac{1}{3}$$

$$\therefore \text{ New output,} \quad V_0 = 200 \frac{1}{1 - \frac{1}{3}} = 330\ \text{V}$$

4.6 A step down d.c. chopper has load resistance of 20 Ω. Chopper input voltage is 200 V (d.c). The chopper switch has the voltage drop of 1.5 V when conducting. If the chopper frequency is 2 kHz. Find the input and output power of the chopper at the duty cycle of 0.5. Also find chopper efficiency.

[10 marks : 2009]

Solution:

When chopper is on, output voltage is (V_s – 1.5) volts and during the time chopper is off, output is zero

$$\therefore \quad \text{Average output voltage} = \left(\frac{(V_S - 1.5)T_{ON}}{T}\right) = (200 - 1.5) \times 0.5 = 99.25 \text{ V}$$

R.M.S. value of output voltage,

$$V_{OR} = \left[(V_s - 1.5)^2 \cdot \frac{T_{on}}{T}\right]^{1/2} = \left[(200 - 1.5)^2 \times 0.5\right]^{1/2} = 140.36 \text{ volt}$$

Power output or power delivered to load,

$$P_0 = \frac{V_{OR}^2}{R} = \frac{140.36^2}{20} = 985 \text{ watts.}$$

$$\text{Power input to chopper,} \quad P_i = V_s \times I_0 = 200 \times \frac{99.25}{20} = 992.5 \text{ W}$$

$$\therefore \quad \text{Chopper efficiency} = \frac{P_0}{P_i} \times 100 = \frac{985}{992.5} \times 100 = 99.24\%$$

4.7 A 1-ϕ circuit for temperature regulation uses ON-OFF control. The ac input is 220 V, 1-ϕ, 50 Hz supply. The circuit has a variable frequency, constant ON time. If the input voltage goes up by 10%, calculate the percentage change required in the triggering frequency of the chopper.

[16 marks : 2012]

Solution:

RMS value of the input voltage, $V_{rms} = 220 \text{ V}$

The rms value of the input voltage when the supply voltage increases by 10%

$$V_{rms\,1} = (220 \times 1.1) \text{ V} = 242 \text{ V}$$

$$V_0 = f\,T_{on} \cdot V_i = f\,T_{on} \times 220$$

When input supply changes, $V_o = f'T_{on}\,V_i' = f'\,T_{on} \times 242$

$$f'T_{on} \times 242 = f\,T_{on} \times 220$$

$$\frac{f'}{f} = \frac{220}{242}$$

$$\frac{f' - f}{f} = \frac{220 - 242}{242} = -\frac{1}{11}$$

$$\% \text{ change} = 9.1\%$$

4.8 Draw a neat diagram for a four quadrant chopper employing self commutated switches, feeding the armature of a DC motor (separately excited type). Explain through voltage and current waveforms the working for both duty ratio greater than and less than 0.5.

[10 marks : 2013]

Solution:

Type-E chopper or Four quadrant chopper:

The power circuit diagram for a four-quadrant chopper is shown in figure. It consists of four semiconductor switches CH_1 to CH_4 and four diodes D_1 to D_4 in antiparallel.

Working of this chopper in the four quadrants is explained as under.

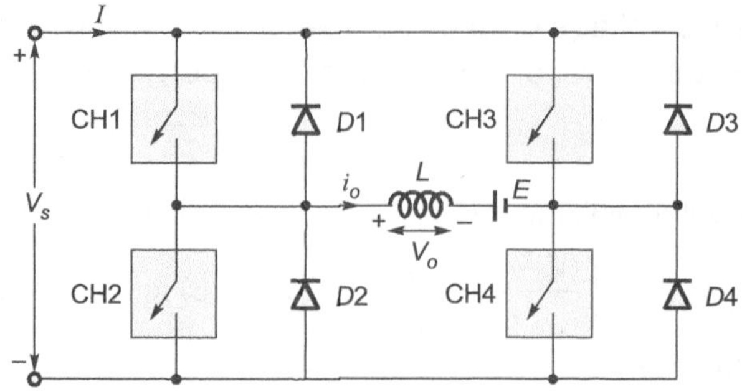

Circuit diagram

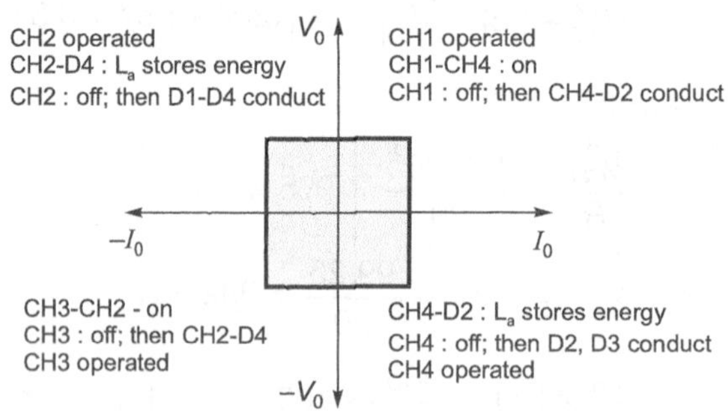

Operation of conducting devices four-quadrant, or Type-E chopper

First quadrant:

$$\left.\begin{aligned} V_o &= +ve \\ c_o &= +ve \end{aligned}\right\} \text{CH}_1\text{, is operated and CH}_4 \text{ is kept on and CH}_3 \text{ is kept off.}$$

$$V_s = Ri_o + \frac{Ldi_o}{dt} + E$$

$$\frac{di_o}{dt} = \frac{V_s - Ri_o - E}{L}$$

$$= V_o,\ i_o \text{ increased and inductor } L$$

Stored energy. $V_0 = V_s$, i_0 is giving first quadrant operation. When CH_1 is turned-off, positive current free-wheels through CH_4, D_2. In this manner, both V_0, i_0 can be controlled in the first quadrant.

Second quadrant: Here CH_2 is operated and CH_1, CH_3 and CH_4 are kept-off with CH_2 on, reverse (or negative) current flows through L, CH_2, D_4 and E. Inductance L stores energy during the time CH_2 is on.
When CH_2 is turned-off, current is fed back to source through diodes D_1, D_4.

Here $\left(\frac{E + Ldi}{dt}\right) > V_s$, as voltage V_0 is positive, and i_0 is negative, it is second quadrant operation of chopper. Also power is fed back from load to source.

Third quadrant: CH_1 is kept off, CH_2 is kept on and CH_3 is operated. Polarity of load emf E must be reversed for this quadrant working with CH_3 on, load gets connected to source V_s so that both V_o, i_o are negative leading to third quadrant operation. When CH_3, D_4. In this manner, V_o and i_o can be controlled in the third quadrant.

Fourth quadrant: Here CH_4 is operated and other devices are kept off. Load emf E must have its polarity reversed for operation in the fourth quadrant. With CH_4 on, positive current flows through CH_4, D_2, L and E. Inductance L stores energy during the time CH_4 is on. When CH_4 is turned-off, current is fed back to source through diodes D_2, D_3. Here load voltage is negative, but load current is positive leading to chopper operation in the fourth quadrant. Also power is fed back from load to source.

4.9 In a voltage commutated chopper DC voltage input $V = 250$ V, constant load current $I_0 = 20$ A, chopper frequency = 250 Hz, commutating components $L = 1.25$ mH and $C = 8$ μF. Calculate the exact minimum average output voltage and circuit turn-off time.

[10 marks : 2014]

Solution:

Voltage commutated chopper circuit,

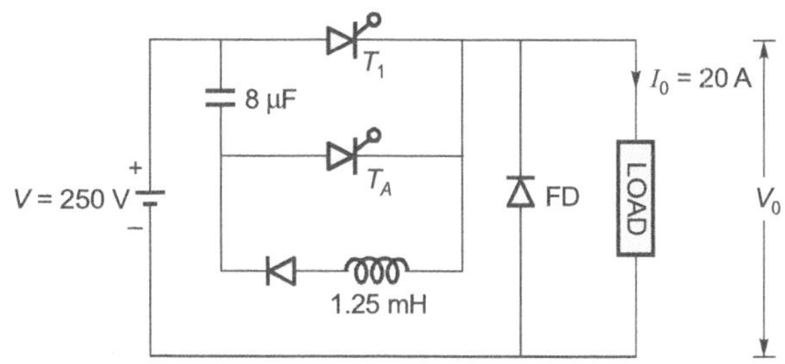

Circuit turn-off time, $t_c = \dfrac{CV_s}{I_0} = \dfrac{8\times10^{-6}\times250}{20}$

$= 1\times10^{-4}$ s

The minimum on period for this chopper is,

$$t_1 = \frac{\pi}{\omega_0} = \pi\sqrt{LC}$$

$$= \pi\sqrt{1.25\times10^{-3}\times8\times10^{-6}}$$

$$= 3.1416\times10^{-4}$$

The minimum average output voltage of the circuit is,

$$V_{0,\,min} = f\,V_s[t_1 + 2t_c]$$

$$= 250\times250\,[3.1416\times10^{-4} + 2\times10^{-4}]$$

$$V_{0,\,min} = 32.135\text{ V}$$

4.10 A 1-quadrant chopper feeds an RL load comprising a resistance of 10 ohms and an inductance of 15 mH and is fed from a 110 V dc. Determine the (i) minimum and maximum values of load current (ii) peak-to-peak ripple (iii) average value of load current. Assume chopper frequency is 500 Hz, duty cycle = 0.5 and current is continuous.

[10 marks : 2015]

Solution:

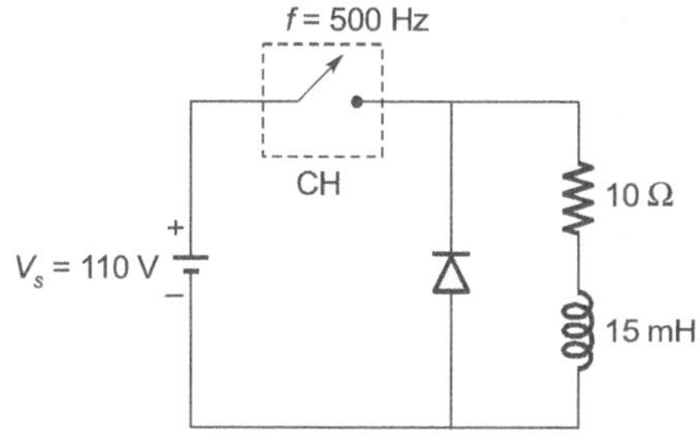

As the above chopper is step down chopper.

(iii) $V_0 = \alpha V_s$

$= 0.5\times110 = 55$ V

$$I_0 = \frac{V_0}{R_1} = \frac{55}{10} = 5.5\text{ A}$$

Hence duty cycle is $\alpha = 0.5$.

(ii) Peak to peak ripple current,

$$\Delta I_{max} = \frac{V_s}{4fL} = \frac{110}{4\times500\times15\times10^{-3}} = 3.666\text{ A}$$

(i) Maximum value of load current $= I_0 + \dfrac{\Delta I_{max}}{2} = 5.5 + 1.833$

$$I_{max} = 7.33\text{ A}$$

Minimum value of load current $= I_0 - \dfrac{\Delta I_{max}}{2} = 5.5 - 1.833$

$$I_{min} = 3.667\text{ A}$$

4.11 Discuss the operation of a Boost dc-dc converter with relevant waveforms. Draw the circuit diagram indicating the voltages across each element in both the operating modes. Derive the expressions for

(i) Average output voltage,

(ii) Minimum inductance for continuous current,

(iii) Output voltage ripple.

[10 marks : 2016]

Solution:

Boost Regulator:

In boost regulator the output voltage is greater than the input voltage hence the name 'boost'.

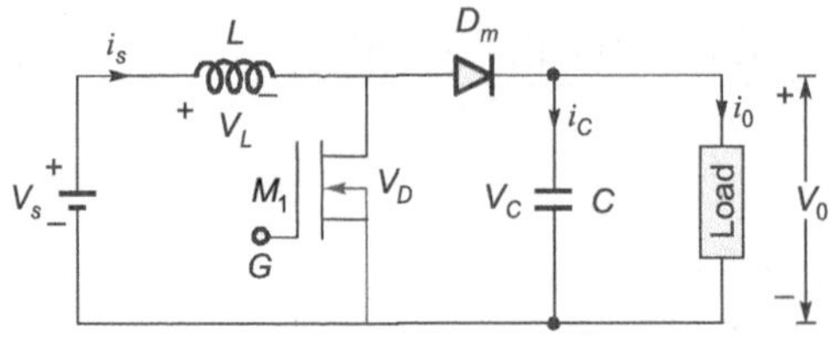

(a)

The circuit operation is divided into two modes.

Mode-1

Begin when MOSFET M_1 is switched ON at $t = 0$.

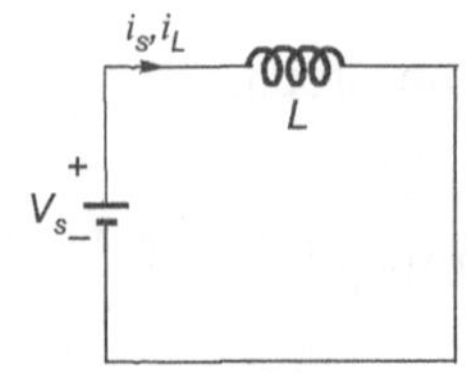

(b)

The input current, which rises, flows through inductor L and MOSFET M_1. Mode 2 begins when MOSFET M_1 is switched off at $t = t_1$.

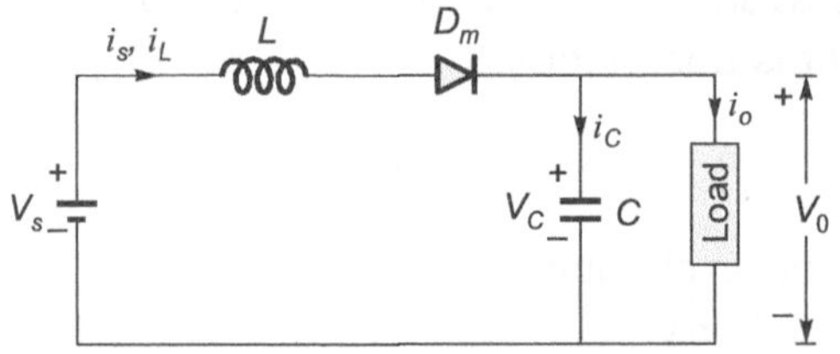

(c)

The current that was flowing through the MOSFET would now flow through L/C, load and diode D_m. The inductor current until MOSFET M_1 is turned on again in the next cycle.

Assuming that the inductor current rises linearly from I_1 to I_2 in time t_1,

$$V_s = L\frac{I_2 - I_1}{t_1} = L\frac{\Delta I}{t_1}$$

$$t_1 = T_{ON} = \frac{\Delta I_L}{V_s}$$

and the inductor current falls linearly from I_2 to I_1 in time t_2.

$$V_s - V_0 = -L\frac{\Delta I}{t_2}$$

$$t_2 = \frac{\Delta IL}{V_0 - V_s}$$

where, $\Delta I = I_2 - I_1$ is peak to peak ripple current of the inductor L.

$$\boxed{\Delta I = \frac{V_s T_{ON}}{L} = \frac{(V_0 - V_s)T_{OFF}}{L}}$$

(i) **The average output voltage,** $V_0 = V_s \frac{T}{T_{OFF}} = \left(\frac{1}{1-\alpha}\right) V_s$

(ii) The peak to peak current ripple is, $\Delta I = \frac{V_s \alpha}{f L}$

(iii) The peak to peak ripple voltage of capacitor, $\Delta V_C = \frac{I_0 \alpha}{f C}$

Condition for Continuous Inductor Current and Capacitor Voltage

If V_C is the average capacitor voltage, the capacitor ripple voltage $\Delta V_C = 2V_0$.

$$\frac{I_0 \alpha}{cf} = 2V_0 = 2 I_0 R \qquad \text{[At the boundary]}$$

Which gives the critical value of the capacitor C_C as $C_C = C = \frac{\alpha}{2fR}$.

Output Waveforms:

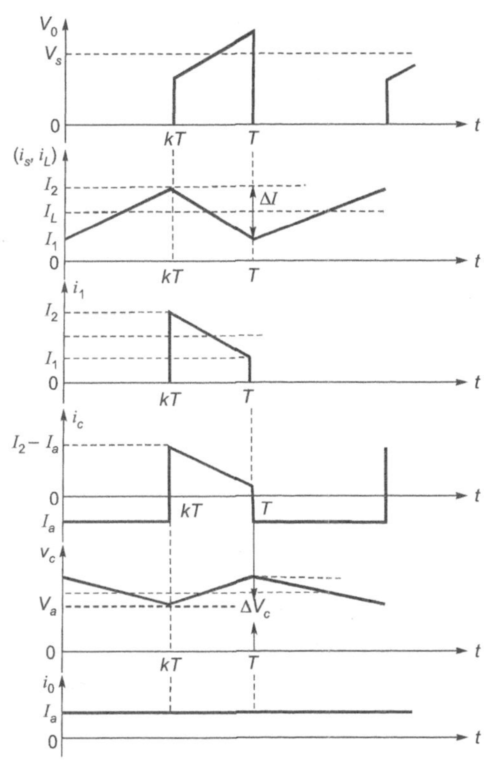

A boost regular can step up the output voltage with out a transformer. Due to a single transistor, it has a high efficiency. The input current is continuous. However a high peak current has to flow through the power transistor. The output voltage is very sensitive to changes in duty cycle a and it might be difficult to stabilize the regulator. The average output current is less than the average inductor current by a factor of (1 – K), and a much higher rms current would flow through the filter capacitor, resulting in the use of a large filter capacitor and a large inductor than those of a buck regulator.

4.12 A buck-boost regulator has an input voltage of 6 V. This produces an output voltage of 15 V while supplying an average load current of 0.5 A. The converter is operated at a frequency of 20 kHz. If the inductance and capacitance of the converter are 250 μH and 440 μF, then determine the duty cycle, ripple current of inductor and ripple voltage of filter capacitor. Draw the waveforms and derive the relationship used for computing ripple in voltage and current.

[20 marks : 2017]

Solution:

Given:

Supply voltage, $V_s = 6$ V

Output voltage, $V_0 = 15$ V

and the given regulator is buck-boost regular.

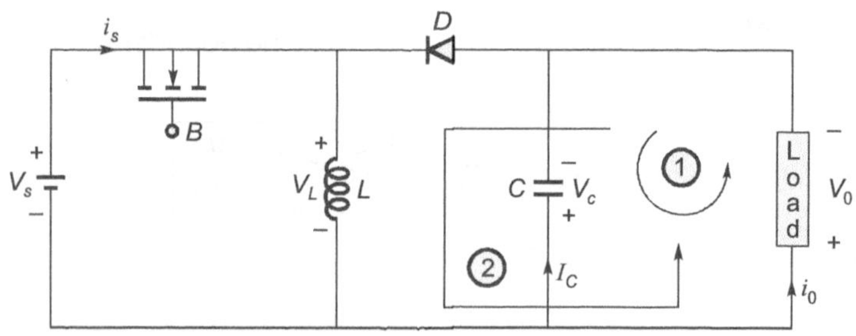

Buck-boost regulator circuit diagram

Now, for Mode-1, $0 \le t \le T_{ON}$ i.e. $T_1 \rightarrow {}_{ON}$, $D \rightarrow$ OFF

When the power MOSFET is switched-ON, the supply current flows through the path, $V_s - T_L - L - V_s$.

Hence, inductor 'L' stores the energy during the T_{ON} period.

During time T_{ON} by assuming that the inductor current rises linearly from I_1 to I_2.

From figure for Mode-1,

$$V_s = V_L$$

$$L\frac{di}{dt} = V_s$$

$$\int_{I_1}^{I_2} di = \frac{V_s}{L}\int_0^{T_{ON}} dt$$

$$\Delta I = (I_2 - I_1) = \frac{V_s}{L}(T_{ON} - 0)$$

$$\Delta I = \frac{V_s T_{ON}}{L} \text{ or } \frac{V_s \alpha}{fL} \qquad \left(\frac{T_{ON}}{T}, T = -\frac{\alpha}{f};\ \therefore\ \alpha = \frac{T_0}{T}\right)$$

Now, for Mode (2), $T_{ON} \le t \le T$; i.e., $T_1 \rightarrow$ OFF, $D \rightarrow$ ON

When the power MOSFET is switched-OFF, the inductor current tends to decrease and as a result the polarity of the emf induced in 'L' is reversed. Thus, the inductance energy discharges in the load through the path L_+ – Load – D – L.

During time T_{OFF}, the inductor current falls linearly from I_2 to I_1,

From figure for Mode (2), $I_L = I_C + I_0 \Rightarrow I_C = I_L - I_0$

Apply KVL in loop-2 (for reference polarity), we get

$$V_L + V_0 = 0$$

or, $$V_L = -V_0$$

and $$(\Delta V_L)_{avg} = 0$$

$$V_s T_{ON} = V_0 T_{OFF}$$

$$V_s(\alpha T) = V_0 T_{OFF}$$

$$\alpha V_s = V_0\left(\frac{T_{OFF}}{T}\right) = V_0(1-\alpha)$$

$$V_0 = \left(\frac{\alpha}{1-\alpha}\right) V_s$$

Now, during T_{ON} period when the power MOSFET is ON. The filter capacitor supplies the load current. Therefore, the average discharging current of the capacitor is

$$I_C = I_0$$

Also, the peak to peak ripple voltage of the capacitor is

$$\Delta V_e = \frac{1}{C}\int_0^{T_{ON}} I_C\, dt = \frac{1}{C}\int_0^{T_{ON}} I_0\, dt = \frac{I_0 T_{ON}}{C}$$

$$\Delta V_e = \frac{I_0 \cdot \alpha}{fC} \qquad \left(\alpha = \frac{T_{ON}}{T} \text{ and } f = \frac{1}{T}\right)$$

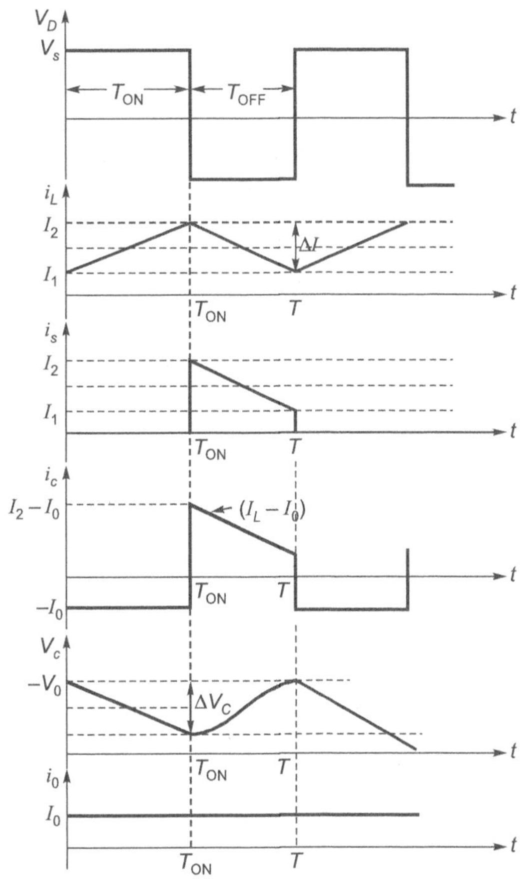

Now,
$$V_0 = \left(\frac{\alpha}{1-\alpha}\right) V_s$$

$$15 = \left(\frac{\alpha}{1-\alpha}\right) 6$$

$$15 - 15\alpha = 6\alpha$$

$$\alpha = \frac{15}{21} = \frac{5}{7}$$

Duty cycle, $\alpha = 0.7143$

The ripple current of inductor,

$$\Delta I = \frac{\alpha V_s}{fL} = \frac{\left(\frac{5}{7}\right) \times 6}{20 \times 10^3 \times 250 \times 10^{-6}} = \frac{6}{7} = 0.8571 \text{ A}$$

The ripple voltage of filter current,

$$\Delta V_C = \frac{\alpha I_0}{fC} = \frac{\left(\frac{5}{7}\right) \times 0.5}{20 \times 10^3 \times 440 \times 10^{-6}} = 0.0406 \text{ V} = 40.60 \text{ mV}$$

4.13 **A boost converter is required to have an output voltage of 48 V and supply a load current of 5 A. The input varies from 12 V - 24 V. A control circuit adjusts the duty ratio to keep the output voltage constant. Select the switching frequency to be 200 kHz. Determine a value of inductor such that the variation in inductor current is no more than 40% of average inductor current for all operation. Prescribe a suitable value of capacitor such that output ripple is no more than 2%.**

[20 marks : 2018]

Solution:

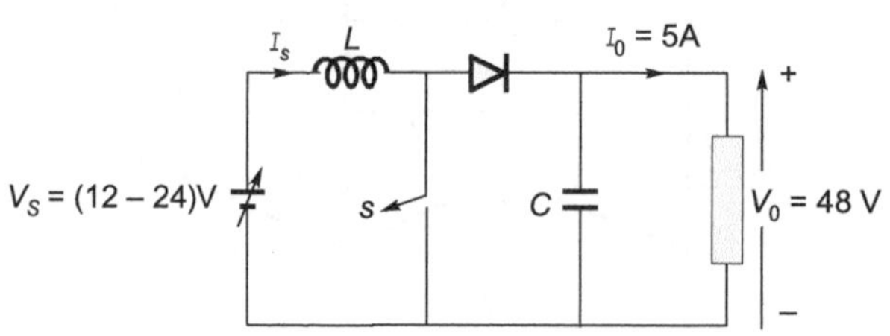

Given, V_0 is constant at 48 V.

$$V_0 = \frac{1}{1-\alpha_1}V_s \qquad V_0 = \frac{1}{1-\alpha_2}V_s$$

$$48 = \frac{1}{1-\alpha_1} \times 12 \qquad 48 = \frac{1}{1-\alpha_2} \times 24$$

$$\alpha_1 = 0.75 \qquad \alpha_2 = 0.5$$

$$\alpha_1 = \frac{T_{on}}{T} = 0.75 \qquad \alpha_2 = \frac{T_{on}}{T} = 0.5$$

$$T_{on} = \frac{0.75}{200 \times 10^3} = 3.75\ \mu\text{s} \qquad T_{on} = \frac{0.5}{200 \times 10^3} = 2.5\ \mu\text{s}$$

$$T = 5\ \mu\text{s}$$

$$I_{L\,avg} = I_{Savg} = \frac{I_0}{1-\alpha_1} \qquad I_{L\,avg} = I_{Savg} = \frac{I_0}{1-\alpha_2}$$

$$\therefore \quad I_{L\,avg} = \frac{5}{1-0.75} = 20 \text{ A} \qquad I_{L\,avg} = \frac{5}{1-0.5} = 10 \text{ A}$$

$$\Delta I = 0.4 \times 20 = \frac{V_s T_{on}}{L} \qquad \Delta I = 0.4 \times 10 = \frac{V_s T_{on}}{L}$$

$$\therefore \quad L = \frac{12 \times 3.75 \times 10^{-6}}{0.4 \times 20} \qquad L = \frac{24 \times 2.5 \times 10^{-6}}{0.4 \times 10}$$

$$L = 5.625\,\mu H \qquad\qquad L = 15\,\mu H$$

∴ Large value of inductor is considered i.e.

$$L = 15\,\mu H$$

$$\Delta V_C = \frac{I_0\alpha}{fC} \qquad\qquad \Delta V_C = \frac{I_0\alpha}{fC}$$

$$0.02 \times 48 = \frac{5 \times 0.75}{200 \times 10^3 \times C} \qquad\qquad 0.02 \times 48 = \frac{5 \times 0.5}{200 \times 10^3 \times C}$$

$$C = 19.53\,\mu F \qquad\qquad C = 13.02\,\mu F$$

∴ Larger value of capacitance is taken (i.e) $C = 19.53\,\mu F$

4.14 **A Buck-Boost converter is operating at 20 kHz with Inductor L = 50 μH. The output capacitor C is sufficiently large and source voltage V_d = 15 V. The output is to be regulated at 10 V and the converter is supplying a load of 10 Ω. Find:**

(i) The duty ratio D, and

(ii) Maximum value of Inductor current. **[20 Marks : 2019]**

Solution:

(i) Initially the mode of conduction is assume to be continuous,

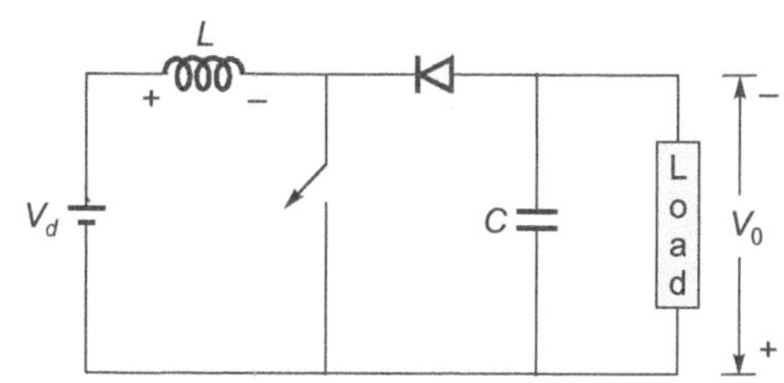

$$V_0 = \frac{\alpha}{1-\alpha} V_d$$

$$10 = \left(\frac{\alpha}{1-\alpha}\right)15$$

$$\left(\frac{\alpha}{1-\alpha}\right) = 1.5$$

$$\alpha = 0.4$$

At the boundary condition,

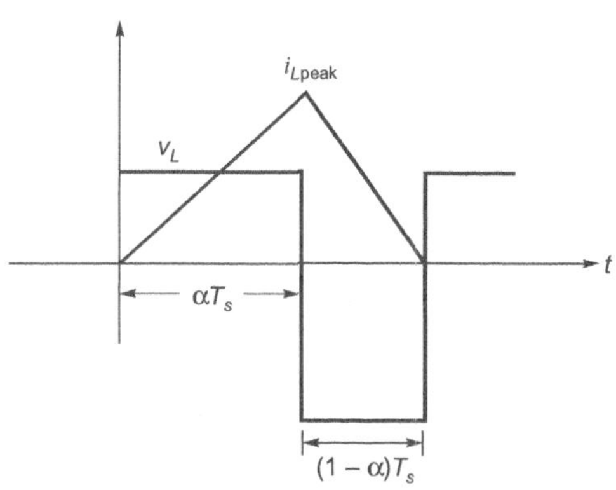

$$I_{OB,\max} = \frac{V_0}{2fL} = \frac{10}{2 \times 20 \times 10^3 \times 50 \times 10^{-6}} = 5\text{ A}$$

$$I_{OB} = I_{OB,\max}\,(1-\alpha)^2 = 5(1-0.4)^2 = 1.8\text{ A}$$

$$P_0 = V_0 I_0$$

$$10 = 10 \times I_0$$

$$I_0 = 1\text{ A}$$

Since the output current I_0 = 1 A, is less than I_{OB}.

∴ It is discontinuous mode.

$$\alpha_1 = \frac{V_0}{V_d}\sqrt{\frac{I_0}{I_{OB,max}}} = \frac{10}{15}\sqrt{\frac{1}{5}} = 0.298$$

(ii) Maximum inductor current,

$$I_{LB,max} = \frac{V_0}{2fL} = \frac{10}{2\times 20\times 10^3\times 50\times 10^{-6}} = 5\text{ A}$$

4.15 The DC–DC converter given below is operating at 30 kHz and drawing an input current of 25 A at 48 V DC.

(i) For a load current of 10 A, find

I. the duty ratio of the switch,

II. output voltage,

III. peak inductor current,

IV. output voltage ripple, and

V. the load current where the inductor current just becomes discontinuous.

(ii) Also find the critical value of L to keep the inductor current just continuous when the input voltage changes to 60 V with output remaining same. (Assume lossless operation of converter components).

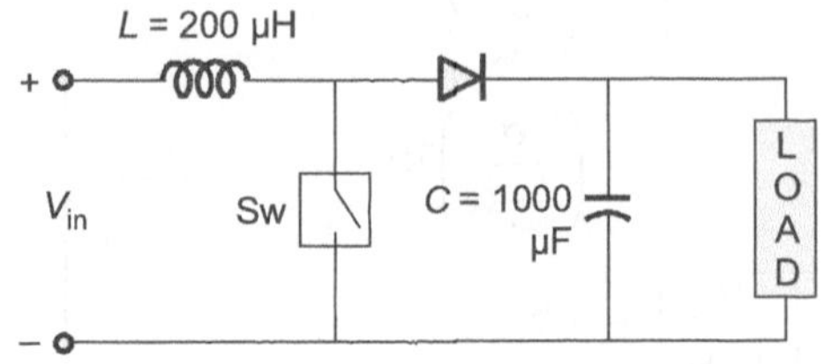

[20 marks : 2020]

Solution:

Boost Converter :

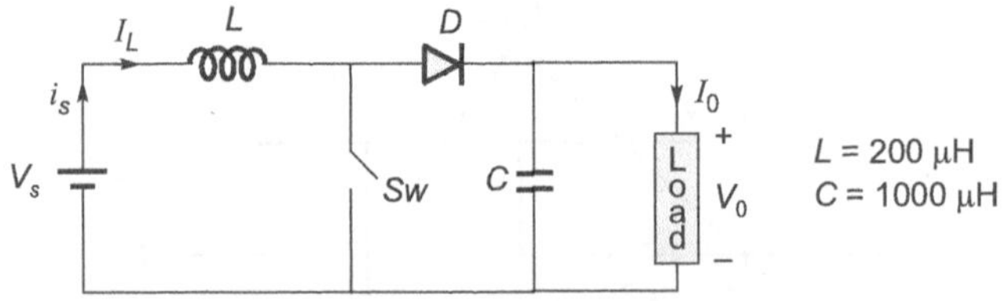

$$f = 30\text{ kHz},\ I_s = 25\text{ A},\ I_o = 10\text{ A},\ V_s = 48\text{ V}$$

I. $$P_o = P_{in}$$

$$V_oI_o = V_s.I_s$$

Output voltage, $$V_o = \frac{V_s\cdot I_s}{I_o} = \frac{48\times 25}{10} = 120\text{ V}$$

Let us assume it is continuous conduction.

$$V_o = \frac{V_s}{1-\alpha}$$

$$120 = \frac{48}{1-\alpha}$$

II. Duty ratio, $\alpha = 0.6$

$$I_{mn} = I_L - \frac{\Delta I_L}{2}$$

$$= I_S - \frac{\alpha V_S}{2fL}$$

$$= 25 - \frac{0.6 \times 48}{2 \times 30.10^3 \times 200.10^{-6}}$$

$$I_{mn} = 22.6 \text{ A}$$

$I_{mn} > 0$ ∴ our assumption is true, i.e., continuous conduction.

III. Peak inductor current,

$$(i_L)_{peak} = I_{mx} = I_L + \frac{\Delta I_L}{2}$$

$$= 25 + \frac{\alpha V_S}{2fL}$$

$$= 25 + \frac{0.6 \times 48}{2 \times 30.10^3 \times 200.10^{-6}}$$

$$= 27.4 \text{ A}$$

IV. Output voltage ripple,

$$\Delta V_o = \Delta V_c = \frac{\alpha I_o}{fC}$$

$$= \frac{0.6 \times 10}{30.10^3 \times 1000.10^{-6}} = 0.2 \text{ V}$$

V. At the Boundary :

$$I_{LB} = \frac{\Delta I_L}{2}$$

$$\frac{I_{OB}}{1-\alpha} = \frac{\alpha V_S}{2fL}$$

$$I_{OB} = \frac{\alpha(1-\alpha)V_S}{2fL}$$

$$= \frac{0.6 \times (1-0.6) \times 48}{2 \times 30.10^3 \times 200.10^{-6}}$$

$$I_{OB} = 0.96 \text{ A}$$

(ii) Supply voltage changes to 60 V.
Output remaining same.

$$V_o = 120 \text{ V}, I_o = 10 \text{ A}$$

$$V_o I_o = V_s I_s$$

$$I_s = \frac{V_o I_o}{V_s} = \frac{120.10}{60}$$

$$I_s = 20 \text{ A}$$

$$V_o = \frac{V_s}{1-\alpha}$$

$$120 = \frac{60}{1-\alpha}$$

$$\therefore \quad 1-\alpha = \frac{60}{120} = 0.5$$

$$\alpha = 0.5$$

At the boundary :

$$I_{LB} = \frac{\Delta I_L}{2}$$

$$I_{SB} = \frac{\alpha V_S}{2fL_C}$$

Here L_C is the critical value of inductance required.

$$\frac{I_{OB}}{1-\alpha} = \frac{\alpha V_S}{2fL_C}$$

$$\frac{10}{1-0.5} = \frac{0.5\times 60}{2\times 30\cdot 10^3\cdot L_C}$$

$$L_C = \frac{0.5\times 0.5\times 60}{10\times 2\times 30\times 10^3} = 0.25\times 10^{-4}\text{ H}$$

$$L_C = 25\,\mu\text{H}$$

4.16 **A buck converter in operating from a 24 V dc input voltage with variation of ±10%. The required output voltage is 9 V dc with allowable voltage ripple of 100 mV. The converter has rated capacity of 20 W and is operating at a switching frequency of 40 kHz. Find the minimum values of inductance and capacitance to be provided in the output filter for (i) keeping the inductor current peak to peak ripple at 0.5 A, and (ii) inductor current to be just continuous.**
(Assume the converter is operating rated power)

[12 marks : 2021]

Solution:

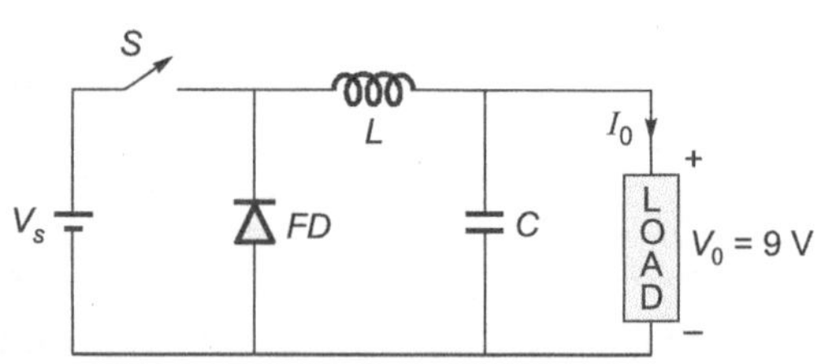

Given Data : Buck converter

Voltage ripple, $\Delta V_0 = 100\text{ mV}$

Supply Voltage, $V_S = 24 \pm 10\%$

Frequency, $f = 40\text{ kHz}$

Output power, $P_0 = 20\text{ W}$

$$V_0 I_0 = 20$$

Output current, $$I_0 = \frac{20}{V_0} = \frac{20}{9} = 2.22\text{ A}$$

For Case (1) : $V_{s1} = 21.6\text{ V}$ $\quad (V_{s1} = 24 - 10\%\text{ of }24)$

$$V_0 = \alpha_1 V_{s1}$$

$$9 = \alpha_1(21.6)$$

Duty cycle, $\alpha_1 = 0.4166$

When SW is ON, $$\Delta I_L = \frac{\alpha_1(1-\alpha_1)V_{s1}}{f\cdot L_1}$$ $(\Delta I_L = \text{charge in inductor current})$

$$0.5 = \frac{0.4166(1-0.4166)\times 21.6}{40\times 10^3\times L_1}$$

Inductance, $L_1 = 262.48\,\mu\text{H}$

For Case (2) :

Input voltage $V_{s2} = 26.4\text{ V}$ $\quad (V_{s2} = 24 + 10\% \text{ of } 24)$

$$V_0 = \alpha_2 \cdot V_{s2}$$

$$9 = \alpha_2 \times 26.4$$

Duty cycle, $\alpha_2 = 0.34$

For buck converter,

$$\Delta I = \frac{\alpha_2(1-\alpha_2)\cdot V_{s2}}{f\cdot L_2}$$

$$0.5 = \frac{0.34(1-0.34)\times 26.4}{40\times 10^3 \times L_2}$$

Inductance, $L_2 = 296.21\ \mu\text{H}$

(i) ∴ Minimum inductance required

$$= 296.21\ \mu\text{H}$$

[Hint : Here must consider maximum inductance considering worst case]

$$\Delta V_0 = \frac{\Delta I_L}{8fC}$$

$$100\times 10^{-3} = \frac{0.5}{8\times 40.10^3 \times C}$$

$$C = 15.625\ \mu\text{F}$$

(ii) Inductor current to be just continuous:

At boundary condition ⇒ $I_{LB} = \dfrac{\Delta I_L}{2}$ → At the boundary

Boundary current, $I_{LB} = \dfrac{\alpha(1-\alpha)V_s}{2fL}$

When $V_{s1} = 21.6\text{ V}$

$$\alpha_1 = 0.4166$$

$$I_{OB} = \frac{\alpha_1(1-\alpha_1)V_{s1}}{2f\cdot L_1}$$

$$2.22 = \frac{0.4166(1-0.4166)\times 21.6}{2\times 40\times 10^3 \cdot L_1}$$

For inductance, $L_1 = 29.5\ \mu\text{H}$

Case 1 : When $V_{s2} = 26.4\text{ V}$,

$$\alpha_2 = 0.34$$

$$I_{OB} = \frac{\alpha_2(1-\alpha_2)V_{s2}}{2f\cdot L_2}$$

$$2.22 = \frac{0.34(1-0.34)\times 26.4}{2\times 40\times 10^3 \times L_2}$$

$$L_2 = 33.36\ \mu\text{H}$$

∴ Minimum inductance required

$$L_2 = 33.36\ \mu\text{H}$$

∴ $$\Delta I_L = \frac{\alpha(1-\alpha)V_s}{f\cdot L}$$

Now:
$$L = 33.36\ \mu H$$
$$V_{s1} = 21.6\ V,$$
$$\alpha_1 = 0.4166$$
$$\Delta I_L = \frac{0.4166(1-0.4166)\times 21.6}{40\times 10^3 \times 33.36\times 10^{-6}}$$
$$\Delta I_{L1} = 3.93\ A$$
$$\Delta V_0 = \frac{\Delta I_{L1}}{8fC_1} \Rightarrow 10\times 10^{-3} = \frac{3.93}{8\times 40\times 10^3 \times C_2}$$
$$C = 122.9\ \mu F$$

Case 2 :
$$V_{s2} = 26.4\ V$$
$$\alpha_2 = 0.34$$
$$\Delta I_{L2} = \frac{\alpha_2(1-\alpha_2)\cdot V_{s2}}{f\cdot L}$$
$$= \frac{0.34(1-0.34)\times 26.4}{40\times 10^3 \times 33.36\times 10^{-6}} = 4.44\ A$$
$$\Delta V_0 = \frac{\Delta I_{L2}}{8f\cdot C_2}$$
$$100\times 10^{-3} = \frac{4.44}{8\times 40\times 10^3 \times C_2}$$

∴ Minimum capacitance required = 138.75 μH

Hint : We must consider maximum capacitance to design for worst case and that is the minimum value required.

4.17 **A separately excited DC motor of 10 hp, 200 V, 1750 rpm is fed from a DC-DC chopper for speed control purpose. The motor has armature resistance r_a = 0.25 Ω and the series inductance is such that the motor current is flat and continuous. The chopper is fed from a 450 V DC source. The schematic diagram is shown in the figure below. Find :**

(i) the duty ratio, transistor rms current rating under rated condition.

(ii) the motor speed under no load condition at rated intput voltage.

(iii) Now the motor is relocated at a distance with a connecting cable of 1.5 Ω resistance and the speed is to be reduced to 1000 rpm at half-rated torque. Find the new duty ratio and converter output voltage.

Assume negligible device losses, a total brush drop of 3.0 V for the motor under operation and a 10 kHz switching frequency for the chopper.

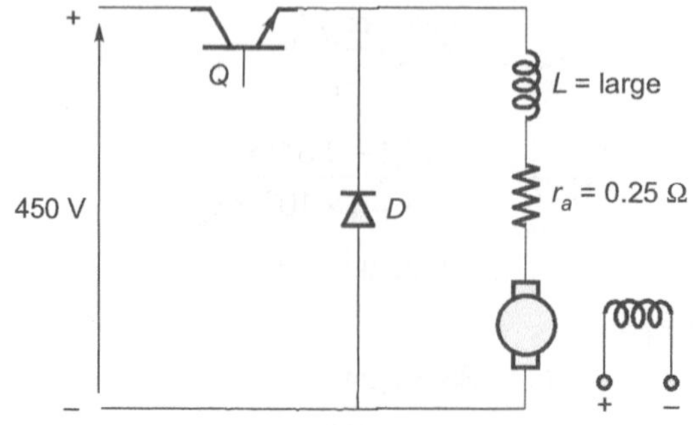

[20 marks : 2022]

Solution:

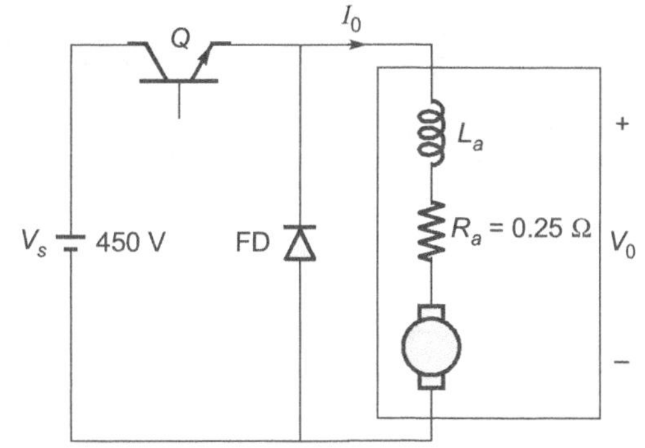

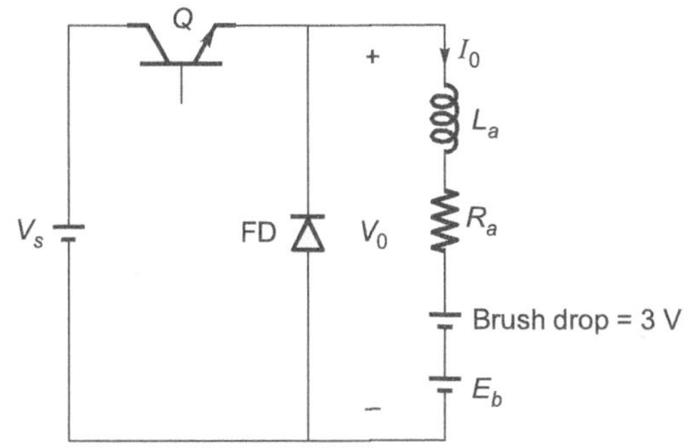

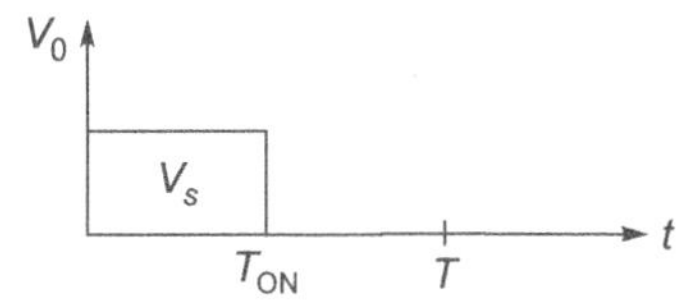

$$V_o = \alpha . V_s$$

$$V_{o(\text{Rated})} = \alpha .450$$

$$\alpha = \frac{200}{450} = 0.444$$

$$P_{o(\text{Rated})} = V_{o(\text{Rated})} . I_{o(\text{Rated})}$$

$$10\text{ HP} = 200 I_{o(\text{Rated})}$$

$$(10 \times 745.699)\text{ W} = 200 I_{o(\text{Rated})}$$

$$I_{o(\text{Rated})} = 37.28\text{ A}$$

$$(I_{\text{Transistor}})_{\text{rms}} = I_{o(\text{Rated})} \left(\frac{T_{ON}}{T}\right)^{1/2}$$

$$= \sqrt{\alpha} I_{o(\text{Rated})}$$

$$= \sqrt{0.44} \times (37.28)$$

$$= 24.85\text{ A}$$

(i)

$$V_{o(\text{Rated})} = E_b + \text{Brush drop voltage} + I_{o(\text{Rated})} R_a$$

$$200 = K_m \cdot \frac{2\pi}{60} N_{\text{Rated}} + 3 + (37.28 \times 0.25)$$

$$200 = K_m \cdot \frac{2\pi}{60} \cdot 1750 + 3 + (37.28 \times 0.25)$$

$$K_m = 1.02\text{ V-S/rad}$$

(ii) At No Load ($I_o = 0$)

$$\therefore \quad V_{o(\text{Rated})} = K_m \cdot \frac{2\pi}{60} N + \text{Brush drop voltage} + I_o R_a$$

$$200 = 1.02 \times \frac{2\pi}{60} N + 3 + (0 \times 0.25)$$

$$N = 1844.32 \text{ rpm}$$

(iii)

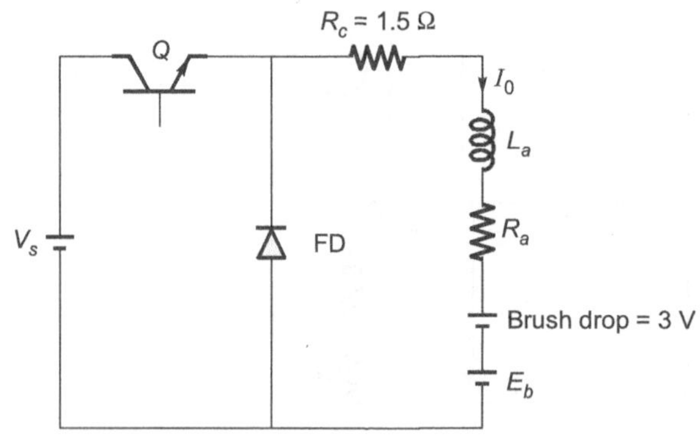

$R_c \rightarrow$ Connecting cable resistance

$$T_a \propto I_o \qquad [\because \phi \rightarrow \text{Const}]$$

At half rated torque,

$$I_o = \frac{I_{o(\text{Rated})}}{2} = \frac{37.28}{2}$$

$$I_o = 18.64 \text{ A}$$

$$V_o = E_b + \text{Brush drop voltage} + I_o(R_a + R_c)$$

$$V_o = K_m \frac{2\pi}{60} N + 3 + I_o(0.25 + 1.5)$$

$$= 1.02 \times \frac{2\pi}{60} \times 1000 + 3 + (18.64 \times 1.75)$$

$$V_o = 106.814 + 3 + 32.62$$

$$V_o = 142.434 \text{ V}$$

$$V_o = \alpha V_s$$

$$142.434 = \alpha \times 450$$

$$\alpha = 0.316$$

4.18 The equivalent circuit and its associated voltage waveform for a switched mode DC power supply is shown below,

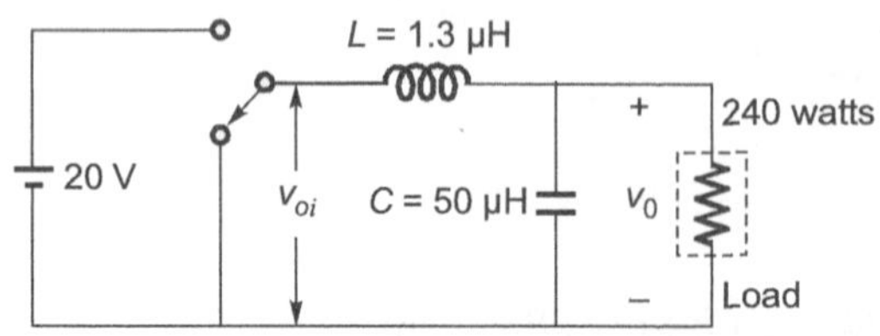

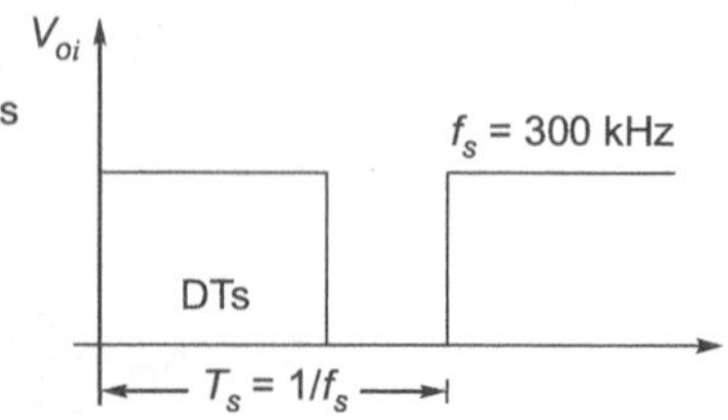

(i) Assuming a pure dc V_0 = 15 V at the output across a load of 240 watts, calculate and draw the waveforms of voltage and current associated with the filter inductor 'L' and current through 'C'. Let switch duty ratio D = 0.75 in this condition.

(ii) Estimate the peak-to-peak ripple in the voltage across capacitor.

(iii) Calculate the harmonic voltage of v_{oi}.

(iv) Calculate the attenuation in decibels of ripple voltage in v_{oi} at harmonic frequency

[20 marks : 2023]

Solution:

(i) Given circuit diagram is :

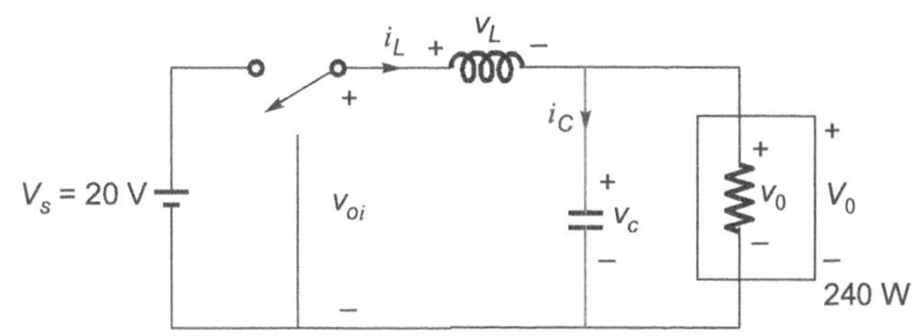

Waveform of current and voltage across inductor and capacitor :

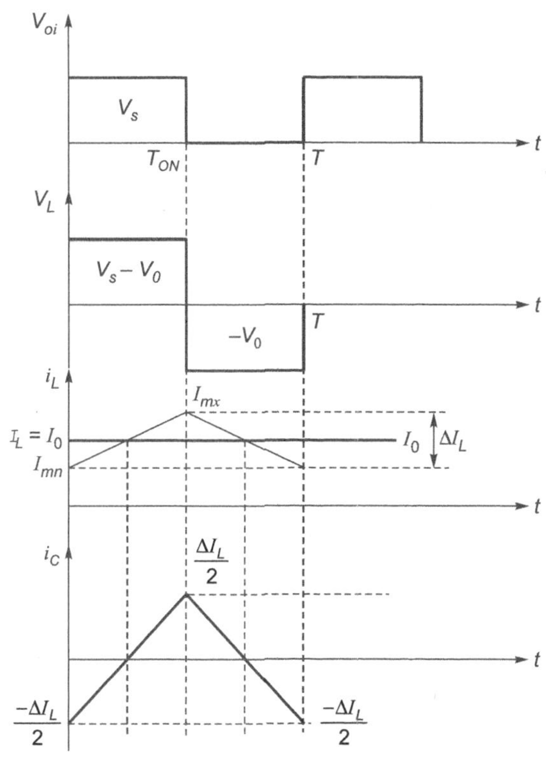

If $V_o = DV_s$, then it is 0.75 × 20, either continuous V_o = 15 V (given) or at the boundary.

$$\therefore \quad V_o = 15 \text{ V} = DV_s \text{ (given)}$$

Output current at boundary condition,

$$I_{OB} = \frac{\alpha(1-\alpha)V_s}{2fL} = \frac{0.75(1-0.75)\times 20}{2\times 300.10^3 \times (1.3\times 10^{-6})}$$

$$I_{OB} = \frac{3.75}{0.78} = 4.8 \text{ A}$$

∴ Output across load is P_o = 240 W

$$V_oI_o = 240$$

$$I_o = \frac{240}{15} = 16 \text{ A}$$

$\because \quad I_o = 16\text{ A} = I_{OB}$

Hence, i_L is continuous.

(ii) Ripple voltage across capacitor is,

$$\Delta V_o = \Delta V_c = \frac{\alpha(1-\alpha)V_s}{8f^2LC}$$

$$= \frac{0.75(1-0.75)\times 20}{8\times(300.10^3)^2\times(1.3\times10^{-6})\times(50.10^{-6})}$$

$$= \frac{3.75}{1560.10^{-2}}$$

$$= 0.24\text{ V}$$

Required peak to peak ripple in the voltage across capacitor,

$$(V_o)_{\text{ripple,harmonic rms}} = \frac{0.24/2}{\sqrt{3}} = \frac{0.12}{\sqrt{3}} = 0.06928$$

(iii)

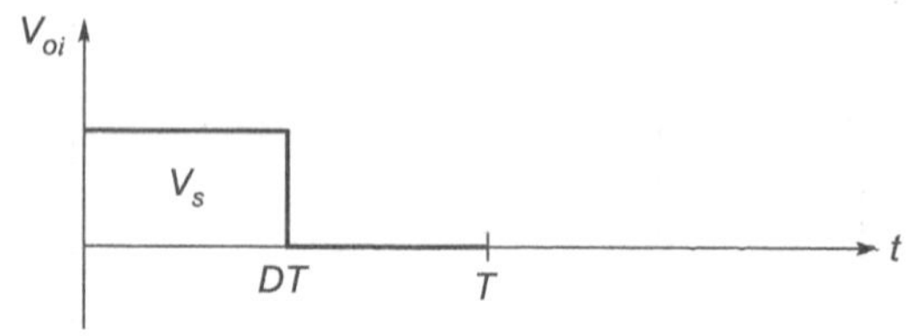

$$V_{oi,\text{Avg}} = DV_s = 0.75 \times 20 = 15\text{ V}$$

$$V_{oi,\text{rms}} = \sqrt{D}\cdot V_s = \sqrt{0.75}\times 20 = 17.32\text{ V}$$

$$V_{oi,\text{harmonic voltage}} = \sqrt{V_{oi,\text{rms}}^2 - V_{oi,\text{avg}}^2}$$

$$= \sqrt{17.32^2 - 15^2}$$

$$= 8.66\text{ V}$$

(iv) Attenuation in decibels of ripples voltage (V_{oi})

$$= 20\log_{10}\left[\frac{(V_{oi})_{\text{Harmonic rms}}}{(V_o)_{\text{Harmonic rms}}}\right]$$

$$= 20\log_{10}\left(\frac{8.66}{0.06928}\right)$$

Required ripple voltage (V_{oi}) in dB is 41.9 dB.

5. Inverters

5.1 What is PWM? Explain sinusoidal-pulse modulation as used in PWM inverters. Discuss the conditions leading to the number of pulses generated per half-cycle as $\frac{f_c}{2f}$ or $\left(\frac{f_c}{2f} - 1\right)$. Here f_c and f are the carrier and reference signal frequency respectively.

Bring out the important features of sinusoidal-pulse modulation.

[16 marks : 2001]

Solution:

PWM (pulse width modulation) is a internal voltage control of inverter. In this method, a fixed dc input voltage is given to the inverter and a controlled output voltage is obtained by, adjusting the on and off periods of the inverter components. In Sine modulation [Sin *M*] the pulse width is a sinusoidal function of the angular position of the pulse in a cycle as shown in figure.

For realizing sin *M*, a high-frequency triangular carrier wave V_c is compared with a sinusoidal reference wave V_r of the desired frequency. The intersection of V_c and V_r waves determines the switching instants and commutation of the modulated pulse. In figure V_C is the peak value of triangular carrier wave and V_r that of the reference, or modulating signal.

The carrier and reference waves are mixed in a comparator. When sinusoidal wave has magnitude higher than the triangular wave, the comparator output is high, otherwise it is low. The comparator output is processed in a trigger pulse generator in such a manner that the output voltage wave of the inverter has a pulse width in agreement with the comparator output pulse width.

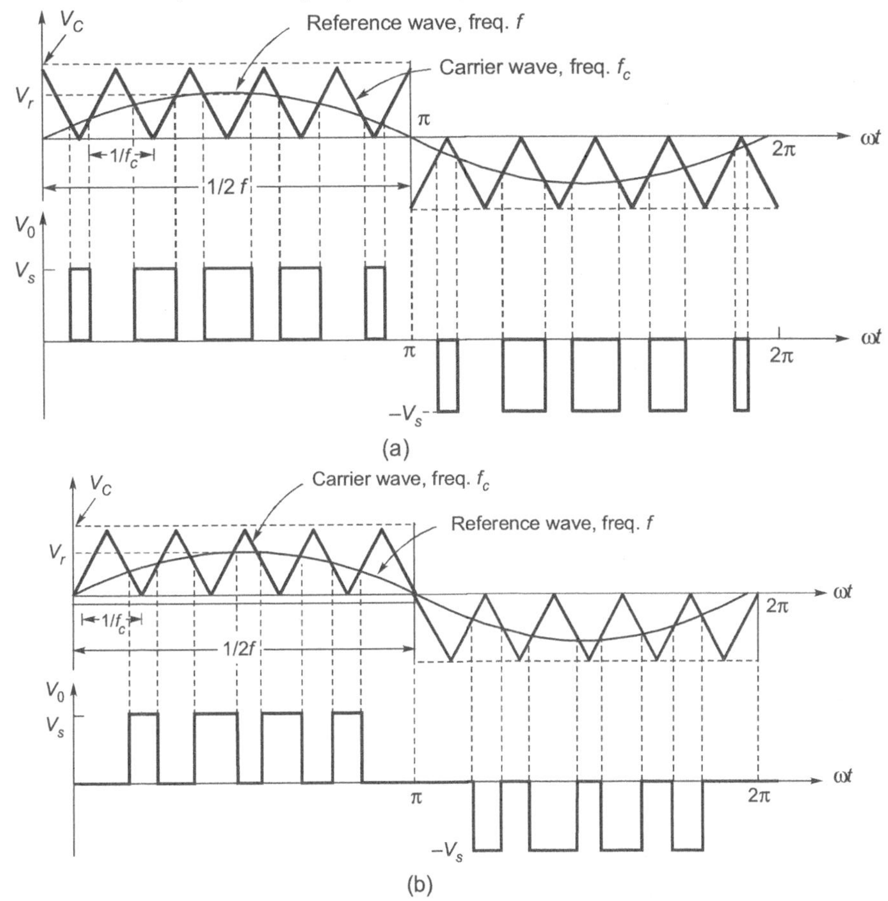

Output voltage waveforms with sinusoidal pulse modulation

When triangular carrier wave has its peak coincident with zero of the reference sinusoid, there are $N = f_c/2f = \dfrac{f_c}{2f}$ pulses per half cycle ; Fig. (a) has five pulses. In case zero of the triangular wave coincides with zero of the reference sinusoid, there are $(N-1)$ pulses per half cycle ; Fig. (b) has $(f_c/2f-1)$, i.e. four, pulses per cycle.

The ratio of V_r/V_c is called the modulation index (MI) and it controls the harmonic content of the output voltage waveform. The magnitude of fundamental component of output voltage is proportional to MI, but MI can never be more than unity. Thus the output voltage is controlled by varying MI.

Harmonic analysis of the output modulated voltage wave reveals that sin *M* has the following important features:

(*i*) For MI less than one, largest harmonic amplitudes in the output voltage are associated with harmonics of order $f_c/f \pm 1$ or $2N \pm 1$, where N is the number of pulses per half cycle. Thus, by increasing the number of pulses per half cycle, the order of dominant harmonic frequency can be raised, which can then be filtered out easily.

It is observed from above that as N is increased, the order of significant harmonic increases and the filtering requirements are accordingly minimised. But higher value of N entails higher switching frequency of thyristors. This amounts to more switching losses and therefore an impaired inverter efficiency. Thus a compromise between the filtering requirements and inverter efficiency should be made.

(*ii*) For MI greater than one, lower order harmonics appear, since for MI > 1, pulse width is no longer a sinusoidal function of the angular position of the pulse.

5.2 **Why the feedback diodes are connected in antiparallel with thyristors in inverter circuits? How do these diodes come into play?**

[5 marks : 2001]

Solution:

When in the inverter circuit, load is other than resistive, then load current i_0 is not in phase with load voltage V_0. For such type of load, diodes are connected in antiparallel with thyristors to allow the current to flow when the main thyristor are turned off.

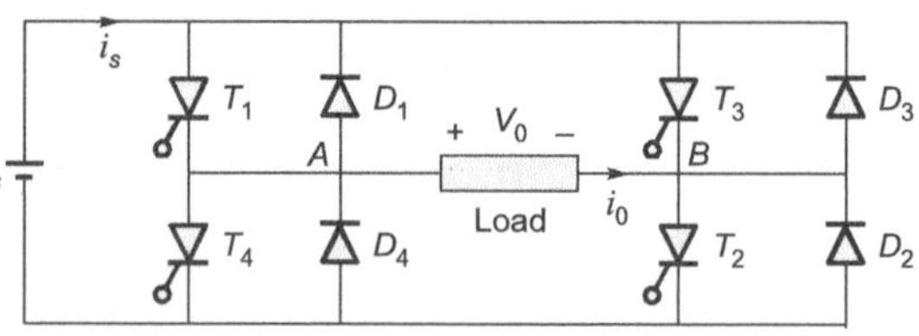

For illustration a single phase full-bridge inverter shown below. Suppose the given load is purely inductive. The load current waveform shown next.

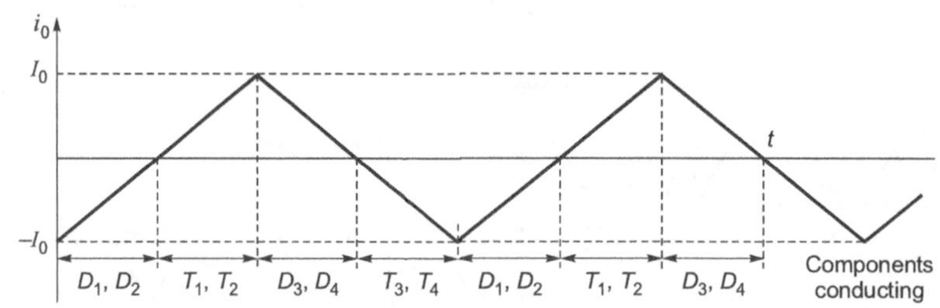

In the load waveform before (t = 0), thyristors T_3, T_4 are conducting and the load current i_0 is flowing from B to A in the negative direction. After T_3, T_4 turned off at (t = 0), current i_0 can't change its direction immediately due to nature of load. As a result Diodes D_1 and D_2 start conducting after (t = 0) and allow i_0 to flow against supply voltage V_1. Also T_1, T_2 are turned off due to reverse-biasing across these by voltage drops across diodes (D_1 and D_2).

When i_0 through D_1, D_2 falls to zero, T_1 and T_2 become forward biased by source voltage V_1, T_1 and T_2 therefore get turned on as these are gated for a period $T/2$ sec. Now the load current I_0 flows in the positive direction from A to B. At $t = T/2$; T_1 and T_2 are turned off by forced commutation and as load current can't reverse immediately, diodes D_3, D_4 come into conduction to allow the flow of current i_0 after $T/2$. Thyristor T_3, T_4 will not turn on as reverse-biasing across it by diodes D_3, D_4. When current in diodes D_3, D_4 reduces to zero, T_3, T_4 are turned on. In this way feedback do their work.

For reactive loads feedback diodes will allow the negative power.

5.3 **In a single-phase DC to AC inverter, using single pulse modulation for control of output voltage, harmonics of the order n can be eliminated by making the pulse width β.**

(a) $4\pi/n$ (b) $2\pi/n$

(c) π/n (d) $\pi/2n$

[2 marks : 2002]

Solution: (b)

For single pulse modulation, output voltage of single phase DC to AC inverter,

$$V_0 = \sum_{n=1,3}^{\infty} \frac{4V_s}{n\pi} \sin\frac{n\pi}{2} \sin(nd)\sin(n\omega t)$$

$\therefore \quad nd = \pi \quad \text{and} \quad \beta = 2d$

or if pulse width made equal to $\left(2d = \frac{2\pi}{n}\right)$ then n^{th} harmonic will absent in the output.

Hence, option (b) is correct.

5.4 With the help of equivalent circuits obtain the nature of waveform of phase voltage of a star connected resistive load fed from a three-phase DC to AC bridge-inverter operating in 180° conduction mode.

[20 marks : 2002]

Solution:

A basic three-phase inverter is a six-step bridge inverter it uses a minimum of six thyristors.

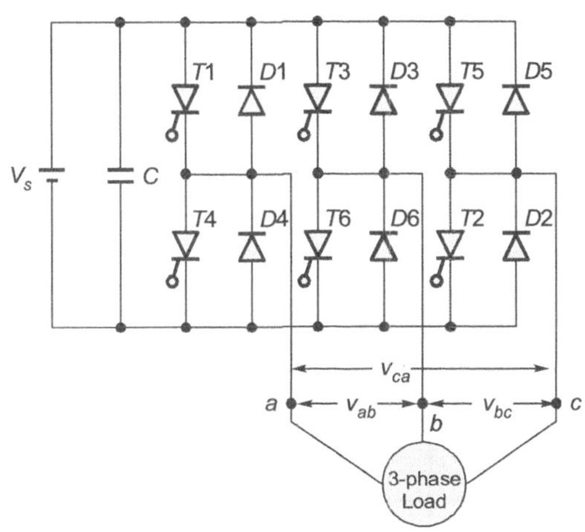

Three-phase bridge inverter using thyristors

In inverter terminology a step is defined as a change in the firing from one thyristor to the next thyristor in proper sequence. For one cycle of 360°, each step would be of 60° interval for a six-step inverter. This mean that thyristors would be gated at regular intervals of 60° in proper sequence so that 3-phase ac voltage is synthesized at the output terminals of a six-step inverter.

In the three-phase inverter of figure each SCR conducts for 180° of a cycle. Thyristor pair in each arm i.e. *T*1, *T*4 ; *T*3, *T*6 and *T*5, *T*2 are turned on with a time interval of 180°.

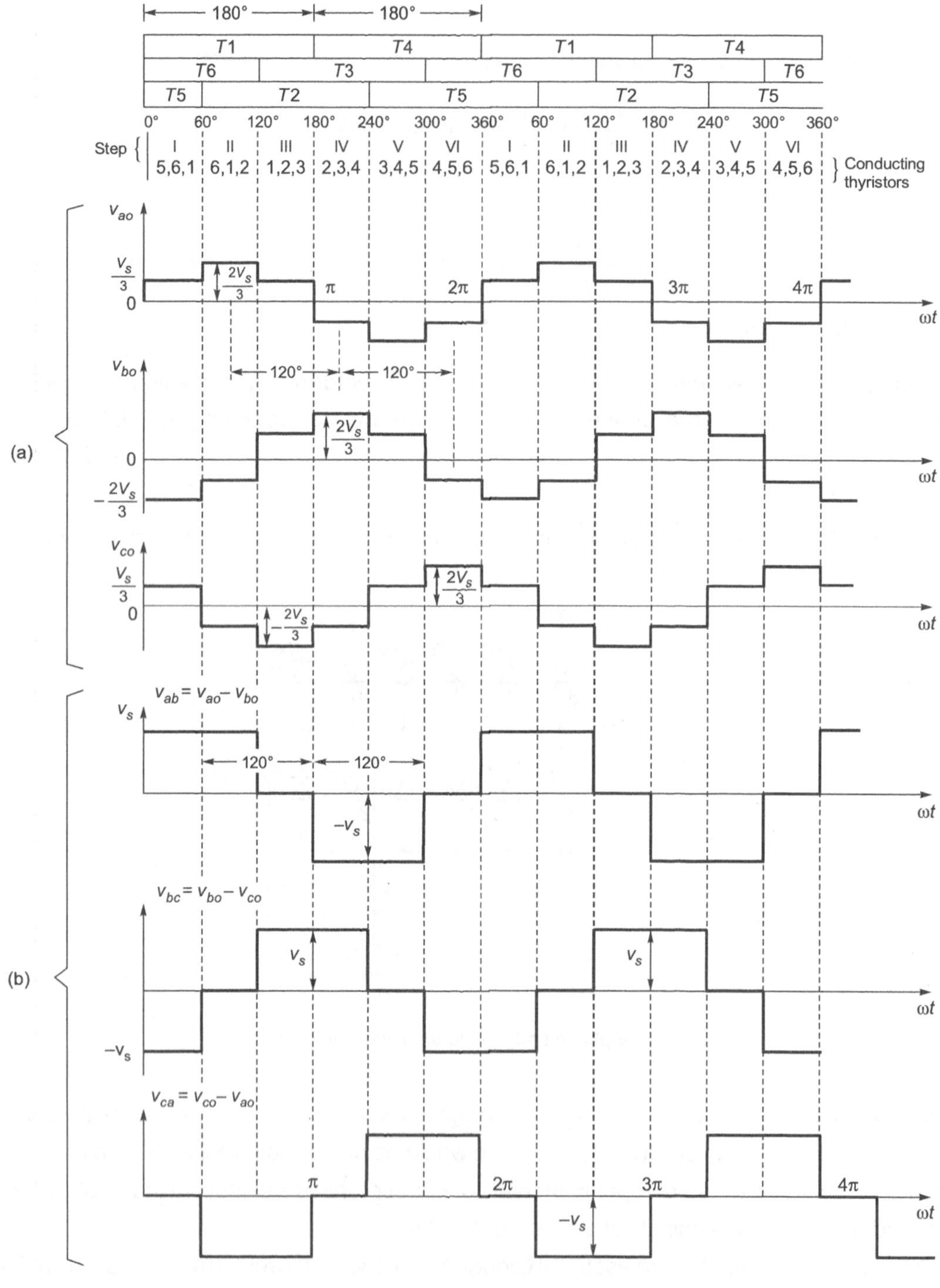

Fig. (2) Voltage waveforms for 180° mode 3-phase VSI.

It means that *T*1 conducts for 180° and *T*4 for the next 180° of a cycle. Thyristors in the upper group, i.e. *T*1, *T*3, T5 conduct at an interval of 120°. It implies that if *T*1 is fired at $\omega t = 0°$, then *T*3 must be fired at $\omega t = 120°$ and *T*5 at $\omega t = 240°$. Same is true for lower group of SCRs. On the basis of this firing scheme, a table is prepared as shown at the top of Fig. In this table, first row shows that *T*1 from upper group conducts for 180°, *T*4 for the next 180° and then again *T*1 for 180° and so on. In the second row, *T*3 from the upper group is shown to start conducting 120° after *T*1 starts conducting. After *T*3 conduction for 180°, *T*6 conducts for the next 180° and again *T*3 for the next 180° and so on. Further in the third row, *T*5 from the upper group starts conducting 120° after *T*3 or 240° after *T*1. After *T*5 conduction for 180°, *T*2 conducts for the next 180°, *T*5 for the next 180° and so on.

These output voltages are plotted in Fig. 2. In this manner, the variation of phase voltages v_{a0}, v_{co} as obtained in Fig. 3 up to step IV and similarly for other steps, is plotted in Fig. 2. It is clear that for each cycle of output voltage of each phase, six steps are required and each step has a duration of 60°.

Step-I

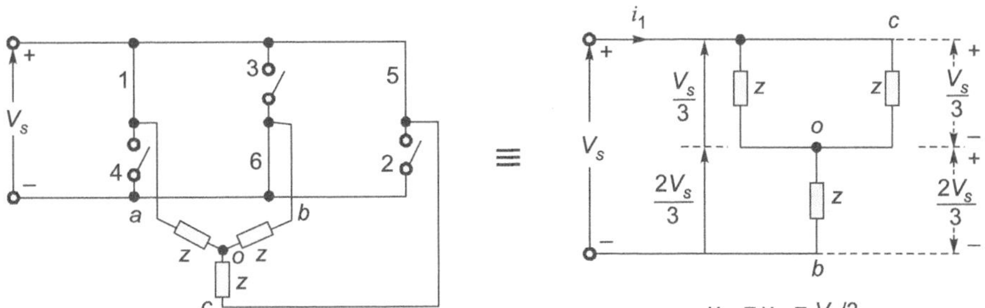

(a) 0 – 60°; 5, 6, 1 closed.

$v_{ao} = v_{co} = V_s/3$
$v_{bo} = -v_{ob} = -2V_s/3$

Step-II

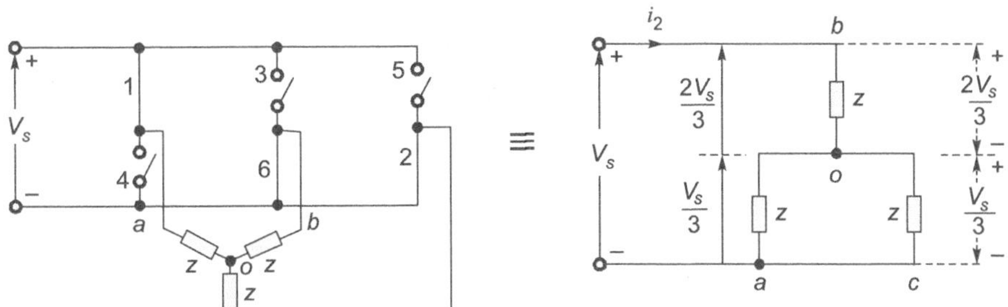

(b) 60 – 120°; 6, 1, 2 closed.

$v_{ao} = 2V_s/3$
$v_{bo} = v_{co} = -V_s/3$

Step-III

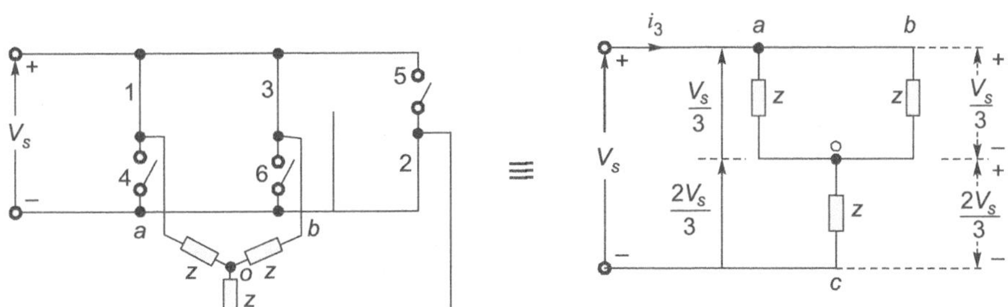

(c) 120 – 180°; 1, 2, 3 closed.

$v_{ao} = v_{bo} = V_s/3$
$v_{co} = -2V_s/3$

Step-IV

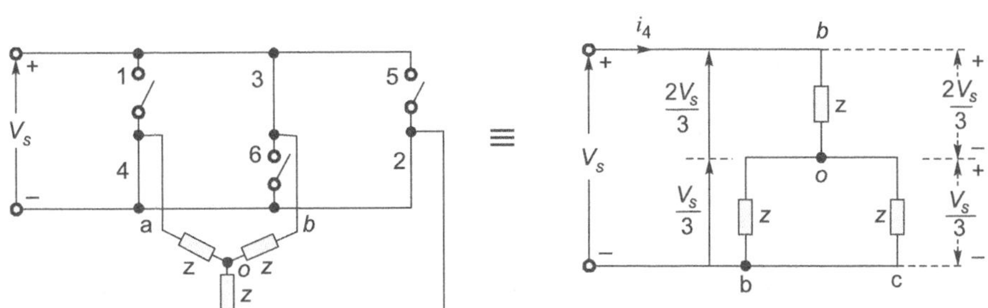

(d) 180 – 240°; 2, 3, 4 closed.

$v_{bo} = 2\,V_s/3$
$v_{ao} = v_{co} = -V_s/3$

Fig. (3) Equivalent circuits for a 3-phase six-step 180° mode inverter with a balanced star-connected load.

5.5 Draw the diagram of connections of 3 phase Bridge Inverter using six Thyristors. It is based on 120° mode of conduction. Draw the Time diagram showing conduction periods of 6 Thyristors and the phase voltages.

[8 + 8 = 16 marks : 2007]

Solution:

A basic three-phase inverter is a six-step bridge inverter it uses a minimum of six thyristors. In inverter terminology a step is defined as a change in the firing from one thyristor to the next thyristor in proper sequence. For one cycle of 360°, each step would be of 60° interval for a six-step inverter. This mean that thyristors would be gated at regular intervals of 60° in proper sequence so that 3-phase ac voltage is synthesized at the output terminals of a six-step inverter.

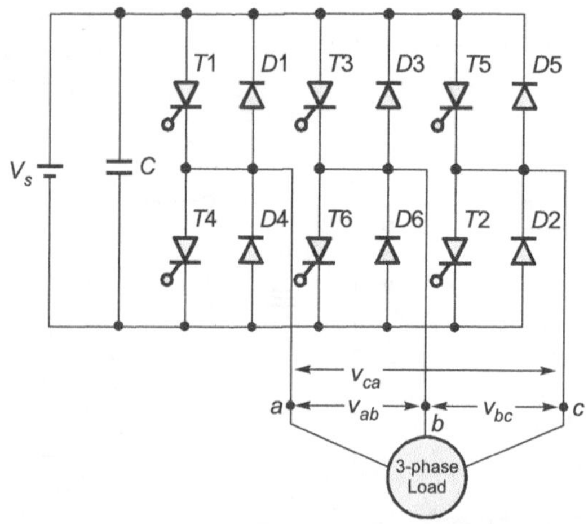

Three-phase bridge inverter using thyristors

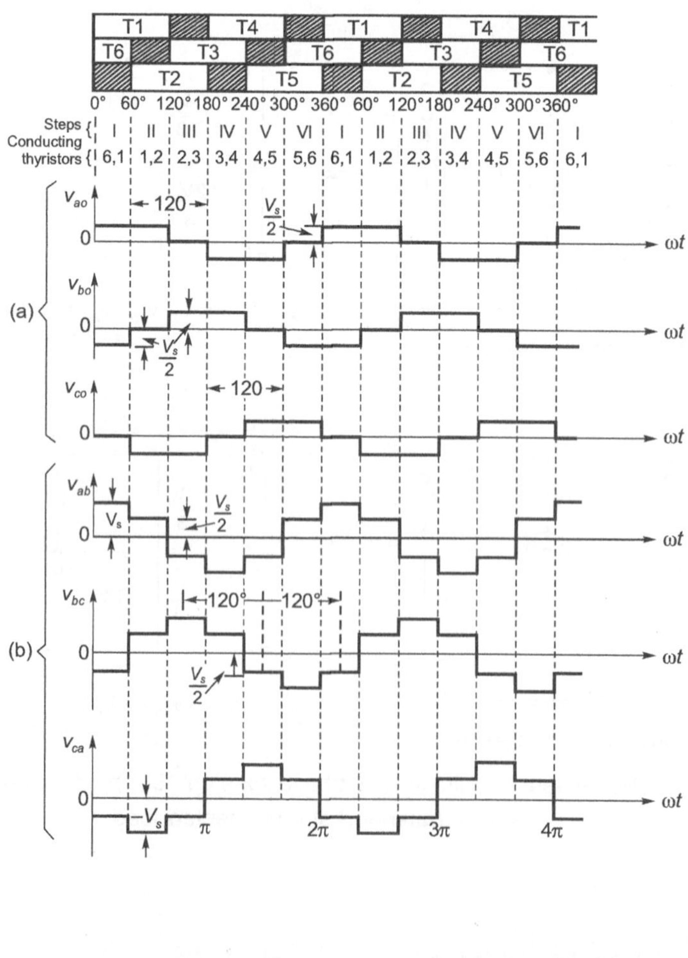

For this inverter , a table giving the sequence of firing the six thyristors is prepared as shown in the top of Fig. In this table, first rows shows that *T*1 conducts for 120° and for the next 60°, neither *T*1 nor *T*4 conducts. Now *T*4 is turned on at ωt = 180° and it further conducts for 120°, i.e. from ωt = 180° to ωt = 300°. This means that for 60° interval from ωt = 120° to ωt = 180°, series connected SCRs do not conduct. At ωt = 300°, *T*4 is turned off, then 60° interval elapses before *T*1 is turned on again at ωt = 360°. In the second row, *T*3 is turned on at ωt = 120° as in 180° mode inverter. Now *T*3 conducts for 120°, then 60° interval elapses during which neither *T*3 nor *T*6 conducts. At ωt = 300°, *T*6 is turned on, it conducts for 120° and then 60° interval elapses after which *T*3 is turned on again. The third row is also completed similarly. This table shows that *T*6, *T*1 should be gated for step-I; *T*1, *T*2 for step-II, *T*2, *T*3 for step-III and so on. During each steps only two thyristors conduct for this inverter – one from the upper group and one from the lower group.

Step-I

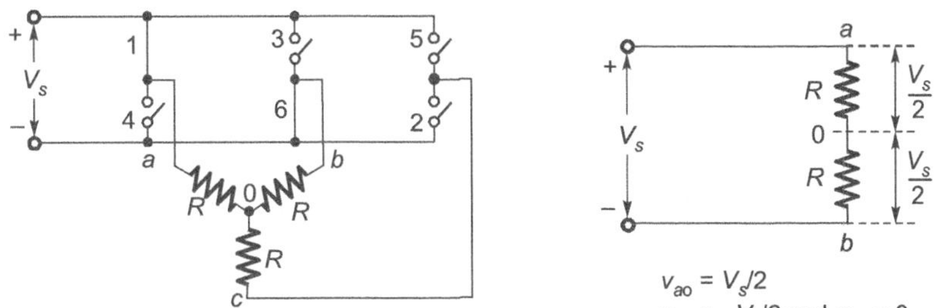

$v_{ao} = V_s/2$
$v_{bo} = -V_s/2$ and $v_{co} = 0$

(a) 0 – 60° ; 6, 1 closed

Step-II

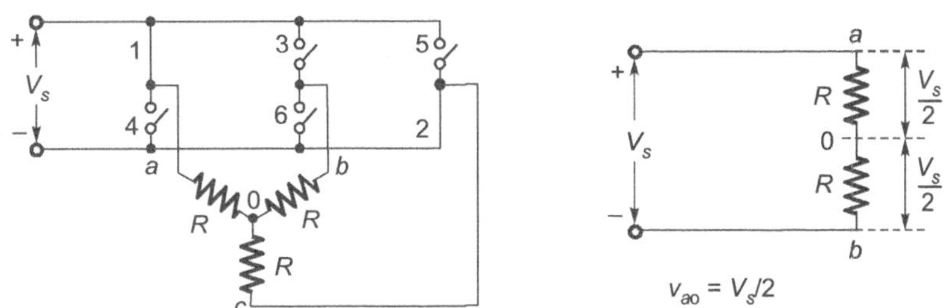

$v_{ao} = V_s/2$
$v_{co} = -V_s/2$ and $v_{bo} = 0$

(b) 60 – 120° ; 1, 2 closed

Step-III

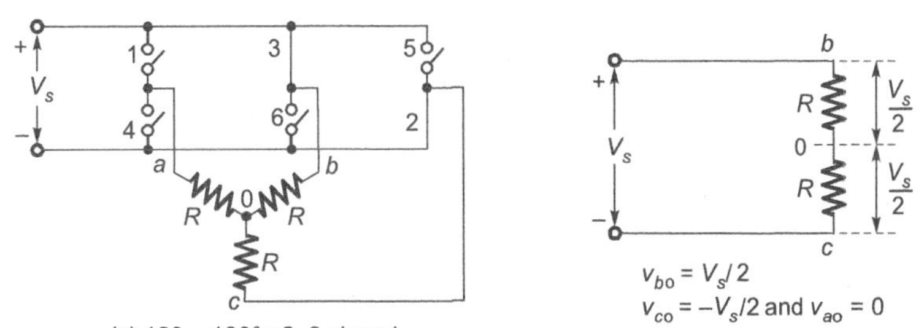

$v_{bo} = V_s/2$
$v_{co} = -V_s/2$ and $v_{ao} = 0$

(c) 120 – 180° ; 2, 3 closed

Step-IV

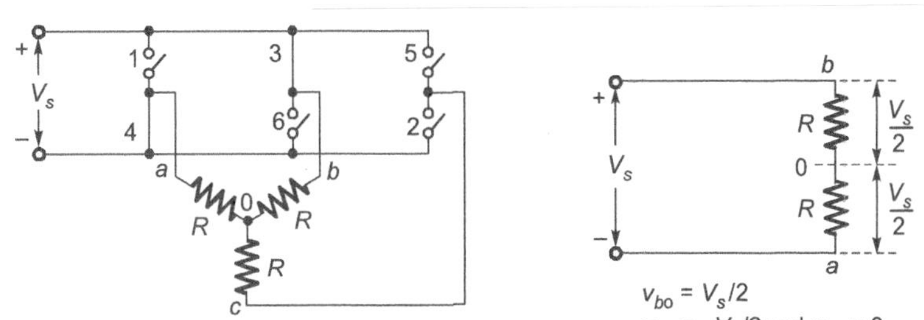

(d) 180 – 240° ; 3, 4 closed

$v_{bo} = V_s/2$
$v_{ao} = -V_s/2$ and $v_{co} = 0$

Equivalent circuits for a 3-phase six-step 120° mode inverter with balanced star-connected resistive load.

5.6 In a sinusoidal PWM inverter, the harmonics are of the form $k_p \pm l$(p is the carrier ratio) where
(a) both k and l are either even or both are odd
(b) k is always even and l is always odd
(c) k is always odd and l is always even
(d) k is odd and l is even or k is even and l is odd

[2 marks : 2009]

Solution: (b)

In sinusoidal PWM inverter, the harmonic are of the form ($kp + l$) where (p is the carrier ratio) then k is always even and 'l' is is always odd.

5.7 For a single pulse-width modulation of a single-phase inverter, what is the distortion factor for pulse width of $\pi/2$?

[5 marks : 2009]

Solution:

In single phase modulation of a 1-ϕ inverter

$$V_0 = \sum_{n=1,3,5}^{\infty} \left(\frac{4V_s}{n\pi}\right) \sin\frac{n\pi}{2} \sin nd \sin n\omega t$$

$$V_0 = \frac{4V_s}{\pi}\left[\sin d \sin \omega t - \frac{1}{3}\sin 3d \sin 3\omega t + \frac{1}{5}\sin 5d \sin 5\omega t + ...\right]$$

peak value of fundamental for $\left(2d = \frac{\pi}{2}\right)$

$$V_{01(\text{peak})} = \frac{4\,V_s}{\pi}\sin\frac{\pi}{4}$$

$$V_{01(\text{rms})} = \frac{4\,V_s}{\pi} \times \frac{1}{\sqrt{2}} \times \frac{1}{\sqrt{2}} = \frac{2V_s}{\pi}$$

where distortion factor $\quad (D:F) = \dfrac{V_{s1(rms)}}{V_{s(rms)}}$

and then, $\quad V_{s(rms)} = V_s\sqrt{\dfrac{\pi/2}{\pi}} = \dfrac{V_s}{\sqrt{2}}$

$$DF = \frac{2\,V_s/\pi}{V_s/\sqrt{2}} = \frac{2\sqrt{2}}{\pi} = 0.9$$

5.8 A single-phase, half-bridge inverter is feeding power into a load of resistance 10 ohms; d.c. input to the inverter is 400 V. Determine the r.m.s. load voltage, load current and power factor.

[10 marks : 2009]

Solution:

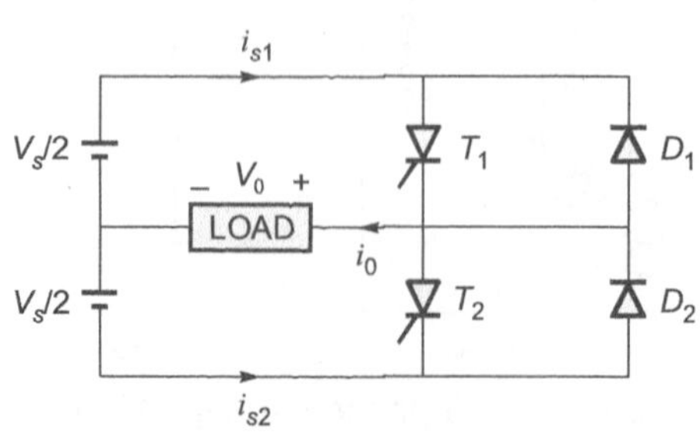

Single phase half-bridge inverter,

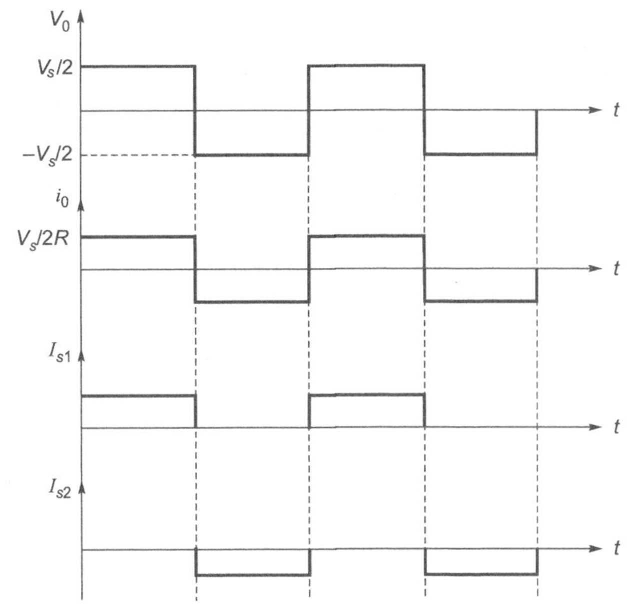

The rms value of output voltage,

$$V_{0(rms)} = \frac{V_s}{2} = \frac{400}{2} = 200 \text{ V}$$

$$I_{0(rms)} = \frac{V_s}{2R} = \frac{400}{2 \times 10} = 20 \text{ A}$$

Power delivered to the load = 200 × 20 = 4000 W

when (T_1) is conducting, power to load is delivered by upper source $\left(\frac{V_s}{2}\right)$ and when 'T_2' is 'ON' lower source deliver power to load.

Power delivered by each source = $\frac{V_s}{2} I_s(av) = \frac{V_s}{2}\left[I_{S1}(av) + I_{S2}(av)\right]$

Here, $$I_{S1} = \left(\frac{V_s}{2R}\right) \times \frac{1}{2} = \frac{V_s}{4R}$$

Similarly, $$I_{S2} = \left(\frac{V_s}{2R}\right) \times \frac{1}{2} = \frac{V_s}{4R}$$

$\therefore$ Power delivered by each source = $\left(\frac{V_s}{2}\right) \times \left(\frac{V_s}{2R}\right)$

$$= \left(\frac{400}{2}\right)\left(\frac{400}{2 \times 10}\right) = 200 \times 20$$

$$= 4000 \text{ W}$$

$\therefore$ $$\text{pf} = \frac{\text{power delivered to load}}{\text{supplied (VI)}} = 1 \text{ (unity power factor)}$$

5.9 **Explain the single pulse width modulation technique to control the output voltage of a 1-φ inverter.**

[16 marks : 2012]

Solution:

The output voltage from single-phase full-bridge inverter is shown in figure (a). When this waveform is modulated, the output voltage is of the form shown in figure (b). It consists of a pulse of width $2d$ located symmetrically about $\pi/2$ and another pulse located symmetrically about $3\pi/2$. The range of pulse width $2d$ varies from 0 to π; i.e. $0 < 2d < \pi$. The output voltage is controlled by varying the pulse-width $2d$.

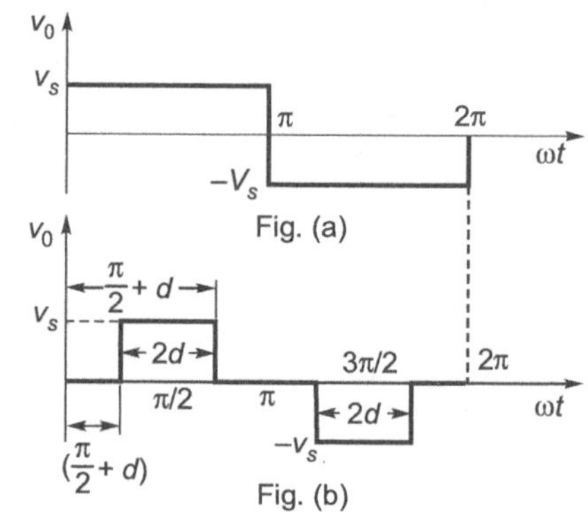

Fig. (a)

Fig. (b)

Fourier analysis of figure (b) is as under

$$v_0 = \sum_{n=1,3,5....}^{\infty} \frac{4V_s}{n\pi} \sin\frac{n\pi}{2} \sin nd \sin n\omega t$$

or, $v_0 = \frac{4V_s}{\pi}[\sin d \sin\omega t - \frac{1}{3}\sin 3d \sin 3\omega t + \frac{1}{5}\sin 5d \sin\omega t......]$

- When pulse width $2d$ is equal to its maximum value of π radians, then the fundamental component of output voltage has a peak value of

$$V_{01m} = \frac{4V_s}{\pi}$$

- If pulse width is equal to $2d = (2\pi/n)$, the nth harmonic is eliminated from the inverter output voltage.
- The peak value of nth harmonic

$$V_{onm} = \frac{4V_s}{n\pi}\sin nd$$

- The rms value of output voltage

$$V_{or} = \left[\frac{V_s^2 \cdot 2d}{\pi}\right]^{1/2} = V_s\left[\frac{2d}{\pi}\right]^{1/2}$$

5.10 **A full bridge inverter (IGBT) has a switching sequence which produces a square wave voltage across a series *R-L* load. For the instant case the switching frequency is 50 Hz. V_{dc} = 100 V, R = 10 Ω and L = 25 mH. Determine the amplitude of the Fourier series terms for load current and the power absorbed by the load. Consider only 3rd, 5th and 7th harmonic terms. Compute THD for voltage and current. If the switching sequence is modified to produce quasi square waveform, what changes will be observed in Fourier coefficients and THD of voltage waveform and currents.**

[20 marks : 2013]

Solution:

(a) Square-wave output:

RMS value of fundamental voltage is

$$V_{01} = \frac{4V_s}{\pi\sqrt{2}} = \frac{4\times 100}{\pi\times\sqrt{2}} = 90.03 \text{ V}$$

Load impedance at fundamental frequency is

$$Z_1 = \left[10^2 + (2\pi\times 50\times 0.025)^2\right]^{1/2} = 12.72\ \Omega$$

$$I_{01} = \frac{90.03}{12.72} = 7.08 \text{ Amp}$$

$$V_{03} = \frac{4V_s}{3\pi\sqrt{2}} = \frac{4\times 100}{3\times\pi\times\sqrt{2}} = 30.01 \text{ V}$$

$$Z_3 = \sqrt{10^2+(2\pi\times 50\times 3\times 0.025)^2} = 25.59\ \Omega$$

$$I_{03} = \frac{V_{03}}{Z_3} = \frac{30.01}{25.59} = 1.17\text{ A}$$

$$V_{05} = \frac{4\times 100}{5\times\pi\times\sqrt{2}} = 18.00\text{ V}$$

$$Z_{05} = \sqrt{(10)^2+(2\pi\times 50\times 5\times 0.25)^2} = 40.52\ \Omega$$

$$I_{05} = \frac{V_{05}}{Z_{05}} = \frac{18.00}{40.52} = 0.44\ A$$

$$V_{07} = \frac{4\times 100}{7\times\pi\times\sqrt{2}} = 12.86\ V$$

$$Z_{07} = \sqrt{(10)^2+(2\pi\times 50\times 7\times 0.025)^2} = 55.88\ \Omega$$

$$I_{07} = \frac{12.86}{55.88} = 0.23\text{ A}$$

RMS value of resultant load current,

$$I_0 = \left[I_{01}^2+I_{03}^2+I_{05}^2+I_{07}^2\right]^{1/2}$$

$$= \left[(7.08)^2+(1.17)^2+(0.44)^2+(0.23)^2\right]^{1/2}$$

$$I_0 = 7.19\text{ A}$$

Power absorbed by the load = $I_0^2\cdot R = (7.19)^2\times 10 = 516.96$ Watt

RMS value of voltage,

$$V_o = \left[V_{01}^2+V_{03}^2+V_{05}^2+V_{07}^2\right]^{1/2}$$

$$= \left[(90.03)^2+(30.01)^2+(18.00)^2+(12.86)^2\right]^{1/2} = 97.44$$

$$\text{T.H.D. of current waveform} = \sqrt{\frac{I_0^2-I_{01}^2}{I_{01}^2}} = \sqrt{\frac{(7.19)^2-(7.08)^2}{(7.08)^2}} = 17.7\%$$

$$\text{T.H.D. of voltage waveform} = \sqrt{\frac{V_0^2-V_{01}^2}{V_{01}^2}} = \sqrt{\frac{(97.44)^2-(90.03)^2}{(90.03)^2}} = 41.40\%$$

(b) **For Quasi-Square Wave:** Let quasi square wave output with an ON period of 0.5 of a cycle. For quasi-square wave or single pulse modulated wave, where pulse width $2d = 0.5\times 180 = 90°$

$$d = 45°$$

The R.M.S. value of fundamental voltage is

$$V_{01} = \frac{4V_s}{\pi\sqrt{2}}\sin d = \frac{4\times 100}{\pi\times\sqrt{2}}\sin 45° = 63.66\text{ V}$$

$$I_{01} = \frac{63.66}{12.72} = 5.00\text{ A}$$

$$V_{03} = \frac{4V_s}{3\times\pi\times\sqrt{2}}\sin(3\times 45°) = 21.22\text{ V}$$

$$I_{03} = \frac{21.22}{25.59} = 0.8292 \text{ A}$$

$$V_{05} = \frac{4V_s}{5 \times \pi \times \sqrt{2}} \sin(5 \times 45°) = -12.72 \text{ V}$$

$$I_{05} = -\frac{12.72}{40.52} = -0.314 \text{ A}$$

$$V_{07} = \frac{4V_s}{7 \times \pi \times \sqrt{2}} \sin(7 \times 45°) = -9.09 \text{ V}$$

$$I_{07} = -\frac{9.09}{55.88} = -0.163 \text{ A}$$

RMS value of resultant load current,

$$I_0 = \left[(5.00)^2 + (0.8292)^2 + (-0.314)^2 + (-0.163)^2\right]^{1/2} = 5.08 \text{ A}$$

Power absorbed by the load = $I_0^2 \times R = (5.08)^2 \times 10 = 258.13\ Watt$

RMS value of voltage,

$$V_o = \left[V_{01}^2 + V_{03}^2 + V_{05}^2 + V_{07}^2\right]^{1/2}$$

$$= \left[(63.66)^2 + (21.22)^2 + (-12.72)^2 + (-9.09)^2\right]^{1/2} = 68.90 \text{ V}$$

T.H.D. of current waveform = $\sqrt{\dfrac{I_0^2 - I_{01}^2}{I_{01}^2}} = \sqrt{\dfrac{(5.08)^2 - (5.00)^2}{(5.00)^2}} = 17.96\%$

T.H.D. of voltage waveform = $\sqrt{\dfrac{(68.90)^2 - (63.66)^2}{(63.66)^2}} = 41.40\%$

5.11 **A line commutated inverter transfers energy into a 440 V, 50 Hz three-phase supply from a battery of 500 V. The battery is linked to the converter through a large filter choke of resistance 12.4 Ω. It is desired to transfer 5 kW power into the system.**

(i) Calculate the firing angle at which inverter is to be operated. Also, determine (a) input power factor, (b) RMS value of fundamental ac current, (c) Efficiency of energy transfer.

(ii) What is the maximum usable value of the SCR firing angle?

(iii) Calculate the SCR voltage and rms current rating.

[15 marks : 2014]

Solution:

(i) Here in this case line commutated inverter means the battery is supplying power to source, since battery is supplying total power which is desired to be transferred i.e. 5000 W and $I_{0,rms}^2 R$ loss so, according to energy balance equation.

$$E_b I_0 = 5000 + I_{0,rms}^2 R$$

$$I_{0'rms} \simeq I_0 \text{ because of large inductor}$$

$$500\, I_0 = 5000 + I_0^2\, 12.4$$

$12.4 I_0^2 - 500 I_0 + 5000 = 0$ is a quadratic equation, the roots of this equation are $I_0 = 21.96$ A or 18.35 A.

Considering the lowest value of load current,

$$I_0 = 18.35\text{ A}$$

$$-E_b + I_0R = \frac{3V_{mL}}{\pi}\cos\alpha$$

$$-500 + (18.35)(12.4) = \frac{3\times\sqrt{2}\times 440}{\pi}\cos\alpha$$

$$\alpha = \cos^{-1}\left(\frac{-272.46\times\pi}{3\times\sqrt{2}\times 440}\right) = 117.2920°$$

(a) $$\text{Input power factor} = \frac{I_{S_1}}{I_S}\times\cos\alpha = \frac{3}{\pi}\cos(117.2920°) = 0.4378\text{ lagging}$$

(b) Rms value of fundamental ac current

$$= I_{S_1} = \frac{2\sqrt{2}}{\pi}I_0\sin 60° = \frac{\sqrt{6}}{\pi}I_0 = \frac{\sqrt{6}}{\pi}(18.35) = 14.307\text{ A}$$

(c) Efficiency of energy transferred

$$= \frac{5000}{E_bI_0} = \frac{5000}{500\times 18.35}\times 100$$

$$\eta = 54.49\%$$

(ii) The maximum usable firing angle is obtained by making load current equal to zero,

$$\frac{3V_{mL}}{\pi}\cos\alpha = -E + I_0R$$

$$\frac{3\times\sqrt{2}\times 440}{\pi}\cos\alpha = 500$$

$$\alpha = 147.29°$$

(iii) Rms current rating of SCR is,

$$I_{T_{rms}} = I_0\sqrt{\frac{1}{3}} = 18.35\sqrt{\frac{1}{3}} = 10.6\text{ A}$$

SCR voltage rating = Maximum value of source voltage

$$= V_m = 440\sqrt{2} = 623\text{ V}$$

5.12 **A 1-phase bridge inverter is feeding an *R-L* load with *R* = 8 Ω, *L* = 0.04 H. Find the load voltage and current expressions for the first two half cycles with rectangular wave output at 50 Hz. The input to the inverter is 220 V.**

[10 marks : 2015]

Solution:

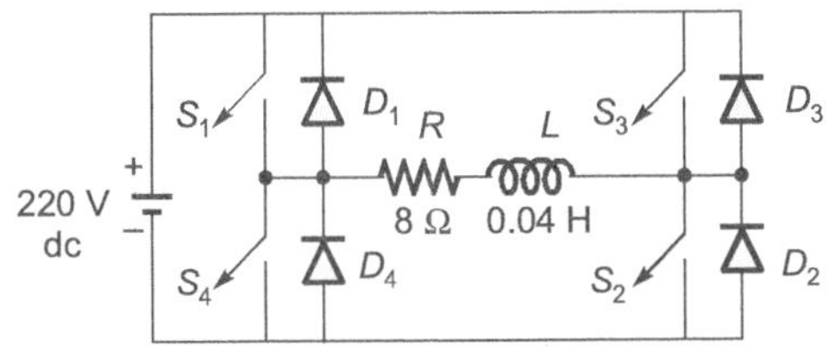

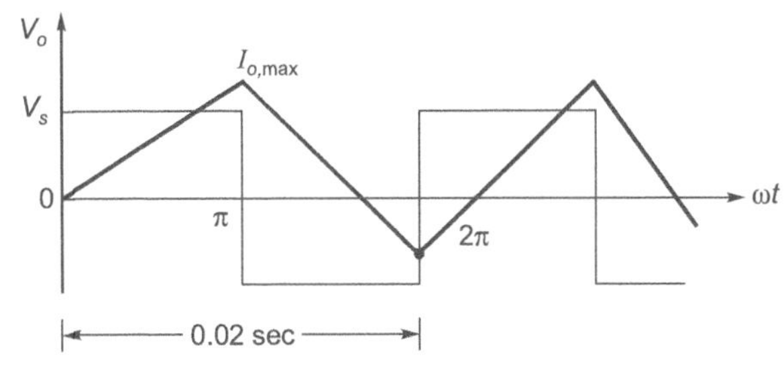

For the first half cycle $0 < t < \frac{T}{2}$

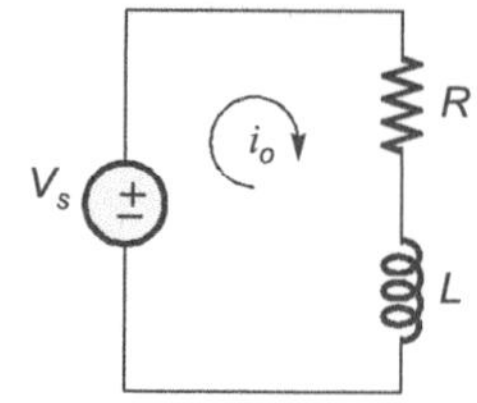

the voltage equation for RL load is

$$V_s = Ri_0 + L\frac{di_0}{dt}$$

$$i_o(t) = \frac{V_s}{R}(1-e^{-t/\tau}) \quad ...(1)$$

This is the expression of current as a function of time for the first half cycle from the instant of switching in $i_o(t) = 0$ at $t = 0$. During second half cycle.

$$I_0 = I_{(\text{initial})} = \frac{V_s}{R}$$

$$I_\infty = I_{(\text{final})} = -\frac{V_s}{R}$$

$$I(t) = (I_\infty - (I_\infty - I_o)e^{-t/\tau}) = \left[\frac{-V_s}{R} - \left(-\frac{V_s}{R} - \frac{V_s}{R}\right)e^{-t/\tau}\right]$$

$$I(t) = -\frac{V_s}{R} + \frac{2V_s}{R}e^{-t/\tau} \quad ...(2)$$

$$\tau = \frac{L}{R} = \frac{0.04}{8} = 0.005\ s.$$

Expression for transient current during first half cycle is from eq. (1)

$$i_o(t) = \frac{V_s}{R}(1-e^{-t/\tau})$$

$$i_o(t) = \frac{220}{8}(1-e^{-t/0.005})$$

$$\boxed{i_o(t) = 27.5(1-e^{-200t})} \text{ A from } 0 < t < \frac{T}{2}$$

Expression for transient current during second half cycle is from equation (2),

$$i_o(t) = \frac{-V_s}{R} + \frac{2V_s}{R}e^{-t/\tau} = \frac{-220}{8} + \frac{2\times 220}{8}e^{-t/0.005}$$

$$\boxed{i_o(t) = -27.5 + 55e^{-200t}} \text{ A from } \frac{T}{2} < t < T$$

5.13 **In a single-phase full bridge inverter, feeding power to an inductive load, each commutating switch is triggered for 2π/3 radian as shown in the following figures. Assuming the load current to the continuous, draw one cycle of the load voltage and current waveforms if the load current passes through zero value at ωt = 0, π, 2π, etc. Mention the conducting elements in the various intervals throughout the cycle.**

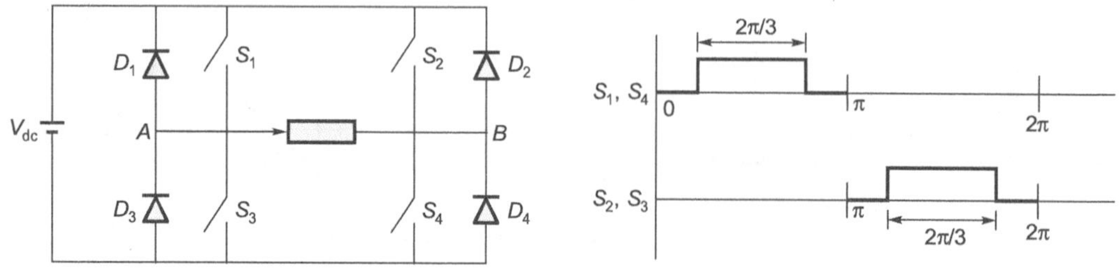

[10 marks : 2016]

Solution:

During the period $0 \le \omega t \le \frac{\pi}{6}$ the triggering pulses are not given to S_1 and S_4, so the current should flow from diodes. The circuit behaves as

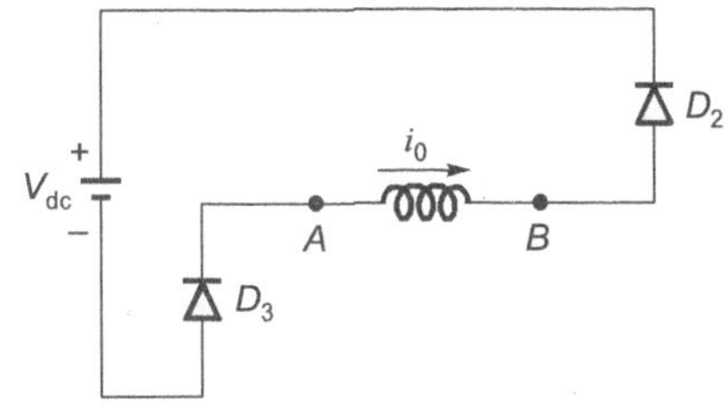

$$\therefore \qquad V_{AB} = -V_{dc} \quad \text{from} \quad 0 \le \omega t \le \frac{\pi}{6}$$

This is also the same thing will happen from $\frac{5\pi}{6} \le \omega t \le \pi$.

During the period $\pi \le \omega t \le \frac{7\pi}{6}$ the triggering pulses are not given to S_2 and S_3, so the current should flow from diodes. The circuit behaves as

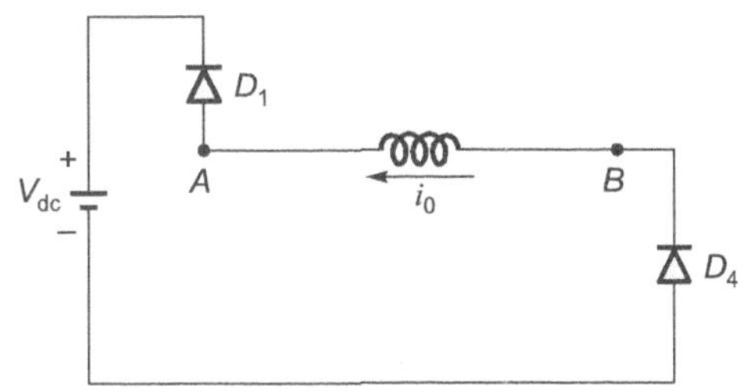

$$\therefore \qquad V_{AB} = V_{dc} \quad \text{from} \quad \pi \le \omega t \le \frac{7\pi}{6}$$

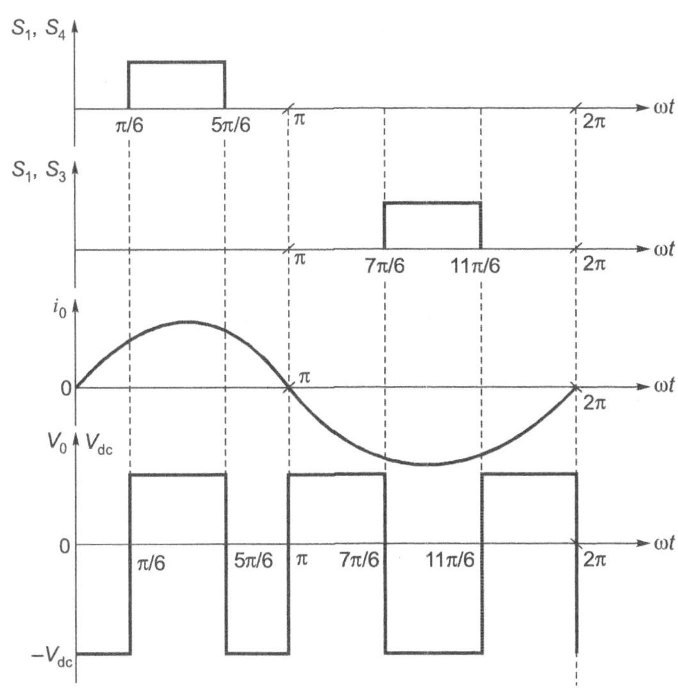

5.14 Discuss the unipolar control of a single-phase sinusoidal PWM inverter. Explain the effect of modulation index and carrier frequency on inverter performance.

[10 marks : 2016]

Solution:

Sinusoidal Pulse-Width Modulation:

$$m_A = \frac{A_{\text{Reference}}}{A_{\text{carrier}}}$$

$$m_F = \frac{f_{\text{carrier}}}{f_{\text{Reference}}}$$

Instead of maintaining the width of all pulses the same as in the case of multiple-pulse modulation, the width of each pulse is varied in proportion to the amplitude of a sine wave evaluated at the center of the same pulse. The DF and LOH are reduced significantly. The gating signals are generated by comparing a sinusoidal reference signal with a triangular carrier wave of frequency f_c. This sinusoidal pulse-width modulation (SPWM) is commonly used in industrial applications. The frequency of reference signal f_r determines the inverter output frequency f_0; and its peak amplitude A_r controls the modulation index M, and then in turn the rms output voltage V_0.

The rms output voltage can be varied by varying the modulation index M_A. It can be observed that the area of each pulse corresponds approximately to the area under the sine wave between the adjacent midpoints of off periods on the gating signals.

The harmonic profile is shown in figure for five pulses per half-cycle. The DF is significantly reduced compared with that of multiple-pulse modulation.

The output voltage of an inverter contains harmonics. The PWM pushes the harmonics into a high-frequency range around the switching frequency f_c and its multiples, that is around harmonics m_f, $2m_f$, $3m_f$, and so on. The frequencies at which the voltage harmonics occur can be related by

$$f_n = (jm_f \pm k)\, f_c$$

where the nth harmonic equals the kth sideband of jth times the frequency to modulation ratio m_f.

$$n = jm_f \pm k$$
$$= 2\,jp \pm k \text{ for}$$

For $j = 1, 2, 3, \ldots$ and $k = 1, 3, 5, \ldots$

The peak fundamental output voltage for PWM and SPWM control can be found approximately from

$$V_{m1} = m_A V_s \text{ for } 0 \le m_A \le 1.0$$

For $m_A = 1$, equation gives the maximum peak amplitude of the fundamental output voltage as $V_{m\,1(\max)} = V_s$. According to equation, $V_{m\,1(\max)}$ could be as high as $4V_s/\pi = 1.273\,V_s$ for a square-wave output. To increase the fundamental output voltage, m_A must be increased beyond 1.0. The operation beyond $m_A = 1.0$ is called overmodulation. The value of m_A at which $V_{m\,1(\max)}$ equals $1.273\,V_s$ is dependent on the number of pulses per half-cycle p and is approximately 3 for $p = 7$, as shown in figure. Overmodulation basically leads to a square-wave operation and adds more harmonics as compared with operation in the linear range (with $m_A \le 1.0$). Overmodulation is normally avoided in applications requiring low distortion (e.g. uninterruptible power supplies [UPS]).

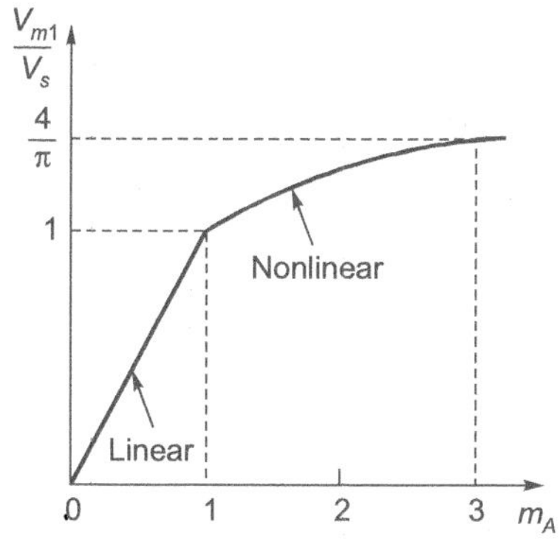

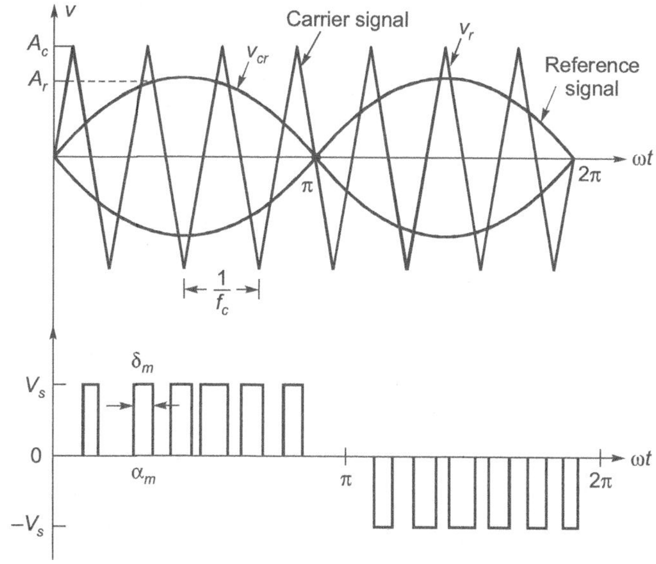

5.15 **A single-phase, full-bridge bipolar PWM inverter employs selective harmonic elimination method. The output voltage waveform of the inverter is shown in the figure below. For $\alpha_1 = 23.62°$ and $\alpha_2 = 33.30°$, find the amplitude of 7th, 9th and 11th harmonics.**

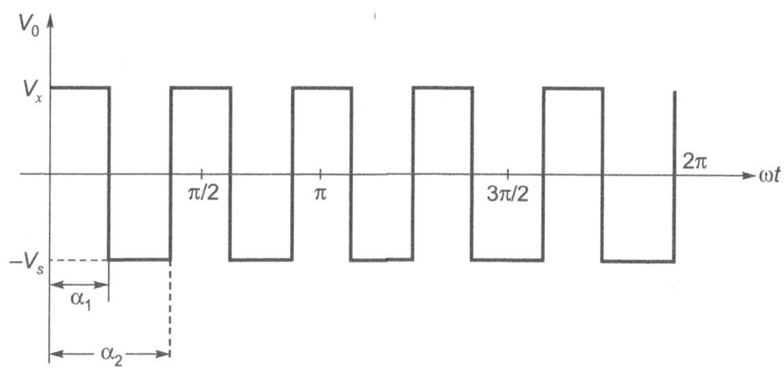

[20 marks : 2017]

Solution:

The voltage waveform of the given figure is symmetrical about π as well as π/2.

As this voltage waveform has quarter wave symmetry,

$$a_n = 0$$

and

$$b_n = \frac{4V_s}{\pi}\left[\int_0^{\alpha_1} \sin\omega t \cdot d\omega(t) - \int_{\alpha_1}^{\alpha_2} \sin n\omega t \cdot d\omega(t) + \int_{\alpha_2}^{\pi/2} \sin n\omega t \cdot d\omega(t)\right]$$

$$b_n = \frac{4V_s}{\pi}\left[\left(-\frac{\cos n\omega t}{n}\right)\Bigg|_0^{\alpha_1} - \left(-\frac{\cos n\omega t}{n}\right)\Bigg|_{\alpha_1}^{\alpha_2} + \left(-\frac{\cos n\omega t}{n}\right)\Bigg|_{\alpha_2}^{\pi/2}\right]$$

$$= \frac{4V_s}{\pi}\left[\frac{1-\cos n\alpha_1}{n} + \frac{\cos\alpha_2 - \cos\alpha_1}{n} + \frac{\cos n\alpha_2}{n}\right]$$

$$b_n = \frac{4V_s}{\pi}\left[\frac{1-2\cos n\alpha_1 + 2\cos n\alpha_2}{n}\right]$$

Now, for the values of $\alpha_1 = 23.62°$ and $\alpha_2 = 33.30°$

The amplitude of 7th harmonics

$$b_7 = \frac{4V_s}{\pi}\left[\frac{1-2\cos(7\times 23.62°)+2\cos(7\times 33.30°)}{7}\right] = 0.3154\ V_s$$

The amplitude of 9th harmonics

$$b_9 = \frac{4V_s}{\pi}\left[\frac{1-2\cos(9\times 23.62°)+2\cos(9\times 33.30°)}{9}\right] = 0.5201\ V_s$$

and the amplitude of 11th harmonics,

$$b_{11} = \frac{4V_s}{\pi}\left[\frac{1-2\cos(11\times 23.62°)+2\cos(11\times 33.30°)}{11}\right] = 0.3867\ V_s$$

5.16 **A single-phase full bridge inverter is used to produce a 50 Hz voltage across a series R-L load (R = 10 Ω and L = 20 mH) using bipolar PWM. The DC input to the bridge is 380 V, the amplitude modulation ratio m_a = 0.8 and frequency modulation ratio m_f = 21. Consider dominant harmonics to be frequency dominant and its nearby side frequencies (both sides). Assume normalized Fourier coefficient for m_a = 0.8 to be 82% for dominant harmonic frequency and 22% for the nearby side frequencies.**

Determine:

(i) Amplitude of 50 Hz component of output voltage and current;

(ii) Power absorbed by the load resistor;

(iii) THD of the load current.

Also compare the amplitude of 50 Hz component of output voltage with square wave and quasi-square wave output.

[20 marks : 2018]

Solution:

(i) Amplitude of 50 Hz component,

$$V_1 = m_a V_{dc}$$
$$= 0.8 \times 380$$
$$V_1 = 304\text{ V}$$
$$V_{1rms} = \frac{V_1}{\sqrt{2}} = 214.96\text{ V}$$
$$Z_1 = R + j\omega L$$
$$= 10 + j2\pi \times 50 \times 20 \times 10^{-3}$$
$$Z_1 = 11.81\angle 32.14°\ \Omega$$
$$I_1 = \frac{V_1}{Z_1} = \frac{304}{11.81\angle 32.14°}$$
$$I_1 = 25.74\angle -32.14°\text{ V}$$
$$I_{1rms} = \frac{25.74}{\sqrt{2}} = 18.201\text{ A}$$

(ii)

$m_f = 21$ first harmonics are at

$$n = 23, 19, 21$$
$$V_{21} = 0.82 \times 380 = 311.6$$
$$V_{21,rms} = 220.33\text{ V}$$

$$V_{19} = V_{23} = 0.22 \times 380 = 83.6 \text{ V}$$

$$V_{19\,rms} = V_{23\,rms} = \frac{83.6}{\sqrt{2}} = 59.11 \text{ V}$$

n	$f_n(Hz)$	$V_n(V)_{rms}$	$Z_n(\Omega)$	$I_n(rms)(A)$
1	50	214.96	11.81∠32.14	18.2
19	950	59.11	119.79∠85.21	0.49
21	1050	220.33	132.33∠85.66	1.66
23	1150	59.11	144.86∠86	0.41

$$I_{rms} = \sqrt{I_1^2 + I_{19}^2 + I_{21}^2 + I_{23}^2}$$

$$= \sqrt{18.2^2 + 0.49^2 + 1.66^2 + 0.41^2} = 18.28\text{A}$$

$$P = I_{rms}^2 R = 18.28^2 \times 10$$

$$P = 3344.04 \text{ watts}$$

(iii)

$$g = \frac{I_{s1}}{I_{sr}} = \frac{18.2}{18.28} = 0.9956$$

$$\text{THD} = \sqrt{\frac{1}{g^2} - 1} = \sqrt{\frac{1}{0.9956^2} - 1} = 0.09412 \text{ or } 9.412\%$$

5.17 The full bridge inverter is used to produce a 50 Hz voltage across a series RL load using Bipolar PWM. The dc input to the bridge is 200 V, the frequency modulation m_f is 21 and amplitude modulation m_a is 0.8. The load has resistance of R = 10 Ω and inductance L = 20 mH. Find:

(i) The amplitude of fundamental voltage and current and

(ii) Total harmonic distortion in load current.

Assume harmonics (> 25th order) are insignificant and normalized voltage is

$m_a = 1$		0.9	0.8	0.7	0.6	0.5
$n = 1$	1.0	0.9	0.8	0.7	0.6	0.5
$n = m_f$	0.6	0.71	0.82	0.92	1.01	1.15
$n = m_f \pm 2$	0.32	0.27	0.22	0.17	0.13	0.09

[20 Marks : 2019]

Solution:

(i)

$$V_1 = m_a V_{dc}$$

$$V_1 = 0.8 \times 200 = 160 \text{ V}$$

$$Z_1 = l + j\omega L$$

$$= 10 + g100\pi \times 20 \times 10^{-3}$$

$$= 11.81\angle 32.142^\circ \ \Omega$$

$$I_1 = \frac{V_1}{Z_1} = \frac{160}{11.81\angle 32.142^\circ} = 13.548\angle -32.142^\circ$$

(ii) For bipolar PWM,

$$f_n = (jm_f \pm k)\, f_L\,; \qquad V_{21} = 0.82 \times 200 = 164 \text{ V}$$
$$f_n = (j21 \pm k) \times 50$$
$$f_{21} = 21 \times 50 = 1050 \text{ Hz}; \qquad V_{23} = 0.22 \times 200 = 44 \text{ V}$$
$$f_{23} = 23 \times 50 = 1150 \text{ Hz}$$
$$f_{19} = 19 \times 50 = 950 \text{ Hz}; \qquad V_{19} = 0.22 \times 200 = 44 \text{ V}$$
$$Z_n = R + j\omega_n L$$
$$= 10 + j2\pi f_n = 0.02 = (10 + 0.04\pi f_n)\ \Omega$$

n	f_n(Hz)	V_n(max)	$Z_n(\Omega)$	I_n(max) A
1	50	160	11.81∠32.14°	13.55∠–32.14°
19	950	44	119.79∠85.2°	0.3673∠–85.2°
21	1050	164	132.32∠85.66°	1.239∠–85.66°
23	1150	44	144.86∠86.04°	0.304∠–86.04°

$$\text{THD} = \frac{\sqrt{\sum_{n+1} I_n^2}}{I_L} = \frac{\sqrt{0.3673^2 + 1.239^2 + 0.304^2}}{13.55} = 0.0979$$

$$\text{THD} = 9.79\%$$

5.18 The configuration of a single phase bridge inverter is shown in the figure below. The DC source voltage is 100 V and the connected load is a pure inductor of 1 H. The switching frequency of the inverter is 50 Hz.

Determine :

(i) the maximum current through the transistors and diodes.

(ii) the rms currents of the diodes and transistors.

(iii) Sketch the load voltage and current waveforms indicating conducting devices.

(Assume ideal devices with no losses and square wave switching for the inverter).

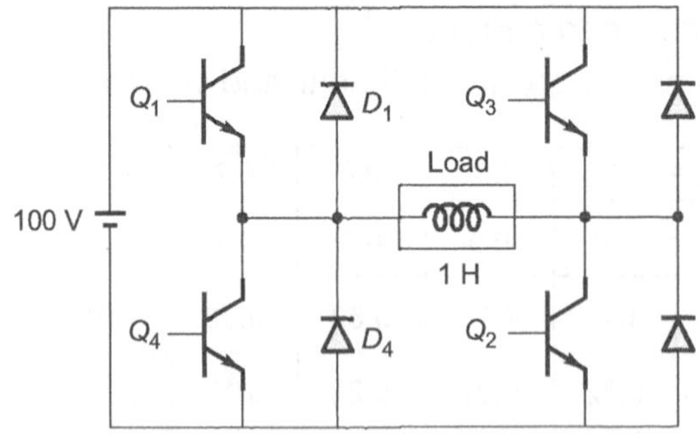

[12 marks : 2022]

Solution:

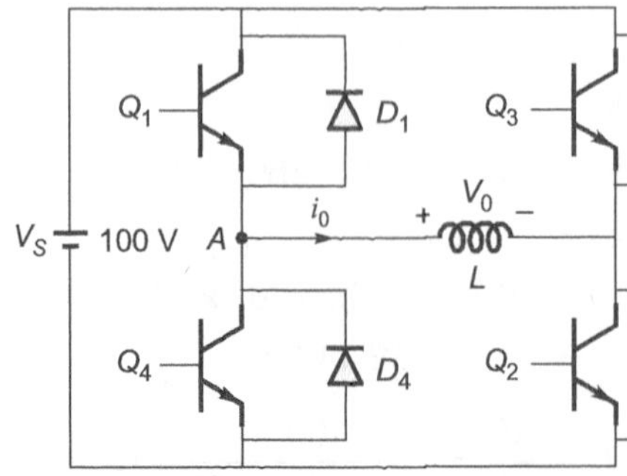

$V_S = 100$ V, $L = 1$ H, $f = 50$ Hz

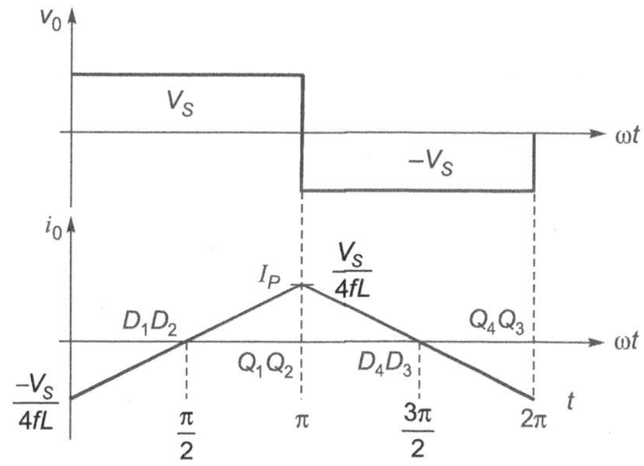

Let peak current passing through load current is I_P (after reaching steady state).

$\frac{\pi}{2}$ to π : $Q_1Q_2 \rightarrow$ ON

$$V_o = V_s$$

$$L\cdot\frac{di}{dt} = V_s$$

$$di = \frac{V_s}{L}\cdot dt$$

$$\int_0^{I_P} di = \frac{V_s}{\omega L}\int_{\pi/2}^{\pi} d(\omega t)$$

$$I_P = \frac{V_s}{\omega L}\cdot\frac{\pi}{2} = \frac{V_s}{4fL}$$

$$= \frac{100}{4\times 50\times 1}$$

$$= 0.5 \text{ A}$$

(i) Maximum current through transistors and diodes

$$= I_P = \frac{V_s}{4fL} = 0.5 \text{ A}$$

(ii)

$$I_{o,rms} = \frac{I_P}{\sqrt{3}} = \frac{0.5}{\sqrt{3}} = 0.2886 \text{ A}$$

$$(I_D)_{rms} = (I_Q)_{rms} = I_{o,rms}\left(\frac{\pi/2}{2\pi}\right)^{1/2} = \frac{I_{o,rms}}{\sqrt{4}}$$

$$= \frac{0.2886}{2} = 0.1443 \text{ A}$$

5.19 Explain the concept of Pulse Width Modulation. How is it used in the reduction of harmonics in a single-phase full bridge. Inverter?

[12 marks : 2023]

Solution:

PWM (Pulse Width Modulation) is an internal voltage control of inverter. In this method, a fixed dc input voltage is given to the inverter and a controlled output voltage is obtained by, adjusting the on and off periods of the inverter component.

In pulse width modulation, the width of the pulse is adjusted to reduce the harmonic. In general, the RMS value of the amplitude of harmonics voltage of a single phase full bridge inverter is given by

$$E_{Ln} = \frac{4E_{dc}}{\sqrt{2}n\pi} \times \sin nP$$

where P is the width of pulse, E_{dc} is the supply dc voltage

If the nth harmonic is to be eliminated,

$$E_{Ln} = 0$$

$$\therefore \quad \frac{4E_{dc}}{\sqrt{2}n\pi} \times \sin nP = 0$$

$$nP = 2\pi$$

$$P = \frac{2\pi}{n} \text{ where } n = 1, 2, 3, 4, ...$$

6. Power Semiconductors Drives

6.1 **A 250 V separately excited DC motor has armature resistance of 2.5 ohms. When driving a load at 600 r.p.m. with constant torque, the armature takes 20 A. The motor is controlled by a DC chopper operating with a frequency of 400 Hz and an input voltage of 250 V DC. What should be the value of duty ratio, if it is desired to reduce the speed from 600 r.pm. to 400 r.p.m.? Also find the motor speed at rated current and a duty ratio of 0.5, if the motor is regenerating.**

[20 marks : 2002]

Solution:

For separately excited dc motor,

$$\text{Armature Resistance} = 2.5\ \Omega$$

$$\therefore \quad \text{back emf } E_{\phi} = k_n \phi N$$

where $E = V_t - I_a R_a = 250 - 20 \times 2.5 = 200$ V

$$\therefore \quad k_n\phi = \frac{200}{600} = \frac{1}{3}$$

Let (δ) be the duty ratio, then, $V_t = \delta V_i$ [where V_i = input voltage]

$$[\delta V_i - I_a R_a] = k_n\phi \times N'$$

Since torque remains constant,

$\therefore$ 'I' should be constant

$$[\delta \times 250 - 20 \times 2.5] = \frac{1}{3} \times 400$$

$$\delta = 0.733$$

At ($\delta = 0.5$), and given, motor is regenerating working as a generator, then

$$N'' = \frac{[\delta V_i + I_a R_a]}{k_n\phi} = 3 \times [125 + 20 \times 2.5] = 525 \text{ rpm}$$

6.2 **A triac-diac used for a stepless fan regulator.** [5 marks : 2003]

Solution:

This is the circuit diagram of the simplest fan regulator. The circuit is based on the principle of power control using a Triac. The circuit works by varying the firing angle of the Triac. The firing angle can be varied by varying the resistance R. By varying the value of R, the firing angle of Triac changes. This directly varies the load power, since load is driven by Triac. The firing pulses are given to the gate of Triac using Diac.

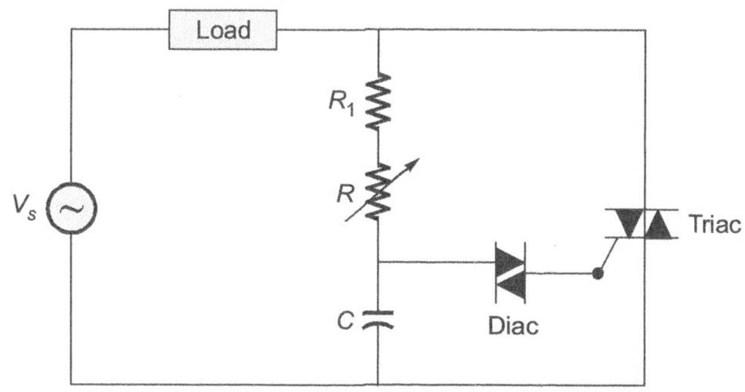

6.3 Which of the following configurations is used for both motoring and regenerative breaking?

(a) First quadrant chopper (b) Second quadrant chopper
(c) Two quadrant chopper (d) Four quadrant chopper [2 marks : 2006]

Solution: (c)

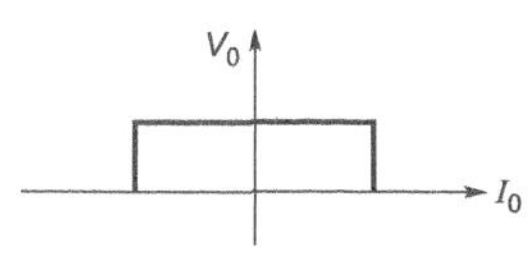

Two quadrant chopper is used for both motoring and regenerative breaking.

6.4 A dc motor is fed from a 220 V DC supply through a chopper circuit operating on constant chopping frequency of 800 Hz. The armature and series field resistances are 0.08 Ω and 0.04 Ω respectively. The back emf of the motor is 170 V. Find the ON and OFF periods of the chopper. Assume armature current is 50 A.

[4 marks : 2015]

Solution:

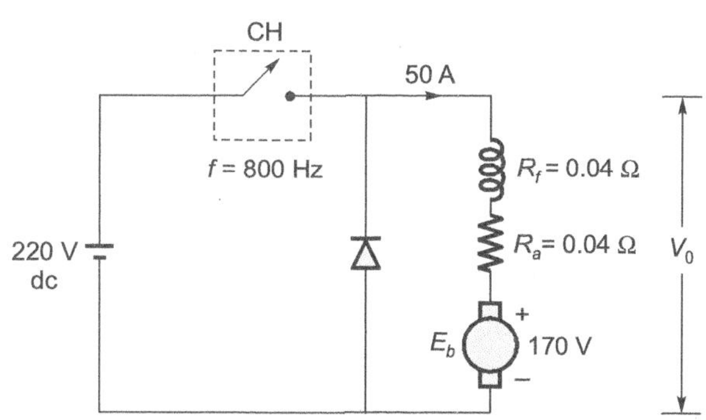

Time period, $$T = \frac{1}{f} = \frac{1}{800} = 1.25 \times 10^{-3} \text{ sec}$$

$$V_0 = I_0(R_a + R_f) + E_b = 50(0.08 + 0.04) + 170 = 176$$

$$\boxed{V_0 = \alpha V_s} \quad \left(\alpha = \frac{T_{ON}}{T}\right)$$ [∵ It is a step down chopper]

$$176 = \frac{T_{on}}{1.25 \times 10^{-3}} \times 220$$

$$T_{on} = 1 \times 10^{-3} \text{ sec and } T_{OFF} = T - T_{ON} = 0.25 \times 10^{-3} \text{ sec}$$

6.5 A DC motor has an armature resistance of 0.5 Ω and $K\phi$ of 3 Vs. The motor is driven by a single-phase thyristorized full converter. The input to the converter is an AC source of 230 V, 50 Hz. The motor is used as a prime mover of a forklift. In the upward direction, the mechanical load is 69 Nm and the triggering angle is $\alpha = 15°$. In the downward direction, the load torque is 180 Nm. Calculate the triggering angle required to keep the downward speed equal in magnitude to upward speed. Assume continuous motor current for all operation. Also calculate the triggering angle to keep the motor at holding position while it was moving upward.

[12 marks : 2018]

Solution:

Given, $R_a = 0.5\ \Omega$, $V = 230$ V,

$f = 50$ Hz, $K\phi = 3$ V-sec

Load torque when operating in upward direction = 69 N-m

$$\alpha_1 = 15°$$

Load torque when operating in downward direction = 180 N-m

Electromagnetic torque T_{em} during upward motion,

$$T_{em1} = (K\phi) I_{a1}$$

$$\Rightarrow \quad 69 = 3 \times I_{a1}$$

$$\Rightarrow \quad I_{a1} = 23 \text{ A}$$

Also we know that, $V_{t1} = E_b + I_{a1} R_a$

$$\Rightarrow \quad \frac{2V_m}{\pi} \cos\alpha_1 = E_{b1} + (23 \times 0.5)$$

$$\Rightarrow \quad \frac{2 \times \sqrt{2} \times 230 \times \cos 15°}{\pi} = E_{b1} + (23 \times 0.5)$$

$$\Rightarrow \quad E_{b1} = 188.5169 \text{ V}$$

Electromagnetic torque during downward motion,

$$T_{em2} = (K\phi) I_{a2}$$

$$\Rightarrow \quad 180 = (K\phi) I_{a2}$$

$$\Rightarrow \quad I_{a2} = \frac{180}{3} = 60 \text{ A}$$

Now as direction of speed is reversed, E_b will become negative

$$V_{t2} = -E_{b2} + I_{a2} R_a$$

Since $E_b \propto N$ as speed is same in both the cases we take the magnitude of E_b as same in both cases.

$$\Rightarrow \quad \frac{2V_m}{\pi} \cos\alpha_2 = -188.5169 + (60 \times 0.5)$$

$$\frac{2 \times \sqrt{2} \times \cos\alpha_2}{\pi} = -158.5169$$

On solving, $\alpha_2 = 140°$

During holding position speed is zero so back emf is zero

$$\therefore \quad V_3 = I_{a1} R_a$$

$$\Rightarrow \quad \frac{2\sqrt{2} \times 230}{\pi} \times \cos\alpha_3 = 23 \times 0.5$$

On solving, $\alpha_3 = 86.82°$

6.6 For a 3-phase, 50 Hz, 415 V, 4-pole induction motor, the standstill resistance and reactance are 3.0 Ω and 5.0 Ω at 50 Hz respectively. The machine has magnetizing inductance of 350 mH and stator resistance of 1.2 Ω. The machine is supplied from a 3-phase voltage source inverter with qausi square wave output voltage waveform per phase as shown in the figure below. The DC bus voltage is 500 V.

If the machine is operating at 4% slip, find (i) the fundamental input current, (ii) harmonic copper losses in the machine up to 13 harmonics, and (iii) input power factor.

Assume negligible core losses, equal distribution of stator and rotor leakage reactances and linear magnetic circuit.

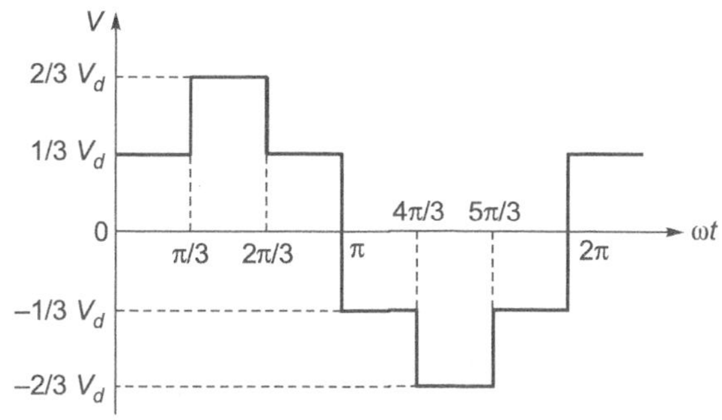

[20 marks : 2020]

Solution:

The per phase equivalent parameters of induction motor is

$$r_1 = 1.2\ \Omega$$

$$r'_2 = 3\ \Omega$$

$$x_1 = j5\ \Omega$$

$$x_2 = j5\ \Omega$$

$$L_m = 350\text{ mH}$$

$$X_m = 2\pi \times 50 \times 350 \times 10^{-3} = j109.95\ \Omega$$

Input supply phase waveform is six step waveform.

$$V_{on} = \sum_{6K\pm I}^{\infty} \frac{2V_d}{n\pi} \sin n\omega t$$

Fundamental output voltage of inverter

$$V_{01} = \frac{2V_d}{\sqrt{2}\pi} = 225.079\text{ V}$$

$$V_{05} = \frac{2V_d}{\sqrt{2}\times 5\times\pi} = 45.0158\text{ V}$$

$$V_{07} = \frac{2V_d}{\sqrt{2}\times 7\times\pi} = 32.154\text{ V}$$

$$V_{011} = \frac{2V_d}{\sqrt{2}\times 11\times\pi} = 20.461\text{ V}$$

$$V_{013} = \frac{2V_d}{\sqrt{2}\times 13\times\pi} = 17.3137\text{ V}$$

Using approximate equivalent circuit of induction motor

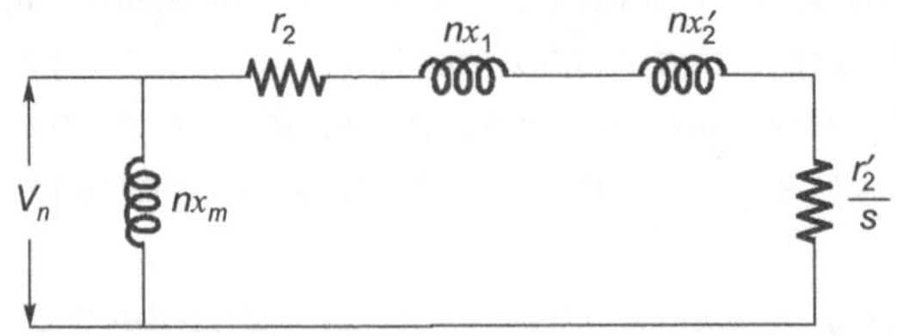

Equivalent impedance at fundamental frequency

$$Z_{eq} = jX_m \times \left[\frac{r_1 + \frac{r_2'}{s} + j(x_1 + x_2')}{jX_m + r_1 + \frac{r_2'}{s} + j(x_1 + x_2')} \right]$$

$$Z_{eq} = 59.46\angle 39.90\Omega$$

(i) Fundamental input current

$$= \frac{V_{01}}{Z_{eq1}} = 3.78\angle{-39.90} \text{ A}$$

(ii) Fundamental input power factor

$$\cos\phi = \cos 39.90 = 0.76714 \text{ lag}$$

(iii) **Induction Motor Equivalent Circuit with respect to Harmonics**

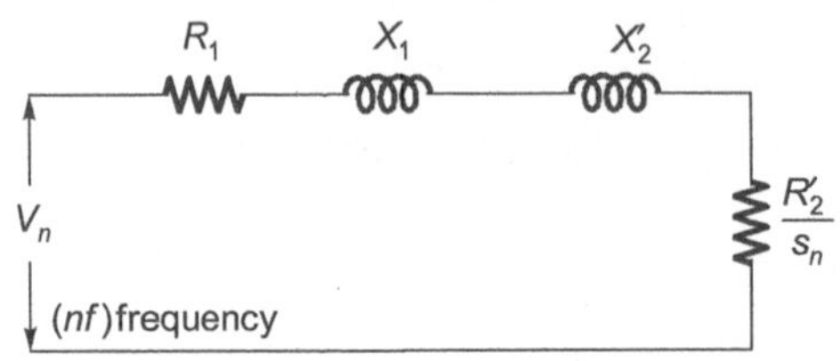

n : Order of harmonic
s : Fundamental slip

Harmonic slip, $$s_n = \frac{N_{sn} \pm N}{N_{sn}}$$

$$N_{sn} = n.N_s$$

$$N = N_s(1 - s)$$

$$s_n = \frac{nN_s \pm N_s(1-s)}{n \cdot N_s}$$

$$s_n = \frac{n \pm (1-s)}{n} \qquad (+ \Rightarrow 6n - 1;\ - \Rightarrow 6n + 1)$$

$n = 1$, Fundamental $$s_n = \frac{1-(1-s)}{1} = s = 0.04$$

For $n = 5$, $$s_5 = \frac{5+(1-s)}{5}$$

$\therefore$ $$s_5 = \frac{6-s}{5} = \frac{6-0.04}{5} = 1.192$$

For $n = 7$, $$s_7 = \frac{7-(1-s)}{7}$$

$$s_7 = \frac{6+s}{7} = \frac{6+0.04}{7} = 0.8628$$

For $n = 11$,
$$s_{11} = \frac{11+(1-s)}{11} = \frac{12-s}{11}$$
$$s_{11} = \frac{12-0.04}{11} = 1.08$$

For $n = 13$,
$$s_{13} = \frac{13-(1-s)}{13} = \frac{12+s}{13}$$
$$s_{13} = \frac{12+0.04}{13} = 0.926$$

Now,
$$I_{05} = \frac{V_{05}}{R_1 + jnX_1 + jnX_2' + \frac{R_2}{s_5}} = 0.897\angle{-85.74°}\text{ A}$$
$$I_{07} = \frac{V_{07}}{R_1 + jnX_1 + jnX_2 + \frac{R_2}{s_7}} = 0.4583\angle{-86.177°}\text{ A}$$
$$I_{011} = \frac{V_{011}}{R_1 + jnX_1 + jnX_2 + \frac{R_2}{s_{11}}} = 0.18588\angle{-87.928}\text{ A}$$
$$I_{013} = \frac{V_{013}}{R_1 + jnX_1 + jnX_2 + \frac{R_2}{s_{13}}} = 0.1331\angle{-88.044}\text{ A}$$
$$P_L = I_{05}^2\left(r_1 + \frac{r_2'}{s_5}\right) + I_{07}^2\left(r_1 + \frac{r_2'}{s_7}\right) + I_{011}^2\left(r_1 + \frac{r_2'}{s_{11}}\right) + I_{013}\left(r_1 + \frac{r_2'}{s_{13}}\right)$$
$$P_L = 2.990 + 0.9823 + 0.1374 + 0.078\text{ W}$$
$$P_L = 4.1877\text{ W}$$

6.7 A 10 kW, 220 V, 1750 rpm dc separately excited motor is controlled by a three-phase fully controlled converter. The connecting cable between motor and converter has a resistance of 1.0 Ω. The input-side of the converter is supplied from a 3-phase 300 V, 50 Hz ac source. The dc motor has armature resistance r_a = 0.5 Ω. The armature current is flat and ripple free. Determine

(i) the triggering angle of the converter when the motor delivers rated power at rated voltage and speed.

(ii) the converter input rms current and power factor under the above condition of (i).

(iii) no load speed of the motor when the triggering angle is same as (i) and the motor lakes 10% of rated current.

(Assume constant field current at rated value for the entire operation)

[20 marks : 2021]

Solution:

Given : 10 kW, 220 V, 1750 rpm dc motor

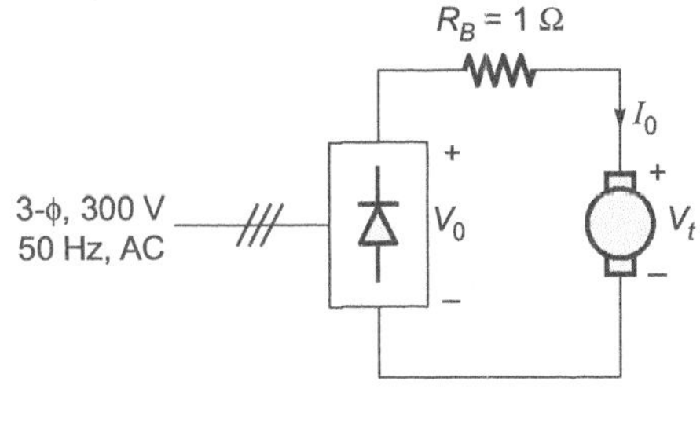

Rectifier input ⇒ 300 V, 50 Hz

Input current, $I_{0\,\text{rated}} = \frac{P_{\text{rated}}}{V_{t\text{rated}}} = \frac{10.10^3}{220}$

∴ $I_{0\,\text{rated}} = 45.45$ A

O/P of rectifier, $V_0 = I_0 \cdot R_b + V_t$

$$\frac{3.300\sqrt{2}}{\pi} \cdot \cos\alpha = (45.45 \times 1) + 220$$

$$\frac{3 \cdot 300\sqrt{2}}{\pi} \cdot \cos\alpha = 265.45 \text{ V}$$

(i) The firing angle, $\alpha = 49°$

(ii) Input supply current, $I_{sr} = \sqrt{\frac{2}{3}} \cdot I_0 = \sqrt{\frac{2}{3}} \times 45.45 = 37.1$ A

Input power factor, $PF = \frac{3}{\pi} \cdot \cos\alpha = \frac{3}{\pi} \cos 49 = 0.626$ lag

(iii) At rated condition, $V_t = E_{b\,\text{rated}} + I_0 R_a$

$$220 = E_{b\,\text{rated}} + (45.45 \times 0.5)$$

∴ Back emf, $E_{b\text{rated}} = 197.275$ V

At no load, $I_0 = 10\%$ of $I_{0\,\text{rated}}$

$I_0 = 10\%$ of (45.45)

Input current, $I_0 = 4.545$ A

$$V_0 = \frac{3V_{mL}}{\pi} \cdot \cos\alpha = \frac{3 \times 300\sqrt{2}}{\pi} \cdot \cos 49$$

$$= 265.79 \text{ V}$$

$$V_0 = I_0(R_b + R_a) + E_{b\,\text{no load}}$$

$$E_{b\,\text{no load}} = 258.9725$$

$$\frac{E_{b\text{rated}}}{E_{b\text{load}}} = \frac{N_{\text{rated}}}{N_{\text{noload}}}$$

$$\frac{197.275}{258.9725} = \frac{1750}{N_{\text{no load}}}$$

$$N_{\text{no load}} = 2297.3 \text{ rpm}$$

7. Miscellaneous

7.1 A purely inductive load is controlled by a single-phase AC voltage controller using back to back connected SCRs. If the firing angle of the SCRs is 75°, the current through the two SCRs will flow for

(a) 285° and 0°
(b) 210° and 0°
(c) 105° and 0°
(d) 105° and 105°

[2 marks : 2002]

Solution: (c)

For RL load, $\sin(\beta - \phi) = \sin(\alpha - \phi)\, e^{\left[\frac{R}{L} \cdot \frac{(\alpha-\beta)}{\omega}\right]}$

where, $\beta \rightarrow$ extinction angle, $\alpha \rightarrow$ firing angle

and conduction angle, $r = \beta - \alpha$, ϕ is *pf* angle

For ($R = 0$), (purely inductive load)

$$\sin(\beta - \phi) = \sin(\alpha - \phi)$$

$$\sin \beta = \sin \alpha$$

$\therefore$ $$\beta = \alpha$$

Then, r = conduction angle $= \beta - \alpha = 0$

For another SCR, $r' = \pi - \alpha = 180 - 75 = 105°$

7.2 **A thyristor-controlled inductor will work as a variable inductor OR as fixed inductor, respectively for firing angles**

(a) less than or equal to 90°, greater than 90°
(b) less than 90°, greater than or equal to 90°
(c) greater than 90°, less than or equal to 90°
(d) less than 90°, greater than 90° [2 marks : 2008]

Solution: (c)

A thyristor controlled inductor work as a fixed inductor when ($\alpha \leq 90°$) and as a variable inductor when ($\alpha > 90°$).

7.3 **Draw the circuit diagram and waveform of load voltage and current of two-stage sequence control of single-phase a.c. voltage regulator feeding resistive load. Assume 1 : 1 transformers are used on the source side. Give sequence of operation of two regulators when voltage control is required from 0 to V and V to 2 V.**

[10 marks : 2009]

Solution:

A two-stage sequence control of ac voltage regulators employs two stages in parallel as shown in Fig. (a). The turns ratio from primary to each secondary is taken as unity. This means that for source voltage $V_s = V_m \sin\omega t$, $V_1 = V_2 = V_m \sin\omega t$ and sum of two secondary voltages is $2V_m \sin\omega t$.

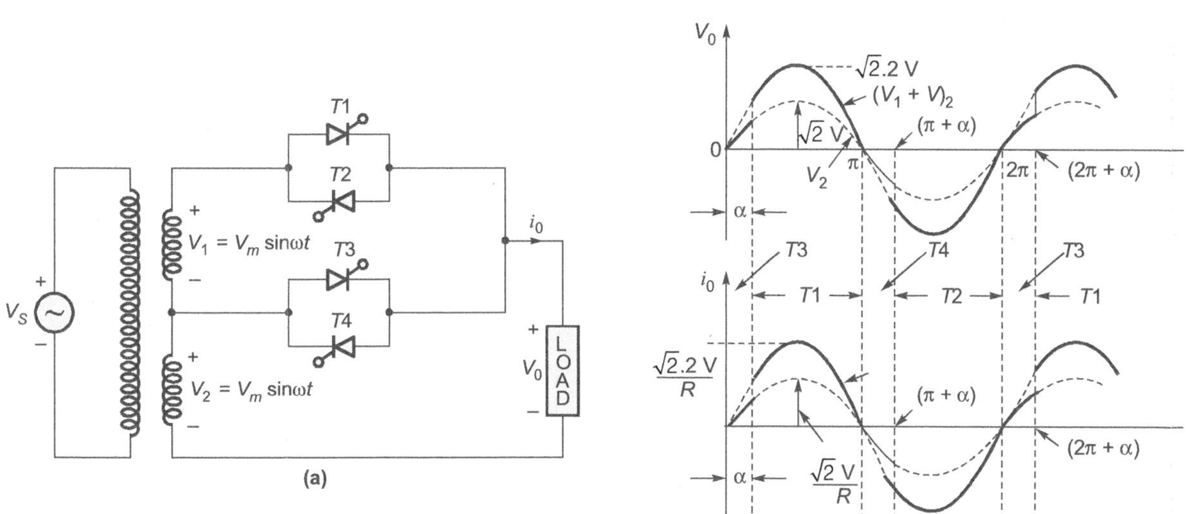

(a) (b)

The load is R for obtaining output voltage control from zero to rms value V, use only thyristor pair $T3$, $T4$ in figure. For zero output voltage α is 180° for $T3$, $T4$ and for V, α is zero. For output voltage control from V to

2 V, α for thyristor pair T3, T4 is always zero and for thyristor pair T1, T2 ; α is varied from zero to 180°.
The main advantage of two-stage sequence control of ac voltage controller over single-phase full-wave ac voltage controller is the reduction of harmonics in the load and line currents.
For resistance load, the load current waveform is identical with output voltage waveform.

7.4 **For a single power a.c. voltage controller, which type of gating signal is more suitable, when the load is inductive? Give reasons for your answer.**

[14 marks : 2010]

Solution:

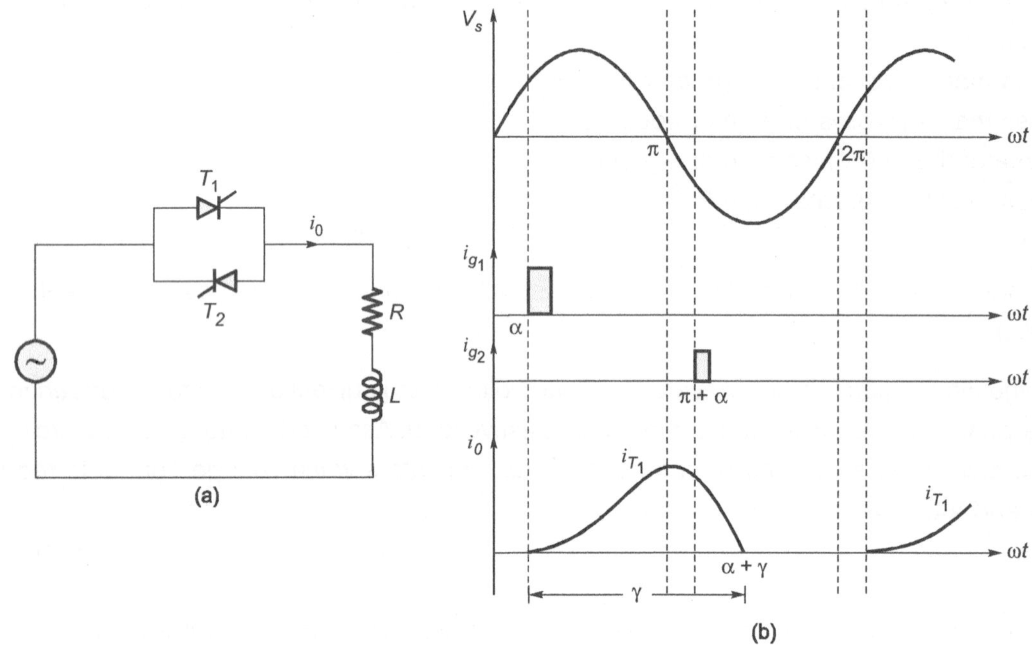

- Pulse gating is not suitable for *RL* loads. The reason for this can be explained by referring to figure (b). At α, T_1 is fixed and the current grows as shown. At π + α, T_1 is fixed. At π + α, T_2 is fired. As T_1 is still conducting, voltage drop across T_1 reverse biases T_2 at π + α, T_2 therefore not turned on.

  At (α + γ), T_0 i_{T_1} decays to zero and T_1 stops conducting, as a result T_2 gets forward biased but the gate pulse i_{g_2} applied to T_2 at π + α is already zero and therefore T_2 does not get turned on.

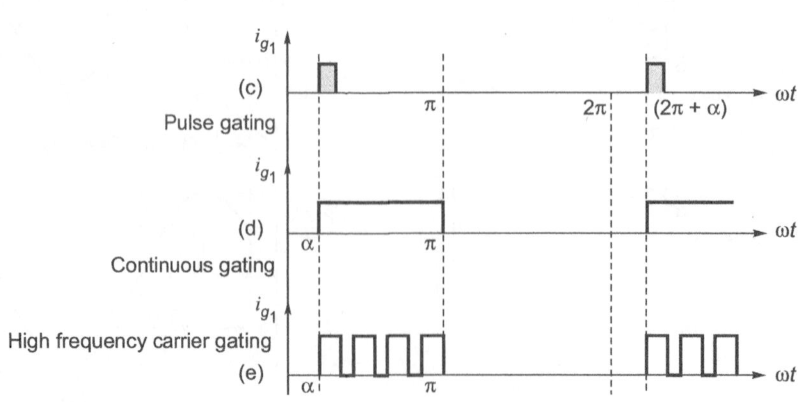

- This difficulty can be overcome by applying continuous gate signal to the SCRs T_1 and T_2 so that when i_{T_1} becomes zero at (α + γ), T_2 get turned on due to the presence of continuous gate signal.

- In practice continuous gating is undesirable as it leads to more heating of the SCR gate and at the same time, it increases the size of the pulse transformer. High frequency carrier gating mitigates the disadvantages of continuous gate signal and ensures thyristor turn on.

7.5 The quality of output a.c. voltage of a cycloconverter is improved with

(a) increase in output voltage at reduced frequency.
(b) increase in output voltage at increased frequency.
(c) decrease in output voltage at reduced frequency.
(d) decreases in output voltage at increased frequency. [2 marks : 2010]

Solution: (b)

Increase in output voltage at increased frequency.

7.6 In a 1-phase AC-AC voltage controller feeding a

(i) Lighting load
(ii) Heating load, suggest a suitable control method.

[5 marks : 2011]

Solution:

(i) Phase control method:

For lighting load, phase control method is used.

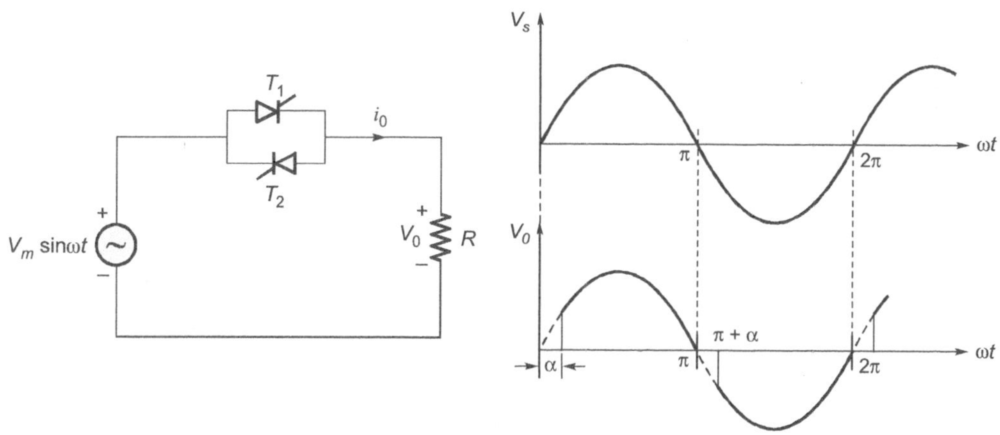

During positive half cycle, T_1 is triggered at firing angle α, it conducts from $\omega t = \alpha$ to π for the load. During negative half cycle T_2 is triggered at $\omega t = \pi + \alpha$, it conducts from $\omega t = \pi + \alpha$ to 2π.

Rms value of output voltage,

$$V_{or} = \left[\frac{1}{\pi}\int_2^{\pi} V_m^2 \sin^2 \omega t \cdot d(\omega t)\right]^{1/2} = \frac{V_m}{\sqrt{2}}\left[\frac{1}{\pi}\left\{(\pi - \alpha) + \frac{\sin 2\alpha}{2}\right\}\right]^{1/2}$$

By varying α, the rms value of the voltage across the lighting load is controlled.

(ii) Integral cycle control:

For heating loads, almost no variation in temperature will be noticed if control is achieved connecting the load to source for some on-cycle and then disconnecting the load for some off-cycles. This form of power control is called integral cycle control. So integral cycle control consists of switching on the supply to load for an integral number of cycles and then switching off the supply for a further number of integral cycles.

The source energies the load for n cycles. When gate pulses are withdrawn, load remains off for m cycles. By varying the number of n and m cycles, power delivered to load can be regulated as desired.

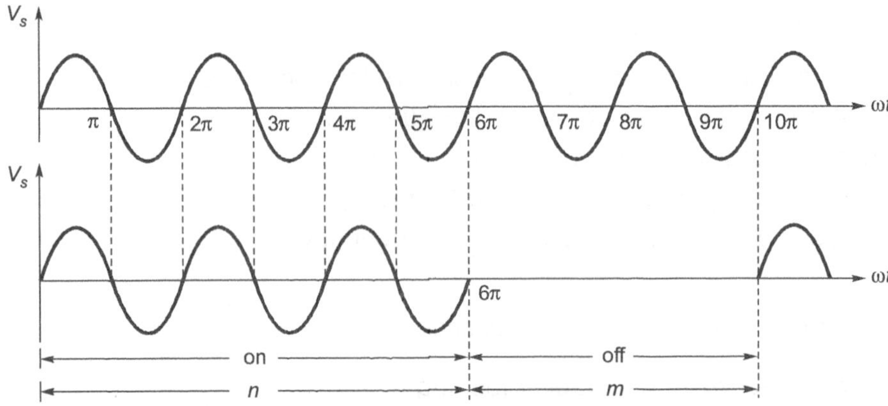

7.7 The single-phase ac voltage regulator has 120 V_{rms}, 50 Hz source. The load resistance is 15 ohm. Determine the

(i) delay angle required to deliver 500 W to the load
(ii) rms source current
(iii) input power factor
(iv) THD of the source current

[10 marks : 2014]

Solution:

(i) Rms load voltage,

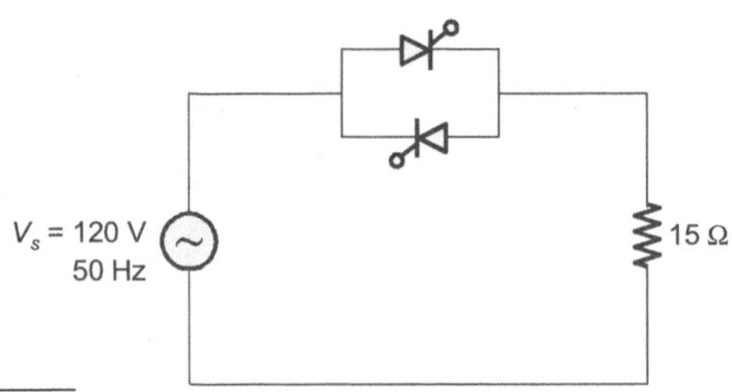

$$V_{0,\,rms} = V_S\sqrt{\left[\frac{1}{\pi}\left\{(\pi-\alpha)+\frac{\sin 2\alpha}{2}\right\}\right]}$$

$$V_{0,rms} = 120\sqrt{\left[\frac{1}{\pi}\left\{(\pi-\alpha)+\frac{\sin 2\alpha}{2}\right\}\right]}$$

$$I_{0,\,rms} = \frac{V_{0,rms}}{R} = \frac{120\sqrt{\left[\frac{1}{\pi}\left\{(\pi-\alpha)+\frac{\sin 2\alpha}{2}\right\}\right]}}{R}$$

$$P_0 = I_{0,rms}^2 \times R$$

$$500 = \frac{(120)^2\left[\frac{1}{\pi}\left\{(\pi-\alpha)+\frac{\sin 2\alpha}{2}\right\}\right]}{15}$$

$$0.521 = \frac{1}{\pi}\left\{(\pi-\alpha)+\frac{\sin 2\alpha}{2}\right\}$$

$$1.6367 = (\pi-\alpha)+\frac{\sin 2\alpha}{2}$$

$$3.2734 = 2\pi - 2\alpha + \sin 2\alpha$$

$$-3.0097 = -2\alpha + \sin 2\alpha$$

Let, $2\alpha = x$

$$-3.0097 = -x + \sin x$$

sin x varies from –1 to 1. So, $x \in (2.0097, 4.0097)$

Now, by trial and error method we get $x \simeq 3.075$

$$2\alpha = 3.075$$

$$\alpha = 1.5375\left(\frac{180°}{\pi}\right)$$

∴ The delay angle required to deliver 500 W to the load is $\alpha = 88.09°$.

(ii) Rms source = $I_{s,\,rms}$ = rms load current = $I_{0,\,rms}$

$$I_{0,rms} = \frac{V_{0,rms}}{R} = \frac{V_s\sqrt{\left[\frac{1}{\pi}\left\{(\pi-\alpha)+\frac{\sin 2\alpha}{2}\right\}\right]}}{R}$$

$$= \frac{120\sqrt{\left[\frac{1}{\pi}\left\{\left(\pi - 88.09\left(\frac{\pi}{180}\right)\right)+\frac{\sin 2(88.09)}{2}\right\}\right]}}{15} = \frac{86.6342}{15}$$

$$I_{s,rms} = I_{0,\,rms} = 5.7756 \text{ A}$$

(iii) Input power factor $= \dfrac{V_{0,rms} \times I_{0,rms}}{V_s \times I_{s,rms}} = \dfrac{V_{0,rms}}{V_s} = \dfrac{86.6342}{120}$

∴ Input power factor = 0.7219 lagging

(iv) Input displacement factor $(DF) = \cos\phi_1$

$$\phi_1 = 31.3844°$$

$$\cos\phi_1 = 0.8537$$

$$\text{Input power factor} = \frac{I_{s1}}{I_s}\cos\phi_1$$

$$\frac{0.7219}{0.8537} = \frac{I_{s1}}{I_s} = 0.8456$$

Total Harmonic Distortion (THD) of the source current

$$= \sqrt{\left(\frac{I_s}{I_{s1}}\right)^2 - 1} = \sqrt{(1.1826)^2 - 1} = 0.631$$

7.8 **Derive an expression for r.m.s. output voltage of 1-phase AC voltage controller feeding an R-L load. Draw the circuit and waveforms.**

[4 marks : 2015]

Solution:

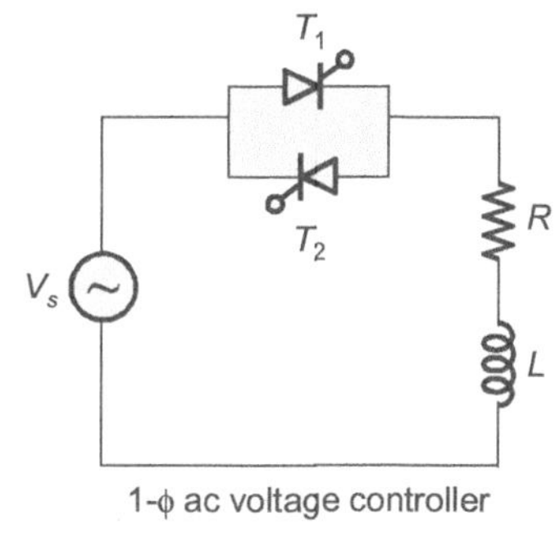

1-ϕ ac voltage controller

Output waveforms:

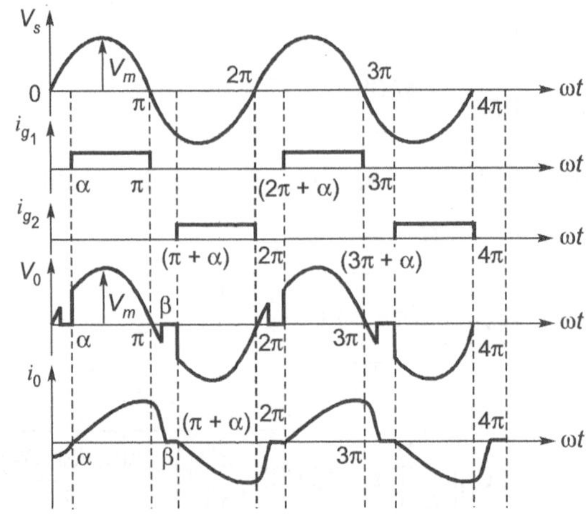

Output voltage waveform for 1-ϕ ac voltage controller is

$$V_{o,\,rms} = \sqrt{\frac{1}{\pi}\int_{\alpha}^{\beta} V_m^2 \sin^2 \omega t \; d(\omega t)} = \sqrt{\frac{V_m^2}{\pi}\int_{\alpha}^{\beta}\left(\frac{1-\cos 2\omega t}{2}\right)^2 d(\omega t)}$$

$$V_{o,rms} = V_m\left[\frac{1}{2\pi}\left\{(\beta-\alpha)+\left(\frac{\sin 2\alpha - \sin 2\beta}{2}\right)\right\}\right]^{1/2}$$

7.9 A single-phase ac regulator is used to control the power output of a heater. The supply voltage is 220 V, 50 Hz and the resistance of the heater is 100 Ω. If the regulator is operated at a firing angle (α) of 90°, draw the voltage waveform across the regulator. Derive the expression for input p.f., power output and input current and determine their values.

[10 marks : 2015]

Solution:

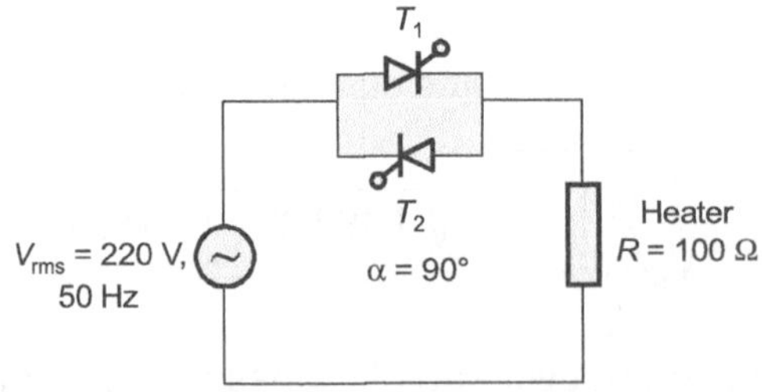

Output wave forms:

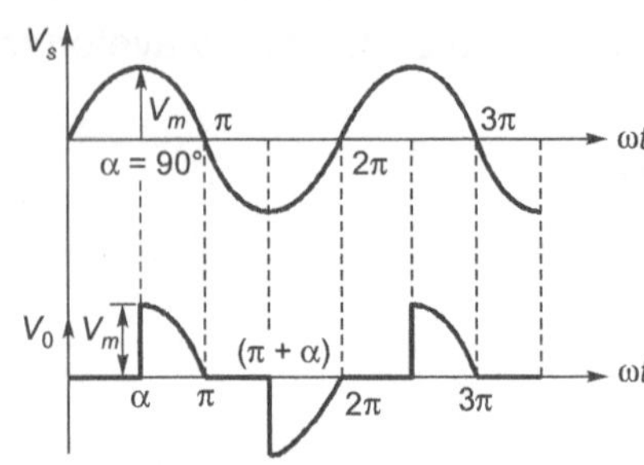

$$V_{0,\,rms} = \sqrt{\frac{1}{\pi}\int_{\alpha}^{\pi} V_m^2 \sin^2 \omega t \, d(\omega t)}$$

$$V_{0,\,rms} = \frac{V_m}{\sqrt{2}}\left[\frac{1}{\pi}\left\{(\pi-\alpha)+\frac{\sin 2\alpha}{2}\right\}\right]^{1/2} = 155.5635 \text{ V}$$

$$I_{0,\,rms} = \frac{V_{0,rms}}{P_r} = \frac{155.5635}{100} = 1.5556 \text{ A}$$

$$\text{power output} = P_o = I_{0,rms}^2 \times R = (1.5556)^2 \times 100$$

$$P_o = 241.9891 \text{ W}$$

Rms value of source current,

$$I_s = \text{Rms value of load current, } I_{0,\text{ rms}}$$
$$I_s = I_{0,\text{ rms}} = 1.5556 \text{ A}$$

$\therefore$ $$\text{Input power factor} = \frac{I_{0,\text{rms}}^2 \times R}{V_s \times I_{0,\text{rms}}} \qquad [\because I_{s,\text{rms}} = I_{0,\text{ rms}}]$$
$$= \frac{241.9891}{220 \times 1.5556} = 0.707 \text{ lagging}$$

7.10 **A d.c. links has a loop resistance of 40 Ω and connected to transformers giving secondary voltage of 120 kV at each end. The bridge connected converters operate as follows:**

Rectifier : α = 15°; X = 15 Ω

Inverter : β = 25°; X = 15 Ω

Calculate the direct current delivered, if the inverter operates on constant ignition angle β control.

[20 marks : 2017]

Solution:

Secondary voltage = 120 kV

Loop resistance, $R_{\text{loop}} = 40\ \Omega$

So, resistance of each dc transmission line,

$$R_d = 20\ \Omega$$

At constant ignition angle β, inverter dc voltage is given by

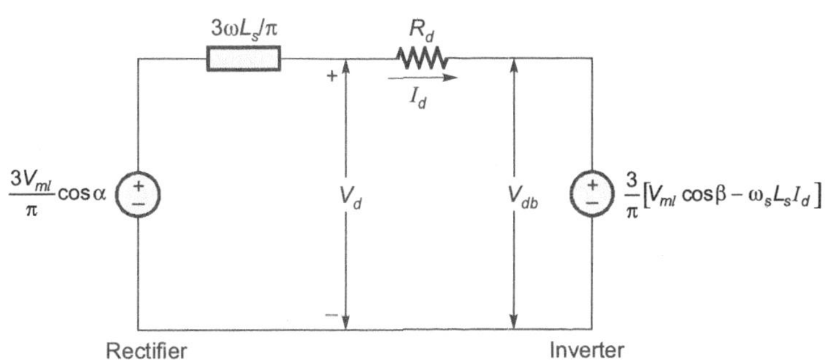

$$V_{db} = \frac{3}{\pi}[V_{ml}\cos\beta - \omega L_s I_d]$$

and the rectifier output V_d is $$V_d = V_{db} + I_d R_d = \frac{3}{\pi}[V_{ml}\cos\beta - \omega L_s I_d] + I_d R_d \qquad \text{...(1)}$$

Also, $$V_d = \frac{3V_{ml}}{\pi}\cos\alpha - \frac{3\omega L_s}{\pi}\cdot I_d \qquad \text{...(2)}$$

From equation (1) and (2), we get

$$\frac{3V_{ml}}{\pi}\cos\alpha - \frac{3\omega L_s}{\pi}\cdot I_d = \frac{3V_{ml}\cos\beta}{\pi} - \frac{3\omega L_s I_d}{\pi} + I_d R_d$$

$$\cos\alpha = \cos\beta + \frac{\pi}{3V_{ml}}\cdot I_d R_d$$

So, $$\cos 15° = \cos 25° + \frac{\pi}{3\times\sqrt{2}\times 120\times 10^3}\times I_d \times 20 = 483.076 \text{ A}$$

Direct current delivered, $I_d = 483.076$ A

7.11 **A single-phase a.c. voltage regulator is made of anti-parallel combination of a thyristor and a diode. This controller is connected to a resistive load of 2 Ω from a 220 V, 50 Hz supply. Determine the average and rms values of thyristor and diode currents for α = 60°.**

[12 marks : 2017]

Solution:

Given that, Supply voltage, $V_s = 220$ V

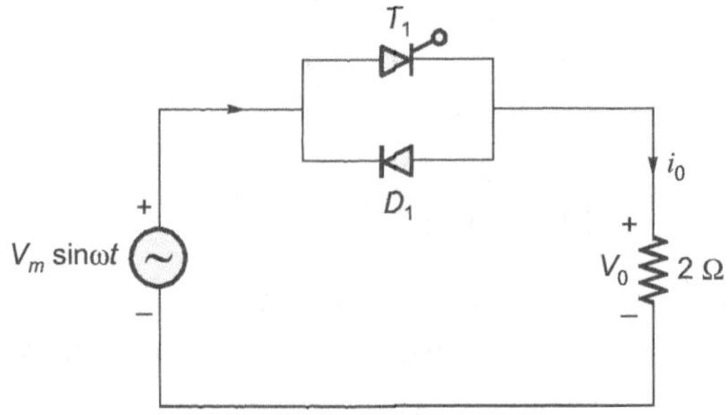

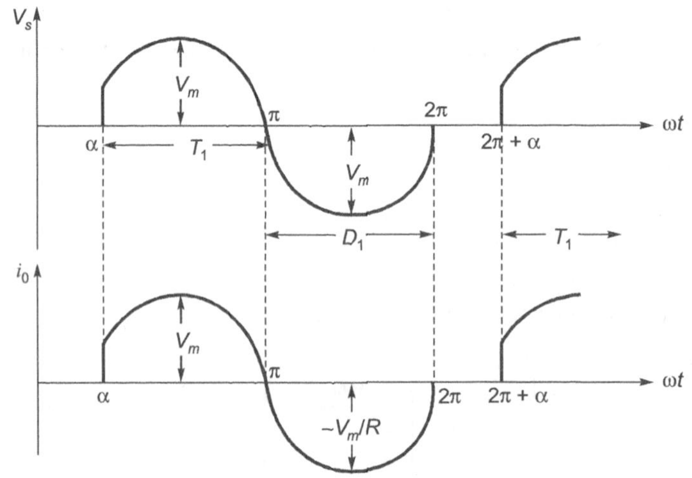

From the above shown figure thyristor T_1 get turn on at $\omega t = \alpha$ and get turned-off at $\omega t = \pi$ for resistive load. After $\omega t = \pi$ negative half cycle forward biases diode D_1, therefore D_1 conducts from $\omega t = \pi$ to 2π.

Now, average thyristor current, $$I_{TA} = \frac{1}{2\pi R}\int_{\alpha}^{\pi} V_m \sin\omega t\, d(\omega t) = \frac{V_m}{2\pi R}(1+\cos\alpha)$$

At $V_s = 220$ V and $\alpha = 60$, $$I_{TA} = \frac{220\sqrt{2}}{2\pi\times 2}(1+\cos 60^\circ) = 37.138\,\text{A}$$

Rms value of thyristor current, $$I_{Tr} = \left[\frac{1}{2\pi R}\int_{\alpha}^{\pi} V_m^2 \sin^2\omega t\, d(\omega t)\right]^{1/2} = \frac{V_m}{2R}\left[\frac{1}{\pi}\left\{(\pi-\alpha)+\frac{\sin 2\alpha}{2}\right\}\right]^{1/2}$$

$$= \frac{220\sqrt{2}}{2\times 2}\left[\frac{1}{\pi}\left\{\left(\pi-\frac{\pi}{3}\right)+\frac{\sin 120^\circ}{2}\right\}\right]^{1/2} = 69.765\text{ A}$$

Now, average diode current, $$I_{DA} = \frac{1}{2\pi R}\int_{\pi}^{2\pi} -V_m \sin\omega t\, d(\omega t) = -\frac{V_m}{2\pi R}[\cos\pi - \cos 2\pi] = \frac{2V_m}{2\pi R} = \frac{V_m}{\pi R}$$

$$I_{DA} = \frac{220\sqrt{2}}{\pi\times 2} = 49.5174\text{ A}$$

and rms value of diode current, $$I_{Dr} = \left[\frac{1}{2\pi R}\int_{\pi}^{2\pi} V_m^2 \sin^2\omega t\, d(\omega t)\right]^{1/2}$$

$$= \frac{V_m}{2R}\left[\frac{1}{\pi}\{(2\pi-\pi)+0\right]^{1/2} = \frac{V_m}{2R} = \frac{220\sqrt{2}}{2\times 2} = 77.782\text{ A}$$

7.12 A single-phase AC voltage controller is feeding a resistive load of 26.45 Ω from an AC source of 230 V, 50 Hz. Compute the firing angle to deliver 1000 W to the load. Also compute the p.f. at which this power is delivered. Draw a neat circuit diagram and waveforms of voltage at load terminals with current flowing in the load.

[12 marks : 2018]

Solution:

$$V_{or} = \sqrt{\frac{1}{\pi}\int_{\alpha}^{\pi} V_m^2 \sin^2 \omega t d\omega t}$$

$$V_{or} = \frac{V_m}{\sqrt{2\pi}}\left[(\pi-\alpha)+\frac{\sin 2\alpha}{2}\right]^{1/2}$$

$$P = \frac{V_{or}^2}{R}$$

$$V_{or} = \sqrt{1000\times 26.45} = 162.635 \text{ V}$$

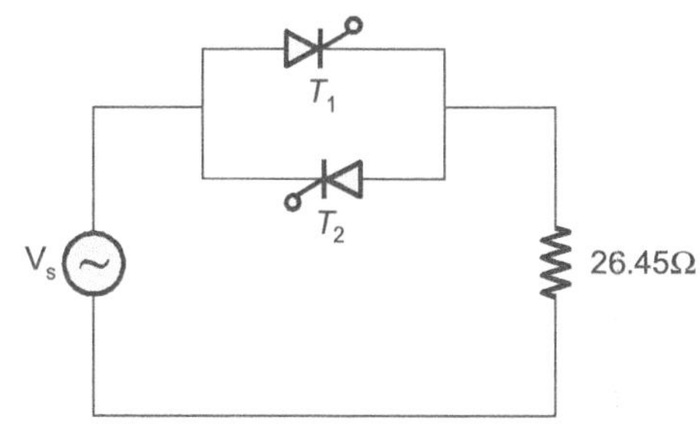

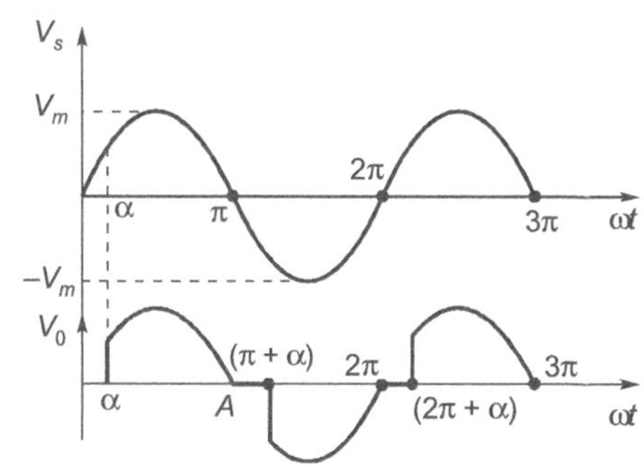

Now, $$162.635 = \frac{230\sqrt{2}}{\sqrt{2\pi}}\left[(\pi-\alpha)+\left(\frac{\sin 2\alpha}{2}\right)\right]^{1/2}$$

$$-\alpha + 0.5\sin 2\alpha + 1.5707 = 0$$

By observing above equation,

$$\alpha = 90°$$

$$\text{Input p.f.} = \frac{P_0}{V_{sr}I_{or}} = \frac{V_{or}I_o}{V_{sr}I_o} = \left(\frac{V_{or}}{V_{sr}}\right)$$

$$\text{Input p.f.} = \frac{162.635}{230} = 0.707 \text{ lag.}$$

7.13 A flyback converter has the following circuit parameters:

$V_s = 24$ V, $\frac{N_1}{N_2} = 3$

$L_m = 500$ μH, $R = 5$ Ω

$C = 200$ μF, $f = 25$ kHz

$V_0 = 10$ V

Find:

(i) The average magnetizing current and

(ii) The critical value of magnetizing inductor.

[12 Marks : 2019]

Solution:

(i)

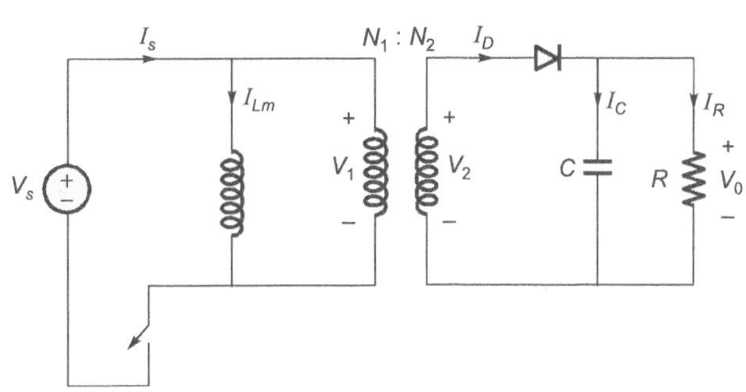

$$V_0 = V_s\left(\frac{\alpha}{1-\alpha}\right)\frac{N_2}{N_1}$$

$$10 = 24\left(\frac{\alpha}{1-\alpha}\right)\frac{1}{3}$$

$$\left(\frac{1}{\alpha}-1\right) = 0.8$$

$$\alpha = 0.555$$

$$V_0 I_0 = V_s I_s$$

$$I_0 = \frac{V_0}{R} = \frac{10}{5} = 2\text{ A}$$

$$I_{Lm} = \frac{I_s}{\alpha} = \frac{10\times 2}{24}\times\frac{1}{0.555} = 1.501\text{ A}$$

(ii)

$$I_{L,\min} = I_{Lm} - \frac{\Delta I_{Lm}}{2} = 0$$

$$\frac{\alpha V_s}{2fL_{mc}} = 1.501$$

$$L_{mc} = 177.48\ \mu\text{H}$$

7.14 The circuit shown in the figure is in steady state with thyristor OFF for a long time. Find the suitable values of L and C for the circuit so that current pulse across the load R = 550 Ω is approximately of 1 ms. The circuit is designed to generate a pulse of 0.75 T, where T is period of resonant circuit, It is assumed that subsequent firing of thyristor occurs after 1 ms and inductor is ideal, i.e., $R_L = 0$. Derive all expressions with $R_L \neq 0$.

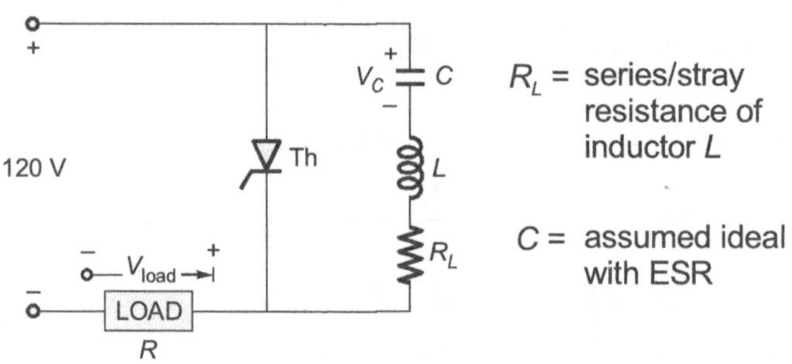

Also, plot the time variation of $V_{C(+)}$ and $V_{Load(+)}$ for one cycle.

[20 marks : 2021]

Solution:

The given circuit in question can be redrawn as :

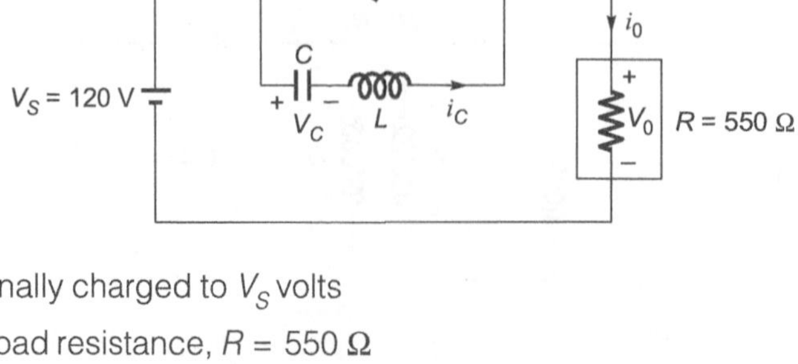

When Th → OFF, V_C finally charged to V_S volts

Given : Load resistance, R = 550 Ω

Pulse width = 1 msec (required)

In above circuit,

i_o = Load current

i_{th} = Thyristor current

i_c = Capacitor current

v_o = Load voltage across load resistance

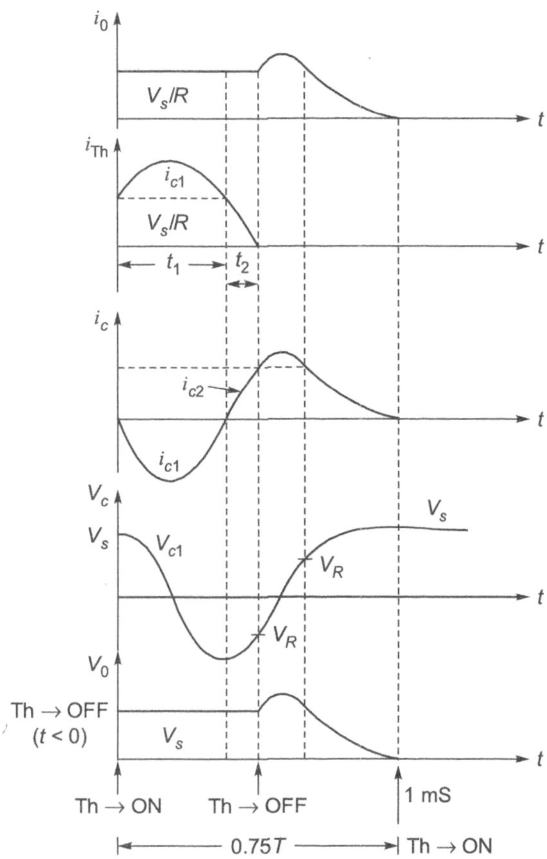

Case 1 : Mode : At $t = 0$

Th → ON

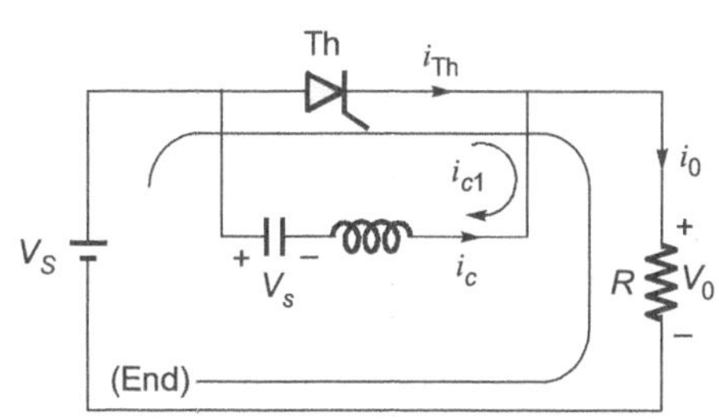

$$i_{Th} = i_0 + i_{C1}$$

$$i_{Th} = \frac{V_0}{R} + I_P \sin\omega_0 t,$$

Peak current,

$$I_p = V_s\sqrt{\frac{C}{L}},$$

$$\omega_0 = \frac{1}{\sqrt{LC}}$$

$$i_c = -I_p \sin\omega_0 t$$

$$V_{c1} = V_s \cdot \cos\omega_0 t$$

$$t_1 = \pi\sqrt{LC}$$

Case 2 : $Th \rightarrow$ OFF

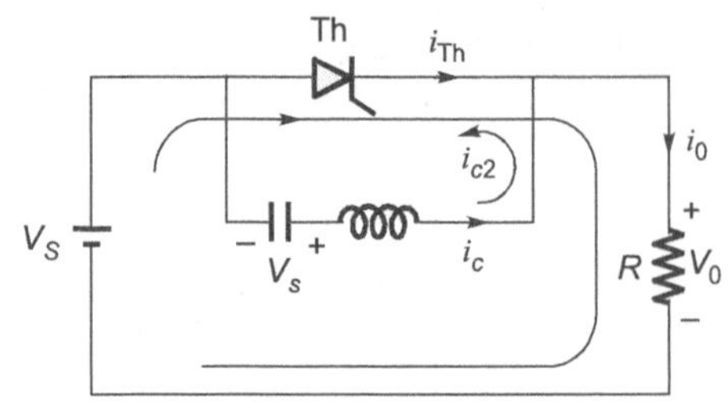

$$i_{c2} = I_p \sin \omega_0 t$$

$$\downarrow i_{Th} = i_0 - i_{c2} \uparrow$$

End : when $i_{c2} = i_0$,

$$i_{Th} = 0$$

$\therefore$ Th $\rightarrow$ OFF

$$I_p \cdot \sin \omega_0 t_2 = \frac{V_S}{R}$$

$$\omega_0 t_2 = \sin^{-1}\left(\frac{V_S / R}{I_P}\right)$$

$$t_2 = \sqrt{LC} \cdot \sin^{-1}\left(\frac{V_S / R}{I_P}\right)$$

In the 2nd mode,

For successful turn off,

$$I_P > I_0$$

Where, $$I_0 = \frac{V_S}{R}$$

Usually $I_P \Rightarrow$ 1.5 to 2 times I_0

Let, $I_P = 2I_0$ (considering safety factor = 2)

$$\Rightarrow \quad \omega_0 t_2 = \sin^{-1}\left(\frac{I_0}{I_p}\right) = \sin^{-1}\left(\frac{1}{2}\right)$$

$$\Rightarrow \quad \omega_0 t_2 = \frac{\pi}{6}$$

$$\Rightarrow \quad t_2 = \frac{\pi}{6 \cdot \omega_0} = \frac{\pi}{6}\sqrt{LC}$$

$$\Rightarrow \quad I_P = 2I_0$$

$$V_s\sqrt{\frac{C}{L}} = 2 \cdot \frac{V_s}{R}$$

$$\Rightarrow \quad \sqrt{\frac{C}{L}} = \frac{2}{R} \quad \text{...(i)}$$

$$\text{Conduction time of Thy} = \pi\sqrt{LC} + \frac{\pi}{6}\sqrt{LC}(t_1 + t_2)$$

$$\text{Duration of current pulse } (t_p) = \frac{7\pi}{6}\sqrt{LC}$$

$$t_p = \frac{7\pi}{6}\sqrt{LC}$$

$$\sqrt{LC} = \frac{6 \cdot t_p}{7\pi} \quad \text{...(ii)}$$

By multiplying equation (1) and (ii)

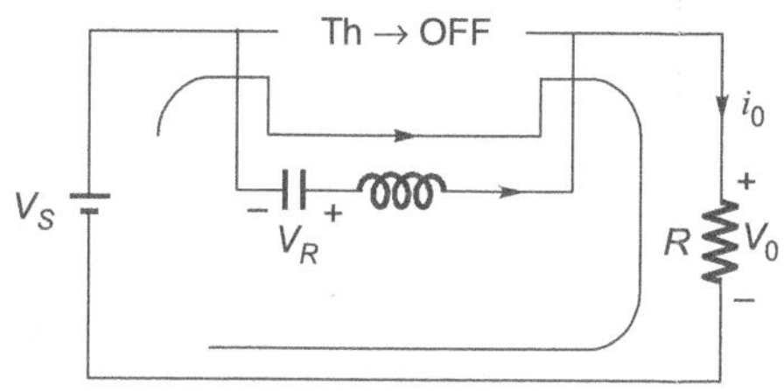

$$\sqrt{\frac{C}{L}} \times \sqrt{LC} = \frac{2}{R} \times \frac{6t_p}{7\pi}$$

$$\text{Capacitance, } C = \frac{12t_p}{7\pi R},$$

$$\text{Inductance, } L = \frac{3t_p.R}{7\pi}$$

$$0.75T = 0.75 \times 2\pi\sqrt{LC} \quad (T = 2\pi\sqrt{LC})$$

$$\therefore \quad 0.75T = 0.75 \times 2\pi\sqrt{LC} = 1 \text{ mS}$$

$$\sqrt{LC} = \frac{1.10^{-3}}{0.75 \times 2\pi} \quad \text{...(iii)}$$

$$I_p = 2I_0$$

$$V_s\sqrt{\frac{C}{L}} = 2 \cdot \frac{V_s}{R}$$

$$\sqrt{\frac{C}{L}} = \frac{2}{R} = \frac{2}{550} \quad \text{...(iv)}$$

From equation (iii) and (iv)

$$\sqrt{LC} = \frac{1 \times 10^{-3}}{0.75 \times 2\pi}$$

$$\sqrt{\frac{C}{L}} = \frac{2}{R} = \frac{2}{550} = \frac{1}{225}$$

$$C = \frac{L}{225^2} \quad \text{...(v)}$$

On substituting equation (v) in equation (iii),

$$L \times \frac{L}{225^2} = \left[\frac{1 \times 10^{-3}}{0.75 \times 2\pi}\right]^2$$

$$\text{Inductance, } L = 225 \times \frac{1 \times 10^{-3}}{0.75 \times 2\pi} = 47.74 \text{ mH}$$

and Capacitance, $C = 0.943\ \mu C$

Here inductor is practical ($R_L \neq 0$), so R_L can be neglected as compared to the reactance of L and C.

7.15 **A single phase ac controller supplied from a source, $V_{in} = 220\sin(314.28t)$ produces an rms output voltage of 110 V for a resistive load of 10 Ω at its firing angle α. Determine**

(i) the value of α,

(ii) the amplitude of the seventh harmonic current for α = π/6, and

(iii) the input power factor,

[4 + 8 + 8 marks : 2021]

Solution:

Given data is :

1-ϕ ac controller supplied from a source,

$$V_{in}(t) = 220\sin(314.28t) \text{ V}$$

An rms o/p voltage of 110 V for a resistive load

$$V_{or} = 110\text{ V}$$

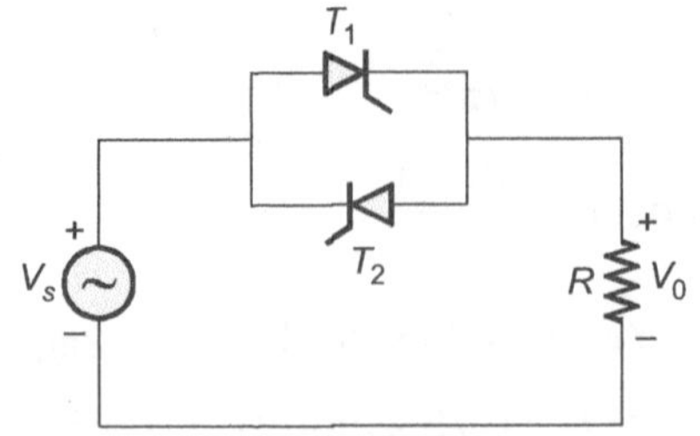

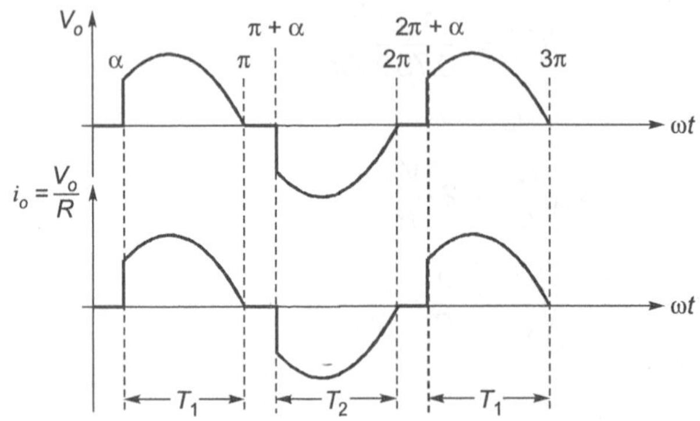

rms voltage :

$$V_{o,\text{rms}} = \left[\frac{1}{\pi}\int_{\alpha}^{\pi} V_m^2 \sin^2 \omega t \cdot d\omega t\right]^{1/2}$$

$$= \left[\frac{V_m^2}{2\pi}\int_{\alpha}^{\pi}(1-\cos 2\omega t)\cdot d\omega t\right]^{1/2}$$

$$= \frac{V_m}{\sqrt{\pi}\sqrt{2}}\left[\omega t\Big|_{\alpha}^{\pi} - \frac{1}{2}\sin 2\omega t\Big|_{\alpha}^{\pi}\right]^{1/2}$$

$$= \frac{V_m}{\sqrt{2}\sqrt{\pi}}\left[(\pi-\alpha) - \frac{1}{2}(\sin 2\pi - \sin 2\alpha)\right]^{1/2}$$

$$= \frac{V_m}{\sqrt{2\pi}}\left[(\pi-\alpha) + \frac{1}{2}\sin 2\alpha\right]^{1/2}$$

$$\Rightarrow \quad 110 = \frac{220}{\sqrt{2\pi}}\left[(\pi-\alpha) + \frac{1}{2}\sin 2\alpha\right]^{1/2}$$

$$\Rightarrow \quad 1.57 = (\pi-\alpha) + \frac{1}{2}\sin 2\alpha$$

[α = 1.57 rad or 90°]

⇒ Harmonics of output quantities and input current

The output volt V_0 can be represented by Fourier series as under,

$$V_0 = \sum_{n=1,3,5}^{\infty} A_n \sin(n\omega t) + \sum_{n=1,3,5}^{\infty} B_n \cos(n\omega t)$$

$$A_n = \frac{2}{\pi}\int_{\alpha}^{\pi}(V_m \sin\omega t)\sin(n\omega t)\cdot d\omega t$$

$$B_n = \frac{2}{\pi}\int_{\alpha}^{\pi}(V_m \sin\omega t)\cos(n\omega t)\cdot d\omega t$$

$$\Rightarrow \quad A_n = \frac{V_m}{\pi}\int_{\alpha}^{\pi}[\cos(n-1)\omega t - \cos(n+1)\omega t]\,d\omega t$$

$$= \frac{V_m}{\pi}\left[\frac{\sin(n+1)\alpha}{(n+1)} - \frac{\sin(n-1)\alpha}{(n-1)}\right]$$

$$\Rightarrow \quad B_n = \frac{V_m}{\pi}\int_{\alpha}^{\pi}[\sin(n+1)\omega t - \sin(n-1)\omega t]\,d\omega t$$

$$= \frac{V_m}{\pi}\left[\frac{\cos(n+1)\alpha - 1}{n+1} - \frac{\cos(n-1)\alpha - 1}{n-1}\right]$$

For $n = 7$, $\cos(n+1)\pi = 1$

$\cos(n-1)\pi = 1$

The amplitude of the 7th harmonic output voltage V_{7m}

$$\Rightarrow \quad V_{7m} = \sqrt{A_7^2 + B_7^2}$$

$$\because \quad A_7 = \frac{V_m}{\pi}\left[\frac{\sin 8\alpha}{8} - \frac{\sin 6\alpha}{6}\right]$$

$$\Rightarrow \quad B_7 = \frac{V_m}{\pi}\left[\frac{\cos 8\alpha - 1}{8} - \frac{\cos 6\alpha - 1}{6}\right]$$

Given, $\alpha = \frac{\pi}{6}$ or $30°$

$$\Rightarrow \quad A_7 = \frac{220}{\pi}\left[\frac{\sin(8\times 30)}{8} - \frac{\sin(6\times 30)}{6}\right]$$

$$\Rightarrow \quad B_7 = \frac{220}{\pi}\left[\frac{\cos(8\times 30) - 1}{8} - \frac{\cos(6\times 30) - 1}{6}\right]$$

$$A_7 = -7.58,\ B_7 = 10.212$$

Now, $V_{7m} = 12.72$

The amplitude of the seventh harmonic current

$$I_{o7} = \frac{V_{7m}}{R} = \frac{12.72}{10} = 1.272 \text{ Amp}$$

(iii) Input power factor

$$\text{Real power delivered to load} = \frac{V_{0rms}^2}{R}$$

$$\text{Apparent power delivered to load} = V_s \cdot I_{0r}$$

$$P_o = V_s \cdot \frac{V_{0r}}{R}$$

Input power factor,

$$\text{IPF} = \frac{\frac{V_{0,rms}^2}{R}}{V_s \cdot \frac{V_{0rms}}{R}} = \frac{V_{0rms}}{V_{srms}}$$

$$\text{IPF} = \left[\frac{1}{\pi}\left\{(\pi - \alpha) + \frac{1}{2}\sin 2\alpha\right\}\right]^{1/2}$$

$$= \left[\frac{1}{\pi}\left\{\left(\pi - \frac{\pi}{6}\right) + \frac{1}{2}\sin 60\right\}\right]^{1/2}$$

Input power factor, $\text{IPF} = 0.985 \text{ (lag) .... for } \alpha = \frac{\pi}{6}$

For firing angle, $\alpha = \frac{\pi}{2}$

Input power factor, $\text{IPF} = \left[\frac{1}{\pi}\left(\pi - \frac{\pi}{2}\right) + \frac{1}{2}\sin(2 \times 90°)\right]^{1/2}$

$$= \frac{1}{\sqrt{2}} = 0.707 \text{ lagging for } \alpha = \frac{\pi}{2}$$

■■■■

9 Systems and Signal Processing

Revised Syllabus of ESE: *Representation of continuous and discrete-time signals, shifting and scaling operations, linear, time-invariant and causal systems, Fourier series representation of continuous periodic signals, sampling theorem, Fourier and Laplace transforms, Z transforms, Discrete Fourier transform, FFT, linear convolution, discrete cosine transform, FIR filter, IIR filter, bilinear transformation.*

1.1 Write down the trigonometric Fourier series representation of the following signal:

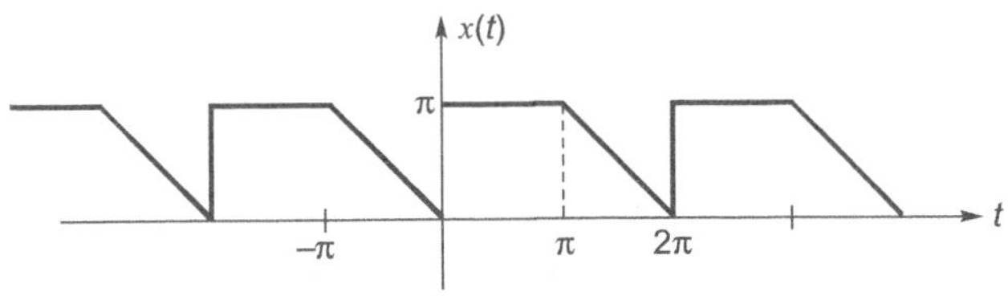

[20 marks : 2017]

Solution:

$$x(t) \text{ for one period } = \begin{cases} \pi, & 0 \le t \le \pi \\ 2\pi - t, & \pi < t \le 2\pi \end{cases}$$

$$\text{Trigonometric Fourier series } = a_0 + \sum_{n=1}^{\infty} a_n \cos n\omega_0 t + \sum_{n=1}^{\infty} b_n \sin n\omega_0 t$$

$$\omega_0 = \frac{2\pi}{T}$$

$$T = 2\pi$$

$$\omega_0 = \frac{2\pi}{2\pi} = 1$$

$$a_0 = \frac{1}{T}\int_0^T x(t)\,dt$$

$$a_n = \frac{2}{T}\int_0^T x(t)\cos n\omega_0 t\,dt$$

$$b_n = \frac{2}{T}\int_0^T x(t)\sin n\omega_0 t\,dt$$

$$a_0 = \frac{1}{2\pi}\int_0^{2\pi} x(t)\,dt = \frac{1}{2\pi}\left[\int_0^{\pi} \pi\,dt + \int_0^{2\pi} (2\pi - t)\,dt\right]$$

$$= \frac{1}{2\pi}\left[[\pi t]_0^{\pi} + \left[2\pi t - \frac{t^2}{2}\right]_{\pi}^{2\pi}\right]$$

$$= \frac{1}{2\pi}\left[(\pi^2 - 0) + \left(4\pi^2 - \frac{4\pi^2}{2}\right) - \left(2\pi^2 - \frac{\pi^2}{2}\right)\right]$$

$$= \frac{1}{2\pi}\left[\pi^2 + \frac{4\pi^2}{2} - \frac{3\pi^2}{2}\right] = \frac{3\pi^2}{2} \times \frac{1}{2\pi} = \frac{3\pi}{4}$$

$$a_n = \frac{2}{2\pi}\int_0^{2\pi} x(t)\cos nt\,dt = \frac{1}{\pi}\left[\int_0^{\pi} \pi\cos nt\,dt + \int_{\pi}^{2\pi} (2\pi - t)\cos nt\,dt\right]$$

$$= \frac{1}{\pi}\left[\left[\frac{\pi\sin nt}{n}\right]_0^{\pi} + \left[\frac{2\pi\sin nt}{n}\right]_{\pi}^{2\pi} + \left[\frac{-t\sin nt}{n}\right]_{\pi}^{2\pi} + \int_{\pi}^{2\pi}\frac{\sin nt}{n}dt\right]$$

$$= \frac{1}{\pi}\left[0 + 0 + 0 - \left[\frac{\cos nt}{n^2}\right]_{\pi}^{2\pi}\right]$$

$$= \frac{1}{\pi}\left[-\left[\frac{1}{n^2} + \frac{1}{n^2}\right]\right] \quad \text{for } n - \text{odd}$$

$$= \frac{1}{\pi}\left[-\left[\frac{1}{n^2} - \frac{1}{n^2}\right]\right] \quad \text{for } n\text{-even}$$

$\therefore$

$$a_n = -\frac{2}{\pi n^2} \quad \text{for } n\text{ - odd}$$

$$0 \quad \text{for } n\text{ - even}$$

$$b_n = \frac{2}{2\pi}\int_0^{2\pi} x(t)\sin nt\,dt = \frac{1}{\pi}\left[\int_0^{\pi} \pi\sin nt\,dt + \int_{\pi}^{2\pi} (2\pi - t)\sin nt\,dt\right]$$

$$= \frac{1}{\pi}\left[-\left[\frac{\pi\cos nt}{n}\right]_0^{\pi} + \left[\frac{-2\pi\cos nt}{n}\right]_{\pi}^{2\pi} + \left[\frac{t\cos nt}{n}\right]_{\pi}^{2\pi} - \int_{\pi}^{2\pi}\frac{\cos nt\,dt}{n}\right]$$

$$= \frac{1}{\pi}\left[-\left[\frac{-\pi}{n} - \frac{\pi}{n}\right] + \left[\frac{-2\pi}{n} - \frac{2\pi}{n}\right] + \left[\frac{2\pi}{n} + \frac{\pi}{n}\right] - \left[\frac{\sin nt}{n^2}\right]_{\pi}^{2\pi}\right] \quad \text{for } n\text{-odd}$$

$$= \frac{1}{\pi}\left[\frac{2\pi}{n} - \frac{4\pi}{n} + \frac{3\pi}{n} - 0\right] = \frac{1}{n} \quad \text{for } n\text{-odd}$$

$$= \frac{1}{\pi}\left[-\left[\frac{\pi}{n} - \frac{\pi}{n}\right] + \left[\frac{-2\pi}{n} + \frac{2\pi}{n}\right] + \left[\frac{2\pi}{n} - \frac{\pi}{n}\right] - 0\right] \quad \text{for } n\text{-even}$$

$$= \frac{1}{\pi}\left[\frac{\pi}{n}\right] = \frac{1}{n} \quad \text{for } n\text{-even}$$

$\therefore$

$$a_0 = \frac{3\pi}{4}$$

$$a_n = \begin{cases} -\dfrac{2}{\pi n^2} & \text{for } n\text{-odd} \\ 0 & \text{for } n\text{-even} \end{cases}$$

$$b_n = \begin{cases} \frac{1}{n} & \text{for } n\text{-odd} \\ \frac{1}{n} & \text{for } n\text{-even} \end{cases}$$

$$\therefore \quad x(t) = \frac{3\pi}{4} + \sum_{n\text{-odd}} -\frac{2}{\pi n^2}\cos nt + \sum_{n=1}^{\infty}\frac{1}{n}\sin nt$$

1.2 Determine the Laplace transform and the ROC of the signal, $x(t) = e^{at}\,u(t-k)$.

[12 marks : 2017]

Solution:

$$x(t) = e^{at}\,u(t-k)$$

$$\text{Laplace transform} = \int_{-\infty}^{\infty} x(t)\,e^{-st}\,dt$$

$$= \int_{-\infty}^{\infty} e^{-at}\,u(t-k)\,e^{-st}\,dt = \int_{k}^{\infty} e^{-(s-a)t}\,dt$$

$$= \left[\frac{e^{-(s-a)t}}{-(s-a)}\right]_k^{\infty} = \left[0 + \frac{e^{-(s-a)k}}{(s-a)}\right]$$

$$= \frac{e^{-(s-a)k}}{(s-a)} \qquad \text{ROC } \sigma > a$$

1.3 Two sequences are defined as:

$$x[n] = \begin{cases} 1, & 0 \le n \le 4 \\ 0, & \text{otherwise} \end{cases} \text{ and } h[n] = \begin{cases} \alpha^n, & 0 \le n \le 6 \\ 0, & \text{otherwise} \end{cases}$$

where α is +ve. Find $x[n] * h[n]$.

[20 marks : 2017]

Solution:

$$x[n] = u[n] - u[n-5]$$

$$h[n] = h[n] * [u[n] - u[n-5]]$$

$$= h[n] * u[n] - h[n] * u[n-5]$$

Let,

$$h(k) = \sum_{k=-\infty}^{+\infty} h[k] - \sum_{k=-\infty}^{+\infty} h[k-5]$$

$$\therefore \quad y[n] = \begin{cases} 0; & n < 0 \\ \sum_{k=0}^{n} a^k; & 0 \le n \le 4 \\ \sum_{k=0}^{n} a^k - \sum_{k=5}^{n} a^{k-5}; & 5 \le n \le 6 \\ \sum_{k=0}^{6} a^k - \sum_{k=5}^{n} a^{k-5}; & 7 \le n \le 11 \\ \sum_{k=0}^{6} a^k - \sum_{k=5}^{11} a^{k-5}; & n \ge 12 \end{cases}$$

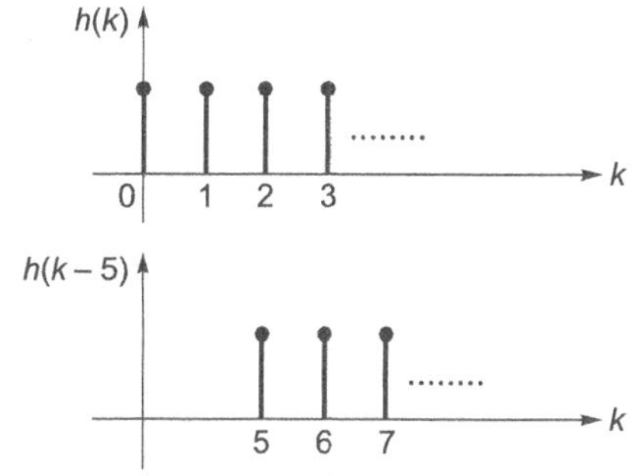

$$\therefore \qquad y[n] = \begin{cases} 0; & n<0 \\ \dfrac{1-a^{n+1}}{1-a}; & 0\le n\le 4 \\ \dfrac{a^{n-4}-a^{n+1}}{1-a}; & 5\le n\le 6 \\ \dfrac{a^{n-4}-a^{7}}{1-a}; & 7\le n\le 11 \\ 0; & n\ge 12 \end{cases}$$

1.4 The continuous-time Fourier transform (CTFT) of a square pulse defined by $x(t) = 1$ for $-0.5 \le t \le 0.5$ is given by

$$X(\omega) = \frac{\sin\left(\frac{\omega}{2}\right)}{\frac{\omega}{2}}$$

Use the properties of CTFT and synthesize the equation, and find the CTFT of the following signals $y(t)$ and $z(t)$:

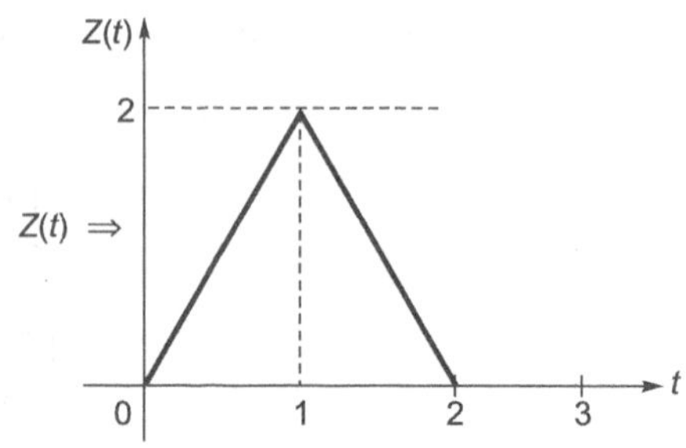

$$y(t) = \begin{cases} 2, & \text{for } 0\le t<1 \\ -2, & \text{for } 1\le t\le 2 \\ 0, & \text{elsewhere} \end{cases}$$

[12 marks : 2018]

Solution:

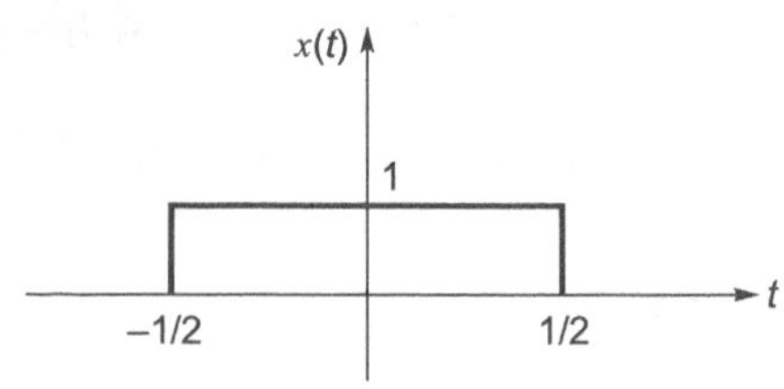

It is given that,
$$X(\omega) = \frac{\sin\left(\frac{\omega}{2}\right)}{\left(\frac{\omega}{2}\right)}$$

$$y(t) = \begin{cases} 2 & \text{for } 0\le t<1 \\ -2 & \text{for } 1\le t\le 2 \\ 0 & \text{elsewhere} \end{cases}$$

Let us represent $y(t)$ graphically,

$y(t)$ can be expressed in terms of $x(t)$ as shown below:

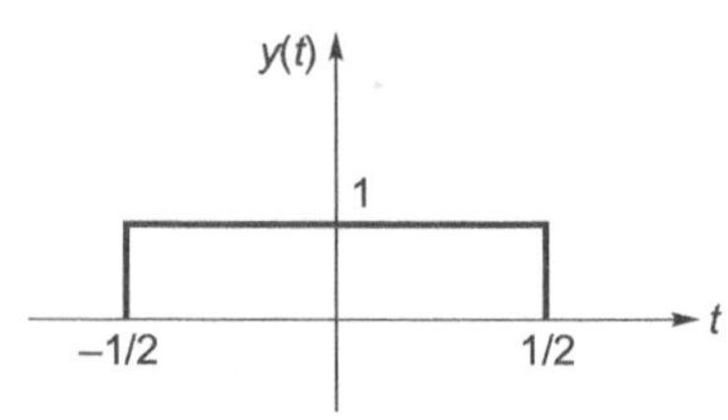

$$y(t) = 2x\left(t-\frac{1}{2}\right)-2x\left(t-\frac{3}{2}\right)$$

Using time shifting property of CTFT:

$$[x(t-t_0) \xrightarrow{F.T.} e^{-j\omega t_0}\, X(\omega)]$$

$$Y(\omega) = \frac{2e^{-\frac{j\omega}{2}}\sin\left(\frac{\omega}{2}\right)}{\left(\frac{\omega}{2}\right)} - \frac{2e^{-\frac{j3\omega}{2}}\sin\left(\frac{\omega}{2}\right)}{\left(\frac{\omega}{2}\right)}$$

$$Y(\omega) = \frac{2\sin\left(\frac{\omega}{2}\right)}{\left(\frac{\omega}{2}\right)}(e^{-j\frac{\omega}{2}} - e^{-\frac{j3\omega}{2}})$$

Let us differentiate $Z(t)$ graphically,

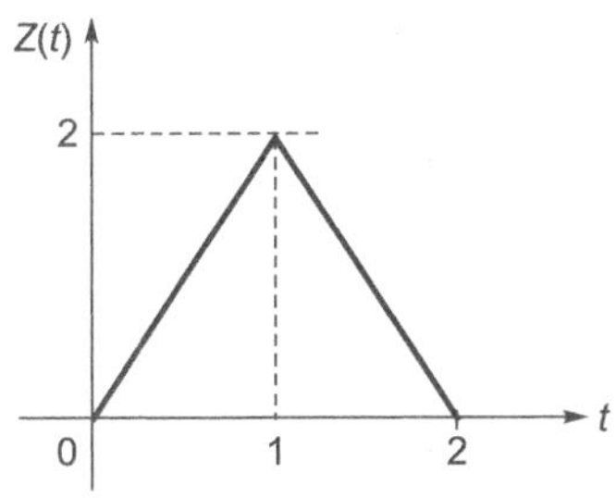

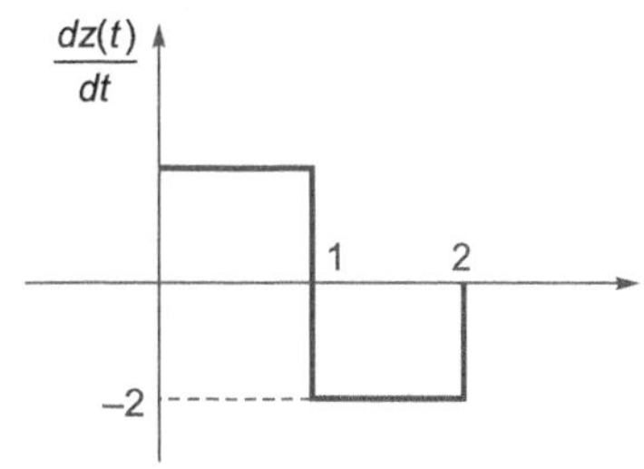

It can be seen that, $\frac{dZ(t)}{dt} = y(t)$

Using the property of CTFT,

i.e. if $Z(t) \xrightarrow{F.T.} j(\omega)\, Z(\omega)$

So, $Y(\omega) = (j\omega)\, Z(\omega)$

$$Z(\omega) = \frac{Y(\omega)}{j\omega} = \frac{2\sin\left(\frac{\omega}{2}\right)}{\left(\frac{\omega}{2}\right)(j\omega)}(e^{-\frac{j\omega}{2}} - e^{-\frac{j3\omega}{2}})$$

1.5 A signal $x_a(t)$ is band-limited to the range 900 Hz ≤ f ≤ 1100 Hz (assume the shape of an isosceles triangle for continuous Fourier transform and $|X_a(f)| = 1$ and f = 1000 Hz.) It is used as an input to the system shown below:

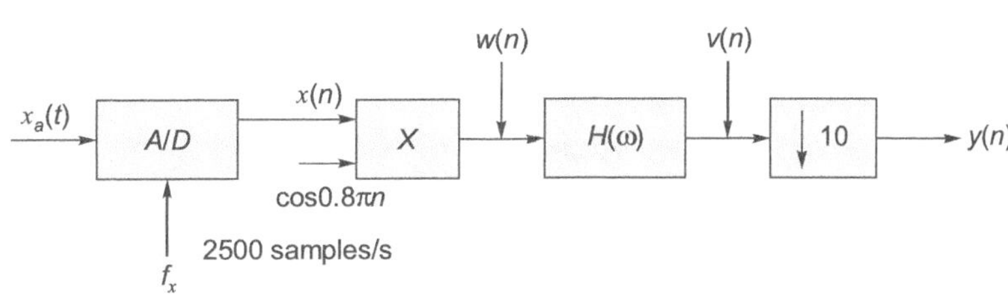

In this system, $H(\omega)$ is a low-pass filter with a discrete cut-off frequency equivalent to f_c = 125 Hz (normalized w.r.t. the sample rate at the point in the block diagram). Determine and sketch the spectra of $X(\omega_x)$, $W(\omega_w)$, $V(\omega_v)$ and $Y(\omega_y)$ w.r.t. ω_x, ω_w, ω_v and ω_y respectively for $-\pi < \omega < \pi$.

[20 marks : 2018]

Solution:

Given that the spectrum of $x_a(t)$ is,

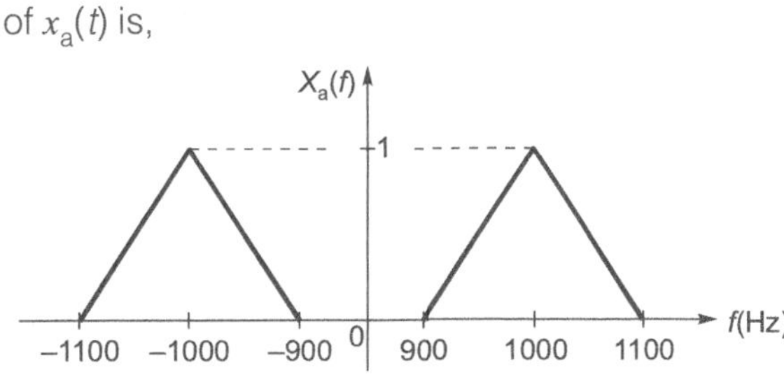

$x(n)$ is the sampled version of $x_a(t)$ with a sampling rate of f_s = 2500 samples/s. Let ω_x is the normalized frequency of the spectrum of $x(n)$ in rad/s.

So,
$$\omega_x = 2\pi\frac{f}{f_s} = \frac{2\pi}{2500}f \text{ rad/s}$$

The spectrum of $x(n)$ is,

$$X(f) = \sum_{k=-\infty}^{\infty}\frac{1}{T_s}X_a(f-kf_s)$$

$$X(\omega_x) = \sum_{k=-\infty}^{\infty}\frac{1}{T_s}X_a(\omega_x-2\pi k)$$

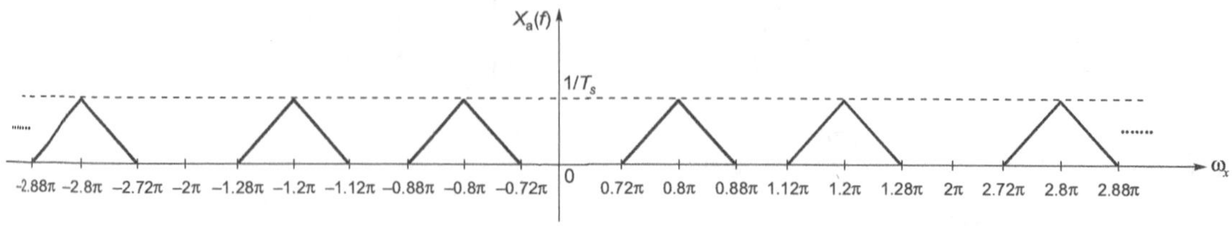

$$W(n) = x(n)\cos(0.8\pi n)$$

$$W(\omega_w) = \frac{1}{2}[X(\omega_x-0.8\pi)+X(\omega_x+0.8\pi)]$$

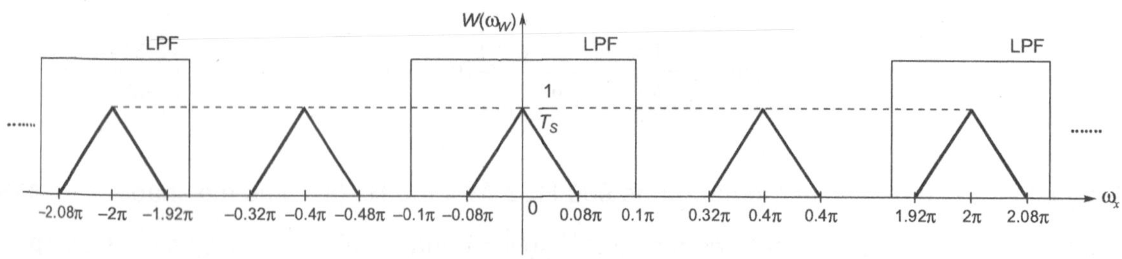

The normalized cut-off frequency of the LPF is,

$$\omega_c = 2\pi\times\frac{f_c}{f_s} = 2\pi\times\frac{125}{2500} = 0.1\pi$$

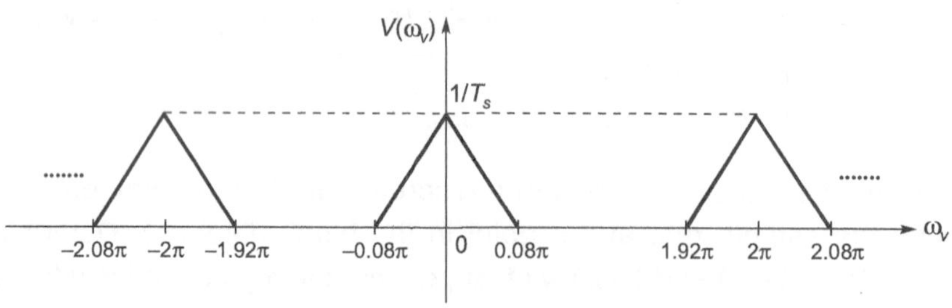

After down conversion of the sampling rate,

$$f_s' = \frac{f_s}{10} \text{ and } \omega_y = \omega\frac{f_s}{f_s'} = 10\omega_v$$

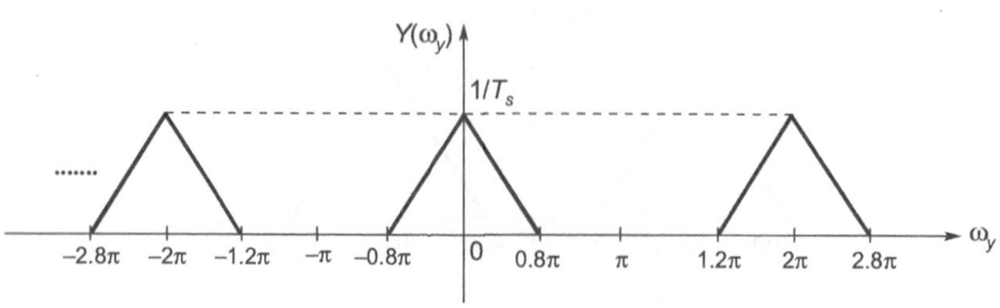

1.6 A signal is given by: $x[t] = \cos(28\pi t) + 2\cos(40\pi t) + 3\cos(70\pi t)$
The signal is sampled at 90 samples/s to get discrete-time signal $x(n)$.

(i) Find the periodicity of the individual components in the signal and hence find the periodicity N_0 of the signal $x(n)$.

(ii) Find the harmonic indices $m(0 \le m \le N_0)$ of the complex DTFS coefficient D_m, where D_m is non-zero.

(iii) By inspection, write the magnitude of the coefficients $|D_m|$ for the indices found above.

[20 marks : 2018]

Solution:

$$N_S = 90 \text{ samples /sec}$$

Sampling,
$$t \to nT_s$$
$$t = \left(\frac{n}{90}\right)$$
$$x(n) = \cos\left(\frac{28\pi n}{90}\right) + 2\cos\left(\frac{40\pi n}{90}\right) + 3\cos\left(\frac{70\pi n}{90}\right)$$

(i) Fundamental frequency,

$$\omega_0 = \text{HCF}\left(\frac{28\pi}{90}, \frac{40\pi}{90}, \frac{70\pi}{90}\right) = \left(\frac{2\pi}{90}\right)$$
$$N_0 = \frac{2\pi}{\omega_0} = \frac{2\pi}{2\pi}\times 90 = 90 \text{ samples/sec}$$

(ii)
$$N_1 = \frac{2\pi}{\omega_1}k = \frac{2\pi}{28\pi}\times 90k = \frac{90}{14}k = \frac{45}{7}k$$

$k = 7$,
$$N_1 = 45 \text{ samples/sec.}$$
$$N_2 = \frac{2\pi}{\omega_2} = \frac{2\pi}{40\pi}\times 90k = \frac{9k}{2}$$
$$k = 2$$
$$N_2 = 9 \text{ sample/sec}$$
$$N_3 = \frac{2\pi}{\omega_3}k = \frac{2\pi\times 90}{70\pi}k = \frac{18}{7}k$$
$$k = 7$$
$$N_3 = 18 \text{ sample/sec}$$
$$m_1 = \frac{N_0}{N_1} = \frac{90}{45} = 2$$
$$m_2 = \frac{N_0}{N_2} = \frac{90}{9} = 10$$
$$m_3 = \frac{N_0}{N_3} = \frac{90}{18} = 5$$

$\therefore$ Indices are 2, 10, 5.

(iii)

$$x(n) = \frac{1}{2}e^{j\frac{28\pi}{90}n} + \frac{1}{2}e^{\frac{-j28\pi}{90}n} + \frac{1}{2}e^{\frac{i40\pi}{90}} + \frac{1}{2}e^{\frac{-i40\pi}{90}} + \frac{3}{2}e^{\frac{i70\pi}{90}n} + \frac{3}{2}e^{\frac{-i70\pi}{90}}$$

$$\therefore \quad |D_2| = |D_{-2}| = \frac{1}{2};\quad |D_{10}| = |D_{-10}| = 1;\quad |D_5| = |D_{-5}| = 1.5$$

1.7 Determine the total energy and average power of the following signal:

$$x(t) = \begin{cases} 2 & -3 \le t \le 3 \\ 5-t & 3 \le t \le 5 \\ 0 & otherwise \end{cases}$$

[12 Marks : 2019]

Solution:

The given signal is energy signal, so energy is finite and power should be zero.

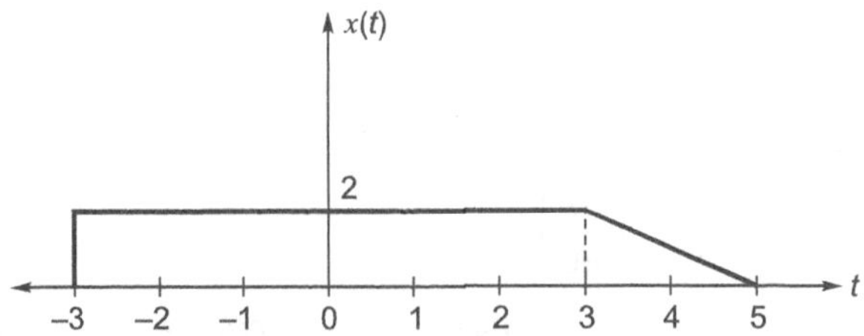

$$\text{Energy} = \int_{-\infty}^{\infty} |x(t)|^2 dt = \int_{-3}^{3} (2)^2 dt + \int_{3}^{5} (5-t)^2 dt$$

$$= 4(t)\Big|_{-3}^{3} + \int_{3}^{5} (25 + t^2 - 10t)\, dt$$

$$= 26.67 \text{ units}$$

1.8 (i) Fourier transform of a periodic signal is given as,

$$X(j\omega) = j\delta\left(\omega - \frac{\pi}{3}\right) + 2\delta\left(\omega - \frac{\pi}{7}\right)$$

Determine the fundamental angular frequency and the Fourier series coefficients. Then determine the corresponding time signal.

(ii) Determine the Laplace transform and the ROC for the signal

$$x(t) = e^{at}\, u(t-k)$$

[20 Marks : 2019]

Solution:

(i) Given Fourier transform of a periodic signal as,

$$X(j\omega) = j\delta\left(\omega - \frac{\pi}{3}\right) + 2\delta\left(\omega - \frac{\pi}{7}\right)$$

$$\delta(t) \xrightleftharpoons{\text{F.T.}} 1$$

$$1 \rightleftharpoons 2\pi\, \delta(\omega)$$

According to frequency shifting property,

$$e^{j\omega_0 t}\, x(t) \rightleftharpoons X(\omega - \omega_0)$$

$$e^{j\left(\frac{\pi}{3}\right)t} \rightleftharpoons 2\pi\delta\left(\omega - \frac{\pi}{3}\right)$$

$$je^{j\left(\frac{\pi}{3}\right)t} \rightleftharpoons j2\pi\delta\left(\omega - \frac{\pi}{3}\right)$$

Similarly, $$2e^{j\left(\frac{\pi}{7}\right)t} \rightleftharpoons 4\pi\delta\left(\omega - \frac{\pi}{7}\right)$$

$$x(t) \rightleftharpoons X(j\omega)$$

$$x(t) = \frac{j}{2\pi} e^{j\left(\frac{\pi}{3}\right)t} + \frac{1}{\pi} e^{j\left(\frac{\pi}{7}\right)t} \qquad ...(1)$$

Fundamental angular frequency,

$$\omega_0 = GCD\left\{\frac{\pi}{3}, \frac{\pi}{7}\right\} = \frac{\pi}{21} \text{ rad/s}$$

$x(t)$ can be represented as,

$$x(t) = \sum_{k=-\infty}^{\infty} C_n e^{jn\omega_0 t} \qquad ...(2)$$

By comparing (1) and (2),

$$x(t) = \frac{j}{2\pi} e^{j7\omega_0 t} + \frac{1}{\pi} e^{j3\omega_0 t}$$

So Fourier series coefficients are,

$$C_3 = \frac{1}{\pi}, \qquad C_7 = \frac{j}{2\pi}$$

(ii) Given signals,
$$x(t) = e^{at}\, u(t-k)$$
$$x(t) = e^{a(t-k+k)} \cdot u(t-k)$$
$$= e^{ak}[e^{a(t-k)} \cdot u(t-k)]$$

By using time shifting property,

$$x(t-t_0) = X(s) \cdot e^{-st_0} \qquad \text{(No change in ROC)}$$

$$X(s) = e^{ak} \cdot \left[\frac{1}{s-a} \cdot e^{-ks}\right] = e^{k(a-s)} \cdot \frac{1}{s-a}$$

ROC of the signal is $\text{Re}\{s\} > a$

Right side of the right most pole.

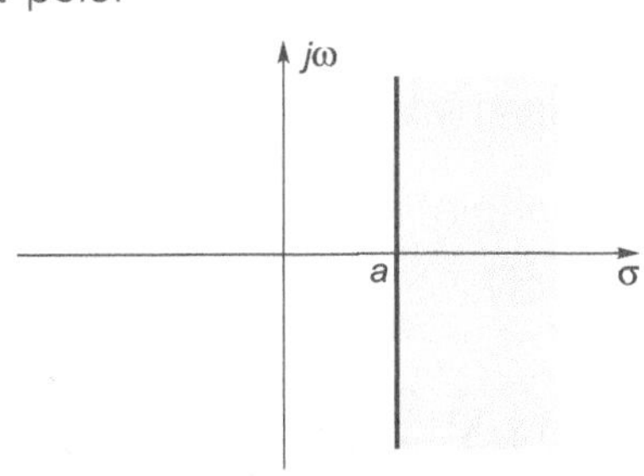

1.9 **For a causal system specified by the transfer function,**

$$H(z) = \frac{z}{z-0.5}$$

Determine the zero state response to the input,

$$r(k) = (0.8)^k u(k) + (2)^{k+1} u\{-(k+1)\}$$

[20 Marks : 2019]

Solution:

Given, $$H(z) = \frac{z}{z-0.5}$$

Input given as, $$r(k) = (0.8)^k u(k) + (2)^{k+1} u\{-(k+1)\}$$

As we know, $$Y(z) = R(z)\,H(z) \quad \text{ROC of } Y(z) : \text{Common ROC of } r(k) \text{ and } h(k)$$

$$R(z) = \frac{1}{1-0.8z^{-1}} - \frac{2}{1-2z^{-1}}$$

$$H(z) = \frac{z}{z-0.5}; \quad \text{ROC: } |z| > 0.5$$

$R(z)$ ROC: $|z| > 0.8$ and $|z| < 2$

Common ROC: $$0.8 < |z| < 2$$

$$Y(z) = H(z) \cdot X(z)$$

$$= \left[\frac{z}{z-0.5}\right]\left[\frac{1}{1-0.8z^{-1}} - \frac{2}{1-2z^{-1}}\right]$$

$$= \left(\frac{z}{z-0.5}\right)\left(\frac{z}{z-0.8} - \frac{2z}{z-2}\right)$$

$$Y(z) = \frac{z^2}{(z-0.5)(z-0.8)} - \frac{2z^2}{(z-0.5)(z-2)}$$

$$\frac{Y(z)}{z} = \frac{z}{(z-0.5)(z-0.8)} - \frac{2z}{(z-0.5)(z-2)}$$

After performing partial fraction,

$$Y(z) = \frac{-\frac{5}{3}z}{z-0.5} + \frac{\frac{8}{3}z}{z-0.8} + \frac{\frac{2}{3}z}{z-0.5} - \frac{\frac{8}{3}z}{z-2}$$

$$= \frac{-z}{z-0.5} + \frac{\frac{8}{3}z}{z-0.8} - \frac{\frac{8}{3}z}{z-2}$$

$$y(k) = -(0.5)^k u(k) + \frac{8}{3}(0.8)^k u(k) + \frac{8}{3}(2)^k u(-k-1)$$

1.10 A signal $g(t)$ band limited to B Hz is sampled by a periodic pulse train $p_T(t)$ made up of a rectangular pulse of width $\frac{1}{8B}$ sec (centered at origin) repeating at the Nyquist rate (2 B pulses per sec.) Show that the sampled signal $g_s(t)$ is given by

$$g_s(t) = \frac{1}{4}g(t) + \sum_{n=1}^{\infty} \frac{2}{n\pi}\sin\left(\frac{n\pi}{4}\right) g(t)\cos(4n\pi Bt)$$

How will you recover $g(t)$ from the signal $g_s(t)$?

[15 + 5 = 20 marks : 2020]

Solution:

$$g_s(t) = g(t)p_T(t)$$

Given that $p_T(t)$ is made up of rectangular pulse of width $\frac{1}{8B}$ sec and repeating at the Nyquist rate 2 B pulses/sec

$$T_s = \frac{1}{2B}$$

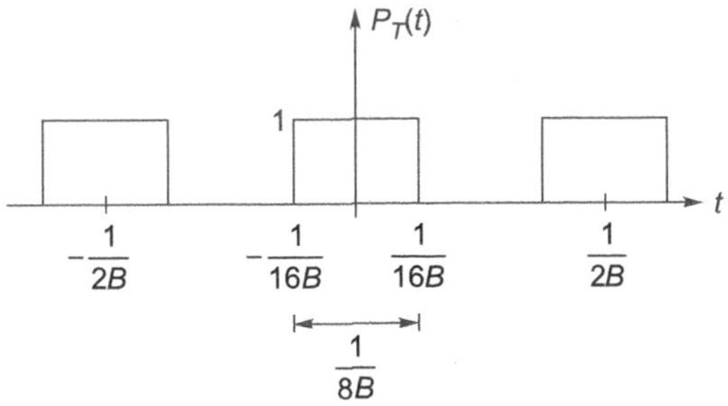

Fourier series of $P_T(t)$ can be written as

$$P_T(t) = a_0 + \sum_{n=1}^{\infty}(a_n \cos n\omega_0 t + b_n \sin n\omega_0 t)$$

As the given signal is even signal,

$$b_n = 0$$

$$P_T(t) = a_0 + \sum_{n=1}^{\infty}(a_n \cos n\omega_0 t)$$

$$a_0 = \frac{1}{T}\int_0^T P_T(t)\cdot dt = \frac{1}{T}\int_{-\frac{1}{16B}}^{1/16B} 1\cdot dt$$

$$a_0 = \frac{1}{\left(\frac{1}{2B}\right)}\left[\frac{1}{16B}+\frac{1}{16B}\right] = \frac{\frac{1}{8B}}{\frac{1}{2B}} = \frac{1}{4}$$

$$a_n = \frac{2}{T}\int_{-T/2}^{T/2} P_T(t)\cdot \cos(n\omega_0 t)\cdot dt$$

$$\omega_0 = \frac{2\pi}{T} = \frac{2\pi}{\left(\frac{1}{2B}\right)} = 4B\pi$$

$$a_n = \frac{2}{\left(\frac{1}{2B}\right)}\int_{-\frac{1}{16B}}^{\frac{1}{16B}} 1\cdot \cos(4B\pi nt)\cdot dt$$

$$a_n = 4B\left[\frac{\sin(4B\pi nt)}{4B\pi n}\right]_{-1/16B}^{1/16B}$$

$$a_n = 4B\left[\frac{\sin\left(\frac{\pi n}{4}\right) - \sin\left(\frac{-\pi n}{4}\right)}{4B\pi n}\right]$$

$$a_n = \frac{2}{\pi n}\sin\left(\frac{\pi n}{4}\right)$$

$$\therefore \quad P_T(t) = \frac{1}{4} + \sum_{n=1}^{\infty} \frac{2}{\pi n}\sin\left(\frac{\pi n}{4}\right)\cos(4B\pi nt)$$

$$\therefore \quad g_s(t) = g(t) \cdot P_T(t)$$

$$\therefore \quad g_s(t) = \frac{g(t)}{4} + \sum_{n=1}^{\infty} \frac{2}{\pi n}\sin\left(\frac{\pi n}{4}\right)g(t)\cdot\cos(4B\pi nt)$$

If we will expand $g_s(t)$,

then we can write $g_s(t) = \dfrac{g(t)}{4} + \dfrac{2}{\pi}\sin\left(\dfrac{\pi}{4}\right)g(t)\cos(4\pi Bt) + \dfrac{1}{\pi}\sin\left(\dfrac{\pi}{2}\right)g(t)\cos(8\pi Bt) + ...$

Suppose $g(t) \xleftrightarrow{F.T.} G(f)$

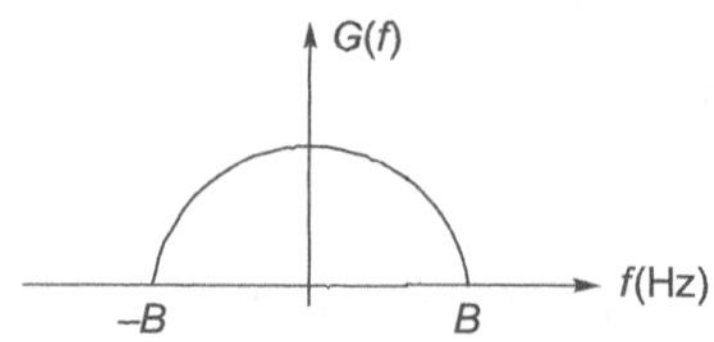

Then for $\dfrac{2}{\pi}\sin\dfrac{\pi}{4}g(t)\cdot\cos(4\pi Bt) \xleftrightarrow{F.T.}$

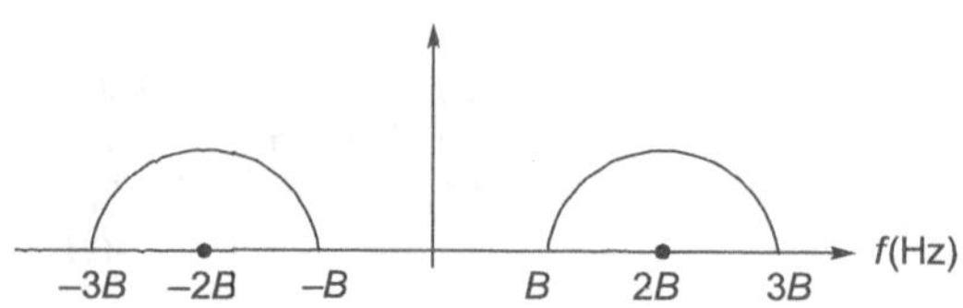

(By using modulation property of fourier transform)

It means to filter out $g(t)$ from $g_s(t)$ and to reject all other terms, we have to pass $g_s(t)$ through an LPF whose cut off frequency should be 'B' Hz and pass band gain should be '4'.

i.e.,

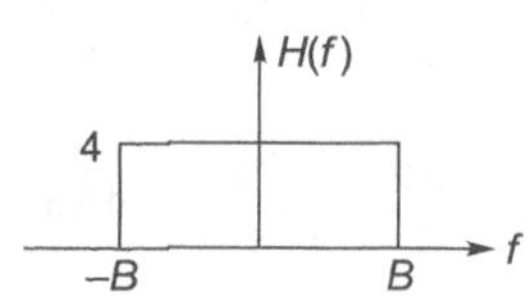

$$H(f) = 4\,\text{rect}\left(\frac{f}{2B}\right)$$

1.11 **A Gaussian pulse is specified by**

$$g(t) = Ae^{-\alpha^2 t^2},$$

where α is an arbitrary attenuation coefficient and A is constant. Show that the Fourier transform of $g(t)$ is also Gaussian.

[12 marks : 2020]

Solution:

$$G(\omega) = A\int_{-\infty}^{\infty} e^{-\alpha^2 t^2} e^{-j\omega t}\cdot dt$$

$$= A\int_{-\infty}^{\infty} e^{-(\alpha^2 t^2 + j\omega t)} dt$$

Substituting, $$\alpha^2 t^2 + j\omega t = \left(\alpha t + \frac{j\omega}{2\alpha}\right)^2 + \frac{\omega^2}{4\alpha^2}$$

$$G(\omega) = A\int_{-\infty}^{\infty} e^{-\left(\alpha t + \frac{j\omega}{2\alpha}\right)^2} \cdot e^{-\frac{\omega^2}{4\alpha^2}} dt$$

$$G(\omega) = Ae^{-\frac{\omega^2}{4\alpha^2}} \int_{-\infty}^{\infty} e^{-\left(\alpha t + j\frac{\omega}{2\alpha}\right)^2} dt$$

Let $$u = \alpha t + j\frac{\omega}{2\alpha}$$

$$du = \alpha\ dt$$

$$dt = \frac{du}{\alpha}$$

As $t \to \infty$, $u \to \infty$

As $t \to -\infty$, $u \to -\infty$

$$G(\omega) = Ae^{-\frac{\omega^2}{4\alpha^2}} \int_{-\infty}^{\infty} e^{-u^2} \cdot \frac{du}{\alpha}$$

$$= Ae^{-\frac{\omega^2}{4\alpha^2}} \cdot \frac{2}{\alpha}\int_{0}^{\infty} e^{-u^2} \cdot du$$

Since $$\int_0^{\infty} e^{-u^2} \cdot du = \frac{\sqrt{\pi}}{2}$$

$$G(\omega) = A\frac{\sqrt{\pi}}{2} \cdot e^{-\frac{\omega^2}{4\alpha^2}}$$

$G(\omega)$ is a Gaussian pulse

∴ Hence proved.

1.12 A continuous-time integrator has a system function $H_a(s) = \frac{1}{s}$.

(i) Design a discrete-time integrator using bilinear transformation and find the difference equation relating the input $x[n]$ to the output $y[n]$ of the discrete-time system.

(ii) Find the frequency response of the discrete-time integrator found in part (i) and determine whether or not this system is a good approximation of the continuous time system.

(For $\theta << 1$, $\sin\theta \approx \theta$ and $\cos\theta \approx 1 - \frac{\theta^2}{2}$)

[10+10 = 20 marks : 2020]

Solution:

Given that, $$H_a(s) = \frac{1}{s}$$

Where, $H_a(s)$ = System function of continuous time integrator

(i) Let $H(z)$ be the system function of discrete time integrator using Bilinear transformation. Hence, we can write

$$H(z) = Ha(s)\Big|_{s=\frac{2}{T}\left[\frac{1-z^{-1}}{1+z^{-1}}\right]}$$

Where T = sampling interval

$$= \frac{1}{s}\Big|_{s=\frac{2}{T}\left[\frac{1-z^{-1}}{1+z^{-1}}\right]}$$

$$\Rightarrow \quad \frac{Y(z)}{X(z)} = \frac{1}{\frac{2}{T}\left[\frac{1-z^{-1}}{1+z^{-1}}\right]}$$

$$\Rightarrow \quad \frac{Y(z)}{X(z)} = \frac{1+z^{-1}}{\frac{2}{T}\left[1-z^{-1}\right]}$$

$$\Rightarrow \quad \frac{2}{T}Y(z) - \frac{2}{T}Z^{-1}Y(z) = X(z) + z^{-1}X(z)$$

By applying inverse Z-T.

$$\frac{2}{T}y(n) - \frac{2}{T}y(n-1) = x(n) + x(n-1)$$

The above difference equation is for the desired discrete time integrator.

(ii) As we have seen that in part (i),

$$H(z) = \frac{1+z^{-1}}{\frac{2}{T}[1-z^{-1}]}$$

Put $z = e^{j\omega}$ in the above function

$$H(e^{j\omega}) = \frac{1+e^{-j\omega}}{\frac{2}{T}[1-e^{-j\omega}]} = \frac{1+\cos\omega - j\sin\omega}{\frac{2}{T}[1-\cos\omega + j\sin\omega]}$$

$$= \frac{(1+\cos\omega) - j\sin\omega}{\frac{2}{T}[(1-\cos\omega) + j\sin\omega]} \times \frac{1-\cos\omega - j\sin\omega}{1-\cos\omega - j\sin\omega}$$

$$\Rightarrow \quad H(e^{j\omega}) = \frac{[(1-j\sin\omega)+\cos\omega][(1-j\sin\omega)-\cos\omega]}{\frac{2}{T}[(1-\cos\omega)^2 + \sin^2\omega]}$$

$$= \frac{T}{2}\cdot\frac{(1-j\sin\omega)^2 - \cos^2\omega}{1+\cos^2\omega - 2\cos\omega + \sin^2\omega}$$

$$= \frac{T}{2}\cdot\frac{1-\sin^2\omega - 2j\sin\omega - \cos^2\omega}{2-2\cos\omega} \qquad \left[\because \sin^2\omega + \cos^2\omega = 1\right]$$

$$= \frac{T}{2}\cdot\frac{-2j\sin\omega}{2(1-\cos\omega)} = \frac{-T}{2}j\cdot\frac{\sin\omega}{1-\cos\omega}$$

$$= -\frac{Tj}{2}\frac{2\sin\frac{\omega}{2}\cos\frac{\omega}{2}}{2\sin^2\frac{\omega}{2}}$$

$$= -\frac{Tj}{2}\cdot\frac{\cos\frac{\omega}{2}}{\sin\frac{\omega}{2}} \quad \text{...(i)}$$

Since it is given that if $\theta << 1$ then $\sin\theta \approx \theta$ and $\cos\theta = 1-\frac{\theta^2}{2}$

So, by using the above approximation,

$$\cos\frac{\omega}{2} = \frac{1-(\omega/2)^2}{2} = 1-\frac{\omega^2}{8}$$

$$\sin\frac{\omega}{2} = \frac{\omega}{2}$$

By using equation (i),

$$H(e^{j\omega}) = -\frac{Tj}{2}\cdot\frac{\left(1-\frac{\omega^2}{8}\right)}{\frac{\omega}{2}} = -Tj\cdot\left[\frac{1-\frac{\omega^2}{8}}{\omega}\right]$$

Assuming, $T = 1$ sec,

$$H(e^{j\omega}) = -j\left[\frac{1-\frac{\omega^2}{8}}{\omega}\right]$$

Desired system function of discrete time integrator.

Now,

ω	$\lvert H(e^{j\omega})\rvert = \left\lvert\frac{1-\omega^2/8}{\omega}\right\rvert$
0	∞
1	7/8
2	1/4
$2\sqrt{2}$	0

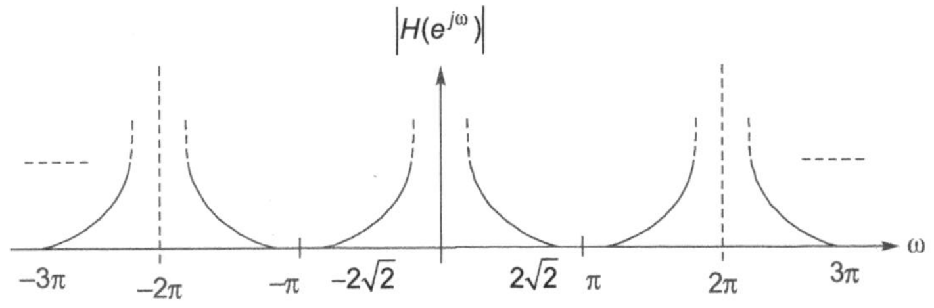

Since, the above magnitude characteristics of discrete time integrator is well approximating the magnitude characteristics of continuous time integrals. Therefore, the obtained discrete time integrator is good approximation of continous time integrators.

1.13 Given the following facts about a real signal $x(t)$ with Laplace transform $X(s)$:

A : $X(s)$ has exactly two poles

B : $X(s)$ has no zeros in the finite s-plane

C : $X(s)$ has a pole at $s = -1 + j$

D : $e^{2t}x(t)$ is not absolutely integrable

E : $X(0) = 8$

Determine $X(s)$ and specify its region of convergence.

[10+10 = 20 marks : 2020]

Solution:

Since $X(s)$ has exactly two poles in the finite s-plane, $X(s)$ can be written as

$$X(s) = \frac{A}{(s-a)(s-b)}$$

Since $x(t)$ is real, the poles of $X(s)$ must occur in conjugate reciprocal pairs.

Therefore $\quad b = a^*$

$$X(s) = \frac{A}{(s-a)(s-a^*)}$$

$$X(s) = \frac{A}{(s+1-j)(s+1+j)} = \frac{A}{(s+1)^2+1}$$

Given that, $\quad X(0) = 8$

$$\frac{A}{1+1} = 8$$

$$A = 16$$

$$\therefore \quad X(s) = \frac{16}{s^2+2s+2}$$

From the pole locations we know that there are two possible choices of ROC, either $\sigma > -1$ (or) $\sigma < -1$.

Given that $e^{2t}x(t)$ is not absolutely integrable,

Let $\quad y(t) = e^{2t}x(t) \xleftrightarrow{L.T.} Y(s) = X(s-2)$

The ROC of $Y(s)$ is the ROC of $X(s)$ shifted by 2 to the right. The poles of $Y(s)$ are located at $-1 + j + 2 = 1 + j$ and $-1 - j + 2 = 1 - j$.

Since it is given that $y(t)$ is not absolutely integrable, the ROC of $Y(s)$ should not include the $j\omega$-axis. This is possible only if ROC of $X(s)$ is $\sigma > -1$.

1.14 Let $x(t)$ be the rectangular pulse as shown in figure (1). Express the signal $y(t)$ shown in figure (2) in terms of rectangular pulse $x(t)$.

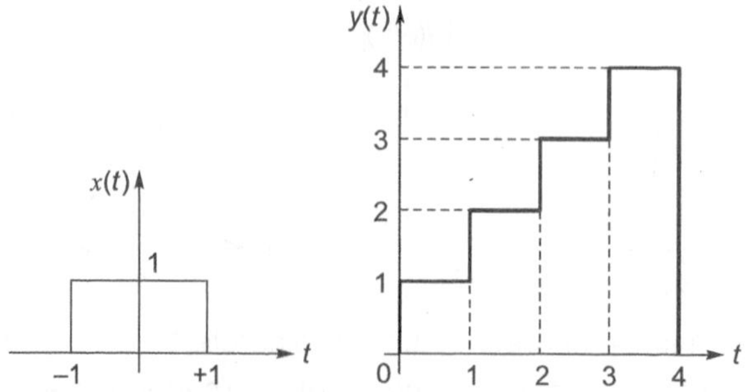

Figure (1) Figure (2)

[20 marks : 2021]

Solution:

Given that, rectangular pulse has width of 2.

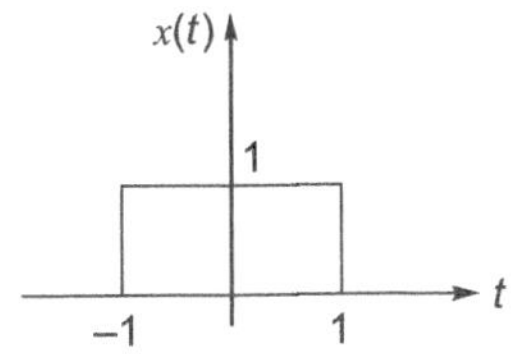

By performing time-scaling by '2', on $x(t)$

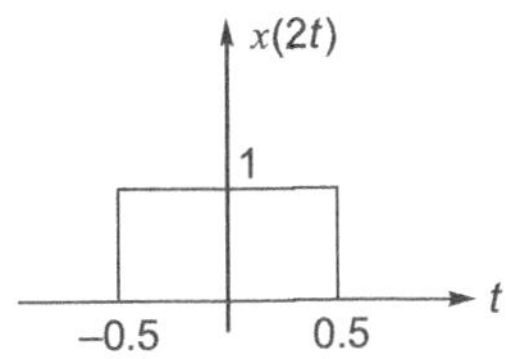

Let, $$p(t) = x(2t) \quad \text{...(i)}$$

It is also given that,

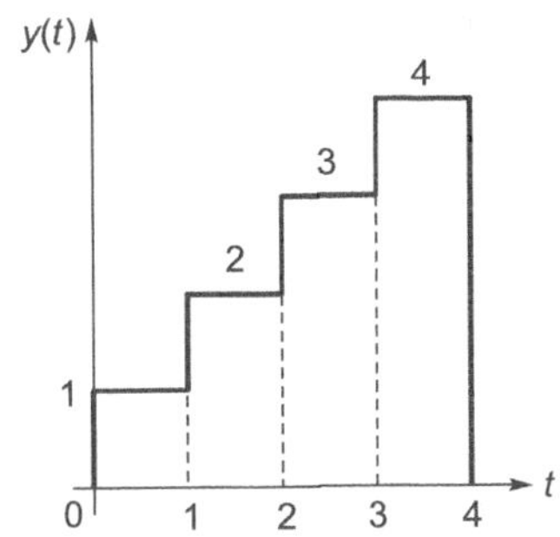

We can write $y(t)$ mathematically in the form mentioned below,

$$y(t) = y_1(t) + y_2(t) + y_3(t) + y_4(t) \quad \text{...(ii)}$$

Where,

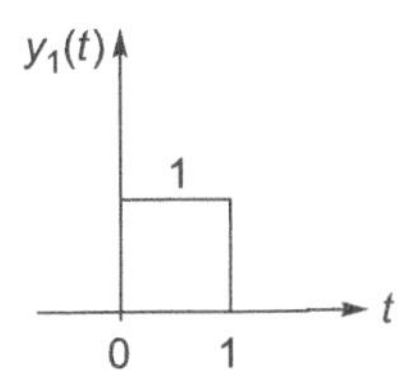

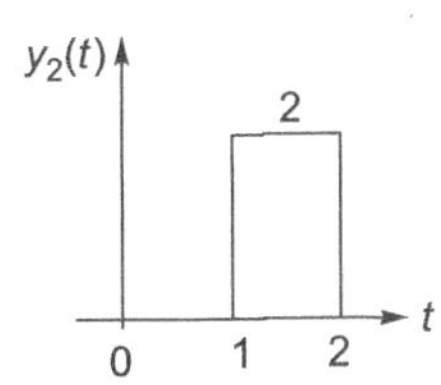

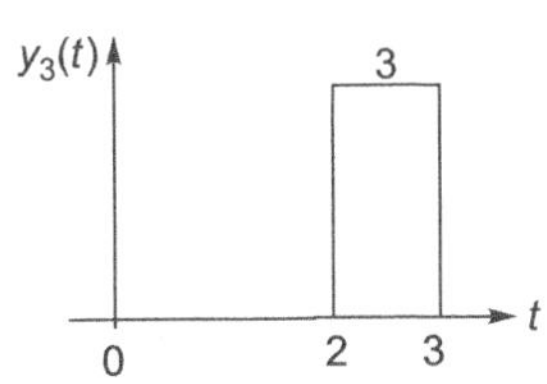

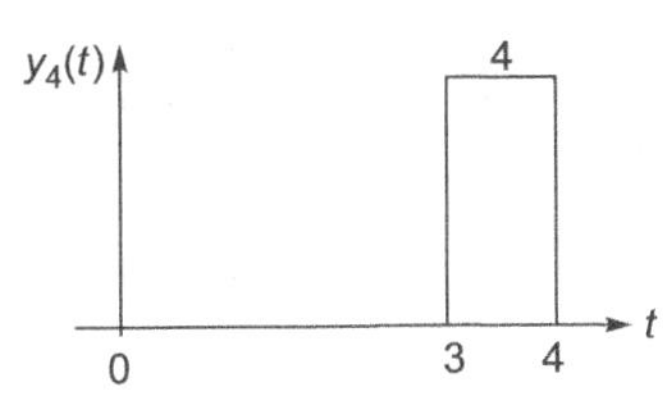

Now, we can relate $y_1(t)$, $y_2(t)$, $y_3(t)$ and $y_4(t)$ with $p(t)$ in the following way,

$$y_1(t) = p(t-0.5)$$
$$y_2(t) = p(t-1.5)$$
$$y_3(t) = p(t-2.5)$$
$$y_4(t) = p(t-3.5)$$

From equation (ii), $y(t)$ can be written as

$$y(t) = p(t-0.5) + p(t-1.5) + p(t-2.5) + p(t-3.5)$$

By using equation (i), $y(t)$ can be expressed in terms of $x(t)$ as follows

$$y(t) = x[2(t-0.5) + x[2(t-1.5)] + x[2(t-2.5)] + x[2(t-3.5)]$$

$$\Rightarrow \quad y(t) = [x(2t-1) + x(2t-3)] + x(2t-5) + x(2t-7)]$$

1.15 Consider the FIR filter described by the equation

$$y(n) = x(n) + x(n-4)$$

Determine its response to the input,

$$x(n) = \cos\left(\frac{\pi}{2}n\right) + \cos\left(\frac{\pi}{4}n\right), -\infty < n < \infty.$$

Comment on the result obtained.

[12 marks : 2021]

Solution:

Given that the difference equation of an FIR filter is

$$y(n) = x(n) + x(n-4) \quad \text{...(i)}$$

System input is given as

$$x(n) = \cos\frac{\pi}{2}n + \cos\frac{\pi}{4}n$$

From (i), we can obtain response in the following way,

$$y(n) = \left(\cos\frac{\pi}{2}n + \cos\frac{\pi}{4}n\right) + \cos\left[\frac{\pi}{4}(n-4)\right] + \cos\left[\frac{\pi}{2}(n-4)\right]$$

$$= \cos\frac{\pi}{2}n + \cos\frac{\pi}{4}n + \cos\left(\frac{\pi}{2}n - 2\pi\right) + \cos\left(\frac{\pi}{4}n - \pi\right)$$

$$= \cos\frac{\pi}{2}n + \cos\frac{\pi}{4}n + \cos\left(2\pi - \frac{\pi}{2}n\right) + \cos\left(\pi - \frac{\pi}{4}n\right) \quad [\because \cos(-\theta) = \cos(\theta)]$$

$$= \cos\frac{\pi}{2}n + \cos\frac{\pi}{4}n + \cos\frac{\pi}{2}n - \cos\frac{\pi}{4}n \quad [\because \cos(2\pi-\theta) = \cos\theta, \cos(\pi-\theta) = -\cos\theta]$$

Thus, $$y(n) = 2\cos\frac{\pi}{2}n$$

Since, output is containing only one frequency component of $\frac{\pi}{2}$ rad/sample whereas input was containing two-frequency components of $\frac{\pi}{4}$ rad/sample and $\frac{\pi}{2}$ rad/sample. Therefore, we can conclude that $\frac{\pi}{2}$ rad/sample is lying in the passband and $\frac{\pi}{4}$ rad/sample is lying in the stopband of given FIR-filter.

1.16 Determine the unilateral Laplace transform of the signals given below. Specify the property used, if any, in each step.

(i) $x(t) = u(t-1) * e^{-2t} u(t-1)$.

(ii) $x(t) = t \cdot \frac{d}{dt}(e^{-t} \cdot \cos(t)u(t))$.

[20 marks : 2021]

Solution:

(i) Given signal :
$$x(t) = u(t-1) * e^{-2t} u(t-1)$$
$$= x_1(t) * x_2(t) \quad \text{...(i)}$$

where,
$$x_1(t) = u(t-1) \rightleftharpoons X_1(s)$$
$$x_2(t) = e^{-2t} u(t-1) \rightleftharpoons X_2(s)$$

Now,
$$u(t) \rightleftharpoons \frac{1}{s}$$
$$u(t-1) \rightleftharpoons \frac{e^{-s}}{s}, \text{ by time shifting property}$$
$$e^{-2t} u(t-1) \rightleftharpoons \frac{e^{-(s+2)}}{s+2}, \text{ by frequency shifting property}$$

By using convolution in time property of unilateral LT on equation,
$$X(s) = X_1(s) \cdot X_2(s)$$
$$= \frac{e^{-s}}{s} \cdot \frac{e^{-(s+2)}}{s+2}$$
$$\Rightarrow \quad X(s) = \frac{e^{-2(s+1)}}{s(s+2)}$$

(ii) Given signal :
$$x(t) = t \cdot \frac{d}{dt}\left[e^{-t} \cdot \cos t\, u(t)\right]$$
$$\Rightarrow \quad x(t) = t\, y(t) \quad \text{...(i)}$$

Where,
$$y(t) = \frac{d}{dt}\left[e^{-t} \cdot \cos t\, u(t)\right]$$

For,
$$\cos t\, u(t) \rightleftharpoons \frac{s}{s^2+1}$$
$$e^{-t} \cos t \cdot u(t) \rightleftharpoons \frac{(s+1)}{(s+1)^2+1} \quad \text{...frequency shifting property}$$
$$y(t) = \frac{d}{dt}\left[e^{-t} \cos t\, u(t)\right] \rightleftharpoons \frac{s(s+1)}{(s+1)^2+1} = Y(s)$$
...differentiation in time property

From (i),
$$x(t) = t\, y(t)$$

By using differentiation in frequency property,

$$X(s) = -\frac{dY(s)}{ds} = -\frac{d}{ds}\left[\frac{s(s+1)}{(s+1)^2+1}\right] = -\frac{d}{ds}\left[\frac{s^2+s}{s^2+2s+2}\right]$$

$$= -\left[\frac{(2s+1)(s^2+2s+2)-(2s+2)(s^2+s)}{(s^2+2s+2)^2}\right]$$

$$\Rightarrow \qquad X(s) = \frac{-(s^2+4s+2)}{(s^2+2s+2)^2}$$

1.17 Let an analog filter have a transfer function

$$H(s) = \frac{s+0.5}{(s+0.5)^2+16}$$

Use bilinear transformation method to convert analog filter into a digital filter.

Assume the resonant frequency of $\omega_r = \frac{\pi}{2}$ for the digital IIR filter.

[12 marks : 2022]

Solution:

Given : $\omega_r = \frac{\pi}{2}$

From the system transfer function, we note that $\Omega_c = 4$. The sampling period can be determined as

$$\Omega_c = \frac{2}{T_s}\tan\frac{\omega_r}{2}$$

$$4 = \frac{2}{T_s}\tan\frac{\pi}{4}$$

$$T_s = \frac{1}{2}\text{sec}$$

Using bilinear transformation

$$H(z) = H(s)\Big|_{s=\frac{2(z-1)}{T(z+1)}}$$

$$H(z) = \frac{\frac{4(z-1)}{(z+1)}+0.5}{\left[\frac{4(z-1)}{(z+1)}+0.5\right]^2+16}$$

$$= \frac{[4(z-1)+0.5(z+1)](z+1)}{[4(z-1)+0.5(z+1)]^2+16(z+1)^2}$$

$$= \frac{(4z-4+0.5z+0.5)(z+1)}{16(z-1)^2+0.25(z+1)^2+4(z-1)(z+1)+16(z+1)^2}$$

$$= \frac{(4.5z-3.5)(z+1)}{16(z^2-2z+1)+16.25(z^2+2z+1)+4z^2-4}$$

$$H(z) = \frac{4.5z^2+z-3.5}{36.25z^2+0.5z+28.25}$$

$$H(z) = \frac{4.5 + z^{-1} - 3.5z^{-2}}{36.25 + 0.5z^{-1} + 28.25z^{-2}} \text{ (Required bilinear transformation)}$$

1.18 The transfer function of a 2nd order filter has a zero at the origin of the *s*-plane while its poles are located at $s = -3 \pm j4$ rad/sec. Identify the filter, if the magnitude of the voltage gain at 5 rad/sec = 1. Also plot the magnitude of the voltage gain as the input signal frequency is varied between $\omega = 0$ to $\omega = \infty$.

[8 marks : 2022]

Solution:

(ii) Poles : $s = -3 \pm j4$

Zeros : $s = 0$

∴ Transfer function of 2nd order is given as

$$H(s) = \frac{K.s}{(s+3)^2 + 16} = \frac{Ks}{s^2 + 6s + 25}$$

$$|H(j\omega)||_{\omega=5} = \left|\frac{K(5)}{-25 + 30j + 2s}\right| = 1$$

$$\frac{5K}{30} = 1$$

$$K = 6$$

∴ $$H(j\omega) = \frac{6(j\omega)}{2s - \omega^2 + 6j\omega}$$

$$|H(j\omega)| = \frac{6\omega}{\sqrt{(2s - \omega^2)^2 + (6\omega)^2}}$$

At $\omega = 0$, $|H(j\omega)| = 0$

At $\omega = 1$, $|H(j\omega)| = 0.242$

At $\omega = 10$, $|H(j\omega)| = 0.624$

At $\omega = 15$, $|H(j\omega)| = 0.410$

At $\omega = 20$, $|H(j\omega)| = 0.304$

At $\omega = 30$, $|H(j\omega)| = 0.2014$

At $\omega = 50$, $|H(j\omega)| = 0.12$

At $\omega = 100$, $|H(j\omega)| = 0.059$

Plot $|H(j\omega)|$ (voltage gain) $V_s\omega$

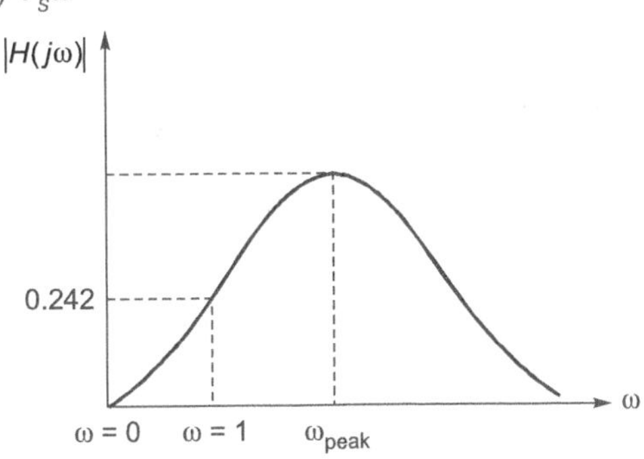

From the plot, we can see that, it is a band pass filter.

1.19 Consider the unilateral Laplace transform pair $\cos(2t)u(t) \xleftrightarrow{Lu} X(s)$. Using the Laplace transform properties, determine the time signals corresponding to the following :

(i) $X(2s)$

(ii) $(s + 4)X(s)$

(iii) $\frac{d}{ds}(e^{-5s}X(s))$

(iv) $s^{-2}X(s)$

[20 marks : 2022]

Solution:

$$x(t) = \cos(2t)u(t) \rightleftharpoons X(s) = \frac{s}{s^2+4}$$

(i) Time-scaling property : $x(at),\ a \neq 0 \rightleftharpoons \frac{1}{|a|}X\left(\frac{s}{a}\right)$

Put $a = \frac{1}{2}$

$$x\left(\frac{t}{2}\right) \rightleftharpoons 2X(2s)$$

$$\frac{1}{2}x\left(\frac{t}{2}\right) \rightleftharpoons X(2s)$$

Let $F(s) = X(2s)$

Therefore, $f(t) = \frac{1}{2}x\left(\frac{t}{2}\right) = \frac{1}{2}\cos 2\left(\frac{t}{2}\right) = \frac{1}{2}\cos t$

(ii) Differentiation in time property :

$$\frac{dx(t)}{dt} \rightleftharpoons sX(s) - x(0^-) \quad \text{...(1)}$$

$\because$ $x(t) = \cos 3t u(t)$

$\therefore$ $x(0^-) = 0$

From (1), $\frac{dx(t)}{dt} \rightleftharpoons sX(s)$

Let $F(s) = (s + 4)X(s) = sX(s) + 4X(s)$

Therefore, $f(t) = \frac{dx(t)}{dt} + 4x(t)$

$$= \frac{d}{dt}[\cos 2t.u(t)] + 4\cos 2tu(t)$$

$\Rightarrow$ $f(t) = [-2\sin 2tu(t) + \cos 2t\delta(t)] + 4\cos 2tu(t)$

$= -2\sin 2t.u(t) + \delta(t) + 4\cos 2t.u(t)$

$\Rightarrow$ $f(t) = [4\cos 2t - 2\sin 2t]u(t) + \delta(t)$ $\quad [\because \cos 2t.\delta(t) = \cos 0\,\delta(t) = \delta(t)]$

(iii) Time-shifting property :

$$x(t - t_o) \rightleftharpoons X(s).e^{-st_o}$$

Put $t_o = 5$

$$x(t-5) \rightleftharpoons X(s).e^{-5s}$$

Let $$F(s) \rightleftharpoons e^{-5s}X(s)$$

Therefore, $$f(t) = x(t-5)$$

By applying differentiation in frequency property,

$$tf(t) \rightleftharpoons \frac{-dF(s)}{ds}$$

$$\Rightarrow \quad -tf(t) \rightleftharpoons \frac{dF(s)}{ds}$$

$$\Rightarrow \quad -tx(t-5) \rightleftharpoons \frac{d}{ds}[e^{-5s}X(s)]$$

(iv) $$s^{-2}X(s) = s^{-2}\cdot\frac{s}{s^2+4}$$

$$= \frac{1}{s(s^2+4)}$$

$$= \frac{A}{s}+\frac{Bs+C}{s^2+4}$$

$$= \frac{As^2+4A+Bs^2+Cs}{s(s^2+4)}$$

$$A + B = 0,\ 4A = 1,\ C = 0$$

$$\Rightarrow \quad B = -\frac{1}{4},\ A = \frac{1}{4}$$

$$\Rightarrow \quad s^{-2}X(s) = \frac{\frac{1}{4}}{s}-\frac{\frac{1}{4}s}{s^2+4}$$

Take laplace inverse of above expression

$$x(t) = \frac{1}{4}u(t)-\frac{1}{4}\cos(2t)u(t)$$

$$= \frac{1}{4}[1-\cos(2t)]u(t)$$

1.20 Consider the trapezoidal function $x(t)$ as shown below. Express $x(t)$ in terms of ramp function and find its Fourier transform. Specify the Fourier transform property used (if any).

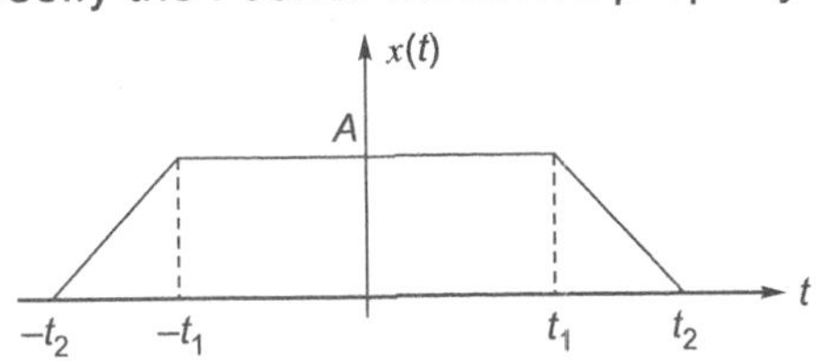

[20 marks : 2022]

Solution:

Given signal $x(t)$ be represented in terms of ramp signal as

$$x(t) = \frac{A}{t_2-t_1}r(t+t_2)-\frac{A}{t_2-t_1}r(t+t_1)-\frac{A}{t_2-t_1}r(t-t_1)+\frac{A}{t_2-t_1}r(t-t_2)$$

$$x(t) = \frac{A}{(t_2 - t_1)}[r(t+t_2) - r(t+t_1) - r(t-t_1) + r(t-t_2)]$$

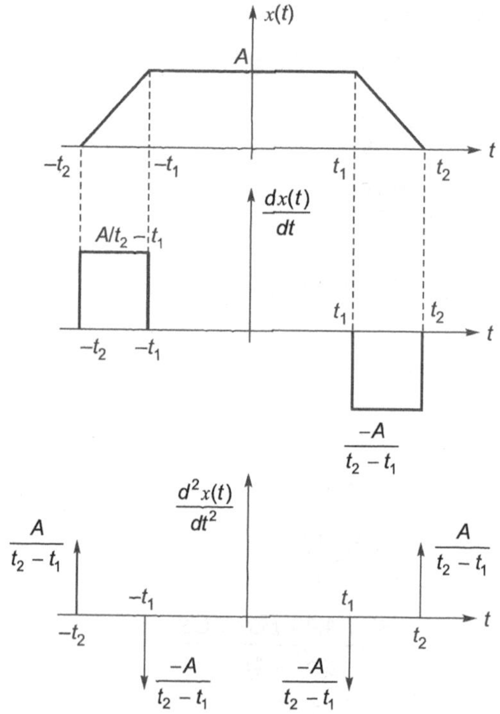

Now,
$$\frac{d^2x(t)}{dt^2} = \frac{A}{(t_2 - t_1)}[\delta(t+t_2) - \delta(t+t_1) - \delta(t-t_1) + \delta(t-t_2)] \quad ...(1)$$

As we know,

$$\delta(t) \xleftrightarrow{F.T.} 1$$

$$\delta(t+t_2) \xleftrightarrow{F.T.} e^{j\omega t_2} \quad \text{(Time shifting property)}$$

$$\delta(t-t_2) \xleftrightarrow{F.T.} e^{-j\omega t_2}$$

$$\delta(t+t_1) \xleftrightarrow{F.T.} e^{j\omega t_1}$$

$$\delta(t-t_1) \xleftrightarrow{F.T.} e^{-j\omega t_1}$$

Also using the differentiation property

$$x(t) \xleftrightarrow{F.T.} X(\omega)$$

$$\frac{dx(t)}{dt} \xleftrightarrow{F.T.} j\omega X(\omega)$$

$$\frac{d^2x(t)}{dt^2} \xleftrightarrow{F.T.} (j\omega)^2 X(\omega)$$

Substituting all the above results in eqn. (1)

$$(j\omega)^2 X(\omega) = \frac{A}{(t_2 - t_1)}[e^{j\omega t_2} - e^{+j\omega t_1} - e^{-j\omega t_1} + e^{-j\omega t_2}]$$

$$X(\omega) = \frac{A}{(j\omega)^2(t_2 - t_1)}[e^{j\omega t_2} + e^{-j\omega t_2} - (e^{j\omega t_1} + e^{-j\omega t_1})]$$

$$= \frac{2A}{\omega^2(t_2 - t_1)}\left[\frac{(e^{j\omega t_1} + e^{-j\omega t_1})}{2} - \frac{(e^{j\omega t_2} + e^{-j\omega t_2})}{2}\right]$$

$$X(\omega) = \frac{2A}{\omega^2(t_2 - t_1)}[\cos\omega t_1 - \cos\omega t_2]$$

1.21 Consider the sequence $x(n) = \left(\frac{1}{2}\right)^n u(n)$ and $y(n) = \left(\frac{1}{3}\right)^{n-2} u(n-2)$. Use the convolution property of Z-transform to find the convolution of the two sequences, $q(n) = x(n)*y(n)$. Validate your result using time-domain method of convolution.

[20 marks : 2022]

Solution:

Given :

$$x(n) = \left(\frac{1}{2}\right)^n u(n)$$

$$y(n) = \left(\frac{1}{3}\right)^{n-2} u(n-2)$$

Given a new signal,

$$q(n) = x(n) * y(n)$$

$$\Updownarrow \text{Z.T.}$$

$$Q(z) = X(z).Y(z) \quad \text{...(1)}$$

As we know,

$$x(n) = \left(\frac{1}{2}\right)^n u(n) \xrightleftharpoons{\text{Z.T.}} X(z) = \frac{z}{z-0.5};\ |z| > 0.5$$

$$y_1(n) = \left(\frac{1}{3}\right)^n u(n) \xrightleftharpoons{\text{Z.T.}} Y_1(z) = \frac{z}{z-\frac{1}{3}};\ |z| > \frac{1}{3} \quad \text{...(2)}$$

Now,

$$y(n) = y_1(n-2)$$

$$\Updownarrow \text{Z.T.}$$

$$y(z) = z^{-2}Y_1(z)$$

Substituting above result in eqn. (2)

$$Y(z) = \frac{z^{-1}}{z-\frac{1}{3}}$$

On putting values of $X(z)$ and $Y(z)$ in eqn. (1)

$$Q(z) = \frac{1}{\left(z-\frac{1}{2}\right)\left(z-\frac{1}{3}\right)}$$

$$Q(z) = \frac{A}{z-\frac{1}{2}} + \frac{B}{z-\frac{1}{3}}$$

$$A = Q(z)\cdot\left(z-\frac{1}{2}\right)\Bigg|_{z=\frac{1}{2}} = \frac{1}{\frac{1}{2}-\frac{1}{3}} = 6$$

$$B = Q(z)\cdot\left(z-\frac{1}{3}\right)\Bigg|_{z=\frac{1}{3}} = \frac{1}{\frac{1}{3}-\frac{1}{2}} = -6$$

Therefore,

$$Q(z) = \frac{6}{z-\frac{1}{2}} - \frac{6}{z-\frac{1}{3}} = z^{-1}\left(\frac{6z}{z-\frac{1}{2}} - \frac{6z}{z-\frac{1}{3}}\right)$$

$\Downarrow\Uparrow$ I.Z.T.

$$q(n) = 6\left(\frac{1}{2}\right)^{n-2} u(n-1) - 6\left(\frac{1}{3}\right)^{n-1} u(n-1) \qquad ...(1)$$

By using time domain approach :

$$q(n) = \sum_{K=-\infty}^{\infty} y(k)\cdot x(n-k)$$

$$= \sum_{K=-\infty}^{\infty} \left(\frac{1}{3}\right)^{K-2} u(K-2)\cdot\left(\frac{1}{2}\right)^{n-K} u(n-K)$$

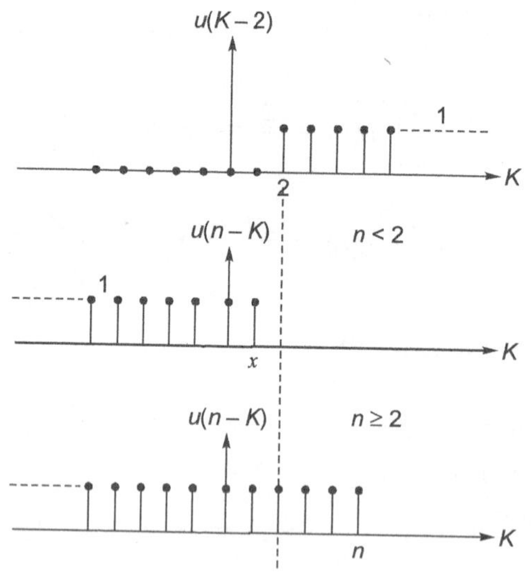

Thus,

$$q(n) = \begin{cases} 0, & \text{for } n < 2 \\ \sum_{K=2}^{n} \left(\frac{1}{3}\right)^{K-2} \cdot \left(\frac{1}{2}\right)^{n-K} & \text{for } n \geq 2 \end{cases}$$

$$= \begin{cases} 0, & \text{for } n < 2 \\ 9\cdot\left(\frac{1}{2}\right)^{n} \sum_{K=2}^{n} \left(\frac{2}{3}\right)^{K} & \text{for } n \geq 2 \end{cases}$$

$$= \begin{cases} 0, & \text{for } n < 2 \\ 9\cdot\left(\frac{1}{2}\right)^n \cdot \dfrac{\left(\frac{2}{3}\right)^2\left[1-\left(\frac{2}{3}\right)^{n-1}\right]}{1-\frac{2}{3}} & \text{for } n \geq 2 \end{cases}$$

$$\Rightarrow \qquad q(n) = \begin{cases} 0, & \text{for } n < 2 \\ \dfrac{9\cdot\left(\frac{1}{2}\right)^n \cdot \frac{4}{9}\left[1-\left(\frac{2}{3}\right)^{n-1}\right]}{\frac{1}{3}} & \text{for } n \geq 2 \end{cases}$$

$$= \begin{cases} 0, & \text{for } n < 2 \\ 3\cdot\left(\frac{1}{2}\right)^{n-2}\left[1-\left(\frac{2}{3}\right)^{n-1}\right] & \text{for } n \geq 2 \end{cases}$$

$$= \begin{cases} 0, & \text{for } n < 2 \\ 3\left[\left(\frac{1}{2}\right)^{n-2} - 2\left(\frac{1}{3}\right)^{n-1}\right] & \text{for } n \geq 2 \end{cases}$$

$$= \begin{cases} 0, & \text{for } n < 2 \\ 6\left[\left(\frac{1}{2}\right)^{n-1} - \left(\frac{1}{3}\right)^{n-1}\right] & \text{for } n \geq 2 \end{cases}$$

$$= 6\left[\left(\frac{1}{2}\right)^{n-1} - \left(\frac{1}{3}\right)^{n-1}\right]u(n-2) \qquad \text{...(1)}$$

Since, $\quad q(n)|_{n=1} = 0$

So, we can write eqn. (1) in the following form also,

$$q(n) = 6\left[\left(\frac{1}{2}\right)^{n-1} - \left(\frac{1}{3}\right)^{n-1}\right]u(n-1)$$

Hence, result obtained from convolution property of z-transform is validated using time domain approach of convolution.

1.22 **Find $x(t) * g(t)$, using graphical convolution.**

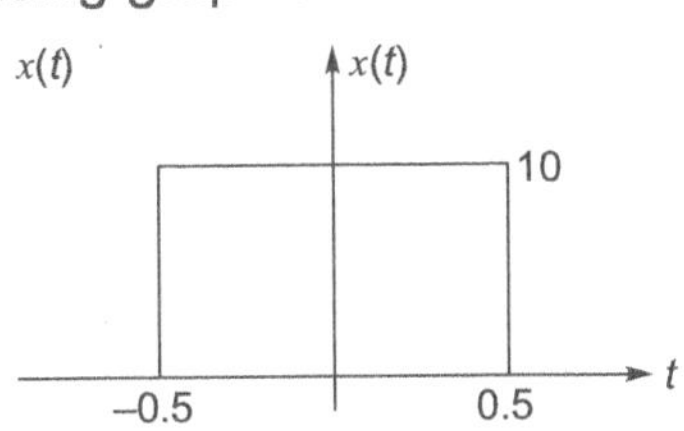

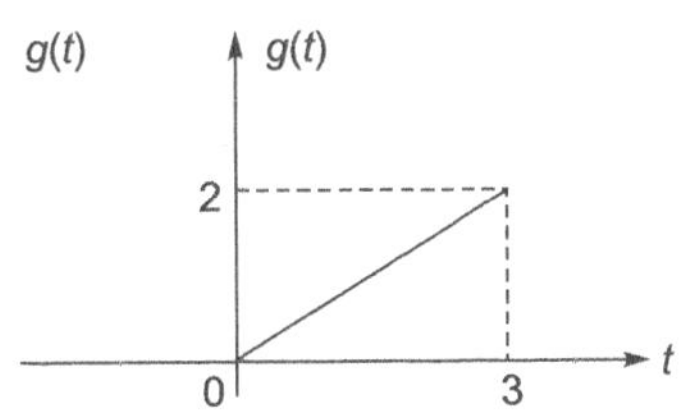

[20 marks : 2023]

Solution:

Given, $\quad y(t) = x(t) * g(t)$

So, $\quad y(t) = \int_{-\infty}^{\infty} g(\tau)\cdot x(t-\tau)d\tau$

Case-I:

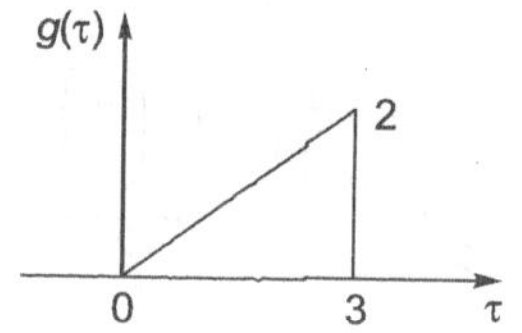

When $0.5 + t < 0$

$\Rightarrow \quad t < -0.5$

then, $\quad y(t) = 0$

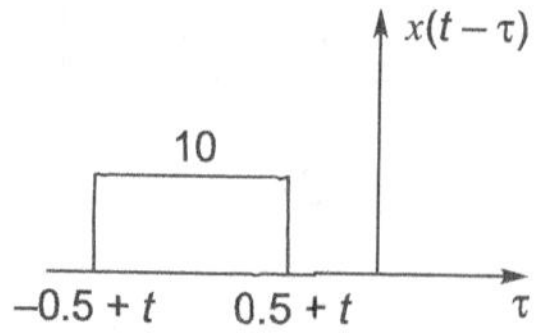

Case-II:

When $-0.5 + t < 0$ but $0.5 + t > 0$

i.e., $-0.5 < t < 0.5$

then,
$$y(t) = \int_0^{0.5+t} 10 \cdot \frac{2}{3}\tau \, d\tau = \frac{20}{3}\left[\frac{\tau^2}{2}\right]_0^{0.5+t} = \frac{10}{3}(0.5+t)^2$$

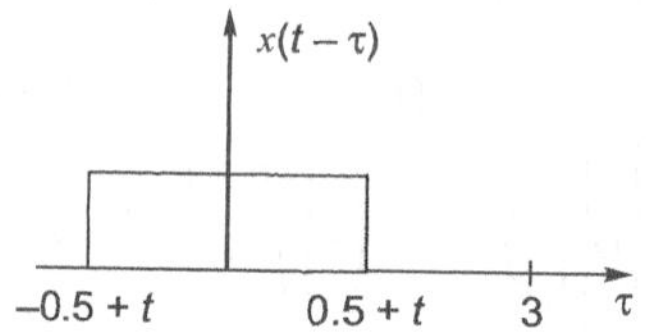

Case-III:

When $-0.5 + t > 0$ but $0.5 + t < 3$

i.e., $\quad 0.5 < t < 2.5$

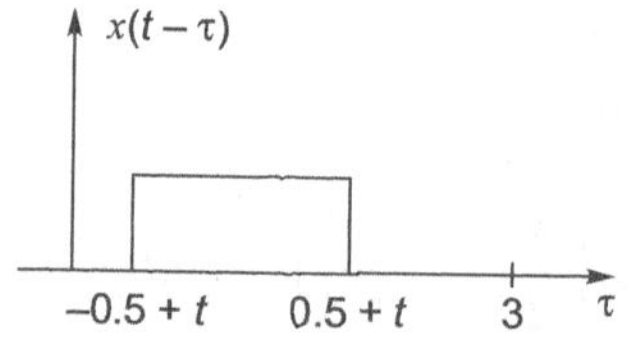

$$y(t) = \int_{-0.5+t}^{0.5+t} 10 \cdot \frac{2}{3}\tau \, d\tau = \frac{20}{3}\left[\frac{\tau^2}{2}\right]_{-0.5+t}^{0.5+t}$$

$$= \frac{10}{3}\left[(0.5+t)^2 - (-0.5+t)^2\right]$$

$$= \frac{20}{3}t$$

Case-IV:

When $-0.5 + t < 3$ but $0.5 + t > 3$

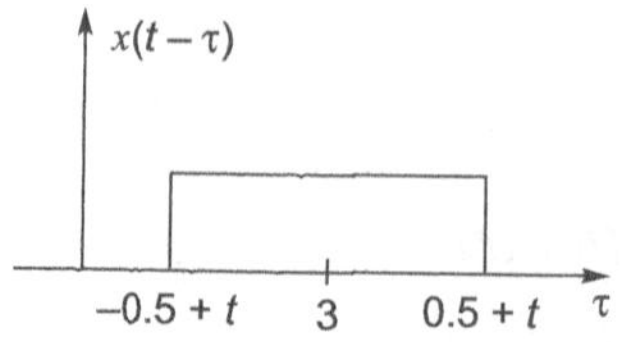

i.e., $2.5 < t < 3.5$

then,
$$y(t) = \int_{-0.5+t}^{3} 10\cdot\frac{2}{3}\tau\, d\tau = \frac{20}{3}\left[\frac{\tau^2}{2}\right]_{-0.5+t}^{3}$$
$$= \frac{10}{3}\left[9-(-0.5+t)^2\right] = \frac{10}{3}\left[8.75-t^2+t\right]$$

Case-V:
When $-0.5 + t > 3$,
i.e., $t > 3.5$

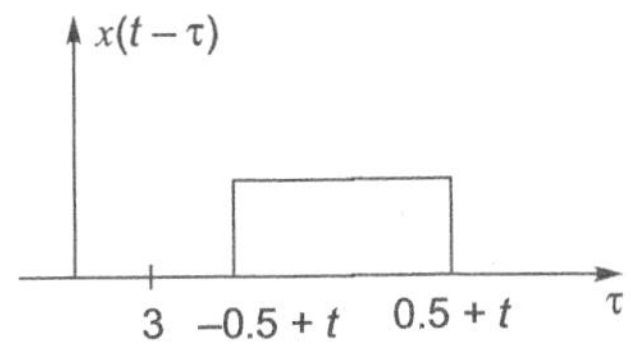

then $y(t) = 0$

Thus,
$$y(t) = \begin{cases} 0, & \text{for } t < -0.5 \\ \frac{10}{3}(0.5+t)^2, & \text{for } -0.5 < t < 0.5 \\ \frac{20t}{3}, & \text{for } 0.5 < t < 2.5 \\ \frac{10}{3}[8.75-t^2+t], & \text{for } 2.5 < t < 3.5 \\ 0, & \text{for } t > 3.5 \end{cases}$$

1.23 Find the Laplace transform of the signal given below.

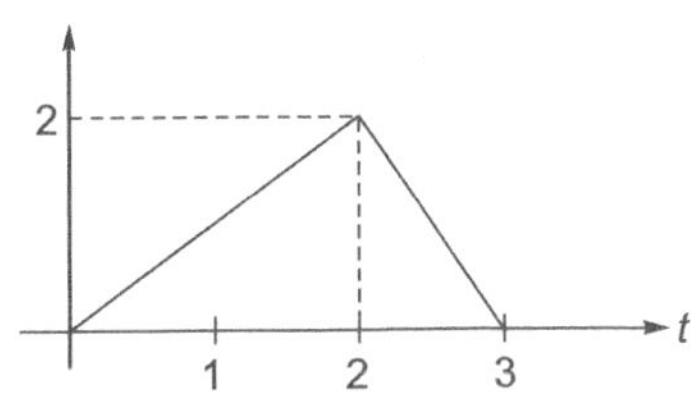

[12 marks : 2023]

Solution:

Given wave form is

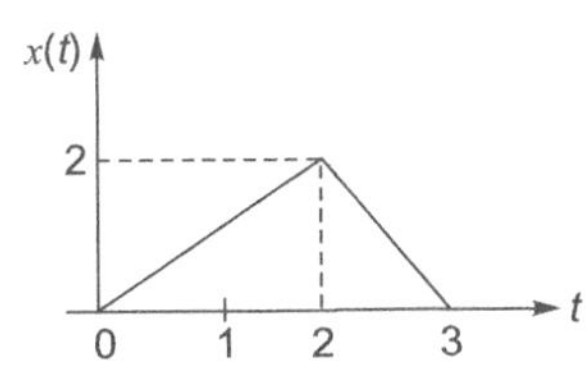

Step-I:
Waveform (i)

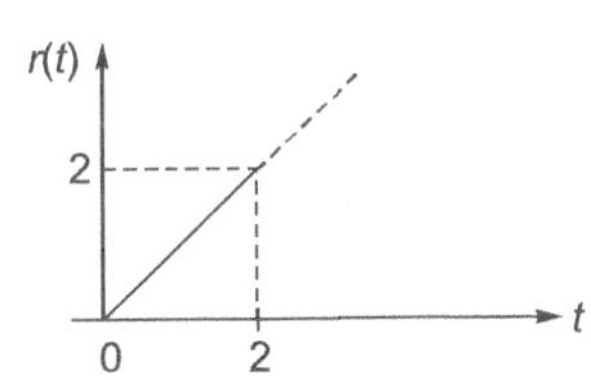

Step-II:

Waveform (ii)

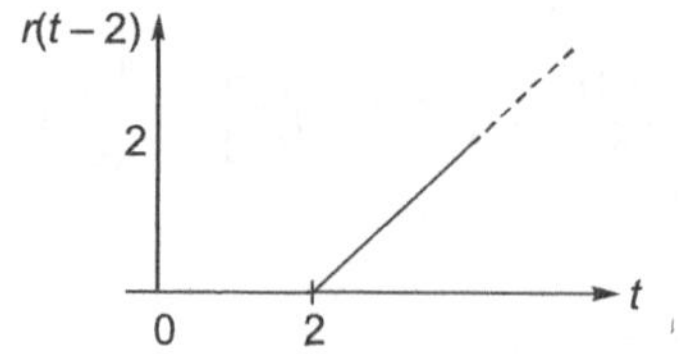

Step-III:

Waveform (iii) = Waveform, (i) - (ii),

$r(t) - r(t-2)$

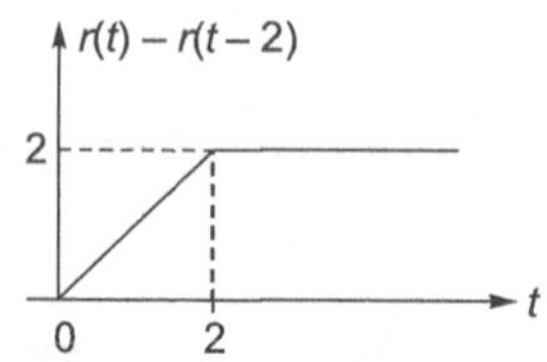

Step-IV:

Waveform (iv)

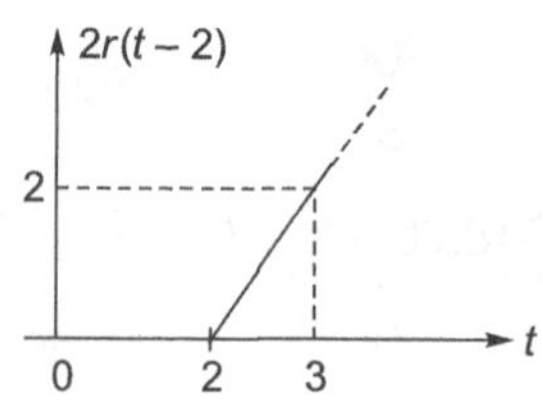

Step-V:

Waveform (v) = Waveform (iii) – (iv)

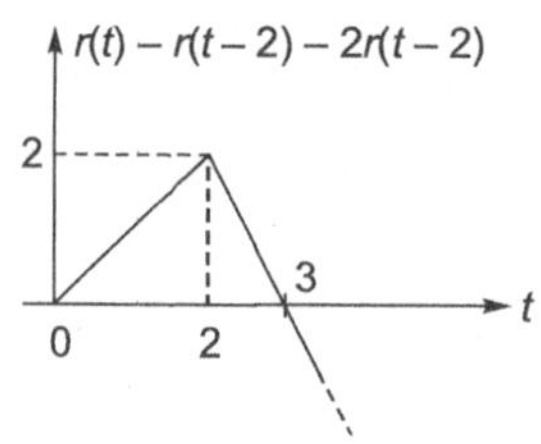

Step-VI:

Waveform (vi)

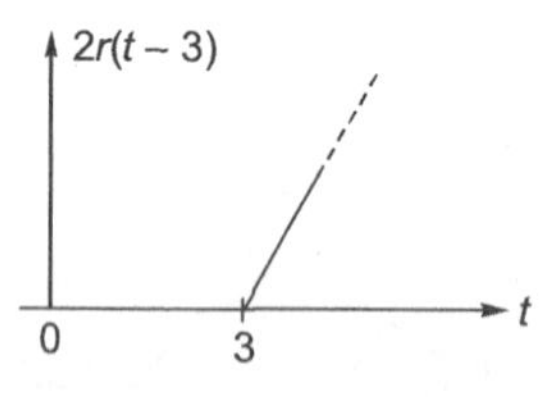

Step-VII:

Waveform (vii) = Waveform (v) + (vi)

$$x(t) = [r(t) - r(t-2) - 2r(t-2)] + 2r(t-3)$$

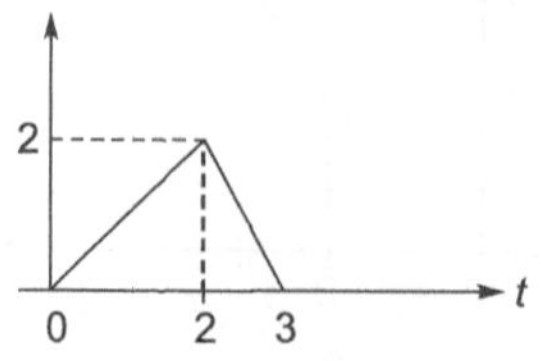

Thus, $$x(t) = r(t) - 3r(t-2) + 2r(t-3)$$

Now, $$r(t) \rightleftharpoons \frac{1}{s^2}$$

$$-3\,r(t-2) \rightleftharpoons \frac{-3}{s^2}e^{-2s}$$ ...by time-shifting property

$$2\,r(t-3) \rightleftharpoons \frac{2}{s^2}e^{-3s}$$ ...by time shifting property

Therefore Laplace transform of $x(t)$ is

$$X(s) = \frac{1}{s^2} - \frac{3}{s^2}e^{-2s} + \frac{2}{s^2}e^{-3s}$$

$$= \frac{1}{s^2}\left[1 - 3e^{-2s} + 2e^{-3s}\right]$$

1.24 **Find the time response, initial value and final value of the given function,**

$$F(s) = \frac{12(s+1)}{s(s+2)^2(s+3)}$$

[12 marks : 2023]

Solution:

Given function is :

$$F(s) = \frac{12(s+1)}{s(s+2)^2(s+3)}$$

For residue of $s = 0$

$$A = 1$$

For residue of $s = -2$.

Put $s = -2$ in $F(s)$

$$B = \frac{12 \times -1}{-2 \times 1} = 6$$

For residue of $s = -3$

$$C = \frac{12 \times -2}{-3 \times 1} = 8$$

For residue of $s = -2$, apply partial fraction

$$\frac{12(s+1)}{s(s+2)^2(s+3)} = \frac{A}{s} + \frac{B}{(s+2)^2} + \frac{C}{(s+3)^2} + \frac{D}{s+2}$$

$$\frac{12(s+1)}{s(s+2)^2(s+3)} = \frac{1}{s} + \frac{6}{(s+2)^2} + \frac{8}{(s+3)^2} + \frac{D}{(s+2)}$$

$$= \frac{(s+2)^2(s+3) + 6(s+3)s + 8s(s+2)^2 + D[s(s+2)(s+3)]}{s(s+3)(s+2)^2}$$

On comparing,

$$16 + 18 + 32 + 6D = 12$$

$$D = -9$$

$$F(s) = \frac{1}{s} + \frac{6}{(s+2)^2} + \frac{8}{(s+3)} - \frac{9}{(s+2)}$$

On taking inverse laplace transform

$$f(t) = 1 + 6te^{-2t} + 8e^{-3t} - 9e^{-2t}$$

By applying initial value theorem

$$f(t)\big|_{t=0} = \lim_{s\to\infty} sF(s) = \lim_{s\to\infty} \frac{12s(s+1)}{s(s+2)^2(s+3)}$$

Required initial value is,

$$\lim_{s\to 0} sF(s) = 0$$

By applying final value theorem

$$f(t)\big|_{t\to\infty} = \lim_{s\to 0} sF(s) = \lim_{s\to 0} \frac{s\cdot 12(s+1)}{s(s+2)^2(s+3)}$$

Required final value is, $\lim_{s\to 0} sF(s) = 1$

1.25 **Determine the Fourier transform of a pulse shown below.**

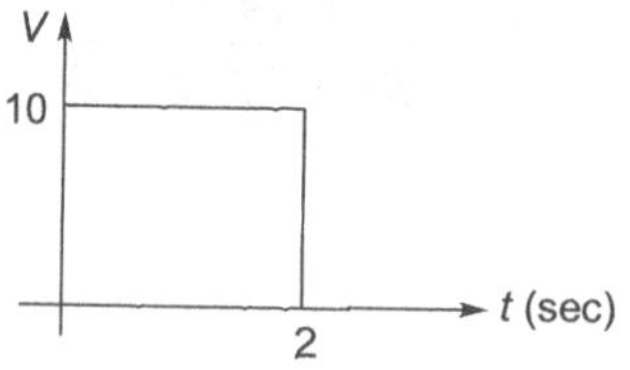

Find the magnitude at ω = 2π.

[20 marks : 2023]

Solution:

Given pulse is

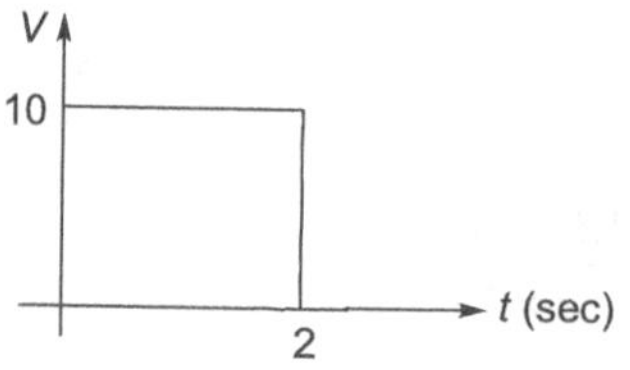

The fourier transform of $V(t)$ is given by,

$$V(\omega) = \int_{-\infty}^{\infty} v(t)\cdot e^{-j\omega t}dt = \int_0^2 10\cdot e^{-j\omega t}dt$$

$$= 10\cdot\left[\frac{e^{-j\omega t}}{-j\omega}\right]_0^2 = 10\cdot\left[\frac{e^{-j2\omega}}{-j\omega} + \frac{1}{j\omega}\right]$$

$$= \frac{-10}{j\omega}\left[e^{-j2\omega} - 1\right] = \frac{10}{j\omega}\left[1 - e^{-j2\omega}\right]$$

At $\omega = 2\pi$,

$$V(2\pi) = \frac{10}{j2\pi}\left[1 - e^{-j4\pi}\right]$$

$$= \frac{10}{j2\pi}[1-1] \qquad \left[\because e^{-j4\pi} = 1\right]$$

$$= 0$$

Thus magnitude of $V(\omega)$ at $\omega = 2\pi$ is 'zero'.

1.26 For a causal system $H(z) = \frac{z}{z-0.5}$, find the zero state response to input

$$x(n) = \left(\frac{1}{4}\right)^n u(n) + 5(3)^n u[-(n+1)].$$

[20 marks : 2023]

Solution:

For causal LTI-system:

$$H(z) = \frac{z}{z-0.5}, \quad |z| > 0.5$$

System input:

$$x(n) = \left(\frac{1}{4}\right)^n u(n) + 5(3)^n u[-(n+1)]$$

Now,

$$\left(\frac{1}{4}\right)^n u(n) \rightleftharpoons \frac{1}{1-\frac{1}{4}z^{-1}}, \qquad |z| > \frac{1}{4}$$

$$-(3)^n u(-n-1) \rightleftharpoons \frac{1}{1-3z^{-1}}, \qquad |z| < 3$$

$$5(3)^n u(-n-1) \rightleftharpoons \frac{-5}{1-3z^{-1}}, \qquad |z| < 3$$

Thus,

$$x(n) \rightleftharpoons X(z) = \frac{1}{1-\frac{1}{4}z^{-1}} - \frac{5}{1-3z^{-1}}, \qquad \frac{1}{4} < |z| < 3$$

For zero-state response:
Initial conditions are zero,
Hence, we can write

$$Y(z) = H(z) \cdot X(z)$$

$$= \frac{1}{1-0.5z^{-1}} \cdot \left[\frac{1}{1-\frac{1}{4}z^{-1}} - \frac{5}{1-3z^{-1}}\right], \qquad 0.5 < |z| < 3$$

$$\Rightarrow \qquad Y(z) = \frac{1}{(1-0.5z^{-1})\left(1-\frac{1}{4}z^{-1}\right)} - \frac{5}{(1-0.5z^{-1})(1-3z^{-1})}$$

By applying partial fraction :

$$= \frac{2}{1-0.5z^{-1}} - \frac{1}{1-\frac{1}{4}z^{-1}} - \left[\frac{-1}{1-0.5z^{-1}} + \frac{6}{1-3z^{-1}}\right]$$

$$= \frac{3}{1-0.5z^{-1}} - \frac{1}{1-\frac{1}{4}z^{-1}} - \frac{6}{1-3z^{-1}}, \qquad 0.5 < |z| < 3$$

By applying inverse ZT,
Required zero state response,

$$y(n) = 3(0.5)^n u(n) - \left(\frac{1}{4}\right)^n u(n) + 6(3)^n u(-n-1)$$

■■■■